THE KORAN

Born in Baghdad, N. J. Dawood came to England as an Iraq State Scholar in 1945 and graduated from London University. In 1959 he founded the Arabic Advertising & Publishing Co. Ltd, London (ARADCO), which is now one of the major producers of Arabic typesetting outside the Middle East. His translation of *Tales from the Thousand and One Nights* was first published as Penguin No. 1001 in 1954 and has since been printed in over twenty various formats and editions.

He is best known for his translation of the Koran, the first in contemporary English idiom, which was first published as a Penguin Classic in 1956 and has since sold over one million copies. An illustrated hardback edition of the Koran was published by Allen Lane in 1978. In the present revised edition the translation follows even more closely the standard Islamic commentaries and interpretations. It includes an introduction and an exhaustive index. The *sūrahs* follow the traditional sequence alongside a parallel calligraphic version of the Arabic original. This translation is also available without the Arabic original in the Penguin Classics series.

As well as contributing book reviews and articles on literary subjects to the national press, N. J. Dawood has retold for children two selections from *The Arabian Nights*, published in the Puffin Classics. He has edited and abridged *The Muqaddimah of Ibn Khaldūn* (Princeton University Press), translated numerous technical works into Arabic, written and spoken radio and film commentaries and contributed to specialized English–Arabic dictionaries.

THE KORAN

WITH A PARALLEL
ARABIC TEXT

TRANSLATED WITH NOTES BY
N. J. DAWOOD

PENGUIN BOOKS

PENGUIN CLASSICS

Published by the Penguin Group
Penguin Books Ltd, 80 Strand, London WC2R 0RL, England
Penguin Group (USA) Inc., 375 Hudson Street, New York, New York 10014, USA
Penguin Group (Canada), 90 Eglinton Avenue East, Suite 700, Toronto, Ontario, Canada M4P 2Y3
(a division of Pearson Penguin Canada Inc.)
Penguin Ireland, 25 St Stephen's Green, Dublin 2, Ireland (a division of Penguin Books Ltd)
Penguin Group (Australia), 707 Collins Street, Melbourne, Victoria 3008, Australia
(a division of Pearson Australia Group Pty Ltd)
Penguin Books India Pvt Ltd, 11 Community Centre, Panchsheel Park, New Delhi – 110 017, India
Penguin Group (NZ), 67 Apollo Drive, Rosedale, Auckland 0632, New Zealand
(a division of Pearson New Zealand Ltd)
Penguin Books (South Africa) (Pty) Ltd, Block D, Rosebank Office Park,
181 Jan Smuts Avenue, Parktown North, Gauteng 2193, South Africa

Penguin Books Ltd, Registered Offices: 80 Strand, London WC2R 0RL, England

www.penguin.com

English translation first published in Penguin Classics 1956
First revised edition 1959
Second revised edition 1966
Third revised edition 1968
Fourth revised edition 1974
Fifth revised edition following the traditional sequence of *sūrahs*,
published in Penguin Classics 1990
This parallel edition first published 1990
Reprinted with revisions 1993
Reprinted with minor revisions 1994
Reprinted with minor revisions and additional notes 1995
Reprinted with further revisions and additional notes 1998
Reprinted with minor revisions 2000
The 50th anniversary edition published with further revisions 2006
This extensively revised edition published with additional notes 2014
001

The Arabic text in this parallel edition is a facsimile of a Koran penned by the calligrapher Hamid al-Amidi and first printed in Istanbul in 1974 in accordance with Decision Number 212 of the Turkish Government's Commission on the Verification of Koranic Texts

Set in 11.5/13pt Garamond MT Std
Typeset by Jouve (UK), Milton Keynes
Printed in Great Britain by Clays Ltd, St Ives plc

ISBN: 978-0-141-39384-1

www.greenpenguin.co.uk

Penguin Books is committed to a sustainable future for our business, our readers and our planet. This book is made from Forest Stewardship Council™ certified paper.

CONTENTS

INTRODUCTION

The Koran[1] is the earliest and by far the finest work of Classical Arabic prose. For Muslims it is the infallible Word of God, a transcript of a tablet preserved in heaven, revealed to the Prophet Muḥammad by the Angel Gabriel. Except in the opening verses and some passages in which the words are clearly those of the Prophet or the Angel, the speaker throughout is God.[2]

The posthumous son of ʿAbdullāh bin ʿAbd al-Muṭṭalib, of the tribe of Quraysh, Muḥammad was born in Mecca about the year 570. His mother Āminah died when he was still a child, and he was brought up by his grandfather and then by his uncle Abū Ṭālib. As a youth he travelled with the trading caravans from Mecca to Syria, and at the age of twenty-five married Khadījah, daughter of Khuwailid, a rich widow fifteen years his senior. Meanwhile he had acquired a reputation for honesty and wisdom, and had come under the influence of Jewish and Christian teachings.

Long before Muḥammad's call, Arabian paganism was showing signs of decay. At the Kaʿbah the Meccans worshipped not only Allāh, the supreme Semitic God, but also a number of female deities whom they regarded as the daughters of Allāh. Among these were Al-Lāt, Al-ʿUzzā, and Manāt, who represented the Sun, Venus, and Fortune respectively. Impressed by Jewish and Christian monotheism, a number of theists, or spiritual fundamentalists, known as ḥanīfs had already rejected idolatry for an ascetic religion of their own. Muḥammad appears to have been influenced by them. It was his habit to retire to a cave in the mountains in order to give himself up to solitary prayer and meditation. According to Muslim tradition, one night in Ramaḍān about the year 610, as he was asleep or in a trance, the Angel Gabriel came to him and said: 'Read!' He replied: 'What shall I read?' The order was repeated three times, until the Angel said:

'Read in the name of your Lord who created; created Man from clots of blood.

'Read! Your Lord is the Most Bountiful One, who by the pen taught Man what he did not know.'

1. The Arabic name (Qur'ān) means 'The Recital'.
2. God speaks in the first person plural, which often changes to the first person singular or the third person singular in the course of the same verse.

When he awoke, these words, we are told, seemed to be 'inscribed upon his heart'.

Muḥammad, who disclaimed power to perform miracles, firmly believed that he was the Apostle of God, sent forth to confirm previous Scriptures. God had revealed His will to the Jews and the Christians through chosen apostles, but they disobeyed God's commandments and divided themselves into schisms. The Koran accuses the Jews of corrupting the Scriptures and the Christians of worshipping Jesus as the son of God, although He had expressly commanded them to worship none but Him. Having thus gone astray, they must be brought back to the right path, to 'the True Religion preached by Abraham'. This was Islām – absolute submission or resignation to the will of God.

The Koran preaches the oneness of God and emphasizes divine mercy and forgiveness. God is almighty and all-knowing, and though compassionate towards His creatures He is stern in retribution. He enjoins justice and fair dealing, kindness to orphans and widows, and charity to the poor. The most important duties of the Muslim are faith in God and His apostle, prayer, almsgiving, fasting, and (if possible) pilgrimage to the Sacred House at Mecca, built, according to the Koran, by Abraham for the worship of the One God.

The Koranic revelations followed each other at brief intervals and were at first committed to memory by professional remembrancers. During Muḥammad's lifetime verses were written on palm-leaves, stones, and any material that came to hand. Their collection is said to have been completed during the caliphate of 'Umar, the second Caliph, and an authorized version was established, according to Muslim scholars, during the caliphate of 'Uthmān, his successor (644–56). To this day this version is regarded by believers as the authoritative Word of God. But, owing to the fact that the kufic script in which the Koran was originally written contained no indication of vowels or diacritical points, variant readings are recognized by Muslims as of equal authority.

In preparing the contents of the Koran for book-form its editor or editors followed no chronological sequence. The *sūrahs*, or chapters, were arranged generally in order of length, the longest coming first and the shortest last. Attempts have been made by Noldeke, Grimme, Rodwell, and Bell to arrange the *sūrahs* in chronological order, but scholars are agreed that a strictly chronological arrangement is impossible without dissecting some into scattered verses, owing to the inclusion of revelations spoken in Medina in *sūrahs* begun several years earlier in Mecca.

In preparing this translation it has been my guiding principle to present the modern reader with an intelligible version of the Koran in contemporary, grammatically correct and natural English. The translation, first published in 1956, has been regularly revised in the light of a life-long study of the style and language of the Koran, and has been brought as close to the original as English idiom and usage will allow. Basic changes include 'God' instead of 'Allāh'; 'Lord of the Universe' instead of 'Lord of the Creation'; and 'alms levy' instead of 'alms tax'.

It is universally acknowledged that the Koran is one of the most influential books of prophetic literature; by Muslims it is also regarded as a literary masterpiece in its own right, flawless and inimitable. In adhering to a rigidly literal rendering of Arabic idioms, previous translations have, in my opinion, failed to convey both the meaning and the rhetorical grandeur of the original. The Koran contains many statements which, if not recognized as altogether obscure, lend themselves to more than one interpretation. I have taken pains to reproduce these ambiguities wherever they occur, and have provided explanatory footnotes in order to avoid turning the text into an interpretation rather than a translation. Throughout this rendering the standard commentaries of Al-Bayḍāwī and Al-Jalālayn have been closely followed.

Here a word should also be said about the cryptic Arabic letters which head certain chapters of the Koran. Various theories have been put forward by Muslim and Western scholars to explain their meaning, but none of them is satisfactory. The fact is that no one knows what they stand for. Traditional commentators dismiss them by saying 'God alone knows what He means by these letters.'

In the foregoing paragraphs I have endeavoured to confine myself to a bare outline of the facts regarding the genesis of the Koran and its subsequent preservation. It is the text itself that matters; and the reader should be allowed to approach it with a free and unprejudiced mind.

N. J. D.

This translation of the Koran, first published in 1956, has since undergone at least eight major revisions over the years. This 50th anniversary edition strives more tenaciously than ever before to combine accuracy with clarity and respect for the English language.

London, 2006 N. J. D.

This revision, the outcome of a further seven years' study of orthodox Koranic commentaries, attempts to reconcile the 'literal' with the 'liberal'. It may help the English-speaking general reader to get a better glimpse of the stylistic mannerisms and distinctive structural patterns characteristic of the Koranic text; it may also help the student to understand the Arabic by direct reference to the English. I have again retained the use of 'God' instead of 'Allāh', although in my view it might be more logical and appropriate to refer to God as Allāh, as Muslims do in daily life. This extensively revised version also takes into its compass the many valid changes over the past fifty-seven years in the connotation and usage of certain English words and expressions.

London, 2013 N. J. D.

NOTE TO THE GENERAL READER

It is recognized that reading the *sūrahs* in their traditional sequence – as presented in this translation – is not essential for an adequate understanding of the Koran. Readers approaching the Koran for the first time may therefore find it helpful to begin with the shorter and more poetic chapters, such as those describing the Day of Judgement, Paradise and Hell (e.g. 'The Cessation' and 'The Merciful') and those with biblical themes (e.g. 'Mary' and 'Joseph'), before attempting the much longer and often more complex chapters in the first half (e.g. 'The Cow' and 'The Table'), which presuppose familiarity with events in the early days of Islām.

CHRONOLOGICAL TABLE OF THE MAIN EVENTS IN THE LIFE OF MUḤAMMAD

c. 570	Birth of Muḥammad (his father having died a few months earlier)
576	Death of his mother Āminah
595	Marriage to Khadījah
c. 610	Beginning of Call
615	Flight of his followers to Ethiopia
619	Death of Khadījah
620	Muḥammad's reputed 'Night Journey' from Mecca to the Temple of Jerusalem, and thence to the Seventh Heaven
622	The *Hijra* (Flight or Migration) of Muḥammad and his followers to Medina, and beginning of the Muslim Era
624	Battle of Badr: the Quraysh defeated by the Muslims
625	Battle of 'Uḥud: the Muslims defeated
626	The Jewish tribe of al-Naḍīr crushed and expelled
627	'The War of the Ditch' – the Meccans' expedition against the Muslims in Medina; attackers driven off
627	The Jewish tribe of Qurayẓah raided and put to the sword
628	The Treaty of Ḥudaybiyya; truce with the Quraysh, who recognize Muḥammad's right to proselytize without hindrance
629	The Jews of Khaybar crushed and expelled Muḥammad sends letters and messengers to the kings of Persia, Yemen, and Ethiopia and the Emperor Heraclius, inviting them to accept Islām

630	Truce broken by the Quraysh. Mecca taken by Muḥammad – the entire population converted, and the Ka‘bah established as the religious centre of Islām
631	'The Year of Embassies' – Islām accepted by the Arabian tribes
632	Muḥammad's Farewell Pilgrimage to Mecca
632, 8 June	Death of Muḥammad, three months after his return to Medina

سورة فاتحة الكتاب مكية

بسم الله الرحمن الرحيم
الحمد لله رب العالمين الرحمن
الرحيم مالك يوم الدين
اياك نعبد واياك نستعين
اهدنا الصراط المستقيم
صراط الذين انعمت عليهم غير
المغضوب عليهم ولا الضالين

وهي سبع آيات

THE EXORDIUM[1]

IN THE NAME OF GOD 1:1
THE MERCIFUL
THE COMPASSIONATE

Praise be to God, Lord of the Universe,
The Merciful, the Compassionate,
Sovereign of the Day of Judgement!
You alone we worship, and to You alone
we turn for help.
Guide us to the straight path,
The path of those whom You have favoured, 1:7
Not of those who have provoked Your ire,
Nor of those who have lost their way.

1. Or: 'Opening Verses'; generally recited as a prayer for the dead, and corresponds to the Lord's Prayer in Christendom.

THE COW

In the Name of God, the Merciful, the Compassionate

ALIF *lām mīm.* This Book is not to be doubted. It is a guide for the righteous, 2:
who believe in the Unseen and are steadfast in prayer; who give[1] from what
We gave them; who believe in what has been revealed to you[2] and what was
revealed before you, and have absolute faith in the life to come. These are
rightly guided by their Lord; these shall surely succeed.

1. Literally, spend. 2. Muḥammad.

2:6 As FOR the unbelievers, it is the same whether or not you forewarn them; they will not have faith. God has set a seal upon their hearts and ears; their sight is dimmed and grievous punishment awaits them.

And some there are who declare: 'We believe in God and the Last Day,' yet they are no true believers. They seek to deceive God and those who believe in Him: but they deceive none save themselves, though they may not perceive it. There is a sickness in their hearts which God has aggravated: grievous punishment awaits them for the lies they ever told.

2:11 If they are told: 'You shall not do evil in the land,' they reply: 'Surely we are doing only what is good.' But it is they who are the evil-doers, though they may not perceive it.

And if they are told: 'Believe as the people believe,' they reply: 'Are we to believe as fools believe?' It is they who are the fools, if they but knew it.

And when they meet the faithful, they declare: 'We, too, are believers.' But when alone with their demons they say to them: 'We follow none but you: we were only mocking.' God will mock them and keep them long in sin, ever straying from the right path.

2:16 Such are those that barter guidance for error: they profit nothing, nor are they on the right path.

إِنَّ الَّذِينَ كَفَرُوا سَوَاءٌ عَلَيْهِمْ أَأَنْذَرْتَهُمْ أَمْ لَمْ تُنْذِرْهُمْ
لَا يُؤْمِنُونَ ﴿٦﴾ خَتَمَ اللَّهُ عَلَىٰ قُلُوبِهِمْ وَعَلَىٰ سَمْعِهِمْ ۖ وَعَلَىٰ
أَبْصَارِهِمْ غِشَاوَةٌ ۖ وَلَهُمْ عَذَابٌ عَظِيمٌ ﴿٧﴾ وَمِنَ النَّاسِ
مَنْ يَقُولُ آمَنَّا بِاللَّهِ وَبِالْيَوْمِ الْآخِرِ وَمَا هُمْ بِمُؤْمِنِينَ
﴿٨﴾ يُخَادِعُونَ اللَّهَ وَالَّذِينَ آمَنُوا وَمَا يَخْدَعُونَ إِلَّا
أَنْفُسَهُمْ وَمَا يَشْعُرُونَ ﴿٩﴾ فِي قُلُوبِهِمْ مَرَضٌ فَزَادَهُمُ
اللَّهُ مَرَضًا ۖ وَلَهُمْ عَذَابٌ أَلِيمٌ بِمَا كَانُوا يَكْذِبُونَ ﴿١٠﴾ وَإِذَا قِيلَ
لَهُمْ لَا تُفْسِدُوا فِي الْأَرْضِ قَالُوا إِنَّمَا نَحْنُ مُصْلِحُونَ ﴿١١﴾ أَلَا إِنَّهُمْ
هُمُ الْمُفْسِدُونَ وَلَٰكِنْ لَا يَشْعُرُونَ ﴿١٢﴾ وَإِذَا قِيلَ لَهُمْ آمِنُوا
كَمَا آمَنَ النَّاسُ قَالُوا أَنُؤْمِنُ كَمَا آمَنَ السُّفَهَاءُ ۗ أَلَا إِنَّهُمْ
هُمُ السُّفَهَاءُ وَلَٰكِنْ لَا يَعْلَمُونَ ﴿١٣﴾ وَإِذَا لَقُوا الَّذِينَ آمَنُوا
قَالُوا آمَنَّا وَإِذَا خَلَوْا إِلَىٰ شَيَاطِينِهِمْ قَالُوا إِنَّا مَعَكُمْ إِنَّمَا نَحْنُ
مُسْتَهْزِئُونَ ﴿١٤﴾ اللَّهُ يَسْتَهْزِئُ بِهِمْ وَيَمُدُّهُمْ فِي
طُغْيَانِهِمْ يَعْمَهُونَ ﴿١٥﴾ أُولَٰئِكَ الَّذِينَ اشْتَرَوُا الضَّلَالَةَ
بِالْهُدَىٰ فَمَا رَبِحَتْ تِجَارَتُهُمْ وَمَا كَانُوا مُهْتَدِينَ ﴿١٦﴾

مثلهم كمثل الذي استوقد نارا فلما أضاءت ما حوله ذهب الله
بنورهم وتركهم في ظلمات لا يبصرون ﴿١٧﴾ صم بكم عمي
فهم لا يرجعون ﴿١٨﴾ أو كصيب من السماء فيه ظلمات
ورعد وبرق يجعلون أصابعهم في آذانهم من الصواعق
حذر الموت والله محيط بالكافرين ﴿١٩﴾ يكاد البرق يخطف
أبصارهم كلما أضاء لهم مشوا فيه وإذا أظلم عليهم
قاموا ولو شاء الله لذهب بسمعهم وأبصارهم إن الله
على كل شيء قدير ﴿٢٠﴾ يا أيها الناس اعبدوا ربكم
الذي خلقكم والذين من قبلكم لعلكم تتقون ﴿٢١﴾ الذي
جعل لكم الأرض فراشا والسماء بناء وأنزل من السماء
ماء فأخرج به من الثمرات رزقا لكم فلا تجعلوا لله
أندادا وأنتم تعلمون ﴿٢٢﴾ وإن كنتم في ريب مما نزلنا على
عبدنا فأتوا بسورة من مثله وادعوا شهداءكم من دون الله
إن كنتم صادقين ﴿٢٣﴾ فإن لم تفعلوا ولن تفعلوا فاتقوا
النار التي وقودها الناس والحجارة أعدت للكافرين ﴿٢٤﴾

THEY ARE like one who 2:17
kindled a fire, but as soon as it
lit up all around him God put it
out and left him in darkness:
they do not see. Deaf, dumb,
and blind, they will never
return to the right path.

Or like those who, beneath
a dark storm-cloud charged with
thunder and lightning, thrust
their fingers into their ears at
the sound of every thunder-
clap for fear of death (God thus
encompasses the unbelievers).
The lightning almost snatches
away their sight: whenever it
flashes upon them they walk
on, but as soon as it darkens
they stand still. Indeed, if God
pleased, He could take away
their hearing and their sight:
God has power over all things.

You people! Worship your 2:21
Lord, who has created you and those who have gone before you, so that you
may guard yourselves against evil; who has made the earth a bed for you and
the sky a dome, and has sent down water from the sky to bring forth fruits
for your sustenance. Do not knowingly set up other deities besides God.

And if you doubt what We have revealed to Our servant, produce one
sūrah comparable to it. Call upon your idols to assist you, if what you say be
true. But if you fail (as you are sure to fail), then guard yourselves against the 2:24
Fire whose fuel is humans and stones, prepared for the unbelievers.

2:25 AND PROCLAIM joyful tidings to those that believe and
do good works. They shall
dwell in Gardens watered by
running brooks: whenever
they are given fruit to eat they
will say: 'This is what we used
to eat before,' for they shall
be given the like. Wedded to
chaste spouses, they shall abide
therein for ever.

Surely God does not disdain
to make comparison with a
gnat or with a larger creature.
The faithful know that it is the
Truth from their Lord, but the
unbelievers ask: 'What could
God mean by this compari-
son?'

By such comparison God
confounds many and enlightens many. But He confounds
2:27 none except the ungodly, who
break God's covenant after accepting it, and put asunder what God has bidden to be united, and perpetrate corruption in the land. It is these who will
surely be the lost ones.

How can you deny God? Did He not give you life when you were dead,
and will He not cause you to die and then restore you to life? Will you not
2:29 return to Him at last? He created for you all that the earth contains; then,
ascending to the sky, He fashioned it into seven heavens. And He has knowledge of all things.

وَبَشِّرِ الَّذِينَ آمَنُوا وَعَمِلُوا الصَّالِحَاتِ أَنَّ لَهُمْ جَنَّاتٍ
تَجْرِي مِنْ تَحْتِهَا الْأَنْهَارُ كُلَّمَا رُزِقُوا مِنْهَا مِنْ
ثَمَرَةٍ رِزْقًا قَالُوا هَٰذَا الَّذِي رُزِقْنَا مِنْ قَبْلُ وَأُتُوا بِهِ
مُتَشَابِهًا وَلَهُمْ فِيهَا أَزْوَاجٌ مُطَهَّرَةٌ وَهُمْ فِيهَا
خَالِدُونَ ﴿٢٥﴾ إِنَّ اللَّهَ لَا يَسْتَحْيِي أَنْ يَضْرِبَ مَثَلًا مَا
بَعُوضَةً فَمَا فَوْقَهَا فَأَمَّا الَّذِينَ آمَنُوا فَيَعْلَمُونَ
أَنَّهُ الْحَقُّ مِنْ رَبِّهِمْ وَأَمَّا الَّذِينَ كَفَرُوا فَيَقُولُونَ
مَاذَا أَرَادَ اللَّهُ بِهَٰذَا مَثَلًا يُضِلُّ بِهِ كَثِيرًا وَيَهْدِي بِهِ
كَثِيرًا وَمَا يُضِلُّ بِهِ إِلَّا الْفَاسِقِينَ ﴿٢٦﴾ الَّذِينَ يَنْقُضُونَ
عَهْدَ اللَّهِ مِنْ بَعْدِ مِيثَاقِهِ وَيَقْطَعُونَ مَا أَمَرَ
اللَّهُ بِهِ أَنْ يُوصَلَ وَيُفْسِدُونَ فِي الْأَرْضِ أُولَٰئِكَ هُمُ الْخَاسِرُونَ
﴿٢٧﴾ كَيْفَ تَكْفُرُونَ بِاللَّهِ وَكُنْتُمْ أَمْوَاتًا فَأَحْيَاكُمْ
ثُمَّ يُمِيتُكُمْ ثُمَّ يُحْيِيكُمْ ثُمَّ إِلَيْهِ تُرْجَعُونَ ﴿٢٨﴾ هُوَ الَّذِي
خَلَقَ لَكُمْ مَا فِي الْأَرْضِ جَمِيعًا ثُمَّ اسْتَوَىٰ إِلَى السَّمَاءِ
فَسَوَّاهُنَّ سَبْعَ سَمَاوَاتٍ وَهُوَ بِكُلِّ شَيْءٍ عَلِيمٌ ﴿٢٩﴾

وإذ قال ربك للملائكة إني جاعل في الأرض خليفة قالوا
أتجعل فيها من يفسد فيها ويسفك الدماء ونحن نسبح
بحمدك ونقدس لك قال إني أعلم ما لا تعلمون ٣٠ وعلم
آدم الأسماء كلها ثم عرضهم على الملائكة فقال أنبئوني
بأسماء هؤلاء إن كنتم صادقين ٣١ قالوا سبحانك
لا علم لنا إلا ما علمتنا إنك أنت العليم الحكيم ٣٢ قال يا
آدم أنبئهم بأسمائهم فلما أنبأهم بأسمائهم قال ألم أقل
لكم إني أعلم غيب السماوات والأرض وأعلم ما تبدون
وما كنتم تكتمون ٣٣ وإذ قلنا للملائكة اسجدوا
لآدم فسجدوا إلا إبليس أبى واستكبر وكان من الكافرين ٣٤ وقلنا يا
آدم اسكن أنت وزوجك الجنة وكلا منها رغدا حيث شئتما
ولا تقربا هذه الشجرة فتكونا من الظالمين ٣٥ فأزلهما الشيطان
عنها فأخرجهما مما كانا فيه وقلنا اهبطوا بعضكم لبعض
عدو ولكم في الأرض مستقر ومتاع إلى حين ٣٦ فتلقى
آدم من ربه كلمات فتاب عليه إنه هو التواب الرحيم ٣٧

AND WHEN your Lord said 2:30
to the angels: 'I am placing on
the earth one that shall rule as
My deputy,' they replied: 'Will
You put there one that will
do evil and shed blood, when
we have for so long sung Your
praises and sanctified Your
name?'

He said: 'I know what you
know not.'

He taught Adam the names
of all things and then set them
before the angels, saying: 'Tell
Me the names of these, if what
you say be true.'

'Glory be to You,' they replied,
'we have no knowledge except
that which You have given us.
You alone are all-knowing and
wise.'

Then said He: 'Adam, tell
them their names.' And when
Adam had named them, He said: 'Did I not tell you that I know the secrets
of the heavens and the earth, and know all that you reveal and all that you
conceal?'

And when We said to the angels: 'Prostrate yourselves before Adam,' they 2:34
all prostrated themselves except Satan, who in his pride refused and became
an unbeliever.

We said: 'Adam, dwell with your spouse in Paradise and both of you eat of
its fruits to your hearts' content wherever you will. But never approach this
tree or you shall both become transgressors.'

But Satan lured them thence and brought about their banishment. 'Get
you down,' We said, 'and be enemies to each other. The earth will provide for
you an abode and comforts for a time.'

Then Adam received commandments from his Lord, and his Lord 2:37
relented towards him. He is the Relenting One, the Compassionate.

2:38 'GET YOU down hence,
all,' We said. 'When My guidance is revealed to you, those
that follow My guidance shall
have nothing to fear or to
regret; but those that deny
and reject Our revelations
shall be the inmates of the
Fire, wherein shall they abide
for ever.'

Children of Israel, remember the favour I have bestowed
upon you. Keep your covenant, and I will be true to Mine.
Dread My power. Have faith
in My revelations, which confirm your Scriptures, and do
not be the first to deny them.
Do not sell My revelations for
a paltry price; fear Me. Do not
confound Truth with falsehood, nor knowingly conceal
2:43 the Truth. Attend to your
prayers, render the alms levy, and kneel with those who kneel. Would you
enjoin people to be charitable and forget yourselves? Yet you recite the
Scriptures. Have you no sense?

Fortify yourselves with patience and with prayer. This may indeed be an
exacting discipline, but not to the devout, who know that they will meet their
Lord and that to Him they will return.

Children of Israel, remember the favour I have bestowed upon you, and
2:48 that I exalted you above the nations. Guard yourselves against a day on which
no soul shall stand for another: when no intercession shall be accepted for it,
no ransom be taken from it, and none shall be helped.

قلنا اهبطوا منها جميعا فإما يأتينكم مني هدى فمن تبع
هداى فلا خوف عليهم ولا هم يحزنون ٣٨ والذين كفروا
وكذبوا بآياتنا أولئك أصحاب النار هم فيها خالدون ٣٩
يا بني إسرائيل اذكروا نعمتي التي أنعمت عليكم وأوفوا بعهدي
أوف بعهدكم وإياى فارهبون ٤٠ وآمنوا بما أنزلت مصدقا
لما معكم ولا تكونوا أول كافر به ولا تشتروا بآياتي ثمنا
قليلا وإياى فاتقون ٤١ ولا تلبسوا الحق بالباطل وتكتموا
الحق وأنتم تعلمون ٤٢ وأقيموا الصلوة وآتوا الزكوة
واركعوا مع الراكعين ٤٣ أتأمرون الناس بالبر
وتنسون أنفسكم وأنتم تتلون الكتاب أفلا تعقلون ٤٤
واستعينوا بالصبر والصلوة وإنها لكبيرة إلا على الخاشعين
٤٥ الذين يظنون أنهم ملاقوا ربهم وأنهم إليه راجعون ٤٦
يا بني إسرائيل اذكروا نعمتي التي أنعمت عليكم وأني فضلتكم
على العالمين ٤٧ واتقوا يوما لا تجزي نفس عن نفس شيئا
ولا يقبل منها شفاعة ولا يؤخذ منها عدل ولا هم ينصرون ٤٨

وإذ نجيناكم من آل فرعون يسومونكم سوء العذاب يذبحون
أبناءكم ويستحيون نساءكم وفي ذلكم بلاء من ربكم
عظيم ﴿٤٩﴾ وإذ فرقنا بكم البحر فأنجيناكم وأغرقنا آل
فرعون وأنتم تنظرون ﴿٥٠﴾ وإذ واعدنا موسى أربعين ليلة
ثم اتخذتم العجل من بعده وأنتم ظالمون ﴿٥١﴾ ثم عفونا
عنكم من بعد ذلك لعلكم تشكرون ﴿٥٢﴾ وإذ آتينا موسى
الكتاب والفرقان لعلكم تهتدون ﴿٥٣﴾ وإذ قال موسى
لقومه يا قوم إنكم ظلمتم أنفسكم باتخاذكم العجل
فتوبوا إلى بارئكم فاقتلوا أنفسكم ذلكم خير
لكم عند بارئكم فتاب عليكم إنه هو التواب الرحيم
﴿٥٤﴾ وإذ قلتم يا موسى لن نؤمن لك حتى نرى الله
جهرة فأخذتكم الصاعقة وأنتم تنظرون ﴿٥٥﴾ ثم بعثناكم
من بعد موتكم لعلكم تشكرون ﴿٥٦﴾ وظللنا عليكم
الغمام وأنزلنا عليكم المن والسلوى كلوا من طيبات
ما رزقناكم وما ظلمونا ولكن كانوا أنفسهم يظلمون ﴿٥٧﴾

AND REMEMBER how We 2:49
delivered you from Pharaoh's
people, who had oppressed
you cruelly, slaying your sons
and sparing only your daughters. Surely that was a great
trial by your Lord. We parted
the sea for you and, taking you
to safety, drowned Pharaoh's
men before your very eyes. We
made a tryst with Moses for
the fortieth night, and in his
absence you took up the calf
and thus committed evil. Yet
after that We pardoned you,
so that you might give thanks.
We gave Moses the Book
and Salvation,[1] so that you
might be rightly guided. Moses 2:54
said to his people: 'You have
wronged yourselves, my people,
in worshipping the calf. Turn
in penitence to your Creator
and slay the culprits among you. That will be best for you in your Creator's
sight.' And He relented towards you. He is the Relenting One, the Compassionate.
When you said to Moses: 'We will not believe in you until we see God[2]
with our own eyes,' the thunderbolt struck you while you were looking on.
Then We revived you from your stupor, so that you might give thanks.
We caused the clouds to draw their shadow over you and sent down for 2:57
you manna and quails,[3] saying: 'Eat of the wholesome things We have given
you.' Indeed, they[4] did not wrong Us, but they wronged themselves.

1. *Al-Furqān*: Variously interpreted by traditional commentators as 'the difference between right and wrong', or 'between good and evil'; the word makes its first appearance in the Koran, and is the Arabicized form of the Aramaic *purqān*, as in the Aramaic Qaddish. See also A. J. Arberry's interpretation.
2. Cf. Exodus 19:21.
3. Cf. Exodus 16.
4. The Israelites.

2:58 'ENTER THIS city,' We said, 'and eat where you will to your hearts' content. Make your way reverently through the gates, saying: "We repent." We shall forgive you your sins and bestow abundance on the righteous.' But that which they were told the wrongdoers replaced with other words; and We let loose on the wrongdoers a scourge from heaven as punishment for their misdeeds.

And when Moses requested water for his people, We said to him: 'Strike the Rock with your staff.'[1] Thereupon twelve springs gushed from the Rock, and each tribe knew their drinking-place. We said: 'Eat and drink of that which God has provided and do not foul the land with evil.'

وإذ قلنا ادخلوا هذه القرية فكلوا منها حيث شئتم رغدا
وادخلوا الباب سجدا وقولوا حطة نغفر لكم خطاياكم
وسنزيد المحسنين ۝ فبدل الذين ظلموا قولا غير الذي
قيل لهم فأنزلنا على الذين ظلموا رجزا من السماء بما
كانوا يفسقون ۝ وإذ استسقى موسى لقومه فقلنا اضرب
بعصاك الحجر فانفجرت منه اثنتا عشرة عينا قد علم
كل أناس مشربهم كلوا واشربوا من رزق الله ولا تعثوا
في الأرض مفسدين ۝ وإذ قلتم يا موسى لن نصبر على
طعام واحد فادع لنا ربك يخرج لنا مما تنبت الأرض
من بقلها وقثائها وفومها وعدسها وبصلها
قال أتستبدلون الذي هو أدنى بالذي هو خير
اهبطوا مصرا فإن لكم ما سألتم وضربت عليهم
الذلة والمسكنة وباءو بغضب من الله ذلك
بأنهم كانوا يكفرون بآيات الله ويقتلون
النبيين بغير الحق ذلك بما عصوا وكانوا يعتدون ۝

2:61 'Moses,' you said, 'we will no longer put up with this monotonous diet. Call on your Lord to give us some of the varied produce of the earth, green herbs and cucumbers, corn[2] and lentils and onions.'

'What!' he answered. 'Would you exchange that which is good for what is worse? Go back to Egypt.[3] There you will find all you have asked for.'

Servility and misery were stamped upon them and they incurred the wrath of God; because they disbelieved God's signs and slew the prophets unjustly; because they were rebels and transgressors.

1. Cf. Numbers 20:8.
2. An alternative reading gives *thūm*, garlic. Cf. Numbers 11:5.
3. Or: to a 'big city', according to another reading (Al-Bayḍāwī).

إن الذين آمنوا والذين هادوا والنصارى والصابئين
من آمن بالله واليوم الآخر وعمل صالحا فلهم أجرهم
عند ربهم ولا خوف عليهم ولا هم يحزنون (٦٢) وإذ
أخذنا ميثاقكم ورفعنا فوقكم الطور خذوا ما آتيناكم
بقوة واذكروا ما فيه لعلكم تتقون (٦٣) ثم توليتم من
بعد ذلك فلولا فضل الله عليكم ورحمته لكنتم من
الخاسرين (٦٤) ولقد علمتم الذين اعتدوا منكم في السبت
فقلنا لهم كونوا قردة خاسئين (٦٥) فجعلناها نكالا لما
بين يديها وما خلفها وموعظة للمتقين (٦٦) وإذ قال موسى
لقومه إن الله يأمركم أن تذبحوا بقرة قالوا أتتخذنا
هزوا قال أعوذ بالله أن أكون من الجاهلين (٦٧) قالوا
ادع لنا ربك يبين لنا ما هي قال إنه يقول إنها بقرة لا فارض
ولا بكر عوان بين ذلك فافعلوا ما تؤمرون (٦٨) قالوا
ادع لنا ربك يبين لنا ما لونها قال إنه يقول إنها بقرة
صفراء فاقع لونها تسر الناظرين (٦٩)

BELIEVERS, THOSE who 2:62
follow the Jewish Faith,[1] Christians, and Sabaeans – whoever believes in God and the Last Day and does what is right – shall be rewarded by their Lord; they have nothing to fear or to regret.

We made a covenant with you[2] and raised the Mount above you, saying: 'Hold fast to what We have given you and bear in mind its precepts, that you may guard yourselves against evil.' Yet after that you turned away, and but for God's grace and mercy you would have surely been among the lost.

You have heard of those of you that broke the Sabbath. We said to them: 'Change into
detested apes!' We made their 2:66
fate an example to their own generation and to those who followed them, and a lesson to the righteous.

And when Moses said to his people: 'God commands you to sacrifice a cow,'[3] they replied: 'Are you mocking us?'

'God forbid that I should be so foolish!' he rejoined.

'Call on your Lord,' they said, 'to make known to us what kind of cow she shall be.'

He replied: 'Your Lord says: "Let her be neither an old cow nor a young heifer, but in between." Do, therefore, as you are bidden.'

'Call on your Lord,' they said, 'to make known to us what her colour 2:69
shall be.'

He replied: 'Your Lord says: "Let the cow be yellow, a rich yellow, pleasing to those that see it."'

1. *Alladhīna hādū*, as distinct from *al-Yahūd* (the Jews), would also include Arabian converts to the Jewish faith.
2. The Israelites.
3. Cf. Numbers 19, which refers merely to a sacrificial 'cow'; it contains none of the verbal exchanges related in this *sūrah*.

2:70 'CALL ON your Lord,' they said, 'to make known to us the exact type of cow she shall be; for to us cows look all alike. If God wills we shall be rightly guided.'

Moses replied: 'Your Lord says: "Let her be a healthy cow, not worn out with ploughing the earth or watering the field; a cow free from any blemish."'

'Now you have told us all,' they answered. And they slaughtered a cow, after they had nearly declined.

And when you slew a man and then fell out with one another concerning him, God made known what you concealed. We said: 'Strike him with a part of it.' Thus God restores the dead to life and shows you His signs, that you may grow in understanding.

2:74 Yet after that your hearts became as hard as rock or even harder; for from some rocks rivers take their course: some break asunder and water gushes from them: and others tumble down through fear of God. God is not unaware of what you do.

Do you[1] then hope that they will believe in you, when some of them have already heard the Word of God and knowingly perverted it, although they understood its meaning?

2:76 And when they meet the faithful they declare: 'We, too, are believers.' But when alone they say to each other: 'Must you declare to them what God has revealed to you? They will only dispute with you about it in your Lord's presence. Have you no sense?'

قالوا ادع لنا ربك يبين لنا ما هي إن البقر تشابه علينا
وإنا إن شاء الله لمهتدون ٧٠ قال إنه يقول إنها بقرة
لا ذلول تثير الأرض ولا تسقي الحرث مسلمة لا شية فيها قالوا الآن
جئت بالحق فذبحوها وما كادوا يفعلون ٧١ وإذ قتلتم نفسا
فادارأتم فيها والله مخرج ما كنتم تكتمون ٧٢ فقلنا اضربوه ببعضها
كذلك يحيي الله الموتى ويريكم آياته لعلكم تعقلون ٧٣
ثم قست قلوبكم من بعد ذلك فهي كالحجارة أو أشد
قسوة وإن من الحجارة لما يتفجر منه الأنهار وإن منها لما
يشقق فيخرج منه الماء وإن منها لما يهبط من خشية
الله وما الله بغافل عما تعملون ٧٤ أفتطمعون
أن يؤمنوا لكم وقد كان فريق منهم يسمعون
كلام الله ثم يحرفونه من بعد ما عقلوه وهم
يعلمون ٧٥ وإذا لقوا الذين آمنوا قالوا آمنا وإذا
خلا بعضهم إلى بعض قالوا أتحدثونهم بما فتح
الله عليكم ليحاجوكم به عند ربكم أفلا تعقلون ٧٦

1. The believers are here addressed.

اولا يعلمون ان الله يعلم ما يسرون وما يعلنون ٧٧ ومنهم
اميون لا يعلمون الكتاب الا اماني وان هم الا يظنون
٧٨ فويل للذين يكتبون الكتاب بايديهم ثم يقولون
هذا من عند الله ليشتروا به ثمنا قليلا فويل لهم
مما كتبت ايديهم وويل لهم مما يكسبون
٧٩ وقالوا لن تمسنا النار الا اياما معدودة قل
اتخذتم عند الله عهدا فلن يخلف الله عهده
ام تقولون على الله ما لا تعلمون ٨٠ بلى من كسب
سيئة واحاطت به خطيئته فاولئك اصحاب النار
هم فيها خالدون ٨١ والذين امنوا وعملوا الصالحات
اولئك اصحاب الجنة هم فيها خالدون ٨٢ واذ اخذنا
ميثاق بني اسرائيل لا تعبدون الا الله وبالوالدين
احسانا وذي القربى واليتامى والمساكين وقولوا
للناس حسنا واقيموا الصلوة واتوا الزكوة
ثم توليتم الا قليلا منكم وانتم معرضون ٨٣

DO THEY not know that 2:77
God has knowledge of all that
they conceal and all that they
reveal?

Some among them are illiterate, ignorant of the Book and know of nothing but wishful fancies and vague conjecture. Woe betide those that write the Book with their own hands and then declare: 'This is from God,' in order to gain some paltry end. Woeful shall be their fate, because of what their hands have written, because of what they did.

They declare: 'The Fire will 2:80
never touch us – except for a
few days.' Say: 'Did God make
you such a promise – God will
not break His promise – or do
you assert of God what you
know not?'

Truly, those that commit evil and become engrossed in sin shall be the inmates of the Fire, wherein shall they abide for ever. But those that have faith and do good works shall be the tenants of Paradise, wherein shall they abide for ever.

And when We made a covenant with the Israelites, We said: 'Serve none 2:83
but God. Show kindness to your parents, to your kin, to orphans, and to the
destitute. Exhort people to righteousness. Attend to your prayers and render
alms.' But you all broke your covenant except a few, and paid no heed.

2:84 AND WHEN We made a
covenant with you, We said:
'You shall not shed your kin's
blood or turn them out of
their dwellings.' To this you
consented and bore witness.
Yet there you were, slaying
your own kin, and turning a
number of you out of their
dwellings, and helping each
other against them with sin
and aggression; though had
they come to you as captives,
you would have ransomed
them. Surely their expulsion
was unlawful. Do you believe
in one part of the Book and
deny another?

So what reward is there for
those of you that act thus but
disgrace in this world and
grievous punishment on the
Day of Resurrection? God is
never heedless of what you do.

وَإِذْ أَخَذْنَا مِيثَاقَكُمْ لَا تَسْفِكُونَ دِمَاءَكُمْ وَلَا تُخْرِجُونَ
أَنْفُسَكُمْ مِنْ دِيَارِكُمْ ثُمَّ أَقْرَرْتُمْ وَأَنْتُمْ تَشْهَدُونَ
(٨٤) ثُمَّ أَنْتُمْ هَٰؤُلَاءِ تَقْتُلُونَ أَنْفُسَكُمْ وَتُخْرِجُونَ
فَرِيقًا مِنْكُمْ مِنْ دِيَارِهِمْ تَظَاهَرُونَ عَلَيْهِمْ بِالْإِثْمِ
وَالْعُدْوَانِ وَإِنْ يَأْتُوكُمْ أُسَارَىٰ تُفَادُوهُمْ وَهُوَ
مُحَرَّمٌ عَلَيْكُمْ إِخْرَاجُهُمْ أَفَتُؤْمِنُونَ بِبَعْضِ الْكِتَابِ
وَتَكْفُرُونَ بِبَعْضٍ فَمَا جَزَاءُ مَنْ يَفْعَلُ ذَٰلِكَ مِنْكُمْ
إِلَّا خِزْيٌ فِي الْحَيَاةِ الدُّنْيَا وَيَوْمَ الْقِيَامَةِ يُرَدُّونَ إِلَىٰ أَشَدِّ
الْعَذَابِ وَمَا اللَّهُ بِغَافِلٍ عَمَّا تَعْمَلُونَ (٨٥) أُولَٰئِكَ الَّذِينَ
اشْتَرَوُا الْحَيَاةَ الدُّنْيَا بِالْآخِرَةِ فَلَا يُخَفَّفُ عَنْهُمُ الْعَذَابُ
وَلَا هُمْ يُنْصَرُونَ (٨٦) وَلَقَدْ آتَيْنَا مُوسَى الْكِتَابَ وَقَفَّيْنَا مِنْ
بَعْدِهِ بِالرُّسُلِ وَآتَيْنَا عِيسَى ابْنَ مَرْيَمَ الْبَيِّنَاتِ وَأَيَّدْنَاهُ بِرُوحِ
الْقُدُسِ أَفَكُلَّمَا جَاءَكُمْ رَسُولٌ بِمَا لَا تَهْوَىٰ أَنْفُسُكُمُ اسْتَكْبَرْتُمْ
فَفَرِيقًا كَذَّبْتُمْ وَفَرِيقًا تَقْتُلُونَ (٨٧) وَقَالُوا قُلُوبُنَا غُلْفٌ
بَلْ لَعَنَهُمُ اللَّهُ بِكُفْرِهِمْ فَقَلِيلًا مَا يُؤْمِنُونَ (٨٨)

2:86 Such are they who buy the life of this world at the price of the life to
come. Their punishment shall not be mitigated, nor shall they be helped.

To Moses We gave the Book and after him We sent other apostles. We
gave Jesus son of Mary veritable signs and strengthened him with the Holy
Spirit. You scorn each apostle who comes to you with whatever does not suit
your fancies, charging some with imposture and slaying others.

2:88 And they say: 'Our hearts are sealed.' But God has cursed them for their
unbelief. They have but little faith.

ولما جاءهم كتاب من عند الله مصدق لما معهم وكانوا
من قبل يستفتحون على الذين كفروا فلما جاءهم
ما عرفوا كفروا به فلعنة الله على الكافرين ﴿٨٩﴾ بئسما
اشتروا به أنفسهم أن يكفروا بما أنزل
الله بغيا أن ينزل الله من فضله على من يشاء من
عباده فباءو بغضب على غضب وللكافرين عذاب مهين ﴿٩٠﴾
وإذا قيل لهم آمنوا بما أنزل الله قالوا نؤمن بما أنزل
علينا ويكفرون بما وراءه وهو الحق مصدقا لما معهم
قل فلم تقتلون أنبياء الله من قبل إن كنتم
مؤمنين ﴿٩١﴾ ولقد جاءكم موسى بالبينات ثم
اتخذتم العجل من بعده وأنتم ظالمون ﴿٩٢﴾ وإذ
أخذنا ميثاقكم ورفعنا فوقكم الطور خذوا
ما آتيناكم بقوة واسمعوا قالوا سمعنا وعصينا
وأشربوا في قلوبهم العجل بكفرهم قل بئسما
يأمركم به إيمانكم إن كنتم مؤمنين ﴿٩٣﴾

AND NOW that a Book con- 2:89
firming their own has come to
them from God, they deny it,
although they know it to be
the Truth and have long prayed
for help against the unbelievers. God's curse be upon the
infidels! Evil is that for which
they have bartered their souls.
To deny God's own revelation,
grudging that He should reveal
His bounty to whom He
chooses from among His servants! They have incurred
God's most inexorable ire. Ignominious punishment awaits
the unbelievers.

And if they are told: 'Believe 2:91
in what God has revealed,' they
reply: 'We believe in what was
revealed to *us*.' And they deny
what has since been revealed,
although it is the Truth, corroborating their own Scriptures.

Say: 'Why did you kill the prophets of God, if you are true believers?
Moses came to you with veritable signs, but in his absence you worshipped
the calf and committed evil.'

And when We made a covenant with you and raised the Mount above you, 2:93
saying: 'Hold fast to what We have given you and hear Our commandments,'
you[1] replied: 'We hear, and will not obey.'

For their unbelief they were made to drink down the calf into their hearts.[2]
Say: 'Evil is that to which your faith prompts you if you are true believers.'

1. Literally, they. 2. Cf. Exodus 32:20.

قل إن كانت لكم الدار الآخرة عند الله خالصة
من دون الناس فتمنوا الموت إن كنتم صادقين
﴿٩٤﴾ ولن يتمنوه أبدا بما قدمت أيديهم والله عليم
بالظالمين ﴿٩٥﴾ ولتجدنهم أحرص الناس على حيوة ومن
الذين أشركوا يود أحدهم لو يعمر ألف سنة وما
هو بمزحزحه من العذاب أن يعمر والله بصير بما
يعملون ﴿٩٦﴾ قل من كان عدوا لجبريل فإنه نزله على
قلبك بإذن الله مصدقا لما بين يديه وهدى
وبشرى للمؤمنين ﴿٩٧﴾ من كان عدوا لله وملئكته
ورسله وجبريل وميكال فإن الله عدو
للكافرين ﴿٩٨﴾ ولقد أنزلنا إليك آيات بينات وما يكفر بها
إلا الفاسقون ﴿٩٩﴾ أوكلما عاهدوا عهدا نبذه فريق منهم
بل أكثرهم لا يؤمنون ﴿١٠٠﴾ ولما جاءهم رسول من عند الله مصدق
لما معهم نبذ فريق من الذين أوتوا الكتاب
كتاب الله وراء ظهورهم كأنهم لا يعلمون ﴿١٠١﴾

2:94 SAY: 'IF God's Abode of
the Hereafter is for yourselves
alone, to the exclusion of
other people, then wish for
death if your claim be true!'
But they will never wish for
death, because of what they
did; and God knows the wrongdoers. Indeed, you will find
that, of all people, they love life
most: more than the pagans do.
Each of them would love to
live a thousand years. And even
if his life were indeed prolonged, that will surely not save
him from the scourge. God is
cognizant of what they do.
Say: 'Whoever is an enemy
of Gabriel' (who has by God's
grace revealed to you[1] the
Koran as a guide and joyful
tidings for the faithful, confirming previous Scriptures)
2:98 'whoever is an enemy of God, His angels, or His apostles, or of Gabriel or
Michael, will surely find that God is the enemy of the unbelievers.'
We have sent down to you clear revelations: none will deny them except
the ungodly. What! Whenever they make a covenant, must some of them
cast it aside? Most of them do not believe.
2:101 And now that an apostle has come to them from God confirming
their own Scriptures, some of those to whom the Book was given cast off
the Book of God over their backs, as though they know nothing of it,

1. Muḥammad.

واتبعوا ما تتلوا الشياطين على ملك سليمن وما كفر سليمن
ولكن الشياطين كفروا يعلمون الناس السحر وما
أنزل على الملكين ببابل هاروت وماروت وما يعلمان
من أحد حتى يقولا إنما نحن فتنة فلا تكفر
فيتعلمون منهما ما يفرقون به بين المرء وزوجه
وما هم بضارين به من أحد إلا بإذن الله ويتعلمون
ما يضرهم ولا ينفعهم ولقد علموا لمن اشتريه
ما له في الآخرة من خلاق ولبئس ما شروا به
أنفسهم لو كانوا يعلمون ﴿١٠٢﴾ ولو أنهم آمنوا
واتقوا لمثوبة من عند الله خير لو كانوا يعلمون
﴿١٠٣﴾ يا أيها الذين آمنوا لا تقولوا راعنا وقولوا انظرنا
واسمعوا وللكافرين عذاب أليم ﴿١٠٤﴾ ما يود الذين
كفروا من أهل الكتاب ولا المشركين أن ينزل
عليكم من خير من ربكم والله يختص
برحمته من يشاء والله ذو الفضل العظيم ﴿١٠٥﴾

and accept what the demons 2:102
tell of Solomon's kingdom. Not that Solomon was an unbeliever: it is the demons who are unbelievers. They teach the people witchcraft and that which was revealed to the angels Hārūt and Mārūt in Babylon. Yet they never instruct any without saying beforehand: 'We have been sent only to tempt you; do not blaspheme.' From these two, they learn that which creates discord between husband and wife, although they can harm none with what they learn except by God's leave. They learn what harms them and does not profit them; yet they knew full well that anyone who engaged in that traffic would have no share in the life to come. Vile is that for which
they have sold their souls, if they but knew it. Had they embraced the Faith 2:103
and feared God, far better for them would God's reward have been, if they but knew it.

Believers, do not say *rā'inā*, but say *unẓurnā*.[1] Take heed; woeful punishment awaits the unbelievers.

The unbelievers among the People of the Book, and the pagans, resent 2:105
that any blessings should have been sent down to you from your Lord. But God chooses whom He will for His mercy. God's grace is infinite.

1. The words mean 'listen to us' and 'look upon us' respectively; but in Judaeo-Arabic the sound of the first conveyed the sense, 'our evil one'.

2:106 ANY VERSE We abrogate or
cause to be forgotten, We will
replace by a better one or one
similar. Did you not know that
God has power over all things?
Did you not know that it is
God who has sovereignty over
the heavens and the earth, and
that there is none besides God
to protect or help you?
Or would you rather demand
of your Apostle that which was
once demanded of Moses? He
that barters faith for unbelief
has surely strayed from the
right path.
2:109 Many among the People of
the Book wish, through envy,
to lead you back to unbelief,
now that you have embraced
the Faith and the Truth has
been made plain to them. Forgive them and bear with them
until God makes known His will. God has power over all things.
Attend to your prayers and render the alms levy. Whatever good you do
shall be recompensed by God: God is watching all your actions.
And they declare: 'None shall enter Paradise but Jews and Christians.'
Such are their wishful fancies. Say: 'Let us have your proof, if what you say
2:112 be true.' Indeed, those that submit to God and do good works shall be recompensed by their Lord: they shall have nothing to fear or to regret.

ما ننسخ من آية او ننسها نأت بخير منها او مثلها الم
تعلم ان الله على كل شيء قدير ١٠٦ الم تعلم ان الله
له ملك السموات والارض وما لكم من دون الله
من ولي ولا نصير ١٠٧ ام تريدون ان تسئلوا رسولكم كما
سئل موسى من قبل ومن يتبدل الكفر بالايمان فقد ضل
سواء السبيل ١٠٨ ود كثير من اهل الكتاب لو يردونكم
من بعد ايمانكم كفارا حسدا من عند انفسهم من بعد
ما تبين لهم الحق فاعفوا واصفحوا حتى يأتي الله
بامره ان الله على كل شيء قدير ١٠٩ واقيموا الصلوة
واتوا الزكوة وما تقدموا لانفسكم من خير تجدوه
عند الله ان الله بما تعملون بصير ١١٠ وقالوا
لن يدخل الجنة الا من كان هودا او نصارى تلك
امانيهم قل هاتوا برهانكم ان كنتم صادقين ١١١
بلى من اسلم وجهه لله وهو محسن فله اجره
عند ربه ولا خوف عليهم ولا هم يحزنون ١١٢

وقالت اليهود ليست النصارى على شيء وقالت النصارى ليست
اليهود على شيء وهم يتلون الكتاب كذلك قال الذين لا يعلمون
مثل قولهم فالله يحكم بينهم يوم القيامة فيما كانوا
فيه يختلفون ﴿١١٣﴾ ومن أظلم ممن منع مساجد الله
أن يذكر فيها اسمه وسعى في خرابها أولئك ما كان لهم أن
يدخلوها إلا خائفين لهم في الدنيا خزي ولهم في الآخرة عذاب
عظيم ﴿١١٤﴾ ولله المشرق والمغرب فأينما تولوا فثم وجه
الله إن الله واسع عليم ﴿١١٥﴾ وقالوا اتخذ الله
ولدا سبحانه بل له ما في السماوات والأرض كل له
قانتون ﴿١١٦﴾ بديع السماوات والأرض وإذا قضى أمرا
فإنما يقول له كن فيكون ﴿١١٧﴾ وقال الذين لا يعلمون
لولا يكلمنا الله أو تأتينا آية كذلك قال الذين
من قبلهم مثل قولهم تشابهت قلوبهم قد بينا
الآيات لقوم يوقنون ﴿١١٨﴾ إنا أرسلناك بالحق
بشيرا ونذيرا ولا تسأل عن أصحاب الجحيم ﴿١١٩﴾

THE JEWS say the Christians 2:113
are misguided, and the Christians say it is the Jews who are misguided. Yet they both recite the Book. And the ignorant say the same of both. God will on the Day of Resurrection judge what they disagreed about.

And who is more wicked than those that forbid God's name to be pronounced in the mosques of God and seek to destroy them, when they should enter them only with fear in their hearts? They shall be held up to shame in this world, and in the world to come grievous punishment awaits them.

To God belongs the East 2:115
and the West. Whichever way you turn there is the Face of God. God is omnipresent and all-knowing.

And they say: 'God has begotten a son.' Glory be to Him! His is what the heavens and the earth contain; all is obedient to Him. Creator of the heavens and the earth! When He decrees a thing, He need only say 'Be,' and it is.

And the ignorant ask: 'Why does God not speak to us or give us a sign?' The same demand was made by those before them: their hearts are all alike. But to those whose faith is firm We have already revealed Our signs.

We have sent you forth to proclaim the Truth and to give warning. You 2:119
shall not be questioned about the heirs of Hell.

2:120 YOU WILL please neither the Jews nor the Christians unless you follow their faith. Say: 'God's guidance is the only guidance.' And if after all the knowledge you have been given you yield to their whims, there shall be none to help or protect you from God's ire. Those to whom We have given the Book, and who recite it as it ought to be recited, truly believe in it; those that dissent from it will surely be lost.

Children of Israel, remember the favour I have bestowed upon you, and that I exalted you above the nations. Guard yourselves against a day on which no soul shall stand in for another: when no ransom shall be accepted from it, no intercession avail it, no help be given it.

وَلَن تَرْضَىٰ عَنكَ الْيَهُودُ وَلَا النَّصَارَىٰ حَتَّىٰ تَتَّبِعَ مِلَّتَهُمْ قُلْ
إِنَّ هُدَى اللَّهِ هُوَ الْهُدَىٰ وَلَئِنِ اتَّبَعْتَ أَهْوَاءَهُم بَعْدَ الَّذِي جَاءَكَ
مِنَ الْعِلْمِ مَا لَكَ مِنَ اللَّهِ مِن وَلِيٍّ وَلَا نَصِيرٍ ﴿١٢٠﴾ الَّذِينَ آتَيْنَاهُمُ
الْكِتَابَ يَتْلُونَهُ حَقَّ تِلَاوَتِهِ أُولَٰئِكَ يُؤْمِنُونَ بِهِ وَمَن يَكْفُرْ بِهِ فَأُولَٰئِكَ
هُمُ الْخَاسِرُونَ ﴿١٢١﴾ يَا بَنِي إِسْرَائِيلَ اذْكُرُوا نِعْمَتِيَ الَّتِي أَنْعَمْتُ عَلَيْكُمْ
وَأَنِّي فَضَّلْتُكُمْ عَلَى الْعَالَمِينَ ﴿١٢٢﴾ وَاتَّقُوا يَوْمًا لَّا تَجْزِي نَفْسٌ عَن نَّفْسٍ
شَيْئًا وَلَا يُقْبَلُ مِنْهَا عَدْلٌ وَلَا تَنفَعُهَا شَفَاعَةٌ وَلَا هُمْ يُنصَرُونَ
﴿١٢٣﴾ وَإِذِ ابْتَلَىٰ إِبْرَاهِيمَ رَبُّهُ بِكَلِمَاتٍ فَأَتَمَّهُنَّ قَالَ إِنِّي جَاعِلُكَ
لِلنَّاسِ إِمَامًا قَالَ وَمِن ذُرِّيَّتِي قَالَ لَا يَنَالُ عَهْدِي الظَّالِمِينَ
﴿١٢٤﴾ وَإِذْ جَعَلْنَا الْبَيْتَ مَثَابَةً لِّلنَّاسِ وَأَمْنًا وَاتَّخِذُوا
مِن مَّقَامِ إِبْرَاهِيمَ مُصَلًّى وَعَهِدْنَا إِلَىٰ إِبْرَاهِيمَ وَإِسْمَاعِيلَ أَن
طَهِّرَا بَيْتِيَ لِلطَّائِفِينَ وَالْعَاكِفِينَ وَالرُّكَّعِ السُّجُودِ
﴿١٢٥﴾ وَإِذْ قَالَ إِبْرَاهِيمُ رَبِّ اجْعَلْ هَٰذَا بَلَدًا آمِنًا وَارْزُقْ أَهْلَهُ مِنَ
الثَّمَرَاتِ مَنْ آمَنَ مِنْهُم بِاللَّهِ وَالْيَوْمِ الْآخِرِ قَالَ وَمَن كَفَرَ
فَأُمَتِّعُهُ قَلِيلًا ثُمَّ أَضْطَرُّهُ إِلَىٰ عَذَابِ النَّارِ وَبِئْسَ الْمَصِيرُ ﴿١٢٦﴾

2:124 When his Lord put Abraham to the proof by enjoining on him certain commandments and Abraham fulfilled them, He said: 'I have appointed you a leader of mankind.'

'And what of my descendants?' Abraham asked.

'My covenant,' said He, 'does not apply to wrongdoers.'

We made the House[1] a resort and a sanctuary for mankind, saying: 'Make the place where Abraham stood a house of worship.' We enjoined Abraham and Ishmael to cleanse My House for those who walk round and round it, who meditate in it, and who kneel and prostrate themselves.

2:126 'Lord,' said Abraham, 'make this a secure land and bestow plenty upon its people, those of them that believe in God and the Last Day.'

'As for those that do not,' He answered, 'I shall let them live awhile, and then shall drag them to the scourge of the Fire: a wretched fate!'

1. The Ka'bah at Mecca.

وَإِذْ يَرْفَعُ إِبْرَٰهِـۧمُ ٱلْقَوَاعِدَ مِنَ ٱلْبَيْتِ وَإِسْمَٰعِيلُ رَبَّنَا تَقَبَّلْ مِنَّآ
إِنَّكَ أَنتَ ٱلسَّمِيعُ ٱلْعَلِيمُ ١٢٧ رَبَّنَا وَٱجْعَلْنَا مُسْلِمَيْنِ لَكَ وَمِن
ذُرِّيَّتِنَآ أُمَّةً مُّسْلِمَةً لَّكَ وَأَرِنَا مَنَاسِكَنَا وَتُبْ عَلَيْنَآ
إِنَّكَ أَنتَ ٱلتَّوَّابُ ٱلرَّحِيمُ ١٢٨ رَبَّنَا وَٱبْعَثْ فِيهِمْ رَسُولًا مِّنْهُمْ
يَتْلُوا۟ عَلَيْهِمْ ءَايَٰتِكَ وَيُعَلِّمُهُمُ ٱلْكِتَٰبَ وَٱلْحِكْمَةَ وَيُزَكِّيهِمْ
إِنَّكَ أَنتَ ٱلْعَزِيزُ ٱلْحَكِيمُ ١٢٩ وَمَن يَرْغَبُ عَن مِّلَّةِ إِبْرَٰهِـۧمَ إِلَّا
مَن سَفِهَ نَفْسَهُۥ وَلَقَدِ ٱصْطَفَيْنَٰهُ فِى ٱلدُّنْيَا وَإِنَّهُۥ فِى ٱلْءَاخِرَةِ
لَمِنَ ٱلصَّٰلِحِينَ ١٣٠ إِذْ قَالَ لَهُۥ رَبُّهُۥٓ أَسْلِمْ قَالَ أَسْلَمْتُ لِرَبِّ ٱلْعَٰلَمِينَ ١٣١
وَوَصَّىٰ بِهَآ إِبْرَٰهِـۧمُ بَنِيهِ وَيَعْقُوبُ يَٰبَنِىَّ إِنَّ ٱللَّهَ ٱصْطَفَىٰ
لَكُمُ ٱلدِّينَ فَلَا تَمُوتُنَّ إِلَّا وَأَنتُم مُّسْلِمُونَ ١٣٢ أَمْ
كُنتُمْ شُهَدَآءَ إِذْ حَضَرَ يَعْقُوبَ ٱلْمَوْتُ إِذْ قَالَ
لِبَنِيهِ مَا تَعْبُدُونَ مِنۢ بَعْدِى قَالُوا۟ نَعْبُدُ إِلَٰهَكَ
وَإِلَٰهَ ءَابَآئِكَ إِبْرَٰهِـۧمَ وَإِسْمَٰعِيلَ وَإِسْحَٰقَ إِلَٰهًا وَٰحِدًا
وَنَحْنُ لَهُۥ مُسْلِمُونَ ١٣٣ تِلْكَ أُمَّةٌ قَدْ خَلَتْ لَهَا مَا كَسَبَتْ
وَلَكُم مَّا كَسَبْتُمْ وَلَا تُسْـَٔلُونَ عَمَّا كَانُوا۟ يَعْمَلُونَ ١٣٤

Abraham and Ishmael laid 2:127
the foundations of the House
and dedicated it, saying: 'Accept
this from us, Lord. You are the
One that hears all and knows
all. Lord, make us submissive
to You; make of our descendants a community that will
submit to You. Teach us our
rites of worship and turn to
us with mercy; You are the
Forgiving One, the Compassionate. Lord, send forth to
them an apostle of their own
who shall declare to them Your
revelations, and shall instruct
them in the Book and in wisdom, and shall purify them of
sin. You are the Mighty, the
Wise One.'

Who but a foolish man
would renounce the faith of
Abraham? We chose him in
this world, and in the world to come he shall abide among the righteous.
When his Lord said to him: 'Submit,' he answered: 'I have submitted to the 2:131
Lord of the Universe.'

Abraham enjoined the Faith on his children, and so did Jacob, saying: 'My children, God has chosen the Faith for you. Do not depart this life except as Muslims.'

Were you present when death came to Jacob? He said to his children: 'What will you worship when I am gone?' They replied: 'We will worship your God and the God of your forefathers Abraham and Ishmael and Isaac: One God. To Him we will submit as Muslims.'

That community has passed away. Theirs is what they did and yours what 2:134
you have done. You shall not be questioned about their actions.

وقالوا كونوا هودا او نصارى تهتدوا قل بل ملة ابراهيم
حنيفا وما كان من المشركين قولوا امنا بالله وما انزل
الينا وما انزل الى ابراهيم واسمعيل واسحق ويعقوب والاسباط
وما اوتي موسى وعيسى وما اوتي النبيون من ربهم
لا نفرق بين احد منهم ونحن له مسلمون فان امنوا بمثل
ما امنتم به فقد اهتدوا وان تولوا فانما هم في شقاق
فسيكفيكهم الله وهو السميع العليم صبغة الله
ومن احسن من الله صبغة ونحن له عابدون
قل اتحاجوننا في الله وهو ربنا وربكم ولنا
اعمالنا ولكم اعمالكم ونحن له مخلصون
ام تقولون ان ابراهيم واسمعيل واسحق ويعقوب والاسباط
كانوا هودا او نصارى قل ءانتم اعلم ام الله
ومن اظلم ممن كتم شهادة عنده من الله وما الله
بغافل عما تعملون تلك امة قد خلت لها ما كسبت
ولكم ما كسبتم ولا تسئلون عما كانوا يعملون

2:135 THEY SAY: 'Follow the Jewish or the Christian Faith and you shall be rightly guided.'

Say: 'By no means! Only the faith of Abraham, the upright one. And he was no idolater.'

Say: 'We believe in God and that which has been revealed to us; in what was revealed to Abraham, Ishmael, Isaac, Jacob, and the tribes; to Moses and Jesus and the other prophets by their Lord. We make no distinction among any of them, and to Him we do submit as Muslims.'

If they believe as you believe, they shall be rightly guided; if they turn away, they shall surely be in schism. Against them God is your all-sufficient defender. And it is He that hears all and knows all.

We take on God's own dye.
And who has a better dye than God's? Him will we worship.
2:139 Say: 'Would you dispute with us about God, who is our Lord and your
Lord? We shall both be judged by our works. To Him alone we are devoted.

'Or do you claim that Abraham, Ishmael, Isaac, Jacob, and the tribes, were all Jews or Christians?' Say: 'Who knows better, you or God? Who is more wicked than he that hides a testimony he has received from God? God is never heedless of what you do.'

2:141 That community has passed away. Theirs is what they did and yours what
you have done. You shall not be questioned about their actions.

سيقول السفهاء من الناس ما ولىهم عن قبلتهم التي
كانوا عليها قل لله المشرق والمغرب يهدي من يشاء
إلى صراط مستقيم ﴿١٤٢﴾ وكذلك جعلناكم أمة وسطا
لتكونوا شهداء على الناس ويكون الرسول عليكم
شهيدا وما جعلنا القبلة التي كنت عليها إلا لنعلم من
يتبع الرسول ممن ينقلب على عقبيه وإن كانت لكبيرة إلا
على الذين هدى الله وما كان الله ليضيع إيمانكم إن
الله بالناس لرءوف رحيم ﴿١٤٣﴾ قد نرى تقلب وجهك
في السماء فلنولينك قبلة ترضىها فول وجهك شطر
المسجد الحرام وحيث ما كنتم فولوا وجوهكم شطره
وإن الذين أوتوا الكتاب ليعلمون أنه الحق من ربهم وما
الله بغافل عما يعملون ﴿١٤٤﴾ ولئن أتيت الذين أوتوا
الكتاب بكل آية ما تبعوا قبلتك وما أنت بتابع قبلتهم
وما بعضهم بتابع قبلة بعض ولئن اتبعت أهواءهم
من بعد ما جاءك من العلم إنك إذا لمن الظالمين ﴿١٤٥﴾

THE FOOLISH will ask: 2:142
'What has made them turn away from their former *qiblah*?'[1]

Say: 'The East and the West are God's. He guides whom He will to a straight path.'

Thus have We made you a just community, so that you may testify against mankind and that your own Apostle may testify against you. We decreed your former *qiblah* only in order that We might know the Apostle's true adherents and those who were to disown him. It was indeed a hard test, but not to those whom God has guided. God's aim was not to make your faith fruitless. God is benignant and compassionate to mankind.

Many a time have We seen 2:144
you[2] turn your face hither and thither towards the sky. We will henceforth make you turn towards a *qiblah* that will please you. Turn your face towards the Holy Mosque; wherever you[3] be, turn your faces towards it.

Those to whom the Book was given know this to be the Truth from their
Lord. God is never heedless of what they do. But even if you gave them 2:145
every proof they would not accept your *qiblah*, nor would you accept theirs; nor would any of them accept the *qiblah* of the other. If, after all the knowledge you have been given, you yield to their desires, then you will surely become a wrongdoer.

1. The direction which the Muslim faces in prayer. At first the believers were ordered to turn towards the 'Holy Temple' (Bayt al-Maqdis) in Jerusalem (thus Al-Bayḍāwī); afterwards to Mecca.
2. Muḥammad.
3. The faithful.

2:146 THOSE TO whom We gave
the Scriptures know him[1] as
they know their own sons.
But some of them deliberately
conceal the Truth. This is the
Truth from your Lord: therefore never doubt it.

Each one has a goal towards
which he turns. But wherever
you are, emulate one another
in good works. God will bring
you all before Him. God has
power over all things.

Whichever way you depart,
face towards the Holy Mosque.
This is surely the Truth from
your Lord. God is never heedless of what you do.

2:150 Whichever way you depart,
face towards the Holy Mosque:
and wherever you are, face
towards it, so that people will
have no cause to reproach
you, except the wrongdoers among them. Have no fear of them; fear Me, so
that I may perfect My favour to you and that you may be rightly guided.

Thus have We sent forth to you an apostle of your own who will recite to
you Our revelations and purify you of sin, who will instruct you in the Book
and in wisdom and teach you what you knew not. Remember Me, then, and
I will remember you. Give thanks to Me and never deny Me.

2:153 Believers, fortify yourselves with patience and with prayer; God is with
those that are patient.

الَّذِينَ آتَيْنَاهُمُ الْكِتَابَ يَعْرِفُونَهُ كَمَا يَعْرِفُونَ أَبْنَاءَهُمْ وَإِنَّ فَرِيقًا
مِنْهُمْ لَيَكْتُمُونَ الْحَقَّ وَهُمْ يَعْلَمُونَ ﴿١٤٦﴾ الْحَقُّ مِنْ رَبِّكَ فَلَا تَكُونَنَّ
مِنَ الْمُمْتَرِينَ ﴿١٤٧﴾ وَلِكُلٍّ وِجْهَةٌ هُوَ مُوَلِّيهَا فَاسْتَبِقُوا
الْخَيْرَاتِ أَيْنَ مَا تَكُونُوا يَأْتِ بِكُمُ اللَّهُ جَمِيعًا إِنَّ اللَّهَ
عَلَىٰ كُلِّ شَيْءٍ قَدِيرٌ ﴿١٤٨﴾ وَمِنْ حَيْثُ خَرَجْتَ فَوَلِّ وَجْهَكَ
شَطْرَ الْمَسْجِدِ الْحَرَامِ وَإِنَّهُ لَلْحَقُّ مِنْ رَبِّكَ وَمَا اللَّهُ
بِغَافِلٍ عَمَّا تَعْمَلُونَ ﴿١٤٩﴾ وَمِنْ حَيْثُ خَرَجْتَ فَوَلِّ وَجْهَكَ
شَطْرَ الْمَسْجِدِ الْحَرَامِ وَحَيْثُ مَا كُنْتُمْ فَوَلُّوا وُجُوهَكُمْ
شَطْرَهُ لِئَلَّا يَكُونَ لِلنَّاسِ عَلَيْكُمْ حُجَّةٌ إِلَّا الَّذِينَ ظَلَمُوا
مِنْهُمْ فَلَا تَخْشَوْهُمْ وَاخْشَوْنِي وَلِأُتِمَّ نِعْمَتِي عَلَيْكُمْ
وَلَعَلَّكُمْ تَهْتَدُونَ ﴿١٥٠﴾ كَمَا أَرْسَلْنَا فِيكُمْ رَسُولًا مِنْكُمْ
يَتْلُو عَلَيْكُمْ آيَاتِنَا وَيُزَكِّيكُمْ وَيُعَلِّمُكُمُ الْكِتَابَ
وَالْحِكْمَةَ وَيُعَلِّمُكُمْ مَا لَمْ تَكُونُوا تَعْلَمُونَ ﴿١٥١﴾ فَاذْكُرُونِي
أَذْكُرْكُمْ وَاشْكُرُوا لِي وَلَا تَكْفُرُونِ ﴿١٥٢﴾ يَا أَيُّهَا الَّذِينَ
آمَنُوا اسْتَعِينُوا بِالصَّبْرِ وَالصَّلَاةِ إِنَّ اللَّهَ مَعَ الصَّابِرِينَ ﴿١٥٣﴾

1. Muḥammad.

وَلَا تَقُولُوا لِمَنْ يُقْتَلُ فِي سَبِيلِ اللَّهِ أَمْوَاتٌ بَلْ أَحْيَاءٌ وَلَٰكِنْ
لَا تَشْعُرُونَ ﴿١٥٤﴾ وَلَنَبْلُوَنَّكُمْ بِشَيْءٍ مِنَ الْخَوْفِ وَالْجُوعِ وَنَقْصٍ
مِنَ الْأَمْوَالِ وَالْأَنْفُسِ وَالثَّمَرَاتِ وَبَشِّرِ الصَّابِرِينَ ﴿١٥٥﴾ الَّذِينَ
إِذَا أَصَابَتْهُمْ مُصِيبَةٌ قَالُوا إِنَّا لِلَّهِ وَإِنَّا إِلَيْهِ رَاجِعُونَ ﴿١٥٦﴾
أُولَٰئِكَ عَلَيْهِمْ صَلَوَاتٌ مِنْ رَبِّهِمْ وَرَحْمَةٌ وَأُولَٰئِكَ هُمُ الْمُهْتَدُونَ
﴿١٥٧﴾ إِنَّ الصَّفَا وَالْمَرْوَةَ مِنْ شَعَائِرِ اللَّهِ فَمَنْ حَجَّ الْبَيْتَ أَوِ اعْتَمَرَ فَلَا
جُنَاحَ عَلَيْهِ أَنْ يَطَّوَّفَ بِهِمَا وَمَنْ تَطَوَّعَ خَيْرًا فَإِنَّ اللَّهَ
شَاكِرٌ عَلِيمٌ ﴿١٥٨﴾ إِنَّ الَّذِينَ يَكْتُمُونَ مَا أَنْزَلْنَا مِنَ
الْبَيِّنَاتِ وَالْهُدَىٰ مِنْ بَعْدِ مَا بَيَّنَّاهُ لِلنَّاسِ فِي
الْكِتَابِ أُولَٰئِكَ يَلْعَنُهُمُ اللَّهُ وَيَلْعَنُهُمُ اللَّاعِنُونَ ﴿١٥٩﴾
إِلَّا الَّذِينَ تَابُوا وَأَصْلَحُوا وَبَيَّنُوا فَأُولَٰئِكَ أَتُوبُ عَلَيْهِمْ
وَأَنَا التَّوَّابُ الرَّحِيمُ ﴿١٦٠﴾ إِنَّ الَّذِينَ كَفَرُوا وَمَاتُوا وَهُمْ
كُفَّارٌ أُولَٰئِكَ عَلَيْهِمْ لَعْنَةُ اللَّهِ وَالْمَلَائِكَةِ وَالنَّاسِ أَجْمَعِينَ
﴿١٦١﴾ خَالِدِينَ فِيهَا لَا يُخَفَّفُ عَنْهُمُ الْعَذَابُ وَلَا هُمْ يُنْظَرُونَ
﴿١٦٢﴾ وَإِلَٰهُكُمْ إِلَٰهٌ وَاحِدٌ لَا إِلَٰهَ إِلَّا هُوَ الرَّحْمَٰنُ الرَّحِيمُ ﴿١٦٣﴾

DO NOT say that those slain in 2:154
the cause of God are dead.
They are alive, but you are not
aware of them.

We shall test your steadfastness with fear and famine, with loss of property and life and crops. Give joyful tidings to those who endure with fortitude; who in adversity say: 'We belong to God, and to Him we shall return.' On such shall be God's blessing and mercy; such are those that are rightly guided.

Ṣafā and Marwa[1] are two of God's beacons. It shall be no offence for the pilgrim or the visitor to the Sacred House to walk around them both. He that does good of his own accord shall be recompensed by God. God has knowledge of all things.

Those that hide the clear proofs and the guidance We have revealed to 2:159
mankind after We had proclaimed them in the Book shall be cursed by God
and cursed by those who invoke damnation; except those that repent and
mend their ways and make known the Truth. Towards them I shall relent. I
am the Relenting One, the Compassionate. But the infidels who die unbelievers shall incur the curse of God, the angels, and people all. Under it they
shall remain for ever; their punishment shall not be mitigated, nor shall they
be reprieved.

Your God is one God. There is no god but Him. He is the Merciful, the 2:163
Compassionate.

1. Two hills near Mecca, held in reverence by pagan Arabs.

2:164 SURELY IN the creation of
the heavens and the earth; in
the alternation of night and
day; in the ships that sail the
ocean with cargoes beneficial
to mankind; in the water which
God sends down from the sky
and with which He revives the
earth after its death, dispers-
ing over it all manner of
beasts; in the disposal of the
winds, and in the clouds that
are driven between sky and
earth: surely in these there are
signs for rational people.

And yet there are some who
worship idols, bestowing on
them the adoration due to God
(though the love of God is
stronger in the faithful). But
when they face their punishment the wrongdoers will learn
that might is God's alone, and
2:166 God is stern in retribution. When they face their punishment those who were
followed will disown their followers, and the bonds which now unite them will
break asunder. Those who followed them will say: 'Could we but live again, we
would disown them as they have now disowned us.'

Thus will God show them their own works. They shall sigh with remorse,
but shall never emerge from the Fire.

You people! Eat of what is lawful and wholesome on the earth and do not
2:169 walk in Satan's footsteps, for he is your veritable foe. He enjoins on you evil
and lewdness, and bids you assert about God what you know not.

إِنَّ فِي خَلْقِ السَّمَاوَاتِ وَالْأَرْضِ وَاخْتِلَافِ اللَّيْلِ وَالنَّهَارِ
وَالْفُلْكِ الَّتِي تَجْرِي فِي الْبَحْرِ بِمَا يَنْفَعُ النَّاسَ وَمَا أَنْزَلَ
اللَّهُ مِنَ السَّمَاءِ مِنْ مَاءٍ فَأَحْيَا بِهِ الْأَرْضَ بَعْدَ مَوْتِهَا
وَبَثَّ فِيهَا مِنْ كُلِّ دَابَّةٍ وَتَصْرِيفِ الرِّيَاحِ وَالسَّحَابِ
الْمُسَخَّرِ بَيْنَ السَّمَاءِ وَالْأَرْضِ لَآيَاتٍ لِقَوْمٍ يَعْقِلُونَ ١٦٤
وَمِنَ النَّاسِ مَنْ يَتَّخِذُ مِنْ دُونِ اللَّهِ أَنْدَادًا يُحِبُّونَهُمْ كَحُبِّ
اللَّهِ وَالَّذِينَ آمَنُوا أَشَدُّ حُبًّا لِلَّهِ وَلَوْ يَرَى الَّذِينَ ظَلَمُوا
إِذْ يَرَوْنَ الْعَذَابَ أَنَّ الْقُوَّةَ لِلَّهِ جَمِيعًا وَأَنَّ اللَّهَ
شَدِيدُ الْعَذَابِ ١٦٥ إِذْ تَبَرَّأَ الَّذِينَ اتُّبِعُوا مِنَ الَّذِينَ اتَّبَعُوا
وَرَأَوُا الْعَذَابَ وَتَقَطَّعَتْ بِهِمُ الْأَسْبَابُ ١٦٦ وَقَالَ الَّذِينَ اتَّبَعُوا
لَوْ أَنَّ لَنَا كَرَّةً فَنَتَبَرَّأَ مِنْهُمْ كَمَا تَبَرَّءُوا مِنَّا كَذَٰلِكَ يُرِيهِمُ اللَّهُ
أَعْمَالَهُمْ حَسَرَاتٍ عَلَيْهِمْ وَمَا هُمْ بِخَارِجِينَ مِنَ النَّارِ ١٦٧ يَا أَيُّهَا
النَّاسُ كُلُوا مِمَّا فِي الْأَرْضِ حَلَالًا طَيِّبًا وَلَا تَتَّبِعُوا خُطُوَاتِ
الشَّيْطَانِ إِنَّهُ لَكُمْ عَدُوٌّ مُبِينٌ ١٦٨ إِنَّمَا يَأْمُرُكُمْ بِالسُّوءِ
وَالْفَحْشَاءِ وَأَنْ تَقُولُوا عَلَى اللَّهِ مَا لَا تَعْلَمُونَ ١٦٩

وَإِذَا قِيلَ لَهُمُ اتَّبِعُوا مَا أَنزَلَ اللَّهُ قَالُوا بَلْ نَتَّبِعُ مَا
أَلْفَيْنَا عَلَيْهِ آبَاءَنَا أَوَلَوْ كَانَ آبَاؤُهُمْ لَا يَعْقِلُونَ شَيْئًا وَلَا
يَهْتَدُونَ ﴿١٧٠﴾ وَمَثَلُ الَّذِينَ كَفَرُوا كَمَثَلِ الَّذِي يَنْعِقُ بِمَا لَا
يَسْمَعُ إِلَّا دُعَاءً وَنِدَاءً صُمٌّ بُكْمٌ عُمْيٌ فَهُمْ لَا يَعْقِلُونَ ﴿١٧١﴾
يَا أَيُّهَا الَّذِينَ آمَنُوا كُلُوا مِن طَيِّبَاتِ مَا رَزَقْنَاكُمْ وَاشْكُرُوا
لِلَّهِ إِن كُنتُمْ إِيَّاهُ تَعْبُدُونَ ﴿١٧٢﴾ إِنَّمَا حَرَّمَ عَلَيْكُمُ الْمَيْتَةَ
وَالدَّمَ وَلَحْمَ الْخِنزِيرِ وَمَا أُهِلَّ بِهِ لِغَيْرِ اللَّهِ فَمَنِ اضْطُرَّ غَيْرَ
بَاغٍ وَلَا عَادٍ فَلَا إِثْمَ عَلَيْهِ إِنَّ اللَّهَ غَفُورٌ رَّحِيمٌ
﴿١٧٣﴾ إِنَّ الَّذِينَ يَكْتُمُونَ مَا أَنزَلَ اللَّهُ مِنَ الْكِتَابِ
وَيَشْتَرُونَ بِهِ ثَمَنًا قَلِيلًا أُولَٰئِكَ مَا يَأْكُلُونَ فِي
بُطُونِهِمْ إِلَّا النَّارَ وَلَا يُكَلِّمُهُمُ اللَّهُ يَوْمَ الْقِيَامَةِ وَلَا
يُزَكِّيهِمْ وَلَهُمْ عَذَابٌ أَلِيمٌ ﴿١٧٤﴾ أُولَٰئِكَ الَّذِينَ اشْتَرَوُا
الضَّلَالَةَ بِالْهُدَىٰ وَالْعَذَابَ بِالْمَغْفِرَةِ فَمَا أَصْبَرَهُمْ
عَلَى النَّارِ ﴿١٧٥﴾ ذَٰلِكَ بِأَنَّ اللَّهَ نَزَّلَ الْكِتَابَ
بِالْحَقِّ وَإِنَّ الَّذِينَ اخْتَلَفُوا فِي الْكِتَابِ لَفِي شِقَاقٍ بَعِيدٍ ﴿١٧٦﴾

IF THEY are told: 'Follow 2:170
what God has revealed,' they say: 'We will follow what our fathers practised,' even though their fathers understood nothing and had no guidance.

The unbelievers are like those that, call out to them as one may, can hear nothing but a shout and a cry. Deaf, dumb, and blind, they do not understand.

Believers, eat of the wholesome things with which We have provided you and give thanks to God, if it is Him you worship.

He has forbidden you car- 2:173
rion, blood, and the flesh of swine;[1] also any flesh that is consecrated other than in the name of God. But whoever is driven by necessity, intending neither to sin nor to transgress, shall incur no guilt. God is forgiving and compassionate.

Those that suppress any part of the Book which God has revealed in order to gain some paltry end shall swallow nothing but fire into their bellies. On the Day of Resurrection God will neither speak to them nor purify them. Woeful punishment awaits them.

Such are those that barter guidance for error and forgiveness for punishment. How steadfastly they seek the Fire! That is because God has revealed 2:176
the Book with the Truth; those that disagree about it are in extreme schism.

1. Cf. Leviticus 17:15; 17:10–12; and 11:7.

2:177 RIGHTEOUSNESS DOES
not consist in whether you
turn your faces to the East or
to the West. The righteous are
those who believe in God and
the Last Day, in the angels
and the Book and the prophets; who, though they love it
dearly, give their wealth to
kin, to orphans, to the destitute, to the traveller in need
and to beggars, and for the
redemption of captives; who
attend to their prayers and
render the alms levy; who are
true to their promises and
steadfast in trial and adversity
and in times of war. Such are
the true believers; such are
the God-fearing.

2:178 Believers, retaliation is decreed for you in bloodshed:
a free man for a free man, a
slave for a slave, and a female for a female. He who is pardoned by his
aggrieved brother shall be prosecuted according to usage and shall pay him
a liberal fine. This is a merciful dispensation from your Lord. Whoever transgresses thereafter, a woeful punishment awaits him.

In retaliation you have a safeguard for your lives – you that are of good
sense possessed; perchance you will fear God.

It is decreed that when death approaches, those of you that leave property
shall bequeath it equitably to parents and kin. This is a duty incumbent on
2:181 the God-fearing. He that alters a will after hearing it shall be accountable for
his crime: God hears all and knows all.

ليس البر أن تولوا وجوهكم قبل المشرق والمغرب
ولكن البر من آمن بالله واليوم الآخر والملائكة
والكتاب والنبيين وآتى المال على حبه ذوي القربى واليتامى
والمساكين وابن السبيل والسائلين وفي الرقاب وأقام
الصلوة وآتى الزكوة والموفون بعهدهم إذا عاهدوا
والصابرين في البأساء والضراء وحين البأس أولئك الذين
صدقوا وأولئك هم المتقون ١٧٧ يا أيها الذين آمنوا كتب
عليكم القصاص في القتلى الحر بالحر والعبد بالعبد والأنثى
بالأنثى فمن عفي له من أخيه شيء فاتباع بالمعروف وأداء إليه
بإحسان ذلك تخفيف من ربكم ورحمة فمن اعتدى بعد
ذلك فله عذاب أليم ١٧٨ ولكم في القصاص حيوة يا أولي
الألباب لعلكم تتقون ١٧٩ كتب عليكم إذا حضر
أحدكم الموت إن ترك خيرا الوصية للوالدين والأقربين
بالمعروف حقا على المتقين ١٨٠ فمن بدله بعد ما سمعه فإنما
إثمه على الذين يبدلونه إن الله سميع عليم ١٨١

فمن خاف من موص جنفا أو إثما فأصلح بينهم
فلا إثم عليه إن الله غفور رحيم ﴿١٨٢﴾ يا أيها
الذين آمنوا كتب عليكم الصيام كما كتب على الذين من
قبلكم لعلكم تتقون ﴿١٨٣﴾ أياما معدودات فمن كان
منكم مريضا أو على سفر فعدة من أيام أخر وعلى الذين
يطيقونه فدية طعام مسكين فمن تطوع خيرا فهو خير له
وأن تصوموا خير لكم إن كنتم تعلمون ﴿١٨٤﴾
شهر رمضان الذي أنزل فيه القرآن هدى للناس
وبينات من الهدى والفرقان فمن شهد منكم
الشهر فليصمه ومن كان مريضا أو على سفر فعدة
من أيام أخر يريد الله بكم اليسر ولا يريد
بكم العسر ولتكملوا العدة ولتكبروا
الله على ما هداكم ولعلكم تشكرون ﴿١٨٥﴾ وإذا
سألك عبادي عني فإني قريب أجيب دعوة الداع إذا دعان
فليستجيبوا لي وليؤمنوا بي لعلهم يرشدون ﴿١٨٦﴾

HE THAT suspects an error 2:182
or an injustice on the part of a
testator and brings about a
settlement among the parties
incurs no guilt. God is forgiving and compassionate.

Believers, fasting is decreed for you as it was decreed for those before you; perchance you will fear God. Fast a certain number of days, but if any one among you is ill or on a journey, let him fast a similar number of days later; and for those that cannot[1] endure it there is a penance ordained: the feeding of a poor man. He that does good of his own accord shall be well rewarded; but to fast is better for you, if you but knew it.

It was in the month of 2:185
Ramaḍān that the Koran was
revealed, a guide for mankind with proofs of guidance and Salvation.[2] Therefore whoever of you is present in that month let him fast. And he who is ill or on a journey shall fast a similar number of days later.

God desires your well-being, not your discomfort. He desires you to fast the whole month so that you may magnify God for His guidance and render thanks.

If My servants question you about Me, tell them that I am near. I answer 2:186
the prayer of the suppliant when he calls to Me; therefore let them answer
My call and put their trust in Me, that they may be rightly guided.

1. Thus Al-Jalālayn; the negative being understood. Alternatively: 'and for those well able to fast there is a penance ordained:'.
2. See p. 7, note 1.

2:187 IT IS now lawful for you to lie with your wives on the night of the fast; they are a comfort to you as you are a comfort to them. God knew that you were deceiving yourselves. He has relented towards you and pardoned you. Therefore you may now lie with them and seek what God has ordained for you. Eat and drink until you can tell a white thread from a black one in the light of the coming dawn. Then resume the fast till nightfall and do not approach them, when you should be preoccupied with your prayers in the mosques.

These are the bounds set by God: do not approach them. Thus God makes known His revelations to mankind that they may guard themselves against evil.

أحل لكم ليلة الصيام الرفث إلى نسائكم هن لباس
لكم وأنتم لباس لهن علم الله أنكم كنتم تختانون
أنفسكم فتاب عليكم وعفا عنكم فالآن
باشروهن وابتغوا ما كتب الله لكم وكلوا واشربوا
حتى يتبين لكم الخيط الأبيض من الخيط الأسود
من الفجر ثم أتموا الصيام إلى الليل ولا تباشروهن
وأنتم عاكفون في المساجد تلك حدود الله
فلا تقربوها كذلك يبين الله آياته للناس لعلهم
يتقون ﴿١٨٧﴾ ولا تأكلوا أموالكم بينكم بالباطل وتدلوا
بها إلى الحكام لتأكلوا فريقا من أموال الناس بالإثم
وأنتم تعلمون ﴿١٨٨﴾ يسألونك عن الأهلة قل هي مواقيت
للناس والحج وليس البر بأن تأتوا البيوت من ظهورها
ولكن البر من اتقى وأتوا البيوت من أبوابها واتقوا الله
لعلكم تفلحون ﴿١٨٩﴾ وقاتلوا في سبيل الله
الذين يقاتلونكم ولا تعتدوا إن الله لا يحب المعتدين ﴿١٩٠﴾

2:188 Do not devour one another's property by unjust means, nor bribe the judges with it in order that you may wrongfully and knowingly devour other people's possessions.

They ask you about the phases of the moon. Say: 'They are times set for the people and for the Pilgrimage.'

Righteousness does not consist in entering your dwellings from the back.[1] The righteous are those that fear God. Enter dwellings by their doors and fear God, so that you may prosper.

2:190 Fight in the cause of God those that fight you, but commit no aggression. God does not love the aggressors.

1. It was the custom of pagan Arabs, on returning from the Pilgrimage, to enter their homes from the back.

وَاقْتُلُوهُمْ حَيْثُ ثَقِفْتُمُوهُمْ وَأَخْرِجُوهُمْ مِنْ حَيْثُ أَخْرَجُوكُمْ وَالْفِتْنَةُ
أَشَدُّ مِنَ الْقَتْلِ وَلَا تُقَاتِلُوهُمْ عِنْدَ الْمَسْجِدِ الْحَرَامِ حَتَّىٰ يُقَاتِلُوكُمْ فِيهِ
فَإِنْ قَاتَلُوكُمْ فَاقْتُلُوهُمْ كَذَٰلِكَ جَزَاءُ الْكَافِرِينَ ﴿١٩١﴾ فَإِنِ انْتَهَوْا فَإِنَّ
اللَّهَ غَفُورٌ رَحِيمٌ ﴿١٩٢﴾ وَقَاتِلُوهُمْ حَتَّىٰ لَا تَكُونَ فِتْنَةٌ وَيَكُونَ الدِّينُ
لِلَّهِ فَإِنِ انْتَهَوْا فَلَا عُدْوَانَ إِلَّا عَلَى الظَّالِمِينَ ﴿١٩٣﴾ الشَّهْرُ الْحَرَامُ بِالشَّهْرِ
الْحَرَامِ وَالْحُرُمَاتُ قِصَاصٌ فَمَنِ اعْتَدَىٰ عَلَيْكُمْ فَاعْتَدُوا عَلَيْهِ بِمِثْلِ
مَا اعْتَدَىٰ عَلَيْكُمْ وَاتَّقُوا اللَّهَ وَاعْلَمُوا أَنَّ اللَّهَ مَعَ الْمُتَّقِينَ ﴿١٩٤﴾
وَأَنْفِقُوا فِي سَبِيلِ اللَّهِ وَلَا تُلْقُوا بِأَيْدِيكُمْ إِلَى التَّهْلُكَةِ وَأَحْسِنُوا إِنَّ
اللَّهَ يُحِبُّ الْمُحْسِنِينَ ﴿١٩٥﴾ وَأَتِمُّوا الْحَجَّ وَالْعُمْرَةَ لِلَّهِ فَإِنْ أُحْصِرْتُمْ فَمَا
اسْتَيْسَرَ مِنَ الْهَدْيِ وَلَا تَحْلِقُوا رُءُوسَكُمْ حَتَّىٰ يَبْلُغَ الْهَدْيُ مَحِلَّهُ
فَمَنْ كَانَ مِنْكُمْ مَرِيضًا أَوْ بِهِ أَذًى مِنْ رَأْسِهِ فَفِدْيَةٌ مِنْ صِيَامٍ
أَوْ صَدَقَةٍ أَوْ نُسُكٍ فَإِذَا أَمِنْتُمْ فَمَنْ تَمَتَّعَ بِالْعُمْرَةِ إِلَى الْحَجِّ فَمَا
اسْتَيْسَرَ مِنَ الْهَدْيِ فَمَنْ لَمْ يَجِدْ فَصِيَامُ ثَلَاثَةِ أَيَّامٍ فِي الْحَجِّ وَسَبْعَةٍ
إِذَا رَجَعْتُمْ تِلْكَ عَشَرَةٌ كَامِلَةٌ ذَٰلِكَ لِمَنْ لَمْ يَكُنْ أَهْلُهُ حَاضِرِي
الْمَسْجِدِ الْحَرَامِ وَاتَّقُوا اللَّهَ وَاعْلَمُوا أَنَّ اللَّهَ شَدِيدُ الْعِقَابِ ﴿١٩٦﴾

SLAY THEM wherever you 2:191
find them. Drive them out of the places from which they drove you. Idolatry[1] is more grievous than bloodshed. But do not fight them within the precincts of the Holy Mosque unless they attack you there; if they attack you, slay them. Thus shall the unbelievers be requited: but if they desist, God is forgiving and compassionate.

Fight them until idolatry is no more and God's religion reigns supreme. But if they desist, attack none except the wrongdoers.

A sacred month for a sacred 2:194
month: sacred things too are subject to retaliation. If anyone attacks you, attack him as he attacked you. Have fear of God, and know that God is with those that fear Him.

Give generously for the cause of God and do not with your own hands cast yourselves into destruction. Be charitable; God loves the charitable.

Make the Pilgrimage and the Visit for His sake. If you cannot, send such 2:196
offerings as you can afford and do not shave your heads until the offerings have reached their destination. But if any of you is ill or suffers from an ailment of the head, he must do penance either by fasting or by almsgiving or by offering a sacrifice.

If in peacetime anyone among you combines the Visit with the Pilgrimage, he must offer such gifts as he can afford; but if he lacks the means let him fast three days during the Pilgrimage and seven when he has returned; that is, ten days in all. That is incumbent on him whose family are not present at the Holy Mosque. Have fear of God, and know that God is stern in retribution.

1. Thus Al-Jalālayn. The noun *fitnah* occurs about thirty times in the Koran and is used in several different senses, according to context. It can also mean sedition, persecution, temptation, etc.

2:197 THE PILGRIMAGE shall be made in the appointed months. He that intends to perform it in those months must abstain from sexual intercourse, obscene language, and acrimonious disputes while on pilgrimage. God is aware of whatever good you do. Provide well for yourselves: the best provision is fear of God. Fear Me, then, you that are of good sense possessed.

It shall be no offence for you to seek the bounty of your Lord. When you come down from 'Arafāt[1] remember God as you approach the Sacred Monument. Remember Him that gave you guidance when you were assuredly among the
2:199 lost. Then go out from the
place whence the pilgrims will go out and implore the forgiveness of God. God is forgiving and compassionate. And when you have fulfilled your sacred duties, remember God as you remember your forefathers or with deeper reverence.

There are some who say: 'Lord, give us a good life in this world.' These shall have no share in the world to come. And there are some who say: 'Lord, give us what is good both in this world and in the world to come, and keep
2:202 us from the torment of the Fire.' These shall have a share, according to what
they did. Swift is God's reckoning.

الحج أشهر معلومات فمن فرض فيهن الحج
فلا رفث ولا فسوق ولا جدال في الحج وما تفعلوا
من خير يعلمه الله وتزودوا فإن خير الزاد
التقوى واتقون يا أولي الألباب ﴿١٩٧﴾ ليس عليكم
جناح أن تبتغوا فضلا من ربكم فإذا أفضتم
من عرفات فاذكروا الله عند المشعر الحرام
واذكروه كما هداكم وإن كنتم من قبله لمن
الضالين ﴿١٩٨﴾ ثم أفيضوا من حيث أفاض الناس
واستغفروا الله إن الله غفور رحيم ﴿١٩٩﴾ فإذا
قضيتم مناسككم فاذكروا الله كذكركم
آباءكم أو أشد ذكرا فمن الناس من يقول
ربنا آتنا في الدنيا وما له في الآخرة من
خلاق ﴿٢٠٠﴾ ومنهم من يقول ربنا آتنا في الدنيا حسنة
وفي الآخرة حسنة وقنا عذاب النار ﴿٢٠١﴾ أولئك
لهم نصيب مما كسبوا والله سريع الحساب ﴿٢٠٢﴾

1. Near Mecca.

وَاذكروا الله في أيام معدودات فمن تعجل في يومين
فلا إثم عليه ومن تأخر فلا إثم عليه لمن اتقى
واتقوا الله واعلموا أنكم إليه تحشرون ٢٠٣ ومن الناس
من يعجبك قوله في الحيوة الدنيا ويشهد الله على ما في قلبه
وهو ألد الخصام ٢٠٤ وإذا تولى سعى في الأرض
ليفسد فيها ويهلك الحرث والنسل والله لا يحب الفساد
٢٠٥ وإذا قيل له اتق الله أخذته العزة بالإثم
فحسبه جهنم ولبئس المهاد ٢٠٦ ومن الناس من يشري
نفسه ابتغاء مرضات الله والله رءوف بالعباد
٢٠٧ يا أيها الذين آمنوا ادخلوا في السلم كافة
ولا تتبعوا خطوات الشيطان إنه لكم عدو
مبين ٢٠٨ فإن زللتم من بعد ما جاءتكم
البينات فاعلموا أن الله عزيز حكيم ٢٠٩ هل
ينظرون إلا أن يأتيهم الله في ظلل من الغمام
والملئكة وقضي الأمر وإلى الله ترجع الأمور ٢١٠

GIVE GLORY to God on 2:203
appointed days. He that departs
in haste after two days incurs
no sin, nor does he who stays
on longer, if he truly fears
God. Have fear of God, then,
and know that before Him you
shall all be herded.

Among people there may
be one whose views on the life
of this world please you: he
even calls on God to vouch for
that which is in his heart;
whereas in fact he is the dead-
liest of adversaries. No sooner
does he turn away than he hastens to perpetrate evil in the
land, destroying crops and cattle; and God does not love evil.

And if he is told: 'Fear 2:206
God,' vanity carries him off to
sin. Sufficient is Hell for him;
an evil resting-place.

And among people there may be one who would give away his soul to find favour with God. God is compassionate to His creatures.

Believers, submit all of you to God and do not follow in Satan's footsteps; he is to you a veritable foe. If you lapse after the conspicuous signs that have come to you, know that God is mighty and wise.

Are they waiting for God to come down to them in the shadow of a 2:210
cloud, with the angels? But judgement has been duly passed, and to God
shall all return.

2:211 Ask the Israelites how many conspicuous signs We gave them. He that tampers with the gift of God after it had been bestowed on him shall find that God is stern in retribution.

For the unbelievers the life of this world is decked with all manner of temptations. They scoff at the faithful, but those that fear God shall be above them on the Day of Resurrection. God gives to whom He will without reckoning.

People were once but one community. Then God sent forth prophets to give them joyful tidings and to warn them, and with these He sent down the Book with the Truth, that it might serve as arbiter in people's disputes. None disputed it save those to whom it was given, and that was through envy of one another, after veritable signs had been vouchsafed them. So God guided by His will those who believed in the Truth which had been disputed. God guides whom He will to a straight path.

2:214 Or did you suppose that you would enter Paradise untouched by the suffering endured by those before you? Affliction and adversity befell them; and so shaken were they that each apostle, and those who shared his faith, cried out: 'When will God's help come?' Surely God's help is ever near.

2:215 They will ask you about almsgiving. Say: 'Whatever you give in charity shall go to parents and to kin, to the orphans and to the destitute, and to the traveller in need. God is fully aware of whatever good you do.'

سَلْ بَنِيٓ إِسْرَٰٓءِيلَ كَمْ ءَاتَيْنَٰهُم مِّنْ ءَايَةٍۭ بَيِّنَةٍ ۗ وَمَن يُبَدِّلْ نِعْمَةَ
ٱللَّهِ مِنۢ بَعْدِ مَا جَآءَتْهُ فَإِنَّ ٱللَّهَ شَدِيدُ ٱلْعِقَابِ ﴿٢١١﴾ زُيِّنَ
لِلَّذِينَ كَفَرُوا۟ ٱلْحَيَوٰةُ ٱلدُّنْيَا وَيَسْخَرُونَ مِنَ ٱلَّذِينَ ءَامَنُوا۟ ۘ وَٱلَّذِينَ
ٱتَّقَوْا۟ فَوْقَهُمْ يَوْمَ ٱلْقِيَٰمَةِ ۗ وَٱللَّهُ يَرْزُقُ مَن يَشَآءُ بِغَيْرِ حِسَابٍ
﴿٢١٢﴾ كَانَ ٱلنَّاسُ أُمَّةً وَٰحِدَةً فَبَعَثَ ٱللَّهُ ٱلنَّبِيِّـۧنَ مُبَشِّرِينَ
وَمُنذِرِينَ وَأَنزَلَ مَعَهُمُ ٱلْكِتَٰبَ بِٱلْحَقِّ لِيَحْكُمَ بَيْنَ ٱلنَّاسِ فِيمَا
ٱخْتَلَفُوا۟ فِيهِ ۚ وَمَا ٱخْتَلَفَ فِيهِ إِلَّا ٱلَّذِينَ أُوتُوهُ مِنۢ بَعْدِ
مَا جَآءَتْهُمُ ٱلْبَيِّنَٰتُ بَغْيًۢا بَيْنَهُمْ ۖ فَهَدَى ٱللَّهُ ٱلَّذِينَ ءَامَنُوا۟ لِمَا
ٱخْتَلَفُوا۟ فِيهِ مِنَ ٱلْحَقِّ بِإِذْنِهِۦ ۗ وَٱللَّهُ يَهْدِى مَن يَشَآءُ إِلَىٰ صِرَٰطٍ
مُّسْتَقِيمٍ ﴿٢١٣﴾ أَمْ حَسِبْتُمْ أَن تَدْخُلُوا۟ ٱلْجَنَّةَ وَلَمَّا يَأْتِكُم مَّثَلُ
ٱلَّذِينَ خَلَوْا۟ مِن قَبْلِكُم ۖ مَّسَّتْهُمُ ٱلْبَأْسَآءُ وَٱلضَّرَّآءُ وَزُلْزِلُوا۟
حَتَّىٰ يَقُولَ ٱلرَّسُولُ وَٱلَّذِينَ ءَامَنُوا۟ مَعَهُۥ مَتَىٰ نَصْرُ ٱللَّهِ ۗ أَلَآ إِنَّ نَصْرَ
ٱللَّهِ قَرِيبٌ ﴿٢١٤﴾ يَسْـَٔلُونَكَ مَاذَا يُنفِقُونَ ۖ قُلْ مَآ أَنفَقْتُم
مِّنْ خَيْرٍ فَلِلْوَٰلِدَيْنِ وَٱلْأَقْرَبِينَ وَٱلْيَتَٰمَىٰ وَٱلْمَسَٰكِينِ
وَٱبْنِ ٱلسَّبِيلِ ۗ وَمَا تَفْعَلُوا۟ مِنْ خَيْرٍ فَإِنَّ ٱللَّهَ بِهِۦ عَلِيمٌ ﴿٢١٥﴾

كتب عليكم القتال وهو كره لكم وعسى أن تكرهوا شيئا
وهو خير لكم وعسى أن تحبوا شيئا وهو شر لكم والله
يعلم وأنتم لا تعلمون ﴿٢١٦﴾ يسئلونك عن الشهر الحرام
قتال فيه قل قتال فيه كبير وصد عن سبيل الله
وكفر به والمسجد الحرام وإخراج أهله منه أكبر عند
الله والفتنة أكبر من القتل ولا يزالون يقاتلونكم
حتى يردوكم عن دينكم إن استطاعوا ومن يرتدد
منكم عن دينه فيمت وهو كافر فأولئك حبطت
أعمالهم في الدنيا والآخرة وأولئك أصحاب النار
هم فيها خالدون ﴿٢١٧﴾ إن الذين آمنوا والذين هاجروا
وجاهدوا في سبيل الله أولئك يرجون رحمت الله
والله غفور رحيم ﴿٢١٨﴾ يسئلونك عن الخمر والميسر
قل فيهما إثم كبير ومنافع للناس وإثمهما أكبر
من نفعهما ويسئلونك ماذا ينفقون قل العفو
كذلك يبين الله لكم الآيات لعلكم تتفكرون ﴿٢١٩﴾

FIGHTING IS obligatory 2:216
for you, much as you dislike it.
But you may hate a thing
although it is good for you,
and love a thing although it is
bad for you. God knows, but
you know not.

They ask you about the
Sacred Month and about
fighting therein. Say: 'To fight
in this month is a grave
offence; but to debar people
from the path of God, to
blaspheme against Him and
against the Holy Mosque, and
to expel its worshippers from
it, is more grievous in God's
sight. Idolatry[1] is more grievous than bloodshed.'

They will not cease to fight
you until they force you to
renounce your religion – if
they are able. But whoever
among you renounces his religion and dies an unbeliever, his works shall
come to nothing in this world and in the world to come. Such shall be the
tenants of the Fire, wherein shall they abide for ever.

Those that have embraced the Faith, and those that have fled their land 2:218
and fought for the cause of God, may hope for God's mercy. God is forgiving and compassionate.

They ask you about drinking and gambling. Say: 'There is great harm in 2:219
both, although they have some benefits for the people; but their harm is far
greater than their benefit.'

They ask you what they should give in alms. Say: 'What you can spare.'
Thus God makes plain to you His revelations so that you may reflect

1. Thus Al-Jalālayn. See p. 29, note 1.

2:220 upon this world and the Hereafter.

They question you concerning orphans. Say: 'To deal justly with them is best. If you mix their affairs with yours: they are your brothers: God knows the unjust from the just. If God pleased, He could afflict you. God is mighty and wise.'

You shall not wed pagan women, unless they embrace the Faith. A believing slave-girl is better than an idolatress, although she may please you. Nor shall you wed idolaters, unless they embrace the Faith. A believing slave is better than an idolater, although he may please you. These call you to the Fire; but God calls you, by His will, to Paradise and to forgiveness. He makes plain His revelations to mankind, so that they may remember.

2:222 They ask you about menstruation. Say: 'It is an indisposition. Keep aloof from women during their menstrual periods and do not approach them until they are clean again; when they are clean, have intercourse with them whence God enjoined you. God loves those that turn to Him in penitence and strive to keep themselves clean.'

Women are your fields: go, then, into your fields whence you please. Do good works and fear God. Know that you shall meet Him. Give joyful tidings to the believers.

2:224 And do not make God, when you swear by Him, a means to prevent you from dealing justly, from fearing Him, and from making peace among people. God hears all and knows all.

فِي الدُّنْيَا وَالْآخِرَةِ ۗ وَيَسْأَلُونَكَ عَنِ الْيَتَامَىٰ ۖ قُلْ إِصْلَاحٌ لَهُمْ خَيْرٌ ۖ
وَإِنْ تُخَالِطُوهُمْ فَإِخْوَانُكُمْ ۚ وَاللَّهُ يَعْلَمُ الْمُفْسِدَ مِنَ الْمُصْلِحِ ۚ
وَلَوْ شَاءَ اللَّهُ لَأَعْنَتَكُمْ ۚ إِنَّ اللَّهَ عَزِيزٌ حَكِيمٌ ﴿٢٢٠﴾ وَلَا
تَنْكِحُوا الْمُشْرِكَاتِ حَتَّىٰ يُؤْمِنَّ ۚ وَلَأَمَةٌ مُؤْمِنَةٌ خَيْرٌ مِنْ مُشْرِكَةٍ
وَلَوْ أَعْجَبَتْكُمْ ۗ وَلَا تُنْكِحُوا الْمُشْرِكِينَ حَتَّىٰ يُؤْمِنُوا ۚ وَلَعَبْدٌ
مُؤْمِنٌ خَيْرٌ مِنْ مُشْرِكٍ وَلَوْ أَعْجَبَكُمْ ۗ أُولَٰئِكَ يَدْعُونَ إِلَى
النَّارِ ۖ وَاللَّهُ يَدْعُو إِلَى الْجَنَّةِ وَالْمَغْفِرَةِ بِإِذْنِهِ ۖ وَيُبَيِّنُ
آيَاتِهِ لِلنَّاسِ لَعَلَّهُمْ يَتَذَكَّرُونَ ﴿٢٢١﴾ وَيَسْأَلُونَكَ عَنِ الْمَحِيضِ ۖ
قُلْ هُوَ أَذًى فَاعْتَزِلُوا النِّسَاءَ فِي الْمَحِيضِ ۖ وَلَا تَقْرَبُوهُنَّ
حَتَّىٰ يَطْهُرْنَ ۖ فَإِذَا تَطَهَّرْنَ فَأْتُوهُنَّ مِنْ حَيْثُ أَمَرَكُمُ
اللَّهُ ۚ إِنَّ اللَّهَ يُحِبُّ التَّوَّابِينَ وَيُحِبُّ الْمُتَطَهِّرِينَ ﴿٢٢٢﴾ نِسَاؤُكُمْ
حَرْثٌ لَكُمْ فَأْتُوا حَرْثَكُمْ أَنَّىٰ شِئْتُمْ ۖ وَقَدِّمُوا لِأَنْفُسِكُمْ ۚ
وَاتَّقُوا اللَّهَ وَاعْلَمُوا أَنَّكُمْ مُلَاقُوهُ ۗ وَبَشِّرِ الْمُؤْمِنِينَ ﴿٢٢٣﴾ وَلَا
تَجْعَلُوا اللَّهَ عُرْضَةً لِأَيْمَانِكُمْ أَنْ تَبَرُّوا وَتَتَّقُوا
وَتُصْلِحُوا بَيْنَ النَّاسِ ۗ وَاللَّهُ سَمِيعٌ عَلِيمٌ ﴿٢٢٤﴾

لا يؤاخذكم الله باللغو في أيمانكم ولكن يؤاخذكم بما كسبت
قلوبكم والله غفور حليم ﴿٢٢٥﴾ للذين يؤلون من نسائهم تربص
أربعة أشهر فإن فاءو فإن الله غفور رحيم ﴿٢٢٦﴾ وإن عزموا
الطلاق فإن الله سميع عليم ﴿٢٢٧﴾ والمطلقات يتربصن بأنفسهن ثلثة
قروء ولا يحل لهن أن يكتمن ما خلق الله في أرحامهن إن كن
يؤمن بالله واليوم الآخر وبعولتهن أحق بردهن في ذلك إن
أرادوا إصلاحا ولهن مثل الذي عليهن بالمعروف وللرجال عليهن
درجة والله عزيز حكيم ﴿٢٢٨﴾ الطلاق مرتان فإمساك بمعروف
أو تسريح بإحسان ولا يحل لكم أن تأخذوا مما آتيتموهن شيئا
إلا أن يخافا ألا يقيما حدود الله فإن خفتم ألا يقيما
حدود الله فلا جناح عليهما فيما افتدت به تلك حدود الله
فلا تعتدوها ومن يتعد حدود الله فأولئك هم الظالمون ﴿٢٢٩﴾
فإن طلقها فلا تحل له من بعد حتى تنكح زوجا غيره
فإن طلقها فلا جناح عليهما أن يتراجعا إن ظنا أن يقيما
حدود الله وتلك حدود الله يبينها لقوم يعلمون ﴿٢٣٠﴾

GOD WILL not call you to 2:225
account for that which is inadvertent in your oaths. But He
will take you to task for that
which is intended in your hearts.
God is forgiving and lenient.

Those that renounce their
wives on oath must wait four
months. If they change their
minds, God is forgiving and
compassionate; but if they
decide to divorce them, know
that God hears all and knows all.

Divorced women must wait, 2:228
keeping themselves from men,
three menstrual courses. It is
unlawful for them, if they
believe in God and the Last Day,
to hide what God has created in
their wombs: in which case their
husbands would do more justly
to take them back, should they
desire reconciliation.

Women shall with justice have rights similar to those exercised against
them, although men have a status above them. God is mighty and wise.

Divorce[1] may be pronounced twice, and then a woman shall be retained in 2:229
honour or allowed to go with kindness. It is unlawful for you to take from
them anything you gave them, unless both fear that they may not be able to
keep within the bounds set by God; in which case it shall be no offence for
either of them if the wife redeems herself.

These are the bounds set by God; do not transgress them. Those that
transgress the bounds of God are assuredly the wrongdoers.

If a man divorces[2] his wife, he shall not remarry her until she has wedded 2:230
another man and been divorced by him; in which case it shall be no offence
for either of them to return to the other, if they think they can keep within
the bounds set by God.

Such are the bounds of God. He makes them plain to those endowed
with knowledge.

1. Revocable divorce, or the renunciation of one's wife on oath.
2. By pronouncing the formula 'I divorce you' for the third time.

2:231 WHEN YOU have renounced your wives and they have reached the end of their waiting period, either retain them in honour or let them go with kindness. But you shall not retain them in order to harm them or to wrong them. Whoever does this wrongs his own soul.

Do not trifle with God's revelations. Remember the favour God has bestowed upon you, and the Book and the wisdom He has revealed for your instruction. Fear God and know that God has knowledge of all things.

When you have renounced your wives and they have reached the end of their waiting period, do not prevent them from remarrying their husbands if they have come to an honourable agreement. This is enjoined on every one of you who believes in God and the Last Day; this is more honourable for you and more chaste. God knows, and you know not.

2:233 Mothers shall give suck to their children for two whole years if the father wishes the sucking to be completed. They must be maintained and clothed in a reasonable manner by the child's father. None shall be charged with more than one can bear. A mother shall not be allowed to suffer on account of her child, nor shall a father on account of his child. The same duties devolve upon the father's heir. But if, by mutual consent and consultation, they choose to wean the child, they shall incur no offence. Nor shall it be any offence for you if you prefer to have a nurse for your children, provided that you pay her what you promise, according to usage. Fear God, and know that God is cognizant of what you do.

وَإِذَا طَلَّقْتُمُ النِّسَاءَ فَبَلَغْنَ أَجَلَهُنَّ فَأَمْسِكُوهُنَّ بِمَعْرُوفٍ
أَوْ سَرِّحُوهُنَّ بِمَعْرُوفٍ وَلَا تُمْسِكُوهُنَّ ضِرَارًا لِتَعْتَدُوا وَمَنْ يَفْعَلْ
ذَٰلِكَ فَقَدْ ظَلَمَ نَفْسَهُ وَلَا تَتَّخِذُوا آيَاتِ اللَّهِ هُزُوًا وَاذْكُرُوا نِعْمَتَ
اللَّهِ عَلَيْكُمْ وَمَا أَنْزَلَ عَلَيْكُمْ مِنَ الْكِتَابِ وَالْحِكْمَةِ
يَعِظُكُمْ بِهِ وَاتَّقُوا اللَّهَ وَاعْلَمُوا أَنَّ اللَّهَ بِكُلِّ شَيْءٍ عَلِيمٌ ﴿٢٣١﴾
وَإِذَا طَلَّقْتُمُ النِّسَاءَ فَبَلَغْنَ أَجَلَهُنَّ فَلَا تَعْضُلُوهُنَّ أَنْ يَنْكِحْنَ
أَزْوَاجَهُنَّ إِذَا تَرَاضَوْا بَيْنَهُمْ بِالْمَعْرُوفِ ذَٰلِكَ يُوعَظُ بِهِ مَنْ
كَانَ مِنْكُمْ يُؤْمِنُ بِاللَّهِ وَالْيَوْمِ الْآخِرِ ذَٰلِكُمْ أَزْكَىٰ لَكُمْ وَأَطْهَرُ
وَاللَّهُ يَعْلَمُ وَأَنْتُمْ لَا تَعْلَمُونَ ﴿٢٣٢﴾ وَالْوَالِدَاتُ يُرْضِعْنَ أَوْلَادَهُنَّ
حَوْلَيْنِ كَامِلَيْنِ لِمَنْ أَرَادَ أَنْ يُتِمَّ الرَّضَاعَةَ وَعَلَى الْمَوْلُودِ لَهُ رِزْقُهُنَّ
وَكِسْوَتُهُنَّ بِالْمَعْرُوفِ لَا تُكَلَّفُ نَفْسٌ إِلَّا وُسْعَهَا لَا تُضَارَّ وَالِدَةٌ
بِوَلَدِهَا وَلَا مَوْلُودٌ لَهُ بِوَلَدِهِ وَعَلَى الْوَارِثِ مِثْلُ ذَٰلِكَ فَإِنْ أَرَادَا
فِصَالًا عَنْ تَرَاضٍ مِنْهُمَا وَتَشَاوُرٍ فَلَا جُنَاحَ عَلَيْهِمَا وَإِنْ أَرَدْتُمْ
أَنْ تَسْتَرْضِعُوا أَوْلَادَكُمْ فَلَا جُنَاحَ عَلَيْكُمْ إِذَا سَلَّمْتُمْ مَا آتَيْتُمْ
بِالْمَعْرُوفِ وَاتَّقُوا اللَّهَ وَاعْلَمُوا أَنَّ اللَّهَ بِمَا تَعْمَلُونَ بَصِيرٌ ﴿٢٣٣﴾

والذين يتوفون منكم ويذرون أزواجا يتربصن بأنفسهن
أربعة أشهر وعشرا فإذا بلغن أجلهن فلا جناح عليكم
فيما فعلن في أنفسهن بالمعروف والله بما تعملون خبير ﴿٢٣٤﴾
ولا جناح عليكم فيما عرضتم به من خطبة النساء
أو أكننتم في أنفسكم علم الله أنكم ستذكرونهن
ولكن لا تواعدوهن سرا إلا أن تقولوا قولا معروفا
ولا تعزموا عقدة النكاح حتى يبلغ الكتاب أجله واعلموا
أن الله يعلم ما في أنفسكم فاحذروه واعلموا
أن الله غفور حليم ﴿٢٣٥﴾ لا جناح عليكم إن طلقتم
النساء ما لم تمسوهن أو تفرضوا لهن فريضة ومتعوهن
على الموسع قدره وعلى المقتر قدره متاعا بالمعروف
حقا على المحسنين ﴿٢٣٦﴾ وإن طلقتموهن من قبل أن تمسوهن
وقد فرضتم لهن فريضة فنصف ما فرضتم إلا أن يعفون
أو يعفو الذي بيده عقدة النكاح وأن تعفوا أقرب للتقوى
ولا تنسوا الفضل بينكم إن الله بما تعملون بصير ﴿٢٣٧﴾

THOSE OF you who die 2:234
and leave wives behind, their
widows shall wait, keeping to
themselves for four months
and ten days. When they have
reached the end of their waiting period, it shall be no
offence for you to let them
do whatever they choose for
themselves, provided that it is
decent. God is cognizant of
what you do.

It shall be no offence for you openly to propose marriage to such women or to cherish them in your hearts. God knows that you will remember them. But do not arrange to meet them in secret, and, if you do, speak to them honourably, and you shall not consummate the marriage before the end of their waiting period. Know that God has knowledge of all that is in your minds. Therefore fear Him and know that God is forgiving and lenient.

It shall be no offence for you to divorce your wives unless the marriage 2:236
has been consummated and the dowry settled. And provide for them; the
rich man according to his means and the poor man according to his: a fair
provision. This is incumbent on men of virtue. And if you divorce them 2:237
before the marriage is consummated, but after their dowry has been settled,
give them the half of their dowry, unless they or the husband agree to waive
it. But it is more proper and decent that the husband should waive it. Do not
forget to show kindness to each other. God is cognizant of what you do.

حافظوا على الصلوات والصلوة الوسطى وقوموا
لله قانتين ﴿٢٣٨﴾ فإن خفتم فرجالا أو ركبانا فإذا
أمنتم فاذكروا الله كما علمكم ما لم تكونوا تعلمون
﴿٢٣٩﴾ والذين يتوفون منكم ويذرون أزواجا وصية
لأزواجهم متاعا إلى الحول غير إخراج فإن خرجن
فلا جناح عليكم في ما فعلن في أنفسهن من معروف
والله عزيز حكيم ﴿٢٤٠﴾ وللمطلقات متاع بالمعروف
حقا على المتقين ﴿٢٤١﴾ كذلك يبين الله لكم آياته
لعلكم تعقلون ﴿٢٤٢﴾ ألم تر إلى الذين خرجوا من
ديارهم وهم ألوف حذر الموت فقال لهم
الله موتوا ثم أحياهم إن الله لذو فضل على
الناس ولكن أكثر الناس لا يشكرون ﴿٢٤٣﴾ وقاتلوا في سبيل
الله واعلموا أن الله سميع عليم ﴿٢٤٤﴾ من ذا الذي يقرض
الله قرضا حسنا فيضاعفه له أضعافا كثيرة
والله يقبض ويبصط وإليه ترجعون ﴿٢٤٥﴾

2:238 ATTEND REGULARLY to
your prayers, including the
middle prayer, and stand up
with all devotion before God.
When you are exposed to
danger pray on foot or while
riding; and when you are
restored to safety remember
God, as He has taught you
what you did not know.

Those of you who die
leaving wives behind shall
bequeath their widows a year's
maintenance without causing
them to leave their homes; but
if they leave of their own
accord, no blame shall be
attached to you for any course
they may deem reasonable to
pursue. God is mighty and
2:241 wise. Reasonable provision
shall also be made for divorced
women; this is incumbent on
those who fear God.

Thus God makes known to you His revelations that you may grow in understanding.

Consider those that fled their homes in their thousands for fear of death. God had said to them: 'You will die,' and then He brought them back to life. Surely God is bountiful to mankind, but most do not give thanks.

Fight for the cause of God, and know that He assuredly hears all and knows all.

2:245 Who will grant God a generous loan? He will repay him many times over. God gives abundantly and in scant measure. To Him shall you be recalled.

الم تر إلى الملإ من بني إسرائيل من بعد موسى إذ قالوا
لنبي لهم ابعث لنا ملكا نقاتل في سبيل الله
قال هل عسيتم إن كتب عليكم القتال ألا
تقاتلوا قالوا وما لنا ألا نقاتل في سبيل الله
وقد أخرجنا من ديارنا وأبنائنا فلما كتب
عليهم القتال تولوا إلا قليلا منهم والله
عليم بالظالمين ﴿٢٤٦﴾ وقال لهم نبيهم إن الله
قد بعث لكم طالوت ملكا قالوا أنى يكون له الملك
علينا ونحن أحق بالملك منه ولم يؤت سعة من
المال قال إن الله اصطفاه عليكم وزاده بسطة في
العلم والجسم والله يؤتي ملكه من يشاء والله
واسع عليم ﴿٢٤٧﴾ وقال لهم نبيهم إن آية
ملكه أن يأتيكم التابوت فيه سكينة من ربكم
وبقية مما ترك آل موسى وآل هارون تحمله الملائكة
إن في ذلك لآية لكم إن كنتم مؤمنين ﴿٢٤٨﴾

HAVE YOU not heard of 2:246
what the leaders of the Israelites demanded of a prophet of theirs after the death of Moses? 'Raise up for us a king,' they said, 'and we will fight for the cause of God.'

He replied: 'What if you refuse, when ordered so to fight?'

'Why should we refuse to fight for the cause of God,' they said, 'when we have been driven from our dwellings and our children?'

But when they were ordered to fight, they all refused, except a few of them. God knows the wrongdoers.

Their prophet said to them: 2:247
'God has appointed Saul to be your king.' They replied: 'Why should he be given the kingship, when we are more deserving of it than he? Besides, he has not been given abundant wealth.'

He said: 'God has chosen him to rule over you and made him grow in knowledge and in stature. God gives His sovereignty to whom He will. God is munificent and all-knowing.'

Their prophet also said to them: 'The portent of his reign shall be the 2:248
advent of the Ark. Therein shall be a Divine Presence[1] from your Lord, and the relics which the House of Moses and the House of Aaron left behind. It will be borne by the angels. That will be a sign for you, if you are true believers.'

1. The Arabic word *sakīnah* derives from the same Semitic root as *shekhīna* = Divine Presence. See also Arberry, who renders *sakīnah* as *Shechina* (without mention of its meaning in English).

2:249 AND WHEN Saul marched out with his warriors, he said: 'God will put you to the test at a certain river. He that drinks from it shall be no soldier of mine, but he that does not drink from it, or scoops a little in the hollow of his hand, shall fight by my side.'[1]

They all drank from it, except a few of them. And when he had crossed the river with those who shared his faith, they said: 'We have no power this day against Goliath and his warriors.'

Those of them who believed that they would meet with God said: 'Many a small band has, by God's grace, vanquished a mighty army. God is with those who endure with fortitude.'

2:250 And when they confronted Goliath and his warriors they said: 'Lord, fill our hearts with steadfastness; make us firm of foot and help us against the unbelievers.'

By God's will they routed them. David slew Goliath,[2] and God bestowed on him sovereignty and wisdom and taught him what He pleased. Had God not defeated some by the might of others, the earth would have been utterly corrupted. But God is bountiful to mankind.

2:252 Such are God's revelations: We recite them to you in all truth; and one of Our emissaries you surely are.

فَلَمَّا فَصَلَ طَالُوتُ بِالْجُنُودِ قَالَ إِنَّ اللَّهَ مُبْتَلِيكُمْ
بِنَهَرٍ فَمَنْ شَرِبَ مِنْهُ فَلَيْسَ مِنِّي وَمَنْ لَمْ يَطْعَمْهُ
فَإِنَّهُ مِنِّي إِلَّا مَنِ اغْتَرَفَ غُرْفَةً بِيَدِهِ فَشَرِبُوا مِنْهُ
إِلَّا قَلِيلًا مِنْهُمْ فَلَمَّا جَاوَزَهُ هُوَ وَالَّذِينَ آمَنُوا
مَعَهُ قَالُوا لَا طَاقَةَ لَنَا الْيَوْمَ بِجَالُوتَ وَجُنُودِهِ
قَالَ الَّذِينَ يَظُنُّونَ أَنَّهُمْ مُلَاقُو اللَّهِ كَمْ مِنْ
فِئَةٍ قَلِيلَةٍ غَلَبَتْ فِئَةً كَثِيرَةً بِإِذْنِ اللَّهِ وَاللَّهُ
مَعَ الصَّابِرِينَ ﴿٢٤٩﴾ وَلَمَّا بَرَزُوا لِجَالُوتَ وَجُنُودِهِ قَالُوا
رَبَّنَا أَفْرِغْ عَلَيْنَا صَبْرًا وَثَبِّتْ أَقْدَامَنَا وَانْصُرْنَا
عَلَى الْقَوْمِ الْكَافِرِينَ ﴿٢٥٠﴾ فَهَزَمُوهُمْ بِإِذْنِ
اللَّهِ وَقَتَلَ دَاوُودُ جَالُوتَ وَآتَاهُ اللَّهُ الْمُلْكَ
وَالْحِكْمَةَ وَعَلَّمَهُ مِمَّا يَشَاءُ وَلَوْلَا دَفْعُ اللَّهِ
النَّاسَ بَعْضَهُمْ بِبَعْضٍ لَفَسَدَتِ الْأَرْضُ وَلَٰكِنَّ
اللَّهَ ذُو فَضْلٍ عَلَى الْعَالَمِينَ ﴿٢٥١﴾ تِلْكَ آيَاتُ اللَّهِ
نَتْلُوهَا عَلَيْكَ بِالْحَقِّ وَإِنَّكَ لَمِنَ الْمُرْسَلِينَ ﴿٢٥٢﴾

1. Cf. Judges 7. 2. 1 Samuel 17.

تلك الرسل فضلنا بعضهم على بعض منهم من كلم الله
ورفع بعضهم درجات وآتينا عيسى ابن مريم البينات
وأيدناه بروح القدس ولو شاء الله ما اقتتل الذين من
بعدهم من بعد ما جاءتهم البينات ولكن اختلفوا فمنهم
من آمن ومنهم من كفر ولو شاء الله ما اقتتلوا ولكن الله
يفعل ما يريد ﴿٢٥٣﴾ يا أيها الذين آمنوا أنفقوا مما رزقناكم
من قبل أن يأتي يوم لا بيع فيه ولا خلة ولا شفاعة
والكافرون هم الظالمون ﴿٢٥٤﴾ الله لا إله إلا هو الحي القيوم
لا تأخذه سنة ولا نوم له ما في السماوات وما في الأرض من
ذا الذي يشفع عنده إلا بإذنه يعلم ما بين أيديهم وما
خلفهم ولا يحيطون بشيء من علمه إلا بما شاء وسع كرسيه
السماوات والأرض ولا يئوده حفظهما وهو العلي
العظيم ﴿٢٥٥﴾ لا إكراه في الدين قد تبين الرشد من الغي
فمن يكفر بالطاغوت ويؤمن بالله فقد استمسك
بالعروة الوثقى لا انفصام لها والله سميع عليم ﴿٢٥٦﴾

OF THESE emissaries We have 2:253
exalted some above others. To
some God spoke; others He
raised to a lofty status. We gave
Jesus son of Mary conspicuous
signs and strengthened him
with the Holy Spirit. Had God
pleased, those who succeeded
them would not have fought
each other after the conspicuous signs had been given them.
But they disagreed among
themselves; some had faith and
others had none. And had God
pleased they would not have
fought each other; but God
does what He will.

Believers, bestow in alms a 2:254
part of what We have given you
before that day arrives when
no commerce or friendship or
intercession shall avail. It is
the unbelievers who are the
wrongdoers.

God: there is no god but Him, the Living, the Eternal One.[1] Neither slumber nor sleep overtakes Him. His is what the heavens and the earth contain. Who can intercede with Him except by His permission? He knows what is before them and behind them. They can grasp only that part of His knowledge which He wills. His throne is as vast as the heavens and the earth, and the preservation of both does not weary Him. He is the Exalted, the Immense One.

There shall be no compulsion in religion. True guidance is now distinct 2:256
from error. He that renounces idol-worship and believes in God shall grasp
a firm handle that will never break. God hears all and knows all.

1. Al-Ḥayyu 'l Qayyūm; cf. Ḥāy wa Qiyyām, in the Old Testament.

2:257 God is the Patron of the faithful; He leads them from darkness to the light. As for the unbelievers, their patrons are false gods, who lead them from the light to darkness. They are the inmates of the Fire, wherein shall they abide for ever.

2:258 Have you not thought of him who argued with Abraham about his Lord because He had bestowed sovereignty upon him? Abraham said: 'My Lord is He who has power over life and death.'

'I, too,' replied the other, 'have power over life and death.'

'God brings up the sun from the east,' said Abraham. 'Bring it up yourself from the west.'

The unbeliever was confounded. God does not guide the wrongdoers.

2:259 Or of him, who, when passing by a ruined and desolate city, remarked: 'How can God give life to this city, now that it is dead?' Thereupon God caused him to die, and after a hundred years brought him back to life.

'How long have you been here?' God asked.

'A day,' he replied, 'or part of a day.'

God said: 'You have been here a hundred years. Yet look at your food and drink: they have not rotted. And look at your ass. We will make of you a sign for the people: and look at the bones, how We will revive them and clothe them with flesh.'

And when it had all become manifest to him, he said: 'Now I know that God has power over all things.'

اللّٰه ولي الذين آمنوا يخرجهم من الظلمات إلى النور
والذين كفروا أولياؤهم الطاغوت يخرجونهم من
النور إلى الظلمات أولئك أصحاب النار هم فيها
خالدون ٢٥٧ ألم تر إلى الذي حاج إبراهيم في ربه أن آتاه
الله الملك إذ قال إبراهيم ربي الذي يحيي ويميت قال
أنا أحيي وأميت قال إبراهيم فإن الله يأتي بالشمس من
المشرق فأت بها من المغرب فبهت الذي كفر
والله لا يهدي القوم الظالمين ٢٥٨ أو كالذي مر على
قرية وهي خاوية على عروشها قال أنى يحيي هذه
الله بعد موتها فأماته الله مائة عام ثم بعثه
قال كم لبثت قال لبثت يوما أو بعض يوم قال بل
لبثت مائة عام فانظر إلى طعامك وشرابك لم يتسنه
وانظر إلى حمارك ولنجعلك آية للناس وانظر
إلى العظام كيف ننشزها ثم نكسوها لحما
فلما تبين له قال أعلم أن الله على كل شيء قدير ٢٥٩

وإذ قال إبراهيم رب أرني كيف تحيي الموتى قال أولم
تؤمن قال بلى ولكن ليطمئن قلبي قال فخذ أربعة
من الطير فصرهن إليك ثم اجعل على كل جبل
منهن جزءا ثم ادعهن يأتينك سعيا واعلم أن الله
عزيز حكيم ٢٦٠ مثل الذين ينفقون أموالهم في سبيل الله
كمثل حبة أنبتت سبع سنابل في كل سنبلة مائة حبة والله
يضاعف لمن يشاء والله واسع عليم ٢٦١ الذين ينفقون
أموالهم في سبيل الله ثم لا يتبعون ما أنفقوا منا ولا
أذى لهم أجرهم عند ربهم ولا خوف عليهم ولا هم يحزنون ٢٦٢
قول معروف ومغفرة خير من صدقة يتبعها أذى والله
غني حليم ٢٦٣ يا أيها الذين آمنوا لا تبطلوا صدقاتكم بالمن
والأذى كالذي ينفق ماله رئاء الناس ولا يؤمن بالله
واليوم الآخر فمثله كمثل صفوان عليه تراب
فأصابه وابل فتركه صلدا لا يقدرون على
شيء مما كسبوا والله لا يهدي القوم الكافرين ٢٦٤

AND WHEN Abraham said: 2:260
'Show me, Lord, how You will raise the dead,' He replied: 'Have you no faith?'

'Yes,' said he, 'but just to reassure my heart.'

He said: 'Take four birds, and cut them to pieces. Scatter them over the mountain-tops, then call them back. They will come swiftly to you. Know that God is mighty and wise.'

Those that give their wealth 2:261
for the cause of God can be compared to a grain of corn which brings forth seven ears, each bearing a hundred grains. God gives more and more to whom He will; God is munificent and all-knowing.

Those that give their wealth for the cause of God and do not follow their almsgiving with taunts and insults shall be rewarded by their Lord; they shall have nothing to fear or to regret.

A kind word with forgiveness is better than charity followed by insult. God is self-sufficient and gracious.

Believers, do not nullify your almsgiving with taunts and mischief-making, 2:264
like him who spends his wealth only to be seen by people, and believes neither in God nor in the Last Day. He can be compared to a rock covered with earth: a shower falls upon it and leaves it hard and bare. They shall gain nothing from their works; and God does not guide the unbelievers.

2:265 BUT THOSE that give their wealth from a desire to please God and to reassure their own souls can be compared to an orchard on a hillside: if a shower falls upon it, it yields up twice its normal produce; and if no shower falls upon it, it's watered by the dew. God is cognizant of what you do.

Would any one of you, being well advanced in age with helpless children to support, wish to have an orchard planted with palm-trees, vines, and all manner of fruits, and watered by running brooks – only to be blasted and consumed by a fiery whirlwind?

Thus God makes plain to you His revelations, so that you may give thought.

2:267 You believers! Give in alms from the wealth you have lawfully earned and from that which We have brought out of the earth for you; not worthless things which you yourselves would but reluctantly accept. Know that God is self-sufficient and worthy of praise.

Satan threatens you with poverty and enjoins lewdness on you. But God promises you His forgiveness and His bounty: God is munificent and all-knowing.

2:269 He gives wisdom to whom He will; and he that receives the gift of wisdom is rich indeed. Yet none remembers but those that are of good sense possessed.

وَمَثَلُ الَّذِينَ يُنفِقُونَ أَمْوَالَهُمُ ابْتِغَاءَ مَرْضَاتِ
اللَّهِ وَتَثْبِيتًا مِّنْ أَنفُسِهِمْ كَمَثَلِ جَنَّةٍ بِرَبْوَةٍ أَصَابَهَا
وَابِلٌ فَآتَتْ أُكُلَهَا ضِعْفَيْنِ فَإِن لَّمْ يُصِبْهَا وَابِلٌ فَطَلٌّ
وَاللَّهُ بِمَا تَعْمَلُونَ بَصِيرٌ ﴿٢٦٥﴾ أَيَوَدُّ أَحَدُكُمْ أَن تَكُونَ لَهُ
جَنَّةٌ مِّن نَّخِيلٍ وَأَعْنَابٍ تَجْرِي مِن تَحْتِهَا الْأَنْهَارُ لَهُ فِيهَا
مِن كُلِّ الثَّمَرَاتِ وَأَصَابَهُ الْكِبَرُ وَلَهُ ذُرِّيَّةٌ ضُعَفَاءُ
فَأَصَابَهَا إِعْصَارٌ فِيهِ نَارٌ فَاحْتَرَقَتْ كَذَٰلِكَ يُبَيِّنُ
اللَّهُ لَكُمُ الْآيَاتِ لَعَلَّكُمْ تَتَفَكَّرُونَ ﴿٢٦٦﴾ يَا أَيُّهَا الَّذِينَ
آمَنُوا أَنفِقُوا مِن طَيِّبَاتِ مَا كَسَبْتُمْ وَمِمَّا أَخْرَجْنَا لَكُم
مِّنَ الْأَرْضِ وَلَا تَيَمَّمُوا الْخَبِيثَ مِنْهُ تُنفِقُونَ وَلَسْتُم
بِآخِذِيهِ إِلَّا أَن تُغْمِضُوا فِيهِ وَاعْلَمُوا أَنَّ اللَّهَ غَنِيٌّ حَمِيدٌ
﴿٢٦٧﴾ الشَّيْطَانُ يَعِدُكُمُ الْفَقْرَ وَيَأْمُرُكُم بِالْفَحْشَاءِ
وَاللَّهُ يَعِدُكُم مَّغْفِرَةً مِّنْهُ وَفَضْلًا وَاللَّهُ وَاسِعٌ عَلِيمٌ
﴿٢٦٨﴾ يُؤْتِي الْحِكْمَةَ مَن يَشَاءُ وَمَن يُؤْتَ الْحِكْمَةَ فَقَدْ
أُوتِيَ خَيْرًا كَثِيرًا وَمَا يَذَّكَّرُ إِلَّا أُولُو الْأَلْبَابِ ﴿٢٦٩﴾

وَمَآ أَنفَقْتُم مِّن نَّفَقَةٍ أَوْ نَذَرْتُم مِّن نَّذْرٍ فَإِنَّ
ٱللَّهَ يَعْلَمُهُۥ ۗ وَمَا لِلظَّٰلِمِينَ مِنْ أَنصَارٍ ﴿٢٧٠﴾ إِن تُبْدُوا۟
ٱلصَّدَقَٰتِ فَنِعِمَّا هِىَ ۖ وَإِن تُخْفُوهَا وَتُؤْتُوهَا ٱلْفُقَرَآءَ
فَهُوَ خَيْرٌ لَّكُمْ ۚ وَيُكَفِّرُ عَنكُم مِّن سَيِّـَٔاتِكُمْ ۗ
وَٱللَّهُ بِمَا تَعْمَلُونَ خَبِيرٌ ﴿٢٧١﴾ لَّيْسَ عَلَيْكَ هُدَىٰهُمْ وَلَٰكِنَّ
ٱللَّهَ يَهْدِى مَن يَشَآءُ ۗ وَمَا تُنفِقُوا۟ مِنْ خَيْرٍ
فَلِأَنفُسِكُمْ ۚ وَمَا تُنفِقُونَ إِلَّا ٱبْتِغَآءَ وَجْهِ
ٱللَّهِ ۚ وَمَا تُنفِقُوا۟ مِنْ خَيْرٍ يُوَفَّ إِلَيْكُمْ وَأَنتُمْ
لَا تُظْلَمُونَ ﴿٢٧٢﴾ لِلْفُقَرَآءِ ٱلَّذِينَ أُحْصِرُوا۟ فِى سَبِيلِ
ٱللَّهِ لَا يَسْتَطِيعُونَ ضَرْبًا فِى ٱلْأَرْضِ يَحْسَبُهُمُ
ٱلْجَاهِلُ أَغْنِيَآءَ مِنَ ٱلتَّعَفُّفِ تَعْرِفُهُم بِسِيمَٰهُمْ
لَا يَسْـَٔلُونَ ٱلنَّاسَ إِلْحَافًا ۗ وَمَا تُنفِقُوا۟ مِنْ خَيْرٍ فَإِنَّ
ٱللَّهَ بِهِۦ عَلِيمٌ ﴿٢٧٣﴾ ٱلَّذِينَ يُنفِقُونَ أَمْوَٰلَهُم بِٱلَّيْلِ
وَٱلنَّهَارِ سِرًّا وَعَلَانِيَةً فَلَهُمْ أَجْرُهُمْ عِندَ
رَبِّهِمْ وَلَا خَوْفٌ عَلَيْهِمْ وَلَا هُمْ يَحْزَنُونَ ﴿٢٧٤﴾

AND WHATEVER alms you 2:270
give and whatever vows you
make are known to God. The
wrongdoers shall have none
to help them.

To be charitable in public is
good, but to give alms to the
poor in private is better for
you and will atone for some
of your sins. God has knowledge of all your actions.

It is not for you to guide
them; God gives guidance to
whom He will.

Whatever alms you give
shall rebound to your own
advantage, provided that you
give them only for the love of
God. And whatever alms you
give shall be repaid to you in
full: you shall not be wronged.

As for the poor who are 2:273
preoccupied with fighting in
the cause of God, and cannot travel the land in quest of a livelihood: the
ignorant take them for men of wealth on account of their modest behav-
iour. But you recognize them by their look – they never importune people
for alms. Whatever alms you give are known to God.

Those that give of their wealth by night and by day, in private and in pub- 2:274
lic, shall be rewarded by their Lord and have nothing to fear or to regret.

2:275 THOSE THAT devour usury shall rise up before God like him that Satan has demented by his touch; for they claim that trading is no different from usury. But God has permitted trading and made usury unlawful. He that has received an admonition from his Lord and mended his ways may keep his previous gains; God will be his judge. Those that turn back shall be the inmates of the Fire, wherein shall they abide for ever.

God has laid His curse on usury and blessed almsgiving with increase. God bears no love for the impious and the sinful.

Those that believe and do good works, attend to their prayers and render the alms levy, shall be rewarded by their Lord and have nothing to fear or to regret.

2:278 Believers, fear God and waive what is still due to you from usury, if your faith be true; or war shall be declared against you by God and His apostle. If you repent, you may retain your principal, suffering no loss and causing loss to none.

If your debtor be in straits, grant him a delay until he can discharge his debt; but if you waive the sum as alms it will be better for you, if you but knew it.

2:281 Fear the day when you shall all return to God; and then every soul shall be paid back for what it did. None shall be wronged.

الَّذِينَ يَأْكُلُونَ الرِّبَوٰا لَا يَقُومُونَ إِلَّا كَمَا يَقُومُ الَّذِي
يَتَخَبَّطُهُ الشَّيْطَانُ مِنَ الْمَسِّ ذَٰلِكَ بِأَنَّهُمْ قَالُوا إِنَّمَا
الْبَيْعُ مِثْلُ الرِّبَوٰا وَأَحَلَّ اللَّهُ الْبَيْعَ وَحَرَّمَ الرِّبَوٰا فَمَن جَاءَهُ
مَوْعِظَةٌ مِّن رَّبِّهِ فَانتَهَىٰ فَلَهُ مَا سَلَفَ وَأَمْرُهُ إِلَى اللَّهِ
وَمَنْ عَادَ فَأُولَٰئِكَ أَصْحَابُ النَّارِ هُمْ فِيهَا خَالِدُونَ ﴿٢٧٥﴾ يَمْحَقُ اللَّهُ
الرِّبَوٰا وَيُرْبِي الصَّدَقَاتِ وَاللَّهُ لَا يُحِبُّ كُلَّ كَفَّارٍ أَثِيمٍ ﴿٢٧٦﴾ إِنَّ الَّذِينَ
آمَنُوا وَعَمِلُوا الصَّالِحَاتِ وَأَقَامُوا الصَّلَوٰةَ وَآتَوُا الزَّكَوٰةَ لَهُمْ
أَجْرُهُمْ عِندَ رَبِّهِمْ وَلَا خَوْفٌ عَلَيْهِمْ وَلَا هُمْ يَحْزَنُونَ ﴿٢٧٧﴾
يَا أَيُّهَا الَّذِينَ آمَنُوا اتَّقُوا اللَّهَ وَذَرُوا مَا بَقِيَ مِنَ الرِّبَوٰا إِن
كُنتُم مُّؤْمِنِينَ ﴿٢٧٨﴾ فَإِن لَّمْ تَفْعَلُوا فَأْذَنُوا بِحَرْبٍ مِّنَ اللَّهِ
وَرَسُولِهِ وَإِن تُبْتُمْ فَلَكُمْ رُءُوسُ أَمْوَالِكُمْ لَا تَظْلِمُونَ
وَلَا تُظْلَمُونَ ﴿٢٧٩﴾ وَإِن كَانَ ذُو عُسْرَةٍ فَنَظِرَةٌ إِلَىٰ
مَيْسَرَةٍ وَأَن تَصَدَّقُوا خَيْرٌ لَّكُمْ إِن كُنتُمْ
تَعْلَمُونَ ﴿٢٨٠﴾ وَاتَّقُوا يَوْمًا تُرْجَعُونَ فِيهِ إِلَى اللَّهِ
ثُمَّ تُوَفَّىٰ كُلُّ نَفْسٍ مَّا كَسَبَتْ وَهُمْ لَا يُظْلَمُونَ ﴿٢٨١﴾

يا أيها الذين آمنوا إذا تداينتم بدين إلى أجل مسمى
فاكتبوه وليكتب بينكم كاتب بالعدل ولا يأب
كاتب أن يكتب كما علمه الله فليكتب وليملل
الذي عليه الحق وليتق الله ربه ولا يبخس منه شيئا
فإن كان الذي عليه الحق سفيها أو ضعيفا أو لا يستطيع
أن يمل هو فليملل وليه بالعدل واستشهدوا شهيدين
من رجالكم فإن لم يكونا رجلين فرجل وامرأتان ممن
ترضون من الشهداء أن تضل إحداهما فتذكر إحداهما
الأخرى ولا يأب الشهداء إذا ما دعوا ولا تسأموا أن
تكتبوه صغيرا أو كبيرا إلى أجله ذلكم أقسط عند
الله وأقوم للشهادة وأدنى ألا ترتابوا إلا أن تكون
تجارة حاضرة تديرونها بينكم فليس عليكم جناح ألا
تكتبوها وأشهدوا إذا تبايعتم ولا يضار كاتب
ولا شهيد وإن تفعلوا فإنه فسوق بكم واتقوا
الله ويعلمكم الله والله بكل شيء عليم ٢٨٢

BELIEVERS, WHEN you 2:282
contract a debt for a fixed period, put it in writing. Let a scribe write it down for you with fairness; no scribe should refuse to write as God has taught him. Therefore let him write; and let the debtor dictate, fearing God his Lord and not diminishing the sum he owes. If the debtor be an ignorant or feeble-minded person, or one who cannot dictate, let his guardian dictate for him in fairness. Call in two male witnesses from among you, but if two men cannot be found, then one man and two women whom you judge fit to act as witnesses; so that if either of them make an error, the other will remind her. Witnesses shall not refuse if called upon to give evidence. So do not fail to put your debts in writing, be they small or large, together with the date of payment. This is more just in the sight of God; it ensures accuracy in testifying and is the best way to remove all doubt. But if the transaction be a bargain concluded on the spot, it shall be no offence for you if you do not put it into writing.

See that witnesses are present when you barter with one another, and let no harm be done to either scribe or witness. If you harm them you will commit a transgression. Have fear of God; God teaches you, and God has knowledge of all things.

2:283 IF YOU are travelling the road and cannot find a scribe, then let pledges be given. If one of you entrusts another with a pledge, let the trustee restore the pledge to its owner; and let him fear God, his Lord.

You shall not withhold testimony; sinful is the heart of him who withholds it. God has knowledge of what you do.

To God belongs all that the heavens and the earth contain. Whether you reveal your thoughts or hide them, God will bring you to account for them. He will forgive whom He will and punish whom He pleases; God has power over all things.

2:285 The Apostle believes in
what has been revealed to
him by his Lord, and so do the faithful. They all believe in God and His
angels, His Scriptures, and His apostles: We discriminate against none of His
apostles. They say: 'We hear and obey. Grant us Your forgiveness, Lord; to
2:286 You shall all return. God does not charge a soul with more than it can bear.
It shall be requited for whatever good and whatever evil it has done. Lord,
do not reproach us if we forget or lapse into error. Lord, do not lay on us a
burden such as You laid on those before us. Lord, do not charge us with
more than we can bear. Pardon us, forgive us our sins, and have mercy upon
us; You alone are our Protector. Give us victory over the unbelievers.'

وإن كنتم على سفر ولم تجدوا كاتبا فرهان مقبوضة فإن
أمن بعضكم بعضا فليؤد الذي اؤتمن أمانته وليتق الله
ربه ولا تكتموا الشهادة ومن يكتمها فإنه آثم قلبه
والله بما تعملون عليم ٢٨٣ لله ما في السماوات وما في الأرض
وإن تبدوا ما في أنفسكم أو تخفوه يحاسبكم به
الله فيغفر لمن يشاء ويعذب من يشاء والله
على كل شيء قدير ٢٨٤ آمن الرسول بما أنزل إليه من
ربه والمؤمنون كل آمن بالله وملائكته وكتبه
ورسله لا نفرق بين أحد من رسله وقالوا
سمعنا وأطعنا غفرانك ربنا وإليك المصير ٢٨٥ لا يكلف
الله نفسا إلا وسعها لها ما كسبت وعليها ما اكتسبت
ربنا لا تؤاخذنا إن نسينا أو أخطأنا ربنا
ولا تحمل علينا إصرا كما حملته على الذين من قبلنا ربنا
ولا تحملنا ما لا طاقة لنا به واعف عنا واغفر لنا وارحمنا
أنت مولانا فانصرنا على القوم الكافرين ٢٨٦

سورة آل عمران مدنية وهي مائتا آية

بسم الله الرحمن الرحيم
الم ١ الله لا إله إلا هو الحي القيوم ٢ نزل عليك الكتاب بالحق
مصدقا لما بين يديه وأنزل التوراة والإنجيل ٣ من قبل هدى للناس
وأنزل الفرقان إن الذين كفروا بآيات الله لهم عذاب شديد
والله عزيز ذو انتقام ٤ إن الله لا يخفى عليه شيء في
الأرض ولا في السماء ٥ هو الذي يصوركم في الأرحام كيف
يشاء لا إله إلا هو العزيز الحكيم ٦ هو الذي أنزل عليك الكتاب
منه آيات محكمات هن أم الكتاب وأخر متشابهات فأما الذين في قلوبهم
زيغ فيتبعون ما تشابه منه ابتغاء الفتنة وابتغاء تأويله وما يعلم
تأويله إلا الله والراسخون في العلم يقولون آمنا به كل من عند
ربنا وما يذكر إلا أولو الألباب ٧ ربنا لا تزغ قلوبنا بعد
إذ هديتنا وهب لنا من لدنك رحمة إنك أنت الوهاب ٨
ربنا إنك جامع الناس ليوم لا ريب فيه إن الله لا يخلف الميعاد ٩

THE HOUSE OF ʻIMRĀN

In the Name of God,
the Merciful, the Compassionate

Alif *lām mīm.* God! There is 3:1
no god but Him, the Living,
the Ever-existent One.
He has revealed to you the
Book with the Truth, confirming that which preceded it; for
He had already revealed the
Torah and the Gospel for the
guidance of mankind, and
revealed Salvation.[1]
Those that deny God's
revelations shall be sternly
punished; God is mighty and
capable of revenge. Nothing
on earth or in heaven is hidden
from God. It is He who shapes your bodies in your mothers' wombs as He 3:6
pleases. There is no god but Him, the Mighty, the Wise One.
It is He who has revealed to you the Book. Some of its verses are precise
in meaning – they are the foundation of the Book – and others ambiguous.
Those whose hearts are infected with disbelief observe the ambiguous part,
so as to create dissension by seeking to explain it. But no one knows its
meaning except God. Those who are well-grounded in knowledge say: 'We
believe in it: it is all from our Lord. Yet none remembers but those that are
of good sense possessed. Lord, do not cause our hearts to go astray after
You have guided us. Grant us mercy through Your own grace; You are the
munificent Giver. Lord, You will surely gather up all mankind upon a day of 3:9
which there is no doubt. God will not fail the time appointed.'

1. See p. 7, note 1.

3:10 As FOR the unbelievers, neither their riches nor their children will in the least save them from God's judgement. They will surely be the fuel of the Fire. Like Pharaoh's people and those before them, they denied Our revelations, and God smote them in their sins: God is stern in retribution.

Say to the unbelievers: 'You shall be overthrown and driven into Hell – an evil resting-place!'

3:13 Indeed, there was a sign for you in the two armies which met on the battlefield.[1] One was fighting for the cause of God, the other being a host of unbelievers. The faithful saw with their very eyes that they were twice their own number. But God strengthens with His aid whom He will. Surely in that there was a lesson for the discerning.

Men are tempted by the lure of women and offspring, of hoarded treasures of gold and silver, of splendid horses, cattle, and plantations. These are the enjoyments of this life, but far better is the return to God.

3:15 Say: 'Shall I tell you of better things than these, with which the God-fearing shall be rewarded by their Lord? Gardens watered by running brooks, wherein shall they abide for ever: spouses of perfect chastity and grace from God.'

God is ever observant of His servants,

إِنَّ الَّذِينَ كَفَرُوا لَنْ تُغْنِيَ عَنْهُمْ أَمْوَالُهُمْ وَلَا أَوْلَادُهُمْ مِنَ
اللَّهِ شَيْئًا وَأُولَٰئِكَ هُمْ وَقُودُ النَّارِ ﴿١٠﴾ كَدَأْبِ آلِ
فِرْعَوْنَ وَالَّذِينَ مِنْ قَبْلِهِمْ كَذَّبُوا بِآيَاتِنَا فَأَخَذَهُمُ
اللَّهُ بِذُنُوبِهِمْ وَاللَّهُ شَدِيدُ الْعِقَابِ ﴿١١﴾ قُلْ لِلَّذِينَ
كَفَرُوا سَتُغْلَبُونَ وَتُحْشَرُونَ إِلَىٰ جَهَنَّمَ وَبِئْسَ الْمِهَادُ ﴿١٢﴾
قَدْ كَانَ لَكُمْ آيَةٌ فِي فِئَتَيْنِ الْتَقَتَا فِئَةٌ تُقَاتِلُ فِي سَبِيلِ
اللَّهِ وَأُخْرَىٰ كَافِرَةٌ يَرَوْنَهُمْ مِثْلَيْهِمْ رَأْيَ الْعَيْنِ
وَاللَّهُ يُؤَيِّدُ بِنَصْرِهِ مَنْ يَشَاءُ إِنَّ فِي ذَٰلِكَ لَعِبْرَةً لِأُولِي
الْأَبْصَارِ ﴿١٣﴾ زُيِّنَ لِلنَّاسِ حُبُّ الشَّهَوَاتِ مِنَ النِّسَاءِ
وَالْبَنِينَ وَالْقَنَاطِيرِ الْمُقَنْطَرَةِ مِنَ الذَّهَبِ وَالْفِضَّةِ
وَالْخَيْلِ الْمُسَوَّمَةِ وَالْأَنْعَامِ وَالْحَرْثِ ذَٰلِكَ مَتَاعُ الْحَيَاةِ الدُّنْيَا
وَاللَّهُ عِنْدَهُ حُسْنُ الْمَآبِ ﴿١٤﴾ قُلْ أَؤُنَبِّئُكُمْ بِخَيْرٍ مِنْ
ذَٰلِكُمْ لِلَّذِينَ اتَّقَوْا عِنْدَ رَبِّهِمْ جَنَّاتٌ تَجْرِي مِنْ
تَحْتِهَا الْأَنْهَارُ خَالِدِينَ فِيهَا وَأَزْوَاجٌ مُطَهَّرَةٌ
وَرِضْوَانٌ مِنَ اللَّهِ وَاللَّهُ بَصِيرٌ بِالْعِبَادِ ﴿١٥﴾

1. In the Battle of Badr. See p. 176, notes 1 and 2.

الذين يقولون ربنا إننا آمنا فاغفر لنا ذنوبنا وقنا
عذاب النار ﴿١٦﴾ الصابرين والصادقين والقانتين والمنفقين
والمستغفرين بالأسحار ﴿١٧﴾ شهد الله أنه لا إله إلا هو
والملائكة وأولوا العلم قائما بالقسط لا إله إلا هو
العزيز الحكيم ﴿١٨﴾ إن الدين عند الله الإسلام
وما اختلف الذين أوتوا الكتاب إلا من بعد ما جاءهم
العلم بغيا بينهم ومن يكفر بآيات الله فإن الله
سريع الحساب ﴿١٩﴾ فإن حاجوك فقل أسلمت وجهي لله
ومن اتبعن وقل للذين أوتوا الكتاب والأميين
أأسلمتم فإن أسلموا فقد اهتدوا وإن تولوا فإنما
عليك البلاغ والله بصير بالعباد ﴿٢٠﴾ إن الذين
يكفرون بآيات الله ويقتلون النبيين بغير حق
ويقتلون الذين يأمرون بالقسط من الناس فبشرهم
بعذاب أليم ﴿٢١﴾ أولئك الذين حبطت أعمالهم
في الدنيا والآخرة وما لهم من ناصرين ﴿٢٢﴾

those who say: 'Lord, we do 3:16
believe: forgive us our sins and
keep us from the torment of
the Fire'; who are steadfast,
sincere, obedient, and charitable;
and who implore
forgiveness at break of day.

God bears witness that
there is no god but Him, and
so do the angels and the sages;
the Executor of Justice, the
Only God, the Almighty, the
Wise One.

The only religion in God's
sight is Islām. Those to whom
the Book was given dissented,
through insolence, only after
knowledge had been vouchsafed
them. He that denies
God's revelations should know
that swift is God's reckoning.

If they argue with you, say: 3:20
'I have submitted my face to
God and so have those that follow me.'

And to those who were given the Book and to the Gentiles say: 'Will you submit to God?' If they embrace Islām, they shall be rightly guided; and if they pay no heed, then your only duty is to warn them. God is ever observant of His creatures.

Those that deny God's revelations, and slay the prophets unjustly, and kill
those among the people who preach fair dealing – warn them of a woeful
scourge. Their works shall come to nothing in this world and in the world to 3:22
come, and there shall be none to help them.

3:23 Do BUT consider those
who have received a portion of the Book: when they are called on to accept the judgement of God's Book, some turn their backs and pay no heed. For they declare: 'We shall endure the Fire for a few days only.' In their religion they are deceived by their own lies.

What will they do when We gather them all together upon a day of which there is no doubt, when every soul will be given what it has earned, with none treated unjustly?

3:26 Say: 'Lord, Sovereign of all
sovereignty, You bestow sovereignty on whom You will and take sovereignty away from whom You please; You exalt whomever You will and abase whomever You please. In Your hand all goodness lies; You have power over all things. You cause the night to pass into the day, and the day to pass into the night; You bring forth the living from the dead and You bring forth the dead from the living. You give without reckoning to whom You will.'

Let not believers take infidels as their friends in preference to the faithful – he that does this has nothing to hope for from God – except in self-defence. God admonishes you to fear Him: for to God shall all return.

3:29 Say: 'Whether you hide what is in your hearts or reveal it, it is known to
God. He knows all that the heavens and the earth contain; and God has power over all things.'

ألم تر إلى الذين أوتوا نصيبا من الكتاب يدعون
إلى كتاب الله ليحكم بينهم ثم يتولى فريق منهم وهم
معرضون ﴿٢٣﴾ ذلك بأنهم قالوا لن تمسنا النار إلا أياما
معدودات وغرهم في دينهم ما كانوا يفترون ﴿٢٤﴾ فكيف
إذا جمعناهم ليوم لا ريب فيه ووفيت كل نفس ما كسبت
وهم لا يظلمون ﴿٢٥﴾ قل اللهم مالك الملك تؤتي الملك
من تشاء وتنزع الملك ممن تشاء وتعز من تشاء وتذل
من تشاء بيدك الخير إنك على كل شيء قدير ﴿٢٦﴾ تولج الليل
في النهار وتولج النهار في الليل وتخرج الحي من الميت وتخرج
الميت من الحي وترزق من تشاء بغير حساب ﴿٢٧﴾ لا يتخذ
المؤمنون الكافرين أولياء من دون المؤمنين ومن يفعل ذلك
فليس من الله في شيء إلا أن تتقوا منهم تقية
ويحذركم الله نفسه وإلى الله المصير ﴿٢٨﴾ قل إن تخفوا ما في
صدوركم أو تبدوه يعلمه الله ويعلم ما في السماوات
وما في الأرض والله على كل شيء قدير ﴿٢٩﴾

يوم تجد كل نفس ما عملت من خير محضرا وما عملت من سوء
تود لو أن بينها وبينه أمدا بعيدا ويحذركم الله نفسه
والله رءوف بالعباد ٣٠ قل إن كنتم تحبون الله فاتبعوني
يحببكم الله ويغفر لكم ذنوبكم والله غفور
رحيم ٣١ قل أطيعوا الله والرسول فإن تولوا فإن الله لا يحب
الكافرين ٣٢ إن الله اصطفى آدم ونوحا وآل إبراهيم
وآل عمران على العالمين ٣٣ ذرية بعضها من بعض
والله سميع عليم ٣٤ إذ قالت امرأت عمران رب إني نذرت
لك ما في بطني محررا فتقبل مني إنك أنت السميع العليم ٣٥
فلما وضعتها قالت رب إني وضعتها أنثى والله أعلم بما
وضعت وليس الذكر كالأنثى وإني سميتها مريم وإني أعيذها بك
وذريتها من الشيطان الرجيم ٣٦ فتقبلها ربها بقبول
حسن وأنبتها نباتا حسنا وكفلها زكريا كلما دخل عليها
زكريا المحراب وجد عندها رزقا قال يا مريم أنى لك هذا قالت
هو من عند الله إن الله يرزق من يشاء بغير حساب ٣٧

THE DAY will surely come 3:30
when each soul will be confronted with whatever good it did. As for its evil deeds, it will wish them far away. God admonishes you to fear Him. God is kindly to His servants.

Say: 'If you love God, follow me. God will love you and forgive you your sins; God is forgiving and compassionate.'

Say: 'Obey God and the Apostle.' If they pay no heed, then, surely, God does not love the unbelievers.

God exalted Adam and Noah, Abraham's descendants and the descendants of 'Imrān[1] above the nations. They were the offspring of one another. God hears all and knows all.

Remember the words of 'Imrān's[2] wife. 'Lord,' she said, 'I dedicate to You that which is in my womb. Accept it from me; You alone hear all and know all.'

And when she was delivered of the child, she said: 'Lord, I have given 3:36
birth to a daughter' – God knew better of what she was delivered: the male is not like the female – 'and have named her Mary. I beseech you to protect her and all her descendants from Satan, the Accursed One.'

Her Lord graciously accepted her. He made her grow a goodly child and 3:37
entrusted her to the care of Zacharias.[3]

Whenever Zacharias visited her in the Shrine he found she had food with her. 'Mary,' he said, 'where is this food from?'

'It is from God,' she answered. 'God gives without reckoning to whom He will.'

1. Amram, the father of Moses and Aaron (Exodus 6:20).
2. In the Koran, 'Imrān (Amram) is also the Virgin Mary's father.
3. Or Zachariah. See Luke 1:12–22 for the accepted spelling of the name.

3:38 THEREUPON ZACHARIAS prayed to his Lord, saying: 'Lord, grant me of Your own grace upright descendants; You hear all prayers.'

And as he stood praying in the Shrine, the angels called out to him, saying: 'God bids you rejoice in the birth of John, who shall confirm the Word of God. He shall be princely and chaste, a prophet and a righteous man.'

'Lord,' he said, 'how shall I have a son when I am now overtaken by old age and my wife is barren?'

'Such is the will of God,' He said. 'He does what He pleases.'

'Lord,' said he, 'vouchsafe me a sign.'

'Your sign is that for three days and three nights,' He replied, 'you shall not speak to people except by symbols. Remember your Lord always; give glory to Him evening and morning.'

هنالك دعا زكريا ربه قال رب هب لى من لدنك ذرية
طيبة إنك سميع الدعاء ﴿٣٨﴾ فنادته الملئكة وهو
قائم يصلى فى المحراب أن الله يبشرك بيحيى مصدقا
بكلمة من الله وسيدا وحصورا ونبيا من
الصالحين ﴿٣٩﴾ قال رب أنى يكون لى غلام وقد بلغنى الكبر
وامرأتى عاقر قال كذلك الله يفعل ما يشاء ﴿٤٠﴾ قال
رب اجعل لى آية قال آيتك ألا تكلم الناس ثلثة أيام
إلا رمزا واذكر ربك كثيرا وسبح بالعشى والإبكار ﴿٤١﴾
وإذ قالت الملئكة يامريم إن الله اصطفيك وطهرك
واصطفيك على نساء العالمين ﴿٤٢﴾ يامريم اقنتى
لربك واسجدى واركعى مع الراكعين ﴿٤٣﴾ ذلك من أنباء الغيب
نوحيه إليك وما كنت لديهم إذ يلقون أقلامهم أيهم
يكفل مريم وما كنت لديهم إذ يختصمون ﴿٤٤﴾ إذ قالت
الملئكة يامريم إن الله يبشرك بكلمة منه اسمه المسيح
عيسى ابن مريم وجيها فى الدنيا والآخرة ومن المقربين ﴿٤٥﴾

3:42 And remember the angels' words to Mary. They said:[1] 'God has chosen you. He has made you pure and exalted you above womankind. Mary, be obedient to your Lord; bow down and worship with the worshippers.'

This is an account of a divine secret: We reveal it to you.[2] You were not present when they cast lots to see which of them should have charge of Mary; nor were you present when they argued about her.

3:45 The angels said: 'Mary, God bids you rejoice in a Word from Him. His name is the Christ, Jesus son of Mary; noble in this world and in the world to come, and one of the favoured.

1. Cf. Luke 1:26–38.
2. Muḥammad.

وَيُكَلِّمُ النَّاسَ فِي الْمَهْدِ وَكَهْلًا وَمِنَ الصَّالِحِينَ ﴿٤٦﴾ قَالَتْ
رَبِّ أَنَّىٰ يَكُونُ لِي وَلَدٌ وَلَمْ يَمْسَسْنِي بَشَرٌ قَالَ كَذَٰلِكِ اللَّهُ
يَخْلُقُ مَا يَشَاءُ إِذَا قَضَىٰ أَمْرًا فَإِنَّمَا يَقُولُ لَهُ كُن فَيَكُونُ
﴿٤٧﴾ وَيُعَلِّمُهُ الْكِتَابَ وَالْحِكْمَةَ وَالتَّوْرَاةَ وَالْإِنجِيلَ
﴿٤٨﴾ وَرَسُولًا إِلَىٰ بَنِي إِسْرَائِيلَ أَنِّي قَدْ جِئْتُكُم بِآيَةٍ مِّن
رَّبِّكُمْ أَنِّي أَخْلُقُ لَكُم مِّنَ الطِّينِ كَهَيْئَةِ الطَّيْرِ فَأَنفُخُ فِيهِ
فَيَكُونُ طَيْرًا بِإِذْنِ اللَّهِ وَأُبْرِئُ الْأَكْمَهَ وَالْأَبْرَصَ
وَأُحْيِي الْمَوْتَىٰ بِإِذْنِ اللَّهِ وَأُنَبِّئُكُم بِمَا تَأْكُلُونَ
وَمَا تَدَّخِرُونَ فِي بُيُوتِكُمْ إِنَّ فِي ذَٰلِكَ لَآيَةً لَّكُمْ إِن
كُنتُم مُّؤْمِنِينَ ﴿٤٩﴾ وَمُصَدِّقًا لِّمَا بَيْنَ يَدَيَّ مِنَ التَّوْرَاةِ
وَلِأُحِلَّ لَكُم بَعْضَ الَّذِي حُرِّمَ عَلَيْكُمْ وَجِئْتُكُم بِآيَةٍ
مِّن رَّبِّكُمْ فَاتَّقُوا اللَّهَ وَأَطِيعُونِ ﴿٥٠﴾ إِنَّ اللَّهَ
رَبِّي وَرَبُّكُمْ فَاعْبُدُوهُ هَٰذَا صِرَاطٌ مُّسْتَقِيمٌ ﴿٥١﴾ فَلَمَّا أَحَسَّ
عِيسَىٰ مِنْهُمُ الْكُفْرَ قَالَ مَنْ أَنصَارِي إِلَى اللَّهِ قَالَ الْحَوَارِيُّونَ
نَحْنُ أَنصَارُ اللَّهِ آمَنَّا بِاللَّهِ وَاشْهَدْ بِأَنَّا مُسْلِمُونَ ﴿٥٢﴾

HE SHALL preach to people 3:46
in his cradle and in the prime of manhood, and shall lead a righteous life.'

'Lord,' she said, 'how can I bear a child when no man has touched me?'

He said: 'Even thus: God creates whom He will. If He decrees a thing He need only say: "Be," and it is. He will instruct him in the Scriptures and in wisdom, in the Torah
and in the Gospel, and send 3:49
him forth an apostle to the Israelites. He will say: "I bring you a sign from your Lord. From clay I will create for you the likeness of a bird. I shall breathe into it and, by God's leave, it shall become a living bird. By God's leave I shall heal the blind man and the leper, and raise the dead to life. I shall tell you what to eat and what to store up in your houses. Surely that will be a sign for you, if you are true believers. I come to confirm the Torah which preceded me and to make lawful for you some of the things you are forbidden. I bring you a sign from your Lord: therefore fear God and obey me. Surely God is my Lord and your Lord: therefore worship Him. That is a straight path."'

And when Jesus observed that they had no faith, he said: 'Who will help 3:52
me in the cause of God?'

The disciples replied: 'We are God's helpers. We believe in God, and bear witness that we are Muslims.

3:53 LORD, WE believe in Your revelations and follow the apostle. Count us among Your witnesses.'

They contrived, and God contrived; God is the supreme Contriver. God said: 'Jesus, I am about to claim you back and lift you up to Me. I shall cleanse you of the unbelievers and exalt your followers above them till the Day of Resurrection. Then to Me you shall all return and I shall judge your dissensions. To the unbelievers I shall mete out grievous punishment in this world and in the world to come: there shall be none to help them. As for those that have faith and do good works, He will give them their rewards in full. God does not love the wrongdoers.'

ربنا امنا بما انزلت واتبعنا الرسول فاكتبنا مع الشاهدين
(٥٣) ومكروا ومكر الله والله خير الماكرين (٥٤) اذ قال
الله يا عيسى اني متوفيك ورافعك الي ومطهرك من الذين
كفروا وجاعل الذين اتبعوك فوق الذين كفروا الى يوم
القيمة ثم الي مرجعكم فاحكم بينكم فيما كنتم
فيه تختلفون (٥٥) فاما الذين كفروا فاعذبهم عذابا
شديدا في الدنيا والاخرة وما لهم من ناصرين (٥٦)
واما الذين امنوا وعملوا الصالحات فيوفيهم اجورهم
والله لا يحب الظالمين (٥٧) ذلك نتلوه عليك من
الايات والذكر الحكيم (٥٨) ان مثل عيسى عند
الله كمثل ادم خلقه من تراب ثم قال له كن فيكون
(٥٩) الحق من ربك فلا تكن من الممترين (٦٠) فمن
حاجك فيه من بعد ما جاءك من العلم فقل تعالوا ندع
ابناءنا وابناءكم ونساءنا ونساءكم وانفسنا وانفسكم
ثم نبتهل فنجعل لعنت الله على الكاذبين (٦١)

3:58 This revelation, and the Wise Admonition, We recite to you. Jesus can be compared to Adam in the sight of God. He created him from dust and then said to him: 'Be,' and he was.

3:61 This is the Truth from your Lord: therefore do not doubt it. To those that dispute with you concerning him after the knowledge you have received, say: 'Come, let us gather our sons and your sons, our wives and your wives, our people and your people. We will then fervently pray and call down the curse of God on the liars.'

إن هذا لهو القصص الحق ۚ وما من إله إلا الله ۚ وإن الله
لهو العزيز الحكيم ﴿٦٢﴾ فإن تولوا فإن الله عليم بالمفسدين
﴿٦٣﴾ قل يا أهل الكتاب تعالوا إلى كلمة سواء بيننا
وبينكم ألا نعبد إلا الله ولا نشرك به شيئا ولا
يتخذ بعضنا بعضا أربابا من دون الله ۚ فإن تولوا
فقولوا اشهدوا بأنا مسلمون ﴿٦٤﴾ يا أهل الكتاب لم تحاجون
في إبراهيم وما أنزلت التوراة والإنجيل إلا من بعده ۚ أفلا
تعقلون ﴿٦٥﴾ ها أنتم هؤلاء حاججتم فيما لكم به علم فلم
تحاجون فيما ليس لكم به علم ۚ والله يعلم وأنتم
لا تعلمون ﴿٦٦﴾ ما كان إبراهيم يهوديا ولا نصرانيا ولكن
كان حنيفا مسلما وما كان من المشركين ﴿٦٧﴾ إن أولى الناس
بإبراهيم للذين اتبعوه وهذا النبي والذين آمنوا ۗ والله
ولي المؤمنين ﴿٦٨﴾ ودت طائفة من أهل الكتاب لو يضلونكم
وما يضلون إلا أنفسهم وما يشعرون ﴿٦٩﴾ يا أهل
الكتاب لم تكفرون بآيات الله وأنتم تشهدون ﴿٧٠﴾

SURELY THIS is the true 3:62
story. There is no deity but God. And surely it is God who is the Almighty, the Wise One.

If they pay no heed, God surely knows the evil-doers.

Say: 'People of the Book, let us come to a fair agreement between us: that we will worship none but God, that we will associate none with Him, and that none of us shall set up mortals as deities besides God.'

If they turn away, say: 'Bear witness, then, that we are Muslims.'

People of the Book, why do you argue about Abraham when both the Torah and the Gospel were not revealed till after him? Have you no sense?

Indeed, you have argued about things of which you have some know- 3:66
ledge; must you now argue about that of which you have no knowledge? God knows, but you know not.

Abraham was neither Jew nor Christian. He was a devout Muslim. And he was no idolater. Surely those who are nearest to Abraham are those who followed him, this Prophet, and the true believers. God is the guardian of the faithful. Some of the People of the Book wish to mislead you; but they mislead none but themselves, unaware though they are.

People of the Book! Why do you deny God's revelations when you can 3:70
clearly see?

3:71 PEOPLE OF the Book! Why
do you confound Truth with
falsehood, and knowingly
hide the Truth?
Some of the People of the
Book say: 'Believe in that
which is revealed to the faithful in the morning and deny it
at the end of the day, so that
they may recant. Believe in
none except those that follow
your own religion.' (Say: 'The
only guidance is God's guidance!') 'Do not believe that
anyone will be given the like
of that which you were given,
or that they will ever dispute
with you in your Lord's presence.'
Say: 'Grace is in the hands
of God: He bestows it on
whom He will. And God is
munificent and all-knowing.
3:74 He is merciful only to whom He will. God is He whose grace is infinite.'
Among the People of the Book there are some who, if you trust them
with a heap of gold, will return it to you intact; and some who, if you trust
them with one dinar, will not hand it back unless you demand it with impor-
tunity. For they say: 'We are not bound to keep faith with Gentiles.' And they
knowingly utter falsehood against God. Indeed, those that are true to their
covenant and fear God know that God loves those that fear Him.
3:77 Those that sell God's covenant and their own oaths for a paltry price shall
have no share in the world to come. God will neither speak to them nor look
at them on the Day of Resurrection; nor will He purify them: woeful punishment awaits them.

يا أهل الكتاب لم تلبسون الحق بالباطل وتكتمون الحق وأنتم
تعلمون ٧١ وقالت طائفة من أهل الكتاب آمنوا بالذي أنزل
على الذين آمنوا وجه النهار واكفروا آخره لعلهم يرجعون
٧٢ ولا تؤمنوا إلا لمن تبع دينكم قل إن الهدى هدى الله
أن يؤتى أحد مثل ما أوتيتم أو يحاجوكم عند ربكم
قل إن الفضل بيد الله يؤتيه من يشاء والله
واسع عليم ٧٣ يختص برحمته من يشاء والله
ذو الفضل العظيم ٧٤ ومن أهل الكتاب من إن تأمنه
بقنطار يؤده إليك ومنهم من إن تأمنه بدينار لا يؤده
إليك إلا ما دمت عليه قائما ذلك بأنهم قالوا ليس علينا في
الأميين سبيل ويقولون على الله الكذب وهم يعلمون ٧٥ بلى
من أوفى بعهده واتقى فإن الله يحب المتقين ٧٦ إن
الذين يشترون بعهد الله وأيمانهم ثمنا قليلا
أولئك لا خلاق لهم في الآخرة ولا يكلمهم الله
ولا ينظر إليهم يوم القيامة ولا يزكيهم ولهم عذاب أليم ٧٧

وإن منهم لفريقا يلوون ألسنتهم بالكتاب لتحسبوه
من الكتاب وما هو من الكتاب ويقولون هو من عند الله
وما هو من عند الله ويقولون على الله الكذب وهم
يعلمون (٧٨) ما كان لبشر أن يؤتيه الله الكتاب والحكم
والنبوة ثم يقول للناس كونوا عبادا لي من دون الله
ولكن كونوا ربانيين بما كنتم تعلمون الكتاب وبما كنتم
تدرسون (٧٩) ولا يأمركم أن تتخذوا الملائكة
والنبيين أربابا أيأمركم بالكفر بعد إذ أنتم مسلمون
(٨٠) وإذ أخذ الله ميثاق النبيين لما آتيتكم من
كتاب وحكمة ثم جاءكم رسول مصدق لما
معكم لتؤمنن به ولتنصرنه قال أأقررتم وأخذتم
على ذلكم إصري قالوا أقررنا قال فاشهدوا وأنا
معكم من الشاهدين (٨١) فمن تولى بعد ذلك فأولئك
هم الفاسقون (٨٢) أفغير دين الله يبغون وله أسلم
من في السماوات والأرض طوعا وكرها وإليه يرجعون (٨٣)

AND THERE are some 3:78
among them who twist their
tongues when quoting the
Scriptures, so that you may
think it from the Scriptures,
whereas it is not from the
Scriptures. They say: 'This is
from God,' whereas it is not
from God. And they know-
ingly utter falsehood against
God.

No mortal to whom God
has given the Book and wisdom and prophethood would
say to people: 'Worship me
instead of God.' But rather:
'Be devoted masters, for you
have taught and studied the
Book.' Nor would he enjoin
you to adopt the angels and
the prophets as deities; for
would he enjoin you to be
unbelievers after you have
become Muslims?

And when God made His covenant with the prophets: 'Here is the Book 3:81
and the wisdom which I have given you. An apostle will then come forth to
confirm them. You shall believe in him and you shall help him.' And He said:
'Will you affirm this and accept the burden I have laid on you in these terms?'

They replied: 'We do affirm.'

'Then bear witness,' He said, 'and I will bear witness with you. He that
hereafter turns away is a transgressor.'

Are they seeking a religion other than God's, when every soul in the heav- 3:83
ens and the earth has submitted as a Muslim, willingly or with reluctance? To
Him shall they be recalled.

3:84 SAY: 'WE believe in God
and what was revealed to us;
in that which was revealed
to Abraham and Ishmael, to
Isaac and Jacob and the tribes;
and in that which was given
to Moses and Jesus and the
prophets by their Lord. We
discriminate against none of
them. To Him we submit as
Muslims.'

He that follows a religion
other than Islām, it will not
save him[1] and in the world to
come he will surely be among
the lost.

How will God guide
people who lapsed into
unbelief after embracing the
Faith and acknowledging the
Apostle as true, and after
receiving veritable proofs?
And God does not guide the
3:87 wrongdoers. Their reward will be the curse of God, the angels, and mankind
all; under it shall they abide for ever. Their punishment shall not be mitigated, nor shall they be reprieved; except those who afterwards repent and
mend their ways; for surely God is forgiving and compassionate.

But those that recant after they had believed and grow in unbelief, their
repentance shall not be accepted; these are the truly erring ones.

3:91 As for those that recant and die unbelievers, no ransom shall be accepted
from any of them: be it as much gold as would fill the earth entire. Woeful
punishment awaits them; and none shall help them.

قل آمنا بالله وما أنزل علينا وما أنزل على إبراهيم
وإسماعيل وإسحق ويعقوب والأسباط وما أوتي
موسى وعيسى والنبيون من ربهم لا نفرق بين أحد
منهم ونحن له مسلمون ﴿٨٤﴾ ومن يبتغ غير الإسلام
دينا فلن يقبل منه وهو في الآخرة من الخاسرين ﴿٨٥﴾ كيف
يهدي الله قوما كفروا بعد إيمانهم وشهدوا أن
الرسول حق وجاءهم البينات والله لا يهدي القوم الظالمين ﴿٨٦﴾
أولئك جزاؤهم أن عليهم لعنة الله والملائكة والناس
أجمعين ﴿٨٧﴾ خالدين فيها لا يخفف عنهم العذاب ولا هم
ينظرون ﴿٨٨﴾ إلا الذين تابوا من بعد ذلك وأصلحوا
فإن الله غفور رحيم ﴿٨٩﴾ إن الذين كفروا بعد إيمانهم
ثم ازدادوا كفرا لن تقبل توبتهم وأولئك هم
الضالون ﴿٩٠﴾ إن الذين كفروا وماتوا وهم كفار
فلن يقبل من أحدهم ملء الأرض ذهبا ولو افتدى به
أولئك لهم عذاب أليم وما لهم من ناصرين ﴿٩١﴾

1. Literally, will not be accepted from him.

لن تنالوا البر حتى تنفقوا مما تحبون وما تنفقوا من شيء فان
الله به عليم ﴿٩٢﴾ كل الطعام كان حلا لبني اسرائيل الا
ما حرم اسرائيل على نفسه من قبل ان تنزل التورية قل فاتوا
بالتورية فاتلوها ان كنتم صادقين ﴿٩٣﴾ فمن افترى على الله
الكذب من بعد ذلك فاولئك هم الظالمون ﴿٩٤﴾ قل صدق الله
فاتبعوا ملة ابرهيم حنيفا وما كان من المشركين ﴿٩٥﴾ ان
اول بيت وضع للناس للذي ببكة مباركا وهدى للعالمين ﴿٩٦﴾
فيه ايات بينات مقام ابرهيم ومن دخله كان امنا ولله
على الناس حج البيت من استطاع اليه سبيلا ومن كفر فان الله
غني عن العالمين ﴿٩٧﴾ قل يا اهل الكتاب لم تكفرون بايات الله
والله شهيد على ما تعملون ﴿٩٨﴾ قل يا اهل الكتاب
لم تصدون عن سبيل الله من امن تبغونها عوجا
وانتم شهداء وما الله بغافل عما تعملون ﴿٩٩﴾
يا ايها الذين امنوا ان تطيعوا فريقا من الذين اوتوا
الكتاب يردوكم بعد ايمانكم كافرين ﴿١٠٠﴾

YOU SHALL never attain 3:92
righteousness until you give in
alms what you dearly cherish.
Whatever you give, it shall be
known to God.

All food was lawful to the
Israelites except what Israel
forbade himself before the
Torah was revealed. Say:
'Bring the Torah and read it, if
what you say be true.'

Those that after this invent
falsehood about God are the
real transgressors.

Say: 'God has declared the
Truth. Follow the faith of
Abraham. He was an upright
man, never an idolater.'

The first temple ever to be
built for mankind was that at
Bakkah,[1] a blessed site, a beacon for the nations. Therein 3:97
are veritable signs and the
spot where Abraham stood. Whoever enters it is safe. Pilgrimage to the
House is a duty to God for all who can make the journey. As for the unbelievers, God can surely do without them all.

Say: 'People of the Book, why do you deny God's revelations? God is
witness of what you do.'

Say: 'People of the Book, why do you debar believers from the path of
God and seek to make it crooked when you have witnessed all? God is never
heedless of what you do.'

Believers, if you obey a group from among those who were given the 3:100
Book, they will turn you back after your faith into unbelievers.

1. Another name for Mecca.

3:101 AND HOW can you disbelieve when God's revelations are recited to you and His own apostle is in your midst? He that holds fast to God shall surely be guided to a straight path.

Believers, fear God as you rightly should, and die only as Muslims. Cling one and all to the Faith[1] of God and never be divided. Remember the favour God has bestowed upon you: how, after your enmity, He united your hearts, so that you are now brothers through His grace; and how, when you were on the brink of an abyss of fire, He delivered you from it. God thus makes plain to you His revelations, that you may be rightly guided.

وكيف تكفرون وأنتم تتلى عليكم آيات الله
وفيكم رسوله ومن يعتصم بالله فقد هدي إلى صراط مستقيم
(١٠١) يا أيها الذين آمنوا اتقوا الله حق تقاته ولا تموتن إلا وأنتم
مسلمون (١٠٢) واعتصموا بحبل الله جميعا ولا تفرقوا واذكروا
نعمت الله عليكم إذ كنتم أعداء فألف بين قلوبكم
فأصبحتم بنعمته إخوانا وكنتم على شفا حفرة من النار
فأنقذكم منها كذلك يبين الله لكم آياته لعلكم تهتدون
(١٠٣) ولتكن منكم أمة يدعون إلى الخير ويأمرون بالمعروف
وينهون عن المنكر وأولئك هم المفلحون (١٠٤) ولا تكونوا
كالذين تفرقوا واختلفوا من بعد ما جاءهم البينات وأولئك
لهم عذاب عظيم (١٠٥) يوم تبيض وجوه وتسود وجوه فأما
الذين اسودت وجوههم أكفرتم بعد إيمانكم فذوقوا العذاب
بما كنتم تكفرون (١٠٦) وأما الذين ابيضت وجوههم ففي
رحمة الله هم فيها خالدون (١٠٧) تلك آيات الله
نتلوها عليك بالحق وما الله يريد ظلما للعالمين (١٠٨)

3:104 And of you let there become a community that shall call for righteousness, enjoin justice, and forbid the reprehensible. Such are those that will surely thrive.

Do not follow the example of those who became divided and opposed to each other after veritable proofs had been given them. Grievous punishment awaits them, on the day when some faces will be bright with joy and other faces blackened. The black-faced will be asked: 'Did you recant after embracing the true Faith? Taste then the scourge, for you were unbelievers!' As for those whose faces will be bright, in God's mercy shall they abide for ever.

3:108 Such are God's revelations; We recite them to you in Truth. God desires no injustice to mankind.

1. Literally, rope.

وَلِلَّهِ مَا فِي السَّمَاوَاتِ وَمَا فِي الْأَرْضِ وَإِلَى اللَّهِ تُرْجَعُ
الْأُمُورُ ﴿١٠٩﴾ كُنْتُمْ خَيْرَ أُمَّةٍ أُخْرِجَتْ لِلنَّاسِ تَأْمُرُونَ
بِالْمَعْرُوفِ وَتَنْهَوْنَ عَنِ الْمُنْكَرِ وَتُؤْمِنُونَ بِاللَّهِ وَلَوْ آمَنَ
أَهْلُ الْكِتَابِ لَكَانَ خَيْرًا لَهُمْ مِنْهُمُ الْمُؤْمِنُونَ وَأَكْثَرُهُمُ
الْفَاسِقُونَ ﴿١١٠﴾ لَنْ يَضُرُّوكُمْ إِلَّا أَذًى وَإِنْ يُقَاتِلُوكُمْ
يُوَلُّوكُمُ الْأَدْبَارَ ثُمَّ لَا يُنْصَرُونَ ﴿١١١﴾ ضُرِبَتْ عَلَيْهِمُ
الذِّلَّةُ أَيْنَ مَا ثُقِفُوا إِلَّا بِحَبْلٍ مِنَ اللَّهِ وَحَبْلٍ
مِنَ النَّاسِ وَبَاءُوا بِغَضَبٍ مِنَ اللَّهِ وَضُرِبَتْ عَلَيْهِمُ الْمَسْكَنَةُ
ذَٰلِكَ بِأَنَّهُمْ كَانُوا يَكْفُرُونَ بِآيَاتِ اللَّهِ وَيَقْتُلُونَ
الْأَنْبِيَاءَ بِغَيْرِ حَقٍّ ذَٰلِكَ بِمَا عَصَوْا وَكَانُوا يَعْتَدُونَ ﴿١١٢﴾
لَيْسُوا سَوَاءً مِنْ أَهْلِ الْكِتَابِ أُمَّةٌ قَائِمَةٌ يَتْلُونَ آيَاتِ
اللَّهِ آنَاءَ اللَّيْلِ وَهُمْ يَسْجُدُونَ ﴿١١٣﴾ يُؤْمِنُونَ بِاللَّهِ وَالْيَوْمِ
الْآخِرِ وَيَأْمُرُونَ بِالْمَعْرُوفِ وَيَنْهَوْنَ عَنِ الْمُنْكَرِ وَيُسَارِعُونَ
فِي الْخَيْرَاتِ وَأُولَٰئِكَ مِنَ الصَّالِحِينَ ﴿١١٤﴾ وَمَا يَفْعَلُوا
مِنْ خَيْرٍ فَلَنْ يُكْفَرُوهُ وَاللَّهُ عَلِيمٌ بِالْمُتَّقِينَ ﴿١١٥﴾

HIS IS all that the heavens and 3:109
the earth contain. To God
shall all things return.

You are the noblest com-
munity ever raised up for
people. You enjoin justice and
forbid the reprehensible and
believe in God.

Had the People of the Book
accepted the Faith, it would
surely have been better for
them. Some are true believers,
but most of them are ungodly.

If they harm you, they can
cause you but little hurt; and
if they fight you they will turn
their backs and run away.
Then there shall be none to
help them. Servility shall be 3:112
stamped upon them wherever
they are found, unless they
make a covenant with God and
a covenant with man. They
have provoked God's ire, and wretchedness is stamped upon them: because
they disbelieved God's revelations and slew the prophets unjustly; and because
they were rebels and transgressors.

Yet they are not all alike. There is among the People of the Book an
upright community who all night long recite God's revelations and bow
down in worship; who believe in God and the Last Day; who enjoin justice,
and forbid the reprehensible, and strive to do good works. These are among
the righteous; whatever good they do, its reward shall not be denied them. 3:115
God well knows those that fear Him.

3:116 As FOR the unbelievers, neither their riches nor their children shall in the least protect them from the scourge of God. They are the inmates of the Fire, wherein shall they abide for ever. The wealth they spend in this world can be compared to a freezing wind that smites the tillage of people who have wronged themselves, laying it waste. God is not unjust to them; they are unjust to their own souls.

Believers, do not make friends with any but your own people. They will spare no pains to corrupt you; they desire nothing but your ruin; their hatred is evident from what they utter with their mouths, but greater is the hatred which their bosoms conceal.

إِنَّ الَّذِينَ كَفَرُوا لَن تُغْنِيَ عَنْهُمْ أَمْوَالُهُمْ وَلَا أَوْلَادُهُم مِّنَ
اللَّهِ شَيْئًا وَأُولَٰئِكَ أَصْحَابُ النَّارِ هُمْ فِيهَا خَالِدُونَ ١١٦ مَثَلُ
مَا يُنفِقُونَ فِي هَٰذِهِ الْحَيَاةِ الدُّنْيَا كَمَثَلِ رِيحٍ فِيهَا صِرٌّ
أَصَابَتْ حَرْثَ قَوْمٍ ظَلَمُوا أَنفُسَهُمْ فَأَهْلَكَتْهُ وَمَا ظَلَمَهُمُ
اللَّهُ وَلَٰكِنْ أَنفُسَهُمْ يَظْلِمُونَ ١١٧ يَا أَيُّهَا الَّذِينَ آمَنُوا لَا تَتَّخِذُوا
بِطَانَةً مِّن دُونِكُمْ لَا يَأْلُونَكُمْ خَبَالًا وَدُّوا مَا عَنِتُّمْ قَدْ
بَدَتِ الْبَغْضَاءُ مِنْ أَفْوَاهِهِمْ وَمَا تُخْفِي صُدُورُهُمْ أَكْبَرُ قَدْ
بَيَّنَّا لَكُمُ الْآيَاتِ إِن كُنتُمْ تَعْقِلُونَ ١١٨ هَا أَنتُمْ أُولَاءِ
تُحِبُّونَهُمْ وَلَا يُحِبُّونَكُمْ وَتُؤْمِنُونَ بِالْكِتَابِ كُلِّهِ وَإِذَا
لَقُوكُمْ قَالُوا آمَنَّا وَإِذَا خَلَوْا عَضُّوا عَلَيْكُمُ الْأَنَامِلَ مِنَ
الْغَيْظِ قُلْ مُوتُوا بِغَيْظِكُمْ إِنَّ اللَّهَ عَلِيمٌ بِذَاتِ الصُّدُورِ
١١٩ إِن تَمْسَسْكُمْ حَسَنَةٌ تَسُؤْهُمْ وَإِن تُصِبْكُمْ سَيِّئَةٌ
يَفْرَحُوا بِهَا وَإِن تَصْبِرُوا وَتَتَّقُوا لَا يَضُرُّكُمْ كَيْدُهُمْ شَيْئًا إِنَّ
اللَّهَ بِمَا يَعْمَلُونَ مُحِيطٌ ١٢٠ وَإِذْ غَدَوْتَ مِنْ أَهْلِكَ تُبَوِّئُ
الْمُؤْمِنِينَ مَقَاعِدَ لِلْقِتَالِ وَاللَّهُ سَمِيعٌ عَلِيمٌ ١٢١

We have made plain to you Our revelations; perchance you will understand.

3:119 Behold how you love them and they do not love you; because you believe in the Book entire.

When they meet you they say: 'We believe.' But when alone, they bite their fingertips with rage. Say: 'May you perish in your rage! God has knowledge of your innermost thoughts.'

If you are blessed with something good it grieves them: but if something bad befalls you they rejoice. If you persevere and fear God, their machinations will not a whit harm you. God has full knowledge of what they do.

3:121 Remember when you[1] left your people at an early hour to lead the faithful to their battle-posts.[2] And God heard all and knew all.

1. Muḥammad.
2. The allusion is to the Battle of 'Uḥud, in which the Muslims were defeated by the Quraysh of Mecca.

إذ همت طائفتان منكم أن تفشلا والله وليهما وعلى
الله فليتوكل المؤمنون ﴿١٢٢﴾ ولقد نصركم الله ببدر وأنتم
أذلة فاتقوا الله لعلكم تشكرون ﴿١٢٣﴾ إذ تقول
للمؤمنين ألن يكفيكم أن يمدكم ربكم بثلثة آلاف
من الملئكة منزلين ﴿١٢٤﴾ بلى إن تصبروا وتتقوا ويأتوكم من فورهم
هذا يمددكم ربكم بخمسة آلاف من الملئكة مسومين ﴿١٢٥﴾ وما جعله
الله إلا بشرى لكم ولتطمئن قلوبكم به وما النصر
إلا من عند الله العزيز الحكيم ﴿١٢٦﴾ ليقطع طرفا من الذين
كفروا أو يكبتهم فينقلبوا خائبين ﴿١٢٧﴾ ليس لك من
الأمر شيء أو يتوب عليهم أو يعذبهم فإنهم ظالمون ﴿١٢٨﴾
ولله ما في السموات وما في الأرض يغفر لمن يشاء ويعذب
من يشاء والله غفور رحيم ﴿١٢٩﴾ يا أيها الذين آمنوا
لا تأكلوا الربوا أضعافا مضاعفة واتقوا الله لعلكم
تفلحون ﴿١٣٠﴾ واتقوا النار التي أعدت للكافرين ﴿١٣١﴾
وأطيعوا الله والرسول لعلكم ترحمون ﴿١٣٢﴾

TWO OF your battalions be- 3:122
came faint-hearted, but God
was their protector. In God let
the faithful put their trust.

God had already given you
victory at Badr when you were
helpless. Therefore fear God.
Perchance you will give thanks.

You said to the believers: ‘Is
it not enough that your Lord
should send down three thousand angels to help you?’

Yes! If you have patience
and fear God; and if they suddenly attack you, your Lord will
send to your aid five thousand
angels splendidly accoutred.

God designed this to be but 3:126
good news for you, so that
your hearts might be com-
forted (victory comes only
from God, the Almighty, the
Wise One) and that He might
cut off the flank of the unbelievers or put them to flight, that they might
withdraw defeated.

It is no concern of yours whether He will forgive or punish them. Wrongdoers they surely are. His is all that the heavens and the earth contain. He
pardons whom He will and punishes whom He pleases. God is forgiving and
compassionate.

Believers, do not live on usury, doubling your wealth many times over.
Have fear of God, that you may prosper. Guard yourselves against the Fire,
prepared for unbelievers. Obey God and the Apostle that you may find 3:132
mercy

3:133 VIE WITH each other to earn forgiveness from your Lord and a Paradise as vast as the heavens and the earth, prepared for the righteous: those who give, alike in prosperity and in adversity; who curb their anger and pardon their fellow men (God loves the charitable); who, if they commit a lewd act or wrong their souls, remember God and seek forgiveness for their sins (for who but God can forgive sins?) and do not knowingly persist in their misdeeds. These shall be rewarded with forgiveness from their Lord and with Gardens watered by running brooks, wherein shall they abide for ever. And blessed is the reward of those who do good works.

وَسَارِعُوٓا إِلَىٰ مَغْفِرَةٍ مِّن رَّبِّكُمْ وَجَنَّةٍ عَرْضُهَا ٱلسَّمَٰوَٰتُ
وَٱلْأَرْضُ أُعِدَّتْ لِلْمُتَّقِينَ ١٣٣ ٱلَّذِينَ يُنفِقُونَ فِى ٱلسَّرَّآءِ وَٱلضَّرَّآءِ
وَٱلْكَٰظِمِينَ ٱلْغَيْظَ وَٱلْعَافِينَ عَنِ ٱلنَّاسِ وَٱللَّهُ يُحِبُّ ٱلْمُحْسِنِينَ
١٣٤ وَٱلَّذِينَ إِذَا فَعَلُوا فَٰحِشَةً أَوْ ظَلَمُوٓا أَنفُسَهُمْ ذَكَرُوا
ٱللَّهَ فَٱسْتَغْفَرُوا لِذُنُوبِهِمْ وَمَن يَغْفِرُ ٱلذُّنُوبَ إِلَّا
ٱللَّهُ وَلَمْ يُصِرُّوا عَلَىٰ مَا فَعَلُوا وَهُمْ يَعْلَمُونَ ١٣٥ أُولَٰٓئِكَ
جَزَآؤُهُم مَّغْفِرَةٌ مِّن رَّبِّهِمْ وَجَنَّٰتٌ تَجْرِى مِن تَحْتِهَا
ٱلْأَنْهَٰرُ خَٰلِدِينَ فِيهَا وَنِعْمَ أَجْرُ ٱلْعَٰمِلِينَ ١٣٦ قَدْ
خَلَتْ مِن قَبْلِكُمْ سُنَنٌ فَسِيرُوا فِى ٱلْأَرْضِ فَٱنظُرُوا
كَيْفَ كَانَ عَٰقِبَةُ ٱلْمُكَذِّبِينَ ١٣٧ هَٰذَا بَيَانٌ لِّلنَّاسِ
وَهُدًى وَمَوْعِظَةٌ لِّلْمُتَّقِينَ ١٣٨ وَلَا تَهِنُوا وَلَا تَحْزَنُوا
وَأَنتُمُ ٱلْأَعْلَوْنَ إِن كُنتُم مُّؤْمِنِينَ ١٣٩ إِن يَمْسَسْكُمْ
قَرْحٌ فَقَدْ مَسَّ ٱلْقَوْمَ قَرْحٌ مِّثْلُهُ وَتِلْكَ ٱلْأَيَّامُ
نُدَاوِلُهَا بَيْنَ ٱلنَّاسِ وَلِيَعْلَمَ ٱللَّهُ ٱلَّذِينَ ءَامَنُوا
وَيَتَّخِذَ مِنكُمْ شُهَدَآءَ وَٱللَّهُ لَا يُحِبُّ ٱلظَّٰلِمِينَ ١٤٠

3:137 Numerous were the cults that came and went before you. Roam the earth and behold what was the fate of those who disbelieved.

This is a declaration to the people: a guide and an admonition to the righteous. Do not waver and do not despair. Have faith and you shall triumph.

3:140 If once a defeat hit you, the foe was hit by a like defeat. These vicissitudes We alternate among people, that God may know the true believers and choose martyrs from among you: God does not love the wrongdoers;

وليمحص الله الذين آمنوا ويمحق الكافرين ﴿١٤١﴾ أم حسبتم
أن تدخلوا الجنة ولما يعلم الله الذين جاهدوا منكم
ويعلم الصابرين ﴿١٤٢﴾ ولقد كنتم تمنون الموت من
قبل أن تلقوه فقد رأيتموه وأنتم تنظرون ﴿١٤٣﴾ وما
محمد إلا رسول قد خلت من قبله الرسل أفإن مات
أو قتل انقلبتم على أعقابكم ومن ينقلب على عقبيه
فلن يضر الله شيئا وسيجزي الله الشاكرين ﴿١٤٤﴾ وما
كان لنفس أن تموت إلا بإذن الله كتابا مؤجلا ومن يرد
ثواب الدنيا نؤته منها ومن يرد ثواب الآخرة نؤته منها
وسنجزي الشاكرين ﴿١٤٥﴾ وكأين من نبي قاتل معه
ربيون كثير فما وهنوا لما أصابهم في سبيل الله
وما ضعفوا وما استكانوا والله يحب الصابرين ﴿١٤٦﴾ وما
كان قولهم إلا أن قالوا ربنا اغفر لنا ذنوبنا وإسرافنا في
أمرنا وثبت أقدامنا وانصرنا على القوم الكافرين ﴿١٤٧﴾ فآتاهم الله
ثواب الدنيا وحسن ثواب الآخرة والله يحب المحسنين ﴿١٤٨﴾

and that God may test the faith- 3:141
ful and annihilate the infidels.

Did you suppose that you would enter Paradise before God knew which of you had fought and which of you endured with fortitude? You used to wish for death before you met it, and now you behold what it is like. Muḥammad is but an apostle: other apostles have passed away before him. If he should die or be slain, will you recant? He that recants will in no way harm God. And God will recompense the thankful.

And it is not for a soul to 3:145
die except with God's will: upon a time decreed. He that desires the reward of this world shall have it; and he that desires the reward of the life to come shall have it also. We will recompense the thankful.

Many a large army fought by the side of its prophet. They were never daunted by whatever befell them on the path of God: they neither weakened nor cringed abjectly. God loves the steadfast. Their only words were: 'Lord, forgive us our sins and our excesses; make us firm of foot and give us victory
over the unbelievers.' Therefore God gave them the reward of this life, and 3:148
the glorious recompense of the life to come; God loves the righteous.

3:149 You BELIEVERS! If you yield to the infidels they will drag you back to unbelief and you will return headlong to perdition. But God is your protector, and He is the best of helpers.

We will cast terror into the hearts of the unbelievers, because they serve other deities besides God for whom He has revealed no sanction. The Fire shall be their dwelling; and evil is the wrongdoers' dwelling.

3:152 Surely God fulfilled His pledge to you when, by His leave, you defeated them. But afterwards your courage failed you; discord reigned among you and you disobeyed the Apostle after he had brought you within sight of what you wished for. Some among you wanted this world; and some wanted the world to come. He allowed you to be defeated in order to test you. But now He has pardoned you, for God is gracious to the faithful.

3:153 Remember how you fled in panic while the Apostle at your rear was calling out to you. Therefore He paid you back with tribulation for every vexation, that you might not grieve for what you missed or what befell you. God is cognizant of what you do.

يا أيها الذين آمنوا إن تطيعوا الذين كفروا
يردوكم على أعقابكم فتنقلبوا
خاسرين ﴿١٤٩﴾ بل الله مولاكم وهو خير
الناصرين ﴿١٥٠﴾ سنلقي في قلوب الذين كفروا
الرعب بما أشركوا بالله ما لم ينزل به سلطانا
ومأواهم النار وبئس مثوى الظالمين ﴿١٥١﴾
ولقد صدقكم الله وعده إذ تحسونهم
بإذنه حتى إذا فشلتم وتنازعتم في الأمر وعصيتم
من بعد ما أراكم ما تحبون منكم من يريد الدنيا
ومنكم من يريد الآخرة ثم صرفكم عنهم ليبتليكم
ولقد عفا عنكم والله ذو فضل على المؤمنين
﴿١٥٢﴾ إذ تصعدون ولا تلوون على أحد والرسول
يدعوكم في أخراكم فأثابكم غما
بغم لكيلا تحزنوا على ما فاتكم
ولا ما أصابكم والله خبير بما تعملون ﴿١٥٣﴾

ثم أنزل عليكم من بعد الغم أمنة نعاسا يغشى طائفة منكم
وطائفة قد أهمتهم أنفسهم يظنون بالله غير الحق ظن
الجاهلية يقولون هل لنا من الأمر من شيء قل إن الأمر كله
لله يخفون في أنفسهم ما لا يبدون لك يقولون لو كان
لنا من الأمر شيء ما قتلنا هاهنا قل لو كنتم في بيوتكم
لبرز الذين كتب عليهم القتل إلى مضاجعهم وليبتلي
الله ما في صدوركم وليمحص ما في قلوبكم والله
عليم بذات الصدور (١٥٤) إن الذين تولوا منكم يوم
التقى الجمعان إنما استزلهم الشيطان ببعض ما كسبوا
ولقد عفا الله عنهم إن الله غفور حليم (١٥٥) يا أيها الذين
آمنوا لا تكونوا كالذين كفروا وقالوا لإخوانهم إذا ضربوا
في الأرض أو كانوا غزى لو كانوا عندنا ما ماتوا وما قتلوا
ليجعل الله ذلك حسرة في قلوبهم والله يحيي ويميت
والله بما تعملون بصير (١٥٦) ولئن قتلتم في سبيل الله
أو متم لمغفرة من الله ورحمة خير مما يجمعون (١٥٧)

THEN, AFTER tribulation, 3:154
He let peace fall upon you – a sleep which overtook some among you, while others lay troubled by their own fancies, thinking unjust and foolish thoughts about God.

'Have we any say in the matter?' they ask.

Say: '*All* is in the hands of God.'

They conceal in their minds what they do not reveal to you.

They complain: 'Had we had any say in the matter, we should not have been slain here.'

Say: 'Had you stayed in your homes, those of you who were destined to be slain would have died in their beds; for it was God's will to test what was in your bosoms and to scrutinize what was in your hearts. God has full knowledge of one's innermost thoughts.'

Those of you who ran away on the day the two armies met[1] must have 3:155
been seduced by Satan on account of some evil they had done. But now God has pardoned them; God is forgiving and lenient.

Believers, do not follow the example of the infidels, who say of their brothers when they meet death abroad or in battle: 'Had they stayed with us they would not have died, nor would they have been killed.' God will turn that into a sigh in their hearts. God has power over life and death, and God is ever observant of what you do.

If you should be slain in the cause of God or die, God's forgiveness and 3:157
His mercy would surely be better than the riches they amass.

1. In the Battle of 'Uḥud.

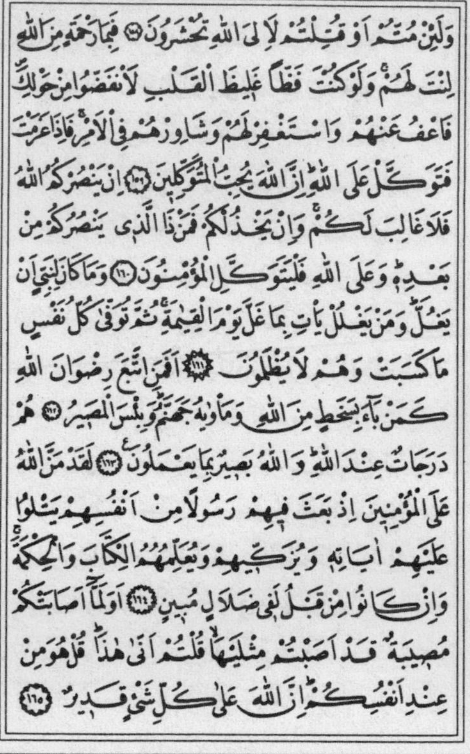

3:158 AND IF you should die or be slain, before God shall you all be herded.

It was thanks to God's mercy that you[1] dealt so leniently with them. Had you been cruel or hard-hearted, they would have surely deserted you. Pardon them and implore God to forgive them. Take counsel with them in the conduct of affairs; and when you are resolved, put your trust in God. God loves those that are trustful.

And if God helps you, none can overcome you; if He abandons you, who then can help you after Him? Therefore in God let the faithful put their trust.

No prophet would steal; for anyone that steals shall on the Day of Resurrection bring with him that which he has stolen. Then shall every soul be paid what it has earned: none shall be wronged.

Can the man who seeks to please God be compared to him who has incurred God's anger? Hell shall be his home, evil his fate.

3:163 Varied are the rewards of God. God is cognizant of all their actions.

God has surely been gracious to the faithful in sending them an apostle of their own to recite to them His revelations, to purify them, and to instruct them in the Book and in wisdom; for before that they surely were in monstrous error.

3:165 When a disaster befell you after you had yourselves inflicted losses twice as heavy, you said: 'Whose fault was that?'

Say: 'It was your own doing. God has power over all things.

1. Muḥammad.

وما اصابكم يوم التقى الجمعان فباذن الله وليعلم المؤمنين
وليعلم الذين نافقوا وقيل لهم تعالوا قاتلوا في سبيل الله ١٦٦
او ادفعوا قالوا لو نعلم قتالا لاتبعناكم هم للكفر
يومئذ اقرب منهم للايمان يقولون بافواههم ما ليس في
قلوبهم والله اعلم بما يكتمون ١٦٧ الذين قالوا لاخوانهم
وقعدوا لو اطاعونا ما قتلوا قل فادرءوا عن انفسكم
الموت ان كنتم صادقين ١٦٨ ولا تحسبن الذين قتلوا
في سبيل الله امواتا بل احياء عند ربهم يرزقون ١٦٩ فرحين
بما اتاهم الله من فضله ويستبشرون بالذين لم
يلحقوا بهم من خلفهم الا خوف عليهم ولا هم
يحزنون ١٧٠ يستبشرون بنعمة من الله وفضل وان الله
لا يضيع اجر المؤمنين ١٧١ الذين استجابوا لله والرسول من بعد
ما اصابهم القرح للذين احسنوا منهم واتقوا اجر عظيم ١٧٢
الذين قال لهم الناس ان الناس قد جمعوا لكم فاخشوهم
فزادهم ايمانا وقالوا حسبنا الله ونعم الوكيل ١٧٣

AND THE misfortune which 3:166
befell you when the two armies met was ordained by God, so that He might know the true believers and know the hypocrites.'

And when they were told: 'Come, fight for the cause of God and defend yourselves,' they said: 'If we only knew how to fight, we would surely follow you.'

On that day they were nearer unbelief than faith. Their words belied their intentions: but God knew their secret thoughts. Such were the men who, as they sat at home, said of their brothers: 'Had they listened to us, they would not have been slain.'

Say: 'Ward off death from yourselves, then, if what you say be true!'

Never think that those who were slain in the cause of God are dead. They 3:169
are alive, and well provided for by their Lord; pleased with what God of His own bounty has given them; and rejoicing that those they left behind, who have not yet joined them, shall have nothing to fear or to regret; rejoicing in God's grace and bounty. God will not deny the faithful their reward.

As for the men who after their defeat answered the call of God and the
Apostle, those of them that do what is right and fear God shall be richly
recompensed. They are those who, when people said to them: 'The people 3:173
have mustered a great force against you: fear them,' grew more tenacious in their faith and said: 'Sufficient for us is God, the best of guardians.'

3:174 THUS DID they earn God's grace and bounty, and no harm befell them. For they had striven to please God, and God's bounty is infinite.

It is Satan that causes his followers to be feared. But have no fear of them, and fear Me, if you are true believers. Do not grieve for those that rush back headlong to disbelief; in no way will they harm God. God intends to give them no share in the Hereafter. And grievous punishment awaits them.

Those that barter their faith for unbelief will in no way harm God. Woeful punishment awaits them.

3:178 Let not the unbelievers think We prolong their days for their own good; We give them respite only that they may commit more grievous sins. Shameful punishment awaits them.

It was not God's aim to leave the faithful in their present plight, but only to tell the evil from the good. Nor was God to reveal to you what is hidden. But God chooses those of His apostles whom He will. Therefore have faith in God and His apostles; for if you have faith and fear God, your recompense shall be rich indeed.

3:180 Let not those who stingily hoard the wealth which God has given them out of His bounty think it good for them: rather it is an evil thing for them. They shall be shackled round with what they hoarded on the Day of Resurrection. It is God who shall inherit the heavens and the earth, and God is cognizant of what you do.

فَانْقَلَبُوا بِنِعْمَةٍ مِنَ اللَّهِ وَفَضْلٍ لَمْ يَمْسَسْهُمْ سُوءٌ
وَاتَّبَعُوا رِضْوَانَ اللَّهِ وَاللَّهُ ذُو فَضْلٍ عَظِيمٍ ﴿١٧٤﴾ إِنَّمَا ذَٰلِكُمُ
الشَّيْطَانُ يُخَوِّفُ أَوْلِيَاءَهُ فَلَا تَخَافُوهُمْ وَخَافُونِ إِنْ كُنْتُمْ مُؤْمِنِينَ
﴿١٧٥﴾ وَلَا يَحْزُنْكَ الَّذِينَ يُسَارِعُونَ فِي الْكُفْرِ إِنَّهُمْ لَنْ يَضُرُّوا اللَّهَ
شَيْئًا يُرِيدُ اللَّهُ أَلَّا يَجْعَلَ لَهُمْ حَظًّا فِي الْآخِرَةِ وَلَهُمْ عَذَابٌ
عَظِيمٌ ﴿١٧٦﴾ إِنَّ الَّذِينَ اشْتَرَوُا الْكُفْرَ بِالْإِيمَانِ لَنْ يَضُرُّوا اللَّهَ
شَيْئًا وَلَهُمْ عَذَابٌ أَلِيمٌ ﴿١٧٧﴾ وَلَا يَحْسَبَنَّ الَّذِينَ كَفَرُوا أَنَّمَا نُمْلِي لَهُمْ
خَيْرٌ لِأَنْفُسِهِمْ إِنَّمَا نُمْلِي لَهُمْ لِيَزْدَادُوا إِثْمًا وَلَهُمْ عَذَابٌ مُهِينٌ
﴿١٧٨﴾ مَا كَانَ اللَّهُ لِيَذَرَ الْمُؤْمِنِينَ عَلَىٰ مَا أَنْتُمْ عَلَيْهِ حَتَّىٰ
يَمِيزَ الْخَبِيثَ مِنَ الطَّيِّبِ وَمَا كَانَ اللَّهُ لِيُطْلِعَكُمْ عَلَى
الْغَيْبِ وَلَٰكِنَّ اللَّهَ يَجْتَبِي مِنْ رُسُلِهِ مَنْ يَشَاءُ فَآمِنُوا بِاللَّهِ
وَرُسُلِهِ وَإِنْ تُؤْمِنُوا وَتَتَّقُوا فَلَكُمْ أَجْرٌ عَظِيمٌ ﴿١٧٩﴾ وَلَا
يَحْسَبَنَّ الَّذِينَ يَبْخَلُونَ بِمَا آتَاهُمُ اللَّهُ مِنْ فَضْلِهِ هُوَ خَيْرًا
لَهُمْ بَلْ هُوَ شَرٌّ لَهُمْ سَيُطَوَّقُونَ مَا بَخِلُوا بِهِ يَوْمَ الْقِيَامَةِ وَلِلَّهِ
مِيرَاثُ السَّمَاوَاتِ وَالْأَرْضِ وَاللَّهُ بِمَا تَعْمَلُونَ خَبِيرٌ ﴿١٨٠﴾

لقد سمع الله قول الذين قالوا إن الله فقير ونحن
أغنياء سنكتب ما قالوا وقتلهم الأنبياء بغير
حق ونقول ذوقوا عذاب الحريق ﴿١٨١﴾ ذلك بما قدمت
أيديكم وأن الله ليس بظلام للعبيد ﴿١٨٢﴾ الذين
قالوا إن الله عهد إلينا ألا نؤمن لرسول حتى يأتينا
بقربان تأكله النار قل قد جاءكم رسل من قبلي
بالبينات وبالذي قلتم فلم قتلتموهم إن كنتم
صادقين ﴿١٨٣﴾ فإن كذبوك فقد كذب رسل من قبلك
جاءو بالبينات والزبر والكتاب المنير ﴿١٨٤﴾ كل نفس
ذائقة الموت وإنما توفون أجوركم يوم القيامة فمن
زحزح عن النار وأدخل الجنة فقد فاز وما الحياة
الدنيا إلا متاع الغرور ﴿١٨٥﴾ لتبلون في أموالكم
وأنفسكم ولتسمعن من الذين أوتوا الكتاب
من قبلكم ومن الذين أشركوا أذى كثيرا وإن
تصبروا وتتقوا فإن ذلك من عزم الأمور ﴿١٨٦﴾

GOD HAS surely heard the 3:181
words of those who said: 'God is poor, but we are rich.' Their words We will record, and their slaying of the prophets unjustly. We shall say: 'Taste now the torment of the Conflagration. This is the reward of your misdeeds. God is never unjust to His servants.'

To those that say: 'God has bidden us believe in no apostle until he bring down for us an offering to be consumed by fire,'[1] say: 'Other apostles before me have come to you with veritable signs and worked the miracle you asked for. Why did you slay them, if what you say be true?'

If they deny you, other 3:184
apostles have been denied before you, although they came with veritable signs, psalms, and the light-giving Book.

Every soul shall taste death. You shall receive your rewards only on the Day of Resurrection. Whoever is spared the Fire and is admitted to Paradise will surely triumph; for the life of this world is but a frivolous show of vanity.

You shall be sorely tried in the matter of your possessions and your per- 3:186
sons, and will hear much that is hurtful from those who were given the Book before you, and from the pagans. But if you endure with fortitude and fear God, your triumph shall be assured.

1. The reference is probably to the story of Elijah and the prophets of Baal (1 Kings 18:17–46).

3:187 AND WHEN God made a
covenant with those to whom
the Book was given He said:
'Proclaim it to the people and
suppress it not.' But they cast
the Book over their backs and
sold it for a paltry price. Evil
was their bargain.

Never think that those who
rejoice in what they did and
wish to be praised for what
they failed to do – never think
they will escape the torment;
woeful torment awaits them.

God has sovereignty over
the heavens and the earth.
And God has power over all
things.

In the creation of the heavens and the earth, and in the
alternation of night and day,
surely there are signs for those
that are of good sense pos-
3:191 sessed; those that remember God when standing, sitting, and lying down,
and reflect on the creation of the heavens and the earth, saying: 'Lord, You
have not created this in vain. Glory be to You! Save us from the torment of
the Fire. Lord, those whom You will cast into the Fire You will disgrace:
none will help the wrongdoers. Lord, we have heard a summoner summoning to the Faith, saying: "Believe in your Lord," and we believed. Lord,
forgive us our sins and purge us of our evil deeds and claim us back with the
3:194 righteous. Lord, grant us what You promised through Your apostles, and do
not hold us up to shame on the Day of Resurrection. You never fail the time
decreed.'

وإذ أخذ الله ميثاق الذين أوتوا الكتاب لتبيننه
للناس ولا تكتمونه فنبذوه وراء ظهورهم
واشتروا به ثمنا قليلا فبئس ما يشترون ﴿١٨٧﴾ لا تحسبن
الذين يفرحون بما أتوا ويحبون أن يحمدوا بما لم يفعلوا
فلا تحسبنهم بمفازة من العذاب ولهم عذاب
أليم ﴿١٨٨﴾ ولله ملك السموات والأرض والله
على كل شيء قدير ﴿١٨٩﴾ إن في خلق السموات والأرض
واختلاف الليل والنهار لآيات لأولي الألباب ﴿١٩٠﴾ الذين
يذكرون الله قياما وقعودا وعلى جنوبهم ويتفكرون
في خلق السموات والأرض ربنا ما خلقت هذا باطلا
سبحانك فقنا عذاب النار ﴿١٩١﴾ ربنا إنك من تدخل النار فقد
أخزيته وما للظالمين من أنصار ﴿١٩٢﴾ ربنا إننا سمعنا مناديا ينادي
للإيمان أن آمنوا بربكم فآمنا ربنا فاغفر لنا ذنوبنا وكفر عنا
سيئاتنا وتوفنا مع الأبرار ﴿١٩٣﴾ ربنا وآتنا ما وعدتنا على
رسلك ولا تخزنا يوم القيامة إنك لا تخلف الميعاد ﴿١٩٤﴾

فاستجاب لهم ربهم أني لا أضيع عمل عامل منكم من ذكر
أو أنثى بعضكم من بعض فالذين هاجروا وأخرجوا من
ديارهم وأوذوا في سبيلي وقاتلوا وقتلوا لأكفرن عنهم
سيئاتهم ولأدخلنهم جنات تجري من تحتها الأنهار
ثوابا من عند الله والله عنده حسن الثواب ١٩٥ لا
يغرنك تقلب الذين كفروا في البلاد ١٩٦ متاع
قليل ثم مأواهم جهنم وبئس المهاد ١٩٧ لكن
الذين اتقوا ربهم لهم جنات تجري من تحتها الأنهار خالدين
فيها نزلا من عند الله وما عند الله خير للأبرار ١٩٨ و
إن من أهل الكتاب لمن يؤمن بالله وما أنزل إليكم وما أنزل
إليهم خاشعين لله لا يشترون بآيات الله ثمنا قليلا أولئك لهم
أجرهم عند ربهم إن الله سريع الحساب ١٩٩ يا أيها الذين
آمنوا اصبروا وصابروا ورابطوا واتقوا الله لعلكم تفلحون ٢٠٠

THEIR LORD will answer 3:195
them: 'I will deny none among
you, male or female, the
reward of their labours. The
one of you is as the other.'

Those that fled their land and were expelled from their homes, and suffered persecution for My sake and fought and were slain: I shall surely acquit them of their evil deeds and admit them into Gardens watered by running brooks, as a recompense from God; God dispenses the richest recompense.

Never be deluded by the 3:196
goings-on of the unbelievers
in the land: a little enjoyment –
then Hell shall be their home:
an evil resting-place. But for
those that fear God, theirs
shall be Gardens watered by
running brooks, wherein shall they abide for ever: a gracious welcome from
God. And that which is in store with God is surely better for the righteous.

Some there are among the People of the Book who truly believe in God, and in what has been revealed to you and what was revealed to them: they humble themselves before God and do not sell God's revelations for a trifling price. These shall be rewarded by their Lord. Swift is God's reckoning.

Believers, be patient and forbear; stand firm in your faith and fear God, 3:200
that you may succeed.

WOMEN

In the Name of God,
the Merciful, the Compassionate

4:1 YOU PEOPLE! Fear your Lord, who created you from a single soul. From that soul He created its spouse and through them He bestrewed the earth with countless men and women.

Fear God, in whose name you plead with one another, and honour the mothers who bore you. God is ever watching you.

Give orphans the property which belongs to them. Do not exchange their valuables for worthless things or cheat them of their possessions; for this would surely be a grievous sin. If you fear that you cannot treat orphans[1] with fairness, then you may marry other women who seem good to you: two, three, or four. But if you fear that you cannot maintain equality among them, marry one only or any slave-girls you may own. This will make it easier for you to avoid injustice.

Give women their dowry as a free gift; but if they willingly choose to make over to you a part of it, you may enjoy it as lawfully yours.

4:5 Do not give the feeble-minded the property with which God has charged you for their support; but maintain and clothe them with its proceeds, and speak kind words to them.

4:6 Put orphans to the test until they reach a marriageable age. If you find them capable of sound judgement, hand over to them their property, and do not cheat them of it by squandering it before they come of age.

Let not the rich guardian touch the property of his orphan ward; and let him who is poor use no more than a fair portion of it for his own advantage.

When you hand over to them their property, call in some witnesses to be present; sufficient is God's reckoning.

بسم الله الرحمن الرحيم
يا أيها الناس اتقوا ربكم الذي خلقكم من نفس واحدة وخلق منها
زوجها وبث منهما رجالا كثيرا ونساء واتقوا الله الذي تساءلون
به والأرحام إن الله كان عليكم رقيبا (١) وآتوا اليتامى أموالهم
ولا تتبدلوا الخبيث بالطيب ولا تأكلوا أموالهم إلى أموالكم إنه كان
حوبا كبيرا (٢) وإن خفتم ألا تقسطوا في اليتامى فانكحوا ما طاب
لكم من النساء مثنى وثلاث ورباع فإن خفتم ألا تعدلوا فواحدة
أو ما ملكت أيمانكم ذلك أدنى ألا تعولوا (٣) وآتوا النساء صدقاتهن
نحلة فإن طبن لكم عن شيء منه نفسا فكلوه هنيئا مريئا (٤)
ولا تؤتوا السفهاء أموالكم التي جعل الله لكم قياما وارزقوهم
فيها واكسوهم وقولوا لهم قولا معروفا (٥) وابتلوا اليتامى
حتى إذا بلغوا النكاح فإن آنستم منهم رشدا فادفعوا
إليهم أموالهم ولا تأكلوها إسرافا وبدارا أن يكبروا ومن كان
غنيا فليستعفف ومن كان فقيرا فليأكل بالمعروف فإذا دفعتم
إليهم أموالهم فأشهدوا عليهم وكفى بالله حسيبا (٦)

1. Orphan girls.

للرجال نصيب مما ترك الوالدان والأقربون وللنساء
نصيب مما ترك الوالدان والأقربون مما قل منه أو كثر
نصيبا مفروضا ۝٧ وإذا حضر القسمة أولوا القربى واليتامى
والمساكين فارزقوهم منه وقولوا لهم قولا معروفا
۝٨ وليخش الذين لو تركوا من خلفهم ذرية ضعافا
خافوا عليهم فليتقوا الله وليقولوا قولا سديدا ۝٩ إن
الذين يأكلون أموال اليتامى ظلما إنما يأكلون في بطونهم نارا
وسيصلون سعيرا ۝١٠ يوصيكم الله في أولادكم للذكر
مثل حظ الأنثيين فإن كن نساء فوق اثنتين فلهن ثلثا
ما ترك وإن كانت واحدة فلها النصف ولأبويه لكل
واحد منهما السدس مما ترك إن كان له ولد فإن لم
يكن له ولد وورثه أبواه فلأمه الثلث فإن كان له
إخوة فلأمه السدس من بعد وصية يوصي بها أو دين
آباؤكم وأبناؤكم لا تدرون أيهم أقرب لكم
نفعا فريضة من الله إن الله كان عليما حكيما ۝١١

MEN SHALL have a share in 4:7
what their parents and kin
leave; and women shall have a
share in what their parents and
kin leave: whether it be little or
much, they shall be entitled to
a share decreed.

If relatives, orphans, or
needy men are present at the
division of an inheritance, give
them, too, a share of it, and
speak kind words to them.

Let those who are solicitous
about the welfare of their
young children after their own
death take care not to wrong
orphans. Let them fear God
and speak for justice.

Those that devour the 4:10
property of orphans unjustly,
do swallow fire into their bellies; they shall burn in a mighty
conflagration.

God has thus enjoined you concerning your children: 4:11

A male shall inherit twice as much as a female. If there be more than two girls, they shall have two-thirds of the inheritance; but if there be one only, she shall inherit the half. Parents shall inherit a sixth each, if the deceased have a child; but if he leave no child and his parents be his heirs, his mother shall have a third. If he have brothers, his mother shall have a sixth after payment of any legacy he may have bequeathed or any debt he may have owed.

You may wonder whether your parents or your children are more beneficial to you. But this is a decree from God; surely God is all-knowing and wise.

4:12 AND YOU shall inherit the half of your wives' estate if they die childless. If they leave children, a quarter of their estate shall be yours after payment of any legacy they may have bequeathed or any debt they may have owed.

Your wives shall inherit one-quarter of your estate if you die childless. If you leave children, they shall inherit one-eighth of your estate, after payment of any legacy you may have bequeathed or any debt you may have owed.

If a man or a woman leave neither children nor parents and have a brother or a sister, they shall each inherit one-sixth. If there be more, they shall equally share the third of the estate, after payment of any legacy he may have bequeathed or any debt he may have owed, without prejudice to the rights of the heirs. That is a commandment from God. God is all-knowing, and gracious.

4:13 Such are the bounds set by God. He that obeys God and His apostle shall
be admitted by Him into Gardens watered by running brooks, wherein shall
4:14 they abide for ever. That is the supreme triumph. But he that defies God and
His apostle and transgresses His bounds, shall be cast into a Fire wherein he
shall abide for ever. Shameful punishment awaits him.

ولكم نصف ما ترك أزواجكم إن لم يكن لهن ولد
فإن كان لهن ولد فلكم الربع مما تركن من بعد
وصية يوصين بها أو دين ولهن الربع مما تركتم
إن لم يكن لكم ولد فإن كان لكم ولد فلهن
الثمن مما تركتم من بعد وصية توصون بها أو دين
وإن كان رجل يورث كلالة أو امرأة وله
أخ أو أخت فلكل واحد منهما السدس
فإن كانوا أكثر من ذلك فهم شركاء في
الثلث من بعد وصية يوصى بها أو دين غير
مضار وصية من الله والله عليم حليم ١٢
تلك حدود الله ومن يطع الله ورسوله يدخله
جنات تجري من تحتها الأنهار
خالدين فيها وذلك الفوز العظيم ١٣
ومن يعص الله ورسوله ويتعد حدوده
يدخله نارا خالدا فيها وله عذاب مهين ١٤

والتي يأتين الفاحشة من نسائكم فاستشهدوا عليهن
أربعة منكم فإن شهدوا فأمسكوهن في البيوت حتى
يتوفاهن الموت أو يجعل الله لهن سبيلا ﴿١٥﴾ واللذان
يأتيانها منكم فآذوهما فإن تابا وأصلحا
فأعرضوا عنهما إن الله كان توابا رحيما
﴿١٦﴾ إنما التوبة على الله للذين يعملون السوء
بجهالة ثم يتوبون من قريب فأولئك يتوب
الله عليهم وكان الله عليما حكيما ﴿١٧﴾ وليست
التوبة للذين يعملون السيئات حتى إذا حضر أحدهم
الموت قال إني تبت الآن ولا الذين يموتون وهم كفار
أولئك أعتدنا لهم عذابا أليما ﴿١٨﴾ يا أيها الذين آمنوا
لا يحل لكم أن ترثوا النساء كرها ولا تعضلوهن
لتذهبوا ببعض ما آتيتموهن إلا أن يأتين بفاحشة
مبينة وعاشروهن بالمعروف فإن كرهتموهن فعسى
أن تكرهوا شيئا ويجعل الله فيه خيرا كثيرا ﴿١٩﴾

IF ANY of your women 4:15
commit a lewd act, call in four witnesses from among yourselves against them; if they testify to their guilt, confine them to their houses till death overtakes them or till God finds another way for them.

If two men among you commit a lewd act, punish them both. If they repent and mend their ways, let them be. Surely God is forgiving and compassionate.

God pardons those who 4:17
commit evil in ignorance and then quickly turn to Him in penitence. These God will pardon. God is all-knowing and wise. But He will not pardon those who do evil and, when death comes to any of them, he says: 'Now I repent!' Nor those who die unbelievers: for them We have prepared a woeful scourge.

Believers, it is unlawful for you to inherit the women of your deceased 4:19
kinsmen against their will, or to bar them from remarrying, in order that you may force them to give up a part of what you have given them, unless they be guilty of a proven lewd act. Live with them in modest conduct; for even if you dislike them, it may well be that you dislike a thing which God has meant for your own abundant good.

4:20 If you wish to replace one wife with another, do not take anything from the dowry you gave her even if it be a talent. That would be improper and a veritable sin; for how can you take it back when you have lain with each other and entered into a firm contract?

You shall not marry the women whom your fathers married: all previous such marriages excepted. That was an evil practice, indecent and abominable.

4:23 Forbidden to you are your mothers, your daughters, your sisters, your paternal and maternal aunts, the daughters of your brothers and sisters, your foster-mothers, your foster-sisters, the mothers of your wives, your stepdaughters who are in your charge, born of the wives with whom you have lain (it is no offence for you to marry your stepdaughters if you have not consummated your marriage with their mothers), and the wives of your own begotten sons.[1] You are forbidden also to marry two sisters at one and the same time: all previous such marriages excepted. Surely God is forgiving and compassionate.

وَإِنْ أَرَدْتُمُ اسْتِبْدَالَ زَوْجٍ مَكَانَ زَوْجٍ وَآتَيْتُمْ
إِحْدَاهُنَّ قِنْطَارًا فَلَا تَأْخُذُوا مِنْهُ شَيْئًا أَتَأْخُذُونَهُ
بُهْتَانًا وَإِثْمًا مُبِينًا ﴿٢٠﴾ وَكَيْفَ تَأْخُذُونَهُ وَقَدْ
أَفْضَىٰ بَعْضُكُمْ إِلَىٰ بَعْضٍ وَأَخَذْنَ مِنْكُمْ مِيثَاقًا غَلِيظًا
﴿٢١﴾ وَلَا تَنْكِحُوا مَا نَكَحَ آبَاؤُكُمْ مِنَ النِّسَاءِ إِلَّا
مَا قَدْ سَلَفَ إِنَّهُ كَانَ فَاحِشَةً وَمَقْتًا وَسَاءَ
سَبِيلًا ﴿٢٢﴾ حُرِّمَتْ عَلَيْكُمْ أُمَّهَاتُكُمْ وَبَنَاتُكُمْ
وَأَخَوَاتُكُمْ وَعَمَّاتُكُمْ وَخَالَاتُكُمْ وَبَنَاتُ الْأَخِ
وَبَنَاتُ الْأُخْتِ وَأُمَّهَاتُكُمُ اللَّاتِي أَرْضَعْنَكُمْ
وَأَخَوَاتُكُمْ مِنَ الرَّضَاعَةِ وَأُمَّهَاتُ نِسَائِكُمْ
وَرَبَائِبُكُمُ اللَّاتِي فِي حُجُورِكُمْ مِنْ نِسَائِكُمُ
اللَّاتِي دَخَلْتُمْ بِهِنَّ فَإِنْ لَمْ تَكُونُوا دَخَلْتُمْ بِهِنَّ
فَلَا جُنَاحَ عَلَيْكُمْ وَحَلَائِلُ أَبْنَائِكُمُ الَّذِينَ
مِنْ أَصْلَابِكُمْ وَأَنْ تَجْمَعُوا بَيْنَ الْأُخْتَيْنِ إِلَّا
مَا قَدْ سَلَفَ إِنَّ اللَّهَ كَانَ غَفُورًا رَحِيمًا ﴿٢٣﴾

1. Cf. Leviticus 18.

والمحصنات من النساء إلا ما ملكت أيمانكم
كتاب الله عليكم وأحل لكم ما وراء ذلكم أن
تبتغوا بأموالكم محصنين غير مسافحين فما استمتعتم
به منهن فآتوهن أجورهن فريضة ولا جناح عليكم فيما
تراضيتم به من بعد الفريضة إن الله كان عليما حكيما
(٢٤) ومن لم يستطع منكم طولا أن ينكح المحصنات
المؤمنات فمن ما ملكت أيمانكم من فتياتكم
المؤمنات والله أعلم بإيمانكم بعضكم من بعض
فانكحوهن بإذن أهلهن وآتوهن أجورهن
بالمعروف محصنات غير مسافحات ولا متخذات
أخدان فإذا أحصن فإن أتين بفاحشة فعليهن نصف
ما على المحصنات من العذاب ذلك لمن خشي العنت منكم
وأن تصبروا خير لكم والله غفور رحيم (٢٥)
يريد الله ليبين لكم ويهديكم سنن الذين
من قبلكم ويتوب عليكم والله عليم حكيم (٢٦)

ALSO MARRIED women, 4:24
except those whom you own
as slaves. Such is the decree of
God. All women other than
these are lawful for you, provided you court them with
your wealth in modest conduct, not in fornication. Give
them their dowry for the
enjoyment you have had of
them as a duty; but it shall be
no offence for you to make
any other agreement among
yourselves after you have fulfilled your duty. Surely God is
all-knowing and wise.
If any one of you cannot 4:25
afford to marry a believing
free woman, let him marry a
slave-girl who is a believer
(God best knows your faith:
you are born one of another).
Marry them with their mas-
ters' permission and give them their dowry in all justice, provided they are
honourable and chaste and have not courted other men. If after marriage
they commit a lewd act, they shall suffer half the penalty inflicted upon free
women. Such is the provision for those of you who fear impropriety: but if
you abstain, it will be better for you. God is forgiving and compassionate.
God desires to make this clear to you and to guide you along the paths of 4:26
those who have gone before you, and to pardon you. God is all-knowing and
wise.

4:27 AND GOD wishes to pardon you, but those who follow their own appetites wish to see you stray grievously into error. God wishes to lighten your burdens, for Man was created weak.

Believers, do not consume your wealth among yourselves in vanity, but rather trade with it by mutual consent.

Do not kill one another.[1] Surely God is compassionate to you, but he that does that through wickedness and injustice We shall burn in fire. Surely that is[2] easy enough for God.

If you avoid the enormities you are forbidden, We shall pardon your misdeeds and
usher you in with all honour.
4:32 Do not covet the favours by
which God has exalted some among you above others. Men shall be rewarded according to their deserts, and women shall be rewarded according to their deserts. Rather implore God to bestow on you His bounty. Surely God has knowledge of all things.

4:33 To every parent and kin We have appointed heirs who will inherit from them. As for those with whom you have entered into agreements, let them, too, have their share. Surely God bears witness to all things.

والله يريد أن يتوب عليكم ويريد الذين
يتبعون الشهوات أن تميلوا ميلا عظيما ٢٧ يريد
الله أن يخفف عنكم وخلق الإنسان ضعيفا ٢٨
يا أيها الذين آمنوا لا تأكلوا أموالكم بينكم
بالباطل إلا أن تكون تجارة عن تراض منكم
ولا تقتلوا أنفسكم إن الله كان بكم رحيما ٢٩ ومن يفعل
ذلك عدوانا وظلما فسوف نصليه نارا وكان ذلك على
الله يسيرا ٣٠ إن تجتنبوا كبائر ما تنهون عنه نكفر
عنكم سيئاتكم وندخلكم مدخلا كريما ٣١
ولا تتمنوا ما فضل الله به بعضكم على بعض للرجال
نصيب مما اكتسبوا وللنساء نصيب مما اكتسبن وسئلوا
الله من فضله إن الله كان بكل شيء عليما ٣٢
ولكل جعلنا موالي مما ترك الوالدان
والأقربون والذين عقدت أيمانكم فآتوهم
نصيبهم إن الله كان على كل شيء شهيدا ٣٣

1. Literally, do not kill yourselves.
2. Literally, was; in the language of the Koran, the use of *kana* is for emphasis, not as a form of past tense.

الرِّجَالُ قَوَّامُونَ عَلَى النِّسَاءِ بِمَا فَضَّلَ اللَّهُ
بَعْضَهُمْ عَلَىٰ بَعْضٍ وَبِمَا أَنْفَقُوا مِنْ أَمْوَالِهِمْ
فَالصَّالِحَاتُ قَانِتَاتٌ حَافِظَاتٌ لِلْغَيْبِ بِمَا حَفِظَ اللَّهُ
وَاللَّاتِي تَخَافُونَ نُشُوزَهُنَّ فَعِظُوهُنَّ وَاهْجُرُوهُنَّ
فِي الْمَضَاجِعِ وَاضْرِبُوهُنَّ فَإِنْ أَطَعْنَكُمْ
فَلَا تَبْغُوا عَلَيْهِنَّ سَبِيلًا إِنَّ اللَّهَ كَانَ عَلِيًّا كَبِيرًا ٣٤
وَإِنْ خِفْتُمْ شِقَاقَ بَيْنِهِمَا فَابْعَثُوا حَكَمًا مِنْ أَهْلِهِ وَحَكَمًا مِنْ
أَهْلِهَا إِنْ يُرِيدَا إِصْلَاحًا يُوَفِّقِ اللَّهُ بَيْنَهُمَا إِنَّ اللَّهَ
كَانَ عَلِيمًا خَبِيرًا ٣٥ وَاعْبُدُوا اللَّهَ وَلَا تُشْرِكُوا بِهِ
شَيْئًا وَبِالْوَالِدَيْنِ إِحْسَانًا وَبِذِي الْقُرْبَىٰ وَالْيَتَامَىٰ
وَالْمَسَاكِينِ وَالْجَارِ ذِي الْقُرْبَىٰ وَالْجَارِ الْجُنُبِ وَالصَّاحِبِ
بِالْجَنْبِ وَابْنِ السَّبِيلِ وَمَا مَلَكَتْ أَيْمَانُكُمْ إِنَّ اللَّهَ
لَا يُحِبُّ مَنْ كَانَ مُخْتَالًا فَخُورًا ٣٦ الَّذِينَ يَبْخَلُونَ
وَيَأْمُرُونَ النَّاسَ بِالْبُخْلِ وَيَكْتُمُونَ مَا آتَاهُمُ اللَّهُ
مِنْ فَضْلِهِ وَأَعْتَدْنَا لِلْكَافِرِينَ عَذَابًا مُهِينًا ٣٧

MEN HAVE authority over women because God has made the one superior to the other, and because they spend their wealth to maintain them. Good women are obedient. They guard their unseen parts because God has guarded them. As for those from whom you fear disobedience, admonish them, and forsake them in beds[1] apart, and beat them. Then if they obey you, take no further action against them. Surely God is high, supreme. 4:34

If you fear a breach between a man and his wife, appoint an arbiter from his people and an arbiter from her people. If they wish to be reconciled, God will bring them together again. Surely God is all-knowing and wise.

Serve God and associate none with Him. Show kindness to parents and to 4:36
kin, to orphans and to the destitute, to near and distant neighbours, to those
that keep company with you, to the traveller in need, and to the slaves you
own. God does not love the arrogant and the boastful, who are themselves 4:37
niggardly and enjoin people to be niggardly; who conceal that which God of
His bounty has given them (We have prepared a shameful punishment for
the unbelievers);

1. Or: bedrooms.

4:38 and who spend their wealth only to be seen by people, believing neither in God nor in the Last Day. He that chooses Satan for his friend, an evil friend has he.

What could harm them if they believed in God and the Last Day and gave in alms from that which God bestowed on them? God surely knows them well.

God will wrong none by as much as the weight of an atom. A good deed He will repay two-fold. Of His own bounty He will bestow a rich recompense.

How will it be when We produce a witness from each community and call upon you to testify against them? On that day those who disbelieved and disobeyed the Apostle will wish that they were levelled with the dust; they cannot hide from God any word that is spoken.

4:43 Believers, do not approach your prayers when you are drunk, until you know what you are saying; nor when you are unclean – unless you are travelling the road – until you have washed yourselves. If you are sick or on a journey, or if, when you have relieved yourselves or had intercourse with women, you can find no water, take some clean sand and rub your faces and your hands with it. God will surely pardon and forgive.

4:44 Consider those to whom a portion of the Book was given. They purchase error for themselves and wish to see you go astray.

والذين ينفقون اموالهم رئاء الناس ولا يؤمنون بالله
ولا باليوم الآخر ومن يكن الشيطان له قرينا فساء قرينا
﴿٣٨﴾ وماذا عليهم لو امنوا بالله واليوم الآخر وانفقوا
مما رزقهم الله وكان الله بهم عليما ﴿٣٩﴾ ان الله
لا يظلم مثقال ذرة وان تك حسنة يضاعفها
ويؤت من لدنه اجرا عظيما ﴿٤٠﴾ فكيف اذا جئنا من
كل امة بشهيد وجئنا بك على هؤلاء شهيدا ﴿٤١﴾ يومئذ
يود الذين كفروا وعصوا الرسول لو تسوى بهم الارض
ولا يكتمون الله حديثا ﴿٤٢﴾ يا ايها الذين امنوا لا تقربوا
الصلوة وانتم سكارى حتى تعلموا ما تقولون ولا جنبا الا
عابري سبيل حتى تغتسلوا وان كنتم مرضى او على سفر
او جاء احد منكم من الغائط او لمستم النساء فلم تجدوا ماء
فتيمموا صعيدا طيبا فامسحوا بوجوهكم وايديكم ان الله
كان عفوا غفورا ﴿٤٣﴾ الم تر الى الذين اوتوا نصيبا من الكتاب
يشترون الضلالة ويريدون ان تضلوا السبيل ﴿٤٤﴾

وَاللَّهُ أَعْلَمُ بِأَعْدَائِكُمْ وَكَفَىٰ بِاللَّهِ وَلِيًّا وَكَفَىٰ بِاللَّهِ
نَصِيرًا ﴿٤٥﴾ مِنَ الَّذِينَ هَادُوا يُحَرِّفُونَ الْكَلِمَ عَنْ مَوَاضِعِهِ
وَيَقُولُونَ سَمِعْنَا وَعَصَيْنَا وَاسْمَعْ غَيْرَ مُسْمَعٍ وَرَاعِنَا لَيًّا
بِأَلْسِنَتِهِمْ وَطَعْنًا فِي الدِّينِ وَلَوْ أَنَّهُمْ قَالُوا سَمِعْنَا وَأَطَعْنَا
وَاسْمَعْ وَانْظُرْنَا لَكَانَ خَيْرًا لَهُمْ وَأَقْوَمَ وَلَٰكِنْ لَعَنَهُمُ
اللَّهُ بِكُفْرِهِمْ فَلَا يُؤْمِنُونَ إِلَّا قَلِيلًا ﴿٤٦﴾ يَا أَيُّهَا الَّذِينَ أُوتُوا
الْكِتَابَ آمِنُوا بِمَا نَزَّلْنَا مُصَدِّقًا لِمَا مَعَكُمْ مِنْ قَبْلِ أَنْ
نَطْمِسَ وُجُوهًا فَنَرُدَّهَا عَلَىٰ أَدْبَارِهَا أَوْ نَلْعَنَهُمْ كَمَا
لَعَنَّا أَصْحَابَ السَّبْتِ وَكَانَ أَمْرُ اللَّهِ مَفْعُولًا ﴿٤٧﴾ إِنَّ اللَّهَ
لَا يَغْفِرُ أَنْ يُشْرَكَ بِهِ وَيَغْفِرُ مَا دُونَ ذَٰلِكَ لِمَنْ يَشَاءُ وَمَنْ يُشْرِكْ
بِاللَّهِ فَقَدِ افْتَرَىٰ إِثْمًا عَظِيمًا ﴿٤٨﴾ أَلَمْ تَرَ إِلَى الَّذِينَ يُزَكُّونَ أَنْفُسَهُمْ بَلِ
اللَّهُ يُزَكِّي مَنْ يَشَاءُ وَلَا يُظْلَمُونَ فَتِيلًا ﴿٤٩﴾ انْظُرْ كَيْفَ يَفْتَرُونَ عَلَى
اللَّهِ الْكَذِبَ وَكَفَىٰ بِهِ إِثْمًا مُبِينًا ﴿٥٠﴾ أَلَمْ تَرَ إِلَى الَّذِينَ أُوتُوا
نَصِيبًا مِنَ الْكِتَابِ يُؤْمِنُونَ بِالْجِبْتِ وَالطَّاغُوتِ وَيَقُولُونَ
لِلَّذِينَ كَفَرُوا هَٰؤُلَاءِ أَهْدَىٰ مِنَ الَّذِينَ آمَنُوا سَبِيلًا ﴿٥١﴾

AND GOD best knows your 4:45
enemies. Sufficient is God as
a protector, and sufficient is
God as a helper.

Among those who follow
the Jewish Faith are some
who take words out of their
context and say:[1] 'We hear,
but will disobey. May you be
bereft of hearing! *Rā'inā!*' –
thus distorting the phrase
with their tongues and reviling the Religion. But if they
said: 'We hear and obey: hear
us and *unẓurnā*,'[2] it would be
better and more proper for
them. But God has cursed
them in their unbelief. They
have no faith, except a few.

You to whom the Book 4:47
was given! Believe in that
which We have revealed, confirming your own, before We
obliterate some faces and turn them backward, or curse them as We cursed
the Sabbath-breakers. What God ordains shall be accomplished.

God will not forgive those who serve other deities besides Him; but He
will forgive whom He will for other sins. He that serves other deities besides
God is guilty of a heinous sin.

Do but consider those who think themselves pure. God purifies whom
He will. They shall not be wronged by as much as the husk of a date-stone.

Behold how they invent falsehoods about God; this in itself is a most
grievous sin.

Consider those to whom a portion of the Book was given. They believe 4:51
in idols and false gods and say of the infidels: 'These are better guided than
those who believe.'

1. To Muḥammad. 2. See p. 15, note 1.

4:52 THESE ARE they whom God has cursed; and he who is cursed by God has none to help him.

Will they have a share in sovereignty? If so, they will not give people so much as the speck on a date-stone.

Or do they envy others what God has of His bounty given them? We gave Abraham's descendants the Book and wisdom, and an illustrious kingdom. Some among them believe in him,[1] and some reject him. Sufficient scourge is the fire of Hell.

Those that deny Our revelations We will burn in fire. No sooner will their skins be consumed than We shall give them other skins, so that they may taste the torment. Surely God is mighty and wise.

اولئك الذين لعنهم الله ومن يلعن الله فلن تجد له نصيرا
٥٢ ام لهم نصيب من الملك فاذا لا يؤتون الناس نقيرا
٥٣ ام يحسدون الناس على ما اتيهم الله من فضله فقد
اتينا ال ابرهيم الكتاب والحكمة واتيناهم ملكا عظيما ٥٤
فمنهم من امن به ومنهم من صد عنه وكفى بجهنم سعيرا ٥٥ ان
الذين كفروا باياتنا سوف نصليهم نارا كلما نضجت جلودهم
بدلناهم جلودا غيرها ليذوقوا العذاب ان الله كان عزيزا حكيما ٥٦
والذين امنوا وعملوا الصالحات سندخلهم جنات تجري من
تحتها الانهار خالدين فيها ابدا لهم فيها ازواج مطهرة
وندخلهم ظلا ظليلا ٥٧ ان الله يامركم ان تؤدوا
الامانات الى اهلها واذا حكمتم بين الناس ان تحكموا
بالعدل ان الله نعما يعظكم به ان الله كان سميعا بصيرا ٥٨
يا ايها الذين امنوا اطيعوا الله واطيعوا الرسول واولي الامر منكم
فان تنازعتم في شيء فردوه الى الله والرسول ان كنتم
تؤمنون بالله واليوم الاخر ذلك خير واحسن تاويلا ٥٩

4:57 As for those that believe and do good works, We shall admit them into Gardens watered by running brooks, wherein, wedded to chaste spouses, shall they abide for ever. To a cool shade shall We admit them.

God commands you to hand back your trusts to their rightful owners, and, when you pass judgement among people, to judge with fairness. Noble is that to which God exhorts you. Surely God hears all and observes all.

4:59 Believers, obey God and obey the Apostle and those in authority among you. Should you disagree about anything refer it to God and the Apostle, if you believe in God and the Last Day. This will in the end be better and more just.

1. Muḥammad.

الم تر الى الذين يزعمون انهم امنوا بما انزل
اليك وما انزل من قبلك يريدون ان يتحاكموا
الى الطاغوت وقد امروا ان يكفروا به ويريد
الشيطان ان يضلهم ضلالا بعيدا ٦٠ واذا قيل لهم
تعالوا الى ما انزل الله والى الرسول رايت المنافقين
يصدون عنك صدودا ٦١ فكيف اذا اصابتهم مصيبة
بما قدمت ايديهم ثم جاؤك يحلفون بالله ان اردنا الا
احسانا وتوفيقا ٦٢ اولئك الذين يعلم الله ما في قلوبهم
فاعرض عنهم وعظهم وقل لهم في انفسهم
قولا بليغا ٦٣ وما ارسلنا من رسول الا ليطاع
باذن الله ولو انهم اذ ظلموا انفسهم
جاؤك فاستغفروا الله واستغفر لهم الرسول
لوجدوا الله توابا رحيما ٦٤ فلا وربك لا يؤمنون
حتى يحكموك فيما شجر بينهم ثم لا يجدوا
في انفسهم حرجا مما قضيت ويسلموا تسليما ٦٥

MARK THOSE who profess 4:60
to believe in what has been
revealed to you and what was
revealed before you. They
seek the judgement of the
devil, although they were bidden to deny him. Satan would
lead them far into error.

If they are told: 'Come to
be judged by that which God
has revealed and by the Apostle,' you see the hypocrites
reject you vehemently. But
how would it be if some disaster befell them on account
of what their hands committed? They would come to you
swearing by God that 'we
desired nothing but amity and
conciliation.' But God knows 4:63
what their hearts conceal. Let
them be. Admonish them and
eloquently rebuke them.

We have sent forth apostles only so that they are obeyed by God's leave.
If, when they wronged themselves, they had come to you imploring God's
forgiveness, and if the Apostle had sought forgiveness for them, they would
have found that God pardons and is compassionate.

But, by your Lord, they will not believe until they seek your arbitration in 4:65
their disputes. Then they will not doubt the justice of your verdicts and will
submit entirely.

4:66 AND HAD We commanded them: 'Lay down your lives,' or 'Flee from your homes,' only a few would have complied. Yet, had they done what they were admonished to do, it would have been better for them and their faith would have been strengthened. We would have bestowed on them of Our grace a rich recompense and guided them to a straight path.

And he that obeys God and the Apostle shall dwell with the prophets and the saints, the martyrs and the righteous whom God has favoured. Gracious companions will be those.

Such is God's bounty; and sufficient is God's infinite knowledge.

ولو أنا كتبنا عليهم أن اقتلوا أنفسكم أو اخرجوا من
ديٰركم ما فعلوه إلا قليل منهم ولو أنهم فعلوا ما يوعظون
به لكان خيرا لهم وأشد تثبيتا ٦٦ وإذا لآتينٰهم
من لدنا أجرا عظيما ٦٧ ولهدينٰهم صرٰطا مستقيما ٦٨
ومن يطع الله والرسول فأولٰئك مع الذين أنعم الله
عليهم من النبيين والصديقين والشهداء والصٰلحين
وحسن أولٰئك رفيقا ٦٩ ذٰلك الفضل من الله
وكفى بالله عليما ٧٠ يٰأيها الذين آمنوا خذوا حذركم
فانفروا ثبات أو انفروا جميعا ٧١ وإن منكم لمن
ليبطئن فإن أصٰبتكم مصيبة قال قد أنعم الله
علي إذ لم أكن معهم شهيدا ٧٢ ولئن أصٰبكم
فضل من الله ليقولن كأن لم تكن بينكم وبينه مودة يٰليتني
كنت معهم فأفوز فوزا عظيما ٧٣ فليقٰتل في سبيل الله
الذين يشرون الحيوٰة الدنيا بالآخرة ومن يقٰتل
في سبيل الله فيقتل أو يغلب فسوف نؤتيه أجرا عظيما ٧٤

4:71 Believers, be ever on your guard: march in detachments or in one body. Someone among you is sure to lag behind, so that if a disaster befell you, he would say: 'God was gracious to me; I was not present with them.' But if, by God's grace, you were successful, he would surely say, as though there was no friendship between you and him: 'Would that I had been with them! I should have won a great victory.'

4:74 Let those who would exchange the life of this world for the Hereafter, fight for the cause of God; whoever fights for the cause of God, whether he be slain or he triumph, on him We shall bestow a rich recompense.

وَمَا لَكُمْ لَا تُقَاتِلُونَ فِي سَبِيلِ اللَّهِ وَالْمُسْتَضْعَفِينَ مِنَ الرِّجَالِ
وَالنِّسَاءِ وَالْوِلْدَانِ الَّذِينَ يَقُولُونَ رَبَّنَا أَخْرِجْنَا مِنْ هَٰذِهِ الْقَرْيَةِ
الظَّالِمِ أَهْلُهَا وَاجْعَلْ لَنَا مِنْ لَدُنْكَ وَلِيًّا وَاجْعَلْ لَنَا مِنْ لَدُنْكَ نَصِيرًا
٧٥ الَّذِينَ آمَنُوا يُقَاتِلُونَ فِي سَبِيلِ اللَّهِ وَالَّذِينَ كَفَرُوا يُقَاتِلُونَ
فِي سَبِيلِ الطَّاغُوتِ فَقَاتِلُوا أَوْلِيَاءَ الشَّيْطَانِ إِنَّ كَيْدَ الشَّيْطَانِ
كَانَ ضَعِيفًا ٧٦ أَلَمْ تَرَ إِلَى الَّذِينَ قِيلَ لَهُمْ كُفُّوا أَيْدِيَكُمْ
وَأَقِيمُوا الصَّلَاةَ وَآتُوا الزَّكَاةَ فَلَمَّا كُتِبَ عَلَيْهِمُ الْقِتَالُ إِذَا فَرِيقٌ
مِنْهُمْ يَخْشَوْنَ النَّاسَ كَخَشْيَةِ اللَّهِ أَوْ أَشَدَّ خَشْيَةً وَقَالُوا
رَبَّنَا لِمَ كَتَبْتَ عَلَيْنَا الْقِتَالَ لَوْلَا أَخَّرْتَنَا إِلَىٰ أَجَلٍ قَرِيبٍ قُلْ مَتَاعُ الدُّنْيَا
قَلِيلٌ وَالْآخِرَةُ خَيْرٌ لِمَنِ اتَّقَىٰ وَلَا تُظْلَمُونَ فَتِيلًا ٧٧ أَيْنَمَا تَكُونُوا
يُدْرِكْكُمُ الْمَوْتُ وَلَوْ كُنْتُمْ فِي بُرُوجٍ مُشَيَّدَةٍ وَإِنْ تُصِبْهُمْ
حَسَنَةٌ يَقُولُوا هَٰذِهِ مِنْ عِنْدِ اللَّهِ وَإِنْ تُصِبْهُمْ سَيِّئَةٌ يَقُولُوا
هَٰذِهِ مِنْ عِنْدِكَ قُلْ كُلٌّ مِنْ عِنْدِ اللَّهِ فَمَالِ هَٰؤُلَاءِ الْقَوْمِ لَا يَكَادُونَ
يَفْقَهُونَ حَدِيثًا ٧٨ مَا أَصَابَكَ مِنْ حَسَنَةٍ فَمِنَ اللَّهِ وَمَا أَصَابَكَ
مِنْ سَيِّئَةٍ فَمِنْ نَفْسِكَ وَأَرْسَلْنَاكَ لِلنَّاسِ رَسُولًا وَكَفَىٰ بِاللَّهِ شَهِيدًا ٧٩

AND HOW should you not 4:75
fight for the cause of God, and for the helpless old men, women, and children[1] who say: 'Deliver us, Lord, from this city of wrongdoers; send forth to us a guardian from Your presence; send to us from Your presence one that will help us'?

The true believers fight for the cause of God, but the infidels fight for the devil. Fight then the friends of Satan; Satan's cunning is weak indeed.

Mark those who were told: 4:77
'Lay down your arms; recite your prayers and render the alms levy.' When they were ordered to fight, some of them feared man as much as they feared God or even more. 'Lord,' they said, 'why do You bid us fight? Could you not give us a brief respite?'

Say: 'Trifling are the pleasures of this life. Better is the life to come for those who fear God. You shall not be wronged by as much as the husk of a date-stone. Wherever you may be, death will overtake you: though you put yourselves in lofty towers.'

When they are blessed with good fortune, they say: 'This is from God.' But when evil befalls them, they say: 'It was your[2] fault.'

Say: 'All is from God!'

What has come over these people that they can hardly understand a word?

Whatever good befalls you,[3] it is from God: and whatever ill befalls you is 4:79
from yourself.

We have sent you forth as an apostle to mankind. Sufficient is God as a witness.

1. In Mecca. 2. Muḥammad's. 3. Man.

4:80 HE THAT obeys the Apostle has assuredly obeyed God. As for those that pay no heed, We have not sent you to be their keeper.

They promise obedience: but as soon as they leave your presence a band of them plot in secret to do otherwise. God takes note of all their plots. Therefore let them be, and put your trust in God. Sufficient is God as a guardian.

Will they not ponder on the Koran? If it had come from other than God, they could have surely found in it many contradictions.

4:83 When they hear any news, good or bad, they at once make it known to all; whereas if they reported it to the Apostle and to those in authority among them, those who sought news could learn it from them. But for God's grace and mercy, all but a few of you would have followed Satan.

Therefore fight for the cause of God. You are accountable for none but yourself. Rouse the faithful: perchance God will overthrow the might of the unbelievers. Mightier is God and more terrible is His retribution.

He that mediates in a good cause shall gain by his mediation; and he that mediates in a bad cause shall be held accountable for its evil. God surely has control over all things.

4:86 If a man greets you, let your greeting be better than his – or at least return it. God surely keeps count of all things.

من يطع الرسول فقد أطاع الله ومن تولى فما أرسلناك
عليهم حفيظا ٨٠ ويقولون طاعة فإذا برزوا من
عندك بيت طائفة منهم غير الذي تقول والله يكتب
ما يبيتون فأعرض عنهم وتوكل على الله وكفى بالله
وكيلا ٨١ أفلا يتدبرون القرآن ولو كان من عند غير الله
لوجدوا فيه اختلافا كثيرا ٨٢ وإذا جاءهم أمر من الأمن
أو الخوف أذاعوا به ولو ردوه إلى الرسول وإلى أولي الأمر منهم
لعلمه الذين يستنبطونه منهم ولولا فضل الله عليكم
ورحمته لاتبعتم الشيطان إلا قليلا ٨٣ فقاتل في سبيل الله
لا تكلف إلا نفسك وحرض المؤمنين عسى الله أن يكف
بأس الذين كفروا والله أشد بأسا وأشد تنكيلا
٨٤ من يشفع شفاعة حسنة يكن له نصيب منها
ومن يشفع شفاعة سيئة يكن له كفل منها وكان الله
على كل شيء مقيتا ٨٥ وإذا حييتم بتحية فحيوا بأحسن
منها أو ردوها إن الله كان على كل شيء حسيبا ٨٦

اللّه لا إله إلا هو ليجمعنكم إلى يوم القيمة لا ريب فيه
ومن أصدق من اللّه حديثا ٨٧ فما لكم في المنافقين فئتين
واللّه أركسهم بما كسبوا أتريدون أن تهدوا من أضل
اللّه ومن يضلل اللّه فلن تجد له سبيلا ٨٨ ودوا لو تكفرون
كما كفروا فتكونون سواء فلا تتخذوا منهم أولياء حتى
يهاجروا في سبيل اللّه فإن تولوا فخذوهم واقتلوهم حيث
وجدتموهم ولا تتخذوا منهم وليا ولا نصيرا ٨٩
إلا الذين يصلون إلى قوم بينكم وبينهم ميثاق
أو جاءوكم حصرت صدورهم أن يقاتلوكم أو يقاتلوا
قومهم ولو شاء اللّه لسلطهم عليكم فلقاتلوكم فإن
اعتزلوكم فلم يقاتلوكم وألقوا إليكم السلم فما جعل
اللّه لكم عليهم سبيلا ٩٠ ستجدون آخرين يريدون أن يأمنوكم
ويأمنوا قومهم كلما ردوا إلى الفتنة أركسوا فيها فإن لم يعتزلوكم
ويلقوا إليكم السلم ويكفوا أيديهم فخذوهم واقتلوهم
حيث ثقفتموهم وأولئكم جعلنا لكم عليهم سلطانا مبينا ٩١

GOD: THERE is no god but 4:87
Him. He will surely gather you
all together on the Day of
Resurrection of which there is
no doubt. And who has a truer
word than God?

Why are you thus divided
concerning the hypocrites,
when God has cast them off
on account of their misdeeds?
Would you guide those whom
God has confounded? He
whom God confounds you
cannot guide.

They would have you disbelieve as they themselves have
disbelieved, so that you may
be all alike. Do not befriend
them until they have fled their
homes in God's cause. If they
desert you, seize them and slay
them wherever you find them.
Look for neither friend nor
helper among them, except those who seek refuge with your allies or come 4:90
over to you because their hearts forbid them to fight you or to fight their
own people. Had God pleased, He would have given them power over you,
so that they would have taken arms against you. Therefore, if they keep away
from you and cease their hostility and offer you peace, God bids you not to
harm them.

Others you will find who seek security from you as well as from their own 4:91
people. Whenever they are called back to sedition they plunge into it headlong. If these do not keep their distance from you, if they neither offer you
peace nor cease their hostilities against you, lay hold of them and slay them
wherever you find them. Over such men We give you absolute authority.

4:92 It is unlawful for a believer to kill another believer, accidents excepted. He that accidentally kills a believer shall free one Muslim slave and pay blood-money to the family of the victim, unless they choose to give it away in alms. If the victim be a Muslim from a hostile tribe, the penalty shall be the freeing of one Muslim slave. But if the victim be a member of an allied tribe, then blood-money shall be paid to his family and a Muslim slave set free. He that lacks the means shall fast two consecutive months. Such is the penance imposed by God: God is all-knowing and wise.

4:93 He that kills a believer by design shall burn in Hell for ever. And he shall incur the ire of God, who will lay His curse on him and prepare for him a mighty scourge.

4:94 Believers, if you go to fight for the cause of God, show discernment and do not say to him that offers you peace: 'You are not a believer,' seeking the chance booty of this world; for with God there are abundant gains. Such was your custom in days gone by, but now God has bestowed on you His grace. Therefore show discernment; God is cognizant of what you do.

وما كان لمؤمن أن يقتل مؤمنا إلا خطأ ومن قتل
مؤمنا خطأ فتحرير رقبة مؤمنة ودية مسلمة إلى
أهله إلا أن يصدقوا فإن كان من قوم
عدو لكم وهو مؤمن فتحرير رقبة مؤمنة وإن
كان من قوم بينكم وبينهم ميثاق فدية
مسلمة إلى أهله وتحرير رقبة مؤمنة فمن
لم يجد فصيام شهرين متتابعين توبة من
الله وكان الله عليما حكيما ﴿٩٢﴾ ومن يقتل
مؤمنا متعمدا فجزاؤه جهنم خالدا فيها وغضب
الله عليه ولعنه وأعد له عذابا عظيما ﴿٩٣﴾
يا أيها الذين آمنوا إذا ضربتم في سبيل الله فتبينوا
ولا تقولوا لمن ألقى إليكم السلام لست مؤمنا
تبتغون عرض الحياة الدنيا فعند الله مغانم
كثيرة كذلك كنتم من قبل فمن الله عليكم
فتبينوا إن الله كان بما تعملون خبيرا ﴿٩٤﴾

لا يستوي القاعدون من المؤمنين غير أولي الضرر والمجاهدون في سبيل
الله بأموالهم وأنفسهم فضل الله المجاهدين بأموالهم وأنفسهم
على القاعدين درجة وكلا وعد الله الحسنى وفضل الله المجاهدين
على القاعدين أجرا عظيما ﴿٩٥﴾ درجات منه ومغفرة ورحمة وكان
الله غفورا رحيما ﴿٩٦﴾ إن الذين توفاهم الملائكة ظالمي أنفسهم قالوا
فيم كنتم قالوا كنا مستضعفين في الأرض قالوا ألم تكن أرض
الله واسعة فتهاجروا فيها فأولئك مأواهم جهنم وساءت
مصيرا ﴿٩٧﴾ إلا المستضعفين من الرجال والنساء والولدان
لا يستطيعون حيلة ولا يهتدون سبيلا ﴿٩٨﴾ فأولئك عسى
الله أن يعفو عنهم وكان الله عفوا غفورا ﴿٩٩﴾ ومن يهاجر في سبيل
الله يجد في الأرض مراغما كثيرا وسعة ومن يخرج من بيته مهاجرا إلى
الله ورسوله ثم يدركه الموت فقد وقع أجره على الله وكان
الله غفورا رحيما ﴿١٠٠﴾ وإذا ضربتم في الأرض فليس عليكم
جناح أن تقصروا من الصلاة إن خفتم أن يفتنكم
الذين كفروا إن الكافرين كانوا لكم عدوا مبينا ﴿١٠١﴾

THE BELIEVERS who stay 4:95
at home – apart from those that suffer from a grave disability – are not the equals of those who fight for the cause of God with their goods and their persons. God has exalted in rank those who fight with their goods and their persons above those who stay at home. God has promised all a good reward; but far richer is the recompense of those who fight for Him: ranks of His own bestowal, forgiveness, and mercy. Surely God is forgiving and compassionate.

The angels will ask those whom they claim back while steeped in sin: 'What were you doing?' 'We were oppressed in the land,' they will reply. They will say: 'Was not the earth of God spacious enough for you to fly for refuge?' Hell shall be the abode of these: a wretched fate!

As for the helpless men, women, and children who have neither the 4:98
strength nor the means to escape, God may pardon them: surely God pardons and forgives.

He that leaves his home in God's cause shall find many a refuge in the land and great abundance. He that leaves his dwelling to fight for God and His apostle and is then overtaken by death shall be recompensed by God. Surely God is forgiving and compassionate.

It is no offence for you to shorten your prayers when travelling the road if 4:101
you fear that the unbelievers may attack you. The unbelievers are your veritable foe.

4:102 WHEN YOU[1] are among them, conducting the prayers, let one party of them rise up to pray with you, armed with their weapons. After making their prostrations, let them withdraw to the rear and then let another party who have not prayed come forward and pray with you; and let these also be on their guard, armed with their weapons. It would much please the unbelievers if you neglected your arms and your baggage, so that they could swoop upon you with one assault. But it is no offence for you to lay aside your arms when overtaken by heavy rain or stricken with an illness, although you must be always on your guard. God has prepared a shameful punishment for the unbelievers.

وَإِذَا كُنتَ فِيهِمْ فَأَقَمْتَ لَهُمُ الصَّلَوٰةَ فَلْتَقُمْ طَائِفَةٌ
مِّنْهُم مَّعَكَ وَلْيَأْخُذُوا أَسْلِحَتَهُمْ فَإِذَا سَجَدُوا فَلْيَكُونُوا
مِن وَرَائِكُمْ وَلْتَأْتِ طَائِفَةٌ أُخْرَىٰ لَمْ يُصَلُّوا فَلْيُصَلُّوا
مَعَكَ وَلْيَأْخُذُوا حِذْرَهُمْ وَأَسْلِحَتَهُمْ وَدَّ الَّذِينَ
كَفَرُوا لَوْ تَغْفُلُونَ عَنْ أَسْلِحَتِكُمْ وَأَمْتِعَتِكُمْ فَيَمِيلُونَ
عَلَيْكُم مَّيْلَةً وَاحِدَةً وَلَا جُنَاحَ عَلَيْكُمْ إِن كَانَ
بِكُمْ أَذًى مِّن مَّطَرٍ أَوْ كُنتُم مَّرْضَىٰ أَن تَضَعُوا أَسْلِحَتَكُمْ
وَخُذُوا حِذْرَكُمْ إِنَّ اللَّهَ أَعَدَّ لِلْكَافِرِينَ عَذَابًا مُّهِينًا
١٠٢ فَإِذَا قَضَيْتُمُ الصَّلَوٰةَ فَاذْكُرُوا اللَّهَ قِيَامًا
وَقُعُودًا وَعَلَىٰ جُنُوبِكُمْ فَإِذَا اطْمَأْنَنتُمْ فَأَقِيمُوا الصَّلَوٰةَ
إِنَّ الصَّلَوٰةَ كَانَتْ عَلَى الْمُؤْمِنِينَ كِتَابًا مَّوْقُوتًا ١٠٣ وَلَا تَهِنُوا
فِي ابْتِغَاءِ الْقَوْمِ إِن تَكُونُوا تَأْلَمُونَ فَإِنَّهُمْ يَأْلَمُونَ كَمَا
تَأْلَمُونَ وَتَرْجُونَ مِنَ اللَّهِ مَا لَا يَرْجُونَ وَكَانَ اللَّهُ عَلِيمًا
حَكِيمًا ١٠٤ إِنَّا أَنزَلْنَا إِلَيْكَ الْكِتَابَ بِالْحَقِّ لِتَحْكُمَ
بَيْنَ النَّاسِ بِمَا أَرَاكَ اللَّهُ وَلَا تَكُن لِّلْخَائِنِينَ خَصِيمًا ١٠٥

4:103 When your prayers are ended, remember God standing, sitting, and lying down. When you are safe, attend to your prayers: for prayer is a duty incumbent on the faithful, to be conducted at appointed times.

Seek out the enemy relentlessly. If you have suffered, they too have suffered as you have: but you at least hope to receive from God what they cannot hope for. Surely God is all-knowing and wise.

4:105 We have revealed to you the Book with the Truth, that you may arbitrate among people by that which God has shown you. You shall not plead for the treacherous.

1. Muḥammad.

واستغفر الله إن الله كان غفورا رحيما ﴿١٠٦﴾ ولا تجادل
عن الذين يختانون أنفسهم إن الله لا يحب من كان خوانا
أثيما ﴿١٠٧﴾ يستخفون من الناس ولا يستخفون من الله
وهو معهم إذ يبيتون ما لا يرضى من القول وكان الله
بما يعملون محيطا ﴿١٠٨﴾ هاأنتم هؤلاء جادلتم عنهم
في الحيوة الدنيا فمن يجادل الله عنهم يوم القيمة
أم من يكون عليهم وكيلا ﴿١٠٩﴾ ومن يعمل سوءا أو يظلم نفسه ثم
يستغفر الله يجد الله غفورا رحيما ﴿١١٠﴾ ومن يكسب إثما
فإنما يكسبه على نفسه وكان الله عليما حكيما ﴿١١١﴾
ومن يكسب خطيئة أو إثما ثم يرم به بريئا
فقد احتمل بهتانا وإثما مبينا ﴿١١٢﴾ ولولا فضل الله
عليك ورحمته لهمت طائفة منهم أن يضلوك
وما يضلون إلا أنفسهم وما يضرونك من
شيء وأنزل الله عليك الكتاب والحكمة وعلمك
ما لم تكن تعلم وكان فضل الله عليك عظيما ﴿١١٣﴾

IMPLORE GOD's forgiveness: 4:106
God is ever forgiving and
compassionate. Nor shall you
plead for those who betray
their own souls; God does not
love the treacherous or the
sinful.

They seek to hide from
people, but they cannot hide
from God. He is with them
when they utter in secret what
does not please Him: God has
knowledge of all their actions.

Yes, you may plead for
them in this life, but who will
plead for them with God on
the Day of Resurrection?
Who will be their defender?

He that does evil or wrongs 4:110
his own soul and then seeks
God's forgiveness, will find
God forgiving and compas-
sionate.

He that commits sin commits it against his own soul. God is all-knowing
and wise.

And he that commits an offence or a crime and charges an innocent man
with it, shall bear the guilt of calumny and gross injustice.

But for God's grace and mercy you would have been led astray by some 4:113
among them. They lead astray none but themselves, nor can they do you any
harm.

God has revealed to you the Book and wisdom and taught you what you
did not know before. God's goodness to you has been great indeed.

4:114 THERE IS no virtue in much of their counsel: only in his who enjoins charity, kindness, or peace among people. He that does this seeking to please God, on him We shall bestow a rich recompense.

He that defies the Apostle after guidance has been revealed to him, and follows a path other than that of the faithful, shall be given by Us what he has chosen. We will burn him in the fire of Hell: a wretched fate!

God will not forgive the worship of other deities besides Him. But He will forgive whom He will all other sins. He that serves other deities besides God has strayed far into error.

لا خير في كثير من نجواهم إلا من أمر بصدقة
أو معروف أو إصلاح بين الناس ومن يفعل ذلك
ابتغاء مرضات الله فسوف نؤتيه أجرا عظيما ﴿١١٤﴾ ومن
يشاقق الرسول من بعد ما تبين له الهدى ويتبع غير
سبيل المؤمنين نوله ما تولى ونصله جهنم وساءت
مصيرا ﴿١١٥﴾ إن الله لا يغفر أن يشرك به ويغفر
ما دون ذلك لمن يشاء ومن يشرك بالله فقد ضل ضلالا
بعيدا ﴿١١٦﴾ إن يدعون من دونه إلا إناثا وإن يدعون
إلا شيطانا مريدا ﴿١١٧﴾ لعنه الله وقال لأتخذن
من عبادك نصيبا مفروضا ﴿١١٨﴾ ولأضلنهم
ولأمنينهم ولآمرنهم فليبتكن آذان الأنعام
ولآمرنهم فليغيرن خلق الله ومن يتخذ الشيطان
وليا من دون الله فقد خسر خسرانا مبينا ﴿١١٩﴾ يعدهم
ويمنيهم وما يعدهم الشيطان إلا غرورا ﴿١٢٠﴾
أولئك مأواهم جهنم ولا يجدون عنها محيصا ﴿١٢١﴾

4:117 Rather than to Him, they pray but to females: they pray but to a rebellious Satan. God laid His curse on him, for he had said: 'I shall entice a determined share of Your servants and shall lead them astray. I shall arouse in them vain desires and order them to slit the ears of cattle. I shall order them to tamper with God's creation.' Indeed, he that chooses Satan rather than God for his protector ruins himself beyond redemption.

He makes promises and stirs up in them vain desires; Satan makes them
4:121 promises only to deceive them. Hell shall be their abode, and from it shall
they find no refuge.

والذين امنوا وعملوا الصالحات سندخلهم جنات
تجري من تحتها الانهار خالدين فيها ابدا وعد الله
حقا ومن اصدق من الله قيلا ﴿١٢٢﴾ ليس بامانيكم
ولا اماني اهل الكتاب من يعمل سوءا يجز به
ولا يجد له من دون الله وليا ولا نصيرا ﴿١٢٣﴾ ومن
يعمل من الصالحات من ذكر او انثى وهو مؤمن فاولئك
يدخلون الجنة ولا يظلمون نقيرا ﴿١٢٤﴾ ومن احسن
دينا ممن اسلم وجهه لله وهو محسن واتبع ملة
ابراهيم حنيفا واتخذ الله ابراهيم خليلا ﴿١٢٥﴾ ولله
ما في السموات وما في الارض وكان الله
بكل شيء محيطا ﴿١٢٦﴾ ويستفتونك في النساء قل الله
يفتيكم فيهن وما يتلى عليكم في الكتاب في يتامى النساء
التي لا تؤتونهن ما كتب لهن وترغبون ان تنكحوهن
والمستضعفين من الولدان وان تقوموا لليتامى بالقسط
وما تفعلوا من خير فان الله كان به عليما ﴿١٢٧﴾

As FOR those that believe 4:122
and do good works, We shall
admit them into Gardens
watered by running brooks,
wherein shall they abide for
ever. Such is God's true promise: and who has a truer word
than God?

It shall not be in accordance with your wishes, nor shall it be as the People of the Book desire. He that does evil shall be requited with evil: he shall find none besides God to protect or help him. But the believers who do good works, be they men or women, shall enter Paradise. They shall not suffer the least injustice.

And who has a nobler reli- 4:125
gion than he who submits to
God, does what is right, and
follows the faith of saintly
Abraham, God having chosen Abraham as His friend?[1]

To God belongs all that the heavens and the earth contain. God encompasses all things.

They consult you concerning women. Say: 'God has instructed you about 4:127
them, and so have the verses proclaimed to you in the Book, concerning the
orphan girls whom you deny their lawful rights and refuse to marry; also
regarding helpless children. He has instructed you to deal justly with orphans.
Of the good you do, surely God has full knowledge.'

1. Cf. Isaiah 41:8.

4:128 IF A woman fear ill-treatment or desertion on the part of her husband, it shall be no offence for them to seek a mutual agreement, for agreement is best. People are prone to avarice. But if you do what is right and guard yourselves against evil, know then that God is cognizant of all your actions.

Try as you may, you cannot treat all your wives impartially. Do not set yourself altogether against any of them, leaving her, as it were, in suspense. If you do what is right and fear God, God is forgiving and compassionate. If they separate, God will compensate each out of His own abundance: God is munificent and wise.

وإن امرأة خافت من بعلها نشوزا أو إعراضا
فلا جناح عليهما أن يصلحا بينهما صلحا والصلح خير
وأحضرت الأنفس الشح وإن تحسنوا وتتقوا فإن الله
كان بما تعملون خبيرا (١٢٨) ولن تستطيعوا أن تعدلوا
بين النساء ولو حرصتم فلا تميلوا كل الميل
فتذروها كالمعلقة وإن تصلحوا وتتقوا فإن الله
كان غفورا رحيما (١٢٩) وإن يتفرقا يغن الله
كلا من سعته وكان الله واسعا حكيما (١٣٠) ولله
ما في السموات وما في الأرض ولقد وصينا الذين أوتوا الكتاب
من قبلكم وإياكم أن اتقوا الله وإن تكفروا فإن لله
ما في السموات وما في الأرض وكان الله غنيا حميدا (١٣١) ولله
ما في السموات وما في الأرض وكفى بالله وكيلا (١٣٢) إن يشأ
يذهبكم أيها الناس ويأت بآخرين وكان الله
على ذلك قديرا (١٣٣) من كان يريد ثواب الدنيا فعند الله
ثواب الدنيا والآخرة وكان الله سميعا بصيرا (١٣٤)

4:131 To God belongs all that the heavens and the earth contain. We exhort you, as We have exhorted those to whom the Book was given before you, to fear God. If you deny Him, know that to God belongs all that the heavens and the earth contain. God is self-sufficient and worthy of praise.

To God belongs all that the heavens and the earth contain. Sufficient is God as a guardian. If He pleased, He could obliterate you all, you people! and replace you by other men. This God has the power to do.

4:134 Let him who seeks the reward of this life know that it is God who dispenses the reward of both this life and the life to come; God hears all and observes all.

يا أيها الذين آمنوا كونوا قوامين بالقسط شهداء لله
ولو على أنفسكم أو الوالدين والأقربين إن يكن غنيا أو فقيرا
فالله أولى بهما فلا تتبعوا الهوى أن تعدلوا وإن تلووا
أو تعرضوا فإن الله كان بما تعملون خبيرا ١٣٥ يا أيها
الذين آمنوا آمنوا بالله ورسوله والكتاب الذي نزل على
رسوله والكتاب الذي أنزل من قبل ومن يكفر بالله
وملائكته وكتبه ورسله واليوم الآخر فقد ضل ضلالا بعيدا
١٣٦ إن الذين آمنوا ثم كفروا ثم آمنوا ثم كفروا ثم ازدادوا
كفرا لم يكن الله ليغفر لهم ولا ليهديهم سبيلا ١٣٧
بشر المنافقين بأن لهم عذابا أليما ١٣٨ الذين يتخذون
الكافرين أولياء من دون المؤمنين أيبتغون عندهم
العزة فإن العزة لله جميعا ۞ وقد نزل عليكم في الكتاب
أن إذا سمعتم آيات الله يكفر بها ويستهزأ بها فلا تقعدوا
معهم حتى يخوضوا في حديث غيره إنكم إذا مثلهم إن
الله جامع المنافقين والكافرين في جهنم جميعا ١٤٠

BELIEVERS, CONDUCT your- 4:135
selves with justice and bear true witness before God, even though it be against yourselves, your parents, or your kin. Be they rich or poor, God knows better about them both. So do not be led by passion, lest you swerve from the truth. If you distort your testimony or decline to give it, know that God is cognizant of all your actions.

Believers, have faith in God and His apostle, in the Book He has revealed to His apostle, and in the Scriptures He formerly revealed. He that denies God, His angels, His Scriptures, His apostles, and the Last Day has strayed far indeed.

Those who accept the Faith 4:137
and then renounce it, who again embrace it and again deny it and grow in unbelief – God will neither forgive them nor rightly guide them.

Give warning to the hypocrites that woeful punishment awaits them: those who choose the unbelievers rather than the faithful for their friends. Are they seeking glory at their hands? Surely all glory belongs to God.

He has instructed you in the Book that if you hear God's revelations being 4:140
blasphemed or ridiculed you shall not sit with them until they engage in other talk; or else you shall yourselves become like them. God will surely gather in Hell the hypocrites and the unbelievers all.

4:141 THEY WATCH your fortunes closely. If God grants you victory, they say: 'Did we not stand on your side?' And if it be the unbelievers' turn, they say to them: 'Were we not mightier than you, and did we not protect you from the faithful?'

God will judge between you on the Day of Resurrection. God will not let the unbelievers triumph over the faithful.

The hypocrites seek to deceive God, but it is He who deceives them. When they rise to pray, they stand up sluggishly: they pray only to be seen by people and remember God but little, wavering between this and that and belonging neither to these nor those. You cannot guide the man whom God has confounded.

الذين يتربصون بكم فإن كان لكم فتح من الله
قالوا ألم نكن معكم وإن كان للكافرين نصيب
قالوا ألم نستحوذ عليكم ونمنعكم من المؤمنين فالله
يحكم بينكم يوم القيامة ولن يجعل الله للكافرين
على المؤمنين سبيلا ﴿١٤١﴾ إن المنافقين يخادعون الله وهو خادعهم
وإذا قاموا إلى الصلوة قاموا كسالى يراءون الناس
ولا يذكرون الله إلا قليلا ﴿١٤٢﴾ مذبذبين بين ذلك لا إلى
هؤلاء ولا إلى هؤلاء ومن يضلل الله فلن تجد له سبيلا
﴿١٤٣﴾ يا أيها الذين آمنوا لا تتخذوا الكافرين أولياء من
دون المؤمنين أتريدون أن تجعلوا لله عليكم سلطانا
مبينا ﴿١٤٤﴾ إن المنافقين في الدرك الأسفل من النار ولن
تجد لهم نصيرا ﴿١٤٥﴾ إلا الذين تابوا وأصلحوا واعتصموا بالله
وأخلصوا دينهم لله فأولئك مع المؤمنين وسوف يؤت الله
المؤمنين أجرا عظيما ﴿١٤٦﴾ ما يفعل الله بعذابكم
إن شكرتم وآمنتم وكان الله شاكرا عليما ﴿١٤٧﴾

4:144 Believers, do not choose the infidels as your allies rather than the faithful. Would you give God clear evidence against yourselves?

The hypocrites shall be cast into the lowest depths of the Fire; and you shall find none to help them: except those who repent and mend their ways, who hold fast to God and are sincere in their devotion to God – they shall be numbered with the faithful, and God will richly recompense the faithful.

4:147 And why should God punish you if you render thanks and truly believe in Him? God will surely recompense your labours, for He has full knowledge of them all.

لا يحب الله الجهر بالسوء من القول إلا من ظلم وكان الله
سميعا عليما ﴿١٤٨﴾ إن تبدوا خيرا أو تخفوه أو تعفوا عن سوء
فإن الله كان عفوا قديرا ﴿١٤٩﴾ إن الذين يكفرون بالله
ورسله ويريدون أن يفرقوا بين الله ورسله ويقولون
نؤمن ببعض ونكفر ببعض ويريدون أن يتخذوا بين ذلك
سبيلا ﴿١٥٠﴾ أولئك هم الكافرون حقا وأعتدنا للكافرين
عذابا مهينا ﴿١٥١﴾ والذين آمنوا بالله ورسله ولم يفرقوا
بين أحد منهم أولئك سوف يؤتيهم أجورهم وكان الله
غفورا رحيما ﴿١٥٢﴾ يسألك أهل الكتاب أن تنزل عليهم كتابا
من السماء فقد سألوا موسى أكبر من ذلك فقالوا أرنا الله
جهرة فأخذتهم الصاعقة بظلمهم ثم اتخذوا العجل
من بعد ما جاءتهم البينات فعفونا عن ذلك وآتينا
موسى سلطانا مبينا ﴿١٥٣﴾ ورفعنا فوقهم الطور
بميثاقهم وقلنا لهم ادخلوا الباب سجدا وقلنا لهم
لا تعدوا في السبت وأخذنا منهم ميثاقا غليظا ﴿١٥٤﴾

GOD DOES not love harsh 4:148
words to be openly uttered,
except by the truly wronged.
God hears all and knows all.
Whether you do good openly
or in private, whether you pardon a wrong – God pardons
and is omnipotent.

Those that deny God and His apostles, and those that discriminate between God and His apostles, saying: 'We believe in some, but deny others,' thus seeking a middle way – these truly are the unbelievers; and for the unbelievers We have prepared a shameful punishment.

As for those that believe in 4:152
God and His apostles and discriminate against none of them,
they shall be recompensed by
Him. God is ever forgiving and
compassionate.

The People of the Book ask you to bring down for them a book from heaven. Of Moses they demanded a harder thing than that; they said to him: 'Show us God openly.' And for their wrongdoing the thunderbolt smote them. Then they took up the calf after clear signs had been revealed to them; yet We pardoned them that, and bestowed on Moses clear authority.

We raised the Mount above them when We made a covenant with them, 4:154
and said to them: 'Enter the gates bowing down.' And We said to them: 'Do
not break the Sabbath.' We took from them a solemn covenant.

4:155 BUT THEY broke their covenant, denied God's revelations, and killed the prophets unjustly. They said: 'Our hearts are sealed.'

It was God who sealed their hearts, on account of their unbelief. They have no faith, except a few.

They denied the Truth and uttered a monstrous falsehood against Mary. They declared: 'We have killed the Christ, Jesus son of Mary, the apostle of God.' They did not kill him, nor did they crucify him, but they thought they did.[1]

Those that disagreed about him were in doubt concerning him; they knew nothing about him that was not sheer conjecture; they did not kill
4:158 him for certain. Rather God lifted him up to Himself; God is Almighty and
wise. There is none among the People of the Book but will believe in him before his death; and on the Day of Resurrection he will bear witness against them.

Because of their iniquity, We forbade those who followed the Jewish Faith wholesome things which were formerly allowed them; because time after time they have debarred many from the path of God; because they practise usury – although they had been forbidden it – and cheat people of their possessions. Woeful punishment have We prepared for those of them that
4:162 disbelieve. But those of them that are well-grounded in knowledge, and the
believers who believe in what has been revealed to you and what was revealed before you; who attend to their prayers and render the alms levy and believe in God and the Last Day – on these We shall bestow a rich recompense.

فبما نقضهم ميثاقهم وكفرهم بآيات الله وقتلهم الأنبياء
بغير حق وقولهم قلوبنا غلف بل طبع الله عليها بكفرهم
فلا يؤمنون إلا قليلا ﴿١٥٥﴾ وبكفرهم وقولهم على مريم بهتانا
عظيما ﴿١٥٦﴾ وقولهم إنا قتلنا المسيح عيسى ابن مريم رسول
الله وما قتلوه وما صلبوه ولكن شبه لهم وإن الذين
اختلفوا فيه لفي شك منه ما لهم به من علم إلا اتباع
الظن وما قتلوه يقينا ﴿١٥٧﴾ بل رفعه الله إليه وكان
الله عزيزا حكيما ﴿١٥٨﴾ وإن من أهل الكتاب إلا ليؤمنن به قبل
موته ويوم القيامة يكون عليهم شهيدا ﴿١٥٩﴾ فبظلم من الذين
هادوا حرمنا عليهم طيبات أحلت لهم وبصدهم عن سبيل
الله كثيرا ﴿١٦٠﴾ وأخذهم الربا وقد نهوا عنه وأكلهم أموال
الناس بالباطل وأعتدنا للكافرين منهم عذابا أليما ﴿١٦١﴾ لكن
الراسخون في العلم منهم والمؤمنون يؤمنون بما أنزل إليك وما
أنزل من قبلك والمقيمين الصلاة والمؤتون الزكاة والمؤمنون
بالله واليوم الآخر أولئك سنؤتيهم أجرا عظيما ﴿١٦٢﴾

1. Or: literally, he was made to resemble another for them.

إنا أوحينا إليك كما أوحينا إلى نوح والنبيين من
بعده وأوحينا إلى إبرهيم وإسمعيل وإسحق ويعقوب
والأسباط وعيسى وأيوب ويونس وهرون وسليمن
وءاتينا داود زبورا ١٦٣ ورسلا قد قصصناهم عليك
من قبل ورسلا لم نقصصهم عليك وكلم الله
موسى تكليما ١٦٤ رسلا مبشرين ومنذرين لئلا يكون للناس
على الله حجة بعد الرسل وكان الله عزيزا حكيما ١٦٥
لكن الله يشهد بما أنزل إليك أنزله بعلمه والملئكة يشهدون
وكفى بالله شهيدا ١٦٦ إن الذين كفروا وصدوا عن سبيل الله
قد ضلوا ضللا بعيدا ١٦٧ إن الذين كفروا وظلموا لم
يكن الله ليغفر لهم ولا ليهديهم طريقا ١٦٨ إلا
طريق جهنم خلدين فيها أبدا وكان ذلك على الله
يسيرا ١٦٩ يأيها الناس قد جاءكم الرسول بالحق
من ربكم فءامنوا خيرا لكم وإن تكفروا فإن لله
ما في السموت والأرض وكان الله عليما حكيما ١٧٠

WE HAVE revealed Our will 4:163
to you as We revealed it to Noah
and to the prophets who came
after him; as We revealed it to
Abraham, Ishmael, Isaac, Jacob,
and the tribes; to Jesus, Job,
Jonah, Aaron and Solomon; to
David We gave Psalms. Apostles of whom We have already
told you, and apostles of whom
We have not yet told you; God
spoke directly to Moses; apostles who brought joyful tidings
as well as warnings, so that
people might have no plea
against God after the apostles'
coming: God is Almighty and
wise.

But God bears witness, by 4:166
that which He has revealed to
you, that He revealed it with
His knowledge; the angels bear
witness, too. And there is no
better witness than God.

Those that disbelieve and debar others from the path of God have strayed far into error. God will not forgive those who disbelieve and act unjustly; nor will He guide them to any path other than the path of Hell, wherein shall they abide for ever. Surely that is easy enough for God.

You people! The Apostle has brought you the Truth from your Lord. 4:170
Have faith and it shall be well with you. If you disbelieve: to God belongs all
that the heavens and the earth contain. God is omniscient and wise.

4:171 People of the Book,[1] do
not transgress the bounds of
your religion. Speak nothing
but the Truth about God. The
Christ, Jesus son of Mary, was
no more than God's apostle
and His Word which He cast
to Mary: a spirit from Him. So
believe in God and His apostles and do not say: 'Three.'
Forbear, and it shall be better
for you. Surely God is but one
God; God forbid that He
should have a son! His is all
that the heavens and the earth
contain. Sufficient is God as a
4:172 patron. Christ does not disdain to be a servant of God,
nor do the angels who are
nearest to Him. Those who
through arrogance disdain to
worship Him shall be herded,
all, before Him.

As for those that believe and do good works, God will bestow their
rewards on them and enrich them from His own abundance. But those who
are scornful and proud He will sternly punish, and they will find none besides
God to protect or succour them.

You people! Clear evidence has come to you from your Lord. We have
4:175 sent down to you a veritable light. Those that believe in God and hold fast to
Him He will admit to His mercy and to His grace; He will guide them to Him
along a straight path.

يَا أَهْلَ الْكِتَابِ لَا تَغْلُوا فِي دِينِكُمْ وَلَا تَقُولُوا عَلَى
اللَّهِ إِلَّا الْحَقَّ إِنَّمَا الْمَسِيحُ عِيسَى ابْنُ مَرْيَمَ رَسُولُ
اللَّهِ وَكَلِمَتُهُ أَلْقَاهَا إِلَى مَرْيَمَ وَرُوحٌ مِنْهُ فَآمِنُوا
بِاللَّهِ وَرُسُلِهِ وَلَا تَقُولُوا ثَلَاثَةٌ انْتَهُوا خَيْرًا لَكُمْ إِنَّمَا
اللَّهُ إِلَٰهٌ وَاحِدٌ سُبْحَانَهُ أَنْ يَكُونَ لَهُ وَلَدٌ لَهُ مَا فِي السَّمَاوَاتِ
وَمَا فِي الْأَرْضِ وَكَفَى بِاللَّهِ وَكِيلًا ﴿١٧١﴾ لَنْ يَسْتَنْكِفَ الْمَسِيحُ
أَنْ يَكُونَ عَبْدًا لِلَّهِ وَلَا الْمَلَائِكَةُ الْمُقَرَّبُونَ وَمَنْ
يَسْتَنْكِفْ عَنْ عِبَادَتِهِ وَيَسْتَكْبِرْ فَسَيَحْشُرُهُمْ إِلَيْهِ جَمِيعًا ﴿١٧٢﴾
فَأَمَّا الَّذِينَ آمَنُوا وَعَمِلُوا الصَّالِحَاتِ فَيُوَفِّيهِمْ أُجُورَهُمْ
وَيَزِيدُهُمْ مِنْ فَضْلِهِ وَأَمَّا الَّذِينَ اسْتَنْكَفُوا وَاسْتَكْبَرُوا
فَيُعَذِّبُهُمْ عَذَابًا أَلِيمًا وَلَا يَجِدُونَ لَهُمْ مِنْ دُونِ
اللَّهِ وَلِيًّا وَلَا نَصِيرًا ﴿١٧٣﴾ يَا أَيُّهَا النَّاسُ قَدْ جَاءَكُمْ
بُرْهَانٌ مِنْ رَبِّكُمْ وَأَنْزَلْنَا إِلَيْكُمْ نُورًا مُبِينًا ﴿١٧٤﴾
فَأَمَّا الَّذِينَ آمَنُوا بِاللَّهِ وَاعْتَصَمُوا بِهِ فَسَيُدْخِلُهُمْ فِي رَحْمَةٍ
مِنْهُ وَفَضْلٍ وَيَهْدِيهِمْ إِلَيْهِ صِرَاطًا مُسْتَقِيمًا ﴿١٧٥﴾

1. Christians.

يستفتونك قل الله يفتيكم في الكلالة إن امرؤا هلك
ليس له ولد وله أخت فلها نصف ما ترك وهو يرثها إن لم
يكن لها ولد فإن كانتا اثنتين فلهما الثلثان مما ترك
وإن كانوا إخوة رجالا ونساء فللذكر مثل حظ
الأنثيين يبين الله لكم أن تضلوا والله بكل شيء عليم ١٧٦

سورة المائدة مدنية وهي مائة وعشرون آية

بسم الله الرحمن الرحيم

يا أيها الذين آمنوا أوفوا بالعقود أحلت لكم بهيمة الأنعام إلا
ما يتلى عليكم غير محلي الصيد وأنتم حرم إن الله يحكم ما يريد ١
يا أيها الذين آمنوا لا تحلوا شعائر الله ولا الشهر الحرام ولا
الهدي ولا القلائد ولا آمين البيت الحرام يبتغون فضلا من ربهم
ورضوانا وإذا حللتم فاصطادوا ولا يجرمنكم شنآن قوم أن
صدوكم عن المسجد الحرام أن تعتدوا وتعاونوا على البر والتقوى ولا
تعاونوا على الإثم والعدوان واتقوا الله إن الله شديد العقاب ٢

THEY SEEK your guidance. 4:176
Say: 'Thus God instructs you regarding those that die childless and without living parents. If a man die childless and he have a sister, she shall inherit the half of his estate. If a woman die childless, her brother shall be her sole heir. If a childless man have two sisters, they shall inherit two-thirds of his estate; but if he have both brothers and sisters, the share of the male shall be that of two females.'

God enlightens you, so that you may not err. God has knowledge of all things.

THE TABLE

In the Name of God, the Merciful, the Compassionate

BELIEVERS, BE true to your obligations. It is lawful for you to eat the flesh 5:1
of all beasts other than that which is hereby announced to you. Game is forbidden while you are on the Pilgrimage. God decrees what He will.

Believers, do not violate the rites of God, or the sacred month, or the 5:2
offerings or their ornaments, or those that repair to the Sacred House seeking their Lord's grace and pleasure. Once your Pilgrimage is ended, you shall be free to go hunting.

Do not allow your hatred for those who would debar you from the Holy Mosque to lead you to commit aggression. Help one another in what is good and pious, and help not one another in sin and belligerence. And fear God; God is stern in retribution.

5:3 YOU ARE forbidden carrion, blood, and the flesh of swine; also any flesh dedicated to any other than God. You are forbidden the flesh of strangled animals and of those beaten or gored to death; of those killed by a fall or mangled by beasts of prey (unless you make it clean by giving the death-stroke yourselves); also of animals sacrificed to idols.

You are forbidden to settle disputes by consulting the Arrows. That is a pernicious practice.

The unbelievers have this day abandoned all hope of vanquishing your religion. Have no fear of them: fear Me.

This day I have perfected your religion for you and completed My favour to you. I have chosen Islām to be your religion.

حرمت عليكم الميتة والدم ولحم الخنزير وما أهل لغير
الله به والمنخنقة والموقوذة والمتردية والنطيحة وما
أكل السبع إلا ما ذكيتم وما ذبح على النصب وأن تستقسموا
بالأزلام ذلكم فسق اليوم يئس الذين كفروا من دينكم
فلا تخشوهم واخشون اليوم أكملت لكم دينكم وأتممت
عليكم نعمتي ورضيت لكم الإسلام دينا فمن اضطر في
مخمصة غير متجانف لإثم فإن الله غفور رحيم ۝٣
يسألونك ماذا أحل لهم قل أحل لكم الطيبات وما علمتم
من الجوارح مكلبين تعلمونهن مما علمكم الله فكلوا
مما أمسكن عليكم واذكروا اسم الله عليه واتقوا الله إن
الله سريع الحساب ۝٤ اليوم أحل لكم الطيبات وطعام الذين
أوتوا الكتاب حل لكم وطعامكم حل لهم والمحصنات من المؤمنات
والمحصنات من الذين أوتوا الكتاب من قبلكم إذا آتيتموهن
أجورهن محصنين غير مسافحين ولا متخذي أخدان ومن يكفر
بالإيمان فقد حبط عمله وهو في الآخرة من الخاسرين ۝٥

He that is constrained by hunger to eat of what is forbidden, not intending to commit sin, will find that God is forgiving and compassionate.

5:4 They ask you what is lawful for them. Say: 'All wholesome things are lawful for you, as well as that which you have taught the birds and beasts of prey to catch, training them as God has taught you. Eat of what they catch for you, pronouncing upon it the name of God. And fear God: swift is God's reckoning.'

5:5 Wholesome things are this day made lawful for you. The food of those to whom the Book was given[1] is lawful for you, and yours for them.

Lawful for you are the believing women and the free women from among those who were given the Book before you, provided that you give them their dowries and live in honour with them, neither committing fornication nor taking them as mistresses.

He that denies the Faith shall gain nothing from his labours; and in the world to come he will surely be among the lost.

1. The Jews (but not the Christians).

يا ايها الذين امنوا اذا قمتم الى الصلوة فاغسلوا
وجوهكم وايديكم الى المرافق وامسحوا برؤسكم
وارجلكم الى الكعبين وان كنتم جنبا فاطهروا
وان كنتم مرضى او على سفر او جاء احد منكم
من الغائط او لمستم النساء فلم تجدوا ماء فتيمموا
صعيدا طيبا فامسحوا بوجوهكم وايديكم منه
ما يريد الله ليجعل عليكم من حرج ولكن يريد
ليطهركم وليتم نعمته عليكم لعلكم
تشكرون ﴿٦﴾ واذكروا نعمة الله عليكم
وميثاقه الذى واثقكم به اذ قلتم سمعنا واطعنا واتقوا
الله ان الله عليم بذات الصدور ﴿٧﴾ يا ايها الذين امنوا كونوا
قوامين لله شهداء بالقسط ولا يجرمنكم شنان قوم
على الا تعدلوا اعدلوا هو اقرب للتقوى واتقوا
الله ان الله خبير بما تعملون ﴿٨﴾ وعد الله الذين امنوا
وعملوا الصالحات لهم مغفرة واجر عظيم ﴿٩﴾

BELIEVERS, WHEN you rise 5:6
to pray wash your faces and
your hands as far as the elbow,
and wipe your heads and your
feet to the ankle. If you are
unclean, cleanse yourselves.
But if you are sick or on a journey, or if, when you have just
relieved yourselves or had
intercourse with women, you
can find no water, take some
clean sand and rub your faces
and your hands with it. God
does not wish to inconveni-
ence you; but He seeks only to
purify you and to perfect His
favour to you, so that you may
give thanks.

Remember God's favour to 5:7
you, and the covenant with
which He bound you when
you said: 'We hear and obey.'
Fear God; God knows your
innermost thoughts.

Believers, fulfil your duties to God and bear true witness. Do not allow
your hatred for other people to turn you away from justice. Deal justly;
that will bring you closer to true piety. Fear God; God is cognizant of what
you do.

God has promised those that believe and do good works forgiveness 5:9
and a rich reward.

5:10 As FOR those who disbelieve
and deny Our revelations, they
are the heirs of Hell.
Believers, remember the
favour God bestowed upon
you when He restrained the
hands of those who sought to
harm you. Fear God; in God
let the faithful put their trust.
5:12 God made a covenant with
the Israelites and We raised
among them twelve chieftains.
And God said: 'I shall be with
you. If you attend to your
prayers and render the alms
levy; if you believe in My apostles and support them and give
God a generous loan, I shall
forgive you your sins and admit
you to Gardens watered by
running brooks. But whoever
of you hereafter disbelieves
will surely stray from the
straight path.'

وَالَّذِينَ كَفَرُوا وَكَذَّبُوا بِآيَاتِنَا أُولَٰئِكَ أَصْحَابُ الْجَحِيمِ
(١٠) يَا أَيُّهَا الَّذِينَ آمَنُوا اذْكُرُوا نِعْمَتَ اللَّهِ عَلَيْكُمْ
إِذْ هَمَّ قَوْمٌ أَنْ يَبْسُطُوا إِلَيْكُمْ أَيْدِيَهُمْ فَكَفَّ
أَيْدِيَهُمْ عَنْكُمْ ۖ وَاتَّقُوا اللَّهَ ۚ وَعَلَى اللَّهِ فَلْيَتَوَكَّلِ
الْمُؤْمِنُونَ (١١) وَلَقَدْ أَخَذَ اللَّهُ مِيثَاقَ بَنِي إِسْرَائِيلَ
وَبَعَثْنَا مِنْهُمُ اثْنَيْ عَشَرَ نَقِيبًا ۖ وَقَالَ اللَّهُ إِنِّي مَعَكُمْ
لَئِنْ أَقَمْتُمُ الصَّلَاةَ وَآتَيْتُمُ الزَّكَاةَ وَآمَنْتُمْ بِرُسُلِي
وَعَزَّرْتُمُوهُمْ وَأَقْرَضْتُمُ اللَّهَ قَرْضًا حَسَنًا لَأُكَفِّرَنَّ
عَنْكُمْ سَيِّئَاتِكُمْ وَلَأُدْخِلَنَّكُمْ جَنَّاتٍ تَجْرِي مِنْ
تَحْتِهَا الْأَنْهَارُ ۚ فَمَنْ كَفَرَ بَعْدَ ذَٰلِكَ مِنْكُمْ فَقَدْ
ضَلَّ سَوَاءَ السَّبِيلِ (١٢) فَبِمَا نَقْضِهِمْ مِيثَاقَهُمْ
لَعَنَّاهُمْ وَجَعَلْنَا قُلُوبَهُمْ قَاسِيَةً ۖ يُحَرِّفُونَ الْكَلِمَ
عَنْ مَوَاضِعِهِ ۙ وَنَسُوا حَظًّا مِمَّا ذُكِّرُوا بِهِ ۚ وَلَا تَزَالُ
تَطَّلِعُ عَلَىٰ خَائِنَةٍ مِنْهُمْ إِلَّا قَلِيلًا مِنْهُمْ ۖ فَاعْفُ
عَنْهُمْ وَاصْفَحْ ۚ إِنَّ اللَّهَ يُحِبُّ الْمُحْسِنِينَ (١٣)

5:13 But because they broke their covenant We laid on them Our curse and
hardened their hearts. They have tampered with words out of their context
and forgotten much of what they were enjoined. You will ever find them
deceitful, except for a few of them. But pardon them and bear with them;
God loves those who do good.

وَمِنَ الَّذِينَ قَالُوا إِنَّا نَصَارَىٰ أَخَذْنَا مِيثَاقَهُمْ
فَنَسُوا حَظًّا مِمَّا ذُكِّرُوا بِهِ فَأَغْرَيْنَا بَيْنَهُمُ
الْعَدَاوَةَ وَالْبَغْضَاءَ إِلَىٰ يَوْمِ الْقِيَامَةِ وَسَوْفَ
يُنَبِّئُهُمُ اللَّهُ بِمَا كَانُوا يَصْنَعُونَ ﴿١٤﴾ يَا أَهْلَ الْكِتَابِ
قَدْ جَاءَكُمْ رَسُولُنَا يُبَيِّنُ لَكُمْ كَثِيرًا مِمَّا كُنْتُمْ
تُخْفُونَ مِنَ الْكِتَابِ وَيَعْفُو عَنْ كَثِيرٍ
قَدْ جَاءَكُمْ مِنَ اللَّهِ نُورٌ وَكِتَابٌ مُبِينٌ ﴿١٥﴾
يَهْدِي بِهِ اللَّهُ مَنِ اتَّبَعَ رِضْوَانَهُ سُبُلَ السَّلَامِ
وَيُخْرِجُهُمْ مِنَ الظُّلُمَاتِ إِلَى النُّورِ بِإِذْنِهِ
وَيَهْدِيهِمْ إِلَىٰ صِرَاطٍ مُسْتَقِيمٍ ﴿١٦﴾ لَقَدْ كَفَرَ
الَّذِينَ قَالُوا إِنَّ اللَّهَ هُوَ الْمَسِيحُ ابْنُ مَرْيَمَ قُلْ
فَمَنْ يَمْلِكُ مِنَ اللَّهِ شَيْئًا إِنْ أَرَادَ أَنْ يُهْلِكَ
الْمَسِيحَ ابْنَ مَرْيَمَ وَأُمَّهُ وَمَنْ فِي الْأَرْضِ
جَمِيعًا وَلِلَّهِ مُلْكُ السَّمَاوَاتِ وَالْأَرْضِ وَمَا بَيْنَهُمَا
يَخْلُقُ مَا يَشَاءُ وَاللَّهُ عَلَىٰ كُلِّ شَيْءٍ قَدِيرٌ ﴿١٧﴾

AND WITH those who 5:14
said they were Christians We made a covenant, but they too have forgotten much of what they were exhorted to do. Therefore We stirred among them enmity and hatred, which shall endure till the Day of Resurrection, when God will declare to them all that they have done.

People of the Book! Our 5:15
apostle has come to reveal to you much of what you have hidden of the Book, and to pardon you much. A light has surely come to you from God and a veritable Book, with which God will guide to the paths of peace those that seek to please Him; He will lead them by His will from darkness to the light; He will guide them to a straight path.

They do blaspheme, who declare: 'God is Christ, the son of Mary.' Say: 5:17
'Who could prevent God, if He so willed, from destroying Christ, the son of Mary, his mother, and all the people of the earth? God has sovereignty over the heavens and the earth and all that lies between them. He creates what He will; and God has power over all things.'

5:18 THE JEWS and the Christians say: 'We are the children of God and His loved ones.' Say: 'Why then does He punish you for your sins? Surely you are mortals of His own creation. He forgives whom He will and punishes whom He pleases. God has sovereignty over the heavens and the earth and all that lies between them. All shall return to Him.'

People of the Book! Our apostle has come to you with revelations after an interval which saw no apostles, lest you say: 'No one has come to give us joyful tidings or to warn us.' Now someone has come to give you joyful tidings and to warn you. God has power over all things.

وقالت اليهود والنصارى نحن أبناء الله وأحباؤه قل
فلم يعذبكم بذنوبكم بل أنتم بشر ممن خلق يغفر لمن يشاء
ويعذب من يشاء ولله ملك السموات والأرض وما بينهما
وإليه المصير ١٨ يا أهل الكتاب قد جاءكم رسولنا
يبين لكم على فترة من الرسل أن تقولوا ما جاءنا
من بشير ولا نذير فقد جاءكم بشير ونذير والله
على كل شيء قدير ١٩ وإذ قال موسى لقومه يا قوم
اذكروا نعمة الله عليكم إذ جعل فيكم أنبياء وجعلكم
ملوكا وآتاكم ما لم يؤت أحدا من العالمين ٢٠ يا قوم
ادخلوا الأرض المقدسة التي كتب الله لكم ولا ترتدوا
على أدباركم فتنقلبوا خاسرين ٢١ قالوا يا موسى إن فيها
قوما جبارين وإنا لن ندخلها حتى يخرجوا منها فإن يخرجوا منها
فإنا داخلون ٢٢ قال رجلان من الذين يخافون أنعم الله
عليهما ادخلوا عليهم الباب فإذا دخلتموه فإنكم
غالبون وعلى الله فتوكلوا إن كنتم مؤمنين ٢٣

5:20 Bear in mind the words of Moses to his people. He had said: 'Remember, my people, the favour God bestowed upon you. He has raised up prophets among you, made you kings, and given you that which He has given to no other nation. Enter, my people, the holy land which God has assigned for you; do not turn back, and thus lose all.'

'Moses,' they said, 'a race of giants dwells in this land; we will not set foot in it till they are gone. As soon as they are gone we will enter.'

5:23 Thereupon two God-fearing men[1] whom God had favoured said: 'Go in to them through the gates, and when you have entered you shall surely be victorious. In God put your trust, if you are true believers.'

1. Cf. Numbers 14:6.

قالوا يا موسى إنا لن ندخلها أبدا ما داموا فيها فاذهب أنت
وربك فقاتلا إنا ههنا قاعدون ﴿٢٤﴾ قال رب
إني لا أملك إلا نفسي وأخي فافرق بيننا وبين القوم
الفاسقين ﴿٢٥﴾ قال فإنها محرمة عليهم أربعين سنة
يتيهون في الأرض فلا تأس على القوم الفاسقين ﴿٢٦﴾ واتل
عليهم نبأ ابني آدم بالحق إذ قربا قربانا فتقبل من أحدهما
ولم يتقبل من الآخر قال لأقتلنك قال إنما يتقبل الله
من المتقين ﴿٢٧﴾ لئن بسطت إلي يدك لتقتلني ما
أنا بباسط يدي إليك لأقتلك إني أخاف الله
رب العالمين ﴿٢٨﴾ إني أريد أن تبوأ بإثمي وإثمك فتكون
من أصحاب النار وذلك جزاؤا الظالمين ﴿٢٩﴾ فطوعت له
نفسه قتل أخيه فقتله فأصبح من الخاسرين ﴿٣٠﴾ فبعث الله
غرابا يبحث في الأرض ليريه كيف يواري سوأة أخيه
قال يا ويلتى أعجزت أن أكون مثل هذا الغراب
فأواري سوأة أخي فأصبح من النادمين ﴿٣١﴾

BUT THEY said: 'Moses, we 5:24
will never go in as long as *they* are in it. Go, you and your Lord, and fight. Here will we stay.'

'Lord,' said Moses, 'I have none but myself and my brother. Keep us apart from the iniquitous people.'

He said: 'They shall be forbidden this land for forty years, during which time they shall wander homeless on the earth. Do not grieve for the iniquitous people.'

Recount to them in all truth the story of Adam's two sons: how they each made an offering, which was accepted from the one and was not accepted from the other. One said: 'I will surely kill you.' The other said: 'God accepts only from
the righteous. If you stretch your hand to kill me, I shall not stretch my hand 5:28
to kill you; for I fear God, Lord of the Universe. I would rather you should add your sin against me to your other sins and thus become an inmate of the Fire. Such is the recompense of the unjust.'

His soul prompted him to slay his brother; he slew him, and thus became
one of the lost. Then God sent down a raven, which clawed the earth to 5:31
show him how to bury the naked corpse of his brother. 'Alas for me!' he said. 'Have I not strength enough to do as this raven has done and so bury my brother's naked corpse?' And he repented.

من اجل ذلك كتبنا على بني اسرائيل انه من قتل نفسا
بغير نفس او فساد في الارض فكانما قتل الناس
جميعا ومن احياها فكانما احيا الناس جميعا ولقد
جاءتهم رسلنا بالبينات ثم ان كثيرا منهم بعد ذلك
في الارض لمسرفون ﴿٣٢﴾ انما جزاؤا الذين يحاربون
الله ورسوله ويسعون في الارض فسادا ان يقتلوا
او يصلبوا او تقطع ايديهم وارجلهم من
خلاف او ينفوا من الارض ذلك لهم خزي في
الدنيا ولهم في الاخرة عذاب عظيم ﴿٣٣﴾ الا الذين
تابوا من قبل ان تقدروا عليهم فاعلموا ان
الله غفور رحيم ﴿٣٤﴾ يا ايها الذين امنوا اتقوا
الله وابتغوا اليه الوسيلة وجاهدوا في سبيله
لعلكم تفلحون ﴿٣٥﴾ ان الذين كفروا لو ان لهم
ما في الارض جميعا ومثله معه ليفتدوا به من
عذاب يوم القيمة ما تقبل منهم ولهم عذاب اليم ﴿٣٦﴾

5:32 THAT WAS why We laid it down for the Israelites that whoever killed a human being, except as punishment for murder or other villainy in the land, it shall be as if he has killed all mankind; and that whoever saved a life, it shall be as if he has saved all mankind.

Indeed, Our apostles brought them veritable proofs: yet many among them after that did prodigious evil in the land.

5:33 The punishment of those that make war against God and His apostle and spread disorder in the land shall be to be slain or crucified or have their hands and feet cut off on alternate sides, or be banished from the land. They shall be held up to opprobrium in this world, and in the world to come grievous punishment awaits them: except those that repent before you reduce them. For you must know that God is forgiving and compassionate.

Believers, have fear of God and seek the right path to Him. Fight valiantly for His cause, that you may triumph.

5:36 As for the unbelievers, if they offered all that the earth contains and as much besides to redeem themselves from the torment of the Day of Resurrection, it shall not be accepted from them. Woeful punishment awaits them.

يريدون أن يخرجوا من النار وما هم بخارجين
منها ولهم عذاب مقيم ٣٧ والسارق والسارقة
فاقطعوا أيديهما جزاء بما كسبا نكالا من الله
والله عزيز حكيم ٣٨ فمن تاب من بعد ظلمه وأصلح فإن
الله يتوب عليه إن الله غفور رحيم ٣٩ ألم تعلم أن
الله له ملك السموات والأرض يعذب من يشاء
ويغفر لمن يشاء والله على كل شيء قدير ٤٠ يا أيها
الرسول لا يحزنك الذين يسارعون في الكفر من
الذين قالوا آمنا بأفواههم ولم تؤمن قلوبهم ومن
الذين هادوا سماعون للكذب سماعون لقوم
آخرين لم يأتوك يحرفون الكلم من بعد مواضعه
يقولون إن أوتيتم هذا فخذوه وإن لم تؤتوه
فاحذروا ومن يرد الله فتنته فلن تملك له من الله
شيئا أولئك الذين لم يرد الله أن يطهر قلوبهم لهم في
الدنيا خزي ولهم في الآخرة عذاب عظيم ٤١

THEY WILL strive to get out 5:37
of the Fire, but get out of it
they shall not. Lasting torment
awaits them.

As for the man or woman
who is guilty of theft, cut off
their hands to punish them for
what they did. That is the
punishment enjoined by God.
And God is Almighty and wise.
But whoever repents after his
wrongdoing, and mends his
ways, shall be pardoned by
God; God is forgiving and
compassionate.

Did you not know that God 5:40
has sovereignty over the heavens and the earth? He punishes
whom He will and forgives
whom He pleases. God has
power over all things.

Apostle, do not grieve for 5:41
those who plunge headlong
into unbelief; those who say with their mouths: 'We believe,' but have no
faith in their hearts, and those of the Jewish Faith who avidly listen to lies
and avidly listen to others who have not come to you. They tamper with
words out of their context and say: 'If such-and-such be given you, accept it;
if it be not given you, beware!'

You cannot help a man if God intends to try him. Those whose hearts
God does not intend to purify shall be held up to shame in this world, and in
the world to come grievous punishment awaits them.

5:42 THEY AVIDLY listen to lies and avidly devour the unlawful. If they come to you, give them your judgement or avoid them. If you avoid them, they can in no way harm you; but if you do act as their judge, judge them with fairness. God loves those that deal justly.

But how will they come to you for judgement when they already have the Torah which enshrines God's own judgement? Soon after, they will turn their backs: they are no believers.

5:44 We have revealed the Torah, in which there is guidance and light. By it the prophets who submitted to God were to judge those of the Jewish Faith, and so would the rabbis and the clerics, according to God's Book which had been committed to their keeping and to which they themselves were witnesses.

Have no fear of people; fear Me, and do not sell My revelations for a paltry sum. Unbelievers are those who do not judge according to God's revelations.

5:45 Therein We decreed for them a life for a life, an eye for an eye, a nose for a nose, an ear for an ear, a tooth for a tooth, and a wound for a wound. But if a man charitably forbears from retaliation, his remission shall atone for him. Wrongdoers are those that do not judge according to what God has revealed.

سَمَّاعُونَ لِلْكَذِبِ أَكَّالُونَ لِلسُّحْتِ فَإِن جَاءُوكَ
فَاحْكُم بَيْنَهُمْ أَوْ أَعْرِضْ عَنْهُمْ وَإِن تُعْرِضْ عَنْهُمْ فَلَن
يَضُرُّوكَ شَيْئًا وَإِنْ حَكَمْتَ فَاحْكُم بَيْنَهُم بِالْقِسْطِ إِنَّ
اللَّهَ يُحِبُّ الْمُقْسِطِينَ ﴿٤٢﴾ وَكَيْفَ يُحَكِّمُونَكَ وَعِندَهُمُ
التَّوْرَاةُ فِيهَا حُكْمُ اللَّهِ ثُمَّ يَتَوَلَّوْنَ مِن بَعْدِ ذَٰلِكَ وَمَا
أُولَٰئِكَ بِالْمُؤْمِنِينَ ﴿٤٣﴾ إِنَّا أَنزَلْنَا التَّوْرَاةَ فِيهَا هُدًى وَنُورٌ
يَحْكُمُ بِهَا النَّبِيُّونَ الَّذِينَ أَسْلَمُوا لِلَّذِينَ هَادُوا
وَالرَّبَّانِيُّونَ وَالْأَحْبَارُ بِمَا اسْتُحْفِظُوا مِن كِتَابِ
اللَّهِ وَكَانُوا عَلَيْهِ شُهَدَاءَ فَلَا تَخْشَوُا النَّاسَ وَاخْشَوْنِ
وَلَا تَشْتَرُوا بِآيَاتِي ثَمَنًا قَلِيلًا وَمَن لَّمْ يَحْكُم بِمَا أَنزَلَ
اللَّهُ فَأُولَٰئِكَ هُمُ الْكَافِرُونَ ﴿٤٤﴾ وَكَتَبْنَا عَلَيْهِمْ
فِيهَا أَنَّ النَّفْسَ بِالنَّفْسِ وَالْعَيْنَ بِالْعَيْنِ وَالْأَنفَ
بِالْأَنفِ وَالْأُذُنَ بِالْأُذُنِ وَالسِّنَّ بِالسِّنِّ وَالْجُرُوحَ
قِصَاصٌ فَمَن تَصَدَّقَ بِهِ فَهُوَ كَفَّارَةٌ لَّهُ وَمَن لَّمْ
يَحْكُم بِمَا أَنزَلَ اللَّهُ فَأُولَٰئِكَ هُمُ الظَّالِمُونَ ﴿٤٥﴾

وقفينا على آثارهم بعيسى ابن مريم مصدقا لما بين يديه من
التوراة وآتيناه الإنجيل فيه هدى ونور ومصدقا لما بين
يديه من التوراة وهدى وموعظة للمتقين (٤٦) وليحكم
أهل الإنجيل بما أنزل الله فيه ومن لم يحكم بما أنزل الله
فأولئك هم الفاسقون (٤٧) وأنزلنا إليك الكتاب
بالحق مصدقا لما بين يديه من الكتاب ومهيمنا عليه
فاحكم بينهم بما أنزل الله ولا تتبع أهواءهم عما جاءك من
الحق لكل جعلنا منكم شرعة ومنهاجا ولو شاء الله
لجعلكم أمة واحدة ولكن ليبلوكم في ما آتاكم
فاستبقوا الخيرات إلى الله مرجعكم جميعا فينبئكم
بما كنتم فيه تختلفون (٤٨) وأن احكم بينهم بما أنزل الله
ولا تتبع أهواءهم واحذرهم أن يفتنوك عن بعض ما أنزل الله
إليك فإن تولوا فاعلم أنما يريد الله أن يصيبهم ببعض ذنوبهم
وإن كثيرا من الناس لفاسقون (٤٩) أفحكم الجاهلية
يبغون ومن أحسن من الله حكما لقوم يوقنون (٥٠)

In their trail We sent forth 5:46
Jesus son of Mary, confirming
the Torah revealed before him;
and We gave him the Gospel, in
which there is guidance and
light, corroborating what was
revealed before him in the
Torah: a guide and an admonition to the righteous. Let those
who follow the Gospel judge
by what God has revealed in it;
ungodly are those that do not
judge by what God has revealed.

And to you We have revealed 5:48
the Book with the Truth. It
confirms the Book which came
before it and supersedes it.
Therefore pronounce judgement among them by what
God has revealed and do not
follow their whims or swerve
from the Truth made known
to you.

For each of you We have ordained a law and assigned a path. Had God pleased, He could have made of you but one community: but it is His wish to prove you by that which He has given you. Vie with each other in good works; to God shall you all return and He will resolve your differences for you.

Pronounce judgement among them by what God has revealed and do not follow their whims. Beware of them, lest they tempt you away from a part of that which God has revealed to you. If they turn away, know that it is God's wish to scourge them for some of their sins. A great many people are ungodly.

Is it the pagan laws that they wish to be judged by? And who is a better 5:50
judge than God for those whose faith is firm?

5:51 BELIEVERS, TAKE neither the Jews nor the Christians for your friends. They are friends to each other. Whoever of you seeks their friendship shall become one of their number. God does not guide the wrong-doing people.

You see the faint-hearted hastening to woo them. They say: 'We fear lest a change of fortune should befall us.' But it may well be that when God grants victory or makes known His will, they will regret their secret plans. Then will the faithful say: 'Are these the men who solemnly swore by God that they would stand by you?' Their works will come to nothing and they will lose all.

5:54 Believers, if any among you renounce their religion, God will replace them by others who love Him and are loved by Him, who are humble towards the faithful and stern towards the unbelievers, zealous for God's cause and fearless of man's censure. Such is the grace of God: He bestows it on whom He will. God is munificent and all-knowing.

Your only protectors are God, His apostle, and the faithful: those who attend to their prayers, render the alms levy, and kneel down in worship. Those who seek the protection of God, His apostle, and the faithful must know that God's party is sure to triumph.

5:57 Believers, do not seek the friendship of those who have mocked and derided your religion, among those who were given the Book before you; nor of the infidels. And fear God, if you are true believers.

يا ايها الذين امنوا لا تتخذوا اليهود والنصارى اولياء بعضهم
اولياء بعض ومن يتولهم منكم فانه منهم ان الله لا يهدي القوم
الظالمين (٥١) فترى الذين في قلوبهم مرض يسارعون فيهم يقولون
نخشى ان تصيبنا دائرة فعسى الله ان يأتي بالفتح او امر من عنده
فيصبحوا على ما اسروا في انفسهم نادمين (٥٢) ويقول الذين
امنوا اهؤلاء الذين اقسموا بالله جهد ايمانهم انهم لمعكم
حبطت اعمالهم فاصبحوا خاسرين (٥٣) يا ايها الذين امنوا من يرتد
منكم عن دينه فسوف يأتي الله بقوم يحبهم ويحبونه اذلة على
المؤمنين اعزة على الكافرين يجاهدون في سبيل الله ولا يخافون
لومة لائم ذلك فضل الله يؤتيه من يشاء والله واسع عليم
(٥٤) انما وليكم الله ورسوله والذين امنوا الذين يقيمون
الصلوة ويؤتون الزكوة وهم راكعون (٥٥) ومن يتول الله ورسوله
والذين امنوا فان حزب الله هم الغالبون (٥٦) يا ايها الذين امنوا
لا تتخذوا الذين اتخذوا دينكم هزوا ولعبا من الذين اوتوا الكتاب من
قبلكم والكفار اولياء واتقوا الله ان كنتم مؤمنين (٥٧)

وإذا ناديتم إلى الصلوة اتخذوها هزوا ولعبا ذلك بأنهم قوم
لا يعقلون ۝٥٨ قل يا أهل الكتاب هل تنقمون منا إلا أن آمنا بالله
وما أنزل إلينا وما أنزل من قبل وأن أكثركم فاسقون ۝٥٩
قل هل أنبئكم بشر من ذلك مثوبة عند الله من لعنه الله
وغضب عليه وجعل منهم القردة والخنازير وعبد الطاغوت
أولئك شر مكانا وأضل عن سواء السبيل ۝٦٠ وإذا جاءوكم
قالوا آمنا وقد دخلوا بالكفر وهم قد خرجوا به والله
أعلم بما كانوا يكتمون ۝٦١ وترى كثيرا منهم يسارعون في الإثم
والعدوان وأكلهم السحت لبئس ما كانوا يعملون ۝٦٢ لولا
ينهاهم الربانيون والأحبار عن قولهم الإثم وأكلهم السحت لبئس
ما كانوا يصنعون ۝٦٣ وقالت اليهود يد الله مغلولة غلت أيديهم
ولعنوا بما قالوا بل يداه مبسوطتان ينفق كيف يشاء وليزيدن
كثيرا منهم ما أنزل إليك من ربك طغيانا وكفرا وألقينا بينهم
العداوة والبغضاء إلى يوم القيامة كلما أوقدوا نارا للحرب أطفأها الله
ويسعون في الأرض فسادا والله لا يحب المفسدين ۝٦٤

IF YOU call them to the prayer, 5:58
they treat it as a jest and a
diversion. This is because they
are a people devoid of understanding.

Say: 'People of the Book, is
it not that you hate us only
because we believe in God
and in what has been revealed
to us and what was formerly
revealed, and because most of
you are ungodly?'

Say: 'Shall I tell you who will
receive a worse reward from
God? Those whom God has
cursed and with whom He has
been angry, transforming them
into apes and swine, and those
who serve the devil. Worse is
the plight of these, and they
have strayed farther from the
right path.'

When they came to you 5:61
they said: 'We are believers.' Indeed, infidels they came and infidels they
departed. God knew best what they concealed.

You see many among them rush headlong into sin and transgression and
practise what is unlawful. Surely evil is what they do.

Why do their rabbis and clerics not forbid them to blaspheme or to practise what is unlawful? Evil indeed are their doings.

The Jews say: 'God's hand is chained.' May their own hands be chained! 5:64
May they be cursed for what they say! By no means. His hands are both outstretched: He bestows as He will.

That which is revealed to you from your Lord will surely increase the
wickedness and unbelief of many among them. We have stirred among them
enmity and hatred, which shall endure till the Day of Resurrection. Whenever they kindle the fire of war, God puts it out. They perpetrate evil in the
land, and God does not love the evil-doers.

5:65 And if the People of the
Book accept the Faith and
fear God, We will pardon
them their misdeeds and
admit them to the Gardens of
Delight. If they observed the
Torah and the Gospel and
what has been revealed to
them from their Lord, they
would enjoy all that is good,
from above, and from beneath
their feet.

Among them there is a righteous community; but many among them are evil-doers.

Apostle, proclaim what has been revealed to you from your Lord; if you do not, you will surely fail to convey His message. God will protect you from all people. God does not guide the unbelievers.

5:68 Say: 'People of the Book,
you will attain nothing until you observe the Torah and the Gospel and that
which has been revealed to you from your Lord.'

That which has been revealed to you from your Lord will surely increase the wickedness and unbelief of many among them. But do not grieve for the unbelievers.

Believers, those who follow the Jewish Faith, Sabaeans, and Christians – whoever believes in God and the Last Day and does what is right – shall have nothing to fear or to regret.

5:70 We made a covenant with the Israelites and sent forth apostles among
them. But whenever an apostle came to them with a message that did not
suit their inclinations, some they accused of lying and some they killed.

ولو أن أهل الكتاب آمنوا واتقوا لكفرنا عنهم سيئاتهم
ولأدخلناهم جنات النعيم ٦٥ ولو أنهم أقاموا التوراة
والإنجيل وما أنزل إليهم من ربهم لأكلوا من فوقهم ومن
تحت أرجلهم منهم أمة مقتصدة وكثير منهم ساء ما
يعملون ٦٦ يا أيها الرسول بلغ ما أنزل إليك من ربك وإن لم
تفعل فما بلغت رسالته والله يعصمك من الناس إن
الله لا يهدي القوم الكافرين ٦٧ قل يا أهل الكتاب
لستم على شيء حتى تقيموا التوراة والإنجيل
وما أنزل إليكم من ربكم وليزيدن كثيرا
منهم ما أنزل إليك من ربك طغيانا وكفرا فلا تأس
على القوم الكافرين ٦٨ إن الذين آمنوا والذين هادوا
والصابئون والنصارى من آمن بالله واليوم الآخر وعمل صالحا
فلا خوف عليهم ولا هم يحزنون ٦٩ لقد أخذنا ميثاق
بني إسرائيل وأرسلنا إليهم رسلا كلما جاءهم رسول بما
لا تهوى أنفسهم فريقا كذبوا وفريقا يقتلون ٧٠

وَحَسِبُوٓا أَلَّا تَكُونَ فِتْنَةٌ فَعَمُوا وَصَمُّوا ثُمَّ تَابَ ٱللَّهُ
عَلَيْهِمْ ثُمَّ عَمُوا وَصَمُّوا كَثِيرٌ مِّنْهُمْ وَٱللَّهُ
بَصِيرٌ بِمَا يَعْمَلُونَ ﴿٧١﴾ لَقَدْ كَفَرَ ٱلَّذِينَ قَالُوٓا إِنَّ ٱللَّهَ
هُوَ ٱلْمَسِيحُ ٱبْنُ مَرْيَمَ وَقَالَ ٱلْمَسِيحُ يَٰبَنِىٓ إِسْرَٰٓءِيلَ ٱعْبُدُوا ٱللَّهَ
رَبِّى وَرَبَّكُمْ إِنَّهُ مَن يُشْرِكْ بِٱللَّهِ فَقَدْ حَرَّمَ ٱللَّهُ
عَلَيْهِ ٱلْجَنَّةَ وَمَأْوَىٰهُ ٱلنَّارُ وَمَا لِلظَّٰلِمِينَ مِنْ أَنصَارٍ ﴿٧٢﴾
لَقَدْ كَفَرَ ٱلَّذِينَ قَالُوٓا إِنَّ ٱللَّهَ ثَالِثُ ثَلَٰثَةٍ وَمَا مِنْ
إِلَٰهٍ إِلَّآ إِلَٰهٌ وَٰحِدٌ وَإِن لَّمْ يَنتَهُوا عَمَّا يَقُولُونَ لَيَمَسَّنَّ
ٱلَّذِينَ كَفَرُوا مِنْهُمْ عَذَابٌ أَلِيمٌ ﴿٧٣﴾ أَفَلَا يَتُوبُونَ إِلَى
ٱللَّهِ وَيَسْتَغْفِرُونَهُ وَٱللَّهُ غَفُورٌ رَّحِيمٌ ﴿٧٤﴾
مَا ٱلْمَسِيحُ ٱبْنُ مَرْيَمَ إِلَّا رَسُولٌ قَدْ خَلَتْ مِن قَبْلِهِ ٱلرُّسُلُ
وَأُمُّهُ صِدِّيقَةٌ كَانَا يَأْكُلَانِ ٱلطَّعَامَ ٱنظُرْ كَيْفَ
نُبَيِّنُ لَهُمُ ٱلْآيَٰتِ ثُمَّ ٱنظُرْ أَنَّىٰ يُؤْفَكُونَ ﴿٧٥﴾
قُلْ أَتَعْبُدُونَ مِن دُونِ ٱللَّهِ مَا لَا يَمْلِكُ لَكُمْ
ضَرًّا وَلَا نَفْعًا وَٱللَّهُ هُوَ ٱلسَّمِيعُ ٱلْعَلِيمُ ﴿٧٦﴾

THEY THOUGHT no punish- 5:71
ment[1] would follow: they were blind and deaf. Then God turned to them in mercy, but many again were blind and deaf. God is ever observant of what they do.

They do blaspheme, that say: 'God is the Christ, the son of Mary.' For Christ himself said: 'Children of Israel, worship God, my Lord and your Lord.' He that worships other deities besides God, God will deny him Paradise, and his abode shall be the Fire. The wrongdoers shall have none to succour them.

They do blaspheme, that say: 'God is one of three.' There is but one God. If they do not desist from so saying, those of them that disbelieve shall be smitten by grievous torment.

Will they not turn to God in penitence and seek forgiveness of Him? God 5:74
is forgiving and compassionate.

Christ, the son of Mary, was no more than an apostle: other apostles passed away before him. His mother was a saintly woman; they both ate earthly food.

Behold how We manifest to them Our revelations. Then behold how they ignore the Truth.

Say: 'Will you serve instead of God that which can neither harm nor help 5:76
you? And God it is who hears all and knows all.'

1. See p. 29, note 1.

5:77 SAY: 'PEOPLE of the Book! Do not transgress the bounds of Truth in your religion. Do not yield to the desires of those who have erred before; who have led many astray and have themselves strayed from the even path.'

Those of the Israelites who disbelieved were cursed by the tongue of David and of Jesus son of Mary for their rebelliousness and transgression. Nor did they reproach each other for any reprehensible act they committed. Evil indeed is what they did.

5:80 You see many among them make friends with unbelievers. Evil is that to which their souls prompt them. They have incurred the wrath of God and shall endure eternal torment. Had they believed in God and the Prophet and that which has been revealed to him, they would not have befriended them. But the greater part of them are ungodly.

5:82 You will assuredly find that the most hostile of people to the faithful are the Jews and the pagans; and you will assuredly find that the nearest in affection to the faithful are those who say: 'We are Christians.' That is because there are priests and monks among them; and because they are free from pride.

قل يا أهل الكتاب لا تغلوا في دينكم غير الحق
ولا تتبعوا أهواء قوم قد ضلوا من قبل وأضلوا
كثيرا وضلوا عن سواء السبيل ﴿٧٧﴾ لعن الذين
كفروا من بني إسرائيل على لسان داود وعيسى
ابن مريم ذلك بما عصوا وكانوا يعتدون ﴿٧٨﴾
كانوا لا يتناهون عن منكر فعلوه لبئس
ما كانوا يفعلون ﴿٧٩﴾ ترى كثيرا منهم يتولون الذين
كفروا لبئس ما قدمت لهم أنفسهم أن سخط
الله عليهم وفي العذاب هم خالدون ﴿٨٠﴾ ولو كانوا يؤمنون
بالله والنبي وما أنزل إليه ما اتخذوهم أولياء
ولكن كثيرا منهم فاسقون ﴿٨١﴾ لتجدن
أشد الناس عداوة للذين آمنوا اليهود والذين
أشركوا ولتجدن أقربهم مودة للذين آمنوا
الذين قالوا إنا نصارى ذلك بأن منهم
قسيسين ورهبانا وأنهم لا يستكبرون ﴿٨٢﴾

وإذا سمعوا ما أنزل إلى الرسول ترى أعينهم تفيض من الدمع
مما عرفوا من الحق يقولون ربنا آمنا فاكتبنا مع الشاهدين
(٨٣) وما لنا لا نؤمن بالله وما جاءنا من الحق ونطمع
أن يدخلنا ربنا مع القوم الصالحين (٨٤) فأثابهم الله
بما قالوا جنات تجري من تحتها الأنهار خالدين فيها
وذلك جزاء المحسنين (٨٥) والذين كفروا وكذبوا
بآياتنا أولئك أصحاب الجحيم (٨٦) يا أيها الذين آمنوا لا
تحرموا طيبات ما أحل الله لكم ولا تعتدوا إن الله
لا يحب المعتدين (٨٧) وكلوا مما رزقكم الله
حلالا طيبا واتقوا الله الذي أنتم به مؤمنون (٨٨)
لا يؤاخذكم الله باللغو في أيمانكم ولكن يؤاخذكم بما
عقدتم الأيمان فكفارته إطعام عشرة مساكين من أوسط
ما تطعمون أهليكم أو كسوتهم أو تحرير رقبة فمن لم يجد
فصيام ثلاثة أيام ذلك كفارة أيمانكم إذا حلفتم واحفظوا
أيمانكم كذلك يبين الله لكم آياته لعلكم تشكرون (٨٩)

WHEN THEY listen to that 5:83
which was revealed to the Apostle, you see their eyes overflow with tears as they recognize its Truth. They say: 'Lord, we believe. Count us among the witnesses. Why should we not believe in God and in the Truth that has come down to us? Why should we not hope our Lord will admit us among the righteous?' And for their words God has rewarded them with Gardens watered by running brooks, wherein shall they abide for ever. Such is the recompense of the righteous. But those that disbelieve and deny Our revelations shall become the inmates of Hell.

Believers, do not forbid the 5:87
wholesome things which God made lawful for you. Do not transgress; God does not love the transgressors. Eat of the lawful and wholesome things which God has given you. And fear God, in whom you do believe.

God will not take you to task for that which is inadvertent in your oaths. 5:89
But He will take you to task over the oaths which you solemnly swear. The penance for a broken oath shall be the feeding of ten needy men with such food as you normally offer to your own people; or fitting them out with clothes; or the freeing of a slave. He that cannot afford any of these shall fast three days. In this way you shall atone for your broken oaths. Therefore be true to that which you have sworn. Thus God manifests to you His revelations, so that you may give thanks.

5:90 YOU THAT believe! Wine and games of chance, idols and divining arrows, are abominations devised by Satan. Avoid them, so that you may prosper. Surely Satan seeks to stir up enmity and hatred among you by means of wine and gambling, and to keep you from the remembrance of God and from your prayers. Will you then desist?

Obey God, and obey the Apostle. Beware; if you pay no heed, know that Our apostle's duty is but to give clear warning.

In regard to any food they may have eaten, no blame shall be attached to those that have embraced the Faith and done good works so long as they fear God and believe in Him and do good works; so long as they fear God and believe in Him; so long as they fear God and do good works. God loves the charitable.

Believers, God will surely put you to the proof by means of the game which you can catch with your hands or with your spears, so that God may know those who fear Him in their hearts. He that transgresses hereafter, woeful punishment awaits him.

5:95 Believers, you shall not kill game while on the Pilgrimage. He that kills game by design, shall present, as an offering to the Ka'bah, an animal equivalent to the one he killed, to be determined by two just men among you; or he shall, in atonement, either feed the destitute or fast, so that he may taste the evil consequences of his deed. God has pardoned what is past; but if anyone relapses God will avenge Himself on him: God is Almighty and capable of revenge.

يا أيها الذين آمنوا إنما الخمر والميسر والأنصاب والأزلام
رجس من عمل الشيطان فاجتنبوه لعلكم تفلحون ﴿٩٠﴾ إنما
يريد الشيطان أن يوقع بينكم العداوة والبغضاء في الخمر
والميسر ويصدكم عن ذكر الله وعن الصلوة فهل أنتم منتهون
﴿٩١﴾ وأطيعوا الله وأطيعوا الرسول واحذروا فإن توليتم فاعلموا
أنما على رسولنا البلاغ المبين ﴿٩٢﴾ ليس على الذين آمنوا وعملوا الصالحات
جناح فيما طعموا إذا ما اتقوا وآمنوا وعملوا الصالحات ثم اتقوا
وآمنوا ثم اتقوا وأحسنوا والله يحب المحسنين ﴿٩٣﴾ يا أيها الذين
آمنوا ليبلونكم الله بشيء من الصيد تناله أيديكم ورما
حكم ليعلم الله من يخافه بالغيب فمن اعتدى بعد ذلك فله
عذاب أليم ﴿٩٤﴾ يا أيها الذين آمنوا لا تقتلوا الصيد وأنتم حرم ومن
قتله منكم متعمدا فجزاء مثل ما قتل من النعم يحكم به ذوا عدل
منكم هديا بالغ الكعبة أو كفارة طعام مساكين أو عدل ذلك
صياما ليذوق وبال أمره عفا الله عما سلف ومن عاد
فينتقم الله منه والله عزيز ذو انتقام ﴿٩٥﴾

أحل لكم صيد البحر وطعامه متاعا لكم وللسيارة
وحرم عليكم صيد البر ما دمتم حرما واتقوا الله
الذي إليه تحشرون ﴿٩٦﴾ جعل الله الكعبة البيت الحرام
قياما للناس والشهر الحرام والهدي والقلائد ذلك
لتعلموا أن الله يعلم ما في السموات وما في الأرض وأن الله
بكل شيء عليم ﴿٩٧﴾ اعلموا أن الله شديد العقاب وأن الله
غفور رحيم ﴿٩٨﴾ ما على الرسول إلا البلاغ والله
يعلم ما تبدون وما تكتمون ﴿٩٩﴾ قل لا يستوي الخبيث
والطيب ولو أعجبك كثرة الخبيث فاتقوا الله
يا أولي الألباب لعلكم تفلحون ﴿١٠٠﴾ يا أيها الذين آمنوا لا تسألوا
عن أشياء إن تبد لكم تسؤكم وإن تسألوا عنها حين ينزل القرآن
تبد لكم عفا الله عنها والله غفور حليم ﴿١٠١﴾ قد
سألها قوم من قبلكم ثم أصبحوا بها كافرين ﴿١٠٢﴾ ما جعل الله
من بحيرة ولا سائبة ولا وصيلة ولا حام ولكن الذين كفروا
يفترون على الله الكذب وأكثرهم لا يعقلون ﴿١٠٣﴾

LAWFUL FOR you is what 5:96
you catch from the sea and the sustenance it provides; wholesome, for you and for the seafarers. But you are forbidden the game of the land while on the Pilgrimage. And fear God, before whom you shall be herded.

God has made the Ka'bah, the Sacred House, a standing shrine for people; also the sacred month, and the sacrificial offerings with their ornaments, so that you may know God has knowledge of all that the heavens and the earth contain; that God has knowledge of all things.

Know that God is stern in retribution, and that God is forgiving and compassionate.

The Apostle's duty is only to give warning. God knows all that you reveal and all that you conceal.

Say: 'Evil and good are not equal, even though the abundance of evil may 5:100
tempt you. Fear God, you that are of good sense possessed, that you may thrive.'

Believers, do not ask questions about things which, if made known to you, would only pain you; but if you ask them when the Koran is being revealed, they shall be made plain to you. God will pardon you for this; God is forgiving and gracious. People asked them before you, only to disbelieve them thereafter.

God demands neither a *baḥīrah*, nor a *sā'ibah*, nor a *waṣīlah*, nor a *ḥāmi*.[1] 5:103
The unbelievers invent falsehoods about God; and most of them are lacking in judgement.

1. Names given by pagan Arabs to sacrificial animals offered at the Ka'bah.

5:104 If they are told: 'Come to
that which God has revealed,
and to the Apostle,' they say:
'Sufficient for us is the faith
of our fathers,' even though
their fathers knew nothing
and did not follow the right
path.

Believers, you are accountable for none but yourselves;
he that strays cannot harm
you if you are on the right
path. To God shall you all
return, and He will declare to
you what you have done.

5:106 Believers, when death approaches you, let two just
men from among you act as
witnesses when you make
your testament; or two men
from another tribe if while
you are travelling the land the
calamity of death overtakes
you. Detain them after prayers, and if you doubt their honesty, let them
swear by God: 'We will not sell our testimony for any price even to kin. We
will not hide the testimony of God; for we should then be sinners.' If both
prove dishonest, replace them by another pair from among those immediately concerned, and let them both swear by God, saying: 'Our testimony is
truer than theirs. We have told no lies, for we should then be wrongdoers.'
5:108 Thus will they be more likely to bear true witness or to fear that the oaths of
others may contradict theirs. Fear God, and be attentive. God does not guide
the ungodly.

وإذا قيل لهم تعالوا إلى ما أنزل الله وإلى الرسول
قالوا حسبنا ما وجدنا عليه آباءنا أولو كان آباؤهم لا يعلمون
شيئا ولا يهتدون ١٠٤ يا أيها الذين آمنوا عليكم أنفسكم
لا يضركم من ضل إذا اهتديتم إلى الله مرجعكم جميعا
فينبئكم بما كنتم تعملون ١٠٥ يا أيها الذين آمنوا شهادة
بينكم إذا حضر أحدكم الموت حين الوصية اثنان ذوا عدل
منكم أو آخران من غيركم إن أنتم ضربتم في الأرض
فأصابتكم مصيبة الموت تحبسونهما من بعد الصلوة فيقسمان
بالله إن ارتبتم لا نشتري به ثمنا ولو كان ذا قربى
ولا نكتم شهادة الله إنا إذا لمن الآثمين ١٠٦ فإن عثر على
أنهما استحقا إثما فآخران يقومان مقامهما من الذين استحق عليهم
الأوليان فيقسمان بالله لشهادتنا أحق من شهادتهما وما
اعتدينا إنا إذا لمن الظالمين ١٠٧ ذلك أدنى أن يأتوا بالشهادة
على وجهها أو يخافوا أن ترد أيمان بعد أيمانهم واتقوا
الله واسمعوا والله لا يهدي القوم الفاسقين ١٠٨

يوم يجمع الله الرسل فيقول ماذا أجبتم قالوا لا علم لنا
إنك أنت علام الغيوب ﴿١٠٩﴾ إذ قال الله يا عيسى ابن مريم
اذكر نعمتي عليك وعلى والدتك إذ أيدتك بروح القدس
تكلم الناس في المهد وكهلا وإذ علمتك الكتاب
والحكمة والتوراة والإنجيل وإذ تخلق من الطين
كهيئة الطير بإذني فتنفخ فيها فتكون طيرا
بإذني وتبرئ الأكمه والأبرص بإذني وإذ تخرج
الموتى بإذني وإذ كففت بني إسرائيل عنك إذ جئتهم
بالبينات فقال الذين كفروا منهم إن هذا إلا سحر
مبين ﴿١١٠﴾ وإذ أوحيت إلى الحواريين أن آمنوا بي وبرسولي
قالوا آمنا واشهد بأننا مسلمون ﴿١١١﴾ إذ قال الحواريون
يا عيسى ابن مريم هل يستطيع ربك أن ينزل علينا
مائدة من السماء قال اتقوا الله إن كنتم مؤمنين
﴿١١٢﴾ قالوا نريد أن نأكل منها وتطمئن قلوبنا ونعلم
أن قد صدقتنا ونكون عليها من الشاهدين ﴿١١٣﴾

ON THE day God gathers 5:109
the apostles and says to them: 'How were you received?' they will say: 'We have no knowledge. You alone know what is hidden.' God will say: 'Jesus son of Mary, remember the favour I bestowed on you and on your mother: how I strengthened you with the Holy Spirit, so that you spoke to people in the cradle and in the prime of manhood; how I instructed you in the Book and in wisdom, in the Torah and in the Gospel; how by My leave you fashioned from clay the likeness of a bird and breathed into it so that, by My leave, it became a living bird; how, by My leave, you healed the blind man and the leper, and, by My leave, restored the dead to life; how I protected you from the Israelites when you had come to them with conspicuous signs: when those of them who disbelieved said: "This is but
sorcery manifest"; how, when I enjoined the disciples to believe in Me and in 5:111
My apostle, they said: "We do believe; bear witness that we are Muslims."'

'Jesus son of Mary,' said the disciples, 'is your Lord able to send down to us from heaven a table spread with food?'

He said: 'Fear God, if you are true believers.'

'We wish to eat of it,' they said, 'so that we may reassure our hearts and 5:113
know that what you said to us is true, and that we may be witnesses of it.'

5:114 'LORD,' SAID Jesus son of
Mary, 'send down to us from
heaven a table spread with
food, that it may mark a feast
for the first of us and for the
last of us: a sign from You.
Give us our sustenance; You
are the best provider.'

God said: 'I am sending
one to you. But whoever of
you disbelieves hereafter shall
be punished as no man will
ever be punished.'

Then God will say: 'Jesus
son of Mary, did you ever say
to the people: "Worship me
and my mother as gods
besides God?"'

'Glory be to You,' he will
answer, 'I could never have
claimed what I have no right
to. If I had ever said so, You
would have surely known it.
You know what is in my mind, but I know not what is in Your mind. You
5:117 alone know what is hidden. I told them only what You bade me: "Worship
God, my Lord and your Lord." I was a witness over them while living in their
midst, and ever since You took me to Yourself, You Yourself have been
watching them. Over all things You are the witness. If You punish them,
they surely are Your creatures; and if You forgive them, surely You are the
Almighty, the Wise One.'

God will say: 'This is the day when their truthfulness will benefit the truthful. They shall for ever dwell in Gardens watered by running brooks. God is pleased with them, and they are pleased with Him. That is the supreme triumph.'

5:120 God it is who has sovereignty over the heavens and the earth and all that
they contain. And He has power over all things.

قال عيسى ابن مريم اللهم ربنا انزل علينا مائدة من السماء
تكون لنا عيدا لاولنا واخرنا واية منك وارزقنا وانت خير
الرازقين ﴿١١٤﴾ قال الله اني منزلها عليكم فمن يكفر بعد منكم
فاني اعذبه عذابا لا اعذبه احدا من العالمين ﴿١١٥﴾ واذ قال الله
يا عيسى ابن مريم ءانت قلت للناس اتخذوني وامي الهين من دون
الله قال سبحانك ما يكون لي ان اقول ما ليس لي بحق ان
كنت قلته فقد علمته تعلم ما في نفسي ولا اعلم ما في
نفسك انك انت علام الغيوب ﴿١١٦﴾ ما قلت لهم الا ما امرتني
به ان اعبدوا الله ربي وربكم وكنت عليهم شهيدا ما دمت
فيهم فلما توفيتني كنت انت الرقيب عليهم وانت على كل شيء شهيد
﴿١١٧﴾ ان تعذبهم فانهم عبادك وان تغفر لهم فانك انت العزيز
الحكيم ﴿١١٨﴾ قال الله هذا يوم ينفع الصادقين صدقهم لهم
جنات تجري من تحتها الانهار خالدين فيها ابدا رضي
الله عنهم ورضوا عنه ذلك الفوز العظيم ﴿١١٩﴾ لله
ملك السموات والارض وما فيهن وهو على كل شيء قدير ﴿١٢٠﴾

بسم الله الرحمن الرحيم
الحمد لله الذي خلق السموات والأرض وجعل الظلمات
والنور ثم الذين كفروا بربهم يعدلون (١) هو الذي خلقكم
من طين ثم قضى أجلا وأجل مسمى عنده ثم أنتم تمترون (٢)
وهو الله في السموات وفي الأرض يعلم سركم وجهركم ويعلم ما تكسبون
(٣) وما تأتيهم من آية من آيات ربهم إلا كانوا عنها معرضين (٤)
فقد كذبوا بالحق لما جاءهم فسوف يأتيهم أنبؤا ما كانوا به
يستهزءون (٥) ألم يروا كم أهلكنا من قبلهم من قرن مكناهم
في الأرض ما لم نمكن لكم وأرسلنا السماء عليهم مدرارا وجعلنا
الأنهار تجري من تحتهم فأهلكناهم بذنوبهم وأنشأنا من
بعدهم قرنا آخرين (٦) ولو نزلنا عليك كتابا في قرطاس فلمسوه
بأيديهم لقال الذين كفروا إن هذا إلا سحر مبين (٧) وقالوا لولا
أنزل عليه ملك ولو أنزلنا ملكا لقضي الأمر ثم لا ينظرون (٨)

CATTLE

In the Name of God,
the Merciful, the Compassionate

PRAISE BE to God, who cre- 6:1
ated the heavens and the earth
and ordained darkness and
light. Yet the unbelievers set
up other gods as equals with
their Lord.

He it was who created you
from clay. Then He decreed a
term for you in this world and
another specified by Him. Yet
you are still in doubt.

God is He in the heavens
and on earth. He knows what
you conceal and what you
reveal; He knows what you do.

Yet every time a revelation
comes to them from their
Lord, they pay no heed to it. Thus do they deny the Truth when it is declared 6:5
to them: but they shall learn the consequences of their scorn.

Can they not see how many generations We have destroyed before them?
We had given them more power in the land than the power We have given
you,[1] We sent down for them abundant water from the sky, and We gave
them rivers that rolled at their feet. Yet because they sinned We obliterated
them, and raised up other generations after them.

If We sent down to you a Book inscribed on real parchment and they
touched it with their own hands, the unbelievers would still assert: 'This is
but sorcery manifest.'

And they ask: 'Why has no angel been sent down to him?' If We had sent 6:8
down an angel, judgement would have been passed and they would have
never been reprieved.

1. The Meccans.

6:9 AND IF We had made him an angel, We would have given him the semblance of a man, and would have thus added to their confusion.

Other apostles have been laughed to scorn before you; but those that scoffed at them were felled by the very scourge they had derided.

Say: 'Roam the earth and see what was the fate of those that disbelieved.'

Say: 'To whom belongs all that the heavens and the earth contain?' Say: 'To God. He has decreed mercy for Himself, and will gather you all on the Day of Resurrection: a day not to be doubted. Those who have forfeited their souls will never believe.'

And His is whatever takes
its rest in the night or in the day. And He it is who hears all and knows all.
6:14 Say: 'Should I take any but God for my Protector? Creator of the heavens
and the earth, He gives nourishment to all and is nourished by none.'

Say: 'I was commanded to be the first of the Muslims. You shall serve no other god besides Him.'

Say: 'I will never disobey my Lord, for I fear the torment of a fateful day.'

He who is spared that day shall have received His mercy. That is the glorious triumph.

If God afflicts you with an evil, none can remove it but Him; and if He blesses you with good fortune, know that He has power over all things.

6:18 He reigns supreme over His servants; and He alone is the Wise One, the
Omniscient.

ولو جعلناه ملكا لجعلناه رجلا وللبسنا عليهم
ما يلبسون (٩) ولقد استهزئ برسل من قبلك فحاق بالذين
سخروا منهم ما كانوا به يستهزئون (١٠) قل سيروا في
الأرض ثم انظروا كيف كان عاقبة المكذبين (١١) قل لمن
ما في السماوات والأرض قل لله كتب على نفسه الرحمة
ليجمعنكم إلى يوم القيامة لا ريب فيه الذين خسروا
أنفسهم فهم لا يؤمنون (١٢) وله ما سكن في الليل والنهار وهو
السميع العليم (١٣) قل أغير الله أتخذ وليا فاطر السماوات
والأرض وهو يطعم ولا يطعم قل إني أمرت أن
أكون أول من أسلم ولا تكونن من المشركين (١٤)
قل إني أخاف إن عصيت ربي عذاب يوم عظيم (١٥)
من يصرف عنه يومئذ فقد رحمه وذلك الفوز
المبين (١٦) وإن يمسسك الله بضر فلا كاشف له إلا هو
وإن يمسسك بخير فهو على كل شيء قدير (١٧) وهو
القاهر فوق عباده وهو الحكيم الخبير (١٨)

قل اي شيء اكبر شهادة قل الله شهيد بيني وبينكم واوحي الي
هذا القران لانذركم به ومن بلغ ائنكم لتشهدون ان مع الله
الهة اخرى قل لا اشهد قل انما هو اله واحد وانني بريء مما تشركون
(١٩) الذين اتيناهم الكتاب يعرفونه كما يعرفون ابناءهم الذين
خسروا انفسهم فهم لا يؤمنون (٢٠) ومن اظلم ممن افترى على الله
كذبا او كذب بآياته انه لا يفلح الظالمون (٢١) ويوم نحشرهم
جميعا ثم نقول للذين اشركوا اين شركاؤكم الذين كنتم
تزعمون (٢٢) ثم لم تكن فتنتهم الا ان قالوا والله
ربنا ما كنا مشركين (٢٣) انظر كيف كذبوا على انفسهم وضل عنهم
ما كانوا يفترون (٢٤) ومنهم من يستمع اليك وجعلنا على قلوبهم
اكنة ان يفقهوه وفي اذانهم وقرا وان يروا كل اية لا يؤمنوا
بها حتى اذا جاءوك يجادلونك يقول الذين كفروا ان هذا الا
اساطير الاولين (٢٥) وهم ينهون عنه وينأون عنه وان يهلكون
الا انفسهم وما يشعرون (٢٦) ولو ترى اذ وقفوا على النار فقالوا
يا ليتنا نرد ولا نكذب بآيات ربنا ونكون من المؤمنين (٢٧)

SAY: 'WHAT counts most in 6:19
testimony?'

Say: 'God is my witness and your witness. This Koran has been revealed to me that I may thereby warn you and all whom it may reach. Will you really testify there are other gods besides God?'

Say: 'I will testify to no such thing!'

Say: 'He is but one God. I disown the gods you serve besides Him.'

Those to whom We have given the Book[1] know him as they know their own children. But those who have forfeited their souls will never have faith.

And who is more wicked than the man who invents a falsehood about God or denies His revelations? The wrongdoers shall never succeed.

On the day We herd them all together We shall say to the pagans: 'Where 6:22
are your idols now, those whom you claimed to be your gods?' They will then have no case to argue, but will only say: 'By God, our Lord, we have never worshipped idols.'

You shall see how they have deceived themselves and how the deities of their own invention will forsake them.

And some among them listen to you. But We have cast veils over their hearts and made them hard of hearing lest they understand your words. They will believe in none of Our signs, even if they see them, one and all.

When they come to argue with you the unbelievers say: 'This is nothing but fables of the ancients.' They forbid it and distance themselves from it. They ruin none but themselves, though they do not perceive it.

If you could see them when they are set before the Fire! They will say: 6:27
'Would that we could return! Then we would not deny the revelations of our Lord and would be true believers.'

1. Christians and Jews.

6:28 INDEED, THAT which they concealed before will manifest itself to them.

But if they were sent back, they would return to that which they had been forbidden; they are surely lying.

They say: 'It is but this, our nether life; nor shall we ever be raised to life again.'

If you could see them when they are set before their Lord! He will say: 'Is this not real?' 'Yes, by our Lord,' they will reply, and He will say: 'Taste then the torment, the reward of your unbelief!'

Lost indeed are those who deny they will ever meet God. When the Hour overtakes them unawares, they will say: 'Alas, we have neglected much in our lifetime!' And they shall bear their burdens on their backs; evil are the burdens they shall bear.

6:32 The life of this world is but a sport and a diversion. Surely better is the life to come for those that fear God. Will you not understand?

We know too well that what they say grieves you. It is not you that they are disbelieving; the wrongdoers deny God's own revelations. Other apostles have been denied before you; but they patiently bore with disbelief and persecution until Our help came down to them: for none can change the decrees of God. You have already heard of those apostles.

6:35 And if you find their aversion hard to bear, seek if you can a tunnel in the earth or a ladder to the sky by which you may bring them a sign. Had God pleased He would have given them guidance, one and all. Do not be foolish, then.

بل بدا لهم ما كانوا يخفون من قبل ولو ردوا لعادوا لما نهوا عنه
وإنهم لكاذبون ۝ وقالوا إن هي إلا حياتنا الدنيا وما نحن
بمبعوثين ۝ ولو ترى إذ وقفوا على ربهم قال أليس هذا بالحق
قالوا بلى وربنا قال فذوقوا العذاب بما كنتم تكفرون ۝
قد خسر الذين كذبوا بلقاء الله حتى إذا جاءتهم الساعة
بغتة قالوا يا حسرتنا على ما فرطنا فيها وهم يحملون
أوزارهم على ظهورهم ألا ساء ما يزرون ۝ وما الحياة
الدنيا إلا لعب ولهو وللدار الآخرة خير للذين يتقون
أفلا تعقلون ۝ قد نعلم إنه ليحزنك الذي يقولون فإنهم
لا يكذبونك ولكن الظالمين بآيات الله يجحدون ۝ ولقد
كذبت رسل من قبلك فصبروا على ما كذبوا وأوذوا حتى
أتاهم نصرنا ولا مبدل لكلمات الله ولقد جاءك من نبإي
المرسلين ۝ وإن كان كبر عليك إعراضهم فإن استطعت
أن تبتغي نفقا في الأرض أو سلما في السماء فتأتيهم بآية
ولو شاء الله لجمعهم على الهدى فلا تكونن من الجاهلين ۝

إِنَّمَا يَسْتَجِيبُ ٱلَّذِينَ يَسْمَعُونَ ۘ وَٱلْمَوْتَىٰ يَبْعَثُهُمُ ٱللَّهُ ثُمَّ إِلَيْهِ
يُرْجَعُونَ ٣٦ وَقَالُوا لَوْلَا نُزِّلَ عَلَيْهِ ءَايَةٌ مِّن رَّبِّهِۦ ۚ قُلْ إِنَّ
ٱللَّهَ قَادِرٌ عَلَىٰٓ أَن يُنَزِّلَ ءَايَةً وَلَٰكِنَّ أَكْثَرَهُمْ لَا يَعْلَمُونَ ٣٧
وَمَا مِن دَآبَّةٍ فِى ٱلْأَرْضِ وَلَا طَٰٓئِرٍ يَطِيرُ بِجَنَاحَيْهِ إِلَّآ أُمَمٌ
أَمْثَالُكُم ۚ مَّا فَرَّطْنَا فِى ٱلْكِتَٰبِ مِن شَىْءٍ ۚ ثُمَّ إِلَىٰ رَبِّهِمْ يُحْشَرُونَ
٣٨ وَٱلَّذِينَ كَذَّبُوا بِـَٔايَٰتِنَا صُمٌّ وَبُكْمٌ فِى ٱلظُّلُمَٰتِ ۗ مَن يَشَإِ
ٱللَّهُ يُضْلِلْهُ وَمَن يَشَأْ يَجْعَلْهُ عَلَىٰ صِرَٰطٍ مُّسْتَقِيمٍ ٣٩ قُلْ
أَرَءَيْتَكُمْ إِنْ أَتَىٰكُمْ عَذَابُ ٱللَّهِ أَوْ أَتَتْكُمُ ٱلسَّاعَةُ أَغَيْرَ
ٱللَّهِ تَدْعُونَ إِن كُنتُمْ صَٰدِقِينَ ٤٠ بَلْ إِيَّاهُ تَدْعُونَ فَيَكْشِفُ
مَا تَدْعُونَ إِلَيْهِ إِن شَآءَ وَتَنسَوْنَ مَا تُشْرِكُونَ ٤١ وَلَقَدْ
أَرْسَلْنَآ إِلَىٰٓ أُمَمٍ مِّن قَبْلِكَ فَأَخَذْنَٰهُم بِٱلْبَأْسَآءِ وَٱلضَّرَّآءِ
لَعَلَّهُمْ يَتَضَرَّعُونَ ٤٢ فَلَوْلَآ إِذْ جَآءَهُم بَأْسُنَا تَضَرَّعُوا وَلَٰكِن
قَسَتْ قُلُوبُهُمْ وَزَيَّنَ لَهُمُ ٱلشَّيْطَٰنُ مَا كَانُوا يَعْمَلُونَ ٤٣
فَلَمَّا نَسُوا مَا ذُكِّرُوا بِهِۦ فَتَحْنَا عَلَيْهِمْ أَبْوَٰبَ كُلِّ شَىْءٍ حَتَّىٰٓ إِذَا
فَرِحُوا بِمَآ أُوتُوٓا أَخَذْنَٰهُم بَغْتَةً فَإِذَا هُم مُّبْلِسُونَ ٤٤

THOSE THAT can hear will 6:36
surely answer. As for the dead, God will bring them back to life. Then to Him shall they be recalled.

They ask: 'Why was no sign sent down to him from his Lord?'

Say: 'God is well able to send down a sign.' But most of them have no knowledge.

All the beasts that roam the earth and all the birds that soar on high are but communities like your own. We have left out nothing in the Book. Then to their Lord they shall be herded all.

Deaf and dumb are those that deny Our revelations: they are in darkness. God confounds whom He will, and whom He pleases He guides on to a straight path.

Say: 'Do but consider. When God's scourge smites you and the Hour sud- 6:40
denly overtakes you, will you call on any but God to help you? Answer me, if you are truthful! No, on Him you will call; and He will relieve your affliction if He pleases. Then you will forget your idols.'

We sent forth apostles before you to other communities, and afflicted them with calamities and misfortunes that they might humble themselves. If only did they humble themselves when Our scourge overtook them! But their hearts hardened, and Satan made their deeds seem fair to them.

And when they had clean forgotten Our Admonition We opened every 6:44
door for them; but just as they were rejoicing in what they were given, We suddenly smote them, and, lo, they were despondent.

6:45 THUS WERE the wrongdoers annihilated. Praise be to God, Lord of the Universe!

Say: 'Do but consider: if God took away your hearing and your sight and set a seal upon your hearts, could any but God restore them to you?'

See how We expound the revelations; and yet they turn away.

Say: 'Do but consider: if the scourge of God overtook you suddenly or predictably, would any perish but the wrongdoers?'

We send forth apostles only to proclaim joyful tidings and to give warning. Those that believe in them and mend their ways shall have nothing to fear or to regret; and those that deny Our revelations shall be punished for their foul deeds.

6:50 Say: 'I do not tell you that I possess God's treasures or know what is hidden, nor do I say to you I am an angel; I follow only that which is revealed to me.'

Say: 'Are the blind and the seeing equal? Will you not reflect?'

Warn those who dread to be herded before their Lord that they have no
6:52 guardian or intercessor besides Him, so that they may fear Him. Do not
drive away those that call on their Lord morning and evening, seeking only
to gain His favour. You are in no way accountable for them, nor are they in
any way accountable for you. If you dismiss them, you shall yourself become
a wrongdoer.

فقطع دابر القوم الذين ظلموا والحمد لله رب العالمين ٤٥ قل
أرأيتم إن أخذ الله سمعكم وأبصاركم وختم على قلوبكم
من إله غير الله يأتيكم به انظر كيف نصرف الآيات ثم هم
يصدفون ٤٦ قل أرأيتكم إن أتاكم عذاب الله بغتة أو جهرة
هل يهلك إلا القوم الظالمون ٤٧ وما نرسل المرسلين إلا
مبشرين ومنذرين فمن آمن وأصلح فلا خوف عليهم
ولا هم يحزنون ٤٨ والذين كذبوا بآياتنا يمسهم
العذاب بما كانوا يفسقون ٤٩ قل لا أقول لكم
عندي خزائن الله ولا أعلم الغيب ولا أقول لكم إني ملك
إن أتبع إلا ما يوحى إلي قل هل يستوي الأعمى والبصير
أفلا تتفكرون ٥٠ وأنذر به الذين يخافون أن
يحشروا إلى ربهم ليس لهم من دونه ولي ولا شفيع لعلهم
يتقون ٥١ ولا تطرد الذين يدعون ربهم بالغداة والعشي
يريدون وجهه ما عليك من حسابهم من شيء وما من حسابك
عليهم من شيء فتطردهم فتكون من الظالمين ٥٢

وَكَذَٰلِكَ فَتَنَّا بَعْضَهُم بِبَعْضٍ لِّيَقُولُوٓا أَهَٰٓؤُلَآءِ مَنَّ ٱللَّهُ
عَلَيْهِم مِّنۢ بَيْنِنَآ أَلَيْسَ ٱللَّهُ بِأَعْلَمَ بِٱلشَّٰكِرِينَ ﴿٥٣﴾ وَإِذَا
جَآءَكَ ٱلَّذِينَ يُؤْمِنُونَ بِـَٔايَٰتِنَا فَقُلْ سَلَٰمٌ عَلَيْكُمْ كَتَبَ رَبُّكُمْ
عَلَىٰ نَفْسِهِ ٱلرَّحْمَةَ أَنَّهُۥ مَنْ عَمِلَ مِنكُمْ سُوٓءًۢا بِجَهَٰلَةٍ
ثُمَّ تَابَ مِنۢ بَعْدِهِۦ وَأَصْلَحَ فَأَنَّهُۥ غَفُورٌ رَّحِيمٌ ﴿٥٤﴾ وَكَذَٰلِكَ
نُفَصِّلُ ٱلْءَايَٰتِ وَلِتَسْتَبِينَ سَبِيلُ ٱلْمُجْرِمِينَ ﴿٥٥﴾ قُلْ إِنِّى
نُهِيتُ أَنْ أَعْبُدَ ٱلَّذِينَ تَدْعُونَ مِن دُونِ ٱللَّهِ
قُل لَّآ أَتَّبِعُ أَهْوَآءَكُمْ قَدْ ضَلَلْتُ إِذًا وَمَآ أَنَا۠ مِنَ ٱلْمُهْتَدِينَ
﴿٥٦﴾ قُلْ إِنِّى عَلَىٰ بَيِّنَةٍ مِّن رَّبِّى وَكَذَّبْتُم بِهِۦ مَا عِندِى مَا
تَسْتَعْجِلُونَ بِهِۦٓ إِنِ ٱلْحُكْمُ إِلَّا لِلَّهِ يَقُصُّ ٱلْحَقَّ وَهُوَ خَيْرُ ٱلْفَٰصِلِينَ
﴿٥٧﴾ قُل لَّوْ أَنَّ عِندِى مَا تَسْتَعْجِلُونَ بِهِۦ لَقُضِىَ
ٱلْأَمْرُ بَيْنِى وَبَيْنَكُمْ وَٱللَّهُ أَعْلَمُ بِٱلظَّٰلِمِينَ ﴿٥٨﴾ وَعِندَهُۥ
مَفَاتِحُ ٱلْغَيْبِ لَا يَعْلَمُهَآ إِلَّا هُوَ وَيَعْلَمُ مَا فِى ٱلْبَرِّ وَٱلْبَحْرِ وَمَا
تَسْقُطُ مِن وَرَقَةٍ إِلَّا يَعْلَمُهَا وَلَا حَبَّةٍ فِى ظُلُمَٰتِ
ٱلْأَرْضِ وَلَا رَطْبٍ وَلَا يَابِسٍ إِلَّا فِى كِتَٰبٍ مُّبِينٍ ﴿٥٩﴾

AND THUS have We made 6:53
some among them a means
for testing others, so that they
should say: 'Are these the ones
God has favoured among us?'
But does not God best know
the thankful?

If those that believe in Our
revelations come to you, say:
'Peace be upon you. Your
Lord has decreed mercy for
Himself. If any one among
you has done a bad deed
through ignorance and then
repented and mended his
ways, he will find God forgiving and compassionate.'

Thus do We expound Our
revelations, so that the path of
the guilty may be laid bare.

Say: 'I am forbidden to wor- 6:56
ship the deities you invoke
besides God.'

Say: 'I will not yield to your wishes, for then I would have strayed and
ceased to be on the right path.'

Say: 'I have received veritable proofs from my Lord, yet you deny Him. I
have no power to hasten that which you challenge; judgement is for God
only. He it is who declares the Truth and is the best of arbiters.'

Say: 'Had I the power to hasten that which you challenge, judgement
would have been passed between myself and you. But God best knows the
wrongdoers. He has the keys to all that is hidden: none knows it but Him. He 6:59
knows all that land and sea contain: every leaf that falls is known to Him.
There is no grain in the darkest bowels of the earth, nor anything green or
sear, but is recorded in a veritable Book.

وهو الذي يتوفاكم بالليل ويعلم ما جرحتم بالنهار ثم
يبعثكم فيه ليقضى أجل مسمى ثم إليه مرجعكم ثم
ينبئكم بما كنتم تعملون ٦٠ وهو القاهر فوق عباده ويرسل
عليكم حفظة حتى إذا جاء أحدكم الموت توفته رسلنا وهم
لا يفرطون ٦١ ثم ردوا إلى الله مولاهم الحق ألا له الحكم
وهو أسرع الحاسبين ٦٢ قل من ينجيكم من ظلمات البر
والبحر تدعونه تضرعا وخفية لئن أنجانا من هذه لنكونن
من الشاكرين ٦٣ قل الله ينجيكم منها ومن كل كرب
ثم أنتم تشركون ٦٤ قل هو القادر على أن يبعث عليكم
عذابا من فوقكم أو من تحت أرجلكم أو يلبسكم شيعا ويذيق
بعضكم بأس بعض انظر كيف نصرف الآيات لعلهم يفقهون
٦٥ وكذب به قومك وهو الحق قل لست عليكم بوكيل ٦٦
لكل نبإ مستقر وسوف تعلمون ٦٧ وإذا رأيت الذين يخوضون
في آياتنا فأعرض عنهم حتى يخوضوا في حديث غيره وإما ينسينك
الشيطان فلا تقعد بعد الذكرى مع القوم الظالمين ٦٨

6:60 'HE IT is who claims you back by night, knowing what you have done by day, and then rouses you up to fulfil your allotted span of life. Then to Him shall you return, and He will then declare to you all that you have done.

'He it is who reigns supreme over His servants. And He sends forth guardians to watch over you, so that when death overtakes any one of you, Our emissaries will claim him back: they never fail. Then are all restored to God, their true Lord. His alone is the Judgement, and most swift is His reckoning.'

Say: 'Who delivers you from the dark perils of land and sea, when you call out to Him humbly and in secret, saying: "Save us from these and we will be truly thankful!"?'

6:64 Say: 'God delivers you from them, and from all afflictions; yet you worship idols.'

Say: 'He it is who has power to let loose a scourge upon you from above your heads and from beneath your feet, and to divide you into discordant factions, causing the one to suffer at the hands of the other.'

See how We expound Our revelations, that they may understand them.

Your people have rejected this[1] although it is the very Truth. Say: 'I am not your keeper. The time will come when every prophecy shall be fulfilled, and you shall learn.'

6:68 If you see those that scoff at Our revelations, withdraw from them till they engage in other talk. And should Satan cause you to forget, take leave of the wrongdoers as soon as you remember.

1. The Koran.

وما على الذين يتقون من حسابهم من شيء ولكن
ذكرى لعلهم يتقون ۝٦٩ وذر الذين اتخذوا دينهم
لعبا ولهوا وغرتهم الحيوة الدنيا وذكر به أن
تبسل نفس بما كسبت ليس لها من دون الله
ولي ولا شفيع وإن تعدل كل عدل لا يؤخذ منها أولئك
الذين أبسلوا بما كسبوا لهم شراب من حميم وعذاب
أليم بما كانوا يكفرون ۝٧٠ قل أندعوا من دون الله
ما لا ينفعنا ولا يضرنا ونرد على أعقابنا بعد إذ هدينا الله
كالذي استهوته الشياطين في الأرض حيران له
أصحاب يدعونه إلى الهدى ائتنا قل إن هدى الله
هو الهدى وأمرنا لنسلم لرب العالمين ۝٧١ وأن أقيموا
الصلوة واتقوه وهو الذي إليه تحشرون ۝٧٢ وهو الذي
خلق السموات والأرض بالحق ويوم يقول كن
فيكون قوله الحق وله الملك يوم ينفخ في الصور
عالم الغيب والشهادة وهو الحكيم الخبير ۝٧٣

THOSE THAT fear God are in 6:69
no way accountable for them.
Remind them only that they
may fear Him.

Avoid those that treat their
faith as a sport and a diversion
and are seduced by the life of
this world. Admonish them
with this lest their souls be
damned by their own actions,
having no guardian or intercessor besides God: and though
they offer every ransom, it shall
not be accepted from them.
Such are those that are damned
by their own actions. Scalding
water shall they drink, and suffer woeful torment for their
unbelief.

Say: 'Are we to call on idols 6:71
which can neither help nor
harm us? Are we to turn upon
our heels after God has guided
us, like him who, being bewitched by demons in the land, blunders along
perplexed, although his friends call him to the right path, shouting: "Come
this way!"?'

Say: 'God's guidance is the only guidance. We are commanded to submit
to the Lord of the Universe, to pray, and to fear Him. Before Him shall you
be herded all.'

He it was who created the heavens and the earth with Truth. On the day 6:73
He says: 'Be,' it shall be. His word is Truth: and sovereignty shall be His
on the day when the Trumpet is blown. He has knowledge of the unknown
and the manifest. He alone is the Wise One, the Omniscient.

6:74 TELL OF Abraham, who
said to Azar, his father: 'Will
you worship idols as your gods?
I can see that you and your
people are in palpable error.'
Thus did We show Abraham
the kingdom of the heavens
and the earth, so that he might
become a firm believer.
When night drew its shadow
over him, he saw a star. 'That,'
he said, 'is surely my God.'
But when it faded away, he
said: 'I have no love for such
that fade.'
When he beheld the rising
moon, he said: 'That is my
God.' But when it set, he said:
'If my Lord does not guide
me, I shall surely go astray.'
Then, when he beheld the
sun rising, he said: 'That must
be my God: it is larger.'
6:79 But when it set, he said to his people: 'I disown your idols. I will turn my
face to Him who has created the heavens and the earth, and will live a righteous life. I am no idolater.'
His people argued with him. He said: 'Will you argue with me about God,
who has given me guidance? I do not fear your idols, unless my Lord so
willed for a purpose. My Lord has prodigious knowledge of all things: will
6:81 you not reflect? And how should I fear your idols when you yourselves are
not afraid of serving idols not sanctioned for you by God? Which of us is
more deserving of salvation? Tell me, if you know.

وإذ قال إبرهيم لأبيه ءازر أتتخذ أصناما ءالهة
إني أرىك وقومك في ضلل مبين ٧٤ وكذلك نري
إبرهيم ملكوت السموت والأرض وليكون من الموقنين
٧٥ فلما جن عليه اليل رءا كوكبا قال هذا ربي
فلما أفل قال لا أحب الأفلين ٧٦ فلما رءا القمر
بازغا قال هذا ربي فلما أفل قال لئن لم يهدني ربي
لأكونن من القوم الضالين ٧٧ فلما رءا الشمس
بازغة قال هذا ربي هذا أكبر فلما أفلت قال يقوم إني
بريء مما تشركون ٧٨ إني وجهت وجهي للذي فطر السموت
والأرض حنيفا وما أنا من المشركين ٧٩ وحاجه قومه
قال أتحجوني في الله وقد هدين ولا أخاف ما تشركون
به إلا أن يشاء ربي شيئا وسع ربي كل شيء علما أفلا
تتذكرون ٨٠ وكيف أخاف ما أشركتم ولا تخافون
أنكم أشركتم بالله ما لم ينزل به عليكم سلطنا
فأي الفريقين أحق بالأمن إن كنتم تعلمون ٨١

الذين آمنوا ولم يلبسوا إيمانهم بظلم أولئك لهم الأمن
وهم مهتدون ﴿٨٢﴾ وتلك حجتنا آتيناها إبراهيم على
قومه نرفع درجات من نشاء إن ربك حكيم عليم ﴿٨٣﴾
ووهبنا له إسحق ويعقوب كلا هدينا ونوحا هدينا
من قبل ومن ذريته داود وسليمن وأيوب ويوسف
وموسى وهرون وكذلك نجزي المحسنين ﴿٨٤﴾ وزكريا
ويحيى وعيسى وإلياس كل من الصالحين ﴿٨٥﴾ وإسمعيل
واليسع ويونس ولوطا وكلا فضلنا على العالمين ﴿٨٦﴾
ومن آبائهم وذرياتهم وإخوانهم واجتبيناهم وهديناهم
إلى صراط مستقيم ﴿٨٧﴾ ذلك هدى الله يهدي به من يشاء
من عباده ولو أشركوا لحبط عنهم ما كانوا يعملون ﴿٨٨﴾
أولئك الذين آتيناهم الكتاب والحكم والنبوة
فإن يكفر بها هؤلاء فقد وكلنا بها قوما ليسوا بها
بكافرين ﴿٨٩﴾ أولئك الذين هدى الله فبهداهم اقتده
قل لا أسألكم عليه أجرا إن هو إلا ذكرى للعالمين ﴿٩٠﴾

THOSE THAT have faith and 6:82
do not taint their faith with
wrongdoing shall surely earn
salvation, and are rightly
guided.'

Such was the argument with which We furnished Abraham against his people. We raise whom We will to an exalted rank. Your Lord is wise and all-knowing.

We gave him Isaac and
Jacob and guided both as We
had guided Noah before them.
Among his descendants were
David and Solomon, Job and
Joseph and Moses and Aaron
(thus do We reward the righteous); Zacharias and John,
Jesus and Elias[1] (all were
upright men); and Ishmael, 6:86
Elisha, Jonah, and Lot. All
these We exalted above the
nations as We had exalted some of their fathers, their children, and their
brothers. We chose them and guided them to a straight path.

Such is God's guidance; He guides those of His servants whom He chooses. Had they served other gods besides Him, their labours would have been vain indeed.

On those We bestowed the Book, wisdom, and prophethood. If these are denied by them, We will entrust them to others who will not deny them.

It was those whom God had guided: follow then their guidance and say: 'I 6:90
demand of you no recompense for this. It is but an admonition to mankind.'

1. Elijah.

6:91 And they have no true
notion of God's glory, those
that say: 'God has never
revealed anything to a mortal.'
Say: 'Who, then, revealed
the Scriptures which Moses
brought down, a light and a
guide for mankind? You have
transcribed them on scraps of
paper, declaring some and
suppressing much, though
now you have been taught
what neither you nor your
fathers knew before.'
Say: 'God!' Then leave
them to amuse themselves
with foolish chatter.
This is a blessed Book
which We have revealed, confirming what came before it,
that you may warn the mother
city[1] and those that dwell
around her. Those who be-
lieve in the life to come believe in it and are steadfast in their prayers.
6:93 Who is more wicked than he who invents a falsehood about God, or says:
'This was revealed to me,' when nothing was revealed to him? Or says: 'I can
reveal the like of what God has revealed'?
Could you but see the wrongdoers when death overwhelms them! With
hands outstretched, the angels will say: 'Yield up your souls this day. You
shall be rewarded with the scourge of shame, for you have said of God what
6:94 is untrue and scorned His revelations. And now you have returned to Us,
one by one, as We created you at first, leaving behind all that We bestowed
on you. Nor do We see with you your intercessors, those whom you claimed
to be God's equals. Broken are the ties which bound you, and that which you
claimed has failed you.'

وما قدروا الله حق قدره إذ قالوا ما أنزل الله على
بشر من شيء قل من أنزل الكتاب الذي جاء به موسى نورا وهدى
للناس تجعلونه قراطيس تبدونها وتخفون كثيرا وعلمتم
ما لم تعلموا أنتم ولا آباؤكم قل الله ثم ذرهم في خوضهم
يلعبون ۝٩١ وهذا كتاب أنزلناه مبارك مصدق الذي بين
يديه ولتنذر أم القرى ومن حولها والذين يؤمنون بالآخرة
يؤمنون به وهم على صلاتهم يحافظون ۝٩٢ ومن أظلم
ممن افترى على الله كذبا أو قال أوحي إلي ولم يوح إليه شيء
ومن قال سأنزل مثل ما أنزل الله ولو ترى إذ الظالمون
في غمرات الموت والملائكة باسطوا أيديهم أخرجوا أنفسكم
اليوم تجزون عذاب الهون بما كنتم تقولون على الله غير
الحق وكنتم عن آياته تستكبرون ۝٩٣ ولقد جئتمونا فرادى
كما خلقناكم أول مرة وتركتم ما خولناكم وراء ظهوركم
وما نرى معكم شفعاءكم الذين زعمتم أنهم فيكم شركاء
لقد تقطع بينكم وضل عنكم ما كنتم تزعمون ۝٩٤

1. Mecca.

إن الله فالق الحب والنوى يخرج الحي من الميت ومخرج
الميت من الحي ذلكم الله فأنى تؤفكون ﴿٩٥﴾ فالق الإصباح
وجعل الليل سكنا والشمس والقمر حسبانا ذلك تقدير
العزيز العليم ﴿٩٦﴾ وهو الذي جعل لكم النجوم لتهتدوا بها
في ظلمات البر والبحر قد فصلنا الآيات لقوم يعلمون ﴿٩٧﴾
وهو الذي أنشأكم من نفس واحدة فمستقر ومستودع
قد فصلنا الآيات لقوم يفقهون ﴿٩٨﴾ وهو الذي أنزل من السماء
ماء فأخرجنا به نبات كل شيء فأخرجنا منه خضرا نخرج
منه حبا متراكبا ومن النخل من طلعها قنوان دانية وجنات
من أعناب والزيتون والرمان مشتبها وغير متشابه انظروا
إلى ثمره إذا أثمر وينعه إن في ذلكم لآيات لقوم
يؤمنون ﴿٩٩﴾ وجعلوا لله شركاء الجن وخلقهم وخرقوا له
بنين وبنات بغير علم سبحانه وتعالى عما يصفون ﴿١٠٠﴾
بديع السموات والأرض أنى يكون له ولد ولم تكن له
صاحبة وخلق كل شيء وهو بكل شيء عليم ﴿١٠١﴾

God it is who splits the 6:95
seed and the fruit-stone. He
brings forth the living from
the dead, and the dead from
the living. Such is God: how
then can you turn away?

He kindles the light of
dawn; He has ordained the
night for rest and the sun and
the moon for reckoning. Such
is the ordinance of the Mighty
One, the All-knowing.

He it was who created for
you the stars, so that you may
be guided by them in the darkness of land and sea. We have
expounded Our revelations
for those endowed with knowledge.

And He it was who created
you from a single soul and
furnished you with a dwelling
and a resting-place. We have
expounded Our revelations for those who understand.

And He it is who sends down water from the sky with which We bring 6:99
forth the buds of every plant. From these We bring forth green foliage and
close-growing grain, palm-trees laden with clusters of dates, vineyards and
olive groves, and pomegranates alike and different. Behold their fruits when
they ripen. Surely in these there are signs for those who truly believe.

And they made the jinn God's partners, though He Himself created them,
and in their ignorance ascribe to Him sons and daughters. Glory be to Him!
Exalted be He above their imputations!

Creator of the heavens and the earth. How should He have a son when 6:101
He had no consort? He created all things, and of all things He has knowledge.

6:102 SUCH IS God, your Lord.
There is no god but Him, Creator of all things. Therefore
serve Him. And of all things
He is the Guardian.

No mortal eyes can see
Him, though He sees all eyes.
He is the Benign One, the
Omniscient.

Momentous portents have
come to you from your Lord.
He that sees them shall himself have much to gain, and he
who is blind to them shall lose
much indeed. I[1] am not your
keeper.

Thus do We expound Our
revelations, that they may say:
'You[1] have studied deep,' and
that We may make it clear for
those endowed with know-
ledge. Therefore follow what
has been revealed to you from
6:107 your Lord; there is no god but Him. Avoid the pagans; had God pleased,
they would not have worshipped idols. We have not made you their keeper,
nor are you their guardian.

Do not revile[2] the idols which they invoke besides God, lest in their ignorance they revile God with rancour. Thus have We made the actions of each
community seem pleasing to itself. Then to their Lord shall they return, and
He will declare to them what they have done.

They solemnly swear by God that if a sign be given them they would
assuredly believe in it. Say: 'Signs are only vouchsafed by God.' And how can
you tell? Even if a sign be given them they may still not believe.
6:110 And We will turn away their hearts and eyes from the Truth, even as
they did not believe in it at first. We will let them blunder about in their
wickedness.

ذلكم الله ربكم لا إله إلا هو خالق كل شيء فاعبدوه
وهو على كل شيء وكيل ﴿١٠٢﴾ لا تدركه الأبصار
وهو يدرك الأبصار وهو اللطيف الخبير ﴿١٠٣﴾ قد جاءكم
بصائر من ربكم فمن أبصر فلنفسه ومن عمي فعليها وما
أنا عليكم بحفيظ ﴿١٠٤﴾ وكذلك نصرف الآيات وليقولوا
درست ولنبينه لقوم يعلمون ﴿١٠٥﴾ اتبع ما أوحي
إليك من ربك لا إله إلا هو وأعرض عن المشركين ﴿١٠٦﴾
ولو شاء الله ما أشركوا وما جعلناك عليهم حفيظا وما
أنت عليهم بوكيل ﴿١٠٧﴾ ولا تسبوا الذين يدعون من
دون الله فيسبوا الله عدوا بغير علم كذلك زينا لكل أمة
عملهم ثم إلى ربهم مرجعهم فينبئهم بما كانوا يعملون ﴿١٠٨﴾
وأقسموا بالله جهد أيمانهم لئن جاءتهم آية ليؤمنن بها
قل إنما الآيات عند الله وما يشعركم أنها إذا جاءت
لا يؤمنون ﴿١٠٩﴾ ونقلب أفئدتهم وأبصارهم كما لم يؤمنوا
به أول مرة ونذرهم في طغيانهم يعمهون ﴿١١٠﴾

1. Muḥammad. 2. These words are addressed to the believers.

ولو أننا نزلنا إليهم الملائكة وكلمهم الموتى وحشرنا
عليهم كل شيء قبلا ما كانوا ليؤمنوا إلا أن يشاء الله
ولكن أكثرهم يجهلون ﴿١١١﴾ وكذلك جعلنا لكل نبي عدوا
شياطين الإنس والجن يوحي بعضهم إلى بعض زخرف القول
غرورا ولو شاء ربك ما فعلوه فذرهم وما يفترون
﴿١١٢﴾ ولتصغى إليه أفئدة الذين لا يؤمنون بالآخرة
وليرضوه وليقترفوا ما هم مقترفون ﴿١١٣﴾ أفغير الله
أبتغي حكما وهو الذي أنزل إليكم الكتاب مفصلا
والذين آتيناهم الكتاب يعلمون أنه منزل من ربك
بالحق فلا تكونن من الممترين ﴿١١٤﴾ وتمت كلمت ربك
صدقا وعدلا لا مبدل لكلماته وهو السميع العليم
﴿١١٥﴾ وإن تطع أكثر من في الأرض يضلوك عن سبيل الله
إن يتبعون إلا الظن وإن هم إلا يخرصون ﴿١١٦﴾ إن ربك
هو أعلم من يضل عن سبيله وهو أعلم بالمهتدين ﴿١١٧﴾ فكلوا
مما ذكر اسم الله عليه إن كنتم بآياته مؤمنين ﴿١١٨﴾

AND IF We sent the angels 6:111
down to them, and caused the dead to speak with them, and ranged all things in front of them, they would still not believe, unless God willed otherwise. But most of them are ignorant men.

Thus have We assigned for every prophet an adversary: the demons of people and of jinn, who inspire each other with vain and varnished falsehoods. And had your Lord pleased, they would not have done so. Therefore leave them to their own inventions, so that the hearts of those who have no faith in the life to come may be inclined to what they say and, being pleased, persist in their sinful ways.

Should I[1] seek a judge other 6:114
than God when He it is who has revealed the Book for you with all its precepts? Those to whom We gave the Book know that it is revealed with Truth from your Lord. Therefore never doubt it.

Perfected are the words of your Lord in Truth and Justice. None can change His words. And He it is who hears all and knows all.

If you obeyed the greater part of those on earth, they would lead you away from God's path. They follow nothing but idle fancies and preach nothing but falsehoods. Surely your Lord is best aware of those who stray from His path, as He best knows the rightly guided.

Eat only of that which has been consecrated in the name of God, if you 6:118
do believe in His revelations.

1. Muḥammad.

6:119 AND WHY should you not eat
of that which has been consecrated in God's name when He
has expounded to you what He
forbade you, except when you
are constrained?
Many are those that are misled through ignorance by their
desires: surely your Lord best
knows the transgressors.
Sin neither openly nor in
secret. Those that commit sin
shall be punished for the sins
they committed.
Therefore do not eat of that
which has not been conse-
crated in the name of God; for
that is ungodly.
The demons will teach their
votaries to argue with you; if
you obey them, you shall yourselves become idolaters.
6:122 Can the dead man We have
raised to life, and given a light to walk with among people, be compared to
him who is in darkness from which he will never emerge? Thus do their deeds
seem fair to the unbelievers.
We have placed in every city arch-transgressors who scheme within its
walls. But they scheme only against themselves, though they may not per-
6:124 ceive it. When a sign is revealed to them they say: 'We will not believe in it
unless we are given the like of what God's apostles were given.' But God
knows best whom to entrust with His message.
God will humiliate the transgressors and mete out to them grievous
torment for their scheming.

وما لكم ألا تأكلوا مما ذكر اسم الله عليه وقد فصل
لكم ما حرم عليكم إلا ما اضطررتم إليه وإن كثيرا
ليضلون بأهوائهم بغير علم إن ربك هو أعلم بالمعتدين
﴿١١٩﴾ وذروا ظاهر الإثم وباطنه إن الذين يكسبون الإثم
سيجزون بما كانوا يقترفون ﴿١٢٠﴾ ولا تأكلوا مما لم يذكر اسم
الله عليه وإنه لفسق وإن الشياطين ليوحون إلى
أوليائهم ليجادلوكم وإن أطعتموهم إنكم لمشركون
﴿١٢١﴾ أومن كان ميتا فأحييناه وجعلنا له نورا يمشي به
في الناس كمن مثله في الظلمات ليس بخارج منها
كذلك زين للكافرين ما كانوا يعملون ﴿١٢٢﴾ وكذلك
جعلنا في كل قرية أكابر مجرميها ليمكروا فيها
وما يمكرون إلا بأنفسهم وما يشعرون ﴿١٢٣﴾ وإذا
جاءتهم آية قالوا لن نؤمن حتى نؤتى مثل ما أوتي رسل
الله الله أعلم حيث يجعل رسالته سيصيب الذين أجرموا صغار
عند الله وعذاب شديد بما كانوا يمكرون ﴿١٢٤﴾

فمن يرد الله ان يهديه يشرح صدره للاسلام ومن
يرد ان يضله يجعل صدره ضيقا حرجا كانما يصعد في السماء
كذلك يجعل الله الرجس على الذين لا يؤمنون ﴿١٢٥﴾ وهذا صراط
ربك مستقيما قد فصلنا الايات لقوم يذكرون ﴿١٢٦﴾
لهم دار السلام عند ربهم وهو وليهم بما كانوا يعملون ﴿١٢٧﴾
ويوم يحشرهم جميعا يا معشر الجن قد استكثرتم من الانس وقال
اولياؤهم من الانس ربنا استمتع بعضنا ببعض وبلغنا اجلنا
الذي اجلت لنا قال النار مثويكم خالدين فيها
الا ما شاء الله ان ربك حكيم عليم ﴿١٢٨﴾ وكذلك نولي
بعض الظالمين بعضا بما كانوا يكسبون ﴿١٢٩﴾ يا معشر
الجن والانس الم يأتكم رسل منكم يقصون عليكم
اياتي وينذرونكم لقاء يومكم هذا قالوا شهدنا
على انفسنا وغرتهم الحيوة الدنيا وشهدوا على
انفسهم انهم كانوا كافرين ﴿١٣٠﴾ ذلك ان لم يكن
ربك مهلك القرى بظلم واهلها غافلون ﴿١٣١﴾

If God intends to guide a 6:125
man, He opens his bosom to Islām; and if He pleases to confound him, He makes his bosom small and narrow as though he were climbing up to the sky. Thus shall God lay the abomination on the unbelievers.

Such is the path of your Lord: a straight path. We have expounded the revelations to people who reflect. They shall dwell in peace with their Lord. He will give them His protection as recompense for what they do.

And on the day He herds them all together, He will say: 'You clans of jinn, you have seduced mankind in great numbers.' And their votaries among mankind will say: 'Lord, we did enjoy each other's fellowship. But now we have reached the end of the term You have decreed for us.'

He will say: 'The Fire shall be your home, therein to abide for ever: unless God ordain otherwise.' Surely your Lord is wise and all-knowing.

Thus do We give the wrongdoers sway over each other as punishment for 6:129
their misdeeds.

'You clans of jinn and humankind! Did there not come to you apostles of your own who proclaimed to you My revelations and warned you of this day?'

They will say: 'We bear witness against our own souls.' The life of this world has seduced them. They will testify against their own souls that they were unbelievers.

Nor would your Lord destroy the cities without just cause, with their 6:131
people unaware.

6:132 FOR EACH there shall be grades, according to their deeds. Your Lord is never heedless of what they do.

Your Lord is the Self-sufficient One, the Merciful. He takes you away if He wills and replaces you with whom He pleases, just as He raised you from the offspring of other people.

That which you are promised is sure to come. Resist it you shall not.

Say: 'My people, do all that is in your power, and I will do what is in mine. You shall learn who is to gain the recompense of the Hereafter; the wrongdoers shall never succeed.'

6:136 They set aside for God a share of their produce and of their cattle, saying: 'This is for God' – so they pretend – 'and this for our idols.' Their idols' share does not reach God, but the share of God is wholly given to their idols. How ill they judge!

6:137 Thus did their idols induce many pagans to kill their children, seeking to ruin them and to confuse them in their religion. Had God pleased they would not have done so. Therefore leave them to their false devices.

ولكل درجات مما عملوا وما ربك بغافل عما
يعملون ﴿١٣٢﴾ وربك الغني ذو الرحمة إن يشأ
يذهبكم ويستخلف من بعدكم ما يشاء
كما أنشأكم من ذرية قوم آخرين ﴿١٣٣﴾ إن
ما توعدون لآت وما أنتم بمعجزين ﴿١٣٤﴾ قل يا قوم
اعملوا على مكانتكم إني عامل فسوف تعلمون
من تكون له عاقبة الدار إنه لا يفلح الظالمون
﴿١٣٥﴾ وجعلوا لله مما ذرأ من الحرث والأنعام نصيبا
فقالوا هذا لله بزعمهم وهذا لشركائنا
فما كان لشركائهم فلا يصل إلى الله وما كان
لله فهو يصل إلى شركائهم ساء ما
يحكمون ﴿١٣٦﴾ وكذلك زين لكثير من
المشركين قتل أولادهم شركاؤهم
ليردوهم وليلبسوا عليهم دينهم ولو شاء
الله ما فعلوه فذرهم وما يفترون ﴿١٣٧﴾

وقالوا هذه أنعام وحرث حجر لا يطعمها إلا من
نشاء بزعمهم وأنعام حرمت ظهورها وأنعام لا
يذكرون اسم الله عليها افتراء عليه سيجزيهم بما
كانوا يفترون ١٣٨ وقالوا ما في بطون هذه الأنعام
خالصة لذكورنا ومحرم على أزواجنا وإن يكن
ميتة فهم فيه شركاء سيجزيهم وصفهم
إنه حكيم عليم ١٣٩ قد خسر الذين قتلوا
أولادهم سفها بغير علم وحرموا ما رزقهم الله
افتراء على الله قد ضلوا وما كانوا مهتدين ١٤٠
وهو الذي أنشأ جنات معروشات وغير معروشات
والنخل والزرع مختلفا أكله والزيتون والرمان
متشابها وغير متشابه كلوا من ثمره إذا أثمر وآتوا
حقه يوم حصاده ولا تسرفوا إنه لا يحب المسرفين ١٤١
ومن الأنعام حمولة وفرشا كلوا مما رزقكم الله
ولا تتبعوا خطوات الشيطان إنه لكم عدو مبين ١٤٢

THEY SAY: 'These animals 6:138
and these crops are forbidden.
None may eat of them save
those whom we permit.' So
they assert. And there are
beasts which they prohibit
men from riding, and others
over which they do not pronounce the name of God,
thus inventing lies against
Him. He will punish them for
the lies they invented.
They also say: 'The off-
spring of these animals is
lawful for our males but forbidden to our females.' But if
it is stillborn, they all partake
of it! He will punish them for
their imputations. Surely He is
wise and all-knowing.
Losers are those that in 6:140
their ignorance have wantonly
slain their own children and
made unlawful what God has given them, inventing falsehoods about God.
They have surely gone astray and are not guided.
And He it is who brings gardens into being: creepers and upright trees, the
palm, and produce of various taste, and olives, and pomegranates alike and
different. Eat of these fruits when they ripen and give away what is due upon
the harvest day. But you shall not be prodigal; He does not love the prodigal.
Of the beasts you have, some are for carrying loads and others for slaugh- 6:142
ter. Eat of that which God has given you and do not walk in Satan's footsteps;
he is your veritable foe.

6:143 EIGHT KINDS of livestock: take a pair of sheep and a pair of goats. Say: 'Has He forbidden you the two males, the two females, or that which is in the wombs of the two females? Tell me with knowledge if you are truthful.' And a pair of camels and a pair of cattle. Say: 'Has He forbidden you the two males, the two females, or that which is in the wombs of the two females? Were you present when God gave you this commandment?'

Who is more wicked than he who, in ignorance, invents a falsehood about God to lead people astray? God does not guide the wrongdoers.

6:145 Say: 'I find nothing in what has been revealed to me that forbids anyone to eat of such food, unless it be carrion, running blood, or the flesh of swine – for that is an abomination – or any profane thing that has been consecrated to other than God. But whoever is driven by necessity, intending neither to sin nor to transgress – surely your Lord is forgiving and compassionate.'

6:146 To those who follow the Jewish Faith We forbade all animals with undivided hoofs[1] and the fat of sheep and oxen, except what is on their backs or their entrails, or what is mixed with the bone. Such is the penance We imposed on them for their misdeeds. What We declare is surely true.

ثَمَانِيَةَ أَزْوَاجٍ مِنَ الضَّأْنِ اثْنَيْنِ وَمِنَ الْمَعْزِ اثْنَيْنِ قُلْ
آلذَّكَرَيْنِ حَرَّمَ أَمِ الْأُنْثَيَيْنِ أَمَّا اشْتَمَلَتْ عَلَيْهِ
أَرْحَامُ الْأُنْثَيَيْنِ نَبِّئُونِي بِعِلْمٍ إِنْ كُنْتُمْ صَادِقِينَ
١٤٣ وَمِنَ الْإِبِلِ اثْنَيْنِ وَمِنَ الْبَقَرِ اثْنَيْنِ قُلْ
آلذَّكَرَيْنِ حَرَّمَ أَمِ الْأُنْثَيَيْنِ أَمَّا اشْتَمَلَتْ عَلَيْهِ
أَرْحَامُ الْأُنْثَيَيْنِ أَمْ كُنْتُمْ شُهَدَاءَ إِذْ وَصَّاكُمُ اللَّهُ
بِهَٰذَا فَمَنْ أَظْلَمُ مِمَّنِ افْتَرَىٰ عَلَى اللَّهِ كَذِبًا لِيُضِلَّ
النَّاسَ بِغَيْرِ عِلْمٍ إِنَّ اللَّهَ لَا يَهْدِي الْقَوْمَ الظَّالِمِينَ
١٤٤ قُلْ لَا أَجِدُ فِي مَا أُوحِيَ إِلَيَّ مُحَرَّمًا عَلَىٰ طَاعِمٍ يَطْعَمُهُ
إِلَّا أَنْ يَكُونَ مَيْتَةً أَوْ دَمًا مَسْفُوحًا أَوْ لَحْمَ خِنْزِيرٍ
فَإِنَّهُ رِجْسٌ أَوْ فِسْقًا أُهِلَّ لِغَيْرِ اللَّهِ بِهِ فَمَنِ اضْطُرَّ
غَيْرَ بَاغٍ وَلَا عَادٍ فَإِنَّ رَبَّكَ غَفُورٌ رَحِيمٌ ١٤٥ وَعَلَى الَّذِينَ
هَادُوا حَرَّمْنَا كُلَّ ذِي ظُفُرٍ وَمِنَ الْبَقَرِ وَالْغَنَمِ حَرَّمْنَا
عَلَيْهِمْ شُحُومَهُمَا إِلَّا مَا حَمَلَتْ ظُهُورُهُمَا أَوِ الْحَوَايَا أَوْ
مَا اخْتَلَطَ بِعَظْمٍ ذَٰلِكَ جَزَيْنَاهُمْ بِبَغْيِهِمْ وَإِنَّا لَصَادِقُونَ ١٤٦

1. Leviticus 11.

فإن كذبوك فقل ربكم ذو رحمة واسعة ولا يرد بأسه
عن القوم المجرمين ﴿١٤٧﴾ سيقول الذين أشركوا لو شاء
الله ما أشركنا ولا آباؤنا ولا حرمنا من شيء كذلك كذب
الذين من قبلهم حتى ذاقوا بأسنا قل هل عندكم من علم
فتخرجوه لنا إن تتبعون إلا الظن وإن أنتم إلا تخرصون ﴿١٤٨﴾ قل
فلله الحجة البالغة فلو شاء لهديكم أجمعين
﴿١٤٩﴾ قل هلم شهداءكم الذين يشهدون أن
الله حرم هذا فإن شهدوا فلا تشهد معهم ولا تتبع
أهواء الذين كذبوا بآياتنا والذين لا يؤمنون
بالآخرة وهم بربهم يعدلون ﴿١٥٠﴾ قل تعالوا أتل ما حرم
ربكم عليكم ألا تشركوا به شيئا وبالوالدين
إحسانا ولا تقتلوا أولادكم من إملاق نحن
نرزقكم وإياهم ولا تقربوا الفواحش ما
ظهر منها وما بطن ولا تقتلوا النفس التي حرم
الله إلا بالحق ذلكم وصيكم به لعلكم تعقلون ﴿١٥١﴾

IF THEY disbelieve in you, 6:147
say: 'All-encompassing is the
mercy of your Lord: and His
punishment cannot be warded
off from those that do wrong.'

The idolaters will say: 'Had
God pleased, neither we nor
our fathers would have served
other gods besides Him; nor
would we have declared anything unlawful.' In like manner
did those who have gone
before them disbelieve until
they felt Our might.

Say: 'Have you any know-
ledge you can put before us?
You believe in nothing but
conjecture and follow nothing
but falsehoods.'

Say: 'God alone has the 6:149
conclusive proof. Had He so
pleased He would have guided
you all.'

Say: 'Bring me those witnesses of yours who can testify that God has forbidden this.' If they so testify, do not testify with them, nor follow the whims of those that deny Our revelations, disbelieve in the life to come, and set up other gods as equals with their Lord.

Say: 'Come, I will tell you what your Lord has made unlawful for you: that 6:151
you shall serve no other gods besides Him; that you shall show kindness to
your parents; that you shall not kill your children because you cannot support them: We provide for you and for them; that you shall not commit lewd
acts, whether openly or in secret; and that you shall not kill – for that is forbidden by God – except for a just cause. Thus does He exhort you, that you
may grow in wisdom.'

6:152 Do not tamper with the
property of orphans, unless
to improve their lot until they
reach maturity. Give just
weight and full measure; We
never charge a soul with more
than it can bear. Speak for
justice, even if it affects your
own kin. And be true to God's
covenant. Thus does He
exhort you, so that you may
take thought.

This path of Mine is
straight. Follow it, and do not
follow other paths, for they
will lead you away from His
path. Thus does He exhort
you, so that you may fear
Him.

6:154 We gave the Book to Moses,
a perfect code for the righteous with precepts about all
things, a guide and a blessing,
so that they might believe in meeting their Lord. And this Book We have now
revealed: truly blessed. Observe it and fear God, so that you may find mercy
and not say: 'The Book was revealed only to two communities[1] before us;
6:157 though of their studies we were surely heedless'; or: 'Had the Book been
revealed to *us*, we would have been better guided than they.'

A veritable sign has now come to you from your Lord, a guide and a blessing. And who is more wicked than he who denies God's revelations and turns away from them? Those that turn away from Our revelations We shall requite with grievous torment for their turning.

ولا تقربوا مال اليتيم إلا بالتي هي أحسن حتى يبلغ
أشده وأوفوا الكيل والميزان بالقسط لا نكلف
نفسا إلا وسعها وإذا قلتم فاعدلوا ولو كان
ذا قربى وبعهد الله أوفوا ذلكم وصاكم به لعلكم
تذكرون ١٥٢ وأن هذا صراطي مستقيما فاتبعوه ولا تتبعوا
السبل فتفرق بكم عن سبيله ذلكم وصاكم به لعلكم
تتقون ١٥٣ ثم آتينا موسى الكتاب تماما على الذي أحسن
وتفصيلا لكل شيء وهدى ورحمة لعلهم بلقاء ربهم
يؤمنون ١٥٤ وهذا كتاب أنزلناه مبارك فاتبعوه واتقوا
لعلكم ترحمون ١٥٥ أن تقولوا إنما أنزل الكتاب على
طائفتين من قبلنا وإن كنا عن دراستهم لغافلين ١٥٦
أو تقولوا لو أنا أنزل علينا الكتاب لكنا أهدى منهم فقد
جاءكم بينة من ربكم وهدى ورحمة فمن أظلم
ممن كذب بآيات الله وصدف عنها سنجزي الذين
يصدفون عن آياتنا سوء العذاب بما كانوا يصدفون ١٥٧

1. Jews and Christians.

هَلْ يَنظُرُونَ إِلَّا أَن تَأْتِيَهُمُ الْمَلَٰٓئِكَةُ أَوْ يَأْتِيَ رَبُّكَ أَوْ يَأْتِيَ
بَعْضُ آيَاتِ رَبِّكَ يَوْمَ يَأْتِي بَعْضُ آيَاتِ رَبِّكَ لَا يَنفَعُ
نَفْسًا إِيمَانُهَا لَمْ تَكُنْ آمَنَتْ مِن قَبْلُ أَوْ كَسَبَتْ فِي إِيمَانِهَا خَيْرًا قُلِ
انتَظِرُوا إِنَّا مُنتَظِرُونَ ﴿١٥٨﴾ إِنَّ الَّذِينَ فَرَّقُوا دِينَهُمْ وَكَانُوا
شِيَعًا لَّسْتَ مِنْهُمْ فِي شَيْءٍ إِنَّمَا أَمْرُهُمْ إِلَى اللَّهِ ثُمَّ يُنَبِّئُهُم بِمَا
كَانُوا يَفْعَلُونَ ﴿١٥٩﴾ مَن جَاءَ بِالْحَسَنَةِ فَلَهُ عَشْرُ أَمْثَالِهَا وَمَن
جَاءَ بِالسَّيِّئَةِ فَلَا يُجْزَىٰ إِلَّا مِثْلَهَا وَهُمْ لَا يُظْلَمُونَ ﴿١٦٠﴾ قُلْ إِنَّنِي هَدَانِي
رَبِّي إِلَىٰ صِرَاطٍ مُّسْتَقِيمٍ دِينًا قِيَمًا مِّلَّةَ إِبْرَاهِيمَ حَنِيفًا وَمَا كَانَ مِنَ الْمُشْرِكِينَ
﴿١٦١﴾ قُلْ إِنَّ صَلَاتِي وَنُسُكِي وَمَحْيَايَ وَمَمَاتِي لِلَّهِ رَبِّ الْعَالَمِينَ
﴿١٦٢﴾ لَا شَرِيكَ لَهُ وَبِذَٰلِكَ أُمِرْتُ وَأَنَا أَوَّلُ الْمُسْلِمِينَ ﴿١٦٣﴾ قُلْ أَغَيْرَ
اللَّهِ أَبْغِي رَبًّا وَهُوَ رَبُّ كُلِّ شَيْءٍ وَلَا تَكْسِبُ كُلُّ نَفْسٍ إِلَّا
عَلَيْهَا وَلَا تَزِرُ وَازِرَةٌ وِزْرَ أُخْرَىٰ ثُمَّ إِلَىٰ رَبِّكُم مَّرْجِعُكُمْ
فَيُنَبِّئُكُم بِمَا كُنتُمْ فِيهِ تَخْتَلِفُونَ ﴿١٦٤﴾ وَهُوَ الَّذِي جَعَلَكُمْ خَلَائِفَ
الْأَرْضِ وَرَفَعَ بَعْضَكُمْ فَوْقَ بَعْضٍ دَرَجَاتٍ لِّيَبْلُوَكُمْ
فِي مَا آتَاكُمْ إِنَّ رَبَّكَ سَرِيعُ الْعِقَابِ وَإِنَّهُ لَغَفُورٌ رَّحِيمٌ ﴿١٦٥﴾

ARE THEY waiting for the 6:158
angels to come to them, or for your Lord to come, or for a sign of your Lord to come? On the day some sign of your Lord does come, faith shall not avail the soul that had no faith before or did not put its faith to good uses.

Say: 'Wait if you will; we too are waiting.'

Have nothing to do with those who have split up their religion into sects. God will call them to account and declare to them what they have done.

He that does a good deed shall be repaid ten of the like of it; and he that does evil shall be rewarded only with the like. None shall be wronged.

Say: 'My Lord has guided 6:161
me to a straight path, to an upright religion, to the faith of saintly Abraham, who was no idolater.'

Say: 'My prayers and my devotions, my life and my death, are all for God, Lord of the Universe: He has no peer. Thus am I commanded, and I am the first of the Muslims.'

Say: 'Should I seek any but God for my Lord, when He is the Lord of all things? Each soul shall reap the fruits only of its own deeds: no burdened soul shall bear another's burden. Then to your Lord shall you return, and He will resolve for you your differences.'

He has given you the earth for your heritage and exalted some of you in 6:165
rank above others, that He might test you with what He has given you. Swift is your Lord in retribution; yet is He forgiving and compassionate.

THE HEIGHTS

سورة الأعراف مكية وهي مائتان وست آيات

بسم الله الرحمن الرحيم

المص ﴿١﴾ كتاب أنزل إليك فلا يكن في صدرك حرج منه لتنذر به
وذكرى للمؤمنين ﴿٢﴾ اتبعوا ما أنزل إليكم من ربكم ولا تتبعوا من
دونه أولياء قليلا ما تذكرون ﴿٣﴾ وكم من قرية أهلكناها
فجاءها بأسنا بياتا أو هم قائلون ﴿٤﴾ فما كان دعواهم
إذ جاءهم بأسنا إلا أن قالوا إنا كنا ظالمين ﴿٥﴾ فلنسألن
الذين أرسل إليهم ولنسألن المرسلين ﴿٦﴾ فلنقصن عليهم
بعلم وما كنا غائبين ﴿٧﴾ والوزن يومئذ الحق فمن ثقلت
موازينه فأولئك هم المفلحون ﴿٨﴾ ومن خفت موازينه فأولئك
الذين خسروا أنفسهم بما كانوا بآياتنا يظلمون ﴿٩﴾ ولقد
مكناكم في الأرض وجعلنا لكم فيها معايش قليلا ما
تشكرون ﴿١٠﴾ ولقد خلقناكم ثم صورناكم ثم قلنا للملائكة
اسجدوا لآدم فسجدوا إلا إبليس لم يكن من الساجدين ﴿١١﴾

In the Name of God,
the Merciful, the Compassionate

7:1 ALIF *lām mīm ṣād.* A Book
has been revealed to you – let
not your heart be troubled
about it – so that you may
thereby give warning and
admonish the faithful.

Observe that which is
brought down to you[1] from
your Lord and follow no
other masters besides Him.
But you seldom take warning.

How many cities have We
obliterated! While sleeping
Our scourge fell upon them,
or at midday, when they were
drowsing.

And when Our scourge
fell upon them, their only cry was: 'We have indeed been wrongdoers.'

7:6 We will surely question those to whom the emissaries were sent, and We
will surely question the emissaries themselves. With knowledge We will
recount to them what they have done, for We were never away from them.

On that day all shall be weighed with justice. Those whose good deeds
weigh heavy in the scales shall prosper, and those whose good deeds are light
shall lose their souls, because they have reviled Our revelations.

We have given you power in the land and provided you with a livelihood:
yet you are seldom thankful.

7:11 We created you and gave you form. Then We said to the angels: 'Prostrate
yourselves before Adam.' They all prostrated themselves except Satan, who
refused to prostrate himself.

1. The Meccans.

قال ما منعك ألا تسجد إذ أمرتك قال أنا خير منه خلقتني من نار
وخلقته من طين ﴿١٢﴾ قال فاهبط منها فما يكون لك أن
تتكبر فيها فاخرج إنك من الصاغرين ﴿١٣﴾ قال أنظرني إلى
يوم يبعثون ﴿١٤﴾ قال إنك من المنظرين ﴿١٥﴾ قال فبما أغويتني
لأقعدن لهم صراطك المستقيم ﴿١٦﴾ ثم لآتينهم من بين أيديهم
ومن خلفهم وعن أيمانهم وعن شمائلهم ولا تجد أكثرهم
شاكرين ﴿١٧﴾ قال اخرج منها مذءوما مدحورا لمن تبعك
منهم لأملأن جهنم منكم أجمعين ﴿١٨﴾ ويا آدم اسكن أنت
وزوجك الجنة فكلا من حيث شئتما ولا تقربا هذه الشجرة
فتكونا من الظالمين ﴿١٩﴾ فوسوس لهما الشيطان ليبدي لهما ما ووري
عنهما من سوآتهما وقال ما نهاكما ربكما عن هذه الشجرة إلا أن
تكونا ملكين أو تكونا من الخالدين ﴿٢٠﴾ وقاسمهما إني لكما لمن الناصحين
﴿٢١﴾ فدلاهما بغرور فلما ذاقا الشجرة بدت لهما سوآتهما وطفقا
يخصفان عليهما من ورق الجنة وناداهما ربهما ألم أنهكما عن
تلكما الشجرة وأقل لكما إن الشيطان لكما عدو مبين ﴿٢٢﴾

'WHY DID you not prostrate 7:12
yourself when I commanded you?' He asked.

'I am nobler than he,' he replied. 'You created me from fire, and You created him from clay.'

He said: 'Get you down hence! This is no place for your contemptuous pride. Away with you! Abject shall you henceforth be.'

He said: 'Reprieve me till the Day of Resurrection.'

'You are reprieved,' said He.

'Because You have led me into sin,' he said, 'I will waylay them as they walk on Your straight path, then spring upon them from before and from behind them, from their right and from their left. Then You will find the greater part of them ungrateful.'

'Get you hence!' He said. 'A despicable outcast shall you be. As for those 7:18
that follow you, I will surely fill Hell with you all.

'And you Adam, dwell with your wife in Paradise, and eat of any fruit you please; but never approach this tree or you shall both become wrongdoers.'

But Satan tempted them, so that he might reveal to them their shameful parts, which they had never seen before. And he said: 'Your Lord has forbidden you both to approach this tree only to prevent you from becoming angels or immortals.' Then he swore to them that he would give them friendly counsel.

Thus did he cunningly seduce them. And when they had eaten of the tree, 7:22
their shame became visible to them, and they both hastened to cover themselves with the leaves of the Garden.

Their Lord called out to them, saying: 'Did I not forbid you both to approach that tree, and say to you that Satan was your veritable foe?'

قالا ربنا ظلمنا أنفسنا وإن لم تغفر لنا وترحمنا لنكونن
من الخاسرين (٢٣) قال اهبطوا بعضكم لبعض عدو ولكم
في الأرض مستقر ومتاع إلى حين (٢٤) قال فيها تحيون وفيها
تموتون ومنها تخرجون (٢٥) يا بني آدم قد أنزلنا عليكم
لباسا يواري سوآتكم وريشا ولباس التقوى ذلك خير ذلك من
آيات الله لعلهم يذكرون (٢٦) يا بني آدم لا يفتننكم الشيطان
كما أخرج أبويكم من الجنة ينزع عنهما لباسهما ليريهما
سوآتهما إنه يراكم هو وقبيله من حيث لا ترونهم
إنا جعلنا الشياطين أولياء للذين لا يؤمنون (٢٧) وإذا
فعلوا فاحشة قالوا وجدنا عليها آباءنا والله أمرنا بها قل
إن الله لا يأمر بالفحشاء أتقولون على الله ما لا تعلمون
(٢٨) قل أمر ربي بالقسط وأقيموا وجوهكم عند كل مسجد
وادعوه مخلصين له الدين كما بدأكم تعودون (٢٩) فريقا
هدى وفريقا حق عليهم الضلالة إنهم اتخذوا الشياطين
أولياء من دون الله ويحسبون أنهم مهتدون (٣٠)

7:23 THEY REPLIED: 'Lord, we have wronged our own souls. Pardon us and have mercy on us, or we shall surely be among the lost.'

He said: 'Get you down hence, and may your descendants be adversaries to each other. The earth will for a certain term provide your dwelling and your comforts. There shall you live and there shall you die, and thence shall you be raised to life.'

Children of Adam! We have given you clothes to cover your shameful parts, and garments pleasing to the eye; but the robe of piety is the finest of them all. That is one of God's revelations. Perchance they will take thought.

Children of Adam! Let not Satan tempt you, as he seduced your parents out of Paradise. He stripped them of their garments to reveal to them both their shameful parts. He and his minions see you whence you cannot see them. We have made the demons patrons of the unbelievers.

7:28 When they commit a lewd act, they say: 'This is what our fathers used to do. God enjoined it.'

Say: 'God does not enjoin lewdness. Would you tell of God what you know not?'

Say: 'My Lord has enjoined justice. Turn your face to Him wherever you kneel down in prayer and call on Him with true devotion. Even as He created you, so shall you return.'

7:30 Some He has guided and some He has justly left in error; for they chose the demons for their patrons instead of God and deemed themselves on the right path.

يَٰبَنِيٓ ءَادَمَ خُذُواْ زِينَتَكُمۡ عِندَ كُلِّ مَسۡجِدٖ وَكُلُواْ وَٱشۡرَبُواْ وَلَا
تُسۡرِفُوٓاْۚ إِنَّهُۥ لَا يُحِبُّ ٱلۡمُسۡرِفِينَ ٣١ قُلۡ مَنۡ حَرَّمَ زِينَةَ ٱللَّهِ ٱلَّتِيٓ
أَخۡرَجَ لِعِبَادِهِۦ وَٱلطَّيِّبَٰتِ مِنَ ٱلرِّزۡقِۚ قُلۡ هِيَ لِلَّذِينَ ءَامَنُواْ
فِي ٱلۡحَيَوٰةِ ٱلدُّنۡيَا خَالِصَةٗ يَوۡمَ ٱلۡقِيَٰمَةِۗ كَذَٰلِكَ نُفَصِّلُ ٱلۡأٓيَٰتِ
لِقَوۡمٖ يَعۡلَمُونَ ٣٢ قُلۡ إِنَّمَا حَرَّمَ رَبِّيَ ٱلۡفَوَٰحِشَ مَا ظَهَرَ مِنۡهَا
وَمَا بَطَنَ وَٱلۡإِثۡمَ وَٱلۡبَغۡيَ بِغَيۡرِ ٱلۡحَقِّ وَأَن تُشۡرِكُواْ بِٱللَّهِ مَا لَمۡ
يُنَزِّلۡ بِهِۦ سُلۡطَٰنٗا وَأَن تَقُولُواْ عَلَى ٱللَّهِ مَا لَا تَعۡلَمُونَ ٣٣ وَلِكُلِّ أُمَّةٍ
أَجَلٞۖ فَإِذَا جَآءَ أَجَلُهُمۡ لَا يَسۡتَـٔۡخِرُونَ سَاعَةٗ وَلَا يَسۡتَقۡدِمُونَ ٣٤
يَٰبَنِيٓ ءَادَمَ إِمَّا يَأۡتِيَنَّكُمۡ رُسُلٞ مِّنكُمۡ يَقُصُّونَ عَلَيۡكُمۡ ءَايَٰتِي فَمَنِ
ٱتَّقَىٰ وَأَصۡلَحَ فَلَا خَوۡفٌ عَلَيۡهِمۡ وَلَا هُمۡ يَحۡزَنُونَ ٣٥ وَٱلَّذِينَ كَذَّبُواْ
بِـَٔايَٰتِنَا وَٱسۡتَكۡبَرُواْ عَنۡهَآ أُوْلَٰٓئِكَ أَصۡحَٰبُ ٱلنَّارِۖ هُمۡ فِيهَا خَٰلِدُونَ
٣٦ فَمَنۡ أَظۡلَمُ مِمَّنِ ٱفۡتَرَىٰ عَلَى ٱللَّهِ كَذِبًا أَوۡ كَذَّبَ بِـَٔايَٰتِهِۦٓۚ
أُوْلَٰٓئِكَ يَنَالُهُمۡ نَصِيبُهُم مِّنَ ٱلۡكِتَٰبِۖ حَتَّىٰٓ إِذَا جَآءَتۡهُمۡ رُسُلُنَا
يَتَوَفَّوۡنَهُمۡ قَالُوٓاْ أَيۡنَ مَا كُنتُمۡ تَدۡعُونَ مِن دُونِ ٱللَّهِۖ قَالُواْ
ضَلُّواْ عَنَّا وَشَهِدُواْ عَلَىٰٓ أَنفُسِهِمۡ أَنَّهُمۡ كَانُواْ كَٰفِرِينَ ٣٧

CHILDREN OF Adam! Dress 7:31
well when you attend your
mosques. Eat and drink, but
do not indulge. He does not
love the indulgent.
Say: 'Who has forbidden
you to wear the decent clothes
or to eat the wholesome things
which God has provided for
His servants?'
Say: 'These are for the
enjoyment of the faithful in
the life of this world, and they
shall be theirs alone on the
Day of Resurrection.'
Thus do We expound Our
revelations to those endowed
with knowledge. Say: 'My Lord
has forbidden all lewd acts,
whether overt or disguised, sin,
and wrongful oppression; and
He has forbidden you to worship what He did not sanction,
or to tell of God what you know not.'
Every community has a term decreed; when their time is come, not for 7:34
one hour shall they hold it back, nor can they go before it.
Children of Adam! When apostles of your own come to proclaim to you
My revelations, those that take warning and mend their ways will have nothing to fear or to regret; but those that deny and scorn Our revelations shall
be the inmates of the Fire, wherein shall they abide for ever.
Who is more wicked than he who invents a falsehood about God or denies 7:37
His revelations? Those shall have their share as destined in the Book, and
when Our emissaries come to claim back their souls they shall say: 'Where
are your idols now, those whom you invoked besides God?' 'They have forsaken us,' they will say, and will impeach themselves as unbelievers.

7:38 He will say: 'Enter, and join communities of jinn and humankind that have gone before you into the Fire.'

As it enters, every community will curse the one that went before it, and when all are gathered there, the last of them will say of the first: 'These, Lord, have led us astray. Let their punishment be doubled in the Fire.'

He will say: 'All shall be doubly punished, though you may know not.'

Then the first will say to the last: 'You were no better than we. Taste then the torment, the penalty of your misdeeds.'

7:40 For those who have denied and scorned Our revelations the gates of heaven shall not be opened; nor shall they enter Paradise until the camel shall pass through the eye of a sewing needle.[1] Thus shall We reward the transgressors.

Hell shall be their couch, and sheets of fire shall cover them. Thus shall We requite the wrongdoers.

As for those that believe and do good works – We never charge a soul with more than it can bear – they are the heirs of Paradise, wherein shall they abide for ever.

7:43 We shall take away all rancour from their hearts. Rivers will roll at their feet and they shall say: 'Praise be to God who has guided us hither. Had He not given us guidance we would not have been rightly guided. Our Lord's apostles have surely preached the Truth.' And a voice will cry out to them: 'This is the Paradise you inherited for what you did.'

قال ادخلوا في أمم قد خلت من قبلكم من الجن
والإنس في النار كلما دخلت أمة لعنت أختها حتى إذا
اداركوا فيها جميعا قالت أخراهم لأولاهم ربنا هؤلاء
أضلونا فآتهم عذابا ضعفا من النار قال لكل ضعف
ولكن لا تعلمون ﴿٣٨﴾ وقالت أولاهم لأخراهم فما كان لكم
علينا من فضل فذوقوا العذاب بما كنتم تكسبون ﴿٣٩﴾
إن الذين كذبوا بآياتنا واستكبروا عنها لا تفتح لهم أبواب
السماء ولا يدخلون الجنة حتى يلج الجمل في سم الخياط وكذلك
نجزي المجرمين ﴿٤٠﴾ لهم من جهنم مهاد ومن فوقهم غواش
وكذلك نجزي الظالمين ﴿٤١﴾ والذين آمنوا وعملوا الصالحات
لا نكلف نفسا إلا وسعها أولئك أصحاب الجنة هم فيها
خالدون ﴿٤٢﴾ ونزعنا ما في صدورهم من غل تجري من
تحتهم الأنهار وقالوا الحمد لله الذي هدانا لهذا وما كنا
لنهتدي لولا أن هدانا الله لقد جاءت رسل ربنا بالحق
ونودوا أن تلكم الجنة أورثتموها بما كنتم تعملون ﴿٤٣﴾

1. Cf. Matthew 19:24; Mark 10:25; Luke 18:25.

وَنَادَىٰٓ أَصْحَٰبُ ٱلْجَنَّةِ أَصْحَٰبَ ٱلنَّارِ أَن قَدْ وَجَدْنَا مَا وَعَدَنَا
رَبُّنَا حَقًّا فَهَلْ وَجَدتُّم مَّا وَعَدَ رَبُّكُمْ حَقًّا قَالُوا۟ نَعَمْ فَأَذَّنَ مُؤَذِّنٌۢ
بَيْنَهُمْ أَن لَّعْنَةُ ٱللَّهِ عَلَى ٱلظَّٰلِمِينَ ﴿٤٤﴾ ٱلَّذِينَ يَصُدُّونَ عَن سَبِيلِ
ٱللَّهِ وَيَبْغُونَهَا عِوَجًا وَهُم بِٱلْءَاخِرَةِ كَٰفِرُونَ ﴿٤٥﴾ وَبَيْنَهُمَا
حِجَابٌ وَعَلَى ٱلْأَعْرَافِ رِجَالٌ يَعْرِفُونَ كُلًّۢا بِسِيمَىٰهُمْ
وَنَادَوْا۟ أَصْحَٰبَ ٱلْجَنَّةِ أَن سَلَٰمٌ عَلَيْكُمْ لَمْ يَدْخُلُوهَا وَهُمْ
يَطْمَعُونَ ﴿٤٦﴾ وَإِذَا صُرِفَتْ أَبْصَٰرُهُمْ تِلْقَآءَ أَصْحَٰبِ ٱلنَّارِ قَالُوا۟
رَبَّنَا لَا تَجْعَلْنَا مَعَ ٱلْقَوْمِ ٱلظَّٰلِمِينَ ﴿٤٧﴾ وَنَادَىٰٓ أَصْحَٰبُ ٱلْأَعْرَافِ
رِجَالًا يَعْرِفُونَهُم بِسِيمَىٰهُمْ قَالُوا۟ مَآ أَغْنَىٰ عَنكُمْ جَمْعُكُمْ وَمَا
كُنتُمْ تَسْتَكْبِرُونَ ﴿٤٨﴾ أَهَٰٓؤُلَآءِ ٱلَّذِينَ أَقْسَمْتُمْ لَا يَنَالُهُمُ
ٱللَّهُ بِرَحْمَةٍ ٱدْخُلُوا۟ ٱلْجَنَّةَ لَا خَوْفٌ عَلَيْكُمْ وَلَآ أَنتُمْ تَحْزَنُونَ
﴿٤٩﴾ وَنَادَىٰٓ أَصْحَٰبُ ٱلنَّارِ أَصْحَٰبَ ٱلْجَنَّةِ أَنْ أَفِيضُوا۟ عَلَيْنَا مِنَ ٱلْمَآءِ
أَوْ مِمَّا رَزَقَكُمُ ٱللَّهُ قَالُوٓا۟ إِنَّ ٱللَّهَ حَرَّمَهُمَا عَلَى ٱلْكَٰفِرِينَ ﴿٥٠﴾
ٱلَّذِينَ ٱتَّخَذُوا۟ دِينَهُمْ لَهْوًا وَلَعِبًا وَغَرَّتْهُمُ ٱلْحَيَوٰةُ ٱلدُّنْيَا فَٱلْيَوْمَ نَنسَىٰهُمْ
كَمَا نَسُوا۟ لِقَآءَ يَوْمِهِمْ هَٰذَا وَمَا كَانُوا۟ بِـَٔايَٰتِنَا يَجْحَدُونَ ﴿٥١﴾

THEN THE heirs of Para- 7:44
dise will cry out to the inmates
of the Fire: 'What our Lord
promised we have found to be
true. Have you, too, found the
promise of your Lord to be
true?'

'Yes,' they will answer, and a
herald will cry out among
them: 'The curse of God be
upon the wrongdoers who
have debarred others from the
path of God and sought to
make it crooked, and who disbelieved in the life to come.'

A screen will divide them,
and on the Heights there will
be men who recognize each
one by his look. To those in
Paradise they shall say: 'Peace
be upon you!' They shall not
yet enter, though they long to
be there.

And when they turn their eyes towards the inmates of the Fire they will 7:47
cry: 'Lord, do not cast us among the wrongdoers!' Then, those on the
Heights will say to men they recognize by their looks: 'Nothing have the
riches you amassed and your scornful pride availed you. Are these the ones 7:49
who you swore would never earn God's mercy? Come into Paradise. You
have nothing to fear or to regret.'

And the inmates of the Fire will cry out to the heirs of Paradise: 'Give us
some water, or some of that which God has given you.' They will say: 'God
has forbidden both to the unbelievers, who made their religion a diversion 7:51
and an idle sport, and who were seduced by their earthly life.'

On that day We will forget them as they forgot they would ever meet that
day, and because they denied Our revelations.

7:52 And We have bestowed on
them a Book We expounded
with knowledge, a guide and a
blessing to true believers. Are
they waiting but for its fulfilment? On the day it is fulfilled,
those that had forgotten it will
say: 'Our Lord's apostles
surely came to us with the
Truth before. Could we but
have intercessors to plead on
our behalf! Could we but live
our lives again, we would not
do as we have done.' They
shall forfeit their souls, and
that which they invented will
forsake them.
7:54 Your Lord is God, who created the heavens and the earth
in six days and then ascended
the throne. He throws the veil
of night over the day; swiftly
they follow one another. And
the sun and the moon and the stars – all subservient to His will. His is the
creation, His the command. Blessed be God, Lord of the Universe!
Pray to your Lord with humility and in secret. He does not love the transgressors.
Do not corrupt the earth after it has been purged of evil. Pray to Him
with fear and hope; His mercy is within reach of the righteous.
7:57 He sends forth the winds as harbingers of His mercy, and when they have
gathered up a heavy cloud, We drive it on to some dead land and let the water
fall upon it, bringing forth all manner of fruit. Thus will We raise the dead to
life. Perchance you will take thought.

ولقد جئناهم بكتاب فصلناه على علم هدى ورحمة
لقوم يؤمنون ۝ هل ينظرون إلا تأويله يوم يأتي
تأويله يقول الذين نسوه من قبل قد جاءت رسل ربنا
بالحق فهل لنا من شفعاء فيشفعوا لنا أو نرد فنعمل غير
الذي كنا نعمل قد خسروا أنفسهم وضل عنهم ما كانوا
يفترون ۝ إن ربكم الله الذي خلق السموات والأرض
في ستة أيام ثم استوى على العرش يغشي الليل النهار يطلبه
حثيثا والشمس والقمر والنجوم مسخرات بأمره ألا له
الخلق والأمر تبارك الله رب العالمين ۝ ادعوا ربكم
تضرعا وخفية إنه لا يحب المعتدين ۝ ولا تفسدوا في
الأرض بعد إصلاحها وادعوه خوفا وطمعا إن رحمت الله
قريب من المحسنين ۝ وهو الذي يرسل الرياح بشرا
بين يدي رحمته حتى إذا أقلت سحابا ثقالا سقناه
لبلد ميت فأنزلنا به الماء فأخرجنا به من كل
الثمرات كذلك نخرج الموتى لعلكم تذكرون ۝

والبلد الطيب يخرج نباته بإذن ربه والذي خبث لا
يخرج إلا نكدا كذلك نصرف الآيات لقوم يشكرون ﴿٥٨﴾
لقد أرسلنا نوحا إلى قومه فقال يا قوم اعبدوا الله
ما لكم من إله غيره إني أخاف عليكم عذاب يوم عظيم ﴿٥٩﴾
قال الملأ من قومه إنا لنراك في ضلال مبين ﴿٦٠﴾ قال يا قوم
ليس بي ضلالة ولكني رسول من رب العالمين ﴿٦١﴾
أبلغكم رسالات ربي وأنصح لكم وأعلم من الله
ما لا تعلمون ﴿٦٢﴾ أوعجبتم أن جاءكم ذكر من ربكم
على رجل منكم لينذركم ولتتقوا ولعلكم ترحمون ﴿٦٣﴾
فكذبوه فأنجيناه والذين معه في الفلك وأغرقنا الذين
كذبوا بآياتنا إنهم كانوا قوما عمين ﴿٦٤﴾ وإلى عاد أخاهم
هودا قال يا قوم اعبدوا الله ما لكم من إله غيره أفلا تتقون
﴿٦٥﴾ قال الملأ الذين كفروا من قومه إنا لنراك في
سفاهة وإنا لنظنك من الكاذبين ﴿٦٦﴾ قال يا قوم
ليس بي سفاهة ولكني رسول من رب العالمين ﴿٦٧﴾

RICH SOIL yields its crop 7:58
by God's will; but poor soil
yields nothing but what is
poor and scant. Thus do We
expound Our revelations to
those who render thanks.

We sent forth Noah to his
people. He said: 'Serve God,
my people, for you have no
god but Him. Beware the torment of a fateful day.'

But the elders of his people
said: 'We can see that you are
in palpable error.'

'I am not in error, my
people,' he said, 'but am sent
forth by the Lord of the Universe to deliver to you my
Lord's messages and to give
you friendly counsel; for I
know of God what you know
not. Do you think it strange 7:63
that an Admonition should
come to you from your Lord through a mortal like yourselves to warn you,
so that you may fear God and be shown mercy?'

They denied him. So We saved him and all who were with him in the ark,
and drowned those that denied Our revelations. Surely they were blind
people.

And to the tribe of 'Ād We sent their kin Hūd. He said: 'Serve God, my
people, for you have no god but Him. Will you not fear Him?'

The unbelievers among the elders of his tribe said: 'We can see you are a
foolish man, and we surely think that you are lying.'

'Foolish I am not, my people,' he replied. 'I am sent forth by the Lord of 7:67
the Universe

7:68 to deliver to you my Lord's
messages and to give you honest counsel. Do you think it
strange that an Admonition has
come to you from your Lord
through a mortal from among
yourselves to warn you? Remember that He has made you
the heirs of Noah's people and
gave you greater power than He
did to other creatures. Remember God's favours, that you may
thrive.'

They said: 'Would you have
us serve God alone and renounce the gods our fathers
worshipped? Bring down the
scourge you threaten us with, if
what you say be true.'

7:71 He said: 'Your Lord's punishment and ire have already
been decreed to visit you.
Would you dispute with me
about names which you and your fathers named, and for which God has
revealed no sanction? Wait if you will; I will wait with you.'

We delivered him and those who were with him through Our mercy, and
annihilated those that denied Our revelations. They were unbelievers all.

7:73 And to Thamūd We sent their kin Ṣaliḥ. He said: 'Serve God, my people,
for you have no god but Him. A veritable proof has come to you from your
Lord. Here is God's she-camel: a sign for you. Leave her to graze at will
in God's own land and do not molest her, lest a woeful scourge should
take you.

أبلغكم رسالات ربي وأنا لكم ناصح أمين ﴿٦٨﴾ أوعجبتم أن
جاءكم ذكر من ربكم على رجل منكم لينذركم
واذكروا إذ جعلكم خلفاء من بعد قوم نوح
وزادكم في الخلق بصطة فاذكروا آلاء الله
لعلكم تفلحون ﴿٦٩﴾ قالوا أجئتنا لنعبد الله
وحده ونذر ما كان يعبد آباؤنا فأتنا بما تعدنا إن
كنت من الصادقين ﴿٧٠﴾ قال قد وقع عليكم من ربكم
رجس وغضب أتجادلونني في أسماء سميتموها أنتم
وآباؤكم ما نزل الله بها من سلطان فانتظروا إني
معكم من المنتظرين ﴿٧١﴾ فأنجيناه والذين معه برحمة
منا وقطعنا دابر الذين كذبوا بآياتنا وما كانوا
مؤمنين ﴿٧٢﴾ وإلى ثمود أخاهم صالحا قال يا قوم اعبدوا الله
ما لكم من إله غيره قد جاءتكم بينة من ربكم
هذه ناقة الله لكم آية فذروها تأكل في أرض الله
ولا تمسوها بسوء فيأخذكم عذاب أليم ﴿٧٣﴾

وَاذْكُرُوا إِذْ جَعَلَكُمْ خُلَفَاءَ مِنْ بَعْدِ عَادٍ
وَبَوَّأَكُمْ فِي الْأَرْضِ تَتَّخِذُونَ مِنْ سُهُولِهَا
قُصُورًا وَتَنْحِتُونَ الْجِبَالَ بُيُوتًا فَاذْكُرُوا آلَاءَ
اللَّهِ وَلَا تَعْثَوْا فِي الْأَرْضِ مُفْسِدِينَ ٧٤ قَالَ الْمَلَأُ الَّذِينَ
اسْتَكْبَرُوا مِنْ قَوْمِهِ لِلَّذِينَ اسْتُضْعِفُوا لِمَنْ آمَنَ
مِنْهُمْ أَتَعْلَمُونَ أَنَّ صَالِحًا مُرْسَلٌ مِنْ رَبِّهِ قَالُوا إِنَّا بِمَا
أُرْسِلَ بِهِ مُؤْمِنُونَ ٧٥ قَالَ الَّذِينَ اسْتَكْبَرُوا إِنَّا بِالَّذِي
آمَنْتُمْ بِهِ كَافِرُونَ ٧٦ فَعَقَرُوا النَّاقَةَ وَعَتَوْا عَنْ أَمْرِ
رَبِّهِمْ وَقَالُوا يَا صَالِحُ ائْتِنَا بِمَا تَعِدُنَا إِنْ كُنْتَ مِنَ
الْمُرْسَلِينَ ٧٧ فَأَخَذَتْهُمُ الرَّجْفَةُ فَأَصْبَحُوا فِي دَارِهِمْ
جَاثِمِينَ ٧٨ فَتَوَلَّىٰ عَنْهُمْ وَقَالَ يَا قَوْمِ لَقَدْ أَبْلَغْتُكُمْ رِسَالَةَ
رَبِّي وَنَصَحْتُ لَكُمْ وَلَٰكِنْ لَا تُحِبُّونَ النَّاصِحِينَ ٧٩ وَلُوطًا
إِذْ قَالَ لِقَوْمِهِ أَتَأْتُونَ الْفَاحِشَةَ مَا سَبَقَكُمْ بِهَا
مِنْ أَحَدٍ مِنَ الْعَالَمِينَ ٨٠ إِنَّكُمْ لَتَأْتُونَ الرِّجَالَ
شَهْوَةً مِنْ دُونِ النِّسَاءِ بَلْ أَنْتُمْ قَوْمٌ مُسْرِفُونَ ٨١

AND REMEMBER, He made 7:74
you the heirs of 'Ād, and gave
you power in the land. You
have built mansions on its
plains and hewn out houses
into the mountains. Remember
God's favours and do not corrupt the earth with wickedness.'
The haughty elders of his
people said to the believers
who were oppressed: 'Do you
really believe that Ṣāliḥ is sent
forth from his Lord?'
They answered: 'We do
believe in the message he has
been sent with.'
The haughty elders said: 7:76
'We deny all that you believe
in.' They hamstrung the she-
camel and defied the com-
mandment of their Lord,
saying to Ṣāliḥ: 'Bring down
the scourge you threaten us
with, if you have truly been sent.'
Thereupon the earthquake felled them, and when morning came they
were crouching lifeless in their dwellings. He left them, saying: 'I conveyed to
you, my people, the message of my Lord and gave you good counsel; but
you had no love for those who give good counsel.'
And Lot, who said to his people: 'Will you persist in these lewd acts which
no other nation has committed before you? You lust after men instead of 7:81
women. Truly, you are a degenerate people.'

7:82 HIS PEOPLE's only answer was: 'Banish them from your city. They are people who would keep themselves chaste.'

We delivered him and all his kin, except his wife, who stayed behind, and let loose a shower upon them. Consider the fate of the transgressors.

7:85 And to Midian, their kin Shu'aib. He said: 'Serve God, my people, for you have no god but Him. A veritable sign has come to you from your Lord. Give just weight and measure and do not defraud people of their possessions; do not corrupt the land after it has been purged of evil. That is best for you, if you are true believers.

'Do not squat down in every highway, threatening and debarring from the path of God those who believe in Him, and seeking to make that path crooked. Remember how He multiplied you when you were few in number. And consider the fate of the evil-doers.

7:87 'If there are some among you who believe in my message and some who disbelieve, be patient till God shall judge between us; He is the best of judges.'

وَمَا كَانَ جَوَابَ قَوْمِهِ إِلَّا أَنْ قَالُوا أَخْرِجُوهُمْ
مِنْ قَرْيَتِكُمْ إِنَّهُمْ أُنَاسٌ يَتَطَهَّرُونَ ﴿٨٢﴾ فَأَنْجَيْنَاهُ
وَأَهْلَهُ إِلَّا امْرَأَتَهُ كَانَتْ مِنَ الْغَابِرِينَ ﴿٨٣﴾ وَأَمْطَرْنَا
عَلَيْهِمْ مَطَرًا فَانْظُرْ كَيْفَ كَانَ عَاقِبَةُ
الْمُجْرِمِينَ ﴿٨٤﴾ وَإِلَىٰ مَدْيَنَ أَخَاهُمْ شُعَيْبًا قَالَ يَا
قَوْمِ اعْبُدُوا اللَّهَ مَا لَكُمْ مِنْ إِلَٰهٍ غَيْرُهُ قَدْ جَاءَتْكُمْ
بَيِّنَةٌ مِنْ رَبِّكُمْ فَأَوْفُوا الْكَيْلَ وَالْمِيزَانَ وَلَا
تَبْخَسُوا النَّاسَ أَشْيَاءَهُمْ وَلَا تُفْسِدُوا فِي الْأَرْضِ
بَعْدَ إِصْلَاحِهَا ذَٰلِكُمْ خَيْرٌ لَكُمْ إِنْ كُنْتُمْ مُؤْمِنِينَ ﴿٨٥﴾
وَلَا تَقْعُدُوا بِكُلِّ صِرَاطٍ تُوعِدُونَ وَتَصُدُّونَ
عَنْ سَبِيلِ اللَّهِ مَنْ آمَنَ بِهِ وَتَبْغُونَهَا عِوَجًا وَاذْكُرُوا
إِذْ كُنْتُمْ قَلِيلًا فَكَثَّرَكُمْ وَانْظُرُوا كَيْفَ كَانَ
عَاقِبَةُ الْمُفْسِدِينَ ﴿٨٦﴾ وَإِنْ كَانَ طَائِفَةٌ مِنْكُمْ آمَنُوا
بِالَّذِي أُرْسِلْتُ بِهِ وَطَائِفَةٌ لَمْ يُؤْمِنُوا فَاصْبِرُوا
حَتَّىٰ يَحْكُمَ اللَّهُ بَيْنَنَا وَهُوَ خَيْرُ الْحَاكِمِينَ ﴿٨٧﴾

قال الملأ الذين استكبروا من قومه لنخرجنك يا شعيب والذين
آمنوا معك من قريتنا أو لتعودن في ملتنا قال أولو كنا
كارهين ﴿٨٨﴾ قد افترينا على الله كذبا إن عدنا في ملتكم
بعد إذ نجانا الله منها وما يكون لنا أن نعود فيها إلا
أن يشاء الله ربنا وسع ربنا كل شيء علما على
الله توكلنا ربنا افتح بيننا وبين قومنا بالحق وأنت خير
الفاتحين ﴿٨٩﴾ وقال الملأ الذين كفروا من قومه لئن اتبعتم
شعيبا إنكم إذا لخاسرون ﴿٩٠﴾ فأخذتهم الرجفة فأصبحوا
في دارهم جاثمين ﴿٩١﴾ الذين كذبوا شعيبا كأن لم يغنوا
فيها الذين كذبوا شعيبا كانوا هم الخاسرين ﴿٩٢﴾ فتولى عنهم
وقال يا قوم لقد أبلغتكم رسالات ربي ونصحت لكم فكيف
آسى على قوم كافرين ﴿٩٣﴾ وما أرسلنا في قرية من نبي إلا
أخذنا أهلها بالبأساء والضراء لعلهم يضرعون ﴿٩٤﴾ ثم
بدلنا مكان السيئة الحسنة حتى عفوا وقالوا قد مس آباءنا
الضراء والسراء فأخذناهم بغتة وهم لا يشعرون ﴿٩٥﴾

THE HAUGHTY elders of his 7:88
tribe said: 'Return to our fold, Shu'aib, or we will banish you from our city, you and all your followers.'

'Even though we are averse to it?' he said. 'If we returned to your faith, from which God has delivered us, we should be false to God; we could only turn to it again by the will of God, our Lord. Our Lord encompasses all things with His knowledge, and in God we have put our trust. Lord, judge rightly between us and our people; You are the best of judges.'

And the infidel chieftains of his people said: 'If you follow Shu'aib, you shall indeed lose out.'

Thereupon the earthquake 7:91
felled them, and when morning came they were crouching lifeless in their dwellings; as if those that denied Shu'aib had never prospered there. It was those that denied Shu'aib who did lose out.

He left them, saying: 'I conveyed to you, my people, the messages of my Lord and gave you good counsel. How can I grieve for an unbelieving people?'

And whenever We sent a prophet to a city We afflicted its people with
calamities and misfortunes so that they might abase themselves. Then We 7:95
changed adversity to good fortune, so that when they had multiplied they said: 'Our fathers also had their sorrows and their joys.' And in their heedlessness We suddenly smote them.

7:96 AND HAD the people of
those cities believed and
feared God, We would have
showered upon them bless-
ings from heaven and earth.
But they disbelieved, and We
punished them for what they
did.
Were the people of those
cities secure from Our power
when it overtook them in
the night while they were
sleeping?
Or were the people of
those cities secure from Our
power when it overtook them
in the morning at their play?
Did they feel themselves
secure from God's cunning?
None feels secure from God's
cunning except the losers.
7:100 Or is it not plain to those
that inherit the land after those
who once possessed it that, if We pleased, We could smite them for their sins
and set a seal upon their hearts, leaving them bereft of hearing?
We have recounted to you the history of those cities. Their apostles came
to them with veritable proofs, yet they persisted in their unbelief. Thus God
seals up the hearts of the unbelievers.
We found the larger part of them untrue to their covenants; indeed, We
found the larger part of them immersed in evil.
Then, after them We sent forth Moses with Our signs to Pharaoh and his
chieftains, but they too spurned them. Consider the fate of the evil-doers.
7:104 Moses said: 'Pharaoh, I am an apostle from the Lord of the Universe,

ولو أن أهل القرى آمنوا واتقوا لفتحنا عليهم بركات
من السماء والأرض ولكن كذبوا فأخذناهم بما
كانوا يكسبون ٩٦ أفأمن أهل القرى أن يأتيهم بأسنا
بياتا وهم نائمون ٩٧ أوأمن أهل القرى أن يأتيهم بأسنا
ضحى وهم يلعبون ٩٨ أفأمنوا مكر الله فلا يأمن مكر
الله إلا القوم الخاسرون ٩٩ أولم يهد للذين يرثون الأرض
من بعد أهلها أن لو نشاء أصبناهم بذنوبهم ونطبع على
قلوبهم فهم لا يسمعون ١٠٠ تلك القرى نقص عليك
من أنبائها ولقد جاءتهم رسلهم بالبينات فما
كانوا ليؤمنوا بما كذبوا من قبل كذلك يطبع
الله على قلوب الكافرين ١٠١ وما وجدنا لأكثرهم
من عهد وإن وجدنا أكثرهم لفاسقين ١٠٢ ثم بعثنا
من بعدهم موسى بآياتنا إلى فرعون وملئه فظلموا
بها فانظر كيف كان عاقبة المفسدين ١٠٣ وقال
موسى يا فرعون إني رسول من رب العالمين ١٠٤

حقيق على أن لا أقول على الله إلا الحق قد جئتكم
ببينة من ربكم فأرسل معي بني إسرائيل ﴿١٠٥﴾ قال إن كنت
جئت بآية فأت بها إن كنت من الصادقين ﴿١٠٦﴾ فألقى
عصاه فإذا هي ثعبان مبين ﴿١٠٧﴾ ونزع يده فإذا هي
بيضاء للناظرين ﴿١٠٨﴾ قال الملأ من قوم فرعون إن هذا
لساحر عليم ﴿١٠٩﴾ يريد أن يخرجكم من أرضكم فماذا
تأمرون ﴿١١٠﴾ قالوا أرجه وأخاه وأرسل في المدائن حاشرين
﴿١١١﴾ يأتوك بكل ساحر عليم ﴿١١٢﴾ وجاء السحرة فرعون
قالوا إن لنا لأجرا إن كنا نحن الغالبين ﴿١١٣﴾ قال نعم وإنكم
لمن المقربين ﴿١١٤﴾ قالوا يا موسى إما أن تلقي وإما أن
نكون نحن الملقين ﴿١١٥﴾ قال ألقوا فلما ألقوا سحروا
أعين الناس واسترهبوهم وجاءوا بسحر عظيم ﴿١١٦﴾
وأوحينا إلى موسى أن ألق عصاك فإذا هي تلقف
ما يأفكون ﴿١١٧﴾ فوقع الحق وبطل ما كانوا يعملون ﴿١١٨﴾
فغلبوا هنالك وانقلبوا صاغرين ﴿١١٩﴾ وألقي السحرة ساجدين ﴿١٢٠﴾

and may tell nothing of God 7:105
but what is true. I bring you a
clear sign from your Lord. Let
the Children of Israel depart
with me.'

He said: 'If you have indeed brought a sign, show it to us if what you say be true.'

So he threw down his staff, and thereupon it changed to a veritable serpent. Then he drew out his hand, and it was white to all who saw it.

The elders of Pharaoh's people said: 'This man is but a skilful sorcerer who seeks to drive you from your land. What would you have us do?'

They said: 'Put them off awhile, him and his brother, and send forth criers to the cities to summon every skilful sorcerer to your presence.'

The sorcerers came to Pharaoh. They said: 'Shall we be rewarded if we 7:113
win?'

'Yes,' he answered. 'And you shall be among the most favoured.'

They said: 'Moses, will you throw first, or are we the first to throw?'

'Throw,' he replied.

And when they threw, they bewitched the people's eyes and terrified them by a display of mighty sorcery.

Then We signalled to Moses: 'Throw down your staff.' And thereupon it swallowed up their false devices.[1]

Thus did the Truth prevail, and all their doings proved vain. Thus were
they defeated and abased, and the sorcerers bowed down, 7:120

1. Cf. Exodus 7:11ff.

7:121 and said: 'We now believe in the Lord of the Universe, the Lord of Moses and Aaron.'

Pharaoh said: 'Do you dare believe in Him before I give you leave? This is a plot you have contrived to turn the people out of their city. But you shall learn. I will cut off your hands and feet on alternate sides and then crucify you all!'

They said: 'We shall surely return to our Lord. You would punish us only because we believed in the signs of our Lord when they came to us. Lord, instil into us patience and let us die as Muslims.'

7:127 And the elders of Pharaoh's people said: 'Will you allow Moses and his people to perpetrate corruption in the land and to forsake you and your gods?'

He said: 'We will put their sons to death[1] and spare only their daughters. We shall surely triumph over them.'

Moses said to his people: 'Seek help in God and be patient. The earth is God's; He gives it to those of His servants whom He chooses. Happy shall be the lot of those that fear Him.'

They said: 'We were oppressed before you came to us, and still are we after your coming.'

He said: 'Your Lord will perchance destroy your enemies and give you the land to inherit. Then will He see how you will act.'

7:130 We afflicted Pharaoh's people with years of famine and dearth of fruitfulness, so that they might reflect.

قَالُوٓا ءَامَنَّا بِرَبِّ ٱلْعَٰلَمِينَ ﴿١٢١﴾ رَبِّ مُوسَىٰ وَهَٰرُونَ ﴿١٢٢﴾ قَالَ
فِرْعَوْنُ ءَامَنتُم بِهِۦ قَبْلَ أَنْ ءَاذَنَ لَكُمْ إِنَّ هَٰذَا لَمَكْرٌ مَّكَرْتُمُوهُ
فِى ٱلْمَدِينَةِ لِتُخْرِجُوا مِنْهَآ أَهْلَهَا فَسَوْفَ تَعْلَمُونَ ﴿١٢٣﴾ لَأُقَطِّعَنَّ
أَيْدِيَكُمْ وَأَرْجُلَكُم مِّنْ خِلَٰفٍ ثُمَّ لَأُصَلِّبَنَّكُمْ أَجْمَعِينَ ﴿١٢٤﴾
قَالُوٓا إِنَّآ إِلَىٰ رَبِّنَا مُنقَلِبُونَ ﴿١٢٥﴾ وَمَا تَنقِمُ مِنَّآ إِلَّآ أَنْ
ءَامَنَّا بِـَٔايَٰتِ رَبِّنَا لَمَّا جَآءَتْنَا رَبَّنَآ أَفْرِغْ عَلَيْنَا صَبْرًا وَتَوَفَّنَا
مُسْلِمِينَ ﴿١٢٦﴾ وَقَالَ ٱلْمَلَأُ مِن قَوْمِ فِرْعَوْنَ أَتَذَرُ مُوسَىٰ
وَقَوْمَهُۥ لِيُفْسِدُوا فِى ٱلْأَرْضِ وَيَذَرَكَ وَءَالِهَتَكَ قَالَ سَنُقَتِّلُ
أَبْنَآءَهُمْ وَنَسْتَحْىِۦ نِسَآءَهُمْ وَإِنَّا فَوْقَهُمْ قَٰهِرُونَ ﴿١٢٧﴾
قَالَ مُوسَىٰ لِقَوْمِهِ ٱسْتَعِينُوا بِٱللَّهِ وَٱصْبِرُوٓا إِنَّ ٱلْأَرْضَ
لِلَّهِ يُورِثُهَا مَن يَشَآءُ مِنْ عِبَادِهِۦ وَٱلْعَٰقِبَةُ لِلْمُتَّقِينَ ﴿١٢٨﴾
قَالُوٓا أُوذِينَا مِن قَبْلِ أَن تَأْتِيَنَا وَمِنۢ بَعْدِ مَا جِئْتَنَا قَالَ عَسَىٰ
رَبُّكُمْ أَن يُهْلِكَ عَدُوَّكُمْ وَيَسْتَخْلِفَكُمْ فِى ٱلْأَرْضِ
فَيَنظُرَ كَيْفَ تَعْمَلُونَ ﴿١٢٩﴾ وَلَقَدْ أَخَذْنَآ ءَالَ فِرْعَوْنَ
بِٱلسِّنِينَ وَنَقْصٍ مِّنَ ٱلثَّمَرَٰتِ لَعَلَّهُمْ يَذَّكَّرُونَ ﴿١٣٠﴾

1. Cf. Exodus 1:22.

فإذا جاءتهم الحسنة قالوا لنا هذه وإن تصبهم سيئة
يطيروا بموسى ومن معه ألا إنما طائرهم عند الله
ولكن أكثرهم لا يعلمون ١٣١ وقالوا مهما تأتنا به
من آية لتسحرنا بها فما نحن لك بمؤمنين ١٣٢ فأرسلنا
عليهم الطوفان والجراد والقمل والضفادع والدم
آيات مفصلات فاستكبروا وكانوا قوما مجرمين ١٣٣
ولما وقع عليهم الرجز قالوا يا موسى ادع لنا ربك
بما عهد عندك لئن كشفت عنا الرجز لنؤمنن لك
ولنرسلن معك بني إسرائيل ١٣٤ فلما كشفنا عنهم الرجز
إلى أجل هم بالغوه إذا هم ينكثون ١٣٥ فانتقمنا منهم
فأغرقناهم في اليم بأنهم كذبوا بآياتنا وكانوا عنها غافلين
١٣٦ وأورثنا القوم الذين كانوا يستضعفون مشارق
الأرض ومغاربها التي باركنا فيها وتمت كلمت ربك
الحسنى على بني إسرائيل بما صبروا ودمرنا ما كان
يصنع فرعون وقومه وما كانوا يعرشون ١٣٧

IF GOOD things came their 7:131
way, they said: 'It is our due,'
but if evil befell them they
ascribed it to Moses and those
who were with him. Yet it was
God who had ordained their
ills, though most of them did
not know it.

And they said: 'Whatever
miracle you work to enchant
us with it, we will never believe
in you.'

So We plagued them with
the flood and with locusts,
with lice and frogs and blood:
miracles manifest, yet they
scorned them all, for they were
a sinful people.

And when each plague 7:134
smote them, they said: 'Moses,
pray to your Lord for us:
invoke the promise He has
made you. If you do lift the
plague from us, we will believe in you and let the Israelites go with you.'

But when We had lifted the plague from them and the appointed time had
come for them, they broke their promise. So We took vengeance on them
and drowned them in the sea, for they had denied Our signs and paid no
heed to them.

We gave the persecuted people dominion over the eastern and the west- 7:137
ern lands which We had blessed. Thus was your Lord's gracious word fulfilled
for the Israelites, because they had endured with fortitude; and We destroyed
the edifices and the towers of Pharaoh and his people.

7:138 AND WE led the Israelites across the sea, and they came upon a people who worshipped idols which they had. They said to Moses: 'Make us a god like the gods they have.'

He said: 'You are indeed an ignorant people. That which they follow is doomed, and all their works are vain. Am I to seek for you a deity other than God, when He has exalted you above the nations? We delivered you from Pharaoh's people, who had oppressed you cruelly, putting your sons to death and sparing only your daughters. Surely that was a great trial by your Lord.'

7:142 And We promised Moses thirty nights, to which We added ten nights more: so that the appointment with his Lord was after forty nights.[1]

وَجَاوَزْنَا بِبَنِي إِسْرَائِيلَ الْبَحْرَ فَأَتَوْا عَلَىٰ قَوْمٍ يَعْكُفُونَ
عَلَىٰ أَصْنَامٍ لَهُمْ قَالُوا يَا مُوسَى اجْعَلْ لَنَا إِلَٰهًا كَمَا لَهُمْ
آلِهَةٌ قَالَ إِنَّكُمْ قَوْمٌ تَجْهَلُونَ ﴿١٣٨﴾ إِنَّ هَٰؤُلَاءِ مُتَبَّرٌ مَا هُمْ فِيهِ
وَبَاطِلٌ مَا كَانُوا يَعْمَلُونَ ﴿١٣٩﴾ قَالَ أَغَيْرَ اللَّهِ أَبْغِيكُمْ
إِلَٰهًا وَهُوَ فَضَّلَكُمْ عَلَى الْعَالَمِينَ ﴿١٤٠﴾ وَإِذْ أَنْجَيْنَاكُمْ
مِنْ آلِ فِرْعَوْنَ يَسُومُونَكُمْ سُوءَ الْعَذَابِ يُقَتِّلُونَ
أَبْنَاءَكُمْ وَيَسْتَحْيُونَ نِسَاءَكُمْ وَفِي ذَٰلِكُمْ بَلَاءٌ
مِنْ رَبِّكُمْ عَظِيمٌ ﴿١٤١﴾ وَوَاعَدْنَا مُوسَىٰ ثَلَاثِينَ لَيْلَةً
وَأَتْمَمْنَاهَا بِعَشْرٍ فَتَمَّ مِيقَاتُ رَبِّهِ أَرْبَعِينَ
لَيْلَةً وَقَالَ مُوسَىٰ لِأَخِيهِ هَارُونَ اخْلُفْنِي فِي قَوْمِي وَأَصْلِحْ وَلَا
تَتَّبِعْ سَبِيلَ الْمُفْسِدِينَ ﴿١٤٢﴾ وَلَمَّا جَاءَ مُوسَىٰ لِمِيقَاتِنَا وَكَلَّمَهُ رَبُّهُ
قَالَ رَبِّ أَرِنِي أَنْظُرْ إِلَيْكَ قَالَ لَنْ تَرَانِي وَلَٰكِنِ انْظُرْ إِلَى
الْجَبَلِ فَإِنِ اسْتَقَرَّ مَكَانَهُ فَسَوْفَ تَرَانِي فَلَمَّا تَجَلَّىٰ رَبُّهُ
لِلْجَبَلِ جَعَلَهُ دَكًّا وَخَرَّ مُوسَىٰ صَعِقًا فَلَمَّا أَفَاقَ
قَالَ سُبْحَانَكَ تُبْتُ إِلَيْكَ وَأَنَا أَوَّلُ الْمُؤْمِنِينَ ﴿١٤٣﴾

And Moses said to his brother Aaron: 'Take my place among my people. Do what is right and do not follow the path of the wrongdoers.'

7:143 And when Moses came at Our appointed time and his Lord communed with him, he said: 'Lord, reveal Yourself to me, that I may look upon You.'

He replied: 'You shall never see Me. But look upon the Mount; if it remains firm upon its base, then only shall you see Me.'

And when his Lord revealed Himself to the Mount, He levelled it to dust. Moses fell down senseless, and, when he had recovered, said: 'Glory be to You! I turn to You in penitence, and am the first of the believers.'

1. Cf. Exodus 24:18.

قَالَ يَا مُوسَىٰٓ إِنِّى ٱصْطَفَيْتُكَ عَلَى ٱلنَّاسِ بِرِسَـٰلَـٰتِى وَبِكَلَـٰمِى
فَخُذْ مَآ ءَاتَيْتُكَ وَكُن مِّنَ ٱلشَّـٰكِرِينَ ﴿١٤٤﴾ وَكَتَبْنَا لَهُۥ
فِى ٱلْأَلْوَاحِ مِن كُلِّ شَىْءٍ مَّوْعِظَةً وَتَفْصِيلًا لِّكُلِّ شَىْءٍ
فَخُذْهَا بِقُوَّةٍ وَأْمُرْ قَوْمَكَ يَأْخُذُوا۟ بِأَحْسَنِهَا ۚ سَأُو۟رِيكُمْ
دَارَ ٱلْفَـٰسِقِينَ ﴿١٤٥﴾ سَأَصْرِفُ عَنْ ءَايَـٰتِىَ ٱلَّذِينَ يَتَكَبَّرُونَ
فِى ٱلْأَرْضِ بِغَيْرِ ٱلْحَقِّ وَإِن يَرَوْا۟ كُلَّ ءَايَةٍ لَّا يُؤْمِنُوا۟ بِهَا
وَإِن يَرَوْا۟ سَبِيلَ ٱلرُّشْدِ لَا يَتَّخِذُوهُ سَبِيلًا وَإِن يَرَوْا۟
سَبِيلَ ٱلْغَىِّ يَتَّخِذُوهُ سَبِيلًا ۚ ذَٰلِكَ بِأَنَّهُمْ كَذَّبُوا۟
بِـَٔايَـٰتِنَا وَكَانُوا۟ عَنْهَا غَـٰفِلِينَ ﴿١٤٦﴾ وَٱلَّذِينَ كَذَّبُوا۟ بِـَٔايَـٰتِنَا
وَلِقَآءِ ٱلْـَٔاخِرَةِ حَبِطَتْ أَعْمَـٰلُهُمْ ۚ هَلْ يُجْزَوْنَ إِلَّا مَا كَانُوا۟
يَعْمَلُونَ ﴿١٤٧﴾ وَٱتَّخَذَ قَوْمُ مُوسَىٰ مِنۢ بَعْدِهِۦ مِنْ حُلِيِّهِمْ
عِجْلًا جَسَدًا لَّهُۥ خُوَارٌ ۚ أَلَمْ يَرَوْا۟ أَنَّهُۥ لَا يُكَلِّمُهُمْ وَلَا يَهْدِيهِمْ
سَبِيلًا ۘ ٱتَّخَذُوهُ وَكَانُوا۟ ظَـٰلِمِينَ ﴿١٤٨﴾ وَلَمَّا سُقِطَ فِىٓ
أَيْدِيهِمْ وَرَأَوْا۟ أَنَّهُمْ قَدْ ضَلُّوا۟ قَالُوا۟ لَئِن لَّمْ يَرْحَمْنَا
رَبُّنَا وَيَغْفِرْ لَنَا لَنَكُونَنَّ مِنَ ٱلْخَـٰسِرِينَ ﴿١٤٩﴾

HE SAID: 'Moses, I have 7:144
chosen you above all man-
kind for My messages and My
commandments. Take there-
fore what I have given you, and
be thankful.'

And We inscribed for him
upon the Tablets all manner of
precepts, and instructions concerning all things, and said to
him: 'Observe these steadfastly, and enjoin your people
to observe what is best in
them. I shall show you the
abode of the ungodly. I will 7:146
turn away from My signs those
who lord it in the land with
arrogance and injustice, so that
even if they witness each and
every sign they shall not believe
them. If they see the right
path, they shall not walk upon
it: but if they see the path of
error, they shall choose it for their path; because they disbelieved Our signs
and paid no heed to them.

'Vain are the deeds of those who disbelieve in Our signs and in the life to come. Shall they not be rewarded according only to their deeds?'

And in his absence the people of Moses made a calf from their ornaments, an image with a hollow sound. Did they not see that it could neither speak to them nor give them guidance? Yet they worshipped it and thus committed evil.

And when they repented and realized that they had strayed, they said: 'If 7:149
our Lord does not have mercy on us and pardon us, we shall surely be among
the lost.'

7:150 AND WHEN Moses returned to his people, angry and sorrowful, he said: 'Evil is the thing you did in my absence! Would you hasten the ordinance of your Lord?'

He threw down the Tablets and, seizing his brother's head, dragged him closer to him.

'Son of my mother,' Aaron said, 'the people overpowered me and almost did me to death. Do not let the enemy gloat over me; do not number me among the wrongdoers.'

7:151 'Lord,' said Moses, 'forgive me and forgive my brother. Admit us into Your mercy, for, of all those that show mercy, You are the most merciful.'

Those that worshipped the calf were to incur the anger of their Lord and servility in this life. Thus shall We reward those who fabricate falsehoods. But to those that do evil and later repent and believe, your Lord is forgiving and compassionate.

When his anger was allayed, Moses took up the Tablets, upon which was
inscribed a pledge of guidance and of mercy to those that fear their Lord.
7:155 And Moses chose from among his people seventy men[1] for Our appointed
time and, when the quake shook them, said: 'Had it been Your will, Lord,
You could have destroyed them long ago, and myself too. But would You
destroy us because of what the fools among us did? That trial was ordained
by You, to confound whom You willed and to guide whom You pleased. You
alone are our guardian. Forgive us and have mercy on us: You are the best of
those who forgive.

ولما رجع موسى إلى قومه غضبان أسفا قال بئسما خلفتموني
من بعدي أعجلتم أمر ربكم وألقى الألواح وأخذ برأس
أخيه يجره إليه قال ابن أم إن القوم استضعفوني وكادوا
يقتلونني فلا تشمت بي الأعداء ولا تجعلني مع القوم
الظالمين ﴿١٥٠﴾ قال رب اغفر لي ولأخي وأدخلنا في
رحمتك وأنت أرحم الراحمين ﴿١٥١﴾ إن الذين اتخذوا العجل
سينالهم غضب من ربهم وذلة في الحيوة الدنيا وكذلك
نجزي المفترين ﴿١٥٢﴾ والذين عملوا السيئات ثم تابوا من
بعدها وآمنوا إن ربك من بعدها لغفور رحيم ﴿١٥٣﴾
ولما سكت عن موسى الغضب أخذ الألواح وفي نسختها
هدى ورحمة للذين هم لربهم يرهبون ﴿١٥٤﴾ واختار موسى
قومه سبعين رجلا لميقاتنا فلما أخذتهم الرجفة قال
رب لو شئت أهلكتهم من قبل وإياي أتهلكنا بما فعل السفهاء
منا إن هي إلا فتنتك تضل بها من تشاء وتهدي من تشاء
أنت ولينا فاغفر لنا وارحمنا وأنت خير الغافرين ﴿١٥٥﴾

1. Cf. Exodus 24:1, 9.

واكتب لنا في هذه الدنيا حسنة وفي الآخرة إنا هدنا
إليك قال عذابي أصيب به من أشاء ورحمتي
وسعت كل شيء فسأكتبها للذين يتقون
ويؤتون الزكوة والذين هم بآياتنا يؤمنون ١٥٦
الذين يتبعون الرسول النبي الأمي الذي يجدونه مكتوبا
عندهم في التورية والإنجيل يأمرهم بالمعروف وينههم
عن المنكر ويحل لهم الطيبات ويحرم عليهم الخبائث
ويضع عنهم إصرهم والأغلال التي كانت عليهم
فالذين آمنوا به وعزروه ونصروه واتبعوا النور
الذي أنزل معه أولئك هم المفلحون ١٥٧ قل يا أيها
الناس إني رسول الله إليكم جميعا الذي له ملك
السموات والأرض لا إله إلا هو يحيي ويميت فآمنوا
بالله ورسوله النبي الأمي الذي يؤمن بالله
وكلماته واتبعوه لعلكم تهتدون ١٥٨ ومن
قوم موسى أمة يهدون بالحق وبه يعدلون ١٥٩

ORDAIN FOR us what is good, 7:156
both in this life and in the life
to come; to You alone we turn.'
He said: 'My scourge I will
visit upon whom I please: yet
My mercy encompasses all
things. I show it to those that
fear God and give alms, and
to those that in Our signs
believe; to those that follow 7:157
the Apostle – the Unlettered[1]
Prophet – whom they shall
find writ down for them in the
Torah and the Gospel. He will
enjoin righteousness on them
and forbid them to do the
reprehensible. He will make
wholesome things lawful for
them and foul things unlawful
for them. He will relieve them
of their burdens and of the
shackles that weigh upon them.
Those that believe in him and
honour him, those that aid him and follow the light sent down with him,
shall surely triumph.'

Say:[2] 'You people! I am God's emissary to you all; He that has sovereignty over the heavens and the earth. There is no god but Him. He ordains life and death. Therefore have faith in God and His apostle, the Unlettered[1] Prophet, who believes in God and His commandments. Follow him, that you may be rightly guided.'

Yet among the people of Moses there are some who preach the Truth and 7:159
act justly.

1. The word can also mean 'Gentile'.
2. These words are addressed to Muḥammad.

7:160 WE DIVIDED them into twelve tribes, each a whole community. And when his people demanded drink of him, We revealed Our will to Moses: 'Strike the rock with your staff.' Thereupon twelve springs gushed from it and each tribe knew its drinking-place.

We caused the clouds to draw their shadow over them and sent down for them manna and quails: 'Eat of the wholesome things We have given you.' They did Us no wrong, but they wronged themselves.

7:161 And when they were told: 'Dwell in this city, and eat from it whatever you please; pray for forgiveness and enter the gates bowing: We will forgive you your sins and bestow abundance on the righteous,' the wrongdoers among them changed what they were told to words that were not said to them; and We let loose on them a scourge from heaven as punishment for their wrongdoing.

7:163 Ask them about the city which overlooked the sea and what befell its people when they broke the Sabbath. On their Sabbath the fish came to them floating on the water, but on weekdays they never came near them. Thus did We test them because of the evil they did.

وقطعناهم اثنتي عشرة أسباطا أمما وأوحينا إلى
موسى إذ استسقىه قومه أن اضرب بعصاك الحجر
فانبجست منه اثنتا عشرة عينا قد علم كل أناس
مشربهم وظللنا عليهم الغمام وأنزلنا عليهم
المن والسلوى كلوا من طيبات ما رزقناكم
وما ظلمونا ولكن كانوا أنفسهم يظلمون ١٦٠
وإذ قيل لهم اسكنوا هذه القرية وكلوا منها حيث
شئتم وقولوا حطة وادخلوا الباب سجدا
نغفر لكم خطيئاتكم سنزيد المحسنين ١٦١ فبدل
الذين ظلموا منهم قولا غير الذي قيل لهم
فأرسلنا عليهم رجزا من السماء بما كانوا
يظلمون ١٦٢ وسئلهم عن القرية التي كانت حاضرة
البحر إذ يعدون في السبت إذ تأتيهم حيتانهم
يوم سبتهم شرعا ويوم لا يسبتون لا تأتيهم
كذلك نبلوهم بما كانوا يفسقون ١٦٣

وإذ قالت أمة منهم لم تعظون قوما الله مهلكهم أو معذبهم
عذابا شديدا قالوا معذرة إلى ربكم ولعلهم يتقون ﴿١٦٤﴾
فلما نسوا ما ذكروا به أنجينا الذين ينهون عن
السوء وأخذنا الذين ظلموا بعذاب بئيس بما كانوا
يفسقون ﴿١٦٥﴾ فلما عتوا عن ما نهوا عنه قلنا لهم كونوا
قردة خاسئين ﴿١٦٦﴾ وإذ تأذن ربك ليبعثن عليهم إلى يوم
القيامة من يسومهم سوء العذاب إن ربك لسريع العقاب وإنه
لغفور رحيم ﴿١٦٧﴾ وقطعناهم في الأرض أمما منهم
الصالحون ومنهم دون ذلك وبلوناهم بالحسنات
والسيئات لعلهم يرجعون ﴿١٦٨﴾ فخلف من بعدهم خلف
ورثوا الكتاب يأخذون عرض هذا الأدنى ويقولون
سيغفر لنا وإن يأتهم عرض مثله يأخذوه ألم يؤخذ عليهم
ميثاق الكتاب أن لا يقولوا على الله إلا الحق ودرسوا ما فيه
والدار الآخرة خير للذين يتقون أفلا تعقلون ﴿١٦٩﴾ والذين
يمسكون بالكتاب وأقاموا الصلوة إنا لا نضيع أجر المصلحين ﴿١٧٠﴾

AND WHEN one of their 7:164
tribes said: 'Why do you
admonish a people for whom
God has ordained destruction
and grievous torment?' they
replied: 'To be blameless in
the sight of your Lord, and
that they may fear God.'
Therefore, when they forgot
the warning they were given,
We delivered those who had
admonished against evil, and
smote the wrongdoers with
punishment for their mis-
deeds. And when they
scornfully persisted in their
forbidden ways, We said to
them: 'Turn into detested
apes.'

Then your Lord declared
that He would raise against
them others who would oppress
them grievously till the Day of
Resurrection. Swift is the retribution of your Lord, yet is He forgiving and
compassionate.

We dispersed them into communities throughout the earth – some were 7:168
righteous, others were not – and tested them with blessings and misfortunes
that they might return to the right path. Then others succeeded them who
inherited the Book and took to these nether vanities. 'We shall be forgiven,'
they said. And if such vanities came their way once more, they would again
take to them.

Are they not committed in the Book to tell nothing of God but what is
true? And they have studied it well; surely the world to come is better for
those that fear God. Have you no sense?

As for those that strictly observe the Book and are steadfast in prayer, We 7:170
shall not deny the righteous their reward.

وإذ نتقنا الجبل فوقهم كأنه ظلة وظنوا أنه واقع بهم خذوا ما
آتيناكم بقوة واذكروا ما فيه لعلكم تتقون ﴿١٧١﴾ وإذ أخذ
ربك من بني آدم من ظهورهم ذريتهم وأشهدهم على أنفسهم ألست
بربكم قالوا بلى شهدنا أن تقولوا يوم القيامة إنا كنا عن هذا
غافلين ﴿١٧٢﴾ أو تقولوا إنما أشرك آباؤنا من قبل وكنا
ذرية من بعدهم أفتهلكنا بما فعل المبطلون ﴿١٧٣﴾
وكذلك نفصل الآيات ولعلهم يرجعون ﴿١٧٤﴾ واتل
عليهم نبأ الذي آتيناه آياتنا فانسلخ منها فأتبعه
الشيطان فكان من الغاوين ﴿١٧٥﴾ ولو شئنا لرفعناه
بها ولكنه أخلد إلى الأرض واتبع هواه فمثله
كمثل الكلب إن تحمل عليه يلهث أو تتركه يلهث
ذلك مثل القوم الذين كذبوا بآياتنا فاقصص
القصص لعلهم يتفكرون ﴿١٧٦﴾ ساء مثلا القوم الذين
كذبوا بآياتنا وأنفسهم كانوا يظلمون ﴿١٧٧﴾ من يهد
الله فهو المهتدي ومن يضلل فأولئك هم الخاسرون ﴿١٧٨﴾

7:171 AND WHEN We suspended the Mount over them as though it were a shadow (they feared that it was falling down on them) We said: 'Hold fast to that which We have given you and bear in mind what it contains, that you may fear God.'

Your Lord brought forth descendants from the loins of Adam's children, and made them testify against their own souls. He said: 'Am I not your Lord?' They replied: 'Yes, we do testify.' Lest you should say on the Day of Resurrection: 'We had no knowledge of that,' or you should say: 'Our forefathers were, indeed, idolaters; but will You destroy us, their descendants, on account of what the followers of falsehood did?'

Thus do We expound Our revelations that they may return to the right path.

7:175 Tell them of the man to whom We vouchsafed Our signs and who turned away from them: how Satan pursued him and he went astray. Had it been Our will, We would have exalted him through Our signs: but he clung to this earthly life and succumbed to his desires. He can be compared to the dog which pants if you chase it away, and pants still if you leave it alone. Such are those that deny Our revelations. Recount to them these parables, so that they may reflect.

Evil is the tale of those that denied Our revelations and were unjust to their own souls.

7:178 He whom God guides is he who is rightly guided; but those whom He confounds are they that will surely be lost.

ولقد ذرأنا لجهنم كثيرا من الجن والإنس لهم قلوب لا يفقهون
بها ولهم أعين لا يبصرون بها ولهم آذان لا يسمعون بها أولئك
كالأنعام بل هم أضل أولئك هم الغافلون ١٧٩ ولله
الأسماء الحسنى فادعوه بها وذروا الذين يلحدون في أسمائه
سيجزون ما كانوا يعملون ١٨٠ وممن خلقنا أمة يهدون
بالحق وبه يعدلون ١٨١ والذين كذبوا بآياتنا سنستدرجهم
من حيث لا يعلمون ١٨٢ وأملي لهم إن كيدي متين ١٨٣ أولم
يتفكروا ما بصاحبهم من جنة إن هو إلا نذير مبين ١٨٤
أولم ينظروا في ملكوت السماوات والأرض وما خلق الله
من شيء وأن عسى أن يكون قد اقترب أجلهم فبأي حديث بعده
يؤمنون ١٨٥ من يضلل الله فلا هادي له ويذرهم في
طغيانهم يعمهون ١٨٦ يسألونك عن الساعة أيان مرساها
قل إنما علمها عند ربي لا يجليها لوقتها إلا هو ثقلت في
السماوات والأرض لا تأتيكم إلا بغتة يسألونك كأنك حفي عنها
قل إنما علمها عند الله ولكن أكثر الناس لا يعلمون ١٨٧

We have predestined for 7:179
Hell a multitude of jinn and
humans. They have hearts they
cannot comprehend with; and
they have eyes they cannot see
with; and they have ears they
cannot hear with. They are like
beasts – indeed, they are more
misguided. Such are the heedless.

God has the Most Excellent Names; call on Him by them and keep away from those that pervert them; they shall receive their due for what they did.

Among those We created there is a community that gives true guidance and acts justly. As for those that deny Our revelations, We will lead them step by step whence they cannot tell; for though I bear with them, My stratagem is sure.

Has it never occurred to them that their compatriot[1] is no madman, but 7:184
one who gives clear warning? Will they not ponder upon the kingdom of the
heavens and the earth, and all the things that God created, and whether their
hour is not drawing near? And in what other words after these will they
believe?

None can guide those whom God confounds. He leaves them in their sinful ways, ever straying from the right path.

They ask you about the Hour: when will it come? Say: 'None but my Lord 7:187
has knowledge of it.[2] Only He will reveal it – at the appointed time. A fateful
hour shall it be, both in the heavens and on earth. It will but suddenly overtake you.'

They will put questions to you as though you were privy to it. Say: 'Only God has knowledge of it, but the greater part of mankind do not know this.'

1. Muḥammad. 2. Cf. Mark 13:32.

7:188 SAY: 'I have not the power to acquire benefits or to avert evil from myself, except by the will of God. Had I possessed knowledge of what is hidden, I would have availed myself of much that is good and no harm would have touched me. But I am no more than one who gives warning and joyful tidings to true believers.'

He it was who created you from a single being.[1] From that being He created his spouse, so that he might find comfort in her. And when he had lain with her, she conceived, and her burden was light. She carried it with ease, but when it grew heavy, they both called out to God their Lord: 'Grant us a goodly child and we will be truly thankful.'

قُلْ لَا أَمْلِكُ لِنَفْسِي نَفْعًا وَلَا ضَرًّا إِلَّا مَا شَاءَ اللَّهُ
وَلَوْ كُنْتُ أَعْلَمُ الْغَيْبَ لَاسْتَكْثَرْتُ مِنَ الْخَيْرِ وَمَا مَسَّنِيَ السُّوءُ
إِنْ أَنَا إِلَّا نَذِيرٌ وَبَشِيرٌ لِقَوْمٍ يُؤْمِنُونَ ﴿١٨٨﴾ هُوَ الَّذِي خَلَقَكُمْ
مِنْ نَفْسٍ وَاحِدَةٍ وَجَعَلَ مِنْهَا زَوْجَهَا لِيَسْكُنَ إِلَيْهَا فَلَمَّا
تَغَشَّاهَا حَمَلَتْ حَمْلًا خَفِيفًا فَمَرَّتْ بِهِ فَلَمَّا أَثْقَلَتْ دَعَوَا اللَّهَ
رَبَّهُمَا لَئِنْ آتَيْتَنَا صَالِحًا لَنَكُونَنَّ مِنَ الشَّاكِرِينَ ﴿١٨٩﴾ فَلَمَّا
آتَاهُمَا صَالِحًا جَعَلَا لَهُ شُرَكَاءَ فِيمَا آتَاهُمَا فَتَعَالَى اللَّهُ
عَمَّا يُشْرِكُونَ ﴿١٩٠﴾ أَيُشْرِكُونَ مَا لَا يَخْلُقُ شَيْئًا وَهُمْ يُخْلَقُونَ
﴿١٩١﴾ وَلَا يَسْتَطِيعُونَ لَهُمْ نَصْرًا وَلَا أَنْفُسَهُمْ يَنْصُرُونَ ﴿١٩٢﴾
وَإِنْ تَدْعُوهُمْ إِلَى الْهُدَى لَا يَتَّبِعُوكُمْ سَوَاءٌ عَلَيْكُمْ أَدَعَوْتُمُوهُمْ
أَمْ أَنْتُمْ صَامِتُونَ ﴿١٩٣﴾ إِنَّ الَّذِينَ تَدْعُونَ مِنْ دُونِ اللَّهِ
عِبَادٌ أَمْثَالُكُمْ فَادْعُوهُمْ فَلْيَسْتَجِيبُوا لَكُمْ إِنْ كُنْتُمْ
صَادِقِينَ ﴿١٩٤﴾ أَلَهُمْ أَرْجُلٌ يَمْشُونَ بِهَا أَمْ لَهُمْ أَيْدٍ يَبْطِشُونَ بِهَا
أَمْ لَهُمْ أَعْيُنٌ يُبْصِرُونَ بِهَا أَمْ لَهُمْ آذَانٌ يَسْمَعُونَ بِهَا قُلِ
ادْعُوا شُرَكَاءَكُمْ ثُمَّ كِيدُونِ فَلَا تُنْظِرُونِ ﴿١٩٥﴾

7:190 Yet when He had granted them a goodly child, they both set up other gods besides Him in return for what He gave them. Exalted be God above their idols!

Will they worship those that can create nothing, and are themselves created? They cannot help them, nor can they help themselves.

If you call them to the true guidance they will not follow you. It is the same whether you call to them or hold your peace.

Those whom you invoke besides God are, like yourselves, His creatures. Call on them, and let them answer you, if what you say be true!

7:195 Have they feet to walk with? Or have they hands to hold with? Or have they eyes to see with? Or have they ears to hear with?

Say: 'Call on your false gods and scheme against me. Give me no respite.

1. Literally, soul.

إن ولي الله الذي نزل الكتاب وهو يتولى الصالحين
﴿١٩٦﴾ والذين تدعون من دونه لا يستطيعون نصركم ولا أنفسهم
ينصرون ﴿١٩٧﴾ وإن تدعوهم إلى الهدى لا يسمعوا وتراهم
ينظرون إليك وهم لا يبصرون ﴿١٩٨﴾ خذ العفو وأمر بالعرف
وأعرض عن الجاهلين ﴿١٩٩﴾ وإما ينزغنك من الشيطان نزغ
فاستعذ بالله إنه سميع عليم ﴿٢٠٠﴾ إن الذين اتقوا إذا
مسهم طائف من الشيطان تذكروا فإذا هم
مبصرون ﴿٢٠١﴾ وإخوانهم يمدونهم في الغي ثم لا
يقصرون ﴿٢٠٢﴾ وإذا لم تأتهم بآية قالوا لولا اجتبيتها
قل إنما أتبع ما يوحى إلي من ربي هذا بصائر من ربكم
وهدى ورحمة لقوم يؤمنون ﴿٢٠٣﴾ وإذا قرئ القرآن
فاستمعوا له وأنصتوا لعلكم ترحمون ﴿٢٠٤﴾ واذكر ربك
في نفسك تضرعا وخيفة ودون الجهر من القول بالغدو والآصال
ولا تكن من الغافلين ﴿٢٠٥﴾ إن الذين عند ربك
لا يستكبرون عن عبادته ويسبحونه وله يسجدون ﴿٢٠٦﴾

SURELY MY guardian is God, 7:196
who has revealed the Book; He acts as guardian of the righteous. Those on whom you call besides Him cannot help you, nor can they help themselves.'

If you call them to the right guidance, they will not hear. You find them looking towards you, but they cannot see.

Be tolerant, speak for what is right, and avoid the ignorant. If Satan presents you with a temptation, seek refuge in God; He hears all and knows all.

If the God-fearing are touched by a hint from Satan, they have but to reflect; and
they shall see the light. As for 7:202
their brothers, they would keep them long in error, nor would they ever desist.

When you have no *sūrah* to give them, they say: 'Have you not yet invented it?' Say: 'I follow only what is revealed to me by my Lord. This Book is a veritable proof from your Lord, a guide and a blessing to true believers.'

When the Koran is recited, listen to it in silence that you may be shown mercy. Remember your Lord deep in your soul with humility and awe, and without ostentation: in the morning and in the evening; and do not be heedless.

Those who dwell with your Lord do not disdain to worship Him; they give 7:206
glory to Him and before Him they prostrate themselves.

THE SPOILS[1]

In the Name of God,
the Merciful, the Compassionate

8:1 THEY ASK you about the
spoils. Say: 'The spoils belong
to God and the Apostle.
Therefore fear God and end
your differences. Obey God
and His apostle, if you are true
believers.'
The true believers are those
whose hearts are filled with
awe at the mention of God,
and whose faith grows
stronger when His revelations
are recited to them. They are
those who put their trust in
their Lord, pray steadfastly,
and give from what We gave
them. Such are the true believ-
ers. They will be exalted to high ranks by their Lord, and forgiveness and a
generous provision await them.
8:5 Just as your Lord bade you leave your home in the cause of Truth, and
some of the faithful were reluctant, they argued with you about the Truth
that had been revealed, as though they were being led to certain death while
they looked on.
While God promised you victory over one of the two bands, it was your
wish to take possession of the one that was unarmed.[2] God wished to vindi-
8:8 cate the Truth by His words and to rout the unbelievers; to vindicate the Truth
and to render falsehood vain, though the transgressors wished otherwise.

سورة الأنفال مدنية وهي خمس وسبعون آية

بسم الله الرحمن الرحيم
يسئلونك عن الأنفال قل الأنفال لله والرسول فاتقوا
الله وأصلحوا ذات بينكم وأطيعوا الله ورسوله إن كنتم
مؤمنين ١ إنما المؤمنون الذين إذا ذكر الله وجلت قلوبهم
وإذا تليت عليهم آياته زادتهم إيمانا وعلى ربهم يتوكلون ٢
الذين يقيمون الصلوة ومما رزقناهم ينفقون ٣ أولئك
هم المؤمنون حقا لهم درجات عند ربهم ومغفرة ورزق
كريم ٤ كما أخرجك ربك من بيتك بالحق وإن فريقا من
المؤمنين لكارهون ٥ يجادلونك في الحق بعد ما تبين كأنما يساقون
إلى الموت وهم ينظرون ٦ وإذ يعدكم الله إحدى الطائفتين
أنها لكم وتودون أن غير ذات الشوكة تكون لكم ويريد
الله أن يحق الحق بكلماته ويقطع دابر الكافرين ٧
ليحق الحق ويبطل الباطل ولو كره المجرمون ٨

1. Of the Battle of Badr, in 624.
2. Muḥammad's plan was to attack an unarmed caravan belonging to the Quraysh of Mecca on its way from Syria to that city. An army of Meccans marched to its assistance. Some of the Muslims wished to attack the caravan, others the Meccan army. Muḥammad's forces, said to have been only 319 strong, routed the Meccans, who were nearly 1,000 in number.

إِذْ تَسْتَغِيثُونَ رَبَّكُمْ فَاسْتَجَابَ لَكُمْ أَنِّي مُمِدُّكُم
بِأَلْفٍ مِّنَ الْمَلَٰٓئِكَةِ مُرْدِفِينَ ﴿٩﴾ وَمَا جَعَلَهُ اللَّهُ إِلَّا بُشْرَىٰ
وَلِتَطْمَئِنَّ بِهِ قُلُوبُكُمْ وَمَا النَّصْرُ إِلَّا مِنْ عِندِ اللَّهِ إِنَّ اللَّهَ
عَزِيزٌ حَكِيمٌ ﴿١٠﴾ إِذْ يُغَشِّيكُمُ النُّعَاسَ أَمَنَةً مِّنْهُ وَيُنَزِّلُ عَلَيْكُم
مِّنَ السَّمَاءِ مَاءً لِّيُطَهِّرَكُم بِهِ وَيُذْهِبَ عَنكُمْ رِجْزَ الشَّيْطَٰنِ
وَلِيَرْبِطَ عَلَىٰ قُلُوبِكُمْ وَيُثَبِّتَ بِهِ الْأَقْدَامَ ﴿١١﴾ إِذْ يُوحِي رَبُّكَ
إِلَى الْمَلَٰٓئِكَةِ أَنِّي مَعَكُمْ فَثَبِّتُوا الَّذِينَ آمَنُوا سَأُلْقِي فِي
قُلُوبِ الَّذِينَ كَفَرُوا الرُّعْبَ فَاضْرِبُوا فَوْقَ الْأَعْنَاقِ
وَاضْرِبُوا مِنْهُمْ كُلَّ بَنَانٍ ﴿١٢﴾ ذَٰلِكَ بِأَنَّهُمْ شَاقُّوا اللَّهَ
وَرَسُولَهُ وَمَن يُشَاقِقِ اللَّهَ وَرَسُولَهُ فَإِنَّ اللَّهَ شَدِيدُ
الْعِقَابِ ﴿١٣﴾ ذَٰلِكُمْ فَذُوقُوهُ وَأَنَّ لِلْكَافِرِينَ عَذَابَ
النَّارِ ﴿١٤﴾ يَا أَيُّهَا الَّذِينَ آمَنُوا إِذَا لَقِيتُمُ الَّذِينَ كَفَرُوا
زَحْفًا فَلَا تُوَلُّوهُمُ الْأَدْبَارَ ﴿١٥﴾ وَمَن يُوَلِّهِمْ يَوْمَئِذٍ
دُبُرَهُ إِلَّا مُتَحَرِّفًا لِّقِتَالٍ أَوْ مُتَحَيِّزًا إِلَىٰ فِئَةٍ فَقَدْ
بَاءَ بِغَضَبٍ مِّنَ اللَّهِ وَمَأْوَاهُ جَهَنَّمُ وَبِئْسَ الْمَصِيرُ ﴿١٦﴾

Remember when you 8:9
prayed to your Lord for help and He answered: 'I am sending to your aid a thousand angels in their ranks.' By this good news God sought to reassure your hearts, for victory comes only from God; surely God is Almighty and wise.

You were overcome by sleep, a token of protection from Him. He sent down water from the sky to cleanse you and to purify you of Satan's abomination, to strengthen your hearts and to steady your footsteps.

Remember when God re- 8:12
vealed His will to the angels: 'I am with you; so give courage to the believers. I shall cast terror into the hearts of the infidels. Strike off their heads, strike off the very tips of their fingers!'

That was because they defied God and His apostle; and he that defies God and His apostle shall be sternly punished by God. 'That is it: taste it.' The scourge of the Fire awaits the unbelievers.

Believers, when you encounter the infidels on the march, do not turn your
backs to them in flight. If anyone on that day turns his back to them, except 8:16
for tactical reasons, or to join another band, he shall incur the ire of God and Hell shall be his shelter: a wretched fate!

فلم تقتلوهم ولكن الله قتلهم وما رميت إذ رميت
ولكن الله رمى وليبلي المؤمنين منه بلاء حسنا إن الله
سميع عليم ۝ ذلكم وأن الله موهن كيد الكافرين ۝
إن تستفتحوا فقد جاءكم الفتح وإن تنتهوا فهو خير
لكم وإن تعودوا نعد ولن تغني عنكم فئتكم
شيئا ولو كثرت وأن الله مع المؤمنين ۝ يا
أيها الذين آمنوا أطيعوا الله ورسوله ولا تولوا عنه وأنتم
تسمعون ۝ ولا تكونوا كالذين قالوا سمعنا وهم لا يسمعون
۝ إن شر الدواب عند الله الصم البكم الذين لا
يعقلون ۝ ولو علم الله فيهم خيرا لأسمعهم
ولو أسمعهم لتولوا وهم معرضون ۝ يا أيها
الذين آمنوا استجيبوا لله وللرسول إذا دعاكم
لما يحييكم واعلموا أن الله يحول بين المرء وقلبه وأنه
إليه تحشرون ۝ واتقوا فتنة لا تصيبن الذين ظلموا
منكم خاصة واعلموا أن الله شديد العقاب ۝

8:17 YOU DID not slay them, but
it was God who slew them.
You did not smite them, but it
was God who smote them so
that He might richly reward
the faithful. God hears all and
knows all. Even so; God will
surely frustrate the designs of
the unbelievers.
If you[1] were seeking a
judgement, now has a judgement come to you. If you
desist, it will be best for you.
And if you resume the fight,
We will fight back, and your
forces shall avail you nothing,
superior though they be in
number: for God is with the
faithful.
Believers, obey God and
His apostle, and do not forsake him, now that you have
8:21 heard all. Do not be like those
who say: 'We hear,' but pay no heed to what they hear.
The meanest beasts in God's sight are those that are deaf, dumb, and
devoid of reason. Had God perceived any virtue in them, He would have
surely made them hear. But even if He had made them hear, they would have
turned away and refused to listen.
Believers, obey God and the Apostle when he calls you to that which gives
you life. Know that God stands between man and his heart, and that in His
presence shall you all be herded.
8:25 Guard yourselves against temptation.[2] The wrongdoers among you are
not the only men who will be tempted; and know that God's punishment is
stern.

1. The Meccans.
2. Thus Al-Jalālayn; *fitnah* can also mean sedition.

واذكروا إذ أنتم قليل مستضعفون في الأرض
تخافون أن يتخطفكم الناس فآواكم وأيدكم بنصره
ورزقكم من الطيبات لعلكم تشكرون ٢٦ يا أيها
الذين آمنوا لا تخونوا الله والرسول وتخونوا أماناتكم
وأنتم تعلمون ۝ واعلموا أنما أموالكم وأولادكم
فتنة وأن الله عنده أجر عظيم ۝ يا أيها الذين آمنوا
إن تتقوا الله يجعل لكم فرقانا ويكفر عنكم
سيئاتكم ويغفر لكم والله ذو الفضل العظيم ۝ وإذ يمكر
بك الذين كفروا ليثبتوك أو يقتلوك أو يخرجوك ويمكرون
ويمكر الله والله خير الماكرين ۝ وإذا تتلى عليهم
آياتنا قالوا قد سمعنا لو نشاء لقلنا مثل هذا إن هذا إلا أساطير
الأولين ۝ وإذ قالوا اللهم إن كان هذا هو الحق من
عندك فأمطر علينا حجارة من السماء أو ائتنا بعذاب
أليم ۝ وما كان الله ليعذبهم وأنت فيهم
وما كان الله معذبهم وهم يستغفرون ٣٣

AND REMEMBER when you 8:26
were few in number and persecuted in the land, ever fearing the onslaught of the people, how He gave you shelter. He made you strong with His help and provided you with wholesome things that you might render thanks.

Believers, do not betray God and the Apostle, nor knowingly betray your trust. Know that your worldly goods and your children are but a temptation, and that God's recompense is great.

Believers, if you fear God He will grant you salvation and cleanse you of your sins and forgive you. Supreme is God's bounty.

And remember how the 8:30
unbelievers plotted against you,[1] seeking to take you captive or to have you slain or banished. They schemed – and God also schemed. God is the most adroit of schemers.

Whenever Our revelations are recited to them, they say: 'We have heard them. If we wished, we could say the like. They are but fables of the ancients.'

They also say: 'Lord, if this be indeed the Truth revealed from You, rain down upon us stones from heaven or bring us some woeful scourge to punish us.'

But God would not punish them while you were present in their midst. 8:33
Nor would God punish them if they sought forgiveness.

1. Muḥammad.

وما لهم ألا يعذبهم الله وهم يصدون عن
المسجد الحرام وما كانوا أولياءه إن أولياؤه إلا
المتقون ولكن أكثرهم لا يعلمون ﴿٣٤﴾ وما كان صلاتهم
عند البيت إلا مكاء وتصدية فذوقوا العذاب بما
كنتم تكفرون ﴿٣٥﴾ إن الذين كفروا ينفقون
أموالهم ليصدوا عن سبيل الله فسينفقونها ثم
تكون عليهم حسرة ثم يغلبون والذين كفروا
إلى جهنم يحشرون ﴿٣٦﴾ ليميز الله الخبيث من الطيب
ويجعل الخبيث بعضه على بعض فيركمه جميعا
فيجعله في جهنم أولئك هم الخاسرون ﴿٣٧﴾ قل للذين
كفروا إن ينتهوا يغفر لهم ما قد سلف وإن يعودوا
فقد مضت سنت الأولين ﴿٣٨﴾ وقاتلوهم حتى لا تكون
فتنة ويكون الدين كله لله فإن انتهوا فإن
الله بما يعملون بصير ﴿٣٩﴾ وإن تولوا فاعلموا أن
الله مولاكم نعم المولى ونعم النصير ﴿٤٠﴾

8:34 AND YET it is but just that God should punish them; for they have debarred others from the Sacred Mosque, although its guardians they are not. Its guardians are only those that fear God, but most of them have no knowledge.

Their prayers at the Sacred House are nothing but whistling and clapping of hands. 'Taste then the scourge, because you disbelieved.'

8:36 The unbelievers expend their riches in debarring others from the path of God. Thus do they dissipate their wealth: but they shall rue it, and in the end be overthrown. The unbelievers shall into Hell be driven.

8:37 God will separate the wicked from the just. He will heap all the wicked one upon another and then cast them into Hell. These will surely be lost.

Tell the unbelievers that if they mend their ways their past shall be forgiven; but if they relapse, then theirs shall be the fate of bygone nations.

Fight them until idolatry[1] shall cease and God's religion shall reign
8:40 supreme.[2] If they desist, God is cognizant of what they do; but if they pay
no heed, know then that God is your protector; the noblest Protector and
the noblest Helper.

1. Thus Al-Jalālayn; see p. 178, note 2.
2. Literally, all religion shall be God's.

واعلموا أنما غنمتم من شيء فأن لله خمسه وللرسول
ولذي القربى واليتامى والمساكين وابن السبيل إن كنتم
آمنتم بالله وما أنزلنا على عبدنا يوم الفرقان يوم التقى
الجمعان والله على كل شيء قدير ٤١ إذ أنتم بالعدوة
الدنيا وهم بالعدوة القصوى والركب أسفل
منكم ولو تواعدتم لاختلفتم في الميعاد ولكن
ليقضي الله أمرا كان مفعولا ليهلك من هلك عن
بينة ويحيى من حي عن بينة وإن الله لسميع عليم ٤٢ إذ
يريكهم الله في منامك قليلا ولو أراكهم كثيرا
لفشلتم ولتنازعتم في الأمر ولكن الله سلم إنه عليم
بذات الصدور ٤٣ وإذ يريكموهم إذ التقيتم
في أعينكم قليلا ويقللكم في أعينهم
ليقضي الله أمرا كان مفعولا وإلى الله ترجع الأمور ٤٤
يا أيها الذين آمنوا إذا لقيتم فئة فاثبتوا
واذكروا الله كثيرا لعلكم تفلحون ٤٥

AND KNOW that if you gain 8:41
any spoils one-fifth of them
shall belong to God, the Apostle, his kin, the orphans, the
destitute, and the traveller in
need: if you truly believe in
God and what We revealed to
Our servant on the Day of
Salvation,[1] the day when the
two armies met. God has
power over all things.

You were on the nearer side
of the valley and the unbelievers on the farther side, with the
caravan below you. Had they
offered battle, you would have
surely declined; but God sought
to accomplish what had been
ordained, so that he that was
destined to perish might by a
clear sign die, and he that was
destined to live might by a clear
sign survive. Surely God hears
all and knows all.

God made them appear to you in a dream as few; had He showed them to 8:43
you as many, your courage would have failed you and discord would have
triumphed in your ranks. But this God spared you. He has knowledge of
man's innermost thoughts.

And when you met them, He made each appear to the other few in number, that God might accomplish what had been ordained. To God shall all
things be returned.

Believers, when you meet a troop stand firm and pray to God at all times, 8:45
so that you may triumph.

1. Or: the day of victory, according to some commentators.

8:46 AND OBEY God and His apostle and do not quarrel among
yourselves, lest you lose courage and your resolve weaken.
Have patience: God is with
those that are patient.

Do not be like those who
left their homes gloating and
to be seen by people. They
debar others from the path of
God: but God has full knowledge of what they do.

Satan had made their deeds
seem fair to them; and he said:
'No one shall conquer you this
day. I shall be at hand to help
you.' But when the two armies
came within sight of each
other, he took to his heels,
saying: 'I am done with you,
for I can see what you cannot.
I fear God. God's punishment
is stern.'

8:49 The hypocrites, and those whose hearts were tainted, said: 'Their religion
has deceived them.' But he that puts his trust in God shall find that God is
mighty and wise.

If you could see the angels when they carry off the souls of the unbelievers! They shall strike them on their faces and their backs, saying: 'Taste the
torment of the Conflagration! This is the punishment for what your hands
committed.' God is never unjust to His servants.

8:52 Like Pharaoh's people and those before them, they disbelieved God's
revelations. Therefore God smote them for their sins; mighty is God and
stern His retribution.

وَأَطِيعُوا اللَّهَ وَرَسُولَهُ وَلَا تَنَازَعُوا فَتَفْشَلُوا وَتَذْهَبَ
رِيحُكُمْ وَاصْبِرُوا إِنَّ اللَّهَ مَعَ الصَّابِرِينَ ٤٦ وَلَا تَكُونُوا
كَالَّذِينَ خَرَجُوا مِنْ دِيَارِهِمْ بَطَرًا وَرِئَاءَ النَّاسِ وَيَصُدُّونَ
عَنْ سَبِيلِ اللَّهِ وَاللَّهُ بِمَا يَعْمَلُونَ مُحِيطٌ ٤٧ وَإِذْ زَيَّنَ
لَهُمُ الشَّيْطَانُ أَعْمَالَهُمْ وَقَالَ لَا غَالِبَ لَكُمُ الْيَوْمَ مِنَ
النَّاسِ وَإِنِّي جَارٌ لَكُمْ فَلَمَّا تَرَاءَتِ الْفِئَتَانِ نَكَصَ
عَلَى عَقِبَيْهِ وَقَالَ إِنِّي بَرِيءٌ مِنْكُمْ إِنِّي أَرَى مَا لَا تَرَوْنَ
إِنِّي أَخَافُ اللَّهَ وَاللَّهُ شَدِيدُ الْعِقَابِ ٤٨ إِذْ يَقُولُ
الْمُنَافِقُونَ وَالَّذِينَ فِي قُلُوبِهِمْ مَرَضٌ غَرَّ هَؤُلَاءِ دِينُهُمْ وَمَنْ
يَتَوَكَّلْ عَلَى اللَّهِ فَإِنَّ اللَّهَ عَزِيزٌ حَكِيمٌ ٤٩ وَلَوْ تَرَى إِذْ
يَتَوَفَّى الَّذِينَ كَفَرُوا الْمَلَائِكَةُ يَضْرِبُونَ وُجُوهَهُمْ
وَأَدْبَارَهُمْ وَذُوقُوا عَذَابَ الْحَرِيقِ ٥٠ ذَلِكَ بِمَا قَدَّمَتْ
أَيْدِيكُمْ وَأَنَّ اللَّهَ لَيْسَ بِظَلَّامٍ لِلْعَبِيدِ ٥١ كَدَأْبِ
آلِ فِرْعَوْنَ وَالَّذِينَ مِنْ قَبْلِهِمْ كَفَرُوا بِآيَاتِ اللَّهِ
فَأَخَذَهُمُ اللَّهُ بِذُنُوبِهِمْ إِنَّ اللَّهَ قَوِيٌّ شَدِيدُ الْعِقَابِ ٥٢

ذلك بأن الله لم يك مغيرا نعمة أنعمها على قوم حتى
يغيروا ما بأنفسهم وأن الله سميع عليم ﴿٥٣﴾ كدأب آل
فرعون والذين من قبلهم كذبوا بآيات ربهم فأهلكناهم
بذنوبهم وأغرقنا آل فرعون وكل كانوا ظالمين ﴿٥٤﴾ إن شر
الدواب عند الله الذين كفروا فهم لا يؤمنون ﴿٥٥﴾ الذين
عاهدت منهم ثم ينقضون عهدهم في كل مرة وهم
لا يتقون ﴿٥٦﴾ فإما تثقفنهم في الحرب فشرد بهم من
خلفهم لعلهم يذكرون ﴿٥٧﴾ وإما تخافن من قوم خيانة
فانبذ إليهم على سواء إن الله لا يحب الخائنين ﴿٥٨﴾ ولا
يحسبن الذين كفروا سبقوا إنهم لا يعجزون ﴿٥٩﴾ وأعدوا
لهم ما استطعتم من قوة ومن رباط الخيل ترهبون
به عدو الله وعدوكم وآخرين من دونهم لا
تعلمونهم الله يعلمهم وما تنفقوا من شيء في سبيل
الله يوف إليكم وأنتم لا تظلمون ﴿٦٠﴾ وإن جنحوا للسلم
فاجنح لها وتوكل على الله إنه هو السميع العليم ﴿٦١﴾

GOD DOES not change the 8:53
blessings He has bestowed
upon a people until they change
what is in their hearts. And God
hears all and knows all.

Like Pharaoh's people and
those before them, they disbelieved their Lord's revelations.
We destroyed them for their
sins, and We drowned Pharaoh's
people. They were wrongdoers all.

Surely the basest creatures in
the sight of God are the blasphemers who will not believe;
those who time after time violate their treaties with you and
have no fear of God. If you 8:57
capture them in battle discriminate between them and those
that follow them, so that their
followers may take warning.

If you fear treachery from
any of your allies, you may fairly retaliate by breaking off your treaty with
them. God does not love the treacherous.

And let not the unbelievers think they will ever get away; they have not the
power so to do. Muster against them all the armed force and cavalry at your
command, that you may strike terror into the enemy of God and your own
enemy, and others besides them who are unknown to you but known to
God. All that you give in the cause of God shall be repaid to you; and you
shall not be wronged.

If they incline to peace, make peace with them, and put your trust in God. 8:61
Surely He it is who hears all and knows all.

8:62 AND SHOULD they seek to
deceive you, all-sufficient is
God for you. He it was who
has made you strong with His
help and rallied the faithful
round you, uniting their hearts.
If you had given away all the
riches of the earth, you could
not have so united them: but
God has united them. He is
mighty and wise.

Prophet, sufficient is God
for you, and sufficient are the
faithful who follow you.

Prophet, rouse the faithful
to arms. If there are twenty
steadfast men among you,
they shall vanquish two hundred; and if there are a
hundred, they shall rout a
thousand unbelievers, for they
are devoid of understanding.

8:66 God has now lightened
your burden, for He knows that you are weak. If there are a hundred steadfast men among you, they shall vanquish two hundred; and if there are a
thousand, they shall, by God's will, defeat two thousand. God is with those
that are steadfast.

A prophet may not take captives until he has fought and triumphed in the
land. You[1] seek the chance gain of this world, but God desires for you the
world to come. God is mighty and wise. Had there not been a previous writ
8:69 from God, you would have been sternly punished for what you took. Enjoy
therefore the good and lawful things which you have gained in war, and fear
God. Surely God is forgiving and compassionate.

وان يريدوا ان يخدعوك فان حسبك الله هو الذي ايدك
بنصره وبالمؤمنين ۝ والف بين قلوبهم لو انفقت ما في الارض
جميعا ما الفت بين قلوبهم ولكن الله الف بينهم انه
عزيز حكيم ۝ يا ايها النبي حسبك الله ومن اتبعك من
المؤمنين ۝ يا ايها النبي حرض المؤمنين على القتال ان
يكن منكم عشرون صابرون يغلبوا مائتين وان يكن
منكم مائة يغلبوا الفا من الذين كفروا بانهم قوم
لا يفقهون ۝ الئن خفف الله عنكم وعلم ان فيكم
ضعفا فان يكن منكم مائة صابرة يغلبوا مائتين وان يكن
منكم الف يغلبوا الفين باذن الله والله مع الصابرين ۝
ما كان لنبي ان يكون له اسرى حتى يثخن في الارض
تريدون عرض الدنيا والله يريد الاخرة والله
عزيز حكيم ۝ لولا كتاب من الله سبق لمسكم
فيما اخذتم عذاب عظيم ۝ فكلوا مما غنمتم
حلالا طيبا واتقوا الله ان الله غفور رحيم ۝

1. Muḥammad's followers.

يا ايها النبي قل لمن في ايديكم من الاسرى ان يعلم
الله في قلوبكم خيرا يؤتكم خيرا مما اخذ منكم ويغفر لكم
والله غفور رحيم ﴿٧٠﴾ وان يريدوا خيانتك فقد خانوا
الله من قبل فامكن منهم والله عليم حكيم ﴿٧١﴾ ان الذين
امنوا وهاجروا وجاهدوا باموالهم وانفسهم في سبيل
الله والذين اووا ونصروا اولئك بعضهم اولياء بعض
والذين امنوا ولم يهاجروا ما لكم من ولايتهم من شيء حتى
يهاجروا وان استنصروكم في الدين فعليكم النصر الا على
قوم بينكم وبينهم ميثاق والله بما تعملون بصير ﴿٧٢﴾ والذين
كفروا بعضهم اولياء بعض الا تفعلوه تكن فتنة في الارض
وفساد كبير ﴿٧٣﴾ والذين امنوا وهاجروا وجاهدوا في سبيل
الله والذين اووا ونصروا اولئك هم المؤمنون حقا لهم
مغفرة ورزق كريم ﴿٧٤﴾ والذين امنوا من بعد وهاجروا
وجاهدوا معكم فاولئك منكم واولوا الارحام بعضهم
اولى ببعض في كتاب الله ان الله بكل شيء عليم ﴿٧٥﴾

PROPHET, SAY to those you 8:70
have taken captive: 'If God
finds goodness in your hearts,
He will give you that which is
better than what was taken
from you, and He will forgive
you. God is forgiving and compassionate.'

But if they seek to betray
you, they have already betrayed
God. Therefore He has made
you triumph over them; God is
all-knowing and wise.

Those that have embraced
the Faith and left their land,
and fought for the cause of
God with their wealth and with
their persons; and those that
sheltered and helped, shall be
as friends to each other.

Those that have embraced
the Faith, but have not left,
shall in no way be your friends
until they leave. But if they seek your help in the cause of the Religion, it is
your duty to assist them, except against a people with whom you have a
treaty. And God is ever observant of what you do.

The unbelievers give aid and comfort to each other. If you fail to do like- 8:73
wise, there will be sedition in the land and great corruption.

Those that have embraced the Faith and fled their land and fought for the
cause of God, and those that sheltered and helped – they are the true believers. Forgiveness and a gracious provision await them.

Those that have since embraced the Faith and left their land and fought 8:75
with you – they too are your brothers; although according to the Book of
God those who are bound by ties of blood are nearest to one another. Surely
God has knowledge of all things.

REPENTANCE[1]

سورة التوبة مدنية وهي مائة وتسع وعشرون آية

براءة من الله ورسوله إلى الذين عاهدتم من المشركين
١ فسيحوا في الأرض أربعة أشهر واعلموا أنكم غير معجزي
الله وأن الله مخزي الكافرين ٢ وأذان من الله ورسوله
إلى الناس يوم الحج الأكبر أن الله بريء من المشركين ورسوله
فإن تبتم فهو خير لكم وإن توليتم فاعلموا أنكم غير معجزي
الله وبشر الذين كفروا بعذاب أليم ٣ إلا الذين عاهدتم
من المشركين ثم لم ينقصوكم شيئا ولم يظاهروا عليكم أحدا فأتموا
إليهم عهدهم إلى مدتهم إن الله يحب المتقين ٤ فإذا انسلخ
الأشهر الحرم فاقتلوا المشركين حيث وجدتموهم وخذوهم
واحصروهم واقعدوا لهم كل مرصد فإن تابوا وأقاموا
الصلاة وآتوا الزكاة فخلوا سبيلهم إن الله غفور رحيم
٥ وإن أحد من المشركين استجارك فأجره حتى يسمع كلام
الله ثم أبلغه مأمنه ذلك بأنهم قوم لا يعلمون ٦

9:1 A DECLARATION of immunity from God and His apostle to the idolaters with whom you have made treaties:

For four months you shall go unmolested in the land. But know that you shall not escape God's judgement, and that God will humble the unbelievers.

A proclamation to the people from God and His apostle on the day of the Greater Pilgrimage:

God and His apostle are under no obligation to the idolaters. If you repent, it shall be well with you; but if you pay no heed, know that you shall not be immune from God's judgement.

9:4 Proclaim a woeful punishment to the unbelievers, except to those idolaters who have honoured their treaties with you in every detail and aided none against you. With these keep faith, until their treaties have run their term. God loves the righteous.

When the sacred months[2] are over kill the idolaters wherever you find them. Arrest them, besiege them, and lie in ambush everywhere for them. If they repent and take to prayer and render the alms levy, allow them to go their way; God is forgiving and compassionate.

9:6 If an idolater seeks asylum with you, give him protection so that he may hear the Word of God, and then convey him to safety; for the idolaters are ignorant people.

1. This is the only *sūrah* in the Koran which does not begin with the invocation 'In the Name of God, etc.' Traditional commentators regard it as a continuation of 'The Spoils'.
2. Shawwāl, Dhūl-Q'adah, Dhūl-Ḥajjah, and Muḥarram.

كَيْفَ يَكُونُ لِلْمُشْرِكِينَ عَهْدٌ عِندَ ٱللَّهِ وَعِندَ
رَسُولِهِ إِلَّا ٱلَّذِينَ عَاهَدتُّمْ عِندَ ٱلْمَسْجِدِ ٱلْحَرَامِ فَمَا
ٱسْتَقَامُوا لَكُمْ فَٱسْتَقِيمُوا لَهُمْ إِنَّ ٱللَّهَ يُحِبُّ
ٱلْمُتَّقِينَ ٧ كَيْفَ وَإِن يَظْهَرُوا عَلَيْكُمْ لَا يَرْقُبُوا فِيكُمْ
إِلًّا وَلَا ذِمَّةً يُرْضُونَكُم بِأَفْوَاهِهِمْ وَتَأْبَىٰ
قُلُوبُهُمْ وَأَكْثَرُهُمْ فَاسِقُونَ ٨ ٱشْتَرَوْا بِآيَاتِ
ٱللَّهِ ثَمَنًا قَلِيلًا فَصَدُّوا عَن سَبِيلِهِ إِنَّهُمْ سَاءَ مَا كَانُوا
يَعْمَلُونَ ٩ لَا يَرْقُبُونَ فِي مُؤْمِنٍ إِلًّا وَلَا ذِمَّةً وَأُولَٰئِكَ
هُمُ ٱلْمُعْتَدُونَ ١٠ فَإِن تَابُوا وَأَقَامُوا ٱلصَّلَوٰةَ وَآتَوُا
ٱلزَّكَوٰةَ فَإِخْوَانُكُمْ فِي ٱلدِّينِ وَنُفَصِّلُ ٱلْآيَاتِ لِقَوْمٍ يَعْلَمُونَ
١١ وَإِن نَّكَثُوا أَيْمَانَهُم مِّن بَعْدِ عَهْدِهِمْ وَطَعَنُوا فِي
دِينِكُمْ فَقَاتِلُوا أَئِمَّةَ ٱلْكُفْرِ إِنَّهُمْ لَا أَيْمَانَ لَهُمْ لَعَلَّهُمْ
يَنتَهُونَ ١٢ أَلَا تُقَاتِلُونَ قَوْمًا نَّكَثُوا أَيْمَانَهُمْ وَهَمُّوا
بِإِخْرَاجِ ٱلرَّسُولِ وَهُم بَدَءُوكُمْ أَوَّلَ مَرَّةٍ أَتَخْشَوْنَهُمْ
فَٱللَّهُ أَحَقُّ أَن تَخْشَوْهُ إِن كُنتُم مُّؤْمِنِينَ ١٣

HOW CAN God and His 9:7
apostle repose trust in the idolaters, save those with whom you have made treaties at the Sacred Mosque? So long as they keep faith with you, keep faith with them. God loves the righteous.

How can you trust them? If they prevail against you, they will respect neither treaties nor ties of kin. They flatter you with their mouths, but their hearts reject you; and most of them are ungodly.

They sell God's revelations for a paltry price and debar others from His path. Evil is what they do; they break faith with the believers and set at nought all ties of kin. Such are the transgressors.

If they repent and take to 9:11
prayer and render the alms levy, they shall become your brothers in the Faith. Thus do We expound Our revelations to those endowed with knowledge.

But if, after coming to terms with you, they break their oaths, and revile your religion, then fight the leaders of unbelief – for no oaths are binding for them – so that they may desist.

Will you not fight against those who have broken their oaths and con- 9:13
spired to banish the Apostle? They were the first to attack you. Do you fear them? Surely God is more deserving of your fear, if you are true believers.

9:14 FIGHT THEM: God will chastise them at your hands and humble them. He will grant you victory over them and heal the spirit of the faithful. He will take away all rancour from their hearts: God shows mercy to whom He pleases. God is all-knowing and wise.

Or did you imagine you would be forsaken before God has recognized those of you who have fought valiantly and served none but God, His apostle, and the faithful? God is cognizant of what you do.

It ill becomes the idolaters to visit the mosques of God, for they are unbelievers, self-confessed. Vain shall be their works, and in the Fire shall they abide for ever.

قاتلوهم يعذبهم الله بأيديكم ويخزهم وينصركم
عليهم ويشف صدور قوم مؤمنين ﴿١٤﴾ ويذهب غيظ
قلوبهم ويتوب الله على من يشاء والله عليم حكيم
﴿١٥﴾ أم حسبتم أن تتركوا ولما يعلم الله الذين جاهدوا
منكم ولم يتخذوا من دون الله ولا رسوله ولا
المؤمنين وليجة والله خبير بما تعملون ﴿١٦﴾ ما كان للمشركين
أن يعمروا مساجد الله شاهدين على أنفسهم بالكفر أولئك
حبطت أعمالهم وفي النار هم خالدون ﴿١٧﴾ إنما يعمر مساجد
الله من آمن بالله واليوم الآخر وأقام الصلوة وآتى
الزكوة ولم يخش إلا الله فعسى أولئك أن يكونوا من المهتدين
﴿١٨﴾ أجعلتم سقاية الحاج وعمارة المسجد الحرام كمن آمن
بالله واليوم الآخر وجاهد في سبيل الله لا يستوون عند
الله والله لا يهدي القوم الظالمين ﴿١٩﴾ الذين آمنوا وهاجروا
وجاهدوا في سبيل الله بأموالهم وأنفسهم أعظم
درجة عند الله وأولئك هم الفائزون ﴿٢٠﴾

9:18 None should visit the mosques of God except those who believe in God and the Last Day, attend to their prayers, and render the alms levy and fear none but God; these shall be rightly guided.

Do you pretend that he who gives a drink to the pilgrims and pays a visit to the Sacred Mosque is as worthy as the man who believes in God and the Last Day, and fights for God's cause? These are not held equal by God; God does not guide the wrongdoers.

9:20 Those that have embraced the Faith, and left their land, and fought for God's cause with their wealth and with their persons, are held in higher esteem by God; and it is they who shall triumph.

يُبَشِّرُهُمْ رَبُّهُم بِرَحْمَةٍ مِّنْهُ وَرِضْوَانٍ وَجَنَّاتٍ لَّهُمْ فِيهَا
نَعِيمٌ مُّقِيمٌ ٢١ خَالِدِينَ فِيهَا أَبَدًا إِنَّ اللَّهَ عِندَهُ أَجْرٌ
عَظِيمٌ ٢٢ يَا أَيُّهَا الَّذِينَ آمَنُوا لَا تَتَّخِذُوا آبَاءَكُمْ وَإِخْوَانَكُمْ
أَوْلِيَاءَ إِنِ اسْتَحَبُّوا الْكُفْرَ عَلَى الْإِيمَانِ وَمَن يَتَوَلَّهُم
مِّنكُمْ فَأُولَٰئِكَ هُمُ الظَّالِمُونَ ٢٣ قُلْ إِن كَانَ آبَاؤُكُمْ
وَأَبْنَاؤُكُمْ وَإِخْوَانُكُمْ وَأَزْوَاجُكُمْ وَعَشِيرَتُكُمْ
وَأَمْوَالٌ اقْتَرَفْتُمُوهَا وَتِجَارَةٌ تَخْشَوْنَ كَسَادَهَا
وَمَسَاكِنُ تَرْضَوْنَهَا أَحَبَّ إِلَيْكُم مِّنَ اللَّهِ وَرَسُولِهِ
وَجِهَادٍ فِي سَبِيلِهِ فَتَرَبَّصُوا حَتَّىٰ يَأْتِيَ اللَّهُ بِأَمْرِهِ وَاللَّهُ
لَا يَهْدِي الْقَوْمَ الْفَاسِقِينَ ٢٤ لَقَدْ نَصَرَكُمُ اللَّهُ فِي مَوَاطِنَ
كَثِيرَةٍ وَيَوْمَ حُنَيْنٍ إِذْ أَعْجَبَتْكُمْ كَثْرَتُكُمْ فَلَمْ
تُغْنِ عَنكُمْ شَيْئًا وَضَاقَتْ عَلَيْكُمُ الْأَرْضُ بِمَا رَحُبَتْ
ثُمَّ وَلَّيْتُم مُّدْبِرِينَ ٢٥ ثُمَّ أَنزَلَ اللَّهُ سَكِينَتَهُ
عَلَىٰ رَسُولِهِ وَعَلَى الْمُؤْمِنِينَ وَأَنزَلَ جُنُودًا لَّمْ تَرَوْهَا
وَعَذَّبَ الَّذِينَ كَفَرُوا وَذَٰلِكَ جَزَاءُ الْكَافِرِينَ ٢٦

THEIR LORD has promised 9:21
them the joy of mercy from
Himself and His pleasure, and
Gardens of eternal bliss,
wherein shall they abide for
ever; God's recompense is
great indeed.

Believers, do not befriend
your fathers or your brothers
if they choose unbelief in
preference to faith; wrongdoers are those of you that
befriend them.

Say: 'If your fathers, your 9:24
sons, your brothers, your wives,
your tribes, the property you
have acquired, the merchandise
you fear may not be sold, and
the homes you love, are dearer
to you than God, His apostle
and the struggle for His cause,
then wait until God shall pass
His judgement. God does not
guide the ungodly.'

God has aided you on many a battlefield. In the Battle of Hunain[1] you set
great store by your numbers, but they availed you nothing: the earth, for all
its vastness, seemed to close in upon you, and you turned your backs and
fled. Then God caused His Divine Presence[2] to descend upon His apostle 9:26
and the faithful: He sent to your aid warriors you did not see and sternly
punished the unbelievers: that was the infidels' recompense.

1. Fought in the year 630. The Muslim army was 12,000 strong, the Meccans 4,000.

2. See p. 39, note 1.

9:27 THEN GOD will after that show mercy to whom He will. God is forgiving and compassionate.

Believers! The idolaters are unclean. Let them not approach the Sacred Mosque after this year is ended. If you fear poverty, God, if He pleases, will enrich you through His own bounty; God is all-knowing and wise.

9:29 Fight those who believe in neither God nor the Last Day, who do not forbid what God and His apostle have forbidden, and do not embrace the Religion of Truth, from among those who were given the Book, until they render the tribute, by hand, in abject submission.

The Jews say Ezra is the son of God, and the Christians say Christ is the son of God. Such are the words they utter with their mouths, by which they emulate the infidels of old. God smite them! How perverse they are!

9:31 They make of their clerics and their monks, and of Christ, the son of Mary, Lords besides God; though they were ordered to serve but one God; there is no God but Him. Exalted be He above those they deify besides Him!

ثم يتوب الله من بعد ذلك على من يشاء والله
غفور رحيم ٢٧ يا أيها الذين آمنوا إنما المشركون
نجس فلا يقربوا المسجد الحرام بعد عامهم هذا
وإن خفتم عيلة فسوف يغنيكم الله من فضله إن
شاء إن الله عليم حكيم ٢٨ قاتلوا الذين لا
يؤمنون بالله ولا باليوم الآخر ولا يحرمون
ما حرم الله ورسوله ولا يدينون دين الحق من
الذين أوتوا الكتاب حتى يعطوا الجزية عن يد
وهم صاغرون ٢٩ وقالت اليهود عزير ابن الله
وقالت النصارى المسيح ابن الله ذلك قولهم
بأفواههم يضاهئون قول الذين كفروا من قبل
قاتلهم الله أنى يؤفكون ٣٠ اتخذوا أحبارهم
ورهبانهم أربابا من دون الله والمسيح ابن
مريم وما أمروا إلا ليعبدوا إلها واحدا
لا إله إلا هو سبحانه عما يشركون ٣١

يريدون أن يطفئوا نور الله بأفواههم ويأبى
الله إلا أن يتم نوره ولو كره الكافرون ﴿٣٢﴾
هو الذي أرسل رسوله بالهدى ودين الحق ليظهره
على الدين كله ولو كره المشركون ﴿٣٣﴾ يا أيها
الذين آمنوا إن كثيرا من الأحبار والرهبان
ليأكلون أموال الناس بالباطل ويصدون عن سبيل
الله والذين يكنزون الذهب والفضة ولا
ينفقونها في سبيل الله فبشرهم بعذاب أليم
﴿٣٤﴾ يوم يحمى عليها في نار جهنم فتكوى بها جباههم
وجنوبهم وظهورهم هذا ما كنزتم لأنفسكم
فذوقوا ما كنتم تكنزون ﴿٣٥﴾ إن عدة الشهور عند
الله اثنا عشر شهرا في كتاب الله يوم خلق السموات
والأرض منها أربعة حرم ذلك الدين القيم فلا
تظلموا فيهن أنفسكم وقاتلوا المشركين كافة كما
يقاتلونكم كافة واعلموا أن الله مع المتقين ﴿٣٦﴾

THEY WOULD extinguish 9:32
the light of God with their
mouths: but God seeks only to
perfect His light, though the
infidels abhor it.

He it was who has sent forth
His apostle with guidance and
the Religion of Truth that he
may exalt it above all religion,
though the idolaters abhor it.

Believers, many are the clerics
and the monks who defraud
the people of their possessions
and debar them from the path
of God. To those that hoard
up gold and silver and do not
spend them in God's cause,
proclaim a woeful punishment:
the day when their treasures 9:35
shall be heated in the fire of
Hell, and their foreheads, sides,
and backs branded with them.
They will be told: 'These are
the treasures that for yourselves you hoarded. Taste then the treasures that
you hoarded.'

God ordained the months twelve in number when He created the heavens 9:36
and the earth. Of these, four are sacred, according to the True Religion.
Therefore do not sin against yourselves by violating them. But fight the idolaters
in all these months, as they themselves fight you in all of them. And
know that God is with the righteous.

9:37 THE POSTPONEMENT of sacred months is a grossly impious practice, in which the unbelievers are misguided. They make it lawful one year and make it unlawful in the next, in order to make up for the months which God has sanctified; thus making lawful what God has forbidden. Their foul acts seem fair to them: God does not guide the unbelievers.

9:38 Believers, why is it that when you are told: 'March in the cause of God,' you linger slothfully in the land? Are you content with this life in preference to the life to come? Few indeed are the blessings of this life, compared with those of the life to come.

If you do not go on the march, He will mete out to you grievous punishment, and will replace you by other people. You will in no way harm Him: for God has power over all things.

9:40 If you do not help him,[1] God did help him when he was driven out by the unbelievers with one other.[2] In the cave he said to his companion: 'Do not despair, God is with us.' God caused His Divine Presence[3] to descend upon him and sent to his aid warriors you did not see, so that He brought low the unbelievers' design: supreme is God's design. God is mighty and wise.

انما النسيء زيادة في الكفر يضل به الذين
كفروا يحلونه عاما ويحرمونه عاما ليواطئوا
عدة ما حرم الله فيحلوا ما حرم الله زين لهم سوء
اعمالهم والله لا يهدي القوم الكافرين ﴿٣٧﴾
يا ايها الذين امنوا ما لكم اذا قيل لكم انفروا
في سبيل الله اثاقلتم الى الارض ارضيتم
بالحيوة الدنيا من الاخرة فما متاع الحيوة الدنيا
في الاخرة الا قليل ﴿٣٨﴾ الا تنفروا يعذبكم
عذابا اليما ويستبدل قوما غيركم ولا
تضروه شيئا والله على كل شيء قدير ﴿٣٩﴾ الا تنصروه
فقد نصره الله اذ اخرجه الذين كفروا ثاني
اثنين اذ هما في الغار اذ يقول لصاحبه
لا تحزن ان الله معنا فانزل الله سكينته عليه
وايده بجنود لم تروها وجعل كلمة الذين كفروا
السفلى وكلمة الله هي العليا والله عزيز حكيم ﴿٤٠﴾

1. Muḥammad.
2. Abū-Bakr, later the first of the Rightly-guided Caliphs.
3. See p. 39, note 1.

انفروا خفافا وثقالا وجاهدوا بأموالكم وأنفسكم
في سبيل الله ذلكم خير لكم إن كنتم تعلمون ٤١ لو
كان عرضا قريبا وسفرا قاصدا لاتبعوك ولكن بعدت
عليهم الشقة وسيحلفون بالله لو استطعنا لخرجنا
معكم يهلكون أنفسهم والله يعلم إنهم لكاذبون
٤٢ عفا الله عنك لم أذنت لهم حتى يتبين لك
الذين صدقوا وتعلم الكاذبين ٤٣ لا يستأذنك الذين
يؤمنون بالله واليوم الآخر أن يجاهدوا بأموالهم
وأنفسهم والله عليم بالمتقين ٤٤ إنما يستأذنك الذين لا
يؤمنون بالله واليوم الآخر وارتابت قلوبهم فهم
في ريبهم يترددون ٤٥ ولو أرادوا الخروج لأعدوا
له عدة ولكن كره الله انبعاثهم فثبطهم
وقيل اقعدوا مع القاعدين ٤٦ لو خرجوا فيكم ما زادوكم
إلا خبالا ولأوضعوا خلالكم يبغونكم الفتنة
وفيكم سماعون لهم والله عليم بالظالمين ٤٧

WHETHER LIGHTLY armed 9:41
or well-equipped, march on and fight for the cause of God, with your wealth and with your persons. This will be best for you, if you but knew it.

Had the gain been immediate or the journey short, they would have followed you:[1] but the distance seemed too far to them. Yet they will swear by God: 'Had we been able, we would have marched with you.' They bring ruin upon themselves. God knows that they are surely lying.

God pardon you! Why did 9:43
you give them leave before you discovered who was speaking the truth, and knew who was lying?

Those that believe in God and the Last Day will not beg you to exempt them from fighting with their possessions and with their persons. God best knows the righteous. Only those seek exemption who disbelieve in God and the Last Day, and whose hearts are filled with doubt. Because they doubt, they waver.

Had they intended to set forth, they would have prepared themselves for the march. But God was loath to let them go, and held them back. They were bidden to stay with those who stayed behind.

Had they taken the field with you, they would have only added to your 9:47
burden. They would have wormed their way through your ranks, seeking to sow discord among you: and among you there were some who would have been willing listeners. God well knows the wrongdoers.

1. Muḥammad.

9:48 THEY HAD sought to sow
dissension before this, and
turned things topsy-turvy for
you until the Truth prevailed
and the will of God became
manifest, averse to it though
they were.
Some among them say:
'Give us leave to stay behind,
and do not expose us to temptation.' Surely they have already
succumbed to temptation. Hell
shall engulf the unbelievers.
If you meet with success, it
grieves them; and if a disaster
befalls you, they say: 'We have
already taken our precautions.'
And they turn away, rejoicing.
9:51 Say: 'Nothing will befall us
except what God has ordained
for us. He is our guardian. In
God let the faithful put their
trust.'
Say: 'Are you waiting for anything to befall us except victory or martyr-
dom? We are waiting for God's scourge to smite you, direct from Him or at
our hands. Wait if you will; we will wait with you.'
Say: 'Whether you give willingly or with reluctance, your offerings shall
not be accepted from you; for you are ungodly people.'
9:54 Their offerings shall not be accepted from them only because they have
denied God and His apostle. They pray but half-heartedly and give only with
reluctance.

لقد ابتغوا الفتنة من قبل وقلبوا لك الأمور
حتى جاء الحق وظهر أمر الله وهم كارهون ٤٨
ومنهم من يقول ائذن لي ولا تفتني ألا في الفتنة
سقطوا وإن جهنم لمحيطة بالكافرين ٤٩ إن
تصبك حسنة تسؤهم وإن تصبك مصيبة يقولوا
قد أخذنا أمرنا من قبل ويتولوا وهم فرحون ٥٠
قل لن يصيبنا إلا ما كتب الله لنا هو مولينا وعلى
الله فليتوكل المؤمنون ٥١ قل هل تربصون بنا إلا
إحدى الحسنيين ونحن نتربص بكم أن يصيبكم
الله بعذاب من عنده أو بأيدينا فتربصوا إنا
معكم متربصون ٥٢ قل أنفقوا طوعا أو كرها لن
يتقبل منكم إنكم كنتم قوما فاسقين ٥٣ وما
منعهم أن تقبل منهم نفقاتهم إلا أنهم كفروا
بالله وبرسوله ولا يأتون الصلوة إلا وهم
كسالى ولا ينفقون إلا وهم كارهون ٥٤

فلا تعجبك اموالهم ولا اولادهم انما يريد الله ليعذبهم
بها في الحيوة الدنيا وتزهق انفسهم وهم كافرون
(٥٥) ويحلفون بالله انهم لمنكم وما هم منكم ولكنهم
قوم يفرقون (٥٦) لو يجدون ملجا او مغارات او مدخلا
لولوا اليه وهم يجمحون (٥٧) ومنهم من يلمزك في
الصدقات فان اعطوا منها رضوا وان لم يعطوا منها
اذا هم يسخطون (٥٨) ولو انهم رضوا ما اتيهم الله ورسوله
وقالوا حسبنا الله سيؤتينا الله من فضله ورسوله انا
الى الله راغبون (٥٩) انما الصدقات للفقراء والمساكين
والعاملين عليها والمؤلفة قلوبهم وفي الرقاب
والغارمين وفي سبيل الله وابن السبيل فريضة
من الله والله عليم حكيم (٦٠) ومنهم الذين
يؤذون النبي ويقولون هو اذن قل اذن خير
لكم يؤمن بالله ويؤمن للمؤمنين ورحمة للذين امنوا
منكم والذين يؤذون رسول الله لهم عذاب اليم (٦١)

So LET neither their riches 9:55
nor their children make you wonder. Through these God seeks to punish them in the life of this world, so that their souls shall perish while they are still in unbelief.

They swear by God that they are believers with you, and they are not with you. But they are afraid. If they could find a shelter or some caves, or any hiding-place, they would run in frantic haste to seek refuge in it.

And there are some among 9:58
them who speak ill of you[1] concerning the distribution of alms. If a share is given them, they are content: but if they are not given a share, they grow resentful.

Would that they were satisfied with what God and His apostle have given them, and said: 'All-sufficient is God for us. God will provide for us from His own bounty, and so will His apostle. To God we will humbly submit.'

Alms shall be only for the poor and the destitute; for those that are engaged in the management of alms and those whose hearts are sympathetic to the Faith; for the freeing of slaves and debtors; for the advancement of God's cause; and for the traveller in need. That is a duty enjoined by God; God is all-knowing and wise.

And there are some among them who speak ill of the Prophet, saying: 'He 9:61
has an ear for everything.' Say: 'He has an ear only for what is good for you. He believes in God and puts his trust in the faithful. He is a blessing to the true believers among you. Those that speak ill of God's apostle have woeful punishment in wait for them.'

1. Muḥammad.

9:62 THEY SWEAR by God in order to please you. But it is more just that they should please God and the Apostle, if they are true believers.

Are they not aware that whoever defies God and His apostle shall abide for ever in the fire of Hell? That surely is the supreme humiliation.

The hypocrites are afraid lest a *sūrah* be revealed to them, telling them what is in their hearts. Say: 'Scoff if you will; God will surely bring to light what you are dreading.'

9:65 If you question them, they will surely say: 'We were only jesting and making merry.' Say: 'Would you mock God, His revelations, and His apostle? Make no excuses. You have renounced the Faith after embracing it. If We pardon some among you, We will punish others, for they were transgressors.'

Be they men or women, the hypocrites are all alike. They enjoin the reprehensible, forbid the just, and tighten their fists. They forgot God, so God forgot them. Surely it is the hypocrites who are the ungodly.

9:68 God has promised the hypocrites, both men and women, and the unbelievers, the fire of Hell. Therein shall they abide for ever: a sufficient recompense. God has cursed them; and lasting torment awaits them.

يَحْلِفُونَ بِاللَّهِ لَكُمْ لِيُرْضُوكُمْ وَاللَّهُ وَرَسُولُهُ
أَحَقُّ أَنْ يُرْضُوهُ إِنْ كَانُوا مُؤْمِنِينَ ﴿٦٢﴾ أَلَمْ يَعْلَمُوا أَنَّهُ
مَنْ يُحَادِدِ اللَّهَ وَرَسُولَهُ فَأَنَّ لَهُ نَارَ جَهَنَّمَ خَالِدًا
فِيهَا ذَٰلِكَ الْخِزْيُ الْعَظِيمُ ﴿٦٣﴾ يَحْذَرُ الْمُنَافِقُونَ أَنْ
تُنَزَّلَ عَلَيْهِمْ سُورَةٌ تُنَبِّئُهُمْ بِمَا فِي قُلُوبِهِمْ قُلِ
اسْتَهْزِئُوا إِنَّ اللَّهَ مُخْرِجٌ مَا تَحْذَرُونَ ﴿٦٤﴾ وَلَئِنْ سَأَلْتَهُمْ
لَيَقُولُنَّ إِنَّمَا كُنَّا نَخُوضُ وَنَلْعَبُ قُلْ أَبِاللَّهِ وَآيَاتِهِ
وَرَسُولِهِ كُنْتُمْ تَسْتَهْزِئُونَ ﴿٦٥﴾ لَا تَعْتَذِرُوا قَدْ كَفَرْتُمْ
بَعْدَ إِيمَانِكُمْ إِنْ نَعْفُ عَنْ طَائِفَةٍ مِنْكُمْ نُعَذِّبْ
طَائِفَةً بِأَنَّهُمْ كَانُوا مُجْرِمِينَ ﴿٦٦﴾ الْمُنَافِقُونَ وَالْمُنَافِقَاتُ
بَعْضُهُمْ مِنْ بَعْضٍ يَأْمُرُونَ بِالْمُنْكَرِ وَيَنْهَوْنَ عَنِ
الْمَعْرُوفِ وَيَقْبِضُونَ أَيْدِيَهُمْ نَسُوا اللَّهَ فَنَسِيَهُمْ
إِنَّ الْمُنَافِقِينَ هُمُ الْفَاسِقُونَ ﴿٦٧﴾ وَعَدَ اللَّهُ الْمُنَافِقِينَ
وَالْمُنَافِقَاتِ وَالْكُفَّارَ نَارَ جَهَنَّمَ خَالِدِينَ فِيهَا
هِيَ حَسْبُهُمْ وَلَعَنَهُمُ اللَّهُ وَلَهُمْ عَذَابٌ مُقِيمٌ ﴿٦٨﴾

كالذين من قبلكم كانوا أشد منكم قوة وأكثر
أموالا وأولادا فاستمتعوا بخلاقهم فاستمتعتم
بخلاقكم كما استمتع الذين من قبلكم بخلاقهم
وخضتم كالذي خاضوا أولئك حبطت أعمالهم في
الدنيا والآخرة وأولئك هم الخاسرون ٦٩ ألم يأتهم
نبأ الذين من قبلهم قوم نوح وعاد وثمود وقوم
إبراهيم وأصحاب مدين والمؤتفكات أتتهم رسلهم
بالبينات فما كان الله ليظلمهم ولكن كانوا أنفسهم
يظلمون ٧٠ والمؤمنون والمؤمنات بعضهم أولياء بعض
يأمرون بالمعروف وينهون عن المنكر ويقيمون الصلوة
ويؤتون الزكوة ويطيعون الله ورسوله أولئك
سيرحمهم الله إن الله عزيز حكيم ٧١ وعد الله
المؤمنين والمؤمنات جنات تجري من تحتها الأنهار
خالدين فيها ومساكن طيبة في جنات عدن
ورضوان من الله أكبر ذلك هو الفوز العظيم ٧٢

Like those before you, 9:69
mightier they were than you,
and had greater riches and
more offspring. Like them, you
have enjoyed your earthly lot
and, like them, you have
engaged in idle talk. But vain
were their works in this life,
and vain shall they be in the
life to come. These will surely
be lost.
Have they not heard the 9:70
histories of those who have
gone before them? The fate
of Noah's people and of 'Ād
and Thamūd; of Abraham's
people and the people of Midian and the Ruined Cities?
Their apostles came to them
with veritable signs. God did
not wrong them, but they
wronged their own souls.

The true believers, both men and women, are friends to one another. They enjoin the just and forbid the reprehensible; they attend to their prayers, and render the alms levy, and obey God and His apostle. On these God will have mercy. God is mighty and wise.

God has promised the men and women who believe in Him Gardens 9:72
watered by running brooks, wherein shall they abide for ever: goodly mansions in the Gardens of Eden: and, what is more, they shall have grace in
God's sight. That is the supreme triumph.

9:73 PROPHET, MAKE war on
the unbelievers and the hypocrites and deal rigorously with
them. Hell shall be their home:
a wretched fate!

They swear by God that
they said nothing. Yet they
uttered the word of blas-
phemy and renounced Islām
after embracing it. They
sought to do what they could
not attain. Yet they had no
reason to be spiteful; except
perhaps because God and His
apostle had enriched them
through His bounty. If they
repent, it will indeed be better
for them; but if they pay no
heed, God will torment them
grievously, in this world and in
the world to come. They shall
have none on earth to protect
or succour them.

يا أيها النبي جاهد الكفار والمنافقين واغلظ
عليهم ومأواهم جهنم وبئس المصير ٧٣ يحلفون
بالله ما قالوا ولقد قالوا كلمة الكفر وكفروا بعد
إسلامهم وهموا بما لم ينالوا وما نقموا إلا أن أغناهم
الله ورسوله من فضله فإن يتوبوا يك خيرا لهم
وإن يتولوا يعذبهم الله عذابا أليما في الدنيا والآخرة
وما لهم في الأرض من ولي ولا نصير ٧٤ ومنهم من عاهد
الله لئن آتانا من فضله لنصدقن ولنكونن من
الصالحين ٧٥ فلما آتاهم من فضله بخلوا به وتولوا
وهم معرضون ٧٦ فأعقبهم نفاقا في قلوبهم إلى يوم
يلقونه بما أخلفوا الله ما وعدوه وبما كانوا يكذبون
٧٧ ألم يعلموا أن الله يعلم سرهم ونجواهم وأن
الله علام الغيوب ٧٨ الذين يلمزون المطوعين من
المؤمنين في الصدقات والذين لا يجدون إلا جهدهم
فيسخرون منهم سخر الله منهم ولهم عذاب أليم ٧٩

9:75 Some among them pledged themselves to God: 'If He is bountiful to us,
we will assuredly give alms and be among the righteous.' But when God had
bestowed His bounty on them they tightened their fists and, turning their
backs, hurried away. He has caused hypocrisy to reign in their hearts till the
day they meet Him, because they have been untrue to the pledge they gave
Him and because of the lies they told.

Are they not aware that God knows what they conceal and what they talk
9:79 about in secret? That God knows what is hidden? As for those that taunt the
believers who give freely, and deride those who give according to their means,
God will deride them. Woeful punishment awaits them.

استغفر لهم او لا تستغفر لهم ان تستغفر لهم سبعين مرة
فلن يغفر الله لهم ذلك بانهم كفروا بالله ورسوله والله
لا يهدي القوم الفاسقين ٨٠ فرح المخلفون بمقعدهم
خلاف رسول الله وكرهوا ان يجاهدوا باموالهم وانفسهم
في سبيل الله وقالوا لا تنفروا في الحر قل نار جهنم اشد
حرا لو كانوا يفقهون ٨١ فليضحكوا قليلا وليبكوا كثيرا
جزاء بما كانوا يكسبون ٨٢ فان رجعك الله الى طائفة منهم
فاستاذنوك للخروج فقل لن تخرجوا معي ابدا ولن تقاتلوا معي
عدوا انكم رضيتم بالقعود اول مرة فاقعدوا مع الخالفين
٨٣ ولا تصل على احد منهم مات ابدا ولا تقم على قبره انهم
كفروا بالله ورسوله وماتوا وهم فاسقون ٨٤ ولا
تعجبك اموالهم واولادهم انما يريد الله ان يعذبهم بها
في الدنيا وتزهق انفسهم وهم كافرون ٨٥ واذا انزلت سورة
ان امنوا بالله وجاهدوا مع رسوله استاذنك اولوا
الطول منهم وقالوا ذرنا نكن مع القاعدين ٨٦

It is the same whether or 9:80
not you beg forgiveness for them. If seventy times you beg forgiveness for them, God will not forgive them, for they have denied God and His apostle. God does not guide the ungodly.

Those that stayed at home were glad that they were left behind by God's apostle, for they had no wish to fight for the cause of God with their wealth and with their persons. They said: 'Do not go to war, the heat is fierce.'

Say: 'More fierce is the heat of Hell-fire!' Would that they understood!

They shall laugh but little and shed many tears. Thus shall they be rewarded for what they did.

If God brings you back in safety and some of them ask leave to march 9:83
with you, say: 'You shall never march with me, nor shall you ever fight with me against an enemy. You chose to stay at home on the first occasion; therefore you shall now stay with those who will remain behind.'

You shall not pray for any of their dead, nor shall you attend their burial. For they denied God and His apostle and remained sinners to the last.

So let neither their riches nor their offspring rouse your envy. Through these God seeks to punish them in the life of this world, so that their souls shall perish while still in unbelief.

Whenever a *sūrah* was revealed, saying: 'Believe in God and fight alongside 9:86
His apostle,' the rich among them excused themselves to you, saying: 'Leave us; we would rather be with those who are to stay behind.'

9:87 THEY WERE content to be
with those who stayed behind:
a seal was set upon their hearts,
leaving them bereft of understanding. But the Apostle and
the men who shared his faith
fought with their wealth and
with their persons. These shall
be rewarded with good things.
These shall surely prosper.
God has prepared for them
Gardens watered by running
brooks, wherein shall they
abide for ever. That is the
supreme triumph.
Some Arabs of the desert
turned up with excuses, beg-
ging to be given leave; while
those who denied God and
His apostle remained idle at
home. A woeful scourge shall
fall on those of them that disbelieved.

رضوا بأن يكونوا مع الخوالف وطبع على قلوبهم فهم
لا يفقهون ﴿٨٧﴾ لكن الرسول والذين آمنوا معه جاهدوا
بأموالهم وأنفسهم وأولئك لهم الخيرات وأولئك هم
المفلحون ﴿٨٨﴾ أعد الله لهم جنات تجري من تحتها الأنهار
خالدين فيها ذلك الفوز العظيم ﴿٨٩﴾ وجاء المعذرون من
الأعراب ليؤذن لهم وقعد الذين كذبوا الله ورسوله
سيصيب الذين كفروا منهم عذاب أليم ﴿٩٠﴾ ليس
على الضعفاء ولا على المرضى ولا على الذين لا
يجدون ما ينفقون حرج إذا نصحوا لله ورسوله
ما على المحسنين من سبيل والله غفور رحيم
﴿٩١﴾ ولا على الذين إذا ما أتوك لتحملهم قلت لا أجد
ما أحملكم عليه تولوا وأعينهم تفيض من الدمع
حزنا ألا يجدوا ما ينفقون ﴿٩٢﴾ إنما السبيل على الذين
يستأذنونك وهم أغنياء رضوا بأن يكونوا مع
الخوالف وطبع الله على قلوبهم فهم لا يعلمون ﴿٩٣﴾

9:91 It shall be no offence for the disabled, the sick, and those lacking the
means, to stay behind: if they are true to God and His apostle. The righteous
shall not be blamed: God is forgiving and compassionate. Nor shall those be
blamed who, when they came to you demanding conveyances to mount to
the battle-front and you said you could find none to carry them, went away
in tears grieving that they could find nothing to contribute.
9:93 The offenders are those that seek exemption although they are men of
wealth. They are content to be with those who stay behind. God has set a
seal upon their hearts so that they are devoid of knowledge.

يعتذرون إليكم إذا رجعتم إليهم قل لا تعتذروا
لن نؤمن لكم قد نبأنا الله من أخباركم وسيرى الله
عملكم ورسوله ثم تردون إلى عالم الغيب والشهادة
فينبئكم بما كنتم تعملون ﴿٩٤﴾ سيحلفون بالله
لكم إذا انقلبتم إليهم لتعرضوا عنهم فأعرضوا عنهم
إنهم رجس ومأواهم جهنم جزاء بما كانوا يكسبون ﴿٩٥﴾
يحلفون لكم لترضوا عنهم فإن ترضوا عنهم فإن الله
لا يرضى عن القوم الفاسقين ﴿٩٦﴾ الأعراب أشد كفرا
ونفاقا وأجدر ألا يعلموا حدود ما أنزل الله
على رسوله والله عليم حكيم ﴿٩٧﴾ ومن الأعراب من يتخذ
ما ينفق مغرما ويتربص بكم الدوائر عليهم دائرة
السوء والله سميع عليم ﴿٩٨﴾ ومن الأعراب
من يؤمن بالله واليوم الآخر ويتخذ ما ينفق
قربات عند الله وصلوات الرسول ألا إنها قربة لهم
سيدخلهم الله في رحمته إن الله غفور رحيم ﴿٩٩﴾

THEY WILL come up to 9:94
you with excuses when you
return to them. Say: 'Make no
excuses: we will not believe
you. God has revealed to us
the truth about you. God will
watch your actions, and so will
His apostle. Then you shall
return to Him who knows
alike the unknown and the
manifest, and He will declare
to you what you have done.'

When you return they will
appeal to you in God's name to
let them be. So let them be:
they are an abomination. Hell
shall be their home, in requital
for their misdeeds.

They will swear to you in 9:96
order to gain your acceptance.
But if you accept them, God
will not accept the ungodly.

The desert Arabs surpass
others in unbelief and hypocrisy, and have more cause to be ignorant of the
laws which God has revealed to His apostle. But God is all-knowing and wise.

Some desert Arabs regard what they give as a compulsory fine and wait
for some misfortune to befall you. May ill-fortune befall them! God hears all
and knows all.

Yet there are some among the desert Arabs who believe in God and the 9:99
Last Day, and regard what they give as a means of bringing them close to
God and to the Apostle's prayers. Indeed, closer they shall be brought; God
will admit them into His mercy; God is forgiving and compassionate.

9:100 As for those who led the way, the first of the *muhājirīn*[1] and the *anṣār*,[2] and those who nobly followed them, God is pleased with them and they are pleased with Him. He has prepared for them Gardens watered by running brooks, wherein shall they abide for ever. That is the supreme triumph.

Some of the desert Arabs around you are hypocrites, and so are some of the citizens of Madīnah, who are indeed fanatical in their hypocrisy. You know them not, but We know them well. Twice We will chastise them: then shall they return to a grievous torment.

9:102 Others there are who have confessed their sins; they intermixed their good works with evil. Perchance God will pardon them: God is forgiving and compassionate. Take alms from their wealth, that they may thereby be cleansed and purified, and pray for them: for your prayers will give them comfort. God hears all and knows all.

Do they know not that God accepts repentance from His servants and welcomes alms, and that God pardons and is compassionate?

Say: 'Act as you will. God will behold your actions, and so will His apostle and the faithful; then shall you return to Him who knows alike the unknown and the manifest, and He will declare to you what you have done.'

9:106 And there are yet others who must await God's decree. He will either punish them or pardon them: God is all-knowing and wise.

وَالسَّابِقُونَ الْأَوَّلُونَ مِنَ الْمُهَاجِرِينَ وَالْأَنْصَارِ وَالَّذِينَ
اتَّبَعُوهُمْ بِإِحْسَانٍ رَضِيَ اللَّهُ عَنْهُمْ وَرَضُوا عَنْهُ وَأَعَدَّ لَهُمْ
جَنَّاتٍ تَجْرِي تَحْتَهَا الْأَنْهَارُ خَالِدِينَ فِيهَا أَبَدًا ذَٰلِكَ الْفَوْزُ
الْعَظِيمُ ﴿١٠٠﴾ وَمِمَّنْ حَوْلَكُمْ مِنَ الْأَعْرَابِ مُنَافِقُونَ
وَمِنْ أَهْلِ الْمَدِينَةِ مَرَدُوا عَلَى النِّفَاقِ لَا تَعْلَمُهُمْ نَحْنُ نَعْلَمُهُمْ
سَنُعَذِّبُهُمْ مَرَّتَيْنِ ثُمَّ يُرَدُّونَ إِلَىٰ عَذَابٍ عَظِيمٍ ﴿١٠١﴾ وَآخَرُونَ
اعْتَرَفُوا بِذُنُوبِهِمْ خَلَطُوا عَمَلًا صَالِحًا وَآخَرَ سَيِّئًا عَسَى اللَّهُ
أَنْ يَتُوبَ عَلَيْهِمْ إِنَّ اللَّهَ غَفُورٌ رَحِيمٌ ﴿١٠٢﴾ خُذْ مِنْ أَمْوَالِهِمْ
صَدَقَةً تُطَهِّرُهُمْ وَتُزَكِّيهِمْ بِهَا وَصَلِّ عَلَيْهِمْ إِنَّ صَلَاتَكَ
سَكَنٌ لَهُمْ وَاللَّهُ سَمِيعٌ عَلِيمٌ ﴿١٠٣﴾ أَلَمْ يَعْلَمُوا أَنَّ اللَّهَ
هُوَ يَقْبَلُ التَّوْبَةَ عَنْ عِبَادِهِ وَيَأْخُذُ الصَّدَقَاتِ وَأَنَّ اللَّهَ
هُوَ التَّوَّابُ الرَّحِيمُ ﴿١٠٤﴾ وَقُلِ اعْمَلُوا فَسَيَرَى اللَّهُ
عَمَلَكُمْ وَرَسُولُهُ وَالْمُؤْمِنُونَ وَسَتُرَدُّونَ إِلَىٰ عَالِمِ الْغَيْبِ وَ
الشَّهَادَةِ فَيُنَبِّئُكُمْ بِمَا كُنْتُمْ تَعْمَلُونَ ﴿١٠٥﴾ وَآخَرُونَ مُرْجَوْنَ لِأَمْرِ اللَّهِ
إِمَّا يُعَذِّبُهُمْ وَإِمَّا يَتُوبُ عَلَيْهِمْ وَاللَّهُ عَلِيمٌ حَكِيمٌ ﴿١٠٦﴾

1. Muḥammad's early followers who fled with him to Medina.
2. Muḥammad's supporters in Medina.

وَالَّذِينَ اتَّخَذُوا مَسْجِدًا ضِرَارًا وَكُفْرًا وَتَفْرِيقًا بَيْنَ
الْمُؤْمِنِينَ وَإِرْصَادًا لِمَنْ حَارَبَ اللَّهَ وَرَسُولَهُ مِنْ
قَبْلُ وَلَيَحْلِفُنَّ إِنْ أَرَدْنَا إِلَّا الْحُسْنَى وَاللَّهُ يَشْهَدُ إِنَّهُمْ
لَكَاذِبُونَ ١٠٧ لَا تَقُمْ فِيهِ أَبَدًا لَمَسْجِدٌ أُسِّسَ عَلَى التَّقْوَى
مِنْ أَوَّلِ يَوْمٍ أَحَقُّ أَنْ تَقُومَ فِيهِ فِيهِ رِجَالٌ يُحِبُّونَ أَنْ
يَتَطَهَّرُوا وَاللَّهُ يُحِبُّ الْمُطَّهِّرِينَ ١٠٨ أَفَمَنْ أَسَّسَ بُنْيَانَهُ عَلَى
تَقْوَى مِنَ اللَّهِ وَرِضْوَانٍ خَيْرٌ أَمْ مَنْ أَسَّسَ بُنْيَانَهُ عَلَى
شَفَا جُرُفٍ هَارٍ فَانْهَارَ بِهِ فِي نَارِ جَهَنَّمَ وَاللَّهُ لَا يَهْدِي الْقَوْمَ
الظَّالِمِينَ ١٠٩ لَا يَزَالُ بُنْيَانُهُمُ الَّذِي بَنَوْا رِيبَةً فِي
قُلُوبِهِمْ إِلَّا أَنْ تَقَطَّعَ قُلُوبُهُمْ وَاللَّهُ عَلِيمٌ حَكِيمٌ
١١٠ إِنَّ اللَّهَ اشْتَرَى مِنَ الْمُؤْمِنِينَ أَنْفُسَهُمْ وَأَمْوَالَهُمْ
بِأَنَّ لَهُمُ الْجَنَّةَ يُقَاتِلُونَ فِي سَبِيلِ اللَّهِ فَيَقْتُلُونَ
وَيُقْتَلُونَ وَعْدًا عَلَيْهِ حَقًّا فِي التَّوْرَاةِ وَالْإِنْجِيلِ
وَالْقُرْآنِ وَمَنْ أَوْفَى بِعَهْدِهِ مِنَ اللَّهِ فَاسْتَبْشِرُوا
بِبَيْعِكُمُ الَّذِي بَايَعْتُمْ بِهِ وَذَلِكَ هُوَ الْفَوْزُ الْعَظِيمُ ١١١

AND THERE are those who 9:107
built a mosque from mischievous motives, to spread unbelief and disunite the faithful, in expectation of him[1] who had made war on God and His apostle. They swear their intentions were nothing but good, and God bears witness that they are lying. You shall not set foot in it; it is more fitting that you should pray in a mosque founded on piety from the very first, wherein you shall find men who love to keep themselves pure; God loves those that are purified.

Who is a better man, he 9:109
who founds his house on the fear of God and His good pleasure, or he who builds on the brink of a crumbling precipice, so that his house will fall with him into the fire of Hell? God does not guide the wrongdoers.

The edifice they built shall ever inspire their hearts with doubt, until their hearts are cut in pieces. God is all-knowing and wise.

God has purchased from the faithful their lives and worldly goods, and in 9:111
return has promised them the Garden. They will fight for the cause of God, they will slay, and be slain. Such is the true promise He made in the Torah, the Gospel, and the Koran; and who is more true to his pledge than God? Rejoice then in the bargain you have made; that is the supreme triumph.

1. Abū ʿĀmir.

9:112 THOSE THAT repent and those that worship and praise Him; those that fast and those that kneel and prostrate themselves; those that enjoin justice, forbid the reprehensible, and observe God's commandments: proclaim joyful tidings to the faithful.

It is not for the Prophet or the believers to beg forgiveness for idolaters, even though they be related, after it has become manifest to them that they have earned the punishment of Hell. Abraham prayed for his father only to fulfil a promise he had made him. But when he realized he was an enemy of God, he disowned him. Yet Abraham was a compassionate and tenderhearted man.

التائبون العابدون الحامدون السائحون الراكعون
الساجدون الآمرون بالمعروف والناهون عن
المنكر والحافظون لحدود الله وبشر المؤمنين
﴿١١٢﴾ ما كان للنبي والذين آمنوا أن يستغفروا
للمشركين ولو كانوا أولي قربى من بعد ما تبين لهم
أنهم أصحاب الجحيم ﴿١١٣﴾ وما كان استغفار إبراهيم
لأبيه إلا عن موعدة وعدها إياه فلما تبين له أنه عدو
لله تبرأ منه إن إبراهيم لأواه حليم ﴿١١٤﴾ وما كان
الله ليضل قوما بعد إذ هداهم حتى يبين لهم ما يتقون إن
الله بكل شيء عليم ﴿١١٥﴾ إن الله له ملك السماوات
والأرض يحيي ويميت وما لكم من دون
الله من ولي ولا نصير ﴿١١٦﴾ لقد تاب الله على النبي
والمهاجرين والأنصار الذين اتبعوه في ساعة
العسرة من بعد ما كاد يزيغ قلوب فريق منهم
ثم تاب عليهم إنه بهم رءوف رحيم ﴿١١٧﴾

9:115 Nor will God confound men after He has given them guidance until He has manifested to them all that they should avoid; God has knowledge of all things.

God has sovereignty over the heavens and the earth; He ordains life and death. You have none besides God to protect or help you.

9:117 God pardoned the Prophet, the *muhājirīn* and the *anṣār*, who stood by him in the hour of adversity, when some among them were on the point of losing heart. He pardoned them; He took pity on them and was compassionate.

وَعَلَى الثَّلَاثَةِ الَّذِينَ خُلِّفُوا حَتَّىٰ إِذَا ضَاقَتْ عَلَيْهِمُ الْأَرْضُ بِمَا رَحُبَتْ
وَضَاقَتْ عَلَيْهِمْ أَنفُسُهُمْ وَظَنُّوا أَن لَّا مَلْجَأَ مِنَ اللَّهِ إِلَّا إِلَيْهِ ثُمَّ
تَابَ عَلَيْهِمْ لِيَتُوبُوا ۚ إِنَّ اللَّهَ هُوَ التَّوَّابُ الرَّحِيمُ ﴿١١٨﴾ يَا أَيُّهَا
الَّذِينَ آمَنُوا اتَّقُوا اللَّهَ وَكُونُوا مَعَ الصَّادِقِينَ ﴿١١٩﴾
مَا كَانَ لِأَهْلِ الْمَدِينَةِ وَمَنْ حَوْلَهُم مِّنَ الْأَعْرَابِ أَن
يَتَخَلَّفُوا عَن رَّسُولِ اللَّهِ وَلَا يَرْغَبُوا بِأَنفُسِهِمْ عَن
نَّفْسِهِ ۚ ذَٰلِكَ بِأَنَّهُمْ لَا يُصِيبُهُمْ ظَمَأٌ وَلَا نَصَبٌ
وَلَا مَخْمَصَةٌ فِي سَبِيلِ اللَّهِ وَلَا يَطَئُونَ مَوْطِئًا يَغِيظُ
الْكُفَّارَ وَلَا يَنَالُونَ مِنْ عَدُوٍّ نَّيْلًا إِلَّا كُتِبَ
لَهُم بِهِ عَمَلٌ صَالِحٌ ۚ إِنَّ اللَّهَ لَا يُضِيعُ أَجْرَ الْمُحْسِنِينَ ﴿١٢٠﴾ وَلَا
يُنفِقُونَ نَفَقَةً صَغِيرَةً وَلَا كَبِيرَةً وَلَا يَقْطَعُونَ وَادِيًا
إِلَّا كُتِبَ لَهُمْ لِيَجْزِيَهُمُ اللَّهُ أَحْسَنَ مَا كَانُوا يَعْمَلُونَ ﴿١٢١﴾
وَمَا كَانَ الْمُؤْمِنُونَ لِيَنفِرُوا كَافَّةً ۚ فَلَوْلَا نَفَرَ مِن كُلِّ
فِرْقَةٍ مِّنْهُمْ طَائِفَةٌ لِّيَتَفَقَّهُوا فِي الدِّينِ وَلِيُنذِرُوا
قَوْمَهُمْ إِذَا رَجَعُوا إِلَيْهِمْ لَعَلَّهُمْ يَحْذَرُونَ ﴿١٢٢﴾

AND TO the three who had 9:118
been left behind. So despondent were they that the earth, for all its vastness, and their own souls, seemed to close in upon them. They knew there was no refuge from God except in Him. Therefore He pardoned them, that they might repent: God pardons and is compassionate.

You believers, fear God and stand firm with those who
uphold the cause of Truth. No 9:120
cause have the people of Madīnah and the desert Arabs around them to forsake God's apostle or to jeopardize his life so as to safeguard their own; for they do not expose themselves to thirst or hunger or to any ordeal in the cause of God, nor do they take any step which may displease the unbelievers, nor do they inflict any loss on an enemy but it shall be noted down for them as a good deed: God will not deny the righteous their reward. Each sum they give, be it small or large, and each valley they traverse, shall be noted down, so that God may requite them for their noblest deeds.

It is not right that all the faithful should go to war at once. A band from 9:122
each community should stay behind to instruct themselves in the Religion and to admonish their people when they return, so that they may be warned.

9:123 BELIEVERS, FIGHT the infidels who dwell around you. Deal firmly with them; and know that God is with those that fear Him.

Whenever a *sūrah* is revealed, some among them ask: 'Which of you has had his faith increased by this?' It will surely increase the believers' faith and give them joy. As for those whose hearts are tainted, it will add abomination to their abomination, so that they shall die while still in unbelief.

9:126 Do they not see how every year they were afflicted once or twice? Yet they neither repent nor take warning. And whenever a *sūrah* is revealed, they glance at each other, asking: 'Is anyone watching you?' Then they turn away. God has turned away their hearts, for they are senseless people.

There has now come to you an apostle of your own, one who grieves at your sinfulness and cares for you; one who is benevolent and compassionate to the believers.

9:129 If they pay no heed, say: 'All-sufficient is God for me. There is no god but Him; in Him I have put my trust. And He is the Lord of the Glorious Throne.'

يا أيها الذين آمنوا قاتلوا الذين يلونكم من الكفار
وليجدوا فيكم غلظة واعلموا أن الله مع المتقين ١٢٣
وإذا ما أنزلت سورة فمنهم من يقول أيكم زادته هذه
إيمانا فأما الذين آمنوا فزادتهم إيمانا وهم يستبشرون
١٢٤ وأما الذين في قلوبهم مرض فزادتهم رجسا إلى
رجسهم وماتوا وهم كافرون ١٢٥ أولا يرون أنهم
يفتنون في كل عام مرة أو مرتين ثم لا يتوبون ولا هم
يذكرون ١٢٦ وإذا ما أنزلت سورة نظر بعضهم إلى بعض
هل يراكم من أحد ثم انصرفوا صرف الله قلوبهم بأنهم
قوم لا يفقهون ١٢٧ لقد جاءكم رسول من أنفسكم
عزيز عليه ما عنتم حريص عليكم بالمؤمنين رءوف
رحيم ١٢٨ فإن تولوا فقل حسبي الله لا إله إلا هو
عليه توكلت وهو رب العرش العظيم ١٢٩

سورة يونس مكية وهي مائة وتسع آيات

بسم الله الرحمن الرحيم
الر تلك آيات الكتاب الحكيم (١) أكان للناس عجبا
أن أوحينا إلى رجل منهم أن أنذر الناس وبشر الذين
آمنوا أن لهم قدم صدق عند ربهم قال الكافرون
إن هذا لساحر مبين (٢) إن ربكم الله الذي خلق
السموات والأرض في ستة أيام ثم استوى على العرش يدبر الأمر
ما من شفيع إلا من بعد إذنه ذلكم الله ربكم فاعبدوه أفلا
تذكرون (٣) إليه مرجعكم جميعا وعد الله حقا إنه يبدؤا
الخلق ثم يعيده ليجزي الذين آمنوا وعملوا الصالحات
بالقسط والذين كفروا لهم شراب من حميم وعذاب أليم
بما كانوا يكفرون (٤) هو الذي جعل الشمس ضياء والقمر
نورا وقدره منازل لتعلموا عدد السنين والحساب ما خلق
الله ذلك إلا بالحق يفصل الآيات لقوم يعلمون
(٥) إن في اختلاف الليل والنهار وما خلق
الله في السموات والأرض لآيات لقوم يتقون (٦)

JONAH

In the Name of God,
the Merciful, the Compassionate

ALIF *lām rā'*. These are the 10:1
revelations of the Wise Book: Does it seem strange to people that We revealed Our will to a mortal from among themselves, saying: 'Give warning to the people, and proclaim joyful tidings to the faithful that they may have a tried and true footing with their Lord'?

The unbelievers say: 'This man[1] is a sorcerer manifest.' Yet your Lord is God, who in six days created the heavens and the earth and then ascended the throne, ordaining all things. None has power to intercede without His sanction. Such is God, your Lord: therefore serve Him. Will you not reflect?

To Him shall you all return: God's promise shall be fulfilled. He brings the 10:4
Creation into being and will then restore it, so that He may justly recompense those who have believed and done good works. As for the unbelievers, scalding water shall they drink, and for their unbelief woeful punishment awaits them.

It was He that gave the sun his brightness and the moon her light, ordaining her phases that you may learn to compute the seasons and the years.[2] God created them only to manifest the Truth. He expounds His revelations to those endowed with knowledge.

In the alternation of night and day, and in all that God has created in the 10:6
heavens and the earth, there are signs for the God-fearing.

1. Muḥammad. 2. Cf. Genesis 1:14.

10:7 THOSE WHO entertain no hope of meeting Us, being pleased and contented with the life of this world, and those who pay no heed to Our revelations, shall have the Fire as their abode in requital for their deeds.

As for those that believe and do good works, their Lord will guide them through their faith. Brooks will run at their feet in the Gardens of Delight. Their prayer will be: 'Glory be to You, Lord!' and their greeting: 'Peace!' 'Praise be to God, Lord of the Universe' will be the burthen of their plea.

10:11 Had God hastened what is ill for people as they would hasten what is good, their fate would have been sealed. Therefore We leave those who entertain no hope of meeting Us to their wrongdoing, ever straying from the right path.

When misfortune befalls man, he prays to Us lying on his side, sitting, or standing on his feet. But as soon as We relieve his affliction he carries on, as though he never prayed to Us to relieve the misfortune that touched him. Thus do their deeds seem fair to the transgressors.

We obliterated generations before you on account of the wrongs they did;
their apostles had come to them with veritable signs, but they would not
10:14 believe. Thus do We requite the transgressors. We then made you their successors in the land, so that We might observe how you would act.

إن الذين لا يرجون لقاءنا ورضوا بالحيوة الدنيا واطمأنوا
بها والذين هم عن آياتنا غافلون ٧ أولئك مأويهم
النار بما كانوا يكسبون ٨ إن الذين آمنوا وعملوا
الصالحات يهديهم ربهم بإيمانهم تجري من تحتهم
الأنهار في جنات النعيم ٩ دعويهم فيها سبحانك اللهم
وتحيتهم فيها سلام وآخر دعويهم أن الحمد لله رب
العالمين ١٠ ولو يعجل الله للناس الشر استعجالهم بالخير
لقضي إليهم أجلهم فنذر الذين لا يرجون لقاءنا في
طغيانهم يعمهون ١١ وإذا مس الإنسان الضر دعانا
لجنبه أو قاعدا أو قائما فلما كشفنا عنه ضره
مر كأن لم يدعنا إلى ضر مسه كذلك زين للمسرفين
ما كانوا يعملون ١٢ ولقد أهلكنا القرون من قبلكم
لما ظلموا وجاءتهم رسلهم بالبينات وما كانوا ليؤمنوا
كذلك نجزي القوم المجرمين ١٣ ثم جعلناكم خلائف
في الأرض من بعدهم لننظر كيف تعملون ١٤

وإذا تتلى عليهم آياتنا بينات قال الذين
لا يرجون لقاءنا ائت بقرآن غير هذا أو بدله قل ما
يكون لي أن أبدله من تلقاي نفسي إن أتبع إلا ما يوحى
إلي إني أخاف إن عصيت ربي عذاب يوم عظيم ﴿١٥﴾ قل لو
شاء الله ما تلوته عليكم ولا أدراكم به فقد
لبثت فيكم عمرا من قبله أفلا تعقلون ﴿١٦﴾ فمن
أظلم ممن افترى على الله كذبا أو كذب بآياته إنه
لا يفلح المجرمون ﴿١٧﴾ ويعبدون من دون الله ما لا
يضرهم ولا ينفعهم ويقولون هؤلاء شفعاؤنا
عند الله قل أتنبئون الله بما لا يعلم في السموات
ولا في الأرض سبحانه وتعالى عما يشركون ﴿١٨﴾
وما كان الناس إلا أمة واحدة فاختلفوا ولولا
كلمة سبقت من ربك لقضي بينهم فيما فيه
يختلفون ﴿١٩﴾ ويقولون لولا أنزل عليه آية من ربه فقل إنما
الغيب لله فانتظروا إني معكم من المنتظرين ﴿٢٠﴾

WHEN OUR clear revela- 10:15
tions are recited to them, those who entertain no hope of meeting Us say to you: 'Give us a Koran different from this, or change it.'

Say: 'It is not for me to change it, of my own accord. I follow only what is revealed to me, for I fear, if I disobey my Lord, the punishment of a fateful day.'

Say: 'Had God pleased, I would never have recited it to you, nor would He have made you aware of it. A whole lifetime I dwelt among you before its coming. Will you not understand?'

Who is more wicked than he who invents a falsehood about God or denies His revelations? Truly, the transgressors shall not succeed.

They worship idols that can neither harm nor help them, and say: 'These 10:18
will intercede for us with God.'

Say: 'Do you presume to tell God of what He knows to exist neither in the heavens nor on earth?' Glory be to Him! Exalted be He above the gods they serve besides Him!

There was a time when mankind were but one community. Then they disagreed among themselves: and but for a Word from your Lord, long since decreed, their differences would have been surely resolved.

And they say: 'Why has no sign been sent down to him from his Lord?' 10:20

Say: 'God alone has knowledge of what is hidden. Wait if you will: I will wait with you.'

10:21 NO SOONER do We let people taste a blessing after some misfortune has afflicted them than they begin to scheme against Our revelations. Say: 'More swift is God's scheming. Our emissaries are recording your intrigues.'

He it is who guides them by land and sea. They embark: and as the ships set sail, rejoicing in a favourable wind, a raging tempest overtakes them. Billows surge upon them from every side and they fear they are encompassed by death. They call out to God, fervently dedicating all religion to Him: 'Deliver us from this peril and we will be truly thankful.'

10:23 Yet when He does deliver them, they perpetrate corruption in the land and act unjustly.

You people! It is your own souls that you are corrupting. Take your enjoyment in this life: to Us shall you then return, and We will declare to you all that you have done.

This present life is like the rich garment with which the earth adorns itself when watered by the rain We send down from the sky. Crops, sustaining man and beast, grow luxuriantly: but, as the earth's tenants begin to think themselves its masters, down comes Our scourge upon it, by night or by day, laying it waste, as though it did not blossom but yesterday. Thus do We expound Our revelations to people who reflect.

10:25 God invites you to the Abode of Peace; He guides whom He will to a straight path.

وإذا أذقنا الناس رحمة من بعد ضراء مستهم إذا لهم
مكر في آياتنا قل الله أسرع مكرا إن رسلنا يكتبون
ما تمكرون ﴿٢١﴾ هو الذي يسيركم في البر والبحر حتى إذا كنتم
في الفلك وجرين بهم بريح طيبة وفرحوا بها جاءتها ريح
عاصف وجاءهم الموج من كل مكان وظنوا أنهم
أحيط بهم دعوا الله مخلصين له الدين لئن أنجيتنا من
هذه لنكونن من الشاكرين ﴿٢٢﴾ فلما أنجاهم إذا هم يبغون في
الأرض بغير الحق يا أيها الناس إنما بغيكم على أنفسكم متاع
الحيوة الدنيا ثم إلينا مرجعكم فننبئكم بما كنتم تعملون ﴿٢٣﴾
إنما مثل الحيوة الدنيا كماء أنزلناه من السماء فاختلط به نبات
الأرض مما يأكل الناس والأنعام حتى إذا أخذت الأرض
زخرفها وازينت وظن أهلها أنهم قادرون عليها
أتاها أمرنا ليلا أو نهارا فجعلناها حصيدا كأن لم تغن
بالأمس كذلك نفصل الآيات لقوم يتفكرون ﴿٢٤﴾ والله
يدعوا إلى دار السلام ويهدي من يشاء إلى صراط مستقيم ﴿٢٥﴾

لِلَّذِينَ أَحْسَنُوا الْحُسْنَىٰ وَزِيَادَةٌ ۖ وَلَا يَرْهَقُ وُجُوهَهُمْ قَتَرٌ
وَلَا ذِلَّةٌ ۚ أُولَٰئِكَ أَصْحَابُ الْجَنَّةِ ۖ هُمْ فِيهَا خَالِدُونَ ﴿٢٦﴾ وَالَّذِينَ
كَسَبُوا السَّيِّئَاتِ جَزَاءُ سَيِّئَةٍ بِمِثْلِهَا وَتَرْهَقُهُمْ
ذِلَّةٌ ۖ مَا لَهُم مِّنَ اللَّهِ مِنْ عَاصِمٍ ۖ كَأَنَّمَا أُغْشِيَتْ وُجُوهُهُمْ
قِطَعًا مِّنَ اللَّيْلِ مُظْلِمًا ۚ أُولَٰئِكَ أَصْحَابُ النَّارِ ۖ هُمْ فِيهَا خَالِدُونَ ﴿٢٧﴾
وَيَوْمَ نَحْشُرُهُمْ جَمِيعًا ثُمَّ نَقُولُ لِلَّذِينَ أَشْرَكُوا مَكَانَكُمْ أَنتُمْ
وَشُرَكَاؤُكُمْ ۚ فَزَيَّلْنَا بَيْنَهُمْ ۖ وَقَالَ شُرَكَاؤُهُم مَّا كُنتُمْ إِيَّانَا
تَعْبُدُونَ ﴿٢٨﴾ فَكَفَىٰ بِاللَّهِ شَهِيدًا بَيْنَنَا وَبَيْنَكُمْ إِن كُنَّا
عَنْ عِبَادَتِكُمْ لَغَافِلِينَ ﴿٢٩﴾ هُنَالِكَ تَبْلُو كُلُّ نَفْسٍ مَّا
أَسْلَفَتْ ۚ وَرُدُّوا إِلَى اللَّهِ مَوْلَاهُمُ الْحَقِّ ۖ وَضَلَّ عَنْهُم مَّا كَانُوا يَفْتَرُونَ
﴿٣٠﴾ قُلْ مَن يَرْزُقُكُم مِّنَ السَّمَاءِ وَالْأَرْضِ أَمَّن يَمْلِكُ السَّمْعَ وَالْأَبْصَارَ
وَمَن يُخْرِجُ الْحَيَّ مِنَ الْمَيِّتِ وَيُخْرِجُ الْمَيِّتَ مِنَ الْحَيِّ وَمَن يُدَبِّرُ
الْأَمْرَ ۚ فَسَيَقُولُونَ اللَّهُ ۚ فَقُلْ أَفَلَا تَتَّقُونَ ﴿٣١﴾ فَذَٰلِكُمُ
اللَّهُ رَبُّكُمُ الْحَقُّ ۖ فَمَاذَا بَعْدَ الْحَقِّ إِلَّا الضَّلَالُ ۖ فَأَنَّىٰ تُصْرَفُونَ ﴿٣٢﴾
كَذَٰلِكَ حَقَّتْ كَلِمَتُ رَبِّكَ عَلَى الَّذِينَ فَسَقُوا أَنَّهُمْ لَا يُؤْمِنُونَ ﴿٣٣﴾

THOSE THAT have done good 10:26
works shall have a good recompense, and more besides. Neither blackness nor misery shall overcast their faces. They are the heirs of Paradise, wherein shall they abide for ever.

As for those that have done evil, evil shall be requited with like evil. Misery will oppress them (they shall have none to protect them from God), as though patches of the night's own darkness veiled their faces. These shall be the tenants of the Fire, wherein shall they abide for ever.

And on the day We herd them all together, We shall say to the idolaters: 'Keep to your places, you and your idols!' We will separate them one from
another, and then their idols will say to them: 'It was not us that you wor-
shipped. Sufficient is God as our witness, and your witness. Nor were we 10:29
aware of your worship.'

Thereupon each soul will know what it did in days gone by. They shall be sent back to God, their true Lord, and the idols they invented will forsake them.

Say: 'Who provides for you from heaven and earth? Who has endowed you with hearing and sight? Who brings forth the living from the dead, and the dead from the living? Who ordains all things?'

They will say: 'God.'

Say: 'Will you not take heed, then? Such is God, your true Lord. That which is not true must needs be false. How then can you turn away?'

Thus is the Word of your Lord made true about the ungodly; they will not 10:33
believe.

قل هل من شركائكم من يبدأ الخلق ثم يعيده قل الله
يبدأ الخلق ثم يعيده فأنى تؤفكون ٣٤ قل هل من شركائكم
من يهدي إلى الحق قل الله يهدي للحق أفمن يهدي إلى
الحق أحق أن يتبع أمن لا يهدي إلا أن يهدى فما لكم
كيف تحكمون ٣٥ وما يتبع أكثرهم إلا ظنا إن الظن
لا يغني من الحق شيئا إن الله عليم بما يفعلون ٣٦ وما كان
هذا القرآن أن يفترى من دون الله ولكن تصديق الذي
بين يديه وتفصيل الكتاب لا ريب فيه من رب العالمين ٣٧ أم يقولون
افتراه قل فأتوا بسورة مثله وادعوا من استطعتم من دون الله
إن كنتم صادقين ٣٨ بل كذبوا بما لم يحيطوا بعلمه ولما يأتهم
تأويله كذلك كذب الذين من قبلهم فانظر كيف كان عاقبة
الظالمين ٣٩ ومنهم من يؤمن به ومنهم من لا يؤمن به وربك
أعلم بالمفسدين ٤٠ وإن كذبوك فقل لي عملي ولكم عملكم
أنتم بريئون مما أعمل وأنا بريء مما تعملون ٤١ ومنهم من
يستمعون إليك أفأنت تسمع الصم ولو كانوا لا يعقلون ٤٢

10:34 SAY: 'CAN any of your idols
bring the Creation into being
and then restore it?' Say: 'God
brings the Creation into being
and will then restore it. How is
it that you are so misled?'
Say: 'Can any of your idols
give guidance to the Truth?'
Say: 'God gives guidance to
the Truth. Who is more worthy to be followed: He that
can give guidance to the Truth,
or he that cannot and is himself in need of guidance?
What has come over you that
you so judge?'
Most of them follow noth-
ing but mere conjecture. But
conjecture is in no way a substitute for Truth. God is
cognizant of what they do.
This Koran could not have
been devised by any but God.
Indeed, its confirmation of what was revealed before it, and its expounding
of the Book, are beyond doubt from the Lord of the Universe.
10:38 If they say: 'He invented it himself,' say: 'Bring one *sūrah* like it. Call on
whom you will besides God to help you, if what you say be true!'
Indeed, they disbelieve what they cannot grasp, for they have not yet seen
its prophecy fulfilled. Likewise did those before them disbelieve. But see
what was the fate of the wrongdoers.
Some among them believe in it, and some among them do not believe in
it. But your Lord best knows the evil-doers.
If they disbelieve you, say: 'My deeds are mine and your deeds are yours.
You are not accountable for my actions, nor am I accountable for what
you do.'
10:42 Some among them listen to you. But can you make the deaf hear you,
incapable as they are of understanding?

ومنهم من ينظر إليك أفأنت تهدي العمي ولو كانوا
لا يبصرون ﴿٤٣﴾ إن الله لا يظلم الناس شيئا ولكن الناس
أنفسهم يظلمون ﴿٤٤﴾ ويوم يحشرهم كأن لم يلبثوا إلا ساعة
من النهار يتعارفون بينهم قد خسر الذين كذبوا بلقاء الله
وما كانوا مهتدين ﴿٤٥﴾ وإما نرينك بعض الذي نعدهم أو نتوفينك
فإلينا مرجعهم ثم الله شهيد على ما يفعلون ﴿٤٦﴾ ولكل
أمة رسول فإذا جاء رسولهم قضي بينهم بالقسط وهم
لا يظلمون ﴿٤٧﴾ ويقولون متى هذا الوعد إن كنتم صادقين
﴿٤٨﴾ قل لا أملك لنفسي ضرا ولا نفعا إلا ما شاء الله
لكل أمة أجل إذا جاء أجلهم فلا يستأخرون ساعة
ولا يستقدمون ﴿٤٩﴾ قل أرأيتم إن أتاكم عذابه بياتا أو نهارا ماذا
يستعجل منه المجرمون ﴿٥٠﴾ أثم إذا ما وقع آمنتم به آلآن وقد
كنتم به تستعجلون ﴿٥١﴾ ثم قيل للذين ظلموا ذوقوا عذاب
الخلد هل تجزون إلا بما كنتم تكسبون ﴿٥٢﴾ ويستنبئونك
أحق هو قل إي وربي إنه لحق وما أنتم بمعجزين ﴿٥٣﴾

SOME AMONG them look upon you; but can you show the way to the blind, bereft as they are of sight? 10:43

Indeed, in no way does God wrong people, but people wrong themselves.

The day He herds them all together, as though they had lingered but for an hour, they will acquaint themselves with each other and realize they shall lose out: those who denied they would ever meet God and did not follow the right path.

Whether We show you but some of the torment We threaten them with, or claim you back to Us before that, to Us they shall return, and God will then be witness to all their actions.

Each community has its own apostle. When their apostle comes, justice is 10:47
done among them; they are not wronged.

They say: 'When will this promise be fulfilled, if what you say be true?'

Say: 'I have no control over any harm or benefit to myself, except by the will of God. A space of time is fixed for each community; when their time is come, not for one hour shall they delay: nor can they go before it.'

Say: 'Do but consider. Should His scourge fall upon you in the night or by the light of day, what punishment would the guilty hasten? Will you believe in it when it does overtake you, although it was your wish to hurry it on?'

Then will the wrongdoers be told: 'Feel the everlasting torment! Shall you not be rewarded according only to what you have earned?'

And they ask you if it is true. Say: 'Yes, by the Lord, it is certainly true! 10:53
And you shall not escape.'

10:54 To REDEEM itself then, each soul would gladly give all that the earth contains if it possessed it. They will rue in secret when they behold the scourge; but judgement shall be fairly passed upon them; they shall not be wronged.

Surely to God belongs all that the heavens and the earth contain. Surely the promise of God is true, but most of them have no knowledge. He it is who ordains life and death, and to Him shall you be recalled.

You people! An Admonition has come to you from your Lord, a cure for the mind, a guide and a blessing to the believers.

10:58 Say: 'In God's grace and mercy let them rejoice, for these are better than the worldly riches they amass.'

Say: 'Do but consider the provision God has sent down for you. Some of it you pronounced unlawful and some, lawful.' Say: 'Was it God who gave you leave, or do you invent falsehood about God?'

What will they think, those who invent falsehood about God, on the Day of Resurrection? God is bountiful to mankind: yet most of them do not give thanks.

10:61 You shall engage in no affair, you shall recite no verse from the Koran, you shall commit no act, but We shall be witnesses over you when you engage in it. Not an atom's weight in earth or heaven escapes your Lord, nor is there any object smaller or greater, but is recorded in a veritable Book.

ولو أن لكل نفس ظلمت ما في الأرض لافتدت به وأسروا
الندامة لما رأوا العذاب وقضي بينهم بالقسط وهم
لا يظلمون ﴿٥٤﴾ ألا إن لله ما في السموات والأرض ألا إن
وعد الله حق ولكن أكثرهم لا يعلمون ﴿٥٥﴾ هو يحيي ويميت
وإليه ترجعون ﴿٥٦﴾ يا أيها الناس قد جاءتكم موعظة
من ربكم وشفاء لما في الصدور وهدى ورحمة للمؤمنين ﴿٥٧﴾ قل
بفضل الله وبرحمته فبذلك فليفرحوا هو خير مما يجمعون ﴿٥٨﴾
قل أرأيتم ما أنزل الله لكم من رزق فجعلتم
منه حراما وحلالا قل آلله أذن لكم أم على الله
تفترون ﴿٥٩﴾ وما ظن الذين يفترون على الله
الكذب يوم القيامة إن الله لذو فضل على الناس ولكن
أكثرهم لا يشكرون ﴿٦٠﴾ وما تكون في شأن وما تتلو منه من
قرآن ولا تعملون من عمل إلا كنا عليكم شهودا إذ تفيضون
فيه وما يعزب عن ربك من مثقال ذرة في الأرض ولا في
السماء ولا أصغر من ذلك ولا أكبر إلا في كتاب مبين ﴿٦١﴾

ألا إن أولياء الله لا خوف عليهم ولا هم يحزنون
٦٢ الذين ءامنوا وكانوا يتقون ٦٣ لهم البشرى في
الحيوة الدنيا وفي الآخرة لا تبديل لكلمات الله
ذلك هو الفوز العظيم ٦٤ ولا يحزنك قولهم
إن العزة لله جميعا هو السميع العليم ٦٥ ألا إن لله
من في السموات ومن في الأرض وما يتبع الذين
يدعون من دون الله شركاء إن يتبعون إلا الظن
وإن هم إلا يخرصون ٦٦ هو الذي جعل لكم
اليل لتسكنوا فيه والنهار مبصرا إن في
ذلك لآيات لقوم يسمعون ٦٧ قالوا اتخذ الله
ولدا سبحانه هو الغني له ما في السموات وما في
الأرض إن عندكم من سلطان بهذا أتقولون على الله
ما لا تعلمون ٦٨ قل إن الذين يفترون على الله
الكذب لا يفلحون ٦٩ متاع في الدنيا ثم إلينا مرجعهم
ثم نذيقهم العذاب الشديد بما كانوا يكفرون ٧٠

BUT SURELY the servants 10:62
of God have nothing to fear or to regret. Those that have faith and fear Him shall rejoice both in this life and in the life to come: the words of God shall never change. That is the supreme triumph.

Let not their words grieve you. All glory belongs to God; He it is who hears all and knows all.

Surely to God belong all who are in the heavens and all who are on the earth. Those that follow what they call gods besides God follow nothing but idle fancies and preach nothing but falsehoods.

He it is who has ordained 10:67
the night for you to rest in and given the day its light for you to see with. Surely in this there are signs for attentive people.

They say: 'God has begotten a son.' Glory be to Him! Self-sufficient is He. His is all that the heavens and the earth contain. Have you any sanction for this? Would you say of God what you know not?

Say: 'Those that invent falsehood about God shall not succeed. They may 10:70
take their ease in this life, but to Us they shall then return, and for their unbelief We will make them taste the grievous torment.'

10:71 AND RECOUNT to them the tale of Noah. He said to his people: 'If it offends you, my people, that I should dwell in your midst and preach to you God's revelations (for in God I have put my trust), muster all your idols and decide on your course of action. Do not intrigue in secret. Execute your judgement and give me no respite. If you turn away, remember I demand of you no recompense. Only God will reward me. I am commanded to be a Muslim.'

But they disbelieved him. Therefore We saved him and those who were with him in the ark, so that they survived, and drowned those that denied Our revelations. Consider, then, the fate of those who were forewarned.

10:74 After him We sent apostles to their descendants. They brought them veritable signs, but they would not have faith in what they disbelieved before. Thus do We seal up the hearts of the transgressors.

Then We sent forth after them Moses and Aaron with Our signs to Pharaoh and his nobles. But they responded with scorn, for they were wicked people. And when the Truth had come to them from Us, they declared: 'Surely this is but sorcery manifest.'

Moses replied: 'Is this what you say of the Truth when it has come to you? Is this sorcery? Sorcerers shall never succeed.'

10:78 They said: 'Have you come to turn us away from the faith of our forefathers, that you two may lord it over the land? We will never believe in the pair of you.'

وَاتْلُ عَلَيْهِمْ نَبَأَ نُوحٍ إِذْ قَالَ لِقَوْمِهِ يَا قَوْمِ إِنْ كَانَ كَبُرَ
عَلَيْكُمْ مَقَامِي وَتَذْكِيرِي بِآيَاتِ اللَّهِ فَعَلَى اللَّهِ تَوَكَّلْتُ
فَأَجْمِعُوا أَمْرَكُمْ وَشُرَكَاءَكُمْ ثُمَّ لَا يَكُنْ أَمْرُكُمْ
عَلَيْكُمْ غُمَّةً ثُمَّ اقْضُوا إِلَيَّ وَلَا تُنْظِرُونِ ﴿٧١﴾ فَإِنْ تَوَلَّيْتُمْ
فَمَا سَأَلْتُكُمْ مِنْ أَجْرٍ إِنْ أَجْرِيَ إِلَّا عَلَى اللَّهِ وَأُمِرْتُ
أَنْ أَكُونَ مِنَ الْمُسْلِمِينَ ﴿٧٢﴾ فَكَذَّبُوهُ فَنَجَّيْنَاهُ وَمَنْ مَعَهُ
فِي الْفُلْكِ وَجَعَلْنَاهُمْ خَلَائِفَ وَأَغْرَقْنَا الَّذِينَ كَذَّبُوا بِآيَاتِنَا
فَانْظُرْ كَيْفَ كَانَ عَاقِبَةُ الْمُنْذَرِينَ ﴿٧٣﴾ ثُمَّ بَعَثْنَا مِنْ بَعْدِهِ رُسُلًا
إِلَى قَوْمِهِمْ فَجَاءُوهُمْ بِالْبَيِّنَاتِ فَمَا كَانُوا لِيُؤْمِنُوا بِمَا كَذَّبُوا بِهِ
مِنْ قَبْلُ كَذَلِكَ نَطْبَعُ عَلَى قُلُوبِ الْمُعْتَدِينَ ﴿٧٤﴾ ثُمَّ بَعَثْنَا مِنْ
بَعْدِهِمْ مُوسَى وَهَارُونَ إِلَى فِرْعَوْنَ وَمَلَئِهِ بِآيَاتِنَا فَاسْتَكْبَرُوا
وَكَانُوا قَوْمًا مُجْرِمِينَ ﴿٧٥﴾ فَلَمَّا جَاءَهُمُ الْحَقُّ مِنْ عِنْدِنَا قَالُوا إِنَّ
هَذَا لَسِحْرٌ مُبِينٌ ﴿٧٦﴾ قَالَ مُوسَى أَتَقُولُونَ لِلْحَقِّ لَمَّا جَاءَكُمْ أَسِحْرٌ هَذَا
وَلَا يُفْلِحُ السَّاحِرُونَ ﴿٧٧﴾ قَالُوا أَجِئْتَنَا لِتَلْفِتَنَا عَمَّا وَجَدْنَا عَلَيْهِ آبَاءَنَا
وَتَكُونَ لَكُمَا الْكِبْرِيَاءُ فِي الْأَرْضِ وَمَا نَحْنُ لَكُمَا بِمُؤْمِنِينَ ﴿٧٨﴾

وقال فرعون ائتوني بكل ساحر عليم ﴿٧٩﴾ فلما جاء
السحرة قال لهم موسى ألقوا ما أنتم ملقون ﴿٨٠﴾ فلما
ألقوا قال موسى ما جئتم به السحر إن الله سيبطله إن
الله لا يصلح عمل المفسدين ﴿٨١﴾ ويحق الله الحق بكلماته
ولو كره المجرمون ﴿٨٢﴾ فما آمن لموسى إلا ذرية من قومه على
خوف من فرعون وملإيهم أن يفتنهم وإن فرعون لعال في
الأرض وإنه لمن المسرفين ﴿٨٣﴾ وقال موسى يا قوم إن كنتم آمنتم
بالله فعليه توكلوا إن كنتم مسلمين ﴿٨٤﴾ فقالوا على
الله توكلنا ربنا لا تجعلنا فتنة للقوم الظالمين ﴿٨٥﴾
ونجنا برحمتك من القوم الكافرين ﴿٨٦﴾ وأوحينا إلى موسى
وأخيه أن تبوآ لقومكما بمصر بيوتا واجعلوا بيوتكم
قبلة وأقيموا الصلوة وبشر المؤمنين ﴿٨٧﴾ وقال موسى ربنا
إنك آتيت فرعون وملأه زينة وأموالا في الحيوة الدنيا ربنا
ليضلوا عن سبيلك ربنا اطمس على أموالهم واشدد على
قلوبهم فلا يؤمنوا حتى يروا العذاب الأليم ﴿٨٨﴾

AND PHARAOH said: 'Bring 10:79
every learned sorcerer to my
presence.'

And when the sorcerers attended, Moses said to them: 'Throw down what you wish to throw.' And when they had thrown, Moses said: 'The sorcery that you have wrought, God will surely bring to nothing. God does not make good the work of those who do evil. By His words God vindicates the Truth, averse to it though the transgressors may be.'

Few of his[1] people believed in Moses, for they feared the persecution of Pharaoh and his nobles. Surely Pharaoh was a tyrant in the land, a man of rampant wickedness.

Moses said: 'If you believe in 10:84
God, my people, in Him alone then put your trust if you are Muslims.'

They replied: 'In God we have put our trust. Lord, do not let us suffer at the hands of the wrongdoers. Deliver us, through Your mercy, from the unbelievers.'

We revealed Our will to Moses and his brother, saying: 'Build houses in Egypt for your people and make your homes places of worship. Conduct prayers and give good tidings to the faithful.'

'Lord,' said Moses, 'You have bestowed on Pharaoh and his nobles splen- 10:88
dour and riches in this life, Lord, so that they may stray from Your path.
Lord, wipe out their riches and harden their hearts, so that they shall persist
in unbelief until they face the woeful scourge.'

1. Pharaoh's.

10:89 HE SAID: 'Your prayer shall
be answered. Follow, both of
you, the straight path and do
not walk in the footsteps of
those that have no know-
ledge.'
And We led the Israelites
across the sea, and Pharaoh
and his legions pursued them
with wickedness and spite.
But as he was drowning, Pharaoh said: 'Now I believe no
god exists except the One in
whom the Israelites believe. I
am now a Muslim.'
'Only now! But before this
you were a rebel and an evil-
doer. We shall today save your
body, so that you may become
a sign for all posterity: a great
many of mankind do not heed
Our signs.'
10:93 We settled the Israelites in a
secure land and provided them with wholesome things. Nor did they disagree among themselves until knowledge was given them. Your Lord will on
the Day of Resurrection judge their differences.
If you doubt what We have revealed to you, ask those who have read the
Book before you. Truth has come to you from your Lord: therefore do not
doubt it. Nor shall you deny God's revelations, for then you will be one of
the lost.
Those for whom the Word of your Lord shall be fulfilled will not believe,
10:97 even if every sign has come to them, until they face the woeful torment.

قال قد أجيبت دعوتكما فاستقيما ولا تتبعان سبيل
الذين لا يعلمون ﴿٨٩﴾ وجاوزنا ببني إسرائيل البحر فأتبعهم
فرعون وجنوده بغيا وعدوا حتى إذا أدركه الغرق
قال آمنت أنه لا إله إلا الذي آمنت به بنوا إسرائيل وأنا
من المسلمين ﴿٩٠﴾ آلآن وقد عصيت قبل وكنت من المفسدين
﴿٩١﴾ فاليوم ننجيك ببدنك لتكون لمن خلفك آية وإن
كثيرا من الناس عن آياتنا لغافلون ﴿٩٢﴾ ولقد بوأنا
بني إسرائيل مبوأ صدق ورزقناهم من الطيبات فما اختلفوا
حتى جاءهم العلم إن ربك يقضي بينهم يوم القيامة فيما
كانوا فيه يختلفون ﴿٩٣﴾ فإن كنت في شك مما أنزلنا
إليك فسئل الذين يقرءون الكتاب من قبلك لقد
جاءك الحق من ربك فلا تكونن من الممترين ﴿٩٤﴾
ولا تكونن من الذين كذبوا بآيات الله فتكون من
الخاسرين ﴿٩٥﴾ إن الذين حقت عليهم كلمت ربك لا يؤمنون ﴿٩٦﴾
ولو جاءتهم كل آية حتى يروا العذاب الأليم ﴿٩٧﴾

فلولا كانت قرية امنت فنفعها ايمانها الا قوم يونس لما
امنوا كشفنا عنهم عذاب الخزي في الحيوة الدنيا ومتعناهم الى
حين ﴿٩٨﴾ ولو شاء ربك لامن من في الارض كلهم جميعا
افانت تكره الناس حتى يكونوا مؤمنين ﴿٩٩﴾ وما كان لنفس
ان تؤمن الا باذن الله ويجعل الرجس على الذين لا
يعقلون ﴿١٠٠﴾ قل انظروا ماذا في السموات والارض
وما تغني الايات والنذر عن قوم لا يؤمنون ﴿١٠١﴾ فهل
ينتظرون الا مثل ايام الذين خلوا من قبلهم قل
فانتظروا اني معكم من المنتظرين ﴿١٠٢﴾ ثم ننجي رسلنا
والذين امنوا كذلك حقا علينا ننج المؤمنين ﴿١٠٣﴾ قل
يا ايها الناس ان كنتم في شك من ديني فلا اعبد الذين
تعبدون من دون الله ولكن اعبد الله الذي يتوفيكم
وامرت ان اكون من المؤمنين ﴿١٠٤﴾ وان اقم وجهك للدين حنيفا
ولا تكونن من المشركين ﴿١٠٥﴾ ولا تدع من دون الله ما لا ينفعك
ولا يضرك فان فعلت فانك اذا من الظالمين ﴿١٠٦﴾

WERE IT otherwise, every 10:98
community, had it believed,
would have profited from its
faith. But it was so only with
Jonah's people. When they
believed, We spared them the
punishment of disgrace in this
nether life and suffered them
to take their ease a while. Had
your Lord pleased, all the
people of the earth would
have believed, one and all.
Would you then force people
to have faith?

None can have faith except
by God's leave. He will visit
abomination upon the senseless.

Say: 'Behold what the heavens and the earth contain!' But
neither signs nor warnings will
avail the unbelievers.

What can they wait for but 10:102
the fate of those who have
gone before them? Say: 'Wait if you will; I will wait with you.'

We shall save Our apostles and those who believe; it is but just that We
should save the faithful.

Say: 'You people! Doubt my religion if you will, but never will I worship
those that you worship besides God. I worship God, who will claim you
back: for I am commanded to be a believer: "Dedicate yourself to the Religion in all uprightness and serve none besides God. You shall not pray to 10:106
idols which can neither help nor harm you; for if you do, you will become a
wrongdoer.

10:107 IF GOD afflicts you with a misfortune, none can remove it but Him; and if He bestows on you a good thing, none can withhold His bounty. He is bountiful to whom He will among His servants. He is the Forgiving One, the Compassionate.'"

Say: 'You people! Truth has come to you from your Lord. He that follows the right path follows it for his own good, and he that strays from the right path strays at his own peril. I am not your keeper.'

10:109 Observe what is revealed to you, and have patience till God make known His judgement. He is the best of judges.

وإن يمسسك الله بضر فلا كاشف له إلا هو وإن يردك بخير فلا
راد لفضله يصيب به من يشاء من عباده وهو الغفور الرحيم ١٠٧
قل يا أيها الناس قد جاءكم الحق من ربكم فمن اهتدى فإنما
يهتدي لنفسه ومن ضل فإنما يضل عليها وما أنا عليكم بوكيل
١٠٨ واتبع ما يوحى إليك واصبر حتى يحكم الله وهو خير الحاكمين ١٠٩

سورة هود مكية وهي مائة وثلاث وعشرون آية

بسم الله الرحمن الرحيم
الر كتاب أحكمت آياته ثم فصلت من لدن حكيم خبير ١
ألا تعبدوا إلا الله إنني لكم منه نذير وبشير ٢ وأن استغفروا
ربكم ثم توبوا إليه يمتعكم متاعا حسنا إلى أجل مسمى ويؤت
كل ذي فضل فضله وإن تولوا فإني أخاف عليكم عذاب يوم
كبير ٣ إلى الله مرجعكم وهو على كل شيء قدير ٤ ألا
إنهم يثنون صدورهم ليستخفوا منه ألا حين يستغشون ثيابهم
يعلم ما يسرون وما يعلنون إنه عليم بذات الصدور ٥

HŪD

In the Name of God, the Merciful, the Compassionate

11:1 ALIF *lām rā'*. A Book, whose verses are perfected and then expounded, from Him who is wise and all-knowing:

Serve none but God. I am sent to you from Him to warn you and to give good tidings.

Seek forgiveness of your Lord and turn to Him in penitence. A goodly provision He will make for you for an appointed term, and will bestow His grace on each that has merit. But if you pay no heed, then beware the torment of a fateful day: to God shall you return. And He has power over all things.

11:5 They cover up their bosoms to conceal their thoughts from Him. But when they put on their garments, does He not know what they conceal and what they reveal? He well knows their innermost thoughts.

وما من دابة في الارض الا على الله رزقها ويعلم مستقرها
ومستودعها كل في كتاب مبين ٦ وهو الذي خلق
السموات والارض في ستة ايام وكان عرشه على الماء
ليبلوكم ايكم احسن عملا ولئن قلت انكم مبعوثون
من بعد الموت ليقولن الذين كفروا ان هذا الا سحر
مبين ٧ ولئن اخرنا عنهم العذاب الى امة معدودة
ليقولن ما يحبسه الا يوم ياتيهم ليس مصروفا عنهم
وحاق بهم ما كانوا به يستهزءون ٨ ولئن اذقنا
الانسان منا رحمة ثم نزعناها منه انه ليئوس كفور
٩ ولئن اذقناه نعماء بعد ضراء مسته ليقولن
ذهب السيات عني انه لفرح فخور ١٠ الا الذين صبروا
وعملوا الصالحات اولئك لهم مغفرة واجر كبير ١١
فلعلك تارك بعض ما يوحى اليك وضائق به صدرك
ان يقولوا لولا انزل عليه كنز او جاء معه
ملك انما انت نذير والله على كل شيء وكيل ١٢

AND THERE is not a creature 11:6
on the earth but God provides
its sustenance. He knows its
dwelling and its final resting-
place. All is recorded in a
veritable Book.

Throned above the waters,
He created the heavens and the
earth in six days, to find out
which of you shall best acquit
yourselves.

When you[1] say: 'After death
you shall be raised to life,' the
unbelievers declare: 'It is but
sorcery manifest.' And if We 11:8
put off their punishment till an
appointed time, they will surely
say: 'Why is it delayed?'

On the day it overtakes them,
they shall not be immune from
it: the terrors at which they
scoffed will encompass them.

If We let man taste a blessing from Ourself and then withhold it from
him, he yields to despair and becomes ungrateful. And if after adversity We
let him taste good fortune, he will surely say: 'Gone are my sorrows from
me,' and grow jubilant and boastful.

Not so the steadfast who do good works; forgiveness and a rich recompense await them.

You may chance to omit a part of what is revealed to you and be dis- 11:12
tressed because they say: 'Why has no treasure been sent down to him? And
why has no angel come with him?'

But you are only to give warning; and God is the guardian of all things.

1. Muḥammad.

أم يقولون افتريه قل فأتوا بعشر سور مثله مفتريت
وادعوا من استطعتم من دون الله إن كنتم صدقين ﴿١٣﴾ فإلم
يستجيبوا لكم فاعلموا أنما أنزل بعلم الله وأن لا إله إلا هو فهل
أنتم مسلمون ﴿١٤﴾ من كان يريد الحيوة الدنيا وزينتها نوف
إليهم أعملهم فيها وهم فيها لا يبخسون ﴿١٥﴾ أولئك الذين
ليس لهم في الآخرة إلا النار وحبط ما صنعوا فيها وبطل
ما كانوا يعملون ﴿١٦﴾ أفمن كان على بينة من ربه ويتلوه
شاهد منه ومن قبله كتب موسى إماما ورحمة أولئك
يؤمنون به ومن يكفر به من الأحزاب فالنار
موعده فلا تك في مرية منه إنه الحق من ربك ولكن
أكثر الناس لا يؤمنون ﴿١٧﴾ ومن أظلم ممن افترى على
الله كذبا أولئك يعرضون على ربهم ويقول
الأشهاد هؤلاء الذين كذبوا على ربهم ألا لعنة
الله على الظلمين ﴿١٨﴾ الذين يصدون عن سبيل
الله ويبغونها عوجا وهم بالآخرة هم كفرون ﴿١٩﴾

11:13 OR DO they say: 'He has
invented it'?[1] Say: 'Produce ten
sūrahs like it, all invented. Call
on whom you will among your
idols, if what you say be true.
If they do not answer you,
know then that it is revealed
with God's knowledge, and
that there is no god but Him.
So will you be Muslims?'

Those that desire the life of
this world and all its finery We
shall reward for their deeds in
their own lifetime: they shall
11:16 not be given less. They are
those who in the world to
come shall have earned nothing but the Fire. Fruitless are
their deeds, and vain are all
their works.

Are they to be compared to
those that have received a
revelation from their Lord,
recited by a witness from Him and heralded by the Book of Moses, a guide
and a blessing? These have faith in it, but the factions who deny it shall be
consigned to the Fire. Therefore do not doubt it. It is the Truth from your
Lord: yet most people do not believe.

And who is more wicked than he who invents a falsehood about God?
These shall be brought before their Lord; and witnesses will say: 'These are
they who lied about their Lord.'

11:19 God's curse is on the wrongdoers, who debar others from the path of
God and seek to make it crooked, and who deny the life to come.

1. The Koran.

أُولَٰئِكَ لَمْ يَكُونُوا مُعْجِزِينَ فِي الْأَرْضِ وَمَا كَانَ لَهُمْ مِنْ دُونِ
اللَّهِ مِنْ أَوْلِيَاءَ ۘ يُضَاعَفُ لَهُمُ الْعَذَابُ ۚ مَا كَانُوا يَسْتَطِيعُونَ
السَّمْعَ وَمَا كَانُوا يُبْصِرُونَ ﴿٢٠﴾ أُولَٰئِكَ الَّذِينَ خَسِرُوا
أَنْفُسَهُمْ وَضَلَّ عَنْهُمْ مَا كَانُوا يَفْتَرُونَ ﴿٢١﴾ لَا جَرَمَ
أَنَّهُمْ فِي الْآخِرَةِ هُمُ الْأَخْسَرُونَ ﴿٢٢﴾ إِنَّ الَّذِينَ آمَنُوا وَعَمِلُوا
الصَّالِحَاتِ وَأَخْبَتُوا إِلَىٰ رَبِّهِمْ أُولَٰئِكَ أَصْحَابُ الْجَنَّةِ ۖ هُمْ فِيهَا
خَالِدُونَ ﴿٢٣﴾ مَثَلُ الْفَرِيقَيْنِ كَالْأَعْمَىٰ وَالْأَصَمِّ وَالْبَصِيرِ
وَالسَّمِيعِ ۚ هَلْ يَسْتَوِيَانِ مَثَلًا ۚ أَفَلَا تَذَكَّرُونَ ﴿٢٤﴾ وَلَقَدْ أَرْسَلْنَا
نُوحًا إِلَىٰ قَوْمِهِ إِنِّي لَكُمْ نَذِيرٌ مُبِينٌ ﴿٢٥﴾ أَنْ لَا تَعْبُدُوا إِلَّا
اللَّهَ ۖ إِنِّي أَخَافُ عَلَيْكُمْ عَذَابَ يَوْمٍ أَلِيمٍ ﴿٢٦﴾ فَقَالَ الْمَلَأُ الَّذِينَ
كَفَرُوا مِنْ قَوْمِهِ مَا نَرَاكَ إِلَّا بَشَرًا مِثْلَنَا وَمَا نَرَاكَ اتَّبَعَكَ
إِلَّا الَّذِينَ هُمْ أَرَاذِلُنَا بَادِيَ الرَّأْيِ وَمَا نَرَىٰ لَكُمْ عَلَيْنَا
مِنْ فَضْلٍ بَلْ نَظُنُّكُمْ كَاذِبِينَ ﴿٢٧﴾ قَالَ يَا قَوْمِ أَرَأَيْتُمْ
إِنْ كُنْتُ عَلَىٰ بَيِّنَةٍ مِنْ رَبِّي وَآتَانِي رَحْمَةً مِنْ عِنْدِهِ فَعُمِّيَتْ
عَلَيْكُمْ أَنُلْزِمُكُمُوهَا وَأَنْتُمْ لَهَا كَارِهُونَ ﴿٢٨﴾

THESE SHALL not be impreg- 11:20
nable in the land; there is none to protect them besides God. Their punishment shall be doubled, for they could neither hear nor see.

Such are those who shall forfeit their souls; their false devices will forsake them, and in the life to come they will assuredly lose most.

As for those that believe and do good works and humble themselves before their Lord, they are the heirs of Paradise, wherein shall they abide for ever.

The two are like the blind 11:24
and the deaf compared with those that can see and hear. Are the two equal? So will you not take thought?

We sent forth Noah to his people. He said: 'I have come to warn you plainly. Serve none but God; beware the torment of a woeful day.'

The unbelieving elders of his people said: 'We see you as but a mortal like ourselves. Nor can we see you being followed by any but the lowliest of our people: rash and undiscerning. We see no superior merit in you: indeed we think that you are lying.'

He said: 'Consider, my people! If my Lord has revealed to me His will and 11:28
bestowed on me a favour of His own, though it be hidden from you, can we impose it on you, and you averse to it?

11:29 I SEEK of you no recompense for this, my people; for none but God can reward me. Nor will I drive away the faithful, for they will surely meet their Lord. But I can see that you are ignorant people. And were I to drive them away, my people, who would protect me from God? Will you not reflect?

'I do not say to you that I possess God's treasures, nor have I knowledge of what is hidden; I do not claim to be an angel, nor do I say to those your eyes disdain that God will not be bountiful to them – God knows best what is in their hearts – for then I should become a wrongdoer.'

11:32 'Noah,' they said, 'you have argued with us, and argued to excess. Bring down the scourge you threaten us with, if what you say be true!'

He said: 'God will bring it down upon you if He pleases: nor shall you be immune. My counsel will not profit you if God intends to confound you, willing though I am to offer you counsel. He is your Lord, and to Him shall you be recalled.'

If they say: 'He has invented it himself,' say: 'If I have indeed invented it, then may I be punished for my sin! I am innocent of your imputations.'

And it was revealed to Noah: 'None of your people will believe in you
11:37 save those who already believe. Do not grieve at what they do. Build the ark
under Our watchful eyes, and with Our inspiration. You shall not plead with
Me for those who have done wrong: they shall assuredly be drowned.'

ويا قوم لا أسألكم عليه مالا إن أجري إلا على الله وما أنا
بطارد الذين آمنوا إنهم ملاقوا ربهم ولكني أراكم قوما
تجهلون ﴿٢٩﴾ ويا قوم من ينصرني من الله إن طردتهم أفلا
تذكرون ﴿٣٠﴾ ولا أقول لكم عندي خزائن الله ولا أعلم
الغيب ولا أقول إني ملك ولا أقول للذين تزدري
أعينكم لن يؤتيهم الله خيرا الله أعلم بما في أنفسهم
إني إذا لمن الظالمين ﴿٣١﴾ قالوا يا نوح قد جادلتنا فأكثرت
جدالنا فأتنا بما تعدنا إن كنت من الصادقين ﴿٣٢﴾
قال إنما يأتيكم به الله إن شاء وما أنتم بمعجزين ﴿٣٣﴾
ولا ينفعكم نصحي إن أردت أن أنصح لكم إن كان الله يريد
أن يغويكم هو ربكم وإليه ترجعون ﴿٣٤﴾ أم يقولون
افتراه قل إن افتريته فعلي إجرامي وأنا بريء مما تجرمون
﴿٣٥﴾ وأوحي إلى نوح أنه لن يؤمن من قومك إلا من قد
آمن فلا تبتئس بما كانوا يفعلون ﴿٣٦﴾ واصنع الفلك بأعيننا
ووحينا ولا تخاطبني في الذين ظلموا إنهم مغرقون ﴿٣٧﴾

وَيَصْنَعُ الْفُلْكَ وَكُلَّمَا مَرَّ عَلَيْهِ مَلَأٌ مِنْ قَوْمِهِ سَخِرُوا مِنْهُ
قَالَ إِنْ تَسْخَرُوا مِنَّا فَإِنَّا نَسْخَرُ مِنْكُمْ كَمَا تَسْخَرُونَ ﴿٣٨﴾
فَسَوْفَ تَعْلَمُونَ مَنْ يَأْتِيهِ عَذَابٌ يُخْزِيهِ وَيَحِلُّ عَلَيْهِ عَذَابٌ
مُقِيمٌ ﴿٣٩﴾ حَتَّىٰ إِذَا جَاءَ أَمْرُنَا وَفَارَ التَّنُّورُ قُلْنَا احْمِلْ فِيهَا
مِنْ كُلٍّ زَوْجَيْنِ اثْنَيْنِ وَأَهْلَكَ إِلَّا مَنْ سَبَقَ عَلَيْهِ الْقَوْلُ
وَمَنْ آمَنَ وَمَا آمَنَ مَعَهُ إِلَّا قَلِيلٌ ﴿٤٠﴾ وَقَالَ ارْكَبُوا فِيهَا
بِسْمِ اللَّهِ مَجْرَاهَا وَمُرْسَاهَا إِنَّ رَبِّي لَغَفُورٌ رَحِيمٌ ﴿٤١﴾ وَهِيَ
تَجْرِي بِهِمْ فِي مَوْجٍ كَالْجِبَالِ وَنَادَىٰ نُوحٌ ابْنَهُ وَكَانَ فِي
مَعْزِلٍ يَا بُنَيَّ ارْكَبْ مَعَنَا وَلَا تَكُنْ مَعَ الْكَافِرِينَ ﴿٤٢﴾ قَالَ
سَآوِي إِلَىٰ جَبَلٍ يَعْصِمُنِي مِنَ الْمَاءِ قَالَ لَا عَاصِمَ الْيَوْمَ
مِنْ أَمْرِ اللَّهِ إِلَّا مَنْ رَحِمَ وَحَالَ بَيْنَهُمَا الْمَوْجُ فَكَانَ مِنَ
الْمُغْرَقِينَ ﴿٤٣﴾ وَقِيلَ يَا أَرْضُ ابْلَعِي مَاءَكِ وَيَا سَمَاءُ أَقْلِعِي وَغِيضَ
الْمَاءُ وَقُضِيَ الْأَمْرُ وَاسْتَوَتْ عَلَى الْجُودِيِّ وَقِيلَ بُعْدًا
لِلْقَوْمِ الظَّالِمِينَ ﴿٤٤﴾ وَنَادَىٰ نُوحٌ رَبَّهُ فَقَالَ رَبِّ إِنَّ ابْنِي مِنْ
أَهْلِي وَإِنَّ وَعْدَكَ الْحَقُّ وَأَنْتَ أَحْكَمُ الْحَاكِمِينَ ﴿٤٥﴾

So HE built the ark. And 11:38
whenever some elders of his people passed by him they mocked him. He said: 'If you mock us, we shall mock you just as you mock us. You shall learn who will be visited by a scourge that shall humiliate him, and be smitten by a scourge everlasting.'

And when Our judgement was passed and water welled out from the Oven, We said: 'Take into the ark a pair from every species, your kin (except for those already doomed), and the true believers.' But none believed with him except a few.

'Embark,' he said. 'In the 11:41
name of God it shall set sail and cast anchor. Surely my Lord is forgiving and compassionate.'

And as the ark moved on with them amid the mountainous waves, Noah cried out to his son, who stood apart: 'Embark with us, my son; do not remain with the unbelievers.'

He replied: 'I shall seek refuge on a mountain, which will protect me from the water.'

He said: 'None shall be secure today from God's judgement but those who shall enjoy His mercy!' And thereupon the billows rolled between them, and Noah's son was drowned.

A voice cried out: 'Earth, swallow up your waters. Heaven, cease your rain!' The flood abated, and judgement was passed. The ark came to rest upon Al-Jūdī, and a voice declared: 'Gone are the wrongdoers.'

Noah called out to his Lord, saying: 'Lord, my son was my own flesh and 11:45
blood. Your promise was surely true; You are the most just of judges.'

11:46 'NOAH,' HE said, 'he was
no kin of yours: he had acted
unjustly. Do not question Me
about things you know nothing of. I admonish you lest
you become an ignorant man.'
He said: 'I seek refuge in
You, Lord, from asking You
about things I know nothing
of. Forgive me and have mercy
on me, or I shall surely be
among the lost.'
A voice said: 'Noah, land
in peace with blessings from
Ourself upon you and on *some*
of the communities that are
with you. Other communities
We will suffer to take their
ease, and will then visit them
with a woeful scourge.'
11:49 That which We now reveal
to you is secret history: it was
unknown to you and to your
people before this. Have patience; a joyful end awaits the righteous.
And to 'Ād We sent their kin Hūd. He said: 'Serve God, my people; you
have no god but Him. False are your fabrications. I demand of you no recompense, my people, for none can reward me except my Creator. Will you
not understand?
'My people, seek forgiveness of your Lord and turn to Him in penitence.
He will send from the sky abundant rain upon you; He will add strength to
your strength. Do not turn away from Him with wrongdoing.'
11:53 They said: 'Hūd, you have given us no evidence. We will not forsake our
gods at your behest, nor will we believe in you.

قَالَ يَا نُوحُ إِنَّهُ لَيْسَ مِنْ أَهْلِكَ إِنَّهُ عَمَلٌ غَيْرُ صَالِحٍ فَلَا تَسْأَلْنِ
مَا لَيْسَ لَكَ بِهِ عِلْمٌ إِنِّي أَعِظُكَ أَنْ تَكُونَ مِنَ الْجَاهِلِينَ
(٤٦) قَالَ رَبِّ إِنِّي أَعُوذُ بِكَ أَنْ أَسْأَلَكَ مَا لَيْسَ لِي بِهِ عِلْمٌ
وَإِلَّا تَغْفِرْ لِي وَتَرْحَمْنِي أَكُنْ مِنَ الْخَاسِرِينَ (٤٧) قِيلَ يَا نُوحُ
اهْبِطْ بِسَلَامٍ مِنَّا وَبَرَكَاتٍ عَلَيْكَ وَعَلَى أُمَمٍ مِمَّنْ مَعَكَ وَأُمَمٌ
سَنُمَتِّعُهُمْ ثُمَّ يَمَسُّهُمْ مِنَّا عَذَابٌ أَلِيمٌ (٤٨) تِلْكَ مِنْ أَنْبَاءِ
الْغَيْبِ نُوحِيهَا إِلَيْكَ مَا كُنْتَ تَعْلَمُهَا أَنْتَ وَلَا قَوْمُكَ مِنْ قَبْلِ
هَذَا فَاصْبِرْ إِنَّ الْعَاقِبَةَ لِلْمُتَّقِينَ (٤٩) وَإِلَى عَادٍ أَخَاهُمْ هُودًا
قَالَ يَا قَوْمِ اعْبُدُوا اللَّهَ مَا لَكُمْ مِنْ إِلَهٍ غَيْرُهُ إِنْ أَنْتُمْ
إِلَّا مُفْتَرُونَ (٥٠) يَا قَوْمِ لَا أَسْأَلُكُمْ عَلَيْهِ أَجْرًا إِنْ
أَجْرِيَ إِلَّا عَلَى الَّذِي فَطَرَنِي أَفَلَا تَعْقِلُونَ (٥١) وَيَا قَوْمِ
اسْتَغْفِرُوا رَبَّكُمْ ثُمَّ تُوبُوا إِلَيْهِ يُرْسِلِ السَّمَاءَ عَلَيْكُمْ
مِدْرَارًا وَيَزِدْكُمْ قُوَّةً إِلَى قُوَّتِكُمْ وَلَا تَتَوَلَّوْا
مُجْرِمِينَ (٥٢) قَالُوا يَا هُودُ مَا جِئْتَنَا بِبَيِّنَةٍ وَمَا نَحْنُ بِتَارِكِي
آلِهَتِنَا عَنْ قَوْلِكَ وَمَا نَحْنُ لَكَ بِمُؤْمِنِينَ (٥٣)

إن نقول إلا اعتراك بعض آلهتنا بسوء قال إني أشهد
الله واشهدوا أني بريء مما تشركون ﴿٥٤﴾ من دونه
فكيدوني جميعا ثم لا تنظرون ﴿٥٥﴾ إني توكلت على
الله ربي وربكم ما من دابة إلا هو آخذ بناصيتها إن ربي على
صراط مستقيم ﴿٥٦﴾ فإن تولوا فقد أبلغتكم ما أرسلت به
إليكم ويستخلف ربي قوما غيركم ولا تضرونه شيئا إن ربي على
كل شيء حفيظ ﴿٥٧﴾ ولما جاء أمرنا نجينا هودا والذين آمنوا معه
برحمة منا ونجيناهم من عذاب غليظ ﴿٥٨﴾ وتلك عاد جحدوا
بآيات ربهم وعصوا رسله واتبعوا أمر كل جبار عنيد ﴿٥٩﴾ وأتبعوا
في هذه الدنيا لعنة ويوم القيامة ألا إن عادا كفروا ربهم ألا
بعدا لعاد قوم هود ﴿٦٠﴾ وإلى ثمود أخاهم صالحا قال يا قوم اعبدوا
الله ما لكم من إله غيره هو أنشأكم من الأرض واستعمركم
فيها فاستغفروه ثم توبوا إليه إن ربي قريب مجيب ﴿٦١﴾ قالوا
يا صالح قد كنت فينا مرجوا قبل هذا أتنهانا أن نعبد
ما يعبد آباؤنا وإننا لفي شك مما تدعونا إليه مريب ﴿٦٢﴾

WE CAN only suppose that 11:54
one of our gods has afflicted you with evil.'

He said: 'God be my witness, and you are my witnesses too: I disown your idols. Scheme against me if you will, and give me no respite. I have put my trust in God, my Lord and your Lord. There is not a creature on the earth whose destiny He does not govern. Straight is the path of my Lord.

'If you pay no heed, I have made known to you what I was sent with, and my Lord will replace you by other people. You will in no way harm Him. My Lord is watching over all things.'

And when Our judgement came to pass, We delivered Hūd through Our mercy, together with those who shared his faith; We delivered them from a mighty scourge.

Such were 'Ād. They denied the revelations of their Lord, disobeyed His 11:59
apostles, and did the bidding of every headstrong reprobate. Cursed were they in this world, and cursed shall they be on the Day of Resurrection.

'Ād denied their Lord. Gone are 'Ād, the people of Hūd.

And to Thamūd We sent their kin Ṣāliḥ. He said: 'Serve God, my people; you have no god but Him. It was He who brought you into being from the earth and gave you means to dwell upon it. Seek forgiveness of Him, and turn to Him in penitence. My Lord is near at hand and answers all.'

'Ṣāliḥ,' they said, 'great were the hopes we placed in you before this. Would 11:62
you now forbid us to serve the gods our fathers worshipped? Truly, we strongly doubt the faith to which you call us.'

11:63 HE SAID: 'Do but consider,
my people! If my Lord has
revealed to me His will and
bestowed on me His grace,
who would protect me from
God if I rebelled against Him?
You would surely aggravate
my ruin.

'My people, here is God's
she-camel, a sign for you.
Leave her to graze at will in
God's own land, and do not
molest her lest an instant
scourge should fall upon you.'

Yet they hamstrung her. He
said: 'You have but three days
to take your ease in your dwellings: this prophecy shall not
prove false.'

11:66 And when Our judgement
came to pass, We delivered
Ṣāliḥ through Our mercy from
the ignominy of that day, to-
gether with those who shared his faith. Mighty is your Lord and all-powerful.
The Cry took the wrongdoers, and when morning came they were crouching
lifeless in their dwellings, as though they had never prospered there.

Thamūd denied their Lord. Gone are Thamūd.

Our messengers came to Abraham with joyful tidings. They said: 'Peace!'
'Peace!' he said, and hastened to bring them a roasted calf. But when he saw
their hands being withheld from it, he mistrusted them and was afraid of
them. They said: 'Have no fear. We are sent forth to the people of Lot.'

11:71 His wife, who was standing by, laughed.[1] We bade her rejoice in Isaac, and
after Isaac, Jacob.

قال يا قوم أرأيتم إن كنت على بينة من ربي وآتاني منه رحمة
فمن ينصرني من الله إن عصيته فما تزيدونني غير تخسير ٦٣
ويا قوم هذه ناقة الله لكم آية فذروها تأكل في أرض الله
ولا تمسوها بسوء فيأخذكم عذاب قريب ٦٤ فعقروها
فقال تمتعوا في داركم ثلاثة أيام ذلك وعد غير مكذوب
٦٥ فلما جاء أمرنا نجينا صالحا والذين آمنوا معه
برحمة منا ومن خزي يومئذ إن ربك هو القوي العزيز
٦٦ وأخذ الذين ظلموا الصيحة فأصبحوا في ديارهم
جاثمين ٦٧ كأن لم يغنوا فيها ألا إن ثمود كفروا ربهم
ألا بعدا لثمود ٦٨ ولقد جاءت رسلنا إبراهيم بالبشرى
قالوا سلاما قال سلام فما لبث أن جاء بعجل حنيذ
٦٩ فلما رأى أيديهم لا تصل إليه نكرهم وأوجس
منهم خيفة قالوا لا تخف إنا أرسلنا إلى قوم
لوط ٧٠ وامرأته قائمة فضحكت فبشرناها
بإسحاق ومن وراء إسحاق يعقوب ٧١

1. Cf. Genesis 18:12.

قَالَتْ يَا وَيْلَتَىٰ أَأَلِدُ وَأَنَا عَجُوزٌ وَهَٰذَا بَعْلِي شَيْخًا إِنَّ
هَٰذَا لَشَيْءٌ عَجِيبٌ ﴿٧٢﴾ قَالُوا أَتَعْجَبِينَ مِنْ أَمْرِ اللَّهِ رَحْمَتُ
اللَّهِ وَبَرَكَاتُهُ عَلَيْكُمْ أَهْلَ الْبَيْتِ إِنَّهُ حَمِيدٌ مَجِيدٌ ﴿٧٣﴾ فَلَمَّا ذَهَبَ
عَنْ إِبْرَاهِيمَ الرَّوْعُ وَجَاءَتْهُ الْبُشْرَىٰ يُجَادِلُنَا فِي قَوْمِ لُوطٍ ﴿٧٤﴾
إِنَّ إِبْرَاهِيمَ لَحَلِيمٌ أَوَّاهٌ مُنِيبٌ ﴿٧٥﴾ يَا إِبْرَاهِيمُ أَعْرِضْ عَنْ هَٰذَا إِنَّهُ
قَدْ جَاءَ أَمْرُ رَبِّكَ وَإِنَّهُمْ آتِيهِمْ عَذَابٌ غَيْرُ مَرْدُودٍ ﴿٧٦﴾ وَلَمَّا جَاءَتْ
رُسُلُنَا لُوطًا سِيءَ بِهِمْ وَضَاقَ بِهِمْ ذَرْعًا وَقَالَ هَٰذَا يَوْمٌ عَصِيبٌ
﴿٧٧﴾ وَجَاءَهُ قَوْمُهُ يُهْرَعُونَ إِلَيْهِ وَمِنْ قَبْلُ كَانُوا يَعْمَلُونَ السَّيِّئَاتِ
قَالَ يَا قَوْمِ هَٰؤُلَاءِ بَنَاتِي هُنَّ أَطْهَرُ لَكُمْ فَاتَّقُوا اللَّهَ وَلَا
تُخْزُونِ فِي ضَيْفِي أَلَيْسَ مِنْكُمْ رَجُلٌ رَشِيدٌ ﴿٧٨﴾ قَالُوا لَقَدْ
عَلِمْتَ مَا لَنَا فِي بَنَاتِكَ مِنْ حَقٍّ وَإِنَّكَ لَتَعْلَمُ مَا نُرِيدُ ﴿٧٩﴾
قَالَ لَوْ أَنَّ لِي بِكُمْ قُوَّةً أَوْ آوِي إِلَىٰ رُكْنٍ شَدِيدٍ ﴿٨٠﴾ قَالُوا
يَا لُوطُ إِنَّا رُسُلُ رَبِّكَ لَنْ يَصِلُوا إِلَيْكَ فَأَسْرِ بِأَهْلِكَ بِقِطْعٍ
مِنَ اللَّيْلِ وَلَا يَلْتَفِتْ مِنْكُمْ أَحَدٌ إِلَّا امْرَأَتَكَ إِنَّهُ مُصِيبُهَا
مَا أَصَابَهُمْ إِنَّ مَوْعِدَهُمُ الصُّبْحُ أَلَيْسَ الصُّبْحُ بِقَرِيبٍ ﴿٨١﴾

'ALAS!' SHE said. 'How shall 11:72
I bear a child when I am old
and this, my husband, is
well advanced in years? This
is indeed a marvel.'

They said: 'Do you marvel at the ways of God? May God's mercy and blessings be upon you, dear hosts! Worthy of praise is He and glorious.'

And when awe left Abraham as he pondered the joyful tidings, he pleaded with Us for the people of Lot. Abraham was gracious, tender-hearted, and devout.

'Abraham, plead no more; Your Lord's will must needs be done. Irrevocable is the scourge which shall smite them.'

And when Our emissaries came to Lot, he grew anxious about them, and was distressed on their account. 'This is indeed a day of woe,' he said.

His people, long addicted to evil practices, came hurrying towards him. 11:78
'My people,' he said, 'here are my daughters:[1] surely they are more wholesome to you. Fear God, and do not shame me by insulting my guests. Is there
not one right-minded man among you?'

They said: 'You well know we have no need of your daughters; and you know full well what we are seeking.'

He said: 'Would that I had power enough to overcome you, or could find refuge in a tower of strength!'

They said: 'Lot, we are the emissaries of your Lord: they shall not touch 11:81
you. Depart with your kin in the dead of night and let none of you turn
back, except your wife; she shall suffer the fate that they shall suffer. In the
morning their hour will come; is not the morning near?'

1. Cf. Genesis 19:8.

فلما جاء أمرنا جعلنا عاليها سافلها وأمطرنا عليها
حجارة من سجيل منضود ﴿٨٢﴾ مسومة عند ربك وما هي
من الظالمين ببعيد ﴿٨٣﴾ وإلى مدين أخاهم شعيبا قال
يا قوم اعبدوا الله ما لكم من إله غيره ولا تنقصوا
المكيال والميزان إني أراكم بخير وإني أخاف عليكم عذاب
يوم محيط ﴿٨٤﴾ ويا قوم أوفوا المكيال والميزان بالقسط
ولا تبخسوا الناس أشياءهم ولا تعثوا في الأرض مفسدين
﴿٨٥﴾ بقيت الله خير لكم إن كنتم مؤمنين وما
أنا عليكم بحفيظ ﴿٨٦﴾ قالوا يا شعيب أصلاتك
تأمرك أن نترك ما يعبد آباؤنا أو أن نفعل في
أموالنا ما نشاء إنك لأنت الحليم الرشيد ﴿٨٧﴾ قال
يا قوم أرأيتم إن كنت على بينة من ربي ورزقني
منه رزقا حسنا وما أريد أن أخالفكم إلى ما
أنهاكم عنه إن أريد إلا الإصلاح ما استطعت
وما توفيقي إلا بالله عليه توكلت وإليه أنيب ﴿٨٨﴾

11:82 AND WHEN Our judge-
ment came to pass, We turned
their city upside down and let
loose upon it a shower of
clay-stones bearing the tokens
of your Lord. The fate of the
wrongdoers was not far off.

And to the people of Mid-
ian We sent their kin Shu‘aib.
He said: ‘Serve God, my
people; you have no god but
Him. Do not give short weight
and measure. Prosperous
though you are, beware the
torment of a fateful day.

11:85 ‘My people, give just weight
and measure in all fairness.
Do not defraud people of
their possessions, nor shall
you corrupt the land with evil.
Better for you is God’s recompense, if you are true believers.
I am not your keeper.’

‘Shu‘aib,’ they said, ‘do your prayers bid you we renounce the gods our
fathers worshipped and not conduct our affairs in the manner we please?
Truly, you are a kind and rightly-guided man!’

11:88 He said: ‘Do but consider, my people! If my Lord has revealed to me His
will and bestowed on me a gracious gift, should I not guide you? I do not
wish to argue with you, only to practise myself what I forbid you. I seek only
to reform you: as far as I am able. Nor can I succeed without God’s help. In
Him I have put my trust and to Him I turn in penitence.

ويا قوم لا يجرمنكم شقاقي أن يصيبكم مثل ما أصاب
قوم نوح أو قوم هود أو قوم صالح وما قوم لوط
منكم ببعيد ﴿٨٩﴾ واستغفروا ربكم ثم توبوا إليه إن ربي
رحيم ودود ﴿٩٠﴾ قالوا يا شعيب ما نفقه كثيرا مما تقول
وإنا لنراك فينا ضعيفا ولولا رهطك لرجمناك وما أنت
علينا بعزيز ﴿٩١﴾ قال يا قوم أرهطي أعز عليكم من الله
واتخذتموه وراءكم ظهريا إن ربي بما تعملون محيط ﴿٩٢﴾
ويا قوم اعملوا على مكانتكم إني عامل سوف تعلمون
من يأتيه عذاب يخزيه ومن هو كاذب وارتقبوا إني
معكم رقيب ﴿٩٣﴾ ولما جاء أمرنا نجينا شعيبا والذين
آمنوا معه برحمة منا وأخذت الذين ظلموا الصيحة
فأصبحوا في ديارهم جاثمين ﴿٩٤﴾ كأن لم يغنوا فيها
ألا بعدا لمدين كما بعدت ثمود ﴿٩٥﴾ ولقد أرسلنا
موسى بآياتنا وسلطان مبين ﴿٩٦﴾ إلى فرعون وملئه
فاتبعوا أمر فرعون وما أمر فرعون برشيد ﴿٩٧﴾

'MY PEOPLE, let your dis- 11:89
pute with me not bring upon you the doom which overtook the people of Noah, the people of Hūd, and the people of Ṣāliḥ; nor is it long since the people of Lot were punished. Seek forgiveness of your Lord and turn to Him in penitence. Compassionate and loving is my Lord.'

They said: 'Shu'aib, much of what you say we cannot comprehend. We surely know how weak you are in our midst. But for your tribe, we should have stoned you. You shall on no account prevail against us.'

He said: 'My people, have you more regard for my tribe than for God? Dare you turn your backs upon Him? My Lord has knowledge of all your
actions. Do what you will, my people, and so will I. You shall learn who will 11:93
be punished and held up to shame, and who is lying. Watch if you will; I will watch with you.'

And when Our judgement was carried out We delivered Shu'aib through Our mercy, together with those who shared his faith. The Cry took the wrongdoers, and when morning came they were crouching lifeless in their dwellings, as though they had never prospered there. Like Thamūd, gone are the people of Midian.

We sent forth Moses with Our signs and with manifest authority to Phar- 11:97
aoh and his nobles. But they followed the behest of Pharaoh; nor was Pharaoh's behest rightly guided.

11:98 HE SHALL stand at the head
of his people on the Day of
Resurrection, and shall lead
them into the Fire. Evil is the
place they shall be led to.
A curse followed them in
this world, and on the Day of
Resurrection an evil gift shall
they receive.
The annals of those com-
munities We recount to you:
some have survived, while
others have ceased to be. We
did not wrong them, but they
wronged themselves. The
gods they called on besides
God availed them nothing
when your Lord's will was
done; they only added to their
ruin.
Such was the scourge with
which your Lord scourged the
communities while they sinned.
Harrowing and relentless is His scourge.
11:103 Surely in this there is a sign for him that dreads the torment of the Hereafter. That will be a day on which all mankind shall be gathered; and that
shall be a fateful day.
We shall defer it only for a time decreed. When that day is come, no soul
shall speak but by His leave. Some shall be damned, and some shall be
blessed. The damned shall be cast into the Fire, where, groaning and wailing,
they shall abide as long as the heavens and the earth endure, unless your
11:108 Lord ordain otherwise: your Lord shall accomplish what He will. As for the
blessed, they shall abide in Paradise as long as the heavens and the earth
endure, unless your Lord ordain otherwise: an endless recompense.

يَقْدُمُ قَوْمَهُ يَوْمَ الْقِيَمَةِ فَأَوْرَدَهُمُ النَّارَ وَبِئْسَ الْوِرْدُ
الْمَوْرُودُ ﴿٩٨﴾ وَأُتْبِعُوا فِي هَذِهِ لَعْنَةً وَيَوْمَ الْقِيَمَةِ بِئْسَ
الرِّفْدُ الْمَرْفُودُ ﴿٩٩﴾ ذَلِكَ مِنْ أَنْبَاءِ الْقُرَى نَقُصُّهُ عَلَيْكَ
مِنْهَا قَائِمٌ وَحَصِيدٌ ﴿١٠٠﴾ وَمَا ظَلَمْنَاهُمْ وَلَكِنْ ظَلَمُوا
أَنْفُسَهُمْ فَمَا أَغْنَتْ عَنْهُمْ آلِهَتُهُمُ الَّتِي يَدْعُونَ مِنْ دُونِ
اللَّهِ مِنْ شَيْءٍ لَمَّا جَاءَ أَمْرُ رَبِّكَ وَمَا زَادُوهُمْ غَيْرَ تَتْبِيبٍ ﴿١٠١﴾
وَكَذَلِكَ أَخْذُ رَبِّكَ إِذَا أَخَذَ الْقُرَى وَهِيَ ظَالِمَةٌ إِنَّ أَخْذَهُ
أَلِيمٌ شَدِيدٌ ﴿١٠٢﴾ إِنَّ فِي ذَلِكَ لَآيَةً لِمَنْ خَافَ عَذَابَ الْآخِرَةِ ذَلِكَ
يَوْمٌ مَجْمُوعٌ لَهُ النَّاسُ وَذَلِكَ يَوْمٌ مَشْهُودٌ ﴿١٠٣﴾ وَمَا نُؤَخِّرُهُ
إِلَّا لِأَجَلٍ مَعْدُودٍ ﴿١٠٤﴾ يَوْمَ يَأْتِ لَا تَكَلَّمُ نَفْسٌ إِلَّا بِإِذْنِهِ فَمِنْهُمْ
شَقِيٌّ وَسَعِيدٌ ﴿١٠٥﴾ فَأَمَّا الَّذِينَ شَقُوا فَفِي النَّارِ لَهُمْ فِيهَا
زَفِيرٌ وَشَهِيقٌ ﴿١٠٦﴾ خَالِدِينَ فِيهَا مَا دَامَتِ السَّمَوَاتُ وَالْأَرْضُ
إِلَّا مَا شَاءَ رَبُّكَ إِنَّ رَبَّكَ فَعَّالٌ لِمَا يُرِيدُ ﴿١٠٧﴾ وَأَمَّا
الَّذِينَ سُعِدُوا فَفِي الْجَنَّةِ خَالِدِينَ فِيهَا مَا دَامَتِ السَّمَوَاتُ
وَالْأَرْضُ إِلَّا مَا شَاءَ رَبُّكَ عَطَاءً غَيْرَ مَجْذُوذٍ ﴿١٠٨﴾

فلا تك في مرية مما يعبد هؤلاء ما يعبدون إلا كما
يعبد آباؤهم من قبل وإنا لموفوهم نصيبهم غير منقوص
(١٠٩) ولقد آتينا موسى الكتاب فاختلف فيه ولولا كلمة
سبقت من ربك لقضي بينهم وإنهم لفي شك منه
مريب (١١٠) وإن كلا لما ليوفينهم ربك أعمالهم إنه بما
يعملون خبير (١١١) فاستقم كما أمرت ومن تاب معك ولا
تطغوا إنه بما تعملون بصير (١١٢) ولا تركنوا إلى الذين ظلموا
فتمسكم النار وما لكم من دون الله من أولياء ثم
لا تنصرون (١١٣) وأقم الصلوة طرفي النهار وزلفا
من الليل إن الحسنات يذهبن السيئات ذلك
ذكرى للذاكرين (١١٤) واصبر فإن الله لا يضيع أجر المحسنين
(١١٥) فلولا كان من القرون من قبلكم أولوا بقية
ينهون عن الفساد في الأرض إلا قليلا ممن أنجينا منهم
واتبع الذين ظلموا ما أترفوا فيه وكانوا مجرمين (١١٦)
وما كان ربك ليهلك القرى بظلم وأهلها مصلحون (١١٧)

HAVE NO doubt as to what 11:109
they worship; they worship
what their fathers worshipped
before them. Their deserts We
shall requite, undiminished.

We gave the Book to Moses,
but differences arose about it.
And but for a Word from your
Lord, already decreed, their
fate would have long been
sealed. Yet this they strongly
doubt.

Your Lord will surely reward
each according to his deeds; He
has full knowledge of what
they do. Follow then the straight
path as you are bidden, together
with those who have repented
with you, and do not transgress.
Surely He is ever observant of
what you do.

Put no trust in the wrong- 11:113
doers, lest the Fire should touch
you. And none but God can protect or help you.

Attend to your prayers at the two ends of the day, and in part of the
night-time too. Good deeds shall make amends for sins. This is an Admonition for those that reflect. And have patience; God will not deny the
righteous their reward.

Was there, among the generations that have gone before you, a remnant
that forbade corruption in the land, except the few We had delivered from
among them? The wrongdoers pursued their worldly pleasures and were sinful. The Lord would not have ruined the cities, without just cause, had their 11:117
inhabitants been upright.

11:118 AND HAD your Lord pleased, He would have united mankind in one community. They are still at odds, except for those to whom your Lord has shown mercy. To this end He has created them. The Word of your Lord shall be fulfilled: 'I will fill Hell with jinn and humans all.'

We recount to you the histories of those apostles to put courage into your heart. Through them Truth shall be revealed to you, with precepts and an Admonition for the faithful.

Say to the infidels: 'Do whatever lies within your power, and so shall we. Wait if you will; we too are waiting.'

11:123 God alone has knowledge of what the heavens and the earth conceal; to Him all things shall be referred. Worship Him, and put your trust in Him; your Lord is never heedless of what you do.

ولو شاء ربك لجعل الناس أمة واحدة ولا يزالون مختلفين ﴿١١٨﴾ إلا
من رحم ربك ولذلك خلقهم وتمت كلمة ربك لأملأن جهنم من
الجنة والناس أجمعين ﴿١١٩﴾ وكلا نقص عليك من أنباء الرسل
ما نثبت به فؤادك وجاءك في هذه الحق وموعظة وذكرى
للمؤمنين ﴿١٢٠﴾ وقل للذين لا يؤمنون اعملوا على مكانتكم إنا عاملون
﴿١٢١﴾ وانتظروا إنا منتظرون ﴿١٢٢﴾ ولله غيب السموات والأرض وإليه
يرجع الأمر كله فاعبده وتوكل عليه وما ربك بغافل عما تعملون ﴿١٢٣﴾

سورة يوسف مكية وهي مائة وإحدى عشرة آية

بسم الله الرحمن الرحيم
الر تلك آيات الكتاب المبين ﴿١﴾ إنا أنزلناه قرآنا عربيا
لعلكم تعقلون ﴿٢﴾ نحن نقص عليك أحسن القصص بما
أوحينا إليك هذا القرآن وإن كنت من قبله لمن الغافلين
﴿٣﴾ إذ قال يوسف لأبيه يا أبت إني رأيت أحد عشر
كوكبا والشمس والقمر رأيتهم لي ساجدين ﴿٤﴾

JOSEPH

In the Name of God, the Merciful, the Compassionate

12:1 ALIF *lām rā'*. These are the revelations of the veritable Book. We have revealed it an Arabic Koran, that you may grow in understanding.

In inspiring you with this Koran We recount to you the best of narratives, though before it you were heedless.

12:4 Joseph said to his father: 'Father, I dreamt of eleven stars and the sun and the moon; I saw them prostrate themselves before me.'[1]

1. Cf. Genesis 37:9.

قال يا بني لا تقصص رءياك على إخوتك فيكيدوا لك كيدا
إن الشيطان للإنسان عدو مبين ٥ وكذلك يجتبيك
ربك ويعلمك من تأويل الأحاديث ويتم نعمته عليك وعلى آل
يعقوب كما أتمها على أبويك من قبل إبرهيم وإسحق إن
ربك عليم حكيم ٦ لقد كان في يوسف وإخوته
ءايت للسائلين ○ إذ قالوا ليوسف وأخوه أحب إلى أبينا منا ونحن
عصبة إن أبانا لفي ضلل مبين ٨ اقتلوا يوسف أو اطرحوه
أرضا يخل لكم وجه أبيكم وتكونوا من بعده قوما
صلحين ٩ قال قائل منهم لا تقتلوا يوسف وألقوه
في غيبت الجب يلتقطه بعض السيارة إن كنتم فعلين
١٠ قالوا يا أبانا ما لك لا تأمنا على يوسف وإنا له
لنصحون ١١ أرسله معنا غدا يرتع ويلعب وإنا له
لحفظون ١٢ قال إني ليحزنني أن تذهبوا به وأخاف
أن يأكله الذئب وأنتم عنه غفلون ١٣ قالوا
لئن أكله الذئب ونحن عصبة إنا إذا لخسرون ١٤

'My son,' he replied, 'say 12:5
nothing of this dream to your brothers, lest they plot evil against you: Satan is the sworn enemy of man. Even thus shall you be chosen by your Lord. He will teach you to interpret visions, and will perfect His favour to you and to the House of Jacob, as He perfected it to your forefathers Abraham and Isaac before you. Your Lord is all-knowing and wise.'

Surely in Joseph and his brothers there are signs for doubting men.

They said to each other: 'Surely Joseph and his brother[1] are dearer to our father than ourselves, though we are many. Truly, our father is much mistaken. Kill Joseph, or cast him away in some far-off land, so that you may have no rival in your father's love, and after that be honourable men.'

One of the brothers said: 'Do not kill Joseph; but, if you must, rather cast 12:10
him into a dark pit. Some caravan will take him up.'

They said: 'Father, why do you not trust us with Joseph? Surely we wish him well. Send him with us tomorrow, that he may play and enjoy himself. We will take good care of him.'

He said: 'It would much grieve me to let him go with you; for I fear lest the wolf should eat him when you are off your guard.'

They said: 'If the wolf could eat him when we are so many, then we should 12:14
surely be lost!'

1. His full brother, Benjamin.

فلما ذهبوا به وأجمعوا أن يجعلوه في غيابت الجب وأوحينا
إليه لتنبئنهم بأمرهم هذا وهم لا يشعرون ﴿١٥﴾ وجاءو أباهم
عشاء يبكون ﴿١٦﴾ قالوا يا أبانا إنا ذهبنا نستبق وتركنا
يوسف عند متاعنا فأكله الذئب وما أنت بمؤمن لنا ولو
كنا صادقين ﴿١٧﴾ وجاءو على قميصه بدم كذب قال بل سولت
لكم أنفسكم أمرا فصبر جميل والله المستعان على
ما تصفون ﴿١٨﴾ وجاءت سيارة فأرسلوا واردهم فأدلى دلوه
قال يا بشرى هذا غلام وأسروه بضاعة والله عليم بما يعملون
﴿١٩﴾ وشروه بثمن بخس دراهم معدودة وكانوا
فيه من الزاهدين ﴿٢٠﴾ وقال الذي اشتراه من
مصر لامرأته أكرمي مثواه عسى أن ينفعنا أو
نتخذه ولدا وكذلك مكنا ليوسف في الأرض
ولنعلمه من تأويل الأحاديث والله غالب على أمره
ولكن أكثر الناس لا يعلمون ﴿٢١﴾ ولما بلغ أشده
آتيناه حكما وعلما وكذلك نجزي المحسنين ﴿٢٢﴾

12:15 SO WHEN they took him with them, they together resolved to cast him into a dark pit. We revealed to him Our will, saying: 'You shall tell them of all this when they will not know you.'

At nightfall they returned to their father, weeping. 'Father,' they said, 'we went off to compete together, and left Joseph with our packs. The wolf devoured him. But you will not believe us, though we speak the truth.' And they brought him their brother's shirt, stained with false blood.

'No!' he cried. 'Your souls have tempted you to something evil. Sweet patience! God alone can help me bear the loss you speak of.'

12:19 And a caravan passed by,
who sent their water-bearer to the pit. And when he had let down his pail, he
cried: 'Rejoice! Here is a boy!'

They concealed him as part of their merchandise. But God knew what they did. They sold him for a trifling price, for a few pieces of silver. They cared nothing for him.

The Egyptian who bought him said to his wife: 'Be kind to him. He may prove useful to us, or we may adopt him as our son.'

Thus We established Joseph in the land, and taught him to interpret
dreams. God has power to accomplish His will, though most may not know
12:22 it. And when he reached maturity We bestowed on him wisdom and knowledge. Thus do We reward the righteous.

وَرَاوَدَتْهُ الَّتِي هُوَ فِي بَيْتِهَا عَنْ نَفْسِهِ وَغَلَّقَتِ الْأَبْوَابَ
وَقَالَتْ هَيْتَ لَكَ قَالَ مَعَاذَ اللَّهِ إِنَّهُ رَبِّي أَحْسَنَ
مَثْوَايَ إِنَّهُ لَا يُفْلِحُ الظَّالِمُونَ ﴿٢٣﴾ وَلَقَدْ هَمَّتْ بِهِ
وَهَمَّ بِهَا لَوْلَا أَنْ رَأَى بُرْهَانَ رَبِّهِ كَذَٰلِكَ لِنَصْرِفَ عَنْهُ
السُّوءَ وَالْفَحْشَاءَ إِنَّهُ مِنْ عِبَادِنَا الْمُخْلَصِينَ ﴿٢٤﴾ وَاسْتَبَقَا
الْبَابَ وَقَدَّتْ قَمِيصَهُ مِنْ دُبُرٍ وَأَلْفَيَا سَيِّدَهَا لَدَا الْبَابِ
قَالَتْ مَا جَزَاءُ مَنْ أَرَادَ بِأَهْلِكَ سُوءًا إِلَّا أَنْ يُسْجَنَ أَوْ
عَذَابٌ أَلِيمٌ ﴿٢٥﴾ قَالَ هِيَ رَاوَدَتْنِي عَنْ نَفْسِي وَشَهِدَ شَاهِدٌ مِنْ
أَهْلِهَا إِنْ كَانَ قَمِيصُهُ قُدَّ مِنْ قُبُلٍ فَصَدَقَتْ وَهُوَ مِنَ الْكَاذِبِينَ
﴿٢٦﴾ وَإِنْ كَانَ قَمِيصُهُ قُدَّ مِنْ دُبُرٍ فَكَذَبَتْ وَهُوَ مِنَ الصَّادِقِينَ
﴿٢٧﴾ فَلَمَّا رَأَى قَمِيصَهُ قُدَّ مِنْ دُبُرٍ قَالَ إِنَّهُ مِنْ كَيْدِكُنَّ
إِنَّ كَيْدَكُنَّ عَظِيمٌ ﴿٢٨﴾ يُوسُفُ أَعْرِضْ عَنْ هَٰذَا
وَاسْتَغْفِرِي لِذَنْبِكِ إِنَّكِ كُنْتِ مِنَ الْخَاطِئِينَ ﴿٢٩﴾ وَقَالَ
نِسْوَةٌ فِي الْمَدِينَةِ امْرَأَتُ الْعَزِيزِ تُرَاوِدُ فَتَاهَا عَنْ نَفْسِهِ
قَدْ شَغَفَهَا حُبًّا إِنَّا لَنَرَاهَا فِي ضَلَالٍ مُبِينٍ ﴿٣٠﴾

THE WOMAN in whose 12:23
house he served attempted to
seduce him. She bolted the
doors and said: 'Come!'

'God forbid!' he replied. 'My lord has treated me with kindness. Wrongdoers shall never prosper.'

She made for him, and he himself would have succumbed to her had he not seen the sign of his Lord. Thus did We shield him from evil-doing and lechery, for he was one of Our faithful servants.

They both rushed to the door. She tore his shirt from behind. And at the door they met her husband.

She said: 'Shall not the man who wished to violate your wife be thrown into prison or sternly punished?'

Joseph said: 'It was she who attempted to seduce me.' 12:26

'If his shirt is torn from the front,' said one of her people who was present, 'she is speaking the truth and he is lying. And if his shirt is torn from behind, then she is lying and he is speaking the truth.'

And when her husband saw that Joseph's shirt was rent from behind, he said to her: 'This is but one of your tricks. Your cunning is great indeed! Joseph, say no more about this. Woman, ask pardon for your sin. You have assuredly done wrong.'

In the city, women were saying: 'The Prince's wife has sought to seduce 12:30
her servant. She has conceived a passion for him. We can see that she has
clearly gone astray.'

12:31 WHEN SHE heard of their intrigues, she invited them to a banquet prepared at her house. To each she gave a knife, and ordered Joseph to present himself before them. When they saw him, they were amazed at him and cut their hands, exclaiming: 'God preserve us! This is no mortal, but a gracious angel.'

'This is he,' she said, 'on whose account you blamed me. I attempted to seduce him, but he was unyielding. If he declines to do my bidding, he shall be thrown into prison and shall be held in scorn.'

'Lord,' said Joseph, 'sooner would I go to prison than give in to their advances. Shield me from their cunning, or I shall yield to them and lapse into folly.'

فَلَمَّا سَمِعَتْ بِمَكْرِهِنَّ أَرْسَلَتْ إِلَيْهِنَّ وَأَعْتَدَتْ لَهُنَّ مُتَّكَأً وَآتَتْ كُلَّ وَاحِدَةٍ
مِنْهُنَّ سِكِّينًا وَقَالَتِ اخْرُجْ عَلَيْهِنَّ فَلَمَّا رَأَيْنَهُ أَكْبَرْنَهُ وَقَطَّعْنَ
أَيْدِيَهُنَّ وَقُلْنَ حَاشَ لِلَّهِ مَا هَٰذَا بَشَرًا إِنْ هَٰذَا إِلَّا مَلَكٌ كَرِيمٌ
٣١ قَالَتْ فَذَٰلِكُنَّ الَّذِي لُمْتُنَّنِي فِيهِ وَلَقَدْ رَاوَدْتُهُ عَنْ نَفْسِهِ
فَاسْتَعْصَمَ وَلَئِنْ لَمْ يَفْعَلْ مَا آمُرُهُ لَيُسْجَنَنَّ وَلَيَكُونًا مِنَ
الصَّاغِرِينَ ٣٢ قَالَ رَبِّ السِّجْنُ أَحَبُّ إِلَيَّ مِمَّا يَدْعُونَنِي إِلَيْهِ
وَإِلَّا تَصْرِفْ عَنِّي كَيْدَهُنَّ أَصْبُ إِلَيْهِنَّ وَأَكُنْ مِنَ الْجَاهِلِينَ
٣٣ فَاسْتَجَابَ لَهُ رَبُّهُ فَصَرَفَ عَنْهُ كَيْدَهُنَّ إِنَّهُ هُوَ السَّمِيعُ
الْعَلِيمُ ٣٤ ثُمَّ بَدَا لَهُمْ مِنْ بَعْدِ مَا رَأَوُا الْآيَاتِ لَيَسْجُنُنَّهُ
حَتَّىٰ حِينٍ ٣٥ وَدَخَلَ مَعَهُ السِّجْنَ فَتَيَانِ قَالَ أَحَدُهُمَا
إِنِّي أَرَانِي أَعْصِرُ خَمْرًا وَقَالَ الْآخَرُ إِنِّي أَرَانِي أَحْمِلُ فَوْقَ رَأْسِي
خُبْزًا تَأْكُلُ الطَّيْرُ مِنْهُ نَبِّئْنَا بِتَأْوِيلِهِ إِنَّا نَرَاكَ مِنَ الْمُحْسِنِينَ
٣٦ قَالَ لَا يَأْتِيكُمَا طَعَامٌ تُرْزَقَانِهِ إِلَّا نَبَّأْتُكُمَا بِتَأْوِيلِهِ
قَبْلَ أَنْ يَأْتِيَكُمَا ذَٰلِكُمَا مِمَّا عَلَّمَنِي رَبِّي إِنِّي تَرَكْتُ
مِلَّةَ قَوْمٍ لَا يُؤْمِنُونَ بِاللَّهِ وَهُمْ بِالْآخِرَةِ هُمْ كَافِرُونَ ٣٧

12:34 His Lord answered his prayer and warded off their cunning from him. Surely He it is who hears all and knows all.

Yet, for all the evidence they had seen, they thought it right to jail him for a time.

Two young men entered the prison with him. One said: 'I dreamt that I was pressing grapes.' And the other: 'I dreamt I was carrying a loaf upon my head, and the birds came and ate of it. Tell us the meaning of these dreams, for we can see you are a man of virtue.'

12:37 He said: 'Whatever food you are provided with, I can divine for you its meaning, even before it reaches you. This knowledge my Lord has given me, for I have left the faith of those that disbelieve in God and deny the life to come.

وَاتَّبَعْتُ مِلَّةَ آبَائِي إِبْرٰهِيمَ وَإِسْحٰقَ وَيَعْقُوبَ مَا كَانَ
لَنَا أَنْ نُشْرِكَ بِاللّٰهِ مِنْ شَيْءٍ ذٰلِكَ مِنْ فَضْلِ اللّٰهِ عَلَيْنَا
وَعَلَى النَّاسِ وَلٰكِنَّ أَكْثَرَ النَّاسِ لَا يَشْكُرُونَ ﴿٣٨﴾
يَا صَاحِبَيِ السِّجْنِ ءَأَرْبَابٌ مُتَفَرِّقُونَ خَيْرٌ أَمِ اللّٰهُ الْوَاحِدُ
الْقَهَّارُ ﴿٣٩﴾ مَا تَعْبُدُونَ مِنْ دُونِهِ إِلَّا أَسْمَاءً سَمَّيْتُمُوهَا أَنْتُمْ
وَآبَاؤُكُمْ مَا أَنْزَلَ اللّٰهُ بِهَا مِنْ سُلْطَانٍ إِنِ الْحُكْمُ إِلَّا لِلّٰهِ أَمَرَ أَلَّا
تَعْبُدُوا إِلَّا إِيَّاهُ ذٰلِكَ الدِّينُ الْقَيِّمُ وَلٰكِنَّ أَكْثَرَ النَّاسِ
لَا يَعْلَمُونَ ﴿٤٠﴾ يَا صَاحِبَيِ السِّجْنِ أَمَّا أَحَدُكُمَا فَيَسْقِي رَبَّهُ خَمْرًا وَأَمَّا
الْآخَرُ فَيُصْلَبُ فَتَأْكُلُ الطَّيْرُ مِنْ رَأْسِهِ قُضِيَ الْأَمْرُ الَّذِي
فِيهِ تَسْتَفْتِيَانِ ﴿٤١﴾ وَقَالَ لِلَّذِي ظَنَّ أَنَّهُ نَاجٍ مِنْهُمَا
اذْكُرْنِي عِنْدَ رَبِّكَ فَأَنْسَاهُ الشَّيْطَانُ ذِكْرَ رَبِّهِ فَلَبِثَ فِي
السِّجْنِ بِضْعَ سِنِينَ ﴿٤٢﴾ وَقَالَ الْمَلِكُ إِنِّي أَرَى سَبْعَ
بَقَرَاتٍ سِمَانٍ يَأْكُلُهُنَّ سَبْعٌ عِجَافٌ وَسَبْعَ
سُنْبُلَاتٍ خُضْرٍ وَأُخَرَ يَابِسَاتٍ يَا أَيُّهَا الْمَلَأُ أَفْتُونِي
فِي رُؤْيَايَ إِنْ كُنْتُمْ لِلرُّؤْيَا تَعْبُرُونَ ﴿٤٣﴾

AND I followed the faith of 12:38
my forefathers, Abraham, Isaac, and Jacob. We are not to serve idols besides God. Such is the grace which God has bestowed on us and on mankind. Yet the larger part of mankind do not give thanks.

'Fellow prisoners! Are sundry gods better than God, the One who conquers all? Those you serve besides Him are nothing but names which you and your fathers have devised and for which God has revealed no sanction. Judgement rests only with God. He has commanded you to worship none but Him. That is the True Religion: but the larger part of mankind have no knowledge.

'Fellow prisoners, one of 12:41
you will serve his lord with wine. The other will be crucified, and the birds will peck at his head. That is the answer to your question.'

And he said to the prisoner who he knew would survive: 'Remember me in the presence of your lord.'

But Satan made him forget to mention Joseph to his lord, so that he stayed in prison for several years.

The King said: 'I saw seven fatted cows which seven lean ones devoured; 12:43
also seven green ears of corn and seven others dry. Tell me the meaning of this vision, my nobles, if you can interpret visions.'

قالوا أضغاث أحلام وما نحن بتأويل الأحلام بعالمين ﴿٤٤﴾
وقال الذي نجا منهما وادكر بعد أمة أنا أنبئكم بتأويله
فأرسلون ﴿٤٥﴾ يوسف أيها الصديق أفتنا في سبع بقرات سمان
يأكلهن سبع عجاف وسبع سنبلات خضر وأخر يابسات لعلي
أرجع إلى الناس لعلهم يعلمون ﴿٤٦﴾ قال تزرعون سبع سنين دأبا
فما حصدتم فذروه في سنبله إلا قليلا مما تأكلون ﴿٤٧﴾ ثم يأتي
من بعد ذلك سبع شداد يأكلن ما قدمتم لهن إلا قليلا مما
تحصنون ﴿٤٨﴾ ثم يأتي من بعد ذلك عام فيه يغاث الناس وفيه
يعصرون ﴿٤٩﴾ وقال الملك ائتوني به فلما جاءه الرسول قال ارجع إلى
ربك فسئله ما بال النسوة التي قطعن أيديهن إن
ربي بكيدهن عليم ﴿٥٠﴾ قال ما خطبكن إذ راودتن يوسف
عن نفسه قلن حاش لله ما علمنا عليه من سوء قالت
امرأت العزيز الآن حصحص الحق أنا راودته عن
نفسه وإنه لمن الصادقين ﴿٥١﴾ ذلك ليعلم أني لم
أخنه بالغيب وأن الله لا يهدي كيد الخائنين ﴿٥٢﴾

12:44 THEY SAID: 'They are but a
medley of dreams; nor are we
skilled in the interpretation of
dreams.'
Thereupon the man who
had been freed remembered
after all that time. He said: 'I
shall bring you what it means.
Give me leave to go.'
'Joseph,' he said, 'man of
truth, tell us of the seven fatted cows which seven lean
ones devoured; also of the
seven green ears of corn and
the other seven which were
dry: so that I may go back to
the people and inform them.'
He said: 'You shall sow for
seven consecutive years. Leave
in the ear the corn you reap,
except a little which you may
eat. There shall follow seven
hungry years which will con-
sume all but a little of what you stored. Then will come a year of abundant
rain, in which the people will press the grape.'
12:50 He said: 'Bring this man before me.'
But when the envoy came to him, Joseph said: 'Go back to your master
and ask him about the women who cut their hands. My master well knows
their cunning.'
The King questioned the women, saying: 'What made you attempt to
seduce Joseph?'
'God forbid!' they said. 'We know no evil of him.'
'Now the truth must come to light,' said the Prince's wife. 'It was I who
attempted to seduce him. He has told the truth.'
12:52 'From this,' said Joseph, 'my lord will know that I did not betray him in his
absence, and that God does not guide the mischief of the treacherous.

وما أبرئ نفسي إن النفس لأمارة بالسوء إلا ما رحم ربي إن ربي
غفور رحيم ﴿٥٣﴾ وقال الملك ائتوني به أستخلصه لنفسي
فلما كلمه قال إنك اليوم لدينا مكين أمين ﴿٥٤﴾ قال اجعلني
على خزائن الأرض إني حفيظ عليم ﴿٥٥﴾ وكذلك مكنا ليوسف
في الأرض يتبوأ منها حيث يشاء نصيب برحمتنا من
نشاء ولا نضيع أجر المحسنين ﴿٥٦﴾ ولأجر الآخرة خير
للذين آمنوا وكانوا يتقون ﴿٥٧﴾ وجاء إخوة يوسف
فدخلوا عليه فعرفهم وهم له منكرون ﴿٥٨﴾ ولما جهزهم
بجهازهم قال ائتوني بأخ لكم من أبيكم ألا ترون أني
أوفي الكيل وأنا خير المنزلين ﴿٥٩﴾ فإن لم تأتوني به فلا كيل
لكم عندي ولا تقربون ﴿٦٠﴾ قالوا سنراود عنه أباه وإنا
لفاعلون ﴿٦١﴾ وقال لفتيانه اجعلوا بضاعتهم في رحالهم
لعلهم يعرفونها إذا انقلبوا إلى أهلهم لعلهم يرجعون
﴿٦٢﴾ فلما رجعوا إلى أبيهم قالوا يا أبانا منع منا الكيل
فأرسل معنا أخانا نكتل وإنا له لحافظون ﴿٦٣﴾

NOT THAT I claim to be free 12:53
from sin: man's soul is prone
to evil, except his to whom my
Lord has shown mercy. My
Lord is forgiving and compassionate.'

The King said: 'Bring him before me. I will choose him for my own.'

And when he had spoken with him, he said: 'You shall henceforth dwell with us, honoured and trusted.'

Joseph said: 'Give me charge of the granaries of the land. I know how to husband them wisely.'

Thus did We establish Joseph in the land, and he dwelt there as he pleased. We bestow Our mercy on whom We will, and never deny the righteous their reward. Surely better is the recompense of the life to come for those who believe in God and fear Him.

Joseph's brothers came and presented themselves before him. He recog- 12:58
nized them, but they knew him not. And when he had given them their
provisions, he said: 'Bring me a brother of yours from your father. Do you
not see that I give just measure and am the best of hosts? If you refuse to
bring him to me, you shall have no measure here, nor shall you come near
me.'

They replied: 'We will endeavour to fetch him from his father. This we will surely do.'

He said to his servants: 'Put their silver[1] into their packs, so that they may discover it when they return to their people. Perchance they will come back.'

When they returned to their father, they said: 'Father, corn is henceforth 12:63
denied us. Send our brother with us and we shall have our measure. We will
take good care of him.'

1. Literally, their merchandise.

قَالَ هَلْ آمَنُكُمْ عَلَيْهِ إِلَّا كَمَا أَمِنتُكُمْ عَلَىٰ أَخِيهِ
مِن قَبْلُ فَاللَّهُ خَيْرٌ حَافِظًا وَهُوَ أَرْحَمُ الرَّاحِمِينَ ﴿٦٤﴾ وَلَمَّا
فَتَحُوا مَتَاعَهُمْ وَجَدُوا بِضَاعَتَهُمْ رُدَّتْ إِلَيْهِمْ قَالُوا يَا أَبَانَا
مَا نَبْغِي هَٰذِهِ بِضَاعَتُنَا رُدَّتْ إِلَيْنَا وَنَمِيرُ أَهْلَنَا وَنَحْفَظُ
أَخَانَا وَنَزْدَادُ كَيْلَ بَعِيرٍ ذَٰلِكَ كَيْلٌ يَسِيرٌ ﴿٦٥﴾ قَالَ لَنْ
أُرْسِلَهُ مَعَكُمْ حَتَّىٰ تُؤْتُونِ مَوْثِقًا مِّنَ اللَّهِ لَتَأْتُنَّنِي بِهِ
إِلَّا أَن يُحَاطَ بِكُمْ فَلَمَّا آتَوْهُ مَوْثِقَهُمْ قَالَ اللَّهُ عَلَىٰ مَا نَقُولُ
وَكِيلٌ ﴿٦٦﴾ وَقَالَ يَا بَنِيَّ لَا تَدْخُلُوا مِن بَابٍ وَاحِدٍ وَادْخُلُوا
مِنْ أَبْوَابٍ مُّتَفَرِّقَةٍ وَمَا أُغْنِي عَنكُم مِّنَ اللَّهِ مِن شَيْءٍ إِنِ
الْحُكْمُ إِلَّا لِلَّهِ عَلَيْهِ تَوَكَّلْتُ وَعَلَيْهِ فَلْيَتَوَكَّلِ الْمُتَوَكِّلُونَ
﴿٦٧﴾ وَلَمَّا دَخَلُوا مِنْ حَيْثُ أَمَرَهُمْ أَبُوهُم مَّا كَانَ يُغْنِي
عَنْهُم مِّنَ اللَّهِ مِن شَيْءٍ إِلَّا حَاجَةً فِي نَفْسِ يَعْقُوبَ قَضَاهَا
وَإِنَّهُ لَذُو عِلْمٍ لِّمَا عَلَّمْنَاهُ وَلَٰكِنَّ أَكْثَرَ النَّاسِ لَا يَعْلَمُونَ
﴿٦٨﴾ وَلَمَّا دَخَلُوا عَلَىٰ يُوسُفَ آوَىٰ إِلَيْهِ أَخَاهُ قَالَ إِنِّي
أَنَا أَخُوكَ فَلَا تَبْتَئِسْ بِمَا كَانُوا يَعْمَلُونَ ﴿٦٩﴾

12:64 He said: 'Am I to trust you
with him as I once trusted you
with his brother? But God is
the best of guardians: and of
all those that show mercy He
is the most merciful.'

When they opened their
packs, they discovered that
their silver had been returned
to them. 'Father,' they said,
'what more can we desire?
Here is our silver returned to
us. We will buy provisions for
our people, and take good care
of our brother. We should
receive an extra camel-load;
a camel-load should be easy
enough.'

12:66 He replied: 'I will not send
him with you until you promise in God's name to bring him
back to me, unless the worst
befall you.'

And when they had given him their pledge, he said: 'God is the witness of
what we say. My sons, do not enter from one gate; enter from different gates.
In no way can I shield you from the might of God; judgement is God's
alone. In Him I have put my trust. In Him let the trustful put their trust.'

And when they entered as their father bade them, he could in no way
shield them from the might of God. It was but a wish in Jacob's soul which
he had thus fulfilled. He was possessed of knowledge which We had given
him. But the greater part of mankind have no knowledge.

12:69 When they went in to Joseph, he embraced his brother, and said: 'I am
your brother. Do not grieve at what they did.'

فلما جهزهم بجهازهم جعل السقاية في رحل أخيه ثم
أذن مؤذن أيتها العير إنكم لسارقون ﴿٧٠﴾ قالوا وأقبلوا
عليهم ماذا تفقدون ﴿٧١﴾ قالوا نفقد صواع الملك ولمن
جاء به حمل بعير وأنا به زعيم ﴿٧٢﴾ قالوا تالله لقد
علمتم ما جئنا لنفسد في الأرض وما كنا سارقين ﴿٧٣﴾ قالوا
فما جزاؤه إن كنتم كاذبين ﴿٧٤﴾ قالوا جزاؤه من
وجد في رحله فهو جزاؤه كذلك نجزي الظالمين
﴿٧٥﴾ فبدأ بأوعيتهم قبل وعاء أخيه ثم استخرجها
من وعاء أخيه كذلك كدنا ليوسف ما كان
ليأخذ أخاه في دين الملك إلا أن يشاء الله نرفع
درجات من نشاء وفوق كل ذي علم عليم ﴿٧٦﴾ قالوا إن
يسرق فقد سرق أخ له من قبل فأسرها يوسف في
نفسه ولم يبدها لهم قال أنتم شر مكانا والله أعلم
بما تصفون ﴿٧٧﴾ قالوا يا أيها العزيز إن له أبا شيخا كبيرا
فخذ أحدنا مكانه إنا نراك من المحسنين ﴿٧٨﴾

AND WHEN he had pro- 12:70
vided them with their
provisions, he hid a drinking-
cup in his brother's pack.

Then a crier called: 'Travellers, you are surely thieves!'

They turned back to them, and said: 'What have you lost?'

'We miss the King's drinking-cup,' they said. 'He that brings it shall have a camel-load. I pledge my word for it.'

'In God's name,' they said, 'you know we did not come to do evil in the land. We are no thieves.'

They said: 'What punishment shall be his, if you prove to be lying?'

They said: 'He in whose pack the cup is found shall penalize himself for what he did. Thus do we punish the wrongdoers.'

He searched their bags before his brother's, and then took out the cup 12:76
from his brother's bag.

Thus did we devise it for Joseph: by the King's law he had no right to seize his brother: but God willed otherwise. We exalt whom We will to a lofty station: and above those that have knowledge there is One who is all-knowing.

They said: 'If he has stolen – know then that a brother of his did steal before him.'

But Joseph kept his secret and revealed nothing to them. He said: 'Your deed was worse. God best knows the things you speak of.'

They said: 'Noble Prince, he has an aged father; take one of us, instead of 12:78
him. We can see you are a man of virtue.'

قال معاذ الله ان نأخذ الا من وجدنا متاعنا عنده
انا اذا لظالمون ۝ فلما استيأسوا منه خلصوا نجيا
قال كبيرهم الم تعلموا ان اباكم قد اخذ عليكم
موثقا من الله ومن قبل ما فرطتم في يوسف فلن ابرح
الارض حتى يأذن لي ابي او يحكم الله لي وهو خير الحاكمين
٨٠ ارجعوا الى ابيكم فقولوا يا ابانا ان ابنك سرق
وما شهدنا الا بما علمنا وما كنا للغيب حافظين
٨١ واسئل القرية التي كنا فيها والعير التي اقبلنا
فيها وانا لصادقون ۝ قال بل سولت لكم انفسكم
امرا فصبر جميل عسى الله ان يأتيني بهم جميعا
انه هو العليم الحكيم ٨٣ وتولى عنهم وقال يا اسفى
على يوسف وابيضت عيناه من الحزن فهو كظيم
۝ قالوا تالله تفتؤا تذكر يوسف حتى تكون حرضا
او تكون من الهالكين ۝ قال انما اشكوا بثي
وحزني الى الله واعلم من الله ما لا تعلمون ٨٦

12:79 HE SAID: 'God forbid that
we should take any but the
man with whom our property
was found: for then we should
surely be unjust.'
When they despaired of
him, they went aside to confer
in private. Their eldest said:
'Do you not know that your
father took from you a pledge
in God's name, and that long
before you did your worst with
Joseph? I will not stir from the
land until my father gives me
leave or God makes known to
me His judgement: He is the
12:81 best of judges. Return to your
father and say to him: "Father,
your son has stolen. We testify
only to what we know: we
could not guard against the
unforeseen. Inquire at the city
wherein we lodged, and from
the caravan we travelled with. We surely speak the truth."'

'No!' cried their father. 'Your souls have tempted you to evil. But I will have sweet patience. God may bring them all to me: He alone is all-knowing and wise.' And he turned away from them, crying: 'Alas for Joseph!' His eyes went white with grief, and he was oppressed with silent sorrow.

They said: 'In God's name, will you not cease to remember Joseph until you ruin your health and die?'

12:86 He said: 'I complain only to God of my sorrow and sadness; God has
made known to me things that you know not.

يا بني اذهبوا فتحسسوا من يوسف وأخيه ولا تيأسوا من روح
الله إنه لا ييأس من روح الله إلا القوم الكافرون
﴿٨٧﴾ فلما دخلوا عليه قالوا يا أيها العزيز مسنا
وأهلنا الضر وجئنا ببضاعة مزجاة فأوف
لنا الكيل وتصدق علينا إن الله يجزي المتصدقين
﴿٨٨﴾ قال هل علمتم ما فعلتم بيوسف وأخيه إذ
أنتم جاهلون ﴿٨٩﴾ قالوا أءنك لأنت يوسف قال أنا
يوسف وهذا أخي قد من الله علينا إنه من
يتق ويصبر فإن الله لا يضيع أجر المحسنين ﴿٩٠﴾ قالوا
تالله لقد آثرك الله علينا وإن كنا لخاطئين ﴿٩١﴾ قال
لا تثريب عليكم اليوم يغفر الله لكم وهو أرحم
الراحمين ﴿٩٢﴾ اذهبوا بقميصي هذا فألقوه على وجه
أبي يأت بصيرا وأتوني بأهلكم أجمعين ﴿٩٣﴾ ولما
فصلت العير قال أبوهم إني لأجد ريح يوسف لولا أن
تفندون ﴿٩٤﴾ قالوا تالله إنك لفي ضلالك القديم ﴿٩٥﴾

GO, MY sons, and seek news 12:87
of Joseph and his brother.
And do not despair of God's
spirit; none but unbelievers
despair of God's spirit.'

And when they went in to
him, they said: 'Noble Prince,
we and our people are scourged
with famine. We have brought
but little money. Give us our
full measure, and be charitable
to us: God surely rewards the
charitable.'

'Do you know,' he said,
'what you did to Joseph and
his brother? You are surely
unaware.'

They said: 'Can you indeed
be Joseph?'

'I am Joseph,' he said, 'and
this is my brother. God has
been gracious to us. Those
that fear God and endure with
fortitude, God will not deny the virtuous their reward.'

'By the Lord,' they said, 'God has exalted you above us all. We have indeed 12:91
done wrong.'

He said: 'None shall reproach you this day. May God forgive you: of all
those that show mercy He is the most merciful. Take this shirt of mine and
throw it over my father's face: he will recover his sight. Then return to me
with your people all.'

When the caravan departed their father said: 'I feel the breath of Joseph,
though you will not believe me.'

'By the Lord,' they said, 'you are surely under your old illusion.' 12:95

فلما ان جاء البشير القيه على وجهه فارتد بصيرا قال الم
اقل لكم اني اعلم من الله ما لا تعلمون ٩٦ قالوا يابانا
استغفر لنا ذنوبنا انا كنا خاطئين ٩٧ قال سوف
استغفر لكم ربي انه هو الغفور الرحيم ٩٨ فلما دخلوا على
يوسف اوى اليه ابويه وقال ادخلوا مصر ان شاء
الله امنين ٩٩ ورفع ابويه على العرش وخروا له سجدا
وقال يابت هذا تاويل رءياى من قبل قد جعلها
ربي حقا وقد احسن بي اذ اخرجني من السجن وجاء بكم
من البدو من بعد ان نزغ الشيطان بيني وبين
اخوتي ان ربي لطيف لما يشاء انه هو العليم الحكيم ١٠٠
رب قد اتيتني من الملك وعلمتني من تاويل الاحاديث
فاطر السموات والارض انت ولي في الدنيا والاخرة
توفني مسلما والحقني بالصالحين ١٠١ ذلك من انباء
الغيب نوحيه اليك وما كنت لديهم اذ اجمعوا امرهم وهم
يمكرون ١٠٢ وما اكثر الناس ولو حرصت بمؤمنين ١٠٣

12:96 AND WHEN the bearer of joyful tidings arrived, he threw Joseph's shirt over the old man's face, and he regained his sight. He said: 'Did I not tell you, God has made known to me what you know not?'

They said: 'Father, implore forgiveness for our sins. We have indeed done wrong.'

He said: 'I shall implore my Lord to forgive you. He it is who is the Forgiving, the Compassionate One.'

And when they went in to Joseph, he embraced his parents and said: 'Welcome to Egypt, safe, if God wills!'

12:100 He helped up his parents to the throne, and they all fell on their knees and prostrated themselves before him.

'This,' he said to his father, 'is the meaning of my old vision: my Lord has fulfilled it. He has been gracious to me; He has released me from prison, and brought you out of the desert after Satan had stirred up strife between me and my brothers. My Lord is gracious to whom He will: He alone is all-knowing and wise.

'Lord, You have given me authority and taught me to interpret dreams. Creator of the heavens and the earth, my guardian in this world and in the world to come! Allow me to die a Muslim, and admit me among the righteous.'

That which We now reveal to you[1] is a tale of the unknown. You were not
present when they conceived their plan, and when they schemed together.
12:103 Yet strive as you may, the greater part of mankind will not believe.

1. Muḥammad.

وَمَا تَسْأَلُهُمْ عَلَيْهِ مِنْ أَجْرٍ إِنْ هُوَ إِلَّا ذِكْرٌ لِلْعَالَمِينَ
(١٠٤) وَكَأَيِّنْ مِنْ آيَةٍ فِي السَّمَاوَاتِ وَالْأَرْضِ يَمُرُّونَ عَلَيْهَا
وَهُمْ عَنْهَا مُعْرِضُونَ (١٠٥) وَمَا يُؤْمِنُ أَكْثَرُهُمْ بِاللَّهِ
إِلَّا وَهُمْ مُشْرِكُونَ (١٠٦) أَفَأَمِنُوا أَنْ تَأْتِيَهُمْ غَاشِيَةٌ مِنْ عَذَابِ اللَّهِ
أَوْ تَأْتِيَهُمُ السَّاعَةُ بَغْتَةً وَهُمْ لَا يَشْعُرُونَ (١٠٧) قُلْ هَذِهِ سَبِيلِي
أَدْعُو إِلَى اللَّهِ عَلَى بَصِيرَةٍ أَنَا وَمَنِ اتَّبَعَنِي وَسُبْحَانَ اللَّهِ
وَمَا أَنَا مِنَ الْمُشْرِكِينَ (١٠٨) وَمَا أَرْسَلْنَا مِنْ قَبْلِكَ إِلَّا
رِجَالًا نُوحِي إِلَيْهِمْ مِنْ أَهْلِ الْقُرَى أَفَلَمْ يَسِيرُوا فِي الْأَرْضِ
فَيَنْظُرُوا كَيْفَ كَانَ عَاقِبَةُ الَّذِينَ مِنْ قَبْلِهِمْ وَلَدَارُ
الْآخِرَةِ خَيْرٌ لِلَّذِينَ اتَّقَوْا أَفَلَا تَعْقِلُونَ (١٠٩) حَتَّى إِذَا
اسْتَيْأَسَ الرُّسُلُ وَظَنُّوا أَنَّهُمْ قَدْ كُذِبُوا جَاءَهُمْ
نَصْرُنَا فَنُجِّيَ مَنْ نَشَاءُ وَلَا يُرَدُّ بَأْسُنَا عَنِ الْقَوْمِ الْمُجْرِمِينَ
(١١٠) لَقَدْ كَانَ فِي قَصَصِهِمْ عِبْرَةٌ لِأُولِي الْأَلْبَابِ مَا كَانَ
حَدِيثًا يُفْتَرَى وَلَكِنْ تَصْدِيقَ الَّذِي بَيْنَ يَدَيْهِ وَتَفْصِيلَ
كُلِّ شَيْءٍ وَهُدًى وَرَحْمَةً لِقَوْمٍ يُؤْمِنُونَ (١١١)

AND YOU demand of them 12:104
no recompense for this: it is
but an Admonition to mankind.

Many are the marvels in the
heavens and the earth; yet they
pass them by and pay no heed
to them. The greater part of
them believe in God only if
they can worship other gods
besides Him.

Are they confident they will
not be overwhelmed by a
scourge from God, or that the
Hour will not overtake them
unawares, without warning?

Say: 'This is my path. With 12:108
sure knowledge I call on you to
have faith in God, I and all my
followers. Glory be to God! I
am no idolater.'

Nor were those We sent
before you other than men We
inspired from people of the cities.

Have they not travelled the land and seen what was the end of those who
disbelieved before them? Surely better is the life to come for those that fear
God. Can you not understand?

And when the apostles despaired and thought they were denied, Our help
came down to them, delivering whom We pleased. The transgressors could
not be saved from Our power. Their annals point a moral to those that are 12:111
of good sense possessed.

This is no invented tale, but a confirmation of what came before it, an
explanation of all things, a guide and a blessing to people who believe.

THUNDER

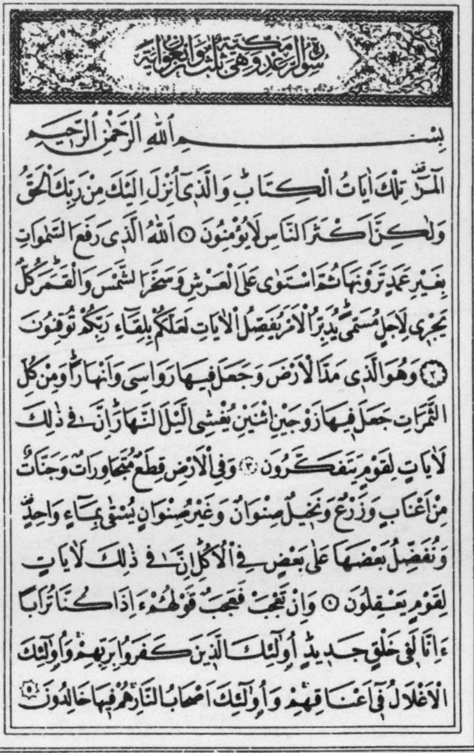
سورة الرعد مكية وهي ثلث واربعون آية

بسم الله الرحمن الرحيم
المر تلك آيات الكتاب والذي أنزل إليك من ربك الحق
ولكن أكثر الناس لا يؤمنون ۝ الله الذي رفع السموات
بغير عمد ترونها ثم استوى على العرش وسخر الشمس والقمر كل
يجري لأجل مسمى يدبر الأمر يفصل الآيات لعلكم بلقاء ربكم توقنون
۝ وهو الذي مد الأرض وجعل فيها رواسي وأنهارا ومن كل
الثمرات جعل فيها زوجين اثنين يغشي الليل النهار إن في ذلك
لآيات لقوم يتفكرون ۝ وفي الأرض قطع متجاورات وجنات
من أعناب وزرع ونخيل صنوان وغير صنوان يسقى بماء واحد
ونفضل بعضها على بعض في الأكل إن في ذلك لآيات
لقوم يعقلون ۝ وإن تعجب فعجب قولهم أإذا كنا ترابا
أإنا لفي خلق جديد أولئك الذين كفروا بربهم وأولئك
الأغلال في أعناقهم وأولئك أصحاب النار هم فيها خالدون ۝

In the Name of God,
the Merciful, the Compassionate

13:1 Alif *lām mīm rā'*. These are
the revelations of the Book:
and that which has been
revealed to you from your
Lord is Truth, yet most do not
believe.
It was God who raised the
heavens without visible pillars.
He then ascended the throne
and pressed the sun and the
moon into service, each pur-
suing an appointed course. He
ordains all things: He makes
plain His revelations, so that
you may firmly believe in
meeting your Lord.
13:3 It was He who spread out
the earth and placed upon it mountains and rivers. He gave all plants their
male and female parts and drew the veil of night over the day. Surely in these
there are signs for people who reflect.
And in the land there are adjoining plots: vineyards and cornfields and
groves of palm, the single and the clustered. Their fruits are nourished by
the same water: yet We make the taste of some more favoured than the taste
of others. Surely in this there are signs for people who understand.
13:5 If anything could make you marvel, then you should surely marvel at
those who say: 'When we are dust, shall we be restored in a new creation?'
Such are those who deny their Lord. Their necks shall be bound with
chains. Those are the tenants of the Fire, wherein shall they abide for ever.

وَيَسْتَعْجِلُونَكَ بِالسَّيِّئَةِ قَبْلَ الْحَسَنَةِ وَقَدْ خَلَتْ
مِنْ قَبْلِهِمُ الْمَثُلَاتُ وَإِنَّ رَبَّكَ لَذُو مَغْفِرَةٍ لِلنَّاسِ عَلَىٰ
ظُلْمِهِمْ وَإِنَّ رَبَّكَ لَشَدِيدُ الْعِقَابِ ﴿٦﴾ وَيَقُولُ الَّذِينَ
كَفَرُوا لَوْلَا أُنْزِلَ عَلَيْهِ آيَةٌ مِنْ رَبِّهِ إِنَّمَا أَنْتَ مُنْذِرٌ وَلِكُلِّ
قَوْمٍ هَادٍ ﴿٧﴾ اللَّهُ يَعْلَمُ مَا تَحْمِلُ كُلُّ أُنْثَىٰ وَمَا تَغِيضُ
الْأَرْحَامُ وَمَا تَزْدَادُ وَكُلُّ شَيْءٍ عِنْدَهُ بِمِقْدَارٍ ﴿٨﴾ عَالِمُ
الْغَيْبِ وَالشَّهَادَةِ الْكَبِيرُ الْمُتَعَالِ ﴿٩﴾ سَوَاءٌ مِنْكُمْ مَنْ
أَسَرَّ الْقَوْلَ وَمَنْ جَهَرَ بِهِ وَمَنْ هُوَ مُسْتَخْفٍ بِاللَّيْلِ وَسَارِبٌ
بِالنَّهَارِ ﴿١٠﴾ لَهُ مُعَقِّبَاتٌ مِنْ بَيْنِ يَدَيْهِ وَمِنْ خَلْفِهِ
يَحْفَظُونَهُ مِنْ أَمْرِ اللَّهِ إِنَّ اللَّهَ لَا يُغَيِّرُ مَا بِقَوْمٍ حَتَّىٰ
يُغَيِّرُوا مَا بِأَنْفُسِهِمْ وَإِذَا أَرَادَ اللَّهُ بِقَوْمٍ سُوءًا فَلَا مَرَدَّ لَهُ
وَمَا لَهُمْ مِنْ دُونِهِ مِنْ وَالٍ ﴿١١﴾ هُوَ الَّذِي يُرِيكُمُ الْبَرْقَ خَوْفًا
وَطَمَعًا وَيُنْشِئُ السَّحَابَ الثِّقَالَ ﴿١٢﴾ وَيُسَبِّحُ الرَّعْدُ بِحَمْدِهِ
وَالْمَلَائِكَةُ مِنْ خِيفَتِهِ وَيُرْسِلُ الصَّوَاعِقَ فَيُصِيبُ بِهَا
مَنْ يَشَاءُ وَهُمْ يُجَادِلُونَ فِي اللَّهِ وَهُوَ شَدِيدُ الْمِحَالِ ﴿١٣﴾

AND THEY bid you hasten 13:6
evil rather than good. Yet many were those who were punished before them. Your Lord is forgiving to people, despite their wrongdoing: yet stern is your Lord in retribution.

And the unbelievers say: 'Why has no sign been sent down to him from his Lord?' But you are only to give warning; every nation has its mentor.

God knows what every female bears: He knows the wombs whose term falls short, and those that signify increase. For everything He has a finite measure.

He knows the unknown 13:9
and the manifest: the Supreme One, the Most High.

It is the same whether you converse in secret or aloud, whether you hide under the cloak of night or walk about in the light of day. Each has guardian angels before him and behind him, who preserve him by God's command.

God does not change a people's lot unless they change what is in their hearts. If God seeks to afflict them with a misfortune, none can ward it off. Besides Him, they have no protector.

He it is who makes the lightning flash upon you, inspiring you with fear
and hope, and gathers up the heavy clouds. The thunder sounds His praises, 13:13
and the angels, too, in awe of Him. He hurls His thunderbolts at whom He pleases. Yet they wrangle about God; and stern is His might.

13:14 To HIM is the prayer of Truth. The idols to which they pray give them no answer. They are like a man who stretches out his hands to the water and bids it rise to his mouth: it cannot reach it. Vain are the prayers of the unbelievers.

All who dwell in the heavens and on the earth shall prostrate themselves before God: some willingly, some perforce; and their very shadows, morning and evening.

13:16 Say: 'Who is the Lord of the heavens and the earth?'

Say: 'God.'

Say: 'Why then have you chosen other gods besides Him, who, even to themselves, can do neither good nor harm?'

Say: 'Are the blind and the seeing equal? Is darkness equal to the light?'

لَهُ دَعْوَةُ الْحَقِّ وَالَّذِينَ يَدْعُونَ مِن دُونِهِ لَا يَسْتَجِيبُونَ لَهُم بِشَيْءٍ
إِلَّا كَبَاسِطِ كَفَّيْهِ إِلَى الْمَاءِ لِيَبْلُغَ فَاهُ وَمَا هُوَ بِبَالِغِهِ وَمَا دُعَاءُ
الْكَافِرِينَ إِلَّا فِي ضَلَالٍ ۝ وَلِلَّهِ يَسْجُدُ مَن فِي السَّمٰوٰتِ وَالْأَرْضِ
طَوْعًا وَكَرْهًا وَظِلَالُهُم بِالْغُدُوِّ وَالْآصَالِ ۝ قُلْ مَن رَّبُّ
السَّمٰوٰتِ وَالْأَرْضِ قُلِ اللَّهُ قُلْ أَفَاتَّخَذْتُم مِّن دُونِهِ
أَوْلِيَاءَ لَا يَمْلِكُونَ لِأَنفُسِهِمْ نَفْعًا وَلَا ضَرًّا قُلْ هَلْ يَسْتَوِي
الْأَعْمَىٰ وَالْبَصِيرُ أَمْ هَلْ تَسْتَوِي الظُّلُمَاتُ وَالنُّورُ أَمْ جَعَلُوا لِلَّهِ
شُرَكَاءَ خَلَقُوا كَخَلْقِهِ فَتَشَابَهَ الْخَلْقُ عَلَيْهِمْ قُلِ اللَّهُ
خَالِقُ كُلِّ شَيْءٍ وَهُوَ الْوَاحِدُ الْقَهَّارُ ۝ أَنزَلَ مِنَ السَّمَاءِ مَاءً
فَسَالَتْ أَوْدِيَةٌ بِقَدَرِهَا فَاحْتَمَلَ السَّيْلُ زَبَدًا رَّابِيًا وَمِمَّا يُوقِدُونَ
عَلَيْهِ فِي النَّارِ ابْتِغَاءَ حِلْيَةٍ أَوْ مَتَاعٍ زَبَدٌ مِّثْلُهُ كَذَٰلِكَ يَضْرِبُ اللَّهُ
الْحَقَّ وَالْبَاطِلَ فَأَمَّا الزَّبَدُ فَيَذْهَبُ جُفَاءً وَأَمَّا مَا يَنفَعُ النَّاسَ فَيَمْكُثُ
فِي الْأَرْضِ كَذَٰلِكَ يَضْرِبُ اللَّهُ الْأَمْثَالَ ۝ لِلَّذِينَ اسْتَجَابُوا لِرَبِّهِمُ
الْحُسْنَىٰ وَالَّذِينَ لَمْ يَسْتَجِيبُوا لَهُ لَوْ أَنَّ لَهُم مَّا فِي الْأَرْضِ جَمِيعًا وَمِثْلَهُ مَعَهُ
لَافْتَدَوْا بِهِ أُولَٰئِكَ لَهُمْ سُوءُ الْحِسَابِ وَمَأْوَاهُمْ جَهَنَّمُ وَبِئْسَ الْمِهَادُ ۝

Or have their idols brought into being a creation like His, so that both creations appear to them alike?

Say: 'God is the Creator of all things; He is the One who conquers all.'

He sends down water from the sky which fills the riverbeds to overflowing, so that the torrent bears a swelling foam, akin to that which rises from smelted ore when men make ornaments and tools. Thus God depicts Truth and falsehood. The scum is cast away, but that which is of use to man remains behind. Even thus God speaks in parables.

13:18 Rich is the recompense of those that obey their Lord. But those that disobey Him – if they possessed all that the earth contains, and as much besides, they would gladly offer it for their ransom. Theirs shall be a baleful reckoning. Hell shall be their home, an evil resting-place.

أَفَمَن يَعْلَمُ أَنَّمَا أُنزِلَ إِلَيْكَ مِن رَّبِّكَ الْحَقُّ كَمَنْ هُوَ أَعْمَىٰ إِنَّمَا يَتَذَكَّرُ
أُولُوا الْأَلْبَابِ ﴿١٩﴾ الَّذِينَ يُوفُونَ بِعَهْدِ اللَّهِ وَلَا يَنقُضُونَ الْمِيثَاقَ
﴿٢٠﴾ وَالَّذِينَ يَصِلُونَ مَا أَمَرَ اللَّهُ بِهِ أَن يُوصَلَ وَيَخْشَوْنَ رَبَّهُمْ وَيَخَافُونَ
سُوءَ الْحِسَابِ ﴿٢١﴾ وَالَّذِينَ صَبَرُوا ابْتِغَاءَ وَجْهِ رَبِّهِمْ وَأَقَامُوا
الصَّلَاةَ وَأَنفَقُوا مِمَّا رَزَقْنَاهُمْ سِرًّا وَعَلَانِيَةً وَيَدْرَءُونَ بِالْحَسَنَةِ
السَّيِّئَةَ أُولَٰئِكَ لَهُمْ عُقْبَى الدَّارِ ﴿٢٢﴾ جَنَّاتُ عَدْنٍ يَدْخُلُونَهَا وَمَن
صَلَحَ مِنْ آبَائِهِمْ وَأَزْوَاجِهِمْ وَذُرِّيَّاتِهِمْ وَالْمَلَائِكَةُ يَدْخُلُونَ
عَلَيْهِم مِّن كُلِّ بَابٍ ﴿٢٣﴾ سَلَامٌ عَلَيْكُم بِمَا صَبَرْتُمْ فَنِعْمَ عُقْبَى الدَّارِ
﴿٢٤﴾ وَالَّذِينَ يَنقُضُونَ عَهْدَ اللَّهِ مِن بَعْدِ مِيثَاقِهِ وَيَقْطَعُونَ مَا أَمَرَ
اللَّهُ بِهِ أَن يُوصَلَ وَيُفْسِدُونَ فِي الْأَرْضِ أُولَٰئِكَ لَهُمُ اللَّعْنَةُ
وَلَهُمْ سُوءُ الدَّارِ ﴿٢٥﴾ اللَّهُ يَبْسُطُ الرِّزْقَ لِمَن يَشَاءُ وَيَقْدِرُ
وَفَرِحُوا بِالْحَيَاةِ الدُّنْيَا وَمَا الْحَيَاةُ الدُّنْيَا فِي الْآخِرَةِ إِلَّا مَتَاعٌ
﴿٢٦﴾ وَيَقُولُ الَّذِينَ كَفَرُوا لَوْلَا أُنزِلَ عَلَيْهِ آيَةٌ مِّن رَّبِّهِ قُلْ إِنَّ
اللَّهَ يُضِلُّ مَن يَشَاءُ وَيَهْدِي إِلَيْهِ مَنْ أَنَابَ ﴿٢٧﴾ الَّذِينَ آمَنُوا
وَتَطْمَئِنُّ قُلُوبُهُم بِذِكْرِ اللَّهِ أَلَا بِذِكْرِ اللَّهِ تَطْمَئِنُّ الْقُلُوبُ ﴿٢٨﴾

Is THEN he who knows 13:19
that the Truth has been revealed to you from your Lord
like him who is blind?

Truly, none will remember but those that are of good sense possessed: those who keep faith with God and do not break their pledge; who join together what God has bidden to be united; who fear their Lord and dread a baleful reckoning; who for the sake of God endure with fortitude, attend to their prayers, and from what We gave them give in private and in public; and who ward off evil with good. These shall have the recompense of Paradise. They shall enter the Gardens of Eden, together with the righteous among their fathers, their spouses, and their descendants. From every gate the angels will come in to them, saying: 'Peace be to you for all that you have steadfastly endured; blessed is the recompense of Paradise.'

As for those who break God's covenant after confirming it, who put asun- 13:25
der what God has bidden to be united and perpetrate corruption in the land,
the curse shall light on them; the scourge of Hell awaits them.

God gives abundantly to whom He will, and sparingly likewise. They rejoice in the life of this world: yet the life of this world is but a brief diversion compared with the life to come.

The unbelievers say: 'Why has no sign been sent down to him from his Lord?'

Say: 'God leaves in error whom He will, and guides to Himself those who
repent and have faith; whose hearts find comfort in the remembrance of 13:28
God. Surely in the remembrance of God all hearts are comforted.

13:29 BLESSED ARE those who believe and do good works; blissful is their final abode.'

Thus have We sent you forth to a community before whom other communities had passed away, that you may recite to them that with which We have inspired you. Yet they deny the Lord of Mercy. Say: 'He is my Lord. There is no god but Him. In Him I have put my trust, and to Him I shall return.'

And even if there be a Koran whereby the mountains could be set in motion, the earth rent asunder, and the dead communed with, surely all things are subject to God's will. Are the faithful unaware that, had God pleased, He could have guided all mankind?

الَّذِينَ آمَنُوا وَعَمِلُوا الصَّالِحَاتِ طُوبَىٰ لَهُمْ وَحُسْنُ مَآبٍ ٢٩ كَذَٰلِكَ
أَرْسَلْنَاكَ فِي أُمَّةٍ قَدْ خَلَتْ مِن قَبْلِهَا أُمَمٌ لِّتَتْلُوَ عَلَيْهِمُ الَّذِي
أَوْحَيْنَا إِلَيْكَ وَهُمْ يَكْفُرُونَ بِالرَّحْمَٰنِ قُلْ هُوَ رَبِّي لَا إِلَٰهَ إِلَّا هُوَ
عَلَيْهِ تَوَكَّلْتُ وَإِلَيْهِ مَتَابِ ٣٠ وَلَوْ أَنَّ قُرْآنًا سُيِّرَتْ بِهِ الْجِبَالُ
أَوْ قُطِّعَتْ بِهِ الْأَرْضُ أَوْ كُلِّمَ بِهِ الْمَوْتَىٰ بَل لِّلَّهِ الْأَمْرُ جَمِيعًا أَفَلَمْ
يَيْأَسِ الَّذِينَ آمَنُوا أَن لَّوْ يَشَاءُ اللَّهُ لَهَدَى النَّاسَ جَمِيعًا وَلَا
يَزَالُ الَّذِينَ كَفَرُوا تُصِيبُهُم بِمَا صَنَعُوا قَارِعَةٌ أَوْ تَحُلُّ قَرِيبًا
مِّن دَارِهِمْ حَتَّىٰ يَأْتِيَ وَعْدُ اللَّهِ إِنَّ اللَّهَ لَا يُخْلِفُ الْمِيعَادَ ٣١
وَلَقَدِ اسْتُهْزِئَ بِرُسُلٍ مِّن قَبْلِكَ فَأَمْلَيْتُ لِلَّذِينَ
كَفَرُوا ثُمَّ أَخَذْتُهُمْ فَكَيْفَ كَانَ عِقَابِ ٣٢ أَفَمَنْ هُوَ
قَائِمٌ عَلَىٰ كُلِّ نَفْسٍ بِمَا كَسَبَتْ وَجَعَلُوا لِلَّهِ شُرَكَاءَ قُلْ
سَمُّوهُمْ أَمْ تُنَبِّئُونَهُ بِمَا لَا يَعْلَمُ فِي الْأَرْضِ أَم بِظَاهِرٍ مِّنَ
الْقَوْلِ بَلْ زُيِّنَ لِلَّذِينَ كَفَرُوا مَكْرُهُمْ وَصُدُّوا عَنِ السَّبِيلِ
وَمَن يُضْلِلِ اللَّهُ فَمَا لَهُ مِنْ هَادٍ ٣٣ لَّهُمْ عَذَابٌ فِي الْحَيَاةِ
الدُّنْيَا وَلَعَذَابُ الْآخِرَةِ أَشَقُّ وَمَا لَهُم مِّنَ اللَّهِ مِن وَاقٍ ٣٤

As for the unbelievers, because of their misdeeds disaster shall not cease to afflict them or to crouch at their very doorstep until God's promise be fulfilled. God will not fail the appointed time.

13:32 Apostles were mocked before you: but, though I bore with the unbelievers, My scourge at length took them; and how terrible was My scourge!

Who is it that watches every soul and all its actions? Yet they set up other deities besides God. Say: 'Name them. Would you tell Him of that which is unknown to Him on the earth? Or are they merely empty words?'

Indeed, their foul devices seem fair to the unbelievers, for they are
debarred from the right path. They have no guide, those whom God has led
13:34 astray. Torment awaits them in this nether life: but more grievous is the
torment of the life to come. From God they have no protector.

مثل الجنة التي وعد المتقون تجري من تحتها الأنهار
أكلها دائم وظلها تلك عقبى الذين اتقوا وعقبى الكافرين
النار ٣٥ والذين آتيناهم الكتاب يفرحون بما أنزل
إليك ومن الأحزاب من ينكر بعضه قل إنما أمرت
أن أعبد الله ولا أشرك به إليه أدعو وإليه مآب ٣٦
وكذلك أنزلناه حكما عربيا ولئن اتبعت أهواءهم
بعد ما جاءك من العلم ما لك من الله من ولي ولا واق
٣٧ ولقد أرسلنا رسلا من قبلك وجعلنا لهم أزواجا وذرية
وما كان لرسول أن يأتي بآية إلا بإذن الله لكل أجل كتاب
٣٨ يمحو الله ما يشاء ويثبت وعنده أم الكتاب ٣٩ وإن
ما نرينك بعض الذي نعدهم أو نتوفينك فإنما عليك البلاغ
وعلينا الحساب ٤٠ أولم يروا أنا نأتي الأرض ننقصها من
أطرافها والله يحكم لا معقب لحكمه وهو سريع الحساب
٤١ وقد مكر الذين من قبلهم فلله المكر جميعا يعلم
ما تكسب كل نفس وسيعلم الكفار لمن عقبى الدار ٤٢

SUCH IS the Paradise the 13:35
righteous have been promised: it is watered by running
brooks: eternal is its fruit, and
eternal is its shade. Such shall
be the end of the righteous;
and the Fire shall be the fate
of the unbelievers.

Those to whom We gave
the Book rejoice in what is
revealed to you, while some
factions deny a part of it. Say:
'I am only commanded to
serve God and to associate
none with Him. To Him I
pray, and to Him I shall return.'

Thus have We revealed it, a
code of judgements in the
Arabic tongue. If you succumb
to their desires after the
knowledge you have been
given, from God you shall
have no guardian or protector.

We sent forth apostles before you and gave them wives and descendants. 13:38
Yet no apostle could work a miracle except by God's leave. Every age has a
term decreed. God abrogates and confirms what He pleases. His is the
Decree Eternal.

Whether We let you glimpse in some measure the scourge We promise
them, or claim you back to Us, your mission is only to give warning: it is for
Us to do the reckoning.

Do they not see how We invade their land and diminish its borders? If
God decrees a thing, none can reverse it. And swift is His reckoning.

Those who have gone before them also schemed, but God is the master 13:42
of all scheming: He knows what every soul has done. And the unbelievers
will then learn for whom the blissful end is destined.

13:43 AND THE unbelievers say: 'You are not sent.' Say: 'Sufficient is God as my witness and your witness, and so are those who know the Book.'

ويقول الذين كفروا لست مرسلا قل كفى بالله
شهيدا بيني وبينكم ومن عنده علم الكتاب ٤٣

سورة ابرهيم مكية وهي اثنتان وخمسون آية

بسم الله الرحمن الرحيم

الر كتاب انزلناه اليك لتخرج الناس من الظلمات
الى النور باذن ربهم الى صراط العزيز الحميد ١ الله
الذى له ما فى السموات وما فى الارض وويل للكافرين
من عذاب شديد ٢ الذين يستحبون الحيوة الدنيا
على الاخرة ويصدون عن سبيل الله ويبغونها عوجا
اولئك فى ضلال بعيد ٣ وما ارسلنا من رسول الا
بلسان قومه ليبين لهم فيضل الله من يشاء ويهدى
من يشاء وهو العزيز الحكيم ٤ ولقد ارسلنا موسى باياتنا
ان اخرج قومك من الظلمات الى النور وذكرهم بايام الله
ان فى ذلك لايات لكل صبار شكور ٥

ABRAHAM

In the Name of God,
the Merciful, the Compassionate

14:1 ALIF *lām rā'*. A Book We have revealed to you so that, by their Lord's leave, you may lead the people from darkness to the light; to the path of the Mighty, the Praiseworthy One: the path of God, to whom belongs all that the heavens and all that the earth contain.

Woe betide the unbelievers, for they shall be grievously punished! Those who love the life of this world more than the life to come; who debar others from the path of God and seek to make it crooked: they have strayed far into error.

14:4 Each apostle We have sent has spoken only in the language of his own people, that he might clearly guide them. But God leaves in error whom He will and gives guidance to whom He pleases; He is the Almighty, the Wise One.

14:5 We sent forth Moses with Our signs: 'Lead your people out of the darkness into the light, and remind them of God's bounty.' Surely in this there are signs for every steadfast, thankful man.

وَاِذْ قَالَ مُوسٰى لِقَوْمِهِ اذْكُرُوا نِعْمَةَ اللّٰهِ عَلَيْكُمْ
اِذْ اَنْجٰيكُمْ مِنْ اٰلِ فِرْعَوْنَ يَسُومُونَكُمْ سُوٓءَ الْعَذَابِ
وَيُذَبِّحُونَ اَبْنَآءَكُمْ وَيَسْتَحْيُونَ نِسَآءَكُمْ وَفِي ذٰلِكُمْ
بَلَآءٌ مِنْ رَبِّكُمْ عَظِيمٌ ۝٦ وَاِذْ تَاَذَّنَ رَبُّكُمْ لَئِنْ شَكَرْتُمْ
لَاَزِيدَنَّكُمْ وَلَئِنْ كَفَرْتُمْ اِنَّ عَذَابِي لَشَدِيدٌ ۝٧ وَقَالَ مُوسٰى
اِنْ تَكْفُرُوٓا اَنْتُمْ وَمَنْ فِي الْاَرْضِ جَمِيعًا فَاِنَّ اللّٰهَ لَغَنِيٌّ حَمِيدٌ
۝٨ اَلَمْ يَاْتِكُمْ نَبَؤُا الَّذِينَ مِنْ قَبْلِكُمْ قَوْمِ نُوحٍ وَعَادٍ
وَثَمُودَ وَالَّذِينَ مِنْ بَعْدِهِمْ لَا يَعْلَمُهُمْ اِلَّا اللّٰهُ جَآءَتْهُمْ
رُسُلُهُمْ بِالْبَيِّنَاتِ فَرَدُّوٓا اَيْدِيَهُمْ فِيٓ اَفْوَاهِهِمْ
وَقَالُوٓا اِنَّا كَفَرْنَا بِمَآ اُرْسِلْتُمْ بِهِ وَاِنَّا لَفِي شَكٍّ مِمَّا
تَدْعُونَنَآ اِلَيْهِ مُرِيبٍ ۝٩ قَالَتْ رُسُلُهُمْ اَفِي اللّٰهِ شَكٌّ فَاطِرِ
السَّمٰوَاتِ وَالْاَرْضِ يَدْعُوكُمْ لِيَغْفِرَ لَكُمْ مِنْ
ذُنُوبِكُمْ وَيُؤَخِّرَكُمْ اِلٰٓى اَجَلٍ مُسَمًّى قَالُوٓا اِنْ
اَنْتُمْ اِلَّا بَشَرٌ مِثْلُنَا تُرِيدُونَ اَنْ تَصُدُّونَا عَمَّا
كَانَ يَعْبُدُ اٰبَآؤُنَا فَاْتُونَا بِسُلْطَانٍ مُبِينٍ ۝١٠

AND WHEN Moses said to 14:6
his people: 'Remember God's
goodness to you when He
delivered you from Pharaoh's
nation, who had oppressed
you cruelly, slaughtering your
sons and sparing only your
daughters; surely that was a
grievous trial by your Lord.
For your Lord had declared:
"If you give thanks, I will
bestow abundance upon you:
but if you are thankless, My
punishment is terrible indeed."'
And Moses said: 'If you and
all who are on earth prove
thankless, God does not need
your thanks, though He de-
serves your praise.'
Have you not heard what 14:9
befell those that have gone
before you? The people of
Noah, 'Ād, and Thamūd, and
those who came after them? God alone knows their number. Their apostles
came to them with veritable signs, but they bit their hands with their mouths[1]
and said: 'We disbelieve your message. Indeed, we strongly doubt the faith to
which you call us.'
Their apostles said: 'Is God, Creator of the heavens and the earth, to be 14:10
doubted? He calls you that He may forgive you your sins and reprieve you till
an appointed time.'

They said: 'You are but mortals like ourselves. You wish to turn us away from the gods our fathers worshipped. Bring us some clear authority.'

1. I.e. with rage; thus Al-Jalālayn. Literally, they thrust their hands into their mouths.

14:11 THEIR APOSTLES said to
them: 'We are indeed but
mortals like yourselves; but
God bestows His grace on
such of His servants as He
chooses. We cannot give you
proof, except by God's leave;
in God let true believers put
their trust. And why should
we not trust in God, when He
has already guided us on to
our paths? We will endure
your persecution patiently. In
God let the trusting put their
trust.'

'Return to our fold,' the
unbelievers said to their apostles, 'or we will banish you
from our land.'

But their Lord revealed His
will to them: 'We shall surely
14:14 destroy the wrongdoers and
shall surely give you the land
to dwell in after them. Let him take heed who dreads My eminence and fears
My threats.'

And they called for help; and every hardened sinner came to grief.

Hell will stretch behind him, and putrid water shall he drink: he will sip,
but scarcely swallow. Death will assail him from every side, yet shall he not
be dead. Harrowing torment awaits him.

14:18 The works of the unbelievers are like ashes which the wind scatters on a
stormy day: they shall gain nothing from what they earn. That is surely the
way to egregious error.

قَالَتْ لَهُمْ رُسُلُهُمْ إِن نَّحْنُ إِلَّا بَشَرٌ مِّثْلُكُمْ وَلَٰكِنَّ اللَّهَ يَمُنُّ عَلَىٰ
مَن يَشَاءُ مِنْ عِبَادِهِ ۖ وَمَا كَانَ لَنَا أَن نَّأْتِيَكُم بِسُلْطَانٍ
إِلَّا بِإِذْنِ اللَّهِ ۚ وَعَلَى اللَّهِ فَلْيَتَوَكَّلِ الْمُؤْمِنُونَ ﴿١١﴾
وَمَا لَنَا أَلَّا نَتَوَكَّلَ عَلَى اللَّهِ وَقَدْ هَدَانَا سُبُلَنَا ۚ وَلَنَصْبِرَنَّ
عَلَىٰ مَا آذَيْتُمُونَا ۚ وَعَلَى اللَّهِ فَلْيَتَوَكَّلِ الْمُتَوَكِّلُونَ ﴿١٢﴾
وَقَالَ الَّذِينَ كَفَرُوا لِرُسُلِهِمْ لَنُخْرِجَنَّكُم مِّنْ أَرْضِنَا
أَوْ لَتَعُودُنَّ فِي مِلَّتِنَا ۖ فَأَوْحَىٰ إِلَيْهِمْ رَبُّهُمْ لَنُهْلِكَنَّ
الظَّالِمِينَ ﴿١٣﴾ وَلَنُسْكِنَنَّكُمُ الْأَرْضَ مِن بَعْدِهِمْ ۚ
ذَٰلِكَ لِمَنْ خَافَ مَقَامِي وَخَافَ وَعِيدِ ﴿١٤﴾ وَاسْتَفْتَحُوا
وَخَابَ كُلُّ جَبَّارٍ عَنِيدٍ ﴿١٥﴾ مِّن وَرَائِهِ جَهَنَّمُ وَيُسْقَىٰ
مِن مَّاءٍ صَدِيدٍ ﴿١٦﴾ يَتَجَرَّعُهُ وَلَا يَكَادُ يُسِيغُهُ وَيَأْتِيهِ
الْمَوْتُ مِن كُلِّ مَكَانٍ وَمَا هُوَ بِمَيِّتٍ ۖ وَمِن وَرَائِهِ
عَذَابٌ غَلِيظٌ ﴿١٧﴾ مَّثَلُ الَّذِينَ كَفَرُوا بِرَبِّهِمْ ۖ أَعْمَالُهُمْ
كَرَمَادٍ اشْتَدَّتْ بِهِ الرِّيحُ فِي يَوْمٍ عَاصِفٍ ۖ لَّا يَقْدِرُونَ
مِمَّا كَسَبُوا عَلَىٰ شَيْءٍ ۚ ذَٰلِكَ هُوَ الضَّلَالُ الْبَعِيدُ ﴿١٨﴾

الم تر ان الله خلق السموات والارض بالحق ان يشا
يذهبكم ويات بخلق جديد ﴿١٩﴾ وما ذلك على الله بعزيز ﴿٢٠﴾
وبرزوا لله جميعا فقال الضعفؤا للذين استكبروا انا
كنا لكم تبعا فهل انتم مغنون عنا من عذاب الله من شيء قالوا
لو هدينا الله لهدينكم سواء علينا اجزعنا ام
صبرنا ما لنا من محيص ﴿٢١﴾ وقال الشيطان لما قضي
الامر ان الله وعدكم وعد الحق ووعدتكم
فاخلفتكم وما كان لي عليكم من سلطان الا ان
دعوتكم فاستجبتم لي فلا تلوموني ولوموا انفسكم
ما انا بمصرخكم وما انتم بمصرخي اني كفرت بما
اشركتمون من قبل ان الظالمين لهم عذاب اليم ﴿٢٢﴾
وادخل الذين امنوا وعملوا الصالحات جنات تجري
من تحتها الانهار خالدين فيها باذن ربهم تحيتهم
فيها سلام ﴿٢٣﴾ الم تر كيف ضرب الله مثلا كلمة
طيبة كشجرة طيبة اصلها ثابت وفرعها في السماء ﴿٢٤﴾

Do YOU not see that God 14:19
created the heavens and the earth with Truth? He can remove you if He will and bring into being a new creation: that is no difficult thing for God.

All shall appear before God. The humble will say to those who thought themselves mighty: 'We were your followers. Can you protect us from God's punishment in any way?'

They will say: 'Had God given us guidance, we would have guided you. Neither panic nor patience will help us now. There is no escape for us.'

And when judgement had 14:22
been passed, Satan will say to them: 'True was the promise which God made you. I too made you a promise, but did not keep it. Yet had I no power over you. I only called you, and you answered me. Do not now blame me, but blame yourselves. I cannot help you, nor can you help me. I never believed in that with which you associated me before.'

Grievous torment awaits the wrongdoers. And those that believe and do good works shall be admitted into Gardens watered by running brooks, wherein, by their Lord's leave, shall they abide for ever. Their greeting shall be: 'Peace!'

Do you not see how God compares a good word to a good tree? Its root 14:24
is firm and its branches are in the sky;

تؤتي أكلها كل حين بإذن ربها ويضرب الله الأمثال
للناس لعلهم يتذكرون ﴿٢٥﴾ ومثل كلمة خبيثة كشجرة
خبيثة اجتثت من فوق الأرض ما لها من قرار ﴿٢٦﴾
يثبت الله الذين آمنوا بالقول الثابت في الحيوة
الدنيا وفي الآخرة ويضل الله الظالمين ويفعل الله
ما يشاء ﴿٢٧﴾ ألم تر إلى الذين بدلوا نعمت الله
كفرا وأحلوا قومهم دار البوار ﴿٢٨﴾ جهنم يصلونها
وبئس القرار ﴿٢٩﴾ وجعلوا لله أندادا ليضلوا عن سبيله
قل تمتعوا فإن مصيركم إلى النار ﴿٣٠﴾ قل لعبادي الذين
آمنوا يقيموا الصلوة وينفقوا مما رزقناهم سرا وعلانية
من قبل أن يأتي يوم لا بيع فيه ولا خلال ﴿٣١﴾ الله الذي
خلق السموات والأرض وأنزل من السماء ماء فأخرج
به من الثمرات رزقا لكم وسخر لكم الفلك لتجري
في البحر بأمره وسخر لكم الأنهار ﴿٣٢﴾ وسخر لكم
الشمس والقمر دائبين وسخر لكم الليل والنهار ﴿٣٣﴾

14:25 it yields its fruit in every sea-
son by its Lord's leave. God
speaks in parables to people
so that they may reflect. But
an evil word is like a rotten
tree torn out of the earth and
shorn of all its roots.

God makes steadfast the
faithful with His steadfast
Word, both in this life and in
the life to come. God leads
the wrongdoers astray; God
accomplishes what He pleases.

Have you not thought of
those who repay the grace of
God with unbelief and drive
their people into the House
of Perdition? In Hell shall
they burn; and evil shall be
their fate.

14:30 They set up equals to God
to lead people away from His
path. Say to them: 'Take your
pleasure now: you are surely destined for the Fire.'

Tell My servants, those who are true believers, to be steadfast in prayer
and from what We gave them to give in private and in public, before that day
arrives when all trading shall cease and friendships be no more.

God it was who created the heavens and the earth. He sends down water
from the sky wherewith He brings forth fruits for your sustenance. He has
subdued the ships which, by His leave, sail the ocean in your service. He has
14:33 subdued for you the rivers, and subdued for you the sun and the moon,
which steadfastly pursue their courses. And He has subdued for you the
night and the day.

وآتاكم من كل ما سألتموه وإن تعدوا نعمت الله لا تحصوها
إن الإنسان لظلوم كفار ﴿٣٤﴾ وإذ قال إبراهيم
رب اجعل هذا البلد آمنا واجنبني وبني أن نعبد
الأصنام ﴿٣٥﴾ رب إنهن أضللن كثيرا من الناس فمن
تبعني فإنه مني ومن عصاني فإنك غفور رحيم ﴿٣٦﴾
ربنا إني أسكنت من ذريتي بواد غير ذي زرع عند
بيتك المحرم ربنا ليقيموا الصلوة فاجعل أفئدة من الناس
تهوي إليهم وارزقهم من الثمرات لعلهم يشكرون ﴿٣٧﴾
ربنا إنك تعلم ما نخفي وما نعلن وما يخفى على
الله من شيء في الأرض ولا في السماء ﴿٣٨﴾ الحمد
لله الذي وهب لي على الكبر إسمعيل وإسحق إن
ربي لسميع الدعاء ﴿٣٩﴾ رب اجعلني مقيم الصلوة ومن ذريتي
ربنا وتقبل دعاء ﴿٤٠﴾ ربنا اغفر لي ولوالدي وللمؤمنين
يوم يقوم الحساب ﴿٤١﴾ ولا تحسبن الله غافلا عما
يعمل الظالمون إنما يؤخرهم ليوم تشخص فيه الأبصار ﴿٤٢﴾

AND OF everything you have asked Him for He has given you some. If you reckoned up God's bounties you could not count them. Truly, man is wicked and thankless. 14:34

Abraham said: 'Lord, make this land[1] secure. Preserve me and my descendants from serving idols. Lord, many have they led astray. He that follows me shall become my brother, and if any turns against me, You are surely forgiving and compassionate.

'Lord, I have settled some of my offspring in a barren valley near Your Sacred House, so that they may observe true worship, Lord. Put in some people's hearts kindness towards them, and provide them with the earth's fruits; perchance they will give thanks. 14:37

'Lord, You have knowledge of all that we conceal and all that we reveal: nothing on earth or in heaven can be concealed from God.

'Praise be to God who has bestowed on me Ishmael and Isaac despite my old age! My Lord well hears all prayers.

'Lord, make me and my descendants steadfast in prayer. Lord, accept my prayer.

'Forgive me, Lord, and forgive my parents and all the faithful on the Day of Reckoning.'

Never think that God is unaware of the wrongdoers' actions. He only gives them respite till the day on which all eyes will stare with consternation. 14:42

1. Mecca.

14:43 THEY SHALL rush in terror with heads uplifted; they shall stare, but see nothing; their hearts utterly vacant.

Forewarn the people of a day when the scourge will overtake them; when the wrongdoers will say: 'Lord, grant us respite for a short while. We will obey Your call, and follow the apostles.'

'Did you not once swear that you would never die away? You lived in the dwellings of those who wronged their souls before you: yet you knew full well how We had dealt with them, and We spoke to you in parables about them.'

14:46 They schemed, but their schemes were known to God, even if their schemes could move mountains.

Never think that God will break the pledge He gave to His apostles. Mighty is God, and capable of revenge.

On the day when the earth is changed into a different earth and the heavens into new heavens, mankind shall stand before God, the One, who conquers all. On that day you shall see the guilty bound with chains, their garments pitch, and their faces covered with flames.

God will surely requite each soul according to what it earned. Swift is God's reckoning.

14:52 This is an exhortation to the people. Let them be warned thereby and know that He is but one God. Let them reflect, those that are of good sense possessed.

مُهْطِعِينَ مُقْنِعِي رُءُوسِهِمْ لَا يَرْتَدُّ إِلَيْهِمْ طَرْفُهُمْ
وَأَفْئِدَتُهُمْ هَوَاءٌ ۝٤٣ وَأَنذِرِ النَّاسَ يَوْمَ يَأْتِيهِمُ الْعَذَابُ
فَيَقُولُ الَّذِينَ ظَلَمُوا رَبَّنَا أَخِّرْنَا إِلَىٰ أَجَلٍ قَرِيبٍ نُّجِبْ
دَعْوَتَكَ وَنَتَّبِعِ الرُّسُلَ أَوَلَمْ تَكُونُوا أَقْسَمْتُم مِّن قَبْلُ
مَا لَكُم مِّن زَوَالٍ ۝٤٤ وَسَكَنتُمْ فِي مَسَاكِنِ الَّذِينَ
ظَلَمُوا أَنفُسَهُمْ وَتَبَيَّنَ لَكُمْ كَيْفَ فَعَلْنَا بِهِمْ وَضَرَبْنَا
لَكُمُ الْأَمْثَالَ ۝٤٥ وَقَدْ مَكَرُوا مَكْرَهُمْ وَعِندَ
اللَّهِ مَكْرُهُمْ وَإِن كَانَ مَكْرُهُمْ لِتَزُولَ مِنْهُ
الْجِبَالُ ۝٤٦ فَلَا تَحْسَبَنَّ اللَّهَ مُخْلِفَ وَعْدِهِ رُسُلَهُ إِنَّ
اللَّهَ عَزِيزٌ ذُو انتِقَامٍ ۝٤٧ يَوْمَ تُبَدَّلُ الْأَرْضُ غَيْرَ الْأَرْضِ
وَالسَّمَاوَاتُ وَبَرَزُوا لِلَّهِ الْوَاحِدِ الْقَهَّارِ ۝٤٨ وَتَرَى الْمُجْرِمِينَ
يَوْمَئِذٍ مُّقَرَّنِينَ فِي الْأَصْفَادِ ۝٤٩ سَرَابِيلُهُم مِّن قَطِرَانٍ وَتَغْشَىٰ
وُجُوهَهُمُ النَّارُ ۝٥٠ لِيَجْزِيَ اللَّهُ كُلَّ نَفْسٍ مَّا كَسَبَتْ إِنَّ
اللَّهَ سَرِيعُ الْحِسَابِ ۝٥١ هَٰذَا بَلَاغٌ لِّلنَّاسِ وَلِيُنذَرُوا
بِهِ وَلِيَعْلَمُوا أَنَّمَا هُوَ إِلَٰهٌ وَاحِدٌ وَلِيَذَّكَّرَ أُولُو الْأَلْبَابِ ۝٥٢

سورة الحجر مكية وهي تسع وتسعون آية

بسم الله الرحمن الرحيم

الر تلك آيات الكتاب وقرآن مبين (١) ربما يود الذين
كفروا لو كانوا مسلمين (٢) ذرهم يأكلوا ويتمتعوا ويلههم
الأمل فسوف يعلمون (٣) وما أهلكنا من قرية إلا ولها كتاب
معلوم (٤) ما تسبق من أمة أجلها وما يستأخرون (٥) وقالوا
يا أيها الذي نزل عليه الذكر إنك لمجنون (٦) لو ما تأتينا
بالملائكة إن كنت من الصادقين (٧) ما ننزل الملائكة
إلا بالحق وما كانوا إذا منظرين (٨) إنا نحن نزلنا الذكر وإنا
له لحافظون (٩) ولقد أرسلنا من قبلك في شيع الأولين (١٠)
وما يأتيهم من رسول إلا كانوا به يستهزئون (١١) كذلك نسلكه
في قلوب المجرمين (١٢) لا يؤمنون به وقد خلت سنة الأولين
(١٣) ولو فتحنا عليهم بابا من السماء فظلوا فيه يعرجون (١٤)
لقالوا إنما سكرت أبصارنا بل نحن قوم مسحورون (١٥)

AL-ḤIJR

In the Name of God,
the Merciful, the Compassionate

ALIF *lām rā'*. These are the 15:1
revelations of the Book, and a
veritable Koran:

The day will surely come
when those who disbelieve
will wish they were Muslims.
Let them feast and make
merry; and let their hopes
beguile them. They shall learn.

Never have We destroyed a
city whose term of life was
not ordained and known
beforehand. Communities
cannot forestall their doom,
nor can they retard it.

They say: 'You to whom 15:6
the Admonition was revealed,
you are surely possessed. Bring down to us the angels, if what you say
be true.'

We shall send down the angels only with the Truth. Then shall they never
be reprieved.

It was We that revealed the Admonition, and shall Ourself preserve it. We
have sent forth apostles before you to the older nations: but they scoffed at
each apostle We sent them. Thus do We put doubt into the hearts of the
guilty: they deny him, despite the example of the ancients.

If We opened for them a gate in heaven and they ascended through it
higher and higher, still would they say: 'Our eyes were dazzled: truly, we must 15:15
have been bewitched.'

15:16 AND WE have decked the
sky with constellations and
made them lovely to behold;
and We guarded them from
every cursèd demon. Eavesdroppers are pursued by a
fiery comet.

We have spread out the earth
and set upon it immovable
mountains. We have planted it
with every seasonable fruit,
providing sustenance for yourselves and for those you do
not provide for. We hold the
store of every blessing and
send it down only in appropriate measure. We let loose the
fertilizing winds and bring
down water from the sky for
you to drink; its stores are
beyond your reach.

15:23 It is surely We who ordain
life and death; We are the
Heirs of all things.

We surely know those who have gone before you, as We surely know those who will come hereafter; and it is your Lord who shall herd them all together. He is wise and all-knowing.

We created man from dry clay, from black moulded loam, and before him Satan from smokeless fire. Your Lord said to the angels: 'I am creating man from dry clay, from black moulded loam. When I have fashioned him and breathed My spirit into him, kneel down and prostrate yourselves before him.'

15:31 The angels, one and all, prostrated themselves, except Satan: he refused to
be with those who prostrated themselves.

وَلَقَدْ جَعَلْنَا فِي السَّمَاءِ بُرُوجًا وَزَيَّنَّاهَا لِلنَّاظِرِينَ ١٦
وَحَفِظْنَاهَا مِنْ كُلِّ شَيْطَانٍ رَجِيمٍ ١٧ إِلَّا مَنِ اسْتَرَقَ
السَّمْعَ فَأَتْبَعَهُ شِهَابٌ مُبِينٌ ١٨ وَالْأَرْضَ مَدَدْنَاهَا وَأَلْقَيْنَا
فِيهَا رَوَاسِيَ وَأَنْبَتْنَا فِيهَا مِنْ كُلِّ شَيْءٍ مَوْزُونٍ ١٩ وَجَعَلْنَا
لَكُمْ فِيهَا مَعَايِشَ وَمَنْ لَسْتُمْ لَهُ بِرَازِقِينَ ٢٠ وَإِنْ مِنْ
شَيْءٍ إِلَّا عِنْدَنَا خَزَائِنُهُ وَمَا نُنَزِّلُهُ إِلَّا بِقَدَرٍ مَعْلُومٍ ٢١
وَأَرْسَلْنَا الرِّيَاحَ لَوَاقِحَ فَأَنْزَلْنَا مِنَ السَّمَاءِ مَاءً فَأَسْقَيْنَاكُمُوهُ
وَمَا أَنْتُمْ لَهُ بِخَازِنِينَ ٢٢ وَإِنَّا لَنَحْنُ نُحْيِي وَنُمِيتُ
وَنَحْنُ الْوَارِثُونَ ٢٣ وَلَقَدْ عَلِمْنَا الْمُسْتَقْدِمِينَ مِنْكُمْ وَلَقَدْ
عَلِمْنَا الْمُسْتَأْخِرِينَ ٢٤ وَإِنَّ رَبَّكَ هُوَ يَحْشُرُهُمْ إِنَّهُ حَكِيمٌ عَلِيمٌ ٢٥
وَلَقَدْ خَلَقْنَا الْإِنْسَانَ مِنْ صَلْصَالٍ مِنْ حَمَإٍ مَسْنُونٍ ٢٦ وَالْجَانَّ خَلَقْنَاهُ مِنْ
قَبْلُ مِنْ نَارِ السَّمُومِ ٢٧ وَإِذْ قَالَ رَبُّكَ لِلْمَلَائِكَةِ إِنِّي خَالِقٌ بَشَرًا
مِنْ صَلْصَالٍ مِنْ حَمَإٍ مَسْنُونٍ ٢٨ فَإِذَا سَوَّيْتُهُ وَنَفَخْتُ فِيهِ
مِنْ رُوحِي فَقَعُوا لَهُ سَاجِدِينَ ٢٩ فَسَجَدَ الْمَلَائِكَةُ كُلُّهُمْ
أَجْمَعُونَ ٣٠ إِلَّا إِبْلِيسَ أَبَى أَنْ يَكُونَ مَعَ السَّاجِدِينَ ٣١

قَالَ يَٰٓإِبْلِيسُ مَا لَكَ أَلَّا تَكُونَ مَعَ ٱلسَّٰجِدِينَ ﴿٣٢﴾ قَالَ لَمْ
أَكُن لِّأَسْجُدَ لِبَشَرٍ خَلَقْتَهُۥ مِن صَلْصَٰلٍ مِّنْ حَمَإٍ مَّسْنُونٍ
﴿٣٣﴾ قَالَ فَٱخْرُجْ مِنْهَا فَإِنَّكَ رَجِيمٌ ﴿٣٤﴾ وَإِنَّ عَلَيْكَ ٱللَّعْنَةَ
إِلَىٰ يَوْمِ ٱلدِّينِ ﴿٣٥﴾ قَالَ رَبِّ فَأَنظِرْنِىٓ إِلَىٰ يَوْمِ يُبْعَثُونَ
﴿٣٦﴾ قَالَ فَإِنَّكَ مِنَ ٱلْمُنظَرِينَ ﴿٣٧﴾ إِلَىٰ يَوْمِ ٱلْوَقْتِ
ٱلْمَعْلُومِ ﴿٣٨﴾ قَالَ رَبِّ بِمَآ أَغْوَيْتَنِى لَأُزَيِّنَنَّ لَهُمْ فِى
ٱلْأَرْضِ وَلَأُغْوِيَنَّهُمْ أَجْمَعِينَ ﴿٣٩﴾ إِلَّا عِبَادَكَ مِنْهُمُ
ٱلْمُخْلَصِينَ ﴿٤٠﴾ قَالَ هَٰذَا صِرَٰطٌ عَلَىَّ مُسْتَقِيمٌ ﴿٤١﴾ إِنَّ عِبَادِى
لَيْسَ لَكَ عَلَيْهِمْ سُلْطَٰنٌ إِلَّا مَنِ ٱتَّبَعَكَ مِنَ ٱلْغَاوِينَ ﴿٤٢﴾ وَإِنَّ
جَهَنَّمَ لَمَوْعِدُهُمْ أَجْمَعِينَ ﴿٤٣﴾ لَهَا سَبْعَةُ أَبْوَٰبٍ لِّكُلِّ بَابٍ مِّنْهُمْ
جُزْءٌ مَّقْسُومٌ ﴿٤٤﴾ إِنَّ ٱلْمُتَّقِينَ فِى جَنَّٰتٍ وَعُيُونٍ ﴿٤٥﴾ ٱدْخُلُوهَا
بِسَلَٰمٍ ءَامِنِينَ ﴿٤٦﴾ وَنَزَعْنَا مَا فِى صُدُورِهِم مِّنْ غِلٍّ إِخْوَٰنًا عَلَىٰ
سُرُرٍ مُّتَقَٰبِلِينَ ﴿٤٧﴾ لَا يَمَسُّهُمْ فِيهَا نَصَبٌ وَمَا هُم مِّنْهَا بِمُخْرَجِينَ
﴿٤٨﴾ نَبِّئْ عِبَادِىٓ أَنِّىٓ أَنَا ٱلْغَفُورُ ٱلرَّحِيمُ ﴿٤٩﴾ وَأَنَّ عَذَابِى هُوَ
ٱلْعَذَابُ ٱلْأَلِيمُ ﴿٥٠﴾ وَنَبِّئْهُمْ عَن ضَيْفِ إِبْرَٰهِيمَ ﴿٥١﴾

HE SAID: 'Satan, how is it 15:32
that you are not with those
who prostrated themselves?'

He said: 'I was not to bow
to a mortal whom You created
of dry clay, of black moulded
loam.'

'Get you hence,' said He, 'you
are accursed: and the curse shall
be on you till Judgement-day.'

'Lord,' he said, 'reprieve me
till the Day of Resurrection.'

He said: 'You are reprieved
till the Appointed Day.'

'Lord,' said Satan, 'since
You have thus tempted me, I
will seduce those on earth: I
will surely tempt them all,
except those among them who
are Your faithful servants.'

He said: 'This is My straight 15:41
path. You shall have no power
over My servants, only the sin-
ners who follow you: they are all destined for Hell. It has seven gates, and
through each gate they shall come in separate bands. The righteous shall
dwell among gardens and fountains; in peace and safety shall they enter
them. We shall remove all rancour from their hearts, and they shall take their
ease on couches face to face, a band of brothers. Toil shall not weary them,
nor shall they ever be driven out.'

Tell My servants that I alone am the Forgiving One, the Compassionate;
and that My scourge is the only woeful scourge.

And tell them of Abraham's guests: 15:51

15:52 WHEN THEY went in to him and said: 'Peace,' he said: 'We fear your intent.'

'Have no fear,' they said. 'We come to you with joyful tidings. You shall have a son endowed with knowledge.'

He said: 'Do you bring me such joyful tidings in my old age? What joyful tidings can you bring me?'

They said: 'We do gladden you with the Truth. Do not despair.'

He said: 'Who but the lost would despair of God's mercy? Envoys,' he said, 'what is your errand?'

They said: 'We are sent forth to a sinful people. The house of Lot alone we shall deliver, except his wife.' We had decreed that she should stay with those who were to stay behind.

15:61 And when the envoys came to the house of Lot, he said: 'No one knows
you.'

'No,' they said. 'We bring you news of that concerning which they are in doubt. We bring you Truth, and what we say is true. Go with your kin in the dead of night; walk in their rear and let none turn round: go where you are commanded.'

Such was the command We gave him; those were to be obliterated next morning.

And the townsfolk came to him rejoicing. He said: 'These are my guests; do not disgrace me. Fear God and do not shame me.'

15:70 They said: 'Did we not forbid you to entertain strangers?'

إذ دخلوا عليه فقالوا سلاما قال إنا منكم وجلون ﴿٥٢﴾ قالوا
لا توجل إنا نبشرك بغلام عليم ﴿٥٣﴾ قال أبشرتموني على أن
مسني الكبر فبم تبشرون ﴿٥٤﴾ قالوا بشرناك بالحق
فلا تكن من القانطين ﴿٥٥﴾ قال ومن يقنط من رحمة
ربه إلا الضالون ﴿٥٦﴾ قال فما خطبكم أيها المرسلون
﴿٥٧﴾ قالوا إنا أرسلنا إلى قوم مجرمين ﴿٥٨﴾ إلا آل لوط إنا
لمنجوهم أجمعين ﴿٥٩﴾ إلا امرأته قدرنا إنها لمن الغابرين
﴿٦٠﴾ فلما جاء آل لوط المرسلون ﴿٦١﴾ قال إنكم قوم
منكرون ﴿٦٢﴾ قالوا بل جئناك بما كانوا فيه يمترون
﴿٦٣﴾ وأتيناك بالحق وإنا لصادقون ﴿٦٤﴾ فأسر بأهلك
بقطع من الليل واتبع أدبارهم ولا يلتفت منكم أحد
وامضوا حيث تؤمرون ﴿٦٥﴾ وقضينا إليه ذلك الأمر أن دابر
هؤلاء مقطوع مصبحين ﴿٦٦﴾ وجاء أهل المدينة يستبشرون
﴿٦٧﴾ قال إن هؤلاء ضيفي فلا تفضحون ﴿٦٨﴾ واتقوا
الله ولا تخزون ﴿٦٩﴾ قالوا أولم ننهك عن العالمين ﴿٧٠﴾

قال هؤلاء بناتي إن كنتم فاعلين ۝ لعمرك إنهم لفي
سكرتهم يعمهون ۝ فأخذتهم الصيحة مشرقين ۝
فجعلنا عاليها سافلها وأمطرنا عليهم حجارة من سجيل ۝
إن في ذلك لآيات للمتوسمين ۝ وإنها لبسبيل مقيم ۝
إن في ذلك لآية للمؤمنين ۝ وإن كان أصحاب الأيكة
لظالمين ۝ فانتقمنا منهم وإنهما لبإمام مبين ۝ ولقد
كذب أصحاب الحجر المرسلين ۝ وآتيناهم آياتنا فكانوا
عنها معرضين ۝ وكانوا ينحتون من الجبال بيوتا آمنين ۝
فأخذتهم الصيحة مصبحين ۝ فما أغنى عنهم ما كانوا
يكسبون ۝ وما خلقنا السموات والأرض وما بينهما إلا
بالحق وإن الساعة لآتية فاصفح الصفح الجميل ۝ إن ربك
هو الخلاق العليم ۝ ولقد آتيناك سبعا من المثاني والقرآن
العظيم ۝ لا تمدن عينيك إلى ما متعنا به أزواجا منهم
ولا تحزن عليهم واخفض جناحك للمؤمنين ۝ وقل إني
أنا النذير المبين ۝ كما أنزلنا على المقتسمين ۝

HE SAID: 'These are my 15:71
daughters: take them, if you
are bent on doing the deed.'
By your life, they were reel-
ing in their frenzy! At sunrise
the Cry took them. We turned
their city upside down and let
loose a shower of clay-stones
upon them.
Surely in this there are signs
for prudent people. The road
on which it stood is trodden
still. Surely in this there is a
sign for true believers.
Surely the dwellers of the
Forest[1] also did wrong. On
them, too, We took vengeance,
and made of both a manifest
example.
The people of Ḥijr[2] also 15:80
denied the apostles. We gave
them Our signs, but they
ignored them. They hewed
their dwellings out of the mountains and led their lives in safety. But one
morning the Cry took them. Nothing did their gains avail them.
It was but to reveal the Truth that We created the heavens and the earth
and all that lies between them. The Hour is sure to come: bear with them
nobly. It is your Lord who is the All-knowing Creator.
We have given you the seven oft-repeated verses[3] and the Glorious Koran.
Do not eye with envy what We have given some among them to enjoy, nor
grieve on their account. Show kindness to the faithful, and say: 'I am he that
gives veritable warning.'
As surely will We punish the schismatics, 15:90

1. The people of Midian.
2. Territory to the north of Medina, where the Thamud are said to have dwelt.
3. The seven verses of the *Fātiḥah*, or Exordium (p. xvii).

15:91 those who have broken up the
Koran into bits and pieces.[1] By
the Lord, We will question
them all about their doings.
Proclaim, then, what you
are bidden and let the idolaters
be. We will Ourself sustain you
against those that mock you
and serve other deities besides
God. They shall learn.
We know you are distressed
by what they say. Give glory in
praise of your Lord and pros-
15:99 trate yourself. Worship your
Lord till the inevitable overtakes you.

THE BEE

In the Name of God, the Merciful, the Compassionate

16:1 GOD'S JUDGEMENT will surely come to pass: do not seek to hurry it on.
Glory be to Him! Exalted be He above their idols!
By His will He sends down the angels with the Spirit to those among His
servants whom He chooses, bidding them give warning: 'There is no god but
Me: therefore fear Me.'
He created the heavens and the earth to manifest the Truth. Exalted be
He above their idols!
He created man from a little germ: and yet is he openly contentious.
He created the beasts which give you warmth and food and other benefits.
16:6 How pleasant they look when you bring them home to rest, and when you
lead them out to pasture!

1. 'Believing in some and denying others', according to Al-Jalālayn.

وتحمل أثقالكم إلى بلد لم تكونوا بالغيه إلا بشق
الأنفس إن ربكم لرءوف رحيم ۝ والخيل والبغال
والحمير لتركبوها وزينة ويخلق ما لا تعلمون
۝ وعلى الله قصد السبيل ومنها جائر ولو شاء
لهديكم أجمعين ۝ هو الذي أنزل من السماء ماء
لكم منه شراب ومنه شجر فيه تسيمون ۝ ينبت
لكم به الزرع والزيتون والنخيل والأعناب ومن
كل الثمرات إن في ذلك لآية لقوم يتفكرون ۝
وسخر لكم الليل والنهار والشمس والقمر
والنجوم مسخرات بأمره إن في ذلك لآيات لقوم
يعقلون ۝ وما ذرأ لكم في الأرض مختلفا ألوانه
إن في ذلك لآية لقوم يذكرون ۝ وهو الذي
سخر البحر لتأكلوا منه لحما طريا وتستخرجوا منه
حلية تلبسونها وترى الفلك مواخر فيه
ولتبتغوا من فضله ولعلكم تشكرون ۝

THEY CARRY your burdens 16:7
to a land you could not otherwise reach except with painful
toil. Surely kindly is your Lord,
and compassionate.

Also horses, mules, and
donkeys, for you to ride or put
on show; and He creates other
things beyond your knowledge.

God alone points to the
right path. Some turn aside
but, had He pleased, He would
have given you guidance all.

It is He who sends down
water from the sky, which provides you with your drink and
brings forth the pasturage on
which your cattle feed. And 16:11
with it He brings forth corn
and olives, dates and grapes
and fruits of every kind. Surely
in this there is a sign for people
who can think.

He has pressed the night and the day, and the sun and the moon, into your service: the stars also serve you by His command. Surely in this there are signs for people who understand.

On the earth He has fashioned for you objects of various hues: surely in this there is a sign for people who reflect.

He it is who has subdued the ocean, so that you may eat from it fresh flesh 16:14
and bring up from its depths ornaments to wear. Behold the ships ploughing
their course through it. All this, that you may seek His bounty and may render thanks.

16:15 HE SET upon the earth firm mountains lest it should move away with you; and rivers and roads, that you may be rightly guided; by landmarks and the stars, too, they are directed.

Is He, then, who has created, like him who cannot create? Will you, then, not ponder?

If you reckoned up God's blessings, you could not count them. Surely God is forgiving and compassionate.

God has knowledge of what you conceal and what you reveal. Those that they invoke besides God create nothing: they are themselves created. Dead, not living; nor do they know when they will be raised to life.

وَأَلْقَىٰ فِي الْأَرْضِ رَوَاسِيَ أَن تَمِيدَ بِكُمْ وَأَنْهَارًا وَسُبُلًا
لَّعَلَّكُمْ تَهْتَدُونَ ﴿١٥﴾ وَعَلَامَاتٍ ۚ وَبِالنَّجْمِ هُمْ يَهْتَدُونَ
﴿١٦﴾ أَفَمَن يَخْلُقُ كَمَن لَّا يَخْلُقُ ۗ أَفَلَا تَذَكَّرُونَ ﴿١٧﴾
وَإِن تَعُدُّوا نِعْمَةَ اللَّهِ لَا تُحْصُوهَا ۗ إِنَّ اللَّهَ لَغَفُورٌ رَّحِيمٌ
﴿١٨﴾ وَاللَّهُ يَعْلَمُ مَا تُسِرُّونَ وَمَا تُعْلِنُونَ ﴿١٩﴾ وَالَّذِينَ
يَدْعُونَ مِن دُونِ اللَّهِ لَا يَخْلُقُونَ شَيْئًا وَهُمْ يُخْلَقُونَ
﴿٢٠﴾ أَمْوَاتٌ غَيْرُ أَحْيَاءٍ ۖ وَمَا يَشْعُرُونَ أَيَّانَ يُبْعَثُونَ ﴿٢١﴾
إِلَٰهُكُمْ إِلَٰهٌ وَاحِدٌ ۚ فَالَّذِينَ لَا يُؤْمِنُونَ بِالْآخِرَةِ قُلُوبُهُم
مُّنكِرَةٌ وَهُم مُّسْتَكْبِرُونَ ﴿٢٢﴾ لَا جَرَمَ أَنَّ اللَّهَ يَعْلَمُ مَا يُسِرُّونَ
وَمَا يُعْلِنُونَ ۚ إِنَّهُ لَا يُحِبُّ الْمُسْتَكْبِرِينَ ﴿٢٣﴾ وَإِذَا قِيلَ لَهُم مَّاذَا
أَنزَلَ رَبُّكُمْ ۙ قَالُوا أَسَاطِيرُ الْأَوَّلِينَ ﴿٢٤﴾ لِيَحْمِلُوا أَوْزَارَهُمْ
كَامِلَةً يَوْمَ الْقِيَامَةِ ۙ وَمِنْ أَوْزَارِ الَّذِينَ يُضِلُّونَهُم بِغَيْرِ
عِلْمٍ ۗ أَلَا سَاءَ مَا يَزِرُونَ ﴿٢٥﴾ قَدْ مَكَرَ الَّذِينَ مِن قَبْلِهِمْ
فَأَتَى اللَّهُ بُنْيَانَهُم مِّنَ الْقَوَاعِدِ فَخَرَّ عَلَيْهِمُ السَّقْفُ
مِن فَوْقِهِمْ وَأَتَاهُمُ الْعَذَابُ مِنْ حَيْثُ لَا يَشْعُرُونَ ﴿٢٦﴾

16:22 Your God is one God. Those that deny the life to come have faithless hearts and are puffed up with pride. God surely knows what they conceal and what they reveal. He does not love the proud.

When they are asked: 'What has your Lord revealed?' they say: 'Fables of the ancients!' They shall bear the full brunt of their burdens on the Day of Resurrection, together with the burdens of those who in their ignorance were misled by them. Evil is that which they shall bear.

16:26 Those who had gone before them also schemed. But God smote their edifice at its foundations, and its roof collapsed upon their heads. The scourge overtook them whence they did not perceive.

ثم يوم القيمة يخزيهم ويقول أين شركاءي الذين كنتم
تشاقون فيهم قال الذين أوتوا العلم إن الخزي اليوم
والسوء على الكافرين ۝٢٧ الذين تتوفيهم الملئكة ظالمي
أنفسهم فألقوا السلم ما كنا نعمل من سوء بلى إن
الله عليم بما كنتم تعملون ۝٢٨ فادخلوا أبواب جهنم خالدين
فيها فلبئس مثوى المتكبرين ۝٢٩ وقيل للذين اتقوا ماذا أنزل
ربكم قالوا خيرا للذين أحسنوا في هذه الدنيا حسنة ولدار
الآخرة خير ولنعم دار المتقين ۝٣٠ جنات عدن يدخلونها
تجري من تحتها الأنهار لهم فيها ما يشاءون كذلك يجزي
الله المتقين ۝٣١ الذين تتوفيهم الملئكة طيبين يقولون
سلام عليكم ادخلوا الجنة بما كنتم تعملون
۝٣٢ هل ينظرون إلا أن تأتيهم الملئكة أو يأتي أمر
ربك كذلك فعل الذين من قبلهم وما ظلمهم
الله ولكن كانوا أنفسهم يظلمون ۝٣٣ فأصابهم
سيئات ما عملوا وحاق بهم ما كانوا به يستهزءون ۝٣٤

THEN, ON the Day of Res- 16:27
urrection He will hold them
up to shame, and He will say:
'Where are your idols now, the
theme of your disputes?' And
those endowed with know-
ledge will say: 'Shame and
sorrow shall this day smite the
unbelievers.'

Those whom the angels
will claim back while steeped
in sin will offer their submission, saying: 'We have done no
wrong!' 'Indeed! God well
knows what you have done.
Enter the gates of Hell,
wherein shall you abide for
ever.' Evil is the abode of the
arrogant.

But when the God-fearing
are asked: 'What has your
Lord revealed?' they will say:
'That which is best.' Good is
the reward of those that do good works in this present life: but better is the
abode of the life to come. Blessed is the abode of the God-fearing. The 16:31
Gardens of Eden they shall enter, wherein brooks will roll at their feet; and
wherein shall they have all that they desire. Thus shall God recompense the
God-fearing, whom the angels will claim, in all their virtue, saying: 'Peace be
on you. Come into Paradise, the reward of your labours.'

Are they only waiting for the angels to come down or for the fulfilment of
your Lord's will? Those who had gone before them also waited. God did not
wrong them, but they wronged their own souls: the evil which they did 16:34
recoiled upon them, and the scourge at which they scoffed encompassed
them.

16:35 THE IDOLATERS say: 'Had God pleased, we would not have worshipped any besides Him, neither we nor our forefathers; nor would we have declared anything unlawful without His sanction.' Such also was the plea of those who had gone before them. Yet what should apostles do but give veritable warning?

We raised an apostle in each community: 'Serve God and keep away from false gods.' Among them were some to whom God gave guidance, and among them were some doomed to go astray. Roam the earth and see what was the fate of the disbelievers!

16:37 Strive as you may to guide them, God will not guide those whom He confounds; there shall be none to help them.

They solemnly swear by God that God will never raise the dead to life. But that is a promise that shall be justly fulfilled, though most may not know it, so that He will resolve for them their differences, and that the unbelievers will know that they were lying. When We decree a thing, We need only say: 'Be,' and it is.

As for those who after persecution fled their homes in the cause of God,
We will reward them well in this nether life: yet better still is the reward of
16:42 the life to come, if they but knew it; those who bore ills with patience and
put their trust in their Lord.

وقال الذين أشركوا لو شاء الله ما عبدنا من دونه
من شيء نحن ولا آباؤنا ولا حرمنا من دونه من شيء
كذلك فعل الذين من قبلهم فهل على الرسل إلا البلاغ
المبين ۝ ولقد بعثنا في كل أمة رسولا أن اعبدوا الله
واجتنبوا الطاغوت فمنهم من هدى الله ومنهم من حقت عليه
الضلالة فسيروا في الأرض فانظروا كيف كان
عاقبة المكذبين ۝ إن تحرص على هداهم فإن الله
لا يهدي من يضل وما لهم من ناصرين ۝ وأقسموا بالله
جهد أيمانهم لا يبعث الله من يموت بلى وعدا
عليه حقا ولكن أكثر الناس لا يعلمون ۝ ليبين لهم
الذي يختلفون فيه وليعلم الذين كفروا أنهم كانوا
كاذبين ۝ إنما قولنا لشيء إذا أردناه أن نقول له كن
فيكون ۝ والذين هاجروا في الله من بعد ما ظلموا
لنبوئنهم في الدنيا حسنة ولأجر الآخرة أكبر لو كانوا
يعلمون ۝ الذين صبروا وعلى ربهم يتوكلون ۝

وَمَآ أَرْسَلْنَا مِن قَبْلِكَ إِلَّا رِجَالًا نُّوحِىٓ إِلَيْهِمْ فَسْـَٔلُوٓا أَهْلَ
الذِّكْرِ إِن كُنتُمْ لَا تَعْلَمُونَ ﴿٤٣﴾ بِالْبَيِّنَاتِ وَالزُّبُرِ وَأَنزَلْنَآ إِلَيْكَ
الذِّكْرَ لِتُبَيِّنَ لِلنَّاسِ مَا نُزِّلَ إِلَيْهِمْ وَلَعَلَّهُمْ يَتَفَكَّرُونَ ﴿٤٤﴾ أَفَأَمِنَ
الَّذِينَ مَكَرُوا السَّيِّـَٔاتِ أَن يَخْسِفَ اللَّهُ بِهِمُ الْأَرْضَ أَوْ يَأْتِيَهُمُ
الْعَذَابُ مِنْ حَيْثُ لَا يَشْعُرُونَ ﴿٤٥﴾ أَوْ يَأْخُذَهُمْ فِى تَقَلُّبِهِمْ
فَمَا هُم بِمُعْجِزِينَ ﴿٤٦﴾ أَوْ يَأْخُذَهُمْ عَلَىٰ تَخَوُّفٍ فَإِنَّ رَبَّكُمْ
لَرَءُوفٌ رَّحِيمٌ ﴿٤٧﴾ أَوَلَمْ يَرَوْا إِلَىٰ مَا خَلَقَ اللَّهُ مِن شَىْءٍ يَتَفَيَّؤُا ظِلَالُهُ
عَنِ الْيَمِينِ وَالشَّمَآئِلِ سُجَّدًا لِّلَّهِ وَهُمْ دَاخِرُونَ ﴿٤٨﴾ وَلِلَّهِ
يَسْجُدُ مَا فِى السَّمَٰوَاتِ وَمَا فِى الْأَرْضِ مِن دَآبَّةٍ وَالْمَلَٰٓئِكَةُ
وَهُمْ لَا يَسْتَكْبِرُونَ ﴿٤٩﴾ يَخَافُونَ رَبَّهُم مِّن فَوْقِهِمْ وَيَفْعَلُونَ
مَا يُؤْمَرُونَ ﴿٥٠﴾ وَقَالَ اللَّهُ لَا تَتَّخِذُوٓا إِلَٰهَيْنِ اثْنَيْنِ إِنَّمَا هُوَ إِلَٰهٌ
وَاحِدٌ فَإِيَّٰىَ فَارْهَبُونِ ﴿٥١﴾ وَلَهُ مَا فِى السَّمَٰوَاتِ وَالْأَرْضِ وَلَهُ
الدِّينُ وَاصِبًا أَفَغَيْرَ اللَّهِ تَتَّقُونَ ﴿٥٢﴾ وَمَا بِكُم مِّن نِّعْمَةٍ فَمِنَ اللَّهِ
ثُمَّ إِذَا مَسَّكُمُ الضُّرُّ فَإِلَيْهِ تَجْـَٔرُونَ ﴿٥٣﴾ ثُمَّ إِذَا كَشَفَ
الضُّرَّ عَنكُمْ إِذَا فَرِيقٌ مِّنكُم بِرَبِّهِمْ يُشْرِكُونَ ﴿٥٤﴾

WE SENT none before you 16:43
but men whom We inspired
with revelations and with
Psalms. Ask the People of the
Admonition, if you know not.
And to you also We have revealed the Admonition, so that
you may proclaim to the people
what was sent down for them,
and that they may reflect.

Are those who plot evil so
certain that God will not cause
the earth to cave in beneath
them, or that the scourge will
not descend on them whence
they do not perceive? Or smite
them in the course of their
journeys when they cannot
escape, or give them over to
slow destruction?[1] Yet is your
Lord kindly and compassionate.

Do they not see how every 16:48
object God created casts its
shadow right and left, prostrating itself before God in all humility? To God
bow all the creatures of the heavens and the earth, and the angels too. They
are not disdainful; they fear their Lord on high and do as they are bidden.

And God has said: 'You shall not serve two gods, for He is but one God.
Fear none but Me.'

His is what the heavens and the earth contain; His is the Religion everlasting. Would you then fear any but God?

There is no blessing you enjoy which does not come from God, and to
Him you turn for help when misfortune befalls you. Yet no sooner does He 16:54
remove your ills than some among you set up other gods besides their Lord,

1. Thus Al-Bayḍāwī; an obscure verse. See also Arberry.

16:55 showing no gratitude for what We gave them. Take your pleasure now, and you shall learn.

To those they know nothing of, they assign a share of what We gave them. By the Lord, you shall be questioned about the lies you fabricated!

They foist daughters upon God (glory be to Him!), but for themselves they choose what they desire. When the birth of a female is announced to one of them, his countenance darkens and he is mightily vexed. On account of the bad news he hides himself from people: should he put up with the shame or bury her in the earth? How ill they judge!

Evil are the ways of those who deny the life to come; and most sublime are the ways of God: He is the Almighty, the Wise One.

لِيَكْفُرُوا بِمَا آتَيْنَاهُمْ فَتَمَتَّعُوا فَسَوْفَ تَعْلَمُونَ ۝ وَيَجْعَلُونَ
لِمَا لَا يَعْلَمُونَ نَصِيبًا مِمَّا رَزَقْنَاهُمْ تَاللَّهِ لَتُسْأَلُنَّ عَمَّا كُنْتُمْ
تَفْتَرُونَ ۝ وَيَجْعَلُونَ لِلَّهِ الْبَنَاتِ سُبْحَانَهُ وَلَهُمْ مَا يَشْتَهُونَ
۝ وَإِذَا بُشِّرَ أَحَدُهُمْ بِالْأُنْثَى ظَلَّ وَجْهُهُ مُسْوَدًّا وَهُوَ كَظِيمٌ
۝ يَتَوَارَى مِنَ الْقَوْمِ مِنْ سُوءِ مَا بُشِّرَ بِهِ أَيُمْسِكُهُ عَلَى هُونٍ
أَمْ يَدُسُّهُ فِي التُّرَابِ أَلَا سَاءَ مَا يَحْكُمُونَ ۝ لِلَّذِينَ لَا يُؤْمِنُونَ
بِالْآخِرَةِ مَثَلُ السَّوْءِ وَلِلَّهِ الْمَثَلُ الْأَعْلَى وَهُوَ الْعَزِيزُ الْحَكِيمُ
۝ وَلَوْ يُؤَاخِذُ اللَّهُ النَّاسَ بِظُلْمِهِمْ مَا تَرَكَ عَلَيْهَا مِنْ
دَابَّةٍ وَلَكِنْ يُؤَخِّرُهُمْ إِلَى أَجَلٍ مُسَمًّى فَإِذَا جَاءَ أَجَلُهُمْ لَا يَسْتَأْخِرُونَ
سَاعَةً وَلَا يَسْتَقْدِمُونَ ۝ وَيَجْعَلُونَ لِلَّهِ مَا يَكْرَهُونَ وَتَصِفُ
أَلْسِنَتُهُمُ الْكَذِبَ أَنَّ لَهُمُ الْحُسْنَى لَا جَرَمَ أَنَّ لَهُمُ النَّارَ
وَأَنَّهُمْ مُفْرَطُونَ ۝ تَاللَّهِ لَقَدْ أَرْسَلْنَا إِلَى أُمَمٍ مِنْ قَبْلِكَ
فَزَيَّنَ لَهُمُ الشَّيْطَانُ أَعْمَالَهُمْ فَهُوَ وَلِيُّهُمُ الْيَوْمَ وَلَهُمْ
عَذَابٌ أَلِيمٌ ۝ وَمَا أَنْزَلْنَا عَلَيْكَ الْكِتَابَ إِلَّا لِتُبَيِّنَ لَهُمُ
الَّذِي اخْتَلَفُوا فِيهِ وَهُدًى وَرَحْمَةً لِقَوْمٍ يُؤْمِنُونَ ۝

16:61 If God punished people for their sins, not one creature would He leave alive. He reprieves them till a time ordained; when their time is come, not for one hour shall they stay behind: nor can they go before it.

They foist upon God what they themselves abhor. Their tongues falsely claim that a good reward awaits them. But let there be no doubt: the Fire awaits them, and they have strayed into egregious error.

By the Lord, We have sent forth before you to other communities. But Satan made their deeds seem fair to them, and to this day he is their patron. Woeful punishment awaits them.

16:64 We have revealed to you the Book only that you may resolve their differences for them: a guide and a blessing to true believers.

والله انزل من السماء ماء فاحيا به الارض بعد موتها ان في
ذلك لاية لقوم يسمعون ٦٥ وان لكم في الانعام لعبرة نسقيكم
مما في بطونه من بين فرث ودم لبنا خالصا سائغا للشاربين ٦٦
ومن ثمرات النخيل والاعناب تتخذون منه سكرا ورزقا حسنا
ان في ذلك لاية لقوم يعقلون ٦٧ واوحى ربك الى النحل ان
اتخذي من الجبال بيوتا ومن الشجر ومما يعرشون ٦٨ ثم
كلي من كل الثمرات فاسلكي سبل ربك ذللا يخرج من
بطونها شراب مختلف الوانه فيه شفاء للناس ان في ذلك لاية
لقوم يتفكرون ٦٩ والله خلقكم ثم يتوفيكم ومنكم من يرد
الى ارذل العمر لكيلا يعلم بعد علم شيئا ان الله عليم قدير ٧٠
والله فضل بعضكم على بعض في الرزق فما الذين فضلوا
برادي رزقهم على ما ملكت ايمانهم فهم فيه سواء افبنعمة
الله يجحدون ٧١ والله جعل لكم من انفسكم ازواجا
وجعل لكم من ازواجكم بنين وحفدة ورزقكم من
الطيبات افبالباطل يؤمنون وبنعمت الله هم يكفرون ٧٢

AND GOD sends down 16:65
water from the sky wherewith
He quickens the earth after its
death. Surely in this there is a
sign for people who can hear.

In cattle too you have a
worthy lesson. We give you to
drink of that which is in their
bellies, between the bowels
and the blood-streams: pure
milk, pleasant for those who
drink it.

And the fruits of the palm
and the vine, from which you
derive intoxicants and wholesome food. Surely in this there
is a sign for those endowed
with reason.

Your Lord inspired the bees,
saying: 'Make your homes in
the mountains, in the trees,
and in the hives which men
shall build for you. Then feed 16:69
on every kind of fruit, and follow the trodden paths of your Lord.'

From its belly comes forth a syrup of different hues, a cure for humans. Surely in this there is a sign for those who would take thought.

God created you, and He will then reclaim you. Some among you shall have their lives prolonged to abject old age, when all that they once knew they shall know no more. All-knowing is God, and Almighty.

In what He has provided, God has favoured some among you above others. Those who are so favoured will not allow their slaves an equal share in what they have. Would they deny God's goodness?

God has given you spouses from among yourselves and, through your 16:72
spouses, children and grandchildren. And He has provided you with wholesome things: will they then in falsehood believe and deny God's bounty?

16:73 AND THEY worship helpless idols which can confer on
them no benefits from the
heavens or the earth. Therefore compare God to none:
God has knowledge, but you
have not.

God makes this compari-
son: one a helpless slave, the
property of his master; and
one on whom We have
bestowed a bounteous provision from which he gives in
private and in public. Are the
two equal? God be praised!
But most of them have no
knowledge.

16:76 And God makes this comparison: two men, one dumb
and helpless, a burden on his
master: wherever he sends
him he comes back with nothing good. Is he equal to him
who enjoins justice and is on a straight path?

To God belong the secrets of the heavens and the earth. The business of
the Hour shall be accomplished in the twinkling of an eye, or in a shorter
time. Surely God has power over all things.

And God brought you out of your mothers' wombs devoid of any knowledge, and gave you ears and eyes and hearts, so that you may give thanks.

16:79 Do they not see the birds that wing their way in heaven's vault? None but
God sustains them. Surely in this there are signs for true believers.

ويعبدون من دون الله ما لا يملك لهم رزقا
من السموات والأرض شيئا ولا يستطيعون ﴿٧٣﴾ فلا
تضربوا لله الأمثال إن الله يعلم وأنتم لا تعلمون ﴿٧٤﴾
ضرب الله مثلا عبدا مملوكا لا يقدر على شيء ومن
رزقناه منا رزقا حسنا فهو ينفق منه سرا وجهرا
هل يستوون الحمد لله بل أكثرهم لا يعلمون ﴿٧٥﴾ و
ضرب الله مثلا رجلين أحدهما أبكم لا يقدر على شيء
وهو كل على مولاه أينما يوجهه لا يأت بخير هل
يستوي هو ومن يأمر بالعدل وهو على صراط مستقيم
﴿٧٦﴾ ولله غيب السموات والأرض وما أمر الساعة إلا كلمح
البصر أو هو أقرب إن الله على كل شيء قدير
﴿٧٧﴾ والله أخرجكم من بطون أمهاتكم لا تعلمون شيئا
وجعل لكم السمع والأبصار والأفئدة لعلكم تشكرون
﴿٧٨﴾ ألم يروا إلى الطير مسخرات في جو السماء ما يمسكهن
إلا الله إن في ذلك لآيات لقوم يؤمنون ﴿٧٩﴾

والله جعل لكم من بيوتكم سكنا وجعل لكم من جلود
الانعام بيوتا تستخفونها يوم ظعنكم ويوم اقامتكم
ومن اصوافها واوبارها واشعارها اثاثا ومتاعا الى حين ﴿٨٠﴾
والله جعل لكم مما خلق ظلالا وجعل لكم من الجبال
اكنانا وجعل لكم سرابيل تقيكم الحر وسرابيل تقيكم
باسكم كذلك يتم نعمته عليكم لعلكم تسلمون
﴿٨١﴾ فان تولوا فانما عليك البلاغ المبين ﴿٨٢﴾ يعرفون نعمت
الله ثم ينكرونها واكثرهم الكافرون ﴿٨٣﴾ ويوم
نبعث من كل امة شهيدا ثم لا يؤذن للذين
كفروا ولا هم يستعتبون ﴿٨٤﴾ واذا را الذين
ظلموا العذاب فلا يخفف عنهم ولا هم ينظرون
﴿٨٥﴾ واذا را الذين اشركوا شركاءهم قالوا
ربنا هؤلاء شركاؤنا الذين كنا ندعوا من دونك
فالقوا اليهم القول انكم لكاذبون ﴿٨٦﴾ والقوا الى
الله يومئذ السلم وضل عنهم ما كانوا يفترون ﴿٨٧﴾

AND GOD has given you 16:80
houses to dwell in, and has
given you animals' skins for
tents, that you may find them
light when you travel and easy
to pitch when you halt for
shelter; while from their wool,
fur, and hair, He has for a
space of time provided you
with comforts and domestic
goods.

By means of that which He
created, God has given you
shelters from the sun; He has
given you refuge in the mountains; He has given you
garments to protect you from
the heat, and coats of armour
to shield you in your wars.
Thus does He perfect His
bounty to you, that you may
turn to Islām.

But if they[1] pay no heed, 16:82
your[2] mission is only to give clear warning.

They recognize God's bounty, yet they deny it. And most of them surely
are ungrateful.

On the day We call to life a witness from each community, their pleas shall
not avail the unbelievers, nor shall they be allowed to make amends. And
when the wrongdoers face the scourge, it shall not be eased for them, nor
shall they ever be reprieved.

When the pagans behold their idols, they will say: 'Lord, these are the
idols to whom we prayed.' But their idols will retort: 'You are surely lying!'
They shall proffer God submission on that day, and the gods of their own 16:87
invention will forsake them.

1. The Meccans. 2. Muḥammad's.

16:88 THOSE THAT disbelieve and debar others from the path of God, We shall chastise all the more for their misdeeds; on the day We call to life a witness in each community from among themselves to testify against them. We shall call *you* to testify against these: for to you We have revealed the Book to manifest the Truth about all things, a guide, a blessing, and joyful tidings for the Muslims.

God enjoins justice, kindness, and charity to kin, and forbids lewdness, reprehensible conduct, and oppression. He admonishes you so that you may take thought.

16:91 Keep faith with God when you make a pledge. And you shall not break your oaths after you have sworn them, having made God thereby your surety. God has knowledge of what you do.

Do not, like the woman who unravels the thread she has firmly spun, take oaths with mutual deceit and break them on finding yourselves superior in numbers. In this, God puts you to the proof. On the Day of Resurrection He will resolve your differences for you.

16:93 Had God pleased, He would have united you into one community. But He confounds whom He will and gives guidance to whom He pleases. And you shall surely be questioned over what you did.

الَّذِينَ كَفَرُوا وَصَدُّوا عَن سَبِيلِ اللَّهِ زِدْنَاهُمْ عَذَابًا
فَوْقَ الْعَذَابِ بِمَا كَانُوا يُفْسِدُونَ ﴿٨٨﴾ وَيَوْمَ نَبْعَثُ فِي كُلِّ
أُمَّةٍ شَهِيدًا عَلَيْهِم مِّنْ أَنفُسِهِمْ وَجِئْنَا بِكَ شَهِيدًا عَلَىٰ
هَٰؤُلَاءِ وَنَزَّلْنَا عَلَيْكَ الْكِتَابَ تِبْيَانًا لِّكُلِّ شَيْءٍ وَهُدًى
وَرَحْمَةً وَبُشْرَىٰ لِلْمُسْلِمِينَ ﴿٨٩﴾ إِنَّ اللَّهَ يَأْمُرُ بِالْعَدْلِ
وَالْإِحْسَانِ وَإِيتَاءِ ذِي الْقُرْبَىٰ وَيَنْهَىٰ عَنِ الْفَحْشَاءِ
وَالْمُنكَرِ وَالْبَغْيِ يَعِظُكُمْ لَعَلَّكُمْ تَذَكَّرُونَ ﴿٩٠﴾ وَأَوْفُوا
بِعَهْدِ اللَّهِ إِذَا عَاهَدتُّمْ وَلَا تَنقُضُوا الْأَيْمَانَ
بَعْدَ تَوْكِيدِهَا وَقَدْ جَعَلْتُمُ اللَّهَ عَلَيْكُمْ كَفِيلًا
إِنَّ اللَّهَ يَعْلَمُ مَا تَفْعَلُونَ ﴿٩١﴾ وَلَا تَكُونُوا كَالَّتِي نَقَضَتْ
غَزْلَهَا مِن بَعْدِ قُوَّةٍ أَنكَاثًا تَتَّخِذُونَ أَيْمَانَكُمْ دَخَلًا بَيْنَكُمْ
أَن تَكُونَ أُمَّةٌ هِيَ أَرْبَىٰ مِنْ أُمَّةٍ إِنَّمَا يَبْلُوكُمُ اللَّهُ بِهِ وَلَيُبَيِّنَنَّ
لَكُمْ يَوْمَ الْقِيَامَةِ مَا كُنتُمْ فِيهِ تَخْتَلِفُونَ ﴿٩٢﴾ وَلَوْ
شَاءَ اللَّهُ لَجَعَلَكُمْ أُمَّةً وَاحِدَةً وَلَٰكِن يُضِلُّ مَن يَشَاءُ
وَيَهْدِي مَن يَشَاءُ وَلَتُسْأَلُنَّ عَمَّا كُنتُمْ تَعْمَلُونَ ﴿٩٣﴾

وَلَا تَتَّخِذُوا أَيْمَانَكُمْ دَخَلًا بَيْنَكُمْ فَتَزِلَّ قَدَمٌ بَعْدَ
ثُبُوتِهَا وَتَذُوقُوا السُّوءَ بِمَا صَدَدْتُمْ عَنْ سَبِيلِ اللَّهِ
وَلَكُمْ عَذَابٌ عَظِيمٌ ﴿٩٤﴾ وَلَا تَشْتَرُوا بِعَهْدِ اللَّهِ
ثَمَنًا قَلِيلًا إِنَّمَا عِنْدَ اللَّهِ هُوَ خَيْرٌ لَكُمْ إِنْ كُنْتُمْ تَعْلَمُونَ ﴿٩٥﴾
مَا عِنْدَكُمْ يَنْفَدُ وَمَا عِنْدَ اللَّهِ بَاقٍ وَلَنَجْزِيَنَّ الَّذِينَ صَبَرُوا
أَجْرَهُمْ بِأَحْسَنِ مَا كَانُوا يَعْمَلُونَ ﴿٩٦﴾ مَنْ عَمِلَ صَالِحًا مِنْ
ذَكَرٍ أَوْ أُنْثَى وَهُوَ مُؤْمِنٌ فَلَنُحْيِيَنَّهُ حَيَوٰةً طَيِّبَةً
وَلَنَجْزِيَنَّهُمْ أَجْرَهُمْ بِأَحْسَنِ مَا كَانُوا يَعْمَلُونَ ﴿٩٧﴾ فَإِذَا
قَرَأْتَ الْقُرْآنَ فَاسْتَعِذْ بِاللَّهِ مِنَ الشَّيْطَانِ الرَّجِيمِ ﴿٩٨﴾
إِنَّهُ لَيْسَ لَهُ سُلْطَانٌ عَلَى الَّذِينَ آمَنُوا وَعَلَى رَبِّهِمْ
يَتَوَكَّلُونَ ﴿٩٩﴾ إِنَّمَا سُلْطَانُهُ عَلَى الَّذِينَ يَتَوَلَّوْنَهُ وَالَّذِينَ
هُمْ بِهِ مُشْرِكُونَ ﴿١٠٠﴾ وَإِذَا بَدَّلْنَا آيَةً مَكَانَ آيَةٍ وَاللَّهُ
أَعْلَمُ بِمَا يُنَزِّلُ قَالُوا إِنَّمَا أَنْتَ مُفْتَرٍ بَلْ أَكْثَرُهُمْ
لَا يَعْلَمُونَ ﴿١٠١﴾ قُلْ نَزَّلَهُ رُوحُ الْقُدُسِ مِنْ رَبِّكَ
بِالْحَقِّ لِيُثَبِّتَ الَّذِينَ آمَنُوا وَهُدًى وَبُشْرَى لِلْمُسْلِمِينَ ﴿١٠٢﴾

AND YOU shall not take 16:94
oaths to deceive each other, lest a foot should slip after being rightly guided, and lest you taste misfortune for debarring others from the path of God: for then indeed you should incur a grievous punishment.

You shall not barter God's covenant for a trifling price. God's recompense is better for you, if you but knew it. Your worldly riches are transitory, but God's recompense is everlasting.

We shall recompense the steadfast according to their noblest deeds. Be they men or women, to those that embrace the Faith and do what is right We will surely grant a happy life; We shall reward them according to their noblest deeds.

When you read the Koran, seek refuge in God from accursèd Satan: no 16:98
power has he over those who believe and who put their trust in their Lord. He has power only over those who befriend him and those who serve partners besides Him.

And if We change one *sūrah* for another (God knows best what He reveals), they say: 'You[1] are but an impostor.' Indeed most of them have no knowledge.

Say: 'The Holy Spirit brought it down from your Lord in Truth to reassure 16:102
the faithful, and to give guidance and joyful tidings to Muslims.'

1. Muḥammad.

16:103 WE DO know that they say:
'A mortal taught him.' But the
man[1] to whom they allude
speaks a foreign tongue, while
this is eloquent Arabic speech.
Those who disbelieve God's
revelations God will not guide.
Woeful punishment awaits
them.
None invents falsehood
save those who disbelieve
God's revelations: it is they
that are the liars.
Those who are forced to
recant while their hearts remain loyal to the Faith shall be
absolved; but those who open
their bosoms to unbelief shall
incur God's ire; and grievous
16:107 punishment awaits them. That
is because they love the life of
this world more than the life to
come; and God does not guide
the unbelievers.
Such are those whose hearts and ears and eyes are sealed by God; such are
the heedless. In the life to come they will assuredly be lost.
16:110 Your Lord – to those who after persecution left their land and fought and
remained constant to the last – your Lord will be forgiving and compassionate

وَلَقَدْ نَعْلَمُ أَنَّهُمْ يَقُولُونَ إِنَّمَا يُعَلِّمُهُ بَشَرٌ
لِسَانُ الَّذِي يُلْحِدُونَ إِلَيْهِ أَعْجَمِيٌّ وَهَٰذَا لِسَانٌ
عَرَبِيٌّ مُبِينٌ ﴿١٠٣﴾ إِنَّ الَّذِينَ لَا يُؤْمِنُونَ بِآيَاتِ اللَّهِ
لَا يَهْدِيهِمُ اللَّهُ وَلَهُمْ عَذَابٌ أَلِيمٌ ﴿١٠٤﴾ إِنَّمَا
يَفْتَرِي الْكَذِبَ الَّذِينَ لَا يُؤْمِنُونَ بِآيَاتِ اللَّهِ
وَأُولَٰئِكَ هُمُ الْكَاذِبُونَ ﴿١٠٥﴾ مَنْ كَفَرَ بِاللَّهِ
مِنْ بَعْدِ إِيمَانِهِ إِلَّا مَنْ أُكْرِهَ وَقَلْبُهُ مُطْمَئِنٌّ
بِالْإِيمَانِ وَلَٰكِنْ مَنْ شَرَحَ بِالْكُفْرِ صَدْرًا فَعَلَيْهِمْ
غَضَبٌ مِنَ اللَّهِ وَلَهُمْ عَذَابٌ عَظِيمٌ ﴿١٠٦﴾ ذَٰلِكَ
بِأَنَّهُمُ اسْتَحَبُّوا الْحَيَاةَ الدُّنْيَا عَلَى الْآخِرَةِ وَأَنَّ اللَّهَ
لَا يَهْدِي الْقَوْمَ الْكَافِرِينَ ﴿١٠٧﴾ أُولَٰئِكَ الَّذِينَ طَبَعَ اللَّهُ
عَلَىٰ قُلُوبِهِمْ وَسَمْعِهِمْ وَأَبْصَارِهِمْ وَأُولَٰئِكَ هُمُ الْغَافِلُونَ
﴿١٠٨﴾ لَا جَرَمَ أَنَّهُمْ فِي الْآخِرَةِ هُمُ الْخَاسِرُونَ ﴿١٠٩﴾ ثُمَّ إِنَّ رَبَّكَ
لِلَّذِينَ هَاجَرُوا مِنْ بَعْدِ مَا فُتِنُوا ثُمَّ جَاهَدُوا
وَصَبَرُوا إِنَّ رَبَّكَ مِنْ بَعْدِهَا لَغَفُورٌ رَحِيمٌ ﴿١١٠﴾

1. Scholars differ as to the identity of this 'foreigner'. Some suppose him to be Salmān the Persian, others Ṣuhaib bin Sinān, and yet others 'Adas the Monk.

يوم تأتي كل نفس تجادل عن نفسها وتوفى كل نفس ما
عملت وهم لا يظلمون ١١١ وضرب الله مثلا قرية كانت
آمنة مطمئنة يأتيها رزقها رغدا من كل مكان
فكفرت بأنعم الله فأذاقها الله لباس الجوع والخوف
بما كانوا يصنعون ١١٢ ولقد جاءهم رسول منهم فكذبوه
فأخذهم العذاب وهم ظالمون ١١٣ فكلوا مما رزقكم الله
حلالا طيبا واشكروا نعمت الله إن كنتم إياه
تعبدون ١١٤ إنما حرم عليكم الميتة والدم ولحم الخنزير
وما أهل لغير الله به فمن اضطر غير باغ ولا عاد فإن الله
غفور رحيم ١١٥ ولا تقولوا لما تصف ألسنتكم
الكذب هذا حلال وهذا حرام لتفتروا على الله
الكذب إن الذين يفترون على الله الكذب لا يفلحون
١١٦ متاع قليل ولهم عذاب أليم ١١٧ وعلى الذين
هادوا حرمنا ما قصصنا عليك من قبل وما
ظلمناهم ولكن كانوا أنفسهم يظلمون ١١٨

on the day when every soul 16:111
will plead for itself; when every soul will be requited for its deeds. They shall not be wronged.

God has made an example of a city[1] which was once safe and peaceful. Its provisions came to it abundantly from every quarter: but it denied God's favours. Therefore God afflicted it with famine and fear as punishment for what they did.

An apostle of their own did come to them, but they denied him; therefore the scourge smote them in their wrongdoing.

Eat of the good and lawful 16:114
things which God bestowed on you, and give thanks for God's bounty if it is Him that you worship.

He has forbidden you carrion, blood, and the flesh of swine; also any flesh consecrated other than in the name of God. But whoever is driven by necessity, intending neither to sin nor to transgress, will find that God is forgiving and compassionate.

You shall not say, when your tongues utter falsehood: 'This is lawful, and that is forbidden,' in order to invent a falsehood about God. Those who invent falsehoods about God shall never succeed. Brief is their enjoyment, and woeful punishment awaits them.

To those who follow the Jewish Faith We have pronounced unlawful what 16:118
We recounted to you before. We never wronged them, but they wronged themselves.

1. Mecca.

16:119 To THOSE who commit
evil through ignorance, and
then repent and mend their
ways, your Lord is forgiving
and compassionate.
Abraham was a paragon of
piety, an upright man obedient
to God: he was no idolater.
He rendered thanks for His
bounty, so that He chose him
and guided him to a straight
path. We bestowed on him a
blessing in this world, and in
the world to come he will
assuredly dwell among the
righteous.
And now We have revealed
to you Our will: that you shall
follow the faith of saintly
Abraham, who was no idolater.
16:124 The Sabbath was ordained
only for those who differed
about it. On the Day of Res-
urrection your Lord will judge their differences.
Call people to the path of your Lord with wisdom and kindly exhortation.
Reason with them in a manner most courteous. Your Lord best knows those
who stray from His path, and He best knows the rightly guided.
If you punish, let your punishment be commensurate with the wrong that
has been done you. But it shall be best for you to endure with patience.
Be patient, then: none but God will grant you patience. Do not grieve for
16:128 them, nor distress yourself at their intrigues. God is with those who fear
Him and do good works.

ثم إن ربك للذين عملوا السوء بجهالة ثم تابوا من
بعد ذلك وأصلحوا إن ربك من بعدها لغفور رحيم ١١٩
إن إبراهيم كان أمة قانتا لله حنيفا ولم يك من المشركين
١٢٠ شاكرا لأنعمه اجتباه وهداه إلى صراط مستقيم
١٢١ وآتيناه في الدنيا حسنة وإنه في الآخرة لمن
الصالحين ١٢٢ ثم أوحينا إليك أن اتبع ملة إبراهيم
حنيفا وما كان من المشركين ١٢٣ إنما جعل السبت على
الذين اختلفوا فيه وإن ربك ليحكم بينهم يوم
القيامة فيما كانوا فيه يختلفون ١٢٤ ادع إلى
سبيل ربك بالحكمة والموعظة الحسنة وجادلهم
بالتي هي أحسن إن ربك هو أعلم بمن ضل عن سبيله
وهو أعلم بالمهتدين ١٢٥ وإن عاقبتم فعاقبوا بمثل ما
عوقبتم به ولئن صبرتم لهو خير للصابرين ١٢٦ واصبر وما
صبرك إلا بالله ولا تحزن عليهم ولا تك في ضيق مما يمكرون
١٢٧ إن الله مع الذين اتقوا والذين هم محسنون ١٢٨

سورة الاسرى مكية وهى مائة واحدى عشرة آية

بسم الله الرحمن الرحيم
سبحان الذى اسرى بعبده ليلا من المسجد الحرام الى المسجد
الاقصا الذى باركنا حوله لنريه من اياتنا انه هو السميع
البصير (١) واتينا موسى الكتاب وجعلناه هدى لبنى اسرائيل
الا تتخذوا من دونى وكيلا (٢) ذرية من حملنا مع
نوح انه كان عبدا شكورا (٣) وقضينا الى بنى اسرائيل
فى الكتاب لتفسدن فى الارض مرتين ولتعلن علوا كبيرا (٤)
فاذا جاء وعد اوليهما بعثنا عليكم عبادا لنا اولى بأس شديد
فجاسوا خلال الديار وكان وعدا مفعولا (٥) ثم رددنا لكم
الكرة عليهم وامددناكم باموال وبنين وجعلناكم اكثر
نفيرا (٦) ان احسنتم احسنتم لانفسكم وان اساتم فلها
فاذا جاء وعد الاخرة ليسوءوا وجوهكم وليدخلوا المسجد
كما دخلوه اول مرة وليتبروا ما علوا تتبيرا (٧)

THE NIGHT JOURNEY

In the Name of God,
the Merciful, the Compassionate

GLORY BE to Him who made 17:1
His servant go by night from
the Sacred Temple[1] to the
farther Temple[2] whose sur-
roundings We have blessed,
that We might show him some
of Our signs. He it is who
hears all and observes all.
We gave Moses the Book
and made it a guide for the
Israelites: 'You shall take no
guardian other than Myself.
You are the descendants of
those We carried in the ark
with Noah: he was a truly
thankful servant.'
In the Book We decreed to the Israelites: 'Twice shall you do evil in the 17:4
land; and you shall commit great transgressions.'
And when the prophecy of the first came to be fulfilled, We sent against
you servants of Ours, a formidable army[3] which ravaged your land and
carried out the punishment that had been promised.
Then We once again granted you victory over them and multiplied your
riches and your descendants, so that once again you grew and multiplied. 'If 17:7
you do good, it shall be to your advantage; and if you do evil, you shall sin
against your own souls.'
And when the prophecy of the second came to be fulfilled, We sent
another[4] to afflict you and to enter the Temple as the former entered it at
first, utterly destroying all that they laid their hands on.

1. Of Mecca.
2. Of Jerusalem (and thence to the Throne of God, accompanied by the Angel Gabriel). Some Muslim commentators give a literal interpretation to this passage, others regard it as a vision.
3. The Assyrians.
4. The Romans.

17:8 'YOUR LORD may yet be merciful to you. If you come back, We shall again come back. We have made Hell a prison-house for the unbelievers.'

Surely this Koran gives guidance to that which is most upright. It promises the faithful who do good works a rich recompense; and for those who deny the life to come We have prepared a woeful scourge. Yet man prays for evil as fervently as he prays for good. Truly, man is ever impatient.

We made the night and the day twin marvels. We enshrouded the marvel of the night with darkness and made the marvel of the day to see with, that you might seek the bounty of your Lord and learn to count the seasons and the years.[1] We have made all things manifestly plain to you.

17:13 And the fate of each man We have bound about his neck. On the Day of Resurrection We shall confront him with a Book he shall find wide open: 'Read your Book: enough for you this day that your own soul should call you to account.'

He that seeks guidance shall have guidance for the good of his own soul, and he that errs shall err at his peril. No burdened soul shall bear another's burden. Nor do We punish until We have sent forth an emissary.

When We resolve to raze a city, We first give warning to its prodigals. If they persist in sin therein, judgement is passed, and We destroy it utterly.

17:17 How many generations have We cut down since Noah's time! Suffice it that your Lord is well aware of His servants' sins and observes them all.

عسى ربكم أن يرحمكم وإن عدتم عدنا وجعلنا جهنم للكافرين
حصيرا ﴿٨﴾ إن هذا القرآن يهدي للتي هي أقوم ويبشر المؤمنين
الذين يعملون الصالحات أن لهم أجرا كبيرا ﴿٩﴾ وأن الذين لا يؤمنون
بالآخرة أعتدنا لهم عذابا أليما ﴿١٠﴾ ويدع الإنسان بالشر دعاءه
بالخير وكان الإنسان عجولا ﴿١١﴾ وجعلنا الليل والنهار آيتين
فمحونا آية الليل وجعلنا آية النهار مبصرة لتبتغوا فضلا
من ربكم ولتعلموا عدد السنين والحساب وكل شيء فصلناه
تفصيلا ﴿١٢﴾ وكل إنسان ألزمناه طائره في عنقه ونخرج له
يوم القيامة كتابا يلقاه منشورا ﴿١٣﴾ اقرأ كتابك كفى
بنفسك اليوم عليك حسيبا ﴿١٤﴾ من اهتدى فإنما يهتدي
لنفسه ومن ضل فإنما يضل عليها ولا تزر وازرة وزر
أخرى وما كنا معذبين حتى نبعث رسولا ﴿١٥﴾ وإذا أردنا
أن نهلك قرية أمرنا مترفيها ففسقوا فيها فحق عليها القول
فدمرناها تدميرا ﴿١٦﴾ وكم أهلكنا من القرون من
بعد نوح وكفى بربك بذنوب عباده خبيرا بصيرا ﴿١٧﴾

1. Literally, and learn the number of the years and how to count.

من كان يريد العاجلة عجلنا له فيها ما نشاء لمن نريد ثم
جعلنا له جهنم يصلاها مذموما مدحورا ١٨ ومن أراد
الآخرة وسعى لها سعيها وهو مؤمن فأولئك كان سعيهم
مشكورا ١٩ كلا نمد هؤلاء وهؤلاء من عطاء ربك
وما كان عطاء ربك محظورا ٢٠ انظر كيف فضلنا بعضهم
على بعض وللآخرة أكبر درجات وأكبر تفضيلا ٢١
لا تجعل مع الله إلها آخر فتقعد مذموما مخذولا
٢٢ وقضى ربك ألا تعبدوا إلا إياه وبالوالدين إحسانا
إما يبلغن عندك الكبر أحدهما أو كلاهما فلا تقل لهما أف
ولا تنهرهما وقل لهما قولا كريما ٢٣ واخفض لهما جناح الذل
من الرحمة وقل رب ارحمهما كما ربياني صغيرا ٢٤ ربكم
أعلم بما في نفوسكم إن تكونوا صالحين فإنه كان
للأوابين غفورا ٢٥ وآت ذا القربى حقه والمسكين
وابن السبيل ولا تبذر تبذيرا ٢٦ إن المبذرين كانوا
إخوان الشياطين وكان الشيطان لربه كفورا ٢٧

WHOEVER DESIRES this 17:18
fleeting life We shall quickly
grant him therein whatever We
will and for whomever We
please. But then We have prepared Hell for him, wherein he
shall burn despised and rejected.

As for him that desires the
life to come and strives for it
as he ought to, being a true
believer, his endeavours shall
be richly recompensed.

On all – on these and
those – We bestow the bounty
of your Lord: none shall be
denied the bounty of your
Lord.

Behold how We have exalted
some above others. Yet the life
to come has higher ranks of
honour and is more exalted.

Set up no other deity besides 17:22
God, lest you incur disgrace
and ruin: your Lord has decreed that you shall worship none but Him. And
that you shall show kindness to your parents: if either or both of them attain
old age in your dwelling, show them no sign of impatience, nor rebuke them;
but speak to them kind words. Treat them with humility and tenderness, and
say: 'Lord, be merciful to them, even as they nursed me when I was an infant.'

Your Lord best knows what is in your hearts, and knows if you are virtuous. He will surely forgive those that turn to Him in penitence.

Give to the near of kin their due, and also to the destitute and to the traveller in need. Do not squander your substance wastefully, for the wasteful are 17:27
Satan's brothers, and Satan is ever ungrateful to his Lord.

17:28 AND IF, while hopefully seeking from your Lord some bounty, you lack the means to assist them, then speak to them kindly.

Be neither miserly nor prodigal, for then you should either earn reproach or be reduced to penury.

Your Lord gives abundantly to whom He will, and sparingly likewise. He knows and observes His servants.

You shall not kill your children for fear of poverty.[1] We will provide for them and for you. To kill them is a grievous sin.

You shall not commit adultery, for it is lewd and the way to evil.

You shall not kill any man God has forbidden you to kill, except for a just cause. If a man is slain unjustly, his heir shall be entitled to satisfaction. But let him not carry his vengeance to excess, for his victim is sure to be assisted and avenged.

17:34 And do not approach the property of orphans except with the best of motives, until they reach maturity. Keep your promises; you are accountable for all that you promise.

And give full measure, when you measure, and weigh with even scales; that is better and fairer in the end.

Do not follow what you know not. Man's eyes, ears, and heart – each of his senses shall be closely questioned.

And do not walk proudly on the earth. You cannot split the earth, nor can you rival the mountains in stature.

17:38 Evil is all this in the sight of your Lord, and odious.

وَإِمَّا تُعْرِضَنَّ عَنْهُمُ ابْتِغَاءَ رَحْمَةٍ مِنْ رَبِّكَ تَرْجُوهَا فَقُلْ لَهُمْ
قَوْلًا مَيْسُورًا ﴿٢٨﴾ وَلَا تَجْعَلْ يَدَكَ مَغْلُولَةً إِلَىٰ عُنُقِكَ وَلَا تَبْسُطْهَا
كُلَّ الْبَسْطِ فَتَقْعُدَ مَلُومًا مَحْسُورًا ﴿٢٩﴾ إِنَّ رَبَّكَ يَبْسُطُ الرِّزْقَ لِمَنْ
يَشَاءُ وَيَقْدِرُ إِنَّهُ كَانَ بِعِبَادِهِ خَبِيرًا بَصِيرًا ﴿٣٠﴾ وَلَا تَقْتُلُوا
أَوْلَادَكُمْ خَشْيَةَ إِمْلَاقٍ نَحْنُ نَرْزُقُهُمْ وَإِيَّاكُمْ إِنَّ قَتْلَهُمْ
كَانَ خِطْئًا كَبِيرًا ﴿٣١﴾ وَلَا تَقْرَبُوا الزِّنَىٰ إِنَّهُ كَانَ فَاحِشَةً وَسَاءَ
سَبِيلًا ﴿٣٢﴾ وَلَا تَقْتُلُوا النَّفْسَ الَّتِي حَرَّمَ اللَّهُ إِلَّا بِالْحَقِّ وَمَنْ
قُتِلَ مَظْلُومًا فَقَدْ جَعَلْنَا لِوَلِيِّهِ سُلْطَانًا فَلَا يُسْرِفْ فِي الْقَتْلِ
إِنَّهُ كَانَ مَنْصُورًا ﴿٣٣﴾ وَلَا تَقْرَبُوا مَالَ الْيَتِيمِ إِلَّا بِالَّتِي هِيَ أَحْسَنُ
حَتَّىٰ يَبْلُغَ أَشُدَّهُ وَأَوْفُوا بِالْعَهْدِ إِنَّ الْعَهْدَ كَانَ مَسْئُولًا ﴿٣٤﴾
وَأَوْفُوا الْكَيْلَ إِذَا كِلْتُمْ وَزِنُوا بِالْقِسْطَاسِ الْمُسْتَقِيمِ ذَٰلِكَ
خَيْرٌ وَأَحْسَنُ تَأْوِيلًا ﴿٣٥﴾ وَلَا تَقْفُ مَا لَيْسَ لَكَ بِهِ عِلْمٌ إِنَّ السَّمْعَ
وَالْبَصَرَ وَالْفُؤَادَ كُلُّ أُولَٰئِكَ كَانَ عَنْهُ مَسْئُولًا ﴿٣٦﴾ وَلَا تَمْشِ
فِي الْأَرْضِ مَرَحًا إِنَّكَ لَنْ تَخْرِقَ الْأَرْضَ وَلَنْ تَبْلُغَ الْجِبَالَ طُولًا ﴿٣٧﴾
كُلُّ ذَٰلِكَ كَانَ سَيِّئُهُ عِنْدَ رَبِّكَ مَكْرُوهًا ﴿٣٨﴾

1. An allusion to the pre-Islamic custom of burying alive unwanted newborn girls.

ذلك مما أوحى إليك ربك من الحكمة ولا تجعل مع الله
إلها آخر فتلقى في جهنم ملوما مدحورا ۝ أفأصفاكم ربكم
بالبنين واتخذ من الملائكة إناثا إنكم لتقولون قولا عظيما
۝ ولقد صرفنا في هذا القرآن ليذكروا وما يزيدهم إلا
نفورا ۝ قل لو كان معه آلهة كما يقولون إذا لابتغوا إلى ذي
العرش سبيلا ۝ سبحانه وتعالى عما يقولون علوا كبيرا ۝ تسبح
له السماوات السبع والأرض ومن فيهن وإن من شيء إلا يسبح بحمده
ولكن لا تفقهون تسبيحهم إنه كان حليما غفورا ۝ وإذا قرأت القرآن
جعلنا بينك وبين الذين لا يؤمنون بالآخرة حجابا مستورا ۝
وجعلنا على قلوبهم أكنة أن يفقهوه وفي آذانهم
وقرا وإذا ذكرت ربك في القرآن وحده ولوا على أدبارهم
نفورا ۝ نحن أعلم بما يستمعون به إذ يستمعون إليك وإذ هم
نجوى إذ يقول الظالمون إن تتبعون إلا رجلا مسحورا ۝ انظر
كيف ضربوا لك الأمثال فضلوا فلا يستطيعون سبيلا ۝ وقالوا
أإذا كنا عظاما ورفاتا أإنا لمبعوثون خلقا جديدا ۝

THESE ARE but some of 17:39
the wise precepts your Lord
has inspired you[1] with. Serve
no other deity besides God,
lest you should be cast into
Hell, condemned and rejected.

What! Has your Lord
favoured *you*[2] with sons and
Himself adopted females from
among the angels? A mon-
strous blasphemy is that which
you utter.

We have expounded Our
revelations in this Koran so
that they may remember. Yet it
has only added to their aversion. Say: 'If, as they claim,
there were other gods besides
God, they would surely seek to
dethrone Him.'

Glory be to Him! Exalted
be He, high above their
falsehoods!

The seven heavens, the earth, and all who dwell in them give glory to Him. 17:44
All creatures celebrate His praises. Yet you cannot understand their praises.
Benevolent is He and forgiving.

And when you recite the Koran, We place between you and those who
deny the life to come a hidden screen. We have cast veils over their hearts lest
they understand it, and made them hard of hearing. When you make mention
of your Lord, alone, in the Koran they turn their backs with much aversion.

We well know what they wish to hear in it when they listen to you, and
what they say when they converse in private; when the wrongdoers declare:
'The man you follow is surely bewitched.'

Behold what epithets they bestow upon you. They have surely gone astray
and cannot find the right path.

And they say: 'What! When we are turned to bones and dust, shall we be 17:49
restored in a new creation?'

1. Muḥammad. 2. The unbelievers.

17:50 SAY: 'WHETHER you turn to stone or iron, or any other substance you may think unlikely to be given life.'

They will say: 'Who will restore us?'

Say: 'He that created you at first.'

They will shake their heads at you and say: 'When will this be?'

Say: 'It may well be near at hand. On that day He will summon you all, and you shall answer Him with praises. You shall think that you have lingered but a little while.'

And tell My servants to be courteous in their speech. Satan would sow discord among them; Satan is surely a veritable enemy of man.

17:54 Your Lord knows you best. He will show you mercy if He will, and punish you if He pleases.

We have not sent you to be their guardian. Your Lord is best aware of all who dwell in the heavens and the earth.

We have exalted some prophets above others. To David We gave Psalms.

Say: 'Pray if you will to those whom you deify besides Him.[1] They cannot relieve your distress, nor can they change it.'

Those to whom they pray, themselves seek to approach their Lord, vying with each other to be near Him. They crave His mercy and fear His punishment; for your Lord's punishment is to be feared indeed.

17:58 There is no city but We shall obliterate it before the Day of Resurrection, or grievously punish it: that is decreed in the Eternal Book.

قل كونوا حجارة او حديدا ۝ او خلقا مما يكبر في صدوركم
فسيقولون من يعيدنا قل الذي فطركم اول مرة فسينغضون
اليك رؤسهم ويقولون متى هو قل عسى ان يكون قريبا
۝ يوم يدعوكم فتستجيبون بحمده وتظنون ان لبثتم
الا قليلا ۝ وقل لعبادي يقولوا التي هي احسن ان
الشيطان ينزغ بينهم ان الشيطان كان للانسان عدوا
مبينا ۝ ربكم اعلم بكم ان يشا يرحمكم او ان يشا يعذبكم
وما ارسلناك عليهم وكيلا ۝ وربك اعلم بمن في السموات
والارض ولقد فضلنا بعض النبيين على بعض وآتينا داود
زبورا ۝ قل ادعوا الذين زعمتم من دونه فلا يملكون
كشف الضر عنكم ولا تحويلا ۝ اولئك الذين يدعون
يبتغون الى ربهم الوسيلة ايهم اقرب ويرجون رحمته
ويخافون عذابه ان عذاب ربك كان محذورا ۝
وان من قرية الا نحن مهلكوها قبل يوم القيمة او معذبوها
عذابا شديدا كان ذلك في الكتاب مسطورا ۝

1. The allusion is to worship of saints.

وما منعنا أن نرسل بالآيات إلا أن كذب بها الأولون
وآتينا ثمود الناقة مبصرة فظلموا بها وما نرسل بالآيات
إلا تخويفا ٥٩ وإذ قلنا لك إن ربك أحاط بالناس
وما جعلنا الرؤيا التي أريناك إلا فتنة للناس
والشجرة الملعونة في القرآن ونخوفهم فما يزيدهم إلا
طغيانا كبيرا ٦٠ وإذ قلنا للملائكة اسجدوا لآدم
فسجدوا إلا إبليس قال أأسجد لمن خلقت طينا ٦١ قال
أرأيتك هذا الذي كرمت علي لئن أخرتن إلى يوم
القيامة لأحتنكن ذريته إلا قليلا ٦٢ قال اذهب فمن
تبعك منهم فإن جهنم جزاؤكم جزاء موفورا ٦٣ واستفزز
من استطعت منهم بصوتك وأجلب عليهم بخيلك
ورجلك وشاركهم في الأموال والأولاد وعدهم وما
يعدهم الشيطان إلا غرورا ٦٤ إن عبادي ليس لك عليهم
سلطان وكفى بربك وكيلا ٦٥ ربكم الذي يزجي لكم
الفلك في البحر لتبتغوا من فضله إنه كان بكم رحيما ٦٦

AND NOTHING hinders Us 17:59
from sending signs except that
the ancients disbelieved them.
To Thamūd We gave the she-
camel as a visible sign, yet they
laid violent hands on her. We
give signs only by way of
warning.

We have told you that your
Lord encompasses mankind.
We have made the vision
which We showed you, as well
as the tree[1] cursed in the
Koran, but a test for people's
faith. We seek to put fear in
their hearts, but this only
makes their wickedness all the
more outrageous.

And when We said to the
angels: 'Prostrate yourselves
before Adam,' they all prostrated themselves, except
Satan, who said: 'Shall I bow
to him whom You have made of clay?' And he said: 'Do You see this being 17:62
whom You have exalted above me? If You give me respite till the Day of
Resurrection, I will exterminate all but a few of his descendants.'

'Go!' said He. 'Hell is your reward, and the reward of those that follow
you. An ample recompense it shall be. Rouse with your voice whomever you
are able. Muster against them your battalions of horse and foot. Be their
partner in riches and in offspring. Promise them what you will. (Satan promises them only to deceive them.) But over My true servants you shall have no
authority. Sufficient is your Lord as a guardian.'

It is your Lord who drives for you the ships across the ocean, that you may 17:66
seek His bounty. Surely He is ever compassionate towards you.

1. The Zaqqūm tree.

17:67 AND WHEN at sea a misfortune befalls you, all but
Him of those to whom you
pray forsake you; yet when
He brings you safe to dry land
you turn your backs: truly,
man is ever thankless.

Are you confident He will not cause the earth to cave in beneath you, or let loose a deadly sandstorm upon you? Then you shall find none to protect you.

Or are you confident that when again He lets you put to sea He will not blast you with a violent tempest and drown you for being thankless? Then you shall find none to prosecute your case against Us.

17:70 We have bestowed bounties on Adam's descendants
and carried them by land and
sea. We have provided them with wholesome things and exalted them above
a great many of Our creatures.

The day will surely come when We shall summon each community with its leader. Those who are given their books in their right hands will read their recorded doings, and shall not in the least be wronged. And those who have been blind in this life shall be blind in the life to come and more misguided.

They sought to entice you from Our revelations – they nearly did – hoping
that you might invent another in Our name, and thus they would adopt you
as an intimate friend. Indeed, had We not strengthened your faith, you might
17:75 have made some compromise with them and We would thus have made you
taste a double punishment in this life and a double punishment after death.
Then you should have found none to help you against Us.

وإذا مسكم الضر في البحر ضل من تدعون إلا إياه فلما
نجاكم إلى البر أعرضتم وكان الإنسان كفورا ٦٧
أفأمنتم أن يخسف بكم جانب البر أو يرسل عليكم حاصبا
ثم لا تجدوا لكم وكيلا ٦٨ أم أمنتم أن يعيدكم فيه تارة
أخرى فيرسل عليكم قاصفا من الريح فيغرقكم بما كفرتم
ثم لا تجدوا لكم علينا به تبيعا ٦٩ ولقد كرمنا بني آدم
وحملناهم في البر والبحر ورزقناهم من الطيبات
وفضلناهم على كثير ممن خلقنا تفضيلا ٧٠ يوم ندعوا
كل أناس بإمامهم فمن أوتي كتابه بيمينه فأولئك
يقرؤن كتابهم ولا يظلمون فتيلا ٧١ ومن كان في
هذه أعمى فهو في الآخرة أعمى وأضل سبيلا ٧٢ وإن كادوا
ليفتنونك عن الذي أوحينا إليك لتفتري علينا غيره
وإذا لاتخذوك خليلا ٧٣ ولولا أن ثبتناك لقد كدت
تركن إليهم شيئا قليلا ٧٤ إذا لأذقناك ضعف الحيوة
وضعف الممات ثم لا تجد لك علينا نصيرا ٧٥

وان كادوا ليستفزونك من الارض ليخرجوك منها واذا
لا يلبثون خلافك الا قليلا ﴿٧٦﴾ سنة من قد ارسلنا قبلك
من رسلنا ولا تجد لسنتنا تحويلا ﴿٧٧﴾ اقم الصلوة لدلوك
الشمس الى غسق اليل وقران الفجر ان قران الفجر كان
مشهودا ﴿٧٨﴾ ومن اليل فتهجد به نافلة لك عسى ان يبعثك ربك
مقاما محمودا ﴿٧٩﴾ وقل رب ادخلني مدخل صدق واخرجني
مخرج صدق واجعل لي من لدنك سلطانا نصيرا ﴿٨٠﴾
وقل جاء الحق وزهق الباطل ان الباطل كان
زهوقا ﴿٨١﴾ وننزل من القران ما هو شفاء ورحمة للمؤمنين
ولا يزيد الظالمين الا خسارا ﴿٨٢﴾ واذا انعمنا على الانسان
اعرض ونا بجانبه واذا مسه الشر كان يؤسا ﴿٨٣﴾ قل
كل يعمل على شاكلته فربكم اعلم بمن هو اهدى سبيلا
﴿٨٤﴾ ويسـٔلونك عن الروح قل الروح من امر ربي
وما اوتيتم من العلم الا قليلا ﴿٨٥﴾ ولئن شئنا لنذهبن
بالذي اوحينا اليك ثم لا تجد لك به علينا وكيلا ﴿٨٦﴾

AND THEY sought to pro- 17:76
voke you – they nearly did – and
thus drive you out of the land:
and they then would have
scarcely survived your departure.
Such was Our way with the
apostles We sent before you.
And you shall find no change
in Our accustomed way.
Perform the prayer at sunset, at nightfall, and at the
dawn recital; the dawn recital
has its witnesses; during the
night as well: an additional
duty, for the fulfilment of
which your Lord may exalt you
to a praiseworthy station.
Say: 'Lord, grant me a
goodly entrance and a goodly
exit, and sustain me with Your
own power.'
And say: 'Truth has come 17:81
and Falsehood has been routed.
Falsehood was bound to be routed.'
That which We reveal in the Koran is a balm and a blessing to true believers, although it only adds to the wrongdoers' prospects of perdition.
When We bestow bounties on man, he turns his back and holds aloof; and
when evil befalls him, he grows despondent.
Say: 'Each man behaves after his own fashion. But your Lord best knows
who is more rightly guided.'
And they put questions to you about the Spirit. Say: 'The Spirit is at my
Lord's command. Little indeed is the knowledge vouchsafed to you.'
If We pleased, We could take away that which We have revealed to you: 17:86
then you should find none to plead with Us on your behalf

17:87 except through a favour from
your Lord. His goodness to
you has been great indeed.
Say: 'If men and jinn combined to produce a book akin
to this Koran, they would
surely fail to produce its like,
though they helped one
another as best they could.'
We have set forth for people
in this Koran all manner of
arguments, yet most of them
17:90 persist in unbelief. They say:
'We will not believe in you
until you make a spring gush
from the earth before our very
eyes, or cause rivers to gush in
a grove of palms and vines;
until you cause the sky to fall
upon us in fragments, as you
have claimed you would, or
bring down God and the
angels in our midst; until you
have for yourself a house of gold, or ascend to heaven: nor will we believe
in your ascent until you have sent down for us a book which we can read.'
Say: 'Glory be to my Lord! Am I not but an emissary, made of flesh and
blood?'
Nothing prevents people from having faith when guidance comes to them
but the excuse: 'Can it be that God has sent a human as an emissary?'
Say: 'Had the earth been safe enough for angels to walk on, We would
have sent down to them an angel from heaven as an emissary.'
17:96 Say: 'Sufficient is God as my witness, and your witness. He well knows and
closely observes His servants.'

إلا رحمة من ربك إن فضله كان عليك كبيرا ﴿٨٧﴾ قل لئن
اجتمعت الإنس والجن على أن يأتوا بمثل هذا القرآن لا يأتون
بمثله ولو كان بعضهم لبعض ظهيرا ﴿٨٨﴾ ولقد صرفنا
للناس في هذا القرآن من كل مثل فأبى أكثر الناس
إلا كفورا ﴿٨٩﴾ وقالوا لن نؤمن لك حتى تفجر لنا
من الأرض ينبوعا ﴿٩٠﴾ أو تكون لك جنة من نخيل
وعنب فتفجر الأنهار خلالها تفجيرا ﴿٩١﴾ أو تسقط
السماء كما زعمت علينا كسفا أو تأتي بالله والملائكة
قبيلا ﴿٩٢﴾ أو يكون لك بيت من زخرف أو ترقى في السماء ولن
نؤمن لرقيك حتى تنزل علينا كتابا نقرؤه
قل سبحان ربي هل كنت إلا بشرا رسولا ﴿٩٣﴾ وما منع الناس
أن يؤمنوا إذ جاءهم الهدى إلا أن قالوا أبعث الله بشرا
رسولا ﴿٩٤﴾ قل لو كان في الأرض ملائكة يمشون مطمئنين
لنزلنا عليهم من السماء ملكا رسولا ﴿٩٥﴾ قل كفى بالله شهيدا
بيني وبينكم إنه كان بعباده خبيرا بصيرا ﴿٩٦﴾

وَمَن يَهْدِ ٱللَّهُ فَهُوَ ٱلْمُهْتَدِ ۖ وَمَن يُضْلِلْ فَلَن تَجِدَ لَهُمْ
أَوْلِيَآءَ مِن دُونِهِۦ ۖ وَنَحْشُرُهُمْ يَوْمَ ٱلْقِيَٰمَةِ عَلَىٰ وُجُوهِهِمْ
عُمْيًا وَبُكْمًا وَصُمًّا ۖ مَّأْوَىٰهُمْ جَهَنَّمُ ۖ كُلَّمَا خَبَتْ زِدْنَٰهُمْ
سَعِيرًا ﴿٩٧﴾ ذَٰلِكَ جَزَآؤُهُم بِأَنَّهُمْ كَفَرُوا۟ بِـَٔايَٰتِنَا وَقَالُوٓا۟ أَءِذَا
كُنَّا عِظَٰمًا وَرُفَٰتًا أَءِنَّا لَمَبْعُوثُونَ خَلْقًا جَدِيدًا ﴿٩٨﴾ أَوَلَمْ
يَرَوْا۟ أَنَّ ٱللَّهَ ٱلَّذِى خَلَقَ ٱلسَّمَٰوَٰتِ وَٱلْأَرْضَ قَادِرٌ عَلَىٰٓ أَن يَخْلُقَ
مِثْلَهُمْ وَجَعَلَ لَهُمْ أَجَلًا لَّا رَيْبَ فِيهِ فَأَبَى ٱلظَّٰلِمُونَ إِلَّا كُفُورًا
﴿٩٩﴾ قُل لَّوْ أَنتُمْ تَمْلِكُونَ خَزَآئِنَ رَحْمَةِ رَبِّىٓ إِذًا لَّأَمْسَكْتُمْ
خَشْيَةَ ٱلْإِنفَاقِ ۚ وَكَانَ ٱلْإِنسَٰنُ قَتُورًا ﴿١٠٠﴾ وَلَقَدْ ءَاتَيْنَا
مُوسَىٰ تِسْعَ ءَايَٰتٍۭ بَيِّنَٰتٍ ۖ فَسْـَٔلْ بَنِىٓ إِسْرَٰٓءِيلَ إِذْ جَآءَهُمْ
فَقَالَ لَهُۥ فِرْعَوْنُ إِنِّى لَأَظُنُّكَ يَٰمُوسَىٰ مَسْحُورًا ﴿١٠١﴾ قَالَ
لَقَدْ عَلِمْتَ مَآ أَنزَلَ هَٰٓؤُلَآءِ إِلَّا رَبُّ ٱلسَّمَٰوَٰتِ وَٱلْأَرْضِ
بَصَآئِرَ وَإِنِّى لَأَظُنُّكَ يَٰفِرْعَوْنُ مَثْبُورًا ﴿١٠٢﴾ فَأَرَادَ أَن يَسْتَفِزَّهُم
مِّنَ ٱلْأَرْضِ فَأَغْرَقْنَٰهُ وَمَن مَّعَهُۥ جَمِيعًا ﴿١٠٣﴾ وَقُلْنَا مِنۢ بَعْدِهِۦ لِبَنِىٓ
إِسْرَٰٓءِيلَ ٱسْكُنُوا۟ ٱلْأَرْضَ فَإِذَا جَآءَ وَعْدُ ٱلْءَاخِرَةِ جِئْنَا بِكُمْ لَفِيفًا ﴿١٠٤﴾

THOSE WHOM God guides 17:97
are rightly guided; and those whom He confounds shall find no guardians besides Him. We shall herd them all on the Day of Resurrection, prostrate upon their faces, blind, dumb, and deaf. Hell shall be their refuge: whenever its flames die down We will rekindle them into a greater conflagration.

Thus shall they be rewarded: because they disbelieved Our revelations and said: 'When we are turned to bones and dust, shall we be restored in a new creation?'

Or do they not see that God, who has created the heavens and the earth, has power to create their like? Their term He preordained beyond all doubt. Yet the wrongdoers persist in unbelief.

Say: 'Had you possessed the treasures of my Lord's mercy, you would 17:100
have covetously hoarded them. How niggardly is man!'

And to Moses We gave nine conspicuous signs. Ask the Israelites how he first appeared among them.

Pharaoh said to him: 'Moses, I can see that you are bewitched.'

'You know full well,' he replied, 'that none but the Lord of the heavens and the earth has revealed these visible signs. Indeed, Pharaoh, I can see that you are doomed.'

He sought to scare them out of the land: but We drowned him, together
with those who were with him all. Then We said to the Israelites: 'Dwell in 17:104
the land. When the promise of the Hereafter comes to be fulfilled, We shall
herd you all together.'

17:105 WITH THE Truth We revealed
it, and with the Truth it has
come down. We have sent you
forth only to proclaim joyful
tidings and to give warning;
with a Koran that We divided
into sections, that you may
read it to the people with de-
liberation. We have imparted
it by gradual revelation.
17:107 Say: 'It is for you to believe
in it or to deny it. Those who
were endowed with know-
ledge before its revelation
prostrate themselves when it
is recited to them and say:
"Glorious is our Lord. Our
Lord's promise has surely been
fulfilled." They fall down upon
their faces, weeping; and as
they listen, their awe increases.'
Say: 'You may call on God
or you may call on the Merci-
ful: by whatever name you call on Him, His are the most gracious names.'
Pray neither with too loud a voice nor in silence, but, between these
17:111 extremes, seek a middle course. Say: 'Praise be to God who has never begotten a son; who has no partner in His Kingdom; who needs none to protect
Him from humiliation.' Proclaim His greatness.

وبالحق أنزلناه وبالحق نزل وما أرسلناك إلا مبشرا ونذيرا
١٠٥ وقرآنا فرقناه لتقرأه على الناس على مكث ونزلناه تنزيلا
١٠٦ قل آمنوا به أو لا تؤمنوا إن الذين أوتوا العلم من قبله إذا يتلى عليهم
يخرون للأذقان سجدا ١٠٧ ويقولون سبحان ربنا إن كان وعد
ربنا لمفعولا ١٠٨ ويخرون للأذقان يبكون ويزيدهم خشوعا ١٠٩ قل
ادعوا الله أو ادعوا الرحمن أيا ما تدعوا فله الأسماء الحسنى
ولا تجهر بصلاتك ولا تخافت بها وابتغ بين ذلك سبيلا ١١٠ وقل
الحمد لله الذي لم يتخذ ولدا ولم يكن له شريك في
الملك ولم يكن له ولي من الذل وكبره تكبيرا ١١١

سورة الكهف مكية ومائة وعشر آيات

بسم الله الرحمن الرحيم
الحمد لله الذي أنزل على عبده الكتاب ولم يجعل له عوجا ١ قيما لينذر
بأسا شديدا من لدنه ويبشر المؤمنين الذين يعملون الصالحات أن لهم أجرا
حسنا ٢ ماكثين فيه أبدا ٣ وينذر الذين قالوا اتخذ الله ولدا ٤

THE CAVE

In the Name of God, the Merciful, the Compassionate

18:1 PRAISE BE to God who has revealed the Book to His servant and made it
flawless, unswerving from the Truth, that he may give warning of a dire
scourge from Himself; proclaim to the faithful who do good works that a
18:4 rich and everlasting recompense awaits them; and admonish those who say
that God has begotten a son.[1]

1. The noun *walad* in Classical Arabic can mean son/sons/daughter/daughters or the collective 'offspring'.

مَا لَهُم بِهِ مِنْ عِلْمٍ وَلَا لِآبَائِهِمْ كَبُرَتْ كَلِمَةً تَخْرُجُ مِنْ
أَفْوَاهِهِمْ إِن يَقُولُونَ إِلَّا كَذِبًا (٥) فَلَعَلَّكَ بَاخِعٌ
نَفْسَكَ عَلَىٰ آثَارِهِمْ إِن لَّمْ يُؤْمِنُوا بِهَٰذَا الْحَدِيثِ أَسَفًا (٦)
إِنَّا جَعَلْنَا مَا عَلَى الْأَرْضِ زِينَةً لَّهَا لِنَبْلُوَهُمْ أَيُّهُمْ أَحْسَنُ عَمَلًا
(٧) وَإِنَّا لَجَاعِلُونَ مَا عَلَيْهَا صَعِيدًا جُرُزًا (٨) أَمْ حَسِبْتَ
أَنَّ أَصْحَابَ الْكَهْفِ وَالرَّقِيمِ كَانُوا مِنْ آيَاتِنَا عَجَبًا (٩) إِذْ
أَوَى الْفِتْيَةُ إِلَى الْكَهْفِ فَقَالُوا رَبَّنَا آتِنَا مِن لَّدُنكَ
رَحْمَةً وَهَيِّئْ لَنَا مِنْ أَمْرِنَا رَشَدًا (١٠) فَضَرَبْنَا عَلَىٰ آذَانِهِمْ
فِي الْكَهْفِ سِنِينَ عَدَدًا (١١) ثُمَّ بَعَثْنَاهُمْ لِنَعْلَمَ أَيُّ
الْحِزْبَيْنِ أَحْصَىٰ لِمَا لَبِثُوا أَمَدًا (١٢) نَّحْنُ نَقُصُّ عَلَيْكَ
نَبَأَهُم بِالْحَقِّ إِنَّهُمْ فِتْيَةٌ آمَنُوا بِرَبِّهِمْ وَزِدْنَاهُمْ هُدًى (١٣)
وَرَبَطْنَا عَلَىٰ قُلُوبِهِمْ إِذْ قَامُوا فَقَالُوا رَبُّنَا رَبُّ السَّمَاوَاتِ
وَالْأَرْضِ لَن نَّدْعُوَ مِن دُونِهِ إِلَٰهًا لَّقَدْ قُلْنَا إِذًا شَطَطًا
(١٤) هَٰؤُلَاءِ قَوْمُنَا اتَّخَذُوا مِن دُونِهِ آلِهَةً لَّوْلَا يَأْتُونَ عَلَيْهِم
بِسُلْطَانٍ بَيِّنٍ فَمَنْ أَظْلَمُ مِمَّنِ افْتَرَىٰ عَلَى اللَّهِ كَذِبًا (١٥)

SURELY OF this they could 18:5
have no knowledge, neither
they nor their forefathers: a
monstrous blasphemy is that
which their mouths utter; they
speak nothing but falsehood.

Yet, if they deny this revelation, you may destroy yourself
with grief, sorrowing over
them.

We have decked the earth
with all manner of ornaments
to test them as to who would
acquit himself best. But We
will surely reduce all that is on
it to barren dust.

Did you think the Sleepers
of the Cave[1] and Al-Raqīm[2] a
wonder among Our signs?

When the youths sought 18:10
refuge in the cave, they said:
'Lord, have mercy on us and
guide us through our ordeal.'

We made them sleep[3] in the cave for many years, and then awakened them
to find out who could best tell the length of their stay.

We recount to you their story in all truth. They were young men who had
faith in their Lord, and on whom We had lavished Our guidance. We put
courage in their hearts when they stood up and said: 'Our Lord is the Lord
of the heavens and the earth. We call on no other god besides Him: for if we
did we should be blaspheming. Our people serve other gods besides Him, 18:15
though they have no convincing proof of their divinity. Who is more wicked
than he who invents a falsehood against God?

1. The allusion is to the story of the Seven Sleepers. Cf. Gibbon's account in *Decline and Fall of the Roman Empire.*
2. This may be the name of their dog, the tablet on which their names were inscribed, or the mountain in which the cave was situated.
3. Literally, We sealed their ears.

18:16 'AND WHEN you forsake
them and those they worship
besides God, go to the cave
for shelter. Your Lord will
extend to you His mercy and
prepare for you a means of
safety.'
You might have seen the
rising sun decline to the right
of their cavern and, as it set,
go past them on the left, while
they stayed within. That was
one of God's signs. He whom
God guides is rightly guided;
but he whom He confounds
shall find no friend to guide
him.
18:18 And you might have
thought them awake, though
they were sleeping. We turned
them about to right and left,
while their dog lay at the
cave's entrance with legs out-
stretched. Had you looked upon them, you would have surely turned your
back and fled in terror.
Thus did We rouse them that they might question one another. One of
them asked: 'How long have you stayed here?' They said: 'We have stayed
one day, or part of a day.' They said: 'Your Lord knows best how long you
have stayed here. Let one of you go to the city with this silver coin and bring
you back whatever food he finds most wholesome there. Let him conduct
18:20 himself with caution and not disclose your whereabouts to anyone. For if
they find you out they will stone you to death, or force you back into their
faith; then will you surely never succeed, ever.'

وَإِذِ اعْتَزَلْتُمُوهُمْ وَمَا يَعْبُدُونَ إِلَّا اللَّهَ فَأْوُوا إِلَى الْكَهْفِ
يَنشُرْ لَكُمْ رَبُّكُم مِّن رَّحْمَتِهِ وَيُهَيِّئْ لَكُم مِّنْ أَمْرِكُم مِّرْفَقًا
١٦ وَتَرَى الشَّمْسَ إِذَا طَلَعَت تَّزَاوَرُ عَن كَهْفِهِمْ ذَاتَ الْيَمِينِ
وَإِذَا غَرَبَت تَّقْرِضُهُمْ ذَاتَ الشِّمَالِ وَهُمْ فِي فَجْوَةٍ مِّنْهُ
ذَٰلِكَ مِنْ آيَاتِ اللَّهِ مَن يَهْدِ اللَّهُ فَهُوَ الْمُهْتَدِ وَمَن يُضْلِلْ
فَلَن تَجِدَ لَهُ وَلِيًّا مُّرْشِدًا ١٧ وَتَحْسَبُهُمْ أَيْقَاظًا وَهُمْ
رُقُودٌ وَنُقَلِّبُهُمْ ذَاتَ الْيَمِينِ وَذَاتَ الشِّمَالِ وَكَلْبُهُم
بَاسِطٌ ذِرَاعَيْهِ بِالْوَصِيدِ لَوِ اطَّلَعْتَ عَلَيْهِمْ لَوَلَّيْتَ مِنْهُمْ
فِرَارًا وَلَمُلِئْتَ مِنْهُمْ رُعْبًا ١٨ وَكَذَٰلِكَ بَعَثْنَاهُمْ لِيَتَسَاءَلُوا
بَيْنَهُمْ قَالَ قَائِلٌ مِّنْهُمْ كَمْ لَبِثْتُمْ قَالُوا لَبِثْنَا يَوْمًا أَوْ بَعْضَ
يَوْمٍ قَالُوا رَبُّكُمْ أَعْلَمُ بِمَا لَبِثْتُمْ فَابْعَثُوا أَحَدَكُم
بِوَرِقِكُمْ هَٰذِهِ إِلَى الْمَدِينَةِ فَلْيَنظُرْ أَيُّهَا أَزْكَىٰ طَعَامًا
فَلْيَأْتِكُم بِرِزْقٍ مِّنْهُ وَلْيَتَلَطَّفْ وَلَا يُشْعِرَنَّ بِكُمْ
أَحَدًا ١٩ إِنَّهُمْ إِن يَظْهَرُوا عَلَيْكُمْ يَرْجُمُوكُمْ
أَوْ يُعِيدُوكُمْ فِي مِلَّتِهِمْ وَلَن تُفْلِحُوا إِذًا أَبَدًا ٢٠

وكذلك أعثرنا عليهم ليعلموا أن وعد الله حق وأن الساعة
لا ريب فيها إذ يتنازعون بينهم أمرهم فقالوا ابنوا
عليهم بنيانا ربهم أعلم بهم قال الذين غلبوا على أمرهم
لنتخذن عليهم مسجدا ﴿٢١﴾ سيقولون ثلاثة رابعهم
كلبهم ويقولون خمسة سادسهم كلبهم رجما بالغيب
ويقولون سبعة وثامنهم كلبهم قل ربي أعلم بعدتهم
ما يعلمهم إلا قليل فلا تمار فيهم إلا مراء ظاهرا ولا
تستفت فيهم منهم أحدا ﴿٢٢﴾ ولا تقولن لشاىء إني
فاعل ذلك غدا ﴿٢٣﴾ إلا أن يشاء الله واذكر ربك
إذا نسيت وقل عسى أن يهدين ربي لأقرب من هذا
رشدا ﴿٢٤﴾ ولبثوا في كهفهم ثلث مائة سنين وازدادوا
تسعا ﴿٢٥﴾ قل الله أعلم بما لبثوا له غيب السموات والأرض
أبصر به وأسمع ما لهم من دونه من ولي ولا يشرك في
حكمه أحدا ﴿٢٦﴾ واتل ما أوحي إليك من كتاب ربك
لا مبدل لكلماته ولن تجد من دونه ملتحدا ﴿٢٧﴾

THUS DID We reveal their 18:21
secret, so that they might know
that God's promise was true
and that the Hour was not to
be doubted.

People argued among themselves concerning them. Some said: 'Build a monument over their remains. Their Lord knows best who they were.' Those who were to win said: 'Let us build a place of worship over them.'

Some will say: 'They were three: their dog was the fourth.' Others, guessing at the unknown, will say: 'They were five: their dog was the sixth.' And yet others: 'Seven: their dog was the eighth.' Say: 'My Lord best knows their number. Only a few know them.'

Therefore, when you dispute about them, adhere only to that which is manifest and do not ask any of these concerning them.

Never say of anything: 'I will do this tomorrow,' without adding: 'If God 18:23
wills.' When you forget, remember your Lord and say: 'May God guide me
and bring me nearer to the Truth.'

Some say they stayed in their cave three hundred years and nine. Say: 'God knows best how long they stayed. His are the secrets of the heavens and the earth. Clear is His sight, and keen His hearing. They have no other guardian besides Him; He allows none to share His sovereignty.'

Proclaim what has been revealed to you from the Book of your Lord. 18:27
None can change His Words. And you shall find no refuge besides Him.

18:28 AND RESTRAIN yourself,
you and those who pray to
their Lord morning and evening, seeking His pleasure. Do
not turn your eyes away from
them in quest of the allure-
ments of this life, nor obey
him whose heart We have
made heedless of Our
remembrance; who follows
his appetite and gives a loose
rein to his desires.

Say: 'This is the Truth from
your Lord. Let him who will,
believe in it, and him who
will, deny it.'

For the wrongdoers We
have prepared a fire which
will encompass them like the
walls of a pavilion. When
they cry out for help they
shall be showered with water
as hot as molten brass, which
will scald their faces; evil the drink, and evil the resting-place.
18:30 As for those that believe and do good works, We shall not deny the recompense of those whose deeds were good. The Gardens of Eden shall be
theirs, wherein brooks will roll at their feet. Reclining there upon soft
couches, they shall be adorned with bracelets of gold, and arrayed in garments of fine green silk and rich brocade: blissful the reward, and happy the
resting-place!

Coin for them a parable: Two men, to one of whom We gave two vineyards set about with palm-trees and watered by a running brook, with a
cornfield lying in between. Each of the vineyards yielded an abundant crop,
18:34 and when their owner had gathered in the harvest, he said to his companion
while conversing with him: 'I am richer than you, and my clan is mightier
than yours.'

واصبر نفسك مع الذين يدعون ربهم بالغدوة والعشي
يريدون وجهه ولا تعد عيناك عنهم تريد زينة الحيوة
الدنيا ولا تطع من أغفلنا قلبه عن ذكرنا واتبع هويه
وكان أمره فرطا ﴿٢٨﴾ وقل الحق من ربكم فمن شاء فليؤمن
ومن شاء فليكفر إنا أعتدنا للظالمين نارا أحاط بهم سرادقها
وإن يستغيثوا يغاثوا بماء كالمهل يشوي الوجوه بئس الشراب
وساءت مرتفقا ۝ إن الذين آمنوا وعملوا الصالحات إنا لا نضيع
أجر من أحسن عملا ۝ أولئك لهم جنات عدن تجري من تحتهم
الأنهار يحلون فيها من أساور من ذهب ويلبسون ثيابا
خضرا من سندس وإستبرق متكئين فيها على
الأرائك نعم الثواب وحسنت مرتفقا ۝ واضرب لهم
مثلا رجلين جعلنا لأحدهما جنتين من أعناب وحففناهما
بنخل وجعلنا بينهما زرعا ۝ كلتا الجنتين آتت أكلها ولم
تظلم منه شيئا وفجرنا خلالهما نهرا ۝ وكان له ثمر فقال
لصاحبه وهو يحاوره أنا أكثر منك مالا وأعز نفرا ﴿٣٤﴾

ودخل جنته وهو ظالم لنفسه قال ما أظن أن تبيد هذه
أبدا ﴿٣٥﴾ وما أظن الساعة قائمة ولئن رددت إلى ربي لأجدن
خيرا منها منقلبا ﴿٣٦﴾ قال له صاحبه وهو يحاوره أكفرت
بالذي خلقك من تراب ثم من نطفة ثم سواك رجلا ﴿٣٧﴾
لكنا هو الله ربي ولا أشرك بربي أحدا ﴿٣٨﴾ ولولا إذ
دخلت جنتك قلت ما شاء الله لا قوة إلا بالله إن ترن
أنا أقل منك مالا وولدا ﴿٣٩﴾ فعسى ربي أن يؤتين خيرا من جنتك
ويرسل عليها حسبانا من السماء فتصبح صعيدا زلقا ﴿٤٠﴾ أو يصبح
ماؤها غورا فلن تستطيع له طلبا ﴿٤١﴾ وأحيط بثمره فأصبح
يقلب كفيه على ما أنفق فيها وهي خاوية على عروشها ويقول
يا ليتني لم أشرك بربي أحدا ﴿٤٢﴾ ولم تكن له فئة ينصرونه
من دون الله وما كان منتصرا ﴿٤٣﴾ هنالك الولاية لله الحق هو
خير ثوابا وخير عقبا ﴿٤٤﴾ واضرب لهم مثل الحياة الدنيا
كماء أنزلناه من السماء فاختلط به نبات الأرض فأصبح
هشيما تذروه الرياح وكان الله على كل شيء مقتدرا ﴿٤٥﴾

AND WHEN, having thus 18:35
wronged his soul, he entered
his vineyard, he said: 'I cannot
think this will ever perish! Nor
do I think the Hour will ever
come. Even if I returned to my
Lord, I should surely find a
better place than this to go
back to.'
His companion replied,
while still conversing with him:
'Have you no faith in Him who
created you from dust, then
from a little germ, and then
fashioned you into a man? As
for myself, God is my Lord,
and I will associate none with
my Lord. When you entered
your garden, why did you not
say: "What God has ordained
must surely come to pass: there
is no strength except in God"?
Though you see me poorer
than yourself and blessed with fewer children, yet my Lord may give me a 18:40
garden better than yours, and send down thunderbolts from heaven upon
your vineyard, turning it into a barren waste, or drain its water deep into the
earth so that you will find none of it.'
And his fruits were destroyed, and he wrung his hands with grief at all
that he had spent on the garden: for the vines had tumbled down upon their
trellises. 'Would that I had served no other gods besides my Lord!' he said.
He had none to help him besides God, nor was he able to defend himself.
In such ordeals protection comes only from God, the true God. His is the
best recompense and His the best requital.
And coin for them a simile about the life of this world. It is like the vege- 18:45
tation of the earth that thrives when watered by the rain We send down from
the sky, soon turning into stubble which the wind scatters abroad. God has
power over all things.

18:46 WEALTH AND children are
the ornament of this life. But
deeds of lasting merit are better rewarded by your Lord
and hold for you a greater
hope of salvation.

Tell of the day when We
shall blot out the mountains
and make the earth a barren
waste; when We shall herd
them all together, leaving not
a soul behind.

They shall be ranged before
your Lord: 'You have returned
to Us as We created you at
first. Yet you supposed We
had not set for you a predestined time.'

The Book will be laid
down, and you shall see the
sinners dismayed at the content. They will say: 'Woe
betide us! What can this Book
mean? It omits nothing small or great: all is noted down!' and they shall find
their deeds recorded there. Your Lord will wrong none.

18:50 And when We said to the angels: 'Prostrate yourselves before Adam,' all
prostrated themselves except Satan, who was a jinnee disobedient to his
Lord. Would you then serve him and his offspring as your masters rather
than Myself, despite their enmity towards you? A sad substitute the wrongdoers have chosen!

I did not call them to witness at the creation of the heavens and the earth,
nor at their own creation; nor was I to seek the aid of those who were to lead
mankind astray.

On that day He will say: 'Call on those you claimed to be My partners.'
They will invoke them, but they will make no answer; for We shall place a
18:53 deadly gulf between them. And when the sinners behold the Fire they will
realize that therein they shall be flung. Nor shall they ever escape from it.

اَلْمَالُ وَالْبَنُونَ زِينَةُ الْحَيٰوةِ الدُّنْيَا وَالْبَاقِيَاتُ الصَّالِحَاتُ خَيْرٌ عِنْدَ
رَبِّكَ ثَوَابًا وَخَيْرٌ اَمَلًا ﴿٤٦﴾ وَيَوْمَ نُسَيِّرُ الْجِبَالَ وَتَرَى الْاَرْضَ
بَارِزَةً وَحَشَرْنَاهُمْ فَلَمْ نُغَادِرْ مِنْهُمْ اَحَدًا ﴿٤٧﴾ وَعُرِضُوا عَلٰى
رَبِّكَ صَفًّا لَقَدْ جِئْتُمُونَا كَمَا خَلَقْنَاكُمْ اَوَّلَ مَرَّةٍ بَلْ زَعَمْتُمْ
اَلَّنْ نَجْعَلَ لَكُمْ مَوْعِدًا ﴿٤٨﴾ وَوُضِعَ الْكِتَابُ فَتَرَى الْمُجْرِمِينَ مُشْفِقِينَ
مِمَّا فِيهِ وَيَقُولُونَ يَا وَيْلَتَنَا مَالِ هٰذَا الْكِتَابِ لَا يُغَادِرُ صَغِيرَةً
وَلَا كَبِيرَةً اِلَّا اَحْصٰيهَا وَوَجَدُوا مَا عَمِلُوا حَاضِرًا وَلَا يَظْلِمُ
رَبُّكَ اَحَدًا ﴿٤٩﴾ وَاِذْ قُلْنَا لِلْمَلٰئِكَةِ اسْجُدُوا لِاٰدَمَ
فَسَجَدُوا اِلَّا اِبْلِيسَ كَانَ مِنَ الْجِنِّ فَفَسَقَ عَنْ اَمْرِ
رَبِّهِ اَفَتَتَّخِذُونَهُ وَذُرِّيَّتَهُ اَوْلِيَاءَ مِنْ دُونِي وَهُمْ لَكُمْ
عَدُوٌّ بِئْسَ لِلظَّالِمِينَ بَدَلًا ﴿٥٠﴾ مَا اَشْهَدْتُهُمْ خَلْقَ السَّمٰوَاتِ
وَالْاَرْضِ وَلَا خَلْقَ اَنْفُسِهِمْ وَمَا كُنْتُ مُتَّخِذَ الْمُضِلِّينَ عَضُدًا
﴿٥١﴾ وَيَوْمَ يَقُولُ نَادُوا شُرَكَائِيَ الَّذِينَ زَعَمْتُمْ فَدَعَوْهُمْ فَلَمْ
يَسْتَجِيبُوا لَهُمْ وَجَعَلْنَا بَيْنَهُمْ مَوْبِقًا ﴿٥٢﴾ وَرَاَ الْمُجْرِمُونَ النَّارَ
فَظَنُّوا اَنَّهُمْ مُوَاقِعُوهَا وَلَمْ يَجِدُوا عَنْهَا مَصْرِفًا ﴿٥٣﴾

وَلَقَدْ صَرَّفْنَا فِي هَٰذَا الْقُرْآنِ لِلنَّاسِ مِن كُلِّ مَثَلٍ وَكَانَ الْإِنسَانُ
أَكْثَرَ شَيْءٍ جَدَلًا ۝ وَمَا مَنَعَ النَّاسَ أَن يُؤْمِنُوا إِذْ جَاءَهُمُ
الْهُدَىٰ وَيَسْتَغْفِرُوا رَبَّهُمْ إِلَّا أَن تَأْتِيَهُمْ سُنَّةُ الْأَوَّلِينَ أَوْ
يَأْتِيَهُمُ الْعَذَابُ قُبُلًا ۝٥٥ وَمَا نُرْسِلُ الْمُرْسَلِينَ إِلَّا مُبَشِّرِينَ
وَمُنذِرِينَ وَيُجَادِلُ الَّذِينَ كَفَرُوا بِالْبَاطِلِ لِيُدْحِضُوا
بِهِ الْحَقَّ وَاتَّخَذُوا آيَاتِي وَمَا أُنذِرُوا هُزُوًا ۝٥٦ وَمَنْ أَظْلَمُ
مِمَّن ذُكِّرَ بِآيَاتِ رَبِّهِ فَأَعْرَضَ عَنْهَا وَنَسِيَ مَا قَدَّمَتْ يَدَاهُ
إِنَّا جَعَلْنَا عَلَىٰ قُلُوبِهِمْ أَكِنَّةً أَن يَفْقَهُوهُ وَفِي
آذَانِهِمْ وَقْرًا وَإِن تَدْعُهُمْ إِلَى الْهُدَىٰ فَلَن يَهْتَدُوا
إِذًا أَبَدًا ۝٥٧ وَرَبُّكَ الْغَفُورُ ذُو الرَّحْمَةِ لَوْ يُؤَاخِذُهُم
بِمَا كَسَبُوا لَعَجَّلَ لَهُمُ الْعَذَابَ بَل لَّهُم مَّوْعِدٌ لَّن يَجِدُوا مِن
دُونِهِ مَوْئِلًا ۝ وَتِلْكَ الْقُرَىٰ أَهْلَكْنَاهُمْ لَمَّا ظَلَمُوا وَجَعَلْنَا
لِمَهْلِكِهِم مَّوْعِدًا ۝ وَإِذْ قَالَ مُوسَىٰ لِفَتَاهُ لَا أَبْرَحُ حَتَّىٰ
أَبْلُغَ مَجْمَعَ الْبَحْرَيْنِ أَوْ أَمْضِيَ حُقُبًا ۝٦٠ فَلَمَّا بَلَغَا مَجْمَعَ
بَيْنِهِمَا نَسِيَا حُوتَهُمَا فَاتَّخَذَ سَبِيلَهُ فِي الْبَحْرِ سَرَبًا ۝٦١

IN THIS Koran We have 18:54
coined for mankind all manner
of parables. But man is exceedingly contentious.

Nothing prevents people from having faith when guidance has been revealed to them, and from seeking their Lord's forgiveness: unless they are waiting for the fate of the ancients to overtake them or to behold the scourge with their own eyes.

We send the apostles only to proclaim joyful tidings and to give warning. But with false arguments the unbelievers seek to confute the Truth, deriding My revelations and My warnings.

Who is more wicked than 18:57
he that, when reminded of his
Lord's revelations, turns away
from them and forgets what his own hands have done? We have cast veils
over their hearts so that they cannot understand it,[1] and made them hard of
hearing. Call them as you may to the right path, they shall never be guided.

And your Lord is the Forgiving One, the Merciful. Had it been His will to scourge them for what they did, He would have hurried on their punishment; but He has set for them a predestined time they cannot evade.

And all those cities! We destroyed them for the wrongs they did, and for their destruction We set a predestined time.

Moses said to his servant: 'I will journey on until I reach the land where the two seas meet, though I may march for ages.'

But when they came to the land where the two seas met, they forgot their 18:61
fish, which made its way into the water, swimming at will.

1. The Koran.

18:62 AND WHEN they had journeyed farther on, he said to his servant: 'Bring us some food; we are worn out with this travelling.'

'Know,' he replied, 'that I forgot the fish when we were resting on the rock. It was only Satan who made me forget to mention this. It made its way miraculously into the sea.'

'This is what we have been seeking,' he said. They went back the way they came, and found one of Our servants to whom We had vouchsafed Our mercy and whom We had endowed with knowledge of Our own. Moses said to him: 'May I follow you, so that you may guide me by that which you have been taught?'

فلما جاوزا قال لفتىه اتنا غداءنا لقد لقينا من سفرنا
هذا نصبا (٦٢) قال أرأيت إذ أوينا إلى الصخرة فإني نسيت
الحوت وما أنسانيه إلا الشيطان أن أذكره واتخذ سبيله
في البحر عجبا (٦٣) قال ذلك ما كنا نبغ فارتدا على آثارهما
قصصا (٦٤) فوجدا عبدا من عبادنا آتيناه رحمة من عندنا
وعلمناه من لدنا علما (٦٥) قال له موسى هل أتبعك على أن
تعلمن مما علمت رشدا (٦٦) قال إنك لن تستطيع معي صبرا
(٦٧) وكيف تصبر على ما لم تحط به خبرا (٦٨) قال ستجدني إن شاء
الله صابرا ولا أعصي لك أمرا (٦٩) قال فإن اتبعتني فلا
تسألني عن شيء حتى أحدث لك منه ذكرا (٧٠) فانطلقا
حتى إذا ركبا في السفينة خرقها قال أخرقتها لتغرق أهلها
لقد جئت شيئا إمرا (٧١) قال ألم أقل إنك لن تستطيع معي
صبرا (٧٢) قال لا تؤاخذني بما نسيت ولا ترهقني من أمري
عسرا (٧٣) فانطلقا حتى إذا لقيا غلاما فقتله قال أقتلت
نفسا زكية بغير نفس لقد جئت شيئا نكرا (٧٤)

'You will not bear with me,' said he. 'For how can you bear with that which is beyond your knowledge?'

Moses said: 'If God wills, you shall find me patient: I shall in no way cross you.'

18:70 He said: 'If you are bent on following me, you must not question me about anything until I mention it to you myself.'

The two set forth, but as soon as they embarked, he bored a hole in the bottom of the ship.

'Is it to drown her passengers that you have bored a hole in her?' he said. 'A strange thing you have done.'

'Did I not tell you,' he said, 'that you would not bear with me?'

'Pardon my forgetfulness,' said Moses. 'Do not be angry with me on account of this.'

18:74 They journeyed on until they fell in with a certain youth. He slew him, and Moses said: 'You have slain an innocent man who has slain no one. Surely you have done a heinous thing.'

قال ألم أقل لك إنك لن تستطيع معي صبرا ﴿٧٥﴾ قال إن سألتك
عن شيء بعدها فلا تصاحبني قد بلغت من لدني عذرا ﴿٧٦﴾ فانطلقا
حتى إذا أتيا أهل قرية استطعما أهلها فأبوا أن يضيفوهما
فوجدا فيها جدارا يريد أن ينقض فأقامه قال لو شئت
لتخذت عليه أجرا ﴿٧٧﴾ قال هذا فراق بيني وبينك سأنبئك
بتأويل ما لم تستطع عليه صبرا ﴿٧٨﴾ أما السفينة فكانت لمساكين
يعملون في البحر فأردت أن أعيبها وكان وراءهم ملك يأخذ
كل سفينة غصبا ﴿٧٩﴾ وأما الغلام فكان أبواه مؤمنين فخشينا
أن يرهقهما طغيانا وكفرا ﴿٨٠﴾ فأردنا أن يبدلهما ربهما
خيرا منه زكوة وأقرب رحما ﴿٨١﴾ وأما الجدار فكان
لغلامين يتيمين في المدينة وكان تحته كنز لهما
وكان أبوهما صالحا فأراد ربك أن يبلغا أشدهما
ويستخرجا كنزهما رحمة من ربك وما فعلته عن أمري
ذلك تأويل ما لم تسطع عليه صبرا ﴿٨٢﴾ ويسألونك
عن ذي القرنين قل سأتلوا عليكم منه ذكرا ﴿٨٣﴾

'DID I not tell you,' he said, 18:75
'that you would not bear with
me?'
He said: 'If ever I question
you again, abandon me; for
then I should deserve it.'
They travelled on until they
came to a city. They asked its
people for some food, but they
declined to receive them as
their guests. There they found
a wall on the point of falling
down. He re-erected it, and
Moses said: 'Had you wished,
you could have demanded
payment.'
'Now has the time arrived
when we must part,' he said.
'But first I will explain to you
those acts of mine which you
could not bear to watch with
patience.
'As for the ship, it belonged 18:79
to some poor fellows who had laboured at sea. I wanted to damage it because
at their rear there was a king who was taking every ship by force.
'As for the youth, his parents both were true believers, and we feared lest
he should plague them with wickedness and unbelief. It was our wish that
their Lord should grant them another in his place, a son more righteous and
more filial.
'As for the wall, it belonged to two orphan boys in the city; beneath it
a treasure of theirs was buried. Their father was an honest man. Your Lord
decreed, as a mercy from your Lord, that they should dig up their treasure
when they grew to manhood. What I did was not done by my will.
'That explains what you could not bear to watch with patience.'
They will ask you about Dhūl-Qarnayn.[1] Say: 'I will give you an account 18:83
of him.

1. Alexander the Great.

18:84 'WE MADE him mighty in the land and gave him means to achieve all things. He journeyed on a certain road until he reached the West and saw the sun setting in a pool of black mud. Hard by he found a certain people.

'"Dhūl-Qarnayn," We said, "you must either punish them or show them kindness."

'He replied: "The wicked we shall surely punish. Then shall they return to their Lord, who will torment them with grievous torment. As for those that have faith and do good works, we shall bestow on them a rich reward and deal indulgently with them."

18:89 'He then journeyed along another road until he reached the East and saw the sun rising upon a people whom We had exposed to its flaming rays.[1] So he did; and We had full knowledge of all the forces at his command.

'Then he journeyed along another road until he came between the Two Mountains and found a people who could barely understand a word. "Dhūl-Qarnayn," they said, "Gog and Magog are ravaging this land. Build a rampart between us, and we will pay you tribute."

'He replied: "The power my Lord has given me is better than any tribute. Lend me a force of men, and I will raise a rampart between you and them. Bring me blocks of iron."

'He dammed up the valley between the Two Mountains, and said: "Ply your bellows." And when the iron blocks were red with heat, he said: "Bring me molten brass to pour on them."

18:97 'Gog and Magog could not scale it, nor could they dig their way through it.

إنا مكنا له في الأرض وآتيناه من كل شيء سببا ﴿٨٤﴾ فأتبع سببا
﴿٨٥﴾ حتى إذا بلغ مغرب الشمس وجدها تغرب في عين حمئة
ووجد عندها قوما قلنا يا ذا القرنين إما أن تعذب وإما أن
تتخذ فيهم حسنا ﴿٨٦﴾ قال أما من ظلم فسوف نعذبه
ثم يرد إلى ربه فيعذبه عذابا نكرا ﴿٨٧﴾ وأما من آمن وعمل صالحا
فله جزاء الحسنى وسنقول له من أمرنا يسرا ﴿٨٨﴾ ثم أتبع سببا
﴿٨٩﴾ حتى إذا بلغ مطلع الشمس وجدها تطلع على قوم لم نجعل لهم من
دونها سترا ﴿٩٠﴾ كذلك وقد أحطنا بما لديه خبرا ﴿٩١﴾ ثم أتبع سببا
﴿٩٢﴾ حتى إذا بلغ بين السدين وجد من دونهما قوما لا يكادون
يفقهون قولا ﴿٩٣﴾ قالوا يا ذا القرنين إن يأجوج ومأجوج مفسدون
في الأرض فهل نجعل لك خرجا على أن تجعل بيننا وبينهم سدا ﴿٩٤﴾ قال
ما مكني فيه ربي خير فأعينوني بقوة أجعل بينكم وبينهم ردما
﴿٩٥﴾ آتوني زبر الحديد حتى إذا ساوى بين الصدفين قال
انفخوا حتى إذا جعله نارا قال آتوني أفرغ عليه قطرا ﴿٩٦﴾ فما
اسطاعوا أن يظهروه وما استطاعوا له نقبا ﴿٩٧﴾

1. Literally, for whom We did not provide a veil to shield them from it.

قال هذا رحمة من ربي فإذا جاء وعد ربي جعله دكاء وكان وعد
ربي حقا (٩٨) وتركنا بعضهم يومئذ يموج في بعض ونفخ في الصور
فجمعناهم جمعا (٩٩) وعرضنا جهنم يومئذ للكافرين عرضا (١٠٠) الذين
كانت أعينهم في غطاء عن ذكري وكانوا لا يستطيعون سمعا
(١٠١) أفحسب الذين كفروا أن يتخذوا عبادي من دوني أولياء إنا
أعتدنا جهنم للكافرين نزلا (١٠٢) قل هل ننبئكم بالأخسرين أعمالا (١٠٣)
الذين ضل سعيهم في الحياة الدنيا وهم يحسبون أنهم يحسنون
صنعا (١٠٤) أولئك الذين كفروا بآيات ربهم ولقائه فحبطت أعمالهم
فلا نقيم لهم يوم القيامة وزنا (١٠٥) ذلك جزاؤهم جهنم بما
كفروا واتخذوا آياتي ورسلي هزوا (١٠٦) إن الذين آمنوا وعملوا
الصالحات كانت لهم جنات الفردوس نزلا (١٠٧) خالدين فيها لا يبغون
عنها حولا (١٠٨) قل لو كان البحر مدادا لكلمات ربي لنفد البحر قبل
أن تنفد كلمات ربي ولو جئنا بمثله مددا (١٠٩) قل إنما أنا بشر
مثلكم يوحى إلي أنما إلهكم إله واحد فمن كان يرجو لقاء
ربه فليعمل عملا صالحا ولا يشرك بعبادة ربه أحدا (١١٠)

HE SAID: "This is a blessing 18:98
from my Lord. But when my
Lord's promise has been fulfilled, He will level it to dust;
the promise of my Lord is
ever true."'

And on that day We will let
them come in tumultuous
throngs. The Trumpet shall be
blown and We will gather them
all together.

On that day We shall lay
Hell bare before the unbelievers, who have turned a blind
eye to My Admonition and a
deaf ear to My warning.

Do the unbelievers think
that they can make My servants patrons besides Me? We
have prepared Hell for the
unbelievers to dwell in.

Say: 'Shall we tell you who
will lose most through their
labours? Those whose endeavours in this world are misguided and who yet 18:104
think that what they do is right; who disbelieve the revelations of their Lord
and deny that they will ever meet Him.' Vain are the works of these. On the
Day of Resurrection We shall give them no consequence.

Hell is their reward: because they disbelieved, and because they mocked
My apostles and My revelations. As for those that have faith and do good
works, they shall for ever dwell in the Gardens of Paradise, desiring no
change.

Say: 'If the sea were ink with which to write the words of my Lord, the sea
would surely run dry before the words of my Lord were finished, though we
found another sea to replenish it.'

Say: 'I am but a mortal like yourselves. It is revealed to me that your God 18:110
is one God. Let him that hopes to meet his Lord do what is right and worship
none besides his Lord.'

MARY

In the Name of God,
the Merciful, the Compassionate

بسم الله الرحمن الرحيم
كهيعص (١) ذكر رحمت ربك عبده زكريا (٢)
إذ نادى ربه نداء خفيا (٣) قال رب إني وهن العظم مني
واشتعل الرأس شيبا ولم أكن بدعائك رب شقيا (٤) وإني
خفت الموالي من ورائي وكانت امرأتي عاقرا فهب لي
من لدنك وليا (٥) يرثني ويرث من آل يعقوب
واجعله رب رضيا (٦) يا زكريا إنا نبشرك بغلام اسمه يحيى
لم نجعل له من قبل سميا (٧) قال رب أنى يكون
لي غلام وكانت امرأتي عاقرا وقد بلغت من الكبر
عتيا (٨) قال كذلك قال ربك هو علي هين وقد
خلقتك من قبل ولم تك شيئا (٩) قال رب اجعل لي آية قال
آيتك ألا تكلم الناس ثلاث ليال سويا (١٠) فخرج على قومه
من المحراب فأوحى إليهم أن سبحوا بكرة وعشيا (١١)

19:1 Kāf *hā' yā' 'ain ṣād.* Remembering your Lord's goodness
to His servant Zacharias:

He invoked his Lord in secret, saying: 'Lord, my bones are enfeebled, and my head glows silver with age. Yet never, Lord, have I prayed to You in vain. I now fear my kin who will succeed me, for my wife is barren. Grant me, from Yourself, a son who will be my heir and an heir to the House of Jacob, and make him worthy, Lord, of Your pleasure.'

'Rejoice, Zacharias. We shall give you a son to rejoice in, and his name shall be John; a name We have given no man before him.'[1]

19:8 'Lord,' said Zacharias, 'how shall I have a son, when my wife is barren, and
I am well advanced in years?'

He replied: 'Thus did your Lord speak. That is easy for Me; even as I brought you into being when you were nothing before.'

'Lord,' said Zacharias, 'give me a sign.'

'Your sign is that for three days and nights,' He replied, 'you shall be bereft of speech, though otherwise sound in body.'

19:11 Then Zacharias came out from the Shrine and exhorted his people to give
glory morning and evening.

1. Cf. Luke 1:61.

يا يحيى خذ الكتاب بقوة وآتيناه الحكم صبيا ﴿١٢﴾ وحنانا
من لدنا وزكاة وكان تقيا ﴿١٣﴾ وبرا بوالديه ولم
يكن جبارا عصيا ﴿١٤﴾ وسلام عليه يوم ولد ويوم
يموت ويوم يبعث حيا ﴿١٥﴾ واذكر في الكتاب مريم
إذ انتبذت من أهلها مكانا شرقيا ﴿١٦﴾ فاتخذت من
دونهم حجابا فأرسلنا إليها روحنا فتمثل لها بشرا
سويا ﴿١٧﴾ قالت إني أعوذ بالرحمن منك إن كنت تقيا
﴿١٨﴾ قال إنما أنا رسول ربك لأهب لك غلاما زكيا ﴿١٩﴾
قالت أنى يكون لي غلام ولم يمسسني بشر ولم أك بغيا
﴿٢٠﴾ قال كذلك قال ربك هو علي هين ولنجعله آية
للناس ورحمة منا وكان أمرا مقضيا ﴿٢١﴾ فحملته فانتبذت
به مكانا قصيا ﴿٢٢﴾ فأجاءها المخاض إلى جذع النخلة قالت
يا ليتني مت قبل هذا وكنت نسيا منسيا ﴿٢٣﴾ فناداها من
تحتها ألا تحزني قد جعل ربك تحتك سريا ﴿٢٤﴾ وهزي
إليك بجذع النخلة تساقط عليك رطبا جنيا ﴿٢٥﴾

TO JOHN We said: 'Observe 19:12
the Book with a firm resolve.'
We bestowed on him from
Ourself wisdom, grace, and
purity while yet a child, and he
grew up a righteous man; honouring his father and mother,
and neither arrogant nor rebellious. Peace be on him on the
day he was born and on the
day of his death and on the
day he is raised to life.

And you shall recount in
the Book the story of Mary:
how she left her people and
betook herself to a solitary
place to the east.

We sent to her Our Spirit in
the semblance of a full-grown
man. And when she saw him
she said: 'May the Merciful 19:18
defend me from you! If you
fear the Lord . . .'

'I am but your Lord's emissary,' he replied, 'and have come to give you a
holy son.'

'How shall I bear a child,' she answered, 'when I have neither been touched
by any man nor ever been unchaste?'

'Thus did your Lord speak,' he replied. '"That is easy enough for Me. We
shall make him a sign to mankind and a blessing from Ourself. Our will shall
be done."'

Thereupon she conceived him, and retired to a far-off place. And when
she felt the throes of childbirth she lay down by the trunk of a palm-tree,
crying: 'Oh, would that I had died before this, and passed into oblivion!'

But a voice from below called out to her: 'Do not despair. Your Lord has
provided a brook that runs at your feet, and if you shake the trunk of the 19:25
palm-tree it will drop fresh ripe dates in your lap.

فكلي واشربي وقري عينا فاما ترين من البشر احدا
فقولي اني نذرت للرحمن صوما فلن اكلم اليوم انسيا
فاتت به قومها تحمله قالوا يا مريم لقد جئت شيئا
فريا ٢٧ يا اخت هرون ما كان ابوك امرا سوء وما
كانت امك بغيا ٢٨ فاشارت اليه قالوا كيف نكلم من
كان في المهد صبيا ٢٩ قال اني عبد الله اتاني الكتاب
وجعلني نبيا ٣٠ وجعلني مباركا اين ما كنت واوصاني
بالصلوة والزكوة ما دمت حيا ٣١ وبرا بوالدتي ولم
يجعلني جبارا شقيا ٣٢ والسلام علي يوم ولدت ويوم اموت
ويوم ابعث حيا ٣٣ ذلك عيسى ابن مريم قول الحق الذي فيه
يمترون ٣٤ ما كان لله ان يتخذ من ولد سبحانه اذا قضى
امرا فانما يقول له كن فيكون ٣٥ وان الله ربي وربكم
فاعبدوه هذا صراط مستقيم ٣٦ فاختلف الاحزاب من بينهم
فويل للذين كفروا من مشهد يوم عظيم ٣٧ اسمع بهم وابصر
يوم ياتوننا لكن الظالمون اليوم في ضلال مبين ٣٨

19:26 THEREFORE EAT and drink and rejoice; and should you meet any mortal say to him: "I have vowed a fast to the Merciful and will not speak with anyone today."'

Carrying the child, she came to her people, who said to her: 'Mary, you have indeed done a shameful deed! Sister of Aaron,[1] your father was never a whoremonger, nor was your mother a harlot.'

She made a sign to them, pointing to the child. But they replied: 'How can we speak with a babe in the cradle?'

19:30 Whereupon he spoke and said: 'I am the servant of God. He has given me the Book and ordained me a prophet. His blessing is upon me wherever I go, and He has exhorted me to be steadfast in prayer and to give alms as long as I shall live. He has exhorted me to honour my mother and has purged me of vanity and wickedness. Peace be on me on the day I was born and on the day of my death and on the day I shall be raised to life.'

Such was Jesus son of Mary. That is the whole truth, which they still doubt. God forbid that He Himself should beget a son! When He decrees a thing He need only say: 'Be,' and it is.

God is my Lord and your Lord: therefore serve Him. That is a straight path.

Yet are the sects at odds among themselves. But when the fateful day
19:38 arrives, woe betide the unbelievers! Their hearing and their sight will be
sharpened on the day they appear before Us. Truly, the wrongdoers are today
in monstrous error.

1. It appears that Miriam, Aaron's sister, and Maryam (Mary), mother of Jesus, were, according to the Koran, one and the same person.

وَأَنذِرْهُمْ يَوْمَ الْحَسْرَةِ إِذْ قُضِيَ الْأَمْرُ وَهُمْ فِي غَفْلَةٍ وَهُمْ
لَا يُؤْمِنُونَ ۝ إِنَّا نَحْنُ نَرِثُ الْأَرْضَ وَمَنْ عَلَيْهَا وَإِلَيْنَا يُرْجَعُونَ
۝٤٠ وَاذْكُرْ فِي الْكِتَابِ إِبْرَاهِيمَ إِنَّهُ كَانَ صِدِّيقًا نَبِيًّا ۝٤١
إِذْ قَالَ لِأَبِيهِ يَا أَبَتِ لِمَ تَعْبُدُ مَا لَا يَسْمَعُ وَلَا يُبْصِرُ وَلَا يُغْنِي عَنكَ
شَيْئًا ۝٤٢ يَا أَبَتِ إِنِّي قَدْ جَاءَنِي مِنَ الْعِلْمِ مَا لَمْ يَأْتِكَ فَاتَّبِعْنِي
أَهْدِكَ صِرَاطًا سَوِيًّا ۝٤٣ يَا أَبَتِ لَا تَعْبُدِ الشَّيْطَانَ إِنَّ الشَّيْطَانَ
كَانَ لِلرَّحْمَٰنِ عَصِيًّا ۝٤٤ يَا أَبَتِ إِنِّي أَخَافُ أَن يَمَسَّكَ عَذَابٌ
مِّنَ الرَّحْمَٰنِ فَتَكُونَ لِلشَّيْطَانِ وَلِيًّا ۝٤٥ قَالَ أَرَاغِبٌ أَنتَ
عَنْ آلِهَتِي يَا إِبْرَاهِيمُ لَئِن لَّمْ تَنتَهِ لَأَرْجُمَنَّكَ وَاهْجُرْنِي مَلِيًّا ۝٤٦
قَالَ سَلَامٌ عَلَيْكَ سَأَسْتَغْفِرُ لَكَ رَبِّي إِنَّهُ كَانَ بِي حَفِيًّا ۝٤٧
وَأَعْتَزِلُكُمْ وَمَا تَدْعُونَ مِن دُونِ اللَّهِ وَأَدْعُو رَبِّي عَسَىٰ أَلَّا أَكُونَ
بِدُعَاءِ رَبِّي شَقِيًّا ۝٤٨ فَلَمَّا اعْتَزَلَهُمْ وَمَا يَعْبُدُونَ مِن
دُونِ اللَّهِ وَهَبْنَا لَهُ إِسْحَاقَ وَيَعْقُوبَ وَكُلًّا جَعَلْنَا نَبِيًّا ۝٤٩
وَوَهَبْنَا لَهُم مِّن رَّحْمَتِنَا وَجَعَلْنَا لَهُمْ لِسَانَ صِدْقٍ عَلِيًّا ۝٥٠
وَاذْكُرْ فِي الْكِتَابِ مُوسَىٰ إِنَّهُ كَانَ مُخْلَصًا وَكَانَ رَسُولًا نَّبِيًّا ۝٥١

AND FOREWARN them of 19:39
that woeful day, when Our decree shall be fulfilled while they heedlessly persist in unbelief. We Ourself shall inherit the earth and all who dwell upon it. And to Us they shall be recalled.

You shall also recount in the Book the story of Abraham:

He was a saintly man and a prophet. He said to his father: 'Why do you worship a worthless idol, a thing that can neither hear nor see?

'Father, things you know nothing of have come to my knowledge: therefore follow me, that I may guide you along an even path.

'Father, do not worship Satan; for Satan has rebelled against the Lord of Mercy.

'Father, I fear that a scourge will fall upon you from the Merciful, and you 19:45
will become one of Satan's minions.'

He said: 'Do you dare renounce my gods, Abraham? Desist, or I will stone you. Leave my house this instant!'

'Peace be with you,' said Abraham. 'I shall implore my Lord to forgive you: for to me He has ever been gracious. But I will not live with you or with your idols. I will pray to my Lord, and may my prayers to my Lord not be in vain.'

And when Abraham had cast off his people and the idols which they worshipped, We bestowed on him Isaac and Jacob. Each of them We made a prophet, and We bestowed on them gracious gifts and high renown.

In the Book tell also of Moses, who was a chosen man, an apostle, and a 19:51
prophet.

19:52 WE CALLED out to him from the right side of the Mount, and when he came near We communed with him in secret. We gave him, of Our mercy, his brother Aaron, himself a prophet.

And in the Book you shall tell of Ishmael: he, too, was a man of his word, an apostle, and a prophet.

He enjoined prayer and almsgiving on his people, and his Lord was pleased with him.

And in the Book tell of Idrīs:[1] he, too, was a saint and a prophet, whom We honoured and exalted.

Those were the men to whom God was gracious: the prophets from among the descendants of Adam and of those whom We carried in the ark with Noah; the descendants of Abraham, of Israel, and of those whom We have guided and chosen. For when the revelations of the Merciful were recited to them they fell down on their knees in tears and adoration.

19:59 But the generations who succeeded them neglected their prayers and succumbed to their desires. These shall assuredly be lost. But those that repent and embrace the Faith and do what is right shall enter Paradise and shall in no way be wronged: the Gardens of Eden, which the Merciful has promised on trust to His servants; His promise shall surely be fulfilled.

Therein shall they hear no idle talk, but only the voice of peace. And their sustenance shall be given them therein morning and evening. Such is the Paradise which We shall give the righteous among Our servants to inherit.

19:64 We descend only at the bidding of your Lord;[2] to Him belongs what is before us and behind us, and all that lies between.

And your Lord never forgets.

وناديناه من جانب الطور الأيمن وقربناه نجيا ۝ ووهبنا له من
رحمتنا أخاه هارون نبيا ۝ واذكر في الكتاب إسماعيل إنه كان
صادق الوعد وكان رسولا نبيا ۝ وكان يأمر أهله بالصلوة
والزكوة وكان عند ربه مرضيا ۝ واذكر في الكتاب
إدريس إنه كان صديقا نبيا ۝ ورفعناه مكانا عليا ۝
أولئك الذين أنعم الله عليهم من النبيين من ذرية آدم وممن
حملنا مع نوح ومن ذرية إبراهيم وإسرائيل وممن هدينا واجتبينا
إذا تتلى عليهم آيات الرحمن خروا سجدا وبكيا ۝ فخلف من
بعدهم خلف أضاعوا الصلوة واتبعوا الشهوات فسوف يلقون
غيا ۝ إلا من تاب وآمن وعمل صالحا فأولئك يدخلون الجنة
ولا يظلمون شيئا ۝ جنات عدن التي وعد الرحمن عباده
بالغيب إنه كان وعده مأتيا ۝ لا يسمعون فيها لغوا إلا سلاما
ولهم رزقهم فيها بكرة وعشيا ۝ تلك الجنة التي نورث من
عبادنا من كان تقيا ۝ وما نتنزل إلا بأمر ربك له ما بين
أيدينا وما خلفنا وما بين ذلك وما كان ربك نسيا ۝

1. Enoch.
2. Commentators say that these are the words of the Angel Gabriel, in reply to Muḥammad's complaint of long intervals elapsing between periods of revelation.

رب السموات والارض وما بينهما فاعبده واصطبر
لعبادته هل تعلم له سميا ﴿٦٥﴾ ويقول الانسان اءذا ما مت
لسوف اخرج حيا ﴿٦٦﴾ اولا يذكر الانسان انا خلقناه
من قبل ولم يك شيئا ﴿٦٧﴾ فوربك لنحشرنهم والشياطين
ثم لنحضرنهم حول جهنم جثيا ﴿٦٨﴾ ثم لننزعن من
كل شيعة ايهم اشد على الرحمن عتيا ﴿٦٩﴾ ثم لنحن اعلم
بالذين هم اولى بها صليا ﴿٧٠﴾ وان منكم الا واردها كان على
ربك حتما مقضيا ﴿٧١﴾ ثم ننجي الذين اتقوا ونذر الظالمين
فيها جثيا ﴿٧٢﴾ واذا تتلى عليهم اياتنا بينات قال الذين
كفروا للذين امنوا اي الفريقين خير مقاما واحسن نديا ﴿٧٣﴾
وكم اهلكنا قبلهم من قرن هم احسن اثاثا ورئيا ﴿٧٤﴾ قل من
كان في الضلالة فليمدد له الرحمن مدا حتى اذا راوا
ما يوعدون اما العذاب واما الساعة فسيعلمون من هو شر
مكانا واضعف جندا ﴿٧٥﴾ ويزيد الله الذين اهتدوا هدى
والباقيات الصالحات خير عند ربك ثوابا وخير مردا ﴿٧٦﴾

THE LORD of the heavens 19:65
and the earth and all that is between them: worship Him, then, and be patient in His service; for do you know any other worthy of His name?

'What!' says man. 'When I am once dead, shall I be raised to life?'

Does man forget that We created him when he was nothing before? By the Lord, We will assuredly herd them in company with the demons and set them on their knees around the fire of Hell: and then from every sect We will carry off its stoutest rebels against the Lord of Mercy. And then We surely know best who deserve most to be burnt in its flames.

There is not one among you 19:71
who shall not pass through it: such is the absolute decree of your Lord. We will deliver those who fear Us, and therein leave the wrongdoers, on their knees.

And when Our revelations are recited to them, manifest, the unbelievers say to the faithful: 'Which of us two will have a finer abode and better companions?'

And how many generations have We destroyed before them, far greater in riches and in splendour!

Say: 'The Merciful will bear long with those in error until they see the fulfilment of His promise: be it a worldly scourge or the Hour itself. Then shall they learn whose is the worse plight and whose the smaller following.'

God will increase His guidance to those that follow the right guidance. 19:76
Deeds of lasting merit shall earn you a better recompense in the sight of your Lord and a more auspicious end.

19:77 MARK THE words of him
who denies Our signs and
who yet boasts: 'I shall surely
be given wealth and children!'
Has the future been re-
vealed to him? Or has the
Merciful made him such a
promise?
By no means! We will re-
cord his words and make his
punishment long and terrible.
All he speaks of he shall leave
behind and come before Us
all alone.
They have chosen deities
other than God to help them.
By no means! They will renounce their worship and turn
against them.
Behold how We send down
to the unbelievers demons
who incite them to evil. Therefore do not hurry them on:
19:85 their days are numbered. The day will surely come when We will gather the
righteous in multitudes before the Lord of Mercy, and drive the guilty to
Hell in thirsty hordes. None has power to intercede for them save him who
has received the sanction of the Merciful.
And they say: 'The Lord of Mercy has begotten a son.' You surely preach
a monstrous falsehood, at which the very heavens might crack, the earth split
asunder, and the mountains crumble to dust. That they should ascribe a son
to the Merciful, when it does not become the Merciful to beget offspring!
There is none in the heavens or on earth but shall return to the Merciful
19:95 in utter submission. He has kept strict count of them all, and one by one
shall they come to Him on the Day of Resurrection.

افرأيت الذي كفر بآياتنا وقال لأوتين مالا وولدا ٧٧ أطلع
الغيب أم اتخذ عند الرحمن عهدا ٧٨ كلا سنكتب ما
يقول ونمد له من العذاب مدا ٧٩ ونرثه ما يقول ويأتينا فردا
٨٠ واتخذوا من دون الله آلهة ليكونوا لهم عزا
٨١ كلا سيكفرون بعبادتهم ويكونون عليهم
ضدا ٨٢ ألم تر أنا أرسلنا الشياطين على الكافرين
تؤزهم أزا ٨٣ فلا تعجل عليهم إنما نعد لهم عدا
٨٤ يوم نحشر المتقين إلى الرحمن وفدا ٨٥ ونسوق
المجرمين إلى جهنم وردا ٨٦ لا يملكون الشفاعة
إلا من اتخذ عند الرحمن عهدا ٨٧ وقالوا اتخذ
الرحمن ولدا ٨٨ لقد جئتم شيئا إدا ٨٩ تكاد السموات
يتفطرن منه وتنشق الأرض وتخر الجبال هدا ٩٠ أن دعوا
للرحمن ولدا ٩١ وما ينبغي للرحمن أن يتخذ ولدا ٩٢ إن كل من
في السموات والأرض إلا آتي الرحمن عبدا ٩٣ لقد أحصيهم
وعدهم عدا ٩٤ وكلهم آتيه يوم القيمة فردا ٩٥

إن الذين آمنوا وعملوا الصالحات سيجعل لهم الرحمن ودا ﴿٩٦﴾ فإنما
يسرناه بلسانك لتبشر به المتقين وتنذر به قوما لدا ﴿٩٧﴾ وكم
أهلكنا قبلهم من قرن هل تحس منهم من أحد أو تسمع لهم ركزا ﴿٩٨﴾

سورة طه مكية وهي مائة وخمس وثلثون آية

بسم الله الرحمن الرحيم
طه ﴿١﴾ ما أنزلنا عليك القرآن لتشقى ﴿٢﴾ إلا تذكرة لمن
يخشى ﴿٣﴾ تنزيلا ممن خلق الأرض والسموات العلى ﴿٤﴾
الرحمن على العرش استوى ﴿٥﴾ له ما في السموات وما في
الأرض وما بينهما وما تحت الثرى ﴿٦﴾ وإن تجهر
بالقول فإنه يعلم السر وأخفى ﴿٧﴾ الله لا إله إلا هو له
الأسماء الحسنى ﴿٨﴾ وهل أتاك حديث موسى ﴿٩﴾ إذ رأى نارا
فقال لأهله امكثوا إني آنست نارا لعلي آتيكم منها بقبس
أو أجد على النار هدى ﴿١٠﴾ فلما أتاها نودي يا موسى ﴿١١﴾ إني أنا
ربك فاخلع نعليك إنك بالواد المقدس طوى ﴿١٢﴾

THE MERCIFUL will cherish 19:96
those who believed and were
charitable in their lifetime.

We have made it easy in
your own tongue that you may
thereby proclaim joyful tidings
to the upright and give warning to a contentious people.

And how many generations 19:98
have We destroyed before
them! Can you find one of
them still alive, or hear so
much as a whisper from them?

ṬĀ' HĀ'

In the Name of God, the Merciful, the Compassionate

Ṭā' hā'. 20:1

It was not to distress you that We revealed the Koran to you, but to admonish the God-fearing. It is a revelation from Him who has created the earth and the lofty heavens, the Merciful who sits enthroned on high.

His is what the heavens and the earth contain, and all that lies between them and underneath the soil. You have no need to speak aloud; for He has knowledge of all that is secret, and all that is hidden.

He is God. There is no god but Him. His are the most gracious names. 20:8

Have you heard the story of Moses?

When he saw a fire, he said to his people: 'Stay here, for I can see a fire. Perchance I can bring you from it a lighted torch, or find a guide hard by the fire.'

When he came near, a voice called out to him: 'Moses, I am your Lord. 20:12
Take off your sandals, for you are now in the sacred valley of Ṭuwā.

20:13 ‘And I have chosen you: so
listen to what shall be revealed.
‘I am God. There is no god
but Me. Worship Me, and
recite your prayers in My
remembrance.
‘The Hour is sure to come.
But I choose to keep it hidden,
so that every soul shall be
rewarded according to its
labours. Let not those who
disbelieve in it and yield to
their desires turn your
thoughts from it, lest you perish. What is it you are carrying
in your right hand, Moses?’
He said: ‘It is my staff; upon
it I lean and with it I beat down
the leaves for my flock. And I
have other uses for it besides.’
He said: ‘Moses, cast it
down.’
Moses threw it down, and
thereupon it turned into a slithering serpent.
‘Take it up and have no fear,’ He said. ‘We will change it back to its former
20:22 state. And now put your hand under your armpit. It shall come out white,
although unharmed: another sign.
‘We shall show you the most wondrous of all Our signs. Go to Pharaoh;
he has transgressed all bounds.’
‘Lord,’ said he, ‘put courage into my heart, and make my task easy. Free
my tongue from its impediment, that men may understand my speech.
Appoint for me a helper from among my kin, Aaron my brother. Grant me
strength through him and let him share my task, so that we may give glory to
You always and remember You always. You are surely watching over us.’
20:37 He said: ‘Your request is granted, Moses. We had already shown you
bounty

وَأَنَا اخْتَرْتُكَ فَاسْتَمِعْ لِمَا يُوحَىٰ (١٣) إِنَّنِي أَنَا اللَّهُ لَا إِلَٰهَ إِلَّا
أَنَا فَاعْبُدْنِي وَأَقِمِ الصَّلَوٰةَ لِذِكْرِي (١٤) إِنَّ السَّاعَةَ آتِيَةٌ
أَكَادُ أُخْفِيهَا لِتُجْزَىٰ كُلُّ نَفْسٍ بِمَا تَسْعَىٰ (١٥) فَلَا يَصُدَّنَّكَ
عَنْهَا مَنْ لَا يُؤْمِنُ بِهَا وَاتَّبَعَ هَوَاهُ فَتَرْدَىٰ (١٦) وَمَا تِلْكَ
بِيَمِينِكَ يَا مُوسَىٰ (١٧) قَالَ هِيَ عَصَايَ أَتَوَكَّؤُا عَلَيْهَا وَأَهُشُّ
بِهَا عَلَىٰ غَنَمِي وَلِيَ فِيهَا مَآرِبُ أُخْرَىٰ (١٨) قَالَ أَلْقِهَا يَا مُوسَىٰ
(١٩) فَأَلْقَاهَا فَإِذَا هِيَ حَيَّةٌ تَسْعَىٰ (٢٠) قَالَ خُذْهَا وَلَا تَخَفْ
سَنُعِيدُهَا سِيرَتَهَا الْأُولَىٰ (٢١) وَاضْمُمْ يَدَكَ إِلَىٰ جَنَاحِكَ
تَخْرُجْ بَيْضَاءَ مِنْ غَيْرِ سُوءٍ آيَةً أُخْرَىٰ (٢٢) لِنُرِيَكَ مِنْ آيَاتِنَا
الْكُبْرَىٰ (٢٣) اذْهَبْ إِلَىٰ فِرْعَوْنَ إِنَّهُ طَغَىٰ (٢٤) قَالَ رَبِّ اشْرَحْ لِي
صَدْرِي (٢٥) وَيَسِّرْ لِي أَمْرِي (٢٦) وَاحْلُلْ عُقْدَةً مِنْ لِسَانِي (٢٧)
يَفْقَهُوا قَوْلِي (٢٨) وَاجْعَلْ لِي وَزِيرًا مِنْ أَهْلِي (٢٩) هَارُونَ أَخِي (٣٠)
اشْدُدْ بِهِ أَزْرِي (٣١) وَأَشْرِكْهُ فِي أَمْرِي (٣٢) كَيْ نُسَبِّحَكَ كَثِيرًا
(٣٣) وَنَذْكُرَكَ كَثِيرًا (٣٤) إِنَّكَ كُنْتَ بِنَا بَصِيرًا (٣٥) قَالَ قَدْ أُوتِيتَ
سُؤْلَكَ يَا مُوسَىٰ (٣٦) وَلَقَدْ مَنَنَّا عَلَيْكَ مَرَّةً أُخْرَىٰ (٣٧)

اذ اوحينا الى امك ما يوحى (٣٨) ان اقذفيه في التابوت فاقذفيه
في اليم فليلقه اليم بالساحل يأخذه عدو لي وعدو له
والقيت عليك محبة مني ولتصنع على عيني (٣٩) اذ تمشي اختك
فتقول هل ادلكم على من يكفله فرجعناك الى امك كي
تقر عينها ولا تحزن وقتلت نفسا فنجيناك من الغم وفتناك
فتونا فلبثت سنين في اهل مدين ثم جئت على قدر يا موسى (٤٠)
واصطنعتك لنفسي (٤١) اذهب انت واخوك باياتي ولا تنيا في
ذكري (٤٢) اذهبا الى فرعون انه طغى (٤٣) فقولا له قولا لينا
لعله يتذكر او يخشى (٤٤) قالا ربنا اننا نخاف ان يفرط
علينا او ان يطغى (٤٥) قال لا تخافا انني معكما اسمع
وارى (٤٦) فأتياه فقولا انا رسولا ربك فارسل معنا بني اسرائيل
ولا تعذبهم قد جئناك باية من ربك والسلام على من اتبع
الهدى (٤٧) انا قد اوحي الينا ان العذاب على من كذب وتولى
(٤٨) قال فمن ربكما يا موسى (٤٩) قال ربنا الذي اعطى كل
شيء خلقه ثم هدى (٥٠) قال فما بال القرون الاولى (٥١)

when we revealed Our will to 20:38
your mother, saying: "Put your child in the ark and let him be carried away by the river. The river will cast him on to the bank, and he shall be taken up by an enemy of Mine and his." I lavished My love on you, so that you might be reared under My eye.

'Your sister went to them and said: "Shall I direct you to one who will nurse him?"

'Thus did We restore you to your mother, so that her mind might be set at ease and that she might not grieve.

'And when you slew a man We delivered you from distress and then proved you by other trials.

'You stayed for years among the people of Midian, and you then came here, Moses, as was ordained. I have chosen you for Myself. Go,
you and your brother, with My signs, and do not cease to remember Me. Go 20:43
both of you to Pharaoh, for he has transgressed all bounds. Speak to him with gentle words; he may yet take thought and fear Us.'

'Lord,' they said, 'we dread his malevolence and tyranny.'

He said: 'Have no fear. I shall be with you. I hear all and see all. Go to him and say: "We are the emissaries of your Lord. Let the Israelites depart with us, and oppress them no more. We have come to you with a revelation from your Lord: peace shall be his that follows the right guidance. It is revealed to us that the scourge will fall on those who deny His signs and turn away from them."'

He said: 'And who is your Lord, Moses?'

'Our Lord,' he said, 'is He that gave all creatures their distinctive form and then rightly guided them.'

'How was it, then, with the early generations?' he said. 20:51

20:52 He said: 'My Lord alone has knowledge of that, recorded in a Book. My Lord does not err, neither does He forget. It is He who has made the earth your cradle and traced on it paths for you to walk on. It is He who sends down water from the sky with which We bring forth every kind of plant, saying: "Eat and graze your cattle. Surely in this there are signs for rational beings. From the earth We have created you, and to the earth We will restore you; and from it We will bring you back to life."'

We showed him all Our signs, but he denied them and paid no heed. He said: 'Have you come to drive us from our land with your sorcery, Moses?
20:58 We will surely confront you with sorcery as powerful as yours. Appoint a day
when both of us can meet, a tryst which neither we nor you shall fail to keep, and a place at an equal distance from us both.'

He said: 'Meet me on the day of the Feast, and let all the people come together before noon.'

Pharaoh withdrew; he gathered his sorcerers and then returned. 'Woe betide you!' said Moses to them. 'Invent no falsehoods against God, or He will obliterate you with a scourge. Those that invent falsehood have ever failed.'

They conferred among themselves, whispering to one another. They said: 'These two are sorcerers who intend to drive you from your land by their
20:64 sorcery and do away with your best traditions. Muster all your forces and
array them in their ranks; those who win today will surely triumph.'

قال علمها عند ربي في كتاب لا يضل ربي ولا ينسى ٥٢
الذي جعل لكم الأرض مهدا وسلك لكم فيها سبلا
وأنزل من السماء ماء فأخرجنا به أزواجا من نبات شتى
٥٣ كلوا وارعوا أنعامكم إن في ذلك لآيات لأولي النهى
٥٤ منها خلقناكم وفيها نعيدكم ومنها نخرجكم تارة أخرى
٥٥ ولقد أريناه آياتنا كلها فكذب وأبى ٥٦ قال أجئتنا
لتخرجنا من أرضنا بسحرك يا موسى ٥٧ فلنأتينك بسحر مثله
فاجعل بيننا وبينك موعدا لا نخلفه نحن ولا أنت مكانا
سوى ٥٨ قال موعدكم يوم الزينة وأن يحشر الناس ضحى
٥٩ فتولى فرعون فجمع كيده ثم أتى ٦٠ قال لهم موسى ويلكم
لا تفتروا على الله كذبا فيسحتكم بعذاب وقد خاب
من افترى ٦١ فتنازعوا أمرهم بينهم وأسروا النجوى ٦٢
قالوا إن هذان لساحران يريدان أن يخرجاكم من أرضكم
بسحرهما ويذهبا بطريقتكم المثلى ٦٣ فأجمعوا كيدكم
ثم ائتوا صفا وقد أفلح اليوم من استعلى ٦٤

قالوا يا موسى إما أن تلقي وإما أن نكون أول من ألقى ۝ قال
بل ألقوا فإذا حبالهم وعصيهم يخيل إليه من سحرهم أنها
تسعى ۝ فأوجس في نفسه خيفة موسى ۝ قلنا لا تخف إنك
أنت الأعلى ۝ وألق ما في يمينك تلقف ما صنعوا إنما صنعوا كيد ساحر
ولا يفلح الساحر حيث أتى ۝ فألقي السحرة سجدا قالوا آمنا برب
هرون وموسى ۝ قال آمنتم له قبل أن آذن لكم إنه لكبيركم
الذي علمكم السحر فلأقطعن أيديكم وأرجلكم من خلاف
ولأصلبنكم في جذوع النخل ولتعلمن أينا أشد عذابا وأبقى
۝ قالوا لن نؤثرك على ما جاءنا من البينات والذي فطرنا
فاقض ما أنت قاض إنما تقضي هذه الحيوة الدنيا ۝ إنا آمنا بربنا
ليغفر لنا خطايانا وما أكرهتنا عليه من السحر والله خير وأبقى
۝ إنه من يأت ربه مجرما فإن له جهنم لا يموت فيها
ولا يحيى ۝ ومن يأته مؤمنا قد عمل الصالحات فأولئك
لهم الدرجات العلى ۝ جنات عدن تجري من تحتها
الأنهار خالدين فيها وذلك جزاء من تزكى ۝

THEY SAID: 'Moses, either 20:65
you throw down, or we shall be the first to throw.'

'Throw you down,' he said.

And lo! by their sorcery their ropes and staffs appeared to Moses' eyes as though they were running.

Moses was much alarmed. We said: 'Have no fear; you shall surely win. Throw that which is in your right hand. It will swallow up their devices, for their devices are but the deceitful show of a sorcerer. And the sorcerer shall never prosper, wherever he has come from.'

The sorcerers prostrated themselves: they said: 'We now believe in the Lord of Aaron and Moses.'

'Do you dare believe in Him before I give you leave?' said Pharaoh. 'This man must be your master, who taught you witchcraft. I will cut off your hands and feet on alternate sides and crucify you on the trunks of palm-trees. You shall learn whose punishment is more terrible, and more lasting.'

They said: 'We cannot have greater faith in you than in the miracles which 20:72
we have witnessed and in Him who has created us. Therefore do your worst;
you can punish us only in this present life. We have put our faith in our Lord
so that He may forgive us our sins and the sorcery you have imposed upon
us. Better is God's recompense, and more lasting. He that comes before his
Lord laden with sin shall be consigned to Hell, wherein he shall neither die
nor live. But they that come before Him with true faith, having done good
works, shall be exalted to the highest ranks: in the Gardens of Eden, watered 20:76
by running brooks, wherein shall they abide for ever. Such shall be the
recompense of those that keep themselves pure.'

20:77 And We revealed Our will
to Moses: 'Set forth with My
servants in the night and strike
for them a dry path across the
sea. Have no fear of being
overtaken, nor let anything
dismay you.'
Pharaoh pursued them with
his warriors, but the waters
of the sea overwhelmed them.
For Pharaoh misled his people:
he did not guide them.
Children of Israel! We delivered you from your enemy and
made a covenant with you on
the right flank of the Mount.
We sent down for you manna
20:81 and quails. 'Eat of the wholesome things with which We
have provided you and do not
transgress, lest you should provoke My ire. He that provokes
My ire shall assuredly be lost;
and I will surely forgive him that repents and believes in Me, does a good
deed, and follows the right path. But, Moses, why have you come with such
haste from your people?'
He said: 'There they are, close behind me. I hastened to You, Lord, that I
might earn Your pleasure.'
He said: 'We proved your people in your absence, but the Sāmirī[1] has led
them astray.'
Moses went back to his people, angry and sorrowful. 'My people,' he said,
'did your Lord not make you a gracious promise? Did my absence seem too
long to you, or was it to incur your Lord's anger that you failed me?'
20:87 They replied: 'We did not fail you of our own free will. We were made to
carry the people's trinkets and cast them into the fire. The Sāmirī threw likewise,

وَلَقَدْ أَوْحَيْنَا إِلَىٰ مُوسَىٰ أَنْ أَسْرِ بِعِبَادِي فَاضْرِبْ لَهُمْ طَرِيقًا فِي
الْبَحْرِ يَبَسًا لَا تَخَافُ دَرَكًا وَلَا تَخْشَىٰ ٧٧ فَأَتْبَعَهُمْ فِرْعَوْنُ
بِجُنُودِهِ فَغَشِيَهُم مِّنَ الْيَمِّ مَا غَشِيَهُمْ ٧٨ وَأَضَلَّ فِرْعَوْنُ قَوْمَهُ
وَمَا هَدَىٰ ٧٩ يَا بَنِي إِسْرَائِيلَ قَدْ أَنجَيْنَاكُم مِّنْ عَدُوِّكُمْ وَوَاعَدْنَاكُمْ
جَانِبَ الطُّورِ الْأَيْمَنَ وَنَزَّلْنَا عَلَيْكُمُ الْمَنَّ وَالسَّلْوَىٰ
٨٠ كُلُوا مِن طَيِّبَاتِ مَا رَزَقْنَاكُمْ وَلَا تَطْغَوْا فِيهِ فَيَحِلَّ عَلَيْكُمْ
غَضَبِي وَمَن يَحْلِلْ عَلَيْهِ غَضَبِي فَقَدْ هَوَىٰ ٨١ وَإِنِّي لَغَفَّارٌ لِّمَن
تَابَ وَآمَنَ وَعَمِلَ صَالِحًا ثُمَّ اهْتَدَىٰ ٨٢ وَمَا أَعْجَلَكَ عَن قَوْمِكَ
يَا مُوسَىٰ ٨٣ قَالَ هُمْ أُولَاءِ عَلَىٰ أَثَرِي وَعَجِلْتُ إِلَيْكَ رَبِّ لِتَرْضَىٰ ٨٤
قَالَ فَإِنَّا قَدْ فَتَنَّا قَوْمَكَ مِن بَعْدِكَ وَأَضَلَّهُمُ السَّامِرِيُّ
٨٥ فَرَجَعَ مُوسَىٰ إِلَىٰ قَوْمِهِ غَضْبَانَ أَسِفًا قَالَ يَا قَوْمِ
أَلَمْ يَعِدْكُمْ رَبُّكُمْ وَعْدًا حَسَنًا أَفَطَالَ عَلَيْكُمُ الْعَهْدُ
أَمْ أَرَدتُّمْ أَن يَحِلَّ عَلَيْكُمْ غَضَبٌ مِّن رَّبِّكُمْ فَأَخْلَفْتُم
مَّوْعِدِي ٨٦ قَالُوا مَا أَخْلَفْنَا مَوْعِدَكَ بِمَلْكِنَا وَلَٰكِنَّا حُمِّلْنَا أَوْزَارًا
مِّن زِينَةِ الْقَوْمِ فَقَذَفْنَاهَا فَكَذَٰلِكَ أَلْقَى السَّامِرِيُّ ٨٧

1. It is not clear who the Sāmirī was.

فَأَخْرَجَ لَهُمْ عِجْلًا جَسَدًا لَهُ خُوَارٌ فَقَالُوا هَٰذَا إِلَٰهُكُمْ وَإِلَٰهُ مُوسَىٰ
فَنَسِيَ ﴿٨٨﴾ أَفَلَا يَرَوْنَ أَلَّا يَرْجِعُ إِلَيْهِمْ قَوْلًا وَلَا يَمْلِكُ لَهُمْ ضَرًّا
وَلَا نَفْعًا ﴿٨٩﴾ وَلَقَدْ قَالَ لَهُمْ هَارُونُ مِنْ قَبْلُ يَا قَوْمِ إِنَّمَا فُتِنْتُمْ
بِهِ وَإِنَّ رَبَّكُمُ الرَّحْمَٰنُ فَاتَّبِعُونِي وَأَطِيعُوا أَمْرِي ﴿٩٠﴾ قَالُوا
لَنْ نَبْرَحَ عَلَيْهِ عَاكِفِينَ حَتَّىٰ يَرْجِعَ إِلَيْنَا مُوسَىٰ ﴿٩١﴾ قَالَ
يَا هَارُونُ مَا مَنَعَكَ إِذْ رَأَيْتَهُمْ ضَلُّوا ﴿٩٢﴾ أَلَّا تَتَّبِعَنِ
أَفَعَصَيْتَ أَمْرِي ﴿٩٣﴾ قَالَ يَا ابْنَ أُمَّ لَا تَأْخُذْ بِلِحْيَتِي وَلَا
بِرَأْسِي إِنِّي خَشِيتُ أَنْ تَقُولَ فَرَّقْتَ بَيْنَ بَنِي إِسْرَائِيلَ وَلَمْ
تَرْقُبْ قَوْلِي ﴿٩٤﴾ قَالَ فَمَا خَطْبُكَ يَا سَامِرِيُّ ﴿٩٥﴾ قَالَ
بَصُرْتُ بِمَا لَمْ يَبْصُرُوا بِهِ فَقَبَضْتُ قَبْضَةً مِنْ أَثَرِ
الرَّسُولِ فَنَبَذْتُهَا وَكَذَٰلِكَ سَوَّلَتْ لِي نَفْسِي ﴿٩٦﴾ قَالَ
فَاذْهَبْ فَإِنَّ لَكَ فِي الْحَيَاةِ أَنْ تَقُولَ لَا مِسَاسَ وَإِنَّ لَكَ
مَوْعِدًا لَنْ تُخْلَفَهُ وَانْظُرْ إِلَىٰ إِلَٰهِكَ الَّذِي ظَلْتَ عَلَيْهِ
عَاكِفًا لَنُحَرِّقَنَّهُ ثُمَّ لَنَنْسِفَنَّهُ فِي الْيَمِّ نَسْفًا ﴿٩٧﴾ إِنَّمَا
إِلَٰهُكُمُ اللَّهُ الَّذِي لَا إِلَٰهَ إِلَّا هُوَ وَسِعَ كُلَّ شَيْءٍ عِلْمًا ﴿٩٨﴾

and forged for them a calf, an 20:88
image with a hollow sound.
"This," they said, "is your god
and the god of Moses whom
he has forgotten."'

Did they not see that it
returned to them no answer,
and that it could neither harm
nor help them?

Aaron had said to them: 'My
people, this is but a test for
you. Your Lord is the Merciful.
Follow me and do as I bid you.'
But they had replied: 'We will
not cease to worship it until
Moses returns.'

He said to Aaron: 'Why did
you not seek me out when you
saw them go astray? Why did
you disobey my bidding?'

'Son of my mother,' he 20:94
replied, 'let go, I pray you, of
my beard and my head. I was
afraid that you might say: "You have sown discord among the Israelites and
did not wait for my orders."'

'Sāmirī,' he said, 'what had come over you?'

He replied: 'I saw what they did not see. I took a handful of dust from the
trail of the Messenger and flung it away: thus did my soul prompt me.'

'Go!' he said. 'An outcast shall you be in this life, nor shall you escape your
appointed doom. Behold this idol which you have served with such devotion: we will burn it to cinders and scatter its ashes far and wide over the sea.'

Your Lord is God, other than whom there is no god. His knowledge 20:98
encompasses all things.

20:99 THUS DO We recount to
you the history of events gone
by. An Admonition of Our
own have We given you: those
that reject it shall bear a heavy
burden on the Day of Resurrection. For ever shall they
bear it: an evil burden on the
Day of Resurrection.
On the day when the Trum-
pet shall be blown; on that day
We shall herd all the sinners
together. Their eyes blue with
terror, they shall murmur
among themselves: 'You lingered on the earth but ten
days.'
We know full well what they
will say. The most upright
among them will say: 'You
lingered but one day.'
20:105 And they ask you about the
mountains. Say: 'My Lord will
crush them to fine dust and reduce them to a desolate waste, with no hollows nor
jutting mounds to be seen.'
On that day men will follow their truthful summoner, their voices hushed
before the Lord of Mercy; and you shall hear only the sound of marching
feet. On that day no intercession will avail except from him that has received
the sanction of the Merciful and whose word was pleasing to Him. He knows
what is before them and behind them, but of Him they have no knowledge.
They will hang their heads with awe before the Living One, the
Ever-existent. Those who are burdened with sin shall come to grief: but
those who have believed and done good works shall fear no tyranny or
injustice.
20:113 And thus have We sent it down: a Koran in the Arabic tongue, and
proclaimed in it warnings and threats, that they may fear God and be
admonished.

كَذَٰلِكَ نَقُصُّ عَلَيْكَ مِنْ أَنبَاءِ مَا قَدْ سَبَقَ ۚ وَقَدْ آتَيْنَاكَ
مِن لَّدُنَّا ذِكْرًا ۝ مَّنْ أَعْرَضَ عَنْهُ فَإِنَّهُ يَحْمِلُ يَوْمَ الْقِيَامَةِ
وِزْرًا ۝ خَالِدِينَ فِيهِ ۖ وَسَاءَ لَهُمْ يَوْمَ الْقِيَامَةِ حِمْلًا ۝١٠١
يَوْمَ يُنفَخُ فِي الصُّورِ ۚ وَنَحْشُرُ الْمُجْرِمِينَ يَوْمَئِذٍ زُرْقًا ۝١٠٢
يَتَخَافَتُونَ بَيْنَهُمْ إِن لَّبِثْتُمْ إِلَّا عَشْرًا ۝١٠٣ نَّحْنُ أَعْلَمُ بِمَا
يَقُولُونَ إِذْ يَقُولُ أَمْثَلُهُمْ طَرِيقَةً إِن لَّبِثْتُمْ إِلَّا يَوْمًا ۝١٠٤
وَيَسْأَلُونَكَ عَنِ الْجِبَالِ فَقُلْ يَنسِفُهَا رَبِّي نَسْفًا ۝ فَيَذَرُهَا قَاعًا
صَفْصَفًا ۝ لَّا تَرَىٰ فِيهَا عِوَجًا وَلَا أَمْتًا ۝١٠٧ يَوْمَئِذٍ يَتَّبِعُونَ
الدَّاعِيَ لَا عِوَجَ لَهُ ۖ وَخَشَعَتِ الْأَصْوَاتُ لِلرَّحْمَٰنِ فَلَا تَسْمَعُ إِلَّا هَمْسًا ۝
يَوْمَئِذٍ لَّا تَنفَعُ الشَّفَاعَةُ إِلَّا مَنْ أَذِنَ لَهُ الرَّحْمَٰنُ وَرَضِيَ لَهُ قَوْلًا ۝١٠٩
يَعْلَمُ مَا بَيْنَ أَيْدِيهِمْ وَمَا خَلْفَهُمْ وَلَا يُحِيطُونَ بِهِ عِلْمًا ۝١١٠
وَعَنَتِ الْوُجُوهُ لِلْحَيِّ الْقَيُّومِ ۖ وَقَدْ خَابَ مَنْ حَمَلَ ظُلْمًا ۝١١١
وَمَن يَعْمَلْ مِنَ الصَّالِحَاتِ وَهُوَ مُؤْمِنٌ فَلَا يَخَافُ ظُلْمًا وَلَا
هَضْمًا ۝١١٢ وَكَذَٰلِكَ أَنزَلْنَاهُ قُرْآنًا عَرَبِيًّا وَصَرَّفْنَا
فِيهِ مِنَ الْوَعِيدِ لَعَلَّهُمْ يَتَّقُونَ أَوْ يُحْدِثُ لَهُمْ ذِكْرًا ۝١١٣

فتعالى الله الملك الحق ولا تعجل بالقرآن من قبل
أن يقضى إليك وحيه وقل رب زدني علما ﴿١١٤﴾ ولقد
عهدنا إلى آدم من قبل فنسي ولم نجد له عزما ﴿١١٥﴾ وإذ
قلنا للملائكة اسجدوا لآدم فسجدوا إلا إبليس أبى ﴿١١٦﴾
فقلنا يا آدم إن هذا عدو لك ولزوجك فلا يخرجنكما
من الجنة فتشقى ﴿١١٧﴾ إن لك ألا تجوع فيها ولا تعرى
﴿١١٨﴾ وأنك لا تظمأ فيها ولا تضحى ﴿١١٩﴾ فوسوس
إليه الشيطان قال يا آدم هل أدلك على شجرة
الخلد وملك لا يبلى ﴿١٢٠﴾ فأكلا منها فبدت لهما
سوآتهما وطفقا يخصفان عليهما من ورق الجنة
وعصى آدم ربه فغوى ﴿١٢١﴾ ثم اجتباه ربه فتاب عليه وهدى
﴿١٢٢﴾ قال اهبطا منها جميعا بعضكم لبعض عدو فإما يأتينكم
مني هدى فمن اتبع هداي فلا يضل ولا يشقى ﴿١٢٣﴾ ومن أعرض
عن ذكري فإن له معيشة ضنكا ونحشره يوم القيامة أعمى
﴿١٢٤﴾ قال رب لم حشرتني أعمى وقد كنت بصيرا ﴿١٢٥﴾

So, EXALTED be God, the 20:114
True King!

Do not be quick to recite the Koran before its revelation is completed, but rather say: 'Lord, increase my knowledge.'

We had made a covenant with Adam, but he forgot, and We found him lacking in steadfastness. And when We said to the angels: 'Prostrate yourselves before Adam,' they all prostrated themselves except Satan, who refused.

'Adam,' We said, 'Satan is an enemy to you and to your wife. Let him not turn you both out of Paradise and plunge you into affliction. Here you shall not hunger or be naked; you shall not thirst, or feel the scorching heat.'

But Satan whispered to him, 20:120
saying: 'Adam, shall I show you the Tree of Immortality and an imperishable
kingdom?'

They both ate from it, so that they saw their shameful parts and began to cover themselves with the leaves of the Garden. Thus did Adam disobey his Lord and stray from the right path.

Then his Lord chose him; He relented towards him and rightly guided him.

'Get you down hence, both, all together,' He said, 'and may you be enemies
to each other. When My guidance is revealed to you, he that follows it shall
neither err nor grieve; but he that forsakes My remembrance shall live in woe
and come before Us blind on the Day of Resurrection. "Lord," he will say, 20:125
"why have You brought me blind before You when I had once been
clear-sighted?"'

20:126 He will say: 'Just as Our
revelations were declared to
you and you forgot them, so
on this day shall you be yourself forgotten.'
Thus shall We reward the
transgressor who denies his
Lord's revelations. But the
scourge of the life to come is
more terrible and more lasting.
Do they not comprehend
how many generations We
have destroyed before them?
They walk amidst the very
ruins wherein once they
dwelt. Surely in this there are
signs for those endowed with
good sense.
But for a Word from your
Lord, long since decreed, their
destruction in this life would
have been certain. Therefore
bear with what they say. Give
glory to your Lord before sunrise and before sunset. Praise Him night and
day, so that you may find comfort.

قال كذلك أتتك آياتنا فنسيتها وكذلك اليوم تنسى ۝
وكذلك نجزي من أسرف ولم يؤمن بآيات ربه ولعذاب الآخرة
أشد وأبقى ۝ أفلم يهد لهم كم أهلكنا قبلهم من القرون
يمشون في مساكنهم إن في ذلك لآيات لأولي النهى ۝ ولولا
كلمة سبقت من ربك لكان لزاما وأجل مسمى ۝ فاصبر على ما
يقولون وسبح بحمد ربك قبل طلوع الشمس وقبل غروبها ومن
آناء الليل فسبح وأطراف النهار لعلك ترضى ۝ ولا تمدن
عينيك إلى ما متعنا به أزواجا منهم زهرة الحيوة الدنيا
لنفتنهم فيه ورزق ربك خير وأبقى ۝ وأمر أهلك بالصلوة
واصطبر عليها لا نسألك رزقا نحن نرزقك والعاقبة
للتقوى ۝ وقالوا لولا يأتينا بآية من ربه أولم تأتهم
بينة ما في الصحف الأولى ۝ ولو أنا أهلكناهم بعذاب
من قبله لقالوا ربنا لولا أرسلت إلينا رسولا فنتبع آياتك
من قبل أن نذل ونخزى ۝ قل كل متربص فتربصوا
فستعلمون من أصحاب الصراط السوي ومن اهتدى ۝

20:131 Do not regard with envy what We have given some among them to enjoy –
the flower of the present life – for with this We seek only to try them. Better
is your Lord's provision, and more lasting.
Enjoin prayer on your people and be diligent in its observance. We
demand of you no provision: We shall Ourself provide for you. Blessed shall
be the end of the devout.
And they say: 'Why does he not bring us a sign from his Lord?' Have they
not been given sufficient proof in previous Scriptures?
Had We destroyed them with a scourge before his[1] coming they would
have said: 'Lord, if only You had sent us an apostle! We would have followed
Your revelations before we were humbled and disgraced.'
20:135 Say: 'All are waiting: so wait if you will. You shall learn who have followed
the even path and who have been rightly guided.'

1. Muḥammad's.

سورة الأنبياء مكية وهي مائة واثنتا عشرة آية

بسم الله الرحمن الرحيم
اقترب للناس حسابهم وهم في غفلة معرضون ١ ما يأتيهم
من ذكر من ربهم محدث إلا استمعوه وهم يلعبون ٢ لاهية
قلوبهم وأسروا النجوى الذين ظلموا هل هذا إلا بشر مثلكم
أفتأتون السحر وأنتم تبصرون ٣ قال ربي يعلم القول في
السماء والأرض وهو السميع العليم ٤ بل قالوا أضغاث
أحلام بل افتراه بل هو شاعر فليأتنا بآية كما أرسل
الأولون ٥ ما آمنت قبلهم من قرية أهلكناها أفهم
يؤمنون ٦ وما أرسلنا قبلك إلا رجالا نوحي إليهم فاسألوا
أهل الذكر إن كنتم لا تعلمون ٧ وما جعلناهم جسدا
لا يأكلون الطعام وما كانوا خالدين ٨ ثم صدقناهم الوعد
فأنجيناهم ومن نشاء وأهلكنا المسرفين ٩ لقد
أنزلنا إليكم كتابا فيه ذكركم أفلا تعقلون ١٠

THE PROPHETS

In the Name of God,
the Merciful, the Compassionate

THE DAY of Reckoning for 21:1
mankind is drawing near, yet
they blithely persist in unbelief.
They listen with ridicule to
each fresh warning that their
Lord gives them: their hearts
are set on pleasure.

In private the wrongdoers
say to each other: 'Is this man
not a mortal like yourselves?
Would you follow witchcraft
with your eyes open?'

Say: 'My Lord has know-
ledge of whatever is said in
heaven and earth. He it is who
hears all and knows all.'

Some say: 'It[1] is but a med- 21:5
ley of dreams.' Others: 'He has invented it himself.' And yet others: 'He is a
poet: let him show us a miracle, as did the apostles in days gone by.'

Communities whom We destroyed before them did not believe either.
Will *they* believe?

The apostles We sent before you were but men whom We inspired. Ask
the People of the Book if you do not know this. The bodies We gave them
could not dispense with food, nor were they immortal. Then We fulfilled for
them Our promise: We delivered them and those We willed, and utterly
destroyed the transgressors.

And now We have revealed a Book for your admonishment. Will you not 21:10
understand?

1. The Koran.

21:11 MANY A sinful city have We
annihilated, and after that replaced by other people. And
when they felt Our might they
took to their heels and ran
away. 'Do not run away; return
to your comforts and to your
habitations: you shall be questioned all.'

'Woe betide us, we have
done wrong!' was their reply.
And this they kept repeating
until We mowed them down
and put out their light.

And it was not in sport that
We created the heaven and the
earth and all that lies between
them. Had it been Our will to
find a diversion, We could have
found one near at hand if such
were Our intent.

21:18 Indeed, We will hurl Truth
at Falsehood, until Truth shall
triumph and Falsehood be no more. Woe betide you, for all the falsehoods
you have uttered.

His are all who dwell in the heavens and on earth. Those who stand in His
presence do not disdain to worship Him, nor are they ever wearied. They
praise Him night and day, tirelessly.

Or have they chosen earthly deities? And can these deities restore the
dead to life? Were there other gods in heaven or earth besides God, both
heaven and earth would be corrupted. Exalted be God, Lord of the Throne,
above their falsehoods!

None shall question Him about His works, but questioned they shall be.
21:24 Or have they chosen other gods besides Him? Say: 'Show us your proof.
Here are the Admonition of today and the Admonition of days gone by.'
But most of them know not the Truth, and this is why they pay no heed.

وكم قصمنا من قرية كانت ظالمة وأنشأنا بعدها قوما آخرين
(١١) فلما أحسوا بأسنا إذا هم منها يركضون (١٢) لا تركضوا
وارجعوا إلى ما أترفتم فيه ومساكنكم لعلكم تسألون (١٣)
قالوا يا ويلنا إنا كنا ظالمين (١٤) فما زالت تلك دعواهم
حتى جعلناهم حصيدا خامدين (١٥) وما خلقنا السماء
والأرض وما بينهما لاعبين (١٦) لو أردنا أن نتخذ لهوا
لاتخذناه من لدنا إن كنا فاعلين (١٧) بل نقذف بالحق على
الباطل فيدمغه فإذا هو زاهق ولكم الويل مما تصفون
(١٨) وله من في السماوات والأرض ومن عنده لا يستكبرون
عن عبادته ولا يستحسرون (١٩) يسبحون الليل والنهار
لا يفترون (٢٠) أم اتخذوا آلهة من الأرض هم ينشرون (٢١)
لو كان فيهما آلهة إلا الله لفسدتا فسبحان الله رب العرش
عما يصفون (٢٢) لا يسأل عما يفعل وهم يسألون (٢٣) أم اتخذوا
من دونه آلهة قل هاتوا برهانكم هذا ذكر من معي وذكر من
قبلي بل أكثرهم لا يعلمون الحق فهم معرضون (٢٤)

وَمَا أَرْسَلْنَا مِن قَبْلِكَ مِن رَسُولٍ إِلَّا نُوحِي إِلَيْهِ أَنَّهُ لَا إِلَٰهَ
إِلَّا أَنَا فَاعْبُدُونِ ۝ وَقَالُوا اتَّخَذَ الرَّحْمَٰنُ وَلَدًا سُبْحَانَهُ بَلْ
عِبَادٌ مُكْرَمُونَ ۝٢٦ لَا يَسْبِقُونَهُ بِالْقَوْلِ وَهُم بِأَمْرِهِ يَعْمَلُونَ
۝٢٧ يَعْلَمُ مَا بَيْنَ أَيْدِيهِمْ وَمَا خَلْفَهُمْ وَلَا يَشْفَعُونَ إِلَّا لِمَنِ
ارْتَضَىٰ وَهُم مِنْ خَشْيَتِهِ مُشْفِقُونَ ۝ وَمَن يَقُلْ مِنْهُمْ إِنِّي إِلَٰهٌ
مِن دُونِهِ فَذَٰلِكَ نَجْزِيهِ جَهَنَّمَ كَذَٰلِكَ نَجْزِي الظَّالِمِينَ
۝٢٩ أَوَلَمْ يَرَ الَّذِينَ كَفَرُوا أَنَّ السَّمَاوَاتِ وَالْأَرْضَ كَانَتَا
رَتْقًا فَفَتَقْنَاهُمَا وَجَعَلْنَا مِنَ الْمَاءِ كُلَّ شَيْءٍ حَيٍّ أَفَلَا يُؤْمِنُونَ
۝٣٠ وَجَعَلْنَا فِي الْأَرْضِ رَوَاسِيَ أَن تَمِيدَ بِهِمْ وَجَعَلْنَا فِيهَا
فِجَاجًا سُبُلًا لَعَلَّهُمْ يَهْتَدُونَ ۝ وَجَعَلْنَا السَّمَاءَ سَقْفًا
مَحْفُوظًا وَهُمْ عَنْ آيَاتِهَا مُعْرِضُونَ ۝٣٢ وَهُوَ الَّذِي خَلَقَ
اللَّيْلَ وَالنَّهَارَ وَالشَّمْسَ وَالْقَمَرَ كُلٌّ فِي فَلَكٍ يَسْبَحُونَ
۝٣٣ وَمَا جَعَلْنَا لِبَشَرٍ مِن قَبْلِكَ الْخُلْدَ أَفَإِن مِتَّ فَهُمُ
الْخَالِدُونَ ۝٣٤ كُلُّ نَفْسٍ ذَائِقَةُ الْمَوْتِ وَنَبْلُوكُم
بِالشَّرِّ وَالْخَيْرِ فِتْنَةً وَإِلَيْنَا تُرْجَعُونَ ۝٣٥

NO APOSTLE have We sent 21:25
before you without inspiring him: 'There is no god but Me. Therefore serve Me.'

And they say: 'The Merciful has begotten children.' God forbid! They are but His honoured servants. They do not speak till He has spoken: they act by His command. He knows what is before them and behind them. They intercede for none save those whom He accepts, and tremble for awe of Him. Whoever of them declares: 'I am a god besides Him,' We shall requite with Hell. Thus shall We requite the wrongdoers.

Are the disbelievers unaware that the heavens and the earth were but one solid mass which We tore asunder, and that We made every living thing from water? Will they not have faith?

We set firm mountains upon the earth lest it should move away with them, 21:31
and hewed out highways in the rock so that they might be rightly guided.

We spread the heaven like a canopy and provided it with strong support: yet of its signs they are heedless.

And He it was who created the night and the day, and the sun and the moon: each moves swiftly in an orbit of its own.

No man before you[1] have We made immortal. If you yourself are doomed to die, will they live on for ever?

Every soul shall taste death. We will test you all with evil and good. And 21:35
to Us shall you be recalled.

1. Muḥammad.

21:36 AND WHEN the unbelievers see you, they only mock
you: 'Is this the one who denies
your gods?' While against the
remembrance of the Merciful
they also blaspheme.

Impatience is the very stuff
man is made of. I shall show
you My signs: do not ask Me to
hurry them on.

And they say: 'When will
this promise be fulfilled, if
what you say be true?'

If only the unbelievers knew
the day when they shall strive
in vain to shield their faces and
their backs from the fire of
Hell; the day when none shall
succour them! Indeed, it will
overtake them unawares and
stupefy them. They shall have
no power to ward it off, nor
shall they be reprieved.

وَإِذَا رَآكَ الَّذِينَ كَفَرُوا إِن يَتَّخِذُونَكَ إِلَّا هُزُوًا
أَهَٰذَا الَّذِي يَذْكُرُ آلِهَتَكُمْ وَهُم بِذِكْرِ الرَّحْمَٰنِ
هُمْ كَافِرُونَ ۝ خُلِقَ الْإِنسَانُ مِنْ عَجَلٍ سَأُرِيكُمْ
آيَاتِي فَلَا تَسْتَعْجِلُونِ ۝٣٧ وَيَقُولُونَ مَتَىٰ هَٰذَا الْوَعْدُ إِن
كُنتُمْ صَادِقِينَ ۝٣٨ لَوْ يَعْلَمُ الَّذِينَ كَفَرُوا حِينَ لَا يَكُفُّونَ
عَن وُجُوهِهِمُ النَّارَ وَلَا عَن ظُهُورِهِمْ وَلَا هُمْ يُنصَرُونَ
۝٣٩ بَلْ تَأْتِيهِم بَغْتَةً فَتَبْهَتُهُمْ فَلَا يَسْتَطِيعُونَ رَدَّهَا
وَلَا هُمْ يُنظَرُونَ ۝٤٠ وَلَقَدِ اسْتُهْزِئَ بِرُسُلٍ مِّن قَبْلِكَ
فَحَاقَ بِالَّذِينَ سَخِرُوا مِنْهُم مَّا كَانُوا بِهِ يَسْتَهْزِئُونَ
۝٤١ قُلْ مَن يَكْلَؤُكُم بِاللَّيْلِ وَالنَّهَارِ مِنَ الرَّحْمَٰنِ
بَلْ هُمْ عَن ذِكْرِ رَبِّهِم مُّعْرِضُونَ ۝٤٢ أَمْ لَهُمْ آلِهَةٌ تَمْنَعُهُم
مِّن دُونِنَا لَا يَسْتَطِيعُونَ نَصْرَ أَنفُسِهِمْ وَلَا هُم مِّنَّا
يُصْحَبُونَ ۝٤٣ بَلْ مَتَّعْنَا هَٰؤُلَاءِ وَآبَاءَهُمْ حَتَّىٰ
طَالَ عَلَيْهِمُ الْعُمُرُ أَفَلَا يَرَوْنَ أَنَّا نَأْتِي الْأَرْضَ
نَنقُصُهَا مِنْ أَطْرَافِهَا أَفَهُمُ الْغَالِبُونَ ۝٤٤

21:41 Other apostles were mocked before you; but those who derided them
were felled by the very scourge they mocked.

Say: 'Who will protect you, by night and by day, from the Lord of Mercy?'
Yet are they unmindful of their Lord's remembrance.

Or have they other gods to defend them? Their idols shall be powerless
over their own salvation, nor shall they be protected from Our scourge.

21:44 Yet have We indulged them and their fathers, so that they have lived too
long. Can they not see how We invade their land and diminish its borders? Is
it they who will triumph?

قل إنما أنذركم بالوحي ولا يسمع الصم الدعاء
إذا ما ينذرون (٤٥) ولئن مستهم نفحة من عذاب ربك
ليقولن يا ويلنا إنا كنا ظالمين (٤٦) ونضع الموازين
القسط ليوم القيامة فلا تظلم نفس شيئا وإن كان
مثقال حبة من خردل أتينا بها وكفى بنا حاسبين (٤٧)
ولقد آتينا موسى وهرون الفرقان وضياء وذكرا
للمتقين (٤٨) الذين يخشون ربهم بالغيب وهم من الساعة
مشفقون (٤٩) وهذا ذكر مبارك أنزلناه أفأنتم له منكرون
(٥٠) ولقد آتينا إبراهيم رشده من قبل وكنا به عالمين (٥١)
إذ قال لأبيه وقومه ما هذه التماثيل التي أنتم لها عاكفون
(٥٢) قالوا وجدنا آباءنا لها عابدين (٥٣) قال لقد كنتم أنتم
وآباؤكم في ضلال مبين (٥٤) قالوا أجئتنا بالحق أم أنت
من اللاعبين (٥٥) قال بل ربكم رب السموات والأرض
الذي فطرهن وأنا على ذلكم من الشاهدين (٥٦) وتالله
لأكيدن أصنامكم بعد أن تولوا مدبرين (٥٧)

SAY: 'I warn you only by 21:45
inspiration.' But the deaf can hear no plea when they are warned.

Yet if the lightest whiff from the vengeance of your Lord touched them, they would surely say: 'Woe betide us: we have done wrong!'

We shall set up just scales for the Day of Resurrection, so that no soul shall in the least be wronged. Actions as small as a grain of mustard seed shall be weighed out. Our reckoning shall suffice.

We bestowed Salvation upon Moses and Aaron, and a light and an Admonition for the righteous: those who fear their Lord, although unseen, and dread the terrors of the Hour.

And this[1] is a blessed Ad- 21:50
monition We have sent down. Will you then reject it?

We formerly bestowed guidance on Abraham, for We knew him well. He said to his father and to his people: 'What are these images to which you are so devoted?'

They said: 'They are the gods our fathers worshipped.'

He said: 'Then you and your fathers have surely been in evident error.'

'Is it the Truth that you are preaching,' they said, 'or is this but a jest?'

'Indeed,' he said, 'your Lord is the Lord of the heavens and the earth. It
was He that made them: to this I bear witness. By the Lord, I will overthrow 21:57
your idols as soon as you have turned your backs.'

1. The Koran.

21:58 So HE broke them all in pieces, except their supreme god, that they might return to him.

'Who has done this to our deities?' said some. 'He must surely be a wrongdoer.'

Others said: 'We have heard a youth called Abraham speak of them.'

They said: 'Then bring him here in sight of all the people, that they may act as witnesses.'

'Abraham,' they said, 'was it you who did this to our deities?'

'No,' he said. 'It was their chief who smote them. Ask *them*, if they can speak.'

Thereupon they turned their thoughts upon themselves and said to each other: 'Surely you are the ones who have done wrong.'

21:65 They were crestfallen: 'You know they cannot speak.'

He said: 'Would you then worship that, instead of God, which can neither help nor harm you? Shame on you and on your idols! Have you no sense?'

They said: 'Burn him and avenge your gods, if you must punish him!'

'Fire,' We said, 'be cool to Abraham and keep him safe.'

They sought to lay a snare for him, but it was they whom We ruined. We delivered him and Lot, and brought them to the land which We had blessed for all mankind.

21:72 We gave him Isaac, and then Jacob for a grandson; and We made each a righteous man.

فجعلهم جذاذا إلا كبيرا لهم لعلهم إليه يرجعون
﴿٥٨﴾ قالوا من فعل هذا بآلهتنا إنه لمن الظالمين ﴿٥٩﴾ قالوا
سمعنا فتى يذكرهم يقال له إبراهيم ﴿٦٠﴾ قالوا
فأتوا به على أعين الناس لعلهم يشهدون ﴿٦١﴾ قالوا
أأنت فعلت هذا بآلهتنا يا إبراهيم ﴿٦٢﴾ قال
بل فعله كبيرهم هذا فاسألوهم إن كانوا ينطقون
﴿٦٣﴾ فرجعوا إلى أنفسهم فقالوا إنكم أنتم الظالمون
﴿٦٤﴾ ثم نكسوا على رءوسهم لقد علمت ما هؤلاء
ينطقون ﴿٦٥﴾ قال أفتعبدون من دون الله ما لا ينفعكم شيئا
ولا يضركم ﴿٦٦﴾ أف لكم ولما تعبدون من دون الله أفلا تعقلون
﴿٦٧﴾ قالوا حرقوه وانصروا آلهتكم إن كنتم فاعلين
﴿٦٨﴾ قلنا يا نار كوني بردا وسلاما على إبراهيم ﴿٦٩﴾ وأرادوا
به كيدا فجعلناهم الأخسرين ﴿٧٠﴾ ونجيناه ولوطا إلى
الأرض التي باركنا فيها للعالمين ﴿٧١﴾ ووهبنا له
إسحاق ويعقوب نافلة وكلا جعلنا صالحين ﴿٧٢﴾

وجعلناهم أئمة يهدون بأمرنا وأوحينا إليهم فعل
الخيرات وإقام الصلوة وإيتاء الزكوة وكانوا لنا
عابدين ۝ ولوطا آتيناه حكما وعلما ونجيناه من القرية
التي كانت تعمل الخبائث إنهم كانوا قوم سوء فاسقين
۝ وأدخلناه في رحمتنا إنه من الصالحين ۝ ونوحا
إذ نادى من قبل فاستجبنا له فنجيناه وأهله من الكرب
العظيم ۝ ونصرناه من القوم الذين كذبوا بآياتنا
إنهم كانوا قوم سوء فأغرقناهم أجمعين ۝ وداود
وسليمن إذ يحكمان في الحرث إذ نفشت فيه
غنم القوم وكنا لحكمهم شاهدين ۝ ففهمناها
سليمن وكلا آتينا حكما وعلما وسخرنا مع داود
الجبال يسبحن والطير وكنا فاعلين ۝ وعلمناه صنعة
لبوس لكم لتحصنكم من بأسكم فهل أنتم شاكرون ۝
ولسليمن الريح عاصفة تجري بأمره إلى الأرض
التي باركنا فيها وكنا بكل شيء عالمين ۝

AND WE ordained them lead- 21:73
ers to give guidance at Our
behest, and enjoined on them
charity, prayer, and almsgiving.
They served none but Ourself.
To Lot We gave wisdom
and knowledge and delivered
him from the city that had
committed deeds of abomination; surely they were men of
iniquity and evil. We admitted
him to Our mercy: he was a
righteous man.
And Noah, who invoked Us
before him; We answered his
prayer, and saved him and all
his kin from the great calamity;
and We delivered him from
those who had denied Our
revelations. Evil were they; We
drowned them all.
And tell of David and 21:78
Solomon: how they passed
judgement regarding the cornfield in which strayed lambs of some people
had grazed by night. We gave Solomon insight into the case and bore witness
to their judgement.
We bestowed on both of them wisdom and knowledge, and caused the
mountains and the birds to join with David in Our praise. All this We did.
We taught him the armourer's craft, so that you might have protection in
your wars. Will you then give thanks?
To Solomon We subjected the raging wind: it sped at his bidding to the 21:81
land which We had blessed. And of all things We had knowledge.

21:82 FROM AMONG the demons
We assigned to him some
who dived for him into the
sea and performed other tasks
besides. We Ourself assured
their preservation.

And tell of Job: how he
called on his Lord, saying: 'I
am sorely afflicted: and of all
those that show mercy You
are the most merciful.'

We answered his prayer
and relieved his affliction. We
restored to him his family and
as many more with them: a
blessing from Ourself and an
Admonition to the devout.

And Ishmael, Idrīs,[1] and
Dhūl-Kifl,[2] who all endured
with patience. To Our mercy
We admitted them, for they
were upright men.

21:87 And of Dhūl-Nūn:[3] how he
went away in anger, thinking We had no power over him. But in the darkness
he cried: 'There is no god but You. Glory be to You! I have done wrong.' We
answered his prayer and delivered him from distress. Thus shall We save the
true believers.

And Zacharias, who invoked his Lord, saying: 'Lord, let me not remain
childless, though of all heirs You are the best.'

21:90 We answered his prayer and gave him John, curing his wife of sterility.
They vied with each other in good works and called on Us with piety, fear,
and awe.

وَمِنَ الشَّيَاطِينِ مَنْ يَغُوصُونَ لَهُ وَيَعْمَلُونَ عَمَلًا
دُونَ ذَٰلِكَ وَكُنَّا لَهُمْ حَافِظِينَ ٨٢ وَأَيُّوبَ إِذْ نَادَىٰ رَبَّهُ
أَنِّي مَسَّنِيَ الضُّرُّ وَأَنْتَ أَرْحَمُ الرَّاحِمِينَ ٨٣ فَاسْتَجَبْنَا لَهُ
فَكَشَفْنَا مَا بِهِ مِنْ ضُرٍّ وَآتَيْنَاهُ أَهْلَهُ وَمِثْلَهُمْ
مَعَهُمْ رَحْمَةً مِنْ عِنْدِنَا وَذِكْرَىٰ لِلْعَابِدِينَ
٨٤ وَإِسْمَاعِيلَ وَإِدْرِيسَ وَذَا الْكِفْلِ كُلٌّ مِنَ
الصَّابِرِينَ ٨٥ وَأَدْخَلْنَاهُمْ فِي رَحْمَتِنَا إِنَّهُمْ مِنَ
الصَّالِحِينَ ٨٦ وَذَا النُّونِ إِذْ ذَهَبَ مُغَاضِبًا فَظَنَّ
أَنْ لَنْ نَقْدِرَ عَلَيْهِ فَنَادَىٰ فِي الظُّلُمَاتِ أَنْ لَا
إِلَٰهَ إِلَّا أَنْتَ سُبْحَانَكَ إِنِّي كُنْتُ مِنَ الظَّالِمِينَ
٨٧ فَاسْتَجَبْنَا لَهُ وَنَجَّيْنَاهُ مِنَ الْغَمِّ وَكَذَٰلِكَ
نُنْجِي الْمُؤْمِنِينَ ٨٨ وَزَكَرِيَّا إِذْ نَادَىٰ رَبَّهُ
رَبِّ لَا تَذَرْنِي فَرْدًا وَأَنْتَ خَيْرُ الْوَارِثِينَ ٨٩ فَاسْتَجَبْنَا لَهُ
وَوَهَبْنَا لَهُ يَحْيَىٰ وَأَصْلَحْنَا لَهُ زَوْجَهُ إِنَّهُمْ كَانُوا يُسَارِعُونَ
فِي الْخَيْرَاتِ وَيَدْعُونَنَا رَغَبًا وَرَهَبًا وَكَانُوا لَنَا خَاشِعِينَ ○

1. Enoch.
2. Ezekiel; his tomb is in the town of Kifl in southern Iraq, and is revered by both Jews and Muslims.
3. Jonah.

وَالَّتِي أَحْصَنَتْ فَرْجَهَا فَنَفَخْنَا فِيهَا مِن رُّوحِنَا وَجَعَلْنَاهَا
وَابْنَهَا آيَةً لِّلْعَالَمِينَ ﴿٩١﴾ إِنَّ هَٰذِهِ أُمَّتُكُمْ أُمَّةً
وَاحِدَةً وَأَنَا رَبُّكُمْ فَاعْبُدُونِ ﴿٩٢﴾ وَتَقَطَّعُوا أَمْرَهُم
بَيْنَهُمْ كُلٌّ إِلَيْنَا رَاجِعُونَ ﴿٩٣﴾ فَمَن يَعْمَلْ مِنَ
الصَّالِحَاتِ وَهُوَ مُؤْمِنٌ فَلَا كُفْرَانَ لِسَعْيِهِ وَإِنَّا لَهُ
كَاتِبُونَ ﴿٩٤﴾ وَحَرَامٌ عَلَىٰ قَرْيَةٍ أَهْلَكْنَاهَا
أَنَّهُمْ لَا يَرْجِعُونَ ﴿٩٥﴾ حَتَّىٰ إِذَا فُتِحَتْ يَأْجُوجُ
وَمَأْجُوجُ وَهُم مِّن كُلِّ حَدَبٍ يَنسِلُونَ ﴿٩٦﴾
وَاقْتَرَبَ الْوَعْدُ الْحَقُّ فَإِذَا هِيَ شَاخِصَةٌ أَبْصَارُ
الَّذِينَ كَفَرُوا يَا وَيْلَنَا قَدْ كُنَّا فِي غَفْلَةٍ مِّنْ
هَٰذَا بَلْ كُنَّا ظَالِمِينَ ﴿٩٧﴾ إِنَّكُمْ وَمَا تَعْبُدُونَ
مِن دُونِ اللَّهِ حَصَبُ جَهَنَّمَ أَنتُمْ لَهَا وَارِدُونَ ﴿٩٨﴾ لَوْ
كَانَ هَٰؤُلَاءِ آلِهَةً مَّا وَرَدُوهَا وَكُلٌّ فِيهَا خَالِدُونَ ﴿٩٩﴾
لَهُمْ فِيهَا زَفِيرٌ وَهُمْ فِيهَا لَا يَسْمَعُونَ ﴿١٠٠﴾ إِنَّ الَّذِينَ
سَبَقَتْ لَهُم مِّنَّا الْحُسْنَىٰ أُولَٰئِكَ عَنْهَا مُبْعَدُونَ ﴿١٠١﴾

AND THE woman who 21:91
kept her chastity; We breathed into her Our spirit, and made her and her son a sign to all mankind.

Your community is but one community, and I am your only Lord. Therefore serve Me. They have divided themselves into factions, but to Us shall they all return. He that does good works in the fullness of his faith, his endeavours shall not be lost: We record them all.

It is ordained that no
community We have destroyed
shall ever rise again. But when 21:96
Gog and Magog are let loose and rush headlong down every hill; when the true promise nears its fulfilment; the unbelievers' eyes shall stare in amazement: 'Woe betide us! Of this we have been heedless. We have assuredly done wrong.'

You and your idols shall be the fuel of Hell; therein shall you all go down. Were they true gods, they would not go there: but therein shall they abide for ever. They shall groan with anguish and be bereft of hearing.

But those to whom We have long since shown Our bounty shall be far 21:101
removed from Hell.

21:102 THEY SHALL not hear its hissing, but shall delight for ever in what their souls desire.

The Supreme Terror shall not grieve them, and the angels will receive them, saying: 'This is the day you have been promised.'

On that day We shall roll up the heaven like a scroll of parchment. Just as We brought the First Creation into being, so will We restore it. This is a promise We shall assuredly fulfil.

We wrote in the Psalms[1] after the Torah was revealed: 'The righteous among My servants shall inherit the earth.'
21:106 That is an Admonition to those who serve Us.

We have sent you forth but as a blessing to mankind. Say: 'It is revealed to me that your God is one God. Will you then be Muslims?'

If they pay no heed, say: 'I have warned you all alike, though I cannot tell whether the scourge you are promised is imminent or far off. He knows your spoken words and knows your hidden thoughts. And for all I know, this may be a test for you and a short reprieve.'

21:112 Say: 'Lord, judge with fairness. Our Lord is the Merciful, whose help We seek against your blasphemies.'

لا يسمعون حسيسها وهم في ما اشتهت أنفسهم
خالدون ﴿١٠٢﴾ لا يحزنهم الفزع الأكبر وتتلقاهم
الملائكة هذا يومكم الذي كنتم توعدون ﴿١٠٣﴾ يوم
نطوي السماء كطي السجل للكتب كما بدأنا أول خلق
نعيده وعدا علينا إنا كنا فاعلين ﴿١٠٤﴾ ولقد كتبنا
في الزبور من بعد الذكر أن الأرض يرثها عبادي
الصالحون ﴿١٠٥﴾ إن في هذا لبلاغا لقوم عابدين ﴿١٠٦﴾
وما أرسلناك إلا رحمة للعالمين ﴿١٠٧﴾ قل إنما يوحى إلي
أنما إلهكم إله واحد فهل أنتم مسلمون ﴿١٠٨﴾ فإن تولوا فقل
آذنتكم على سواء وإن أدري أقريب أم بعيد ما توعدون ﴿١٠٩﴾
إنه يعلم الجهر من القول ويعلم ما تكتمون ﴿١١٠﴾ وإن أدري
لعله فتنة لكم ومتاع إلى حين ﴿١١١﴾ قال رب احكم
بالحق وربنا الرحمن المستعان على ما تصفون ﴿١١٢﴾

سورة الحج مدنية وهي ثمان وسبعون آية

1. Psalm 37:29.

بسم الله الرحمن الرحيم
يا أيها الناس اتقوا ربكم إن زلزلة الساعة شيء عظيم
(١) يوم ترونها تذهل كل مرضعة عما أرضعت
وتضع كل ذات حمل حملها وترى الناس سكارى
وما هم بسكارى ولكن عذاب الله شديد (٢) ومن
الناس من يجادل في الله بغير علم ويتبع كل شيطان
مريد (٣) كتب عليه أنه من تولاه فأنه يضله ويهديه
إلى عذاب السعير (٤) يا أيها الناس إن كنتم في ريب من
البعث فإنا خلقناكم من تراب ثم من نطفة ثم من علقة
ثم من مضغة مخلقة وغير مخلقة لنبين لكم ونقر في
الأرحام ما نشاء إلى أجل مسمى ثم نخرجكم طفلا
ثم لتبلغوا أشدكم ومنكم من يتوفى ومنكم من
يرد إلى أرذل العمر لكيلا يعلم من بعد علم شيئا
وترى الأرض هامدة فإذا أنزلنا عليها الماء
اهتزت وربت وأنبتت من كل زوج بهيج (٥)

THE PILGRIMAGE

In the Name of God,
the Merciful, the Compassionate

YOU PEOPLE! Have fear of 22:1
your Lord. The catastrophe
of the Hour shall be terrible
indeed.

The day you witness it, every
suckling mother shall forsake
her infant, every pregnant
female shall cast her burden,
and you shall see people reel-
ing like drunkards although
not drunk: but such shall be
the horror of God's torment.

Yet there are some who in 22:3
their ignorance dispute about
God, and follow every rebelli-
ous demon doomed to seduce his follower and lead him to the scourge of
the Conflagration.

You people! If you doubt the Resurrection remember that We had created 22:5
you from dust, then from a living germ, then from a clot of blood,[1] and then
from a half-formed lump of flesh, so that We might manifest to you Our
power.

We cause to remain in the wombs whatever We please for an appointed term, and then We bring you forth as infants, that you may grow up and reach your prime. Some among you die young, and some live on to abject old age when all that they once knew they know no more.

You sometimes see the earth dry and barren: but no sooner do We send the water down upon it than it begins to stir and swell, putting forth every kind of radiant bloom.

1. *Alaq* can also mean a leech or a little worm.

22:6 THAT IS because God is Truth: He resurrects the dead and has power over all things.

The Hour is sure to come – of this there is no doubt. And those who are in their graves God will raise to life.

Some wrangle about God, though they have neither knowledge nor guidance nor illuminating scripture. They turn away in scorn, to lead others astray from God's path: they shall incur disgrace in this life, and on the Day of Resurrection taste the torment of the Conflagration. 'This is the reward of your handiwork. God is never unjust to His servants.'

22:11 And among people there are some who profess to serve God and yet stand on the very fringe of the true faith. When blessed with good fortune they are content, but when an ordeal befalls them they turn upon their heels, forfeiting this life and the Hereafter. That way true perdition lies.

They call on idols which can neither harm nor help them. That is the extreme error.

They call on that which would sooner harm than help them: an evil master and an evil friend.

As for those that have faith and do good works, God will admit them to Gardens watered by running brooks. God's will is ever done.

22:15 If anyone thinks that God will not aid him in this world and in the world to come, let him stretch up a rope to the sky and hang himself. Then let him ponder if his cunning has done away with that which has enraged him.

ذَٰلِكَ بِأَنَّ اللَّهَ هُوَ الْحَقُّ وَأَنَّهُ يُحْيِي الْمَوْتَىٰ وَأَنَّهُ عَلَىٰ كُلِّ شَيْءٍ
قَدِيرٌ ٦ وَأَنَّ السَّاعَةَ آتِيَةٌ لَّا رَيْبَ فِيهَا وَأَنَّ اللَّهَ يَبْعَثُ مَن فِي
الْقُبُورِ ٧ وَمِنَ النَّاسِ مَن يُجَادِلُ فِي اللَّهِ بِغَيْرِ عِلْمٍ وَلَا هُدًى
وَلَا كِتَابٍ مُّنِيرٍ ٨ ثَانِيَ عِطْفِهِ لِيُضِلَّ عَن سَبِيلِ اللَّهِ لَهُ فِي الدُّنْيَا
خِزْيٌ وَنُذِيقُهُ يَوْمَ الْقِيَامَةِ عَذَابَ الْحَرِيقِ ٩ ذَٰلِكَ بِمَا قَدَّمَتْ
يَدَاكَ وَأَنَّ اللَّهَ لَيْسَ بِظَلَّامٍ لِّلْعَبِيدِ ١٠ وَمِنَ النَّاسِ
مَن يَعْبُدُ اللَّهَ عَلَىٰ حَرْفٍ فَإِنْ أَصَابَهُ خَيْرٌ اطْمَأَنَّ بِهِ وَإِنْ
أَصَابَتْهُ فِتْنَةٌ انقَلَبَ عَلَىٰ وَجْهِهِ خَسِرَ الدُّنْيَا وَالْآخِرَةَ ذَٰلِكَ
هُوَ الْخُسْرَانُ الْمُبِينُ ١١ يَدْعُو مِن دُونِ اللَّهِ مَا لَا يَضُرُّهُ وَمَا
لَا يَنفَعُهُ ذَٰلِكَ هُوَ الضَّلَالُ الْبَعِيدُ ١٢ يَدْعُو لَمَن ضَرُّهُ أَقْرَبُ
مِن نَّفْعِهِ لَبِئْسَ الْمَوْلَىٰ وَلَبِئْسَ الْعَشِيرُ ١٣ إِنَّ اللَّهَ يُدْخِلُ الَّذِينَ
آمَنُوا وَعَمِلُوا الصَّالِحَاتِ جَنَّاتٍ تَجْرِي مِن تَحْتِهَا
الْأَنْهَارُ إِنَّ اللَّهَ يَفْعَلُ مَا يُرِيدُ ١٤ مَن كَانَ يَظُنُّ أَن
لَّن يَنصُرَهُ اللَّهُ فِي الدُّنْيَا وَالْآخِرَةِ فَلْيَمْدُدْ بِسَبَبٍ إِلَى السَّمَاءِ
ثُمَّ لْيَقْطَعْ فَلْيَنظُرْ هَلْ يُذْهِبَنَّ كَيْدُهُ مَا يَغِيظُ ١٥

وكذلك أنزلناه آيات بينات وأن الله يهدي من يريد ١٦
إن الذين آمنوا والذين هادوا والصابئين والنصارى
والمجوس والذين أشركوا إن الله يفصل بينهم يوم القيامة
إن الله على كل شيء شهيد ١٧ ألم تر أن الله يسجد له من في
السماوات ومن في الأرض والشمس والقمر والنجوم
والجبال والشجر والدواب وكثير من الناس
وكثير حق عليه العذاب ومن يهن الله فما له من مكرم
إن الله يفعل ما يشاء ١٨ هذان خصمان اختصموا
في ربهم فالذين كفروا قطعت لهم ثياب من نار يصب
من فوق رءوسهم الحميم ١٩ يصهر به ما في بطونهم
والجلود ٢٠ ولهم مقامع من حديد ٢١ كلما أرادوا أن
يخرجوا منها من غم أعيدوا فيها وذوقوا عذاب الحريق ٢٢
إن الله يدخل الذين آمنوا وعملوا الصالحات جنات
تجري من تحتها الأنهار يحلون فيها من أساور
من ذهب ولؤلؤا ولباسهم فيها حرير ٢٣

AND THUS have We sent it 22:16
down in clear revelations: God gives guidance to whom He will.

The true believers, those who follow the Jewish Faith, the Sabaeans, the Christians, the Magians, and the pagans, God will surely judge on the Day of Resurrection. Surely God is witness of all things.

Do you not see that those in the heavens and on the earth, and the sun and the moon and the stars, the mountains and the trees, the beasts, and countless people – all do homage to God? Yet many have deserved the scourge. He who is humbled by God has none to honour him: God's will is ever done.

Here are two antagonists 22:19
who contend about their Lord. Garments of fire have been prepared for the unbelievers. Scalding water shall be poured upon their heads, melting their skins and that which is in their bellies. They shall be lashed with rods of iron.

Whenever, in their anguish, they strive to escape from it, back shall they be dragged, and: 'Taste you the torment of the Conflagration!'

As for those that have faith and do good works, God will admit them to 22:23
Gardens watered by running brooks. They shall be adorned with bracelets of gold and pearls, and arrayed therein in garments of silk.

22:24 FOR THEY have been guided
to the noblest of words; they
have been guided to the path
of Him who is worthy of
praise.
The unbelievers who debar
others from the path of God
and from the Sacred Mosque
which We provided for the
people, natives and strangers
alike, and those who seek to
violate it sinfully – We shall
make them taste a grievous
torment.
When We prepared for
Abraham the site of the Sacred
Mosque We said: 'Worship
none besides Me. Keep My
House clean for those who
walk around it, and those who
stand upright, or kneel down
in worship.'
22:27 Exhort all people to make
the Pilgrimage. They will come to you on foot and on the backs of swift
camels from every distant quarter; they will come to avail themselves of
many a benefit, and to pronounce on the appointed days the name of God
over the cattle which He has given them for food. Eat of their flesh, and feed
the poor and the unfortunate.
Then let the pilgrims tidy themselves, make their vows, and circle the
22:30 Ancient House. Such is God's commandment. He that reveres the sacred
rites of God shall fare better in the sight of his Lord.
The flesh of cattle is lawful for you, except for that which has been specified before. Guard yourselves against the abomination of idols; and avoid
the utterance of falsehood.

وَهُدُوٓا إِلَى ٱلطَّيِّبِ مِنَ ٱلْقَوْلِ وَهُدُوٓا إِلَىٰ صِرَٰطِ ٱلْحَمِيدِ
٢٤ إِنَّ ٱلَّذِينَ كَفَرُوا وَيَصُدُّونَ عَن سَبِيلِ ٱللَّهِ وَٱلْمَسْجِدِ
ٱلْحَرَامِ ٱلَّذِى جَعَلْنَٰهُ لِلنَّاسِ سَوَآءً ٱلْعَٰكِفُ فِيهِ
وَٱلْبَادِ وَمَن يُرِدْ فِيهِ بِإِلْحَادٍ بِظُلْمٍ نُّذِقْهُ مِنْ عَذَابٍ
أَلِيمٍ ٢٥ وَإِذْ بَوَّأْنَا لِإِبْرَٰهِيمَ مَكَانَ ٱلْبَيْتِ أَن لَّا تُشْرِكْ
بِى شَيْـًٔا وَطَهِّرْ بَيْتِىَ لِلطَّآئِفِينَ وَٱلْقَآئِمِينَ وَٱلرُّكَّعِ
ٱلسُّجُودِ ٢٦ وَأَذِّن فِى ٱلنَّاسِ بِٱلْحَجِّ يَأْتُوكَ رِجَالًا
وَعَلَىٰ كُلِّ ضَامِرٍ يَأْتِينَ مِن كُلِّ فَجٍّ عَمِيقٍ ٢٧
لِّيَشْهَدُوا مَنَٰفِعَ لَهُمْ وَيَذْكُرُوا ٱسْمَ ٱللَّهِ فِىٓ أَيَّامٍ
مَّعْلُومَٰتٍ عَلَىٰ مَا رَزَقَهُم مِّنۢ بَهِيمَةِ ٱلْأَنْعَٰمِ فَكُلُوا
مِنْهَا وَأَطْعِمُوا ٱلْبَآئِسَ ٱلْفَقِيرَ ٢٨ ثُمَّ لْيَقْضُوا
تَفَثَهُمْ وَلْيُوفُوا نُذُورَهُمْ وَلْيَطَّوَّفُوا بِٱلْبَيْتِ
ٱلْعَتِيقِ ٢٩ ذَٰلِكَ وَمَن يُعَظِّمْ حُرُمَٰتِ ٱللَّهِ فَهُوَ خَيْرٌ
لَّهُۥ عِندَ رَبِّهِۦ وَأُحِلَّتْ لَكُمُ ٱلْأَنْعَٰمُ إِلَّا مَا يُتْلَىٰ عَلَيْكُمْ
فَٱجْتَنِبُوا ٱلرِّجْسَ مِنَ ٱلْأَوْثَٰنِ وَٱجْتَنِبُوا قَوْلَ ٱلزُّورِ ٣٠

حنفاء لله غير مشركين به ومن يشرك بالله فكأنما
خر من السماء فتخطفه الطير أو تهوي به الريح في
مكان سحيق ﴿٣١﴾ ذلك ومن يعظم شعائر الله فإنها
من تقوى القلوب ﴿٣٢﴾ لكم فيها منافع إلى أجل مسمى ثم محلها
إلى البيت العتيق ﴿٣٣﴾ ولكل أمة جعلنا منسكا ليذكروا
اسم الله على ما رزقهم من بهيمة الأنعام فإلهكم إله واحد
فله أسلموا وبشر المخبتين ﴿٣٤﴾ الذين إذا ذكر الله وجلت
قلوبهم والصابرين على ما أصابهم والمقيمي الصلوة ومما
رزقناهم ينفقون ﴿٣٥﴾ والبدن جعلناها لكم من شعائر الله لكم
فيها خير فاذكروا اسم الله عليها صواف فإذا وجبت
جنوبها فكلوا منها وأطعموا القانع والمعتر كذلك
سخرناها لكم لعلكم تشكرون ﴿٣٦﴾ لن ينال الله لحومها
ولا دماؤها ولكن يناله التقوى منكم كذلك سخرها لكم
لتكبروا الله على ما هدىكم وبشر المحسنين ﴿٣٧﴾ إن الله يدافع
عن الذين آمنوا إن الله لا يحب كل خوان كفور ﴿٣٨﴾

DEDICATED TO God, and 22:31
serving none besides Him:
he that serves other deities
besides God is like him who
falls from heaven and is
snatched off by the birds or
carried away by the wind to
some far-off region. Even such
is he.

He that reveres the offerings
made to God shows the piety
of his heart. They are beneficial to you until a time decreed,
then their place of sacrifice is
by the Ancient House.

For every community We
have ordained a ritual, that
they may pronounce the name
of God over the cattle which
He has given them for food.
Your God is one God: to Him
submit. Give joyful tidings to
the humble, whose hearts are
filled with awe at the mention of God; who endure adversity with fortitude,
attend to their prayers, and give from what We gave them.

And the camels We have made a part of God's rites. They are of much use 22:36
to you. Pronounce over them the name of God as you draw them up in line
for slaughter; and when they have fallen to the ground eat of their flesh and
feed the uncomplaining beggar and the demanding supplicant. Thus have
We subjected them to your service, so that you may give thanks.

Their flesh and blood does not reach God; it is your piety that reaches
Him. Thus has He subjected them to your service, so that you may give glory
to God for guiding you.

Give joyful tidings to the righteous. God will ward off evil from true 22:38
believers; God does not love the treacherous and the thankless.

22:39 PERMISSION TO take up arms is hereby given to those who are attacked, because they have been wronged. Surely God has power to grant them victory: those who have been unjustly driven from their homes, only because they said: 'Our Lord is God.' Had God not defended some by the might of others, monasteries and churches, synagogues and mosques in which His praise is daily celebrated, would have been utterly destroyed. But whoever helps God shall surely be helped by Him: God is powerful and mighty: those who, if We make them masters in the land, will attend to their prayers and render the alms levy, enjoin justice and forbid the reprehensible. God governs the destiny of all things.

22:42 If they disbelieve you, before them the people of Noah, 'Ād and Thamūd, the people of Abraham and the people of Lot, and the dwellers of Midian had also disbelieved: Moses was likewise disbelieved. I bore long with the unbelievers, and then I smote them. How awesome was the way I smote them!

How many cities, teeming with sin, have We laid waste! They lie in desolate ruin, their wells abandoned and their proud palaces empty.

22:46 Have they never journeyed through the land? Have they no hearts to reason with, or ears to hear with? It is their hearts, and not their eyes, that are blind.

أُذِنَ لِلَّذِينَ يُقَاتَلُونَ بِأَنَّهُمْ ظُلِمُوا ۚ وَإِنَّ اللَّهَ عَلَىٰ نَصْرِهِمْ
لَقَدِيرٌ ﴿٣٩﴾ الَّذِينَ أُخْرِجُوا مِنْ دِيَارِهِمْ بِغَيْرِ حَقٍّ إِلَّا أَنْ يَقُولُوا
رَبُّنَا اللَّهُ ۗ وَلَوْلَا دَفْعُ اللَّهِ النَّاسَ بَعْضَهُمْ بِبَعْضٍ
لَهُدِّمَتْ صَوَامِعُ وَبِيَعٌ وَصَلَوَاتٌ وَمَسَاجِدُ يُذْكَرُ فِيهَا
اسْمُ اللَّهِ كَثِيرًا ۗ وَلَيَنْصُرَنَّ اللَّهُ مَنْ يَنْصُرُهُ ۗ إِنَّ اللَّهَ لَقَوِيٌّ عَزِيزٌ
﴿٤٠﴾ الَّذِينَ إِنْ مَكَّنَّاهُمْ فِي الْأَرْضِ أَقَامُوا الصَّلَاةَ وَآتَوُا
الزَّكَاةَ وَأَمَرُوا بِالْمَعْرُوفِ وَنَهَوْا عَنِ الْمُنْكَرِ ۗ وَلِلَّهِ عَاقِبَةُ
الْأُمُورِ ﴿٤١﴾ وَإِنْ يُكَذِّبُوكَ فَقَدْ كَذَّبَتْ قَبْلَهُمْ قَوْمُ
نُوحٍ وَعَادٌ وَثَمُودُ ﴿٤٢﴾ وَقَوْمُ إِبْرَاهِيمَ وَقَوْمُ لُوطٍ ﴿٤٣﴾ وَأَصْحَابُ
مَدْيَنَ ۖ وَكُذِّبَ مُوسَىٰ فَأَمْلَيْتُ لِلْكَافِرِينَ ثُمَّ أَخَذْتُهُمْ ۖ
فَكَيْفَ كَانَ نَكِيرِ ﴿٤٤﴾ فَكَأَيِّنْ مِنْ قَرْيَةٍ أَهْلَكْنَاهَا
وَهِيَ ظَالِمَةٌ فَهِيَ خَاوِيَةٌ عَلَىٰ عُرُوشِهَا وَبِئْرٍ مُعَطَّلَةٍ
وَقَصْرٍ مَشِيدٍ ﴿٤٥﴾ أَفَلَمْ يَسِيرُوا فِي الْأَرْضِ فَتَكُونَ لَهُمْ
قُلُوبٌ يَعْقِلُونَ بِهَا أَوْ آذَانٌ يَسْمَعُونَ بِهَا ۖ فَإِنَّهَا لَا تَعْمَى
الْأَبْصَارُ وَلَٰكِنْ تَعْمَى الْقُلُوبُ الَّتِي فِي الصُّدُورِ ﴿٤٦﴾

وَيَسْتَعْجِلُونَكَ بِالْعَذَابِ وَلَن يُخْلِفَ اللَّهُ وَعْدَهُ وَإِنَّ يَوْمًا عِندَ
رَبِّكَ كَأَلْفِ سَنَةٍ مِّمَّا تَعُدُّونَ ﴿٤٧﴾ وَكَأَيِّن مِّن قَرْيَةٍ
أَمْلَيْتُ لَهَا وَهِيَ ظَالِمَةٌ ثُمَّ أَخَذْتُهَا وَإِلَيَّ الْمَصِيرُ ﴿٤٨﴾ قُلْ
يَا أَيُّهَا النَّاسُ إِنَّمَا أَنَا لَكُمْ نَذِيرٌ مُّبِينٌ ﴿٤٩﴾ فَالَّذِينَ آمَنُوا
وَعَمِلُوا الصَّالِحَاتِ لَهُم مَّغْفِرَةٌ وَرِزْقٌ كَرِيمٌ ﴿٥٠﴾ وَالَّذِينَ
سَعَوْا فِي آيَاتِنَا مُعَاجِزِينَ أُولَٰئِكَ أَصْحَابُ الْجَحِيمِ ﴿٥١﴾ وَمَا
أَرْسَلْنَا مِن قَبْلِكَ مِن رَّسُولٍ وَلَا نَبِيٍّ إِلَّا إِذَا تَمَنَّىٰ أَلْقَى
الشَّيْطَانُ فِي أُمْنِيَّتِهِ فَيَنسَخُ اللَّهُ مَا يُلْقِي الشَّيْطَانُ
ثُمَّ يُحْكِمُ اللَّهُ آيَاتِهِ وَاللَّهُ عَلِيمٌ حَكِيمٌ ﴿٥٢﴾ لِّيَجْعَلَ
مَا يُلْقِي الشَّيْطَانُ فِتْنَةً لِّلَّذِينَ فِي قُلُوبِهِم مَّرَضٌ وَالْقَاسِيَةِ
قُلُوبُهُمْ وَإِنَّ الظَّالِمِينَ لَفِي شِقَاقٍ بَعِيدٍ ﴿٥٣﴾ وَلِيَعْلَمَ
الَّذِينَ أُوتُوا الْعِلْمَ أَنَّهُ الْحَقُّ مِن رَّبِّكَ فَيُؤْمِنُوا بِهِ فَتُخْبِتَ لَهُ
قُلُوبُهُمْ وَإِنَّ اللَّهَ لَهَادِ الَّذِينَ آمَنُوا إِلَىٰ صِرَاطٍ مُّسْتَقِيمٍ
﴿٥٤﴾ وَلَا يَزَالُ الَّذِينَ كَفَرُوا فِي مِرْيَةٍ مِّنْهُ حَتَّىٰ تَأْتِيَهُمُ
السَّاعَةُ بَغْتَةً أَوْ يَأْتِيَهُمْ عَذَابُ يَوْمٍ عَقِيمٍ ﴿٥٥﴾

THEY BID you hasten the 22:47
scourge. And God will never
fail His promise. Each day of
your Lord's is like a thousand
years in your reckoning.[1]

I bore long with many cities, teeming though they were with sin, and in the end I smote them. To Me shall all return.

Say: 'You people, I have been sent to warn you plainly. Those that accept the true faith and do good works shall be forgiven and richly provided for; and those that seek to confute Our revelations shall be the tenants of Hell.'

Never have We sent a single 22:52
prophet or apostle before you
with whose wishes Satan did
not tamper. But God abrogates the interjections of Satan and God confirms His own revelations. God is all-knowing and wise. He makes Satan's interjections a temptation for those whose hearts are tainted, whose hearts are hardened – this is why the wrongdoers are in open schism – so that those who are endowed with knowledge may realize that this[2] is the Truth from your Lord and thus believe in it and humble their hearts towards Him. God will surely guide the faithful to a straight path.

Yet will the unbelievers never cease to doubt it, until the Hour overtakes 22:55
them unawares, or the scourge of a baleful day descends upon them.

1. Cf. Psalm 90:4. 2. The Koran.

22:56 ON THAT day God will reign supreme; He will judge them all. Those that believed and did good works shall enter the Gardens of Delight; but the unbelievers who have denied Our revelations shall receive an ignominious punishment.

And for those that have left their land in the cause of God and then died or were slain, God will surely make a generous provision: God is the most munificent Provider. He will surely admit them with a welcome that will please them. Omniscient is God, and gracious.

22:60 Thus shall it be. He that repays an injury in kind and then is wronged again shall be helped by God. God is merciful and forgiving.

Thus shall it be. God causes the night to pass into day, and the day to pass into night. God hears all and observes all.

Thus shall it be. God is Truth, and Falsehood all that they invoke besides Him. God alone is the Most High, the Supreme One.

Do you not see how God sends down water from the sky and forthwith the earth turns green? Gracious is God and all-knowing.

22:64 His is all that the heavens and the earth contain. Surely God is the Self-sufficient, the Praiseworthy One.

الْمُلْكُ يَوْمَئِذٍ لِلَّهِ يَحْكُمُ بَيْنَهُمْ فَالَّذِينَ آمَنُوا وَعَمِلُوا
الصَّالِحَاتِ فِي جَنَّاتِ النَّعِيمِ ٥٦ وَالَّذِينَ كَفَرُوا وَكَذَّبُوا
بِآيَاتِنَا فَأُولَٰئِكَ لَهُمْ عَذَابٌ مُهِينٌ ٥٧ وَالَّذِينَ هَاجَرُوا
فِي سَبِيلِ اللَّهِ ثُمَّ قُتِلُوا أَوْ مَاتُوا لَيَرْزُقَنَّهُمُ اللَّهُ
رِزْقًا حَسَنًا وَإِنَّ اللَّهَ لَهُوَ خَيْرُ الرَّازِقِينَ ٥٨ لَيُدْخِلَنَّهُمْ
مُدْخَلًا يَرْضَوْنَهُ وَإِنَّ اللَّهَ لَعَلِيمٌ حَلِيمٌ ٥٩ ذَٰلِكَ
وَمَنْ عَاقَبَ بِمِثْلِ مَا عُوقِبَ بِهِ ثُمَّ بُغِيَ عَلَيْهِ
لَيَنْصُرَنَّهُ اللَّهُ إِنَّ اللَّهَ لَعَفُوٌّ غَفُورٌ ٦٠
ذَٰلِكَ بِأَنَّ اللَّهَ يُولِجُ اللَّيْلَ فِي النَّهَارِ وَيُولِجُ النَّهَارَ
فِي اللَّيْلِ وَأَنَّ اللَّهَ سَمِيعٌ بَصِيرٌ ٦١ ذَٰلِكَ بِأَنَّ اللَّهَ
هُوَ الْحَقُّ وَأَنَّ مَا يَدْعُونَ مِنْ دُونِهِ هُوَ
الْبَاطِلُ وَأَنَّ اللَّهَ هُوَ الْعَلِيُّ الْكَبِيرُ ٦٢
أَلَمْ تَرَ أَنَّ اللَّهَ أَنْزَلَ مِنَ السَّمَاءِ مَاءً فَتُصْبِحُ الْأَرْضُ
مُخْضَرَّةً إِنَّ اللَّهَ لَطِيفٌ خَبِيرٌ ٦٣ لَهُ مَا فِي السَّمَاوَاتِ وَمَا
فِي الْأَرْضِ وَإِنَّ اللَّهَ لَهُوَ الْغَنِيُّ الْحَمِيدُ ٦٤

الم تر ان الله سخر لكم ما في الارض والفلك تجري
في البحر بامره ويمسك السماء ان تقع على الارض
الا باذنه ان الله بالناس لرءوف رحيم ٦٥ وهو الذي احياكم
ثم يميتكم ثم يحييكم ان الانسان لكفور ٦٦ لكل
امة جعلنا منسكا هم ناسكوه فلا ينازعنك في الامر
وادع الى ربك انك لعلى هدى مستقيم ٦٧ وان جادلوك
فقل الله اعلم بما تعملون ٦٨ الله يحكم
بينكم يوم القيمة فيما كنتم فيه تختلفون ٦٩
الم تعلم ان الله يعلم ما في السماء والارض ان ذلك في كتاب
ان ذلك على الله يسير ٧٠ ويعبدون من دون الله ما لم
ينزل به سلطانا وما ليس لهم به علم وما للظالمين من
نصير ٧١ واذا تتلى عليهم اياتنا بينات تعرف في وجوه
الذين كفروا المنكر يكادون يسطون بالذين يتلون
عليهم اياتنا قل افانبئكم بشر من ذلكم النار
وعدها الله الذين كفروا وبئس المصير ٧٢

Do you not see that God 22:65
has subdued for you all that is in
the earth? And the ships which
sail the sea at His bidding? He
holds the sky from falling down
upon the earth: this it shall not
do except by His own leave.
Kindly is God, and compassionate to mankind.

It is He who has given you
life, and He who will cause you
to die and make you live again.
Surely man is ungrateful.

For every community We
have ordained a ritual which
they observe. Let them not
dispute with you concerning
this. Call them to the path of
your Lord: you are rightly
guided. If they argue with you,
say: 'God knows best all that
you do. On the Day of Resurrection God will judge your
differences.'

Are you not aware that God has knowledge of what heaven and earth 22:70
contain? All is recorded in a Book. That is easy enough for God.

Yet they worship besides God that for which no sanction is revealed and
of which they know nothing. The wrongdoers shall have none to help them.

And when Our revelations are recited to them in all their clarity, you will 22:72
note denial in the faces of the unbelievers. Barely can they restrain themselves from assaulting those who recite Our revelations.

Say: 'Shall I tell you what is worse than that? The Fire which God has
promised those who deny Him. A wretched fate!'

يا أيها الناس ضرب مثل فاستمعوا له إن الذين تدعون
من دون الله لن يخلقوا ذبابا ولو اجتمعوا له وإن يسلبهم
الذباب شيئا لا يستنقذوه منه ضعف الطالب والمطلوب ۝٧٣
ما قدروا الله حق قدره إن الله لقوي عزيز ۝٧٤ الله
يصطفي من الملائكة رسلا ومن الناس إن الله
سميع بصير ۝٧٥ يعلم ما بين أيديهم وما خلفهم وإلى الله
ترجع الأمور ۝٧٦ يا أيها الذين آمنوا اركعوا واسجدوا
واعبدوا ربكم وافعلوا الخير لعلكم تفلحون ۝٧٧
وجاهدوا في الله حق جهاده هو اجتباكم وما جعل عليكم
في الدين من حرج ملة أبيكم إبراهيم هو سماكم المسلمين
من قبل وفي هذا ليكون الرسول شهيدا عليكم وتكونوا
شهداء على الناس فأقيموا الصلاة وآتوا الزكاة
واعتصموا بالله هو مولاكم فنعم المولى ونعم النصير ۝٧٨

سورة المؤمنين مكية وهي مائة وثماني عشرة آية

22:73 YOU PEOPLE! Listen to this aphorism. Those whom you invoke besides God could never create a fly though they combined their forces. And if a fly stole aught from them, they could never retrieve it. Powerless is the supplicant, and powerless he whom he supplicates.

They do not render to God the homage due to Him; yet God is powerful and mighty.

22:75 God chooses emissaries from the angels and from people. Surely God hears all and observes all; He knows what is before them and behind them. And to God shall all things be recalled.

You that are true believers, kneel down and prostrate yourselves. Worship your Lord and do good works, so that you may succeed.

22:78 Fight for the cause of God with the devotion due to Him. *He* has chosen you, and laid on you no burdens in the observance of your Religion, the faith of your father Abraham. In this, as in former Scriptures, He has given you the name of Muslims, so that the Apostle may testify against you, and that you may yourselves testify against people.

Therefore attend to your prayers, render the alms levy, and hold fast to God; for He is your guardian. A gracious guardian and a gracious helper!

بسم الله الرحمن الرحيم
قد أفلح المؤمنون (١) الذين هم في صلاتهم خاشعون
(٢) والذين هم عن اللغو معرضون (٣) والذين هم للزكوة
فاعلون (٤) والذين هم لفروجهم حافظون (٥) إلا على
أزواجهم أو ما ملكت أيمانهم فإنهم غير ملومين (٦)
فمن ابتغى وراء ذلك فأولئك هم العادون (٧) والذين
هم لأماناتهم وعهدهم راعون (٨) والذين هم على
صلواتهم يحافظون (٩) أولئك هم الوارثون (١٠) الذين
يرثون الفردوس هم فيها خالدون (١١) ولقد خلقنا
الإنسان من سلالة من طين (١٢) ثم جعلناه نطفة في قرار
مكين (١٣) ثم خلقنا النطفة علقة فخلقنا العلقة
مضغة فخلقنا المضغة عظاما فكسونا العظام لحما
ثم أنشأناه خلقا آخر فتبارك الله أحسن الخالقين (١٤) ثم
إنكم بعد ذلك لميتون (١٥) ثم إنكم يوم القيمة تبعثون (١٦)
ولقد خلقنا فوقكم سبع طرائق وما كنا عن الخلق غافلين (١٧)

THE BELIEVERS

In the Name of God,
the Merciful, the Compassionate

SUCCESSFUL ARE the believ- 23:1
ers, who are humble in their prayers; who avoid profane talk, and give alms in earnest; who restrain their carnal desires (except with their wives and slave-girls, for with them they are blameless: transgressors are those who lust after other than these); who are true to their trusts and promises, and diligent in their prayers. These are the heirs of Paradise, wherein shall they abide for ever.

We first created man from 23:12
an essence of clay: then placed him, a living germ, in a secure enclosure.[1] The germ We made a clot of blood,[2] and the clot a lump of flesh. This We fashioned into bones, then clothed the bones with flesh, thus bringing forth another creation. Blessed be God, the noblest of creators.

Then you shall surely die hereafter, and then be restored to life on the Day
of Resurrection. We have created seven heavens[3] above you; of Our creation 23:17
We were never heedless.

1. The womb. 2. See p. 331, note 1.
3. Literally, highways (Al-Jalālayn).

23:18 WE SENT down water from the sky in due measure, and lodged it into the earth; but if We please, We can take it all away.

With it We caused palm-groves and vineyards to spring up, yielding abundant fruit for your sustenance. The tree[1] which grows on Mount Sinai gives oil and a condiment for all to eat.

In cattle, too, you have but an example and a lesson. We give you to drink of that which is in their bellies, you eat their flesh, and gain other benefits from them besides. By them, as by the ships that sail the sea, you are carried.

23:23 We sent forth Noah to his people. 'Serve God, my people,' he said, 'for you have no god but Him. Will you not take heed?'

The unbelieving elders of his people said: 'This man is but a mortal like yourselves, feigning to be your superior. Had God willed, He could have sent down angels. Nor did we hear that such a thing ever happened to our forefathers. He is surely but a man possessed. Keep an eye on him awhile.'

He said: 'Help me, Lord, for they disbelieve me.'

23:27 We revealed Our will to him, saying: 'Build the ark under Our watchful eyes, according to Our instructions. When Our judgement comes to pass and water wells out from the Oven, take aboard a pair from every species and the members of your household, except those of them already doomed. Do not plead with Me for those who have done wrong: they shall be drowned.

وأنزلنا من السماء ماء بقدر فأسكناه في الأرض وإنا على
ذهاب به لقادرون ﴿١٨﴾ فأنشأنا لكم به جنات من نخيل وأعناب
لكم فيها فواكه كثيرة ومنها تأكلون ﴿١٩﴾ وشجرة تخرج
من طور سيناء تنبت بالدهن وصبغ للآكلين ﴿٢٠﴾ وإن لكم
في الأنعام لعبرة نسقيكم مما في بطونها ولكم فيها منافع
كثيرة ومنها تأكلون ﴿٢١﴾ وعليها وعلى الفلك تحملون
﴿٢٢﴾ ولقد أرسلنا نوحا إلى قومه فقال يا قوم اعبدوا الله
ما لكم من إله غيره أفلا تتقون ﴿٢٣﴾ فقال الملأ الذين كفروا
من قومه ما هذا إلا بشر مثلكم يريد أن يتفضل عليكم ولو شاء الله
لأنزل ملائكة ما سمعنا بهذا في آبائنا الأولين ﴿٢٤﴾ إن هو
إلا رجل به جنة فتربصوا به حتى حين ﴿٢٥﴾ قال رب
انصرني بما كذبون ﴿٢٦﴾ فأوحينا إليه أن اصنع الفلك
بأعيننا ووحينا فإذا جاء أمرنا وفار التنور فاسلك فيها
من كل زوجين اثنين وأهلك إلا من سبق عليه القول
منهم ولا تخاطبني في الذين ظلموا إنهم مغرقون ﴿٢٧﴾

1. The olive.

فإذا استويت أنت ومن معك على الفلك فقل الحمد
لله الذى نجىنا من القوم الظالمين ۝ وقل رب أنزلنى منزلا
مباركا وأنت خير المنزلين ۝ إن فى ذلك لآيات وإن كنا
لمبتلين ۝ ثم أنشأنا من بعدهم قرنا آخرين ۝
فأرسلنا فيهم رسولا منهم أن اعبدوا الله ما لكم
من إله غيره أفلا تتقون ۝ وقال الملأ من قومه الذين كفروا
وكذبوا بلقاء الآخرة وأترفناهم فى الحيوة الدنيا ما هذا إلا
بشر مثلكم يأكل مما تأكلون منه ويشرب مما تشربون ۝ ولئن أطعتم
بشرا مثلكم إنكم إذا لخاسرون ۝ أيعدكم أنكم إذا متم وكنتم ترابا
وعظاما أنكم مخرجون ۝ هيهات هيهات لما توعدون ۝ إن هى إلا
حياتنا الدنيا نموت ونحيا وما نحن بمبعوثين ۝ إن هو إلا رجل افترى على
الله كذبا وما نحن له بمؤمنين ۝ قال رب انصرنى بما
كذبون ۝ قال عما قليل ليصبحن نادمين ۝
فأخذتهم الصيحة بالحق فجعلناهم غثاء فبعدا للقوم
الظالمين ۝ ثم أنشأنا من بعدهم قرونا آخرين ۝

AND WHEN you and your fol- 23:28
lowers have gone aboard, say:
"Praise be to God who has
delivered us from the sinful
people. Lord, let my landing
be blessed. You alone can
make me land in safety." '
Surely in that there were
veritable signs. Thus did We
put mankind to the test.
Then We raised a new gen-
eration, and sent forth to them
an apostle of their own. 'Serve
God,' he said, 'for you have no
god but Him. Will you not
take heed?'
But the unbelieving elders
of his people, who denied the
life to come and on whom We
had lavished the good things
of this life, said: 'This man is
but a mortal like yourselves,
nourished by the same food
and drink. If you obey a mortal like yourselves, you shall indeed be lost. 23:34
Does he promise you, when you are dead and turned to dust and bones, you
will be raised to life? A foolish promise, indeed. There is no other life but
this, our earthly life: we die and live, never to be restored to life. He is but a
man who tells of God what is untrue. Never will we believe in him.'
He said: 'Help me, Lord, for they disbelieve me.'
He replied: 'Before long they shall rue it.' The Cry took them in all justice,
and We swept them away like withered leaves. Gone are the sinful people.
After them We raised other generations – 23:42

23:43 no community can delay its doom or go before it – and sent forth Our apostles in succession. Yet time after time each community disbelieved its apostle, so that We destroyed them one by one and held them up as an example. Gone are a people who disbelieved.

Then We sent Moses and his brother Aaron, with Our signs and with clear authority, to Pharaoh and his nobles. But they received them with contempt, for they were arrogant men. 'What!' said they. 'Are we to believe in two men like ourselves, whose people are our slaves?' They denied them, and thus incurred destruction. And We gave Moses the Book, that they might be rightly guided.

ما تسبق من امة اجلها وما يستأخرون ۝ ثم ارسلنا رسلنا
تترا كلما جاء امة رسولها كذبوه فاتبعنا بعضهم بعضا
وجعلناهم احاديث فبعدا لقوم لا يؤمنون ۝ ثم ارسلنا
موسى واخاه هرون باياتنا وسلطان مبين ۝ الى فرعون
وملايه فاستكبروا وكانوا قوما عالين ۝ فقالوا انؤمن
لبشرين مثلنا وقومهما لنا عابدون ۝ فكذبوهما فكانوا من
المهلكين ۝ ولقد اتينا موسى الكتاب لعلهم يهتدون ۝
وجعلنا ابن مريم وامه اية واويناهما الى ربوة ذات قرار
ومعين ۝ يا ايها الرسل كلوا من الطيبات واعملوا صالحا اني
بما تعملون عليم ۝ وان هذه امتكم امة واحدة وانا
ربكم فاتقون ۝ فتقطعوا امرهم بينهم زبرا كل حزب بما
لديهم فرحون ۝ فذرهم في غمرتهم حتى حين ۝ ايحسبون انما
نمدهم به من مال وبنين ۝ نسارع لهم في الخيرات بل لا يشعرون
۝ ان الذين هم من خشية ربهم مشفقون ۝ والذين هم بايات
ربهم يؤمنون ۝ والذين هم بربهم لا يشركون ۝

23:50 We made the son of Mary and his mother a sign, and gave them a shelter
on a peaceful hillside watered by a fresh spring.
Apostles! Eat of that which is wholesome, and do good works: I have
knowledge of all your actions. Your community is but one community, and
I am your only Lord: therefore fear Me.
Yet they have divided themselves into factions, each rejoicing in its own
doctrines. Leave them in their error till a time appointed.
Do they think that, in giving them wealth and children, We are solicitous
for their welfare? By no means! They lack perception.
Those who walk in fear of their Lord; who believe in the revelations of
23:59 their Lord; who worship none besides their Lord;

والذين يؤتون ما آتوا وقلوبهم وجلة أنهم إلى ربهم راجعون
﴿٦٠﴾ أولئك يسارعون في الخيرات وهم لها سابقون ﴿٦١﴾ ولا
نكلف نفسا إلا وسعها ولدينا كتاب ينطق بالحق وهم لا
يظلمون ﴿٦٢﴾ بل قلوبهم في غمرة من هذا ولهم أعمال من دون
ذلك هم لها عاملون ﴿٦٣﴾ حتى إذا أخذنا مترفيهم بالعذاب
إذا هم يجأرون ﴿٦٤﴾ لا تجأروا اليوم إنكم منا لا تنصرون ﴿٦٥﴾
قد كانت آياتي تتلى عليكم فكنتم على أعقابكم تنكصون ﴿٦٦﴾
مستكبرين به سامرا تهجرون ﴿٦٧﴾ أفلم يدبروا القول أم جاءهم
ما لم يأت آباءهم الأولين ﴿٦٨﴾ أم لم يعرفوا رسولهم فهم له
منكرون ﴿٦٩﴾ أم يقولون به جنة بل جاءهم بالحق وأكثرهم
للحق كارهون ﴿٧٠﴾ ولو اتبع الحق أهواءهم لفسدت السماوات
والأرض ومن فيهن بل أتيناهم بذكرهم فهم عن
ذكرهم معرضون ﴿٧١﴾ أم تسألهم خرجا فخراج ربك خير وهو
خير الرازقين ﴿٧٢﴾ وإنك لتدعوهم إلى صراط مستقيم ﴿٧٣﴾
وإن الذين لا يؤمنون بالآخرة عن الصراط لناكبون ﴿٧٤﴾

who give from what they were 23:60
given with hearts filled with
awe, knowing that they will
return to their Lord: these
vie with each other for salvation and shall be the first to
attain it.

We charge no soul with
more than it can bear. We have
a Book which speaks the Truth:
and none shall be wronged.

But their hearts are blind to
all this; their deeds are of a different sort, and they are bent on
doing them. But when We visit
Our scourge upon those among
them that live in affluence, they
will howl for help. We shall say:
'Do not howl this day, for from
Us you shall receive no help.
My revelations were recited to
you many a time, but you turned
your backs in scorn, and passed
the nights reviling them.'

Should they not heed the Word? 23:68

Was anything revealed to them that had not been revealed to their
forefathers?

Or is it because they do not know their apostle that they deny him?

Do they say he is possessed?

Surely he has come to them with the Truth. But most of them abhor the
Truth. Had the Truth followed their appetites, the heavens, the earth, and all
who dwell in them, would have surely been corrupted. We have given them
their Admonition: yet to their Admonition they pay no heed.

Are you seeking a recompense from them? Far better is your Lord's recompense: He is the most munificent Giver.

You have surely called them to a straight path, but those who deny the life 23:74
to come will ever stray from the path.

23:75 AND IF We showed them
mercy and relieved their misfortunes, they would persist in
their insolent ways, ever straying blindly from the right
path. We punished them, but
they neither entreated their
Lord nor humbled themselves
before Him. And when We
smote them with a grievous
scourge, they yielded to utter
despair.

He it was who gave you
ears, eyes, and hearts: yet you
are seldom thankful.

He it was who placed you
on the earth, and before Him
shall you be herded.

And He it is who ordains
life and death, and He who
alternates the night with the
day. Can you not understand?

23:81 Indeed, they say what the
ancients said before them. 'After our death, when we are dust and bones,' they
say, 'shall we be raised to life? This we have been promised before, we and our
forefathers. It is but a fable of the ancients.'

Say: 'Whose is the earth and all that it contains? If you really know?'

'God's,' they will say.

Say: 'Then will you not reflect?'

Say: 'Who is the Lord of the seven heavens, and of the Glorious Throne?'

'God,' they will say.

Say: 'Will you not fear Him, then?'

Say: 'In whose hands is the sovereignty of all things, protecting all, while
against Him there is no protection? If you really know?'

23:89 'In God's,' they will say.

Say: 'How then can you be so bewitched?'

وَلَوْ رَحِمْنَاهُمْ وَكَشَفْنَا مَا بِهِمْ مِنْ ضُرٍّ لَلَجُّوا فِي طُغْيَانِهِمْ يَعْمَهُونَ
(٧٥) وَلَقَدْ أَخَذْنَاهُمْ بِالْعَذَابِ فَمَا اسْتَكَانُوا لِرَبِّهِمْ وَمَا
يَتَضَرَّعُونَ (٧٦) حَتَّىٰ إِذَا فَتَحْنَا عَلَيْهِمْ بَابًا ذَا عَذَابٍ شَدِيدٍ
إِذَا هُمْ فِيهِ مُبْلِسُونَ (٧٧) وَهُوَ الَّذِي أَنْشَأَ لَكُمُ السَّمْعَ وَالْأَبْصَارَ
وَالْأَفْئِدَةَ قَلِيلًا مَا تَشْكُرُونَ (٧٨) وَهُوَ الَّذِي ذَرَأَكُمْ فِي الْأَرْضِ
وَإِلَيْهِ تُحْشَرُونَ (٧٩) وَهُوَ الَّذِي يُحْيِي وَيُمِيتُ وَلَهُ اخْتِلَافُ
اللَّيْلِ وَالنَّهَارِ أَفَلَا تَعْقِلُونَ (٨٠) بَلْ قَالُوا مِثْلَ مَا قَالَ الْأَوَّلُونَ
(٨١) قَالُوا أَإِذَا مِتْنَا وَكُنَّا تُرَابًا وَعِظَامًا أَإِنَّا لَمَبْعُوثُونَ
(٨٢) لَقَدْ وُعِدْنَا نَحْنُ وَآبَاؤُنَا هَٰذَا مِنْ قَبْلُ إِنْ هَٰذَا إِلَّا
أَسَاطِيرُ الْأَوَّلِينَ (٨٣) قُلْ لِمَنِ الْأَرْضُ وَمَنْ فِيهَا إِنْ كُنْتُمْ
تَعْلَمُونَ (٨٤) سَيَقُولُونَ لِلَّهِ قُلْ أَفَلَا تَذَكَّرُونَ (٨٥)
قُلْ مَنْ رَبُّ السَّمَاوَاتِ السَّبْعِ وَرَبُّ الْعَرْشِ
الْعَظِيمِ (٨٦) سَيَقُولُونَ لِلَّهِ قُلْ أَفَلَا تَتَّقُونَ (٨٧) قُلْ مَنْ
بِيَدِهِ مَلَكُوتُ كُلِّ شَيْءٍ وَهُوَ يُجِيرُ وَلَا يُجَارُ عَلَيْهِ إِنْ كُنْتُمْ
تَعْلَمُونَ (٨٨) سَيَقُولُونَ لِلَّهِ قُلْ فَأَنَّىٰ تُسْحَرُونَ (٨٩)

بل آتيناهم بالحق وإنهم لكاذبون ۝٩٠ ما اتخذ الله من ولد وما
كان معه من إله إذا لذهب كل إله بما خلق ولعلا بعضهم
على بعض سبحان الله عما يصفون ۝٩١ عالم الغيب
والشهادة فتعالى عما يشركون ۝٩٢ قل رب إما تريني
ما يوعدون ۝٩٣ رب فلا تجعلني في القوم الظالمين ۝٩٤
وإنا على أن نريك ما نعدهم لقادرون ۝٩٥ ادفع بالتي هي
أحسن السيئة نحن أعلم بما يصفون ۝٩٦ وقل رب أعوذ بك
من همزات الشياطين ۝٩٧ وأعوذ بك رب أن يحضرون
۝٩٨ حتى إذا جاء أحدهم الموت قال رب ارجعون ۝٩٩
لعلي أعمل صالحا فيما تركت كلا إنها كلمة هو قائلها
ومن ورائهم برزخ إلى يوم يبعثون ۝١٠٠ فإذا نفخ في
الصور فلا أنساب بينهم يومئذ ولا يتساءلون ۝١٠١ فمن
ثقلت موازينه فأولئك هم المفلحون ۝١٠٢ ومن خفت
موازينه فأولئك الذين خسروا أنفسهم في جهنم خالدون
۝١٠٣ تلفح وجوههم النار وهم فيها كالحون ۝١٠٤

BUT WE have revealed to 23:90
them the Truth, and they are
surely lying.

Never has God begotten a
son, nor is there any other
god besides Him. Were this
otherwise, each god would
govern his own creation, each
holding himself above the
other. Exalted be God above
their falsehoods!

He knows alike the unknown
and the manifest. Exalted be
He above the gods they serve
besides Him!

Say: 'Lord, if You will indeed
let me see the scourge they are
promised, do not abandon me,
Lord, among these wrong-
doing people.' Indeed, We do
have power enough to let you
see the scourge We promise
them.

Requite evil with good. We know their slanders well. And say: 'Lord, I 23:96
seek refuge in You from the promptings of the demons. Lord, I seek refuge
in You from their presence.'

When death comes to one among them, he will say: 'Lord, let me go back,
that I may do good works in the world I have left behind.'

Never! These are the very words which he will speak. Behind them there
shall stand a barrier till the Day of Resurrection. And when the Trumpet is
blown, on that day their ties of kin shall be broken, nor shall they ask help
of one another.

Those whose good deeds weigh heavy in the scales shall triumph, but
those whose good deeds are light shall forfeit their souls and abide in Hell
for ever. The fire will scorch their faces and they will writhe in anguish. 23:104

ألم تكن آياتي تتلى عليكم فكنتم بها تكذبون ﴿١٠٥﴾ قالوا ربنا
غلبت علينا شقوتنا وكنا قوما ضالين ﴿١٠٦﴾ ربنا أخرجنا منها
فإن عدنا فإنا ظالمون ﴿١٠٧﴾ قال اخسئوا فيها ولا تكلمون
﴿١٠٨﴾ إنه كان فريق من عبادي يقولون ربنا آمنا فاغفر لنا
وارحمنا وأنت خير الراحمين ﴿١٠٩﴾ فاتخذتموهم سخريا حتى
أنسوكم ذكري وكنتم منهم تضحكون ﴿١١٠﴾ إني جزيتهم اليوم
بما صبروا أنهم هم الفائزون ﴿١١١﴾ قال كم لبثتم في الأرض
عدد سنين ﴿١١٢﴾ قالوا لبثنا يوما أو بعض يوم فاسأل العادين ﴿١١٣﴾
قال إن لبثتم إلا قليلا لو أنكم كنتم تعلمون ﴿١١٤﴾ أفحسبتم
أنما خلقناكم عبثا وأنكم إلينا لا ترجعون ﴿١١٥﴾ فتعالى الله
الملك الحق لا إله إلا هو رب العرش الكريم ﴿١١٦﴾ ومن يدع مع الله
إلها آخر لا برهان له به فإنما حسابه عند ربه إنه لا يفلح
الكافرون ﴿١١٧﴾ وقل رب اغفر وارحم وأنت خير الراحمين ﴿١١٨﴾

سورة النور مدنية وهي اربع وستون اية

23:105 'Were My revelations not
recited to you, and did you not
deny them?'
'Lord,' they will say, 'fortune betrayed us and we were
people gone astray. Lord, deliver us from it; if we relapse,
then shall we indeed be
wrongdoers.'
He will say: 'Stay here in
shame and do not plead with
Me. Among My servants there
were those who said: "Lord,
we now believe. Forgive us and
have mercy on us: You are the
best of those that show
mercy." But you derided them
until they caused you to forget
My warning; and you laughed
23:111 at them. Today I shall requite
them for their fortitude, for it
is they who have triumphed.'
He will say: 'How many years
did you linger on the earth?'
They will say: 'A day, or possibly less. Ask those who have kept count.'
He will say: 'Brief indeed was your sojourn, if you but knew it! Did you
think We created you in vain and to Us you would never be recalled?'
Exalted be God, the True King. There is no god but Him, the Lord of the
Glorious Throne.
He that invokes another god with God – a god of whose divinity he has
no proof – his Lord will surely bring him to account. The unbelievers shall
never succeed.
23:118 Say: 'Lord, forgive and have mercy. You are the best of those that show
mercy.'

بسم الله الرحمن الرحيم
سورة أنزلناها وفرضناها وأنزلنا فيها آيات بينات لعلكم تذكرون (١)
الزانية والزاني فاجلدوا كل واحد منهما مائة جلدة ولا تأخذكم
بهما رأفة في دين الله إن كنتم تؤمنون بالله واليوم الآخر وليشهد
عذابهما طائفة من المؤمنين (٢) الزاني لا ينكح إلا زانية أو مشركة
والزانية لا ينكحها إلا زان أو مشرك وحرم ذلك على المؤمنين (٣)
والذين يرمون المحصنات ثم لم يأتوا بأربعة شهداء فاجلدوهم
ثمانين جلدة ولا تقبلوا لهم شهادة أبدا وأولئك هم الفاسقون (٤)
إلا الذين تابوا من بعد ذلك وأصلحوا فإن الله غفور رحيم (٥)
والذين يرمون أزواجهم ولم يكن لهم شهداء إلا أنفسهم
فشهادة أحدهم أربع شهادات بالله إنه لمن الصادقين (٦)
والخامسة أن لعنت الله عليه إن كان من الكاذبين (٧) ويدرأ عنها
العذاب أن تشهد أربع شهادات بالله إنه لمن الكاذبين (٨)
والخامسة أن غضب الله عليها إن كان من الصادقين (٩)
ولولا فضل الله عليكم ورحمته وأن الله تواب حكيم (١٠)

LIGHT

In the Name of God,
the Merciful, the Compassionate

A *SŪRAH* We have revealed 24:1
and sanctioned, proclaiming
therein clear revelations, so
that you may reflect.

The adulteress and the
adulterer you shall give each a
hundred lashes. Let no pity
for either cause you to disobey
God's Religion, if you truly
believe in God and the Last
Day; and let their punishment
be witnessed by a number of
believers.

The adulterer may marry
only an adulteress or an idolatress; and the adulteress may
marry only an adulterer or an
idolater. This is forbidden to true believers.

Those that defame honourable women and cannot produce four wit- 24:4
nesses you shall give eighty lashes. Do not accept their testimony ever after,
for it is they who are the transgressors – except those among them that afterwards repent and mend their ways: God is forgiving and compassionate.

Those who accuse their wives but have no witnesses except themselves,
shall each swear four times by God that his charge is true and in a fifth time
call down upon himself the curse of God if he is lying. But if his wife swears
four times by God that his charge is false and in a fifth time calls down His
curse upon herself if it be true, she shall receive no punishment.[1]

And but for God's grace and compassion for you, His forgiveness and His 24:10
wisdom . . .

1. Cf. Numbers 5:11-31.

24:11 THOSE WHO concocted that slander[1] were surely a clique from among your own people. Do not regard it as a misfortune, for it has proved an advantage. Each one of them shall be punished according to his sin. As for him who had the greater share in it among them, his punishment shall be terrible indeed.

When you heard it, why did the faithful, men and women, not think well of their own people, and say: 'This is an evident falsehood'? Why did they not produce four witnesses? If they could not produce the witnesses, then they were surely lying in the sight of God.

But for God's grace and mercy towards you in this life
and in the life to come, you would have been grievously punished for your
24:15 scandalmongering. You carried with your tongues and uttered with your
mouths what you knew not. You may have thought it a trifle, but in the sight of God it was a grave offence.

And when you heard it, why did you not say: 'It is not proper for us to speak of this; glory be to God: this is a monstrous slander'?

God bids you never to repeat the like, if you are true believers. God makes plain to you the revelations. God is omniscient and wise.

Those who delight in spreading salacious slander against the faithful shall be grievously punished in this life and in the life to come. God knows, but you know not.

24:20 And but for God's grace and compassion for you, His kindliness and mercy . . .

إن الذين جاءو بالإفك عصبة منكم لا تحسبوه شرا لكم بل هو
خير لكم لكل امرئ منهم ما اكتسب من الإثم والذي تولى
كبره منهم له عذاب عظيم ١١ لولا إذ سمعتموه ظن المؤمنون
والمؤمنات بأنفسهم خيرا وقالوا هذا إفك مبين ١٢ لولا جاءو
عليه بأربعة شهداء فإذ لم يأتوا بالشهداء فأولئك عند
الله هم الكاذبون ١٣ ولولا فضل الله عليكم ورحمته في
الدنيا والآخرة لمسكم في ما أفضتم فيه عذاب عظيم ١٤ إذ تلقونه
بألسنتكم وتقولون بأفواهكم ما ليس لكم به علم وتحسبونه
هينا وهو عند الله عظيم ١٥ ولولا إذ سمعتموه قلتم ما
يكون لنا أن نتكلم بهذا سبحانك هذا بهتان عظيم ١٦ يعظكم
الله أن تعودوا لمثله أبدا إن كنتم مؤمنين ١٧ ويبين
الله لكم الآيات والله عليم حكيم ١٨ إن الذين يحبون
أن تشيع الفاحشة في الذين آمنوا لهم عذاب أليم في
الدنيا والآخرة والله يعلم وأنتم لا تعلمون ١٩ ولولا فضل
الله عليكم ورحمته وأن الله رءوف رحيم ٢٠

1. The reference is to the scandal instigated by the Prophet's political opponents involving Muḥammad's wife 'Ā'ishah with Ṣafwān b. al-Mu'aṭṭal.

يا أيها الذين آمنوا لا تتبعوا خطوات الشيطان ومن يتبع خطوات
الشيطان فإنه يأمر بالفحشاء والمنكر ولولا فضل الله
عليكم ورحمته ما زكى منكم من أحد أبدا ولكن الله
يزكي من يشاء والله سميع عليم (٢١) ولا يأتل أولوا الفضل منكم
والسعة أن يؤتوا أولي القربى والمساكين والمهاجرين في سبيل الله
وليعفوا وليصفحوا ألا تحبون أن يغفر الله لكم والله
غفور رحيم (٢٢) إن الذين يرمون المحصنات الغافلات المؤمنات
لعنوا في الدنيا والآخرة ولهم عذاب عظيم (٢٣) يوم تشهد عليهم
ألسنتهم وأيديهم وأرجلهم بما كانوا يعملون (٢٤)
يومئذ يوفيهم الله دينهم الحق ويعلمون أن الله هو الحق المبين
(٢٥) الخبيثات للخبيثين والخبيثون للخبيثات والطيبات
للطيبين والطيبون للطيبات أولئك مبرءون مما يقولون
لهم مغفرة ورزق كريم (٢٦) يا أيها الذين آمنوا
لا تدخلوا بيوتا غير بيوتكم حتى تستأنسوا وتسلموا على
أهلها ذلكم خير لكم لعلكم تذكرون (٢٧)

You that are true believ- 24:21
ers, do not follow Satan's
footsteps. He that walks in
Satan's footsteps is incited by
him to lewdness and everything reprehensible. But for
God's grace and mercy, none
of you would ever have kept
himself pure. But God purifies whom He will; God hears
all and knows all.

Let not the honourable and
the rich among you swear to
withhold their gifts from their
kin, the destitute, and those
who have fled their homes in
the cause of God. Rather let
them pardon and forgive. Do
you not wish God to forgive
you? God is forgiving and
compassionate.

Those who defame hon- 24:23
ourable but careless believing
women shall be cursed in this world and in the world to come. Grievous
punishment awaits them on the day when their own tongues, hands, and feet
will testify to what they did. On that day God will justly requite them in full;
and they shall know that God is the veritable Truth.

Unclean women are for unclean men, and unclean men for unclean women. But good women are for good men, and good men for good women. These shall be cleared of calumny. Forgiveness, and a generous provision, await them.

Believers, do not enter dwellings other than your own until you have asked 24:27
their owners' permission and wished them peace. That will be best for you;
perchance you will remember.

24:28 If you find no one in them,
do not go in till you are given
leave. If you are refused
admission, it is but more
proper that you should go
away. God has knowledge of
all your actions.
It shall be no offence for
you to seek shelter in empty
dwellings. God knows what
you reveal and what you hide.
24:30 Enjoin believing men to
turn their eyes away from
temptation and to preserve
their chastity. This will make
their lives purer. God has
knowledge of all their actions.
24:31 Enjoin believing women to
turn their eyes away from
temptation and to preserve
their chastity; not to display
their adornments (except such
as are normally revealed); to
draw their veils over their bosoms and not to display their finery except to
their husbands, their fathers, their husbands' fathers, their sons, their step-
sons, their brothers, their brothers' sons, their sisters' sons, their
women-servants, and their slave-girls; male attendants lacking in natural vig-
our, and children who have no carnal knowledge of women. And let them
not stamp their feet[1] when walking so as to reveal their hidden trinkets.
Believers, turn to God in penitence, all, that you may succeed.

فإن لم تجدوا فيها أحدا فلا تدخلوها حتى يؤذن لكم
وإن قيل لكم ارجعوا فارجعوا هو أزكى لكم
والله بما تعملون عليم ٢٨ ليس عليكم جناح أن تدخلوا بيوتا
غير مسكونة فيها متاع لكم والله يعلم ما تبدون وما تكتمون
٢٩ قل للمؤمنين يغضوا من أبصارهم ويحفظوا
فروجهم ذلك أزكى لهم إن الله خبير بما يصنعون
٣٠ وقل للمؤمنات يغضضن من أبصارهن ويحفظن
فروجهن ولا يبدين زينتهن إلا ما ظهر منها وليضربن بخمرهن
على جيوبهن ولا يبدين زينتهن إلا لبعولتهن أو آبائهن
أو آباء بعولتهن أو أبنائهن أو أبناء بعولتهن أو إخوانهن
أو بني إخوانهن أو بني أخواتهن أو نسائهن أو ما ملكت
أيمانهن أو التابعين غير أولي الإربة من الرجال أو الطفل
الذين لم يظهروا على عورات النساء ولا يضربن
بأرجلهن ليعلم ما يخفين من زينتهن وتوبوا إلى
الله جميعا أيه المؤمنون لعلكم تفلحون ٣١

1. Cf. Isaiah 3:16, 18.

وانكحوا الأيامى منكم والصالحين من عبادكم وإمائكم إن
يكونوا فقراء يغنهم الله من فضله والله واسع عليم ﴿٣٢﴾
وليستعفف الذين لا يجدون نكاحا حتى يغنيهم الله
من فضله والذين يبتغون الكتاب مما ملكت أيمانكم فكاتبوهم
إن علمتم فيهم خيرا وآتوهم من مال الله الذي آتاكم ولا
تكرهوا فتياتكم على البغاء إن أردن تحصنا لتبتغوا عرض
الحيوة الدنيا ومن يكرههن فإن الله من بعد إكراههن
غفور رحيم ﴿٣٣﴾ ولقد أنزلنا إليكم آيات مبينات ومثلا من الذين
خلوا من قبلكم وموعظة للمتقين ﴿٣٤﴾ الله نور السموات والأرض
مثل نوره كمشكوة فيها مصباح المصباح في زجاجة الزجاجة
كأنها كوكب دري يوقد من شجرة مباركة زيتونة لا
شرقية ولا غربية يكاد زيتها يضيء ولو لم تمسسه نار نور
على نور يهدي الله لنوره من يشاء ويضرب الله
الأمثال للناس والله بكل شيء عليم ﴿٣٥﴾ في بيوت أذن الله
أن ترفع ويذكر فيها اسمه يسبح له فيها بالغدو والآصال ﴿٣٦﴾

AND TAKE in marriage 24:32
those among you who are single and those of your male and female slaves who are honest. If they are poor, God will enrich them from His own bounty; God is munificent and all-knowing.

And let those who cannot afford to marry live in continence until God shall enrich them from His own bounty. As for those of your slaves who wish to buy their liberty, free them if you find in them any promise and bestow on them a part of the riches which God has given you.

And you shall not force your slave-girls into prostitution in order that you may enrich yourselves, if they wish to preserve their chastity. If anyone compels them, God will after their compulsion be forgiving and compassionate.

We have sent down to you discerning revelations; an account of those who have gone before you, and an Admonition to the righteous.

God is the light of the heavens and the earth. His light may be compared 24:35
to a niche that enshrines a lamp, the lamp within a crystal of star-like brilliance. It is lit from a blessed olive tree neither eastern nor western. Its very oil would almost shine forth, though no fire touched it. Light upon light; God guides to His light whom He will.

God speaks in parables to mankind. God has knowledge of all things.

His light is found in temples God has sanctioned to be built for the remem- 24:36
brance of His name. In them, His praise is sung morning and evening,

24:37 by men whom neither trade nor profit can divert from remembering God, from offering prayers, or from giving alms; who dread the day when hearts and eyes shall writhe with anguish; who hope that God will requite them for their noblest deeds and lavish His grace upon them. God gives without reckoning to whom He will.

As for the unbelievers, their works are like a mirage in a desert. The thirsty traveller thinks it is water, but when he comes near he finds that it is nothing. He finds God there, who pays him back in full. Swift is God's reckoning.

24:40 Or like darkness on a bottomless ocean spread with clashing billows and overcast with clouds: darkness upon darkness. If he stretches out his hand he can scarcely see it. Indeed the man from whom God withholds His light shall find no light at all.

Do you not see how God is praised by those in the heavens and those on earth? The very birds praise Him as they wing their way. He notes the prayers and praises of all His creatures; God has knowledge of all their actions.

It is God who has sovereignty over the heavens and the earth. To God shall all return.

24:43 Do you not see how God drives the clouds, then gathers and piles them up in masses through which you see the rain pour down in torrents? And from heaven's mountains He sends down the hail, pelting with it whom He will and turning it away from whom He pleases. The flash of His lightning almost snatches out men's eyes.

رجال لا تلهيهم تجارة ولا بيع عن ذكر الله واقام الصلوة وايتاء
الزكوة يخافون يوما تتقلب فيه القلوب والابصار ﴿٣٧﴾ ليجزيهم
الله احسن ما عملوا ويزيدهم من فضله والله يرزق من يشاء
بغير حساب ﴿٣٨﴾ والذين كفروا اعمالهم كسراب بقيعة
يحسبه الظمان ماء حتى اذا جاءه لم يجده شيئا ووجد
الله عنده فوفيه حسابه والله سريع الحساب ﴿٣٩﴾ او كظلمات
في بحر لجي يغشيه موج من فوقه موج من فوقه سحاب ظلمات
بعضها فوق بعض اذا اخرج يده لم يكد يريها ومن لم يجعل
الله له نورا فما له من نور ﴿٤٠﴾ الم تر ان الله يسبح له من في
السموات والارض والطير صافات كل قد علم صلاته وتسبيحه
والله عليم بما يفعلون ﴿٤١﴾ ولله ملك السموات والارض والى
الله المصير ﴿٤٢﴾ الم تر ان الله يزجي سحابا ثم يؤلف
بينه ثم يجعله ركاما فترى الودق يخرج من خلاله وينزل من
السماء من جبال فيها من برد فيصيب به من يشاء ويصرفه
عن من يشاء يكاد سنا برقه يذهب بالابصار ﴿٤٣﴾

يقلب الله الليل والنهار إن في ذلك لعبرة لأولي الأبصار
٤٤ والله خلق كل دابة من ماء فمنهم من يمشي على بطنه
ومنهم من يمشي على رجلين ومنهم من يمشي على أربع
يخلق الله ما يشاء إن الله على كل شيء قدير ٤٥ لقد أنزلنا آيات
مبينات والله يهدي من يشاء إلى صراط مستقيم ٤٦ ويقولون
آمنا بالله وبالرسول وأطعنا ثم يتولى فريق منهم من بعد ذلك
وما أولئك بالمؤمنين ٤٧ وإذا دعوا إلى الله ورسوله ليحكم
بينهم إذا فريق منهم معرضون ٤٨ وإن يكن لهم الحق يأتوا
إليه مذعنين ٤٩ أفي قلوبهم مرض أم ارتابوا أم يخافون أن
يحيف الله عليهم ورسوله بل أولئك هم الظالمون ٥٠
إنما كان قول المؤمنين إذا دعوا إلى الله ورسوله ليحكم
بينهم أن يقولوا سمعنا وأطعنا وأولئك هم المفلحون ٥١ ومن
يطع الله ورسوله ويخش الله ويتقه فأولئك هم الفائزون ٥٢
وأقسموا بالله جهد أيمانهم لئن أمرتهم ليخرجن قل لا تقسموا
طاعة معروفة إن الله خبير بما تعملون ٥٣

GOD MAKES the night 24:44
succeed the day: surely in this
there is a lesson for the
clear-sighted.

God created every beast from water. Some creep upon their bellies, others walk on two legs, and others yet on four. God creates what He pleases. Surely God has power over all things.

We have sent down revelations demonstrating the Truth. God guides whom He will to a straight path.

They say: 'We believe in God and the Apostle and obey.' But soon thereafter some among them turn their backs. Surely these are no believers.

And when they are called
to God and His apostle that
he may judge between them, some among them turn away. Had Truth been 24:49
on their side they would have come to him in all obedience.

Is there a sickness in their hearts, or are they full of doubt? Do they fear that God and His apostle may deny them justice? Surely they are themselves the wrongdoers.

But when true believers are called to God and His apostle that he may judge between them, their only reply is: 'We hear and obey.' It is they that will surely succeed.

Those that obey God and His apostle, revere God and fear Him, will surely triumph.

They solemnly swear by God that if you order them, they will march 24:53
forth. Say: 'Do not swear: your obedience, not your oaths, will count. Surely
God is cognizant of what you do.'

24:54 SAY: 'OBEY God and obey the Apostle. If you do not, he is still bound to fulfil his obligations, and you are still bound to fulfil yours. If you obey him, you shall be rightly guided. The apostle's duty is but to give the veritable warning.'

24:55 God has promised those of you who believe and do good works to make them masters in the land as He made those who went before them, to strengthen the Religion He chose for them, and to change their fears to safety. Let them worship Me and serve none besides Me. Wicked indeed are they who after this deny Me.

And attend to your prayers, render the alms levy, and obey the Apostle, so that you may be shown mercy.

قل اطيعوا الله واطيعوا الرسول فان تولوا فانما عليه
ما حمل وعليكم ما حملتم وان تطيعوه تهتدوا وما على
الرسول الا البلاغ المبين (٥٤) وعد الله الذين امنوا منكم
وعملوا الصالحات ليستخلفنهم في الارض كما استخلف الذين
من قبلهم وليمكنن لهم دينهم الذي ارتضى لهم وليبدلنهم
من بعد خوفهم امنا يعبدونني لا يشركون بي شيئا ومن
كفر بعد ذلك فاولئك هم الفاسقون (٥٥) واقيموا الصلوة
واتوا الزكوة واطيعوا الرسول لعلكم ترحمون (٥٦) لا تحسبن
الذين كفروا معجزين في الارض ومأويهم النار ولبئس
المصير (٥٧) يا ايها الذين امنوا ليستاذنكم الذين ملكت
ايمانكم والذين لم يبلغوا الحلم منكم ثلث مرات من قبل
صلوة الفجر وحين تضعون ثيابكم من الظهيرة ومن بعد
صلوة العشاء ثلث عورات لكم ليس عليكم ولا عليهم
جناح بعدهن طوافون عليكم بعضكم على بعض
كذلك يبين الله لكم الايات والله عليم حكيم (٥٨)

Never think that the unbelievers are immune on the earth. The Fire shall be their shelter: a wretched fate!

24:58 Believers, let your slaves and those who are under the age of puberty among you ask your leave on three occasions: before the dawn prayer, when you have put off your garments in the heat of noon, and after the evening prayer. These are the three occasions when none may intrude upon your privacy. At other times, it shall be no offence for you, or them, to go around visiting one another. Thus God makes plain to you the revelations: God is omniscient and wise.

وإذا بلغ الأطفال منكم الحلم فليستأذنوا كما
استأذن الذين من قبلهم كذلك يبين الله
لكم آياته والله عليم حكيم ﴿٥٩﴾ والقواعد من النساء
اللاتي لا يرجون نكاحا فليس عليهن جناح أن يضعن ثيابهن
غير متبرجات بزينة وأن يستعففن خير لهن والله
سميع عليم ﴿٦٠﴾ ليس على الأعمى حرج ولا على الأعرج
حرج ولا على المريض حرج ولا على أنفسكم أن تأكلوا
من بيوتكم أو بيوت آبائكم أو بيوت أمهاتكم
أو بيوت إخوانكم أو بيوت أخواتكم أو بيوت أعمامكم
أو بيوت عماتكم أو بيوت أخوالكم أو بيوت خالاتكم
أو ما ملكتم مفاتحه أو صديقكم ليس عليكم
جناح أن تأكلوا جميعا أو أشتاتا فإذا دخلتم
بيوتا فسلموا على أنفسكم تحية من عند الله
مباركة طيبة كذلك يبين الله
لكم الآيات لعلكم تعقلون ﴿٦١﴾

AND WHEN they have 24:59
reached the age of puberty, let your children still ask your leave as their elders do. Thus God makes plain to you His revelations: God is all-knowing and wise.

It shall be no offence for 24:60
old spinsters who have no hope of marriage to discard their cloaks without revealing their adornments. Better if they do not discard them. God hears all and knows all.

It shall be no offence for 24:61
the blind, the lame, the sick, and for yourselves to eat in your houses or the houses of your fathers, the houses of your mothers, the houses of your brothers, the houses of your sisters, the houses of your paternal uncles, the houses of your paternal aunts, the houses of your maternal uncles, the houses of your maternal aunts, or of your friends; or in houses with the keys of which you are entrusted. Nor shall it be an offence for you to eat together or apart.

And when you enter a house, salute one another with a greeting from God, devout and kindly. Thus God makes clear to you the revelations, that you may understand.

24:62 THEY ONLY are true believers who have faith in God and His apostle, and who, when gathered with him upon a grave occasion, do not depart till they have begged his leave. Those who ask your leave are those who truly believe in God and His apostle. When they ask your leave to go away on any business of their own, grant it to whomever you please and implore God to forgive them; God is forgiving and compassionate.

24:63 Do not address the Apostle in the manner you address one another. God knows those of you who steal away, concealing themselves behind others. Let those who disobey his orders beware, lest some affliction or some woeful scourge be visited upon them.

إِنَّمَا الْمُؤْمِنُونَ الَّذِينَ آمَنُوا بِاللَّهِ وَرَسُولِهِ وَإِذَا كَانُوا مَعَهُ عَلَىٰ أَمْرٍ
جَامِعٍ لَمْ يَذْهَبُوا حَتَّىٰ يَسْتَأْذِنُوهُ إِنَّ الَّذِينَ يَسْتَأْذِنُونَكَ أُولَٰئِكَ الَّذِينَ
يُؤْمِنُونَ بِاللَّهِ وَرَسُولِهِ فَإِذَا اسْتَأْذَنُوكَ لِبَعْضِ شَأْنِهِمْ فَأْذَنْ
لِمَنْ شِئْتَ مِنْهُمْ وَاسْتَغْفِرْ لَهُمُ اللَّهَ إِنَّ اللَّهَ غَفُورٌ رَحِيمٌ ٦٢
لَا تَجْعَلُوا دُعَاءَ الرَّسُولِ بَيْنَكُمْ كَدُعَاءِ بَعْضِكُمْ بَعْضًا
قَدْ يَعْلَمُ اللَّهُ الَّذِينَ يَتَسَلَّلُونَ مِنْكُمْ لِوَاذًا فَلْيَحْذَرِ الَّذِينَ
يُخَالِفُونَ عَنْ أَمْرِهِ أَنْ تُصِيبَهُمْ فِتْنَةٌ أَوْ يُصِيبَهُمْ عَذَابٌ أَلِيمٌ ٦٣
أَلَا إِنَّ لِلَّهِ مَا فِي السَّمَاوَاتِ وَالْأَرْضِ قَدْ يَعْلَمُ مَا أَنْتُمْ عَلَيْهِ وَيَوْمَ
يُرْجَعُونَ إِلَيْهِ فَيُنَبِّئُهُمْ بِمَا عَمِلُوا وَاللَّهُ بِكُلِّ شَيْءٍ عَلِيمٌ ٦٤

سورة الفرقان مكية وسبع وسبعون آية

بِسْمِ اللَّهِ الرَّحْمَٰنِ الرَّحِيمِ
تَبَارَكَ الَّذِي نَزَّلَ الْفُرْقَانَ عَلَىٰ عَبْدِهِ لِيَكُونَ لِلْعَالَمِينَ نَذِيرًا
١ الَّذِي لَهُ مُلْكُ السَّمَاوَاتِ وَالْأَرْضِ وَلَمْ يَتَّخِذْ وَلَدًا وَلَمْ يَكُنْ
لَهُ شَرِيكٌ فِي الْمُلْكِ وَخَلَقَ كُلَّ شَيْءٍ فَقَدَّرَهُ تَقْدِيرًا ٢

24:64 Surely to God belongs what the heavens and the earth contain. He has knowledge of all you are up to. On the day when they return to Him, He will declare to them all that they have done. God has knowledge of all things.

SALVATION[1]

In the Name of God, the Merciful, the Compassionate

25:1 BLESSED BE He who has revealed Salvation to His servant, that he may warn the nations; Sovereign of the heavens and the earth, who has begotten no children and has no partner in His sovereignty; who has created all things and ordained them in due proportion.

1. See p. 7, note 1.

وَاتَّخَذُوا مِن دُونِهِ آلِهَةً لَا يَخْلُقُونَ شَيْئًا وَهُمْ يُخْلَقُونَ
وَلَا يَمْلِكُونَ لِأَنفُسِهِمْ ضَرًّا وَلَا نَفْعًا وَلَا يَمْلِكُونَ
مَوْتًا وَلَا حَيَاةً وَلَا نُشُورًا (٣) وَقَالَ الَّذِينَ كَفَرُوا
إِنْ هَٰذَا إِلَّا إِفْكٌ افْتَرَاهُ وَأَعَانَهُ عَلَيْهِ قَوْمٌ آخَرُونَ
فَقَدْ جَاءُوا ظُلْمًا وَزُورًا (٤) وَقَالُوا أَسَاطِيرُ الْأَوَّلِينَ
اكْتَتَبَهَا فَهِيَ تُمْلَىٰ عَلَيْهِ بُكْرَةً وَأَصِيلًا (٥) قُلْ أَنزَلَهُ
الَّذِي يَعْلَمُ السِّرَّ فِي السَّمَاوَاتِ وَالْأَرْضِ إِنَّهُ كَانَ غَفُورًا
رَحِيمًا (٦) وَقَالُوا مَالِ هَٰذَا الرَّسُولِ يَأْكُلُ الطَّعَامَ
وَيَمْشِي فِي الْأَسْوَاقِ لَوْلَا أُنزِلَ إِلَيْهِ مَلَكٌ فَيَكُونَ مَعَهُ
نَذِيرًا (٧) أَوْ يُلْقَىٰ إِلَيْهِ كَنزٌ أَوْ تَكُونُ لَهُ جَنَّةٌ يَأْكُلُ
مِنْهَا وَقَالَ الظَّالِمُونَ إِن تَتَّبِعُونَ إِلَّا رَجُلًا مَسْحُورًا (٨) انظُرْ
كَيْفَ ضَرَبُوا لَكَ الْأَمْثَالَ فَضَلُّوا فَلَا يَسْتَطِيعُونَ سَبِيلًا (٩)
تَبَارَكَ الَّذِي إِن شَاءَ جَعَلَ لَكَ خَيْرًا مِن ذَٰلِكَ جَنَّاتٍ تَجْرِي
مِن تَحْتِهَا الْأَنْهَارُ وَيَجْعَل لَكَ قُصُورًا (١٠) بَلْ كَذَّبُوا
بِالسَّاعَةِ وَأَعْتَدْنَا لِمَن كَذَّبَ بِالسَّاعَةِ سَعِيرًا (١١)

AND YET the unbelievers 25:3
serve, besides Him, other gods which can create nothing and were themselves created: which can neither harm nor help themselves, and which have no power over death or life, or the raising of the dead.

The unbelievers say: 'This[1] is but a forgery of his own invention, in which others have helped him.' Unjust is what they say and false.

And they say: 'Fables of the ancients he has written: they are dictated to him morning and evening.'

Say: 'It is revealed by Him who knows the secrets of the heavens and the earth. He is surely forgiving and compassionate.'

They also say: 'How is it that this apostle eats food and walks about the 25:7
market-squares? Why has no angel been sent down to him to give warning with him? Why has no treasure been given him, no garden to provide his sustenance?'

And the wrongdoers say: 'The man you follow is surely bewitched.'

See what epithets they bestow upon you![2] They have gone astray, and cannot return to the true path.

Blessed be He who, if He wills, can make for you better things than these: Gardens watered by running brooks; and He can make palaces for you.

Indeed, they deny the Hour. For those who deny the Hour We have pre- 25:11
pared a Conflagration.

1. The Koran. 2. Muḥammad.

25:12 FROM FAR away they shall
hear it raging and roaring. And
when, chained together, they
are flung into some narrow
space, they will fervently call
for death. But they will be
told: 'Do not call today for
one death; call for many
deaths!'

Say: 'Which is better, this or
the Paradise of Immortality
which the righteous have been
promised? It is their recompense and their retreat. Abiding
there for ever, they shall find
therein all that they desire. That
is a promise which your Lord
must needs fulfil.'

25:17 On the day He herds them
together with their idols, He
will say: 'Was it you who misled these My servants, or did
they choose to go astray?'

They will answer: 'Glory be to You! We should never have chosen other
guardians besides You. But You allowed them and their fathers the enjoyments of this life, so that they forgot the Admonition and became a people
utterly extinct.'

'Your idols have denied your charges. You cannot avert your doom, nor
can you be helped. Those of you who have done wrong We will grievously
punish.'

25:20 And We have sent no apostles before you who did not eat food or walk
about the market-squares. We test you by means of one another. Will you
not have patience? Surely your Lord observes all.

إذا رأتهم من مكان بعيد سمعوا لها تغيظا وزفيرا
(١٢) وإذا ألقوا منها مكانا ضيقا مقرنين دعوا
هنالك ثبورا (١٣) لا تدعوا اليوم ثبورا واحدا وادعوا
ثبورا كثيرا (١٤) قل أذلك خير أم جنة الخلد التي
وعد المتقون كانت لهم جزاء ومصيرا (١٥) لهم
فيها ما يشاءون خالدين كان على ربك وعدا مسئولا
(١٦) ويوم يحشرهم وما يعبدون من دون الله فيقول ءأنتم
أضللتم عبادي هؤلاء أم هم ضلوا السبيل (١٧) قالوا
سبحانك ما كان ينبغي لنا أن نتخذ من دونك من أولياء
ولكن متعتهم وآباءهم حتى نسوا الذكر وكانوا
قوما بورا (١٨) فقد كذبوكم بما تقولون فما تستطيعون
صرفا ولا نصرا ومن يظلم منكم نذقه عذابا كبيرا
(١٩) وما أرسلنا قبلك من المرسلين إلا إنهم ليأكلون
الطعام ويمشون في الأسواق وجعلنا بعضكم
لبعض فتنة أتصبرون وكان ربك بصيرا (٢٠)

وقال الذين لا يرجون لقاءنا لولا أنزل علينا الملائكة
أو نرى ربنا لقد استكبروا في أنفسهم وعتو عتوا كبيرا
﴿٢١﴾ يوم يرون الملائكة لا بشرى يومئذ للمجرمين ويقولون
حجرا محجورا ﴿٢٢﴾ وقدمنا إلى ما عملوا من عمل فجعلناه هباء
منثورا ﴿٢٣﴾ أصحاب الجنة يومئذ خير مستقرا وأحسن
مقيلا ﴿٢٤﴾ ويوم تشقق السماء بالغمام ونزل الملائكة
تنزيلا ﴿٢٥﴾ الملك يومئذ الحق للرحمن وكان يوما على
الكافرين عسيرا ﴿٢٦﴾ ويوم يعض الظالم على يديه يقول
يا ليتني اتخذت مع الرسول سبيلا ﴿٢٧﴾ يا ويلتى ليتني
لم أتخذ فلانا خليلا ﴿٢٨﴾ لقد أضلني عن الذكر بعد
إذ جاءني وكان الشيطان للإنسان خذولا ﴿٢٩﴾ وقال
الرسول يا رب إن قومي اتخذوا هذا القرآن مهجورا ﴿٣٠﴾ وكذلك
جعلنا لكل نبي عدوا من المجرمين وكفى بربك هاديا ونصيرا ﴿٣١﴾
وقال الذين كفروا لولا نزل عليه القرآن جملة واحدة
كذلك لنثبت به فؤادك ورتلناه ترتيلا ﴿٣٢﴾

THOSE WHO entertain no 25:21
hope of meeting Us ask: 'Why
have not the angels been sent
down upon us? Why can we
not see our Lord?' Arrogant
they are, and mightily iniquitous.

On the day they behold the
angels, the transgressors will
not rejoice that day. The
angels will say to them: 'You
shall never cross that barrier.'
Then We shall turn to that
which they have done and
render it as vain as scattered
dust.

As for the heirs of Para-
dise, they shall on that day
lodge in a more auspicious
dwelling, and in a cooler
resting-place.

On that day the sky with all
its clouds shall be rent asun-
der and the angels sent down in their ranks. On that day the Merciful will 25:26
truly reign supreme. A day of woe it shall be to the unbelievers.

On that day the wrongdoer will bite his hands and say: 'Would that I had
walked in the Apostle's path! Oh, would that I had never chosen so-and-so
for my companion! It was he that made me stray from the Admonition after
it had come to me. Satan is ever treacherous to man.'

And the Apostle says: 'Lord, my people have forsaken this Koran.' Thus
to every prophet We have assigned adversaries among the transgressors: but
you need none besides your Lord to guide and help you.

And the unbelievers say: 'Why was the Koran not revealed to him entire 25:32
in a single revelation?'

We have revealed it thus so that We may sustain your heart. We have
imparted it by gradual revelation.

25:33 NO SOONER will they come to
you with an argument than We
shall reveal to you the Truth,
better expounded. Those who
are dragged upon their faces
into Hell shall have a viler
place to dwell in, having
strayed farther from the right
path.
We gave the Book to Moses
and assigned to him his
brother Aaron as a helper. We
sent them to those who had
denied Our signs, and utterly
destroyed them.
And Noah's people: when
they denied the emissaries, We
drowned them and made of
them an example to mankind;
for the wrongdoers We prepared a woeful scourge.
25:38 And 'Ād and Thamūd, and
those who dwelt in Al-Rass,
and many generations in between: to each of them We gave examples, and
each of them We exterminated.
They must surely have passed by the city which was destroyed by the fatal
rain: have they never seen its ruins? Yet have they no faith in the Resurrection.
Whenever they see you they only deride you: 'Is this the man God has sent
as an emissary? Had we not stood firm, he would have made us stray from
our gods.' But when they face the scourge they shall realize who has strayed
farther from the right path.
25:43 Have you considered him who has made a god of his own appetite?
Would *you* be a guardian over him?

ولا يأتونك بمثل إلا جئناك بالحق وأحسن تفسيرا ٣٣
الذين يحشرون على وجوههم إلى جهنم أولئك شر
مكانا وأضل سبيلا ٣٤ ولقد آتينا موسى الكتاب
وجعلنا معه أخاه هرون وزيرا ٣٥ فقلنا اذهبا إلى
القوم الذين كذبوا بآياتنا فدمرناهم تدميرا ٣٦ وقوم
نوح لما كذبوا الرسل أغرقناهم وجعلناهم للناس
آية وأعتدنا للظالمين عذابا أليما ٣٧ وعادا وثمود
وأصحاب الرس وقرونا بين ذلك كثيرا ٣٨ وكلا
ضربنا له الأمثال وكلا تبرنا تتبيرا ٣٩ ولقد أتوا على
القرية التي أمطرت مطر السوء أفلم يكونوا يرونها
بل كانوا لا يرجون نشورا ٤٠ وإذا رأوك إن يتخذونك
إلا هزوا أهذا الذي بعث الله رسولا ٤١ إن كاد
ليضلنا عن آلهتنا لولا أن صبرنا عليها وسوف يعلمون
حين يرون العذاب من أضل سبيلا ٤٢ أرأيت من
اتخذ إلهه هويه أفأنت تكون عليه وكيلا ٤٣

أم تحسب أن أكثرهم يسمعون أو يعقلون إن
هم إلا كالأنعام بل هم أضل سبيلا ۝٤٤ ألم تر إلى
ربك كيف مد الظل ولو شاء لجعله ساكنا ثم جعلنا
الشمس عليه دليلا ۝٤٥ ثم قبضناه إلينا قبضا يسيرا ۝٤٦
وهو الذي جعل لكم الليل لباسا والنوم سباتا وجعل النهار
نشورا ۝٤٧ وهو الذي أرسل الرياح بشرا بين يدي رحمته
وأنزلنا من السماء ماء طهورا ۝٤٨ لنحيي به بلدة ميتا
ونسقيه مما خلقنا أنعاما وأناسي كثيرا ۝٤٩ ولقد صرفناه
بينهم ليذكروا فأبى أكثر الناس إلا كفورا ۝٥٠ ولو شئنا
لبعثنا في كل قرية نذيرا ۝٥١ فلا تطع الكافرين وجاهدهم
به جهادا كبيرا ۝٥٢ وهو الذي مرج البحرين هذا عذب فرات
وهذا ملح أجاج وجعل بينهما برزخا وحجرا محجورا ۝٥٣
وهو الذي خلق من الماء بشرا فجعله نسبا وصهرا وكان
ربك قديرا ۝٥٤ ويعبدون من دون الله ما لا ينفعهم
ولا يضرهم وكان الكافر على ربه ظهيرا ۝٥٥

OR DO you think most of 25:44
them can hear or understand? They are but like cattle; indeed, even more misguided.

Do you not see how your Lord lengthens the shadow? Had it been His will He could have made it constant. But We make the sun its guide; little by little We shorten it.

And He it was who made the night a mantle for you, and sleep a rest. He made each day a resurrection.

And He it is who drives the winds as harbingers of His mercy; and We send down pure water from the sky, so that We may give life to a dead land and quench the thirst of countless beasts and men We have created.

We have made it flow freely 25:50
among them, that they may remember. Yet most decline to render thanks.

And had it been Our will, We could have sent to every city someone to give warning. So do not yield to the unbelievers, but fight them vigorously with this.[1]

And He it was who sent the two seas rolling, the one sweet and fresh, the other salt and bitter, and set a rampart between them, an insurmountable barrier.

And He it was who created man from water, and gave him kin of blood and of marriage. All-powerful is your Lord.

Yet they worship idols which can neither help nor harm them. Surely the 25:55
unbeliever is an enemy to his Lord.

1. The Koran.

25:56 AND WE have sent you only to proclaim joyful tidings and to give warning. Say: 'I demand of you no recompense for this. Let him who will, take the right path to his Lord.'

Put your trust in the Ever-living who never dies. Celebrate His praise: He well knows all His servants' sins. In six days He created the heavens and the earth and all that lies between them, and then ascended the throne. He is the Lord of Mercy. Ask those who know, concerning Him.

When they are told: 'Bow down before the Merciful,' they ask: 'Who is the Merciful? Would you have us bow down to whatever you will?' And they grow more rebellious.

25:61 Blessed be He who decked the sky with constellations and therein set a
lamp and a shining moon. And He it is who makes the night succeed the day:
for those who would remember and render thanks.

True servants of the Merciful are those who walk humbly on the earth
and say: 'Peace!' to the ignorant who accost them; who pass the night standing and on their knees in adoration of their Lord; who say: 'Lord, ward off
from us the torment of Hell, for its torment is everlasting: an evil dwelling
25:67 and an evil resting-place'; who when they spend are neither extravagant nor
niggardly, but keep the golden mean;

وما ارسلناك الا مبشرا ونذيرا (٥٦) قل ما اسألكم عليه
من اجر الا من شاء ان يتخذ الى ربه سبيلا (٥٧) وتوكل
على الحي الذي لا يموت وسبح بحمده وكفى به بذنوب
عباده خبيرا (٥٨) الذي خلق السموات والارض
وما بينهما في ستة ايام ثم استوى على العرش
الرحمن فسئل به خبيرا (٥٩) واذا قيل لهم اسجدوا
للرحمن قالوا وما الرحمن انسجد لما تأمرنا وزادهم
نفورا (٦٠) تبارك الذي جعل في السماء بروجا وجعل
فيها سراجا وقمرا منيرا (٦١) وهو الذي جعل الليل والنهار
خلفة لمن اراد ان يذكر او اراد شكورا (٦٢) وعباد
الرحمن الذين يمشون على الارض هونا واذا خاطبهم الجاهلون
قالوا سلاما (٦٣) والذين يبيتون لربهم سجدا وقياما (٦٤)
والذين يقولون ربنا اصرف عنا عذاب جهنم ان عذابها
كان غراما (٦٥) انها ساءت مستقرا ومقاما (٦٦) والذين اذا
انفقوا لم يسرفوا ولم يقتروا وكان بين ذلك قواما (٦٧)

وَالَّذِينَ لَا يَدْعُونَ مَعَ اللَّهِ إِلَٰهًا آخَرَ وَلَا يَقْتُلُونَ
النَّفْسَ الَّتِي حَرَّمَ اللَّهُ إِلَّا بِالْحَقِّ وَلَا يَزْنُونَ ۚ وَمَن يَفْعَلْ
ذَٰلِكَ يَلْقَ أَثَامًا ﴿٦٨﴾ يُضَاعَفْ لَهُ الْعَذَابُ يَوْمَ الْقِيَامَةِ وَيَخْلُدْ فِيهِ
مُهَانًا ﴿٦٩﴾ إِلَّا مَن تَابَ وَآمَنَ وَعَمِلَ عَمَلًا صَالِحًا فَأُولَٰئِكَ يُبَدِّلُ اللَّهُ
سَيِّئَاتِهِمْ حَسَنَاتٍ ۗ وَكَانَ اللَّهُ غَفُورًا رَّحِيمًا ﴿٧٠﴾ وَمَن تَابَ وَعَمِلَ
صَالِحًا فَإِنَّهُ يَتُوبُ إِلَى اللَّهِ مَتَابًا ﴿٧١﴾ وَالَّذِينَ لَا يَشْهَدُونَ
الزُّورَ وَإِذَا مَرُّوا بِاللَّغْوِ مَرُّوا كِرَامًا ﴿٧٢﴾ وَالَّذِينَ
إِذَا ذُكِّرُوا بِآيَاتِ رَبِّهِمْ لَمْ يَخِرُّوا عَلَيْهَا صُمًّا وَعُمْيَانًا
﴿٧٣﴾ وَالَّذِينَ يَقُولُونَ رَبَّنَا هَبْ لَنَا مِنْ أَزْوَاجِنَا وَذُرِّيَّاتِنَا
قُرَّةَ أَعْيُنٍ وَاجْعَلْنَا لِلْمُتَّقِينَ إِمَامًا ﴿٧٤﴾ أُولَٰئِكَ يُجْزَوْنَ
الْغُرْفَةَ بِمَا صَبَرُوا وَيُلَقَّوْنَ فِيهَا تَحِيَّةً وَسَلَامًا ﴿٧٥﴾ خَالِدِينَ
فِيهَا ۚ حَسُنَتْ مُسْتَقَرًّا وَمُقَامًا ﴿٧٦﴾ قُلْ مَا يَعْبَأُ بِكُمْ رَبِّي
لَوْلَا دُعَاؤُكُمْ ۖ فَقَدْ كَذَّبْتُمْ فَسَوْفَ يَكُونُ لِزَامًا ﴿٧٧﴾

سورة الشعراء مكية وهي مائتان وسبع وعشرون آية

who invoke no other deity 25:68
besides God, and do not kill
except for a just cause:
manslaughter is forbidden by
God; who do not commit
adultery (he that does shall
meet with evil: his punishment
shall be doubled on the Day
of Resurrection and in disgrace shall he abide for
ever – unless he repent and
believe and do good works,
for then God will change his
sins to good actions: God is
forgiving and compassionate:
he that repents and does good 25:71
works shall truly return to
God); who do not bear false
witness, and who maintain
their dignity when hearing
profane abuse; who do not
turn a deaf ear and a blind eye
to the revelations of their
Lord when they are reminded of them; who say: 'Lord, give us joy in our
wives and children, and make us examples to those who fear You.' These
shall be rewarded for their fortitude with the loftiest abode in Paradise.
Therein shall they find a greeting and a welcome, and therein shall they abide
for ever: a pleasant dwelling and a pleasant resting-place.

Say: 'Little cares my Lord if you do not invoke Him. Now that you have 25:77
denied His revelations, His punishment is bound to overtake you.'

THE POETS

بسم الله الرحمن الرحيم
طسم (١) تلك آيات الكتاب المبين (٢) لعلك باخع نفسك ألا
يكونوا مؤمنين (٣) إن نشأ ننزل عليهم من السماء آية فظلت
أعناقهم لها خاضعين (٤) وما يأتيهم من ذكر من الرحمن محدث إلا
كانوا عنه معرضين (٥) فقد كذبوا فسيأتيهم أنبؤا ما كانوا
به يستهزءون (٦) أولم يروا إلى الأرض كم أنبتنا فيها من كل
زوج كريم (٧) إن في ذلك لآية وما كان أكثرهم مؤمنين
(٨) وإن ربك لهو العزيز الرحيم (٩) وإذ نادى ربك موسى أن ائت
القوم الظالمين (١٠) قوم فرعون ألا يتقون (١١) قال رب إني أخاف
أن يكذبون (١٢) ويضيق صدري ولا ينطلق لساني فأرسل إلى
هرون (١٣) ولهم علي ذنب فأخاف أن يقتلون (١٤) قال كلا
فاذهبا بآياتنا إنا معكم مستمعون (١٥) فأتيا فرعون فقولا
إنا رسول رب العالمين (١٦) أن أرسل معنا بني إسرائيل (١٧)
قال ألم نربك فينا وليدا ولبثت فينا من عمرك سنين (١٨)
وفعلت فعلتك التي فعلت وأنت من الكافرين (١٩)

In the Name of God,
the Merciful, the Compassionate

26:1 *Ṭā' sīn mīm.* These are the revelations of the veritable Book: you will perhaps fret yourself to death on account of their unbelief. If We will, We can reveal to them a sign from heaven before which they will bow their necks in utter humility.

They turned their backs on each fresh Admonition they received from the Merciful: they disbelieved, but the truth of that which they have laughed to scorn will dawn upon them.

Do they not see the earth, how We have planted on it all kinds of beneficial plants? Surely in this there is a sign; yet most of them do not believe.

26:10 And surely your Lord is the Mighty One, the Compassionate. Your Lord called out to Moses, saying: 'Go to those wicked people, the people of Pharaoh. Will they not take heed?'

'Lord,' he said, 'I fear they will deny me. I may become impatient and stammer in my speech. Send for Aaron. They accuse me of a crime,[1] and I fear that they may put me to death.'

'Never fear,' said He. 'Go both of you with Our signs; We shall be with you and shall hear all. Go to Pharaoh and say to him: "We are messengers from the Lord of the Universe. Let the Israelites depart with us."'

Pharaoh said: 'Did we not bring you up when you were an infant? And did
26:19 you not stay in our midst several years of your life? Yet you have done the
deed you did; surely you are ungrateful.'

1. Moses had killed an Egyptian.

قال فعلتها إذا وأنا من الضالين ﴿٢٠﴾ ففررت منكم لما
خفتكم فوهب لي ربي حكما وجعلني من المرسلين ﴿٢١﴾ وتلك
نعمة تمنها علي أن عبدت بني إسرائيل ﴿٢٢﴾ قال فرعون وما رب
العالمين ﴿٢٣﴾ قال رب السموات والأرض وما بينهما إن كنتم
موقنين ﴿٢٤﴾ قال لمن حوله ألا تستمعون ﴿٢٥﴾ قال ربكم ورب
آبائكم الأولين ﴿٢٦﴾ قال إن رسولكم الذي أرسل إليكم
لمجنون ﴿٢٧﴾ قال رب المشرق والمغرب وما بينهما إن كنتم
تعقلون ﴿٢٨﴾ قال لئن اتخذت إلها غيري لأجعلنك من
المسجونين ﴿٢٩﴾ قال أولو جئتك بشيء مبين ﴿٣٠﴾ قال فأت به
إن كنت من الصادقين ﴿٣١﴾ فألقى عصاه فإذا هي ثعبان
مبين ﴿٣٢﴾ ونزع يده فإذا هي بيضاء للناظرين ﴿٣٣﴾ قال للملإ
حوله إن هذا لساحر عليم ﴿٣٤﴾ يريد أن يخرجكم من أرضكم
بسحره فماذا تأمرون ﴿٣٥﴾ قالوا أرجه وأخاه وابعث في
المدائن حاشرين ﴿٣٦﴾ يأتوك بكل سحار عليم ﴿٣٧﴾ فجمع السحرة
لميقات يوم معلوم ﴿٣٨﴾ وقيل للناس هل أنتم مجتمعون ﴿٣٩﴾

HE SAID: 'I did that when I 26:20
had gone astray. I fled from
you because I feared you. But
my Lord has given me wisdom
and made me an apostle. And
this is the favour with which
you taunt me: you have made
the Israelites your bondsmen.'
'Who is the Lord of the
Universe?' said Pharaoh.
He said: 'The Lord of the
heavens and the earth and all
that lies between them. If only
you believed!'
'Do you hear?' said he to
those around him.
'Your Lord,' he went on,
'and the Lord of your forefathers.'
He said: 'The apostle who
has been sent to you is surely
possessed!'
'The Lord of the East and 26:28
of the West,' said Moses, 'and all that lies between them. If only you could
understand!'
'If you serve any other god but myself,' he said, 'I shall have you thrown
into prison.'
'Even if I showed you a convincing sign?' he said.
He replied: 'Show it to us, if what you say be true.'
He threw down his staff and thereupon it changed to a veritable serpent.
Then he drew out his hand, and it was white to all who saw it.
'This man,' he said to the nobles around him, 'is a skilful sorcerer who
seeks to drive you from your land by his sorcery. What is your counsel?'
They said: 'Put them off awhile, him and his brother, and send forth criers
to the cities to bring every skilled enchanter to your presence.'
The sorcerers were gathered on an appointed day, and the people were 26:39
asked: 'Are you all assembled?

26:40 WE MAY follow the sorcerers if *they* win the day.'

And when the sorcerers came they said to Pharaoh: 'Shall we be rewarded if we win?'

'Yes,' he answered, 'and you shall become my favoured friends.'

Moses said to them: 'Throw down all that you wish to throw.'

They threw down their ropes and staffs, saying: 'By Pharaoh's glory, we shall surely win!'

Then Moses threw down his staff, and it swallowed up their false devices. The sorcerers prostrated themselves, saying: 'We now believe in the Lord of the Universe, the Lord of Moses and Aaron.'

لعلنا نتبع السحرة إن كانوا هم الغالبين ﴿٤٠﴾ فلما جاء السحرة
قالوا لفرعون أئن لنا لأجرا إن كنا نحن الغالبين ﴿٤١﴾ قال نعم
وإنكم إذا لمن المقربين ﴿٤٢﴾ قال لهم موسى ألقوا ما أنتم ملقون
﴿٤٣﴾ فألقوا حبالهم وعصيهم وقالوا بعزة فرعون إنا لنحن
الغالبون ﴿٤٤﴾ فألقى موسى عصاه فإذا هي تلقف ما يأفكون
﴿٤٥﴾ فألقي السحرة ساجدين ﴿٤٦﴾ قالوا آمنا برب العالمين ﴿٤٧﴾
رب موسى وهرون ﴿٤٨﴾ قال آمنتم له قبل أن آذن لكم إنه
لكبيركم الذي علمكم السحر فلسوف تعلمون لأقطعن أيديكم
وأرجلكم من خلاف ولأصلبنكم أجمعين ﴿٤٩﴾ قالوا لا ضير إنا إلى
ربنا منقلبون ﴿٥٠﴾ إنا نطمع أن يغفر لنا ربنا خطايانا أن
كنا أول المؤمنين ﴿٥١﴾ وأوحينا إلى موسى أن أسر بعبادي إنكم
متبعون ﴿٥٢﴾ فأرسل فرعون في المدائن حاشرين ﴿٥٣﴾ إن هؤلاء
لشرذمة قليلون ﴿٥٤﴾ وإنهم لنا لغائظون ﴿٥٥﴾ وإنا لجميع حاذرون
﴿٥٦﴾ فأخرجناهم من جنات وعيون ﴿٥٧﴾ وكنوز ومقام كريم ﴿٥٨﴾
كذلك وأورثناها بني إسرائيل ﴿٥٩﴾ فأتبعوهم مشرقين ﴿٦٠﴾

26:49 He said: 'Do you dare believe in Him before I give you leave? He must surely be your master, who has taught you witchcraft. But you shall see. I will cut off your hands and feet on alternate sides and crucify you all.'

'That cannot harm us,' they replied, 'for to our Lord we shall return. We hope our Lord will forgive us our sins, since we are the first who have believed.'

Then We revealed Our will to Moses, saying: 'Set forth with My servants in the night, for you will be pursued.'

Pharaoh sent forth criers to the cities. 'These,' they said, 'are but a puny band, who have provoked us much. But we are a numerous army, well prepared.'

Thus did We make them leave their gardens and their fountains, their treasures and their sumptuous dwellings. Even thus; and to the Israelites We gave those.

26:60 At sunrise the Egyptians followed them.

فلما تراءا الجمعان قال أصحاب موسى إنا لمدركون ﴿٦١﴾ قال كلا إن
معي ربي سيهدين ﴿٦٢﴾ فأوحينا إلى موسى أن اضرب بعصاك
البحر فانفلق فكان كل فرق كالطود العظيم ﴿٦٣﴾ وأزلفنا
ثم الآخرين ﴿٦٤﴾ وأنجينا موسى ومن معه أجمعين ﴿٦٥﴾ ثم أغرقنا
الآخرين ﴿٦٦﴾ إن في ذلك لآية وما كان أكثرهم مؤمنين ﴿٦٧﴾
وإن ربك لهو العزيز الرحيم ﴿٦٨﴾ واتل عليهم نبأ إبرهيم
﴿٦٩﴾ إذ قال لأبيه وقومه ما تعبدون ﴿٧٠﴾ قالوا نعبد أصناما
فنظل لها عاكفين ﴿٧١﴾ قال هل يسمعونكم إذ تدعون
﴿٧٢﴾ أو ينفعونكم أو يضرون ﴿٧٣﴾ قالوا بل وجدنا آباءنا
كذلك يفعلون ﴿٧٤﴾ قال أفرأيتم ما كنتم تعبدون
﴿٧٥﴾ أنتم وآباؤكم الأقدمون ﴿٧٦﴾ فإنهم عدو لي
إلا رب العالمين ﴿٧٧﴾ الذي خلقني فهو يهدين ﴿٧٨﴾ والذي
هو يطعمني ويسقين ﴿٧٩﴾ وإذا مرضت فهو يشفين ﴿٨٠﴾ والذي
يميتني ثم يحيين ﴿٨١﴾ والذي أطمع أن يغفر لي خطيئتي يوم الدين
﴿٨٢﴾ رب هب لي حكما وألحقني بالصالحين ﴿٨٣﴾

AND WHEN the two multi- 26:61
tudes came within sight of each other, Moses' companions said: 'We are surely undone!'

'No,' he said, 'my Lord is with me, and He will guide me.'

We bade Moses strike the sea with his staff, and the sea was cleft asunder, each part as high as a massive mountain. In between We made the others follow. We delivered Moses and all who were with him; and the others We drowned.

Surely in that there was a sign; yet most of them did not believe.

Surely your Lord is the Mighty One, the Compassionate. Recount to them the story of Abraham. He said to his father and to his people: 'What is that which you worship?'

They said: 'We worship idols and pray to them with all fervour.' 26:71

'Do they hear you when you pray?' he asked. 'Can they help you or do you harm?'

They said: 'This was what our forefathers did before us.'

He said: 'Do you see those you have worshipped, you and your forefathers of old? They are my enemies. Not so the Lord of the Universe, who has created me; who gives me guidance, food and drink; who, when I am sick, restores me; who will cause me to die and bring me back to life hereafter; who, I hope, will forgive me my sins on the Day of Judgement.

'Lord, bestow wisdom upon me, and admit me among the righteous. 26:83

26:84 ENDOW ME with a tongue of truthfulness among posterity and count me among the heirs of the Blissful Garden. Forgive my father, for he has gone astray. Do not hold me up to shame on the Day of Resurrection; the day when wealth and offspring will be of no avail, and when none shall be saved but him who comes before his Lord with a pure heart; when Paradise shall be brought within sight of the righteous and Hell be revealed to the erring. They will be asked: "Where are the idols which you worshipped besides God? Can they help you or help themselves?" And into Hell they shall be hurled, they and those who misled them, and Satan's legions all. "By the Lord," they
will say, as they contend with them, "we clearly erred when we made you equals
26:99 with the Lord of the Universe. It was but the transgressors who led us astray.
We have no intercessors now, no loving friend. Could we but live our lives
again we would be true believers."'

Surely in that there was a sign, yet most of them did not believe.

Surely your Lord is the Mighty One, the Compassionate. The people of Noah disbelieved the emissaries. 'Will you not fear God?' said Noah, their kin, to them. 'I am indeed your truthful apostle. Fear God, then, and follow me. For this I demand of you no recompense, for none can reward me except the Lord of the Universe. Fear God, and follow me.'

26:111 They said: 'Are we to believe in you when your followers are but the
lowest of the low?'

واجعل لي لسان صدق في الآخرين ﴿٨٤﴾ واجعلني من ورثة جنة
النعيم ﴿٨٥﴾ واغفر لأبي إنه كان من الضالين ﴿٨٦﴾ ولا تخزني
يوم يبعثون ﴿٨٧﴾ يوم لا ينفع مال ولا بنون ﴿٨٨﴾ إلا من أتى الله
بقلب سليم ﴿٨٩﴾ وأزلفت الجنة للمتقين ﴿٩٠﴾ وبرزت الجحيم
للغاوين ﴿٩١﴾ وقيل لهم أين ما كنتم تعبدون ﴿٩٢﴾ من دون الله
هل ينصرونكم أو ينتصرون ﴿٩٣﴾ فكبكبوا فيها هم والغاوون ﴿٩٤﴾
وجنود إبليس أجمعون ﴿٩٥﴾ قالوا وهم فيها يختصمون ﴿٩٦﴾ تالله
إن كنا لفي ضلال مبين ﴿٩٧﴾ إذ نسويكم برب العالمين ﴿٩٨﴾ وما أضلنا
إلا المجرمون ﴿٩٩﴾ فما لنا من شافعين ﴿١٠٠﴾ ولا صديق حميم ﴿١٠١﴾
فلو أن لنا كرة فنكون من المؤمنين ﴿١٠٢﴾ إن في ذلك لآية وما
كان أكثرهم مؤمنين ﴿١٠٣﴾ وإن ربك لهو العزيز الرحيم ﴿١٠٤﴾
كذبت قوم نوح المرسلين ﴿١٠٥﴾ إذ قال لهم أخوهم نوح ألا تتقون
﴿١٠٦﴾ إني لكم رسول أمين ﴿١٠٧﴾ فاتقوا الله وأطيعون ﴿١٠٨﴾ وما أسألكم
عليه من أجر إن أجري إلا على رب العالمين ﴿١٠٩﴾ فاتقوا الله
وأطيعون ﴿١١٠﴾ قالوا أنؤمن لك واتبعك الأرذلون ﴿١١١﴾

قال وما علمي بما كانوا يعملون ١١٢ إن حسابهم إلا على ربي
لو تشعرون ١١٣ وما أنا بطارد المؤمنين ١١٤ إن أنا إلا نذير مبين
١١٥ قالوا لئن لم تنته يا نوح لتكونن من المرجومين ١١٦ قال رب
إن قومي كذبون ١١٧ فافتح بيني وبينهم فتحا ونجني ومن
معي من المؤمنين ١١٨ فأنجيناه ومن معه في الفلك المشحون
١١٩ ثم أغرقنا بعد الباقين ١٢٠ إن في ذلك لآية وما كان
أكثرهم مؤمنين ١٢١ وإن ربك لهو العزيز الرحيم ١٢٢
كذبت عاد المرسلين ١٢٣ إذ قال لهم أخوهم هود ألا تتقون
١٢٤ إني لكم رسول أمين ١٢٥ فاتقوا الله وأطيعون ١٢٦ وما أسألكم
عليه من أجر إن أجري إلا على رب العالمين ١٢٧ أتبنون بكل ريع
آية تعبثون ١٢٨ وتتخذون مصانع لعلكم تخلدون ١٢٩ وإذا
بطشتم بطشتم جبارين ١٣٠ فاتقوا الله وأطيعون ١٣١ واتقوا الذي
أمدكم بما تعلمون ١٣٢ أمدكم بأنعام وبنين ١٣٣ وجنات
وعيون ١٣٤ إني أخاف عليكم عذاب يوم عظيم ١٣٥
قالوا سواء علينا أوعظت أم لم تكن من الواعظين ١٣٦

'I HAVE no knowledge of 26:112
what they did,' he said. 'My Lord alone can bring them to account. Would that you understood! Nor will I drive away the true believers. I am sent forth only to give plain warning.'

'Noah,' they said, 'desist, or you shall be stoned to death.'

He said: 'Lord, my people disbelieve me. Judge rightly between us. Save me and the believers who are with me.'

So We delivered him and those who were with him in the laden ark, and drowned the others thereafter.

Surely in that there was a sign; yet most of them did not believe.

Surely your Lord is the 26:122
Mighty One, the Compassionate. 'Ād disbelieved the apostles. Their kin Hūd had said to them: 'Will you not fear God? I am indeed your truthful apostle. Fear God, then, and follow me. For this I demand of you no recompense; none can reward me except the Lord of the Universe. Will you erect a monument on every hill? Vain is your work. You build strong fortresses, hoping that you may last for ever. When you exercise your power, you act like cruel tyrants. Fear God, and follow me. Fear Him who has given you all the things you know. He has given you flocks and children, gardens and fountains. Beware the torment of a fateful day.'

They said: 'We care nothing whether or not you preach to us. 26:136

26:137 THIS IS but a myth of the
ancients. Surely we shall not
be punished.'
They denied him, and thus
We utterly destroyed them.
Surely in that there was a sign;
yet most of them did not
believe.
Surely your Lord is the
Mighty One, the Compassionate. Thamūd disbelieved the
apostles. Their kin Ṣāliḥ had
said to them: 'Will you not
fear God? I am indeed your
truthful apostle. Fear God and
follow me. For this I demand
of you no recompense; none
can reward me except the
Lord of the Universe. Are you
to be left secure in this land,
26:147 amidst gardens and fountains,
cornfields and palm-trees
laden with fine fruit, hewing
your dwellings out of the mountains and leading a wanton life? Have fear of
God and follow me. Do not obey the bidding of transgressors who perpetrate corruption in the land and do no good at all.'
They said: 'Surely you are bewitched. You are but a mortal like ourselves.
Show us a sign, if what you say be true.'
'Here,' he said, 'is this she-camel. She shall have her share of water as you
have yours, each drinking on an appointed day. Do not harm her, or the
scourge of a fateful day shall take you.'
Yet they hamstrung her, and in the morning were repentant. The scourge
took them.
Surely in that there was a sign. Yet most of them did not believe.
26:159 Surely your Lord is the Mighty One, the Compassionate.

إن هذا إلا خلق الأولين ﴿١٣٧﴾ وما نحن بمعذبين ﴿١٣٨﴾
فكذبوه فأهلكناهم إن في ذلك لآية وما كان
أكثرهم مؤمنين ﴿١٣٩﴾ وإن ربك لهو العزيز الرحيم ﴿١٤٠﴾
كذبت ثمود المرسلين ﴿١٤١﴾ إذ قال لهم أخوهم صالح ألا تتقون ﴿١٤٢﴾
إني لكم رسول أمين ﴿١٤٣﴾ فاتقوا الله وأطيعون ﴿١٤٤﴾ وما أسألكم
عليه من أجر إن أجري إلا على رب العالمين ﴿١٤٥﴾ أتتركون في ما
هاهنا آمنين ﴿١٤٦﴾ في جنات وعيون ﴿١٤٧﴾ وزروع ونخل طلعها هضيم ﴿١٤٨﴾ وتنحتون
من الجبال بيوتا فارهين ﴿١٤٩﴾ فاتقوا الله وأطيعون ﴿١٥٠﴾ ولا تطيعوا
أمر المسرفين ﴿١٥١﴾ الذين يفسدون في الأرض ولا يصلحون
﴿١٥٢﴾ قالوا إنما أنت من المسحرين ﴿١٥٣﴾ ما أنت إلا بشر مثلنا
فأت بآية إن كنت من الصادقين ﴿١٥٤﴾ قال هذه ناقة لها
شرب ولكم شرب يوم معلوم ﴿١٥٥﴾ ولا تمسوها بسوء
فيأخذكم عذاب يوم عظيم ﴿١٥٦﴾ فعقروها فأصبحوا
نادمين ﴿١٥٧﴾ فأخذهم العذاب إن في ذلك لآية وما كان
أكثرهم مؤمنين ﴿١٥٨﴾ وإن ربك لهو العزيز الرحيم ﴿١٥٩﴾

كذبت قوم لوط المرسلين ﴿١٦٠﴾ إذ قال لهم أخوهم لوط ألا تتقون
﴿١٦١﴾ إني لكم رسول أمين ﴿١٦٢﴾ فاتقوا الله وأطيعون ﴿١٦٣﴾ وما أسألكم
عليه من أجر إن أجري إلا على رب العالمين ﴿١٦٤﴾ أتأتون
الذكران من العالمين ﴿١٦٥﴾ وتذرون ما خلق لكم ربكم
من أزواجكم بل أنتم قوم عادون ﴿١٦٦﴾ قالوا لئن لم تنته يا لوط
لتكونن من المخرجين ﴿١٦٧﴾ قال إني لعملكم من القالين ﴿١٦٨﴾ رب
نجني وأهلي مما يعملون ﴿١٦٩﴾ فنجيناه وأهله أجمعين ﴿١٧٠﴾
إلا عجوزا في الغابرين ﴿١٧١﴾ ثم دمرنا الآخرين ﴿١٧٢﴾ وأمطرنا
عليهم مطرا فساء مطر المنذرين ﴿١٧٣﴾ إن في ذلك لآية وما
كان أكثرهم مؤمنين ﴿١٧٤﴾ وإن ربك لهو العزيز الرحيم ﴿١٧٥﴾
كذب أصحاب ليكة المرسلين ﴿١٧٦﴾ إذ قال لهم شعيب ألا تتقون
﴿١٧٧﴾ إني لكم رسول أمين ﴿١٧٨﴾ فاتقوا الله وأطيعون ﴿١٧٩﴾ وما أسألكم
عليه من أجر إن أجري إلا على رب العالمين ﴿١٨٠﴾ أوفوا الكيل
ولا تكونوا من المخسرين ﴿١٨١﴾ وزنوا بالقسطاس المستقيم ﴿١٨٢﴾
ولا تبخسوا الناس أشياءهم ولا تعثوا في الأرض مفسدين ﴿١٨٣﴾

LOT'S PEOPLE disbelieved the 26:160
apostles. Their kin Lot had said to them: 'Will you not fear God? I am indeed your truthful apostle. Fear God and follow me. For this I demand of you no recompense; none can reward me except the Lord of the Universe. Will you fornicate with the males of humans and eschew the wives whom God has created for you? Surely you are a sinful people.'

'Lot,' they said, 'desist or you shall be banished.'

He said: 'I abhor your ways. Lord, deliver me and my kin from their practices.'

We delivered him and his kindred all, save for one old woman who stayed behind, and the others We utterly
destroyed. We pelted them with rain, and evil was the rain which fell on 26:173
those who were forewarned.

Surely in that there was a sign. Yet most of them did not believe.

Your Lord is the Mighty One, the Compassionate. The dwellers of the Forest[1] disbelieved the apostles. Shu'aib had said to them: 'Will you not fear God? I am indeed your truthful apostle. Fear God and follow me. For this I demand of you no recompense: none can reward me except the Lord of the Universe. Give just measure and defraud none. Weigh with even scales and
do not cheat the people of what is rightly theirs; nor shall you corrupt the 26:183
land with evil.

1. The people of Midian.

26:184 AND FEAR Him who created you and the earlier generations.'

They said: 'You are surely bewitched. You are but a mortal like ourselves. Indeed, we believe that you are lying. Bring down upon us a fragment of the sky if what you say be true.'

He said: 'My Lord has better knowledge of what you do.' They disbelieved him, and thus the scourge of the Day of Darkness smote them; it was surely the scourge of a fateful day.

Surely in that there was a sign; yet most of them did not believe.

Your Lord is the Mighty One, the Compassionate. This is surely revealed by the Lord
26:193 of the Universe. The Faithful Spirit has brought it down into your heart, that
you may give warning in eloquent Arabic speech. It was surely foretold in the
Scriptures of the ancients. Is it not sufficient proof for them that the doctors
of the Israelites recognize it? If We had revealed it to a foreign man, and he
had recited it to them, they still would not have believed. Thus do We put
unbelief in the hearts of the guilty: they shall not believe in it until they see
the woeful scourge, which shall suddenly smite them when they are heedless.
And then they will say: 'Shall we ever be reprieved?'

Is it their wish to hurry on Our scourge? Think! If We let them live in ease
26:206 for many years, and then the promised scourge does fall upon them,

واتقوا الذي خلقكم والجبلة الأولين ﴿١٨٤﴾ قالوا إنما أنت من
المسحرين ﴿١٨٥﴾ وما أنت إلا بشر مثلنا وإن نظنك لمن الكاذبين
﴿١٨٦﴾ فأسقط علينا كسفا من السماء إن كنت من الصادقين
﴿١٨٧﴾ قال ربي أعلم بما تعملون ﴿١٨٨﴾ فكذبوه فأخذهم عذاب
يوم الظلة إنه كان عذاب يوم عظيم ﴿١٨٩﴾ إن في ذلك لآية
وما كان أكثرهم مؤمنين ﴿١٩٠﴾ وإن ربك لهو العزيز الرحيم ﴿١٩١﴾
وإنه لتنزيل رب العالمين ﴿١٩٢﴾ نزل به الروح الأمين ﴿١٩٣﴾ على
قلبك لتكون من المنذرين ﴿١٩٤﴾ بلسان عربي مبين ﴿١٩٥﴾ وإنه
لفي زبر الأولين ﴿١٩٦﴾ أولم يكن لهم آية أن يعلمه علماء
بني إسرائيل ﴿١٩٧﴾ ولو نزلناه على بعض الأعجمين ﴿١٩٨﴾ فقرأه
عليهم ما كانوا به مؤمنين ﴿١٩٩﴾ كذلك سلكناه في قلوب
المجرمين ﴿٢٠٠﴾ لا يؤمنون به حتى يروا العذاب الأليم ﴿٢٠١﴾
فيأتيهم بغتة وهم لا يشعرون ﴿٢٠٢﴾ فيقولوا هل نحن
منظرون ﴿٢٠٣﴾ أفبعذابنا يستعجلون ﴿٢٠٤﴾ أفرأيت إن
متعناهم سنين ﴿٢٠٥﴾ ثم جاءهم ما كانوا يوعدون ﴿٢٠٦﴾

ما أغنى عنهم ما كانوا يمتعون ٢٠٧ وما أهلكنا من قرية إلا
لها منذرون ٢٠٨ ذكرى وما كنا ظالمين ٢٠٩ وما تنزلت
به الشياطين ٢١٠ وما ينبغي لهم وما يستطيعون ٢١١ إنهم
عن السمع لمعزولون ٢١٢ فلا تدع مع الله إلها آخر فتكون من
المعذبين ٢١٣ وأنذر عشيرتك الأقربين ٢١٤ واخفض جناحك
لمن اتبعك من المؤمنين ٢١٥ فإن عصوك فقل إني بريء مما تعملون ٢١٦
وتوكل على العزيز الرحيم ٢١٧ الذي يراك حين تقوم ٢١٨ وتقلبك
في الساجدين ٢١٩ إنه هو السميع العليم ٢٢٠ هل أنبئكم على من
تنزل الشياطين ٢٢١ تنزل على كل أفاك أثيم ٢٢٢ يلقون السمع
وأكثرهم كاذبون ٢٢٣ والشعراء يتبعهم الغاوون ٢٢٤ ألم تر
أنهم في كل واد يهيمون ٢٢٥ وأنهم يقولون ما لا يفعلون ٢٢٦
إلا الذين آمنوا وعملوا الصالحات وذكروا الله كثيرا وانتصروا من
بعد ما ظلموا وسيعلم الذين ظلموا أي منقلب ينقلبون ٢٢٧

سورة النمل مكية وهي ثلاث وتسعون آية

of what avail will their past 26:207
enjoyments be to them?

Never have We destroyed a
city We did not warn and
admonish beforehand. We are
never unjust.

It was not the demons who
brought this down: it is neither in their interest nor in
their power. Indeed, they are
too far away to overhear it.

Therefore call on no other
god besides God, lest you suffer torment. Admonish your
nearest kin and show kindness
to those of the believers who
follow you. If they disobey 26:216
you, say: 'I am not accountable for what you do.'

Put your trust in the Mighty
One, the Compassionate, who
observes you when you stand
upright and when you walk
among the worshippers. He it is who hears all and knows all.

Shall I tell you on whom the demons descend? They descend on every
lying sinner. They eagerly listen, but most of them are liars.

Poets are followed by erring men. Behold how aimlessly they rove in every
valley, preaching what they never practise. Not so the true believers, who do 26:227
good works and remember God with fervour and defend themselves only
when wronged. The wrongdoers will then learn to what end they will be
overturned.

THE ANT

In the Name of God,
the Merciful, the Compassionate

بسم الله الرحمن الرحيم
طس تلك آيات القرآن وكتاب مبين ﴿١﴾ هدى وبشرى للمؤمنين
﴿٢﴾ الذين يقيمون الصلوة ويؤتون الزكوة وهم بالآخرة هم يوقنون
﴿٣﴾ إن الذين لا يؤمنون بالآخرة زينا لهم أعمالهم فهم يعمهون
﴿٤﴾ أولئك الذين لهم سوء العذاب وهم في الآخرة هم الأخسرون
﴿٥﴾ وإنك لتلقى القرآن من لدن حكيم عليم ﴿٦﴾ إذ قال موسى
لأهله إني آنست نارا سآتيكم منها بخبر أو آتيكم بشهاب
قبس لعلكم تصطلون ﴿٧﴾ فلما جاءها نودي أن بورك
من في النار ومن حولها وسبحان الله رب العالمين ﴿٨﴾
يا موسى إنه أنا الله العزيز الحكيم ﴿٩﴾ وألق عصاك فلما
رآها تهتز كأنها جان ولى مدبرا ولم يعقب يا موسى لا تخف إني
لا يخاف لدي المرسلون ﴿١٠﴾ إلا من ظلم ثم بدل حسنا بعد سوء
فإني غفور رحيم ﴿١١﴾ وأدخل يدك في جيبك تخرج بيضاء من
غير سوء في تسع آيات إلى فرعون وقومه إنهم كانوا قوما فاسقين
﴿١٢﴾ فلما جاءتهم آياتنا مبصرة قالوا هذا سحر مبين ﴿١٣﴾

27:1 *Ṭā' sīn.* These are the revelations of the Koran, a veritable Book; a guide and joyful tidings to true believers, who attend to their prayers and render the alms levy and firmly believe in the life to come.

As for those that deny the life to come, We make their deeds seem fair to them, so that they blindly stray from the right path. Such are those who shall be grievously punished and in the life to come lose most.

You have surely received the Koran from Himself, from Him who is wise and all-knowing. Tell of Moses, who said to his people: 'I can descry a fire. I will go and bring you news and a lighted torch to warm yourselves with.'

27:8 And when he came near, a voice called out to him: 'Blessed be He who is in the fire and all around it! Glory to God, Lord of the Universe! Moses, I am God, the Almighty, the Wise One. Throw down your staff.'

And when he saw it slithering like a serpent, he turned and fled, without a backward glance.

'Moses, do not be afraid,' said He. 'My apostles are never afraid in My presence. As for those who sin and then do good after evil, I am forgiving and compassionate.

'Put your hand into your pocket. It will come out white, although unharmed. This is but one of the nine signs for Pharaoh and his people; surely they are a sinful people.'

27:13 But when Our visible signs did come to them, they said: 'This is sorcery manifest.'

وجحدوا بها واستيقنتها أنفسهم ظلما وعلوا فانظر كيف
كان عاقبة المفسدين ﴿١٤﴾ ولقد آتينا داود وسليمن علما
وقالا الحمد لله الذى فضلنا على كثير من عباده المؤمنين
﴿١٥﴾ وورث سليمن داود وقال يا أيها الناس علمنا منطق
الطير وأوتينا من كل شىء إن هذا لهو الفضل المبين ﴿١٦﴾
وحشر لسليمن جنوده من الجن والإنس والطير فهم
يوزعون ﴿١٧﴾ حتى إذا أتوا على واد النمل قالت نملة يا
أيها النمل ادخلوا مساكنكم لا يحطمنكم سليمن
وجنوده وهم لا يشعرون ﴿١٨﴾ فتبسم ضاحكا من
قولها وقال رب أوزعنى أن أشكر نعمتك التى أنعمت
على وعلى والدى وأن أعمل صالحا ترضيه وأدخلنى برحمتك
فى عبادك الصالحين ﴿١٩﴾ وتفقد الطير فقال مالى لا أرى
الهدهد أم كان من الغائبين ﴿٢٠﴾ لأعذبنه عذابا شديدا
أو لأاذبحنه أو ليأتينى بسلطان مبين ﴿٢١﴾ فمكث غير بعيد
فقال أحطت بما لم تحط به وجئتك من سبإ بنبإ يقين ﴿٢٢﴾

THEY DENIED them in their 27:14
wickedness and their pride,
although their souls knew
them to be true. Consider the
fate of the evil-doers.

We bestowed knowledge
on David and Solomon. The
two said: 'Praise be to God
who has exalted us above
many of His believing servants.'

And Solomon succeeded
David. He said: 'Know, you
people, we have been taught
the tongue of birds and endowed with all good things.
Surely this is the signal favour.'

His forces of jinn and men
and birds were called to Solomon's presence, and ranged in
battle array. When they came to 27:18
the Valley of the Ants, an ant
said: 'Go into your dwellings,
ants, lest Solomon and his warriors should unwittingly crush you.'

He smiled, laughing at her words, and said: 'Inspire me, Lord, to render
thanks for the favours with which You have favoured me and my parents,
and to do good works that will please You. Admit me, through Your mercy,
among Your righteous servants.'

He inspected the birds and said: 'Why is it that I do not see the lapwing?
Is he not here? I shall grievously punish him or even slay him if he does not
offer me a veritable excuse.'

The bird, who was not long in coming, said: 'Things have come to my 27:22
knowledge that are unknown to you. With truthful news I come to you from
Sheba,

27:23 where I found a woman reigning over them. She is possessed of every virtue and has a splendid throne. I found that she and her subjects worship the sun instead of God. Satan has seduced them and debarred them from the right path, so that they might not be guided to the worship of God, who brings to light all that is hidden in the heavens and the earth and knows what you conceal and what you reveal. God; there is no god but Him, the Lord of the Glorious Throne.'

He said: 'We shall soon see if what you say be true or false. Go and deliver to them this message of mine. Then turn aside and await their answer.'

إِنِّي وَجَدتُّ امْرَأَةً تَمْلِكُهُمْ وَأُوتِيَتْ مِن كُلِّ شَيْءٍ وَلَهَا عَرْشٌ
عَظِيمٌ ﴿٢٣﴾ وَجَدتُّهَا وَقَوْمَهَا يَسْجُدُونَ لِلشَّمْسِ مِن دُونِ اللَّهِ
وَزَيَّنَ لَهُمُ الشَّيْطَانُ أَعْمَالَهُمْ فَصَدَّهُمْ عَنِ السَّبِيلِ فَهُمْ
لَا يَهْتَدُونَ ﴿٢٤﴾ أَلَّا يَسْجُدُوا لِلَّهِ الَّذِي يُخْرِجُ الْخَبْءَ فِي
السَّمَاوَاتِ وَالْأَرْضِ وَيَعْلَمُ مَا تُخْفُونَ وَمَا تُعْلِنُونَ ﴿٢٥﴾ اللَّهُ
لَا إِلَٰهَ إِلَّا هُوَ رَبُّ الْعَرْشِ الْعَظِيمِ ﴿٢٦﴾ قَالَ سَنَنظُرُ أَصَدَقْتَ أَمْ كُنتَ
مِنَ الْكَاذِبِينَ ﴿٢٧﴾ اذْهَب بِّكِتَابِي هَٰذَا فَأَلْقِهْ إِلَيْهِمْ ثُمَّ تَوَلَّ عَنْهُمْ
فَانظُرْ مَاذَا يَرْجِعُونَ ﴿٢٨﴾ قَالَتْ يَا أَيُّهَا الْمَلَأُ إِنِّي أُلْقِيَ إِلَيَّ كِتَابٌ
كَرِيمٌ ﴿٢٩﴾ إِنَّهُ مِن سُلَيْمَانَ وَإِنَّهُ بِسْمِ اللَّهِ الرَّحْمَٰنِ الرَّحِيمِ ﴿٣٠﴾ أَلَّا
تَعْلُوا عَلَيَّ وَأْتُونِي مُسْلِمِينَ ﴿٣١﴾ قَالَتْ يَا أَيُّهَا الْمَلَأُ أَفْتُونِي فِي
أَمْرِي مَا كُنتُ قَاطِعَةً أَمْرًا حَتَّىٰ تَشْهَدُونِ ﴿٣٢﴾ قَالُوا نَحْنُ
أُولُو قُوَّةٍ وَأُولُو بَأْسٍ شَدِيدٍ وَالْأَمْرُ إِلَيْكِ فَانظُرِي مَاذَا
تَأْمُرِينَ ﴿٣٣﴾ قَالَتْ إِنَّ الْمُلُوكَ إِذَا دَخَلُوا قَرْيَةً أَفْسَدُوهَا
وَجَعَلُوا أَعِزَّةَ أَهْلِهَا أَذِلَّةً وَكَذَٰلِكَ يَفْعَلُونَ ﴿٣٤﴾ وَإِنِّي
مُرْسِلَةٌ إِلَيْهِم بِهَدِيَّةٍ فَنَاظِرَةٌ بِمَ يَرْجِعُ الْمُرْسَلُونَ ﴿٣٥﴾

27:29 The Queen of Sheba said: 'Know, my nobles, that I have received a gracious message. It is from Solomon: "In the Name of God, the Merciful, the Compassionate. Do not exalt yourselves above me, but come to me as Muslims." Nobles, let me hear your counsel, for I make no decision without your consent.'

They said: 'We are a valiant and mighty people. It is for you to decide; so consider what you should command.'

She said: 'When kings invade a city they ravage it and abase the mightiest
27:35 of its people. These men will do the same. But I shall send them a present
and see with what reply the envoys will return.'

فَلَمَّا جَاءَ سُلَيْمَانَ قَالَ أَتُمِدُّونَنِ بِمَالٍ فَمَا آتَانِيَ اللَّهُ خَيْرٌ مِمَّا آتَاكُمْ
بَلْ أَنْتُمْ بِهَدِيَّتِكُمْ تَفْرَحُونَ ۝٣٦ ارْجِعْ إِلَيْهِمْ فَلَنَأْتِيَنَّهُمْ بِجُنُودٍ لَا قِبَلَ
لَهُمْ بِهَا وَلَنُخْرِجَنَّهُمْ مِنْهَا أَذِلَّةً وَهُمْ صَاغِرُونَ ۝٣٧ قَالَ يَا أَيُّهَا
الْمَلَأُ أَيُّكُمْ يَأْتِينِي بِعَرْشِهَا قَبْلَ أَنْ يَأْتُونِي مُسْلِمِينَ ۝٣٨ قَالَ عِفْرِيتٌ
مِنَ الْجِنِّ أَنَا آتِيكَ بِهِ قَبْلَ أَنْ تَقُومَ مِنْ مَقَامِكَ وَإِنِّي عَلَيْهِ لَقَوِيٌّ
أَمِينٌ ۝٣٩ قَالَ الَّذِي عِنْدَهُ عِلْمٌ مِنَ الْكِتَابِ أَنَا آتِيكَ بِهِ قَبْلَ أَنْ
يَرْتَدَّ إِلَيْكَ طَرْفُكَ فَلَمَّا رَآهُ مُسْتَقِرًّا عِنْدَهُ قَالَ هَٰذَا مِنْ فَضْلِ رَبِّي
لِيَبْلُوَنِي أَأَشْكُرُ أَمْ أَكْفُرُ وَمَنْ شَكَرَ فَإِنَّمَا يَشْكُرُ لِنَفْسِهِ وَمَنْ كَفَرَ فَإِنَّ رَبِّي
غَنِيٌّ كَرِيمٌ ۝٤٠ قَالَ نَكِّرُوا لَهَا عَرْشَهَا نَنْظُرْ أَتَهْتَدِي أَمْ تَكُونُ
مِنَ الَّذِينَ لَا يَهْتَدُونَ ۝٤١ فَلَمَّا جَاءَتْ قِيلَ أَهَٰكَذَا عَرْشُكِ
قَالَتْ كَأَنَّهُ هُوَ وَأُوتِينَا الْعِلْمَ مِنْ قَبْلِهَا وَكُنَّا مُسْلِمِينَ ۝٤٢
وَصَدَّهَا مَا كَانَتْ تَعْبُدُ مِنْ دُونِ اللَّهِ إِنَّهَا كَانَتْ مِنْ
قَوْمٍ كَافِرِينَ ۝٤٣ قِيلَ لَهَا ادْخُلِي الصَّرْحَ فَلَمَّا رَأَتْهُ حَسِبَتْهُ لُجَّةً
وَكَشَفَتْ عَنْ سَاقَيْهَا قَالَ إِنَّهُ صَرْحٌ مُمَرَّدٌ مِنْ قَوَارِيرَ قَالَتْ رَبِّ
إِنِّي ظَلَمْتُ نَفْسِي وَأَسْلَمْتُ مَعَ سُلَيْمَانَ لِلَّهِ رَبِّ الْعَالَمِينَ ۝٤٤

AND WHEN her envoy came 27:36
to Solomon, he said: 'Is it gold that you would give me? That which God has bestowed on me is better than all the riches He has given you. Yet you glory in your gift. Go back to them: we will march against them with forces they cannot oppose, and drive them from their land humbled and in abject submission.'

And to his nobles he said: 'Which of you will bring to me her throne, before they sue for peace?'

An ifrit from among the jinn said: 'I will bring it to you before you rise from your seat. I am strong enough and faithful.'

But he who was deeply versed in the Book,[1] said: 'I will bring it to you in a twinkling of your eye.'

And when he saw it set before him, he said: 'This is a bounty from my Lord with which He would test my gratitude. He that gives thanks gives them for his own soul; but he who is ungrateful . . . All-sufficient and gracious is my Lord.'

Then he said: 'Let her throne be altered, so that we may see whether she 27:41
will recognize it or be at a loss.'

And when she came to Solomon, she was asked: 'Is your throne like this?' And she said: 'It looks as though it were the same.'

He said: 'Before her we were endowed with knowledge, and were assuredly Muslims. Her false gods have debarred her, for she comes from an unbelieving people.'

She was bidden to enter the palace; and when she saw it she thought it was 27:44
a pool of water, and bared her legs. But Solomon said: 'It is a palace paved with glass.'

'Lord,' she said, 'I have sinned against my own soul. Now I submit with Solomon to God, Lord of the Universe.'

1. Assaf ben Berachia, according to the commentators.

27:45 AND TO Thamūd We sent their kin Ṣāliḥ. He said: 'Serve none but God.' But they divided themselves into two discordant factions.

'My people,' he said, 'why do you wish to hasten evil rather than good? If you seek forgiveness of God, you may be shown mercy.'

They said: 'We presage evil from you and from those who are with you.'

He said: 'The evil you presage can come only from God; you are a people put to the proof.'

27:48 In the town there was a band of nine men, who did evil in the land and nothing that was good. They said: 'Let us swear in the name of God to kill him in the night, together with all his household. And we will say to his next of kin: "We did not witness his family's murder. It is the truth we are telling."'

Thus they plotted: but We too plotted, while they were unaware. And behold the consequence of their plot! We destroyed them utterly, together with their people all. Because they sinned, their dwellings are desolate ruins. Surely in this there is a sign for prudent people. And We delivered the true believers and those who kept from evil.

And tell of Lot. He said to his people: 'Do you commit lewdness with
27:55 your eyes open, lustfully seeking men instead of women? Surely you are an
ignorant people.'

وَلَقَدْ أَرْسَلْنَا إِلَىٰ ثَمُودَ أَخَاهُمْ صَالِحًا أَنِ اعْبُدُوا اللَّهَ
فَإِذَا هُمْ فَرِيقَانِ يَخْتَصِمُونَ ﴿٤٥﴾ قَالَ يَا قَوْمِ لِمَ
تَسْتَعْجِلُونَ بِالسَّيِّئَةِ قَبْلَ الْحَسَنَةِ لَوْلَا تَسْتَغْفِرُونَ اللَّهَ
لَعَلَّكُمْ تُرْحَمُونَ ﴿٤٦﴾ قَالُوا اطَّيَّرْنَا بِكَ وَبِمَن مَّعَكَ قَالَ
طَائِرُكُمْ عِندَ اللَّهِ بَلْ أَنتُمْ قَوْمٌ تُفْتَنُونَ ﴿٤٧﴾ وَكَانَ فِي
الْمَدِينَةِ تِسْعَةُ رَهْطٍ يُفْسِدُونَ فِي الْأَرْضِ وَلَا يُصْلِحُونَ ﴿٤٨﴾
قَالُوا تَقَاسَمُوا بِاللَّهِ لَنُبَيِّتَنَّهُ وَأَهْلَهُ ثُمَّ لَنَقُولَنَّ لِوَلِيِّهِ
مَا شَهِدْنَا مَهْلِكَ أَهْلِهِ وَإِنَّا لَصَادِقُونَ ﴿٤٩﴾ وَمَكَرُوا
مَكْرًا وَمَكَرْنَا مَكْرًا وَهُمْ لَا يَشْعُرُونَ ﴿٥٠﴾ فَانظُرْ
كَيْفَ كَانَ عَاقِبَةُ مَكْرِهِمْ أَنَّا دَمَّرْنَاهُمْ وَقَوْمَهُمْ
أَجْمَعِينَ ﴿٥١﴾ فَتِلْكَ بُيُوتُهُمْ خَاوِيَةً بِمَا ظَلَمُوا إِنَّ
فِي ذَٰلِكَ لَآيَةً لِّقَوْمٍ يَعْلَمُونَ ﴿٥٢﴾ وَأَنجَيْنَا الَّذِينَ
آمَنُوا وَكَانُوا يَتَّقُونَ ﴿٥٣﴾ وَلُوطًا إِذْ قَالَ لِقَوْمِهِ أَتَأْتُونَ
الْفَاحِشَةَ وَأَنتُمْ تُبْصِرُونَ ﴿٥٤﴾ أَئِنَّكُمْ لَتَأْتُونَ الرِّجَالَ
شَهْوَةً مِّن دُونِ النِّسَاءِ بَلْ أَنتُمْ قَوْمٌ تَجْهَلُونَ ﴿٥٥﴾

فما كان جواب قومه إلا أن قالوا أخرجوا آل لوط من
قريتكم إنهم أناس يتطهرون ٥٦ فأنجيناه وأهله إلا
امرأته قدرناها من الغابرين ٥٧ وأمطرنا عليهم مطرا
فساء مطر المنذرين ٥٨ قل الحمد لله وسلام على عباده
الذين اصطفى آلله خير أما يشركون ٥٩ أمن خلق
السموات والأرض وأنزل لكم من السماء ماء فأنبتنا
به حدائق ذات بهجة ما كان لكم أن تنبتوا شجرها
أءله مع الله بل هم قوم يعدلون ٦٠ أمن جعل
الأرض قرارا وجعل خلالها أنهارا وجعل لها رواسي وجعل
بين البحرين حاجزا أءله مع الله بل أكثرهم لا يعلمون
٦١ أمن يجيب المضطر إذا دعاه ويكشف السوء
ويجعلكم خلفاء الأرض أءله مع الله قليلا ما تذكرون
٦٢ أمن يهديكم في ظلمات البر والبحر
ومن يرسل الرياح بشرا بين يدي رحمته
أءله مع الله تعالى الله عما يشركون ٦٣

YET THIS was his people's 27:56
only reply: 'Banish the house
of Lot from your city. They
are people who would keep
themselves chaste.'
So We delivered him and
his household, except his
wife, whom We caused to stay
behind, and pelted the others
with pouring rain; and evil
was the rain which fell on
those who were forewarned.
Say: 'Praise be to God, and
peace upon His servants
whom He has chosen! Who is
more worthy, God or the idols
they serve besides Him? He
who created the heavens and
the earth, and sent down
water from the sky for you,
bringing forth gardens of
delight? Try as you may, you
cannot cause such trees to
grow.' Another god besides God? Yet they make other deities His equals.
He who has established the earth and watered it with running rivers; who 27:61
has set mountains upon it and placed a barrier between the two seas?[1]
Another god besides God? Indeed, the greater part of them have no knowledge.
He who answers the oppressed when they cry out to Him, and relieves
their affliction? He who has given you the earth to inherit? Another god
besides God? How little you reflect!
He who guides you in the darkness of land and sea, and sends the winds 27:63
as harbingers of His mercy? Another god besides God? Exalted be God
above their idols!

1. Salt water and fresh water.

27:64 He who brought the Creation into being and will then restore it; who gives you sustenance from heaven and earth? Another god besides God? Say: 'Give us your proof, if what you say be true!'

Say: 'No one in the heavens or on earth has knowledge of what is hidden except God. Nor shall they ever know when they will be raised to life.'

Have they attained a knowledge of the life to come? By no means! They are in doubt about it and their eyes are sealed.

And the unbelievers say: 'When we and our fathers are turned to dust, shall we be raised to life? We were promised this once before, we and our fathers. It is but a fable of the ancients.'

27:69 Say: 'Roam the earth and see what was the fate of the transgressors.' Do not grieve for them, nor be distressed at their intrigues.

And they say: 'When will this promise be fulfilled, if what you say be true?'

Say: 'A part of what you challenge may well be near at hand.'

Surely your Lord is bountiful to mankind: yet most of them do not give thanks.

Your Lord surely knows what their bosoms hide and what they say in public. There is no secret in heaven or earth but is recorded in a veritable Book.

27:76 Surely this Koran expounds to the Israelites most of that over which they disagree.

أمن يبدؤا الخلق ثم يعيده ومن يرزقكم من السماء والأرض
ءاله مع الله قل هاتوا برهانكم إن كنتم
صادقين ٦٤ قل لا يعلم من في السموات والأرض
الغيب إلا الله وما يشعرون أيان يبعثون ٦٥ بل ادارك
علمهم في الآخرة بل هم في شك منها بل هم منها عمون ٦٦
وقال الذين كفروا أءذا كنا ترابا وآباؤنا أئنا لمخرجون
٦٧ لقد وعدنا هذا نحن وآباؤنا من قبل إن هذا إلا
أساطير الأولين ٦٨ قل سيروا في الأرض فانظروا كيف
كان عاقبة المجرمين ٦٩ ولا تحزن عليهم ولا تكن في ضيق
مما يمكرون ٧٠ ويقولون متى هذا الوعد إن كنتم صادقين ٧١
قل عسى أن يكون ردف لكم بعض الذي تستعجلون ٧٢ وإن ربك
لذو فضل على الناس ولكن أكثرهم لا يشكرون ٧٣ وإن ربك
ليعلم ما تكن صدورهم وما يعلنون ٧٤ وما من غائبة في
السماء والأرض إلا في كتاب مبين ٧٥ إن هذا القرآن
يقص على بني إسرائيل أكثر الذي هم فيه يختلفون ٧٦

وانه لهدى ورحمة للمؤمنين ﴿٧٧﴾ إن ربك يقضي بينهم
بحكمه وهو العزيز العليم ﴿٧٨﴾ فتوكل على الله إنك على الحق
المبين ﴿٧٩﴾ إنك لا تسمع الموتى ولا تسمع الصم الدعاء إذا
ولوا مدبرين ﴿٨٠﴾ وما أنت بهادي العمي عن ضلالتهم إن تسمع
إلا من يؤمن بآياتنا فهم مسلمون ﴿٨١﴾ وإذا وقع القول
عليهم أخرجنا لهم دابة من الأرض تكلمهم أن الناس
كانوا بآياتنا لا يوقنون ﴿٨٢﴾ ويوم نحشر من كل أمة فوجا ممن
يكذب بآياتنا فهم يوزعون ﴿٨٣﴾ حتى إذا جاءو قال أكذبتم بآياتي
ولم تحيطوا بها علما أماذا كنتم تعملون ﴿٨٤﴾ ووقع القول
عليهم بما ظلموا فهم لا ينطقون ﴿٨٥﴾ ألم يروا أنا جعلنا
الليل ليسكنوا فيه والنهار مبصرا إن في ذلك لآيات
لقوم يؤمنون ﴿٨٦﴾ ويوم ينفخ في الصور ففزع من في
السموات ومن في الأرض إلا من شاء الله وكل أتوه
داخرين ﴿٨٧﴾ وترى الجبال تحسبها جامدة وهي تمر مر السحاب
صنع الله الذي أتقن كل شيء إنه خبير بما تفعلون ﴿٨٨﴾

It is surely a guide and a 27:77
blessing to true believers.
Your Lord will rightly judge
them. He is the Almighty, the
All-knowing. Therefore put
your trust in God; yours is
surely the path to the veritable
Truth.

You cannot make the dead hear you, nor can you make the deaf hear your call if they turn their backs and pay no heed; nor can you guide the blind out of their error. None shall give ear to you save those who believe in Our revelations, and have become Muslims.

On the day when the Judgement smites them, We will bring out from the earth a monster that shall speak to them. Truly, people had no faith in Our revelations.

On that day We shall herd from each community a multitude of those 27:83
who disbelieved Our revelations. They shall be led in separate bands, and,
when they come, He will say: 'You denied My revelations although you knew
nothing about them. What was it you were doing?' The Judgement will smite
them in their sins, and they shall be dumbfounded.

Do they not see how We have made the night for them to rest in, and the day to give them light? Surely there are signs in this for true believers.

On that day the Trumpet shall be blown and all who dwell in the heavens and on earth shall be seized with consternation, except for those whom God will choose to spare. And all shall come to Him in utter humility.

The mountains, solid though you may think them, will pass by as the 27:88
clouds pass by. Such is the handiwork of God, who has perfected all things.
He surely has full knowledge of what you do.

من جاء بالحسنة فله خير منها وهم من فزع يومئذ آمنون
٨٩ ومن جاء بالسيئة فكبت وجوههم في النار هل
تجزون إلا ما كنتم تعملون ٩٠ إنما أمرت أن أعبد رب
هذه البلدة الذي حرمها وله كل شيء وأمرت أن أكون من
المسلمين ٩١ وأن أتلو القرآن فمن اهتدى فإنما يهتدي
لنفسه ومن ضل فقل إنما أنا من المنذرين ٩٢ وقل الحمد لله
سيريكم آياته فتعرفونها وما ربك بغافل عما تعملون ٩٣

سورة القصص مكية وهي ثمان وثمانون آية

بسم الله الرحمن الرحيم

طسم ١ تلك آيات الكتاب المبين ٢ نتلوا عليك من نبإ
موسى وفرعون بالحق لقوم يؤمنون ٣ إن فرعون علا في الأرض
وجعل أهلها شيعا يستضعف طائفة منهم يذبح أبناءهم
ويستحيي نساءهم إنه كان من المفسدين ٤ ونريد أن نمن على الذين
استضعفوا في الأرض ونجعلهم أئمة ونجعلهم الوارثين ٥

27:89 THOSE THAT come with a
good deed shall have what is
better, and from the terrors of
that day they shall be secure.
But those that come with a
vile deed shall be hurled headlong into the Fire. Shall you
not be rewarded according
only to your deeds?

I am commanded to serve
the Lord of this City, which
He has made sacred. All things
are His. And I am commanded
27:92 to be a Muslim, and to proclaim the Koran. He that takes
the right path shall take it for
the good of his own soul.
And to him who strays from
the right path, say: 'I am only
to give warning.'
27:93 And say: 'Praise be to God!
He will show you His signs
and you will recognize them.
Your Lord is never heedless of what you do.'

THE STORY

In the Name of God, the Merciful, the Compassionate

28:1 *Ṭā' sīn mīm*. These are the revelations of the veritable Book. In all truth We
shall recount to you the tale of Moses and Pharaoh for the instruction of the
faithful.

Now Pharaoh made himself a tyrant in the land. He divided his people
into castes, one group of which he oppressed, slaughtering their sons and
sparing only their daughters. Surely he was an evil-doer.
28:5 But it was Our will to favour those who were oppressed in the land
and to make them leaders among men, to bestow on them a heritage

وَنُمَكِّنَ لَهُمْ فِي الْأَرْضِ وَنُرِيَ فِرْعَوْنَ وَهَامَانَ وَجُنُودَ
هُمَا مِنْهُمْ مَا كَانُوا يَحْذَرُونَ ﴿٦﴾ وَأَوْحَيْنَا إِلَى
أُمِّ مُوسَى أَنْ أَرْضِعِيهِ فَإِذَا خِفْتِ عَلَيْهِ فَأَلْقِيهِ فِي الْيَمِّ
وَلَا تَخَافِي وَلَا تَحْزَنِي إِنَّا رَادُّوهُ إِلَيْكِ وَجَاعِلُوهُ مِنَ الْمُرْسَلِينَ
﴿٧﴾ فَالْتَقَطَهُ آلُ فِرْعَوْنَ لِيَكُونَ لَهُمْ عَدُوًّا وَحَزَنًا إِنَّ
فِرْعَوْنَ وَهَامَانَ وَجُنُودَهُمَا كَانُوا خَاطِئِينَ ﴿٨﴾ وَقَالَتِ
امْرَأَتُ فِرْعَوْنَ قُرَّتُ عَيْنٍ لِي وَلَكَ لَا تَقْتُلُوهُ عَسَى أَنْ يَنْفَعَنَا
أَوْ نَتَّخِذَهُ وَلَدًا وَهُمْ لَا يَشْعُرُونَ ﴿٩﴾ وَأَصْبَحَ فُؤَادُ
أُمِّ مُوسَى فَارِغًا إِنْ كَادَتْ لَتُبْدِي بِهِ لَوْلَا أَنْ رَبَطْنَا
عَلَى قَلْبِهَا لِتَكُونَ مِنَ الْمُؤْمِنِينَ ﴿١٠﴾ وَقَالَتْ
لِأُخْتِهِ قُصِّيهِ فَبَصُرَتْ بِهِ عَنْ جُنُبٍ وَهُمْ لَا يَشْعُرُونَ ﴿١١﴾
وَحَرَّمْنَا عَلَيْهِ الْمَرَاضِعَ مِنْ قَبْلُ فَقَالَتْ هَلْ أَدُلُّكُمْ
عَلَى أَهْلِ بَيْتٍ يَكْفُلُونَهُ لَكُمْ وَهُمْ لَهُ نَاصِحُونَ ﴿١٢﴾
فَرَدَدْنَاهُ إِلَى أُمِّهِ كَيْ تَقَرَّ عَيْنُهَا وَلَا تَحْزَنَ وَلِتَعْلَمَ
أَنَّ وَعْدَ اللَّهِ حَقٌّ وَلَكِنَّ أَكْثَرَهُمْ لَا يَعْلَمُونَ ﴿١٣﴾

and to give them power in 28:6
the land; and to show Pharaoh, Haman,[1] and their warriors the very scourge they dreaded.

We revealed Our will to Moses' mother, saying: 'Give him suck, but if you are concerned about his safety, then put him down on to the river. Have no fear, nor be dismayed; for We shall restore him to you and shall invest him with a mission.'

Pharaoh's household picked him up, though he was to become their adversary and their scourge. For Pharaoh, Haman, and their warriors were sinners all.

His wife said to Pharaoh: 28:9
'This child may bring joy to us both. Do not slay him. He may show promise, and we may adopt him as a son.' But they little knew what they were doing.

Moses' mother's heart was sorely troubled. She would have revealed who he was, had We not strengthened her heart so that she might become a true believer. She said to his sister: 'Go, and follow him.'

She watched him from a distance, unseen by others. We had earlier caused him to refuse the nurses' breasts, so his sister said: 'Shall I direct you to a family who will bring him up for you and take good care of him?'

Thus did We restore him to his mother, so that she might rejoice in him 28:13
and grieve no more, and that she might know that God's promise was true. But most of them had no knowledge.

1. In the Koran, Haman is one of Pharaoh's ministers; in the Bible (Esther 3:8), Haman is Chief Minister of Ahasuerus (Xerxes I), king of Persia.

28:14 AND WHEN he had reached maturity and grown to manhood We bestowed on him wisdom and knowledge. Thus do We reward the righteous.

He entered the town unnoticed by its people, and found two men at each other's throats, the one of his own race, the other an enemy. The Israelite appealed for Moses' help against his enemy, so that Moses struck him with his fist and killed him. 'This is the work of Satan,' he said. 'He is a veritable enemy of man and seeks to lead him astray. Forgive me, Lord,' he said, 'for I have sinned against my soul.'

And God forgave him; for He it is who is the Forgiving One, the Compassionate. He said: 'By the favour You have shown me, Lord, I vow that I will never lend a helping hand to wrongdoers.'

28:18 Next morning he was walking in the town in fear and caution, when lo, the man who sought his help the day before cried out to him again for help. 'Clearly,' said Moses, 'you are a quarrelsome man.'

And when he was about to lay his hands on him who was an enemy of them both, he said: 'Moses, would you kill me as you killed a man yesterday? You are surely seeking to be a tyrant in the land, not seeking to be an upright man.'

And a man came running from the farthest quarter of the city. 'Moses,' he said, 'the elders are plotting to kill you. Fly for your life; I am one that gives you good counsel!'

28:21 He left it in fear and caution, saying: 'Lord, deliver me from the wrongdoing people.'

ولما بلغ اشده واستوى اتيناه حكما وعلما وكذلك
نجزي المحسنين ﴿١٤﴾ ودخل المدينة على حين غفلة من اهلها
فوجد فيها رجلين يقتتلان هذا من شيعته وهذا من
عدوه فاستغاثه الذي من شيعته على الذي من عدوه
فوكزه موسى فقضى عليه قال هذا من عمل الشيطان
انه عدو مضل مبين ﴿١٥﴾ قال رب اني ظلمت نفسي فاغفر لي فغفر له
انه هو الغفور الرحيم ﴿١٦﴾ قال رب بما انعمت علي فلن اكون ظهيرا
للمجرمين ﴿١٧﴾ فاصبح في المدينة خائفا يترقب فاذا الذي
استنصره بالامس يستصرخه قال له موسى انك لغوي مبين
﴿١٨﴾ فلما ان اراد ان يبطش بالذي هو عدو لهما قال يا موسى
اتريد ان تقتلني كما قتلت نفسا بالامس ان تريد الا ان
تكون جبارا في الارض وما تريد ان تكون من المصلحين
﴿١٩﴾ وجاء رجل من اقصا المدينة يسعى قال يا موسى ان
الملا يأتمرون بك ليقتلوك فاخرج اني لك من الناصحين ﴿٢٠﴾
فخرج منها خائفا يترقب قال رب نجني من القوم الظالمين ﴿٢١﴾

وَلَمَّا تَوَجَّهَ تِلْقَاءَ مَدْيَنَ قَالَ عَسَىٰ رَبِّي أَن يَهْدِيَنِي سَوَاءَ السَّبِيلِ
﴿٢٢﴾ وَلَمَّا وَرَدَ مَاءَ مَدْيَنَ وَجَدَ عَلَيْهِ أُمَّةً مِّنَ النَّاسِ يَسْقُونَ
وَوَجَدَ مِن دُونِهِمُ امْرَأَتَيْنِ تَذُودَانِ قَالَ مَا خَطْبُكُمَا
قَالَتَا لَا نَسْقِي حَتَّىٰ يُصْدِرَ الرِّعَاءُ وَأَبُونَا شَيْخٌ كَبِيرٌ ﴿٢٣﴾ فَسَقَىٰ
لَهُمَا ثُمَّ تَوَلَّىٰ إِلَى الظِّلِّ فَقَالَ رَبِّ إِنِّي لِمَا أَنزَلْتَ إِلَيَّ مِنْ
خَيْرٍ فَقِيرٌ ﴿٢٤﴾ فَجَاءَتْهُ إِحْدَاهُمَا تَمْشِي عَلَى اسْتِحْيَاءٍ
قَالَتْ إِنَّ أَبِي يَدْعُوكَ لِيَجْزِيَكَ أَجْرَ مَا سَقَيْتَ لَنَا
فَلَمَّا جَاءَهُ وَقَصَّ عَلَيْهِ الْقَصَصَ قَالَ لَا تَخَفْ نَجَوْتَ مِنَ
الْقَوْمِ الظَّالِمِينَ ﴿٢٥﴾ قَالَتْ إِحْدَاهُمَا يَا أَبَتِ اسْتَأْجِرْهُ إِنَّ
خَيْرَ مَنِ اسْتَأْجَرْتَ الْقَوِيُّ الْأَمِينُ ﴿٢٦﴾ قَالَ إِنِّي أُرِيدُ أَنْ
أُنكِحَكَ إِحْدَى ابْنَتَيَّ هَاتَيْنِ عَلَىٰ أَن تَأْجُرَنِي ثَمَانِيَ حِجَجٍ
فَإِنْ أَتْمَمْتَ عَشْرًا فَمِنْ عِندِكَ وَمَا أُرِيدُ أَنْ أَشُقَّ
عَلَيْكَ سَتَجِدُنِي إِن شَاءَ اللَّهُ مِنَ الصَّالِحِينَ ﴿٢٧﴾ قَالَ
ذَٰلِكَ بَيْنِي وَبَيْنَكَ أَيَّمَا الْأَجَلَيْنِ قَضَيْتُ
فَلَا عُدْوَانَ عَلَيَّ وَاللَّهُ عَلَىٰ مَا نَقُولُ وَكِيلٌ ﴿٢٨﴾

AND AS he made his way 28:22
towards Midian, he said: 'May the Lord guide me to an even path.'

When he came to the well of Midian he found around it a multitude of people watering their flocks, and beside them he found two women keeping back their sheep. 'What is it that troubles you both?' he asked.

They said: 'We cannot draw water until the shepherds have driven away their flocks. Our father is an elderly man, well advanced in years.'

He drew water for them and then retired to the shade, saying: 'Lord, I surely stand badly in need of the blessing You have sent me.'

One of the two girls came 28:25
bashfully towards him and said: 'My father calls you. He wishes to reward you for drawing water for us.'

And when he went and recounted to him his story, the old man said: 'Fear nothing. You are now safe from the wrongdoing people.'

One of the girls said: 'Father, take him into your service. A man who is strong and honest is the best that you can hire.'

He said: 'I wish to give you in marriage one of these two daughters of mine if you stay eight years in my service; but if you wish it, you may stay ten. I shall not deal harshly with you; you shall find me, God willing, an upright man.'

He said: 'So be it between us. Whichever term I shall fulfil, I trust I shall 28:28
not be wronged. God is witness of what we say.'

28:29 AND WHEN he had fulfilled his term and was
journeying with his family,
Moses descried a fire on the
mountainside. He said to his
people: 'Stay here, for I can
see a fire. Perhaps I can bring
you news of it, or a torch
from the fire to warm yourselves with.'
When he came near it, a
voice called out to him from a
bush in a blessed spot on the
right side of the valley, saying:
'Moses, I am God, Lord of
the Universe. Throw down
your staff.'
And when he saw it slithering like a serpent, he turned
and fled without a backward
glance.
'Moses, approach and fear
28:32 not; you are safe. Put your
hand into your pocket: it will come out white, although unharmed. Now
draw back your arm, and do not stretch it out in terror. These are two proofs
from your Lord for Pharaoh and his elders. Surely they are an ungodly
people.'
'Lord,' said he, 'I have killed one of their number and fear that they will
kill me. Aaron my brother is more fluent of tongue than I; send him with me
that he may help me and confirm my words, for I fear they will reject me.'
28:35 He replied: 'We will strengthen your arm with your brother, and will
bestow such power on you both, that none shall reach you. Set forth, with
Our signs. You, and those who follow you, shall surely triumph.'

فلما قضى موسى الأجل وسار بأهله آنس من جانب الطور
نارا قال لأهله امكثوا إني آنست نارا لعلي آتيكم
منها بخبر أو جذوة من النار لعلكم تصطلون ٢٩
فلما أتاها نودي من شاطئ الواد الأيمن في البقعة
المباركة من الشجرة أن يا موسى إني أنا الله رب العالمين
٣٠ وأن ألق عصاك فلما رآها تهتز كأنها جان ولى مدبرا
ولم يعقب يا موسى أقبل ولا تخف إنك من الآمنين ٣١ اسلك
يدك في جيبك تخرج بيضاء من غير سوء واضمم إليك
جناحك من الرهب فذانك برهانان من ربك إلى فرعون
وملئه إنهم كانوا قوما فاسقين ٣٢ قال رب إني قتلت
منهم نفسا فأخاف أن يقتلون ٣٣ وأخي هارون هو
أفصح مني لسانا فأرسله معي ردءا يصدقني إني
أخاف أن يكذبون ٣٤ قال سنشد عضدك
بأخيك ونجعل لكما سلطانا فلا يصلون إليكما
بآياتنا أنتما ومن اتبعكما الغالبون ٣٥

فَلَمَّا جَاءَهُم مُّوسَىٰ بِآيَاتِنَا بَيِّنَاتٍ قَالُوا مَا هَٰذَا إِلَّا
سِحْرٌ مُّفْتَرًى وَمَا سَمِعْنَا بِهَٰذَا فِي آبَائِنَا الْأَوَّلِينَ
٣٦ وَقَالَ مُوسَىٰ رَبِّي أَعْلَمُ بِمَن جَاءَ بِالْهُدَىٰ مِنْ عِندِهِ
وَمَن تَكُونُ لَهُ عَاقِبَةُ الدَّارِ إِنَّهُ لَا يُفْلِحُ الظَّالِمُونَ ٣٧
وَقَالَ فِرْعَوْنُ يَا أَيُّهَا الْمَلَأُ مَا عَلِمْتُ لَكُم مِّنْ إِلَٰهٍ غَيْرِي
فَأَوْقِدْ لِي يَا هَامَانُ عَلَى الطِّينِ فَاجْعَل لِّي صَرْحًا لَّعَلِّي
أَطَّلِعُ إِلَىٰ إِلَٰهِ مُوسَىٰ وَإِنِّي لَأَظُنُّهُ مِنَ الْكَاذِبِينَ ٣٨
وَاسْتَكْبَرَ هُوَ وَجُنُودُهُ فِي الْأَرْضِ بِغَيْرِ الْحَقِّ وَظَنُّوا
أَنَّهُمْ إِلَيْنَا لَا يُرْجَعُونَ ٣٩ فَأَخَذْنَاهُ وَجُنُودَهُ فَنَبَذْنَا
هُمْ فِي الْيَمِّ فَانظُرْ كَيْفَ كَانَ عَاقِبَةُ الظَّالِمِينَ ٤٠
وَجَعَلْنَاهُمْ أَئِمَّةً يَدْعُونَ إِلَى النَّارِ وَيَوْمَ الْقِيَامَةِ
لَا يُنصَرُونَ ٤١ وَأَتْبَعْنَاهُمْ فِي هَٰذِهِ الدُّنْيَا لَعْنَةً
وَيَوْمَ الْقِيَامَةِ هُم مِّنَ الْمَقْبُوحِينَ ٤٢ وَلَقَدْ آتَيْنَا مُوسَى
الْكِتَابَ مِن بَعْدِ مَا أَهْلَكْنَا الْقُرُونَ الْأُولَىٰ بَصَائِرَ
لِلنَّاسِ وَهُدًى وَرَحْمَةً لَّعَلَّهُمْ يَتَذَكَّرُونَ ٤٣

AND WHEN Moses came 28:36
to them with Our veritable signs, they said: 'This is nothing but sorcery contrived; nor have we heard of the like among our forefathers.'

Moses said: 'My Lord knows best the man who brings guidance from His presence and gains the recompense of the life to come. The wrongdoers shall never succeed.'

'Nobles,' said Pharaoh, 'you have no other god that I know of except myself. Make me, Haman, bricks of clay, and build for me a tower that I may climb up to the god of Moses. I am convinced that he is lying.'

Pharaoh and his warriors 28:39
conducted themselves with arrogance and injustice in the land, thinking they would never be recalled to Us. But We seized him and his warriors, and We cast them into the sea. Consider the fate of the wrongdoers.

We made them leaders who invited to the Fire, but on the Day of Resurrection they shall not be helped. In this world We laid a curse on them, and on the Day of Resurrection they shall be among the damned.

After We had destroyed the early generations We gave Moses the Book as 28:43
a beacon for mankind, a guide and a blessing, so that they might take thought.

28:44 You[1] WERE not present on
the western side when We
charged Moses with his commission, nor did you witness
the event. But We raised many
generations after him whose
lives were prolonged. You did
not dwell among the people
of Midian, nor did you recite
to them Our revelations; but it
was We who sent you forth.
28:46 You were not present on
the mountainside when We
called out. Yet have We sent
you forth, as a blessing from
your Lord, to forewarn a
nation to whom no one before
you had been sent to warn
them, so that they may reflect
and may not say, when evil
befalls them on account of
their misdeeds: 'Lord, had
You sent us an apostle, we
should have obeyed Your revelations and believed in them.'

وَمَا كُنْتَ بِجَانِبِ الْغَرْبِيِّ إِذْ قَضَيْنَا إِلَى مُوسَى الْأَمْرَ
وَمَا كُنْتَ مِنَ الشَّاهِدِينَ ﴿٤٤﴾ وَلَٰكِنَّا أَنْشَأْنَا قُرُونًا
فَتَطَاوَلَ عَلَيْهِمُ الْعُمُرُ وَمَا كُنْتَ ثَاوِيًا فِي أَهْلِ مَدْيَنَ
تَتْلُو عَلَيْهِمْ آيَاتِنَا وَلَٰكِنَّا كُنَّا مُرْسِلِينَ ﴿٤٥﴾
وَمَا كُنْتَ بِجَانِبِ الطُّورِ إِذْ نَادَيْنَا وَلَٰكِنْ رَحْمَةً مِنْ
رَبِّكَ لِتُنْذِرَ قَوْمًا مَا أَتَاهُمْ مِنْ نَذِيرٍ مِنْ قَبْلِكَ لَعَلَّهُمْ يَتَذَكَّرُونَ
﴿٤٦﴾ وَلَوْلَا أَنْ تُصِيبَهُمْ مُصِيبَةٌ بِمَا قَدَّمَتْ أَيْدِيهِمْ فَيَقُولُوا
رَبَّنَا لَوْلَا أَرْسَلْتَ إِلَيْنَا رَسُولًا فَنَتَّبِعَ آيَاتِكَ وَنَكُونَ مِنَ الْمُؤْمِنِينَ
﴿٤٧﴾ فَلَمَّا جَاءَهُمُ الْحَقُّ مِنْ عِنْدِنَا قَالُوا لَوْلَا أُوتِيَ مِثْلَ مَا
أُوتِيَ مُوسَىٰ أَوَلَمْ يَكْفُرُوا بِمَا أُوتِيَ مُوسَىٰ مِنْ قَبْلُ قَالُوا سِحْرَانِ
تَظَاهَرَا وَقَالُوا إِنَّا بِكُلٍّ كَافِرُونَ ﴿٤٨﴾ قُلْ فَأْتُوا بِكِتَابٍ
مِنْ عِنْدِ اللَّهِ هُوَ أَهْدَىٰ مِنْهُمَا أَتَّبِعْهُ إِنْ كُنْتُمْ
صَادِقِينَ ﴿٤٩﴾ فَإِنْ لَمْ يَسْتَجِيبُوا لَكَ فَاعْلَمْ أَنَّمَا يَتَّبِعُونَ
أَهْوَاءَهُمْ وَمَنْ أَضَلُّ مِمَّنِ اتَّبَعَ هَوَاهُ بِغَيْرِ هُدًى مِنَ
اللَّهِ إِنَّ اللَّهَ لَا يَهْدِي الْقَوْمَ الظَّالِمِينَ ﴿٥٠﴾

28:48 And now that they have received the Truth from Us, they ask: 'Why is he
not given the like of what was given to Moses?' But did they not deny what
was formerly given to Moses? They say: 'Two works[2] of sorcery comple-
menting one another!' And they declare: 'We will believe in neither of them.'
Say: 'Bring down from God a scripture that is a better guide than these
and I will follow it, if what you say be true!'
28:50 If they make you no answer, know that they are led by their desires. And
who is in greater error than he who is led by his desires, without guidance
from God? God does not guide the wrongdoers.

1. Muḥammad. 2. The Torah and the Koran.

ولقد وصلنا لهم القول لعلهم يتذكرون ٥١ الذين
آتيناهم الكتاب من قبله هم به يؤمنون ۝ وإذا
يتلى عليهم قالوا آمنا به إنه الحق من ربنا إنا كنا
من قبله مسلمين ٥٣ أولئك يؤتون أجرهم مرتين
بما صبروا ويدرءون بالحسنة السيئة ومما رزقناهم
ينفقون ٥٤ وإذا سمعوا اللغو أعرضوا عنه وقالوا لنا
أعمالنا ولكم أعمالكم سلام عليكم لا نبتغي الجاهلين
٥٥ إنك لا تهدي من أحببت ولكن الله يهدي من
يشاء وهو أعلم بالمهتدين ٥٦ وقالوا إن نتبع الهدى معك
نتخطف من أرضنا أولم نمكن لهم حرما آمنا يجبى إليه ثمرات
كل شيء رزقا من لدنا ولكن أكثرهم لا يعلمون ٥٧ وكم أهلكنا
من قرية بطرت معيشتها فتلك مساكنهم لم تسكن من بعدهم
إلا قليلا وكنا نحن الوارثين ٥٨ وما كان ربك مهلك
القرى حتى يبعث في أمها رسولا يتلو عليهم آياتنا
وما كنا مهلكي القرى إلا وأهلها ظالمون ٥٩

WE HAVE caused the Word 28:51
to reach them so that they may take thought. Those to whom We gave the Book before this believe in it. When it is recited to them they say: 'We believe in it; it is the Truth from our Lord. Before its coming we were Muslims.'

Twice shall their reward be given them, because they have endured with fortitude, requiting evil with good and giving from what We gave them; and because they pay no heed to profane talk, and say: 'We have our actions and you have yours. We wish you peace. We will have nothing to do with ignorant men.'

You cannot guide whom- 28:56
ever you please: but it is God who guides whom He will. He best knows those who yield to guidance.

And they say: 'If we follow your guidance, we shall be dispossessed of our land.' But have We not given them a sanctuary of safety[1] to which fruits of every kind are brought as a provision from Ourself? But most of them have no knowledge.

How many cities have We destroyed that once flourished in wanton ease! The dwellings they left behind are but scarcely inhabited; We Ourself were the only heirs.

Nor did your Lord obliterate the cities until He had sent apostles to their 28:59
capital proclaiming to them Our revelations. Nor did We obliterate the cities unless their inhabitants were wrongdoers.

1. At the Ka'bah.

28:60 THAT WHICH you have
been given is but the enjoyment and the gaudy show of
this present life. Better is
God's recompense and more
lasting. Have you no sense to
reason with?

Can he who has received
Our gracious promise, and will
see it fulfilled, be compared
with him to whom We have
given the enjoyment of this life
and who will be summoned on
the Day of Resurrection?

On that day He will call to
them, saying: 'Where are the
gods whom you alleged to be
My partners?'

Those on whom the Judge-
ment has been passed will say:
'Lord, these are the men
whom we misled. We led them
astray as we ourselves were led
astray. We disown them before You; it was not us that they worshipped.'
28:64 Then they will be told: 'Call to your idols!' And they will call to them, but
they shall get no answer. They shall behold the scourge and wish that they
were rightly guided.

On that day He will call to them, saying: 'What answer did you give those
who were sent?' And on that day they will be so confused that they will ask
no questions. But those that repented and embraced the Faith and did what
was right may hope for salvation.

Your Lord creates what He will and chooses freely, but they have no
power to choose. Glorified and exalted be He above their false gods!

And your Lord knows what their bosoms hide and what they say in public.
28:70 He is God: there is no god but Him. Praise be His in the first world and in
the last. His is the Judgement, and to Him shall you be recalled.

وَمَآ أُوتِيتُم مِّن شَيْءٍ فَمَتَاعُ الْحَيَوٰةِ الدُّنْيَا وَزِينَتُهَا وَمَا عِندَ
اللَّهِ خَيْرٌ وَأَبْقَىٰٓ أَفَلَا تَعْقِلُونَ ٦٠ أَفَمَن وَعَدْنَاهُ وَعْدًا
حَسَنًا فَهُوَ لَاقِيهِ كَمَن مَّتَّعْنَاهُ مَتَاعَ الْحَيَوٰةِ الدُّنْيَا ثُمَّ هُوَ
يَوْمَ الْقِيَامَةِ مِنَ الْمُحْضَرِينَ ٦١ وَيَوْمَ يُنَادِيهِمْ فَيَقُولُ أَيْنَ
شُرَكَآئِيَ الَّذِينَ كُنتُمْ تَزْعُمُونَ ٦٢ قَالَ الَّذِينَ حَقَّ عَلَيْهِمُ الْقَوْلُ
رَبَّنَا هَٰٓؤُلَآءِ الَّذِينَ أَغْوَيْنَآ أَغْوَيْنَاهُمْ كَمَا غَوَيْنَا تَبَرَّأْنَآ إِلَيْكَ
مَا كَانُوٓا إِيَّانَا يَعْبُدُونَ ٦٣ وَقِيلَ ادْعُوا شُرَكَآءَكُمْ فَدَعَوْهُمْ
فَلَمْ يَسْتَجِيبُوا لَهُمْ وَرَأَوُا الْعَذَابَ لَوْ أَنَّهُمْ كَانُوا يَهْتَدُونَ
٦٤ وَيَوْمَ يُنَادِيهِمْ فَيَقُولُ مَاذَآ أَجَبْتُمُ الْمُرْسَلِينَ ٦٥ فَعَمِيَتْ
عَلَيْهِمُ الْأَنۢبَآءُ يَوْمَئِذٍ فَهُمْ لَا يَتَسَآءَلُونَ ٦٦ فَأَمَّا مَن تَابَ
وَءَامَنَ وَعَمِلَ صَٰلِحًا فَعَسَىٰٓ أَن يَكُونَ مِنَ الْمُفْلِحِينَ ٦٧
وَرَبُّكَ يَخْلُقُ مَا يَشَآءُ وَيَخْتَارُ مَا كَانَ لَهُمُ الْخِيَرَةُ سُبْحَٰنَ
اللَّهِ وَتَعَٰلَىٰ عَمَّا يُشْرِكُونَ ٦٨ وَرَبُّكَ يَعْلَمُ مَا تُكِنُّ
صُدُورُهُمْ وَمَا يُعْلِنُونَ ٦٩ وَهُوَ اللَّهُ لَآ إِلَٰهَ إِلَّا هُوَ لَهُ
الْحَمْدُ فِي الْأُولَىٰ وَالْآخِرَةِ وَلَهُ الْحُكْمُ وَإِلَيْهِ تُرْجَعُونَ ٧٠

قُلْ أَرَأَيْتُمْ إِن جَعَلَ ٱللَّهُ عَلَيْكُمُ ٱلَّيْلَ سَرْمَدًا إِلَىٰ يَوْمِ
ٱلْقِيَٰمَةِ مَنْ إِلَٰهٌ غَيْرُ ٱللَّهِ يَأْتِيكُم بِضِيَآءٍ أَفَلَا تَسْمَعُونَ ٧١
قُلْ أَرَأَيْتُمْ إِن جَعَلَ ٱللَّهُ عَلَيْكُمُ ٱلنَّهَارَ سَرْمَدًا إِلَىٰ يَوْمِ
ٱلْقِيَٰمَةِ مَنْ إِلَٰهٌ غَيْرُ ٱللَّهِ يَأْتِيكُم بِلَيْلٍ تَسْكُنُونَ فِيهِ أَفَلَا
تُبْصِرُونَ ٧٢ وَمِن رَّحْمَتِهِۦ جَعَلَ لَكُمُ ٱلَّيْلَ وَٱلنَّهَارَ لِتَسْكُنُوا۟
فِيهِ وَلِتَبْتَغُوا۟ مِن فَضْلِهِۦ وَلَعَلَّكُمْ تَشْكُرُونَ ٧٣ وَيَوْمَ
يُنَادِيهِمْ فَيَقُولُ أَيْنَ شُرَكَآءِىَ ٱلَّذِينَ كُنتُمْ تَزْعُمُونَ ٧٤
وَنَزَعْنَا مِن كُلِّ أُمَّةٍ شَهِيدًا فَقُلْنَا هَاتُوا۟ بُرْهَٰنَكُمْ
فَعَلِمُوٓا۟ أَنَّ ٱلْحَقَّ لِلَّهِ وَضَلَّ عَنْهُم مَّا كَانُوا۟ يَفْتَرُونَ ٧٥
إِنَّ قَٰرُونَ كَانَ مِن قَوْمِ مُوسَىٰ فَبَغَىٰ عَلَيْهِمْ وَءَاتَيْنَٰهُ مِنَ
ٱلْكُنُوزِ مَآ إِنَّ مَفَاتِحَهُۥ لَتَنُوٓأُ بِٱلْعُصْبَةِ أُو۟لِى ٱلْقُوَّةِ إِذْ قَالَ
لَهُۥ قَوْمُهُۥ لَا تَفْرَحْ إِنَّ ٱللَّهَ لَا يُحِبُّ ٱلْفَرِحِينَ ٧٦
وَٱبْتَغِ فِيمَآ ءَاتَىٰكَ ٱللَّهُ ٱلدَّارَ ٱلْءَاخِرَةَ وَلَا تَنسَ نَصِيبَكَ مِنَ
ٱلدُّنْيَا وَأَحْسِن كَمَآ أَحْسَنَ ٱللَّهُ إِلَيْكَ وَلَا تَبْغِ ٱلْفَسَادَ
فِى ٱلْأَرْضِ إِنَّ ٱللَّهَ لَا يُحِبُّ ٱلْمُفْسِدِينَ ٧٧

SAY: 'THINK! If God 28:71
should enshroud you in perpetual night till the Day of Resurrection, what other god could give you light? Will you not hear?'

Say: 'Think! If God should give you perpetual day until the Day of Resurrection, what other god could bring you a night to rest in? Will you not see?'

Of His mercy He has given you the night to rest in, and the day that you may seek His bounty and give thanks.

On that day He will call out to them, saying: 'Where are
the gods whom you alleged to
be My partners?' From each 28:75
community We will seize a witness, and We shall say: 'Show Us your proof.' Then shall they learn that the Truth is God's, and the deities of their own invention will forsake them.

Korah[1] was one of Moses' people, but he treated them unjustly. We had given him such treasures that their very keys would have weighed down a
band of sturdy men. His people said to him: 'Do not exult; God does not
love the exultant. But seek, by means of that which God has given you, to 28:77
attain the Abode of the Hereafter. Do not forget your share in this world. Be good to others as God has been good to you, and do not strive for evil in the land, for God does not love the evil-doers.'

1. Cf. Numbers 16.

28:78 He said: 'I was given this
on account of the knowledge
I possess.'

Did he not know that, from among the generations gone before him, God had obliterated some who were mightier and possessed of much more wealth than he? The wrongdoers shall not be questioned about their sins.

And when he went out among his people in all his finery, those who loved this nether life said: 'Would that we had the like of what Korah has been given! He is indeed a man of great good fortune.'

But those who were endowed with knowledge said: 'Alas for you! Better is God's recompense for him that has faith and does good works; but none shall attain it save those who have endured with fortitude.'

28:81 We caused the earth to swallow him up, him and his dwelling, so that he
found none besides God to help him; nor was he able to help himself. And
those who on the day before had coveted his lot next morning said: 'Behold!
God gives abundantly to whom He will among His servants, and sparingly
also. But for the grace of God to us, He could have caused the earth to swallow us. Behold! The ungrateful shall never succeed.'

That Final Abode We shall assign to those who seek neither grandeur on the earth nor evil-doing. The righteous shall have a blessed end.

28:84 He that comes with a good deed shall have what is better; and they that
commit vile deeds shall be requited only according to what they did.

قال إنما أوتيته على علم عندي أولم يعلم أن الله قد أهلك
من قبله من القرون من هو أشد منه قوة وأكثر جمعا
ولا يسأل عن ذنوبهم المجرمون ٧٨ فخرج على قومه في زينته
قال الذين يريدون الحياة الدنيا يا ليت لنا مثل ما أوتي
قارون إنه لذو حظ عظيم ٧٩ وقال الذين أوتوا العلم
ويلكم ثواب الله خير لمن آمن وعمل صالحا ولا
يلقاها إلا الصابرون ٨٠ فخسفنا به وبداره الأرض
فما كان له من فئة ينصرونه من دون الله وما كان
من المنتصرين ٨١ وأصبح الذين تمنوا مكانه بالأمس
يقولون ويكأن الله يبسط الرزق لمن يشاء من عباده
ويقدر لولا أن من الله علينا لخسف بنا ويكأنه لا يفلح
الكافرون ٨٢ تلك الدار الآخرة نجعلها للذين لا يريدون
علوا في الأرض ولا فسادا والعاقبة للمتقين ٨٣ من
جاء بالحسنة فله خير منها ومن جاء بالسيئة فلا يجزى
الذين عملوا السيئات إلا ما كانوا يعملون ٨٤

إن الذي فرض عليك القرآن لرادك إلى معاد قل ربي أعلم من
جاء بالهدى ومن هو في ضلال مبين ۝ وما كنت ترجوا أن يلقى إليك
الكتاب إلا رحمة من ربك فلا تكونن ظهيرا للكافرين ۝ ولا
يصدنك عن آيات الله بعد إذ أنزلت إليك وادع إلى ربك ولا
تكونن من المشركين ۝ ولا تدع مع الله إلها آخر لا إله إلا
هو كل شيء هالك إلا وجهه له الحكم وإليه ترجعون ۝

سورة العنكبوت مكية وهي تسع وستون آية

بسم الله الرحمن الرحيم
الم ۝ أحسب الناس أن يتركوا أن يقولوا آمنا وهم
لا يفتنون ۝ ولقد فتنا الذين من قبلهم فليعلمن
الله الذين صدقوا وليعلمن الكاذبين ۝ أم حسب الذين يعملون
السيئات أن يسبقونا ساء ما يحكمون ۝ من كان يرجوا لقاء
الله فإن أجل الله لآت وهو السميع العليم ۝ ومن
جاهد فإنما يجاهد لنفسه إن الله لغني عن العالمين ۝

He who has committed 28:85
the Koran to your keeping will
surely bring you home[1] again.
Say: 'My Lord best knows him
who has brought guidance
and him who is in manifest
error.'

Never did you expect the
Book to be revealed to you
except through your Lord's
mercy. Therefore give no support to the unbelievers. Let no
one turn you away from God's
revelations, now that they
have been revealed to you.
Call men to your Lord, and
serve none besides Him.

Invoke no other god to- 28:88
gether with God. There is no
god but Him. All things shall
perish except His Face. His is
the Judgement, and to Him
shall you be recalled.

THE SPIDER

In the Name of God, the Merciful, the Compassionate

Alif *lām mīm*. Do people think that once they say: 'We are believers,' they 29:1
will be left alone and not be tested?

We tested those who have gone before them. God surely knows the truthful, and He surely knows the liars.

Or do the evil-doers think they will escape Our reach? How ill they judge!

He that aspires to meet God must know that God's appointed time is sure
to come. He alone hears all and knows all.

He that fights for God's cause fights for himself. God needs the help of 29:6
none.

1. To Mecca.

29:7 THOSE THAT have faith and do good works We shall surely cleanse of their sins and requite according to their noblest deeds.

We have enjoined man to show kindness to his parents. But if they bid you serve besides Me deities you know nothing of, do not obey them. To Me you will all return, and I shall declare to you all that you have done. Those that believe and do good works We shall assuredly admit among the righteous.

29:10 Some profess to believe in God, yet when they suffer in God's cause they confuse the persecution of man with the punishment of God. But if your Lord gives you victory, they are sure to say: 'We were on your side.'

والذين آمنوا وعملوا الصالحات لنكفرن عنهم سيئاتهم
ولنجزينهم أحسن الذي كانوا يعملون ٧ ووصينا الإنسان
بوالديه حسنا وإن جاهداك لتشرك بي ما ليس لك به علم
فلا تطعهما إلي مرجعكم فأنبئكم بما كنتم تعملون ٨
والذين آمنوا وعملوا الصالحات لندخلنهم في الصالحين
٩ ومن الناس من يقول آمنا بالله فإذا أوذي في الله
جعل فتنة الناس كعذاب الله ولئن جاء نصر من ربك
ليقولن إنا كنا معكم أوليس الله بأعلم بما في صدور
العالمين ١٠ وليعلمن الله الذين آمنوا وليعلمن
المنافقين ١١ وقال الذين كفروا للذين آمنوا اتبعوا
سبيلنا ولنحمل خطاياكم وما هم بحاملين من خطاياهم
من شيء إنهم لكاذبون ١٢ وليحملن أثقالهم وأثقالا مع
أثقالهم وليسألن يوم القيامة عما كانوا يفترون ١٣
ولقد أرسلنا نوحا إلى قومه فلبث فيهم ألف سنة
إلا خمسين عاما فأخذهم الطوفان وهم ظالمون ١٤

Does not God know best the thoughts of people? God well knows the true believers, and He well knows the hypocrites.

The unbelievers say to the faithful: 'Follow us, and we will bear the burden of your sins.' But they will bear none of their sins. They are surely lying.

They shall bear their own burdens, and other burdens besides their burdens; and on the Day of Resurrection they shall surely be questioned about the lies they fabricated.

29:14 We sent forth Noah to his people, and he dwelt among them for a thousand years less fifty.[1] Then in their sinfulness the Flood took them.

1. Cf. Genesis 9:29.

فأنجيناه وأصحاب السفينة وجعلناها آية للعالمين ١٥
وإبراهيم إذ قال لقومه اعبدوا الله واتقوه ذلكم خير
لكم إن كنتم تعلمون ١٦ إنما تعبدون من دون الله أوثانا وتخلقون
إفكا إن الذين تعبدون من دون الله لا يملكون
لكم رزقا فابتغوا عند الله الرزق واعبدوه
واشكروا له إليه ترجعون ١٧ وإن تكذبوا فقد
كذب أمم من قبلكم وما على الرسول إلا البلاغ
المبين ١٨ أولم يروا كيف يبدئ الله الخلق ثم يعيده
إن ذلك على الله يسير ١٩ قل سيروا في الأرض
فانظروا كيف بدأ الخلق ثم الله ينشئ النشأة
الآخرة إن الله على كل شيء قدير ٢٠ يعذب من يشاء
ويرحم من يشاء وإليه تقلبون ٢١ وما أنتم بمعجزين في
الأرض ولا في السماء وما لكم من دون الله من ولي ولا
نصير ٢٢ والذين كفروا بآيات الله ولقائه أولئك
يئسوا من رحمتي وأولئك لهم عذاب أليم ٢٣

BUT WE delivered him and 29:15
those who were in the ark, and made the event a sign for mankind.

And tell of Abraham. He said to his people: 'Serve God and fear Him. That would be best for you, if you but knew it. You worship idols besides God and fabricate falsehoods. Those whom you serve besides God cannot give you your daily bread. Therefore seek your daily bread from God, and worship Him. Give thanks to Him, for to Him you shall return.

'If you disbelieve, other communities before you likewise disbelieved. Yet the apostle's duty is only to render the warning.'

Do they not see how God 29:19
brings the Creation into being, and then restores it? Surely that is easy enough for God.

Say: 'Roam the earth and see how God has brought the Creation into being. Then will God initiate the Latter Creation. God has power over all things; He punishes whom He will and shows mercy to whom He pleases. To Him shall you be recalled.'

Neither on earth nor in heaven shall you escape His reach: nor have you any besides God to protect or help you.

Those that disbelieve God's revelations and deny that they will ever meet 29:23
Him shall despair of My mercy. Woeful punishment awaits them.

29:24 HIS PEOPLE's only reply was: 'Kill him!' or 'Burn him!'

But from the fire God delivered him. Surely in this there are signs for true believers.

He said: 'You have chosen idols instead of God, but your love of them will last only in this nether life. On the Day of Resurrection you shall disown one another, and you shall curse one another. Your abode shall be the Fire, and none shall succour you.'

Lot believed in him. He said: 'I will fly this land whither my Lord bids me.[1] He is the Almighty, the Wise One.'

29:27 We gave him Isaac and Jacob and bestowed on his descendants prophethood and the Book. We gave him his reward in this life, and in the life to come he shall dwell among the righteous.

And Lot: he said to his people: 'You commit lewd acts which no other nation has committed before you. You lust after men and assault them on your highways. At your gatherings you perpetrate abominations.'

But his people's only answer was: 'Bring down the scourge of God upon us, if what you say be true.'

29:30 'Lord,' said he, 'deliver me from these degenerate people.'

فما كان جواب قومه إلا أن قالوا اقتلوه أو
حرقوه فأنجاه الله من النار إن في ذلك لآيات لقوم
يؤمنون ٢٤ وقال إنما اتخذتم من دون الله أوثانا مودة
بينكم في الحياة الدنيا ثم يوم القيامة يكفر بعضكم
ببعض ويلعن بعضكم بعضا ومأواكم النار
وما لكم من ناصرين ٢٥ فآمن له لوط وقال
إني مهاجر إلى ربي إنه هو العزيز الحكيم ٢٦
ووهبنا له إسحاق ويعقوب وجعلنا في ذريته
النبوة والكتاب وآتيناه أجره في الدنيا وإنه
في الآخرة لمن الصالحين ٢٧ ولوطا إذ قال لقومه
إنكم لتأتون الفاحشة ما سبقكم بها من أحد من
العالمين ٢٨ أئنكم لتأتون الرجال وتقطعون السبيل
وتأتون في ناديكم المنكر فما كان جواب
قومه إلا أن قالوا ائتنا بعذاب الله إن كنت من
الصادقين ٢٩ قال رب انصرني على القوم المفسدين ٣٠

1. Thus Al-Jalālayn.

ولما جاءت رسلنا ابرهيم بالبشرى قالوا انا
مهلكوا اهل هذه القرية ان اهلها كانوا ظالمين
(٣١) قال ان فيها لوطا قالوا نحن اعلم بمن فيها
لننجينه واهله الا امرأته كانت من الغابرين (٣٢)
ولما ان جاءت رسلنا لوطا سيء بهم وضاق بهم
ذرعا وقالوا لا تخف ولا تحزن انا منجوك واهلك
الا امرأتك كانت من الغابرين (٣٣) انا منزلون
على اهل هذه القرية رجزا من السماء بما كانوا
يفسقون (٣٤) ولقد تركنا منها اية بينة لقوم
يعقلون (٣٥) والى مدين اخاهم شعيبا فقال يا
قوم اعبدوا الله وارجوا اليوم الاخر ولا تعثوا في
الارض مفسدين (٣٦) فكذبوه فاخذتهم الرجفة
فاصبحوا في دارهم جاثمين (٣٧) وعادا وثمود وقد
تبين لكم من مساكنهم وزين لهم الشيطان
اعمالهم فصدهم عن السبيل وكانوا مستبصرين (٣٨)

AND WHEN Our emissaries 29:31
brought Abraham the joyful
tidings,[1] they said: 'We are to
destroy the people of this city,
for its people have done
wrong.'

He said: 'But Lot dwells in
it.'

'We well know who dwells
in it,' they said. 'We shall
deliver him and all his household, except his wife, who
shall remain behind.'

And when Our emissaries
came to Lot, he was troubled
and distressed on their account.
They said: 'Have no fear, and
do not grieve. We shall deliver
you and all your household,
except your wife, who shall
remain behind. We shall bring 29:34
down a scourge from heaven
upon the people of this city to
punish them for their sins.'

Surely the ruins We left of that city are a veritable sign for those that can
understand.

And to the people of Midian, their kin Shu'aib. He said: 'Serve God,
my people. Look forward to the Last Day. Do not corrupt the earth with
wickedness.'

But they denied him. The earthquake took them, and when morning came
they were crouching lifeless in their homes.

And 'Ād and Thamūd: this is vouched for by their dwellings. Satan had 29:38
made their deeds seem fair to them and debarred them from the right path,
keen-sighted though they were.

1. The birth of a son in his old age.

29:39 AND KORAH, Pharaoh, and
Haman! Moses came to them
with veritable signs, but they
behaved arrogantly in the land,
powerless though they were to
escape Us: and in their sinfulness, one and all, We smote
them. On some We sent down
a violent whirlwind; others the
Cry overtook; some We caused
to be swallowed up by the
earth, and yet others We overwhelmed by the Flood. God
did not wrong them, but they
wronged themselves.

Those who serve other
masters besides God may be
compared to the spider which
builds a cobweb for itself.
Surely the spider's is the frailest
of all dwellings, if they but
29:42 knew it. God knows whatever
they invoke besides Him; He is
the Almighty, the Wise One.

وقارون وفرعون وهامان ولقد جاءهم موسى
بالبينات فاستكبروا في الأرض وما كانوا سابقين ٣٩
فكلا أخذنا بذنبه فمنهم من أرسلنا عليه حاصبا
ومنهم من أخذته الصيحة ومنهم من خسفنا به الأرض
ومنهم من أغرقنا وما كان الله ليظلمهم ولكن
كانوا أنفسهم يظلمون ٤٠ مثل الذين اتخذوا
من دون الله أولياء كمثل العنكبوت اتخذت
بيتا وإن أوهن البيوت لبيت العنكبوت
لو كانوا يعلمون ٤١ إن الله يعلم ما يدعون
من دونه من شيء وهو العزيز الحكيم ٤٢ وتلك
الأمثال نضربها للناس وما يعقلها إلا العالمون
٤٣ خلق الله السماوات والأرض بالحق إن في ذلك
لآية للمؤمنين ٤٤ اتل ما أوحي إليك من الكتاب وأقم
الصلاة إن الصلاة تنهى عن الفحشاء والمنكر
ولذكر الله أكبر والله يعلم ما تصنعون ٤٥

Such are the comparisons We make for the instruction of people; but
none will grasp their meaning save those that have knowledge.

God created the heavens and the earth with Truth. Surely in this there is a
sign for true believers.

29:45 Proclaim the portions of the Book that have been revealed to you and be
steadfast in prayer: prayer fends off all that is foul and reprehensible. But
your foremost duty is to remember God. God has knowledge of what
you do.

ولا تجادلوا أهل الكتاب إلا بالتي هي أحسن إلا الذين
ظلموا منهم وقولوا آمنا بالذي أنزل إلينا وأنزل إليكم
وإلهنا وإلهكم واحد ونحن له مسلمون ۝ وكذلك
أنزلنا إليك الكتاب فالذين آتيناهم الكتاب يؤمنون
به ومن هؤلاء من يؤمن به وما يجحد بآياتنا إلا
الكافرون ۝ وما كنت تتلوا من قبله من كتاب
ولا تخطه بيمينك إذا لارتاب المبطلون ۝ بل هو آيات
بينات في صدور الذين أوتوا العلم وما يجحد بآياتنا
إلا الظالمون ۝ وقالوا لولا أنزل عليه آيات من ربه
قل إنما الآيات عند الله وإنما أنا نذير مبين ۝
أولم يكفهم أنا أنزلنا عليك الكتاب يتلى
عليهم إن في ذلك لرحمة وذكرى لقوم
يؤمنون ۝ قل كفى بالله بيني وبينكم شهيدا
يعلم ما في السماوات والأرض والذين آمنوا
بالباطل وكفروا بالله أولئك هم الخاسرون ۝

AND BE courteous when 29:46
you argue with the People of
the Book, except with those
among them who do wrong.
Say: 'We believe in that which
has been revealed to us and
was revealed to you. Our God
and your God is one. To Him
we submit as Muslims.'

Thus have We revealed the
Book to you. Those to whom
We gave the Book believe in
it, as do some of your own
people. Only the unbelievers
deny Our signs.

Never have you[1] read a
book before this, nor have you
ever transcribed one with your
right hand. Had you done
either, the unbelievers might
have doubted. But to those 29:49
who were given knowledge it
is a veritable sign. Only the
wrongdoers deny Our signs.

They say: 'Why have no signs been sent down to him from his Lord?' Say: 'Signs are in the hands of God. My mission is only to give clear warning.'

Is it not sufficient for them that We have revealed to you the Book for their instruction?[2] Surely in this there is a blessing and an Admonition for true believers.

Say: 'Sufficient is God as my witness, and your witness. He knows all that 29:52
is in the heavens and the earth. Those who believe in falsehood and deny
God will surely be the losers.'

1. Muḥammad. 2. Literally, to be recited to them.

29:53 AND THEY challenge you
to hasten on the scourge. Had
there not been a time ap-
pointed, the scourge would
have long since taken them.
Indeed, it will come down
upon them suddenly, and catch
them unawares.
They challenge you to hasten on the scourge. But Hell
will encompass the unbelievers, when the scourge will assail
them from above and from
beneath their feet, and God
will say: 'Taste the reward of
your own deeds.'
You that are true believers
among My servants, My earth
is vast. Therefore serve Me.
Every soul shall taste death,
and then to Us shall you be
recalled.
29:58 Those that embrace the true
Faith and do good works We shall lodge for ever in the mansions of Paradise, where rivers will roll at their feet. Blessed is the reward of those who
labour patiently and put their trust in their Lord.
Countless are the beasts that cannot fend for themselves. God provides
for them, as He provides for you. He alone hears all and knows all.
If you ask them who it is that has created the heavens and the earth, and
subdued the sun and the moon, they will surely say: 'God.' How then can
they turn away from Him?
God gives abundantly to whom He will among His servants, and sparingly
also. God has full knowledge of all things.
29:63 And if you ask them who it is that sends down water from the sky and
thus resurrects the earth after its death, they will surely say: 'God.' Say:
'Praise, then, be to God!' But the greater part of them are senseless.

ويستعجلونك بالعذاب ولولا أجل مسمى لجاءهم العذاب
وليأتينهم بغتة وهم لا يشعرون ٥٣ يستعجلونك بالعذاب
وإن جهنم لمحيطة بالكافرين ٥٤ يوم يغشاهم العذاب
من فوقهم ومن تحت أرجلهم ويقول ذوقوا ما كنتم تعملون
٥٥ يا عبادي الذين آمنوا إن أرضي واسعة فإياي فاعبدون
٥٦ كل نفس ذائقة الموت ثم إلينا ترجعون ٥٧ والذين
آمنوا وعملوا الصالحات لنبوئنهم من الجنة غرفا تجري من تحتها
الأنهار خالدين فيها نعم أجر العاملين ٥٨ الذين صبروا وعلى
ربهم يتوكلون ٥٩ وكأين من دابة لا تحمل رزقها
الله يرزقها وإياكم وهو السميع العليم ٦٠ ولئن سألتهم
من خلق السماوات والأرض وسخر الشمس والقمر ليقولن
الله فأنى يؤفكون ٦١ الله يبسط الرزق لمن يشاء من
عباده ويقدر له إن الله بكل شيء عليم ٦٢ ولئن سألتهم
من نزل من السماء ماء فأحيا به الأرض من بعد موتها ليقولن
الله قل الحمد لله بل أكثرهم لا يعقلون ٦٣

وما هذه الحيوة الدنيا الا لهو ولعب وان الدار الاخرة
لهي الحيوان لو كانوا يعلمون ٦٤ فاذا ركبوا في الفلك دعوا
الله مخلصين له الدين فلما نجيهم الى البر اذا هم يشركون ٦٥
ليكفروا بما اتينهم وليتمتعوا فسوف يعلمون ٦٦ اولم يروا انا جعلنا
حرما امنا ويتخطف الناس من حولهم افبالباطل يؤمنون وبنعمة
الله يكفرون ٦٧ ومن اظلم ممن افترى على الله كذبا او كذب
بالحق لما جاءه اليس في جهنم مثوى للكافرين ٦٨ والذين
جاهدوا فينا لنهدينهم سبلنا وان الله لمع المحسنين ٦٩

سورة الروم مكية وهي ستون اية

بسم الله الرحمن الرحيم
الم ١ غلبت الروم ٢ في ادنى الارض وهم من بعد
غلبهم سيغلبون ٣ في بضع سنين لله الامر من قبل
ومن بعد ويومئذ يفرح المؤمنون ٤ بنصر
الله ينصر من يشاء وهو العزيز الرحيم ٥

THE LIFE of this world is 29:64
but a sport and a diversion. It is the life to come that is the true life: if they but knew it.

When they embark they pray to God with all religious fervour; but when He brings them safe to land, behold how they serve other gods besides Him, showing ingratitude for what We gave them and revelling in wanton ease. But they shall learn.

Do they not see how We 29:67
have given them a sanctuary of safety,[1] while all around them people are carried off by force? Would they believe in falsehood and deny God's goodness?

And who is more wicked than the man who invents a falsehood about God and denies the Truth when it is declared to him? Is there not in Hell a resting-place for the unbelievers?

Those that fight for Our cause We will surely guide to Our own paths. 29:69
Surely God is with the righteous.

THE GREEKS OF BYZANTIUM

In the Name of God, the Merciful, the Compassionate

ALIF *lām mīm.* The Greeks have been defeated[2] in a neighbouring land. But 30:1
in a few years they shall themselves gain victory: such being the will of God before and after.

On that day the believers will rejoice in God's help. He gives victory to 30:5
whom He will. And He is the Mighty One, the Compassionate.

1. At the Ka'bah.
2. By the Persians, in Syria – in 615. Muḥammad's sympathies were with the Christians, not with the idolatrous Persians.

30:6 THAT IS God's promise;
God will never break His
promise. Yet most do not
know it.
They know the outward
show of this nether life, but
of the life to come they are
heedless. Have they not pondered within their own minds
that God created the heavens
and the earth and all that lies
between them only for a worthy end, and for an appointed
term? Yet many deny they will
ever meet their Lord.
Have they never journeyed
through the land and seen
what was the fate of their
forebears? Far mightier were
they; they tilled the land and
built upon it more than these
have ever built. And to them,
too, their apostles came with
undoubted signs. God did not wrong them but they wronged themselves.
30:10 Evil was the end of those who did evil, because they had disbelieved God's
revelations and derided them.
God brings the Creation into being and will then restore it. To Him shall
you be recalled.
On the day the Hour strikes, the wrongdoers will be speechless with despair. None of their idols will intercede for them: indeed, they will deny their
idols.
30:15 On the day the Hour strikes, mankind will divide. Those who have
embraced the Faith and done good works will rejoice in a fair Garden;

وَعْدَ اللَّهِ لَا يُخْلِفُ اللَّهُ وَعْدَهُ وَلَٰكِنَّ أَكْثَرَ النَّاسِ
لَا يَعْلَمُونَ ٦ يَعْلَمُونَ ظَاهِرًا مِنَ الْحَيَوٰةِ الدُّنْيَا وَهُمْ عَنِ
الْآخِرَةِ هُمْ غَافِلُونَ ٧ أَوَلَمْ يَتَفَكَّرُوا فِي أَنْفُسِهِمْ مَا
خَلَقَ اللَّهُ السَّمَٰوَاتِ وَالْأَرْضَ وَمَا بَيْنَهُمَا إِلَّا بِالْحَقِّ وَأَجَلٍ مُسَمًّى
وَإِنَّ كَثِيرًا مِنَ النَّاسِ بِلِقَاءِ رَبِّهِمْ لَكَافِرُونَ ٨ أَوَلَمْ يَسِيرُوا فِي
الْأَرْضِ فَيَنْظُرُوا كَيْفَ كَانَ عَاقِبَةُ الَّذِينَ مِنْ قَبْلِهِمْ
كَانُوا أَشَدَّ مِنْهُمْ قُوَّةً وَأَثَارُوا الْأَرْضَ وَعَمَرُوهَا أَكْثَرَ
مِمَّا عَمَرُوهَا وَجَاءَتْهُمْ رُسُلُهُمْ بِالْبَيِّنَاتِ فَمَا كَانَ اللَّهُ
لِيَظْلِمَهُمْ وَلَٰكِنْ كَانُوا أَنْفُسَهُمْ يَظْلِمُونَ ٩ ثُمَّ
كَانَ عَاقِبَةَ الَّذِينَ أَسَاءُوا السُّوأَىٰ أَنْ كَذَّبُوا بِآيَاتِ اللَّهِ
وَكَانُوا بِهَا يَسْتَهْزِئُونَ ١٠ اللَّهُ يَبْدَأُ الْخَلْقَ ثُمَّ يُعِيدُهُ ثُمَّ
إِلَيْهِ تُرْجَعُونَ ١١ وَيَوْمَ تَقُومُ السَّاعَةُ يُبْلِسُ الْمُجْرِمُونَ ١٢ وَلَمْ
يَكُنْ لَهُمْ مِنْ شُرَكَائِهِمْ شُفَعَاءُ وَكَانُوا بِشُرَكَائِهِمْ كَافِرِينَ
١٣ وَيَوْمَ تَقُومُ السَّاعَةُ يَوْمَئِذٍ يَتَفَرَّقُونَ ١٤ فَأَمَّا الَّذِينَ
آمَنُوا وَعَمِلُوا الصَّالِحَاتِ فَهُمْ فِي رَوْضَةٍ يُحْبَرُونَ ١٥

وأما الذين كفروا وكذبوا بآياتنا ولقاي الآخرة
فأولئك في العذاب محضرون ﴿١٦﴾ فسبحان الله حين تمسون
وحين تصبحون ﴿١٧﴾ وله الحمد في السموات والأرض وعشيا
وحين تظهرون ﴿١٨﴾ يخرج الحي من الميت ويخرج الميت
من الحي ويحيي الأرض بعد موتها وكذلك تخرجون
﴿١٩﴾ ومن آياته أن خلقكم من تراب ثم إذا أنتم
بشر تنتشرون ﴿٢٠﴾ ومن آياته أن خلق لكم من
أنفسكم أزواجا لتسكنوا إليها وجعل بينكم
مودة ورحمة إن في ذلك لآيات لقوم يتفكرون
﴿٢١﴾ ومن آياته خلق السموات والأرض واختلاف ألسنتكم
وألوانكم إن في ذلك لآيات للعالمين ﴿٢٢﴾ ومن آياته
منامكم بالليل والنهار وابتغاؤكم من فضله إن في ذلك لآيات
لقوم يسمعون ﴿٢٣﴾ ومن آياته يريكم البرق خوفا
وطمعا وينزل من السماء ماء فيحيي به الأرض
بعد موتها إن في ذلك لآيات لقوم يعقلون ﴿٢٤﴾

but those who have disbelieved 30:16
and denied Our revelations
and the life to come, shall be
delivered up for punishment.

So glory be to God in your evenings and in your mornings; and to Him be praise in the heavens and the earth, at your twilights and at your noons.

He brings forth the living from the dead, and brings forth the dead from the living: He resurrects the earth after its death. Likewise shall you be raised to life.

By one of His signs He
created you from dust; and,
behold, you became humans
and multiplied throughout the
earth. By another of His signs 30:21
He created for you spouses
from among yourselves, that
you might live in peace with them, and between you planted love and kindness. Surely there are signs in this for people who reflect.

And among His signs are the creation of the heavens and the earth, and the diversity of your tongues and colours. Surely in this there are signs for all mankind.

By another sign of His you sleep at night and seek by day His bounty. Surely there are signs in this for those who can hear.

Lightning is yet another of His signs, inspiring you with fear and hope. He 30:24
sends down water from the sky, and with it He quickens the earth after its death. Surely in this there are signs for those that are of sense possessed.

30:25 And by another of His signs heaven and earth stand firm at His bidding. Then, when with one shout He summons you out of the earth, lo, you shall be raised.

To Him belongs whosoever is in the heavens and the earth: all are obedient to Him.

And He it is who brings the Creation into being, and will then restore it: that is easier for Him.

His is the most exalted attribute in the heavens and the earth; and He is the Almighty, the Wise One.

He makes you this comparison, drawn from your own lives. Do your slaves share with you on equal terms what We have given you? Do you fear them as you fear one another? Thus do We expound Our revelations to people who understand.

ومن آياته أن تقوم السماء والأرض بأمره ثم إذا دعاكم
دعوة من الأرض إذا أنتم تخرجون ۝ وله من في السموات
والأرض كل له قانتون ۝ وهو الذي يبدأ الخلق ثم
يعيده وهو أهون عليه وله المثل الأعلى في السموات
والأرض وهو العزيز الحكيم ۝ ضرب لكم مثلا من
أنفسكم هل لكم من ما ملكت أيمانكم من شركاء
في ما رزقناكم فأنتم فيه سواء تخافونهم كخيفتكم
أنفسكم كذلك نفصل الآيات لقوم يعقلون ۝ بل اتبع
الذين ظلموا أهواءهم بغير علم فمن يهدي من أضل
الله وما لهم من ناصرين ۝ فأقم وجهك للدين حنيفا فطرت
الله التي فطر الناس عليها لا تبديل لخلق
الله ذلك الدين القيم ولكن أكثر الناس
لا يعلمون ۝ منيبين إليه واتقوه وأقيموا الصلوة
ولا تكونوا من المشركين ۝ من الذين فرقوا دينهم
وكانوا شيعا كل حزب بما لديهم فرحون ۝

30:29 Indeed, the wrongdoers are led unwittingly by their own appetites. And who can guide those whom God has led astray? There shall be none to succour them.

Therefore, stand firm in your devotion to the True Religion, which God created for mankind to embrace. God's Creation cannot be changed. This is surely the Upright Religion, but most do not know it.

Turn to Him and fear Him; be steadfast in prayer and serve no other god
30:32 besides Him. Do not divide your Religion into sects, each exulting in its own
doctrines.

وإذا مس الناس ضر دعوا ربهم منيبين إليه ثم إذا أذاقهم
منه رحمة إذا فريق منهم بربهم يشركون ۝ ليكفروا
بما آتيناهم فتمتعوا فسوف تعلمون ۝ أم أنزلنا عليهم
سلطانا فهو يتكلم بما كانوا به يشركون ۝ وإذا أذقنا الناس
رحمة فرحوا بها وإن تصبهم سيئة بما قدمت أيديهم إذا هم
يقنطون ۝ أولم يروا أن الله يبسط الرزق لمن يشاء
ويقدر إن في ذلك لآيات لقوم يؤمنون ۝ فآت ذا القربى
حقه والمسكين وابن السبيل ذلك خير للذين يريدون وجه
الله وأولئك هم المفلحون ۝ وما آتيتم من ربا ليربوا في
أموال الناس فلا يربوا عند الله وما آتيتم من زكوة تريدون وجه
الله فأولئك هم المضعفون ۝ الله الذي خلقكم ثم رزقكم
ثم يميتكم ثم يحييكم هل من شركائكم من
يفعل من ذلكم من شيء سبحانه وتعالى عما يشركون
۝ ظهر الفساد في البر والبحر بما كسبت أيدي الناس
ليذيقهم بعض الذي عملوا لعلهم يرجعون ۝

AND WHEN a misfortune 30:33
befalls people, they turn in
prayer to their Lord. But no
sooner does He let them taste
a blessing from Himself than
some among them take up
other gods besides their Lord,
showing no gratitude for what
We gave them. Take your
pleasure now, and you shall
learn.

Have We revealed to them
a sanction enjoining them to
serve idols?

And when We give people
the taste of a good thing they
rejoice in it, but when evil
befalls them through their
own fault, they grow des-
pondent. Do they not see that
God gives abundantly to
whom He will, and sparingly
also? Surely there are signs in
this for true believers.

Therefore give their due to the next of kin, to the destitute, and to the 30:38
traveller in need. That is best for those that strive to please God; such men
will surely prosper.

People's wealth you seek to increase by usury will not increase in the sight
of God; but the alms you give for the love of God shall be repaid many
times over.

God it is who has created you and given you your daily bread. He will
cause you to die hereafter and will then bring you back to life. Can any of
your idols do the least of these? God forbid! Glory to Him, and exalted be
He above their false gods!

Corruption is now manifest on land and at sea in consequence of what 30:41
the hands of mankind did: that they may taste the fruit of what they did and
mend their ways.

30:42 SAY: 'ROAM the earth and
see what was the fate of those
who came before you. The
greater part of them worshipped idols.'

Therefore stand firm in your devotion to the Upright Religion before that day arrives which none may put off against the will of God. On that day mankind will be parted in two: the unbelievers shall answer for their unbelief, and the righteous will have done well for themselves: for then He will of His bounty recompense those who have believed and done good works. He does not love the unbelievers.

30:46 By another of His signs He
sends the winds as bearers of good tidings, so that He may give you a taste of His mercy and that the ships may sail at His bidding; so that you may seek His bounty and render thanks.

We sent before you apostles to their peoples, and they brought them veritable signs. We took vengeance on those who sinned, and rightly succoured the true believers.

God it is who drives the winds that stir the clouds. He spreads them as He will in the heavens and breaks them up, so that you can see the rain falling from their midst. When He sends it down on such of His servants as He chooses, behold, they are elated with joy, though before its coming they had lost all hope.

30:50 Behold then the tokens of God's mercy; how He resurrects the earth after
its death. It is He who will assuredly resurrect the dead; He has power over
all things.

قل سيروا في الأرض فانظروا كيف كان عاقبة الذين من قبل
كان أكثرهم مشركين ۝ فأقم وجهك للدين القيم من قبل
أن يأتي يوم لا مرد له من الله يومئذ يصدعون ۝ من كفر
فعليه كفره ومن عمل صالحا فلأنفسهم يمهدون ۝ ليجزي
الذين آمنوا وعملوا الصالحات من فضله إنه لا يحب الكافرين
۝ ومن آياته أن يرسل الرياح مبشرات وليذيقكم من
رحمته ولتجري الفلك بأمره ولتبتغوا من فضله ولعلكم
تشكرون ۝ ولقد أرسلنا من قبلك رسلا إلى قومهم
فجاءوهم بالبينات فانتقمنا من الذين أجرموا وكان حقا
علينا نصر المؤمنين ۝ الله الذي يرسل الرياح فتثير سحابا
فيبسطه في السماء كيف يشاء ويجعله كسفا فترى الودق يخرج
من خلاله فإذا أصاب به من يشاء من عباده إذا هم يستبشرون
۝ وإن كانوا من قبل أن ينزل عليهم من قبله لمبلسين
۝ فانظر إلى آثار رحمت الله كيف يحيي الأرض بعد موتها
إن ذلك لمحيي الموتى وهو على كل شيء قدير ۝

وَلَئِنْ أَرْسَلْنَا رِيحًا فَرَأَوْهُ مُصْفَرًّا لَظَلُّوا مِنْ بَعْدِهِ يَكْفُرُونَ ٥١ فَإِنَّكَ
لَا تُسْمِعُ الْمَوْتَىٰ وَلَا تُسْمِعُ الصُّمَّ الدُّعَاءَ إِذَا وَلَّوْا مُدْبِرِينَ ٥٢ وَمَا أَنْتَ
بِهَادِ الْعُمْيِ عَنْ ضَلَالَتِهِمْ إِنْ تُسْمِعُ إِلَّا مَنْ يُؤْمِنُ بِآيَاتِنَا فَهُمْ مُسْلِمُونَ
٥٣ اللَّهُ الَّذِي خَلَقَكُمْ مِنْ ضَعْفٍ ثُمَّ جَعَلَ مِنْ بَعْدِ ضَعْفٍ
قُوَّةً ثُمَّ جَعَلَ مِنْ بَعْدِ قُوَّةٍ ضَعْفًا وَشَيْبَةً يَخْلُقُ مَا يَشَاءُ
وَهُوَ الْعَلِيمُ الْقَدِيرُ ٥٤ وَيَوْمَ تَقُومُ السَّاعَةُ يُقْسِمُ
الْمُجْرِمُونَ مَا لَبِثُوا غَيْرَ سَاعَةٍ كَذَٰلِكَ كَانُوا يُؤْفَكُونَ ٥٥
وَقَالَ الَّذِينَ أُوتُوا الْعِلْمَ وَالْإِيمَانَ لَقَدْ لَبِثْتُمْ فِي
كِتَابِ اللَّهِ إِلَىٰ يَوْمِ الْبَعْثِ فَهَٰذَا يَوْمُ الْبَعْثِ وَلَٰكِنَّكُمْ
كُنْتُمْ لَا تَعْلَمُونَ ٥٦ فَيَوْمَئِذٍ لَا يَنْفَعُ الَّذِينَ ظَلَمُوا
مَعْذِرَتُهُمْ وَلَا هُمْ يُسْتَعْتَبُونَ ٥٧ وَلَقَدْ ضَرَبْنَا لِلنَّاسِ فِي
هَٰذَا الْقُرْآنِ مِنْ كُلِّ مَثَلٍ وَلَئِنْ جِئْتَهُمْ بِآيَةٍ لَيَقُولَنَّ
الَّذِينَ كَفَرُوا إِنْ أَنْتُمْ إِلَّا مُبْطِلُونَ ٥٨ كَذَٰلِكَ
يَطْبَعُ اللَّهُ عَلَىٰ قُلُوبِ الَّذِينَ لَا يَعْلَمُونَ ٥٩ فَاصْبِرْ إِنَّ
وَعْدَ اللَّهِ حَقٌّ وَلَا يَسْتَخِفَّنَّكَ الَّذِينَ لَا يُوقِنُونَ ٦٠

YET IF We let loose a sear- 30:51
ing wind, and they beheld their
crops turn yellow, they would
after that persist in unbelief.

You surely cannot make the
dead hear you, nor can you
make the deaf hear your call if
they turn their backs and pay
no heed; nor can you guide the
blind out of their error. None
shall give ear to you save those
who believe in Our revelations,
and are now Muslims.

God creates you weak: after
weakness He gives you strength,
and after strength infirmity and
grey hairs. He creates whatever
He will: He is the Omniscient,
the Almighty.

On the day the Hour strikes, 30:55
the wrongdoers will swear that
they had lingered but one hour.
Thus are they ever deceived.

But those to whom knowledge and faith have been given will say: 'You
lingered there, as God ordained, till the Day of Resurrection. This is the Day
of Resurrection: yet you did not know it.'

On that day their pleas shall not avail the wrongdoers, nor shall they be
asked to make amends.

In this Koran we have set forth for people all manner of arguments. Yet
if you recite to them a single verse, the unbelievers will surely say: 'You
preach nothing but falsehoods.' Thus God seals the hearts of the ignorant.

Therefore have patience. God's promise is true. Let not those who dis- 30:60
believe drive you to despair.

LUQMĀN

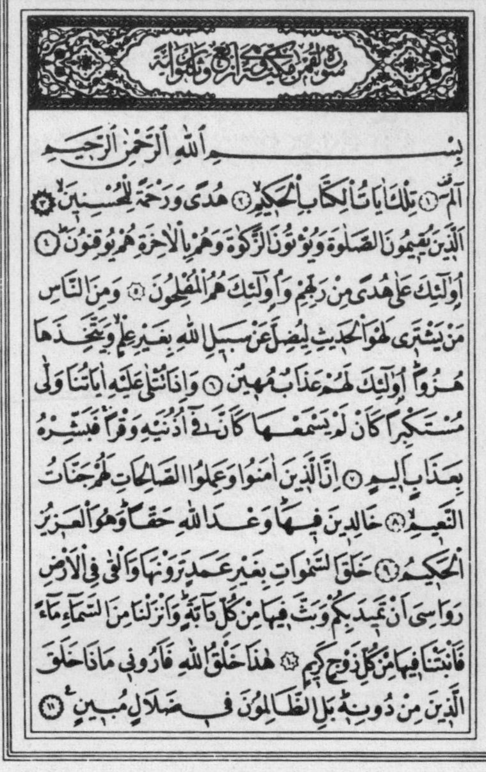
سورة لقمان مكية أربع وثلاثون آية
بسم الله الرحمن الرحيم
الم ١ تلك آيات الكتاب الحكيم ٢ هدى ورحمة للمحسنين ٣
الذين يقيمون الصلوة ويؤتون الزكوة وهم بالآخرة هم يوقنون ٤
أولئك على هدى من ربهم وأولئك هم المفلحون ٥ ومن الناس
من يشتري لهو الحديث ليضل عن سبيل الله بغير علم ويتخذها
هزوا أولئك لهم عذاب مهين ٦ وإذا تتلى عليه آياتنا ولى
مستكبرا كأن لم يسمعها كأن في أذنيه وقرا فبشره
بعذاب أليم ٧ إن الذين آمنوا وعملوا الصالحات لهم جنات
النعيم ٨ خالدين فيها وعد الله حقا وهو العزيز
الحكيم ٩ خلق السموات بغير عمد ترونها وألقى في الأرض
رواسي أن تميد بكم وبث فيها من كل دابة وأنزلنا من السماء ماء
فأنبتنا فيها من كل زوج كريم ١٠ هذا خلق الله فأروني ماذا خلق
الذين من دونه بل الظالمون في ضلال مبين ١١

In the Name of God,
the Merciful, the Compassionate

31:1 Alif *lām mīm.* These are the
revelations of the Wise Book,
a guide and a blessing to the
righteous, who attend to their
prayers, render the alms levy,
and firmly believe in the life to
come. These are rightly guided
by their Lord, and will surely
succeed.

Some there are who would
indulge in frivolous talk, so
that they may without knowledge lead men away from the
path of God and hold it up to
ridicule. For these there shall
be shameful punishment.

When Our revelations are
recited to them, they turn their backs in scorn, as though they never heard
them: as though their ears were sealed. To these proclaim a woeful punishment.

31:8 But those that believe and do good works shall enter the Gardens of
Delight, wherein shall they abide for ever. God's promise shall be fulfilled:
He is the Almighty, the Wise One.

He raised the heavens with no visible pillars, and set firm mountains on
the earth lest it should shake with you. He dispersed upon it all manner of
beasts; and We sent down water from the sky with which We caused all kinds
of goodly plants to grow.

31:11 Such is God's Creation: now show Me what your other gods created.
Surely, the unbelievers are in evident error.

وَلَقَدْ آتَيْنَا لُقْمَانَ الْحِكْمَةَ أَنِ اشْكُرْ لِلَّهِ وَمَنْ يَشْكُرْ
فَإِنَّمَا يَشْكُرُ لِنَفْسِهِ وَمَنْ كَفَرَ فَإِنَّ اللَّهَ غَنِيٌّ حَمِيدٌ
١٢ وَإِذْ قَالَ لُقْمَانُ لِابْنِهِ وَهُوَ يَعِظُهُ يَا بُنَيَّ لَا تُشْرِكْ بِاللَّهِ
إِنَّ الشِّرْكَ لَظُلْمٌ عَظِيمٌ ١٣ وَوَصَّيْنَا الْإِنْسَانَ بِوَالِدَيْهِ حَمَلَتْهُ
أُمُّهُ وَهْنًا عَلَىٰ وَهْنٍ وَفِصَالُهُ فِي عَامَيْنِ أَنِ اشْكُرْ لِي وَلِوَالِدَيْكَ
إِلَيَّ الْمَصِيرُ ١٤ وَإِنْ جَاهَدَاكَ عَلَىٰ أَنْ تُشْرِكَ بِي مَا لَيْسَ لَكَ
بِهِ عِلْمٌ فَلَا تُطِعْهُمَا وَصَاحِبْهُمَا فِي الدُّنْيَا مَعْرُوفًا وَاتَّبِعْ سَبِيلَ
مَنْ أَنَابَ إِلَيَّ ثُمَّ إِلَيَّ مَرْجِعُكُمْ فَأُنَبِّئُكُمْ بِمَا كُنْتُمْ تَعْمَلُونَ ١٥
يَا بُنَيَّ إِنَّهَا إِنْ تَكُ مِثْقَالَ حَبَّةٍ مِنْ خَرْدَلٍ فَتَكُنْ فِي صَخْرَةٍ
أَوْ فِي السَّمَاوَاتِ أَوْ فِي الْأَرْضِ يَأْتِ بِهَا اللَّهُ إِنَّ اللَّهَ
لَطِيفٌ خَبِيرٌ ١٦ يَا بُنَيَّ أَقِمِ الصَّلَاةَ وَأْمُرْ بِالْمَعْرُوفِ وَانْهَ عَنِ
الْمُنْكَرِ وَاصْبِرْ عَلَىٰ مَا أَصَابَكَ إِنَّ ذَٰلِكَ مِنْ عَزْمِ الْأُمُورِ ١٧
وَلَا تُصَعِّرْ خَدَّكَ لِلنَّاسِ وَلَا تَمْشِ فِي الْأَرْضِ مَرَحًا إِنَّ اللَّهَ
لَا يُحِبُّ كُلَّ مُخْتَالٍ فَخُورٍ ١٨ وَاقْصِدْ فِي مَشْيِكَ وَاغْضُضْ
مِنْ صَوْتِكَ إِنَّ أَنْكَرَ الْأَصْوَاتِ لَصَوْتُ الْحَمِيرِ ١٩

WE BESTOWED wisdom on 31:12
Luqmān,[1] saying: 'Give thanks
to God. He that gives thanks
has much to gain for his own
soul, but if anyone is thankless, God is self-sufficient and
worthy of praise.'

Tell of Luqmān, who admonished his son, saying: 'My son, serve no other deity besides God, for idolatry is an abominable sin.'

We enjoined man to show kindness to his parents, for with much pain his mother bears him, and he is not weaned before he is two years of age. We said: 'Give thanks to Me and to your parents. To Me shall all return. But if they press you to serve besides Me deities you know nothing of, do not obey them. Be kind to them in this world, and follow the path of those who turn to Me. To Me shall you return, and I will declare to you what you have done.'

'My son, if it be as small as a grain of mustard seed, be it hidden inside 31:16
a rock or in the heavens or in the earth, God will bring it to light. Surely
gracious is God and all-knowing.

'My son, be steadfast in prayer, enjoin justice, and forbid the reprehensible. Endure with fortitude whatever befalls you. That is a duty incumbent on all.

'Do not treat people with scorn, nor walk exultant on the earth: surely
God does not love the arrogant and the vainglorious. Rather let your stride 31:19
be modest and your voice low: the most hideous of voices is the braying of
the ass.'

1. A sage who, we are told, was a grandson of a sister or an aunt of Job.

31:20 Do you not see how God
has subjected to you all that
the heavens and the earth contain, and lavished on you His
bounty, visible and unseen?
Yet some among people still
argue about God, without
knowledge or guidance or
illuminating scripture.

And when they are told:
'Follow what God has revealed,'
they say: 'We will follow the
faith our fathers practised.'
Yes, even though Satan invites
them to the torment of the
Conflagration.

He that submits his face to
God and leads a righteous life
stands on the firmest ground.[1]
To God shall all return. As for
those that disbelieve, let not
their disbelief grieve you. To
Us shall they return and We
will declare to them what they have done. God has knowledge of their innermost thoughts.

31:24 We suffer them to take their ease awhile, and will then subject them to a
grievous scourge.

If you say to them: 'Who has created the heavens and the earth?' they will
surely say: 'God.' Say: 'Praise, then, be to God!' But the greater part of them
have no knowledge.

His is what the heavens and the earth contain. Surely God alone is
self-sufficient and worthy of praise.

If all the trees of the earth were pens, and the sea, replenished by seven
other seas, were ink, the words of God could not be finished still. Almighty
is God, and wise.

31:28 You were created but as one soul, and as one soul you shall be raised to
life. God hears all and observes all.

ألم تروا أن الله سخر لكم ما في السموات وما في الأرض
وأسبغ عليكم نعمه ظاهرة وباطنة ومن الناس من يجادل في
الله بغير علم ولا هدى ولا كتاب منير ۝ وإذا قيل لهم
اتبعوا ما أنزل الله قالوا بل نتبع ما وجدنا عليه آباءنا
أولو كان الشيطان يدعوهم إلى عذاب السعير ۝ ومن يسلم
وجهه إلى الله وهو محسن فقد استمسك بالعروة الوثقى وإلى
الله عاقبة الأمور ۝ ومن كفر فلا يحزنك كفره إلينا مرجعهم
فننبئهم بما عملوا إن الله عليم بذات الصدور ۝ نمتعهم قليلا
ثم نضطرهم إلى عذاب غليظ ۝ ولئن سألتهم من خلق السموات
والأرض ليقولن الله قل الحمد لله بل أكثرهم
لا يعلمون ۝ لله ما في السموات والأرض إن
الله هو الغني الحميد ۝ ولو أن ما في الأرض من شجرة
أقلام والبحر يمده من بعده سبعة أبحر ما نفدت
كلمات الله إن الله عزيز حكيم ۝ ما خلقكم
ولا بعثكم إلا كنفس واحدة إن الله سميع بصير ۝

1. Literally, grasps the firmest handle.

الم تر ان الله يولج الليل في النهار ويولج النهار في الليل وسخر
الشمس والقمر كل يجري الى اجل مسمى وان الله بما تعملون خبير ٢٩
ذلك بان الله هو الحق وان ما يدعون من دونه الباطل وان الله
هو العلي الكبير ٣٠ الم تر ان الفلك تجري في البحر بنعمت الله
ليريكم من اياته ان في ذلك لايات لكل صبار شكور ٣١
واذا غشيهم موج كالظلل دعوا الله مخلصين له الدين
فلما نجاهم الى البر فمنهم مقتصد وما يجحد باياتنا الا كل
ختار كفور ٣٢ يا ايها الناس اتقوا ربكم واخشوا يوما لا
يجزي والد عن ولده ولا مولود هو جاز عن والده شيئا
ان وعد الله حق فلا تغرنكم الحيوة الدنيا ولا
يغرنكم بالله الغرور ٣٣ ان الله عنده علم الساعة
وينزل الغيث ويعلم ما في الارحام وما تدري نفس ماذا تكسب
غدا وما تدري نفس باي ارض تموت ان الله عليم خبير ٣٤

سورة السجدة مكية وهي ثلثون اية

Do you not see how God 31:29
causes the night to pass into
the day and the day to pass
into the night? And He has
pressed the sun and the moon
into His service, each running
for an appointed term. God
is cognizant of what you do.
Because God is the Truth, and
false are the idols they invoke
besides Him. And surely God
is the Most High, the Supreme
One.

Do you not see how the
ships speed upon the ocean by
God's grace, so that He may
reveal to you some of His
wonders? Surely in this there
are signs for every steadfast,
thankful person.

When the waves, like a giant 31:32
shadow, envelop them, they
pray to God, consecrating
their religion to Him. But no sooner does He bring them safe to land than
some among them falter between faith and unbelief. None denies Our
revelations except the treacherous and the ungrateful.

You people! Fear your Lord, and fear the day when no parent shall avail
his child nor any child his parent. God's promise is surely true. Let the life of
this world never deceive you, nor let the Dissembler trick you about God.

God alone has knowledge of the Hour. He sends down the abundant rain 31:34
and knows what every womb contains.

No mortal knows what he will earn tomorrow; no mortal knows on which
ground he will breathe his last. God alone is omniscient and well aware.

PROSTRATION

بسم الله الرحمن الرحيم
الم ۝ تنزيل الكتاب لا ريب فيه من رب العالمين ۝ أم
يقولون افتراه بل هو الحق من ربك لتنذر قوما ما أتاهم
من نذير من قبلك لعلهم يهتدون ۝ الله الذي خلق السموات
والأرض وما بينهما في ستة أيام ثم استوى على العرش
ما لكم من دونه من ولي ولا شفيع أفلا تتذكرون
۝ يدبر الأمر من السماء إلى الأرض ثم يعرج إليه
في يوم كان مقداره ألف سنة مما تعدون ۝
ذلك عالم الغيب والشهادة العزيز الرحيم ۝
الذي أحسن كل شيء خلقه وبدأ خلق الإنسان من طين
۝ ثم جعل نسله من سلالة من ماء مهين ۝ ثم سواه
ونفخ فيه من روحه وجعل لكم السمع والأبصار والأفئدة
قليلا ما تشكرون ۝ وقالوا أإذا ضللنا في الأرض أإنا
لفي خلق جديد بل هم بلقاء ربهم كافرون ۝ قل يتوفاكم
ملك الموت الذي وكل بكم ثم إلى ربكم ترجعون ۝

In the Name of God,
the Merciful, the Compassionate

32:1 ALIF *lām mīm.* The revelation
of the Book, of which there is
no doubt, is from the Lord of
the Universe.
Do they say: 'He[1] has
invented it himself'?
Surely it is the Truth from
your Lord, that you may forewarn a people none has
warned before you, and that
they may be rightly guided.
It was God who in six days
created the heavens and the
earth and all that lies between
them, and then ascended the
throne. You have no guardian
or intercessor besides Him.
Will you not reflect?
He governs all, from heaven to earth. And all will ascend to Him in a
single day, a day whose space is a thousand years by your reckoning.
32:6 He knows the unknown and the manifest. He is the Almighty, the Merciful, who excelled in everything He created. He first created man from clay,
then made his offspring from a drop of humble fluid. Then He moulded him
and breathed His spirit into him. He made for you ears and eyes and hearts:
yet you are seldom thankful.
And they say: 'Once lost into the earth, shall we be in a new creation?'
Indeed, they deny they will ever meet their Lord.
32:11 Say: 'The angel of death in charge of you will claim you back. Then to
your Lord shall you be recalled.'

1. Muḥammad.

ولو ترى إذ المجرمون ناكسوا رءوسهم عند ربهم
ربنا أبصرنا وسمعنا فارجعنا نعمل صالحا إنا موقنون ١٢
ولو شئنا لآتينا كل نفس هداها ولكن حق القول
مني لأملأن جهنم من الجنة والناس أجمعين ١٣ فذوقوا
بما نسيتم لقاء يومكم هذا إنا نسيناكم وذوقوا
عذاب الخلد بما كنتم تعملون ١٤ إنما يؤمن بآياتنا
الذين إذا ذكروا بها خروا سجدا وسبحوا بحمد ربهم
وهم لا يستكبرون ١٥ تتجافى جنوبهم عن المضاجع يدعون
ربهم خوفا وطمعا ومما رزقناهم ينفقون ١٦ فلا
تعلم نفس ما أخفي لهم من قرة أعين جزاء بما كانوا
يعملون ١٧ أفمن كان مؤمنا كمن كان فاسقا لا يستوون
١٨ أما الذين آمنوا وعملوا الصالحات فلهم جنات
المأوى نزلا بما كانوا يعملون ١٩ وأما الذين فسقوا
فمأواهم النار كلما أرادوا أن يخرجوا منها أعيدوا فيها
وقيل لهم ذوقوا عذاب النار الذي كنتم به تكذبون ٢٠

WOULD THAT you could see 32:12
the wrongdoers when they
hang their heads before their
Lord! They will say: 'Lord, we
now see and hear. Send us back
and we will do good works.
Now we are firm believers.'

Had it been Our will, We
could have given every soul its
guidance. But My Judgement
shall be fulfilled: 'I will surely
fill Hell with jinn and humans
all. Taste this, for you forgot
you would ever meet this day.
We, too, will forget you. Taste
the eternal torment, which you
have earned by what you did.'

Indeed, none believes in
Our revelations save those
who, when reminded of them,
prostrate themselves in adoration and give glory to their
Lord in all humility; who for- 32:16
sake their beds to pray to their Lord in fear and hope; who give from what
We gave them. No mortal knows what bliss will be in store for these as a
reward for their labours.

Can he, then, who is a true believer, be compared to him who is ungodly?
Surely they are not equal.

As for those that believe and do good works, they shall be lodged in the
Gardens of Paradise in recompense for their labours. But those that do evil, 32:20
the Fire shall be their home. Whenever they wish to emerge from it they shall
be driven back, and shall be told: 'Taste the torment of the Fire, which you
persistently denied.'

32:21 WE WILL surely make them taste the lighter torment of this world before the greater torment of the world to come, that they may perchance return to the right path. And who is more wicked than he that pays no heed to the revelations of his Lord when he is reminded of them? We will surely take vengeance on the transgressors.

We gave the Book to Moses (never doubt that you[1] will meet him) and made it a guide for the Israelites. And when they grew steadfast and firmly believed in Our revelations, We appointed leaders from among them who gave guidance at Our bidding. On the Day of Resurrection your Lord will resolve their differences for them.

ولنذيقنهم من العذاب الأدنى دون العذاب الأكبر لعلهم
يرجعون ٢١ ومن أظلم ممن ذكر بآيات ربه ثم أعرض عنها
إنا من المجرمين منتقمون ٢٢ ولقد آتينا موسى الكتاب
فلا تكن في مرية من لقائه وجعلناه هدى لبني إسرائيل
٢٣ وجعلنا منهم أئمة يهدون بأمرنا لما صبروا
وكانوا بآياتنا يوقنون ٢٤ إن ربك هو يفصل بينهم
يوم القيامة فيما كانوا فيه يختلفون ٢٥ أولم يهد لهم كم
أهلكنا من قبلهم من القرون يمشون في مساكنهم إن في ذلك
لآيات أفلا يسمعون ٢٦ أولم يروا أنا نسوق الماء إلى الأرض
الجرز فنخرج به زرعا تأكل منه أنعامهم وأنفسهم أفلا
يبصرون ٢٧ ويقولون متى هذا الفتح إن كنتم صادقين
٢٨ قل يوم الفتح لا ينفع الذين كفروا إيمانهم ولا هم
ينظرون ٢٩ فأعرض عنهم وانتظر إنهم منتظرون ٣٠

سورة الأحزاب مدنية وهي ثلث وسبعون آية

32:26 Or do they not know how many generations We have destroyed before
them? They walk among their ruined dwellings. Surely in this there are conspicuous signs. Have they no ears to hear with?

Do they not see how We drive the water to the parched land and bring forth crops which they and their cattle eat? Have they no eyes to see with?

They say: 'When will this judgement[2] come, if what you say be true?'

Say: 'On the Day of Judgement their faith shall not avail the unbelievers, nor shall they be reprieved.'

32:30 Therefore pay no heed to them, and wait as they are waiting.

1. Muḥammad. 2. Or: victory.

بسم الله الرحمن الرحيم
يا أيها النبي اتق الله ولا تطع الكافرين والمنافقين إن الله
كان عليما حكيما ۝١ واتبع ما يوحى إليك من ربك إن الله
كان بما تعملون خبيرا ۝٢ وتوكل على الله وكفى بالله
وكيلا ۝٣ ما جعل الله لرجل من قلبين في جوفه وما جعل
أزواجكم اللائي تظاهرون منهن أمهاتكم وما جعل
أدعياءكم أبناءكم ذلكم قولكم بأفواهكم والله
يقول الحق وهو يهدي السبيل ۝٤ ادعوهم لآبائهم
هو أقسط عند الله فإن لم تعلموا آباءهم فإخوانكم
في الدين ومواليكم وليس عليكم جناح فيما أخطأتم به
ولكن ما تعمدت قلوبكم وكان الله غفورا رحيما ۝٥
النبي أولى بالمؤمنين من أنفسهم وأزواجه أمهاتهم
وأولو الأرحام بعضهم أولى ببعض في كتاب الله
من المؤمنين والمهاجرين إلا أن تفعلوا إلى أوليائكم
معروفا كان ذلك في الكتاب مسطورا ۝٦

THE CONFEDERATES

In the Name of God,
the Merciful, the Compassionate

PROPHET, HAVE fear of God 33:1
and do not yield to the unbelievers and the hypocrites.
God is all-knowing and wise.
Obey what is revealed to
you from your Lord, for God
is cognizant of all your actions,
and put your trust in God. Sufficient is God as a guardian.
God has never put two hearts
within one man's body. He does
not regard the wives whom you
divorce as your mothers,[1] nor
your adopted sons as your own
sons. These are mere words
which you utter with your
mouths: but God speaks the Truth and gives guidance to the right path.
Name your adopted sons after their fathers; that is more just in the sight 33:5
of God. If you do not know their fathers, regard them as your brothers in
the Faith and as your cousins. Your unintentional errors shall be overlooked,
but not the errors your hearts intended. God is ever forgiving and compassionate.
The Prophet has a greater claim on the faithful than they have on each 33:6
other. His wives are their mothers.
God ordains that blood relations are closer to one another than to other
believers or *muhājirīn*,[2] although you are permitted to do your friends a kindness.[3] That is in the Book decreed.

1. An allusion to the formula: 'Be to me as my mother's back', accepted among pagan Arabs as a declaration of divorce.
2. See p. 202, note 1.
3. By leaving them bequests.

33:7 TELL OF the covenant We made with the prophets; with you, with Noah and Abraham, with Moses and Jesus son of Mary. A solemn covenant We made with them, that He might question the truthful about their truthfulness. But for the unbelievers He has prepared a woeful punishment.

Believers, remember God's goodness to you when you were attacked by your enemy's army. We unleashed against them a violent wind and invisible warriors: God observed all that you were doing.

They attacked you from above and from below, so that your eyes were blurred, your hearts leapt up to your throats, and you thought ill of God's
design. There the faithful were put to the proof; there they were grievously
33:12 shaken. The hypocrites and the faint-hearted said: 'God and His apostle
made us promises only to deceive us.' Some among them said: 'People of
Yathrib,[1] you cannot stand much longer. Go back to your city.' And yet others
sought the Prophet's leave, saying: 'Our homes are defenceless,' while
defenceless they were not. They only wished to flee.

Had the city been entered from every quarter, and had they been roused to rebellion, they would have surely rebelled. But they would have occupied it only for a little while.

33:15 Surely before that, they swore to God never to turn their backs in flight. And an oath to God must needs be answered for.

وَإِذْ أَخَذْنَا مِنَ النَّبِيِّينَ مِيثَاقَهُمْ وَمِنكَ وَمِن نُّوحٍ وَإِبْرَاهِيمَ
وَمُوسَىٰ وَعِيسَى ابْنِ مَرْيَمَ وَأَخَذْنَا مِنْهُم مِّيثَاقًا غَلِيظًا ﴿٧﴾
لِّيَسْأَلَ الصَّادِقِينَ عَن صِدْقِهِمْ وَأَعَدَّ لِلْكَافِرِينَ عَذَابًا أَلِيمًا
﴿٨﴾ يَا أَيُّهَا الَّذِينَ آمَنُوا اذْكُرُوا نِعْمَةَ اللَّهِ عَلَيْكُمْ إِذْ جَاءَتْكُمْ
جُنُودٌ فَأَرْسَلْنَا عَلَيْهِمْ رِيحًا وَجُنُودًا لَّمْ تَرَوْهَا وَكَانَ اللَّهُ
بِمَا تَعْمَلُونَ بَصِيرًا ﴿٩﴾ إِذْ جَاءُوكُم مِّن فَوْقِكُمْ وَمِنْ أَسْفَلَ مِنكُمْ
وَإِذْ زَاغَتِ الْأَبْصَارُ وَبَلَغَتِ الْقُلُوبُ الْحَنَاجِرَ وَتَظُنُّونَ بِاللَّهِ
الظُّنُونَا ﴿١٠﴾ هُنَالِكَ ابْتُلِيَ الْمُؤْمِنُونَ وَزُلْزِلُوا زِلْزَالًا شَدِيدًا ﴿١١﴾
وَإِذْ يَقُولُ الْمُنَافِقُونَ وَالَّذِينَ فِي قُلُوبِهِم مَّرَضٌ مَّا وَعَدَنَا اللَّهُ
وَرَسُولُهُ إِلَّا غُرُورًا ﴿١٢﴾ وَإِذْ قَالَت طَّائِفَةٌ مِّنْهُمْ يَا أَهْلَ يَثْرِبَ
لَا مُقَامَ لَكُمْ فَارْجِعُوا وَيَسْتَأْذِنُ فَرِيقٌ مِّنْهُمُ النَّبِيَّ يَقُولُونَ إِنَّ
بُيُوتَنَا عَوْرَةٌ وَمَا هِيَ بِعَوْرَةٍ إِن يُرِيدُونَ إِلَّا فِرَارًا ﴿١٣﴾ وَلَوْ
دُخِلَتْ عَلَيْهِم مِّنْ أَقْطَارِهَا ثُمَّ سُئِلُوا الْفِتْنَةَ لَآتَوْهَا
وَمَا تَلَبَّثُوا بِهَا إِلَّا يَسِيرًا ﴿١٤﴾ وَلَقَدْ كَانُوا عَاهَدُوا اللَّهَ
مِن قَبْلُ لَا يُوَلُّونَ الْأَدْبَارَ وَكَانَ عَهْدُ اللَّهِ مَسْئُولًا ﴿١٥﴾

1. The old name of Medina.

قل لن ينفعكم الفرار إن فررتم من الموت أو القتل وإذا
لا تمتعون إلا قليلا ﴿١٦﴾ قل من ذا الذي يعصمكم من
الله إن أراد بكم سوءا أو أراد بكم رحمة ولا يجدون لهم من دون
الله وليا ولا نصيرا ﴿١٧﴾ قد يعلم الله المعوقين منكم
والقائلين لإخوانهم هلم إلينا ولا يأتون البأس إلا قليلا
﴿١٨﴾ أشحة عليكم فإذا جاء الخوف رأيتهم ينظرون إليك
تدور أعينهم كالذي يغشى عليه من الموت فإذا ذهب الخوف
سلقوكم بألسنة حداد أشحة على الخير أولئك لم يؤمنوا فأحبط
الله أعمالهم وكان ذلك على الله يسيرا ﴿١٩﴾ يحسبون
الأحزاب لم يذهبوا وإن يأت الأحزاب يودوا لو أنهم بادون
في الأعراب يسألون عن أنبائكم ولو كانوا فيكم ما قاتلوا إلا
قليلا ﴿٢٠﴾ لقد كان لكم في رسول الله أسوة حسنة لمن كان يرجوا
الله واليوم الآخر وذكر الله كثيرا ﴿٢١﴾ ولما رأى
المؤمنون الأحزاب قالوا هذا ما وعدنا الله ورسوله وصدق
الله ورسوله وما زادهم إلا إيمانا وتسليما ﴿٢٢﴾

SAY: 'NOTHING will your 33:16
flight avail you. If you escaped
from death or slaughter you
would enjoy this world only
for a little while.'
Say: 'Who can protect you
from God if it is His will to
scourge you? And who can
prevent Him from showing
you mercy?' They shall find
none besides God to protect
or help them.
God well knows those of
you who hold the others back;
who say to their comrades:
'Join our side,' and seldom
take part in the fighting, being 33:19
ever reluctant to assist you.
When fear overtakes them
they look to you[1] for help,
their eyes rolling, like someone
in the agony of death. But
once they are out of danger
they assail you with their sharp tongues, covetously demanding the richest
part of the booty. Those never had faith, and God will bring their acts to
nothing: that is easy enough for God.
They thought the confederates would never withdraw. Indeed, if the confederates should come again, they would sooner be in the desert among the
wandering Arabs. There they would ask news of you, but were they with you
they would take but little part in the fighting.
There is a good example in God's apostle for those of you who look to
God and the Last Day and remember God always.
When the true believers saw the confederates, they said: 'This is what God 33:22
and His apostle have promised us; God and His apostle have spoken the
Truth.' And this only increased their faith and submission.

1. Muḥammad.

33:23 AMONG THE believers there are men who have been true to their covenants with God. Some have died, and some await their end, yielding to no change. God will surely requite the faithful for their faith and sternly punish the hypocrites – or show them mercy if He will: God is ever forgiving and compassionate.

God turned back the unbelievers in their rage, and they went away empty-handed. God helped the faithful in the stress of war: Almighty is God, and all-powerful.

He brought down from their strongholds those who had supported them from among the People of the Book[1] and cast terror into their hearts, so that some you slew and some you took captive.

من المؤمنين رجال صدقوا ما عاهدوا الله عليه فمنهم
من قضى نحبه ومنهم من ينتظر وما بدلوا تبديلا
٢٣ ليجزي الله الصادقين بصدقهم ويعذب المنافقين إن شاء أو يتوب
عليهم إن الله كان غفورا رحيما ٢٤ ورد الله الذين كفروا
بغيظهم لم ينالوا خيرا وكفى الله المؤمنين القتال
وكان الله قويا عزيزا ٢٥ وأنزل الذين ظاهروهم من
أهل الكتاب من صياصيهم وقذف في قلوبهم الرعب فريقا
تقتلون وتأسرون فريقا ٢٦ وأورثكم أرضهم وديارهم
وأموالهم وأرضا لم تطئوها وكان الله على كل شيء
قديرا ٢٧ يا أيها النبي قل لأزواجك إن كنتن تردن
الحيوة الدنيا وزينتها فتعالين أمتعكن وأسرحكن
سراحا جميلا ٢٨ وإن كنتن تردن الله ورسوله والدار
الآخرة فإن الله أعد للمحسنات منكن أجرا عظيما ٢٩
يا نساء النبي من يأت منكن بفاحشة مبينة يضاعف لها
العذاب ضعفين وكان ذلك على الله يسيرا ٣٠

33:27 He made you heirs of their land, their houses, and their goods, and of yet another land[2] on which you had never set foot before. Truly, God has power over all things.

Prophet, say to your wives: 'If you seek this nether life and its vanities, come, I will make provision for you and release you honourably. But if you seek God and His apostle and the Abode of the Hereafter, God has prepared a rich recompense for those of you who do good works.'

33:30 Wives of the Prophet! Those of you who commit a veritable lewd act shall be doubly punished. That is easy enough for God.

1. The Jews of Banī Qurayẓah; 600–900 men were beheaded and the women and children sold into slavery (Al-Bayḍāwī). 2. Khaybar.

وَمَن يَقْنُتْ مِنكُنَّ لِلَّهِ وَرَسُولِهِ وَتَعْمَلْ صَالِحًا نُّؤْتِهَا
أَجْرَهَا مَرَّتَيْنِ وَأَعْتَدْنَا لَهَا رِزْقًا كَرِيمًا ٣١ يَا نِسَاءَ النَّبِيِّ
لَسْتُنَّ كَأَحَدٍ مِّنَ النِّسَاءِ إِنِ اتَّقَيْتُنَّ فَلَا تَخْضَعْنَ بِالْقَوْلِ
فَيَطْمَعَ الَّذِي فِي قَلْبِهِ مَرَضٌ وَقُلْنَ قَوْلًا مَّعْرُوفًا ٣٢
وَقَرْنَ فِي بُيُوتِكُنَّ وَلَا تَبَرَّجْنَ تَبَرُّجَ الْجَاهِلِيَّةِ
الْأُولَىٰ وَأَقِمْنَ الصَّلَاةَ وَآتِينَ الزَّكَاةَ وَأَطِعْنَ اللَّهَ
وَرَسُولَهُ إِنَّمَا يُرِيدُ اللَّهُ لِيُذْهِبَ عَنكُمُ الرِّجْسَ أَهْلَ
الْبَيْتِ وَيُطَهِّرَكُمْ تَطْهِيرًا ٣٣ وَاذْكُرْنَ مَا يُتْلَىٰ فِي
بُيُوتِكُنَّ مِنْ آيَاتِ اللَّهِ وَالْحِكْمَةِ إِنَّ اللَّهَ
كَانَ لَطِيفًا خَبِيرًا ٣٤ إِنَّ الْمُسْلِمِينَ وَالْمُسْلِمَاتِ وَالْمُؤْمِنِينَ
وَالْمُؤْمِنَاتِ وَالْقَانِتِينَ وَالْقَانِتَاتِ وَالصَّادِقِينَ وَالصَّادِقَاتِ
وَالصَّابِرِينَ وَالصَّابِرَاتِ وَالْخَاشِعِينَ وَالْخَاشِعَاتِ
وَالْمُتَصَدِّقِينَ وَالْمُتَصَدِّقَاتِ وَالصَّائِمِينَ وَالصَّائِمَاتِ
وَالْحَافِظِينَ فُرُوجَهُمْ وَالْحَافِظَاتِ وَالذَّاكِرِينَ اللَّهَ
كَثِيرًا وَالذَّاكِرَاتِ أَعَدَّ اللَّهُ لَهُم مَّغْفِرَةً وَأَجْرًا عَظِيمًا ٣٥

BUT THOSE of you who obey 33:31
God and His apostle and do
good works shall be doubly
recompensed; for them We
have made a rich provision.
Wives of the Prophet! You
are not like other women. If
you fear God, do not be too
complaisant in your speech, lest
the lecherous-hearted should
lust after you. Show discretion
in what you say. Stay in your 33:33
homes and do not display your
finery as women used to do in
the days of ignorance.[1] Attend
to your prayers, give alms, and
obey God and His apostle.
Women of the Household,
God seeks only to remove
abomination from you and to
purify you. Commit to memory the revelations of God
and the wise sayings that are
recited in your dwellings. Gracious is God and all-knowing.
Be they men or women, those who are Muslims and have faith; who are 33:35
devout, sincere, patient, humble, charitable, and chaste; who fast and are ever
mindful of God – on these God will bestow forgiveness and a rich recompense.

1. Pre-Islamic days.

33:36 It is not for true believers – men or women – to order their own affairs if God and His apostle decree otherwise. He that disobeys God and His apostle strays grievously into error.

You[1] said to the man[2] whom God and yourself have favoured: 'Keep your wife and have fear of God.' You sought to hide in your heart what God was to reveal.[3] You were afraid of man, although it would have been more proper for you to fear God. And when Zayd divorced her, We gave her to you in marriage, so that it should become legitimate for true believers to wed the wives of their adopted sons if they had divorced them. God's will must needs be done.

وما كان لمؤمن ولا مؤمنة إذا قضى الله ورسوله أمرا أن
يكون لهم الخيرة من أمرهم ومن يعص الله ورسوله فقد ضل
ضلالا مبينا ۝ وإذ تقول للذي أنعم الله عليه وأنعمت
عليه أمسك عليك زوجك واتق الله وتخفي في نفسك ما
الله مبديه وتخشى الناس والله أحق أن تخشاه فلما
قضى زيد منها وطرا زوجناكها لكي لا يكون على المؤمنين حرج في أزواج
أدعيائهم إذا قضوا منهن وطرا وكان أمر الله مفعولا ۝ ما
كان على النبي من حرج فيما فرض الله له سنة الله
في الذين خلوا من قبل وكان أمر الله قدرا مقدورا
۝ الذين يبلغون رسالات الله ويخشونه ولا
يخشون أحدا إلا الله وكفى بالله حسيبا ۝ ما كان
محمد أبا أحد من رجالكم ولكن رسول الله وخاتم النبيين وكان
الله بكل شيء عليما ۝ يا أيها الذين آمنوا اذكروا الله ذكرا كثيرا ۝
وسبحوه بكرة وأصيلا ۝ هو الذي يصلي عليكم وملائكته
ليخرجكم من الظلمات إلى النور وكان بالمؤمنين رحيما ۝

33:38 No blame shall be attached to the Prophet for doing what is sanctioned for him by God. Such was the way of God with those who went before him: God's decrees are ever preordained; those who convey God's commandments, fearing Him and fearing none besides God. Sufficient is God's reckoning.

Muḥammad is the father of no man among you.[4] He is the Apostle of God and the Seal of the Prophets. Surely God has knowledge of all things.

33:43 Believers, be ever mindful of God: praise Him morning and evening. It is He and His angels that bless you, so that He may lead you from darkness to the light. To believers He is ever compassionate.

1. Muḥammad. 2. Zayd, Muḥammad's adopted son.
3. Your intention to marry Zayd's wife.
4. Muḥammad left no male heirs.

تَحِيَّتُهُمْ يَوْمَ يَلْقَوْنَهُ سَلَامٌ وَأَعَدَّ لَهُمْ أَجْرًا كَرِيمًا ٤٤
يَا أَيُّهَا النَّبِيُّ إِنَّا أَرْسَلْنَاكَ شَاهِدًا وَمُبَشِّرًا وَنَذِيرًا ٤٥
وَدَاعِيًا إِلَى اللَّهِ بِإِذْنِهِ وَسِرَاجًا مُنِيرًا ٤٦ وَبَشِّرِ الْمُؤْمِنِينَ
بِأَنَّ لَهُمْ مِنَ اللَّهِ فَضْلًا كَبِيرًا ٤٧ وَلَا تُطِعِ الْكَافِرِينَ
وَالْمُنَافِقِينَ وَدَعْ أَذَاهُمْ وَتَوَكَّلْ عَلَى اللَّهِ وَكَفَى بِاللَّهِ
وَكِيلًا ٤٨ يَا أَيُّهَا الَّذِينَ آمَنُوا إِذَا نَكَحْتُمُ الْمُؤْمِنَاتِ ثُمَّ
طَلَّقْتُمُوهُنَّ مِنْ قَبْلِ أَنْ تَمَسُّوهُنَّ فَمَا لَكُمْ عَلَيْهِنَّ مِنْ عِدَّةٍ
تَعْتَدُّونَهَا فَمَتِّعُوهُنَّ وَسَرِّحُوهُنَّ سَرَاحًا جَمِيلًا ٤٩ يَا أَيُّهَا النَّبِيُّ
إِنَّا أَحْلَلْنَا لَكَ أَزْوَاجَكَ اللَّاتِي آتَيْتَ أُجُورَهُنَّ وَمَا مَلَكَتْ
يَمِينُكَ مِمَّا أَفَاءَ اللَّهُ عَلَيْكَ وَبَنَاتِ عَمِّكَ وَبَنَاتِ عَمَّاتِكَ
وَبَنَاتِ خَالِكَ وَبَنَاتِ خَالَاتِكَ اللَّاتِي هَاجَرْنَ مَعَكَ
وَامْرَأَةً مُؤْمِنَةً إِنْ وَهَبَتْ نَفْسَهَا لِلنَّبِيِّ إِنْ أَرَادَ النَّبِيُّ أَنْ
يَسْتَنْكِحَهَا خَالِصَةً لَكَ مِنْ دُونِ الْمُؤْمِنِينَ قَدْ عَلِمْنَا
مَا فَرَضْنَا عَلَيْهِمْ فِي أَزْوَاجِهِمْ وَمَا مَلَكَتْ أَيْمَانُهُمْ
لِكَيْلَا يَكُونَ عَلَيْكَ حَرَجٌ وَكَانَ اللَّهُ غَفُورًا رَحِيمًا ٥٠

THEIR GREETING on the 33:44
day they meet Him shall be: 'Peace!' A rich reward He has prepared for them.

Prophet, We have sent you forth as a witness, a bearer of joyful tidings, and an emissary to warn them; one who shall call men to God by His leave and by a shining light.

Tell the faithful that God
has prodigious blessings in
store for them. Do not yield to 33:48
the unbelievers and the hypocrites: disregard their insolence. Put your trust in God; sufficient is God as a guardian.

Believers, if you marry believing women and divorce them before the marriage is consummated, you are not required to observe a waiting period. Provide well for them and release them honourably.

Prophet, We have made lawful for you the wives to whom you have 33:50
granted dowries and the slave-girls whom God has given you as booty; the daughters of your paternal and maternal uncles and of your paternal and maternal aunts who fled with you; and any believing woman who gives herself to the Prophet and whom the Prophet wishes to take in marriage. This privilege is yours alone, being granted to no other believer.

We well know the duties We have imposed on them concerning their wives and their slave-girls: so that none may blame you. God is ever forgiving and compassionate.

33:51 YOU MAY put off any of
your wives you please and take
to your bed any of them you
please. Nor is it an offence for
you to receive any of those
whom you have temporarily
set aside. That is more proper,
so that they may be contented
and not vexed, and may all be
pleased with what you give
them.

God knows what is in your[1]
hearts. Surely God is all-
knowing and gracious.

It shall be unlawful for you[2]
to take more wives or to
change your present wives for
other women, though their
beauty please you, unless they
are slave-girls whom you own.
God takes cognizance of all
things.

33:53 Believers, do not enter the
houses of the Prophet for a meal without waiting for the proper time, unless
you are given leave. But if you are invited, enter; and when you have eaten,
disperse. Do not engage in familiar talk, for this would annoy the Prophet
and he would be ashamed to bid you go; but of the truth God is not ashamed.
If you ask his wives for anything, speak to them from behind a curtain. This
is more chaste for your hearts and their hearts.

You must not speak ill of God's apostle, nor shall you ever wed his wives
33:54 after him; this would surely be a grave offence in the sight of God. Whether
you reveal a thing or conceal it, God has knowledge of all things.

تُرْجِي مَن تَشَاءُ مِنْهُنَّ وَتُؤْوِي إِلَيْكَ مَن تَشَاءُ وَمَنِ ابْتَغَيْتَ مِمَّنْ
عَزَلْتَ فَلَا جُنَاحَ عَلَيْكَ ذَٰلِكَ أَدْنَىٰ أَن تَقَرَّ أَعْيُنُهُنَّ وَلَا يَحْزَنَّ
وَيَرْضَيْنَ بِمَا آتَيْتَهُنَّ كُلُّهُنَّ وَاللَّهُ يَعْلَمُ مَا فِي قُلُوبِكُمْ
وَكَانَ اللَّهُ عَلِيمًا حَلِيمًا ۝ لَا يَحِلُّ لَكَ النِّسَاءُ مِن بَعْدُ وَلَا أَن
تَبَدَّلَ بِهِنَّ مِنْ أَزْوَاجٍ وَلَوْ أَعْجَبَكَ حُسْنُهُنَّ إِلَّا مَا مَلَكَتْ يَمِينُكَ
وَكَانَ اللَّهُ عَلَىٰ كُلِّ شَيْءٍ رَقِيبًا ۝ يَا أَيُّهَا الَّذِينَ آمَنُوا
لَا تَدْخُلُوا بُيُوتَ النَّبِيِّ إِلَّا أَن يُؤْذَنَ لَكُمْ إِلَىٰ طَعَامٍ غَيْرَ
نَاظِرِينَ إِنَاهُ وَلَٰكِنْ إِذَا دُعِيتُمْ فَادْخُلُوا فَإِذَا طَعِمْتُمْ
فَانتَشِرُوا وَلَا مُسْتَأْنِسِينَ لِحَدِيثٍ إِنَّ ذَٰلِكُمْ كَانَ يُؤْذِي
النَّبِيَّ فَيَسْتَحْيِي مِنكُمْ وَاللَّهُ لَا يَسْتَحْيِي مِنَ الْحَقِّ وَإِذَا
سَأَلْتُمُوهُنَّ مَتَاعًا فَاسْأَلُوهُنَّ مِن وَرَاءِ حِجَابٍ ذَٰلِكُمْ
أَطْهَرُ لِقُلُوبِكُمْ وَقُلُوبِهِنَّ وَمَا كَانَ لَكُمْ أَن تُؤْذُوا
رَسُولَ اللَّهِ وَلَا أَن تَنكِحُوا أَزْوَاجَهُ مِن بَعْدِهِ أَبَدًا
إِنَّ ذَٰلِكُمْ كَانَ عِندَ اللَّهِ عَظِيمًا ۝ إِن
تُبْدُوا شَيْئًا أَوْ تُخْفُوهُ فَإِنَّ اللَّهَ كَانَ بِكُلِّ شَيْءٍ عَلِيمًا ۝

1. The believers'. 2. Muḥammad.

لا جناح عليهن في آبائهن ولا أبنائهن ولا إخوانهن
ولا أبناء إخوانهن ولا أبناء أخواتهن ولا نسائهن
ولا ما ملكت أيمانهن واتقين الله إن الله كان
على كل شيء شهيدا ٥٥ إن الله وملائكته يصلون على
النبي يا أيها الذين آمنوا صلوا عليه وسلموا تسليما
٥٦ إن الذين يؤذون الله ورسوله لعنهم الله في
الدنيا والآخرة وأعد لهم عذابا مهينا ٥٧ والذين يؤذون
المؤمنين والمؤمنات بغير ما اكتسبوا فقد احتملوا بهتانا
وإثما مبينا ٥٨ يا أيها النبي قل لأزواجك وبناتك ونساء
المؤمنين يدنين عليهن من جلابيبهن ذلك أدنى أن
يعرفن فلا يؤذين وكان الله غفورا رحيما ٥٩ لئن لم
ينته المنافقون والذين في قلوبهم مرض والمرجفون في المدينة
لنغرينك بهم ثم لا يجاورونك فيها إلا قليلا ٦٠ ملعونين
أينما ثقفوا أخذوا وقتلوا تقتيلا ٦١ سنة الله في
الذين خلوا من قبل ولن تجد لسنة الله تبديلا ٦٢

IT SHALL be no offence for 33:55
the Prophet's wives to be seen unveiled by their fathers, their sons, their brothers, their brothers' sons, their sisters' sons, their women, or their slave-girls. Women, have fear of God; surely God observes all things.

The Prophet is blessed by God and His angels. Bless him, then, you that are true believers, and greet him with a worthy salutation.

Those who speak ill of God and His apostle shall be cursed by God in this life and in the life to come. And He has prepared for them a shameful punishment.

Those who traduce believing 33:58
men and believing women undeservedly shall bear the guilt of slander and grievous sin.

Prophet, enjoin your wives, your daughters, and the wives of true believers to draw their veils close round them. That is more proper, so that they may be recognized and not be molested. God is ever forgiving and compassionate.

If the hypocrites and those who have tainted hearts and the scandalmongers of Madīnah do not desist, We will rouse you against them, and their days therein will be numbered. Cursed wherever they are found, they shall be seized and put to death without mercy.

Such has been God's way with those who have gone before them. And 33:62
you shall find no change in the way of God.

33:63 PEOPLE ASK you about the Hour. Say: 'God alone has knowledge of it. And how are you to know? The Hour may well be near at hand.'

God has laid His curse upon the unbelievers and prepared for them a Conflagration. Abiding therein for ever, they shall find none to protect or help them.

On the day when their heads roll about in the Fire, they shall say: 'Would that we had obeyed God and obeyed the Apostle!' And they shall say: 'Lord, we obeyed our masters and our great ones, but they led us away from the right path. Lord, mete out to them a double scourge; lay on them a mighty curse.'

33:69 Believers, do not behave like those who slandered Moses. God cleared him of their calumny, and he was exalted by God. Believers, fear God and speak the Truth. He will bless your works and forgive you your sins. Those who obey God and His apostle shall win a signal victory.

We offered Our trust to the heavens, to the earth, and to the mountains, but they refused the burden and were afraid to receive it. Man undertook to bear it, but he has proved a sinner and a fool.

33:73 God will surely punish the hypocrites and the idolaters, both men and women; but to believing men and to believing women He will turn in mercy. God is ever forgiving and compassionate.

يَسْـَٔلُكَ النَّاسُ عَنِ السَّاعَةِ قُلْ اِنَّمَا عِلْمُهَا عِنْدَ
اللّٰهِ وَمَا يُدْرٖيكَ لَعَلَّ السَّاعَةَ تَكُونُ قَرٖيبًا ﴿٦٣﴾ اِنَّ
اللّٰهَ لَعَنَ الْكَافِرٖينَ وَاَعَدَّ لَهُمْ سَعٖيرًا ﴿٦٤﴾ خَالِدٖينَ فٖيهَا اَبَدًا لَا يَجِدُونَ
وَلِيًّا وَلَا نَصٖيرًا ﴿٦٥﴾ يَوْمَ تُقَلَّبُ وُجُوهُهُمْ فِي النَّارِ يَقُولُونَ يَا لَيْتَنَا اَطَعْنَا
اللّٰهَ وَاَطَعْنَا الرَّسُولَا ﴿٦٦﴾ وَقَالُوا رَبَّنَا اِنَّا اَطَعْنَا سَادَتَنَا
وَكُبَرَاءَنَا فَاَضَلُّونَا السَّبٖيلَا ﴿٦٧﴾ رَبَّنَا اٰتِهِمْ ضِعْفَيْنِ مِنَ
الْعَذَابِ وَالْعَنْهُمْ لَعْنًا كَبٖيرًا ﴿٦٨﴾ يَا اَيُّهَا الَّذٖينَ اٰمَنُوا
لَا تَكُونُوا كَالَّذٖينَ اٰذَوْا مُوسٰى فَبَرَّاَهُ اللّٰهُ مِمَّا قَالُوا وَكَانَ عِنْدَ
اللّٰهِ وَجٖيهًا ﴿٦٩﴾ يَا اَيُّهَا الَّذٖينَ اٰمَنُوا اتَّقُوا اللّٰهَ وَقُولُوا قَوْلًا سَدٖيدًا
﴿٧٠﴾ يُصْلِحْ لَكُمْ اَعْمَالَكُمْ وَيَغْفِرْ لَكُمْ ذُنُوبَكُمْ وَمَنْ يُطِعِ
اللّٰهَ وَرَسُولَهُ فَقَدْ فَازَ فَوْزًا عَظٖيمًا ﴿٧١﴾ اِنَّا عَرَضْنَا الْاَمَانَةَ عَلَى
السَّمٰوَاتِ وَالْاَرْضِ وَالْجِبَالِ فَاَبَيْنَ اَنْ يَحْمِلْنَهَا وَاَشْفَقْنَ
مِنْهَا وَحَمَلَهَا الْاِنْسَانُ اِنَّهُ كَانَ ظَلُومًا جَهُولًا ﴿٧٢﴾ لِيُعَذِّبَ
اللّٰهُ الْمُنَافِقٖينَ وَالْمُنَافِقَاتِ وَالْمُشْرِكٖينَ وَالْمُشْرِكَاتِ وَيَتُوبَ
اللّٰهُ عَلَى الْمُؤْمِنٖينَ وَالْمُؤْمِنَاتِ وَكَانَ اللّٰهُ غَفُورًا رَحٖيمًا ﴿٧٣﴾

سورة سبأ مكية وهي اربع وخمسون آية

بسم الله الرحمن الرحيم
الحمد لله الذي له ما في السموات وما في الأرض وله
الحمد في الآخرة وهو الحكيم الخبير ﴿١﴾ يعلم ما يلج في الأرض
وما يخرج منها وما ينزل من السماء وما يعرج فيها وهو الرحيم
الغفور ﴿٢﴾ وقال الذين كفروا لا تأتينا الساعة قل
بلى وربي لتأتينكم عالم الغيب لا يعزب عنه مثقال ذرة في
السموات ولا في الأرض ولا أصغر من ذلك ولا أكبر إلا في
كتاب مبين ﴿٣﴾ ليجزي الذين آمنوا وعملوا الصالحات أولئك لهم
مغفرة ورزق كريم ﴿٤﴾ والذين سعو في آياتنا معاجزين أولئك
لهم عذاب من رجز أليم ﴿٥﴾ ويرى الذين أوتوا العلم الذي أنزل إليك
من ربك هو الحق ويهدي إلى صراط العزيز الحميد ﴿٦﴾
وقال الذين كفروا هل ندلكم على رجل ينبئكم إذا
مزقتم كل ممزق إنكم لفي خلق جديد ﴿٧﴾

SHEBA

In the Name of God,
the Merciful, the Compassionate

PRAISE BE to God, to whom 34:1
belongs all that the heavens
and the earth contain! Praise
be to Him in the world to
come. He is the Wise One, the
All-knowing.

He has knowledge of all
that goes into the earth and all
that springs up from it; all that
comes down from heaven and
all that ascends to it. He is the
Compassionate, the Forgiving
One.

The unbelievers say: 'The
Hour will never come upon
us.' Say: 'Yes, by the Lord, it is
surely coming! He knows all
that is hidden. Not an atom's weight in the heavens or the earth escapes Him;
nor is there anything smaller or greater but is recorded in a veritable Book.
He will surely recompense those who have faith and do good works; they 34:4
shall be forgiven and a rich provision shall be made for them. But those who
strive to confute Our revelations shall suffer the torment of a harrowing
scourge.'

Those endowed with knowledge can see that what has been revealed to
you from your Lord is the Truth, leading to the path of the Almighty, the
Praised One.

The unbelievers say: 'Shall we show you a man[1] who would have you know 34:7
that when you have been torn into shreds you will be raised in a new creation?

1. Muhammad.

34:8 HAS HE invented a falsehood
about God, or is he a man
possessed?' Truly, those who
deny the life to come are
doomed to torment, and they
have strayed far into error.

Do they not see what is
before them and behind them
in heaven and earth? If We
will, We can cause the earth to
cave in beneath their feet or
let fragments of the sky fall
upon them. Surely there is a
sign in this for every penitent
man.

On David We bestowed Our
bounty. We said: 'Mountains,
and you birds, echo his songs
of praise.' We made iron pliant
to him, saying: 'Make coats of
mail and measure their links
with care. Do what is right: I
am watching all your actions.'

افترى على الله كذبا أم به جنة بل الذين لا يؤمنون
بالآخرة في العذاب والضلال البعيد (٨) أفلم يروا
إلى ما بين أيديهم وما خلفهم من السماء والأرض إن
نشأ نخسف بهم الأرض أو نسقط عليهم كسفا من السماء
إن في ذلك لآية لكل عبد منيب (٩) ولقد آتينا داود
منا فضلا يا جبال أوبي معه والطير وألنا له الحديد
(١٠) أن اعمل سابغات وقدر في السرد واعملوا صالحا
إني بما تعملون بصير (١١) ولسليمان الريح غدوها شهر
ورواحها شهر وأسلنا له عين القطر ومن الجن من يعمل بين
يديه بإذن ربه ومن يزغ منهم عن أمرنا نذقه من عذاب
السعير (١٢) يعملون له ما يشاء من محاريب وتماثيل وجفان
كالجواب وقدور راسيات اعملوا آل داود شكرا وقليل من
عبادي الشكور (١٣) فلما قضينا عليه الموت ما دلهم على
موته إلا دابة الأرض تأكل منسأته فلما خر تبينت الجن
أن لو كانوا يعلمون الغيب ما لبثوا في العذاب المهين (١٤)

34:12 And to Solomon We subjected the wind, travelling a month's journey on
a morning and a month's journey on an evening. We gave him a spring flowing with molten brass, and jinn who served him by leave of his Lord. Those
of them who did not do Our bidding We shall chasten with the torment of
the Conflagration. They made for him whatever he pleased: shrines and
statues, basins as large as watering-troughs, and built-in cauldrons. We said:
'Give thanks, House of David.' Yet few of My servants are truly thankful.
34:14 And when We had decreed his death, they did not know that he was dead
until they saw a worm eating away his staff. And when his corpse fell down,
the jinn realized that had they had knowledge of the unknown, they would
not have remained in shameful torment.

لقد كان لسبإ في مسكنهم آية جنتان عن يمين وشمال كلوا
من رزق ربكم واشكروا له بلدة طيبة ورب غفور ﴿١٥﴾
فأعرضوا فأرسلنا عليهم سيل العرم وبدلناهم بجنتيهم
جنتين ذواتي أكل خمط وأثل وشيء من سدر قليل ﴿١٦﴾
ذلك جزيناهم بما كفروا وهل نجازي إلا الكفور ﴿١٧﴾
وجعلنا بينهم وبين القرى التي باركنا فيها قرى ظاهرة
وقدرنا فيها السير سيروا فيها ليالي وأياما آمنين ﴿١٨﴾
فقالوا ربنا باعد بين أسفارنا وظلموا أنفسهم فجعلنا
هم أحاديث ومزقناهم كل ممزق إن في ذلك لآيات
لكل صبار شكور ﴿١٩﴾ ولقد صدق عليهم إبليس ظنه
فاتبعوه إلا فريقا من المؤمنين ﴿٢٠﴾ وما كان له عليهم
من سلطان إلا لنعلم من يؤمن بالآخرة ممن هو منها
في شك وربك على كل شيء حفيظ ﴿٢١﴾ قل ادعوا الذين زعمتم
من دون الله لا يملكون مثقال ذرة في السماوات ولا في
الأرض وما لهم فيهما من شرك وما له منهم من ظهير ﴿٢٢﴾

FOR THE natives of Sheba 34:15
there was indeed a sign in their dwelling-place: a garden on their right and a garden on their left. We said to them: 'Eat of what your Lord has given you and render thanks to Him. Pleasant is your land and forgiving is your Lord.'

But they paid no heed. So We let loose upon them the waters of the dam and replaced their gardens by two others bearing bitter fruit, tamarisks, and a few nettles. Thus did We punish them for their ingratitude: do We punish any but the ungrateful?

Between them and the cities that We have blessed, We placed roadside hamlets so that they could journey to and fro in measured stages. We said: 'Travel through them by night and by day in safety.'

But they said: 'Lord, make the stages of our travel longer.' They sinned 34:19
against their souls; so We held them up as an example and tore them into shreds. Surely there is a sign in this for every steadfast, thankful person.

Satan had judged them rightly; they followed him all, except for a band of true believers. Yet had he no power over them: Our only aim was to recognize those who believed in the life to come and those who were in doubt. Your Lord takes cognizance of all things.

Say: 'Call on those whom you deify besides God. They do not control an 34:22
atom's weight in the heavens nor on the earth; nor have they any share in either. Nor has He any helpers among them.'

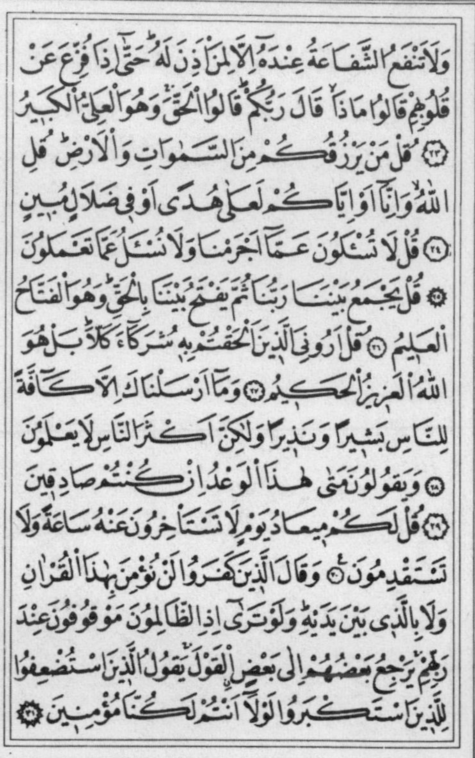
ولا تنفع الشفاعة عنده إلا لمن أذن له حتى إذا فزع عن
قلوبهم قالوا ماذا قال ربكم قالوا الحق وهو العلي الكبير
٢٣ قل من يرزقكم من السموات والأرض قل
الله وإنا أو إياكم لعلى هدى أو في ضلال مبين
٢٤ قل لا تسألون عما أجرمنا ولا نسأل عما تعملون
٢٥ قل يجمع بيننا ربنا ثم يفتح بيننا بالحق وهو الفتاح
العليم ٢٦ قل أروني الذين ألحقتم به شركاء كلا بل هو
الله العزيز الحكيم ٢٧ وما أرسلناك إلا كافة
للناس بشيرا ونذيرا ولكن أكثر الناس لا يعلمون
٢٨ ويقولون متى هذا الوعد إن كنتم صادقين
٢٩ قل لكم ميعاد يوم لا تستأخرون عنه ساعة ولا
تستقدمون ٣٠ وقال الذين كفروا لن نؤمن بهذا القرآن
ولا بالذي بين يديه ولو ترى إذ الظالمون موقوفون عند
ربهم يرجع بعضهم إلى بعض القول يقول الذين استضعفوا
للذين استكبروا لولا أنتم لكنا مؤمنين ٣١

34:23 NONE CAN intercede with
God save him who has
received His sanction. When
fear is banished from their
hearts, they shall ask each
other: 'What has your Lord
ordained?' 'The Truth,' they
shall answer. 'He is the Most
High, the Supreme One.'
Say: 'Who provides for you
from the heavens and the
earth?'
Say: 'God. Either we or you
are right, or clearly in the
wrong.'
Say: 'You are not accountable for our sins, nor are we
accountable for your actions.'
Say: 'Our Lord will bring
us all together, then He will
rightly judge between us. He is
the All-knowing Judge.'
34:27 Say: 'Show me those whom
you have named with Him as partners. Never. God alone is the Almighty, the
Wise One.'
We have sent you forth to all mankind, that you may give them joyful tidings and forewarn them. But the larger part of mankind have no knowledge.
And they say: 'When will this promise be fulfilled, if what you say be true?'
Say: 'Your day is already appointed. Not for one hour can you hold it back,
nor can you hurry it on.'
34:31 And the unbelievers say: 'We will never believe in this Koran, nor in what
had come before it.'
If only you could see the wrongdoers when they are brought before their
Lord! Bandying charges with one another, those who were despised will say
to those who deemed themselves mighty: 'But for you, we would have been
believers.'

قال الذين استكبروا للذين استضعفوا أنحن صددناكم
عن الهدى بعد إذ جاءكم بل كنتم مجرمين (٣٢) وقال الذين
استضعفوا للذين استكبروا بل مكر الليل والنهار إذ تأمروننا
أن نكفر بالله ونجعل له أندادا وأسروا الندامة لما
رأوا العذاب وجعلنا الأغلال في أعناق الذين كفروا هل
يجزون إلا ما كانوا يعملون (٣٣) وما أرسلنا في قرية
من نذير إلا قال مترفوها إنا بما أرسلتم به كافرون (٣٤)
وقالوا نحن أكثر أموالا وأولادا وما نحن بمعذبين (٣٥)
قل إن ربي يبسط الرزق لمن يشاء ويقدر ولكن أكثر
الناس لا يعلمون (٣٦) وما أموالكم ولا أولادكم بالتي
تقربكم عندنا زلفى إلا من آمن وعمل صالحا فأولئك لهم
جزاء الضعف بما عملوا وهم في الغرفات آمنون (٣٧) والذين
يسعون في آياتنا معاجزين أولئك في العذاب محضرون (٣٨)
قل إن ربي يبسط الرزق لمن يشاء من عباده ويقدر له وما
أنفقتم من شيء فهو يخلفه وهو خير الرازقين (٣٩)

THEN THOSE who deemed 34:32
themselves mighty will say to
those who were despised: 'Was it we who debarred you from God's guidance after it was given you? No! You yourselves were wrongdoers.'

'By no means,' the others will rejoin. 'You have plotted, night and day, bidding us disbelieve in God and set up rivals to Him.'

And they will repent in secret when they see the scourge. We will put chains round the necks of the unbelievers. Shall they not be rewarded but according to their deeds?

We have sent no apostle to any city whose message was not denied by its affluent people. The unbelievers say: 'We have been given greater wealth and more children than the faithful. Surely we shall not be punished.'

Say: 'My Lord gives abundantly to whom He will, and sparingly also. But 34:36
most do not know it.'

Neither your riches nor your children shall bring you one jot nearer to Us. Those that have faith and do what is right shall be doubly rewarded for their deeds: in the High Pavilions they shall dwell in peace. But those that strive to confute Our revelations shall be summoned up.

Say: 'My Lord gives abundantly to whom He will of His creatures, and 34:39
sparingly also. Whatever you give in alms He will recompense you for it. He is the most munificent Provider.'

34:40 ON THE day He herds them all together, He will say to the angels: 'Was it you that they worshipped?'

'Glory be to You!' they will say. 'You are our defender against them! They worshipped jinn, and it was in jinn that most of them believed.'

On that day you shall be powerless to help or harm one another. To the wrongdoers We shall say: 'Taste the torment of the Fire, which you persistently denied.'

When Our clear revelations are recited to them, they say: 'This is but a man who would turn you away from the gods your fathers worshipped.' And they say: 'This[1] is nothing but an invented falsehood.' While those who denied the Truth when it was given them say: 'This is but sorcery manifest.'

34:44 Yet have We given them no scriptures to study, nor have We sent before you any apostle to warn them.

Those who have gone before them likewise denied Our revelations. They were ten times as prosperous and mighty:[2] yet they rejected My apostles. And then how terrible was the way I rejected them!

Say: 'With one thing I admonish you: stand up before God in pairs or singly and ponder whether your compatriot[3] is indeed possessed. He is sent forth only to forewarn you of a grievous scourge.'

Say: 'I demand no recompense of you: keep it for yourselves. None but God can reward me; and He is the witness of all things.'

34:48 Say: 'My Lord hurls forth the Truth. He has knowledge of all that is hidden.'

ويوم يحشرهم جميعا ثم يقول للملئكة اهؤلاء اياكم كانوا
يعبدون ﴿٤٠﴾ قالوا سبحانك انت ولينا من دونهم بل كانوا
يعبدون الجن اكثرهم بهم مؤمنون ﴿٤١﴾ فاليوم لا يملك بعضكم
لبعض نفعا ولا ضرا ونقول للذين ظلموا ذوقوا عذاب النار
التي كنتم بها تكذبون ﴿٤٢﴾ واذا تتلى عليهم اياتنا بينات قالوا
ما هذا الا رجل يريد ان يصدكم عما كان يعبد اباؤكم وقالوا
ما هذا الا افك مفترى وقال الذين كفروا للحق لما جاءهم ان
هذا الا سحر مبين ﴿٤٣﴾ وما اتيناهم من كتب يدرسونها وما
ارسلنا اليهم قبلك من نذير ﴿٤٤﴾ وكذب الذين من قبلهم
وما بلغوا معشار ما اتيناهم فكذبوا رسلي فكيف كان نكير
﴿٤٥﴾ قل انما اعظكم بواحدة ان تقوموا لله مثنى وفرادى
ثم تتفكروا ما بصاحبكم من جنة ان هو الا
نذير لكم بين يدي عذاب شديد ﴿٤٦﴾ قل ما سالتكم
من اجر فهو لكم ان اجري الا على الله وهو على كل
شيء شهيد ﴿٤٧﴾ قل ان ربي يقذف بالحق علام الغيوب ﴿٤٨﴾

1. The Koran.
2. Literally, they (the Meccans) scarcely possess one-tenth of what We gave them (their predecessors).
3. Muḥammad.

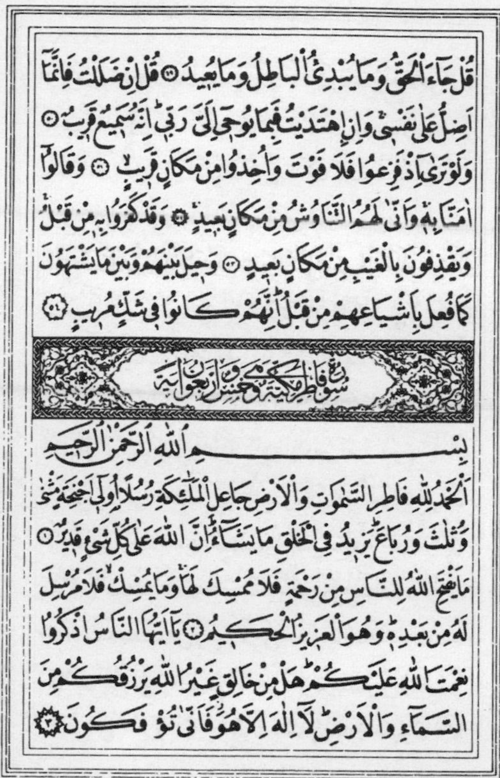

قُلْ جَاءَ الْحَقُّ وَمَا يُبْدِئُ الْبَاطِلُ وَمَا يُعِيدُ ۝ قُلْ إِن ضَلَلْتُ فَإِنَّمَا
أَضِلُّ عَلَىٰ نَفْسِي وَإِنِ اهْتَدَيْتُ فَبِمَا يُوحِي إِلَيَّ رَبِّي إِنَّهُ سَمِيعٌ قَرِيبٌ ۝
وَلَوْ تَرَىٰ إِذْ فَزِعُوا فَلَا فَوْتَ وَأُخِذُوا مِن مَّكَانٍ قَرِيبٍ ۝ وَقَالُوا
آمَنَّا بِهِ وَأَنَّىٰ لَهُمُ التَّنَاوُشُ مِن مَّكَانٍ بَعِيدٍ ۝ وَقَدْ كَفَرُوا بِهِ مِن قَبْلُ
وَيَقْذِفُونَ بِالْغَيْبِ مِن مَّكَانٍ بَعِيدٍ ۝ وَحِيلَ بَيْنَهُمْ وَبَيْنَ مَا يَشْتَهُونَ
كَمَا فُعِلَ بِأَشْيَاعِهِم مِّن قَبْلُ إِنَّهُمْ كَانُوا فِي شَكٍّ مُّرِيبٍ ۝

سورة فاطر مكية وهي خمس وأربعون آية

بِسْمِ اللَّهِ الرَّحْمَٰنِ الرَّحِيمِ

الْحَمْدُ لِلَّهِ فَاطِرِ السَّمَاوَاتِ وَالْأَرْضِ جَاعِلِ الْمَلَائِكَةِ رُسُلًا أُولِي أَجْنِحَةٍ مَّثْنَىٰ
وَثُلَاثَ وَرُبَاعَ يَزِيدُ فِي الْخَلْقِ مَا يَشَاءُ إِنَّ اللَّهَ عَلَىٰ كُلِّ شَيْءٍ قَدِيرٌ ۝
مَّا يَفْتَحِ اللَّهُ لِلنَّاسِ مِن رَّحْمَةٍ فَلَا مُمْسِكَ لَهَا وَمَا يُمْسِكْ فَلَا مُرْسِلَ
لَهُ مِن بَعْدِهِ وَهُوَ الْعَزِيزُ الْحَكِيمُ ۝ يَا أَيُّهَا النَّاسُ اذْكُرُوا
نِعْمَتَ اللَّهِ عَلَيْكُمْ هَلْ مِنْ خَالِقٍ غَيْرُ اللَّهِ يَرْزُقُكُم مِّنَ
السَّمَاءِ وَالْأَرْضِ لَا إِلَٰهَ إِلَّا هُوَ فَأَنَّىٰ تُؤْفَكُونَ ۝

SAY: 'TRUTH has come. 34:49
Falsehood has vanished and
shall return no more.'[1]

Say: 'If I am in error, the loss
is surely mine; but if I am in the
right, it is thanks to that which
my Lord has revealed to me. He
hears all and is near at hand.'

If you could only see the 34:51
unbelievers when they are
seized with terror! There shall
be no escape; they shall be
taken from their graves.[2] They
will say: 'We believe in Him.'
But how will they attain the
Faith when they are far away,
since they at first denied it,
and sneered at the unseen
when they were far away?

They shall be barred from 34:54
their desires, as were those
before them; they, too, were
perplexed with doubt.

THE CREATOR

In the Name of God, the Merciful, the Compassionate

PRAISE BE to God, Creator of the heavens and the earth. He sends forth the 35:1
angels as His messengers, with two, three, or four pairs of wings. He multi-
plies His creatures according to His will. And God has power over all things.

The blessings God bestows on people none can withhold; and what He
withholds none can bestow after Him. He is the Almighty, the Wise One.

You people! Bear in mind God's goodness to you. Is there any other 35:3
creator who provides for you from heaven and earth? There is no god but
Him. How then can you turn away?

1. Thus Al-Jalālayn. Or: Falsehood cannot bring aught into being, neither can it restore it.
2. Literally, from a place near at hand (Al-Jalālayn).

35:4 IF THEY deny you, other apostles have been denied before you. To God shall all things revert.

You people! The promise of God is true. Let not the life of this world ever deceive you, nor let the Dissembler ever deceive you about God. Satan is your foe: therefore treat him as a foe. He tempts his followers, that they may become the heirs of the Conflagration.

The unbelievers shall have grievous torment, but those that believe and do good works shall have forgiveness and a rich recompense.

And what of him whose foul deeds are made to seem fair to him? God leaves in error whom He will and guides whom He pleases. Do not destroy yourself[1] with sighs on their account: God has full knowledge of what they do.

35:9 God it is who sends forth the winds which set the clouds in motion. We drive them on to some dead land and give fresh life to the earth after it has died. Such is the Resurrection.

If anyone seeks glory, let him know that glory is God's alone. The good word ascends to Him, and the good deed is exalted by Him. But those that plot evil shall be grievously punished; and their plots shall come to nothing.

35:11 God created you from dust, then from a little germ. Into two sexes He divided you. No female conceives or gives birth without His knowledge. No one grows old or has his life cut short but in accordance with what a Book decrees. This is easy enough for God.

وَإِن يُكَذِّبُوكَ فَقَدْ كُذِّبَتْ رُسُلٌ مِّن قَبْلِكَ وَإِلَى اللَّهِ تُرْجَعُ الْأُمُورُ ﴿٤﴾
يَا أَيُّهَا النَّاسُ إِنَّ وَعْدَ اللَّهِ حَقٌّ فَلَا تَغُرَّنَّكُمُ الْحَيَوٰةُ الدُّنْيَا وَلَا يَغُرَّنَّكُم
بِاللَّهِ الْغَرُورُ ﴿٥﴾ إِنَّ الشَّيْطَانَ لَكُمْ عَدُوٌّ فَاتَّخِذُوهُ عَدُوًّا إِنَّمَا
يَدْعُوا حِزْبَهُ لِيَكُونُوا مِنْ أَصْحَابِ السَّعِيرِ ﴿٦﴾ الَّذِينَ كَفَرُوا لَهُمْ
عَذَابٌ شَدِيدٌ وَالَّذِينَ آمَنُوا وَعَمِلُوا الصَّالِحَاتِ لَهُم مَّغْفِرَةٌ وَأَجْرٌ
كَبِيرٌ ﴿٧﴾ أَفَمَن زُيِّنَ لَهُ سُوءُ عَمَلِهِ فَرَآهُ حَسَنًا فَإِنَّ اللَّهَ يُضِلُّ مَن يَشَاءُ
وَيَهْدِي مَن يَشَاءُ فَلَا تَذْهَبْ نَفْسُكَ عَلَيْهِمْ حَسَرَاتٍ إِنَّ
اللَّهَ عَلِيمٌ بِمَا يَصْنَعُونَ ﴿٨﴾ وَاللَّهُ الَّذِي أَرْسَلَ الرِّيَاحَ فَتُثِيرُ سَحَابًا
فَسُقْنَاهُ إِلَى بَلَدٍ مَّيِّتٍ فَأَحْيَيْنَا بِهِ الْأَرْضَ بَعْدَ مَوْتِهَا كَذَٰلِكَ
النُّشُورُ ﴿٩﴾ مَن كَانَ يُرِيدُ الْعِزَّةَ فَلِلَّهِ الْعِزَّةُ جَمِيعًا
إِلَيْهِ يَصْعَدُ الْكَلِمُ الطَّيِّبُ وَالْعَمَلُ الصَّالِحُ يَرْفَعُهُ وَالَّذِينَ
يَمْكُرُونَ السَّيِّئَاتِ لَهُمْ عَذَابٌ شَدِيدٌ وَمَكْرُ أُولَٰئِكَ هُوَ يَبُورُ ﴿١٠﴾
وَاللَّهُ خَلَقَكُم مِّن تُرَابٍ ثُمَّ مِن نُّطْفَةٍ ثُمَّ جَعَلَكُمْ أَزْوَاجًا
وَمَا تَحْمِلُ مِنْ أُنثَى وَلَا تَضَعُ إِلَّا بِعِلْمِهِ وَمَا يُعَمَّرُ مِن مُّعَمَّرٍ وَلَا
يُنقَصُ مِنْ عُمُرِهِ إِلَّا فِي كِتَابٍ إِنَّ ذَٰلِكَ عَلَى اللَّهِ يَسِيرٌ ﴿١١﴾

1. Muḥammad.

وما يستوي البحران هذا عذب فرات سائغ شرابه وهذا
ملح اجاج ومن كل تأكلون لحما طريا وتستخرجون حلية
تلبسونها وترى الفلك فيه مواخر لتبتغوا من فضله
ولعلكم تشكرون ١٢ يولج الليل في النهار ويولج النهار
في الليل وسخر الشمس والقمر كل يجري لأجل مسمى
ذلكم الله ربكم له الملك والذين تدعون من دونه
ما يملكون من قطمير ١٣ إن تدعوهم لا يسمعوا دعاءكم
ولو سمعوا ما استجابوا لكم ويوم القيامة يكفرون
بشرككم ولا ينبئك مثل خبير ١٤ يا أيها الناس أنتم الفقراء
إلى الله والله هو الغني الحميد ١٥ إن يشأ يذهبكم
ويأت بخلق جديد ١٦ وما ذلك على الله بعزيز ١٧
ولا تزر وازرة وزر أخرى وإن تدع مثقلة إلى حملها
لا يحمل منه شيء ولو كان ذا قربى إنما تنذر الذين
يخشون ربهم بالغيب وأقاموا الصلاة ومن
تزكى فإنما يتزكى لنفسه وإلى الله المصير ١٨

THE TWO seas are not alike. 35:12
The one is fresh, sweet, and
pleasant to drink from, and
the other is salt and bitter.
From both you eat fresh fish
and from both you bring out
ornaments to wear. Behold
how the ships plough their
course through them as you
sail away to seek His bounty.
Perchance you will give thanks.
He causes the night to pass
into the day, and He causes
the day to pass into the night.
He has pressed the sun and
the moon into His service,
each running for an appointed
term. Such is God, your Lord.
His is the sovereignty: the
idols whom you invoke be-
sides Him have power over
nothing. If you pray to them 35:14
they cannot hear your prayer,
and even if they hear you they cannot answer you. On the Day of Resurrection they will deny that you ever served them. None can make known to you
the Truth like the One who is all-knowing.

You people! It is you who stand in need of God. God it is who needs none and is worthy of praise. He can do away with you if He will and replace you with a new creation; this is no impossible thing for God.

No burdened soul shall bear another's burden. If a laden soul cries out for 35:18
help, not even a near relation shall share its burden.

You shall admonish none but those who fear their Lord though they cannot see Him, and are steadfast in prayer. He that keeps himself pure surely keeps pure for his own soul. To God is the final return.

35:19 THE BLIND and the seeing are not equal, nor are the darkness and the light. The shade and the heat are not equal, nor are the living and the dead. God can cause whom He will to hear Him, but you cannot make those who are in their graves hear you.

Your only duty is to give warning. We have sent you with the Truth to proclaim joyful tidings and to give warning; for there is no community that has not had an emissary to warn it. If they disbelieve you, those who have gone before them also disbelieved. Their apostles came to them with veritable signs, with Scriptures, and with the light-giving Book. But in the end I smote the unbelievers: and how terrible was the way I disowned them!

وَمَا يَسْتَوِي الْأَعْمَىٰ وَالْبَصِيرُ ۝ وَلَا الظُّلُمَاتُ وَلَا النُّورُ ۝
وَلَا الظِّلُّ وَلَا الْحَرُورُ ۝ وَمَا يَسْتَوِي الْأَحْيَاءُ وَلَا الْأَمْوَاتُ ۚ إِنَّ
اللَّهَ يُسْمِعُ مَن يَشَاءُ ۖ وَمَا أَنتَ بِمُسْمِعٍ مَّن فِي الْقُبُورِ ۝ إِنْ
أَنتَ إِلَّا نَذِيرٌ ۝ إِنَّا أَرْسَلْنَاكَ بِالْحَقِّ بَشِيرًا وَنَذِيرًا ۚ وَإِن
مِّنْ أُمَّةٍ إِلَّا خَلَا فِيهَا نَذِيرٌ ۝ وَإِن يُكَذِّبُوكَ فَقَدْ كَذَّبَ
الَّذِينَ مِن قَبْلِهِمْ جَاءَتْهُمْ رُسُلُهُم بِالْبَيِّنَاتِ وَبِالزُّبُرِ
وَبِالْكِتَابِ الْمُنِيرِ ۝ ثُمَّ أَخَذْتُ الَّذِينَ كَفَرُوا ۖ فَكَيْفَ
كَانَ نَكِيرِ ۝ أَلَمْ تَرَ أَنَّ اللَّهَ أَنزَلَ مِنَ السَّمَاءِ مَاءً
فَأَخْرَجْنَا بِهِ ثَمَرَاتٍ مُّخْتَلِفًا أَلْوَانُهَا ۚ وَمِنَ الْجِبَالِ جُدَدٌ بِيضٌ
وَحُمْرٌ مُّخْتَلِفٌ أَلْوَانُهَا وَغَرَابِيبُ سُودٌ ۝ وَمِنَ النَّاسِ
وَالدَّوَابِّ وَالْأَنْعَامِ مُخْتَلِفٌ أَلْوَانُهُ كَذَٰلِكَ ۗ إِنَّمَا يَخْشَى
اللَّهَ مِنْ عِبَادِهِ الْعُلَمَاءُ ۗ إِنَّ اللَّهَ عَزِيزٌ غَفُورٌ ۝ إِنَّ
الَّذِينَ يَتْلُونَ كِتَابَ اللَّهِ وَأَقَامُوا الصَّلَاةَ وَأَنفَقُوا
مِمَّا رَزَقْنَاهُمْ سِرًّا وَعَلَانِيَةً يَرْجُونَ تِجَارَةً لَّن تَبُورَ ۝
لِيُوَفِّيَهُمْ أُجُورَهُمْ وَيَزِيدَهُم مِّن فَضْلِهِ ۚ إِنَّهُ غَفُورٌ شَكُورٌ ۝

35:27 Do you not see that God has sent down water from the sky with which We bring forth fruits of different hues? In the mountains there are streaks of various shades of white and red, and jet-black rocks. Humans, beasts, and cattle have their different colours, too.

From among His servants, only those fear God who know that God is mighty and forgiving.

Surely those who recite the Book of God and attend to their prayers and
give from what We gave them, in private and in public, may hope for imper-
35:30 ishable gain. He will give them their rewards and enrich them from His own
abundance. He is forgiving and bountiful in His rewards.

والذي أوحينا إليك من الكتاب هو الحق مصدقا لما
بين يديه إن الله بعباده لخبير بصير ٣١ ثم أورثنا
الكتاب الذين اصطفينا من عبادنا فمنهم ظالم لنفسه
ومنهم مقتصد ومنهم سابق بالخيرات بإذن الله
ذلك هو الفضل الكبير ٣٢ جنات عدن يدخلونها يحلون
فيها من أساور من ذهب ولؤلؤا ولباسهم فيها حرير
٣٣ وقالوا الحمد لله الذي أذهب عنا الحزن إن ربنا
لغفور شكور ٣٤ الذي أحلنا دار المقامة من فضله
لا يمسنا فيها نصب ولا يمسنا فيها لغوب ٣٥ والذين
كفروا لهم نار جهنم لا يقضى عليهم فيموتوا ولا يخفف
عنهم من عذابها كذلك نجزي كل كفور ٣٦ وهم
يصطرخون فيها ربنا أخرجنا نعمل صالحا غير الذي كنا
نعمل أولم نعمركم ما يتذكر فيه من تذكر وجاءكم
النذير فذوقوا فما للظالمين من نصير ٣٧ إن الله
عالم غيب السماوات والأرض إنه عليم بذات الصدور ٣٨

WHAT WE have revealed to 35:31
you in the Book is the Truth
confirming what had come
before it. God knows and
observes His servants.

Then We bestowed the
Book on those of Our ser-
vants whom We have chosen.
Some among them sin against
their souls, some follow a
middle course, and some, by
God's leave, vie with each
other in charitable works: this
is the supreme virtue.

The Gardens of Eden they
shall enter, wherein they shall
be decked with bracelets of
gold and pearls, and arrayed in
robes of silk. They will say:
'Praise be to God who has
taken away from us all sorrow;
our Lord is forgiving and
bountiful in His rewards.
Through His grace He has admitted us into the Eternal Mansion, wherein
we shall endure no toil, and shall endure no weariness.'

As for the unbelievers, the fire of Hell awaits them. Death shall not deliver 35:36
them; and its torment shall never be eased for them. Thus shall We requite
the thankless.

Therein they will cry out: 'Lord, get us out, and we will do good works
unlike what we used to do.' 'Did We not make your lives long enough for
anyone who would be warned to take warning? Besides, someone *did* come
to warn you: have a taste of it then. None shall succour the wrongdoers.'

God knows the mysteries of the heavens and the earth. He well knows 35:38
people's innermost thoughts.

35:39 He it is who has given you the earth to inherit. He that disbelieves shall bear the burden of his disbelief. In disbelieving, the unbelievers earn nothing but odium in the sight of their Lord; their disbelief earns the unbelievers nothing but perdition.

Say: 'Behold your other gods on whom you call besides God. Show me what part of the earth they have created! Have they a share in the heavens?'

Or have We given them a scripture affording them a veritable proof? Truly, vain are the promises the wrongdoers give each other.

It is God who keeps the heavens and the earth from falling asunder. Should they fall, none could hold them back after Him. Gracious is He, and forgiving.

35:42 They solemnly swore by God that if someone came to warn them, they would accept his guidance more readily than did other communities. Yet when someone did come to warn them, they turned away from him with greater aversion, behaving arrogantly in the land and plotting evil. But evil shall recoil only on those that plot evil.

Are they awaiting any but the way the ancients were dealt with? But you will find no change in the ways of God; nor will you find in the ways of God any alteration.

35:44 Have they never journeyed through the land and seen the fate of those who went before them, who were far mightier than they?

Surely there is nothing in the heavens or the earth beyond the power of God. All-knowing is He, and mighty.

هو الذي جعلكم خلائف في الارض فمن كفر فعليه كفره ولا يزيد
الكافرين كفرهم عند ربهم الا مقتا ولا يزيد الكافرين كفرهم الا
خسارا ۝٣٩ قل ارايتم شركاءكم الذين تدعون من دون الله اروني
ماذا خلقوا من الارض ام لهم شرك في السموات ام اتيناهم
كتابا فهم على بينت منه بل ان يعد الظالمون بعضهم بعضا
الا غرورا ۝٤٠ ان الله يمسك السموات والارض ان تزولا
ولئن زالتا ان امسكهما من احد من بعده انه كان حليما
غفورا ۝٤١ واقسموا بالله جهد ايمانهم لئن جاءهم نذير
ليكونن اهدى من احدى الامم فلما جاءهم نذير ما زادهم
الا نفورا ۝٤٢ استكبارا في الارض ومكر السيئ ولا يحيق
المكر السيئ الا باهله فهل ينظرون الا سنت الاولين
فلن تجد لسنت الله تبديلا ولن تجد لسنت الله تحويلا
۝٤٣ اولم يسيروا في الارض فينظروا كيف كان عاقبة الذين
من قبلهم وكانوا اشد منهم قوة وما كان الله ليعجزه
من شيء في السموات ولا في الارض انه كان عليما قديرا ۝٤٤

وَلَوْ يُؤَاخِذُ اللَّهُ النَّاسَ بِمَا كَسَبُوا مَا تَرَكَ عَلَىٰ ظَهْرِهَا مِن دَابَّةٍ وَلَٰكِن
يُؤَخِّرُهُمْ إِلَىٰ أَجَلٍ مُّسَمًّى فَإِذَا جَاءَ أَجَلُهُمْ فَإِنَّ اللَّهَ كَانَ بِعِبَادِهِ بَصِيرًا ٤٥

سورة يس مكية ثلث وثمانون آية

بِسْمِ اللَّهِ الرَّحْمَٰنِ الرَّحِيمِ

يس ١ وَالْقُرْآنِ الْحَكِيمِ ٢ إِنَّكَ لَمِنَ الْمُرْسَلِينَ ٣ عَلَىٰ
صِرَاطٍ مُّسْتَقِيمٍ ٤ تَنزِيلَ الْعَزِيزِ الرَّحِيمِ ٥ لِتُنذِرَ
قَوْمًا مَّا أُنذِرَ آبَاؤُهُمْ فَهُمْ غَافِلُونَ ٦ لَقَدْ حَقَّ الْقَوْلُ
عَلَىٰ أَكْثَرِهِمْ فَهُمْ لَا يُؤْمِنُونَ ٧ إِنَّا جَعَلْنَا فِي أَعْنَاقِهِمْ
أَغْلَالًا فَهِيَ إِلَى الْأَذْقَانِ فَهُم مُّقْمَحُونَ ٨ وَجَعَلْنَا مِن بَيْنِ
أَيْدِيهِمْ سَدًّا وَمِنْ خَلْفِهِمْ سَدًّا فَأَغْشَيْنَاهُمْ فَهُمْ لَا
يُبْصِرُونَ ٩ وَسَوَاءٌ عَلَيْهِمْ أَأَنذَرْتَهُمْ أَمْ لَمْ تُنذِرْهُمْ لَا
يُؤْمِنُونَ ١٠ إِنَّمَا تُنذِرُ مَنِ اتَّبَعَ الذِّكْرَ وَخَشِيَ الرَّحْمَٰنَ بِالْغَيْبِ
فَبَشِّرْهُ بِمَغْفِرَةٍ وَأَجْرٍ كَرِيمٍ ١١ إِنَّا نَحْنُ نُحْيِي الْمَوْتَىٰ وَنَكْتُبُ
مَا قَدَّمُوا وَآثَارَهُمْ وَكُلَّ شَيْءٍ أَحْصَيْنَاهُ فِي إِمَامٍ مُّبِينٍ ١٢

WERE IT God's will to 35:45
bring people to account for
what they did, not one creature would He have left on the
earth's surface. But He res-
pites them till an appointed
time. And when their time is
come, God has been watching
all His servants.

YĀ' SĪN

In the Name of God,
the Merciful, the Compassionate

Yā' sīn. By the Wise Koran, 36:1
you are surely one sent forth
upon a straight path.

A revelation from the
Almighty, the Forgiving: that
you may forewarn a people
who, because their fathers were not warned before them, are now heedless.
On most of them judgement has been passed; yet still they disbelieve.

We have bound their necks with chains of iron reaching up to their chins, 36:8
so that they cannot bow their heads. We have put a barrier before them and
a barrier behind them and covered them over, so that they cannot see.

It is the same for them whether or not you warn them: they will not
believe. You shall warn only those who observe the Admonition and fear the
Merciful, though they cannot see Him. To these give joyful tidings of pardon
and a rich reward.

It is We who will resurrect the dead. We record their deeds and the ves- 36:12
tiges they leave behind: We keep account of all things in a veritable Book.

وَاضْرِبْ لَهُم مَّثَلًا أَصْحَابَ الْقَرْيَةِ إِذْ جَاءَهَا الْمُرْسَلُونَ
﴿١٣﴾ إِذْ أَرْسَلْنَا إِلَيْهِمُ اثْنَيْنِ فَكَذَّبُوهُمَا فَعَزَّزْنَا
بِثَالِثٍ فَقَالُوا إِنَّا إِلَيْكُم مُّرْسَلُونَ ﴿١٤﴾ قَالُوا مَا أَنتُمْ إِلَّا
بَشَرٌ مِّثْلُنَا وَمَا أَنزَلَ الرَّحْمَٰنُ مِن شَيْءٍ إِنْ أَنتُمْ إِلَّا تَكْذِبُونَ ﴿١٥﴾
قَالُوا رَبُّنَا يَعْلَمُ إِنَّا إِلَيْكُمْ لَمُرْسَلُونَ ﴿١٦﴾ وَمَا عَلَيْنَا إِلَّا الْبَلَاغُ
الْمُبِينُ ﴿١٧﴾ قَالُوا إِنَّا تَطَيَّرْنَا بِكُمْ لَئِن لَّمْ تَنتَهُوا لَنَرْجُمَنَّكُمْ
وَلَيَمَسَّنَّكُم مِّنَّا عَذَابٌ أَلِيمٌ ﴿١٨﴾ قَالُوا طَائِرُكُم مَّعَكُمْ
أَئِن ذُكِّرْتُم بَلْ أَنتُمْ قَوْمٌ مُّسْرِفُونَ ﴿١٩﴾ وَجَاءَ مِنْ
أَقْصَا الْمَدِينَةِ رَجُلٌ يَسْعَىٰ قَالَ يَا قَوْمِ اتَّبِعُوا الْمُرْسَلِينَ
﴿٢٠﴾ اتَّبِعُوا مَن لَّا يَسْأَلُكُمْ أَجْرًا وَهُم مُّهْتَدُونَ ﴿٢١﴾
وَمَا لِيَ لَا أَعْبُدُ الَّذِي فَطَرَنِي وَإِلَيْهِ تُرْجَعُونَ ﴿٢٢﴾ أَأَتَّخِذُ مِن
دُونِهِ آلِهَةً إِن يُرِدْنِ الرَّحْمَٰنُ بِضُرٍّ لَّا تُغْنِ عَنِّي شَفَاعَتُهُمْ شَيْئًا
وَلَا يُنقِذُونِ ﴿٢٣﴾ إِنِّي إِذًا لَّفِي ضَلَالٍ مُّبِينٍ ﴿٢٤﴾ إِنِّي
آمَنتُ بِرَبِّكُمْ فَاسْمَعُونِ ﴿٢٥﴾ قِيلَ ادْخُلِ الْجَنَّةَ قَالَ يَا لَيْتَ قَوْمِي
يَعْلَمُونَ ﴿٢٦﴾ بِمَا غَفَرَ لِي رَبِّي وَجَعَلَنِي مِنَ الْمُكْرَمِينَ ﴿٢٧﴾

36:13 YOU SHALL cite, as a case in point, the people of the city[1] to which the emissaries made their way. We first sent to them two, but when they rejected both We strengthened them with a third. They said: 'We have been sent to you as emissaries.' But they said: 'You are but mortals like ourselves. The Merciful has revealed nothing: you are only lying.'

They said: 'Our Lord knows that we are true emissaries. Our only duty is to give clear warning.'

They said: 'Your presence bodes but evil for us. Desist, or we will stone you or inflict on you a painful scourge.'

36:19 They said: 'The evil you forebode can come only from yourselves. Will you not take heed? Surely you are great transgressors.'

Thereupon a man came running from the far quarter of the city. 'My people,' he said, 'follow those who have been sent to you. Follow those who ask no recompense of you and are rightly guided. Why should I not serve Him who has created me and to whom you shall be recalled? Should I serve other gods than Him? If it is the will of the Merciful to afflict me, their intercession will avail me nothing, nor will they save me. Indeed, I should then be in evident error. I believe in your Lord; so hear me.'

He was told: 'Enter Paradise'; and he said: 'Would that my people knew
36:27 how gracious my Lord has been to me, how highly He has honoured me!'

1. Probably Antioch, to which, we are told, Jesus sent two disciples, and then a third.

وَمَا أَنزَلْنَا عَلَىٰ قَوْمِهِ مِن بَعْدِهِ مِن جُندٍ مِّنَ السَّمَاءِ وَمَا
كُنَّا مُنزِلِينَ ﴿٢٨﴾ إِن كَانَتْ إِلَّا صَيْحَةً وَاحِدَةً فَإِذَا هُمْ
خَامِدُونَ ﴿٢٩﴾ يَا حَسْرَةً عَلَى الْعِبَادِ مَا يَأْتِيهِم مِّن رَّسُولٍ إِلَّا
كَانُوا بِهِ يَسْتَهْزِئُونَ ﴿٣٠﴾ أَلَمْ يَرَوْا كَمْ أَهْلَكْنَا قَبْلَهُم
مِّنَ الْقُرُونِ أَنَّهُمْ إِلَيْهِمْ لَا يَرْجِعُونَ ﴿٣١﴾ وَإِن كُلٌّ لَّمَّا جَمِيعٌ
لَّدَيْنَا مُحْضَرُونَ ﴿٣٢﴾ وَآيَةٌ لَّهُمُ الْأَرْضُ الْمَيْتَةُ أَحْيَيْنَاهَا وَأَخْرَجْنَا
مِنْهَا حَبًّا فَمِنْهُ يَأْكُلُونَ ﴿٣٣﴾ وَجَعَلْنَا فِيهَا جَنَّاتٍ مِّن نَّخِيلٍ
وَأَعْنَابٍ وَفَجَّرْنَا فِيهَا مِنَ الْعُيُونِ ﴿٣٤﴾ لِيَأْكُلُوا مِن ثَمَرِهِ
وَمَا عَمِلَتْهُ أَيْدِيهِمْ أَفَلَا يَشْكُرُونَ ﴿٣٥﴾ سُبْحَانَ الَّذِي
خَلَقَ الْأَزْوَاجَ كُلَّهَا مِمَّا تُنبِتُ الْأَرْضُ وَمِنْ أَنفُسِهِمْ
وَمِمَّا لَا يَعْلَمُونَ ﴿٣٦﴾ وَآيَةٌ لَّهُمُ اللَّيْلُ نَسْلَخُ مِنْهُ النَّهَارَ
فَإِذَا هُم مُّظْلِمُونَ ﴿٣٧﴾ وَالشَّمْسُ تَجْرِي لِمُسْتَقَرٍّ لَّهَا ذَٰلِكَ
تَقْدِيرُ الْعَزِيزِ الْعَلِيمِ ﴿٣٨﴾ وَالْقَمَرَ قَدَّرْنَاهُ مَنَازِلَ حَتَّىٰ
عَادَ كَالْعُرْجُونِ الْقَدِيمِ ﴿٣٩﴾ لَا الشَّمْسُ يَنبَغِي لَهَا أَن تُدْرِكَ
الْقَمَرَ وَلَا اللَّيْلُ سَابِقُ النَّهَارِ وَكُلٌّ فِي فَلَكٍ يَسْبَحُونَ ﴿٤٠﴾

AFTER HIM, We sent down 36:28
no host from heaven against his people: this We never do. There was but one shout – and, behold, they were lifeless.

Alas for My bondsmen! They laugh to scorn every apostle that comes to them. Do they not see how many generations We have destroyed before them? Never shall they return to them: all shall be brought before Us.

Let the once-dead earth be a sign for them. We gave it life, and from it produced grain for their sustenance. We planted it with gardens of the palm and the vine, and watered it with gushing springs, that they might feed on its fruit. It was not their hands that made all this.[1] Should they not give thanks?

Glory be to Him who made all things in pairs: the plants of the earth, 36:36
mankind themselves, and things they know nothing of.

Another sign for them is the night. From the night We sheer off the day – and lo, they are plunged in darkness.

And the sun hastens to its own resting-place: its course is laid by the Almighty, the All-knowing.

And for the moon We have ordained phases; it wanes, until it returns like a bent old twig.

The sun is not to overtake the moon, nor does the night outpace the day. 36:40
Each in its own orbit swims.

1. Or: so that they might feed on its fruit and what their hands have made.

36:41 ANOTHER SIGN for them
is that We carried their offspring in the laden ark. And
similar vessels We have made
for them to ride on. We drown
them if We will: none can
help or rescue them, except
through Our mercy and unless
enjoyment is allowed for a
time.

When they are told: 'Have
fear of that which is before
you and behind you, that you
may be shown mercy,' they
turn away from every sign that
comes to them from their
Lord.

And when they are told:
'Give from that which God
has given you,' the unbelievers
say to the faithful: 'Are we to
feed those whom God can
feed if He chooses? Surely
36:48 you are in glaring error.' And they say: 'When will this promise be fulfilled, if
what you say be true?'

They must be waiting but for a single blast, which will take them while
they are still disputing. They will have no time to make a will, nor shall they
return to their kin.

The Trumpet will be blown and, behold, from the graves they will stand
before their Lord. 'Woe betide us!' they will say. 'Who has roused us from our
resting-place? This is what the Lord of Mercy promised: the apostles have
told the truth!' And with but one blast they shall be gathered all before Us.
36:54 On that day no soul shall suffer the least injustice. You shall be rewarded
only according to your deeds.

وآية لهم أنا حملنا ذريتهم في الفلك المشحون ۝ وخلقنا
لهم من مثله ما يركبون ۝ وإن نشأ نغرقهم فلا صريخ لهم
ولا هم ينقذون ۝ إلا رحمة منا ومتاعا إلى حين
۝ وإذا قيل لهم اتقوا ما بين أيديكم وما خلفكم
لعلكم ترحمون ۝ وما تأتيهم من آية من آيات
ربهم إلا كانوا عنها معرضين ۝ وإذا قيل لهم أنفقوا مما رزقكم
الله قال الذين كفروا للذين آمنوا أنطعم من لو يشاء
الله أطعمه إن أنتم إلا في ضلال مبين ۝ ويقولون متى
هذا الوعد إن كنتم صادقين ۝ ما ينظرون إلا صيحة واحدة
تأخذهم وهم يخصمون ۝ فلا يستطيعون توصية ولا إلى
أهلهم يرجعون ۝ ونفخ في الصور فإذا هم من الأجداث إلى
ربهم ينسلون ۝ قالوا يا ويلنا من بعثنا من مرقدنا هذا ما وعد
الرحمن وصدق المرسلون ۝ إن كانت إلا صيحة واحدة
فإذا هم جميع لدينا محضرون ۝ فاليوم لا تظلم نفس
شيئا ولا تجزون إلا ما كنتم تعملون ۝

إِنَّ أَصْحَابَ الْجَنَّةِ الْيَوْمَ فِي شُغُلٍ فَاكِهُونَ ﴿٥٥﴾ هُمْ
وَأَزْوَاجُهُمْ فِي ظِلَالٍ عَلَى الْأَرَائِكِ مُتَّكِئُونَ ﴿٥٦﴾ لَهُمْ
فِيهَا فَاكِهَةٌ وَلَهُمْ مَا يَدَّعُونَ ﴿٥٧﴾ سَلَامٌ قَوْلًا مِنْ رَبٍّ
رَحِيمٍ ﴿٥٨﴾ وَامْتَازُوا الْيَوْمَ أَيُّهَا الْمُجْرِمُونَ ﴿٥٩﴾ أَلَمْ أَعْهَدْ
إِلَيْكُمْ يَا بَنِي آدَمَ أَنْ لَا تَعْبُدُوا الشَّيْطَانَ إِنَّهُ لَكُمْ عَدُوٌّ
مُبِينٌ ﴿٦٠﴾ وَأَنِ اعْبُدُونِي هَٰذَا صِرَاطٌ مُسْتَقِيمٌ ﴿٦١﴾ وَلَقَدْ
أَضَلَّ مِنْكُمْ جِبِلًّا كَثِيرًا أَفَلَمْ تَكُونُوا تَعْقِلُونَ ﴿٦٢﴾ هَٰذِهِ
جَهَنَّمُ الَّتِي كُنْتُمْ تُوعَدُونَ ﴿٦٣﴾ اصْلَوْهَا الْيَوْمَ بِمَا كُنْتُمْ
تَكْفُرُونَ ﴿٦٤﴾ الْيَوْمَ نَخْتِمُ عَلَىٰ أَفْوَاهِهِمْ وَتُكَلِّمُنَا أَيْدِيهِمْ
وَتَشْهَدُ أَرْجُلُهُمْ بِمَا كَانُوا يَكْسِبُونَ ﴿٦٥﴾ وَلَوْ نَشَاءُ لَطَمَسْنَا
عَلَىٰ أَعْيُنِهِمْ فَاسْتَبَقُوا الصِّرَاطَ فَأَنَّىٰ يُبْصِرُونَ ﴿٦٦﴾ وَلَوْ نَشَاءُ
لَمَسَخْنَاهُمْ عَلَىٰ مَكَانَتِهِمْ فَمَا اسْتَطَاعُوا مُضِيًّا وَلَا يَرْجِعُونَ
﴿٦٧﴾ وَمَنْ نُعَمِّرْهُ نُنَكِّسْهُ فِي الْخَلْقِ أَفَلَا يَعْقِلُونَ ﴿٦٨﴾ وَمَا
عَلَّمْنَاهُ الشِّعْرَ وَمَا يَنْبَغِي لَهُ إِنْ هُوَ إِلَّا ذِكْرٌ وَقُرْآنٌ مُبِينٌ
﴿٦٩﴾ لِيُنْذِرَ مَنْ كَانَ حَيًّا وَيَحِقَّ الْقَوْلُ عَلَى الْكَافِرِينَ ﴿٧٠﴾

ON THAT day the tenants 36:55
of Paradise will be busy with
their joys. They and their
spouses in shady groves upon
soft couches they shall recline;
therein shall they have fruits,
and all that they call for.

'Peace!' shall be the word
from a compassionate God.
'Keep yourselves apart, you
sinners, this day! Children of
Adam, did I not charge you
never to worship Satan, your
veritable foe, but to worship
Me? That is a straight path. Yet
has he led from among you
many a generation astray. Had
you no sense? This is the Hell
you have been promised. Burn
therein this day on account of
your disbelief.'

On that day We shall seal 36:65
their mouths. Their hands will
speak to Us, and their very feet will testify to what they did. Had it been Our
will, We could have put out their eyes: yet even then they would have rushed
headlong upon their wonted path. But how could they see their error?

Had it been Our will, We could have transformed them where they stood,
so that they could neither go forward nor retrace their steps.

We reverse the growth of those to whom We give long life. Have they no
sense?

We have taught him[1] no poetry, nor would poetry befit him. This is but an
Admonition: an eloquent Koran to exhort the living and to pass judgement 36:70
on the unbelievers.

1. Muḥammad.

36:71 Or have they not considered how, among the things Our hands have made, We have created for them the beasts of which they are masters? We have subjected these to them, that they may ride on some and eat the flesh of others; they drink their milk and put them to other uses. Will they not give thanks?

They have set up other gods besides God, hoping they may be helped. They cannot help them: yet they stand like warriors ready to defend their idols.

So let not their words grieve you. We have knowledge of what they conceal and what they reveal.

اولم يروا انا خلقنا لهم مما عملت ايدينا انعاما فهم لها
مالكون ۝ وذللناها لهم فمنها ركوبهم ومنها ياكلون
۝ ولهم فيها منافع ومشارب افلا يشكرون ۝ واتخذوا
من دون الله الهة لعلهم ينصرون ۝ لا يستطيعون نصرهم
وهم لهم جند محضرون ۝ فلا يحزنك قولهم انا نعلم ما
يسرون وما يعلنون ۝ اولم ير الانسان انا خلقناه من
نطفة فاذا هو خصيم مبين ۝ وضرب لنا مثلا ونسي خلقه
قال من يحيي العظام وهي رميم ۝ قل يحييها الذي
انشاها اول مرة وهو بكل خلق عليم ۝ الذي جعل لكم من
الشجر الاخضر نارا فاذا انتم منه توقدون ۝ اوليس الذي
خلق السموات والارض بقادر على ان يخلق مثلهم بلى وهو
الخلاق العليم ۝ انما امره اذا اراد شيئا ان يقول له كن فيكون
۝ فسبحان الذي بيده ملكوت كل شيء واليه ترجعون ۝

36:77 Has not man considered that We created him from a little germ? Yet is he brazenly contentious. He answers Us back with arguments, and forgets his own creation. He says: 'Who will give life to rotten bones?'

Say: 'He who first brought them into being will give them life again: He has knowledge of every creature; He who gives you from the green tree a flame, and lo! you light a fire.'

Or has He who created the heavens and the earth no power to create others like them? That He surely has. He is the all-knowing Creator. When He decrees a thing He need only say: 'Be,' and it is.

36:83 So glory be to Him who with His hands holds sovereignty over all things, and to whom shall you be recalled.

بسم الله الرحمن الرحيم
والصافات صفا ﴿١﴾ فالزاجرات زجرا ﴿٢﴾ فالتاليات ذكرا ﴿٣﴾ إن
إلهكم لواحد ﴿٤﴾ رب السموات والأرض وما بينهما ورب
المشارق ﴿٥﴾ إنا زينا السماء الدنيا بزينة الكواكب ﴿٦﴾ وحفظا
من كل شيطان مارد ﴿٧﴾ لا يسمعون إلى الملإ الأعلى ويقذفون
من كل جانب ﴿٨﴾ دحورا ولهم عذاب واصب ﴿٩﴾ إلا من خطف
الخطفة فأتبعه شهاب ثاقب ﴿١٠﴾ فاستفتهم أهم أشد خلقا
أم من خلقنا إنا خلقناهم من طين لازب ﴿١١﴾ بل عجبت ويسخرون
﴿١٢﴾ وإذا ذكروا لا يذكرون ﴿١٣﴾ وإذا رأوا آية يستسخرون ﴿١٤﴾
وقالوا إن هذا إلا سحر مبين ﴿١٥﴾ أءذا متنا وكنا ترابا وعظاما
أءنا لمبعوثون ﴿١٦﴾ أوآباؤنا الأولون ﴿١٧﴾ قل نعم وأنتم داخرون
﴿١٨﴾ فإنما هي زجرة واحدة فإذا هم ينظرون ﴿١٩﴾ وقالوا يا ويلنا
هذا يوم الدين ﴿٢٠﴾ هذا يوم الفصل الذي كنتم به تكذبون ﴿٢١﴾
احشروا الذين ظلموا وأزواجهم وما كانوا يعبدون ﴿٢٢﴾ من دون الله
فاهدوهم إلى صراط الجحيم ﴿٢٣﴾ وقفوهم إنهم مسؤلون ﴿٢٤﴾

THE RANKS

In the Name of God,
the Merciful, the Compassionate

BY THOSE who range them- 37:1
selves in ranks; by those who cast out demons;[1] and by those who recite an Admonition: your God is One: the Lord of the heavens and the earth and all that lies between them: the Lord of the Eastern Regions.

We have decked the lower heaven with constellations, guarding it against every rebellious demon, so that they may not listen in to those on high. Meteors are hurled at them from every side; then, driven away, they are consigned to an eternal scourge. Eavesdroppers are pursued by fiery comets.

Ask them if they deem themselves of a nobler make than the rest of Our 37:11
creation. Of coarse clay We created them.

You marvel, while they scoff. When they are warned they heed no warning. When they are shown a sign they mock at it and say: 'This is but sorcery manifest. What! When we have died and turned to dust and bones, shall we be raised to life, we and our forefathers?'

Say: 'Yes. And you shall be utterly humbled.'

One blast will sound, and they shall see it all. 'Woe betide us!' they will say. 'This is the Day of Reckoning; this is the Judgement-day which you denied.'

But We shall say: 'Herd up the sinners, their spouses, and the deities they
worshipped besides God, and lead them to the path of Hell. Hold them 37:24
there for questioning.

1. One of the interpretations given by Al-Bayḍāwī.

37:25 'WHAT HAS come over you that you cannot help each other?'

But on that day they will submit. They will reproach each other, saying: 'You have imposed upon us!' – 'No! It was you who would not be believers. We had no power over you: you were sinners all. Just is the verdict our Lord has passed upon us; we shall surely taste the scourge. We seduced you, but we ourselves have been seduced.'

On that day they will all share in the torment. Thus shall We deal with the wrong-doers, for when they were told: 'There is no deity but God,' they said with scorn: 'Are we to renounce our gods for the sake of a mad poet?'

ما لكم لا تناصرون ۝ بل هم اليوم مستسلمون ۝ وأقبل بعضهم
على بعض يتساءلون ۝ قالوا إنكم كنتم تأتوننا عن اليمين
۝ قالوا بل لم تكونوا مؤمنين ۝ وما كان لنا عليكم من سلطان
بل كنتم قوما طاغين ۝ فحق علينا قول ربنا إنا لذائقون ۝
فأغويناكم إنا كنا غاوين ۝ فإنهم يومئذ في العذاب مشتركون
۝ إنا كذلك نفعل بالمجرمين ۝ إنهم كانوا إذا قيل لهم لا إله إلا
الله يستكبرون ۝ ويقولون أئنا لتاركو آلهتنا لشاعر مجنون
۝ بل جاء بالحق وصدق المرسلين ۝ إنكم لذائقو العذاب
الأليم ۝ وما تجزون إلا ما كنتم تعملون ۝ إلا عباد
الله المخلصين ۝ أولئك لهم رزق معلوم ۝ فواكه
وهم مكرمون ۝ في جنات النعيم ۝ على سرر متقابلين ۝
يطاف عليهم بكأس من معين ۝ بيضاء لذة للشاربين ۝
لا فيها غول ولا هم عنها ينزفون ۝ وعندهم قاصرات
الطرف عين ۝ كأنهن بيض مكنون ۝ فأقبل بعضهم على
بعض يتساءلون ۝ قال قائل منهم إني كان لي قرين ۝

37:37 Surely he has brought the Truth, confirming those who were sent before. You shall all taste the grievous torment: you shall be requited only according to your deeds.

But God's true servants shall be well provided for, feasting on fruits, and honoured in the Gardens of Delight. Reclining face to face upon soft couches, there shall be passed among them a goblet filled at a gushing fountain, white, and delicious to those who drink it. It will neither dull their senses nor befuddle them. They shall sit with bashful, dark-eyed virgins, as chaste as hidden pearls.[1]

37:51 With questions they will approach each other. One will say: 'I had a friend

1. As 'if they were the sheltered eggs of ostriches' is another interpretation.

يَقُولُ أَئِنَّكَ لَمِنَ الْمُصَدِّقِينَ ۝ أَإِذَا مِتْنَا وَكُنَّا تُرَابًا وَعِظَامًا
أَإِنَّا لَمَدِينُونَ ۝ قَالَ هَلْ أَنْتُمْ مُطَّلِعُونَ ۝ فَاطَّلَعَ فَرَآهُ
فِي سَوَاءِ الْجَحِيمِ ۝ قَالَ تَاللَّهِ إِنْ كِدْتَ لَتُرْدِينِ
۝ وَلَوْلَا نِعْمَةُ رَبِّي لَكُنْتُ مِنَ الْمُحْضَرِينَ ۝ أَفَمَا نَحْنُ بِمَيِّتِينَ
۝ إِلَّا مَوْتَتَنَا الْأُولَىٰ وَمَا نَحْنُ بِمُعَذَّبِينَ ۝ إِنَّ هَٰذَا لَهُوَ
الْفَوْزُ الْعَظِيمُ ۝ لِمِثْلِ هَٰذَا فَلْيَعْمَلِ الْعَامِلُونَ ۝ أَذَٰلِكَ خَيْرٌ
نُزُلًا أَمْ شَجَرَةُ الزَّقُّومِ ۝ إِنَّا جَعَلْنَاهَا فِتْنَةً لِلظَّالِمِينَ ۝
إِنَّهَا شَجَرَةٌ تَخْرُجُ فِي أَصْلِ الْجَحِيمِ ۝ طَلْعُهَا كَأَنَّهُ رُءُوسُ
الشَّيَاطِينِ ۝ فَإِنَّهُمْ لَآكِلُونَ مِنْهَا فَمَالِئُونَ مِنْهَا الْبُطُونَ
۝ ثُمَّ إِنَّ لَهُمْ عَلَيْهَا لَشَوْبًا مِنْ حَمِيمٍ ۝ ثُمَّ إِنَّ مَرْجِعَهُمْ
لَإِلَى الْجَحِيمِ ۝ إِنَّهُمْ أَلْفَوْا آبَاءَهُمْ ضَالِّينَ ۝ فَهُمْ عَلَىٰ
آثَارِهِمْ يُهْرَعُونَ ۝ وَلَقَدْ ضَلَّ قَبْلَهُمْ أَكْثَرُ الْأَوَّلِينَ ۝
وَلَقَدْ أَرْسَلْنَا فِيهِمْ مُنْذِرِينَ ۝ فَانْظُرْ كَيْفَ كَانَ عَاقِبَةُ
الْمُنْذَرِينَ ۝ إِلَّا عِبَادَ اللَّهِ الْمُخْلَصِينَ ۝ وَلَقَدْ نَادَانَا
نُوحٌ فَلَنِعْمَ الْمُجِيبُونَ ۝ وَنَجَّيْنَاهُ وَأَهْلَهُ مِنَ الْكَرْبِ الْعَظِيمِ ۝

who used to say: "Do you 37:52
really believe? When we have
died and turned to dust and
bones, shall we ever be brought
to judgement?"' And he will
say: 'Come, will you look
down?' He will look down and
see his friend in the very midst
of Hell. 'By the Lord,' he will
say, 'you almost ruined me!
But for the grace of my Lord I
should have surely been summoned myself. Shall we never
die again, having died once,
and shall we never be scourged
at all?'

Surely that is the supreme
triumph. To this end let everyone labour.

Is this not a better welcome
than the Zaqqūm tree? We
have made this tree a scourge
for the unjust. It grows in the 37:64
nethermost part of Hell, bearing fruit like demons' heads: on it they shall
feed, and with it they shall cram their bellies, together with draughts of scalding water. Then to Hell shall they surely return.

They found their fathers erring, yet they eagerly followed in their footsteps. Most of the ancients went astray before them, though We had sent
emissaries to give them warning. So consider the fate of those who had been
warned: except God's true servants.

Noah called to Us, and he was graciously answered. We delivered him, and 37:76
his household, from the great calamity,

37:77 and made his descendants the sole survivors. We bestowed on him the praise of later generations: 'Peace be on Noah among all mankind!'

Thus do We reward the righteous: he was one of Our believing servants. The others We peremptorily drowned.

Of the selfsame faith was Abraham, who came to his Lord with a pure heart. He said to his father and to his people: 'What are these that you worship? Would you serve false deities instead of God? What think you of the Lord of the Universe?'

He lifted up his eyes to the stars and said: 'I am sick!' And his people turned their backs and went off.

37:91 He stole away to their idols and said: 'Will you not eat? Why do you not speak?' With that he fell upon them, striking them down with his right hand.

The people came running to the scene. 'Would you worship that which you have carved with your own hands,' he said, 'when it was God who created you and all that you have made?'

They said: 'Build up a pyre and cast him into the blazing hell.' Thus did they scheme against him: but We abased them all.

He said: 'I will take refuge with my Lord; He will give me guidance. Lord, grant me a righteous son.'

37:102 We gave him joyful tidings of a gentle son. And when he reached the age when he could work with him, his father said to him: 'My son, I dreamt that I was sacrificing you. Tell me what you think.'

He said: 'Father, do as you are bidden. God willing, you shall find me steadfast.'

وجعلنا ذريته هم الباقين ۝ وتركنا عليه في الآخرين ۝٧٨
سلام على نوح في العالمين ۝ إنا كذلك نجزي المحسنين ۝ إنه
من عبادنا المؤمنين ۝ ثم أغرقنا الآخرين ۝ وإن من شيعته
لإبراهيم ۝٨٣ إذ جاء ربه بقلب سليم ۝ إذ قال لأبيه وقومه
ماذا تعبدون ۝ أئفكا آلهة دون الله تريدون ۝ فما ظنكم
برب العالمين ۝ فنظر نظرة في النجوم ۝ فقال إني سقيم ۝
فتولوا عنه مدبرين ۝ فراغ إلى آلهتهم فقال ألا تأكلون ۝٩١
ما لكم لا تنطقون ۝ فراغ عليهم ضربا باليمين ۝ فأقبلوا إليه
يزفون ۝ قال أتعبدون ما تنحتون ۝ والله خلقكم وما تعملون
۝٩٦ قالوا ابنوا له بنيانا فألقوه في الجحيم ۝ فأرادوا
به كيدا فجعلناهم الأسفلين ۝ وقال إني ذاهب إلى
ربي سيهدين ۝ رب هب لي من الصالحين ۝ فبشرناه
بغلام حليم ۝١٠١ فلما بلغ معه السعي قال يا بني إني
أرى في المنام أني أذبحك فانظر ماذا ترى قال يا أبت
افعل ما تؤمر ستجدني إن شاء الله من الصابرين ۝١٠٢

فلما اسلما وتله للجبين ﴿١٠٣﴾ ونادينه ان يا ابرهيم ﴿١٠٤﴾ قد
صدقت الرءيا انا كذلك نجزي المحسنين ﴿١٠٥﴾ ان هذا لهو
البلؤا المبين ﴿١٠٦﴾ وفدينه بذبح عظيم ﴿١٠٧﴾ وتركنا عليه في
الاخرين ﴿١٠٨﴾ سلم على ابرهيم ﴿١٠٩﴾ كذلك نجزي المحسنين
﴿١١٠﴾ انه من عبادنا المؤمنين ﴿١١١﴾ وبشرنه باسحق نبيا من
الصلحين ﴿١١٢﴾ وبركنا عليه وعلى اسحق ومن ذريتهما
محسن وظالم لنفسه مبين ﴿١١٣﴾ ولقد مننا على موسى
وهرون ﴿١١٤﴾ ونجينهما وقومهما من الكرب العظيم
﴿١١٥﴾ ونصرنهم فكانوا هم الغلبين ﴿١١٦﴾ واتينهما
الكتب المستبين ﴿١١٧﴾ وهدينهما الصرط المستقيم
﴿١١٨﴾ وتركنا عليهما في الاخرين ﴿١١٩﴾ سلم على موسى
وهرون ﴿١٢٠﴾ انا كذلك نجزي المحسنين ﴿١٢١﴾ انهما من
عبادنا المؤمنين ﴿١٢٢﴾ وان الياس لمن المرسلين ﴿١٢٣﴾ اذ قال
لقومه الا تتقون ﴿١٢٤﴾ اتدعون بعلا وتذرون احسن
الخلقين ﴿١٢٥﴾ الله ربكم ورب ابائكم الاولين ﴿١٢٦﴾

AND WHEN they had both 37:103
submitted, and he had laid him
down upon his brow, We called
out to him, saying: 'Abraham,
you have confirmed the vision.'
Thus do We reward the righteous. That was indeed the
veritable test. We ransomed
him with a noble sacrifice and
left for him the praise of later
generations: 'Peace be on Abraham!'

Thus do We reward the
righteous. He was one of Our
believing servants.

We gladdened him with the
news of Isaac, a saintly prophet,
and blessed him and Isaac.
Among their descendants were
some who did good works and
some who clearly sinned
against their souls.

We showed favour to Moses 37:114
and to Aaron and delivered them both, with their people, from the great
calamity. We succoured them, and it was they who were the victors. We gave
them the Illuminating Book and guided them to the straight path. We left for
them both the praise of later generations: 'Peace be on Moses and Aaron!'

Thus do We reward the righteous. They were two of Our believing
servants.

Elias[1] also was one of those sent forth. He said to his people: 'Have you
no fear? Would you invoke Baal and forsake the most gracious of creators?
God is your Lord and the Lord of your forefathers.' 37:126

1. Elijah. Cf. 1 Kings 18:17–21.

37:127 But they rejected him,
and will thus be called to
account. Not so God's true
servants. We bestowed on him
the praise of later generations:
'Peace be on Elias!'

Thus do We reward the
righteous. He was one of Our
believing servants.

Lot also was one of those
sent forth. We delivered him
and his kindred all, except for
an old woman who stayed
behind, and utterly destroyed
the others. You pass by their
ruins in the morning and at
night: have you no sense?

Jonah also was one of those
sent forth. He fled to the laden
ship, cast lots, and was con-
37:142 demned. The whale swallowed
him, for he had sinned; and
had he not devoutly praised
the Lord he would have stayed in its belly till the Day of Resurrection. We
cast him, gravely ill, upon a desolate shore and caused a gourd-tree to grow
over him. We sent him to a hundred thousand, or even more; they believed
in him, and We let them live in ease for a certain time.

Ask them if it be true that your Lord has daughters, and they sons. Or did
We create the angels females; and were they witnesses? Surely they lie when
they assert: 'God has given birth.'

37:153 Would He choose daughters, rather than sons?

فكذبوه فإنهم لمحضرون ﴿١٢٧﴾ إلا عباد الله المخلصين
﴿١٢٨﴾ وتركنا عليه في الآخرين ﴿١٢٩﴾ سلام على إل ياسين
﴿١٣٠﴾ إنا كذلك نجزي المحسنين ﴿١٣١﴾ إنه من عبادنا المؤمنين
﴿١٣٢﴾ وإن لوطا لمن المرسلين ﴿١٣٣﴾ إذ نجيناه وأهله أجمعين
﴿١٣٤﴾ إلا عجوزا في الغابرين ﴿١٣٥﴾ ثم دمرنا الآخرين
﴿١٣٦﴾ وإنكم لتمرون عليهم مصبحين ﴿١٣٧﴾ وبالليل أفلا تعقلون
﴿١٣٨﴾ وإن يونس لمن المرسلين ﴿١٣٩﴾ إذ أبق إلى الفلك المشحون
﴿١٤٠﴾ فساهم فكان من المدحضين ﴿١٤١﴾ فالتقمه الحوت وهو مليم
﴿١٤٢﴾ فلولا أنه كان من المسبحين ﴿١٤٣﴾ للبث في بطنه إلى يوم
يبعثون ﴿١٤٤﴾ فنبذناه بالعراء وهو سقيم ﴿١٤٥﴾ وأنبتنا عليه
شجرة من يقطين ﴿١٤٦﴾ وأرسلناه إلى مائة ألف أو يزيدون
﴿١٤٧﴾ فآمنوا فمتعناهم إلى حين ﴿١٤٨﴾ فاستفتهم ألربك البنات
ولهم البنون ﴿١٤٩﴾ أم خلقنا الملائكة إناثا وهم شاهدون
﴿١٥٠﴾ ألا إنهم من إفكهم ليقولون ﴿١٥١﴾ ولد الله وإنهم
لكاذبون ﴿١٥٢﴾ أصطفى البنات على البنين ﴿١٥٣﴾

ما لكم كيف تحكمون ﴿١٥٤﴾ أفلا تذكرون ﴿١٥٥﴾ أم لكم سلطان مبين ﴿١٥٦﴾
فأتوا بكتابكم إن كنتم صادقين ﴿١٥٧﴾ وجعلوا بينه وبين الجنة نسبا
ولقد علمت الجنة إنهم لمحضرون ﴿١٥٨﴾ سبحان الله عما يصفون ﴿١٥٩﴾
إلا عباد الله المخلصين ﴿١٦٠﴾ فإنكم وما تعبدون ﴿١٦١﴾ ما أنتم
عليه بفاتنين ﴿١٦٢﴾ إلا من هو صال الجحيم ﴿١٦٣﴾ وما منا إلا له مقام
معلوم ﴿١٦٤﴾ وإنا لنحن الصافون ﴿١٦٥﴾ وإنا لنحن المسبحون ﴿١٦٦﴾
وإن كانوا ليقولون ﴿١٦٧﴾ لو أن عندنا ذكرا من الأولين ﴿١٦٨﴾
لكنا عباد الله المخلصين ﴿١٦٩﴾ فكفروا به فسوف يعلمون ﴿١٧٠﴾ ولقد
سبقت كلمتنا لعبادنا المرسلين ﴿١٧١﴾ إنهم لهم المنصورون ﴿١٧٢﴾ وإن
جندنا لهم الغالبون ﴿١٧٣﴾ فتول عنهم حتى حين ﴿١٧٤﴾ وأبصرهم
فسوف يبصرون ﴿١٧٥﴾ أفبعذابنا يستعجلون ﴿١٧٦﴾ فإذا نزل
بساحتهم فساء صباح المنذرين ﴿١٧٧﴾ وتول عنهم حتى حين
﴿١٧٨﴾ وأبصر فسوف يبصرون ﴿١٧٩﴾ سبحان ربك رب العزة عما
يصفون ﴿١٨٠﴾ وسلام على المرسلين ﴿١٨١﴾ والحمد لله رب العالمين ﴿١٨٢﴾

سورة ص مكية وهي ثمان وثمانون آية

WHAT HAS come over you that 37:154
you should so judge?

Will you not take thought? Have you a veritable proof? Bring us your scripture, if what you say be true!

They assert kinship between Him and the jinn. But the jinn well know that they will be called up to account. Exalted be God above their imputations! Not so God's true servants.

Neither you nor your idols shall deceive any about God save him who is destined to be burnt in Hell. We[1] each have our appointed place. It is we who range ourselves in ranks, and we are they that give glory.

And they say: 'Had we 37:168
received an admonition from the ancients, we would have become God's true servants.' Yet they disbelieve; and they shall learn.

Before then We promised Our servants who were sent forth they would be helped and Our armies would surely be the victors. So pay no heed to them awhile: you will surely see their downfall as they shall see your triumph.

Do they wish to hurry on Our scourge? Evil shall be that morning when it smites them in their courtyards, forewarned though they have been.

So pay no heed to them awhile. You will surely see their downfall as they shall see your triumph. Exalted be your Lord, the Lord of Glory, above their imputations!

And peace be on those who were sent forth, and praise to God, Lord of 37:182
the Universe!

1. The angels.

ṢĀD

In the Name of God,
the Merciful, the Compassionate

بسم الله الرحمن الرحيم
ص والقرآن ذي الذكر ۝ بل الذين كفروا في عزة وشقاق ۝٢
كم أهلكنا من قبلهم من قرن فنادوا ولات حين مناص ۝ وعجبوا
أن جاءهم منذر منهم وقال الكافرون هذا ساحر كذاب ۝٤
أجعل الآلهة إلها واحدا إن هذا لشيء عجاب ۝ وانطلق الملأ
منهم أن امشوا واصبروا على آلهتكم إن هذا لشيء يراد ۝٦ ما سمعنا
بهذا في الملة الآخرة إن هذا إلا اختلاق ۝ أأنزل عليه
الذكر من بيننا بل هم في شك من ذكري بل لما يذوقوا عذاب ۝٨
أم عندهم خزائن رحمة ربك العزيز الوهاب ۝٩ أم لهم ملك
السماوات والأرض وما بينهما فليرتقوا في الأسباب ۝١٠ جند
ما هنالك مهزوم من الأحزاب ۝١١ كذبت قبلهم قوم
نوح وعاد وفرعون ذو الأوتاد ۝١٢ وثمود وقوم لوط
وأصحاب لئيكة أولئك الأحزاب ۝ إن كل إلا كذب الرسل
فحق عقاب ۝١٤ وما ينظر هؤلاء إلا صيحة واحدة ما لها
من فواق ۝ وقالوا ربنا عجل لنا قطنا قبل يوم الحساب ۝١٦

38:1 *Ṣād.* By the Koran, proclaiming the Admonition! Surely the unbelievers are imbued with arrogance and perverseness.

How many generations have We destroyed before them! They all cried out for mercy, when it was too late to escape.

They marvel that one of their own should come to warn them. 'This is a sorcerer, a teller of lies,' the unbelievers say. 'Does he claim the gods are one god? This is indeed a strange thing.'

Their elders go about saying: 'Go, and stand firm in the worship of your gods: it is a binding duty. We have not heard of this[1] in the Christian Faith.[2] It is nothing but a false invention. What! Was the Admonition sent down to him alone among us?'

Indeed, they are in doubt about My Admonition; indeed, they have not yet tasted My scourge.

38:9 Do they possess the treasures of the mercy of your Lord, the Almighty, the Munificent One? Is theirs the sovereignty over the heavens and the earth and all that lies between them? Then let them climb up to the sky by ropes! There, none shall be found but factions of defeated warriors.

Before them the people of Noah, 'Ād, and Pharaoh, who impaled his victims upon the stakes; Thamūd, the people of Lot, and the dwellers of the Forest[3] – they disbelieved, they were all those factions: all charged the apostles with imposture. And My punishment justly smote them.

38:16 Yet these are waiting but for a single cry – which none may retard. They say: 'Lord, hasten our doom before the Day of Reckoning!'

1. Monotheism. 2. Literally, the last Faith.
3. The people of Midian.

اصبر على ما يقولون واذكر عبدنا داود ذا الأيد إنه أواب
(١٧) إنا سخرنا الجبال معه يسبحن بالعشي والإشراق (١٨)
والطير محشورة كل له أواب (١٩) وشددنا ملكه وآتيناه
الحكمة وفصل الخطاب (٢٠) وهل أتاك نبأ الخصم إذ تسوروا
المحراب (٢١) إذ دخلوا على داود ففزع منهم قالوا لا تخف خصمان
بغى بعضنا على بعض فاحكم بيننا بالحق ولا تشطط واهدنا
إلى سواء الصراط (٢٢) إن هذا أخي له تسع وتسعون نعجة ولي
نعجة واحدة فقال أكفلنيها وعزني في الخطاب (٢٣) قال لقد
ظلمك بسؤال نعجتك إلى نعاجه وإن كثيرا من الخلطاء ليبغي
بعضهم على بعض إلا الذين آمنوا وعملوا الصالحات وقليل ما هم
وظن داود أنما فتناه فاستغفر ربه وخر راكعا وأناب (٢٤)
فغفرنا له ذلك وإن له عندنا لزلفى وحسن مآب (٢٥) يا داود
إنا جعلناك خليفة في الأرض فاحكم بين الناس بالحق
ولا تتبع الهوى فيضلك عن سبيل الله إن الذين يضلون
عن سبيل الله لهم عذاب شديد بما نسوا يوم الحساب (٢٦)

BEAR WITH what they say, 38:17
and remember Our servant
David, who was both a mighty
and a penitent man. We made
the mountains[1] join with him in
praise evening and morning,
and the birds, too, in all their
flocks; all were obedient to him.
We made his kingdom strong,
and gave him wisdom and dis-
criminating judgement.

Have you heard the story of
the litigants who entered his
chamber by climbing over the
wall? When they went in to
David and saw that he was
alarmed, they said: 'Fear not.
We are two litigants, one of
whom has wronged the other.
Judge rightly between us and
do not be unjust; guide us to
the right path.

'My brother here has 38:23
ninety-nine ewes, but I have only one ewe.[2] He demanded that I should
entrust it to him, and got the better of me in the dispute.'

He said: 'He has certainly wronged you in seeking to add your ewe to his
flock. Many partners are unjust to one another; but not so those that have
faith and do good works, and they are few indeed.'

David realized that We were only testing him. He sought forgiveness of
his Lord and fell down penitently on his knees. We forgave him that, and in
Our presence he shall be honoured and well received. 'David, We have made 38:26
you master in the land. Rule with justice among the people and do not yield
to lust, lest it turn you away from God's path. Because they forget the Day of
Reckoning, those that stray from God's path shall be grievously punished.'

1. Cf. Psalm 148:9–10.
2. The allusion is to Uriah's wife.

38:27 It was not in vain that We
created heaven and earth and
all that lies between them.
That is what the unbelievers
think. But woe betide the
unbelievers when they are cast
into the Fire!
Are We to equate those that
have faith and do good works
with those that perpetrate corruption in the land? Are We to
equate the righteous with the
ungodly?
This Book We have revealed
to you with Our blessing, that
those that are of good sense
possessed might ponder its
revelations and take warning.
And We gave Solomon to
David; and he was a good and
penitent servant. When, one
evening, his prancing steeds
were ranged before him, he
said: 'My love for good things has distracted me from the remembrance of
my Lord, until the sun disappeared behind the veil of darkness. Bring me
back my chargers!' And with this he fell to hacking their legs and necks.
38:34 We put Solomon to the proof and placed a body upon his throne, so that
he at length repented. He said: 'Forgive me, Lord, and bestow upon me such
sovereignty as shall belong to none after me. You are the Bountiful Giver.'
We subjected the wind to him, so that it blew softly at his bidding wherever he directed it; and the demons, too, every builder and diver and others
bound with chains. 'This is Our giving. It is for you to bestow or to withhold,
without reckoning.' In Our presence he shall be honoured and well received.
And tell of Our servant Job. He called out to his Lord, saying: 'Satan has
afflicted me with anguish and torment.'
38:42 'Stamp your feet; here is a cool spring for you to wash in and to drink from.'

وما خلقنا السماء والأرض وما بينهما باطلا ذلك ظن الذين
كفروا فويل للذين كفروا من النار ٢٧ أم نجعل الذين آمنوا وعملوا
الصالحات كالمفسدين في الأرض أم نجعل المتقين كالفجار ٢٨
كتاب أنزلناه إليك مبارك ليدبروا آياته وليتذكر أولوا
الألباب ٢٩ ووهبنا لداود سليمن نعم العبد إنه أواب ٣٠
إذ عرض عليه بالعشي الصافنات الجياد ٣١ فقال إني أحببت
حب الخير عن ذكر ربي حتى توارت بالحجاب ٣٢ ردوها علي فطفق
مسحا بالسوق والأعناق ٣٣ ولقد فتنا سليمن وألقينا على كرسيه
جسدا ثم أناب ٣٤ قال رب اغفر لي وهب لي ملكا لا ينبغي لأحد
من بعدي إنك أنت الوهاب ٣٥ فسخرنا له الريح تجري بأمره
رخاء حيث أصاب ٣٦ والشياطين كل بناء وغواص ٣٧ وآخرين
مقرنين في الأصفاد ٣٨ هذا عطاؤنا فامنن أو أمسك بغير
حساب ٣٩ وإن له عندنا لزلفى وحسن مآب ٤٠ واذكر
عبدنا أيوب إذ نادى ربه أني مسني الشيطان بنصب وعذاب
٤١ اركض برجلك هذا مغتسل بارد وشراب ٤٢

ووهبنا له أهله ومثلهم معهم رحمة منا وذكرى لأولي
الألباب ۝٤٣ وخذ بيدك ضغثا فاضرب به ولا تحنث إنا
وجدناه صابرا نعم العبد إنه أواب ۝٤٤ واذكر عبادنا
إبرهيم وإسحق ويعقوب أولي الأيدي والأبصار ۝٤٥ إنا أخلصنا
هم بخالصة ذكرى الدار ۝٤٦ وإنهم عندنا لمن المصطفين
الأخيار ۝٤٧ واذكر إسمعيل واليسع وذا الكفل وكل من
الأخيار ۝٤٨ هذا ذكر وإن للمتقين لحسن مآب ۝٤٩ جنات عدن
مفتحة لهم الأبواب ۝٥٠ متكئين فيها يدعون فيها بفاكهة
كثيرة وشراب ۝٥١ وعندهم قاصرات الطرف أتراب ۝٥٢
هذا ما توعدون ليوم الحساب ۝٥٣ إن هذا لرزقنا ما له من نفاد ۝٥٤
هذا وإن للطاغين لشر مآب ۝٥٥ جهنم يصلونها فبئس المهاد ۝٥٦
هذا فليذوقوه حميم وغساق ۝٥٧ وآخر من شكله أزواج ۝٥٨
هذا فوج مقتحم معكم لا مرحبا بهم إنهم صالوا النار
۝٥٩ قالوا بل أنتم لا مرحبا بكم أنتم قدمتموه لنا فبئس القرار
۝٦٠ قالوا ربنا من قدم لنا هذا فزده عذابا ضعفا في النار ۝٦١

WE RESTORED to him his 38:43
household and as many more with them: a blessing from Ourself and an Admonition to those that are of good sense possessed.

'Take a bunch of twigs and beat with it; do not break your oath.'[1] We found him steadfast; a good and penitent man.

And tell of Our servants Abraham, Isaac, and Jacob: men of might and vision We made pure with the thought of the Hereafter. They shall dwell with Us among the chosen and the righteous.

And tell of Ishmael, Elisha, and Dhūl-Kifl,[2] who were all among the just.

This is but an Admonition. The righteous shall return to a blessed retreat: to the Gardens
of Eden, whose gates shall open wide to receive them. Reclining therein, they 38:51
will call for abundant fruit and drink with bashful virgins for companions.

All this you are promised for the Day of Reckoning; this is Our gift: a gift unending.

But doleful shall be the return of the transgressors. In Hell shall they burn, an evil resting-place. Therein let them taste their drink: scalding water, festering blood, coupled with other putrid things.

'This band shall be thrown in headlong with you. No welcome shall await them; they shall be promptly cast into the Fire.'

'No welcome for you either! It was you who prepared this for us, an evil plight.'

Then will they say: 'Lord, inflict on those who brought this fate upon us a 38:61
twofold torment in the Fire.'

1. Job had sworn to give his wife a hundred blows. The oath was kept by his giving her one blow with a bunch of a hundred twigs. Commentators quote this passage as permitting any similar release from an oath rashly taken.
2. Ezekiel; see p. 328, note 2.

38:62 AND THEY will say: 'But why do we not see men whom we deemed wicked and whom we laughed to scorn? Or have our eyes missed them?'

All this shall come to pass. The inmates of the Fire will wrangle among themselves.

Say: 'I am only to give warning. There is no divinity but God, the One who conquers all. He is the Lord of the heavens and the earth and all that lies between them: the Almighty, the Forgiving One.'

Say: 'This is a fateful message: yet you pay no heed to it. I had no knowledge of those on high when they wrangled among themselves. It was revealed to me, only that I might warn you plainly.'

Tell of your Lord when He said to the angels: 'I am creating man from clay. When I have fashioned him and breathed My spirit into him, kneel down and prostrate yourselves before him.'

38:73 The angels prostrated themselves one and all, except Satan, who was too proud and was an unbeliever.

'Satan,' said He, 'what prevented you from bowing to him whom I created with My own hands? Are you too proud, or do you deem yourself superior?'

He said: 'I am nobler than he. You created me from fire, but him from clay.'

'Get you out hence, you are accursed!' said He. 'And My curse shall remain on you until the Day of Reckoning.'

He said: 'Reprieve me, Lord, till the Day of Resurrection.'

He said: 'Reprieved you shall be till the Day of the time appointed.'

38:83 'I swear by Your glory,' said he, 'that I will seduce them all except Your faithful servants.'

وَقَالُوا مَا لَنَا لَا نَرَىٰ رِجَالًا كُنَّا نَعُدُّهُم مِّنَ الْأَشْرَارِ ﴿٦٢﴾
أَتَّخَذْنَاهُمْ سِخْرِيًّا أَمْ زَاغَتْ عَنْهُمُ الْأَبْصَارُ ﴿٦٣﴾ إِنَّ ذَٰلِكَ لَحَقٌّ
تَخَاصُمُ أَهْلِ النَّارِ ﴿٦٤﴾ قُلْ إِنَّمَا أَنَا مُنذِرٌ وَمَا مِنْ إِلَٰهٍ إِلَّا اللَّهُ
الْوَاحِدُ الْقَهَّارُ ﴿٦٥﴾ رَبُّ السَّمَاوَاتِ وَالْأَرْضِ وَمَا بَيْنَهُمَا الْعَزِيزُ الْغَفَّارُ
﴿٦٦﴾ قُلْ هُوَ نَبَأٌ عَظِيمٌ ﴿٦٧﴾ أَنتُمْ عَنْهُ مُعْرِضُونَ ﴿٦٨﴾ مَا كَانَ لِيَ مِنْ
عِلْمٍ بِالْمَلَإِ الْأَعْلَىٰ إِذْ يَخْتَصِمُونَ ﴿٦٩﴾ إِن يُوحَىٰ إِلَيَّ إِلَّا أَنَّمَا أَنَا نَذِيرٌ
مُّبِينٌ ﴿٧٠﴾ إِذْ قَالَ رَبُّكَ لِلْمَلَائِكَةِ إِنِّي خَالِقٌ بَشَرًا مِّن طِينٍ ﴿٧١﴾
فَإِذَا سَوَّيْتُهُ وَنَفَخْتُ فِيهِ مِن رُّوحِي فَقَعُوا لَهُ سَاجِدِينَ ﴿٧٢﴾ فَسَجَدَ
الْمَلَائِكَةُ كُلُّهُمْ أَجْمَعُونَ ﴿٧٣﴾ إِلَّا إِبْلِيسَ اسْتَكْبَرَ وَكَانَ مِنَ الْكَافِرِينَ
﴿٧٤﴾ قَالَ يَا إِبْلِيسُ مَا مَنَعَكَ أَن تَسْجُدَ لِمَا خَلَقْتُ بِيَدَيَّ أَسْتَكْبَرْتَ
أَمْ كُنتَ مِنَ الْعَالِينَ ﴿٧٥﴾ قَالَ أَنَا خَيْرٌ مِّنْهُ خَلَقْتَنِي مِن نَّارٍ وَخَلَقْتَهُ مِن
طِينٍ ﴿٧٦﴾ قَالَ فَاخْرُجْ مِنْهَا فَإِنَّكَ رَجِيمٌ ﴿٧٧﴾ وَإِنَّ عَلَيْكَ لَعْنَتِي إِلَىٰ
يَوْمِ الدِّينِ ﴿٧٨﴾ قَالَ رَبِّ فَأَنظِرْنِي إِلَىٰ يَوْمِ يُبْعَثُونَ ﴿٧٩﴾ قَالَ
فَإِنَّكَ مِنَ الْمُنظَرِينَ ﴿٨٠﴾ إِلَىٰ يَوْمِ الْوَقْتِ الْمَعْلُومِ ﴿٨١﴾ قَالَ فَبِعِزَّتِكَ
لَأُغْوِيَنَّهُمْ أَجْمَعِينَ ﴿٨٢﴾ إِلَّا عِبَادَكَ مِنْهُمُ الْمُخْلَصِينَ ﴿٨٣﴾

قال فالحق والحق أقول (٨٤) لأملأن جهنم منك وممن تبعك منهم
أجمعين (٨٥) قل ما أسألكم عليه من أجر وما أنا من المتكلفين
(٨٦) إن هو إلا ذكر للعالمين (٨٧) ولتعلمن نبأه بعد حين (٨٨)

سورة الزمر مكية وآياتها خمس وسبعون آية

بسم الله الرحمن الرحيم
تنزيل الكتاب من الله العزيز الحكيم (١) إنا أنزلنا
إليك الكتاب بالحق فاعبد الله مخلصا له الدين (٢) ألا
لله الدين الخالص والذين اتخذوا من دونه أولياء ما نعبدهم
إلا ليقربونا إلى الله زلفى إن الله يحكم بينهم في ما هم
فيه يختلفون إن الله لا يهدي من هو كاذب كفار (٣) لو أراد
الله أن يتخذ ولدا لاصطفى مما يخلق ما يشاء سبحانه هو
الله الواحد القهار (٤) خلق السماوات والأرض بالحق يكور
الليل على النهار ويكور النهار على الليل وسخر الشمس والقمر
كل يجري لأجل مسمى ألا هو العزيز الغفار (٥)

HE SAID: 'Learn the Truth, 38:84
then, and I speak nothing but
the Truth: I will surely fill Hell
with your offspring and those
from among your followers,
all.'

Say: 'I demand of you for
this no recompense. Nor do I
pretend to be what I am not.
This is but an Admonition to
mankind; in a while you shall 38:88
learn about it all.'

THE THRONGS

In the Name of God,
the Merciful, the Compassionate

THE REVELATION of the 39:1
Book is from God, the
Almighty, the Wise One. We
have revealed to you the Book with the Truth: therefore worship God, consecrating your religion to Him.

Is it not to God that True Religion belongs? As for those who set up other patrons[1] besides Him, saying: 'We serve them only that they may bring us nearer to God,' God Himself will resolve their differences for them. God does not guide the disbelieving liar.

Had it been God's will to adopt a son, He would have chosen whom He pleased out of His own Creation. Exalted be He! He is God, the One, who vanquishes all.

It was with Truth that He created the heavens and the earth. He causes the 39:5
night to succeed the day and causes the day to overtake the night. He made
the sun and the moon subservient to Him, each running for an appointed
term. He is surely the Almighty, the Forgiving One.

1. The allusion is to the worship of saints, and to Christian doctrines.

39:6 He created you from a single soul, then from it He created its spouse. He sent down to you four different pairs of cattle.[1] He moulds you in your mothers' wombs by stages in threefold darkness.

Such is God, your Lord. His is the sovereignty; there is no god but Him. How, then, can you be turned away from Him?

If you render Him no thanks, God does not need you; yet His servants' ingratitude does not please Him; if you are thankful, your thanks will please Him.

No burdened soul shall bear another's burden. To your Lord shall you then return and He will declare to you what you have done. He well knows one's innermost thoughts.

خَلَقَكُم مِّن نَّفْسٍ وَاحِدَةٍ ثُمَّ جَعَلَ مِنْهَا زَوْجَهَا وَأَنزَلَ
لَكُم مِّنَ الْأَنْعَامِ ثَمَانِيَةَ أَزْوَاجٍ يَخْلُقُكُمْ فِي بُطُونِ
أُمَّهَاتِكُمْ خَلْقًا مِّن بَعْدِ خَلْقٍ فِي ظُلُمَاتٍ ثَلَاثٍ ذَٰلِكُمُ اللَّهُ
رَبُّكُمْ لَهُ الْمُلْكُ لَا إِلَٰهَ إِلَّا هُوَ فَأَنَّىٰ تُصْرَفُونَ ﴿٦﴾ إِن تَكْفُرُوا فَإِنَّ اللَّهَ
غَنِيٌّ عَنكُمْ وَلَا يَرْضَىٰ لِعِبَادِهِ الْكُفْرَ وَإِن تَشْكُرُوا يَرْضَهُ لَكُمْ وَلَا تَزِرُ
وَازِرَةٌ وِزْرَ أُخْرَىٰ ثُمَّ إِلَىٰ رَبِّكُم مَّرْجِعُكُمْ فَيُنَبِّئُكُم بِمَا كُنتُمْ
تَعْمَلُونَ إِنَّهُ عَلِيمٌ بِذَاتِ الصُّدُورِ ﴿٧﴾ وَإِذَا مَسَّ الْإِنسَانَ ضُرٌّ دَعَا
رَبَّهُ مُنِيبًا إِلَيْهِ ثُمَّ إِذَا خَوَّلَهُ نِعْمَةً مِّنْهُ نَسِيَ مَا كَانَ يَدْعُو
إِلَيْهِ مِن قَبْلُ وَجَعَلَ لِلَّهِ أَندَادًا لِّيُضِلَّ عَن سَبِيلِهِ قُلْ تَمَتَّعْ
بِكُفْرِكَ قَلِيلًا إِنَّكَ مِنْ أَصْحَابِ النَّارِ ﴿٨﴾ أَمَّنْ هُوَ قَانِتٌ
آنَاءَ اللَّيْلِ سَاجِدًا وَقَائِمًا يَحْذَرُ الْآخِرَةَ وَيَرْجُو رَحْمَةَ
رَبِّهِ قُلْ هَلْ يَسْتَوِي الَّذِينَ يَعْلَمُونَ وَالَّذِينَ لَا يَعْلَمُونَ إِنَّمَا
يَتَذَكَّرُ أُولُو الْأَلْبَابِ ﴿٩﴾ قُلْ يَا عِبَادِ الَّذِينَ آمَنُوا اتَّقُوا
رَبَّكُمْ لِلَّذِينَ أَحْسَنُوا فِي هَٰذِهِ الدُّنْيَا حَسَنَةٌ وَأَرْضُ اللَّهِ
وَاسِعَةٌ إِنَّمَا يُوَفَّى الصَّابِرُونَ أَجْرَهُم بِغَيْرِ حِسَابٍ ﴿١٠﴾

39:8 When evil befalls man, he prays to his Lord and turns to Him in penitence; yet no sooner does He bestow on him a favour than he forgets what he had prayed for and makes other deities God's equals, in order to lead others away from His path.

Say: 'Enjoy your unbelief awhile; but you shall be among the tenants of the Fire. Can he who passes the night in adoration, standing or on his knees, who bewares the life to come and hopes to earn the mercy of his Lord, . . . ?' Say: 'Are they equals, those that have knowledge and those that have none?' Truly, none will take thought but those that are of good sense possessed.

39:10 Say: 'You, My servants, that are true believers, fear your Lord. Those who do good in this life shall receive a good reward. God's earth is vast. But those that endure with fortitude He will recompense without reckoning.'

1. Camels, cows, sheep, and goats, according to the commentators.

قُلْ إِنِّي أُمِرْتُ أَنْ أَعْبُدَ اللَّهَ مُخْلِصًا لَهُ الدِّينَ ﴿١١﴾ وَأُمِرْتُ لِأَنْ أَكُونَ أَوَّلَ
الْمُسْلِمِينَ ﴿١٢﴾ قُلْ إِنِّي أَخَافُ إِنْ عَصَيْتُ رَبِّي عَذَابَ يَوْمٍ عَظِيمٍ ﴿١٣﴾ قُلِ
اللَّهَ أَعْبُدُ مُخْلِصًا لَهُ دِينِي ﴿١٤﴾ فَاعْبُدُوا مَا شِئْتُمْ مِنْ دُونِهِ ۗ قُلْ
إِنَّ الْخَاسِرِينَ الَّذِينَ خَسِرُوا أَنْفُسَهُمْ وَأَهْلِيهِمْ يَوْمَ الْقِيَامَةِ ۗ أَلَا
ذَٰلِكَ هُوَ الْخُسْرَانُ الْمُبِينُ ﴿١٥﴾ لَهُمْ مِنْ فَوْقِهِمْ ظُلَلٌ مِنَ النَّارِ
وَمِنْ تَحْتِهِمْ ظُلَلٌ ۚ ذَٰلِكَ يُخَوِّفُ اللَّهُ بِهِ عِبَادَهُ ۚ يَا عِبَادِ فَاتَّقُونِ
﴿١٦﴾ وَالَّذِينَ اجْتَنَبُوا الطَّاغُوتَ أَنْ يَعْبُدُوهَا وَأَنَابُوا إِلَى
اللَّهِ لَهُمُ الْبُشْرَىٰ ۚ فَبَشِّرْ عِبَادِ ﴿١٧﴾ الَّذِينَ يَسْتَمِعُونَ الْقَوْلَ فَيَتَّبِعُونَ
أَحْسَنَهُ ۚ أُولَٰئِكَ الَّذِينَ هَدَاهُمُ اللَّهُ ۖ وَأُولَٰئِكَ هُمْ أُولُو الْأَلْبَابِ
﴿١٨﴾ أَفَمَنْ حَقَّ عَلَيْهِ كَلِمَةُ الْعَذَابِ أَفَأَنْتَ تُنْقِذُ مَنْ فِي النَّارِ ﴿١٩﴾
لَٰكِنِ الَّذِينَ اتَّقَوْا رَبَّهُمْ لَهُمْ غُرَفٌ مِنْ فَوْقِهَا غُرَفٌ مَبْنِيَّةٌ تَجْرِي مِنْ
تَحْتِهَا الْأَنْهَارُ ۖ وَعْدَ اللَّهِ ۖ لَا يُخْلِفُ اللَّهُ الْمِيعَادَ ﴿٢٠﴾ أَلَمْ تَرَ أَنَّ
اللَّهَ أَنْزَلَ مِنَ السَّمَاءِ مَاءً فَسَلَكَهُ يَنَابِيعَ فِي الْأَرْضِ ثُمَّ
يُخْرِجُ بِهِ زَرْعًا مُخْتَلِفًا أَلْوَانُهُ ثُمَّ يَهِيجُ فَتَرَاهُ مُصْفَرًّا ثُمَّ
يَجْعَلُهُ حُطَامًا ۚ إِنَّ فِي ذَٰلِكَ لَذِكْرَىٰ لِأُولِي الْأَلْبَابِ ﴿٢١﴾

SAY: 'I am commanded to 39:11
worship God, consecrating my religion to Him; I am commanded to be the first of Muslims.'

Say: 'I fear, if I disobey my Lord, the torment of a fateful day.'

Say: 'God I worship, consecrating my religion to Him. As for yourselves, worship what you will besides Him.'

Say: 'They shall lose much, those who will forfeit their souls and their kin on the Day of Resurrection. That will surely be the ultimate loss. Above them there shall be sheets of fire, and sheets of fire shall be beneath them. By this, God puts fear into His servants' hearts.' Fear Me, then, My servants.

But those who keep from idol-worship and turn to God in penitence shall 39:17
rejoice; give joyful tidings to My servants who listen to precepts and follow what is best in them. It is these whom God has guided; it is these that are of good sense possessed.

Can you rescue from the Fire those on whom the Word of torment was pronounced? As for those who truly fear their Lord, they shall be lodged in mansions towering high, set about with running brooks. Such is God's promise: God never fails His promise.

Do you not see how God sends down water from the sky which pene- 39:21
trates the earth and gathers in springs beneath? With it He then brings forth plants of various hues. They wither, they turn yellow, and then He turns them into dust. Surely in this there is an admonition for those that are of good sense possessed.

افمن شرح الله صدره للاسلام فهو على نور من ربه
فويل للقاسية قلوبهم من ذكر الله اولئك في ضلال مبين ٢٢
الله نزل احسن الحديث كتابا متشابها مثاني تقشعر
منه جلود الذين يخشون ربهم ثم تلين جلودهم وقلوبهم
الى ذكر الله ذلك هدى الله يهدي به من يشاء ومن يضلل
الله فما له من هاد ٢٣ افمن يتقي بوجهه سوء العذاب يوم القيمة
وقيل للظالمين ذوقوا ما كنتم تكسبون ٢٤ كذب الذين
من قبلهم فاتيهم العذاب من حيث لا يشعرون ٢٥ فاذاقهم
الله الخزي في الحيوة الدنيا ولعذاب الاخرة اكبر لو
كانوا يعلمون ٢٦ ولقد ضربنا للناس في هذا القران
من كل مثل لعلهم يتذكرون ٢٧ قرانا عربيا غير ذي عوج
لعلهم يتقون ٢٨ ضرب الله مثلا رجلا فيه شركاء
متشاكسون ورجلا سلما لرجل هل يستويان مثلا الحمد
لله بل اكثرهم لا يعلمون ٢٩ انك ميت وانهم ميتون
٣٠ ثم انكم يوم القيمة عند ربكم تختصمون ٣١

39:22 HE WHOSE bosom God has
opened to Islām shall receive
light from his Lord. But woe
betide those whose hearts are
hardened against the remembrance of God! They are in
evident error.

God has now revealed the
best of Scriptures, a Book
uniform in style proclaiming
promises and warnings. Those
who fear their Lord tremble
with awe at its revelations, and
their skins and hearts melt
at the remembrance of God.
Such is God's guidance: He
guides whom He will. But he
whom God confounds shall
have none to guide him.

Can he who with his face
strives to ward off the terrors
of the Resurrection . . . ? And
the wrongdoers will be told:
'Taste the punishment which you have earned.'

Those who have gone before them also disbelieved, so that the scourge
overtook them unawares. God made them taste dishonour in this life, but
the torment of the life to come shall be more terrible, if they but knew it.

39:27 We have given mankind in this Koran all manner of parables, that they
may take thought: a Koran in the Arabic tongue, free from any flaw, that they
may fear God.

God makes this comparison: a man who has many masters who are ever
at odds among themselves; and a man devoted to one master. Are they to be
held equal? God be praised! But most of them have no knowledge.

39:31 You[1] are doomed to die, and they are doomed to die. Then, on the Day of
Resurrection, in your Lord's presence you[2] shall still dispute.

1. Muḥammad. 2. The unbelievers.

فمن أظلم ممن كذب على الله وكذب بالصدق
إذ جاءه أليس في جهنم مثوى للكافرين ٣٢ والذي
جاء بالصدق وصدق به أولئك هم المتقون ٣٣
لهم ما يشاءون عند ربهم ذلك جزاء المحسنين ٣٤
ليكفر الله عنهم أسوأ الذي عملوا ويجزيهم
أجرهم بأحسن الذي كانوا يعملون ٣٥ أليس الله
بكاف عبده ويخوفونك بالذين من دونه ومن
يضلل الله فما له من هاد ٣٦ ومن يهد الله
فما له من مضل أليس الله بعزيز ذي انتقام ٣٧
ولئن سألتهم من خلق السموات والأرض ليقولن الله
قل أفرأيتم ما تدعون من دون الله إن أرادني الله
بضر هل هن كاشفات ضره أو أرادني برحمة هل هن
ممسكات رحمته قل حسبي الله عليه يتوكل المتوكلون
٣٨ قل يا قوم اعملوا على مكانتكم إني عامل فسوف تعلمون
٣٩ من يأتيه عذاب يخزيه ويحل عليه عذاب مقيم ٤٠

So WHO is more wicked 39:32
than he who invents a falsehood about God and denies
the Truth when it is declared
to him? Is there not a home in
Hell for the unbelievers?

Those who proclaim the Truth, and those who give credence to it – they surely are the God-fearing. Their Lord will give them all that they desire. Thus shall the righteous be rewarded.

God will expunge their foulest deeds and reward them according to their noblest actions.

Is God not all-sufficient for
His servant? Yet they threaten
you with those they serve
besides Him. He whom God
confounds has none to guide
him; and he whom God guides 39:37
none can lead astray. Is God not mighty and capable of revenge?

And if you ask them who created the heavens and the earth, they will surely reply: 'God.' Say: 'Do you think then that, if God be pleased to afflict me, your idols could relieve my affliction; or that if He be pleased to show me mercy, they could withhold His mercy?'

Say: 'God is my all-sufficient patron. In Him let the trustful put their trust.'

Say: 'My people, do as best you can and so will I. You shall learn who will 39:40
be seized by a scourge that will disgrace him, and be smitten by a scourge
everlasting.'

39:41 WE HAVE revealed to you
the Book with the Truth, for
the instruction of the people.
He that follows the right path
shall follow it for his own
good; and he that strays shall
do so at his own peril. You are
not their keeper.

God claims back every soul upon its death, and the souls of the living when they are asleep. Those that are doomed to die He keeps, and lets the others go for a time ordained. Surely in this there are signs for people that reflect.

Have they chosen others besides God to intercede for them? Say: 'Even though they have no power nor understanding?'

39:44 Say: 'Intercession is wholly
in the hands of God. His is the
sovereignty over the heavens and the earth. Then to Him shall you be
recalled.'

When God alone is named, the hearts of those who deny the Hereafter shrink with aversion; but when their other gods are named, they are filled with joy.

Say: 'Lord, Creator of the heavens and the earth, who has knowledge of the unknown and the manifest, You alone can judge Your servants' differences.'

39:47 If the wrongdoers possessed all the treasures of the earth and as much
besides, they would gladly offer it to redeem their souls from the harrowing
scourge on the Day of Resurrection. For God will show them what they
have never reckoned with.

إِنَّا أَنزَلْنَا عَلَيْكَ الْكِتَابَ لِلنَّاسِ بِالْحَقِّ فَمَنِ اهْتَدَىٰ
فَلِنَفْسِهِ وَمَن ضَلَّ فَإِنَّمَا يَضِلُّ عَلَيْهَا وَمَا أَنتَ عَلَيْهِم
بِوَكِيلٍ ﴿٤١﴾ اللَّهُ يَتَوَفَّى الْأَنفُسَ حِينَ مَوْتِهَا وَالَّتِي لَمْ تَمُتْ
فِي مَنَامِهَا فَيُمْسِكُ الَّتِي قَضَىٰ عَلَيْهَا الْمَوْتَ وَيُرْسِلُ الْأُخْرَىٰ
إِلَىٰ أَجَلٍ مُّسَمًّى إِنَّ فِي ذَٰلِكَ لَآيَاتٍ لِّقَوْمٍ يَتَفَكَّرُونَ ﴿٤٢﴾ أَمِ اتَّخَذُوا
مِن دُونِ اللَّهِ شُفَعَاءَ قُلْ أَوَلَوْ كَانُوا لَا يَمْلِكُونَ شَيْئًا
وَلَا يَعْقِلُونَ ﴿٤٣﴾ قُل لِّلَّهِ الشَّفَاعَةُ جَمِيعًا لَّهُ مُلْكُ
السَّمٰوَاتِ وَالْأَرْضِ ثُمَّ إِلَيْهِ تُرْجَعُونَ ﴿٤٤﴾
وَإِذَا ذُكِرَ اللَّهُ وَحْدَهُ اشْمَأَزَّتْ قُلُوبُ الَّذِينَ لَا يُؤْمِنُونَ
بِالْآخِرَةِ وَإِذَا ذُكِرَ الَّذِينَ مِن دُونِهِ إِذَا هُمْ يَسْتَبْشِرُونَ
﴿٤٥﴾ قُلِ اللَّهُمَّ فَاطِرَ السَّمٰوَاتِ وَالْأَرْضِ عَالِمَ الْغَيْبِ
وَالشَّهَادَةِ أَنتَ تَحْكُمُ بَيْنَ عِبَادِكَ فِيمَا كَانُوا
فِيهِ يَخْتَلِفُونَ ﴿٤٦﴾ وَلَوْ أَنَّ لِلَّذِينَ ظَلَمُوا مَا فِي الْأَرْضِ
جَمِيعًا وَمِثْلَهُ مَعَهُ لَافْتَدَوْا بِهِ مِن سُوءِ الْعَذَابِ يَوْمَ
الْقِيٰمَةِ وَبَدَا لَهُم مِّنَ اللَّهِ مَا لَمْ يَكُونُوا يَحْتَسِبُونَ ﴿٤٧﴾

وَبَدَا لَهُمْ سَيِّئَاتُ مَا كَسَبُوا وَحَاقَ بِهِم مَّا كَانُوا بِهِ يَسْتَهْزِئُونَ
﴿٤٨﴾ فَإِذَا مَسَّ الْإِنسَانَ ضُرٌّ دَعَانَا ثُمَّ إِذَا خَوَّلْنَاهُ نِعْمَةً
مِّنَّا قَالَ إِنَّمَا أُوتِيتُهُ عَلَىٰ عِلْمٍ بَلْ هِيَ فِتْنَةٌ وَلَٰكِنَّ أَكْثَرَهُمْ
لَا يَعْلَمُونَ ﴿٤٩﴾ قَدْ قَالَهَا الَّذِينَ مِن قَبْلِهِمْ فَمَا أَغْنَىٰ عَنْهُم
مَّا كَانُوا يَكْسِبُونَ ﴿٥٠﴾ فَأَصَابَهُمْ سَيِّئَاتُ مَا كَسَبُوا وَالَّذِينَ ظَلَمُوا
مِنْ هَٰؤُلَاءِ سَيُصِيبُهُمْ سَيِّئَاتُ مَا كَسَبُوا وَمَا هُم بِمُعْجِزِينَ ﴿٥١﴾
أَوَلَمْ يَعْلَمُوا أَنَّ اللَّهَ يَبْسُطُ الرِّزْقَ لِمَن يَشَاءُ وَيَقْدِرُ
إِنَّ فِي ذَٰلِكَ لَآيَاتٍ لِّقَوْمٍ يُؤْمِنُونَ ﴿٥٢﴾ قُلْ يَا عِبَادِيَ الَّذِينَ
أَسْرَفُوا عَلَىٰ أَنفُسِهِمْ لَا تَقْنَطُوا مِن رَّحْمَةِ اللَّهِ إِنَّ اللَّهَ
يَغْفِرُ الذُّنُوبَ جَمِيعًا إِنَّهُ هُوَ الْغَفُورُ الرَّحِيمُ ﴿٥٣﴾
وَأَنِيبُوا إِلَىٰ رَبِّكُمْ وَأَسْلِمُوا لَهُ مِن قَبْلِ أَن يَأْتِيَكُمُ
الْعَذَابُ ثُمَّ لَا تُنصَرُونَ ﴿٥٤﴾ وَاتَّبِعُوا أَحْسَنَ مَا أُنزِلَ
إِلَيْكُم مِّن رَّبِّكُم مِّن قَبْلِ أَن يَأْتِيَكُمُ الْعَذَابُ بَغْتَةً
وَأَنتُمْ لَا تَشْعُرُونَ ﴿٥٥﴾ أَن تَقُولَ نَفْسٌ يَا حَسْرَتَىٰ عَلَىٰ
مَا فَرَّطتُ فِي جَنبِ اللَّهِ وَإِن كُنتُ لَمِنَ السَّاخِرِينَ ﴿٥٦﴾

AND THE evil of their deeds 39:48
will manifest itself to them, and that which they derided will encompass them.

And when evil befalls man he calls out to Us; but when, instead, We vouchsafe him a favour from Ourself, he says: 'It is my due.' By no means! It is but a test: yet most of them do not know it.

The same was said by those before them: but they gained nothing from what they did, and the very evil of their deeds recoiled upon them.

And the wrongdoers among these[1] shall also have the evil of their deeds recoil upon them: nor shall they ever be immune.

Do they not know that God gives abundantly to whom He will, and sparingly also? Surely in this there are signs for true believers.

Say: 'You that serve Me, who have sinned against your souls, do not des- 39:53
pair of God's mercy; assuredly God forgives all sins. He it is who is the Forgiving One, the Compassionate. Turn in penitence to your Lord, and submit to Him before the scourge overtakes you; for then there will be none to help you. Follow the best of what is revealed to you by your Lord before
the scourge suddenly smites you, when you are unaware; lest any soul should 39:56
say: "Alas! I neglected my duty to God and scoffed with the scoffers."

1. The Meccans.

39:57 OR SHOULD say: "If God had
guided me I would have feared
Him." Or should say, when it
sees the scourge: "Could I but
live again, I would lead a righteous life."
'"Yes, indeed. My revela-
tions did come to you; but you
denied them. You were arrogant and a blasphemer."'
And on the Day of Resur-
rection you shall see their faces
blackened, those who uttered
falsehoods about God. Is there
not in Hell a resting-place for
the arrogant?
But God will deliver those
who fear Him, for they have
earned salvation. Evil shall not
strike them, nor shall they ever
grieve.
God is the Creator of all
things, and of all things He is
39:63 the Guardian. His are the keys of the heavens and the earth. And those that
deny God's revelations will surely be lost.
Say: 'Would you bid me serve a deity other than God, you ignorant people?'
You have been warned, you and those who have gone before you, that if
you worship other deities besides God, your works will come to nothing and
you will surely be among the lost. Therefore serve God and render thanks.
39:67 They underrate the might of God. But on the Day of Resurrection He
will hold the entire earth in His grasp and fold up the heavens in His right
hand. Glory be to Him! Exalted be He above their idols!

أو تقول لو أن الله هدىني لكنت من المتقين ٥٧ أو تقول
حين ترى العذاب لو أن لي كرة فأكون من المحسنين
٥٨ بلى قد جاءتك آياتي فكذبت بها واستكبرت
وكنت من الكافرين ٥٩ ويوم القيمة ترى الذين كذبوا على
الله وجوههم مسودة أليس في جهنم مثوى للمتكبرين ٦٠ وينجي
الله الذين اتقوا بمفازتهم لا يمسهم السوء ولا هم
يحزنون ٦١ الله خالق كل شيء وهو على كل شيء وكيل
٦٢ له مقاليد السموات والأرض والذين كفروا بآيات
الله أولئك هم الخاسرون ٦٣ قل أفغير الله
تأمروني أعبد أيها الجاهلون ٦٤ ولقد أوحي
إليك وإلى الذين من قبلك لئن أشركت
ليحبطن عملك ولتكونن من الخاسرين ٦٥ بل الله
فاعبد وكن من الشاكرين ٦٦ وما قدروا الله
حق قدره والأرض جميعا قبضته يوم القيمة والسموات
مطويات بيمينه سبحانه وتعالى عما يشركون ٦٧

وَنُفِخَ فِي الصُّورِ فَصَعِقَ مَنْ فِي السَّمٰوَاتِ وَمَنْ فِي الْأَرْضِ
إِلَّا مَنْ شَاءَ اللّٰهُ ثُمَّ نُفِخَ فِيهِ أُخْرَىٰ فَإِذَا هُمْ قِيَامٌ
يَنْظُرُونَ ﴿٦٨﴾ وَأَشْرَقَتِ الْأَرْضُ بِنُورِ رَبِّهَا وَوُضِعَ
الْكِتَابُ وَجِيءَ بِالنَّبِيِّينَ وَالشُّهَدَاءِ وَقُضِيَ بَيْنَهُمْ بِالْحَقِّ
وَهُمْ لَا يُظْلَمُونَ ﴿٦٩﴾ وَوُفِّيَتْ كُلُّ نَفْسٍ مَا عَمِلَتْ وَهُوَ
أَعْلَمُ بِمَا يَفْعَلُونَ ﴿٧٠﴾ وَسِيقَ الَّذِينَ كَفَرُوا إِلَىٰ جَهَنَّمَ
زُمَرًا حَتَّىٰ إِذَا جَاءُوهَا فُتِحَتْ أَبْوَابُهَا وَقَالَ لَهُمْ خَزَنَتُهَا
أَلَمْ يَأْتِكُمْ رُسُلٌ مِنْكُمْ يَتْلُونَ عَلَيْكُمْ آيَاتِ رَبِّكُمْ وَيُنْذِرُونَكُمْ
لِقَاءَ يَوْمِكُمْ هَٰذَا قَالُوا بَلَىٰ وَلَٰكِنْ حَقَّتْ كَلِمَةُ الْعَذَابِ
عَلَى الْكَافِرِينَ ﴿٧١﴾ قِيلَ ادْخُلُوا أَبْوَابَ جَهَنَّمَ خَالِدِينَ فِيهَا فَبِئْسَ
مَثْوَى الْمُتَكَبِّرِينَ ﴿٧٢﴾ وَسِيقَ الَّذِينَ اتَّقَوْا رَبَّهُمْ إِلَى الْجَنَّةِ
زُمَرًا حَتَّىٰ إِذَا جَاءُوهَا وَفُتِحَتْ أَبْوَابُهَا وَقَالَ لَهُمْ خَزَنَتُهَا
سَلَامٌ عَلَيْكُمْ طِبْتُمْ فَادْخُلُوهَا خَالِدِينَ ﴿٧٣﴾
وَقَالُوا الْحَمْدُ لِلّٰهِ الَّذِي صَدَقَنَا وَعْدَهُ وَأَوْرَثَنَا الْأَرْضَ
نَتَبَوَّأُ مِنَ الْجَنَّةِ حَيْثُ نَشَاءُ فَنِعْمَ أَجْرُ الْعَامِلِينَ ﴿٧٤﴾

AND THE Trumpet shall be 39:68
blown, and all who are in the
heavens and on earth shall fall
down in shock, except those
that shall be spared by God.
Then the Trumpet will be blown
again, and lo! they shall rise and
gaze around them. The earth
will shine with the light of her
Lord, and the Book will be laid
open. The prophets and the witnesses shall be brought in, and
all shall be judged with fairness:
none shall be wronged. Every
soul shall be recompensed
according to its deeds, for He
best knows all that they did.

And in throngs the un- 39:71
believers shall be led to Hell.
When they draw near, its gates
will be opened, and its keepers
will say to them: 'Did there not
come to you apostles of your
own who proclaimed to you the revelations of your Lord and forewarned
you of this day?'

'Yes,' they will say. And thus the promised scourge will smite the unbelievers. They will be told: 'Enter the gates of Hell and stay therein for ever.' Evil
is the dwelling-place of the arrogant.

And in throngs those who fear their Lord shall be led to Paradise. When
they draw near, its gates will be opened, and its keepers will say to them:
'Peace be to you; you have led good lives. Enter Paradise and abide therein
for ever.'

And they will say: 'Praise be to God who has made good to us His prom- 39:74
ise and given us the earth to inherit, that we may dwell in Paradise wherever
we please.' Blessed is the reward of the righteous.

39:75 AND YOU shall behold the
angels circling about the Throne,
giving glory to their Lord. They
shall be judged with fairness,
and all shall say: 'Praise be to
God, Lord of the Universe!'

THE BELIEVER[1]

In the Name of God,
the Merciful, the Compassionate

40:1 *Ḥā' mīm.* The revelation of
the Book is from God, the
Mighty One, the All-knowing,
who forgives sin and accepts
repentance; whose punish-
ment is stern, and bounty
infinite. There is no god but
Him. All shall return to Him.

وَتَرَى الْمَلَائِكَةَ حَافِّينَ مِنْ حَوْلِ الْعَرْشِ يُسَبِّحُونَ بِحَمْدِ
رَبِّهِمْ وَقُضِيَ بَيْنَهُمْ بِالْحَقِّ وَقِيلَ الْحَمْدُ لِلَّهِ رَبِّ الْعَالَمِينَ ﴿٧٥﴾

سورة المؤمن مكية وهي خمس وثمانون آية

بِسْمِ اللَّهِ الرَّحْمَٰنِ الرَّحِيمِ
حم ﴿١﴾ تَنْزِيلُ الْكِتَابِ مِنَ اللَّهِ الْعَزِيزِ الْعَلِيمِ ﴿٢﴾ غَافِرِ الذَّنْبِ وَقَابِلِ
التَّوْبِ شَدِيدِ الْعِقَابِ ذِي الطَّوْلِ لَا إِلَٰهَ إِلَّا هُوَ إِلَيْهِ الْمَصِيرُ ﴿٣﴾
مَا يُجَادِلُ فِي آيَاتِ اللَّهِ إِلَّا الَّذِينَ كَفَرُوا فَلَا يَغْرُرْكَ تَقَلُّبُهُمْ
فِي الْبِلَادِ ﴿٤﴾ كَذَّبَتْ قَبْلَهُمْ قَوْمُ نُوحٍ وَالْأَحْزَابُ مِنْ بَعْدِهِمْ وَهَمَّتْ
كُلُّ أُمَّةٍ بِرَسُولِهِمْ لِيَأْخُذُوهُ وَجَادَلُوا بِالْبَاطِلِ لِيُدْحِضُوا
بِهِ الْحَقَّ فَأَخَذْتُهُمْ فَكَيْفَ كَانَ عِقَابِ ﴿٥﴾ وَكَذَٰلِكَ حَقَّتْ كَلِمَتُ
رَبِّكَ عَلَى الَّذِينَ كَفَرُوا أَنَّهُمْ أَصْحَابُ النَّارِ ﴿٦﴾ الَّذِينَ يَحْمِلُونَ
الْعَرْشَ وَمَنْ حَوْلَهُ يُسَبِّحُونَ بِحَمْدِ رَبِّهِمْ وَيُؤْمِنُونَ بِهِ
وَيَسْتَغْفِرُونَ لِلَّذِينَ آمَنُوا رَبَّنَا وَسِعْتَ كُلَّ شَيْءٍ رَحْمَةً وَعِلْمًا
فَاغْفِرْ لِلَّذِينَ تَابُوا وَاتَّبَعُوا سَبِيلَكَ وَقِهِمْ عَذَابَ الْجَحِيمِ ﴿٧﴾

None but unbelievers dispute God's revelations. Do not be deceived by their prosperous dealings in the land. Before them Noah's people also disbelieved, and so did the factions after them. Each community strove to lay hands on their apostle, seeking with false arguments to refute the Truth; but I smote them, and how stern was My retribution! Thus shall your Lord's judgement be passed on the unbelievers: they are assuredly the inmates of the Fire.

40:7 Those who bear the Throne and those who stand around it give glory to
their Lord and believe in Him. They implore forgiveness for the faithful, saying: 'Lord, You embrace all things with Your mercy and Your knowledge.
Forgive those that have repented and followed Your path. Shield them from
the scourge of Hell.

1. This *sūrah* is also known by another title: 'The Forgiving One'.

رَبَّنَا وَأَدْخِلْهُمْ جَنَّاتِ عَدْنٍ الَّتِي وَعَدْتَهُمْ وَمَنْ صَلَحَ
مِنْ آبَائِهِمْ وَأَزْوَاجِهِمْ وَذُرِّيَّاتِهِمْ إِنَّكَ أَنْتَ الْعَزِيزُ
الْحَكِيمُ ﴿٨﴾ وَقِهِمُ السَّيِّئَاتِ وَمَنْ تَقِ السَّيِّئَاتِ يَوْمَئِذٍ
فَقَدْ رَحِمْتَهُ وَذَٰلِكَ هُوَ الْفَوْزُ الْعَظِيمُ ﴿٩﴾ إِنَّ
الَّذِينَ كَفَرُوا يُنَادَوْنَ لَمَقْتُ اللَّهِ أَكْبَرُ مِنْ مَقْتِكُمْ
أَنْفُسَكُمْ إِذْ تُدْعَوْنَ إِلَى الْإِيمَانِ فَتَكْفُرُونَ ﴿١٠﴾ قَالُوا
رَبَّنَا أَمَتَّنَا اثْنَتَيْنِ وَأَحْيَيْتَنَا اثْنَتَيْنِ فَاعْتَرَفْنَا
بِذُنُوبِنَا فَهَلْ إِلَىٰ خُرُوجٍ مِنْ سَبِيلٍ ﴿١١﴾ ذَٰلِكُمْ بِأَنَّهُ إِذَا دُعِيَ
اللَّهُ وَحْدَهُ كَفَرْتُمْ وَإِنْ يُشْرَكْ بِهِ تُؤْمِنُوا فَالْحُكْمُ
لِلَّهِ الْعَلِيِّ الْكَبِيرِ ﴿١٢﴾ هُوَ الَّذِي يُرِيكُمْ آيَاتِهِ وَيُنَزِّلُ
لَكُمْ مِنَ السَّمَاءِ رِزْقًا وَمَا يَتَذَكَّرُ إِلَّا مَنْ يُنِيبُ ﴿١٣﴾ فَادْعُوا
اللَّهَ مُخْلِصِينَ لَهُ الدِّينَ وَلَوْ كَرِهَ الْكَافِرُونَ ﴿١٤﴾ رَفِيعُ الدَّرَجَاتِ
ذُو الْعَرْشِ يُلْقِي الرُّوحَ مِنْ أَمْرِهِ عَلَىٰ مَنْ يَشَاءُ مِنْ عِبَادِهِ
لِيُنْذِرَ يَوْمَ التَّلَاقِ ﴿١٥﴾ يَوْمَ هُمْ بَارِزُونَ لَا يَخْفَىٰ عَلَى
اللَّهِ مِنْهُمْ شَيْءٌ لِمَنِ الْمُلْكُ الْيَوْمَ لِلَّهِ الْوَاحِدِ الْقَهَّارِ ﴿١٦﴾

ADMIT THEM, Lord, into the 40:8
Gardens of Eden which You
have promised them, together
with all the righteous among
their forefathers, their spouses,
and their descendants. You are
the Mighty One, the Wise
One. Shield them from all evil;
he whom You shield from evil
on that day will surely earn
Your mercy. That is the
supreme triumph.'

To the unbelievers a voice
will call: 'God's abhorrence of
you is greater than your abhor-
ence of yourselves. You were
called to the Faith, but you
denied it.'

They shall say: 'Lord, twice
You made us die, and twice You
gave us life. We now confess
our sins. Is there no way out?'

'This is because when God 40:12
was invoked alone, you disbelieved; but when bidden to serve other gods
besides Him you did believe. Today judgement rests with God, the Most
High, the Supreme One.'

It is He who reveals His signs to you, and sends down sustenance from
the sky for you. Yet none takes thought except the repentant. Pray, then, to
God and consecrate your religion to Him, however much the unbelievers
may dislike it.

Exalted and throned on high, He lets the Spirit descend at His behest on
those of His servants whom He chooses, that He may warn them of the day
when they shall meet Him; the day when they shall rise up from their graves 40:16
with nothing hidden from God. And who shall reign supreme on that day?
God, the One, who vanquishes all.

40:17 On that day every soul
shall be recompensed according to what it did; on that day
none shall be wronged. Swift
is God's reckoning.
Forewarn them of the
approaching day, when men's
hearts will leap up to their
throats and choke them; when
the wrongdoers will have neither friend nor intercessor to
be listened to. He knows the
furtive look and the hidden
thought. God will judge with
fairness, but the idols to which
they pray besides Him can
judge nothing. Surely God
alone hears all and observes all.
40:21 Have they never journeyed
through the land and seen
what was the fate of those
who have gone before them,
far greater in prowess? God
smote them for their sins, and from God they had no protector. That was
because their apostles had come to them with veritable signs and they disbelieved. So God smote them. Mighty is God, and stern His retribution.
We sent forth Moses with Our signs and with veritable authority to Pharaoh, Haman, and Korah. But they said: 'A sorcerer, a teller of lies.'
40:25 And when he brought them the Truth from Ourself, they said: 'Put to
death the sons of those who share his faith, and spare only their daughters.'
Futile were the schemes of the unbelievers.

اليوم تجزى كل نفس بما كسبت لا ظلم اليوم إن الله
سريع الحساب ﴿١٧﴾ وأنذرهم يوم الآزفة إذ القلوب
لدى الحناجر كاظمين ما للظالمين من حميم ولا شفيع
يطاع ﴿١٨﴾ يعلم خائنة الأعين وما تخفي الصدور ﴿١٩﴾ والله
يقضي بالحق والذين يدعون من دونه لا يقضون بشيء إن الله
هو السميع البصير ﴿٢٠﴾ أولم يسيروا في الأرض فينظروا
كيف كان عاقبة الذين كانوا من قبلهم كانوا هم
أشد منهم قوة وآثارا في الأرض فأخذهم الله
بذنوبهم وما كان لهم من الله من واق ﴿٢١﴾ ذلك بأنهم
كانت تأتيهم رسلهم بالبينات فكفروا فأخذهم الله
إنه قوي شديد العقاب ﴿٢٢﴾ ولقد أرسلنا موسى
بآياتنا وسلطان مبين ﴿٢٣﴾ إلى فرعون وهامان وقارون
فقالوا ساحر كذاب ﴿٢٤﴾ فلما جاءهم بالحق من
عندنا قالوا اقتلوا أبناء الذين آمنوا معه واستحيوا
نساءهم وما كيد الكافرين إلا في ضلال ﴿٢٥﴾

وَقَالَ فِرْعَوْنُ ذَرُونِىٓ أَقْتُلْ مُوسَىٰ وَلْيَدْعُ رَبَّهُۥٓ إِنِّىٓ أَخَافُ
أَن يُبَدِّلَ دِينَكُمْ أَوْ أَن يُظْهِرَ فِى ٱلْأَرْضِ ٱلْفَسَادَ ﴿٢٦﴾ وَقَالَ
مُوسَىٰٓ إِنِّى عُذْتُ بِرَبِّى وَرَبِّكُم مِّن كُلِّ مُتَكَبِّرٍ لَّا يُؤْمِنُ بِيَوْمِ
ٱلْحِسَابِ ﴿٢٧﴾ وَقَالَ رَجُلٌ مُّؤْمِنٌ مِّنْ ءَالِ فِرْعَوْنَ يَكْتُمُ إِيمَٰنَهُۥٓ
أَتَقْتُلُونَ رَجُلًا أَن يَقُولَ رَبِّىَ ٱللَّهُ وَقَدْ جَآءَكُم بِٱلْبَيِّنَٰتِ
مِن رَّبِّكُمْ وَإِن يَكُ كَٰذِبًا فَعَلَيْهِ كَذِبُهُۥ وَإِن يَكُ صَادِقًا
يُصِبْكُم بَعْضُ ٱلَّذِى يَعِدُكُمْ إِنَّ ٱللَّهَ لَا يَهْدِى مَنْ هُوَ
مُسْرِفٌ كَذَّابٌ ﴿٢٨﴾ يَٰقَوْمِ لَكُمُ ٱلْمُلْكُ ٱلْيَوْمَ ظَٰهِرِينَ
فِى ٱلْأَرْضِ فَمَن يَنصُرُنَا مِنۢ بَأْسِ ٱللَّهِ إِن جَآءَنَا قَالَ فِرْعَوْنُ
مَآ أُرِيكُمْ إِلَّا مَآ أَرَىٰ وَمَآ أَهْدِيكُمْ إِلَّا سَبِيلَ ٱلرَّشَادِ ﴿٢٩﴾
وَقَالَ ٱلَّذِىٓ ءَامَنَ يَٰقَوْمِ إِنِّىٓ أَخَافُ عَلَيْكُم مِّثْلَ يَوْمِ ٱلْأَحْزَابِ
﴿٣٠﴾ مِثْلَ دَأْبِ قَوْمِ نُوحٍ وَعَادٍ وَثَمُودَ وَٱلَّذِينَ مِنۢ بَعْدِهِمْ
وَمَا ٱللَّهُ يُرِيدُ ظُلْمًا لِّلْعِبَادِ ﴿٣١﴾ وَيَٰقَوْمِ إِنِّىٓ أَخَافُ
عَلَيْكُمْ يَوْمَ ٱلتَّنَادِ ﴿٣٢﴾ يَوْمَ تُوَلُّونَ مُدْبِرِينَ مَا لَكُم
مِّنَ ٱللَّهِ مِنْ عَاصِمٍ وَمَن يُضْلِلِ ٱللَّهُ فَمَا لَهُۥ مِنْ هَادٍ ﴿٣٣﴾

AND PHARAOH said: 'Let 40:26
me kill Moses, and then let
him invoke his god! I fear that
he will change your religion
and spread disorder in the
land.'

Moses said: 'I take refuge in
my Lord and your Lord from
every tyrant who denies the
Day of Reckoning.'

And one of Pharaoh's kin,
who in secret was a true
believer, said: 'Would you kill a
man merely because he says:
"My Lord is God"? He has
brought you veritable signs
from your Lord. If he is lying,
may his lie be on his head; but
if he is speaking the truth,
some of what he threatens
you with will smite you. God
does not guide a lying transgressor. Today you are the 40:29
masters, my people, illustrious throughout the land. But who will save us
from the might of God when it bears down upon us?'

Pharaoh said: 'I have told you what I think. I will surely guide you to the
right path.'

And he who was a true believer said: 'I warn you, my people, against the
fate which overtook the factions: the people of Noah, 'Ād, and Thamūd, and
those that came after them. God does not seek to wrong His servants.

'I warn you, my people, against the day when you will cry out to one
another, the day when you will turn and flee, with none to defend you against 40:33
God. And he whom God confounds will have none to guide him.

40:34 BEFORE THIS, Joseph came to
you with veritable signs, but
you never ceased to doubt
them; and when he died you
said: "After him God will never
send another apostle." Thus
God confounds the doubting
transgressor. Those who dispute God's revelations, with
no authority vouchsafed to
them, are held in deep abhorrence by God and by the
faithful. Thus God seals up
the heart of every scornful
tyrant.'
And Pharaoh said: 'Haman,
build me a tower that I may
40:37 reach the highways – the very
highways – of the heavens,
and look upon the god of
Moses. I am convinced that he
is lying.'
Thus was Pharaoh seduced
by his foul deeds and was turned away from the right path; Pharaoh's cunning led only to perdition.
And he who was a true believer said: 'Follow me, my people, and I shall
guide you to the right path. My people, the life of this world is but a fleeting
40:40 pleasure; the life to come is the everlasting mansion. Those that do evil shall
be rewarded with like evil; but those that have faith and do good works, be
they men or women, shall enter Paradise and therein receive blessings without number.

ولقد جاءكم يوسف من قبل بالبينات فما زلتم في شك
مما جاءكم به حتى إذا هلك قلتم لن يبعث الله من بعده
رسولا كذلك يضل الله من هو مسرف مرتاب (٣٤) الذين
يجادلون في آيات الله بغير سلطان أتاهم كبر مقتا
عند الله وعند الذين آمنوا كذلك يطبع الله على كل
قلب متكبر جبار (٣٥) وقال فرعون يا هامان ابن لي
صرحا لعلي أبلغ الأسباب (٣٦) أسباب السموات فأطلع
إلى إله موسى وإني لأظنه كاذبا وكذلك زين
لفرعون سوء عمله وصد عن السبيل وما كيد
فرعون إلا في تباب (٣٧) وقال الذي آمن يا قوم
اتبعون أهدكم سبيل الرشاد (٣٨) يا قوم إنما
هذه الحيوة الدنيا متاع وإن الآخرة هي دار
القرار (٣٩) من عمل سيئة فلا يجزى إلا مثلها ومن
عمل صالحا من ذكر أو أنثى وهو مؤمن فأولئك
يدخلون الجنة يرزقون فيها بغير حساب (٤٠)

ويا قوم ما لي أدعوكم إلى النجاة وتدعونني إلى النار
﴿٤١﴾ تدعونني لأكفر بالله وأشرك به ما ليس لي به
علم وأنا أدعوكم إلى العزيز الغفار ﴿٤٢﴾ لا جرم
أنما تدعونني إليه ليس له دعوة في الدنيا ولا في
الآخرة وأن مردنا إلى الله وأن المسرفين هم أصحاب
النار ﴿٤٣﴾ فستذكرون ما أقول لكم وأفوض
أمري إلى الله إن الله بصير بالعباد ﴿٤٤﴾ فوقاه الله
سيئات ما مكروا وحاق بآل فرعون سوء العذاب
﴿٤٥﴾ النار يعرضون عليها غدوا وعشيا ويوم تقوم
الساعة أدخلوا آل فرعون أشد العذاب ﴿٤٦﴾ وإذ يتحاجون
في النار فيقول الضعفاء للذين استكبروا إنا
كنا لكم تبعا فهل أنتم مغنون عنا نصيبا من
النار ﴿٤٧﴾ قال الذين استكبروا إنا كل فيها إن الله
قد حكم بين العباد ﴿٤٨﴾ وقال الذين في النار لخزنة جهنم
ادعوا ربكم يخفف عنا يوما من العذاب ﴿٤٩﴾

'MY PEOPLE, how is it that I 40:41
call you to salvation, and you
call me to the Fire? You bid me
deny God and serve other
gods I know nothing of; and I
call you to the Mighty One, the
Forgiving One. Indeed, the
gods to whom you call me can
be invoked neither in this
world nor in the world to
come. Our return shall be to
God. The transgressors shall
be the inmates of the Fire.

'Bear in mind what I have
told you. To God I commend
myself. God is cognizant of all
His servants.'

God delivered him from the 40:45
evils which they plotted, and a
grievous scourge encompassed
Pharaoh's people. To the Fire
they shall be exposed morning
and evening, and on the day
the Hour strikes, a voice will cry: 'Admit Pharaoh's people to the most grievous torment.'

And when they argue in the Fire, the humble will say to those who deemed
themselves mighty: 'We have been your followers: will you now ward off
from us some of the flames?' But those who deemed themselves mighty will
say: 'We are all in it now; God has judged His servants.'

And those in the Fire will say to the keepers of Hell: 'Implore your Lord 40:49
to relieve our torment for a single day!'

قالوا أولم تك تأتيكم رسلكم بالبينات قالوا بلى
قالوا فادعوا وما دعاء الكافرين إلا في ضلال ۝
إنا لننصر رسلنا والذين آمنوا في الحياة الدنيا ويوم
يقوم الأشهاد ۝ يوم لا ينفع الظالمين معذرتهم
ولهم اللعنة ولهم سوء الدار ۝ ولقد آتينا
موسى الهدى وأورثنا بني إسرائيل الكتاب ۝ هدى
وذكرى لأولي الألباب ۝ فاصبر إن وعد الله حق
واستغفر لذنبك وسبح بحمد ربك بالعشي
والإبكار ۝ إن الذين يجادلون في آيات الله بغير
سلطان أتاهم إن في صدورهم إلا كبر ما هم
ببالغيه فاستعذ بالله إنه هو السميع البصير ۝
لخلق السماوات والأرض أكبر من خلق الناس
ولكن أكثر الناس لا يعلمون ۝ وما
يستوي الأعمى والبصير والذين آمنوا وعملوا
الصالحات ولا المسيء قليلا ما تتذكرون ۝

40:50 THEY WILL say: 'But did
your apostles not come to you
with veritable signs?'
'Yes,' they will say. Their
keepers will say: 'Then offer
your prayers.' But vain shall
be the prayers of the un-
believers.
We will surely help Our
apostles and the true believers
both in this world and on the
day when the witnesses rise to
testify; the day when no excuse
avails the wrongdoers. The
Curse shall be their lot, and
theirs the evil abode.
We gave Moses Our guid-
ance and the Israelites the
Book to inherit: a guide and
an Admonition to those that
are of good sense possessed.
40:55 Therefore have patience;
God's promise is surely true.
Implore forgiveness for your sins, and celebrate the praise of your Lord
evening and morning.
As for those who dispute God's revelations, with no authority vouchsafed
to them, they nurture in their hearts ambitions they shall never attain. Therefore seek refuge in God; He it is who hears all and observes all.
Surely, the creation of the heavens and the earth is greater than the
creation of man; yet most have no knowledge.
40:58 The blind and the seeing are not equal, nor are the wicked the equals of
those that have faith and do good works. Yet do you seldom take thought.

إن الساعة لآتية لا ريب فيها ولكن أكثر الناس لا يؤمنون
٥٩ وقال ربكم ادعوني أستجب لكم إن الذين
يستكبرون عن عبادتي سيدخلون جهنم داخرين
٦٠ الله الذي جعل لكم الليل لتسكنوا فيه والنهار
مبصرا إن الله لذو فضل على الناس ولكن أكثر
الناس لا يشكرون ٦١ ذلكم الله ربكم خالق
كل شيء لا إله إلا هو فأنى تؤفكون ٦٢ كذلك
يؤفك الذين كانوا بآيات الله يجحدون
٦٣ الله الذي جعل لكم الأرض قرارا والسماء بناء
وصوركم فأحسن صوركم ورزقكم من الطيبات
ذلكم الله ربكم فتبارك الله رب العالمين ٦٤
هو الحي لا إله إلا هو فادعوه مخلصين له الدين
الحمد لله رب العالمين ٦٥ قل إني نهيت أن أعبد
الذين تدعون من دون الله لما جاءني البينات
من ربي وأمرت أن أسلم لرب العالمين ٦٦

THE HOUR is sure to come: 40:59
of this there is no doubt; yet
most do not believe.

And your Lord has said:
'Call on Me and I will answer
you. Those that disdain My
worship shall enter Hell in
abject humility.'

It was God who made for
you the night to rest in and the
day to give you light. God is
bountiful to people, yet the
larger part of the people do
not give thanks.

Such is God, your Lord, the
Creator of all things. There is
no god but Him. How then
are you led astray? Yet, even
thus, those who deny God's
revelations are led astray.

God it is who has made the 40:64
earth a dwelling-place for you,
and the sky a ceiling. He has
moulded your bodies into comely shapes and provided you with wholesome
things.

Such is God, your Lord. Blessed be God, Lord of the Universe.

He is the Living One; there is no god but Him. Pray to Him, then, consecrating your religion to Him. Praise be to God, Lord of the Universe!

Say: 'I am forbidden to serve your idols, now that veritable proofs have 40:66
come to me from my Lord. I am commanded to submit to the Lord of the
Universe.'

40:67 He it was who created you
from dust, then from a little
germ, and then from a clot of
blood.[1] He brings you out as
infants into the world; you reach
manhood, then decline into old
age though some of you die
young, that you may serve your
appointed term and perchance
grow in understanding.
He it is who ordains life and
death; if He decrees a thing,
He need only say: 'Be,' and it is.
Do you not see how those
who dispute God's revelations
are turned away from the right
path? Those who have denied
the Book and the message We
sent through Our apostles will
learn hereafter: when, with
shackles and chains round their
necks, they shall be dragged
through scalding water and then
burnt in the Fire.
40:73 Then they will be told: 'Where are the gods whom you have served besides
God?'
'They have forsaken us,' they will say. 'Indeed, they were nothing, those
gods to whom we prayed.' Thus God confounds the unbelievers.
And they will be told: 'That is because on earth you took delight in falsehoods, and led a wanton life. Enter the gates of Hell and stay therein for
ever. Evil is the home of the arrogant.'
40:77 Therefore have patience: God's promise is surely true. Whether We let
you[2] glimpse in some measure the scourge We promise them, or claim you
back before We smite them, to Us shall they be recalled.

هُوَ الَّذِي خَلَقَكُم مِّن تُرَابٍ ثُمَّ مِن نُّطْفَةٍ ثُمَّ مِنْ عَلَقَةٍ
ثُمَّ يُخْرِجُكُمْ طِفْلًا ثُمَّ لِتَبْلُغُوا أَشُدَّكُمْ ثُمَّ لِتَكُونُوا
شُيُوخًا وَمِنكُم مَّن يُتَوَفَّىٰ مِن قَبْلُ وَلِتَبْلُغُوا أَجَلًا
مُّسَمًّى وَلَعَلَّكُمْ تَعْقِلُونَ ٦٧ هُوَ الَّذِي يُحْيِي وَيُمِيتُ
فَإِذَا قَضَىٰ أَمْرًا فَإِنَّمَا يَقُولُ لَهُ كُن فَيَكُونُ ٦٨ أَلَمْ تَرَ
إِلَى الَّذِينَ يُجَادِلُونَ فِي آيَاتِ اللَّهِ أَنَّىٰ يُصْرَفُونَ ٦٩ الَّذِينَ
كَذَّبُوا بِالْكِتَابِ وَبِمَا أَرْسَلْنَا بِهِ رُسُلَنَا فَسَوْفَ
يَعْلَمُونَ ٧٠ إِذِ الْأَغْلَالُ فِي أَعْنَاقِهِمْ وَالسَّلَاسِلُ يُسْحَبُونَ
٧١ فِي الْحَمِيمِ ثُمَّ فِي النَّارِ يُسْجَرُونَ ٧٢ ثُمَّ قِيلَ لَهُمْ أَيْنَ مَا
كُنتُمْ تُشْرِكُونَ ٧٣ مِن دُونِ اللَّهِ قَالُوا ضَلُّوا عَنَّا بَل لَّمْ نَكُن
نَّدْعُو مِن قَبْلُ شَيْئًا كَذَٰلِكَ يُضِلُّ اللَّهُ الْكَافِرِينَ ٧٤ ذَٰلِكُم
بِمَا كُنتُمْ تَفْرَحُونَ فِي الْأَرْضِ بِغَيْرِ الْحَقِّ وَبِمَا كُنتُمْ تَمْرَحُونَ
٧٥ ادْخُلُوا أَبْوَابَ جَهَنَّمَ خَالِدِينَ فِيهَا فَبِئْسَ مَثْوَى
الْمُتَكَبِّرِينَ ٧٦ فَاصْبِرْ إِنَّ وَعْدَ اللَّهِ حَقٌّ فَإِمَّا نُرِيَنَّكَ بَعْضَ
الَّذِي نَعِدُهُمْ أَوْ نَتَوَفَّيَنَّكَ فَإِلَيْنَا يُرْجَعُونَ ٧٧

1. See p. 331, note 1. 2. Muḥammad.

ولقد أرسلنا رسلا من قبلك منهم من قصصنا عليك
ومنهم من لم نقصص عليك وما كان لرسول أن يأتي
بآية إلا بإذن الله فإذا جاء أمر الله قضي بالحق
وخسر هنالك المبطلون ٧٨ الله الذي جعل
لكم الأنعام لتركبوا منها ومنها تأكلون ٧٩ ولكم
فيها منافع ولتبلغوا عليها حاجة في صدوركم وعليها
وعلى الفلك تحملون ٨٠ ويريكم آياته فأي آيات الله
تنكرون ٨١ أفلم يسيروا في الأرض فينظروا كيف كان
عاقبة الذين من قبلهم كانوا أكثر منهم وأشد قوة
وآثارا في الأرض فما أغنى عنهم ما كانوا يكسبون ٨٢
فلما جاءتهم رسلهم بالبينات فرحوا بما عندهم من
العلم وحاق بهم ما كانوا به يستهزئون ٨٣ فلما رأوا
بأسنا قالوا آمنا بالله وحده وكفرنا بما كنا به مشركين
٨٤ فلم يك ينفعهم إيمانهم لما رأوا بأسنا سنت الله
التي قد خلت في عباده وخسر هنالك الكافرون ٨٥

WE SENT forth apostles 40:78
before you; of some We have
already told you, of others We
have not yet told you. None of
those apostles could bring a
sign except by God's leave.
And when God's will was
done, justice prevailed, and
there and then the deniers lost.

It is God who has provided
you with beasts, that you may
ride on some and eat the
flesh of others. You put them
to many uses; they take you
where you wish to go, carrying
you by land as ships carry you
by sea.

And He reveals to you His
signs. Which of God's signs
do you deny?

Have they never journeyed 40:82
through the land and seen
what was the fate of those
who have gone before them? They were more numerous than them, and far
greater in prowess and in splendour in the land; yet all their gains proved of
no avail to them.

When their apostles brought them veritable signs they proudly boasted of
their own knowledge; but soon the scourge they mocked encompassed
them. And when they beheld Our might they said: 'We now believe in God
alone. We deny the idols which we served besides Him.'

But their new faith was of no avail to them, when they beheld Our might: 40:85
such being the way of God with His creatures; and there and then the unbelievers lost.

WELL EXPOUNDED

In the Name of God,
the Merciful, the Compassionate

41:1 *Ḥā' mīm.* Sent down from the
Merciful, the Compassionate:
a Book of revelations well
expounded, an Arabic Koran
for those endowed with knowledge.

It proclaims joyful tidings
and a warning: yet most of
them turn their backs and hear
not. They say: 'Our hearts are
proof against that to which you
call us. Our ears are stopped,
and a veil stands between ourselves and you. Do as you will,
and so will we.'

سورة فصلت مكية وهي أربع وخمسون آية

بسم الله الرحمن الرحيم
حمٓ ۝١ تنزيل من الرحمن الرحيم ۝٢ كتاب فصلت آياته قرآنا عربيا
لقوم يعلمون ۝٣ بشيرا ونذيرا فأعرض أكثرهم فهم
لا يسمعون ۝٤ وقالوا قلوبنا في أكنة مما تدعونا إليه وفي
آذاننا وقر ومن بيننا وبينك حجاب فاعمل إننا عاملون ۝٥
قل إنما أنا بشر مثلكم يوحى إلي أنما إلهكم إله واحد فاستقيموا
إليه واستغفروه وويل للمشركين ۝٦ الذين لا يؤتون الزكاة
وهم بالآخرة هم كافرون ۝٧ إن الذين آمنوا وعملوا الصالحات
لهم أجر غير ممنون ۝٨ قل أئنكم لتكفرون بالذي خلق الأرض
في يومين وتجعلون له أندادا ذلك رب العالمين ۝٩ وجعل
فيها رواسي من فوقها وبارك فيها وقدر فيها أقواتها في أربعة
أيام سواء للسائلين ۝١٠ ثم استوى إلى السماء وهي دخان فقال
لها وللأرض ائتيا طوعا أو كرها قالتا أتينا طائعين ۝١١

Say: 'I am but a mortal like yourselves. It is revealed to me that your God
is one God. Therefore take the straight path to Him and implore His for-
41:7 giveness. Woe betide those who serve other gods besides Him; who give no
alms and disbelieve in the life to come. As for those who have faith and do
good works, an endless recompense awaits them.'

Say: 'Do you indeed disbelieve in Him who created the earth in two days?
And do you make other gods His equals? The Lord of the Universe is He.'

He set therein mountains towering high above it; He pronounced His
blessing upon it, and in four days provided it with sustenance for all alike.
41:11 Then, turning to the sky, which was but a cloud of vapour, He said to it and
to the earth: 'Come forward both, willingly or perforce.'

And they both said: 'Come we will, obediently.'

فقضاهن سبع سموات في يومين وأوحى في كل سماء أمرها
وزينا السماء الدنيا بمصابيح وحفظا ذلك تقدير العزيز
العليم ﴿١٢﴾ فإن أعرضوا فقل أنذرتكم صاعقة مثل صاعقة
عاد وثمود ﴿١٣﴾ إذ جاءتهم الرسل من بين أيديهم ومن خلفهم ألا
تعبدوا إلا الله قالوا لو شاء ربنا لأنزل ملئكة فإنا
بما أرسلتم به كافرون ﴿١٤﴾ فأما عاد فاستكبروا
في الأرض بغير الحق وقالوا من أشد منا قوة أولم
يروا أن الله الذي خلقهم هو أشد منهم قوة وكانوا
بآياتنا يجحدون ﴿١٥﴾ فأرسلنا عليهم ريحا صرصرا في أيام
نحسات لنذيقهم عذاب الخزي في الحيوة الدنيا ولعذاب الآخرة
أخزى وهم لا ينصرون ﴿١٦﴾ وأما ثمود فهدينهم فاستحبوا
العمى على الهدى فأخذتهم صاعقة العذاب الهون بما كانوا
يكسبون ﴿١٧﴾ ونجينا الذين آمنوا وكانوا يتقون ﴿١٨﴾ ويوم
يحشر أعداء الله إلى النار فهم يوزعون ﴿١٩﴾ حتى إذا ما جاءوها شهد
عليهم سمعهم وأبصارهم وجلودهم بما كانوا يعملون ﴿٢٠﴾

HE DECREED them to be 41:12
seven heavens in two days,
and to each heaven He
assigned its task. We decked
the lowest heaven with lamps
and guarded them. Such is the
design of the Mighty One, the
All-knowing.

If they pay no heed, say: 'I
have given you warning of a
thunderbolt, like the thunderbolt which struck 'Ād and
Thamūd. When apostles came
to them from before them
and from behind them, saying: "Serve none but God,"
they said: "Had it been our
Lord's will He would have
sent down angels. We will
never believe in your message."'

And as for 'Ād, they 41:15
conducted themselves with
arrogance in the land, without justice. 'Who is mightier than we?' they used
to say. Could they not see that God, who had created them, was mightier
than they? Yet they denied Our revelations.

So, over a few ill-omened days We let loose on them a howling gale, to
make them taste the scourge of shame in this nether life; but more shameful
still will be the scourge of the life to come. There shall be none to succour
them.

And as for Thamūd, We offered them Our guidance, but they preferred
blindness to guidance. Therefore the thunderbolt of a humiliating scourge
struck them for their misdeeds; and We delivered those who believed and
those who feared God.

Forewarn them of the day when God's enemies will be herded into the
Fire, so that when they are sorted out, their ears, their eyes, and their very 41:20
skins will testify to what they did.

41:21 And to their skins they will
say: 'Why did you testify against
us?' and their skins will say:
'God, who gives speech to all
things, has made us speak. It
was He who in the beginning
created you, and to Him shall
you be recalled. You did not
hide yourselves, so that your
ears and eyes and skins could
not be made to testify against
you; yet you thought that God
did not know much of what
you did. It was the thoughts
you entertained about your
Lord that ruined you, so that
you are now among the lost.'

If they persist, the Fire shall
be their home: and if they sue
for pardon, their suit shall not
be granted.

41:25 We have assigned to them
companions who make their
past and present seem fair and right to them. Well have they deserved the
fate of bygone races of jinn and humans. They shall assuredly be lost.

The unbelievers say: 'Do not listen to this Koran. Cut short its recital with
frivolous chatter, so that you may gain the upper hand.'

We will surely make the unbelievers taste grievous torment, and pay them
back for the worst of their misdeeds. Thus shall God's enemies be recompensed. The Fire shall for ever be their home, because they have denied Our
revelations.

41:29 And the unbelievers will say: 'Lord, show us those among the jinn and
humans who made us go astray. We will trample them under our feet and
make them the lowest of the low.'

وَقَالُوا لِجُلُودِهِمْ لِمَ شَهِدتُّمْ عَلَيْنَا قَالُوا أَنطَقَنَا اللَّهُ الَّذِي
أَنطَقَ كُلَّ شَيْءٍ وَهُوَ خَلَقَكُمْ أَوَّلَ مَرَّةٍ وَإِلَيْهِ تُرْجَعُونَ ٢١
وَمَا كُنتُمْ تَسْتَتِرُونَ أَن يَشْهَدَ عَلَيْكُمْ سَمْعُكُمْ وَلَا
أَبْصَارُكُمْ وَلَا جُلُودُكُمْ وَلَٰكِن ظَنَنتُمْ أَنَّ اللَّهَ لَا يَعْلَمُ
كَثِيرًا مِّمَّا تَعْمَلُونَ ٢٢ وَذَٰلِكُمْ ظَنُّكُمُ الَّذِي ظَنَنتُم بِرَبِّكُمْ
أَرْدَاكُمْ فَأَصْبَحْتُم مِّنَ الْخَاسِرِينَ ٢٣ فَإِن يَصْبِرُوا فَالنَّارُ مَثْوًى
لَّهُمْ وَإِن يَسْتَعْتِبُوا فَمَا هُم مِّنَ الْمُعْتَبِينَ ٢٤ وَقَيَّضْنَا لَهُمْ قُرَنَاءَ
فَزَيَّنُوا لَهُم مَّا بَيْنَ أَيْدِيهِمْ وَمَا خَلْفَهُمْ وَحَقَّ عَلَيْهِمُ الْقَوْلُ فِي
أُمَمٍ قَدْ خَلَتْ مِن قَبْلِهِم مِّنَ الْجِنِّ وَالْإِنسِ إِنَّهُمْ كَانُوا خَاسِرِينَ
٢٥ وَقَالَ الَّذِينَ كَفَرُوا لَا تَسْمَعُوا لِهَٰذَا الْقُرْآنِ وَالْغَوْا فِيهِ لَعَلَّكُمْ
تَغْلِبُونَ ٢٦ فَلَنُذِيقَنَّ الَّذِينَ كَفَرُوا عَذَابًا شَدِيدًا وَلَنَجْزِيَنَّهُمْ
أَسْوَأَ الَّذِي كَانُوا يَعْمَلُونَ ٢٧ ذَٰلِكَ جَزَاءُ أَعْدَاءِ اللَّهِ النَّارُ
لَهُمْ فِيهَا دَارُ الْخُلْدِ جَزَاءً بِمَا كَانُوا بِآيَاتِنَا يَجْحَدُونَ ٢٨
وَقَالَ الَّذِينَ كَفَرُوا رَبَّنَا أَرِنَا الَّذَيْنِ أَضَلَّانَا مِنَ الْجِنِّ
وَالْإِنسِ نَجْعَلْهُمَا تَحْتَ أَقْدَامِنَا لِيَكُونَا مِنَ الْأَسْفَلِينَ ٢٩

إن الذين قالوا ربنا الله ثم استقاموا تتنزل عليهم
الملائكة ألا تخافوا ولا تحزنوا وأبشروا بالجنة
التي كنتم توعدون ٣٠ نحن أولياؤكم في الحيوة
الدنيا وفي الآخرة ولكم فيها ما تشتهي أنفسكم
ولكم فيها ما تدعون ٣١ نزلا من غفور رحيم ٣٢ ومن
أحسن قولا ممن دعا إلى الله وعمل صالحا وقال إنني من
المسلمين ٣٣ ولا تستوي الحسنة ولا السيئة ادفع بالتي
هي أحسن فإذا الذي بينك وبينه عداوة كأنه ولي
حميم ٣٤ وما يلقيها إلا الذين صبروا وما يلقيها
إلا ذو حظ عظيم ٣٥ وإما ينزغنك من الشيطان
نزغ فاستعذ بالله إنه هو السميع العليم ٣٦ ومن
آياته الليل والنهار والشمس والقمر لا تسجدوا للشمس
ولا للقمر واسجدوا لله الذي خلقهن إن كنتم
إياه تعبدون ٣٧ فإن استكبروا فالذين عند ربك
يسبحون له بالليل والنهار وهم لا يسئمون ٣٨

As FOR those who say: 41:30
'Our Lord is God,' and then follow the straight path, the angels will descend upon them, saying: 'Fear not, and do not grieve. Rejoice in the Paradise you have been promised. We are your guardians in this world and in the world to come. Therein shall you have all that your souls desire and shall have all that you can ask for: a rich provision from a God forgiving and compassionate.'

And who speaks better than he who calls others to the worship of God, does what is right, and says: 'I am a Muslim'?

Good deeds and evil deeds are not equal. Requite evil with what is better and lo, he
who is your enemy now will become as if your intimate friend. But none will 41:35
attain this attribute save those who patiently endure; and none will attain it save those who are immensely fortunate.

If Satan tempts you, seek refuge in God. He it is who hears all and knows all.

Among His signs are the night and the day, and the sun and the moon. But do not prostrate yourselves before the sun or the moon; rather prostrate yourselves before God, who created them both, if you would truly serve Him.

If they[1] disdain His service, let them remember that those who dwell with 41:38
God give glory to Him night and day and are never wearied.

1. The pagans.

41:39 AND YET another of His signs is that you behold the earth humble and desolate: but when We send down the rain upon it, it stirs and swells. He that gives it life will surely raise the dead to life. He has power over all things.

Those that deny Our revelations are not hidden from Our view. Is he who is cast into the Fire better off than he who emerges safe on the Day of Resurrection? Do as you will, He observes whatever you do.

Those who deny the Admonition when it is preached to them – and surely it is a momentous Book: falsehood cannot reach it from before or from behind. It is a revelation from a wise and praiseworthy God.

ومن آياته أنك ترى الأرض خاشعة فإذا أنزلنا عليها
الماء اهتزت وربت إن الذي أحياها لمحي الموتى إنه على
كل شيء قدير ۝ إن الذين يلحدون في آياتنا لا يخفون علينا
أفمن يلقى في النار خير أم من يأتي آمنا يوم القيامة اعملوا
ما شئتم إنه بما تعملون بصير ۝ إن الذين كفروا بالذكر
لما جاءهم وإنه لكتاب عزيز ۝ لا يأتيه الباطل من بين
يديه ولا من خلفه تنزيل من حكيم حميد ۝ ما يقال لك
إلا ما قد قيل للرسل من قبلك إن ربك لذو مغفرة وذو
عقاب أليم ۝ ولو جعلناه قرآنا أعجميا لقالوا لولا فصلت
آياته أأعجمي وعربي قل هو للذين آمنوا هدى وشفاء
والذين لا يؤمنون في آذانهم وقر وهو عليهم عمى
أولئك ينادون من مكان بعيد ۝ ولقد آتينا
موسى الكتاب فاختلف فيه ولولا كلمة سبقت من
ربك لقضي بينهم وإنهم لفي شك منه مريب ۝ من عمل صالحا
فلنفسه ومن أساء فعليها وما ربك بظلام للعبيد ۝

Nothing is said to you that has not been said to other apostles before you. Your Lord is forgiving, but stern in retribution.

41:44 Had We revealed it a Koran in a foreign tongue they would have said: 'If only its verses were expounded! Why in a foreign tongue, and he an Arabian?'

Say: 'To true believers it is a guide and a healing balm. But those who deny it are deaf and blind: they are called to from a far-off place.'

We gave the Book to Moses, but contentions arose about it. And but for a Word from your Lord, long since decreed, judgement would have been passed among them; grave is their doubt about it.

41:46 He that does good does it for his own soul; and he that commits evil does so at his own peril. Never is your Lord unjust to mortals.

اليه يرد علم الساعة وما تخرج من ثمرات من اكمامها
وما تحمل من انثى ولا تضع الا بعلمه ويوم يناديهم
اين شركاءي قالوا اذنك ما منا من شهيد ﴿٤٧﴾ وضل
عنهم ما كانوا يدعون من قبل وظنوا ما لهم من محيص
﴿٤٨﴾ لا يسٔم الانسان من دعاء الخير وان مسه الشر فئوس
قنوط ﴿٤٩﴾ ولئن اذقناه رحمة منا من بعد ضراء مسته
ليقولن هذا لي وما اظن الساعة قائمة ولئن رجعت الى
ربي ان لي عنده للحسنى فلننبئن الذين كفروا بما عملوا
ولنذيقنهم من عذاب غليظ ﴿٥٠﴾ واذا انعمنا على الانسان
اعرض ونا بجانبه واذا مسه الشر فذو دعاء عريض ﴿٥١﴾ قل
ارءيتم ان كان من عند الله ثم كفرتم به من اضل ممن
هو في شقاق بعيد ﴿٥٢﴾ سنريهم ءاياتنا في الافاق
وفي انفسهم حتى يتبين لهم انه الحق اولم يكف
بربك انه على كل شيء شهيد ﴿٥٣﴾ الا انهم في
مرية من لقاء ربهم الا انه بكل شيء محيط ﴿٥٤﴾

He alone has knowledge 41:47
of the Hour. No fruits come
out of their pods, no female
conceives or is delivered, but
with His knowledge.

On the day He calls out to
them: 'Where are those
fellow-gods of Mine?' 'We
confess,' they will say, 'that
none of us can vouch for
them.' The idols to which they
prayed before will vanish from
them, and they shall learn
there is no escape.

Man never wearies of praying for good things. But when
evil befalls him he loses hope
and grows despondent. And 41:50
if after affliction We vouchsafe him a favour from
Ourself, he is sure to say: 'This
is my own. I do not think the
Hour will ever come. And
even if I do return to my Lord, He will surely reward me well.' We shall tell
the unbelievers what they did, and We will surely visit upon them a grievous
scourge.

When We show favour to man, he turns his back and holds aloof; but
when evil befalls him he is loud in prayer.

Say: 'Do but consider: if this Koran is indeed from God and you deny it,
who can err more than he who openly defies Him?'

We will show them Our signs across the horizons and in their own souls,
until they clearly see that it is the Truth. Does it not suffice that your Lord is
the witness of all things?

Yet they still doubt that they will ever meet their Lord. Yet surely He 41:54
encompasses all things.

COUNSEL

سورة الشورى مكية وهي ثلث وخمسون آية

بسم الله الرحمن الرحيم
حم ۝ عسق ۝ كذلك يوحي إليك وإلى الذين من قبلك الله
العزيز الحكيم ۝ له ما في السموات وما في الأرض وهو العلي
العظيم ۝ تكاد السموات يتفطرن من فوقهن والملئكة
يسبحون بحمد ربهم ويستغفرون لمن في الأرض ألا إن الله
هو الغفور الرحيم ۝ والذين اتخذوا من دونه أولياء الله
حفيظ عليهم وما أنت عليهم بوكيل ۝ وكذلك أوحينا إليك قرآنا
عربيا لتنذر أم القرى ومن حولها وتنذر يوم الجمع لا ريب فيه فريق
في الجنة وفريق في السعير ۝ ولو شاء الله لجعلهم أمة واحدة
ولكن يدخل من يشاء في رحمته والظالمون ما لهم من ولي ولا
نصير ۝ أم اتخذوا من دونه أولياء فالله هو الولي وهو يحيي الموتى
وهو على كل شيء قدير ۝ وما اختلفتم فيه من شيء فحكمه إلى الله
ذلكم الله ربي عليه توكلت وإليه أنيب ۝

In the Name of God,
the Merciful, the Compassionate

42:1 *Ḥā' mīm: 'ain sīn qāf.* Thus God, the Mighty One, the Wise One, inspires you as He inspired those before you.

His is what the heavens and the earth contain. And He is the Most High, the Almighty, the Supreme One.

The heavens above well-nigh split asunder as the angels give glory to their Lord and beg forgiveness for those on earth. Surely God is the Forgiving One, the Compassionate.

As for those that serve other masters besides Him, God Himself is watching them; you are not their keeper.

42:7 Thus have We revealed to you an Arabic Koran, that you may warn the mother-city[1] and those who dwell around it; that you may forewarn them of the day that shall indubitably come: when all are brought together, some in Paradise and some in the Conflagration.

Had it been God's will, He could have united them into one community. But God admits whom He will into His mercy; the wrongdoers have none to befriend or succour them.

Or have they set up other guardians besides Him? But surely it is God who is the Guardian. He resurrects the dead, and He has power over all things.

42:10 Whatever the subject of your disputes, the final word belongs to God. Such is God, my Lord: in Him I have put my trust, and to Him I turn in penitence.

1. Mecca.

فاطر السموات والأرض جعل لكم من أنفسكم أزواجا
ومن الأنعام أزواجا يذرؤكم فيه ليس كمثله شيء
وهو السميع البصير ﴿١١﴾ له مقاليد السموات والأرض
يبسط الرزق لمن يشاء ويقدر إنه بكل شيء عليم
﴿١٢﴾ شرع لكم من الدين ما وصى به نوحا والذي
أوحينا إليك وما وصينا به إبراهيم وموسى وعيسى
أن أقيموا الدين ولا تتفرقوا فيه كبر على المشركين
ما تدعوهم إليه الله يجتبي إليه من يشاء ويهدي إليه من
ينيب ﴿١٣﴾ وما تفرقوا إلا من بعد ما جاءهم العلم بغيا بينهم
ولولا كلمة سبقت من ربك إلى أجل مسمى لقضي بينهم وإن الذين
أورثوا الكتاب من بعدهم لفي شك منه مريب ﴿١٤﴾ فلذلك
فادع واستقم كما أمرت ولا تتبع أهواءهم وقل
آمنت بما أنزل الله من كتاب وأمرت لأعدل بينكم
الله ربنا وربكم لنا أعمالنا ولكم أعمالكم لا حجة
بيننا وبينكم الله يجمع بيننا وإليه المصير ﴿١٥﴾

CREATOR OF the heavens 42:11
and the earth, He has given
you spouses from among
yourselves, and cattle male and
female; it is thus that He multi-
plies you. Nothing can be
compared to Him. He alone
hears all and sees all.

His are the keys of the heavens and the earth. He gives
abundantly to whom He will,
and sparingly also. He has
knowledge of all things.

He has ordained for you
such religion as He enjoined
on Noah, which We have now
revealed to you; which We
enjoined on Abraham, Moses,
and Jesus: 'Observe the Religion and do not divide.' Hard
for the pagans is that to which
you call them. God chooses
for it whom He will, and
guides to it those that repent.

Yet they did not divide themselves, through their own wickedness, until 42:14
knowledge was given them. And but for a Word that had already gone forth
from your Lord reprieving them for an appointed term, judgement would
have surely been passed among them. And those who inherited the Book
after them have their grave doubts too.

Therefore preach and keep to the straight path as you are commanded. 42:15
Do not be led by their desires, but say: 'I believe in all the Scriptures that God
has revealed. I am commanded to exercise justice among you. God is our
Lord and your Lord. We have our works and you have your works; let there
be no argument between us. God will bring us all together, and to Him shall
be the final return.'

42:16 As FOR those who argue
about God after pledging
obedience to Him, their arguments will have no weight
with their Lord. Ire will fall
upon them, and grievous punishment awaits them.

God it is who has revealed
the Book with Truth and
Justice. And how do you
know? The Hour may be fast
approaching.

Those who deny it seek to
hurry it on; but the true believers dread its coming, and
know it is the Truth. Indeed,
those who doubt the Hour
have strayed far into error.

Benign is God towards His
servants; He is bountiful to
whom He will. He is the Invincible One, the Almighty.

42:20 Whoever seeks the harvest
of the world to come, to him We will give in great abundance; and whoever
desires the harvest of this world, a share of it shall We give him: but in the
world to come he shall have no share at all.

Have they idols which in the practice of their faith have made lawful to
them what God has not allowed? Had the Decisive Word not been pronounced already, judgement would have surely been passed among them.
Woeful punishment awaits the wrongdoers.

42:22 You shall behold the wrongdoers aghast at what they earned, which will
surely smite them. But those that have faith and do good works shall dwell
in the fair Gardens of Paradise, and shall receive in their Lord's presence all
that they desire. That will be the supreme grace.

والذين يحاجون في الله من بعد ما استجيب له
حجتهم داحضة عند ربهم وعليهم غضب ولهم
عذاب شديد ﴿١٦﴾ الله الذي أنزل الكتاب بالحق
والميزان وما يدريك لعل الساعة قريب ﴿١٧﴾ يستعجل
بها الذين لا يؤمنون بها والذين آمنوا مشفقون منها
ويعلمون أنها الحق ألا إن الذين يمارون في الساعة
لفي ضلال بعيد ﴿١٨﴾ الله لطيف بعباده يرزق من
يشاء وهو القوي العزيز ﴿١٩﴾ من كان يريد حرث الآخرة
نزد له في حرثه ومن كان يريد حرث الدنيا نؤته منها
وما له في الآخرة من نصيب ﴿٢٠﴾ أم لهم شركاء شرعوا لهم
من الدين ما لم يأذن به الله ولولا كلمة الفصل لقضي
بينهم وإن الظالمين لهم عذاب أليم ﴿٢١﴾ ترى الظالمين
مشفقين مما كسبوا وهو واقع بهم والذين
آمنوا وعملوا الصالحات في روضات الجنات
لهم ما يشاؤون عند ربهم ذلك هو الفضل الكبير ﴿٢٢﴾

ذَٰلِكَ الَّذِي يُبَشِّرُ اللَّهُ عِبَادَهُ الَّذِينَ آمَنُوا وَعَمِلُوا الصَّالِحَاتِ ۗ قُل
لَّا أَسْأَلُكُمْ عَلَيْهِ أَجْرًا إِلَّا الْمَوَدَّةَ فِي الْقُرْبَىٰ ۗ وَمَن يَقْتَرِفْ حَسَنَةً
نَّزِدْ لَهُ فِيهَا حُسْنًا ۚ إِنَّ اللَّهَ غَفُورٌ شَكُورٌ ﴿٢٣﴾ أَمْ يَقُولُونَ افْتَرَىٰ
عَلَى اللَّهِ كَذِبًا ۖ فَإِن يَشَإِ اللَّهُ يَخْتِمْ عَلَىٰ قَلْبِكَ ۗ
وَيَمْحُ اللَّهُ الْبَاطِلَ وَيُحِقُّ الْحَقَّ بِكَلِمَاتِهِ ۚ إِنَّهُ عَلِيمٌ بِذَاتِ
الصُّدُورِ ﴿٢٤﴾ وَهُوَ الَّذِي يَقْبَلُ التَّوْبَةَ عَنْ عِبَادِهِ وَيَعْفُو عَنِ
السَّيِّئَاتِ وَيَعْلَمُ مَا تَفْعَلُونَ ﴿٢٥﴾ وَيَسْتَجِيبُ الَّذِينَ آمَنُوا وَعَمِلُوا
الصَّالِحَاتِ وَيَزِيدُهُم مِّن فَضْلِهِ ۚ وَالْكَافِرُونَ لَهُمْ عَذَابٌ شَدِيدٌ
﴿٢٦﴾ وَلَوْ بَسَطَ اللَّهُ الرِّزْقَ لِعِبَادِهِ لَبَغَوْا فِي الْأَرْضِ وَلَٰكِن
يُنَزِّلُ بِقَدَرٍ مَّا يَشَاءُ ۚ إِنَّهُ بِعِبَادِهِ خَبِيرٌ بَصِيرٌ ﴿٢٧﴾ وَهُوَ الَّذِي
يُنَزِّلُ الْغَيْثَ مِن بَعْدِ مَا قَنَطُوا وَيَنشُرُ رَحْمَتَهُ ۚ وَهُوَ الْوَلِيُّ الْحَمِيدُ
﴿٢٨﴾ وَمِنْ آيَاتِهِ خَلْقُ السَّمَاوَاتِ وَالْأَرْضِ وَمَا بَثَّ فِيهِمَا مِن
دَابَّةٍ ۚ وَهُوَ عَلَىٰ جَمْعِهِمْ إِذَا يَشَاءُ قَدِيرٌ ﴿٢٩﴾ وَمَا أَصَابَكُم مِّن
مُّصِيبَةٍ فَبِمَا كَسَبَتْ أَيْدِيكُمْ وَيَعْفُو عَن كَثِيرٍ ﴿٣٠﴾ وَمَا أَنتُم بِمُعْجِزِينَ
فِي الْأَرْضِ ۖ وَمَا لَكُم مِّن دُونِ اللَّهِ مِن وَلِيٍّ وَلَا نَصِيرٍ ﴿٣١﴾

SUCH IS God's joyful 42:23
promise to His servants who believe and do good works. Say: 'For this I ask of you no recompense, except to love your kin.' He that does a good deed We shall repay many times over. Surely God is forgiving and bountiful in His rewards.

Or do they say: 'He has framed a falsehood about God'? But if God pleased, He could set a seal upon your heart. God will bring falsehood to nothing and vindicate the Truth by His Words. He surely knows one's innermost thoughts.

He it is who accepts His servants' repentance, and pardons their sins. He has knowledge of what you do.

And he answers those who believe and do good works, and enriches them through His bounty. But grievous punishment awaits the unbelievers.

Had God bestowed abundance upon His servants, they would have com- 42:27
mitted much injustice in the land. But He gives what He will in due measure; He well knows and observes His servants.

He it is who sends down the rain when they have lost all hope, and spreads abroad His mercy. He is the Guardian worthy of praise.

And among His signs is the creation of the heavens and the earth, and the living things He has dispersed over them. If He will, He can gather them all together.

Whatever misfortune befalls you, it is the fruit of your own labours. He forgives much.

And on the earth you cannot escape, nor have you any besides God to 42:31
protect or help you.

42:32 AND AMONG His signs are the ships which sail like mountains upon the ocean. If He will, He calms the wind, so that they lie motionless upon its bosom:[1] surely there are signs in this for the steadfast who render thanks; or He causes them to founder as punishment for their misdeeds.[2] Yet He forgives much.

Those who dispute Our revelations shall realize that they have no escape.

That which you have been given is but the fleeting pleasure of this life. Better and more enduring is God's recompense to those who believe and put their trust in their Lord; who eschew grievous sins and lewd acts and, when angered,
42:38 are willing to forgive; who obey
their Lord, attend to their prayers, and conduct their affairs by mutual counsel; who give in alms from what We gave them and, when oppressed, seek to redress their wrongs.

Let evil be requited with like evil. But he that forgives and seeks reconcilement shall be recompensed by God. He does not love the wrongdoers.

Those who seek to redress their wrongs incur no guilt. But great is the guilt of those who oppress their fellow men and conduct themselves with wickedness and injustice in the land. Woeful punishment awaits them.

42:44 To endure with fortitude and to forgive is a duty incumbent on all. He whom God confounds has no protector after Him.

And you shall see the wrongdoers when they behold the scourge, say: 'Is there no way back?'

وَمِنْ ءَايَٰتِهِ ٱلْجَوَارِ فِى ٱلْبَحْرِ كَٱلْأَعْلَٰمِ ﴿٣٢﴾ إِن يَشَأْ يُسْكِنِ ٱلرِّيحَ
فَيَظْلَلْنَ رَوَاكِدَ عَلَىٰ ظَهْرِهِۦٓ إِنَّ فِى ذَٰلِكَ لَءَايَٰتٍ لِّكُلِّ صَبَّارٍ شَكُورٍ
﴿٣٣﴾ أَوْ يُوبِقْهُنَّ بِمَا كَسَبُوا۟ وَيَعْفُ عَن كَثِيرٍ ﴿٣٤﴾ وَيَعْلَمَ ٱلَّذِينَ
يُجَٰدِلُونَ فِىٓ ءَايَٰتِنَا مَا لَهُم مِّن مَّحِيصٍ ﴿٣٥﴾ فَمَآ أُوتِيتُم مِّن شَىْءٍ
فَمَتَٰعُ ٱلْحَيَوٰةِ ٱلدُّنْيَا وَمَا عِندَ ٱللَّهِ خَيْرٌ وَأَبْقَىٰ لِلَّذِينَ ءَامَنُوا۟ وَعَلَىٰ رَبِّهِمْ
يَتَوَكَّلُونَ ﴿٣٦﴾ وَٱلَّذِينَ يَجْتَنِبُونَ كَبَٰٓئِرَ ٱلْإِثْمِ وَٱلْفَوَٰحِشَ
وَإِذَا مَا غَضِبُوا۟ هُمْ يَغْفِرُونَ ﴿٣٧﴾ وَٱلَّذِينَ ٱسْتَجَابُوا۟ لِرَبِّهِمْ
وَأَقَامُوا۟ ٱلصَّلَوٰةَ وَأَمْرُهُمْ شُورَىٰ بَيْنَهُمْ وَمِمَّا رَزَقْنَٰهُمْ يُنفِقُونَ
﴿٣٨﴾ وَٱلَّذِينَ إِذَآ أَصَابَهُمُ ٱلْبَغْىُ هُمْ يَنتَصِرُونَ ﴿٣٩﴾ وَجَزَٰٓؤُا۟ سَيِّئَةٍ سَيِّئَةٌ
مِّثْلُهَا فَمَنْ عَفَا وَأَصْلَحَ فَأَجْرُهُۥ عَلَى ٱللَّهِ إِنَّهُۥ لَا يُحِبُّ ٱلظَّٰلِمِينَ ﴿٤٠﴾ وَلَمَنِ
ٱنتَصَرَ بَعْدَ ظُلْمِهِۦ فَأُو۟لَٰٓئِكَ مَا عَلَيْهِم مِّن سَبِيلٍ ﴿٤١﴾ إِنَّمَا ٱلسَّبِيلُ
عَلَى ٱلَّذِينَ يَظْلِمُونَ ٱلنَّاسَ وَيَبْغُونَ فِى ٱلْأَرْضِ بِغَيْرِ ٱلْحَقِّ أُو۟لَٰٓئِكَ
لَهُمْ عَذَابٌ أَلِيمٌ ﴿٤٢﴾ وَلَمَن صَبَرَ وَغَفَرَ إِنَّ ذَٰلِكَ لَمِنْ عَزْمِ
ٱلْأُمُورِ ﴿٤٣﴾ وَمَن يُضْلِلِ ٱللَّهُ فَمَا لَهُۥ مِن وَلِىٍّ مِّنۢ بَعْدِهِۦ وَتَرَى
ٱلظَّٰلِمِينَ لَمَّا رَأَوُا۟ ٱلْعَذَابَ يَقُولُونَ هَلْ إِلَىٰ مَرَدٍّ مِّن سَبِيلٍ ﴿٤٤﴾

1. Literally, back.
2. The misdeeds of those who sail in them.

وترىهم يعرضون عليها خاشعين من الذل ينظرون
من طرف خفي وقال الذين آمنوا إن الخاسرين الذين
خسروا أنفسهم وأهليهم يوم القيامة ألا إن الظالمين
في عذاب مقيم ۝٤٥ وما كان لهم من أولياء ينصرونهم
من دون الله ومن يضلل الله فما له من سبيل ۝٤٦
استجيبوا لربكم من قبل أن يأتي يوم لا مرد له من الله
ما لكم من ملجإ يومئذ وما لكم من نكير ۝٤٧ فإن
أعرضوا فما أرسلناك عليهم حفيظا إن عليك إلا البلاغ
وإنا إذا أذقنا الإنسان منا رحمة فرح بها وإن تصبهم
سيئة بما قدمت أيديهم فإن الإنسان كفور ۝٤٨ لله
ملك السماوات والأرض يخلق ما يشاء يهب لمن يشاء إناثا
ويهب لمن يشاء الذكور ۝٤٩ أو يزوجهم ذكرانا وإناثا
ويجعل من يشاء عقيما إنه عليم قدير ۝٥٠ وما كان لبشر
أن يكلمه الله إلا وحيا أو من وراء حجاب أو يرسل
رسولا فيوحي بإذنه ما يشاء إنه علي حكيم ۝٥١

AND YOU shall see them 42:45
ranged before it: awed and humiliated, they shall look with furtive glances. And the true believers will say: 'The lost are those who lost their souls and all their kin on the Day of Resurrection.'

The wrongdoers shall surely suffer everlasting torment; they shall have no friends besides God to help them. He whom God confounds shall be lost indeed.

Obey your Lord before a day arrives which none can put off against the will of God. There shall be no refuge for you on that day, nor can there be any denials.

If they pay no heed, know 42:48
that We have not sent you[1] to be their keeper. Your only duty is to give warning.

When We give man a taste of Our mercy, he rejoices in it; but when evil befalls him because of what his hands committed, man is ungrateful.

God's is the sovereignty over the heavens and the earth. He creates what He will; He gives daughters to whom He will and sons to whom He pleases. Or He gives both sons and daughters, and He makes sterile whom He will. Omniscient is God, and Almighty.

It is not vouchsafed to any mortal that God should speak to him except 42:51
by inspiration, or from behind a veil, or through a messenger sent and authorized by Him to make known His will. Exalted is He, and wise.

1. Muḥammad.

42:52 AND THUS have We inspired you[1] with a spirit of
Our will when you knew nothing of the Book or belief; but
We made it a light whereby We
guide those of Our servants
whom We please. You will
surely guide them to a straight
42:53 path: the path of God, to
whom belongs all that is in the
heavens and all that is in the
earth. Surely to God shall all
things in the end return.

وكذلك أوحينا إليك روحا من أمرنا ما كنت تدري ما الكتاب
ولا الإيمان ولكن جعلناه نورا نهدي به من نشاء من عبادنا وإنك
لتهدي إلى صراط مستقيم (٥٢) صراط الله الذي له ما في
السموات وما في الأرض ألا إلى الله تصير الأمور (٥٣)

سورة الزخرف مكية وهي تسع وثمانون آية

بسم الله الرحمن الرحيم
حم (١) والكتاب المبين (٢) إنا جعلناه قرآنا عربيا لعلكم
تعقلون (٣) وإنه في أم الكتاب لدينا لعلي حكيم (٤) أفنضرب
عنكم الذكر صفحا أن كنتم قوما مسرفين (٥) وكم أرسلنا
من نبي في الأولين (٦) وما يأتيهم من نبي إلا كانوا به
يستهزئون (٧) فأهلكنا أشد منهم بطشا ومضى مثل
الأولين (٨) ولئن سألتهم من خلق السموات والأرض
ليقولن خلقهن العزيز العليم (٩) الذي جعل لكم الأرض
مهدا وجعل لكم فيها سبلا لعلكم تهتدون (١٠)

ORNAMENTS

In the Name of God,
the Merciful, the Compassionate

43:1 *Ḥā' mīm.* By the veritable
Book!
We have revealed it an Arabic Koran, that perchance you may understand
it. It is a transcript of the Eternal Book in Our keeping, sublime, and full of
wisdom.
Should We hold back the Admonition from you simply because you are a
43:7 prodigal people? Many a prophet did We send forth to the ancients: but no
prophet did arise among them that they did not mock. We obliterated them,
though they were mightier than these.[2]
Such then, was the example of the ancients. Yet, if you ask them[2] who
created the heavens and the earth, they are bound to say: 'The Almighty, the
All-knowing, created them.'
43:10 He it is who has made the earth a cradle for you and traced out routes
upon it that you may find your way;

1. Muḥammad. 2. The Meccans.

والذي نزل من السماء ماء بقدر فانشرنا به بلدة ميتا
كذلك تخرجون (١١) والذي خلق الازواج كلها وجعل
لكم من الفلك والانعام ما تركبون (١٢) لتستووا على ظهوره
ثم تذكروا نعمة ربكم اذا استويتم عليه وتقولوا
سبحان الذي سخر لنا هذا وما كنا له مقرنين
(١٣) وانا الى ربنا لمنقلبون (١٤) وجعلوا له من عباده
جزءا ان الانسان لكفور مبين (١٥) ام اتخذ مما يخلق بنات
واصفيكم بالبنين (١٦) واذا بشر احدهم بما ضرب للرحمن مثلا ظل
وجهه مسودا وهو كظيم (١٧) اومن ينشؤا في الحلية
وهو في الخصام غير مبين (١٨) وجعلوا الملئكة
الذين هم عباد الرحمن اناثا اشهدوا خلقهم ستكتب
شهادتهم ويسئلون (١٩) وقالوا لو شاء الرحمن ما عبدناهم
ما لهم بذلك من علم ان هم الا يخرصون (٢٠) ام اتيناهم
كتابا من قبله فهم به مستمسكون (٢١) بل قالوا انا
وجدنا اباءنا على امة وانا على اثارهم مهتدون (٢٢)

who sends down water from 43:11
the sky in due measure and thereby We resurrect a dead land: even thus shall you be raised to life; who has created all living things in pairs and made for you the ships and beasts on which you ride, so that, as you rest upon their backs, you may recall the goodness of your Lord and say: 'Glory to Him who has subjected these to us. But for Him we could not be their masters. To our Lord we shall surely return.'

Yet they[1] assign to Him some from among His servants. Surely man is monstrously ungrateful. Would God choose daughters for Himself from what He created and favour you with sons?[2]

And yet when the birth of a female[3] is announced to any of them his
countenance darkens and he is grievously vexed. Or would they ascribe 43:18
to God females who adorn themselves with trinkets and are powerless in disputation?

They make females the angels who are the Merciful's servants: did they witness their creation? Their testimony shall be noted down; and they shall be closely questioned.

They say: 'Had it been the will of the Merciful, we should never have worshipped them.' Surely of this they have no knowledge: they are only lying.

Or have We given them a scripture before this, so that they should hold fast to it?

Indeed, they say: 'This was the faith our fathers practised; and we are 43:22
merely guided by their footsteps.'

1. The Meccans.
2. The pagan Arabs believed that the angels, and their own goddesses, were daughters of Allāh.
3. Literally, the birth of what they liken to the Merciful.

43:23 THUS, NEVER did We send forth before you to a city one to give warning, but those therein who lived in opulence said: 'This was the faith our fathers practised; and we are merely following in their footsteps.'

Each of them said: 'What if I bring you a faith more enlightened than your fathers'?' But they said: 'We reject the message you have been sent with.' So We took vengeance on them; and consider the fate of those who disbelieved.

And tell of Abraham, who said to his father and to his people: 'I renounce the gods you worship, except Him who created me, for He will rightly guide me.' He made this an abiding precept among his descendants, that they might for ever turn to Him.

43:29 Indeed, I made things pleasant for these and for their fathers until there came to them the Truth and an undoubted Apostle. But now that the Truth has come to them, they say: 'This is sorcery. We utterly reject it.' They also say: 'Why has this Koran not been revealed to some important man from the two cities?'[1]

Is it they who apportion your Lord's blessings? It is We who deal out to them their livelihood in this world, exalting some in rank above others, so that the one may take the other into his service. Better is your Lord's mercy than all their hoarded treasures.

43:33 But for the chance that humankind might have become one race of unbelievers, We would have given those who denied the Lord of Mercy mansions with silver roofs, and stairs to ascend on;

وَكَذَٰلِكَ مَآ أَرْسَلْنَا مِن قَبْلِكَ فِى قَرْيَةٍ مِّن نَّذِيرٍ إِلَّا قَالَ
مُتْرَفُوهَآ إِنَّا وَجَدْنَآ ءَابَآءَنَا عَلَىٰٓ أُمَّةٍ وَإِنَّا عَلَىٰٓ ءَاثَٰرِهِم مُّقْتَدُونَ
٢٣ قَٰلَ أَوَلَوْ جِئْتُكُم بِأَهْدَىٰ مِمَّا وَجَدتُّمْ عَلَيْهِ ءَابَآءَكُمْ
قَالُوٓا إِنَّا بِمَآ أُرْسِلْتُم بِهِۦ كَٰفِرُونَ ٢٤ فَٱنتَقَمْنَا مِنْهُمْ فَٱنظُرْ
كَيْفَ كَانَ عَٰقِبَةُ ٱلْمُكَذِّبِينَ ٢٥ وَإِذْ قَالَ إِبْرَٰهِيمُ لِأَبِيهِ
وَقَوْمِهِۦٓ إِنَّنِى بَرَآءٌ مِّمَّا تَعْبُدُونَ ٢٦ إِلَّا ٱلَّذِى فَطَرَنِى فَإِنَّهُۥ
سَيَهْدِينِ ٢٧ وَجَعَلَهَا كَلِمَةًۢ بَاقِيَةً فِى عَقِبِهِۦ لَعَلَّهُمْ يَرْجِعُونَ
٢٨ بَلْ مَتَّعْتُ هَٰٓؤُلَآءِ وَءَابَآءَهُمْ حَتَّىٰ جَآءَهُمُ ٱلْحَقُّ وَرَسُولٌ
مُّبِينٌ ٢٩ وَلَمَّا جَآءَهُمُ ٱلْحَقُّ قَالُوا هَٰذَا سِحْرٌ وَإِنَّا بِهِۦ كَٰفِرُونَ
٣٠ وَقَالُوا لَوْلَا نُزِّلَ هَٰذَا ٱلْقُرْءَانُ عَلَىٰ رَجُلٍ مِّنَ ٱلْقَرْيَتَيْنِ عَظِيمٍ
٣١ أَهُمْ يَقْسِمُونَ رَحْمَتَ رَبِّكَ نَحْنُ قَسَمْنَا بَيْنَهُم مَّعِيشَتَهُمْ
فِى ٱلْحَيَوٰةِ ٱلدُّنْيَا وَرَفَعْنَا بَعْضَهُمْ فَوْقَ بَعْضٍ دَرَجَٰتٍ لِّيَتَّخِذَ بَعْضُهُم
بَعْضًا سُخْرِيًّا وَرَحْمَتُ رَبِّكَ خَيْرٌ مِّمَّا يَجْمَعُونَ ٣٢ وَلَوْلَآ أَن
يَكُونَ ٱلنَّاسُ أُمَّةً وَٰحِدَةً لَّجَعَلْنَا لِمَن يَكْفُرُ بِٱلرَّحْمَٰنِ
لِبُيُوتِهِمْ سُقُفًا مِّن فِضَّةٍ وَمَعَارِجَ عَلَيْهَا يَظْهَرُونَ ٣٣

1. Mecca and Medina.

وَلِبُيُوتِهِمْ أَبْوَابًا وَسُرُرًا عَلَيْهَا يَتَّكِـُٔونَ ﴿٣٤﴾ وَزُخْرُفًا
وَإِن كُلُّ ذَٰلِكَ لَمَّا مَتَاعُ الْحَيَوٰةِ الدُّنْيَا وَالْاٰخِرَةُ عِندَ
رَبِّكَ لِلْمُتَّقِينَ ﴿٣٥﴾ وَمَن يَعْشُ عَن ذِكْرِ الرَّحْمَٰنِ نُقَيِّضْ لَهُ شَيْطَانًا
فَهُوَ لَهُ قَرِينٌ ﴿٣٦﴾ وَإِنَّهُمْ لَيَصُدُّونَهُمْ عَنِ السَّبِيلِ وَيَحْسَبُونَ
أَنَّهُم مُّهْتَدُونَ ﴿٣٧﴾ حَتَّىٰ إِذَا جَاءَنَا قَالَ يَا لَيْتَ بَيْنِي وَبَيْنَكَ
بُعْدَ الْمَشْرِقَيْنِ فَبِئْسَ الْقَرِينُ ﴿٣٨﴾ وَلَن يَنفَعَكُمُ الْيَوْمَ
إِذ ظَّلَمْتُمْ أَنَّكُمْ فِي الْعَذَابِ مُشْتَرِكُونَ ﴿٣٩﴾ أَفَأَنتَ تُسْمِعُ
الصُّمَّ أَوْ تَهْدِي الْعُمْيَ وَمَن كَانَ فِي ضَلَالٍ مُّبِينٍ ﴿٤٠﴾
فَإِمَّا نَذْهَبَنَّ بِكَ فَإِنَّا مِنْهُم مُّنتَقِمُونَ ﴿٤١﴾ أَوْ نُرِيَنَّكَ الَّذِي
وَعَدْنَاهُمْ فَإِنَّا عَلَيْهِم مُّقْتَدِرُونَ ﴿٤٢﴾ فَاسْتَمْسِكْ بِالَّذِي
أُوحِيَ إِلَيْكَ إِنَّكَ عَلَىٰ صِرَاطٍ مُّسْتَقِيمٍ ﴿٤٣﴾ وَإِنَّهُ لَذِكْرٌ
لَّكَ وَلِقَوْمِكَ وَسَوْفَ تُسْأَلُونَ ﴿٤٤﴾ وَسْئَلْ مَنْ أَرْسَلْنَا مِن
قَبْلِكَ مِن رُّسُلِنَا أَجَعَلْنَا مِن دُونِ الرَّحْمَٰنِ آلِهَةً يُعْبَدُونَ ﴿٤٥﴾
وَلَقَدْ أَرْسَلْنَا مُوسَىٰ بِآيَاتِنَا إِلَىٰ فِرْعَوْنَ وَمَلَإِيْهِ فَقَالَ إِنِّي رَسُولُ
رَبِّ الْعَالَمِينَ ﴿٤٦﴾ فَلَمَّا جَاءَهُم بِآيَاتِنَا إِذَا هُم مِّنْهَا يَضْحَكُونَ ﴿٤٧﴾

mansions with silver gates and 43:34
silver couches to recline on;
and ornaments of gold: for all
these are but the baubles of
this life. It is the life to come
that your Lord reserves for
those who fear Him.

He that does not observe
the remembrance of the Merciful shall have a demon for his
companion: they turn people
away from the right path,
though they may think themselves rightly guided. And
when he comes before Us, he
will say:[1] 'Would that we were
as far apart as the East is from
the West.' Evil indeed is that
companion.

But on that day, because
you have done wrong, the
thought that you will share the
scourge with others will not
console you.

Can you make the deaf hear, or guide the blind or those in grievous error? 43:40
Whether We take you hence or let you live to see Our promises fulfilled, of
them We shall surely be avenged: for We have power absolute over them.

Therefore hold fast to that which was revealed to you: you are surely on a
straight path. It is an Admonition to you and to your people: and you shall
be questioned all.

Ask those of Our apostles whom We sent before you if We ever appointed
gods besides the Merciful to be worshipped.

We sent forth Moses with Our signs to Pharaoh and his nobles. He said:
'I am the apostle of the Lord of the Universe.' But when he came to them 43:47
with Our signs they laughed at them;

1. To his companion.

43:48 yet each fresh sign We revealed to them was but more powerful than the one that came before it. We therefore smote them with the scourge, so that they might return to the right path.

'You, sorcerer,' they said, 'pray for us to your Lord and invoke the promise He has made you. We will accept your guidance.'

But when We removed the scourge from them, they broke their pledge.

And Pharaoh made a proclamation to his people. 'My people,' said he, 'is the kingdom of Egypt not mine, and are these rivers which flow at my feet not mine also? Can you not see? Am I not better than this despicable wretch,
43:53 who can scarcely make his utterance clear? Why have no bracelets of gold been given him, or angels sent down to accompany him?'

Thus did he incite his people: and they obeyed him, for they were degenerate people. And when they provoked Us, We took vengeance on them and drowned them all, as a precedent and an example to those who succeeded them.

And when Mary's son is cited as an example, your people turn away and say: 'Who is better, he or our gods?' They cite him to you merely to provoke you. They are indeed a contentious people.

He was but a mortal whom We favoured and made an example to the
43:60 Israelites. Had it been Our will, We could have turned you into angels, your successors on the earth.

وما نريهم من آية إلا هي أكبر من أختها وأخذناهم
بالعذاب لعلهم يرجعون ﴿٤٨﴾ وقالوا يا أيه الساحر ادع لنا
ربك بما عهد عندك إننا لمهتدون ﴿٤٩﴾ فلما كشفنا عنهم
العذاب إذا هم ينكثون ﴿٥٠﴾ ونادى فرعون في قومه قال
يا قوم أليس لي ملك مصر وهذه الأنهار تجري من تحتي
أفلا تبصرون ﴿٥١﴾ أم أنا خير من هذا الذي هو مهين
ولا يكاد يبين ﴿٥٢﴾ فلولا ألقي عليه أسورة من ذهب
أو جاء معه الملائكة مقترنين ﴿٥٣﴾ فاستخف قومه
فأطاعوه إنهم كانوا قوما فاسقين ﴿٥٤﴾ فلما آسفونا
انتقمنا منهم فأغرقناهم أجمعين ﴿٥٥﴾ فجعلناهم سلفا
ومثلا للآخرين ﴿٥٦﴾ ولما ضرب ابن مريم مثلا إذا قومك
منه يصدون ﴿٥٧﴾ وقالوا أآلهتنا خير أم هو ما ضربوه
لك إلا جدلا بل هم قوم خصمون ﴿٥٨﴾ إن هو إلا عبد
أنعمنا عليه وجعلناه مثلا لبني إسرائيل ﴿٥٩﴾ ولو نشاء
لجعلنا منكم ملائكة في الأرض يخلفون ﴿٦٠﴾

وإنه لعلم للساعة فلا تمترن بها واتبعون هذا صراط
مستقيم ﴿٦١﴾ ولا يصدنكم الشيطان إنه لكم
عدو مبين ﴿٦٢﴾ ولما جاء عيسى بالبينات قال قد جئتكم
بالحكمة ولأبين لكم بعض الذي تختلفون فيه
فاتقوا الله وأطيعون ﴿٦٣﴾ إن الله هو ربي وربكم
فاعبدوه هذا صراط مستقيم ﴿٦٤﴾ فاختلف الأحزاب من
بينهم فويل للذين ظلموا من عذاب يوم أليم ﴿٦٥﴾ هل
ينظرون إلا الساعة أن تأتيهم بغتة وهم لا يشعرون ﴿٦٦﴾
الأخلاء يومئذ بعضهم لبعض عدو إلا المتقين ﴿٦٧﴾
يا عباد لا خوف عليكم اليوم ولا أنتم تحزنون ﴿٦٨﴾ الذين
آمنوا بآياتنا وكانوا مسلمين ﴿٦٩﴾ ادخلوا الجنة أنتم
وأزواجكم تحبرون ﴿٧٠﴾ يطاف عليهم بصحاف من ذهب
وأكواب وفيها ما تشتهيه الأنفس وتلذ الأعين وأنتم
فيها خالدون ﴿٧١﴾ وتلك الجنة التي أورثتموها بما كنتم
تعملون ﴿٧٢﴾ لكم فيها فاكهة كثيرة منها تأكلون ﴿٧٣﴾

He is a portent of the 43:61
Hour: have no doubt about its
coming and follow Me. This is
a straight path: let not Satan
debar you, for he is your veritable foe.

And when Jesus came with
evident signs, he said: 'I have
come to give you wisdom, and
to make plain to you some of
the things you differ about.
Fear God and follow me. God
is my Lord and your Lord:
therefore serve Him. That is a
straight path.'

Yet the factions disagreed
among themselves. But woe
betide the wrongdoers, for
they shall suffer the anguish of
a woeful day.

Are they only waiting for 43:66
the Hour to overtake them
suddenly when they are un-
aware? Friends shall on that day become enemies to one another, except the
God-fearing.

But you, My servants, who have believed in Our revelations and are
become Muslims, shall on that day have nothing to fear or to regret. Enter
Paradise, you and your spouses, rejoicing. You shall be served around with
golden dishes and golden goblets. Therein shall abound what every soul
desires and every eye delights in; and therein shall you abide for ever.

And such is the Paradise you shall inherit by virtue of your good deeds.
Therein your sustenance shall be abundant fruit. 43:73

43:74 BUT THE transgressors shall endure for ever the torment of Hell, which for them shall not be assuaged; they shall be speechless with despair. We did not wrong them, but it was they who did wrong.

'Mālik,'[1] they will call out, 'let your Lord make an end of us!' But he will say: 'Here you shall remain!'

We have made known to you the Truth, but most of you the Truth abhor.

If they are resolved to ruin you,[2] We are resolved to ruin them. Or do they think We cannot hear their secret talk and private converse? Yes! Our emissaries, at their side, record it all.

Say:[3] 'If the Lord of Mercy had a son, I would be the first to worship him.'

إِنَّ الْمُجْرِمِينَ فِي عَذَابِ جَهَنَّمَ خَالِدُونَ ٧٤ لَا يُفَتَّرُ عَنْهُمْ وَهُمْ فِيهِ
مُبْلِسُونَ ۝ وَمَا ظَلَمْنَاهُمْ وَلَٰكِن كَانُوا هُمُ الظَّالِمِينَ ٧٦ وَنَادَوْا
يَا مَالِكُ لِيَقْضِ عَلَيْنَا رَبُّكَ قَالَ إِنَّكُم مَّاكِثُونَ ٧٧ لَقَدْ جِئْنَاكُم
بِالْحَقِّ وَلَٰكِنَّ أَكْثَرَكُمْ لِلْحَقِّ كَارِهُونَ ٧٨ أَمْ أَبْرَمُوا أَمْرًا فَإِنَّا
مُبْرِمُونَ ٧٩ أَمْ يَحْسَبُونَ أَنَّا لَا نَسْمَعُ سِرَّهُمْ وَنَجْوَاهُم بَلَىٰ
وَرُسُلُنَا لَدَيْهِمْ يَكْتُبُونَ ٨٠ قُلْ إِن كَانَ لِلرَّحْمَٰنِ وَلَدٌ فَأَنَا أَوَّلُ
الْعَابِدِينَ ۝ سُبْحَانَ رَبِّ السَّمَاوَاتِ وَالْأَرْضِ رَبِّ الْعَرْشِ عَمَّا
يَصِفُونَ ٨٢ فَذَرْهُمْ يَخُوضُوا وَيَلْعَبُوا حَتَّىٰ يُلَاقُوا يَوْمَهُمُ
الَّذِي يُوعَدُونَ ٨٣ وَهُوَ الَّذِي فِي السَّمَاءِ إِلَٰهٌ وَفِي الْأَرْضِ إِلَٰهٌ
وَهُوَ الْحَكِيمُ الْعَلِيمُ ٨٤ وَتَبَارَكَ الَّذِي لَهُ مُلْكُ السَّمَاوَاتِ
وَالْأَرْضِ وَمَا بَيْنَهُمَا وَعِندَهُ عِلْمُ السَّاعَةِ وَإِلَيْهِ تُرْجَعُونَ
٨٥ وَلَا يَمْلِكُ الَّذِينَ يَدْعُونَ مِن دُونِهِ الشَّفَاعَةَ إِلَّا مَن
شَهِدَ بِالْحَقِّ وَهُمْ يَعْلَمُونَ ٨٦ وَلَئِن سَأَلْتَهُم مَّنْ خَلَقَهُمْ
لَيَقُولُنَّ اللَّهُ فَأَنَّىٰ يُؤْفَكُونَ ۝ وَقِيلِهِ يَا رَبِّ إِنَّ هَٰؤُلَاءِ قَوْمٌ
لَّا يُؤْمِنُونَ ٨٨ فَاصْفَحْ عَنْهُمْ وَقُلْ سَلَامٌ فَسَوْفَ يَعْلَمُونَ ٨٩

Exalted be the Lord of the heavens and the earth, the Lord of the Throne,
43:83 above their falsehoods! Let them paddle, let them play, until they face the day
they are promised.

And He it is who in heaven is God and on earth is God; He is the Wise One, the All-knowing. Blessed be He who has sovereignty over the heavens and the earth and all that lies between them! He alone has knowledge of the Hour, and to Him shall you be recalled.

Those to whom they pray besides Him have not the power to intercede for them, save those who testify to the Truth and have knowledge of it.

Yet if you ask them who created them, they will surely say, 'God.' How then can they be so misled?

And he can only say: 'Lord, these are surely people that do not believe.'

43:89 So bear with them and wish them peace; they shall learn.

1. One of the keepers of Hell. 2. Muḥammad.
3. To the Christians.

سورة الدخان مكية وهي تسع وخمسون آية

بسم الله الرحمن الرحيم
حم ۝١ والكتاب المبين ۝٢ إنا أنزلناه في ليلة مباركة إنا
كنا منذرين ۝٣ فيها يفرق كل أمر حكيم ۝٤ أمرا من عندنا
إنا كنا مرسلين ۝٥ رحمة من ربك إنه هو السميع العليم
۝٦ رب السموات والأرض وما بينهما إن كنتم موقنين ۝٧
لا إله إلا هو يحيي ويميت ربكم ورب آبائكم الأولين ۝٨ بل هم
في شك يلعبون ۝٩ فارتقب يوم تأتي السماء بدخان مبين ۝١٠
يغشى الناس هذا عذاب أليم ۝١١ ربنا اكشف عنا العذاب إنا
مؤمنون ۝١٢ أنى لهم الذكرى وقد جاءهم رسول مبين ۝١٣
ثم تولوا عنه وقالوا معلم مجنون ۝١٤ إنا كاشفو العذاب
قليلا إنكم عائدون ۝١٥ يوم نبطش البطشة الكبرى إنا
منتقمون ۝١٦ ولقد فتنا قبلهم قوم فرعون وجاءهم رسول
كريم ۝١٧ أن أدوا إلي عباد الله إني لكم رسول أمين ۝١٨

SMOKE

In the Name of God,
the Merciful, the Compassionate

Ḥa' mīm. By the veritable 44:1
Book, We revealed it[1] on a
blessed night, intending to give
warning; on a night when
every wise commandment was
expounded as a commandment from Ourself. We it was
who sent it down as a blessing
from your Lord; surely He it is
who hears all and knows all:
the Lord of the heavens and
the earth and all that lies
between them. Mark this, if
you are true believers. There is
no god but Him. He ordains
life and death; He is your
God and the God of your
forefathers. Yet they divert themselves with doubt.
Watch for the day when the sky will pour down palpable smoke, envelop- 44:10
ing mankind: a woeful scourge. Then will they say: 'Lord, lift the scourge
from us. We are now believers.' But how will their remembrance help them,
when a true apostle did come to them and they denied him, and said: 'A
well-taught madman!'

Yet if We but slightly ease your torment, you will return to unbelief. On the day We bring down the supreme scourge We will surely be avenged.

Before them, We tested Pharaoh's people. A gracious apostle had come
to them, saying: 'Hand over to me God's servants. I am an honest emissary. 44:18

1. The Koran.

44:19 AND DO not hold yourselves
above God. I bring you clear
authority. I adjure you by Him
who is my Lord and your
Lord not to stone me. If you
have no faith in me, leave me
well alone.'
Then he cried out to his
Lord, saying: 'Surely these are
a sinful people.'
'Set forth with My servants
in the night, for you will be
pursued. Leave the sea at rest
behind you. They are warriors
doomed to be drowned.'
How many gardens and
fountains they left behind!
Cornfields, and noble palaces,
and good things in which they
took delight. All this We gave
to others to inherit. Neither
heaven nor earth shed tears
for them; nor were they
44:30 reprieved. We saved the Israelites from the degrading scourge, from Pharaoh, who surely was a tyrant and a transgressor, and chose them knowingly
above the nations. We showed them such miracles as manifestly tested them.
Yet there are those who say: 'We shall die but one death, nor shall we ever
be raised to life again. Bring back to us our forefathers, if what you say be
true.'
Are they better than the people of Tubba'[1] and those who thrived before
them? We destroyed them all, for they too were wicked men.
It was not in jest that We created the heavens and the earth and all that lies
44:39 between them. We created them both only to reveal the Truth. But of this
the larger part of them have no knowledge.

وَأَن لَّا تَعْلُوا عَلَى اللَّهِ ۖ إِنِّي آتِيكُم بِسُلْطَانٍ مُّبِينٍ ﴿١٩﴾
وَإِنِّي عُذْتُ بِرَبِّي وَرَبِّكُمْ أَن تَرْجُمُونِ ﴿٢٠﴾ وَإِن لَّمْ تُؤْمِنُوا لِي
فَاعْتَزِلُونِ ﴿٢١﴾ فَدَعَا رَبَّهُ أَنَّ هَٰؤُلَاءِ قَوْمٌ مُّجْرِمُونَ ﴿٢٢﴾ فَأَسْرِ
بِعِبَادِي لَيْلًا إِنَّكُم مُّتَّبَعُونَ ﴿٢٣﴾ وَاتْرُكِ الْبَحْرَ رَهْوًا ۖ إِنَّهُمْ
جُندٌ مُّغْرَقُونَ ﴿٢٤﴾ كَمْ تَرَكُوا مِن جَنَّاتٍ وَعُيُونٍ ﴿٢٥﴾ وَزُرُوعٍ
وَمَقَامٍ كَرِيمٍ ﴿٢٦﴾ وَنَعْمَةٍ كَانُوا فِيهَا فَاكِهِينَ ﴿٢٧﴾ كَذَٰلِكَ ۖ
وَأَوْرَثْنَاهَا قَوْمًا آخَرِينَ ﴿٢٨﴾ فَمَا بَكَتْ عَلَيْهِمُ السَّمَاءُ وَالْأَرْضُ
وَمَا كَانُوا مُنظَرِينَ ﴿٢٩﴾ وَلَقَدْ نَجَّيْنَا بَنِي إِسْرَائِيلَ مِنَ الْعَذَابِ الْمُهِينِ
﴿٣٠﴾ مِن فِرْعَوْنَ ۚ إِنَّهُ كَانَ عَالِيًا مِّنَ الْمُسْرِفِينَ ﴿٣١﴾ وَلَقَدِ اخْتَرْنَاهُمْ
عَلَىٰ عِلْمٍ عَلَى الْعَالَمِينَ ﴿٣٢﴾ وَآتَيْنَاهُم مِّنَ الْآيَاتِ مَا فِيهِ بَلَاءٌ مُّبِينٌ
﴿٣٣﴾ إِنَّ هَٰؤُلَاءِ لَيَقُولُونَ ﴿٣٤﴾ إِنْ هِيَ إِلَّا مَوْتَتُنَا الْأُولَىٰ وَمَا نَحْنُ
بِمُنشَرِينَ ﴿٣٥﴾ فَأْتُوا بِآبَائِنَا إِن كُنتُمْ صَادِقِينَ ﴿٣٦﴾ أَهُمْ خَيْرٌ أَمْ
قَوْمُ تُبَّعٍ وَالَّذِينَ مِن قَبْلِهِمْ ۚ أَهْلَكْنَاهُمْ ۖ إِنَّهُمْ كَانُوا مُجْرِمِينَ
﴿٣٧﴾ وَمَا خَلَقْنَا السَّمَاوَاتِ وَالْأَرْضَ وَمَا بَيْنَهُمَا لَاعِبِينَ ﴿٣٨﴾
مَا خَلَقْنَاهُمَا إِلَّا بِالْحَقِّ وَلَٰكِنَّ أَكْثَرَهُمْ لَا يَعْلَمُونَ ﴿٣٩﴾

1. The people of Himyar, in Arabia.

إن يوم الفصل ميقاتهم أجمعين ٤٠ يوم لا يغني مولى
عن مولى شيئا ولا هم ينصرون ٤١ إلا من رحم الله
إنه هو العزيز الرحيم ٤٢ إن شجرت الزقوم ٤٣ طعام
الأثيم ٤٤ كالمهل يغلي في البطون ٤٥ كغلي الحميم ٤٦
خذوه فاعتلوه إلى سواء الجحيم ٤٧ ثم صبوا فوق رأسه
من عذاب الحميم ٤٨ ذق إنك أنت العزيز الكريم ٤٩
إن هذا ما كنتم به تمترون ٥٠ إن المتقين في مقام أمين
٥١ في جنات وعيون ٥٢ يلبسون من سندس وإستبرق
متقابلين ٥٣ كذلك وزوجناهم بحور عين ٥٤ يدعون
فيها بكل فاكهة آمنين ٥٥ لا يذوقون فيها الموت إلا
الموتة الأولى ووقاهم عذاب الجحيم ٥٦ فضلا من ربك
ذلك هو الفوز العظيم ٥٧ فإنما يسرناه بلسانك
لعلهم يتذكرون ٥٨ فارتقب إنهم مرتقبون ٥٩

سورة الجاثية مكية وهي سبع وثلاثون آية

THE DAY of Judgement is 44:40
the appointed time for them all.
On that day no friend shall help
a friend; none shall be helped
save those to whom God shows
mercy. He is the Mighty One,
the Compassionate.

The Zaqqūm tree shall provide the sinner's food. Like
dregs of oil, like scalding water,
it shall simmer in his belly.
'Seize him and drag him into
the depths of Hell. Then pour
out the scourge of scalding
water over his head: "Taste 44:49
this, you illustrious and honourable man! This is the very
fate you always doubted."'

Surely the righteous shall be
lodged in a mansion secure
amid gardens and fountains
face to face, arrayed in rich
silks and fine brocade. Even
thus; and We shall wed them to dark-eyed houris. Secure against all ills, they
shall call for every kind of fruit; and, having died once, they shall never die
again. Your Lord will in His mercy shield them from the scourge of Hell.
That will be the supreme triumph.

We have made it easy in your own tongue, that they may remember. Wait, 44:59
then; they too are waiting.

KNEELING

In the Name of God,
the Merciful, the Compassionate

45:1 *Ḥā' mīm.* The revelation of the
Book is from God, the Mighty
One, the Wise One.
Surely in the heavens and the
earth there are signs for the
faithful; in your own creation,
and in the beasts He scatters far
and near, signs for firm believers; in the alternation of night
and day, in the sustenance God
sends down from the sky with
which He resurrects the earth
after its death, and in the mar-
shalling of the winds, signs for
those who can understand.
Such are God's revelations:
We recite them to you in all
Truth. But in what words will they believe, if not in God Himself and all His
signs?
45:7 Woe betide every untruthful sinner! He hears God's revelations recited to
him and then, as though he never heard them, persists in scorn. Forewarn
him of a woeful scourge. And if he knew a little of Our signs, he would
deride them: such men shall suffer degrading torment.
Hell is at their rear. Their gains shall not avail them, nor shall the masters
they have served besides God. Grievous punishment awaits them.
This is true guidance. Those that deny their Lord's revelations shall suffer
the anguish of a woeful scourge.
God it is who has subdued for you the ocean, that the ships may sail upon
it at His bidding; that you may seek His bounty and render thanks.
45:13 He has subjected to you what the heavens and the earth contain; all is
from Him. Surely in this there are signs for people who reflect.

بسم الله الرحمن الرحيم
حم ١ تنزيل الكتاب من الله العزيز الحكيم ٢ إن في السموات
والأرض لآيات للمؤمنين ٣ وفي خلقكم وما يبث من دابة
آيات لقوم يوقنون ٤ واختلاف الليل والنهار وما أنزل
الله من السماء من رزق فأحيا به الأرض بعد موتها وتصريف
الرياح آيات لقوم يعقلون ٥ تلك آيات الله نتلوها عليك
بالحق فبأي حديث بعد الله وآياته يؤمنون ٦ ويل لكل
أفاك أثيم ٧ يسمع آيات الله تتلى عليه ثم يصر مستكبرا كأن لم
يسمعها فبشره بعذاب أليم ٨ وإذا علم من آياتنا شيئا اتخذها هزوا
أولئك لهم عذاب مهين ٩ من ورائهم جهنم ولا يغني عنهم ما كسبوا
شيئا ولا ما اتخذوا من دون الله أولياء ولهم عذاب عظيم ١٠ هذا
هدى والذين كفروا بآيات ربهم لهم عذاب من رجز أليم ١١
الله الذي سخر لكم البحر لتجري الفلك فيه بأمره ولتبتغوا
من فضله ولعلكم تشكرون ١٢ وسخر لكم ما في السموات
وما في الأرض جميعا منه إن في ذلك لآيات لقوم يتفكرون ١٣

قل للذين ءامنوا يغفروا للذين لا يرجون أيام الله ليجزي
قوما بما كانوا يكسبون ﴿١٤﴾ من عمل صالحا فلنفسه ومن أساء
فعليها ثم إلى ربكم ترجعون ﴿١٥﴾ ولقد ءاتينا بني إسرائيل
الكتاب والحكم والنبوة ورزقناهم من الطيبات
وفضلناهم على العالمين ﴿١٦﴾ وءاتيناهم بينات من
الأمر فما اختلفوا إلا من بعد ما جاءهم العلم بغيا
بينهم إن ربك يقضي بينهم يوم القيامة فيما كانوا فيه
يختلفون ﴿١٧﴾ ثم جعلناك على شريعة من الأمر فاتبعها ولا تتبع
أهواء الذين لا يعلمون ﴿١٨﴾ إنهم لن يغنوا عنك من الله شيئا
وإن الظالمين بعضهم أولياء بعض والله ولي المتقين ﴿١٩﴾
هذا بصائر للناس وهدى ورحمة لقوم يوقنون ﴿٢٠﴾ أم
حسب الذين اجترحوا السيئات أن نجعلهم كالذين
ءامنوا وعملوا الصالحات سواء محياهم ومماتهم
ساء ما يحكمون ﴿٢١﴾ وخلق الله السماوات والأرض
بالحق ولتجزى كل نفس بما كسبت وهم لا يظلمون ﴿٢٢﴾

TELL THE believers to par- 45:14
don those who cannot wish
for the days of God,[1] when He
will requite people according
to what they did. He that does
a good deed does it for his
own soul; and he that commits
evil does so at his own peril.
Then to your Lord shall you be
recalled.

To the Israelites We gave the Book and bestowed on them judgement and prophethood. We provided them with wholesome things and exalted them above the nations. We gave them explicit commandments: yet it was not till knowledge had been vouchsafed them that they disagreed, maliciously, among themselves. Your Lord will on the Day of Resurrection judge what they differ about.

We then set for you a law to the right path. Follow it, and do not yield to 45:18
the desires of those that are devoid of knowledge; for they can in no way
shelter you from God. The wrongdoers are protectors of each other; but the
righteous have God Himself for their protector.

This is an Admonition to mankind; a guide and a blessing to firm believers.

Or do those who committed evil deeds think they are equal in Our sight to those who believe and do good works, and likewise their lives and deaths? How ill they judge!

God created the heavens and the earth to manifest the Truth, and to 45:22
recompense each soul according to its deeds. They shall not be wronged.

1. I.e. the days of victory.

45:23 DO BUT consider: who,
besides God, can guide him
who makes his lust his god,
whom God deliberately confounds, setting a seal upon his
ears and heart, and drawing a
veil over his eyes? Will you not
take thought?
They say: 'There is but one
life in this world and no other.
We die and live; nothing but
Time destroys us.' Surely of
this they have no knowledge.
They are merely guessing.
And when Our veritable
revelations are recited to them,
their only argument is: 'Bring
back our forefathers, if what
you say be true!'
Say: 'God it is who gives
you life and then causes you to
die; He will then gather you all
on the Day of Resurrection,
of which there is no doubt; yet most do not know it.'
45:27 God it is who has sovereignty over the heavens and the earth. On the day
the Hour strikes, those who have denied His revelations will assuredly
lose all.
You shall see each community on its knees. Each community shall be
summoned to its Book: 'You shall this day be requited for your deeds. This
Book of Ours speaks with Truth against you. We have recorded what you
did.'
As for those who believe and do good works, their Lord will usher them
into His mercy. That shall be the veritable triumph.
As for the unbelievers: 'Were My revelations not declared to you? Did you
45:32 not scorn them and commit evil? When you were told: "God's promise is
true: the Hour is sure to come," you said: "We know nothing of the Hour. It
is but a vain conjecture, nor are we convinced."'

أَفَرَأَيْتَ مَنِ اتَّخَذَ إِلَٰهَهُ هَوَاهُ وَأَضَلَّهُ اللَّهُ عَلَىٰ عِلْمٍ وَخَتَمَ عَلَىٰ سَمْعِهِ
وَقَلْبِهِ وَجَعَلَ عَلَىٰ بَصَرِهِ غِشَاوَةً فَمَن يَهْدِيهِ مِن بَعْدِ اللَّهِ
أَفَلَا تَذَكَّرُونَ ٢٣ وَقَالُوا مَا هِيَ إِلَّا حَيَاتُنَا الدُّنْيَا نَمُوتُ وَنَحْيَا وَمَا
يُهْلِكُنَا إِلَّا الدَّهْرُ وَمَا لَهُم بِذَٰلِكَ مِنْ عِلْمٍ إِنْ هُمْ إِلَّا يَظُنُّونَ ٢٤
وَإِذَا تُتْلَىٰ عَلَيْهِمْ آيَاتُنَا بَيِّنَاتٍ مَا كَانَ حُجَّتَهُمْ إِلَّا أَن قَالُوا ائْتُوا
بِآبَائِنَا إِن كُنتُمْ صَادِقِينَ ٢٥ قُلِ اللَّهُ يُحْيِيكُمْ ثُمَّ يُمِيتُكُمْ ثُمَّ يَجْمَعُكُمْ
إِلَىٰ يَوْمِ الْقِيَامَةِ لَا رَيْبَ فِيهِ وَلَٰكِنَّ أَكْثَرَ النَّاسِ لَا يَعْلَمُونَ ٢٦ وَلِلَّهِ
مُلْكُ السَّمَاوَاتِ وَالْأَرْضِ وَيَوْمَ تَقُومُ السَّاعَةُ يَوْمَئِذٍ يَخْسَرُ الْمُبْطِلُونَ
٢٧ وَتَرَىٰ كُلَّ أُمَّةٍ جَاثِيَةً كُلُّ أُمَّةٍ تُدْعَىٰ إِلَىٰ كِتَابِهَا الْيَوْمَ تُجْزَوْنَ مَا
كُنتُمْ تَعْمَلُونَ ٢٨ هَٰذَا كِتَابُنَا يَنطِقُ عَلَيْكُم بِالْحَقِّ إِنَّا كُنَّا نَسْتَنسِخُ مَا
كُنتُمْ تَعْمَلُونَ ٢٩ فَأَمَّا الَّذِينَ آمَنُوا وَعَمِلُوا الصَّالِحَاتِ فَيُدْخِلُهُمْ رَبُّهُمْ
فِي رَحْمَتِهِ ذَٰلِكَ هُوَ الْفَوْزُ الْمُبِينُ ٣٠ وَأَمَّا الَّذِينَ كَفَرُوا
أَفَلَمْ تَكُنْ آيَاتِي تُتْلَىٰ عَلَيْكُمْ فَاسْتَكْبَرْتُمْ وَكُنتُمْ قَوْمًا
مُجْرِمِينَ ٣١ وَإِذَا قِيلَ إِنَّ وَعْدَ اللَّهِ حَقٌّ وَالسَّاعَةُ لَا رَيْبَ فِيهَا
قُلْتُم مَا نَدْرِي مَا السَّاعَةُ إِن نَظُنُّ إِلَّا ظَنًّا وَمَا نَحْنُ بِمُسْتَيْقِنِينَ ٣٢

وبدا لهم سيئات ما عملوا وحاق بهم ما كانوا به يستهزءون ٣٣ وقيل
اليوم ننسيكم كما نسيتم لقاء يومكم هذا ومأويكم النار وما لكم
من ناصرين ٣٤ ذلكم بأنكم اتخذتم آيات الله هزوا وغرتكم
الحيوة الدنيا فاليوم لا يخرجون منها ولا هم يستعتبون ٣٥ فلله
الحمد رب السموات ورب الأرض رب العالمين ٣٦ وله
الكبرياء في السموات والأرض وهو العزيز الحكيم ٣٧

سورة الأحقاف مكية وهي خمس وثلاثون آية

بسم الله الرحمن الرحيم

حم ١ تنزيل الكتاب من الله العزيز الحكيم ٢ ما خلقنا السموات
والأرض وما بينهما إلا بالحق وأجل مسمى والذين كفروا عما أنذروا
معرضون ٣ قل أرأيتم ما تدعون من دون الله أروني ماذا خلقوا
من الأرض أم لهم شرك في السموات ائتوني بكتاب من قبل هذا أو أثارة
من علم إن كنتم صادقين ٤ ومن أضل ممن يدعوا من دون الله
من لا يستجيب له إلى يوم القيمة وهم عن دعائهم غافلون ٥

THE EVIL of their deeds 45:33
will manifest itself to them,
and the scourge at which they
scoffed will encompass them.
They will be told: 'We will this
day forget you, as you yourselves forgot you would meet
this day. The Fire shall be your
shelter, and none will help
you. That is because you 45:35
scoffed at God's revelations
and were seduced by your
earthly life.'

On that day there shall be
no way out for them; nor shall
they be asked to make amends.

Praise, then, be to God, Lord
of the heavens and Lord of the
earth, Lord of the Universe.
Supremacy be His in the heav- 45:37
ens and on earth. He it is who is
the Mighty One, the Wise One.

THE SAND DUNES

In the Name of God, the Merciful, the Compassionate

Ḥā' mīm. The revelation of the Book is from God, the Mighty One, the Wise 46:1
One.

It was but to manifest the Truth that We created the heavens and the earth and all that lies between them: to last for an appointed term. Yet the unbelievers pay no heed to Our warning.

Say: 'Have you pondered on those whom you invoke besides God? Show me what part of the earth they have created! Have they a share in the heavens? Bring me a scripture revealed before this, or some other vestige of divine knowledge, if what you say be true.'

Who is in greater error than he who prays to idols which will never hear 46:5
him till the Day of Resurrection – which are, indeed, unaware of his prayers;

46:6 which, when mankind are
herded up together, will
declare themselves their enemies and will disown their
worship?
When Our revelations are
recited to them, veritable as
they are, the unbelievers say
of the Truth when it is
declared to them: 'This is
sorcery manifest.'
Or do they say: 'He has
fabricated it[1] himself'?
Say: 'If I have indeed fabricated it, then there is nothing
you can do to shield me from
the ire of God. He well knows
the way you fulminate about
it. Sufficient is He as my witness and your witness. And it
is He who is the Forgiving
One, the Compassionate.'
Say: 'I am nothing new
among the apostles; nor do I know what will be done with me or you. I follow
only what is revealed to me, and my only duty is to give clear warning.'
46:10 Say: 'Do but consider: if it[1] is indeed from God and you reject it; if an
Israelite[2] has vouched for it and believed in it, while you yourselves deny it
with disdain: surely God does not guide the wrongdoers.'
And the unbelievers say of the faithful: 'Had there been any good in it[1]
they would not have believed in it before us.' And since they reject its guidance, they say: 'This is an ancient falsehood.'
And before it, was the Book of Moses: a guide and a blessing. And this
Book confirms it in the Arabic tongue, to forewarn the wrongdoers and to
give joyful tidings to the righteous.
Those that say: 'Our Lord is God,' and follow the straight path shall have
46:14 nothing to fear or to regret. They are the heirs of Paradise, therein to abide
for ever as a reward for their labours.

1. The Koran.
1. 'Abdullāh b. Salām, according to the commentators.

ووصينا الإنسان بوالديه إحسانا حملته أمه كرها ووضعته
كرها وحمله وفصاله ثلثون شهرا حتى إذا بلغ أشده وبلغ أربعين
سنة قال رب أوزعني أن أشكر نعمتك التي أنعمت علي وعلى
والدي وأن أعمل صالحا ترضيه وأصلح لي في ذريتي إني
تبت إليك وإني من المسلمين ١٥ أولئك الذين نتقبل عنهم
أحسن ما عملوا ونتجاوز عن سيئاتهم في أصحاب الجنة وعد
الصدق الذي كانوا يوعدون ١٦ والذي قال لوالديه
أف لكما أتعدانني أن أخرج وقد خلت القرون من قبلي وهما
يستغيثان الله ويلك آمن إن وعد الله حق فيقول ما هذا
إلا أساطير الأولين ١٧ أولئك الذين حق عليهم القول في أمم
قد خلت من قبلهم من الجن والإنس إنهم كانوا خاسرين ١٨ ولكل
درجات مما عملوا وليوفيهم أعمالهم وهم لا يظلمون ١٩ ويوم
يعرض الذين كفروا على النار أذهبتم طيباتكم في حياتكم
الدنيا واستمتعتم بها فاليوم تجزون عذاب الهون بما كنتم
تستكبرون في الأرض بغير الحق وبما كنتم تفسقون ٢٠

AND WE have enjoined man to show kindness to his parents. With much pain his mother bears him, and with much pain she brings him into the world. He is born and weaned in thirty months. When he grows to manhood and attains his fortieth year, let him say: 'Inspire me, Lord, to give thanks for the favours You have bestowed on me and on my parents, and to do good works that will please You. Grant me good descendants. To You I turn and to You I submit as a Muslim.' 46:15

Such are those from whom We will accept their noblest works and whose misdeeds We shall overlook. We shall admit them among the heirs of Paradise: true is the promise that has been given them.

But he that says to his parents: 'Fie on you both! Do you threaten me with 46:17
a resurrection, when generations have passed away before me?' – he that, when they pray for God's help and say: 'Woe betide you! Have faith; the promise of God is true,' says: 'This is but a fable of the ancients' – these shall justly deserve the fate of bygone races of jinn and humans: they shall assuredly be lost.

There are rewards for all, according to their deeds, that He may duly requite them for their works. They shall not be wronged.

The day the unbelievers are exposed before the Fire, We shall say to them: 46:20
'You squandered away your precious gifts in your earthly life, and took your fill of pleasure from them. Today your recompense will be degrading torment, because you acted with arrogance and injustice in the land and committed evil.'

46:21 AND TELL of 'Ād's kin
who warned his people in the
Valley of the Sand Dunes; and
there have been other emissaries before and since his
time, saying: 'Serve none but
God. Beware the torment of a
fateful day.'

They said: 'Have you come
to turn us falsely away from
our gods? Bring down what
you threaten us with, if what
you say be true!'

He said: 'God alone has
knowledge of it. I am here
only to deliver to you the message I have been sent with.
But I can see that you are
ignorant people.'

And when they saw a pass-
ing cloud heading for their
valleys, they said: 'This is a passing cloud that will bring us rain.'

'By no means!' he said. 'It is what you have sought to hasten: a hurricane
46:25 bringing a woeful scourge; it shall lay everything waste at the bidding of its
Lord.'

And when morning came there was nothing to be seen besides their
ruined dwellings. Thus do We reward the wrongdoers.

We had made them as powerful as yourselves,[1] and given them ears and
eyes and hearts. Yet nothing did their ears, their eyes, or their hearts avail
them since they denied the revelations of God. That which they mocked
encompassed them.

We destroyed the cities which had once flourished around you, and made
46:28 plain the revelations, that they might return to the right path. Why did their
gods not help them, gods they had set up besides God to bring them close
to Him? Indeed, they utterly forsook them. Such were their lies, and such
their false inventions.

وَاذْكُرْ أَخَا عَادٍ إِذْ أَنذَرَ قَوْمَهُ بِالْأَحْقَافِ وَقَدْ خَلَتِ
النُّذُرُ مِن بَيْنِ يَدَيْهِ وَمِنْ خَلْفِهِ أَلَّا تَعْبُدُوا إِلَّا اللَّهَ إِنِّي أَخَافُ
عَلَيْكُمْ عَذَابَ يَوْمٍ عَظِيمٍ ﴿٢١﴾ قَالُوا أَجِئْتَنَا لِتَأْفِكَنَا عَنْ آلِهَتِنَا فَأْتِنَا بِمَا
تَعِدُنَا إِن كُنتَ مِنَ الصَّادِقِينَ ﴿٢٢﴾ قَالَ إِنَّمَا الْعِلْمُ عِندَ اللَّهِ وَأُبَلِّغُكُم
مَّا أُرْسِلْتُ بِهِ وَلَٰكِنِّي أَرَاكُمْ قَوْمًا تَجْهَلُونَ ﴿٢٣﴾ فَلَمَّا رَأَوْهُ عَارِضًا
مُّسْتَقْبِلَ أَوْدِيَتِهِمْ قَالُوا هَٰذَا عَارِضٌ مُّمْطِرُنَا بَلْ هُوَ مَا اسْتَعْجَلْتُم
بِهِ رِيحٌ فِيهَا عَذَابٌ أَلِيمٌ ﴿٢٤﴾ تُدَمِّرُ كُلَّ شَيْءٍ بِأَمْرِ رَبِّهَا فَأَصْبَحُوا
لَا يُرَىٰ إِلَّا مَسَاكِنُهُمْ كَذَٰلِكَ نَجْزِي الْقَوْمَ الْمُجْرِمِينَ ﴿٢٥﴾
وَلَقَدْ مَكَّنَّاهُمْ فِيمَا إِن مَّكَّنَّاكُمْ فِيهِ وَجَعَلْنَا لَهُمْ سَمْعًا
وَأَبْصَارًا وَأَفْئِدَةً فَمَا أَغْنَىٰ عَنْهُمْ سَمْعُهُمْ وَلَا أَبْصَارُهُمْ
وَلَا أَفْئِدَتُهُم مِّن شَيْءٍ إِذْ كَانُوا يَجْحَدُونَ بِآيَاتِ اللَّهِ وَحَاقَ بِهِم
مَّا كَانُوا بِهِ يَسْتَهْزِئُونَ ﴿٢٦﴾ وَلَقَدْ أَهْلَكْنَا مَا حَوْلَكُم
مِّنَ الْقُرَىٰ وَصَرَّفْنَا الْآيَاتِ لَعَلَّهُمْ يَرْجِعُونَ ﴿٢٧﴾ فَلَوْلَا
نَصَرَهُمُ الَّذِينَ اتَّخَذُوا مِن دُونِ اللَّهِ قُرْبَانًا آلِهَةً
بَلْ ضَلُّوا عَنْهُمْ وَذَٰلِكَ إِفْكُهُمْ وَمَا كَانُوا يَفْتَرُونَ ﴿٢٨﴾

1. The Meccans.

وإذ صرفنا إليك نفرا من الجن يستمعون القرآن فلما حضروه
قالوا أنصتوا فلما قضي ولوا إلى قومهم منذرين ٢٩ قالوا يا قومنا
إنا سمعنا كتابا أنزل من بعد موسى مصدقا لما بين يديه يهدي إلى
الحق وإلى طريق مستقيم ٣٠ يا قومنا أجيبوا داعي الله وآمنوا به
يغفر لكم من ذنوبكم ويجركم من عذاب أليم ٣١
ومن لا يجب داعي الله فليس بمعجز في الأرض وليس له من دونه
أولياء أولئك في ضلال مبين ٣٢ أولم يروا أن الله الذي خلق
السماوات والأرض ولم يعي بخلقهن بقادر على أن يحيي الموتى بلى إنه
على كل شيء قدير ٣٣ ويوم يعرض الذين كفروا على النار أليس هذا
بالحق قالوا بلى وربنا قال فذوقوا العذاب بما كنتم تكفرون
٣٤ فاصبر كما صبر أولو العزم من الرسل ولا تستعجل لهم
كأنهم يوم يرون ما يوعدون لم يلبثوا إلا ساعة من
نهار بلاغ فهل يهلك إلا القوم الفاسقون ٣٥

AND TELL how We dis- 46:29
patched to you a band of jinn who, when they came and listened to the Koran, said to each other: 'Hush! Hush!' And as soon as it was ended they betook themselves to their people to give them warning. 'Our people,' they said, 'we have just been listening to a Book revealed since the time of Moses, confirming what had come before it and guiding to the Truth and to a straight path. Our people, answer the call of God's summoner and believe in Him. He will forgive you your sins and deliver you from a woeful scourge. Those that pay no heed to God's summoner shall not go unpunished on the earth. There shall be none to protect them besides Him. Surely they are in evident error.'

Do they not see that God, who created the heavens and the earth and was 46:33
not wearied by their creation, has power to raise the dead to life? Yes. He has power over all things.

The day the unbelievers are arrayed before the Fire they shall be asked: 'Is this not real?' 'Yes, by the Lord,' they will say. 'Then taste the torment,' He will say, 'for you did not believe.'

Bear up then with patience, as did the steadfast apostles before you, and 46:35
do not seek to hurry on their doom. The day they behold the scourge they are promised, their life on earth will seem to them no longer than one hour of a day.

That is a warning. Shall any be destroyed but the ungodly?

MUḤAMMAD

بسم الله الرحمن الرحيم
الذين كفروا وصدوا عن سبيل الله أضل أعمالهم ۝١ والذين آمنوا وعملوا
الصالحات وآمنوا بما نزل على محمد وهو الحق من ربهم كفر عنهم سيئاتهم
وأصلح بالهم ۝٢ ذلك بأن الذين كفروا اتبعوا الباطل وأن الذين آمنوا
اتبعوا الحق من ربهم كذلك يضرب الله للناس أمثالهم ۝٣
فإذا لقيتم الذين كفروا فضرب الرقاب حتى إذا أثخنتموهم
فشدوا الوثاق فإما منا بعد وإما فداء حتى تضع الحرب
أوزارها ذلك ولو يشاء الله لانتصر منهم ولكن ليبلو بعضكم
ببعض والذين قتلوا في سبيل الله فلن يضل أعمالهم ۝٤ سيهديهم
ويصلح بالهم ۝٥ ويدخلهم الجنة عرفها لهم ۝٦ يا أيها
الذين آمنوا إن تنصروا الله ينصركم ويثبت أقدامكم ۝٧
والذين كفروا فتعسا لهم وأضل أعمالهم ۝٨ ذلك بأنهم
كرهوا ما أنزل الله فأحبط أعمالهم ۝٩ أفلم يسيروا في الأرض
فينظروا كيف كان عاقبة الذين من قبلهم دمر الله عليهم وللكافرين أمثالها ۝١٠
ذلك بأن الله مولى الذين آمنوا وأن الكافرين لا مولى لهم ۝١١

In the Name of God,
the Merciful, the Compassionate

47:1 THOSE WHO disbelieve and
debar others from God's path
He will bring their deeds to
nothing. And the faithful who
do good works and believe in
what has been revealed to
Muḥammad – which is the
Truth from their Lord – He
will forgive their sins and
ennoble their estate.

This, because the unbelievers follow falsehood, while the faithful follow the Truth from their Lord. Thus God lays down for mankind their rules of conduct.

When you meet the unbelievers strike off their heads and, when you have wreaked widespread slaughter among them, bind your captives firmly. Then either grant them their freedom or take a ransom from them, until War shall lay down her burdens.

Thus shall you do. Had God willed, He could Himself have punished them; but thus shall it be that He may test you, the one by the other.

As for those who are slain in the cause of God, He will not bring their
47:5 deeds to nothing. He will vouchsafe them guidance and ennoble their estate;
He will admit them into the Paradise He has made known to them.

Believers, if you help God, He will help you and make you strong. But the unbelievers shall be consigned to perdition, and He will bring their deeds to nothing. Because they have abhorred God's revelations, He will frustrate their works.

Have they never journeyed through the land and seen what was the fate
of those who have gone before them? God destroyed them utterly; and a
47:11 similar fate awaits the unbelievers, because God is the protector of the faithful: and because the unbelievers have no protector.

إن الله يدخل الذين آمنوا وعملوا الصالحات جنات تجري من تحتها
الأنهار والذين كفروا يتمتعون ويأكلون كما تأكل الأنعام
والنار مثوى لهم ﴿١٢﴾ وكأين من قرية هي أشد قوة من قريتك
التي أخرجتك أهلكناهم فلا ناصر لهم ﴿١٣﴾ أفمن كان على بينة
من ربه كمن زين له سوء عمله واتبعوا أهواءهم ﴿١٤﴾ مثل الجنة
التي وعد المتقون فيها أنهار من ماء غير آسن وأنهار من لبن لم
يتغير طعمه وأنهار من خمر لذة للشاربين وأنهار من عسل مصفى
ولهم فيها من كل الثمرات ومغفرة من ربهم كمن هو خالد في النار
وسقوا ماء حميما فقطع أمعاءهم ﴿١٥﴾ ومنهم من يستمع إليك
حتى إذا خرجوا من عندك قالوا للذين أوتوا العلم ماذا قال
آنفا أولئك الذين طبع الله على قلوبهم واتبعوا أهواءهم ﴿١٦﴾
والذين اهتدوا زادهم هدى وآتاهم تقواهم ﴿١٧﴾ فهل ينظرون
إلا الساعة أن تأتيهم بغتة فقد جاء أشراطها فأنى لهم إذا
جاءتهم ذكراهم ﴿١٨﴾ فاعلم أنه لا إله إلا الله واستغفر لذنبك
وللمؤمنين والمؤمنات والله يعلم متقلبكم ومثواكم ﴿١٩﴾

GOD WILL surely admit 47:12
those who believe and do good works to Gardens watered by running brooks. The unbelievers take their fill of pleasure and eat as cattle eat: but the Fire shall be their resting-place.

How many cities were mightier than your own city, which has cast you[1] out! We obliterated them, and there was none to succour them.

Can he who follows the guidance of his Lord be compared to him who is led by his desires and whose foul deeds seem fair to him?

Such is the Paradise which the righteous have been promised: therein shall flow rivers of water undefiled, and rivers of milk for ever fresh; rivers of wine delectable to those that drink it, and rivers of clarified honey. Therein shall they have of every fruit, and forgiveness from their Lord. Are they to be compared to those who shall abide in Hell for ever, and drink scalding water that will tear their bowels to pieces?

Some of them indeed listen to you, but no sooner do they leave your pres- 47:16
ence than they ask those endowed with knowledge: 'What did he say just now?' Such are those whose hearts are sealed by God, and who follow their base desires.

As for those who follow the right path, He will increase their guidance and show them the way to righteousness.

Are they waiting for the Hour to overtake them suddenly? Its portents have already come. How else will they be reminded when it does overtake them?

Know that there is no deity but God. Implore Him to forgive your sins 47:19
and to forgive the true believers, men and women. God knows your busy haunts and resting-places.

1. Muḥammad.

47:20 AND THE faithful say: 'If
only a *sūrah* were revealed!' But
when a forthright *sūrah* is
revealed and fighting is mentioned therein, you see the
infirm of heart staring at you
as though they are fainting
away for fear of death. Yet
obedience and courteous speech
would become them better.
Indeed, should fighting be
ordained, it would be better
for them to be true to God.
If you[1] renounced the Faith,
would you not do evil in the
land and violate the ties of
blood? Such are those whom
God has cursed, leaving them
deaf and sightless.
Will they not ponder on the
Koran? Or are there locks
upon their hearts?
47:25 Those who return to un-
belief after God's guidance has been revealed to them are seduced by Satan
and inspired by him. That is because they say to those who abhor the Word
of God: 'We shall obey you in *some* matters.' God knows their secret talk.
What will they do when the angels carry off their souls, striking their faces
and their backs?
Because they follow what has provoked the ire of God and abhor what
pleases Him, He will bring their works to nothing.
47:29 Or do the feeble-hearted think that God will not reveal their malice?

وَيَقُولُ الَّذِينَ آمَنُوا لَوْلَا نُزِّلَتْ سُورَةٌ فَإِذَا أُنزِلَتْ سُورَةٌ مُّحْكَمَةٌ
وَذُكِرَ فِيهَا الْقِتَالُ رَأَيْتَ الَّذِينَ فِي قُلُوبِهِم مَّرَضٌ يَنظُرُونَ إِلَيْكَ
نَظَرَ الْمَغْشِيِّ عَلَيْهِ مِنَ الْمَوْتِ فَأَوْلَىٰ لَهُمْ ﴿٢٠﴾ طَاعَةٌ وَقَوْلٌ
مَّعْرُوفٌ فَإِذَا عَزَمَ الْأَمْرُ فَلَوْ صَدَقُوا اللَّهَ لَكَانَ خَيْرًا لَّهُمْ
﴿٢١﴾ فَهَلْ عَسَيْتُمْ إِن تَوَلَّيْتُمْ أَن تُفْسِدُوا فِي الْأَرْضِ وَتُقَطِّعُوا
أَرْحَامَكُمْ ﴿٢٢﴾ أُولَٰئِكَ الَّذِينَ لَعَنَهُمُ اللَّهُ فَأَصَمَّهُمْ وَأَعْمَىٰ
أَبْصَارَهُمْ ﴿٢٣﴾ أَفَلَا يَتَدَبَّرُونَ الْقُرْآنَ أَمْ عَلَىٰ قُلُوبٍ أَقْفَالُهَا
﴿٢٤﴾ إِنَّ الَّذِينَ ارْتَدُّوا عَلَىٰ أَدْبَارِهِم مِّن بَعْدِ مَا تَبَيَّنَ
لَهُمُ الْهُدَى الشَّيْطَانُ سَوَّلَ لَهُمْ وَأَمْلَىٰ لَهُمْ ﴿٢٥﴾
ذَٰلِكَ بِأَنَّهُمْ قَالُوا لِلَّذِينَ كَرِهُوا مَا نَزَّلَ اللَّهُ
سَنُطِيعُكُمْ فِي بَعْضِ الْأَمْرِ وَاللَّهُ يَعْلَمُ إِسْرَارَهُمْ
﴿٢٦﴾ فَكَيْفَ إِذَا تَوَفَّتْهُمُ الْمَلَائِكَةُ يَضْرِبُونَ وُجُوهَهُمْ
وَأَدْبَارَهُمْ ﴿٢٧﴾ ذَٰلِكَ بِأَنَّهُمُ اتَّبَعُوا مَا أَسْخَطَ اللَّهَ
وَكَرِهُوا رِضْوَانَهُ فَأَحْبَطَ أَعْمَالَهُمْ ﴿٢٨﴾ أَمْ حَسِبَ الَّذِينَ
فِي قُلُوبِهِم مَّرَضٌ أَن لَّن يُخْرِجَ اللَّهُ أَضْغَانَهُمْ ﴿٢٩﴾

1. The hypocrites.

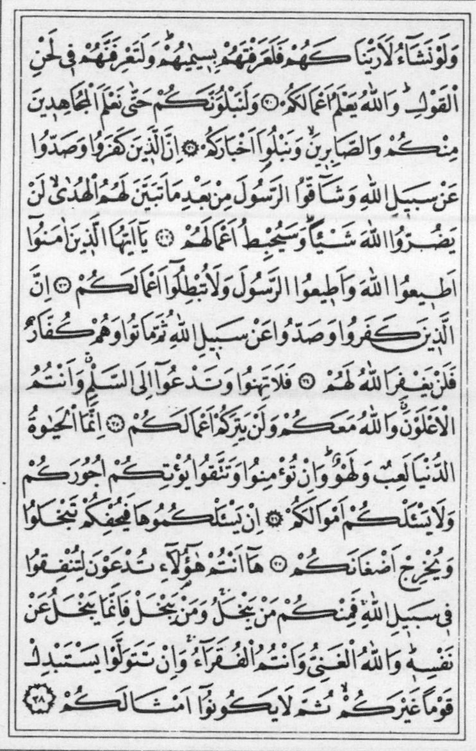

وَلَوْ نَشَاءُ لَأَرَيْنَاكَهُمْ فَلَعَرَفْتَهُم بِسِيمَاهُمْ وَلَتَعْرِفَنَّهُمْ فِي لَحْنِ
الْقَوْلِ وَاللَّهُ يَعْلَمُ أَعْمَالَكُمْ ۝ وَلَنَبْلُوَنَّكُمْ حَتَّىٰ نَعْلَمَ الْمُجَاهِدِينَ
مِنكُمْ وَالصَّابِرِينَ وَنَبْلُوَا أَخْبَارَكُمْ ۝ إِنَّ الَّذِينَ كَفَرُوا وَصَدُّوا
عَن سَبِيلِ اللَّهِ وَشَاقُّوا الرَّسُولَ مِن بَعْدِ مَا تَبَيَّنَ لَهُمُ الْهُدَىٰ لَن
يَضُرُّوا اللَّهَ شَيْئًا وَسَيُحْبِطُ أَعْمَالَهُمْ ۝ يَا أَيُّهَا الَّذِينَ آمَنُوا
أَطِيعُوا اللَّهَ وَأَطِيعُوا الرَّسُولَ وَلَا تُبْطِلُوا أَعْمَالَكُمْ ۝ إِنَّ
الَّذِينَ كَفَرُوا وَصَدُّوا عَن سَبِيلِ اللَّهِ ثُمَّ مَاتُوا وَهُمْ كُفَّارٌ
فَلَن يَغْفِرَ اللَّهُ لَهُمْ ۝ فَلَا تَهِنُوا وَتَدْعُوا إِلَى السَّلْمِ وَأَنتُمُ
الْأَعْلَوْنَ وَاللَّهُ مَعَكُمْ وَلَن يَتِرَكُمْ أَعْمَالَكُمْ ۝ إِنَّمَا الْحَيٰوةُ
الدُّنْيَا لَعِبٌ وَلَهْوٌ وَإِن تُؤْمِنُوا وَتَتَّقُوا يُؤْتِكُمْ أُجُورَكُمْ
وَلَا يَسْأَلْكُمْ أَمْوَالَكُمْ ۝ إِن يَسْأَلْكُمُوهَا فَيُحْفِكُمْ تَبْخَلُوا
وَيُخْرِجْ أَضْغَانَكُمْ ۝ هَا أَنتُمْ هَٰؤُلَاءِ تُدْعَوْنَ لِتُنفِقُوا
فِي سَبِيلِ اللَّهِ فَمِنكُم مَّن يَبْخَلُ وَمَن يَبْخَلْ فَإِنَّمَا يَبْخَلُ عَن
نَّفْسِهِ وَاللَّهُ الْغَنِيُّ وَأَنتُمُ الْفُقَرَاءُ وَإِن تَتَوَلَّوْا يَسْتَبْدِلْ
قَوْمًا غَيْرَكُمْ ثُمَّ لَا يَكُونُوا أَمْثَالَكُمْ ۝٣٨

If We pleased, We could point 47:30
them out to you and you would
recognize them promptly by
their looks: but you will surely
recognize them from the tenor
of their speech. God has
knowledge of all your actions.

We shall put you to the
proof until We know the valiant and the resolute among
you; and We will test all that is
said about you.

The unbelievers who debar
others from the path of God
and disobey the Apostle after
they have seen the light shall in
no way harm God. He will
bring their works to nothing.

Believers, obey God and
obey the Apostle, and let not
your labours come to nothing.

Those that disbelieve and 47:34
debar others from the path of
God and in the end die unbelievers God will never forgive. Therefore do not falter or sue for peace when you have gained the upper hand. God is on your side and will not grudge you the recompense of your labours.

The life of this world is but a sport and a diversion. He will give you your deserts if you believe in Him and fear Him. He does not demand your wealth; if He demanded all and strongly pressed you, you would grow niggardly, and this would show your malice.

It is you who are being called upon to give in the cause of God. Some 47:38
among you are ungenerous; yet whoever is ungenerous to His cause is ungenerous only to his own soul. Indeed, God does not need you, but you need Him. If you pay no heed, He will replace you by other people unlike you.

VICTORY

In the Name of God,
the Merciful, the Compassionate

سورة الفتح مدنية وهي تسع وعشرون آية

بسم الله الرحمن الرحيم

إنا فتحنا لك فتحا مبينا (١) ليغفر لك الله ما تقدم من ذنبك
وما تأخر ويتم نعمته عليك ويهديك صراطا مستقيما
(٢) وينصرك الله نصرا عزيزا (٣) هو الذي أنزل السكينة في قلوب
المؤمنين ليزدادوا إيمانا مع إيمانهم ولله جنود السموات
والأرض وكان الله عليما حكيما (٤) ليدخل المؤمنين والمؤمنات
جنات تجري من تحتها الأنهار خالدين فيها ويكفر عنهم سيئاتهم
وكان ذلك عند الله فوزا عظيما (٥) ويعذب المنافقين والمنافقات
والمشركين والمشركات الظانين بالله ظن السوء عليهم دائرة
السوء وغضب الله عليهم ولعنهم وأعد لهم جهنم وساءت
مصيرا (٦) ولله جنود السموات والأرض وكان الله عزيزا حكيما
(٧) إنا أرسلناك شاهدا ومبشرا ونذيرا (٨) لتؤمنوا بالله ورسوله
وتعزروه وتوقروه وتسبحوه بكرة وأصيلا (٩)

48:1 WE HAVE given you[1] a signal
victory,[2] so that God may forgive you your past and future
sins, and perfect His goodness
to you; that He may guide you
on to a straight path; and that
God may bestow on you His
mighty help.

He it was who sent down
the Divine Presence[3] into the
hearts of the faithful, so that
their faith might grow stronger –
God's are the legions of the
heavens and the earth: God is
all-knowing and wise; that He
may admit the believers, both
men and women, into Gardens
watered by running brooks, therein to abide for ever; that He may forgive
48:6 them their sins – this, in God's sight, is a glorious triumph; and that He may
punish the hypocrites and the idolaters, men and women, who think evil
thoughts about God. A turn of evil shall befall them, for God is angry with
them. He has laid on them His curse and made Hell ready for them: a
wretched fate!

God's are the legions of the heavens and the earth. God is mighty and
wise.

We have sent you[1] forth as a witness and as a bearer of joyful tidings and
48:9 warnings, so that you[4] may have faith in God and His apostle and that you
may assist Him, honour Him, and praise Him morning and evening.

1. Muḥammad.
2. The taking of Mecca in 630, or the Jewish settlement of Khaybar a year earlier.
3. See p. 39, note 1. 4. The Meccans.

إن الذين يبايعونك إنما يبايعون الله يد الله فوق أيديهم
فمن نكث فإنما ينكث على نفسه ومن أوفى بما عاهد عليه الله
فسيؤتيه أجرا عظيما ﴿١٠﴾ سيقول لك المخلفون من الأعراب شغلتنا
أموالنا وأهلونا فاستغفر لنا يقولون بألسنتهم ما ليس في
قلوبهم قل فمن يملك لكم من الله شيئا إن أراد بكم ضرا
أو أراد بكم نفعا بل كان الله بما تعملون خبيرا ﴿١١﴾
بل ظننتم أن لن ينقلب الرسول والمؤمنون إلى أهليهم أبدا
وزين ذلك في قلوبكم وظننتم ظن السوء وكنتم
قوما بورا ﴿١٢﴾ ومن لم يؤمن بالله ورسوله فإنا أعتدنا
للكافرين سعيرا ﴿١٣﴾ ولله ملك السموات والأرض
يغفر لمن يشاء ويعذب من يشاء وكان الله غفورا رحيما
﴿١٤﴾ سيقول المخلفون إذا انطلقتم إلى مغانم لتأخذوها
ذرونا نتبعكم يريدون أن يبدلوا كلام الله
قل لن تتبعونا كذلكم قال الله من قبل فسيقولون بل
تحسدوننا بل كانوا لا يفقهون إلا قليلا ﴿١٥﴾

48:10 Those that swear fealty to you, surely swear fealty to God Himself. The Hand of God is above their hands. He that breaks his oath breaks it at his own peril, but he that keeps his pledge to God shall be richly recompensed by Him.

The desert Arabs who stayed behind[1] will say to you: 'We were occupied with our goods and families. Implore God to pardon us.' They will say with their tongues what they do not mean in their hearts.

Say: 'Who can intervene on your behalf with God if it be His will to do you harm or good? Indeed, God is ever cognizant of what you do.'

48:12 No! You[2] thought the Apostle and the believers would never return to their people; and with this fancy your hearts were delighted. You harboured evil thoughts and thus incurred damnation.

As for those that disbelieve in God and His apostle, for the unbelievers We have prepared a Conflagration. It is God who has sovereignty over the heavens and the earth; He pardons whom He will and punishes whom He pleases. And God is ever forgiving and compassionate.

48:15 Those that stayed behind when you set forth to take some spoils will say: 'Let us come with you.'

They seek to change the Word of God. Say: 'You shall not come with us. So God has said beforehand.'

They will say: 'You are surely jealous of us.' But how little they understand!

1. Away from the fighting. 2. The desert Arabs.

قل للمخلفين من الاعراب ستدعون الى قوم اولي باس شديد
تقاتلونهم او يسلمون فان تطيعوا يؤتكم الله اجرا حسنا وان
تتولوا كما توليتم من قبل يعذبكم عذابا اليما ١٦ ليس على
الاعمى حرج ولا على الاعرج حرج ولا على المريض حرج ومن يطع
الله ورسوله يدخله جنات تجري من تحتها الانهار ومن
يتول يعذبه عذابا اليما ١٧ لقد رضي الله عن المؤمنين
اذ يبايعونك تحت الشجرة فعلم ما في قلوبهم فانزل السكينة
عليهم واثابهم فتحا قريبا ١٨ ومغانم كثيرة ياخذونها وكان
الله عزيزا حكيما ١٩ وعدكم الله مغانم كثيرة
تاخذونها فعجل لكم هذه وكف ايدي الناس عنكم
ولتكون اية للمؤمنين ويهديكم صراطا مستقيما
٢٠ واخرى لم تقدروا عليها قد احاط الله بها وكان
الله على كل شيء قديرا ٢١ ولو قاتلكم الذين كفروا
لولوا الادبار ثم لا يجدون وليا ولا نصيرا ٢٢ سنة
الله التي قد خلت من قبل ولن تجد لسنة الله تبديلا ٢٣

48:16 SAY TO those of the desert Arabs who stayed behind: 'You shall be called upon to fight a people possessed of overwhelming might, unless they willingly embrace Islām. If you prove obedient, God will reward you well. But if you turn away, as you did turn away before this, He will inflict on you a woeful punishment.'

It shall be no offence for the blind, no offence for the lame, and no offence for the sick to stay behind. He that obeys God and His apostle shall be admitted into Gardens watered by running brooks; but on him that turns and flees He will inflict a woeful punishment.

God was well pleased with the faithful when they swore allegiance to you under the tree; He knew what was in their hearts. Therefore He sent down the Divine Presence[1] upon them, and rewarded them with a speedy victory and with abundant spoils to take. Almighty is God and wise.

48:20 God has promised you abundant spoils to take, and has given you this[2] with all promptness. He has stayed your enemies' hands, so that He may make your victory a sign to true believers and guide you along a straight path.

And God knows of other spoils which you have not yet taken. God has power over all things.

If the unbelievers join battle with you, they shall be put to flight. They shall find none to protect or help them.

48:23 Such was the way of God in days gone by: nor shall you ever find change in the way of God.

1. See p. 39, note 1. 2. The spoils taken at Khaybar.

وهو الذي كف أيديهم عنكم وأيديكم عنهم ببطن
مكة من بعد أن أظفركم عليهم وكان الله بما تعملون
بصيرا ٢٤ هم الذين كفروا وصدوكم عن المسجد الحرام
والهدي معكوفا أن يبلغ محله ولولا رجال مؤمنون ونساء
مؤمنات لم تعلموهم أن تطئوهم فتصيبكم منهم معرة
بغير علم ليدخل الله في رحمته من يشاء لو تزيلوا لعذبنا
الذين كفروا منهم عذابا أليما ٢٥ إذ جعل الذين كفروا
في قلوبهم الحمية حمية الجاهلية فأنزل الله سكينته
على رسوله وعلى المؤمنين وألزمهم كلمة التقوى
وكانوا أحق بها وأهلها وكان الله بكل شيء عليما
٢٦ لقد صدق الله رسوله الرؤيا بالحق لتدخلن المسجد
الحرام إن شاء الله آمنين محلقين رءوسكم ومقصرين
لا تخافون فعلم ما لم تعلموا فجعل من دون ذلك فتحا
قريبا ٢٧ هو الذي أرسل رسوله بالهدى ودين
الحق ليظهره على الدين كله وكفى بالله شهيدا ٢٨

AND HE it was who ended 48:24
hostilities between you in the Valley of Mecca[1] after He had given you victory over them. God was watching all your actions.

It was they who disbelieved and debarred you from the Sacred Mosque and prevented your offerings from reaching their destination. But for the fear that you might have trampled underfoot believing men and women unknown to you and thus incurred unwitting guilt on their account, He ordained it thus that He might admit whom He will into His mercy. Had they stood apart from them, We would have inflicted a woeful punishment on those of them who were unbelievers.

And while bigotry – the bigotry of ignorance – was holding sway in the 48:26
hearts of the unbelievers, God sent down His Divine Presence[2] on His apostle and on the faithful and made the word of piety binding on them, for they were most worthy and deserving of it. God has knowledge of all things.

God has in all truth fulfilled His apostle's vision: 'If God wills, you shall enter the Sacred Mosque secure and fearless, with hair cropped or shaven.' He knew what you knew not; and what is more, He granted you a speedy victory.

He it is that has sent forth His apostle with guidance and the Religion of 48:28
Truth, that he may exalt it above all religion. Sufficient is God as a witness.

1. The allusion is probably to the Peace of Ḥudaybiyya, in 628.

2. See p. 39, note 1.

48:29 MUHAMMAD IS God's apostle. And those who follow him are ruthless to the unbelievers but merciful to one another. You behold them worshipping on their knees, seeking grace from God and His good will. Their marks are on their faces, the traces of their prostrations. Thus are they described in the Torah, and are described in the Gospel:[1] they are like the seed which puts forth its shoot and strengthens it, so that it rises stout and firm upon its stalk, delighting the sowers. Through them He seeks to enrage the unbelievers. Yet to those of them who will embrace the Faith and do good works God has promised forgiveness and a rich recompense.

محمد رسول الله والذين معه أشداء على الكفار رحماء بينهم
تراهم ركعا سجدا يبتغون فضلا من الله ورضوانا سيماهم
في وجوههم من أثر السجود ذلك مثلهم في التوراة ومثلهم
في الإنجيل كزرع أخرج شطأه فآزره فاستغلظ فاستوى
على سوقه يعجب الزراع ليغيظ بهم الكفار وعد
الله الذين آمنوا وعملوا الصالحات منهم مغفرة وأجرا عظيما ٢٩

سورة الحجرات مدنية وهي ثماني عشرة آية

بسم الله الرحمن الرحيم

يا أيها الذين آمنوا لا تقدموا بين يدي الله ورسوله واتقوا
الله إن الله سميع عليم ١ يا أيها الذين آمنوا لا ترفعوا أصواتكم
فوق صوت النبي ولا تجهروا له بالقول كجهر بعضكم لبعض أن تحبط
أعمالكم وأنتم لا تشعرون ٢ إن الذين يغضون أصواتهم عند رسول
الله أولئك الذين امتحن الله قلوبهم للتقوى لهم مغفرة وأجر عظيم
٣ إن الذين ينادونك من وراء الحجرات أكثرهم لا يعقلون ٤

THE CHAMBERS

In the Name of God, the Merciful, the Compassionate

49:1 BELIEVERS, DO not behave presumptuously in the presence of God and His apostle. And fear God: surely God hears all and knows all.

Believers, do not raise your voices above the voice of the Prophet, nor shout aloud when speaking to him as you do to one another, lest your labours should come to nothing without your knowledge. Those who speak softly in the presence of God's apostle are those whose hearts God has tested for piety. Forgiveness and a rich reward await them.

49:4 Those who call out to you[2] while you are in your chambers are for the most part devoid of understanding.

1. Cf. Mark 4:26–9. 2. Muḥammad.

ولو انهم صبروا حتى تخرج اليهم لكان خيرا لهم والله
غفور رحيم ٥ يا ايها الذين امنوا ان جاءكم فاسق بنبا
فتبينوا ان تصيبوا قوما بجهالة فتصبحوا على ما فعلتم نادمين
٦ واعلموا ان فيكم رسول الله لو يطيعكم في كثير من
الامر لعنتم ولكن الله حبب اليكم الايمان وزينه في قلوبكم
وكره اليكم الكفر والفسوق والعصيان اولئك هم الراشدون
٧ فضلا من الله ونعمة والله عليم حكيم ٨ وان طائفتان
من المؤمنين اقتتلوا فاصلحوا بينهما فان بغت احديهما على الاخرى
فقاتلوا التي تبغي حتى تفيء الى امر الله فان فاءت فاصلحوا
بينهما بالعدل واقسطوا ان الله يحب المقسطين ٩
انما المؤمنون اخوة فاصلحوا بين اخويكم واتقوا الله
لعلكم ترحمون ١٠ يا ايها الذين امنوا لا يسخر قوم من قوم عسى
ان يكونوا خيرا منهم ولا نساء من نساء عسى ان يكن خيرا منهن
ولا تلمزوا انفسكم ولا تنابزوا بالالقاب بئس الاسم الفسوق
بعد الايمان ومن لم يتب فاولئك هم الظالمون ١١

IF THEY waited until you went 49:5
out to them, it would be better for them. But God is forgiving and compassionate.

Believers, if a mischief maker brings you a piece of news, inquire first into its truth, lest you should wrong people unwittingly and then regret your action.

And be aware that God's apostle is among you. If he obeyed you in many matters, you would surely come to grief. But God has endeared the Faith to you and beautified it in your hearts, making unbelief, wrongdoing, and disobedience abhorrent to you. Such are those who are rightly guided through God's grace and bounty. God is all-knowing and wise.

If two parties of believers take up arms the one against the other, make 49:9
peace between them. If either of them unjustly attacks the other, fight the aggressors till they submit to God's judgement. When they have submitted, make peace between them in equity and fairness; God loves those who exercise fairness.

The believers are a band of brothers. Make peace among your brothers and fear God, that you may be shown mercy.

Believers, let no people mock other people, who may perhaps be better 49:11
than themselves. And let no women mock other women, who may perhaps be better than themselves. Do not defame one another, nor call one another by nicknames. It is an evil thing to be called by a bad name after embracing the Faith. Those that do not repent are themselves the wrongdoers.

49:12 BELIEVERS, AVOID im-
moderate suspicion, for in
some cases suspicion is a
crime. Do not spy on one
another, nor backbite one
another. Would any of you
like to eat the flesh of his
dead brother? Surely you
would loathe it. And fear
God; God pardons and is
compassionate.

You people! We have cre-
ated you from a male and a
female, and made you into
communities and tribes, that
you might get to know one
another. The noblest of you
in God's sight is he who fears
Him. God is all-knowing and
conversant with all.

The Arabs of the desert
say: 'We are believers.' Say:
'Believers you are not. Rather
say: "We profess Islām," for faith has not yet found its way into your hearts.
If you obey God and His apostle, He will in no way deny you the reward of
your labours. Surely God is forgiving and compassionate.'

49:15 The true believers are those that believe in God and His apostle, and
never doubt afterwards; and who fight with their wealth and with their
persons in the cause of God. Such are those whose faith is true.

Say: 'Would you instruct God in your religion, when God knows what the
heavens and the earth contain? When God has knowledge of all things?'

They think they have conferred on you a favour by embracing Islām. Say:
'In accepting Islām you have conferred on me no favour. It was God who
bestowed a favour on you in guiding you to the true Faith. Admit this, if you
49:18 are truthful. God knows all that is hidden in the heavens and the earth. God
is cognizant of what you do.'

يا أيها الذين آمنوا اجتنبوا كثيرا من الظن إن بعض الظن إثم
ولا تجسسوا ولا يغتب بعضكم بعضا أيحب أحدكم أن يأكل لحم
أخيه ميتا فكرهتموه واتقوا الله إن الله تواب رحيم
(١٢) يا أيها الناس إنا خلقناكم من ذكر وأنثى وجعلناكم
شعوبا وقبائل لتعارفوا إن أكرمكم عند الله أتقاكم إن الله
عليم خبير (١٣) قالت الأعراب آمنا قل لم تؤمنوا ولكن قولوا
أسلمنا ولما يدخل الإيمان في قلوبكم وإن تطيعوا الله
ورسوله لا يلتكم من أعمالكم شيئا إن الله غفور رحيم
(١٤) إنما المؤمنون الذين آمنوا بالله ورسوله ثم لم
يرتابوا وجاهدوا بأموالهم وأنفسهم في سبيل الله
أولئك هم الصادقون (١٥) قل أتعلمون الله بدينكم والله
يعلم ما في السماوات وما في الأرض والله بكل شيء عليم
(١٦) يمنون عليك أن أسلموا قل لا تمنوا علي إسلامكم بل الله
يمن عليكم أن هداكم للإيمان إن كنتم صادقين (١٧) إن الله
يعلم غيب السماوات والأرض والله بصير بما تعملون (١٨)

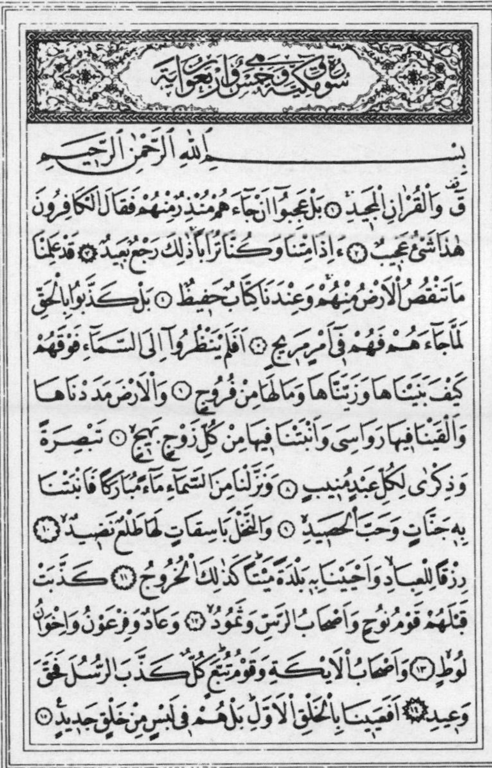
سورة ق مكية وخمس وأربعون آية
بسم الله الرحمن الرحيم
ق والقرآن المجيد ۝ بل عجبوا أن جاءهم منذر منهم فقال الكافرون
هذا شيء عجيب ۝٢ أإذا متنا وكنا ترابا ذلك رجع بعيد ۝ قد علمنا
ما تنقص الأرض منهم وعندنا كتاب حفيظ ۝ بل كذبوا بالحق
لما جاءهم فهم في أمر مريج ۝ أفلم ينظروا إلى السماء فوقهم
كيف بنيناها وزيناها وما لها من فروج ۝ والأرض مددناها
وألقينا فيها رواسي وأنبتنا فيها من كل زوج بهيج ۝ تبصرة
وذكرى لكل عبد منيب ۝ ونزلنا من السماء ماء مباركا فأنبتنا
به جنات وحب الحصيد ۝ والنخل باسقات لها طلع نضيد ۝١٠
رزقا للعباد وأحيينا به بلدة ميتا كذلك الخروج ۝١١ كذبت
قبلهم قوم نوح وأصحاب الرس وثمود ۝١٢ وعاد وفرعون وإخوان
لوط ۝١٣ وأصحاب الأيكة وقوم تبع كل كذب الرسل فحق
وعيد ۝١٤ أفعيينا بالخلق الأول بل هم في لبس من خلق جديد ۝١٥

QĀF

In the Name of God,
the Merciful, the Compassionate

Qāf. By the Glorious Koran! 50:1
They indeed marvel that one of their own has come to warn them; so that the unbelievers say: 'This is indeed a wondrous thing. When we are dead and turned to dust . . . ?[1] Such a return is most improbable!'

We know how the earth consumes them. We hold a Book which records all.

Indeed, they denied the Truth when it had come to them, and now they are perplexed. Have they never observed the sky above them, how We built it up and furnished it with ornaments, leaving no crack in its expanse?

And We spread out the earth and set upon it immovable mountains. We brought forth from it all kinds of delectable plants. A lesson and an Admonition to every penitent mortal.

We send down blessed water from the sky with which We bring forth 50:9
gardens and the harvest grain, and tall palm-trees laden with clusters of dates, a sustenance for humankind; thereby giving new life to a dead land. Such shall be the Resurrection.

Long before these the people of Noah and the dwellers of Al-Rass[2] denied the Truth; and so did Thamūd and 'Ād, Pharaoh and the kin of Lot, the dwellers of the Forest[3] and the people of Tubba';[4] all disbelieved the apostles and were thus visited by My threatened scourge.

Were We worn out by the First Creation? Yet they are in doubt about a 50:15
new creation.[5]

1. '[. . . shall we be raised to life]?'
2. Commentators are disagreed as to the identity of this place name. Some say it is a town in Yamāmah, others a well in Midian.
3. The people of Midian.
4. The people of Himyar, whose kings bore the title of Tubba'.
5. The Resurrection.

50:16 *We* created man; We know the promptings of his soul, and are closer to him than his jugular vein.

When the twin keepers receive him, seated on his right, and on his left, no word he utters but shall be noted down by a vigilant guard.

And when the agony of death comes upon him with the Truth, they will say: 'This is the fate you endeavoured to avoid.' And the Trumpet shall be blown: that is the promised day.

Each soul shall come attended by one who will drive it on, and another to testify against it: 'Of this you have been heedless; now we have removed your veil, so that today your sight is keen.' And his companion will say: 'My testimony is ready to hand.'

'Cast, you two, into Hell every hardened unbeliever, every opponent of good, every doubting transgressor who has set up another deity besides God. Hurl him, you two, into the harrowing scourge!'

50:27 His companion[1] will say: 'Lord, I did not mislead him. He had already strayed far into error.'

He will say: 'Do not dispute in My presence. I did forewarn you; My word cannot be changed, nor am I unjust to mortals.'

On that day, We shall say to Hell: 'Are you now full?' And Hell will say: 'Are there any more?'

And, not far thence, Paradise shall be brought close to the righteous: 'Here is what you were promised: for every penitent and honest man, who fears the Merciful though unseen, and comes before Him with a contrite heart. Enter it in peace. This is the day of immortality.'

50:35 Therein shall they have all that they desire; and We have yet more.

ولقد خلقنا الإنسان ونعلم ما توسوس به نفسه ونحن أقرب إليه
من حبل الوريد ١٦ إذ يتلقى المتلقيان عن اليمين وعن الشمال
قعيد ١٧ ما يلفظ من قول إلا لديه رقيب عتيد ١٨ وجاءت سكرة
الموت بالحق ذلك ما كنت منه تحيد ١٩ ونفخ في الصور ذلك يوم
الوعيد ٢٠ وجاءت كل نفس معها سائق وشهيد ٢١ لقد كنت في
غفلة من هذا فكشفنا عنك غطاءك فبصرك اليوم حديد ٢٢ وقال
قرينه هذا ما لدي عتيد ٢٣ ألقيا في جهنم كل كفار عنيد ٢٤
مناع للخير معتد مريب ٢٥ الذي جعل مع الله إلها آخر
فألقياه في العذاب الشديد ٢٦ قال قرينه ربنا ما أطغيته
ولكن كان في ضلال بعيد ٢٧ قال لا تختصموا لدي وقد قدمت
إليكم بالوعيد ٢٨ ما يبدل القول لدي وما أنا بظلام للعبيد
٢٩ يوم نقول لجهنم هل امتلأت وتقول هل من مزيد ٣٠ وأزلفت
الجنة للمتقين غير بعيد ٣١ هذا ما توعدون لكل أواب حفيظ ٣٢
من خشي الرحمن بالغيب وجاء بقلب منيب ٣٣ ادخلوها بسلام
ذلك يوم الخلود ٣٤ لهم ما يشاءون فيها ولدينا مزيد ٣٥

1. The demon who is chained to him.

وكم أهلكنا قبلهم من قرن هم أشد منهم بطشا فنقبوا
في البلاد هل من محيص ٣٦ إن في ذلك لذكرى لمن كان له
قلب أو ألقى السمع وهو شهيد ٣٧ ولقد خلقنا السموات
والأرض وما بينهما في ستة أيام وما مسنا من لغوب ٣٨
فاصبر على ما يقولون وسبح بحمد ربك قبل طلوع الشمس
وقبل الغروب ٣٩ ومن الليل فسبحه وأدبار السجود ٤٠ واستمع
يوم يناد المناد من مكان قريب ٤١ يوم يسمعون الصيحة بالحق ذلك
يوم الخروج ٤٢ إنا نحن نحيي ونميت وإلينا المصير ٤٣ يوم تشقق
الأرض عنهم سراعا ذلك حشر علينا يسير ٤٤ نحن أعلم بما
يقولون وما أنت عليهم بجبار فذكر بالقرآن من يخاف وعيد ٤٥

سورة الذاريات مكية وهي ستون آية

بسم الله الرحمن الرحيم

والذاريات ذروا ١ فالحاملات وقرا ٢ فالجاريات يسرا ٣
فالمقسمات أمرا ٤ إنما توعدون لصادق ٥ وإن الدين لواقع ٦

How many generations, 50:36
far greater in prowess, have
We wiped out before them!
They searched the entire land:
but could they find a refuge?
Surely in this there is a lesson
for everyone who is of a heart
possessed, and can hear and
see.

In six days We created the
heavens and the earth and all
that lies between them; nor
were We ever wearied.

Bear then with what they[1]
say. Give glory to your Lord
before sunrise and before sunset. In the night praise Him,
and make the additional prostrations.

Listen on the day when 50:41
the Crier will call from near;
the day when they will hear the
cry of Truth. On that day they
will rise up from their graves. It is We who ordain life and death; and to Us
shall all return.

On that day the earth will be rent asunder over them, and from it they
shall emerge in haste. To herd them all is easy enough for Us.

We well know what they say. You shall not use coercion with them. 50:45
Admonish with the Koran whoever fears My threat.

THE WINDS

In the Name of God, the Merciful, the Compassionate

By the dust-scattering winds and the heavily-laden clouds; by the 51:1
smoothly-gliding ships, and by the angels who deal out as commanded; that
which you are promised shall truly be fulfilled, and the Last Judgement shall 51:6
surely come to pass!

1. The unbelievers.

51:7 BY THE heaven with its starry highways, the words you utter are inconsistent! None but the perverse turn away from the Truth. Perish the liars, who dwell in darkness and are heedless of the life to come!

'When will the Day of Judgement be?' they ask. On that day they shall be scourged in the Fire: 'Taste this, the punishment you sought to hasten!'

The righteous shall dwell amidst gardens and fountains, and shall receive what their Lord will give them. For they did good works before, sleeping but little in the night-time, praying at dawn for God's pardon, and sharing their goods with the beggars and the dispossessed.

وَالسَّمَاءِ ذَاتِ الْحُبُكِ ۝ إِنَّكُمْ لَفِي قَوْلٍ مُّخْتَلِفٍ ۝ يُؤْفَكُ عَنْهُ
مَنْ أُفِكَ ۝ قُتِلَ الْخَرَّاصُونَ ۝ الَّذِينَ هُمْ فِي غَمْرَةٍ سَاهُونَ ۝
يَسْأَلُونَ أَيَّانَ يَوْمُ الدِّينِ ۝ يَوْمَ هُمْ عَلَى النَّارِ يُفْتَنُونَ ۝ ذُوقُوا
فِتْنَتَكُمْ هَٰذَا الَّذِي كُنتُم بِهِ تَسْتَعْجِلُونَ ۝ إِنَّ الْمُتَّقِينَ فِي
جَنَّاتٍ وَعُيُونٍ ۝ آخِذِينَ مَا آتَاهُمْ رَبُّهُمْ إِنَّهُمْ كَانُوا قَبْلَ ذَٰلِكَ
مُحْسِنِينَ ۝ كَانُوا قَلِيلًا مِّنَ اللَّيْلِ مَا يَهْجَعُونَ ۝ وَبِالْأَسْحَارِ هُمْ
يَسْتَغْفِرُونَ ۝ وَفِي أَمْوَالِهِمْ حَقٌّ لِّلسَّائِلِ وَالْمَحْرُومِ ۝ وَفِي
الْأَرْضِ آيَاتٌ لِّلْمُوقِنِينَ ۝ وَفِي أَنفُسِكُمْ أَفَلَا تُبْصِرُونَ ۝ وَفِي
السَّمَاءِ رِزْقُكُمْ وَمَا تُوعَدُونَ ۝ فَوَرَبِّ السَّمَاءِ وَالْأَرْضِ إِنَّهُ لَحَقٌّ
مِّثْلَ مَا أَنَّكُمْ تَنطِقُونَ ۝ هَلْ أَتَاكَ حَدِيثُ ضَيْفِ إِبْرَاهِيمَ الْمُكْرَمِينَ
۝ إِذْ دَخَلُوا عَلَيْهِ فَقَالُوا سَلَامًا قَالَ سَلَامٌ قَوْمٌ مُّنكَرُونَ
۝ فَرَاغَ إِلَىٰ أَهْلِهِ فَجَاءَ بِعِجْلٍ سَمِينٍ ۝ فَقَرَّبَهُ إِلَيْهِمْ قَالَ أَلَا
تَأْكُلُونَ ۝ فَأَوْجَسَ مِنْهُمْ خِيفَةً قَالُوا لَا تَخَفْ وَبَشَّرُوهُ بِغُلَامٍ
عَلِيمٍ ۝ فَأَقْبَلَتِ امْرَأَتُهُ فِي صَرَّةٍ فَصَكَّتْ وَجْهَهَا وَقَالَتْ عَجُوزٌ
عَقِيمٌ ۝ قَالُوا كَذَٰلِكِ قَالَ رَبُّكِ إِنَّهُ هُوَ الْحَكِيمُ الْعَلِيمُ ۝

On earth there are signs for firm believers and in your own souls. Can you not see?

51:23 Heaven holds your sustenance and all that you are promised. I swear by
the Lord of heaven and earth that this is true, as true as you are speaking now!

Have you heard the story of Abraham's honoured guests?[1]

They went in to him and said: 'Peace!' 'Peace!' he said and, seeing that they were strangers, betook himself to his family and returned with a fatted calf. He placed it before them, saying: 'Will you not eat?'

He grew afraid of them, but they said, 'Have no fear,' and told him he was to have a son endowed with knowledge.

His wife came crying and beating her face. 'Surely I am a barren old woman,' she said.

51:30 'Such is the will of your Lord,' they said. 'He surely is the Wise One, the
All-knowing.'

1. Cf. Genesis 18.

قال فما خطبكم أيها المرسلون ۝ قالوا إنا أرسلنا إلى قوم
مجرمين ۝ لنرسل عليهم حجارة من طين ۝ مسومة عند ربك
للمسرفين ۝ فأخرجنا من كان فيها من المؤمنين ۝ فما وجدنا فيها
غير بيت من المسلمين ۝ وتركنا فيها آية للذين يخافون العذاب
الأليم ۝ وفي موسى إذ أرسلناه إلى فرعون بسلطان مبين ۝
فتولى بركنه وقال ساحر أو مجنون ۝ فأخذناه وجنوده
فنبذناهم في اليم وهو مليم ۝ وفي عاد إذ أرسلنا عليهم الريح
العقيم ۝ ما تذر من شيء أتت عليه إلا جعلته كالرميم ۝
وفي ثمود إذ قيل لهم تمتعوا حتى حين ۝ فعتوا عن أمر ربهم
فأخذتهم الصاعقة وهم ينظرون ۝ فما استطاعوا من قيام
وما كانوا منتصرين ۝ وقوم نوح من قبل إنهم كانوا قوما فاسقين
۝ والسماء بنيناها بأيد وإنا لموسعون ۝ والأرض فرشناها
فنعم الماهدون ۝ ومن كل شيء خلقنا زوجين لعلكم
تذكرون ۝ ففروا إلى الله إني لكم منه نذير مبين ۝
ولا تجعلوا مع الله إلها آخر إني لكم منه نذير مبين ۝

'MESSENGERS,' SAID he, 51:31
'what is your errand?'

They said: 'We are sent forth to a perverted people, that we may bring down on them a shower of clay-stones marked by your Lord for the destruction of the sinful.'

We led all the believers out of the town – We found but one household of true Muslims – and left therein a sign for those who fear the woeful scourge.

And in Moses there was a sign. We sent him forth to Pharaoh with manifest authority, but he turned his back, he and his nobles, saying: 'A sorcerer, or a man possessed.' So We seized him and his warriors, and cast them into the sea. Indeed, he deserved much blame.

In the fate of 'Ād there was another sign. We let loose on them a blighting wind, which pounded into dust all that it swept before it.

And in Thamūd. They had been told: 'Enjoy yourselves till a time decreed';
but they disobeyed the commandment of their Lord. The thunderbolt struck 51:44
them as they looked on; they could not rise up from their fall, nor did they gain their end.

And the people of Noah before them. Surely they too were a degenerate people.

The heaven We built with mighty hands, giving it a vast expanse, and stretched the earth beneath it: gracious is He who spread it out. And all things We have made in pairs, so that you may take thought.

Therefore seek God. From Him I come to you with a clear warning. You 51:51
shall not set up another deity besides God. From Him I come to you with a clear warning.

51:52 THUS NO apostle ever came
to those before them[1] but that
they said: 'Sorcerer!' or 'A man
possessed!' Have they handed
this down from one generation to the next? Surely they
are transgressors all.

Pay no heed to them; you shall incur no blame. Exhort them; exhortation helps the true believers.

51:56 I created the jinn and mankind only that they might
worship Me. I demand no livelihood of them, nor do I ask that they should feed Me.

God alone is the Munificent Giver, the Mighty One, the Invincible. The wrongdoers' sins are like the sins of those that sinned before them; so let them not hurry Me on.
51:60 Woe betide then the unbeliev-
ers when their promised day is come!

كذلك ما أتى الذين من قبلهم من رسول إلا قالوا ساحر أو
مجنون ﴿٥٢﴾ أتواصوا به بل هم قوم طاغون ﴿٥٣﴾ فتول عنهم
فما أنت بملوم ﴿٥٤﴾ وذكر فإن الذكرى تنفع المؤمنين ﴿٥٥﴾
وما خلقت الجن والإنس إلا ليعبدون ﴿٥٦﴾ ما أريد منهم من
رزق وما أريد أن يطعمون ﴿٥٧﴾ إن الله هو الرزاق ذو
القوة المتين ﴿٥٨﴾ فإن للذين ظلموا ذنوبا مثل ذنوب أصحابهم فلا
يستعجلون ﴿٥٩﴾ فويل للذين كفروا من يومهم الذي يوعدون ﴿٦٠﴾

سورة الطور مكية وهي تسع وأربعون آية

بسم الله الرحمن الرحيم

والطور ﴿١﴾ وكتاب مسطور ﴿٢﴾ في رق منشور ﴿٣﴾ والبيت المعمور ﴿٤﴾
والسقف المرفوع ﴿٥﴾ والبحر المسجور ﴿٦﴾ إن عذاب ربك لواقع ﴿٧﴾ ما له من
دافع ﴿٨﴾ يوم تمور السماء مورا ﴿٩﴾ وتسير الجبال سيرا ﴿١٠﴾ فويل يومئذ
للمكذبين ﴿١١﴾ الذين هم في خوض يلعبون ﴿١٢﴾ يوم يدعون إلى
نار جهنم دعا ﴿١٣﴾ هذه النار التي كنتم بها تكذبون ﴿١٤﴾

THE MOUNT

In the Name of God, the Merciful, the Compassionate

52:1 BY THE Mount,[2] and by a Book penned on unrolled parchment; by the
Visited House,[3] the Lofty Vault,[4] and the swelling sea, your Lord's punishment shall surely come to pass! No power shall ward it off.

On that day the heaven will shake and reel, and the mountains move and pass away. Woe betide on that day the unbelievers, who now divert themselves with profane talk.

52:14 On that day they shall be hurled into the fire of Hell: 'This is the Fire
which you denied.

1. The Meccans.
2. Mount Sinai.
3. The Ka'bah.
4. The sky.

أَفَسِحْرٌ هَٰذَا أَمْ أَنتُمْ لَا تُبْصِرُونَ ﴿١٥﴾ اصْلَوْهَا فَاصْبِرُوا
أَوْ لَا تَصْبِرُوا سَوَاءٌ عَلَيْكُمْ إِنَّمَا تُجْزَوْنَ مَا كُنتُمْ تَعْمَلُونَ ﴿١٦﴾
إِنَّ الْمُتَّقِينَ فِي جَنَّاتٍ وَنَعِيمٍ ﴿١٧﴾ فَاكِهِينَ بِمَا آتَاهُمْ رَبُّهُمْ
وَوَقَاهُمْ رَبُّهُمْ عَذَابَ الْجَحِيمِ ﴿١٨﴾ كُلُوا وَاشْرَبُوا هَنِيئًا بِمَا كُنتُمْ
تَعْمَلُونَ ﴿١٩﴾ مُتَّكِئِينَ عَلَىٰ سُرُرٍ مَّصْفُوفَةٍ وَزَوَّجْنَاهُم بِحُورٍ عِينٍ
﴿٢٠﴾ وَالَّذِينَ آمَنُوا وَاتَّبَعَتْهُمْ ذُرِّيَّتُهُم بِإِيمَانٍ أَلْحَقْنَا بِهِمْ
ذُرِّيَّتَهُمْ وَمَا أَلَتْنَاهُم مِّنْ عَمَلِهِم مِّن شَيْءٍ كُلُّ امْرِئٍ بِمَا كَسَبَ
رَهِينٌ ﴿٢١﴾ وَأَمْدَدْنَاهُم بِفَاكِهَةٍ وَلَحْمٍ مِّمَّا يَشْتَهُونَ ﴿٢٢﴾
يَتَنَازَعُونَ فِيهَا كَأْسًا لَّا لَغْوٌ فِيهَا وَلَا تَأْثِيمٌ ﴿٢٣﴾ وَيَطُوفُ عَلَيْهِمْ
غِلْمَانٌ لَّهُمْ كَأَنَّهُمْ لُؤْلُؤٌ مَّكْنُونٌ ﴿٢٤﴾ وَأَقْبَلَ بَعْضُهُمْ عَلَىٰ
بَعْضٍ يَتَسَاءَلُونَ ﴿٢٥﴾ قَالُوا إِنَّا كُنَّا قَبْلُ فِي أَهْلِنَا مُشْفِقِينَ
﴿٢٦﴾ فَمَنَّ اللَّهُ عَلَيْنَا وَوَقَانَا عَذَابَ السَّمُومِ ﴿٢٧﴾ إِنَّا كُنَّا مِن قَبْلُ
نَدْعُوهُ إِنَّهُ هُوَ الْبَرُّ الرَّحِيمُ ﴿٢٨﴾ فَذَكِّرْ فَمَا أَنتَ بِنِعْمَتِ رَبِّكَ
بِكَاهِنٍ وَلَا مَجْنُونٍ ﴿٢٩﴾ أَمْ يَقُولُونَ شَاعِرٌ نَّتَرَبَّصُ بِهِ رَيْبَ
الْمَنُونِ ﴿٣٠﴾ قُلْ تَرَبَّصُوا فَإِنِّي مَعَكُم مِّنَ الْمُتَرَبِّصِينَ ﴿٣١﴾

'Is THIS sorcery, or can you not see? Burn in its flames. It is the same whether or not you show forbearance. You shall be recompensed according only to your deeds.' 52:15

But in fair Gardens the righteous shall dwell in bliss, rejoicing in what their Lord will give them. Their Lord will shield them from the scourge of Hell. 'Eat and drink to your hearts' content, in recompense for what you did.'

They shall recline on couches ranged in rows. To dark-eyed houris We shall wed them.

We shall unite the true believers with those of their descendants who follow them in their faith, and shall not deny them the reward of their good works; each man is the hostage of his own deeds.

Fruits We shall give them, and such meats as they desire. They will pass 52:23
from hand to hand a cup inspiring no idle talk, no sinful urge; and there shall wait on them young boys of their own, as fair as virgin pearls.

They will approach one another, asking questions. 'When we were living among our kin,' they will say, 'we were troubled by many fears. But God has been gracious to us; He has preserved us from the fiery scourge, for we prayed to Him in days gone by. He alone is the Beneficent One, the Compassionate.'

Therefore give warning. By the grace of God, you are neither soothsayer nor madman.

Or do they say: 'He is but a poet: we are waiting for the uncertainty of
Fate to befall him'? Say: 'Wait if you will; I will wait with you.' 52:31

52:32 Or does their reason bid them say this? Or is it that they are wicked people?

Or do they say: 'He has invented it[1] himself'? Indeed, they have no faith. Let them produce a scripture like it, if what they say be true!

Or were they created out of the void? Or were they their own creators?

Or did *they* create the heavens and the earth? Surely they have no faith!

Or do they hold the treasures of your Lord, and have control absolute?

Or have they a ladder by means of which they overhear Him? Let their eavesdropper bring a positive proof!

Is He to have the daughters and you[2] the sons?

Or are you[3] demanding payment of them, that they should fear to be weighed down with debts?

Or have they knowledge of what is hidden? Can they write it down?

52:42 Or are they scheming? It is the unbelievers' schemes that shall come to nothing.

Or have they a deity other than God? Exalted be God above their idols!

And if they saw a piece of heaven falling down, they would still say: 'It is but a pile of clouds!'

So let them be, until they face the day when they shall stand dumbfounded; the day when their schemes shall be of no avail to them; and they shall not be helped.

And besides this a scourge awaits the wrongdoers, though most of them do not know it.

Await with patience the judgement of your Lord: you are ever in Our sight.
52:49 And give glory to your Lord when you rise, in the night-time praise Him, and
at the setting of the stars.

1. The Koran. 2. The unbelievers. 3. Muḥammad.

THE STAR

بسم الله الرحمن الرحيم
والنجم إذا هوى ﴿١﴾ ما ضل صاحبكم وما غوى ﴿٢﴾ وما ينطق عن
الهوى ﴿٣﴾ إن هو إلا وحي يوحى ﴿٤﴾ علمه شديد القوى ﴿٥﴾ ذو مرة
فاستوى ﴿٦﴾ وهو بالأفق الأعلى ﴿٧﴾ ثم دنا فتدلى ﴿٨﴾ فكان
قاب قوسين أو أدنى ﴿٩﴾ فأوحى إلى عبده ما أوحى ﴿١٠﴾ ما كذب
الفؤاد ما رأى ﴿١١﴾ أفتمارونه على ما يرى ﴿١٢﴾ ولقد رآه نزلة
أخرى ﴿١٣﴾ عند سدرة المنتهى ﴿١٤﴾ عندها جنة المأوى ﴿١٥﴾ إذ يغشى
السدرة ما يغشى ﴿١٦﴾ ما زاغ البصر وما طغى ﴿١٧﴾ لقد رأى من
آيات ربه الكبرى ﴿١٨﴾ أفرأيتم اللات والعزى ﴿١٩﴾ ومنوة
الثالثة الأخرى ﴿٢٠﴾ ألكم الذكر وله الأنثى ﴿٢١﴾ تلك إذا
قسمة ضيزى ﴿٢٢﴾ إن هي إلا أسماء سميتموها أنتم وآباؤكم ما
أنزل الله بها من سلطان إن يتبعون إلا الظن وما تهوى
الأنفس ولقد جاءهم من ربهم الهدى ﴿٢٣﴾ أم للإنسان ما تمنى
﴿٢٤﴾ فلله الآخرة والأولى ﴿٢٥﴾ وكم من ملك في السموات لا تغني
شفاعتهم شيئا إلا من بعد أن يأذن الله لمن يشاء ويرضى ﴿٢٦﴾

In the Name of God,
the Merciful, the Compassionate

By THE star when it declines, 53:1
your compatriot[1] is not in
error, nor is he deceived!

He does not speak out of his own fancy. This is a revelation inspired. He is taught by one who is powerful and mighty.[2]

He stood on the uppermost horizon; then, drawing near, he came down within two bows' length or even closer, and revealed to His servant that which He revealed.

His[3] own heart did not deny his vision. Do you[4] doubt, then, what he beholds?

He beheld him once again at the sidra tree, beyond which no one may pass. Nearby is the Garden of Repose.

When that tree was covered with what covered it, his eyes did not wander, nor did they turn aside: he beheld some of his Lord's mightiest signs.

Have you thought on Al-Lāt and Al-'Uzzā, and on Manāt, the third other?[5] 53:20
Are you to have the male, and He the female? This is indeed an unfair
distinction!

They are but names which you and your forefathers have invented: God has vested no authority in them. The unbelievers follow but vain conjectures and the whims of their own souls, although the guidance of their Lord had long since come to them.

Or is man to attain all that he desires? To God belongs the life to come, and this first life.

Numerous are the angels in the heavens; yet their intercession shall avail 53:26
nothing until God give leave to whom He wills and accepts.

1. Muḥammad. 2. Gabriel.
3. Muḥammad's. 4. The unbelievers.
5. Names of Arabian idols, claimed by the pagans of Mecca to be daughters of God.

53:27 THOSE THAT disbelieve in
the Hereafter call the angels by
the names of females. Yet of
this they have no knowledge:
they follow mere conjecture,
and conjecture is no substitute
for Truth.

Pay no heed, then, to those
who ignore Our Admonition
and seek only the life of this
world. This is the sum of their
knowledge. Your Lord best
knows who has strayed from
His path, and He best knows
who has followed the right
guidance.

And to God belongs what
the heavens and the earth
contain. He will requite the
evil-doers according to their
deeds, and richly recompense
those who do good works.

53:32 To those who avoid the
grossest sins and indecencies and commit only small offences, your Lord will
show abundant forgiveness. He knew you well when He created you from
earth and when you were still in your mothers' wombs. Do not pretend to
purity; He best knows those who fear Him.

Have you considered him who turns his back, giving little at first and then
nothing at all? Does he know, and can he see, what is hidden? Or has he not
been told of what is writ in the Scriptures of Moses and Abraham, who was
true to his covenant: that no burdened soul shall bear another's burden, and
that man shall be judged only by his labours; that his labours shall be scruti-
nized, and that he shall be justly requited for them; that all things shall in the
53:44 end return to your Lord; that it is He who moves to laughter and to tears, and
He who ordains death and life;

إن الذين لا يؤمنون بالآخرة ليسمون الملائكة تسمية الأنثى
٢٧ وما لهم به من علم إن يتبعون إلا الظن وإن الظن لا يغني من
الحق شيئا ٢٨ فأعرض عن من تولى عن ذكرنا ولم يرد إلا
الحياة الدنيا ٢٩ ذلك مبلغهم من العلم إن ربك هو أعلم
بمن ضل عن سبيله وهو أعلم بمن اهتدى ٣٠ ولله
ما في السماوات وما في الأرض ليجزي الذين أساءوا بما
عملوا ويجزي الذين أحسنوا بالحسنى ٣١ الذين يجتنبون
كبائر الإثم والفواحش إلا اللمم إن ربك واسع المغفرة
هو أعلم بكم إذ أنشأكم من الأرض وإذ أنتم أجنة في بطون
أمهاتكم فلا تزكوا أنفسكم هو أعلم بمن اتقى ٣٢ أفرأيت
الذي تولى ٣٣ وأعطى قليلا وأكدى ٣٤ أعنده علم الغيب فهو يرى
٣٥ أم لم ينبأ بما في صحف موسى ٣٦ وإبراهيم الذي وفى ٣٧ ألا
تزر وازرة وزر أخرى ٣٨ وأن ليس للإنسان إلا ما سعى ٣٩ وأن
سعيه سوف يرى ٤٠ ثم يجزاه الجزاء الأوفى ٤١ وأن إلى ربك
المنتهى ٤٢ وأنه هو أضحك وأبكى ٤٣ وأنه هو أمات وأحيا ٤٤

وأنه خلق الزوجين الذكر والأنثى ﴿٤٥﴾ من نطفة إذا تمنى ﴿٤٦﴾
وأن عليه النشأة الأخرى ﴿٤٧﴾ وأنه هو أغنى وأقنى ﴿٤٨﴾ وأنه هو
رب الشعرى ﴿٤٩﴾ وأنه أهلك عادا الأولى ﴿٥٠﴾ وثمود فما أبقى ﴿٥١﴾
وقوم نوح من قبل إنهم كانوا هم أظلم وأطغى ﴿٥٢﴾ والمؤتفكة
أهوى ﴿٥٣﴾ فغشاها ما غشى ﴿٥٤﴾ فبأي آلاء ربك تتمارى ﴿٥٥﴾ هذا
نذير من النذر الأولى ﴿٥٦﴾ أزفت الآزفة ﴿٥٧﴾ ليس لها من دون
الله كاشفة ﴿٥٨﴾ أفمن هذا الحديث تعجبون ﴿٥٩﴾ وتضحكون
ولا تبكون ﴿٦٠﴾ وأنتم سامدون ﴿٦١﴾ فاسجدوا لله واعبدوا ﴿٦٢﴾

سورة القمر مكية وهي خمس وخمسون آية

بسم الله الرحمن الرحيم
اقتربت الساعة وانشق القمر ﴿١﴾ وإن يروا آية يعرضوا ويقولوا
سحر مستمر ﴿٢﴾ وكذبوا واتبعوا أهواءهم وكل أمر مستقر ﴿٣﴾
ولقد جاءهم من الأنباء ما فيه مزدجر ﴿٤﴾ حكمة بالغة فما
تغن النذر ﴿٥﴾ فتول عنهم يوم يدع الداع إلى شيء نكر ﴿٦﴾

that God created the two sexes, 53:45
the male and the female, from
a drop of ejaculated semen,
and will bring about the other
creation; that it is He who
bestows and enriches, He who
is the Lord of Sirius;[1] that it
was He who obliterated 'Ad at
first and then Thamūd, sparing
no one, and before them the
people of Noah, who were
more sinful and more rebellious. The Mu'tafikah[2] He also
doomed, so that they were 53:54
smitten by the scourge that
smote them.

Which then of your Lord's
blessings would you deny? He
that now warns you is just like
those who warned the others
before you. That which is coming is near at hand; none but
God can disclose the Hour.

Do you marvel then at this revelation, and laugh instead of weeping?
Making merry still? Rather prostrate yourselves before God, and worship. 53:62

THE MOON

In the Name of God, the Merciful, the Compassionate

The Hour is drawing near, and the moon is cleft in two. Yet, when they 54:1
behold a sign, the unbelievers turn their backs and say: 'Sorcery unceasing!'

They deny the truth, and follow their own fancies. But in the end all issues
shall be laid to rest.

Cautionary tales, profound in wisdom, have been narrated to them: but
warnings are unavailing.

Let them be. The day the Crier summons them to the dread account, 54:6

1. The Dog Star, worshipped by the pagan Arabs.
2. The Ruined Cities, where Lot's people lived.

54:7 they shall come out from their graves with downcast eyes, and rush towards him like swarming locusts. The unbelievers will say: 'This is indeed a doleful day!'

Before them, the people of Noah disbelieved. They disbelieved Our servant, and called him madman. Rejected and contemned, he cried out to his Lord, saying: 'Help me, I am overcome!'

We opened the gates of heaven with pouring rain and caused the earth to burst with gushing springs, so that the waters met for a predestined end. We carried him in a vessel built with planks and nails, which drifted on under Our eyes: a recompense for him who had been disbelieved.

خشعا ابصارهم يخرجون من الاجداث كانهم جراد منتشر ۝
مهطعين الى الداع يقول الكافرون هذا يوم عسر ۝ كذبت
قبلهم قوم نوح فكذبوا عبدنا وقالوا مجنون وازدجر ۝
فدعا ربه اني مغلوب فانتصر ۝ ففتحنا ابواب السماء بماء
منهمر ۝ وفجرنا الارض عيونا فالتقى الماء على امر قد قدر
۝ وحملناه على ذات الواح ودسر ۝ تجري باعيننا جزاء
لمن كان كفر ۝ ولقد تركناها اية فهل من مدكر ۝
فكيف كان عذابي ونذر ۝ ولقد يسرنا القران للذكر فهل من مدكر
۝ كذبت عاد فكيف كان عذابي ونذر ۝ انا ارسلنا عليهم ريحا
صرصرا في يوم نحس مستمر ۝ تنزع الناس كانهم اعجاز نخل منقعر ۝
فكيف كان عذابي ونذر ۝ ولقد يسرنا القران للذكر فهل من مدكر
۝ كذبت ثمود بالنذر ۝ فقالوا ابشرا منا واحدا نتبعه انا اذا
لفي ضلال وسعر ۝ االقي الذكر عليه من بيننا بل هو كذاب
اشر ۝ سيعلمون غدا من الكذاب الاشر ۝ انا
مرسلوا الناقة فتنة لهم فارتقبهم واصطبر ۝

This We have left as a sign: but is there any that will remember? How grievous was My scourge, and warning!

We have made the Koran easy to remember: but is there any that will remember?

54:19 'Ād, too, did not believe. How grievous was My scourge, and warning! On a day of unremitting woe, We let loose on them a howling wind which snapped people off like trunks of uprooted palm-trees. How grievous was My scourge, and warning!

We have made the Koran easy to remember: but is there any that will remember?

Thamūd, too, disbelieved the warnings. They said: 'Are we to follow a mortal, alone among us? That would surely be error and madness. Did he alone among us receive the Admonition? He is indeed an impudent liar.'

54:27 'Tomorrow they shall learn who is the impudent liar. We are sending the she-camel to test them. Observe them closely and have patience.

ونبئهم أن الماء قسمة بينهم كل شرب محتضر ﴿٢٨﴾ فنادوا
صاحبهم فتعاطى فعقر ﴿٢٩﴾ فكيف كان عذابي ونذر
﴿٣٠﴾ إنا أرسلنا عليهم صيحة واحدة فكانوا كهشيم المحتظر
﴿٣١﴾ ولقد يسرنا القرآن للذكر فهل من مدكر ﴿٣٢﴾ كذبت قوم لوط بالنذر
﴿٣٣﴾ إنا أرسلنا عليهم حاصبا إلا آل لوط نجيناهم بسحر ﴿٣٤﴾ نعمة من
عندنا كذلك نجزي من شكر ﴿٣٥﴾ ولقد أنذرهم بطشتنا فتماروا
بالنذر ﴿٣٦﴾ ولقد راودوه عن ضيفه فطمسنا أعينهم فذوقوا عذابي
ونذر ﴿٣٧﴾ ولقد صبحهم بكرة عذاب مستقر ﴿٣٨﴾ فذوقوا عذابي ونذر
﴿٣٩﴾ ولقد يسرنا القرآن للذكر فهل من مدكر ﴿٤٠﴾ ولقد جاء آل فرعون
النذر ﴿٤١﴾ كذبوا بآياتنا كلها فأخذناهم أخذ عزيز مقتدر ﴿٤٢﴾
أكفاركم خير من أولئكم أم لكم براءة في الزبر ﴿٤٣﴾ أم
يقولون نحن جميع منتصر ﴿٤٤﴾ سيهزم الجمع ويولون الدبر ﴿٤٥﴾
بل الساعة موعدهم والساعة أدهى وأمر ﴿٤٦﴾ إن المجرمين
في ضلال وسعر ﴿٤٧﴾ يوم يسحبون في النار على وجوههم
ذوقوا مس سقر ﴿٤٨﴾ إنا كل شيء خلقناه بقدر ﴿٤٩﴾

TELL THEM they must share 54:28
their drink with her, and that for every draught they must attend in person.'

They called their friend, who took a knife and hamstrung her. How grievous was My scourge, and warning! A single cry was heard, and they became like the dry twigs of the sheepfold builder.

We have made the Koran easy to remember: but is there any that will remember?

The people of Lot disbelieved the warnings. We let loose on them a stone-charged whirlwind: only the house of Lot at dawn did We deliver, through Our mercy. Thus do We reward the thankful.

He had warned them of Our onslaught, but they
doubted the warnings. They demanded his guests of him; so We put out 54:37
their eyes: 'Taste My punishment, now that you have scorned My warnings!' And at daybreak a long-lasting scourge smote them. 'Taste My punishment, now that you have scorned My warnings!'

We have made the Koran easy to remember: but is there any that will remember?

To Pharaoh's people came the warnings. But they disbelieved all Our signs, and We smote them with the scourge of the Almighty, the Omnipotent.

Are your unbelievers better than those? Or have you immunity in the Scriptures?

Or do they say: 'We are a victorious army'? The army shall be routed and put to flight.

The Hour is their time appointed; and more calamitous, and more doleful, shall be the Hour.

Yet the wrongdoers persist in error and madness. On the day they are dragged into the Fire with faces down: 'Feel the touch of Hell!'

We have surely created all things according to a measure. 54:49

وما أمرنا إلا واحدة كلمح بالبصر ۝ ولقد أهلكنا
أشياعكم فهل من مدكر ۝ وكل شيء فعلوه في
الزبر ۝ وكل صغير وكبير مستطر ۝ إن المتقين
في جنات ونهر ۝ في مقعد صدق عند مليك مقتدر ۝

سورة الرحمن مكية وهي ثمان وسبعون آية

بسم الله الرحمن الرحيم
الرحمن ۝ علم القرآن ۝ خلق الإنسان ۝ علمه البيان
۝ الشمس والقمر بحسبان ۝ والنجم والشجر يسجدان ۝
والسماء رفعها ووضع الميزان ۝ ألا تطغوا في الميزان ۝
وأقيموا الوزن بالقسط ولا تخسروا الميزان ۝ والأرض
وضعها للأنام ۝ فيها فاكهة والنخل ذات الأكمام ۝
والحب ذو العصف والريحان ۝ فبأي آلاء ربكما تكذبان ۝
خلق الإنسان من صلصال كالفخار ۝ وخلق
الجان من مارج من نار ۝ فبأي آلاء ربكما تكذبان ۝

54:50 WE COMMAND but once: Our
will is done in the twinkling of
an eye.
We have destroyed many a
people like yourselves: is there
any that will remember?
All they did is in the Scriptures: every action, small or
great, is noted down. The
righteous shall dwell in Gardens watered by running
54:55 brooks, honourably seated in
the presence of a Mighty King.

THE MERCIFUL[1]

In the Name of God,
the Merciful, the Compassionate

55:1 IT IS the Merciful who has
taught the Koran.
He created man and taught him articulate speech. The sun and the moon
pursue their ordered course. The plants and the trees bow down in adoration.
The heaven He raised on high and set the Balance of all things, that you
might not transgress that Balance. Give just weight and full measure, and do
not cheat the Balance.
And the earth He laid for His creatures, with all its fruits and
blossom-bearing palm, chaff-covered grain, and scented herbs. So which of
your Lord's blessings would you[2] deny?
He created man from potter's clay, and the jinn from smokeless fire.
55:16 So which of your Lord's blessings would you deny?

1. Cf. this *sūrah* with Psalm 136.
2. The pronoun is in the dual number (i.e. the two of you), the words being addressed to mankind and the jinn. This refrain is repeated no fewer than 31 times.

رب المشرقين ورب المغربين ۝ فبأي آلاء ربكما تكذبان ۝
مرج البحرين يلتقيان ۝ بينهما برزخ لا يبغيان ۝
فبأي آلاء ربكما تكذبان ۝ يخرج منهما اللؤلؤ والمرجان ۝
فبأي آلاء ربكما تكذبان ۝ وله الجوار المنشآت في البحر كالأعلام ۝
فبأي آلاء ربكما تكذبان ۝ كل من عليها فان ۝ ويبقى وجه
ربك ذو الجلال والإكرام ۝ فبأي آلاء ربكما تكذبان ۝
يسأله من في السماوات والأرض كل يوم هو في شأن ۝
فبأي آلاء ربكما تكذبان ۝ سنفرغ لكم أيه الثقلان ۝
فبأي آلاء ربكما تكذبان ۝ يا معشر الجن والإنس إن استطعتم
أن تنفذوا من أقطار السماوات والأرض فانفذوا لا تنفذون إلا بسلطان ۝
فبأي آلاء ربكما تكذبان ۝ يرسل عليكما شواظ من
نار ونحاس فلا تنتصران ۝ فبأي آلاء ربكما تكذبان ۝
فإذا انشقت السماء فكانت وردة كالدهان ۝
فبأي آلاء ربكما تكذبان ۝ فيومئذ لا يسأل عن
ذنبه إنس ولا جان ۝ فبأي آلاء ربكما تكذبان ۝

THE LORD of the two 55:17
easts[1] is He, and the Lord of
the two wests. So which of your
Lord's blessings would you
deny?

He has let loose the two seas:[2] they meet one another. Yet between them stands a barrier which they cannot overrun. So which of your Lord's blessings would you deny?

Pearls and corals come out from both. So which of your Lord's blessings would you deny?

His are the ships that sail like mountains upon the ocean. So which of your Lord's blessings would you deny?

All that live on earth are doomed to die. But the Face of your Lord will abide for ever, in all its majesty and glory. So which of your Lord's blessings would you deny?

All who dwell in heaven and earth entreat Him. Each day some mighty 55:29
task engages Him. So which of your Lord's blessings would you deny?

Jinn and mankind, We shall surely find the time to judge you. So which of your Lord's blessings would you deny?

You race of jinn and mankind, if you have power to penetrate the confines of heaven and earth, then penetrate them. But this you shall not do except with Our own authority. So which of your Lord's blessings would you deny?

Flames of fire shall be lashed at you, and molten brass. There shall be none to help you. So which of your Lord's blessings would you deny?

When the sky splits asunder, and reddens like a rose or stainèd leather (so
which of your Lord's blessings would you deny?), on that day neither man
nor jinnee will be asked about his sins. So which of your Lord's blessings 55:40
would you deny?

1. The points at which the sun rises in summer and in winter.
2. Salt water and fresh water.

55:41 THE TRANSGRESSORS will be known by their looks; they shall be seized by their forelocks and their feet. So which of your Lord's blessings would you deny?

That is the Hell the transgressors deny. They shall wander between fire and water fiercely seething. So which of your Lord's blessings would you deny?

But for those that fear the majesty of their Lord there are two Gardens (so which of your Lord's blessings would you deny?) planted with shady trees. So which of your Lord's blessings would you deny?

Each is watered by a flowing spring. So which of your Lord's blessings would you deny?

55:52 Each bears every kind of fruit in pairs. So which of your Lord's blessings would you deny?

They shall recline on couches lined with rich brocade, and within reach will hang the fruits of both Gardens. So which of your Lord's blessings would you deny?

Therein are bashful virgins whom neither man nor jinnee will have touched before. So which of your Lord's blessings would you deny?

Virgins as fair as corals and rubies. So which of your Lord's blessings would you deny?

Shall the reward of goodness be anything but good? So which of your Lord's blessings would you deny?

And beside these there shall be two other Gardens (so which of your Lord's blessings would you deny?) of darkest green. So which of your Lord's blessings would you deny?

55:67 A gushing fountain shall flow in each. So which of your Lord's blessings would you deny?

يعرف المجرمون بسيمٰهم فيؤخذ بالنواصي والاقدام ۝
فباي الاء ربكما تكذبان ۝ هذه جهنم التي يكذب بها المجرمون
۝ يطوفون بينها وبين حميم ان ۝ فباي الاء ربكما تكذبان ۝
ولمن خاف مقام ربه جنتان ۝ فباي الاء ربكما تكذبان ۝
ذواتا افنان ۝ فباي الاء ربكما تكذبان ۝
فيهما عينان تجريان ۝ فباي الاء ربكما تكذبان ۝
فيهما من كل فاكهة زوجان ۝ فباي الاء ربكما تكذبان ۝
متكئين على فرش بطائنها من استبرق وجنا الجنتين دان ۝
فباي الاء ربكما تكذبان ۝ فيهن قاصرات الطرف لم
يطمثهن انس قبلهم ولا جان ۝ فباي الاء ربكما تكذبان ۝
كانهن الياقوت والمرجان ۝ فباي الاء ربكما تكذبان ۝
هل جزاء الاحسان الا الاحسان ۝ فباي الاء ربكما تكذبان ۝
ومن دونهما جنتان ۝ فباي الاء ربكما تكذبان ۝
مدهامتان ۝ فباي الاء ربكما تكذبان ۝
فيهما عينان نضاختان ۝ فباي الاء ربكما تكذبان ۝

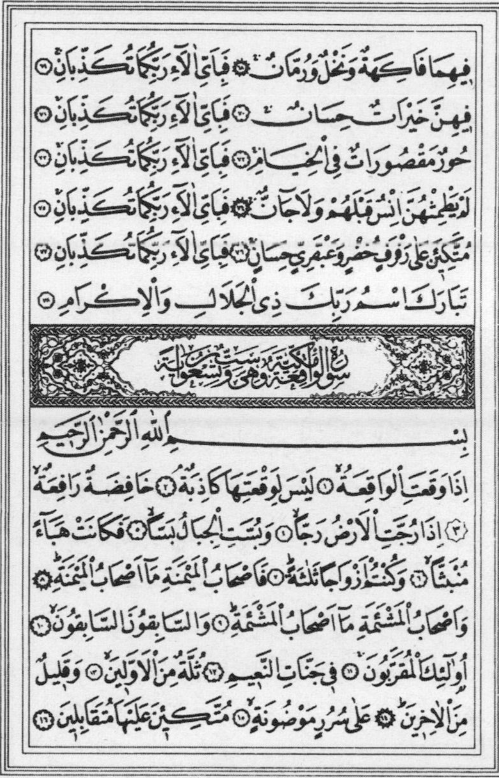

فِيهِمَا فَاكِهَةٌ وَنَخْلٌ وَرُمَّانٌ ۝ فَبِأَيِّ آلَاءِ رَبِّكُمَا تُكَذِّبَانِ ۝
فِيهِنَّ خَيْرَاتٌ حِسَانٌ ۝ فَبِأَيِّ آلَاءِ رَبِّكُمَا تُكَذِّبَانِ ۝
حُورٌ مَقْصُورَاتٌ فِي الْخِيَامِ ۝ فَبِأَيِّ آلَاءِ رَبِّكُمَا تُكَذِّبَانِ ۝
لَمْ يَطْمِثْهُنَّ إِنْسٌ قَبْلَهُمْ وَلَا جَانٌّ ۝ فَبِأَيِّ آلَاءِ رَبِّكُمَا تُكَذِّبَانِ ۝
مُتَّكِئِينَ عَلَىٰ رَفْرَفٍ خُضْرٍ وَعَبْقَرِيٍّ حِسَانٍ ۝ فَبِأَيِّ آلَاءِ رَبِّكُمَا تُكَذِّبَانِ ۝
تَبَارَكَ اسْمُ رَبِّكَ ذِي الْجَلَالِ وَالْإِكْرَامِ ۝

سورة الواقعة مكية وهي ست وتسعون آية

بِسْمِ اللَّهِ الرَّحْمَٰنِ الرَّحِيمِ

إِذَا وَقَعَتِ الْوَاقِعَةُ ۝ لَيْسَ لِوَقْعَتِهَا كَاذِبَةٌ ۝ خَافِضَةٌ رَافِعَةٌ
۝ إِذَا رُجَّتِ الْأَرْضُ رَجًّا ۝ وَبُسَّتِ الْجِبَالُ بَسًّا ۝ فَكَانَتْ هَبَاءً
مُنْبَثًّا ۝ وَكُنْتُمْ أَزْوَاجًا ثَلَاثَةً ۝ فَأَصْحَابُ الْمَيْمَنَةِ مَا أَصْحَابُ الْمَيْمَنَةِ ۝
وَأَصْحَابُ الْمَشْأَمَةِ مَا أَصْحَابُ الْمَشْأَمَةِ ۝ وَالسَّابِقُونَ السَّابِقُونَ ۝
أُولَٰئِكَ الْمُقَرَّبُونَ ۝ فِي جَنَّاتِ النَّعِيمِ ۝ ثُلَّةٌ مِنَ الْأَوَّلِينَ ۝ وَقَلِيلٌ
مِنَ الْآخِرِينَ ۝ عَلَىٰ سُرُرٍ مَوْضُونَةٍ ۝ مُتَّكِئِينَ عَلَيْهَا مُتَقَابِلِينَ ۝

EACH PLANTED with 55:68
fruit-trees, the palm and the
pomegranate. So which of
your Lord's blessings would
you deny?
In each there shall be virgins chaste and fair. So which
of your Lord's blessings would
you deny?
Dark-eyed virgins, shel-
tered in their tents (so which
of your Lord's blessings would
you deny?), whom neither
man nor jinnee will have
touched before. So which of
your Lord's blessings would
you deny?
They shall recline on green
cushions and fine carpets. So
which of your Lord's blessings would you deny?
Blessed be the name of 55:78
your Lord, the Lord of Majesty
and Glory!

THAT WHICH IS COMING

In the Name of God, the Merciful, the Compassionate

WHEN THAT which is coming comes – and no soul shall then deny its 56:1
coming – some shall be abased and others exalted.
When the earth shakes and quivers, and the mountains crumble away and
scatter abroad into fine dust, you shall be divided into three multitudes: those
on the right (blessed shall be those on the right); those on the left (damned
shall be those on the left); and those to the fore (foremost shall be those).
Such are they that shall be brought near to their Lord in the Gardens of
Delight: a whole multitude from ages past, and but a few from the latter age.
They shall recline on jewelled couches face to face, 56:16

يَطُوفُ عَلَيْهِمْ وِلْدَانٌ مُخَلَّدُونَ ۝ بِأَكْوَابٍ وَأَبَارِيقَ وَكَأْسٍ مِنْ مَعِينٍ
۝ لَا يُصَدَّعُونَ عَنْهَا وَلَا يُنْزِفُونَ ۝ وَفَاكِهَةٍ مِمَّا يَتَخَيَّرُونَ ۝
وَلَحْمِ طَيْرٍ مِمَّا يَشْتَهُونَ ۝ وَحُورٌ عِينٌ ۝ كَأَمْثَالِ اللُّؤْلُؤِ الْمَكْنُونِ
۝ جَزَاءً بِمَا كَانُوا يَعْمَلُونَ ۝ لَا يَسْمَعُونَ فِيهَا لَغْوًا وَلَا تَأْثِيمًا ۝
إِلَّا قِيلًا سَلَامًا سَلَامًا ۝ وَأَصْحَابُ الْيَمِينِ مَا أَصْحَابُ الْيَمِينِ ۝
فِي سِدْرٍ مَخْضُودٍ ۝ وَطَلْحٍ مَنْضُودٍ ۝ وَظِلٍّ مَمْدُودٍ ۝ وَمَاءٍ
مَسْكُوبٍ ۝ وَفَاكِهَةٍ كَثِيرَةٍ ۝ لَا مَقْطُوعَةٍ وَلَا مَمْنُوعَةٍ
۝ وَفُرُشٍ مَرْفُوعَةٍ ۝ إِنَّا أَنْشَأْنَاهُنَّ إِنْشَاءً ۝ فَجَعَلْنَاهُنَّ
أَبْكَارًا ۝ عُرُبًا أَتْرَابًا ۝ لِأَصْحَابِ الْيَمِينِ ۝ ثُلَّةٌ مِنَ الْأَوَّلِينَ
۝ وَثُلَّةٌ مِنَ الْآخِرِينَ ۝ وَأَصْحَابُ الشِّمَالِ مَا أَصْحَابُ الشِّمَالِ
۝ فِي سَمُومٍ وَحَمِيمٍ ۝ وَظِلٍّ مِنْ يَحْمُومٍ ۝ لَا بَارِدٍ وَلَا كَرِيمٍ
۝ إِنَّهُمْ كَانُوا قَبْلَ ذَٰلِكَ مُتْرَفِينَ ۝ وَكَانُوا يُصِرُّونَ عَلَى
الْحِنْثِ الْعَظِيمِ ۝ وَكَانُوا يَقُولُونَ أَئِذَا مِتْنَا وَكُنَّا تُرَابًا
وَعِظَامًا أَإِنَّا لَمَبْعُوثُونَ ۝ أَوَآبَاؤُنَا الْأَوَّلُونَ ۝ قُلْ إِنَّ
الْأَوَّلِينَ وَالْآخِرِينَ ۝ لَمَجْمُوعُونَ إِلَىٰ مِيقَاتِ يَوْمٍ مَعْلُومٍ ۝

56:17 and there shall wait on them immortal youths with bowls and ewers and a cup of purest wine (that will neither pain their heads nor take away their reason); with fruits of their own choice and flesh of fowls that they relish. And theirs shall be dark-eyed houris, chaste as virgin pearls: a guerdon for what they did.

Therein they shall hear no idle talk, no sinful speech, but only the greeting, 'Peace! Peace!'

Those on the right hand – happy shall be those on the right hand! They shall recline on couches raised on high in the shade of thornless sidrs and clusters of ṭalḥ;[1] amidst gushing waters and abundant fruits, never-ending, unforbidden.

56:35 We created the houris and made them virgins, loving companions for those on the right hand: a multitude from ages past, and a multitude from the latter age.

As for those on the left hand (wretched shall be those on the left hand!) they shall dwell amidst scorching winds and seething water: in the shade of pitch-black smoke, neither cool nor refreshing. For they have lived in comfort and persisted in the heinous sin,[2] saying: 'What! When we are dead and turned to dust and bones, shall we be raised to life? And our forefathers, too?'

56:50 Say: 'Those from ages past, and those from the latter age, shall be brought together at the time of an appointed day.

1. Probably the banana tree. 2. Idolatry.

ثم انكم ايها الضالون المكذبون ۝ لاكلون من شجر من
زقوم ۝ فمالـٔون منها البطون ۝ فشاربون عليه من
الحميم ۝ فشاربون شرب الهيم ۝ هذا نزلهم يوم الدين
۝ نحن خلقناكم فلولا تصدقون ۝ افرءيتم ما تمنون ۝
ءانتم تخلقونه ام نحن الخالقون ۝ نحن قدرنا بينكم الموت
وما نحن بمسبوقين ۝ على ان نبدل امثالكم وننشئكم في
ما لا تعلمون ۝ ولقد علمتم النشاة الاولى فلولا تذكرون
۝ افرءيتم ما تحرثون ۝ ءانتم تزرعونه ام نحن الزارعون
۝ لو نشاء لجعلناه حطاما فظلتم تفكهون ۝ انا لمغرمون
۝ بل نحن محرومون ۝ افرءيتم الماء الذي تشربون ۝
ءانتم انزلتموه من المزن ام نحن المنزلون ۝ لو نشاء جعلناه
اجاجا فلولا تشكرون ۝ افرءيتم النار التي تورون ۝
ءانتم انشاتم شجرتها ام نحن المنشـٔون ۝ نحن جعلناها
تذكرة ومتاعا للمقوين ۝ فسبح باسم ربك العظيم ۝ فلا
اقسم بمواقع النجوم ۝ وانه لقسم لو تعلمون عظيم ۝

THEN, AS for you who err and 56:51
disbelieve, you shall eat from
the Zaqqūm tree and fill your
bellies with its fruit. You shall
drink scalding water: yet you
shall drink it as the thirsty
camel drinks.'

Such shall be their fare on the Day of Reckoning.

We created you: why then will you not believe?

Behold the semen you discharge: did you create it, or were We its Creators?

It was We that ordained death among you. Nothing can hinder Us from replacing you by others like yourselves or transforming you into beings you know nothing of.

You surely know of the First 56:62
Creation. Why, then, do you
not reflect? Consider the earth
you till. Is it you that sow the seeds, or are We the Sowers? If We pleased, We
could turn your harvest into chaff, so that you would keep forlornly jesting:
'We are laden with debt! Why, we have been robbed!'

Consider the water which you drink. Was it you that sent it down from the cloud, or were We the Senders? If We pleased, We could turn it bitter. Why, then, do you not give thanks?

Consider the fire which you light. Was it you that made the timber, or were We the Makers? A reminder for man We made it, and for the traveller a comfort.

Praise, then, the name of your Lord, the Supreme One.

I swear by the shelters of the stars (a mighty oath, if you but knew it) 56:76

56:77 that this is a holy Koran, safe-
guarded in a Book which none
may touch except the purified;
a revelation sent down from
the Lord of the Universe.

Would you scorn a Scrip-
ture such as this, and earn your
daily bread denying it?

When under your very eyes
a dying man's soul leaps up to
56:85 his throat (We are nearer to
him than you, although you
cannot see), why do you not
restore it, if you are not to be
judged hereafter? If what you
say be true?

Thus, if he is favoured, his
lot will be repose and plenty,
and a Garden of Delight. If he
is one of those on the right
hand, he will be greeted with
'Peace be with you!' by those
on the right hand.

إنه لقرآن كريم ۝ في كتاب مكنون ۝ لا يمسه إلا المطهرون ۝ تنزيل
من رب العالمين ۝ أفبهذا الحديث أنتم مدهنون ۝ وتجعلون
رزقكم أنكم تكذبون ۝ فلولا إذا بلغت الحلقوم ۝ وأنتم
حينئذ تنظرون ۝ ونحن أقرب إليه منكم ولكن لا تبصرون ۝ فلولا
إن كنتم غير مدينين ۝ ترجعونها إن كنتم صادقين ۝ فأما إن كان
من المقربين ۝ فروح وريحان وجنت نعيم ۝ وأما إن كان
من أصحاب اليمين ۝ فسلام لك من أصحاب اليمين ۝ وأما إن كان
من المكذبين الضالين ۝ فنزل من حميم ۝ وتصلية جحيم
۝ إن هذا لهو حق اليقين ۝ فسبح باسم ربك العظيم ۝

سورة الحديد مدنية وهي تسع وعشرون آية

بسم الله الرحمن الرحيم

سبح لله ما في السموات والأرض وهو العزيز الحكيم ۝ له
ملك السموات والأرض يحيي ويميت وهو على كل شيء قدير ۝
هو الأول والآخر والظاهر والباطن وهو بكل شيء عليم ۝

But if he is an erring disbeliever, his welcome shall be a downpour of
scalding water, and incineration in a hell.
56:96 This is surely the veritable Truth. Praise, then, the name of your Lord, the
Supreme One.

IRON

In the Name of God, the Merciful, the Compassionate

57:1 ALL THAT is in the heavens and on the earth gives glory to God. He is the
Almighty, the Wise One.
He it is that has sovereignty over the heavens and the earth. He ordains
life and death, and has power over all things.
57:3 He is the First and the Last, the Visible and the Unseen. He has knowledge of all things.

هو الذي خلق السموات والأرض في ستة أيام ثم استوى على العرش
يعلم ما يلج في الأرض وما يخرج منها وما ينزل من السماء وما يعرج
فيها وهو معكم أين ما كنتم والله بما تعملون بصير ۝ له ملك
السموات والأرض وإلى الله ترجع الأمور ۝ يولج الليل في النهار
ويولج النهار في الليل وهو عليم بذات الصدور ۝ آمنوا بالله
ورسوله وأنفقوا مما جعلكم مستخلفين فيه فالذين آمنوا
منكم وأنفقوا لهم أجر كبير ۝ وما لكم لا تؤمنون بالله
والرسول يدعوكم لتؤمنوا بربكم وقد أخذ ميثاقكم إن
كنتم مؤمنين ۝ هو الذي ينزل على عبده آيات بينات ليخرجكم
من الظلمات إلى النور وإن الله بكم لرءوف رحيم ۝ وما
لكم ألا تنفقوا في سبيل الله ولله ميراث السموات والأرض
لا يستوي منكم من أنفق من قبل الفتح وقاتل أولئك أعظم
درجة من الذين أنفقوا من بعد وقاتلوا وكلا وعد الله
الحسنى والله بما تعملون خبير ۝ من ذا الذي يقرض الله
قرضا حسنا فيضاعفه له وله أجر كريم ۝١١

HE IT was who created the 57:4
heavens and the earth in six days, and then seated Himself upon the throne. He knows all that goes into the earth and all that comes out from it, all that descends from heaven and all that ascends to it. And He is with you wherever you are. God is cognizant of what you do.

He has sovereignty over the heavens and the earth. To God shall all things return. He causes the night to pass into the day, and causes the day to pass into the night. He has knowledge of one's innermost thoughts.

Have faith in God and His 57:7
apostle and give from that which He has made your inheritance; for whoever of you believes and gives shall be richly recompensed.

And what cause have you not to believe in God, when the Apostle calls on you to believe in your Lord, with whom you have made a covenant, if you are true believers?

He it is who sends down clear revelations to His servant, that he may lead you out of darkness into the light. Surely God is benignant to you and compassionate.

And why should you not give in the cause of God, when God alone will inherit the heavens and the earth? Those of you that gave before the victory, and took part in the fighting, shall receive greater honour than those who gave and fought thereafter. Yet God has promised you all a good reward; God has knowledge of what you do.

Who will give a generous loan to God? He will pay him back twofold, and 57:11
his shall be a noble recompense.

يَوْمَ تَرَى الْمُؤْمِنِينَ وَالْمُؤْمِنَاتِ يَسْعَىٰ نُورُهُمْ بَيْنَ أَيْدِيهِمْ وَبِأَيْمَانِهِمْ
بُشْرَاكُمُ الْيَوْمَ جَنَّاتٌ تَجْرِي مِنْ تَحْتِهَا الْأَنْهَارُ خَالِدِينَ فِيهَا
ذَٰلِكَ هُوَ الْفَوْزُ الْعَظِيمُ ﴿١٢﴾ يَوْمَ يَقُولُ الْمُنَافِقُونَ وَالْمُنَافِقَاتُ
لِلَّذِينَ آمَنُوا انْظُرُونَا نَقْتَبِسْ مِنْ نُورِكُمْ قِيلَ ارْجِعُوا وَرَاءَكُمْ
فَالْتَمِسُوا نُورًا فَضُرِبَ بَيْنَهُمْ بِسُورٍ لَهُ بَابٌ بَاطِنُهُ فِيهِ الرَّحْمَةُ وَظَاهِرُهُ
مِنْ قِبَلِهِ الْعَذَابُ ﴿١٣﴾ يُنَادُونَهُمْ أَلَمْ نَكُنْ مَعَكُمْ قَالُوا بَلَىٰ وَلَٰكِنَّكُمْ
فَتَنْتُمْ أَنْفُسَكُمْ وَتَرَبَّصْتُمْ وَارْتَبْتُمْ وَغَرَّتْكُمُ الْأَمَانِيُّ حَتَّىٰ
جَاءَ أَمْرُ اللَّهِ وَغَرَّكُمْ بِاللَّهِ الْغَرُورُ ﴿١٤﴾ فَالْيَوْمَ لَا يُؤْخَذُ
مِنْكُمْ فِدْيَةٌ وَلَا مِنَ الَّذِينَ كَفَرُوا مَأْوَاكُمُ النَّارُ هِيَ مَوْلَاكُمْ
وَبِئْسَ الْمَصِيرُ ﴿١٥﴾ أَلَمْ يَأْنِ لِلَّذِينَ آمَنُوا أَنْ تَخْشَعَ قُلُوبُهُمْ
لِذِكْرِ اللَّهِ وَمَا نَزَلَ مِنَ الْحَقِّ وَلَا يَكُونُوا كَالَّذِينَ أُوتُوا
الْكِتَابَ مِنْ قَبْلُ فَطَالَ عَلَيْهِمُ الْأَمَدُ فَقَسَتْ قُلُوبُهُمْ وَكَثِيرٌ مِنْهُمْ
فَاسِقُونَ ﴿١٦﴾ اعْلَمُوا أَنَّ اللَّهَ يُحْيِي الْأَرْضَ بَعْدَ مَوْتِهَا قَدْ
بَيَّنَّا لَكُمُ الْآيَاتِ لَعَلَّكُمْ تَعْقِلُونَ ﴿١٧﴾ إِنَّ الْمُصَّدِّقِينَ وَالْمُصَّدِّقَاتِ
وَأَقْرَضُوا اللَّهَ قَرْضًا حَسَنًا يُضَاعَفُ لَهُمْ وَلَهُمْ أَجْرٌ كَرِيمٌ ﴿١٨﴾

57:12 THE DAY when you behold the believers, men and women, with their light shining before them and on their right hands: 'Rejoice this day, in Gardens watered by running brooks, wherein shall you abide for ever.' That is the supreme triumph.

On that day the hypocrites, men and women, will say to the believers: 'Wait for us, that we may borrow some of your light.' They will be told: 'Go back, and seek a light!'

A wall with a gate shall be set before them. Inside there shall be mercy, and without, to the fore, the torment. They will call out to them, saying: 'Were we not on your side?' 'Yes,' they will reply, 'but you tempted yourselves, you bided
your time, you doubted, and were seduced by vain desires until God's will
57:15 was done and the Dissembler misled you about God. Today no ransom shall
be accepted from you, nor from the unbelievers. The Fire shall be your refuge: justly have you earned it, a wretched end!'

Is it not time for true believers to submit with humble hearts to God's remembrance and to the Truth He has revealed, that they may not be like those who were given the Book before this, whose days were prolonged and whose hearts were hardened? Many of them are ungodly.

Know that God restores the earth to life after its death. We have made Our revelations clear to you, that you may understand.

57:18 Those that give alms, be they men or women, and those that give a generous loan to God, shall be repaid twofold. Theirs shall be a noble recompense.

والذين آمنوا بالله ورسله أولئك هم الصديقون
والشهداء عند ربهم لهم أجرهم ونورهم والذين كفروا
وكذبوا بآياتنا أولئك أصحاب الجحيم (19) اعلموا أنما الحياة
الدنيا لعب ولهو وزينة وتفاخر بينكم وتكاثر في
الأموال والأولاد كمثل غيث أعجب الكفار نباته ثم يهيج
فتراه مصفرا ثم يكون حطاما وفي الآخرة عذاب شديد
ومغفرة من الله ورضوان وما الحياة الدنيا إلا متاع
الغرور (20) سابقوا إلى مغفرة من ربكم وجنة عرضها
كعرض السماء والأرض أعدت للذين آمنوا بالله ورسله
ذلك فضل الله يؤتيه من يشاء والله ذو الفضل
العظيم (21) ما أصاب من مصيبة في الأرض ولا في أنفسكم إلا في
كتاب من قبل أن نبرأها إن ذلك على الله يسير (22) لكيلا تأسوا
على ما فاتكم ولا تفرحوا بما آتاكم والله لا يحب
كل مختال فخور (23) الذين يبخلون ويأمرون
الناس بالبخل ومن يتول فإن الله هو الغني الحميد (24)

AND THOSE that believe in 57:19
God and His apostles are the
men of Truth who shall testify
in their Lord's presence. They
shall have their guerdon and
their light. But those that disbelieve Our revelations and deny
them are the heirs of Hell.

Know that the life of this
world is but a sport and a
diversion, a show and an empty
boast among you, a quest for
greater riches and more children. It is like the plants that
flourish after rain: the unbelievers rejoice to see them
grow; but then they wither
and turn yellow, soon becoming worthless stubble. In the
life to come there is a grievous
scourge, forgiveness from
God and good pleasure. The
life of this world is but a
pleasurable delusion.

Therefore vie for the pardon of your Lord, and for a Paradise as vast as 57:21
heaven and earth, prepared for those who believe in God and His apostles.
Such is the grace of God: He bestows it on whom He will. God's grace is
infinite.

No misfortune befalls the earth, or your own persons, but is ordained
before We bring it into being. That is easy enough for God; so that you may
not grieve for the good things you miss, or be overjoyed at what you gain.
God does not love the haughty, the vainglorious; nor those who, being 57:24
niggardly themselves, enjoin people to be niggardly. As for him that pays
no heed – God alone is self-sufficient and worthy of praise.

57:25 WE HAVE sent Our apostles
with signs manifest, and with
them sent down the Book and
the Balance, that people might
conduct themselves with fairness. We have sent down iron,
with its mighty strength and
diverse uses for mankind, that
God may recognize those who
aid Him, though unseen, and
His apostles. Strong is God,
and mighty.

We sent forth Noah and
Abraham, and bestowed on
their offspring prophethood
and the Book. Some were
rightly guided, but many were
57:27 degenerate. In their trail We
sent Our apostles, and after
those Jesus son of Mary. We
gave him the Gospel, and put
compassion and mercy in the
hearts of his followers. As for
monasticism, they instituted it themselves (for We had not enjoined it on
them), seeking thereby to please God; but they did not observe it faithfully.
We rewarded only those who believed; many of them were degenerate.

Believers, fear God and put your trust in His apostle. He will grant you a
double share of His mercy, He will bestow on you a light to walk in, and He
will forgive you: God is forgiving and compassionate.

57:29 Let the People of the Book recognize that they have no control over anything within the grace of God, and that grace is in His hands alone; He
vouchsafes it to whom He will, and God's grace is infinite.

لَقَدْ أَرْسَلْنَا رُسُلَنَا بِالْبَيِّنَاتِ وَأَنزَلْنَا مَعَهُمُ الْكِتَابَ وَالْمِيزَانَ
لِيَقُومَ النَّاسُ بِالْقِسْطِ وَأَنزَلْنَا الْحَدِيدَ فِيهِ بَأْسٌ شَدِيدٌ
وَمَنَافِعُ لِلنَّاسِ وَلِيَعْلَمَ اللَّهُ مَن يَنصُرُهُ وَرُسُلَهُ بِالْغَيْبِ إِنَّ
اللَّهَ قَوِيٌّ عَزِيزٌ ۝ وَلَقَدْ أَرْسَلْنَا نُوحًا وَإِبْرَاهِيمَ وَجَعَلْنَا فِي
ذُرِّيَّتِهِمَا النُّبُوَّةَ وَالْكِتَابَ فَمِنْهُم مُّهْتَدٍ وَكَثِيرٌ مِّنْهُمْ
فَاسِقُونَ ۝ ثُمَّ قَفَّيْنَا عَلَىٰ آثَارِهِم بِرُسُلِنَا وَقَفَّيْنَا بِعِيسَى
ابْنِ مَرْيَمَ وَآتَيْنَاهُ الْإِنجِيلَ وَجَعَلْنَا فِي قُلُوبِ الَّذِينَ
اتَّبَعُوهُ رَأْفَةً وَرَحْمَةً وَرَهْبَانِيَّةً ابْتَدَعُوهَا مَا كَتَبْنَاهَا
عَلَيْهِمْ إِلَّا ابْتِغَاءَ رِضْوَانِ اللَّهِ فَمَا رَعَوْهَا حَقَّ رِعَايَتِهَا
فَآتَيْنَا الَّذِينَ آمَنُوا مِنْهُمْ أَجْرَهُمْ وَكَثِيرٌ مِّنْهُمْ فَاسِقُونَ ۝
يَا أَيُّهَا الَّذِينَ آمَنُوا اتَّقُوا اللَّهَ وَآمِنُوا بِرَسُولِهِ يُؤْتِكُمْ
كِفْلَيْنِ مِن رَّحْمَتِهِ وَيَجْعَل لَّكُمْ نُورًا تَمْشُونَ بِهِ وَيَغْفِرْ لَكُمْ
وَاللَّهُ غَفُورٌ رَّحِيمٌ ۝ لِّئَلَّا يَعْلَمَ أَهْلُ الْكِتَابِ أَلَّا
يَقْدِرُونَ عَلَىٰ شَيْءٍ مِّن فَضْلِ اللَّهِ وَأَنَّ الْفَضْلَ بِيَدِ
اللَّهِ يُؤْتِيهِ مَن يَشَاءُ وَاللَّهُ ذُو الْفَضْلِ الْعَظِيمِ ۝

سورة المجادلة مدنية وهي اثنتان وعشرون آية

بسم الله الرحمن الرحيم
قد سمع الله قول التي تجادلك في زوجها وتشتكي الى الله
والله يسمع تحاوركما ان الله سميع بصير ۝ الذين يظاهرون
منكم من نسائهم ما هن امهاتهم ان امهاتهم الا الائي ولدنهم
وانهم ليقولون منكرا من القول وزورا وان الله لعفو غفور ۝٢
والذين يظاهرون من نسائهم ثم يعودون لما قالوا فتحرير رقبة
من قبل ان يتماسا ذلكم توعظون به والله بما تعملون خبير ۝٣
فمن لم يجد فصيام شهرين متتابعين من قبل ان يتماسا فمن لم
يستطع فاطعام ستين مسكينا ذلك لتؤمنوا بالله ورسوله وتلك حدود
الله وللكافرين عذاب اليم ۝ ان الذين يحادون الله ورسوله كبتوا كما
كبت الذين من قبلهم وقد انزلنا آيات بينات وللكافرين
عذاب مهين ۝ يوم يبعثهم الله جميعا فينبئهم بما عملوا
احصيه الله ونسوه والله على كل شيء شهيد ۝٦

SHE WHO PLEADED

In the Name of God,
the Merciful, the Compassionate

GOD HAS surely heard the 58:1
words of her[1] who pleaded
with you against her husband
and made her plaint to God.
God has heard what you two
said to each other. Surely God
hears all and observes all.

Those of you who divorce
their wives by declaring them
to be their mothers' backs
should know that they are *not*
their mothers. Their mothers
are only those who bore them.
The words they utter are unjust
and false: but God pardons
and forgives.

Those that divorce their wives by so saying, and afterwards retract their
words, shall free a slave[2] before they touch each other again. This you are
enjoined to do: God is cognizant of what you do. He that has no slave shall 58:4
fast two successive months before they touch one another. He that cannot
shall feed sixty of the destitute. Thus it is, so that you may believe in God
and His apostle. Such are the bounds set by God. Woeful punishment awaits
the unbelievers.

Those that oppose God and His apostle shall be brought low, as have
been those before them. We have sent down distinct revelations. Shameful
punishment awaits the unbelievers.

On the day when God restores them all to life He will tell them what they 58:6
did. God had counted their deeds, and they forgot them. God is witness of
all things.

1. Khawlah, daughter of Tha'labah, who had been divorced by the formula: 'Be to me as my mother's back', which was accepted as a declaration of divorce among pagan Arabs.
2. As a penalty.

58:7 ARE YOU not aware that God knows what the heavens and the earth contain? If three confer in secret, He is their fourth; if five, He is their sixth; whether fewer or more, He is with them wherever they be. Then, on the Day of Resurrection, He will inform them of their doings. God has knowledge of all things.

Have you not seen those who, though forbidden to intrigue in secret, defiantly intrigue together in sin and enmity and disobedience to the Apostle? When they come to you, they salute you in words which God does not greet you with, and ask themselves: 'Why does God not punish us for what we say?' Hell is scourge enough for them: in its flames they shall burn, a wretched fate!

الم تر ان الله يعلم ما في السموات وما في الارض ما يكون
من نجوى ثلثة الا هو رابعهم ولا خمسة الا هو سادسهم
ولا ادنى من ذلك ولا اكثر الا هو معهم اين ما كانوا
ثم ينبئهم بما عملوا يوم القيمة ان الله بكل شيء
عليم ۝٧ الم تر الى الذين نهوا عن النجوى ثم يعودون لما نهوا عنه
ويتناجون بالاثم والعدوان ومعصيت الرسول واذا جاؤك حيوك بما لم
يحيك به الله ويقولون في انفسهم لولا يعذبنا الله بما نقول
حسبهم جهنم يصلونها فبئس المصير ۝٨ يا ايها الذين
امنوا اذا تناجيتم فلا تتناجوا بالاثم والعدوان ومعصيت
الرسول وتناجوا بالبر والتقوى واتقوا الله الذي اليه
تحشرون ۝٩ انما النجوى من الشيطان ليحزن الذين امنوا
وليس بضارهم شيئا الا باذن الله وعلى الله فليتوكل
المؤمنون ۝١٠ يا ايها الذين امنوا اذا قيل لكم تفسحوا في المجالس فافسحوا
يفسح الله لكم واذا قيل انشزوا فانشزوا يرفع الله الذين امنوا
منكم والذين اوتوا العلم درجات والله بما تعملون خبير ۝١١

58:9 Believers, when you converse in private do not speak in sin and enmity and disobedience to the Apostle, but with justice and with piety; and fear God, before whom you shall be herded.

Intrigue is the work of Satan, who means to vex the faithful. Yet he can harm them not at all, except by the will of God. In God let the faithful put their trust.

58:11 Believers, make room[1] in your assemblies when you are bidden so to do: God will make room for you hereafter. Again, rise up when you are told to rise: God will raise to high ranks those of you that believe and those endowed with knowledge. God is cognizant of what you do.

1. For the Prophet, or for your fellow-Muslims.

يا أيها الذين آمنوا إذا ناجيتم الرسول فقدموا بين يدي نجواكم
صدقة ذلك خير لكم وأطهر فإن لم تجدوا فإن الله غفور رحيم ١٢
ءأشفقتم أن تقدموا بين يدي نجواكم صدقات فإذ لم تفعلوا وتاب الله
عليكم فأقيموا الصلوة وآتوا الزكوة وأطيعوا الله ورسوله والله
خبير بما تعملون ١٣ ألم تر إلى الذين تولوا قوما غضب الله
عليهم ما هم منكم ولا منهم ويحلفون على الكذب وهم
يعلمون ١٤ أعد الله لهم عذابا شديدا إنهم ساء ما كانوا يعملون
١٥ اتخذوا أيمانهم جنة فصدوا عن سبيل الله فلهم عذاب
مهين ١٦ لن تغني عنهم أموالهم ولا أولادهم من الله
شيئا أولئك أصحاب النار هم فيها خالدون ١٧ يوم يبعثهم الله
جميعا فيحلفون له كما يحلفون لكم ويحسبون أنهم على شيء
ألا إنهم هم الكاذبون ١٨ استحوذ عليهم الشيطان
فأنساهم ذكر الله أولئك حزب الشيطان ألا إن حزب الشيطان
هم الخاسرون ١٩ إن الذين يحادون الله ورسوله أولئك في
الأذلين ٢٠ كتب الله لأغلبن أنا ورسلي إن الله قوي عزيز ٢١

YOU BELIEVERS, when you 58:12
confer with the Apostle, give alms before such conference. That is better and more righteous for you. But if you lack the means, God is forgiving and compassionate.

Do you hesitate to offer alms before you confer with him? If you do not (and God will pardon your offence), then at least recite your prayers and render the alms levy and obey God and His apostle. God is cognizant of what you do.

Do you see those that have befriended a people with whom God is angry? They belong neither to you nor to them. They knowingly swear to falsehood. God has prepared for them a grievous scourge. Evil indeed is that which they have done.

They use their faith as a disguise, and debar others from the path of God. 58:16
Shameful punishment awaits them.

Their wealth and children shall in no way protect them from God. They are the inmates of the Fire, wherein shall they abide for ever.

On the day when God restores them all to life, they will swear to Him as they now swear to you, imagining that their oaths will help them. Surely it is they who are lying.

Satan has gained possession of them, and caused them to forget God's Admonition. They are the confederates of Satan; but Satan's confederates will surely be the losers.

Those that oppose God and His apostle shall be brought low. God has 58:21
decreed: 'I will surely triumph, Myself and My apostles.' Powerful is God, and mighty.

لا تجد قوما يؤمنون بالله واليوم الآخر يوادون من حاد الله ورسوله
ولو كانوا آباءهم أو أبناءهم أو إخوانهم أو عشيرتهم
أولئك كتب في قلوبهم الإيمان وأيدهم بروح منه ويدخلهم
جنات تجري من تحتها الأنهار خالدين فيها رضي الله عنهم
ورضوا عنه أولئك حزب الله ألا إن حزب الله هم المفلحون ٢٢

سورة الحشر مدنية وهي أربع وعشرون آية

بسم الله الرحمن الرحيم
سبح لله ما في السموات وما في الأرض وهو العزيز الحكيم ١ هو
الذي أخرج الذين كفروا من أهل الكتاب من ديارهم لأول
الحشر ما ظننتم أن يخرجوا وظنوا أنهم مانعتهم حصونهم
من الله فأتاهم الله من حيث لم يحتسبوا وقذف في
قلوبهم الرعب يخربون بيوتهم بأيديهم وأيدي المؤمنين
فاعتبروا يا أولي الأبصار ٢ ولولا أن كتب الله عليهم
الجلاء لعذبهم في الدنيا ولهم في الآخرة عذاب النار ٣

58:22 YOU SHALL find no believers in God and in the Last Day on friendly terms with those who oppose God and His apostle, even though they be their fathers, their sons, their brothers, or their nearest kin. God has inscribed the Faith in their very hearts, and strengthened them with a spirit of His own. He will usher them into Gardens watered by running brooks, wherein shall they abide for ever. God is well pleased with them, and they are well pleased with Him. They are the confederates of God: and God's confederates will surely triumph.

EXILE

In the Name of God, the Merciful, the Compassionate

59:1 ALL THAT is in the heavens and on the earth gives glory to God. He is the
Omnipotent, the Wise One.
He it was that drove the unbelievers among the People of the Book out
of their dwellings into the first exile.[1] You did not think that they would go;
and they, for their part, fancied that their strongholds would protect them
from God. But God smote them whence they did not expect, casting such
terror into their hearts that their dwellings were destroyed by their own
hands as well as by the faithful. Learn from their example, you that have eyes.
59:3 Had God not decreed exile[2] for them, He would have surely punished them
in this world. But in the world to come the torment of the Fire awaits them,

1. An allusion to Muḥammad's expedition against the Jews of Banu al-Naḍīr in Arabia.
2. Mostly to Syria.

ذلك بأنهم شاقوا الله ورسوله ومن يشاق الله فإن الله
شديد العقاب ﴿٤﴾ ما قطعتم من لينة أو تركتموها قائمة
على أصولها فبإذن الله وليخزي الفاسقين ﴿٥﴾ وما أفاء الله
على رسوله منهم فما أوجفتم عليه من خيل ولا ركاب
ولكن الله يسلط رسله على من يشاء والله على كل شيء
قدير ﴿٦﴾ ما أفاء الله على رسوله من أهل القرى فلله
وللرسول ولذي القربى واليتامى والمساكين وابن السبيل
كي لا يكون دولة بين الأغنياء منكم وما آتاكم الرسول
فخذوه وما نهاكم عنه فانتهوا واتقوا الله إن الله
شديد العقاب ﴿٧﴾ للفقراء المهاجرين الذين أخرجوا
من ديارهم وأموالهم يبتغون فضلا من الله ورضوانا
وينصرون الله ورسوله أولئك هم الصادقون ﴿٨﴾ والذين تبوءوا
الدار والإيمان من قبلهم يحبون من هاجر إليهم ولا يجدون
في صدورهم حاجة مما أوتوا ويؤثرون على أنفسهم ولو كان
بهم خصاصة ومن يوق شح نفسه فأولئك هم المفلحون ﴿٩﴾

because they had set them- 59:4
selves against God and His
apostle; and he that sets himself against God should know
that God is stern in retribution.
It was by God's leave that
you cut down or spared their
palm-trees, so that He might
humiliate the ungodly. As for
those spoils of theirs which
God has assigned to His apostle, you spurred neither horse
nor camel to capture them:
but God gives His apostles
authority over whom He will;
and God has power over all
things.
The spoils taken from the 59:7
town-dwellers and assigned
by God to His apostle shall
belong to God, to the Apostle
and his kin, to orphans, to the
destitute and to the traveller in
need; they shall not become the property of the rich among you. Whatever
the Apostle gives you, take it; and whatever he forbids you, abstain from it.
Fear God; God is stern in retribution.
They shall also be for the poor among the *muhājirīn*[1] who have been driven
from their homes and their possessions, who seek God's grace and pleasure
and who help God and His apostle; these are the true believers.
Those who stayed in their own city[2] and embraced the Faith before them, 59:9
love those who have sought refuge with them; they do not covet what they
are given, but rather prize them above themselves, though they are in want.
Those that preserve themselves from their own greed shall surely prosper.

1. See p. 202, note 1. 2. Medina.

59:10 THOSE THAT came after them say: 'Forgive us, Lord, and forgive our brothers who embraced the Faith before us. Remove from our hearts any rancour towards the faithful. Lord, You are benignant and compassionate.'

Do but consider the hypocrites. They say to their fellow-unbelievers among the People of the Book: 'If you are driven out, we will go with you. We will never obey anyone who seeks to harm you. If you are attacked, we will certainly help you.'

God bears witness that they are lying. If they are driven out, they will not go with them, nor, if they are attacked, will they help them. Indeed, if they do go to their help, they will take to their heels and leave them in the lurch.

Their dread of you is more intense in their hearts than their fear of God: so devoid are they of understanding.

59:14 They will never fight against you in a body except in fortified cities and from behind walls. Great is their valour among themselves; you think of them as one band, yet their hearts are divided; for they are surely lacking in judgement.

Like those who were but recently punished before them, they tasted the fruit of their own deeds. And woeful punishment awaits them.

59:16 They may be compared to Satan, who, when he ordered man to disbelieve and he did his bidding, said to him: 'I do disown you. I fear God, Lord of the Universe.'

وَالَّذِينَ جَاءُوا مِن بَعْدِهِمْ يَقُولُونَ رَبَّنَا اغْفِرْ لَنَا وَلِإِخْوَانِنَا
الَّذِينَ سَبَقُونَا بِالْإِيمَانِ وَلَا تَجْعَلْ فِي قُلُوبِنَا غِلًّا لِّلَّذِينَ
آمَنُوا رَبَّنَا إِنَّكَ رَءُوفٌ رَّحِيمٌ ﴿١٠﴾ أَلَمْ تَرَ إِلَى الَّذِينَ نَافَقُوا
يَقُولُونَ لِإِخْوَانِهِمُ الَّذِينَ كَفَرُوا مِنْ أَهْلِ الْكِتَابِ لَئِنْ
أُخْرِجْتُمْ لَنَخْرُجَنَّ مَعَكُمْ وَلَا نُطِيعُ فِيكُمْ أَحَدًا أَبَدًا
وَإِن قُوتِلْتُمْ لَنَنصُرَنَّكُمْ وَاللَّهُ يَشْهَدُ إِنَّهُمْ لَكَاذِبُونَ
﴿١١﴾ لَئِنْ أُخْرِجُوا لَا يَخْرُجُونَ مَعَهُمْ وَلَئِن قُوتِلُوا لَا يَنصُرُونَهُمْ
وَلَئِن نَّصَرُوهُمْ لَيُوَلُّنَّ الْأَدْبَارَ ثُمَّ لَا يُنصَرُونَ ﴿١٢﴾ لَأَنتُمْ
أَشَدُّ رَهْبَةً فِي صُدُورِهِم مِّنَ اللَّهِ ذَٰلِكَ بِأَنَّهُمْ قَوْمٌ لَّا
يَفْقَهُونَ ﴿١٣﴾ لَا يُقَاتِلُونَكُمْ جَمِيعًا إِلَّا فِي قُرًى مُّحَصَّنَةٍ
أَوْ مِن وَرَاءِ جُدُرٍ بَأْسُهُم بَيْنَهُمْ شَدِيدٌ تَحْسَبُهُمْ جَمِيعًا
وَقُلُوبُهُمْ شَتَّىٰ ذَٰلِكَ بِأَنَّهُمْ قَوْمٌ لَّا يَعْقِلُونَ ﴿١٤﴾ كَمَثَلِ
الَّذِينَ مِن قَبْلِهِمْ قَرِيبًا ذَاقُوا وَبَالَ أَمْرِهِمْ وَلَهُمْ عَذَابٌ
أَلِيمٌ ﴿١٥﴾ كَمَثَلِ الشَّيْطَانِ إِذْ قَالَ لِلْإِنسَانِ اكْفُرْ فَلَمَّا كَفَرَ
قَالَ إِنِّي بَرِيءٌ مِّنكَ إِنِّي أَخَافُ اللَّهَ رَبَّ الْعَالَمِينَ ﴿١٦﴾

فكان عاقبتهما أنهما في النار خالدين فيها وذلك
جزؤا الظالمين ١٧ يا أيها الذين آمنوا اتقوا الله ولتنظر
نفس ما قدمت لغد واتقوا الله إن الله خبير بما
تعملون ١٨ ولا تكونوا كالذين نسوا الله فأنسيهم
أنفسهم أولئك هم الفاسقون ١٩ لا يستوي أصحاب النار وأصحاب
الجنة أصحاب الجنة هم الفائزون ٢٠ لو أنزلنا هذا القرآن
على جبل لرأيته خاشعا متصدعا من خشية الله وتلك
الأمثال نضربها للناس لعلهم يتفكرون ٢١ هو الله الذي لا
إله إلا هو عالم الغيب والشهادة هو الرحمن الرحيم ٢٢
هو الله الذي لا إله إلا هو الملك القدوس السلام المؤمن المهيمن
العزيز الجبار المتكبر سبحان الله عما يشركون ٢٣
هو الله الخالق البارئ المصور له الأسماء الحسنى
يسبح له ما في السموات والأرض وهو العزيز الحكيم ٢٤

سورة الممتحنة مدنية وهي ثلث عشرة آية

THEY SHALL both end in 59:17
the Fire and therein abide for ever. Thus shall the wrongdoers be rewarded.

Believers, have fear of God. Let every soul look to what it offers for the morrow. Fear God; God is cognizant of what you do.

Do not act like those who forgot God, so that He caused them to forget themselves. Such are the ungodly.

The heirs of the Fire and the heirs of Paradise shall not be held equal. The heirs of Paradise alone shall be triumphant.

Had We brought down this 59:21
Koran upon a mountain, you would have seen it humble itself and break asunder for fear of God.

In such parables We speak to people, that they may take thought.

He is God, besides whom there is no other deity. He knows the unknown and the manifest. He is the Merciful, the Compassionate.

He is God, besides whom there is no other deity. He is the Sovereign Lord, the Holy One, the Giver of Peace, the Keeper of Faith; the Preserver, the Almighty, the All-powerful, the Most High. Exalted be God above their idols.

He is God, the Creator, the Originator, the Modeller. His are the most 59:24
gracious names. All that is in the heavens and the earth gives glory to Him. He is the Almighty, the Wise One.

SHE WHO IS TESTED

بسم الله الرحمن الرحيم
يا أيها الذين آمنوا لا تتخذوا عدوي وعدوكم أولياء
تلقون إليهم بالمودة وقد كفروا بما جاءكم من الحق
يخرجون الرسول وإياكم أن تؤمنوا بالله ربكم إن كنتم خرجتم
جهادا في سبيلي وابتغاء مرضاتي تسرون إليهم بالمودة وأنا أعلم
بما أخفيتم وما أعلنتم ومن يفعله منكم فقد ضل سواء السبيل
(١) إن يثقفوكم يكونوا لكم أعداء ويبسطوا إليكم أيديهم
وألسنتهم بالسوء وودوا لو تكفرون (٢) لن تنفعكم أرحامكم
ولا أولادكم يوم القيامة يفصل بينكم والله بما تعملون بصير (٣)
قد كانت لكم أسوة حسنة في إبراهيم والذين معه إذ قالوا لقومهم
إنا برآء منكم ومما تعبدون من دون الله كفرنا بكم وبدا بيننا
وبينكم العداوة والبغضاء أبدا حتى تؤمنوا بالله وحده إلا قول إبراهيم
لأبيه لأستغفرن لك وما أملك لك من الله من شيء ربنا عليك
توكلنا وإليك أنبنا وإليك المصير (٤) ربنا لا تجعلنا فتنة
للذين كفروا واغفر لنا ربنا إنك أنت العزيز الحكيم (٥)

In the Name of God,
the Merciful, the Compassionate

60:1 BELIEVERS, DO not make friends with those who are enemies of Mine and yours. Would you show them affection, when they have denied the Truth that has been revealed to you and driven out the Apostle and yourselves, because you believe in God, your Lord?

If it was indeed to fight for My cause, and out of a desire to please Me, that you left your city, how can you be friendly to them in secret? I well know all that you conceal, and all that you reveal. Whoever of you does this will stray from the right path.

If they gain ascendancy over you, they will prove themselves your enemies, and stretch out their hands and tongues to you with evil. They long to see you unbelievers.

On the Day of Resurrection, neither your kin nor your children shall avail you. He will separate you, and God is cognizant of what you do.

60:4 You have a good example in Abraham and those who followed him. They said to their people: 'We disown you and the idols which you worship besides God. We renounce you: enmity and hate shall reign between us until you believe in God alone.' But do not emulate the words of Abraham to his father: 'I shall implore forgiveness for you, although I can in no way protect you from God.'

'Lord, in You we have put our trust; to You we turn and to You we shall
60:5 come at last. Lord, do not expose us to the designs of the unbelievers. Forgive us, Lord; You are the Almighty, the Wise One.'

لقد كان لكم فيهم أسوة حسنة لمن كان يرجوا الله واليوم الآخر
ومن يتول فإن الله هو الغني الحميد ٦ عسى الله أن يجعل بينكم
وبين الذين عاديتم منهم مودة والله قدير والله غفور رحيم
٧ لا ينهيكم الله عن الذين لم يقاتلوكم في الدين ولم يخرجوكم
من دياركم أن تبروهم وتقسطوا إليهم إن الله يحب المقسطين
٨ إنما ينهيكم الله عن الذين قاتلوكم في الدين وأخرجوكم من
دياركم وظاهروا على إخراجكم أن تولوهم ومن يتولهم فأولئك
هم الظالمون ٩ يا أيها الذين آمنوا إذا جاءكم المؤمنات مهاجرات
فامتحنوهن الله أعلم بإيمانهن فإن علمتموهن مؤمنات فلا
ترجعوهن إلى الكفار لا هن حل لهم ولا هم يحلون لهن وآتوهم
ما أنفقوا ولا جناح عليكم أن تنكحوهن إذا آتيتموهن أجورهن
ولا تمسكوا بعصم الكوافر وسئلوا ما أنفقتم وليسئلوا ما أنفقوا
ذلكم حكم الله يحكم بينكم والله عليم حكيم ١٠ وإن فاتكم
شيء من أزواجكم إلى الكفار فعاقبتم فآتوا الذين ذهبت
أزواجهم مثل ما أنفقوا واتقوا الله الذي أنتم به مؤمنون ١١

SURELY IN those there is 60:6
a good example for you; for
everyone who puts his hopes
in God and in the Last Day.
As for him that pays no heed,
God alone is self-sufficient
and worthy of praise.

It may well be that God
will put good will between
you and those with whom you
have hitherto been at odds.
God is mighty; God is forgiving and compassionate.

God does not forbid you
to be kind and equitable to
those who have neither fought
you on account of your Religion nor driven you from
your homes; God loves the
equitable. But He forbids you
to make friends with those
who have fought you on
account of your religion and
driven you from your homes or abetted others to drive you out. Those that
make friends with them are the wrongdoers.

Believers, when believing women seek refuge with you, test them. God 60:10
best knows their faith. If you find them true believers, do not return them to
the infidels; they are not lawful for the infidels, nor are the infidels lawful for
them. Hand back to them the dowries they gave; nor is it an offence for you
to marry such women, if you give them their dowries. Do not maintain your
marriages with unbelieving women: demand the dowries you gave and let
them demand the dowries they gave. Such is the judgement which God lays
down among you. God is all-knowing and wise.

And if any of your wives go over to the infidels and you subsequently 60:11
gain victory over them, pay those whose wives have deserted the equivalent
of the dowries they gave them. And fear God, in whom you do believe.

60:12 PROPHET, IF believing women come to you and pledge themselves to serve no other deity besides God, to commit neither theft, nor adultery, nor child-murder, to utter no monstrous falsehoods of their own invention, and to disobey you in nothing reasonable, accept their allegiance and implore God to forgive them. Surely God is forgiving and compassionate.

60:13 Believers, do not make friends with people who have provoked the wrath of God; for they have despaired of the life to come, just as the infidels have despaired of the buried dead.

يا أيها النبي إذا جاءك المؤمنات يبايعنك على أن لا
يشركن بالله شيئا ولا يسرقن ولا يزنين ولا يقتلن أولادهن ولا
يأتين ببهتان يفترينه بين أيديهن وأرجلهن ولا يعصينك في
معروف فبايعهن واستغفر لهن الله إن الله غفور رحيم ۝١٢
يا أيها الذين آمنوا لا تتولوا قوما غضب الله عليهم قد يئسوا من
الآخرة كما يئس الكفار من أصحاب القبور ۝١٣

سورة الصف مدنية وهي أربع عشرة آية

بسم الله الرحمن الرحيم
سبح لله ما في السماوات وما في الأرض وهو العزيز الحكيم ۝١
يا أيها الذين آمنوا لم تقولون ما لا تفعلون ۝٢ كبر مقتا
عند الله أن تقولوا ما لا تفعلون ۝٣ إن الله يحب الذين يقاتلون
في سبيله صفا كأنهم بنيان مرصوص ۝٤ وإذ قال موسى لقومه يا
قوم لم تؤذونني وقد تعلمون أني رسول الله إليكم فلما زاغوا
أزاغ الله قلوبهم والله لا يهدي القوم الفاسقين ۝٥

BATTLE ARRAY

In the Name of God, the Merciful, the Compassionate

61:1 ALL THAT is in the heavens and on the earth gives glory to God. He is the Almighty, the Wise One.

Believers, why do you profess what you never do? It is most odious in God's sight that you should say one thing and do another.

God loves those who fight for His cause in ranks as firm as a mighty edifice.

61:5 Tell of Moses, who said to his people: 'Why do you seek to harm me, my people, when you know that I am sent to you by God?' And when they went astray, God led their very hearts astray. God does not guide the ungodly.

وإذ قال عيسى ابن مريم يا بني إسرائيل إني رسول الله إليكم مصدقا لما بين يدي
من التوراة ومبشرا برسول يأتي من بعدي اسمه أحمد فلما جاءهم بالبينات قالوا
هذا سحر مبين ٦ ومن أظلم ممن افترى على الله الكذب وهو يدعى إلى
الإسلام والله لا يهدي القوم الظالمين ٧ يريدون ليطفئوا نور الله
بأفواههم والله متم نوره ولو كره الكافرون ٨ هو الذي أرسل
رسوله بالهدى ودين الحق ليظهره على الدين كله ولو كره المشركون
٩ يا أيها الذين آمنوا هل أدلكم على تجارة تنجيكم من عذاب أليم ١٠
تؤمنون بالله ورسوله وتجاهدون في سبيل الله بأموالكم وأنفسكم
ذلكم خير لكم إن كنتم تعلمون ١١ يغفر لكم ذنوبكم
ويدخلكم جنات تجري من تحتها الأنهار ومساكن طيبة في
جنات عدن ذلك الفوز العظيم ١٢ وأخرى تحبونها نصر من الله
وفتح قريب وبشر المؤمنين ١٣ يا أيها الذين آمنوا كونوا أنصار الله
كما قال عيسى ابن مريم للحواريين من أنصاري إلى الله قال الحواريون نحن
أنصار الله فآمنت طائفة من بني إسرائيل وكفرت طائفة
فأيدنا الذين آمنوا على عدوهم فأصبحوا ظاهرين ١٤

And of Jesus son of Mary, 61:6
who said to the Israelites: 'I am sent forth to you from God to confirm the Torah already revealed, and to give joyful tidings of an apostle that will come after me whose name is Aḥmad.'[1] Yet when he brought them conspicuous signs, they said: 'This is sorcery manifest.'

And who is more wicked than he that invents a falsehood about God when called to Islām? God does not guide the wrongdoers.

They seek to extinguish the light of God with their mouths; but God will perfect His light, much as the infidels may dislike it.

He it is who has sent forth His apostle with guidance and the Religion of Truth that he may exalt it above all religion, much as the idolaters may dislike it.

Believers! Shall I point out to you a profitable course that will save you 61:10
from a woeful scourge? Have faith in God and His apostle, and fight for God's cause with your wealth and with your persons; that would be best for you, if you but knew it.

He will forgive you your sins and admit you into Gardens watered by running brooks; He will lodge you in goodly mansions in the Gardens of Eden. That is the supreme triumph.

And He will bestow upon you other blessings which you desire: help from God and a speedy victory. Proclaim the joyful tidings to the faithful.

Believers, be God's helpers. When Jesus son of Mary said to the disciples: 61:14
'Who will come with me to the help of God?' the disciples replied: '*We* are God's helpers.'

Some among the Israelites believed, while some did not believe. We aided the believers against their enemies, and when morning came they were triumphant.

1. Another name of Muḥammad's, also meaning 'The Praised One'.

FRIDAY, OR THE DAY OF CONGREGATION

سورة الجمعة مدنية وهي احدى عشرة آية

بسم الله الرحمن الرحيم
يسبح لله ما في السموات وما في الارض الملك القدوس العزيز
الحكيم (١) هو الذي بعث في الاميين رسولا منهم يتلوا عليهم اياته
ويزكيهم ويعلمهم الكتاب والحكمة وان كانوا من قبل لفي ضلال
مبين (٢) واخرين منهم لما يلحقوا بهم وهو العزيز الحكيم (٣) ذلك
فضل الله يؤتيه من يشاء والله ذو الفضل العظيم
(٤) مثل الذين حملوا التورية ثم لم يحملوها كمثل الحمار يحمل اسفارا
بئس مثل القوم الذين كذبوا بايات الله والله لا يهدي القوم
الظالمين (٥) قل يا ايها الذين هادوا ان زعمتم انكم
اولياء لله من دون الناس فتمنوا الموت ان كنتم صادقين (٦)
ولا يتمنونه ابدا بما قدمت ايديهم والله عليم بالظالمين
(٧) قل ان الموت الذي تفرون منه فانه ملاقيكم ثم تردون
الى عالم الغيب والشهادة فينبئكم بما كنتم تعملون (٨)

In the Name of God, the Merciful, the Compassionate

62:1 ALL THAT is in the heavens and on the earth gives glory to God, the Sovereign Lord, the Holy One, the Almighty, the Wise One.

He it is that has sent forth among the Gentiles an apostle of their own to recite to them His revelations, to purify them, and to instruct them in the Book and in wisdom, though they have hitherto been in evident error, together with others of their own kin who have not yet followed them. He is the Almighty, the Wise One.

Such is the grace of God: He bestows it on whom He will. His grace is infinite.

62:5 Those to whom the burden of the Torah was entrusted and yet refused to bear it are like a donkey laden with books. Wretched is the example of those who deny God's revelations; and God does not guide the wrongdoers.

Say: 'You that follow the Jewish Faith, if you claim that of all people you alone are God's friends, then you should wish for death, if what you say be true!' But, because of what their hands have done, they will never wish for death; God knows the wrongdoers.

62:8 Say: 'The death from which you flee is sure to overtake you. Then shall you be sent back to Him who knows the unknown and the manifest, and He will declare to you what you have done.'

يا أيها الذين آمنوا إذا نودي للصلوة من يوم الجمعة فاسعوا إلى ذكر الله
وذروا البيع ذلكم خير لكم إن كنتم تعلمون ٩ فإذا قضيت
الصلوة فانتشروا في الأرض وابتغوا من فضل الله واذكروا الله
كثيرا لعلكم تفلحون ١٠ وإذا رأوا تجارة أو لهوا انفضوا إليها وتركوك قائما
قل ما عند الله خير من اللهو ومن التجارة والله خير الرازقين ١١
سورة المنافقون مدنية وهي احدى عشرة آية
بسم الله الرحمن الرحيم
إذا جاءك المنافقون قالوا نشهد إنك لرسول الله والله يعلم إنك
لرسوله والله يشهد إن المنافقين لكاذبون ١ اتخذوا
أيمانهم جنة فصدوا عن سبيل الله إنهم ساء ما كانوا
يعملون ٢ ذلك بأنهم آمنوا ثم كفروا فطبع على قلوبهم
فهم لا يفقهون ٣ وإذا رأيتهم تعجبك أجسامهم وإن يقولوا
تسمع لقولهم كأنهم خشب مسندة يحسبون كل صيحة
عليهم هم العدو فاحذرهم قاتلهم الله أنى يؤفكون ٤

Believers, when you are 62:9
summoned to Friday prayers
hasten to the remembrance of
God and cease your trading.
That would be best for you, if
you but knew it. Then, when
the prayers are ended, disperse
and go your ways in quest of
God's bounty. Remember God
much, that you may prosper.
Yet no sooner do they see 62:11
some commerce or merriment
afoot than they flock
eagerly to it, leaving you[1]
standing.
Say: 'That which God has
in store is far better than any
merriment or any commerce.
And God is the Most Munificent
Giver.'

THE HYPOCRITES

In the Name of God, the Merciful, the Compassionate

When the hypocrites come to you they say: 'We bear witness that you are 63:1
assuredly God's apostle.' God knows that you are indeed His apostle; and
God bears witness that the hypocrites are surely lying.
They use their faith as a disguise, and debar others from the path of God.
Evil is what they ever do.
They believed and then renounced the Faith: their hearts are sealed, so
that they are devoid of understanding.
When you see them, their good looks please you; and when they speak, 63:4
you listen to what they say. Yet they are like propped-up beams of timber.
Every shout they hear they take to be against them. *They* are the enemy.
Guard yourself against them. God smite them! How perverse they are!

1. Muḥammad.

63:5 WHEN THEY are told: 'Come, God's apostle will beg forgiveness for you,' they turn their heads and you see them go away in scorn.

It is the same for them whether or not you ask forgiveness for them: God will not forgive them. God does not guide the ungodly.

It is they who say: 'Give nothing to those that follow God's apostle until they have deserted.' God's are the treasures of the heavens and the earth: but the hypocrites cannot understand.

63:8 They say: 'If we return to Madīnah,[1] the strong will soon drive out the weak.' But strength belongs to God and to His apostle and to the faithful: yet the hypocrites do not know it.

وإذا قيل لهم تعالوا يستغفر لكم رسول الله لووا رءوسهم ورأيتهم
يصدون وهم مستكبرون (٥) سواء عليهم أستغفرت لهم أم لم
تستغفر لهم لن يغفر الله لهم إن الله لا يهدي القوم
الفاسقين (٦) هم الذين يقولون لا تنفقوا على من عند رسول
الله حتى ينفضوا ولله خزائن السموات والأرض ولكن
المنافقين لا يفقهون (٧) يقولون لئن رجعنا إلى المدينة ليخرجن
الأعز منها الأذل ولله العزة ولرسوله وللمؤمنين و
لكن المنافقين لا يعلمون (٨) يا أيها الذين آمنوا لا تلهكم
أموالكم ولا أولادكم عن ذكر الله ومن يفعل ذلك
فأولئك هم الخاسرون (٩) وأنفقوا مما رزقناكم من
قبل أن يأتي أحدكم الموت فيقول رب لولا أخرتني إلى أجل
قريب فأصدق وأكن من الصالحين (١٠) ولن يؤخر
الله نفسا إذا جاء أجلها والله خبير بما تعملون (١١)

سورة التغابن مدنية وهي ثماني عشرة آية

Believers, let neither your riches nor your children divert you from remembering God. Those that are so diverted will surely be the losers.

Give, then, of that which We have given you before death befalls any of you and he should say: 'Reprieve me, Lord, for a short time, that I may give in charity and be among the righteous.'

63:11 But God reprieves no soul when its term expires. And God is cognizant of what you do.

1. To which the Prophet and his followers had fled from Mecca.

بسم الله الرحمن الرحيم
يسبح لله ما في السموات وما في الارض له الملك وله الحمد وهو
على كل شيء قدير ١ هو الذي خلقكم فمنكم كافر ومنكم
مؤمن والله بما تعملون بصير ٢ خلق السموات والارض بالحق
وصوركم فاحسن صوركم واليه المصير ٣ يعلم ما في السموات
والارض ويعلم ما تسرون وما تعلنون والله عليم بذات الصدور
٤ الم ياتكم نبؤا الذين كفروا من قبل فذاقوا وبال امرهم
ولهم عذاب اليم ٥ ذلك بانه كانت تاتيهم رسلهم
بالبينات فقالوا ابشر يهدوننا فكفروا وتولوا واستغنى
الله والله غني حميد ٦ زعم الذين كفروا ان لن يبعثوا قل بلى
وربي لتبعثن ثم لتنبؤن بما عملتم وذلك على الله يسير ٧ فامنوا
بالله ورسوله والنور الذي انزلنا والله بما تعملون خبير
٨ يوم يجمعكم ليوم الجمع ذلك يوم التغابن ومن يؤمن
بالله ويعمل صالحا يكفر عنه سياته ويدخله جنات تجري من
تحتها الانهار خالدين فيها ابدا ذلك الفوز العظيم ٩

CHEATING

In the Name of God,
the Merciful, the Compassionate

ALL THAT is in the heavens 64:1
and on the earth gives glory to
God. His is the sovereignty,
and His all praise. And He has
power over all things.

He it was that created you:
yet some among you are unbelievers, and some have faith.
God observes what you do.

He created the heavens
and the earth to manifest the
Truth, and fashioned you into
a comely shape. To Him shall
all return.

He knows what the heav-
ens and the earth contain; He
knows what you conceal and
what you reveal. God well knows your innermost thoughts.

Have you not heard of those who disbelieved before you? They tasted the
baleful consequences of their unbelief, and grievous punishment is yet in store
for them. That is because, when their apostles brought them veritable signs, 64:6
they said: 'Shall mortals be our guides?' They disbelieved and paid no heed. But
God was in no need of them: God is self-sufficient and worthy of praise.

The unbelievers say they will not be raised to life. Say: 'Yes, by the Lord,
you shall assuredly be raised to life! Then you shall be told of all that you
have done. That is easy enough for God.'

Believe then in God and in His apostle, and in the light We have revealed.
God is cognizant of what you do.

The day He gathers you, the day on which you shall all be gathered – that 64:9
shall be a day of cheating.[1] Those that believe in God and do what is
right shall be forgiven their sins and ushered into Gardens watered by running brooks, wherein shall they abide for ever. That is the supreme triumph.

1. I.e. when the blessed will 'cheat' the damned of their places in Paradise which would have been theirs had they been true believers (Al-Bayḍāwī).

64:10 BUT THOSE that disbelieve
and deny Our revelations shall
be the inmates of the Fire,
wherein shall they abide for
ever: a wretched fate!

No misfortune strikes except
by God's leave. He guides the
hearts of those who believe in
Him; God has knowledge of
all things.

And obey God and obey the
Apostle. If you pay no heed,
Our apostle's duty is only to
give the veritable warning.

God – there is no god but
Him; in God let the faithful
put their trust.

64:14 Believers, in your spouses
and in your children you have
an enemy: beware of them. But
if you overlook their offences
and forgive and pardon them,
then know that God is forgiving and compassionate.

والذين كفروا وكذبوا بآياتنا أولئك أصحاب النار
خالدين فيها وبئس المصير ﴿١٠﴾ ما أصاب من مصيبة إلا بإذن
الله ومن يؤمن بالله يهد قلبه والله بكل شيء عليم
﴿١١﴾ وأطيعوا الله وأطيعوا الرسول فإن توليتم
فإنما على رسولنا البلاغ المبين ﴿١٢﴾ الله لا إله إلا هو وعلى
الله فليتوكل المؤمنون ﴿١٣﴾ يا أيها الذين آمنوا إن من
أزواجكم وأولادكم عدوا لكم فاحذروهم وإن
تعفوا وتصفحوا وتغفروا فإن الله غفور رحيم ﴿١٤﴾
إنما أموالكم وأولادكم فتنة والله عنده أجر عظيم
﴿١٥﴾ فاتقوا الله ما استطعتم واسمعوا وأطيعوا وأنفقوا
خيرا لأنفسكم ومن يوق شح نفسه فأولئك هم المفلحون ﴿١٦﴾
إن تقرضوا الله قرضا حسنا يضاعفه لكم ويغفر لكم
والله شكور حليم ﴿١٧﴾ عالم الغيب والشهادة العزيز الحكيم ﴿١٨﴾

سورة الطلاق مدنية وهي اثنتا عشرة آية

Your wealth and your children are but a temptation. God's recompense is
great: therefore fear God with all your hearts, and be attentive, obedient, and
charitable. That will be best for you.

Those that preserve themselves from their own greed will surely prosper.
If you give a generous loan to God, He will pay you back twofold and will
forgive you. Gracious is God, and benignant.

64:18 He has knowledge of the unknown and the manifest. He is the Almighty,
the Wise One.

بسم الله الرحمن الرحيم
يا أيها النبي إذا طلقتم النساء فطلقوهن لعدتهن
وأحصوا العدة واتقوا الله ربكم لا تخرجوهن من بيوتهن
ولا يخرجن إلا أن يأتين بفاحشة مبينة وتلك حدود الله
ومن يتعد حدود الله فقد ظلم نفسه لا تدري لعل الله
يحدث بعد ذلك أمرا ١ فإذا بلغن أجلهن فأمسكوهن
بمعروف أو فارقوهن بمعروف وأشهدوا ذوي عدل منكم
وأقيموا الشهادة لله ذلكم يوعظ به من كان يؤمن بالله
واليوم الآخر ومن يتق الله يجعل له مخرجا ٢ ويرزقه من
حيث لا يحتسب ومن يتوكل على الله فهو حسبه إن الله
بالغ أمره قد جعل الله لكل شيء قدرا ٣ واللائي يئسن
من المحيض من نسائكم إن ارتبتم فعدتهن ثلاثة
أشهر واللائي لم يحضن وأولات الأحمال أجلهن أن يضعن
حملهن ومن يتق الله يجعل له من أمره يسرا ٤ ذلك أمر الله
أنزله إليكم ومن يتق الله يكفر عنه سيئاته ويعظم له أجرا ٥

DIVORCE

In the Name of God,
the Merciful, the Compassionate

PROPHET (AND you believ- 65:1
ers), if you divorce your wives,
divorce them at the end of
their waiting period. Compute
their waiting period and fear
God, your Lord. You shall not
expel them from their homes,
nor shall they go away, unless
they have committed a proven
lewd act. Such are the bounds
set by God; he that transgresses God's bounds wrongs
his own soul. You never know;
after that, God may bring
about some new event.

When their waiting term is
ended, either keep them hon-
ourably or part with them in honour. Call to witness two honest men among
you and give your testimony before God. Whoever believes in God and the
Last Day is exhorted to do this. He that fears God, He will give him a means
of salvation and will provide for him whence he does not reckon: God is 65:3
all-sufficient for whoever puts his trust in Him. God will surely bring about
what He decrees. God has set a measure for all things.

If you are in doubt concerning those of your wives who have ceased
menstruating, know that their waiting period shall be three months. The
same shall apply to those who have not yet menstruated.[1] As for pregnant
women, their term shall end with their confinement. God will ease the hardship of the man who fears Him.

Such is the commandment God has revealed to you. He that fears God 65:5
shall be forgiven his sins and richly recompensed.

1. On account of their young age. Child marriages were common.

65:6 LODGE THEM in your own
homes, according to your
means, and you shall not har-
ass them so as to make life
intolerable for them. If they
are with child, maintain them
until the end of their confinement; and if, after that, they
give suck to the infants they
bore you, give them their pay
and consult together in all rea-
sonableness. But if you cannot
tolerate each other, let other
women suckle for you.

Let the rich man spend
according to his wealth, and
the poor man according to
what God has given him. God
does not charge a soul with
more than He has given it;
God, after hardship, will bring
ease.

65:8 How many communities
have rebelled against the commandments of their Lord and His apostles!
Stern was Our reckoning with them, and harrowing was Our scourge. They
tasted the baleful consequence of their misdeeds: and the consequence of
their misdeeds was perdition. God has prepared for them a grievous scourge.
So fear God, you that are of good sense possessed.

God has now sent down to you an Admonition; an apostle proclaiming to
you God's revelations in all plainness, so that he may lead the faithful who
do good works from darkness to the light. He that believes in God and
does good works shall be admitted to Gardens watered by running brooks,
wherein shall he abide for ever. God has made for him a rich provision.

65:12 God it was who created seven heavens, and earths as many. The commandment descends through them, that you may learn that God has power
over all things, and that God encompasses all things with His knowledge.

أسكنوهن من حيث سكنتم من وجدكم ولا تضاروهن لتضيقوا
عليهن وإن كن أولات حمل فأنفقوا عليهن حتى يضعن حملهن
فإن أرضعن لكم فآتوهن أجورهن وأتمروا بينكم بمعروف
وإن تعاسرتم فسترضع له أخرى ﴿٦﴾ لينفق ذو سعة من
سعته ومن قدر عليه رزقه فلينفق مما آتاه الله لا يكلف الله
نفسا إلا ما آتاها سيجعل الله بعد عسر يسرا ﴿٧﴾ وكأين من قرية
عتت عن أمر ربها ورسله فحاسبناها حسابا شديدا وعذبناها عذابا
نكرا ﴿٨﴾ فذاقت وبال أمرها وكان عاقبة أمرها خسرا ﴿٩﴾ أعد الله
لهم عذابا شديدا فاتقوا الله يا أولي الألباب الذين آمنوا قد أنزل الله
إليكم ذكرا ﴿١٠﴾ رسولا يتلو عليكم آيات الله مبينات ليخرج
الذين آمنوا وعملوا الصالحات من الظلمات إلى النور ومن يؤمن بالله
ويعمل صالحا يدخله جنات تجري من تحتها الأنهار خالدين
فيها أبدا قد أحسن الله له رزقا ﴿١١﴾ الله الذي خلق سبع
سماوات ومن الأرض مثلهن يتنزل الأمر بينهن لتعلموا أن الله
على كل شيء قدير وأن الله قد أحاط بكل شيء علما ﴿١٢﴾

سورة التحريم مدنية اثنتا عشرة آية

بسم الله الرحمن الرحيم
يا أيها النبي لم تحرم ما أحل الله لك تبتغي مرضات أزواجك والله
غفور رحيم ۝١ قد فرض الله لكم تحلة أيمانكم والله مولاكم وهو
العليم الحكيم ۝٢ وإذ أسر النبي إلى بعض أزواجه حديثا فلما نبأت
به وأظهره الله عليه عرف بعضه وأعرض عن بعض فلما نبأها به
قالت من أنبأك هذا قال نبأني العليم الخبير ۝٣ إن تتوبا إلى الله
فقد صغت قلوبكما وإن تظاهرا عليه فإن الله هو مولاه وجبريل
وصالح المؤمنين والملائكة بعد ذلك ظهير ۝٤ عسى ربه إن طلقكن
أن يبدله أزواجا خيرا منكن مسلمات مؤمنات قانتات تائبات
عابدات سائحات ثيبات وأبكارا ۝٥ يا أيها الذين آمنوا قوا أنفسكم
وأهليكم نارا وقودها الناس والحجارة عليها ملائكة غلاظ شداد
لا يعصون الله ما أمرهم ويفعلون ما يؤمرون ۝٦ يا أيها الذين
كفروا لا تعتذروا اليوم إنما تجزون ما كنتم تعملون ۝٧

PROHIBITION

In the Name of God,
the Merciful, the Compassionate

PROPHET, WHY do you pro- 66:1
hibit that which God has made
lawful for you, in seeking to
please your wives?[1] And God is
forgiving and compassionate.

God has given you absolu-
tion from such oaths. God is
your Master. He is the Omniscient One, the Wise One.

When the Prophet confided
a secret to one of his wives;
and when she disclosed it and
God informed him of this, he
made known one part of it
and said nothing about the
other. And when he had
acquainted her with it she said:
'Who told you this?' He said: 'The All-knowing, the Wise One, told me.'

If you two[2] turn to God in repentance, for your hearts have sinned, you 66:4
shall be pardoned; but if you conspire against him, know that God is his
protector, and Gabriel, and the righteous among the faithful. The angels too
are his helpers.

It may well be that, if he divorce you, his Lord will give him in your place
better wives than yourselves, submissive to God and full of faith, obedient,
penitent, devout, and given to fasting; both formerly-wedded and virgins.

Believers, guard yourselves and your kin against a Fire fuelled with men
and stones, in the charge of stern and mighty angels who never disobey
God's command and promptly do whatever they are bidden. 'You that dis- 66:7
believe, make no excuses for yourselves this day. You shall be rewarded but
according to what you did.'

1. Muḥammad, according to the Muslim commentators, was once found by his wife Ḥafṣah with a Coptic slave from whom he had promised her to separate. Of this Ḥafṣah secretly informed 'Ā'ishah, another wife of his. To free Muḥammad from his promise to Ḥafṣah was the object of this *sūrah*. Some of the references are obscure.
2. Ḥafṣah and 'Ā'ishah.

66:8 Believers, turn to God
in true repentance. Your Lord
may pardon you your sins
and admit you into Gardens
watered by running brooks, on
a day when the Prophet and
those who believe with him
will suffer no disgrace at the
hands of God. Their light will
shine in front of them and on
their right, and they will say:
'Lord, perfect our light for
us and forgive us; You have
power over all things.'

Prophet, make war on the
unbelievers and the hypocrites,
and deal sternly with them.
Hell shall be their home, evil
their fate.

66:10 God gave an example to the
unbelievers in the wife of
Noah and the wife of Lot.
They were married to two of
Our righteous servants and betrayed them. Their husbands could in no way
protect them from God; they were told: 'Enter the Fire with those that shall
enter it.'

But to the faithful God gave an example in Pharaoh's wife, who said:
'Lord, build me a house with You in Paradise and deliver me from Pharaoh
and his misdeeds. Deliver me from the wrongdoing people.'

66:12 And in Mary, 'Imrān's daughter, who preserved her chastity and into
whose womb We breathed Our spirit; who put her trust in the words of her
Lord and His Scriptures, and was truly devout.

يا أيها الذين آمنوا توبوا إلى الله توبة نصوحا عسى ربكم
أن يكفر عنكم سيئاتكم ويدخلكم جنات تجري من
تحتها الأنهار يوم لا يخزي الله النبي والذين آمنوا معه
نورهم يسعى بين أيديهم وبأيمانهم يقولون ربنا
أتمم لنا نورنا واغفر لنا إنك على كل شيء قدير ٨ يا أيها
النبي جاهد الكفار والمنافقين واغلظ عليهم ومأواهم
جهنم وبئس المصير ٩ ضرب الله مثلا للذين كفروا
امرأت نوح وامرأت لوط كانتا تحت عبدين من
عبادنا صالحين فخانتاهما فلم يغنيا عنهما من الله
شيئا وقيل ادخلا النار مع الداخلين ١٠ وضرب الله
مثلا للذين آمنوا امرأت فرعون إذ قالت رب
ابن لي عندك بيتا في الجنة ونجني من فرعون وعمله
ونجني من القوم الظالمين ١١ ومريم ابنت عمران التي
أحصنت فرجها فنفخنا فيه من روحنا وصدقت
بكلمات ربها وكتبه وكانت من القانتين ١٢

سورة الملك مكية وهي ثلثون آية

بسم الله الرحمن الرحيم

تبارك الذي بيده الملك وهو على كل شيء قدير ۝١ الذي خلق الموت
والحيوة ليبلوكم أيكم أحسن عملا وهو العزيز الغفور ۝٢ الذي خلق سبع
سموات طباقا ما ترى في خلق الرحمن من تفاوت فارجع البصر هل ترى
من فطور ۝٣ ثم ارجع البصر كرتين ينقلب إليك البصر خاسئا وهو
حسير ۝٤ ولقد زينا السماء الدنيا بمصابيح وجعلناها رجوما للشياطين
وأعتدنا لهم عذاب السعير ۝٥ وللذين كفروا بربهم عذاب جهنم وبئس
المصير ۝٦ إذا ألقوا فيها سمعوا لها شهيقا وهي تفور ۝٧ تكاد تميز
من الغيظ كلما ألقي فيها فوج سألهم خزنتها ألم يأتكم نذير ۝٨ قالوا
بلى قد جاءنا نذير فكذبنا وقلنا ما نزل الله من شيء إن أنتم
إلا في ضلال كبير ۝٩ وقالوا لو كنا نسمع أو نعقل ما كنا في
أصحاب السعير ۝١٠ فاعترفوا بذنبهم فسحقا لأصحاب السعير
۝١١ إن الذين يخشون ربهم بالغيب لهم مغفرة وأجر كبير ۝١٢

SOVEREIGNTY

In the Name of God,
the Merciful, the Compassionate

BLESSED BE He who in His 67:1
hand holds sovereignty: He has power over all things; who created death and life that He might put you to the proof as to which of you acquitted themselves best: He is the Almighty, the Forgiving One; who created seven heavens, one above the other. You will not see a flaw in the Merciful's creation; turn up your eyes: can you detect a single crack?

Then look once more and yet again: your eyes will in the end grow dim and weary.

We have adorned the low- 67:5
est heaven with lamps, missiles to pelt the demons with. For these We have prepared the torment of the Conflagration, and for those who deny their Lord the scourge of Hell: a wretched fate!

When they are flung therein, they shall hear it roaring and seething, as though bursting with rage. Every time a multitude is thrown in, its keepers will ask them: 'Did no one come to warn you?' 'Yes,' they will say, 'he did come, but we disbelieved and said: "God has revealed nothing: you are but in grievous error."' And they will say: 'If only we had listened and understood, we should not now be among the inmates of the Conflagration.' Thus shall they confess their sin. Cursed be the inmates of the Conflagration!

But those that fear their Lord although unseen shall be forgiven and richly 67:12
recompensed.

67:13 WHETHER YOU speak in private or aloud, He surely knows your innermost thoughts. Shall He who has created all, not know them all? Gracious is He and all-knowing.

He it is who has made the earth subservient to you. Walk about its regions and eat of His provisions. To Him shall all return at the Resurrection.

Are you confident that He who is in heaven will not cause the earth to cave in beneath you, so that it will shake to pieces?

Are you confident that He who is in heaven will not let loose on you a sandy whirlwind? You will surely learn then what My warning was like.

Those who have gone before them likewise disbelieved: but how grievous was the way I rejected them!

Do they not see the birds above their heads, spreading their wings and folding them? None save the Merciful sustains them. He surely observes all things.

Who is it that will defend you like an army, if not the Merciful? Truly, the unbelievers are in error.

67:21 Who will provide for you if *He* withholds His sustenance? Yet they persist in arrogance and in rebellion.

Is he that goes grovelling on his face more rightly guided than he that walks upright upon a straight path?

Say: 'He it was who brought you into being, and gave you ears and eyes and hearts. Yet you are seldom thankful.'

Say: 'He it was who placed you on the earth, and to Him shall you be herded.'

And they say: 'When will this promise be fulfilled, if what you say be true?'

67:26 Say: 'God alone has knowledge of that. I am only to give a veritable warning.'

وأسروا قولكم أو اجهروا به إنه عليم بذات الصدور ﴿١٣﴾
ألا يعلم من خلق وهو اللطيف الخبير ﴿١٤﴾ هو الذي جعل لكم
الأرض ذلولا فامشوا في مناكبها وكلوا من رزقه وإليه
النشور ﴿١٥﴾ ءأمنتم من في السماء أن يخسف بكم الأرض فإذا
هي تمور ﴿١٦﴾ أم أمنتم من في السماء أن يرسل عليكم حاصبا
فستعلمون كيف نذير ﴿١٧﴾ ولقد كذب الذين من قبلهم
فكيف كان نكير ﴿١٨﴾ أولم يروا إلى الطير فوقهم صافات
ويقبضن ما يمسكهن إلا الرحمن إنه بكل شيء بصير ﴿١٩﴾ أمن هذا الذي
هو جند لكم ينصركم من دون الرحمن إن الكافرون إلا في غرور ﴿٢٠﴾
أمن هذا الذي يرزقكم إن أمسك رزقه بل لجوا في عتو ونفور
﴿٢١﴾ أفمن يمشي مكبا على وجهه أهدى أمن يمشي سويا على صراط
مستقيم ﴿٢٢﴾ قل هو الذي أنشأكم وجعل لكم السمع والأبصار
والأفئدة قليلا ما تشكرون ﴿٢٣﴾ قل هو الذي ذرأكم في الأرض
وإليه تحشرون ﴿٢٤﴾ ويقولون متى هذا الوعد إن كنتم صادقين
﴿٢٥﴾ قل إنما العلم عند الله وإنما أنا نذير مبين ﴿٢٦﴾

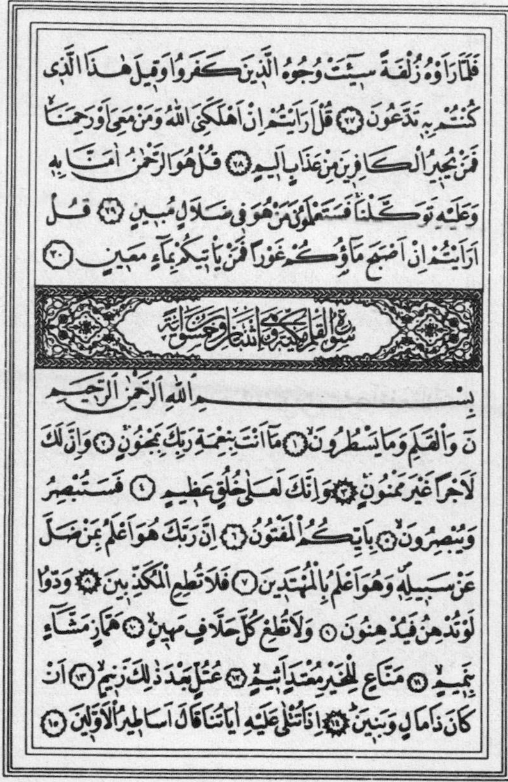

فلما رأوه زلفة سيئت وجوه الذين كفروا وقيل هذا الذي
كنتم به تدعون ﴿٢٧﴾ قل أرأيتم إن أهلكني الله ومن معي أو رحمنا
فمن يجير الكافرين من عذاب أليم ﴿٢٨﴾ قل هو الرحمن آمنا به
وعليه توكلنا فستعلمون من هو في ضلال مبين ﴿٢٩﴾ قل
أرأيتم إن أصبح ماؤكم غورا فمن يأتيكم بماء معين ﴿٣٠﴾

سورة القلم مكية وهي اثنتان وخمسون آية

بسم الله الرحمن الرحيم

ن والقلم وما يسطرون ﴿١﴾ ما أنت بنعمة ربك بمجنون ﴿٢﴾ وإن لك
لأجرا غير ممنون ﴿٣﴾ وإنك لعلى خلق عظيم ﴿٤﴾ فستبصر
ويبصرون ﴿٥﴾ بأييكم المفتون ﴿٦﴾ إن ربك هو أعلم بمن ضل
عن سبيله وهو أعلم بالمهتدين ﴿٧﴾ فلا تطع المكذبين ﴿٨﴾ ودوا
لو تدهن فيدهنون ﴿٩﴾ ولا تطع كل حلاف مهين ﴿١٠﴾ هماز مشاء
بنميم ﴿١١﴾ مناع للخير معتد أثيم ﴿١٢﴾ عتل بعد ذلك زنيم ﴿١٣﴾ أن
كان ذا مال وبنين ﴿١٤﴾ إذا تتلى عليه آياتنا قال أساطير الأولين ﴿١٥﴾

BUT WHEN they see it draw- 67:27
ing near, the unbelievers' faces
will be contorted with woe,
and a voice will say: 'This is
the doom which you have
challenged.'

Say: 'Consider: whether
God destroys me and all my
followers or has mercy upon
us, who will protect the
unbelievers from a woeful
scourge?'

Say: 'He is the Lord of
Mercy: in Him we believe, and
in Him we put our trust. You
shall soon learn who is in
evident error.'

Say: 'Consider: if all the 67:30
water that you have were to
sink down into the earth, who
would give you running water
in its place?'

THE PEN

In the Name of God, the Merciful, the Compassionate

Nūn. BY the Pen, and what they[1] write, you[2] are not a man possessed: thanks 68:1
to the favour of your Lord! A lasting recompense awaits you, for yours is a
sublime nature. You shall before long see – as they will see – which of you is
enchanted.

Your Lord knows best those who stray from His path, as He knows best
those who are rightly guided. Yield not to the disbelievers: they desire you to 68:9
overlook their doings that they may overlook yours. Nor yield to the wretch
of many oaths, the mischief-making slanderer, the opponent of good, the
sinful transgressor, the bully who is of doubtful birth to boot. Though such
a man be blessed with wealth and children, when Our revelations are recited 68:15
to him, he says: 'Fables of the ancients.'

1. The angels. 2. Muḥammad.

68:16 ON THE nose We will brand him!

We have afflicted them[1] as We afflicted the owners of the orchard who had declared that they would pluck its fruit next morning, without adding any reservation.[2] A visitant from your Lord came down upon it while they slept, and in the morning it was as black as midnight.

In the morning they called out to one another: 'Hurry to your orchard, if you would pick its fruit.' And off they went, whispering to one another: 'No beggar shall enter it today.'

Thus they went out, fixed in their resolve. But when they saw it they said: 'We have erred indeed; we are bereft.'

The most upright among them said: 'Did I not bid you give praise?'

سَنَسِمُهُۥ عَلَى ٱلْخُرْطُومِ ﴿١٦﴾ إِنَّا بَلَوْنَٰهُمْ كَمَا بَلَوْنَآ أَصْحَٰبَ ٱلْجَنَّةِ إِذْ أَقْسَمُوا۟
لَيَصْرِمُنَّهَا مُصْبِحِينَ ﴿١٧﴾ وَلَا يَسْتَثْنُونَ ﴿١٨﴾ فَطَافَ عَلَيْهَا طَآئِفٌ مِّن رَّبِّكَ
وَهُمْ نَآئِمُونَ ﴿١٩﴾ فَأَصْبَحَتْ كَٱلصَّرِيمِ ﴿٢٠﴾ فَتَنَادَوْا۟ مُصْبِحِينَ ﴿٢١﴾ أَنِ ٱغْدُوا۟
عَلَىٰ حَرْثِكُمْ إِن كُنتُمْ صَٰرِمِينَ ﴿٢٢﴾ فَٱنطَلَقُوا۟ وَهُمْ يَتَخَٰفَتُونَ ﴿٢٣﴾ أَن لَّا
يَدْخُلَنَّهَا ٱلْيَوْمَ عَلَيْكُم مِّسْكِينٌ ﴿٢٤﴾ وَغَدَوْا۟ عَلَىٰ حَرْدٍ قَٰدِرِينَ ﴿٢٥﴾ فَلَمَّا رَأَوْهَا
قَالُوٓا۟ إِنَّا لَضَآلُّونَ ﴿٢٦﴾ بَلْ نَحْنُ مَحْرُومُونَ ﴿٢٧﴾ قَالَ أَوْسَطُهُمْ أَلَمْ أَقُل لَّكُمْ
لَوْلَا تُسَبِّحُونَ ﴿٢٨﴾ قَالُوا۟ سُبْحَٰنَ رَبِّنَآ إِنَّا كُنَّا ظَٰلِمِينَ ﴿٢٩﴾ فَأَقْبَلَ بَعْضُهُمْ
عَلَىٰ بَعْضٍ يَتَلَٰوَمُونَ ﴿٣٠﴾ قَالُوا۟ يَٰوَيْلَنَآ إِنَّا كُنَّا طَٰغِينَ ﴿٣١﴾ عَسَىٰ رَبُّنَآ
أَن يُبْدِلَنَا خَيْرًا مِّنْهَآ إِنَّآ إِلَىٰ رَبِّنَا رَٰغِبُونَ ﴿٣٢﴾ كَذَٰلِكَ ٱلْعَذَابُ
وَلَعَذَابُ ٱلْءَاخِرَةِ أَكْبَرُ لَوْ كَانُوا۟ يَعْلَمُونَ ﴿٣٣﴾ إِنَّ لِلْمُتَّقِينَ عِندَ رَبِّهِمْ
جَنَّٰتِ ٱلنَّعِيمِ ﴿٣٤﴾ أَفَنَجْعَلُ ٱلْمُسْلِمِينَ كَٱلْمُجْرِمِينَ ﴿٣٥﴾ مَا لَكُمْ كَيْفَ تَحْكُمُونَ
﴿٣٦﴾ أَمْ لَكُمْ كِتَٰبٌ فِيهِ تَدْرُسُونَ ﴿٣٧﴾ إِنَّ لَكُمْ فِيهِ لَمَا تَخَيَّرُونَ ﴿٣٨﴾ أَمْ لَكُمْ
أَيْمَٰنٌ عَلَيْنَا بَٰلِغَةٌ إِلَىٰ يَوْمِ ٱلْقِيَٰمَةِ إِنَّ لَكُمْ لَمَا تَحْكُمُونَ ﴿٣٩﴾ سَلْهُمْ أَيُّهُم
بِذَٰلِكَ زَعِيمٌ ﴿٤٠﴾ أَمْ لَهُمْ شُرَكَآءُ فَلْيَأْتُوا۟ بِشُرَكَآئِهِمْ إِن كَانُوا۟ صَٰدِقِينَ
﴿٤١﴾ يَوْمَ يُكْشَفُ عَن سَاقٍ وَيُدْعَوْنَ إِلَى ٱلسُّجُودِ فَلَا يَسْتَطِيعُونَ ﴿٤٢﴾

'Glory be to our Lord,' they said. 'We have assuredly done wrong.' And they began to blame one another.

'Woe betide us!' they said. 'We have been great transgressors. Perchance our Lord will give us a better one in its place; to our Lord we will turn.'

68:33 Such was their torment. But the torment of the life to come is more terrible, if they but knew it.

In the Gardens of Delight the righteous shall be with their Lord. Are We to treat the Muslims and the sinners alike? What has come over you[3] that you should judge so ill?

Or have you a scripture to study promising you whatever you choose? Or have We sworn a covenant with you – a covenant binding till the Day of Resurrection – that you shall have what you yourselves ordain? Ask if any of them[3] will vouch for that!

Or have they other deities besides God? Let them produce their deities, if what they say be true!

68:42 On the day the dread event unfolds and they are told to prostrate themselves, they will not be able.

1. The Meccans. 2. Without saying: 'If God wills.' 3. The unbelievers.

خاشعة أبصارهم ترهقهم ذلة وقد كانوا يدعون إلى السجود وهم
سالمون ﴿٤٣﴾ فذرني ومن يكذب بهذا الحديث سنستدرجهم من حيث لا
يعلمون ﴿٤٤﴾ وأملي لهم إن كيدي متين ﴿٤٥﴾ أم تسألهم أجرا فهم من مغرم مثقلون
﴿٤٦﴾ أم عندهم الغيب فهم يكتبون ﴿٤٧﴾ فاصبر لحكم ربك ولا تكن
كصاحب الحوت إذ نادى وهو مكظوم ﴿٤٨﴾ لولا أن تداركه نعمة
من ربه لنبذ بالعراء وهو مذموم ﴿٤٩﴾ فاجتباه ربه فجعله من
الصالحين ﴿٥٠﴾ وإن يكاد الذين كفروا ليزلقونك بأبصارهم لما سمعوا
الذكر ويقولون إنه لمجنون ﴿٥١﴾ وما هو إلا ذكر للعالمين ﴿٥٢﴾

سورة الحاقة مكية وآياتها اثنتان وخمسون

بسم الله الرحمن الرحيم

الحاقة ﴿١﴾ ما الحاقة ﴿٢﴾ وما أدراك ما الحاقة ﴿٣﴾ كذبت ثمود وعاد
بالقارعة ﴿٤﴾ فأما ثمود فأهلكوا بالطاغية ﴿٥﴾ وأما عاد فأهلكوا بريح
صرصر عاتية ﴿٦﴾ سخرها عليهم سبع ليال وثمانية أيام حسوما فترى القوم
فيها صرعى كأنهم أعجاز نخل خاوية ﴿٧﴾ فهل ترى لهم من باقية ﴿٨﴾

UTTERLY HUMBLED, they shall 68:43
stand with eyes downcast; for
they had long since been bidden
to prostrate themselves when
they were safe and sound.

Therefore leave to Me those that
deny this revelation. We will lead
them on step by step, in ways
beyond their knowledge. I shall
bear long with them: My stratagem
is sure.

Are you demanding pay of
them, so that they are burdened
with debt?

Or have they knowledge of
what is hidden? Can they write it
down?

Wait, then, the judgement of 68:48
your Lord and do not act like him[1]
who was swallowed by the whale
when he called out in despair.
Had his Lord not bestowed on him His grace, he would have been abandoned in the open to be blamed by all. But his Lord chose him for His own
and made of him a righteous man.

The unbelievers well-nigh devour you with their eyes when they hear the
Admonition. 'He is assuredly possessed,' they say.

Yet it is but an Admonition to mankind. 68:52

THE CATASTROPHE

In the Name of God, the Merciful, the Compassionate

THE CATASTROPHE: and what is the Catastrophe? Would that you knew 69:1
what the Catastrophe is!

Thamūd and 'Ād denied the Last Judgement. By a deafening shout was
Thamūd destroyed, and 'Ād by a howling, violent gale which He let loose on
them for seven nights and eight successive days: you might have seen the
people lying dead as though they had been hollow trunks of palm-trees. Can 69:8
you see even one of them still around?

1. Jonah.

69:9 PHARAOH, AND those before him, and the inhabitants of the Ruined Cities, also committed sin and disobeyed their Lord's apostle. With a terrible scourge He smote them.

When the Flood rose high We carried you[1] in the floating ark, making it a memorable event, that all attentive ears might heed it.

When the Trumpet sounds a single blast; when earth and mountains are raised high and with one mighty crash are flattened into dust – on that day the Dread Event will come to pass.

The sky will be rent asunder on that day, frail and tottering; and the angels will stand on every side with eight of them carrying the Throne of your Lord above their heads. On that day you shall be utterly exposed, and nothing that you hid shall be hidden.

69:19 He who is given his Book in his right hand will say: 'Here it is, read my Book!
I knew I should come face to face with my account!' His shall be a blissful
state in a lofty Garden, with clusters of fruit within his reach. 'Eat and drink
to your heart's content: your recompense for what you did in days gone by.'

But he who is given his Book in his left hand will say: 'Would that I were not given my Book! Would that I knew nothing of my account! Would that my death had ended all! Nothing has my wealth availed me, and bereft am I of all my power.'

'Lay hold of him and bind him. Then burn him in the fire of Hell, and
then fasten him with a chain seventy cubits long. For he did not believe in
69:34 God, the Most Great, nor did he care to feed the destitute.

وجاء فرعون ومن قبله والمؤتفكات بالخاطئة ۝٩ فعصوا
رسول ربهم فأخذهم أخذة رابية ۝١٠ إنا لما طغا الماء حملناكم
في الجارية ۝١١ لنجعلها لكم تذكرة وتعيها أذن واعية ۝١٢
فإذا نفخ في الصور نفخة واحدة ۝١٣ وحملت الأرض والجبال
فدكتا دكة واحدة ۝١٤ فيومئذ وقعت الواقعة ۝١٥ وانشقت
السماء فهي يومئذ واهية ۝١٦ والملك على أرجائها ويحمل
عرش ربك فوقهم يومئذ ثمانية ۝١٧ يومئذ تعرضون لا تخفى منكم
خافية ۝١٨ فأما من أوتي كتابه بيمينه فيقول هاؤم اقرءوا كتابيه
۝١٩ إني ظننت أني ملاق حسابيه ۝٢٠ فهو في عيشة راضية ۝٢١ في جنة
عالية ۝٢٢ قطوفها دانية ۝٢٣ كلوا واشربوا هنيئا بما أسلفتم في الأيام
الخالية ۝٢٤ وأما من أوتي كتابه بشماله فيقول يا ليتني لم أوت كتابيه
۝٢٥ ولم أدر ما حسابيه ۝٢٦ يا ليتها كانت القاضية ۝٢٧ ما أغنى عني
ماليه ۝٢٨ هلك عني سلطانيه ۝٢٩ خذوه فغلوه ۝٣٠ ثم الجحيم صلوه
۝٣١ ثم في سلسلة ذرعها سبعون ذراعا فاسلكوه ۝٣٢ إنه كان
لا يؤمن بالله العظيم ۝٣٣ ولا يحض على طعام المسكين ۝٣٤

1. I.e. your forefathers.

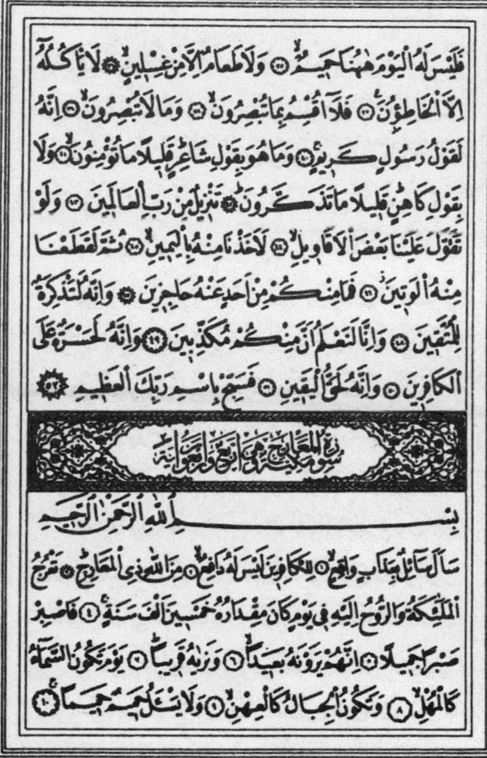

فَلَيْسَ لَهُ الْيَوْمَ هَاهُنَا حَمِيمٌ ۝ وَلَا طَعَامٌ إِلَّا مِنْ غِسْلِينٍ ۝ لَا يَأْكُلُهُ
إِلَّا الْخَاطِئُونَ ۝ فَلَا أُقْسِمُ بِمَا تُبْصِرُونَ ۝ وَمَا لَا تُبْصِرُونَ ۝ إِنَّهُ
لَقَوْلُ رَسُولٍ كَرِيمٍ ۝ وَمَا هُوَ بِقَوْلِ شَاعِرٍ قَلِيلًا مَا تُؤْمِنُونَ ۝ وَلَا
بِقَوْلِ كَاهِنٍ قَلِيلًا مَا تَذَكَّرُونَ ۝ تَنْزِيلٌ مِنْ رَبِّ الْعَالَمِينَ ۝ وَلَوْ
تَقَوَّلَ عَلَيْنَا بَعْضَ الْأَقَاوِيلِ ۝ لَأَخَذْنَا مِنْهُ بِالْيَمِينِ ۝ ثُمَّ لَقَطَعْنَا
مِنْهُ الْوَتِينَ ۝ فَمَا مِنْكُمْ مِنْ أَحَدٍ عَنْهُ حَاجِزِينَ ۝ وَإِنَّهُ لَتَذْكِرَةٌ
لِلْمُتَّقِينَ ۝ وَإِنَّا لَنَعْلَمُ أَنَّ مِنْكُمْ مُكَذِّبِينَ ۝ وَإِنَّهُ لَحَسْرَةٌ عَلَى
الْكَافِرِينَ ۝ وَإِنَّهُ لَحَقُّ الْيَقِينِ ۝ فَسَبِّحْ بِاسْمِ رَبِّكَ الْعَظِيمِ ۝

سُورَةُ الْمَعَارِجِ مَكِّيَّةٌ وَهِيَ أَرْبَعٌ وَأَرْبَعُونَ آيَةً

بِسْمِ اللَّهِ الرَّحْمَٰنِ الرَّحِيمِ

سَأَلَ سَائِلٌ بِعَذَابٍ وَاقِعٍ ۝ لِلْكَافِرِينَ لَيْسَ لَهُ دَافِعٌ ۝ مِنَ اللَّهِ ذِي الْمَعَارِجِ ۝ تَعْرُجُ
الْمَلَائِكَةُ وَالرُّوحُ إِلَيْهِ فِي يَوْمٍ كَانَ مِقْدَارُهُ خَمْسِينَ أَلْفَ سَنَةٍ ۝ فَاصْبِرْ
صَبْرًا جَمِيلًا ۝ إِنَّهُمْ يَرَوْنَهُ بَعِيدًا ۝ وَنَرَاهُ قَرِيبًا ۝ يَوْمَ تَكُونُ السَّمَاءُ
كَالْمُهْلِ ۝ وَتَكُونُ الْجِبَالُ كَالْعِهْنِ ۝ وَلَا يَسْأَلُ حَمِيمٌ حَمِيمًا ۝

TODAY HE shall be friendless 69:35
here; only filth shall be his food,
the filth which only sinners eat.'
I swear by all that you can see,
and all that is hidden from your
view, that this is the utterance of
a noble messenger. It is no poet's
speech: scant is your faith! It is
no soothsayer's divination: how
little you reflect! It is a revelation 69:43
from the Lord of the Universe.

Had he invented lies concerning Us, We would have seized him by the right hand and severed his heart's vein: not one of you could have protected him!

It[1] is but an Admonition to the righteous. We well know that there are some among you who will deny it.

It is the despair of the unbelievers. It is the indubitable
Truth. Praise, then, the name of your Lord, the Almighty. 69:52

THE STAIRWAYS

In the Name of God, the Merciful, the Compassionate

A SCEPTIC[2] once demanded that punishment be visited forthwith upon the 70:1
unbelievers.

No power can hinder God from punishing them. He is the Lord of the Stairways, whereby the angels and the Spirit shall ascend to Him in one day whose space is fifty thousand years.

Therefore conduct yourself with becoming patience. They think the Day of Judgement is far off: but We see it near at hand.

On that day the sky shall become like molten brass, and the mountains like
tufts of wool scattered in the wind. No bosom friend shall ask a bosom friend 70:10

1. The Koran. 2. Literally, a questioner.

70:11 when eye meets eye. To
redeem himself from the torment of that day the sinner
will gladly sacrifice his children, his consort, his brother,
his kin who gave him shelter,
and all that are on the earth,
if then this might deliver him.

But no! The fire of Hell
shall drag him down by the
scalp, shall claim him who
had turned his back and
amassed riches and covet-
ously hoarded them.

Indeed, man was created
impatient. When evil befalls
him he is despondent; but,
blessed with good fortune, he
grows niggardly.

70:22 Not so the worshippers
who are steadfast in prayer;
who set aside a due portion
of their wealth for the beggar
and for the dispossessed; who truly believe in the Day of Reckoning, and
dread the punishment of their Lord (for none is secure from the punishment of their Lord); who restrain their carnal desire (save with their wives
and slave-girls, for with these they are blameless: transgressors are those who
lust after other than these); who keep their trusts and promises and bear true
witness; and who attend to their prayers with promptitude. These shall be
laden with honours in fair Gardens.

But what has befallen the unbelievers, that they scramble towards you in
multitudes from right and left?

Are they each seeking to enter a Garden of Delight?

70:39 No! Of what We created them they know full well.

يُبَصَّرُونَهُمْ يَوَدُّ الْمُجْرِمُ لَوْ يَفْتَدِي مِنْ عَذَابِ يَوْمِئِذٍ بِبَنِيهِ ﴿١١﴾
وَصَاحِبَتِهِ وَأَخِيهِ ﴿١٢﴾ وَفَصِيلَتِهِ الَّتِي تُؤْوِيهِ ﴿١٣﴾ وَمَنْ فِي الْأَرْضِ
جَمِيعًا ثُمَّ يُنْجِيهِ ﴿١٤﴾ كَلَّا إِنَّهَا لَظَىٰ ﴿١٥﴾ نَزَّاعَةً لِلشَّوَىٰ ﴿١٦﴾ تَدْعُو مَنْ
أَدْبَرَ وَتَوَلَّىٰ ﴿١٧﴾ وَجَمَعَ فَأَوْعَىٰ ﴿١٨﴾ إِنَّ الْإِنْسَانَ خُلِقَ هَلُوعًا ﴿١٩﴾ إِذَا
مَسَّهُ الشَّرُّ جَزُوعًا ﴿٢٠﴾ وَإِذَا مَسَّهُ الْخَيْرُ مَنُوعًا ﴿٢١﴾ إِلَّا الْمُصَلِّينَ ﴿٢٢﴾ الَّذِينَ
هُمْ عَلَىٰ صَلَاتِهِمْ دَائِمُونَ ﴿٢٣﴾ وَالَّذِينَ فِي أَمْوَالِهِمْ حَقٌّ مَعْلُومٌ ﴿٢٤﴾
لِلسَّائِلِ وَالْمَحْرُومِ ﴿٢٥﴾ وَالَّذِينَ يُصَدِّقُونَ بِيَوْمِ الدِّينِ ﴿٢٦﴾ وَالَّذِينَ
هُمْ مِنْ عَذَابِ رَبِّهِمْ مُشْفِقُونَ ﴿٢٧﴾ إِنَّ عَذَابَ رَبِّهِمْ غَيْرُ مَأْمُونٍ ﴿٢٨﴾
وَالَّذِينَ هُمْ لِفُرُوجِهِمْ حَافِظُونَ ﴿٢٩﴾ إِلَّا عَلَىٰ أَزْوَاجِهِمْ أَوْ مَا مَلَكَتْ
أَيْمَانُهُمْ فَإِنَّهُمْ غَيْرُ مَلُومِينَ ﴿٣٠﴾ فَمَنِ ابْتَغَىٰ وَرَاءَ ذَٰلِكَ فَأُولَٰئِكَ
هُمُ الْعَادُونَ ﴿٣١﴾ وَالَّذِينَ هُمْ لِأَمَانَاتِهِمْ وَعَهْدِهِمْ رَاعُونَ ﴿٣٢﴾ وَالَّذِينَ
هُمْ بِشَهَادَاتِهِمْ قَائِمُونَ ﴿٣٣﴾ وَالَّذِينَ هُمْ عَلَىٰ صَلَاتِهِمْ يُحَافِظُونَ ﴿٣٤﴾
أُولَٰئِكَ فِي جَنَّاتٍ مُكْرَمُونَ ﴿٣٥﴾ فَمَالِ الَّذِينَ كَفَرُوا قِبَلَكَ مُهْطِعِينَ
﴿٣٦﴾ عَنِ الْيَمِينِ وَعَنِ الشِّمَالِ عِزِينَ ﴿٣٧﴾ أَيَطْمَعُ كُلُّ امْرِئٍ مِنْهُمْ
أَنْ يُدْخَلَ جَنَّةَ نَعِيمٍ ﴿٣٨﴾ كَلَّا إِنَّا خَلَقْنَاهُمْ مِمَّا يَعْلَمُونَ ﴿٣٩﴾

فلا أقسم برب المشارق والمغارب إنا لقادرون ﴿٤٠﴾ على أن نبدل خيرا
منهم وما نحن بمسبوقين ﴿٤١﴾ فذرهم يخوضوا ويلعبوا حتى يلاقوا يومهم
الذي يوعدون ﴿٤٢﴾ يوم يخرجون من الأجداث سراعا كأنهم إلى نصب يوفضون
﴿٤٣﴾ خاشعة أبصارهم ترهقهم ذلة ذلك اليوم الذي كانوا يوعدون ﴿٤٤﴾

سورة نوح مكية وهي ثمان وعشرون آية

بسم الله الرحمن الرحيم
إنا أرسلنا نوحا إلى قومه أن أنذر قومك من قبل أن يأتيهم عذاب أليم ﴿١﴾
قال يا قوم إني لكم نذير مبين ﴿٢﴾ أن اعبدوا الله واتقوه وأطيعون
﴿٣﴾ يغفر لكم من ذنوبكم ويؤخركم إلى أجل مسمى إن أجل الله
إذا جاء لا يؤخر لو كنتم تعلمون ﴿٤﴾ قال رب إني دعوت قومي ليلا
ونهارا ﴿٥﴾ فلم يزدهم دعائي إلا فرارا ﴿٦﴾ وإني كلما دعوتهم
لتغفر لهم جعلوا أصابعهم في آذانهم واستغشوا ثيابهم وأصروا
واستكبروا استكبارا ﴿٧﴾ ثم إني دعوتهم جهارا ﴿٨﴾ ثم إني أعلنت لهم
وأسررت لهم إسرارا ﴿٩﴾ فقلت استغفروا ربكم إنه كان غفارا ﴿١٠﴾

I SWEAR by the Lord of the 70:40
easts and of the wests that We
have power to replace them by
others better than they: nothing can hinder Us from so
doing. So let them paddle, let
them play, until they face the
day they are promised; the day
when they shall rush headlong
from their graves, like men
rallying to a standard, with 70:44
downcast eyes and counte-
nances distorted and abject.

Such is the day they are promised.

NOAH

In the Name of God,
the Merciful, the Compassionate

WE SENT forth Noah to his people, saying: 'Give warning to your people 71:1
before a woeful scourge overtakes them.'

He said: 'My people, I come to warn you clearly. Worship God and fear Him, and obey me. He will forgive you some of your sins and give you respite to an appointed time. When God's time is come, none shall put it back. Would you but knew!'

'Lord,' said Noah, 'night and day have I pleaded with my people, but my pleas have only aggravated their aversion. Each time I call on them to seek Your pardon, they thrust their fingers into their ears and draw their cloaks over their heads, persisting in sin and bearing themselves with insolent pride. Then I called out loud to them, and appealed to them in public and in private.
"Seek forgiveness of your Lord," I said. "He is ever ready to forgive. 71:10

يرسل السماء عليكم مدرارا ۝ ويمددكم بأموال وبنين
ويجعل لكم جنات ويجعل لكم أنهارا ۝ ما لكم لا ترجون
لله وقارا ۝ وقد خلقكم أطوارا ۝ ألم تروا كيف خلق
الله سبع سماوات طباقا ۝ وجعل القمر فيهن نورا وجعل الشمس سراجا ۝
والله أنبتكم من الأرض نباتا ۝ ثم يعيدكم فيها ويخرجكم إخراجا ۝
والله جعل لكم الأرض بساطا ۝ لتسلكوا منها سبلا فجاجا
۝ قال نوح رب إنهم عصوني واتبعوا من لم يزده ماله وولده
إلا خسارا ۝ ومكروا مكرا كبارا ۝ وقالوا لا تذرن
آلهتكم ولا تذرن ودا ولا سواعا ولا يغوث ويعوق ونسرا
۝ وقد أضلوا كثيرا ولا تزد الظالمين إلا ضلالا ۝ مما
خطيئاتهم أغرقوا فأدخلوا نارا فلم يجدوا لهم من دون
الله أنصارا ۝ وقال نوح رب لا تذر على الأرض من الكافرين
ديارا ۝ إنك إن تذرهم يضلوا عبادك ولا يلدوا إلا فاجرا
كفارا ۝ رب اغفر لي ولوالدي ولمن دخل بيتي مؤمنا
وللمؤمنين والمؤمنات ولا تزد الظالمين إلا تبارا ۝

71:11 HE SENDS down abundant
water from the sky for you
and bestows upon you wealth
and children. He has provided
you with gardens and with
running brooks. Why do you
deny the greatness of God
when He created you in gradual stages? Can you not see
how God created the seven
heavens one above the other,
placing in them the moon for
a light and the sun for a lan-
tern? God has brought you
forth from the earth like a
plant, and to the earth He will
restore you. Then He will
bring you back from it afresh.
And God has made the earth
a vast expanse for you, that
you may roam its spacious
paths."'
71:21 Noah said: 'Lord, they dis-
obey me, and follow those whose wealth and offspring will only hasten their
perdition. They have devised an outrageous plot, and said to each other:
"Do not renounce your gods. Do not forsake Wadd or Suwā' or Yaghūth or
Ya'ūq or Nasr."[1] They have led many astray; and You surely drive the wrongdoers to further error.'
Because of their sins they were drowned and cast into the Fire. They
found none besides God to help them.
And Noah said: 'Lord, do not leave a single unbeliever on the earth. If
You spare them, they will mislead Your servants and beget none but sinners
71:28 and unbelievers. Forgive me, Lord, and forgive my parents and whoever
enters my house a true believer. Forgive all the faithful, men and women, and
hasten the wrongdoers' destruction.'

1. Names of idols.

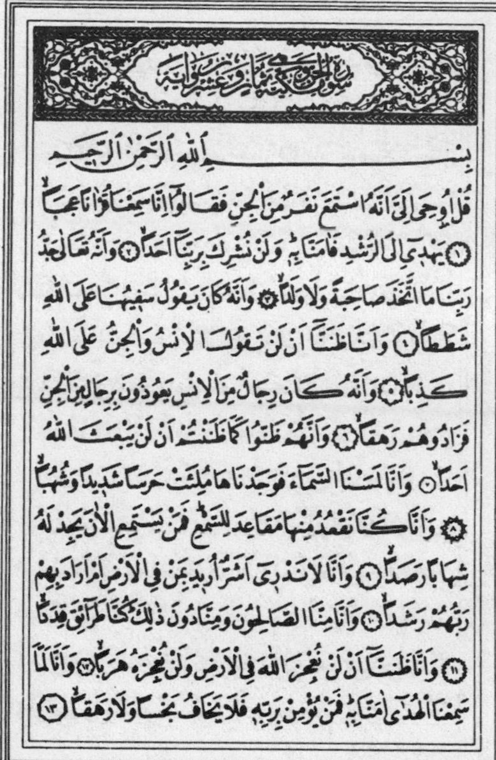
سورة الجن مكية وهي ثمان وعشرون آية
بسم الله الرحمن الرحيم
قل أوحي إلي أنه استمع نفر من الجن فقالوا إنا سمعنا قرآنا عجبا
(١) يهدي إلى الرشد فآمنا به ولن نشرك بربنا أحدا (٢) وأنه تعالى جد
ربنا ما اتخذ صاحبة ولا ولدا (٣) وأنه كان يقول سفيهنا على الله
شططا (٤) وأنا ظننا أن لن تقول الإنس والجن على الله
كذبا (٥) وأنه كان رجال من الإنس يعوذون برجال من الجن
فزادوهم رهقا (٦) وأنهم ظنوا كما ظننتم أن لن يبعث الله
أحدا (٧) وأنا لمسنا السماء فوجدناها ملئت حرسا شديدا وشهبا
(٨) وأنا كنا نقعد منها مقاعد للسمع فمن يستمع الآن يجد له
شهابا رصدا (٩) وأنا لا ندري أشر أريد بمن في الأرض أم أراد بهم
ربهم رشدا (١٠) وأنا منا الصالحون ومنا دون ذلك كنا طرائق قددا
(١١) وأنا ظننا أن لن نعجز الله في الأرض ولن نعجزه هربا (١٢) وأنا لما
سمعنا الهدى آمنا به فمن يؤمن بربه فلا يخاف بخسا ولا رهقا (١٣)

THE JINN

In the Name of God,
the Merciful, the Compassionate

SAY: 'IT is revealed to me that 72:1
a band of jinn listened and
said: "We have heard a wondrous Koran giving true
guidance. We believed in it
and shall henceforth serve
none besides our Lord. He
(exalted be the glory of our
Lord!) has taken up neither
consort, nor son. The Blaspheming One among us has
uttered a wanton falsehood
against God, although we had
supposed no man or jinnee
could tell of God what is
untrue."'
Some men have sought the
help of jinn, but they misled them into further error. Like you, they thought 72:7
that God could never resurrect the dead.
'"We made our way to high heaven, and found it filled with mighty war-
dens and fiery comets. We sat eavesdropping, but eavesdroppers find comets
in wait for them. We know not whether this bodes evil to those on earth or
if their Lord intends to guide them.
'"Some among us are righteous, while others are not; we follow different
ways. We know we cannot escape on earth from God, nor can we elude His
grasp by flight. When we heard His guidance we believed in Him: he that 72:13
believes in his Lord shall fear neither dishonesty nor injustice.

72:14 '"SOME AMONG us are
Muslims and some of us
are wrongdoers. Those that
embrace Islām pursue the
right path; but those that do
wrong shall become the fuel
of Hell."'
If they[1] pursue the straight
path We shall vouchsafe them
abundant rain, and thereby
put them to the proof. He that
pays no heed to his Lord's
Admonition shall be thrust
into grievous torment.
Mosques are for God's
worship; invoke in them no
other deity besides Him.
When God's servant[2] rose to
pray to Him, they pressed
around him in multitudes.
Say: 'I will pray to my Lord
and worship none besides
Him.'

وأنا منا المسلمون ومنا القاسطون فمن أسلم فأولئك تحروا
رشدا ۝ وأما القاسطون فكانوا لجهنم حطبا ۝ وأن لو
استقاموا على الطريقة لأسقيناهم ماء غدقا ۝ لنفتنهم
فيه ومن يعرض عن ذكر ربه يسلكه عذابا صعدا ۝ وأن المساجد
لله فلا تدعوا مع الله أحدا ۝ وأنه لما قام عبد
الله يدعوه كادوا يكونون عليه لبدا ۝ قل إنما أدعوا
ربي ولا أشرك به أحدا ۝ قل إني لا أملك لكم ضرا ولا رشدا
۝ قل إني لن يجيرني من الله أحد ولن أجد من دونه
ملتحدا ۝ إلا بلاغا من الله ورسالاته ومن يعص
الله ورسوله فإن له نار جهنم خالدين فيها أبدا ۝ حتى إذا رأوا
ما يوعدون فسيعلمون من أضعف ناصرا وأقل عددا ۝ قل إن أدري
أقريب ما توعدون أم يجعل له ربي أمدا ۝ عالم الغيب فلا يظهر
على غيبه أحدا ۝ إلا من ارتضى من رسول فإنه يسلك من بين
يديه ومن خلفه رصدا ۝ ليعلم أن قد أبلغوا رسالات
ربهم وأحاط بما لديهم وأحصى كل شيء عددا ۝

Say: 'I have no control over any evil or good that befalls you.'
72:22 Say: 'None can protect me from God, nor can I find any refuge besides
Him. My mission is only to communicate God's messages; those that disobey God and His apostle shall for ever abide in the fire of Hell.'
When they behold the scourge they are promised, they shall realize who
had the less powerful protector, and who were the fewer in number.
Say: 'I cannot tell whether the scourge you are promised is imminent, or
whether my Lord has set for it a far-off day. Cognizant of the Unseen, His
secrets He reveals to none, except to the apostles He has chosen. He sends
72:28 down guardians who walk before them and behind them, that He may ascer-
tain if they have indeed delivered their Lord's messages. He has knowledge
of all they have, and keeps strict count of all things.'

1. The Meccans. 2. Muḥammad.

سورة المزمل مكية وهي عشرون آية

بسم الله الرحمن الرحيم
يا أيها المزمل ﴿١﴾ قم الليل إلا قليلا ﴿٢﴾ نصفه أو انقص منه قليلا ﴿٣﴾
أو زد عليه ورتل القرآن ترتيلا ﴿٤﴾ إنا سنلقي عليك قولا ثقيلا ﴿٥﴾ إن
ناشئة الليل هي أشد وطئا وأقوم قيلا ﴿٦﴾ إن لك في النهار سبحا طويلا
﴿٧﴾ واذكر اسم ربك وتبتل إليه تبتيلا ﴿٨﴾ رب المشرق والمغرب
لا إله إلا هو فاتخذه وكيلا ﴿٩﴾ واصبر على ما يقولون واهجرهم
هجرا جميلا ﴿١٠﴾ وذرني والمكذبين أولي النعمة ومهلهم قليلا
﴿١١﴾ إن لدينا أنكالا وجحيما ﴿١٢﴾ وطعاما ذا غصة وعذابا أليما
﴿١٣﴾ يوم ترجف الأرض والجبال وكانت الجبال كثيبا مهيلا ﴿١٤﴾
إنا أرسلنا إليكم رسولا شاهدا عليكم كما أرسلنا إلى فرعون رسولا
﴿١٥﴾ فعصى فرعون الرسول فأخذناه أخذا وبيلا ﴿١٦﴾ فكيف تتقون
إن كفرتم يوما يجعل الولدان شيبا ﴿١٧﴾ السماء منفطر به كان وعده
مفعولا ﴿١٨﴾ إن هذه تذكرة فمن شاء اتخذ إلى ربه سبيلا ﴿١٩﴾

THE MANTLED ONE

In the Name of God,
the Merciful, the Compassionate

YOU[1] THAT are wrapped up in 73:1
your mantle, keep vigil all
night, save for a few hours;
half the night, or even less: or
a little more – and with measured tone recite the Koran, for
We are about to address to you
words of surpassing gravity. It
is in the watches of the night
that impressions are strongest
and words most eloquent; in
the daytime you are hard-pressed for long.

And remember the name of
your Lord and dedicate yourself to Him utterly. He is the Lord of the East and of the West: there is no
god but Him. Take Him for your Protector.

Bear patiently with what they[2] say, and take leave of them courteously.
Leave to Me those that deny the Truth, those that enjoy the comforts of this
life; bear with them yet a little while. We have in store for them heavy fetters 73:12
and a blazing fire, choking food and harrowing torment: on the day when the
earth shall quiver with all the mountains, and the mountains crumble into
heaps of shifting sand.

We have sent forth to you an apostle to testify against you, just as We sent forth an apostle to Pharaoh. Pharaoh disobeyed the messenger, so that with a baleful scourge We smote him.

If you persist in unbelief, how will you escape the day that will make children grey-haired, the day the sky will split asunder? God's promise shall surely be fulfilled.

This is but an Admonition. Let him who will, take the right path to his 73:19
Lord.

1. Muḥammad. 2. The unbelievers.

73:20 YOUR LORD knows that you[1] sometimes keep vigil well-nigh two-thirds of the night, and sometimes half or one-third of it, as do others among your followers. God measures the night and the day. He knows you[2] cannot count its length, and turned to you mercifully. Recite from the Koran as many verses as you are able; He knows that among you there are sick men and others roaming the land in search of God's bounty; and yet others fighting for the cause of God. Recite from it, then, as many verses as you are able. Attend to your prayers, render the alms levy, and give God a generous loan. Whatever good you do for your own souls you shall surely find it with God, ennobled and more richly rewarded. And implore God to forgive you; surely God is forgiving and compassionate.

إن ربك يعلم أنك تقوم أدنى من ثلثي الليل ونصفه وثلثه وطائفة من
الذين معك والله يقدر الليل والنهار علم أن لن تحصوه فتاب عليكم
فاقرءوا ما تيسر من القرآن علم أن سيكون منكم مرضى وآخرون يضربون
في الأرض يبتغون من فضل الله وآخرون يقاتلون في سبيل الله
فاقرءوا ما تيسر منه وأقيموا الصلوة وآتوا الزكوة وأقرضوا الله
قرضا حسنا وما تقدموا لأنفسكم من خير تجدوه عند الله
هو خيرا وأعظم أجرا واستغفروا الله إن الله غفور رحيم ٢٠

سورة المدثر مكية

بسم الله الرحمن الرحيم
يا أيها المدثر ١ قم فأنذر ٢ وربك فكبر ٣ وثيابك فطهر ٤ والرجز
فاهجر ٥ ولا تمنن تستكثر ٦ ولربك فاصبر ٧ فإذا نقر في الناقور ٨
فذلك يومئذ يوم عسير ٩ على الكافرين غير يسير ١٠ ذرني ومن خلقت
وحيدا ١١ وجعلت له مالا ممدودا ١٢ وبنين شهودا ١٣ ومهدت له تمهيدا
١٤ ثم يطمع أن أزيد ١٥ كلا إنه كان لآياتنا عنيدا ١٦ سأرهقه صعودا ١٧

THE CLOAKED ONE

In the Name of God, the Merciful, the Compassionate

74:1 YOU THAT are wrapped up in your cloak, arise and give warning.
Magnify your Lord, purify your garments, and keep away from uncleanness.
Bestow no favours expecting gain. Be patient for your Lord's sake.
The day the Trumpet sounds shall be a hard and joyless day for the unbelievers. Leave to Me the man whom I created helpless and endowed with
vast riches and thriving children. I have made his progress smooth and easy:
yet he greedily hopes that I should give him more. By no means! Because he
74:17 has stubbornly denied Our revelations, I will lay on him a mounting torment.

1. Muḥammad. 2. The believers.

إِنَّهُ فَكَّرَ وَقَدَّرَ ۝ فَقُتِلَ كَيْفَ قَدَّرَ ۝ ثُمَّ قُتِلَ كَيْفَ قَدَّرَ ۝ ثُمَّ نَظَرَ
۝ ثُمَّ عَبَسَ وَبَسَرَ ۝ ثُمَّ أَدْبَرَ وَاسْتَكْبَرَ ۝ فَقَالَ إِنْ هَٰذَا إِلَّا سِحْرٌ يُؤْثَرُ
۝ إِنْ هَٰذَا إِلَّا قَوْلُ الْبَشَرِ ۝ سَأُصْلِيهِ سَقَرَ ۝ وَمَا أَدْرَاكَ مَا سَقَرُ
۝ لَا تُبْقِي وَلَا تَذَرُ ۝ لَوَّاحَةٌ لِّلْبَشَرِ ۝ عَلَيْهَا تِسْعَةَ عَشَرَ ۝
وَمَا جَعَلْنَا أَصْحَابَ النَّارِ إِلَّا مَلَائِكَةً وَمَا جَعَلْنَا عِدَّتَهُمْ إِلَّا فِتْنَةً لِّلَّذِينَ
كَفَرُوا لِيَسْتَيْقِنَ الَّذِينَ أُوتُوا الْكِتَابَ وَيَزْدَادَ الَّذِينَ آمَنُوا إِيمَانًا وَلَا
يَرْتَابَ الَّذِينَ أُوتُوا الْكِتَابَ وَالْمُؤْمِنُونَ وَلِيَقُولَ الَّذِينَ فِي قُلُوبِهِم مَّرَضٌ
وَالْكَافِرُونَ مَاذَا أَرَادَ اللَّهُ بِهَٰذَا مَثَلًا كَذَٰلِكَ يُضِلُّ اللَّهُ مَن يَشَاءُ
وَيَهْدِي مَن يَشَاءُ وَمَا يَعْلَمُ جُنُودَ رَبِّكَ إِلَّا هُوَ وَمَا هِيَ إِلَّا ذِكْرَىٰ
لِلْبَشَرِ ۝ كَلَّا وَالْقَمَرِ ۝ وَاللَّيْلِ إِذْ أَدْبَرَ ۝ وَالصُّبْحِ إِذَا أَسْفَرَ ۝
إِنَّهَا لَإِحْدَى الْكُبَرِ ۝ نَذِيرًا لِّلْبَشَرِ ۝ لِمَن شَاءَ مِنكُمْ أَن يَتَقَدَّمَ
أَوْ يَتَأَخَّرَ ۝ كُلُّ نَفْسٍ بِمَا كَسَبَتْ رَهِينَةٌ ۝ إِلَّا أَصْحَابَ الْيَمِينِ ۝
فِي جَنَّاتٍ يَتَسَاءَلُونَ ۝ عَنِ الْمُجْرِمِينَ ۝ مَا سَلَكَكُمْ فِي سَقَرَ ۝ قَالُوا
لَمْ نَكُ مِنَ الْمُصَلِّينَ ۝ وَلَمْ نَكُ نُطْعِمُ الْمِسْكِينَ ۝ وَكُنَّا نَخُوضُ مَعَ
الْخَائِضِينَ ۝ وَكُنَّا نُكَذِّبُ بِيَوْمِ الدِّينِ ۝ حَتَّىٰ أَتَانَا الْيَقِينُ ۝

HE PONDERED, and he 74:18
schemed. Confound him,
how he schemed! Again, confound him, how he schemed!
He looked around him,
frowning and scowling; then
he turned away in scornful
pride and said: 'This is but
sorcery counterfeited; this is
but the utterance of a mortal!'
I will surely cast him into
the Fire. Would that you knew
what the Fire is like! It leaves
nothing, it spares no one; it
burns the skins of mortals. It is
guarded by nineteen keepers.
We have appointed none
but angels to guard the Fire,
and made their number a subject for dispute among the
unbelievers, so that those to
whom the Book was given
may be convinced and the
true believers strengthened in their faith; that those to whom the Book was
given, and the true believers, may have no doubts; and that those whose
hearts are tainted and unbelievers may say: 'What could God mean by this as
an example?' Thus God confounds whom He will and guides whom He
pleases. None knows the warriors of your Lord but Himself. This is no more
than an Admonition to mankind.
No, by the moon! By the departing night and the coming dawn, it is a dire 74:35
scourge, a warning to mankind; alike to those of you that would march on
and those that would remain behind.
Each soul is the hostage of its own deeds. Those on the right hand will in
Gardens ask the sinners: 'What has brought you into Hell?' They will say:
'We were never of those who prayed, nor did we ever feed the destitute. We
engaged in vain discourse with those who engaged in it and denied the Day
of Reckoning, till the Inevitable claimed us.' 74:47

فما تنفعهم شفاعة الشافعين ۝ فما لهم عن التذكرة معرضين ۝ كأنهم
حمر مستنفرة ۝ فرت من قسورة ۝ بل يريد كل امرئ منهم أن يؤتى صحفا
منشرة ۝ كلا بل لا يخافون الآخرة ۝ كلا إنه تذكرة ۝ فمن شاء ذكره
۝ وما يذكرون إلا أن يشاء الله هو أهل التقوى وأهل المغفرة ۝

سورة القيامة مكية وهي أربعون آية

بسم الله الرحمن الرحيم

لا أقسم بيوم القيامة ۝ ولا أقسم بالنفس اللوامة ۝ أيحسب الإنسان
ألن نجمع عظامه ۝ بلى قادرين على أن نسوي بنانه ۝ بل يريد الإنسان
ليفجر أمامه ۝ يسأل أيان يوم القيامة ۝ فإذا برق البصر ۝
وخسف القمر ۝ وجمع الشمس والقمر ۝ يقول الإنسان يومئذ أين
المفر ۝ كلا لا وزر ۝ إلى ربك يومئذ المستقر ۝ ينبأ الإنسان
يومئذ بما قدم وأخر ۝ بل الإنسان على نفسه بصيرة ۝ ولو ألقى
معاذيره ۝ لا تحرك به لسانك لتعجل به ۝ إن علينا جمعه وقرآنه
۝ فإذا قرأناه فاتبع قرآنه ۝ ثم إن علينا بيانه ۝

74:48 NO INTERCESSOR'S plea shall save them. Why then do they turn away from this reminder, like frightened asses fleeing from a lion?

Indeed, each one of them demands a scripture of his own to be unrolled before him. No, they have no fear of the Hereafter.

No! This is an Admonition. Let him who will, be admon-
74:56 ished. But none is admonished except by the will of God. It is God who is the Lord of Goodness and Forgiveness.

THE RESURRECTION

In the Name of God,
the Merciful, the Compassionate

75:1 I SWEAR by the Day of Resurrection, and by the self-reproaching soul!
Does man think We shall never put his bones together again? Indeed, We
can remould his very fingers!
Yet man would ever deny what is to come. 'When will this be,' he asks,
'this Day of Resurrection?'
But when the sight of mortals is confounded and the moon eclipsed;
75:10 when sun and moon are joined together – on that day man will ask: 'Whither
shall I flee?'
No, there shall be no refuge; for to your Lord, on that day, all shall be
restored.
Indeed, man shall on that day be told of all he did, from first to last. Indeed,
man shall bear witness against himself, plead as he may with his excuses.
(You[1] need not move your tongue too fast to learn this revelation. We
Ourself shall see to its collection and recital. When We read it, follow its
75:19 words attentively; We shall Ourself explain its meaning.)

1. Muḥammad.

كلا بل تحبون العاجلة (٢٠) وتذرون الآخرة (٢١) وجوه يومئذ ناضرة
(٢٢) إلى ربها ناظرة (٢٣) ووجوه يومئذ باسرة (٢٤) تظن أن يفعل
بها فاقرة (٢٥) كلا إذا بلغت التراقي (٢٦) وقيل من راق (٢٧) وظن أنه
الفراق (٢٨) والتفت الساق بالساق (٢٩) إلى ربك يومئذ المساق (٣٠)
فلا صدق ولا صلى (٣١) ولكن كذب وتولى (٣٢) ثم ذهب إلى أهله يتمطى (٣٣)
أولى لك فأولى (٣٤) ثم أولى لك فأولى (٣٥) أيحسب الإنسان أن يترك سدى (٣٦)
ألم يك نطفة من مني يمنى (٣٧) ثم كان علقة فخلق فسوى (٣٨) فجعل منه
الزوجين الذكر والأنثى (٣٩) أليس ذلك بقادر على أن يحيي الموتى (٤٠)

سورة الدهر مدنية وهي إحدى وثلاثون آية

بسم الله الرحمن الرحيم
هل أتى على الإنسان حين من الدهر لم يكن شيئا مذكورا (١) إنا خلقنا
الإنسان من نطفة أمشاج نبتليه فجعلناه سميعا بصيرا (٢) إنا هديناه
السبيل إما شاكرا وإما كفورا (٣) إنا أعتدنا للكافرين سلاسل وأغلالا
وسعيرا (٤) إن الأبرار يشربون من كأس كان مزاجها كافورا (٥)

No! But you[1] love this 75:20
fleeting life, and ignore the life
to come.
On that day there shall be
joyous faces, looking towards
their Lord. On that day there
shall be mournful faces, dreading some great affliction.
No! But when a man's soul is
about to leave him and those
around him say: 'Will no one
save him?' When he knows it is
the final parting and leg and leg
are twined – on that day to your
Lord he shall be driven. For in 75:31
this life he neither believed nor
prayed; he denied the Truth
and, turning his back, went to
his kin elated with pride.
Well have you deserved
this doom; well have you
deserved it.
Well have you deserved this
doom; too well have you deserved it!
Does man think he will be left alone, to no purpose? Was he not a drop of
ejaculated semen? He became a clot of blood;[2] then God formed and
moulded him, and gave him male and female parts. Has He no power, then, 75:40
to raise the dead to life?

MAN

In the Name of God, the Merciful, the Compassionate

Does there not pass over man a space of time when his life is a blank?[3] 76:1
We have created man from the union of the two sexes, that We may put
him to the proof. We have endowed him with hearing and sight and, be he
thankful or oblivious of Our favours, We have shown him the right path.
For the unbelievers We have prepared chains and fetters, and a Conflagra- 76:5
tion. But the righteous shall drink of a cup tempered at the Camphor Fountain,

1. The Meccans. 2. See p. 331, note 1. 3. In the womb.

76:6 a gushing spring at which the
worshippers of God refresh
themselves: they who keep
their vows and dread the
far-flung terrors of a certain
day; who, though they hold it
dear, give sustenance to the
destitute, the orphan, and the
captive: 'We feed you for God's
sake only; we seek of you no
recompense nor thanks: for we
fear from our Lord a day of
anguish and of woe.'
God will deliver them from
the evil of that day, and make
their faces shine with joy. He
will reward them for their
steadfastness with Paradise and
robes of silk. Reclining therein
on soft couches, they shall feel
neither the scorching heat nor
the biting cold. Trees will
spread their shade around
them, and fruits will hang in clusters over them.
76:15 They shall be served on silver dishes, and beakers as large as goblets; silver
goblets which they themselves shall measure: and cups brim-full with
ginger-flavoured water from a fount called Salsabīl. They shall be attended
by boys graced with eternal youth, who to the beholder's eyes will seem like
sprinkled pearls. When you gaze and gaze upon that scene, you shall behold
a kingdom blissful and glorious.
They shall be arrayed in garments of fine green silk and rich brocade, and
adorned with bracelets of silver. Their Lord will give them pure nectar to
drink.
Thus shall you be rewarded; your endeavours shall earn much thanks.
It was We who sent down to you the Koran by gradual revelation; therefore await with patience the judgement of your Lord, and yield to none of
76:25 them, sinner or blasphemer. Remember the name of your Lord morning and
evening;

عينا يشرب بها عباد الله يفجرونها تفجيرا ٦ يوفون بالنذر ويخافون
يوما كان شره مستطيرا ٧ ويطعمون الطعام على حبه مسكينا ويتيما وأسيرا
٨ إنما نطعمكم لوجه الله لا نريد منكم جزاء ولا شكورا ٩ إنا نخاف من
ربنا يوما عبوسا قمطريرا ١٠ فوقاهم الله شر ذلك اليوم ولقاهم
نضرة وسرورا ١١ وجزاهم بما صبروا جنة وحريرا ١٢ متكئين
فيها على الأرائك لا يرون فيها شمسا ولا زمهريرا ١٣ ودانية عليهم
ظلالها وذللت قطوفها تذليلا ١٤ ويطاف عليهم بآنية من فضة
وأكواب كانت قواريرا ١٥ قوارير من فضة قدروها تقديرا ١٦
ويسقون فيها كأسا كان مزاجها زنجبيلا ١٧ عينا فيها تسمى سلسبيلا
١٨ ويطوف عليهم ولدان مخلدون إذا رأيتهم حسبتهم لؤلؤا منثورا
١٩ وإذا رأيت ثم رأيت نعيما وملكا كبيرا ٢٠ عاليهم ثياب سندس
خضر وإستبرق وحلوا أساور من فضة وسقاهم ربهم شرابا طهورا
٢١ إن هذا كان لكم جزاء وكان سعيكم مشكورا ٢٢ إنا نحن
نزلنا عليك القرآن تنزيلا ٢٣ فاصبر لحكم ربك ولا تطع
منهم آثما أو كفورا ٢٤ واذكر اسم ربك بكرة وأصيلا ٢٥

ومن الليل فاسجد له وسبحه ليلا طويلا ٢٦ إن هؤلاء يحبون العاجلة ويذرون
وراءهم يوما ثقيلا ٢٧ نحن خلقناهم وشددنا أسرهم وإذا شئنا
بدلنا أمثالهم تبديلا ٢٨ إن هذه تذكرة فمن شاء اتخذ إلى ربه سبيلا
٢٩ وما تشاءون إلا أن يشاء الله إن الله كان عليما حكيما ٣٠
يدخل من يشاء في رحمته والظالمين أعد لهم عذابا أليما ٣١

سورة المرسلات مكية وهي خمسون آية

بسم الله الرحمن الرحيم

والمرسلات عرفا ١ فالعاصفات عصفا ٢ والناشرات نشرا ٣
فالفارقات فرقا ٤ فالملقيات ذكرا ٥ عذرا أو نذرا ٦ إنما
توعدون لواقع ٧ فإذا النجوم طمست ٨ وإذا السماء فرجت ٩ وإذا
الجبال نسفت ١٠ وإذا الرسل أقتت ١١ لأي يوم أجلت ١٢ ليوم الفصل
١٣ وما أدراك ما يوم الفصل ١٤ ويل يومئذ للمكذبين ١٥
ألم نهلك الأولين ١٦ ثم نتبعهم الآخرين ١٧
كذلك نفعل بالمجرمين ١٨ ويل يومئذ للمكذبين ١٩

in the night-time bow to Him: 76:26
and praise Him all night long.

Surely the unbelievers love this fleeting life too well, and leave behind them a heavy day of woe. *We* created them, and endowed their limbs and joints with strength; but if We please, We can replace them by others like them.

This is indeed an Admonition. Let him that will, take the right path to his Lord. Yet you cannot will, except by the will of God. God is omniscient and wise.

He admits into His mercy 76:31
whom He will: and for the wrongdoers He has prepared a woeful punishment.

THOSE THAT ARE SENT FORTH

In the Name of God, the Merciful, the Compassionate

BY THE gales, sent forth in swift succession; by the raging tempests and the 77:1
rain-spreading winds; by those that send down the revelations discerning good from evil and admonishing by plea and warning: that which you are promised shall be fulfilled!

When the stars are blotted out; when the sky is rent asunder and the mountains crumble into dust; when the apostles are brought together on an appointed day – when will all this be? Upon the Day of Judgement.

Would that you knew what the Day of Judgement is! On that day woe betide the disbelievers! Did We not obliterate the early generations and cause the latter ones to follow them? Thus shall We deal with the transgressors.

On that day woe betide the disbelievers! 77:19

77:20 Did We not create you from a humble fluid, which We kept in a safe receptacle[1] for an appointed term? All this We did; how excellent is Our work!

On that day woe betide the disbelievers! Have We not made the earth an abode for the living and for the dead? Have We not placed lofty mountains upon it, and given you fresh water for your drink?

On that day woe betide the disbelievers! Begone to that which you deny! Depart into the shadow that will rise high in three columns, giving neither shade nor shelter from the flames, and throwing up sparks as huge as towers, as bright as yellow camels!

On that day woe betide the disbelievers! On that day they shall not speak, nor shall their pleas be heeded.

77:38 On that day woe betide the disbelievers! Such is the Day of Judgement. We will herd you all, together with past generations. If then you are cunning, try your spite against Me!

On that day woe betide the disbelievers! The righteous shall dwell amidst cool shades and fountains, and feed on such fruits as they desire. 'Eat and drink, and may every joy attend you! This is the guerdon of your labours.' Thus shall We recompense the righteous.

On that day woe betide the disbelievers! Eat and enjoy yourselves awhile. Surely you are sinners all.

On that day woe betide the disbelievers! If they are bidden to kneel down, they do not kneel.

77:50 On that day woe betide the disbelievers! In what revelation, after this, will they believe?

أَلَمْ نَخْلُقكُّم مِّن مَّآءٍ مَّهِينٍ ۝ فَجَعَلْنَٰهُ فِى قَرَارٍ مَّكِينٍ ۝ إِلَىٰ قَدَرٍ
مَّعْلُومٍ ۝ فَقَدَرْنَا فَنِعْمَ ٱلْقَٰدِرُونَ ۝ وَيْلٌ يَوْمَئِذٍ لِّلْمُكَذِّبِينَ ۝
أَلَمْ نَجْعَلِ ٱلْأَرْضَ كِفَاتًا ۝ أَحْيَآءً وَأَمْوَٰتًا ۝ وَجَعَلْنَا فِيهَا رَوَٰسِىَ
شَٰمِخَٰتٍ وَأَسْقَيْنَٰكُم مَّآءً فُرَاتًا ۝ وَيْلٌ يَوْمَئِذٍ لِّلْمُكَذِّبِينَ ۝
ٱنطَلِقُوٓا۟ إِلَىٰ مَا كُنتُم بِهِۦ تُكَذِّبُونَ ۝ ٱنطَلِقُوٓا۟ إِلَىٰ ظِلٍّ ذِى ثَلَٰثِ
شُعَبٍ ۝ لَّا ظَلِيلٍ وَلَا يُغْنِى مِنَ ٱللَّهَبِ ۝ إِنَّهَا تَرْمِى بِشَرَرٍ
كَٱلْقَصْرِ ۝ كَأَنَّهُۥ جِمَٰلَتٌ صُفْرٌ ۝ وَيْلٌ يَوْمَئِذٍ لِّلْمُكَذِّبِينَ ۝
هَٰذَا يَوْمُ لَا يَنطِقُونَ ۝ وَلَا يُؤْذَنُ لَهُمْ فَيَعْتَذِرُونَ ۝
وَيْلٌ يَوْمَئِذٍ لِّلْمُكَذِّبِينَ ۝ هَٰذَا يَوْمُ ٱلْفَصْلِ جَمَعْنَٰكُمْ وَٱلْأَوَّلِينَ
۝ فَإِن كَانَ لَكُمْ كَيْدٌ فَكِيدُونِ ۝ وَيْلٌ يَوْمَئِذٍ لِّلْمُكَذِّبِينَ ۝
إِنَّ ٱلْمُتَّقِينَ فِى ظِلَٰلٍ وَعُيُونٍ ۝ وَفَوَٰكِهَ مِمَّا يَشْتَهُونَ ۝ كُلُوا۟
وَٱشْرَبُوا۟ هَنِيٓـًٔا بِمَا كُنتُمْ تَعْمَلُونَ ۝ إِنَّا كَذَٰلِكَ نَجْزِى ٱلْمُحْسِنِينَ ۝
وَيْلٌ يَوْمَئِذٍ لِّلْمُكَذِّبِينَ ۝ كُلُوا۟ وَتَمَتَّعُوا۟ قَلِيلًا إِنَّكُم مُّجْرِمُونَ ۝
وَيْلٌ يَوْمَئِذٍ لِّلْمُكَذِّبِينَ ۝ وَإِذَا قِيلَ لَهُمُ ٱرْكَعُوا۟ لَا يَرْكَعُونَ ۝
وَيْلٌ يَوْمَئِذٍ لِّلْمُكَذِّبِينَ ۝ فَبِأَىِّ حَدِيثٍ بَعْدَهُۥ يُؤْمِنُونَ ۝

1. The womb.

سورة النبا مكية وهي اربعون آية

بسم الله الرحمن الرحيم

عم يتساءلون (١) عن النبإ العظيم (٢) الذي هم فيه مختلفون
(٣) كلا سيعلمون (٤) ثم كلا سيعلمون (٥) ألم نجعل الأرض
مهادا (٦) والجبال أوتادا (٧) وخلقناكم أزواجا (٨) وجعلنا
نومكم سباتا (٩) وجعلنا الليل لباسا (١٠) وجعلنا النهار معاشا (١١)
وبنينا فوقكم سبعا شدادا (١٢) وجعلنا سراجا وهاجا (١٣) وأنزلنا
من المعصرات ماء ثجاجا (١٤) لنخرج به حبا ونباتا (١٥) وجنات ألفافا
(١٦) إن يوم الفصل كان ميقاتا (١٧) يوم ينفخ في الصور فتأتون أفواجا (١٨)
وفتحت السماء فكانت أبوابا (١٩) وسيرت الجبال فكانت سرابا (٢٠) إن
جهنم كانت مرصادا (٢١) للطاغين مآبا (٢٢) لابثين فيها أحقابا (٢٣)
لا يذوقون فيها بردا ولا شرابا (٢٤) إلا حميما وغساقا (٢٥) جزاء وفاقا
(٢٦) إنهم كانوا لا يرجون حسابا (٢٧) وكذبوا بآياتنا كذابا (٢٨) وكل
شيء أحصيناه كتابا (٢٩) فذوقوا فلن نزيدكم إلا عذابا (٣٠)

THE TIDINGS

In the Name of God,
the Merciful, the Compassionate

ABOUT WHAT are they ask- 78:1
ing?

About the fateful tidings –
the theme of their disputes.

But they shall learn; then
they shall surely learn.

Did We not spread the
earth like a bed, and raise
the mountains like supporting
pillars?

We created you in pairs, and
gave you rest in sleep. We
made the night a mantle, and
ordained the day for work. We
built above you seven mighty
heavens and placed in them a
glowing lamp. We sent down
abundant water from the clouds to bring forth grain and varied plants, and
gardens thick with foliage.

Fixed is the Day of Judgement. On that day the Trumpet shall be blown, 78:18
and you shall come in multitudes. The gates of heaven shall swing open, and
the mountains shall pass away into a mirage.

Hell will lie in ambush, a home for the transgressors. Therein shall they abide long ages; therein they shall taste neither refreshment nor any drink, save scalding water and decaying filth: a fitting recompense.

They never expected a reckoning, and roundly denied Our revelations.
But We kept account of what they did and wrote it down. 'So taste this: for 78:30
We shall give you nothing but mounting torment!'

78:31 As FOR the righteous, there
shall surely be a triumph:
gardens and vineyards, and
tender-bosomed maidens for
companions: a truly overflowing cup.
Therein shall they hear no
idle talk, nor any falsehood.
Such is the recompense from
your Lord – a gift that will
78:37 suffice them: the Lord of the
heavens and the earth and all
that lies between them; the
Merciful, from whom they
have no power to speak.
On the day when the Spirit
and the angels stand up in
their ranks, they shall not
speak; except him who shall
receive the sanction of the
Merciful and declare what is
right.
That day is sure to come.
78:40 Let him who will, seek a way back to his Lord. We have forewarned you of
an imminent scourge: the day when man will look upon his works and the
unbeliever say: 'Would that I were dust!'

إن للمتقين مفازا ۝٣١ حدائق وأعنابا ۝٣٢ وكواعب أترابا ۝٣٣ وكأسا دهاقا
۝٣٤ لا يسمعون فيها لغوا ولا كذابا ۝٣٥ جزاء من ربك عطاء
حسابا ۝٣٦ رب السموات والأرض وما بينهما الرحمن لا يملكون
منه خطابا ۝٣٧ يوم يقوم الروح والملئكة صفا لا يتكلمون إلا
من أذن له الرحمن وقال صوابا ۝٣٨ ذلك اليوم الحق فمن شاء
اتخذ إلى ربه مابا ۝٣٩ إنا أنذرناكم عذابا قريبا يوم ينظر
المرء ما قدمت يداه ويقول الكافر يا ليتني كنت ترابا ۝٤٠

سورة النازعات مكية وهي ست وأربعون آية

بسم الله الرحمن الرحيم
والنازعات غرقا ۝١ والناشطات نشطا ۝٢ والسابحات سبحا ۝٣
فالسابقات سبقا ۝٤ فالمدبرات أمرا ۝٥ يوم ترجف الراجفة ۝٦ تتبعها
الرادفة ۝٧ قلوب يومئذ واجفة ۝٨ أبصارها خاشعة ۝٩ يقولون أءنا
لمردودون في الحافرة ۝١٠ أءذا كنا عظاما نخرة ۝١١ قالوا تلك إذا كرة
خاسرة ۝١٢ فإنما هي زجرة واحدة ۝١٣ فإذا هم بالساهرة ۝١٤

THE SOUL-SNATCHERS

In the Name of God, the Merciful, the Compassionate

79:1 BY THOSE who snatch away men's souls, and those who gently release them;
by those who float at will, and those who speed headlong; by those who govern the affairs of this world! On the day the Trumpet sounds its first and
second blast: hearts shall on that day be filled with terror, and eyes shall stare
with awe.
They say: 'When we are turned to hollow bones, shall we be restored to
life?' And they say: 'So it is a fruitless transformation!' But with one blast
79:14 they shall return to the earth's surface.

هل اتيك حديث موسى ﴿١٥﴾ اذ ناديه ربه بالواد المقدس طوى ﴿١٦﴾
اذهب الى فرعون انه طغى ﴿١٧﴾ فقل هل لك الى ان تزكى ﴿١٨﴾ واهديك الى
ربك فتخشى ﴿١٩﴾ فاريه الاية الكبرى ﴿٢٠﴾ فكذب وعصى ﴿٢١﴾ ثم
ادبر يسعى ﴿٢٢﴾ فحشر فنادى ﴿٢٣﴾ فقال انا ربكم الاعلى ﴿٢٤﴾ فاخذه
الله نكال الاخرة والاولى ﴿٢٥﴾ ان في ذلك لعبرة لمن يخشى ﴿٢٦﴾
ءانتم اشد خلقا ام السماء بنيها ﴿٢٧﴾ رفع سمكها فسويها ﴿٢٨﴾ واغطش
ليلها واخرج ضحيها ﴿٢٩﴾ والارض بعد ذلك دحيها ﴿٣٠﴾ اخرج منها
ماءها ومرعيها ﴿٣١﴾ والجبال ارسيها ﴿٣٢﴾ متاعا لكم ولانعامكم
﴿٣٣﴾ فاذا جاءت الطامة الكبرى ﴿٣٤﴾ يوم يتذكر الانسان ما سعى
﴿٣٥﴾ وبرزت الجحيم لمن يرى ﴿٣٦﴾ فاما من طغى ﴿٣٧﴾ واثر الحيوة
الدنيا ﴿٣٨﴾ فان الجحيم هي المأوى ﴿٣٩﴾ واما من خاف مقام
ربه ونهى النفس عن الهوى ﴿٤٠﴾ فان الجنة هي المأوى ﴿٤١﴾
يسئلونك عن الساعة ايان مرسيها ﴿٤٢﴾ فيم انت من ذكريها ﴿٤٣﴾ الى
ربك منتهيها ﴿٤٤﴾ انما انت منذر من يخشيها ﴿٤٥﴾
كانهم يوم يرونها لم يلبثوا الا عشية او ضحيها ﴿٤٦﴾

HAVE YOU heard the story 79:15
of Moses?

His Lord called out to him in the sacred valley of Ṭuwā, saying: 'Go to Pharaoh: he has transgressed all bounds; and say: "Will you reform yourself? I will guide you to your Lord, that you may fear Him."'

He showed Pharaoh the mightiest sign, but he denied it and rebelled. He quickly went away and, summoning all his men, made to them a proclamation. 'I am your supreme Lord,' he said.

So God smote him with the scourge of the life to come, and of this life. Surely in this there is a lesson for the God-fearing.

Are you harder to create or
the heaven He has built? He
raised it high and fashioned it, giving darkness to its night and brightness to 79:29
its day.

After that He spread the earth, and, drawing water from its depth, brought forth its pastures. He set down the mountains, for you and for your cattle to delight in.

But when the supreme calamity strikes – the day when man will call to mind his labours – when Hell appears to those with eyes to see – he that transgressed and chose this present life shall have his home in Hell; and he that feared to stand before his Lord and curbed his soul's desire shall have his home in Paradise.

They question you about the Hour: 'When will it come?' But how are you to know? Only your Lord knows when the end will come. Your duty is but to warn those that fear it.

On the day they see it, it will seem as if they had lingered but one evening, 79:46
or one morning.

HE FROWNED

سورة عبس مكية وهي اثنتان واربعون آية

بسم الله الرحمن الرحيم

عبس وتولى ١ ان جاءه الاعمى ٢ وما يدريك لعله يزكى ٣
او يذكر فتنفعه الذكرى ٤ اما من استغنى ٥ فانت له
تصدى ٦ وما عليك الا يزكى ٧ واما من جاءك يسعى ٨
وهو يخشى ٩ فانت عنه تلهى ١٠ كلا انها تذكرة ١١ فمن
شاء ذكره ١٢ في صحف مكرمة ١٣ مرفوعة مطهرة ١٤
بايدي سفرة ١٥ كرام بررة ١٦ قتل الانسان ما اكفره ١٧
من اي شيء خلقه ١٨ من نطفة خلقه فقدره ١٩ ثم السبيل
يسره ٢٠ ثم اماته فاقبره ٢١ ثم اذا شاء انشره ٢٢ كلا
لما يقض ما امره ٢٣ فلينظر الانسان الى طعامه ٢٤ انا صببنا
الماء صبا ٢٥ ثم شققنا الارض شقا ٢٦ فانبتنا فيها حبا ٢٧
وعنبا وقضبا ٢٨ وزيتونا ونخلا ٢٩ وحدائق غلبا ٣٠ وفاكهة
وابا ٣١ متاعا لكم ولانعامكم ٣٢ فاذا جاءت الصاخة ٣٣

In the Name of God,
the Merciful, the Compassionate

80:1 HE[1] FROWNED and turned his back when the blind man came to him.

How could you[1] tell? He might have sought to purify himself. He might have remembered, and remembrance might have done him good.

But to the wealthy man you were all attention: although the fault would not be yours if he remained uncleansed. Yet to him that came to you with zeal and awe, you paid no heed.

No! This is an Admonition; let him who will, bear it in mind. It is set down on honoured pages, exalted and purified, by the hands of devout and gracious scribes.

Let man perish! How ungrateful he is!

80:19 From what did He create him? From a little germ He created him and
gave him due proportion. He made his path smooth for him, then caused him to die and stowed him in a grave. He will surely bring him back to life when He pleases. Yet he declines to do His bidding.

Let man reflect on the food he eats: how We pour down the rain in torrents and cleave the earth asunder; how We bring forth the corn, the grapes, and the fresh vegetation; the olive and the palm, the thickets, the fruit-trees, and the green pasture, for you and for your cattle to delight in.

80:33 But when the dread blast is sounded,

1. Muḥammad.

يوم يفر المرء من أخيه (٣٤) وأمه وأبيه (٣٥) وصاحبته وبنيه
(٣٦) لكل امرئ منهم يومئذ شأن يغنيه (٣٧) وجوه يومئذ
مسفرة (٣٨) ضاحكة مستبشرة (٣٩) ووجوه يومئذ عليها غبرة
(٤٠) ترهقها قترة (٤١) أولئك هم الكفرة الفجرة (٤٢)

سورة التكوير مكية وهي تسع وعشرون آية

بسم الله الرحمن الرحيم

إذا الشمس كورت (١) وإذا النجوم انكدرت (٢) وإذا الجبال
سيرت (٣) وإذا العشار عطلت (٤) وإذا الوحوش حشرت (٥)
وإذا البحار سجرت (٦) وإذا النفوس زوجت (٧) وإذا الموءودة
سئلت (٨) بأي ذنب قتلت (٩) وإذا الصحف نشرت (١٠)
وإذا السماء كشطت (١١) وإذا الجحيم سعرت (١٢) وإذا الجنة
أزلفت (١٣) علمت نفس ما أحضرت (١٤) فلا أقسم بالخنس (١٥)
الجوار الكنس (١٦) والليل إذا عسعس (١٧) والصبح إذا تنفس (١٨)
إنه لقول رسول كريم (١٩) ذي قوة عند ذي العرش مكين (٢٠)

on that day each man will 80:34
forsake his brother, his mother
and his father, his consort and
his children: for each one of
them will on that day have
enough sorrow of his own.

On that day there shall be
beaming faces, laughing and
joyful. On that day there shall
be faces covered with dust,
veiled with darkness. These 80:42
shall be the faces of the degenerate blasphemers.

THE CESSATION

In the Name of God,
the Merciful, the Compassionate

WHEN THE sun ceases to 81:1
shine; when the stars fall and the mountains are blown away; when camels big with young are left untended, and the wild beasts are together herded; when the seas are set ablaze and souls are reunited; when the infant girl,[1] buried alive, is asked for what crime she was slain; when the records of men's deeds are laid open, and heaven is stripped bare; when Hell turns into a Conflagration and Paradise is brought near: then each soul shall learn what it has done.

I swear by the turning planets, and by the stars that rise and set; by the
night, when it darkens, and the first breath of morning: this is the Word of a
messenger gracious and mighty, held in honour by the Lord of the Throne, 81:20

[1] See p. 284, note 1.

81:21 obeyed, and faithful to his
trust.

No, your countryman[1] is
not possessed. He saw him[2]
on the clear horizon. He does
not grudge the secrets of the
unseen; nor is this the utterance of an accursèd demon.

Whither then are you
going?

This is but an Admonition
to mankind: to those among
you that have the will to be
81:29 upright. Yet you cannot will,
except by the will of God,
Lord of the Universe.

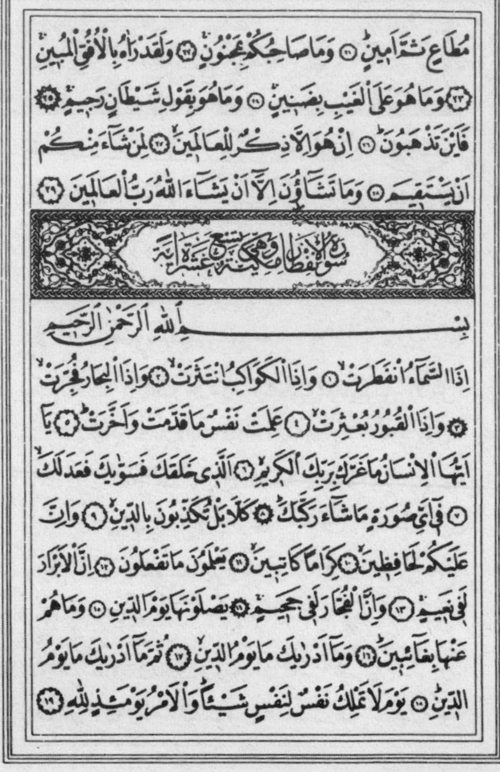
مطاع ثم أمين ۝ وما صاحبكم بمجنون ۝ ولقد رآه بالأفق المبين
۝ وما هو على الغيب بضنين ۝ وما هو بقول شيطان رجيم ۝
فأين تذهبون ۝ إن هو إلا ذكر للعالمين ۝ لمن شاء منكم
أن يستقيم ۝ وما تشاءون إلا أن يشاء الله رب العالمين ۝

سورة الانفطار مكية وهي تسع عشرة آية

بسم الله الرحمن الرحيم

إذا السماء انفطرت ۝ وإذا الكواكب انتثرت ۝ وإذا البحار فجرت
۝ وإذا القبور بعثرت ۝ علمت نفس ما قدمت وأخرت ۝ يا
أيها الإنسان ما غرك بربك الكريم ۝ الذي خلقك فسواك فعدلك
۝ في أي صورة ما شاء ركبك ۝ كلا بل تكذبون بالدين ۝ وإن
عليكم لحافظين ۝ كراما كاتبين ۝ يعلمون ما تفعلون ۝ إن الأبرار
لفي نعيم ۝ وإن الفجار لفي جحيم ۝ يصلونها يوم الدين ۝ وما هم
عنها بغائبين ۝ وما أدراك ما يوم الدين ۝ ثم ما أدراك ما يوم
الدين ۝ يوم لا تملك نفس لنفس شيئا والأمر يومئذ لله ۝

THE CATACLYSM

In the Name of God,
the Merciful, the Compassionate

82:1 When the sky is rent asunder; when the stars scatter and the oceans surge
together; when the graves are hurled about: each soul shall know what it has
done and what it has failed to do.

O man! What evil has enticed you from your gracious Lord who created
you, and gave you due proportions and an upright form? In whatever shape
He willed He could have moulded you.

82:10 No! But you deny the Last Judgement. Surely there are guardians watching over you, noble recorders who know of what you do.

The righteous will surely be in bliss. And the wicked shall be in Hell, burn-
ing therein upon the Judgement-day: nor shall they ever escape from it.

Would that you knew what the Day of Judgement is! Again, would that
82:19 you knew what the Day of Judgement is! It is the day when no soul shall
have power to help another soul and God will reign supreme.

1. Muḥammad. 2. Gabriel.

سورة المطففين مكية وهي ست وثلاثون آية

بسم الله الرحمن الرحيم

ويل للمطففين (١) الذين إذا اكتالوا على الناس يستوفون (٢) وإذا كالوهم أو وزنوهم يخسرون (٣) ألا يظن أولئك أنهم مبعوثون (٤) ليوم عظيم (٥) يوم يقوم الناس لرب العالمين (٦) كلا إن كتاب الفجار لفي سجين (٧) وما أدراك ما سجين (٨) كتاب مرقوم (٩) ويل يومئذ للمكذبين (١٠) الذين يكذبون بيوم الدين (١١) وما يكذب به إلا كل معتد أثيم (١٢) إذا تتلى عليه آياتنا قال أساطير الأولين (١٣) كلا بل ران على قلوبهم ما كانوا يكسبون (١٤) كلا إنهم عن ربهم يومئذ لمحجوبون (١٥) ثم إنهم لصالوا الجحيم (١٦) ثم يقال هذا الذي كنتم به تكذبون (١٧) كلا إن كتاب الأبرار لفي عليين (١٨) وما أدراك ما عليون (١٩) كتاب مرقوم (٢٠) يشهده المقربون (٢١) إن الأبرار لفي نعيم (٢٢) على الأرائك ينظرون (٢٣) تعرف في وجوههم نضرة النعيم (٢٤) يسقون من رحيق مختوم (٢٥) ختامه مسك وفي ذلك فليتنافس المتنافسون (٢٦)

THE UNJUST

In the Name of God,
the Merciful, the Compassionate

WOE BETIDE the unjust who, 83:1
when people measure for
them, exact in full, but when
they measure or weigh for
them, defraud them!

Do they not think they will
be raised to life upon a fateful
day, the day when mankind
will stand before the Lord of
the Universe?

No! The record of the sinners is in Sijjīn. Would that you knew what Sijjīn is! It is a sealed book.

On that day woe betide the
disbelievers who deny the Last
Judgement! None denies it 83:12
except the sinful transgressor who, when Our revelations are recited to him,
says: 'Fables of the ancients!'

No! But their own deeds have drawn a veil over their hearts.

No! A screen shall on that day be set between them and their Lord. Then shall they burn in Hell, and shall be told: 'This is what you denied!'

No! But the record of the righteous shall be in 'Illiyyūn. Would that you knew what 'Illiyyūn is! It is a sealed book, seen only by the favoured ones.

The righteous will surely be in bliss. Reclining on soft couches they will
gaze around: and in their faces you shall mark the glow of joy. They shall be
served with pure nectar to drink, securely sealed, whose very dregs are musk: 83:26
for this let all contenders emulously strive;

83:27 tempered with the waters of
Tasnīm, a spring at which the
favoured will refresh themselves.

Those who transgress laugh at the faithful and wink at one another as they pass by them. When they meet their own kin they speak of them with jests, and when they see them say: 'These have surely lost their way.' Yet they were not sent to
be their keepers.

But on that day the faithful will at the infidels laugh as they recline upon the couches and
gaze around.
83:36 Shall not the infidels be
rewarded according to what
they did?

ومزاجه من تسنيم ٢٧ عينا يشرب بها المقربون ٢٨ إن الذين
أجرموا كانوا من الذين آمنوا يضحكون ٢٩ وإذا مروا بهم
يتغامزون ٣٠ وإذا انقلبوا إلى أهلهم انقلبوا فكهين ٣١ وإذا
رأوهم قالوا إن هؤلاء لضالون ٣٢ وما أرسلوا عليهم
حافظين ٣٣ فاليوم الذين آمنوا من الكفار يضحكون ٣٤ على
الأرائك ينظرون ٣٥ هل ثوب الكفار ما كانوا يفعلون ٣٦

سورة الانشقاق

بسم الله الرحمن الرحيم

إذا السماء انشقت ١ وأذنت لربها وحقت ٢ وإذا الأرض مدت
٣ وألقت ما فيها وتخلت ٤ وأذنت لربها وحقت ٥ يا أيها
الإنسان إنك كادح إلى ربك كدحا فملاقيه ٦ فأما من أوتي
كتابه بيمينه ٧ فسوف يحاسب حسابا يسيرا ٨ وينقلب إلى أهله
مسرورا ٩ وأما من أوتي كتابه وراء ظهره ١٠ فسوف يدعوا
ثبورا ١١ ويصلى سعيرا ١٢ إنه كان في أهله مسرورا ١٣

THE RENDING

In the Name of God, the Merciful, the Compassionate

84:1 WHEN THE sky is rent apart, obeying her Lord in true submission; when the
earth expands and casts out all that is within her and becomes empty, obeying her Lord in true submission; then, O man, who labour constantly to
meet your Lord, shall you meet Him.
He that is given his Book in his right hand shall have a lenient reckoning,
and shall go back rejoicing to his people. But he that is given his Book behind
his back shall call down destruction on himself and burn in the Conflagra-
84:13 tion; for he lived rejoicing among his people

انه ظن ان لن يحور ۝ بلى ان ربه كان به بصيرا ۝ فلا اقسم
بالشفق ۝ والليل وما وسق ۝ والقمر اذا اتسق ۝ لتركبن طبقا
عن طبق ۝ فما لهم لا يؤمنون ۝ واذا قرئ عليهم القران لا يسجدون
۝ بل الذين كفروا يكذبون ۝ والله اعلم بما يوعون ۝
فبشرهم بعذاب اليم ۝ الا الذين امنوا وعملوا الصالحات لهم اجر غير ممنون ۝

سورة البروج مكية وهي اثنتا عشرون آية

بسم الله الرحمن الرحيم
والسماء ذات البروج ۝ واليوم الموعود ۝ وشاهد ومشهود ۝ قتل
اصحاب الاخدود ۝ النار ذات الوقود ۝ اذ هم عليها قعود ۝ وهم
على ما يفعلون بالمؤمنين شهود ۝ وما نقموا منهم الا ان يؤمنوا بالله
العزيز الحميد ۝ الذي له ملك السموات والارض والله على كل شيء شهيد
۝ ان الذين فتنوا المؤمنين والمؤمنات ثم لم يتوبوا فلهم عذاب
جهنم ولهم عذاب الحريق ۝ ان الذين امنوا وعملوا الصالحات لهم
جنات تجري من تحتها الانهار ذلك الفوز الكبير ۝

and thought he would never 84:14
turn back. Yes; but his Lord
was ever watching him.

I swear by the glow of sunset; by the night, and all that it
envelops; by the moon, in her
full perfection: that you shall
march onwards from stage to
stage.

Why then do they not
believe, or kneel down in
prayer when the Koran is read
to them?

The unbelievers indeed are
in denial; but God knows best
the falsehoods they believe in.

Therefore proclaim to them
a woeful scourge, save those 84:25
who believe and do good works;
for theirs is an unfailing recompense.

THE CONSTELLATIONS

In the Name of God, the Merciful, the Compassionate

By the heaven with its constellations! By the Promised Day! By the Wit- 85:1
ness, and that which is witnessed!

Cursed[1] be the diggers of the trench with its consuming fire as they sat
around it to witness what they did to the faithful! Nor did they avenge themselves on them for aught but that they believed in God, the Almighty, the
Praised One, who has sovereignty over the heavens and the earth. And God 85:9
is the Witness of all things.

Those that persecute believers, men or women, and never repent shall
have the torment of Hell, the torment of the blazing fire. But those that 85:11
believe and do good works shall have Gardens watered by running brooks.
That is the supreme triumph.

1. Literally, slain.

85:12 STERN INDEED is the vengeance of your Lord. He it is
who brings into being and
then restores to life. Forgiving
and loving, He is the Lord
of the Glorious Throne, the
Executor of His own will.
Have you not heard the
story of the warriors, of Pharaoh and of Thamūd? Yet the
unbelievers are still in denial.
God surrounds them from
behind. Surely this is a glorious
85:22 Koran, on a Tablet preserved.

THE NIGHTLY VISITANT

In the Name of God,
the Merciful, the Compassionate

إن بطش ربك لشديد ۝ إنه هو يبدئ ويعيد ۝ وهو الغفور
الودود ۝ ذو العرش المجيد ۝ فعال لما يريد ۝ هل أتاك حديث الجنود
۝ فرعون وثمود ۝ بل الذين كفروا في تكذيب ۝ والله من ورائهم
محيط ۝ بل هو قرآن مجيد ۝ في لوح محفوظ ۝

سورة الطارق مكية وهي سبع عشرة آية

بسم الله الرحمن الرحيم
والسماء والطارق ۝ وما أدراك ما الطارق ۝ النجم الثاقب ۝
إن كل نفس لما عليها حافظ ۝ فلينظر الإنسان مم خلق ۝ خلق من
ماء دافق ۝ يخرج من بين الصلب والترائب ۝ إنه على رجعه لقادر
۝ يوم تبلى السرائر ۝ فما له من قوة ولا ناصر ۝ والسماء ذات الرجع
۝ والأرض ذات الصدع ۝ إنه لقول فصل ۝ وما هو بالهزل ۝
إنهم يكيدون كيدا ۝ وأكيد كيدا ۝ فمهل الكافرين أمهلهم رويدا ۝

سورة الأعلى مكية وهي تسع عشرة آية

86:1 BY THE heaven, and by the nightly visitant!
Would that you knew what the nightly visitant is!
It is the star of piercing brightness.
For every soul there is a guardian. Let man reflect from what he is created:
he was created from an ejaculated fluid that issues from between the loins
and the ribs.
Surely He has power to bring him back, on the day when consciences are
searched. Helpless shall he be, with none to succour him.
86:12 By the heaven with its recurring cycles, and by the earth, ever bursting
with new growth; this[1] is a discerning utterance, no flippant jest.
86:17 They scheme and scheme: and I, too, scheme and scheme. Therefore bear
with the unbelievers, and let them be awhile.

1. The Koran.

بسم الله الرحمن الرحيم
سبح اسم ربك الأعلى الذي خلق فسوى والذي قدر فهدى
والذي أخرج المرعى فجعله غثاء أحوى سنقرئك فلا تنسى
إلا ما شاء الله إنه يعلم الجهر وما يخفى ونيسرك لليسرى فذكر
إن نفعت الذكرى سيذكر من يخشى ويتجنبها الأشقى الذي
يصلى النار الكبرى ثم لا يموت فيها ولا يحيى قد أفلح من تزكى
وذكر اسم ربه فصلى بل تؤثرون الحياة الدنيا والآخرة خير
وأبقى إن هذا لفي الصحف الأولى صحف إبراهيم وموسى
سورة الغاشية مكية وهي ست وعشرون آية
بسم الله الرحمن الرحيم
هل أتاك حديث الغاشية وجوه يومئذ خاشعة عاملة ناصبة
تصلى نارا حامية تسقى من عين آنية ليس لهم طعام إلا
من ضريع لا يسمن ولا يغني من جوع وجوه يومئذ ناعمة
لسعيها راضية في جنة عالية لا تسمع فيها لاغية

THE MOST HIGH

In the Name of God,
the Merciful, the Compassionate

PRAISE THE Name of your Lord, 87:1
the Most High, who created all
things and gave them due proportion; who ordained their destinies
and guided them; who brings
forth the green pasture, then turns
it to withered grass.

We shall make you read, so that
you shall never forget except as
God pleases. He has knowledge
of the manifest and the hidden.

We shall guide you to the
smoothest path. Therefore admonish, if admonishment will
avail. He that fears God will pay
heed, but the wretched sinner
will flout it. He shall burn in the 87:12
gigantic Fire, wherein shall he then neither die nor live. Happy shall be he
that keeps himself pure, that remembers the name of his Lord and prays.

Yet you[1] prefer the life of this world, although the life to come is better
and more lasting.

This is surely set down in the earlier Scriptures; the Scriptures of Abra- 87:19
ham and Moses.

THE OVERWHELMING EVENT

In the Name of God, the Merciful, the Compassionate

HAVE YOU heard of the Event that shall overwhelm all? 88:1

On that day there shall be downcast faces, haggard and worn out, burnt
by a scorching fire, drinking from a seething fountain. Their only food shall
be bitter thorns, which will neither sustain them nor satisfy their hunger.

On that day there shall be radiant faces, well pleased with their labours, in
a lofty Garden. Therein shall they hear no idle talk; 88:11

1. The unbelievers of Mecca.

88:12 therein shall be a gushing fountain; therein shall be raised soft couches with goblets placed before them; silken cushions ranged in order and carpets richly spread.

88:17 Do they never reflect on the camels, how they were created? On the heaven, how it was raised on high? On the mountains, how they were set down? On the earth, how it was flattened?

Therefore admonish; your duty is only to admonish: you are not their keeper. As for those that turn their backs and disbelieve, God will torment them with the supreme torment. To Us shall they return,
88:26 and then We will Ourself bring them to account.

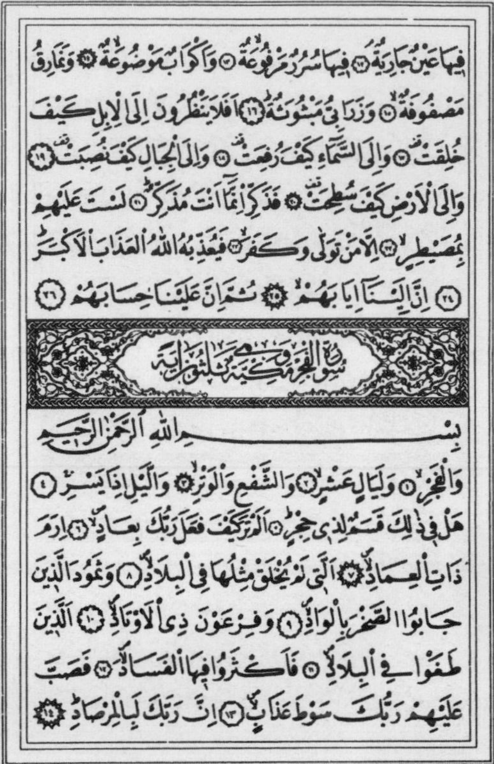

فيها عين جارية ﴿١٢﴾ فيها سرر مرفوعة ﴿١٣﴾ وأكواب موضوعة ﴿١٤﴾ ونمارق
مصفوفة ﴿١٥﴾ وزرابي مبثوثة ﴿١٦﴾ أفلا ينظرون إلى الإبل كيف
خلقت ﴿١٧﴾ وإلى السماء كيف رفعت ﴿١٨﴾ وإلى الجبال كيف نصبت ﴿١٩﴾
وإلى الأرض كيف سطحت ﴿٢٠﴾ فذكر إنما أنت مذكر ﴿٢١﴾ لست عليهم
بمصيطر ﴿٢٢﴾ إلا من تولى وكفر ﴿٢٣﴾ فيعذبه الله العذاب الأكبر
﴿٢٤﴾ إن إلينا إيابهم ﴿٢٥﴾ ثم إن علينا حسابهم ﴿٢٦﴾

سورة الفجر مكية وهي ثلاثون آية

بسم الله الرحمن الرحيم

والفجر ﴿١﴾ وليال عشر ﴿٢﴾ والشفع والوتر ﴿٣﴾ والليل إذا يسر ﴿٤﴾
هل في ذلك قسم لذي حجر ﴿٥﴾ ألم تر كيف فعل ربك بعاد ﴿٦﴾ إرم
ذات العماد ﴿٧﴾ التي لم يخلق مثلها في البلاد ﴿٨﴾ وثمود الذين
جابوا الصخر بالواد ﴿٩﴾ وفرعون ذي الأوتاد ﴿١٠﴾ الذين
طغوا في البلاد ﴿١١﴾ فأكثروا فيها الفساد ﴿١٢﴾ فصب
عليهم ربك سوط عذاب ﴿١٣﴾ إن ربك لبالمرصاد ﴿١٤﴾

THE DAWN

In the Name of God, the Merciful, the Compassionate

89:1 BY THE Dawn and the Ten Nights;[1] by that which is dual, and that which is
single; by the night, as it journeys on!
Is there not in this a mighty oath for a man of sense?
Have you not considered how your Lord dealt with ʿĀd? The
many-columned city of Iram, whose like has never been created in the land?
And Thamūd, who hewed out their dwellings among the rocks of the valley?
And Pharaoh, who impaled his victims upon the stakes?
They had all led sinful lives, and made the land teem with wickedness.
89:14 Therefore your Lord let loose on them the scourge of a torment; for from
His eminence your Lord observes all.

1. The first ten nights of the sacred month of Dhūl-Ḥajjah.

فاما الانسان اذا ما ابتلىه ربه فاكرمه ونعمه فيقول ربي
اكرمن ۝ واما اذا ما ابتلىه فقدر عليه رزقه فيقول ربي
اهانن ۝ كلا بل لا تكرمون اليتيم ۝ ولا تحاضون على طعام المسكين
۝ وتاكلون التراث اكلا لما ۝ وتحبون المال حبا جما ۝ كلا اذا
دكت الارض دكا دكا ۝ وجاء ربك والملك صفا صفا ۝ وجيء يومئذ
بجهنم يومئذ يتذكر الانسان وانى له الذكرى ۝ يقول يا ليتني
قدمت لحياتي ۝ فيومئذ لا يعذب عذابه احد ۝ ولا يوثق
وثاقه احد ۝ يا ايتها النفس المطمئنة ۝ ارجعي الى ربك
راضية مرضية ۝ فادخلي في عبادي ۝ وادخلي جنتي ٣٠

سورة البلد مكية وهي عشرون آية

بسم الله الرحمن الرحيم
لا اقسم بهذا البلد ١ وانت حل بهذا البلد ٢ ووالد وما ولد
٣ لقد خلقنا الانسان في كبد ٤ ايحسب ان لن يقدر عليه احد
٥ يقول اهلكت مالا لبدا ٦ ايحسب ان لم يره احد ٧

AS FOR man, when his Lord 89:15
tests him by honouring him
and bestowing blessings on
him, he says: 'My Lord has
honoured me.' But when He
tests him by diminishing his
provision, he says: 'My Lord
despises me.'

No! But you show no kind-
ness to the orphan, nor do you
vie with each other in feeding
the destitute. Greedily you lay
your hands on the inheritance
of the weak, and you love
riches with all your hearts.

No! But when the earth is 89:21
crushed to fine dust, and your
Lord comes down with the
angels, in their ranks, and Hell
is on that day brought near –
on that day man will remember.
And what will remembrance
avail him?

He will say: 'Would that I had been charitable in my lifetime!' But on
that day none will punish as He will punish, and none will bind with chains
like His.

O serene soul! Return to your Lord, well pleased, and pleasing in His
sight. Join My servants, and enter My Paradise. 89:30

THE CITY

In the Name of God, the Merciful, the Compassionate

I SWEAR by this city (and you[1] are a resident of this city), by the begetter[2] 90:1
and all whom he begot: We created Man to try him with affliction.

Does he think that none has power over him? 'I have squandered vast
riches!' he says. Does he think that none observed him? 90:7

1. Muḥammad. 2. Adam.

90:8 HAVE WE not given him two eyes, a tongue, and two lips, and shown him the two paths?[1] Yet he would not scale the Height.

Would that you knew what the Height is. It is the freeing of a slave; the feeding, in a day of famine, of an orphaned relation or a needy man in distress; to have faith and to enjoin fortitude and mercy.

Such are those that shall stand on the right hand; but those that deny Our revelations
90:20 shall stand on the left, with a Fire close above them.

الم نجعل له عينين ۝ ولسانا وشفتين ۝ وهديناه النجدين ۝
فلا اقتحم العقبة ۝ وما ادريك ما العقبة ۝ فك رقبة ۝
او اطعام في يوم ذي مسغبة ۝ يتيما ذا مقربة ۝ او مسكينا
ذا متربة ۝ ثم كان من الذين امنوا وتواصوا بالصبر وتواصوا
بالمرحمة ۝ اولئك اصحاب الميمنة ۝ والذين كفروا
باياتنا هم اصحاب المشئمة ۝ عليهم نار مؤصدة ۝

سورة الشمس مكية وهي خمس عشرة اية

بسم الله الرحمن الرحيم

والشمس وضحيها ۝ والقمر اذا تليها ۝ والنهار اذا جليها ۝ واليل
اذا يغشيها ۝ والسماء وما بنيها ۝ والارض وما طحيها ۝ ونفس وما
سويها ۝ فالهمها فجورها وتقويها ۝ قد افلح من زكيها ۝ وقد خاب
من دسيها ۝ كذبت ثمود بطغويها ۝ اذ انبعث اشقيها ۝ فقال
لهم رسول الله ناقة الله وسقيها ۝ فكذبوه فعقروها فدمدم
عليهم ربهم بذنبهم فسويها ۝ ولا يخاف عقبيها ۝

THE SUN

In the Name of God,
the Merciful, the Compassionate

91:1 BY THE sun and his midday brightness; by the moon, when she rises after
him; by the day, when it reveals his splendour; by the night, when it veils him!
91:6 By the heaven and Him that built it; by the earth and Him that spread it;
by the soul and Him that moulded it and inspired it with knowledge of sin
and piety: blessed shall be he that has kept it pure, and ruined he that has
corrupted it!
In its presumptuous pride Thamūd denied its apostle when its arch-sinner
rose against him. God's apostle said: 'This is God's own she-camel. Let her
drink.'
They disbelieved him, and hamstrung her. And for their sin their Lord let
91:15 loose His scourge upon them and razed their city to the ground. He did not
fear the consequences.

1. Of right and wrong.

سورة الليل مكية وهي إحدى وعشرون آية
بسم الله الرحمن الرحيم
والليل إذا يغشى (١) والنهار إذا تجلى (٢) وما خلق الذكر والأنثى
إن سعيكم لشتى (٤) فأما من أعطى واتقى (٥) وصدق بالحسنى
(٦) فسنيسره لليسرى (٧) وأما من بخل واستغنى (٨) وكذب بالحسنى
(٩) فسنيسره للعسرى (١٠) وما يغني عنه ماله إذا تردى (١١) إن علينا
للهدى (١٢) وإن لنا للآخرة والأولى (١٣) فأنذرتكم نارا تلظى (١٤)
لا يصلاها إلا الأشقى (١٥) الذي كذب وتولى (١٦) وسيجنبها الأتقى
(١٧) الذي يؤتي ماله يتزكى (١٨) وما لأحد عنده من نعمة تجزى
(١٩) إلا ابتغاء وجه ربه الأعلى (٢٠) ولسوف يرضى (٢١)
سورة الضحى مكية وهي إحدى عشرة آية
بسم الله الرحمن الرحيم
والضحى (١) والليل إذا سجى (٢) ما ودعك ربك وما قلى (٣)

THE NIGHT

In the Name of God,
the Merciful, the Compassionate

BY THE night, when she lets 92:1
fall her darkness, and by the
radiant day! By Him that created the male and the female,
your endeavours have varied
ends!
For him that gives and fears
God and believes in goodness,
We shall smooth the path of
salvation; but for him that
gives nothing and strives to
enrich himself and disbelieves
in goodness, We shall smooth
the path of affliction. When he
breathes his last, his riches will
not avail him.
It is for Us to give guidance. 92:12
Ours is the life to come, Ours the life of this world. I warn you, then, of a
blazing Fire, in which none shall burn save the hardened sinner, who disbelieves and turns away. But the good man who keeps himself pure by
almsgiving shall keep away from it: and so shall he that does good works for
the sake of his Lord the Most High only, seeking no recompense. He will 92:21
surely be well pleased.

THE DAYLIGHT

In the Name of God, the Merciful, the Compassionate

BY THE light of day, and by the night when she spreads her darkness, your 93:1
Lord has not forsaken you,[1] nor does He abhor you.

1. Muḥammad.

93:4 THE LIFE to come holds a
richer prize for you than this
present life; and you shall be
gratified with what your Lord
will give you.
Did He not find you an
orphan and give you shelter?
And did He not find you in
error and guide you?
And did He not find you
poor and enrich you?
Therefore do not wrong
the orphan, nor chide away
93:11 the beggar. But proclaim the
goodness of your Lord.

COMFORT

In the Name of God,
the Merciful, the Compassionate

94:1 HAVE WE not lifted up your
heart and relieved you[1] of the
burden which weighed down your back?
And have We not given you high renown?
With every hardship there comes ease. With every hardship there comes
ease.
94:8 When your prayers are ended resume your toil, and seek your Lord with
all fervour.

THE FIG

In the Name of God, the Merciful, the Compassionate

95:1 BY THE Fig, and by the Olive!
By Mount Sinai, and by this inviolate city:[2]
95:5 We created Man in a most noble image, and then We shall reduce him to
the lowest of the low:

1. Muḥammad. 2. Mecca.

إلا الذين آمنوا وعملوا الصالحات فلهم أجر غير ممنون
فما يكذبك بعد بالدين ألیس الله بأحكم الحاكمين

سورة العلق مكية وهي تسع عشرة آية

بسم الله الرحمن الرحيم
اقرأ باسم ربك الذي خلق خلق الإنسان من علق
اقرأ وربك الأكرم الذي علم بالقلم علم الإنسان
ما لم يعلم كلا إن الإنسان ليطغى أن رآه استغنى
إن إلى ربك الرجعى أرأيت الذي ينهى عبدا
إذا صلى أرأيت إن كان على الهدى أو أمر بالتقوى
أرأيت إن كذب وتولى ألم يعلم بأن الله يرى كلا لئن لم
ينته لنسفعا بالناصية ناصية كاذبة خاطئة فليدع
ناديه سندع الزبانية كلا لا تطعه واسجد واقترب

سورة القدر مكية وهي خمس آيات

except those who believe and 95:6
do good works, for theirs shall
be a boundless recompense.

What then after this can
make you deny the Last Judgement?

Is God not the most just of 95:8
judges?

CLOTS OF BLOOD[1]

In the Name of God,
the Merciful, the Compassionate

READ IN the name of your 96:1
Lord who created; created
Man from clots of blood.

Read! Your Lord is the Most
Bountiful One, who by the
pen taught Man what he did
not know.

No! Man transgresses in thinking himself his own master:[2] for to your
Lord shall all return.

Consider the man who rebukes Our servant when he prays. Consider:
does he follow the right guidance or enjoin true piety?

Do but consider: if he denies the Truth and pays no heed, does he not 96:13
realize that God sees all?

No! Let him desist, or We will drag him by the forelock, his lying, sinful
forelock.

Then let him call his helpmates: We will call the guards of Hell.

No, never obey him! Prostrate yourself and come nearer. 96:19

1. See p. 331, note 1.
2. Or: in thinking himself wealthy.

QADR

In the Name of God,
the Merciful, the Compassionate

بسم الله الرحمن الرحيم
إنا أنزلناه في ليلة القدر ١ وما أدراك ما ليلة القدر ٢
ليلة القدر خير من ألف شهر ٣ تنزل الملائكة والروح
فيها بإذن ربهم من كل أمر ٤ سلام هي حتى مطلع الفجر ٥
سورة البينة مدنية وهي ثمان آيات
بسم الله الرحمن الرحيم
لم يكن الذين كفروا من أهل الكتاب والمشركين منفكين حتى تأتيهم البينة
١ رسول من الله يتلوا صحفا مطهرة ٢ فيها كتب قيمة ٣ وما تفرق
الذين أوتوا الكتاب إلا من بعد ما جاءتهم البينة ٤ وما أمروا إلا ليعبدوا
الله مخلصين له الدين حنفاء ويقيموا الصلوة ويؤتوا الزكوة وذلك دين القيمة
٥ إن الذين كفروا من أهل الكتاب والمشركين في نار جهنم خالدين فيها أولئك هم
شر البرية ٦ إن الذين آمنوا وعملوا الصالحات أولئك هم خير البرية ٧
جزاؤهم عند ربهم جنات عدن تجري من تحتها الأنهار خالدين فيها
أبدا رضي الله عنهم ورضوا عنه ذلك لمن خشي ربه ٨

97:1 WE REVEALED it on the Night
of Qadr.[1] Would that you
knew what the Night of Qadr
is like!
Better is the Night of Qadr
than a thousand months.
On that night the angels
and the Spirit by their Lord's
leave come down with each
command.
97:5 Peace it is, till break of
dawn.

THE PROOF

In the Name of God,
the Merciful, the Compassionate

98:1 THE UNBELIEVERS among the People of the Book[2] and the pagans did not
desist from unbelief until the Proof was given them: an apostle from God
reciting from purified pages infallible decrees.
Nor did those who were vouchsafed the Book divide themselves until the
Proof was given them. Yet they were enjoined only to worship God and to
consecrate their religion to Him, to attend to their prayers and to render the
alms levy. That, surely, is the infallible faith.
The unbelievers among the People of the Book and the pagans shall in
the fire of Hell abide for ever. They are the vilest of all creatures.
But of all creatures those that believe and do good works are the noblest.
98:8 Their recompense, in their Lord's presence, shall be the Gardens of Eden,
watered by running brooks, wherein shall they abide for ever.
God is well pleased with them, and they are well pleased with Him. Thus
shall the God-fearing be rewarded.

1. Literally, glory. 2. Jews and Christians.

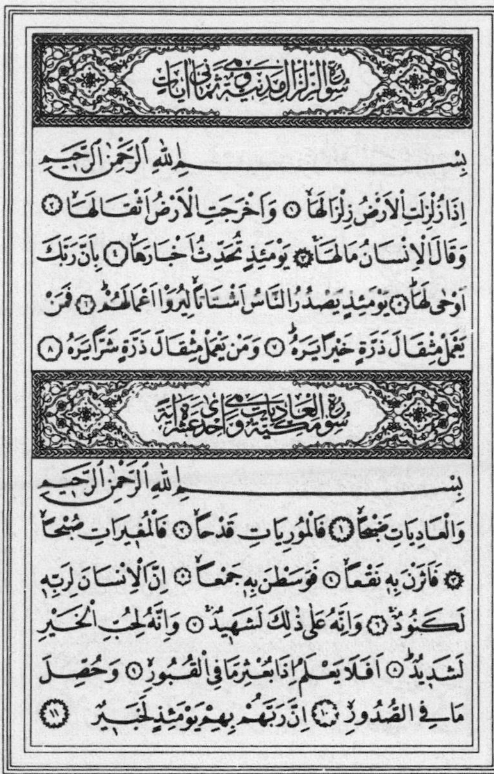
سورة الزلزال مدنية وهي ثمان آيات

بسم الله الرحمن الرحيم

إذا زلزلت الأرض زلزالها ۝١ وأخرجت الأرض أثقالها ۝٢
وقال الإنسان ما لها ۝٣ يومئذ تحدث أخبارها ۝٤ بأن ربك
أوحى لها ۝٥ يومئذ يصدر الناس أشتاتا ليروا أعمالهم ۝٦ فمن
يعمل مثقال ذرة خيرا يره ۝٧ ومن يعمل مثقال ذرة شرا يره ۝٨

سورة العاديات مكية وهي احدى عشرة آية

بسم الله الرحمن الرحيم

والعاديات ضبحا ۝١ فالموريات قدحا ۝٢ فالمغيرات صبحا
۝٣ فأثرن به نقعا ۝٤ فوسطن به جمعا ۝٥ إن الإنسان لربه
لكنود ۝٦ وإنه على ذلك لشهيد ۝٧ وإنه لحب الخير
لشديد ۝٨ أفلا يعلم إذا بعثر ما في القبور ۝٩ وحصل
ما في الصدور ۝١٠ إن ربهم بهم يومئذ لخبير ۝١١

THE EARTHQUAKE

In the Name of God,
the Merciful, the Compassionate

WHEN EARTH is rocked in 99:1
her last convulsion; when
Earth shakes off her burdens
and Man says, 'What may this
mean?' – on that day she will
proclaim her tidings, for your
Lord will have inspired her.
On that day mankind will
come out in broken bands to
be shown their labours. Whoever did an atom's weight of
good shall see it, and whoever 99:8
did an atom's weight of evil
shall also see it.

THE WAR STEEDS

In the Name of God, the Merciful, the Compassionate

BY THE snorting war steeds, which strike fire with their hoofs as they gallop 100:1
to the raid at morn and with a trail of dust cleave a massed army: Man is
ungrateful to his Lord! To this he himself shall bear witness.
He loves riches with all his heart. But is he not aware that when the dead
are thrown out from their graves and their once-hidden thoughts are laid
bare, their Lord will on that day have full knowledge of them all? 100:11

THE DISASTER

In the Name of God,
the Merciful, the Compassionate

101:1 THE DISASTER! What is the
Disaster?
Would that you knew what
the Disaster is!
On that day people shall
become like scattered moths
and the mountains like tufts of
carded wool.
Then he whose good deeds
weigh heavy in the scales shall
live in bliss; but he whose good
deeds are light, the Abyss shall
be his home.
Would that you knew what
this is like!
101:11 It is a scorching Fire.

سورة القارعة مكية وهي احدى عشرة آية
بسم الله الرحمن الرحيم
القارعة ۝ ما القارعة ۝ وما أدراك ما القارعة ۝ يوم يكون
الناس كالفراش المبثوث ۝ وتكون الجبال كالعهن المنفوش ۝
فأما من ثقلت موازينه ۝ فهو في عيشة راضية ۝ وأما من خفت
موازينه ۝ فأمه هاوية ۝ وما أدراك ما هيه ۝ نار حامية ۝
سورة التكاثر مكية وهي ثماني آيات
بسم الله الرحمن الرحيم
ألهاكم التكاثر ۝ حتى زرتم المقابر ۝ كلا سوف تعلمون ۝ ثم
كلا سوف تعلمون ۝ كلا لو تعلمون علم اليقين ۝ لترون الجحيم ۝
ثم لترونها عين اليقين ۝ ثم لتسألن يومئذ عن النعيم ۝
سورة العصر مكية وهي ثلاث آيات

WORLDLY GAIN

In the Name of God, the Merciful, the Compassionate

102:1 YOUR HEARTS are taken up with worldly gain from the cradle to the grave.
No! But you shall learn. No! You then shall surely learn.
No! If you knew the Truth with certainty, you would witness Hell: you
would then witness it with the certainty of your very eyes.
102:8 Then, on that day, you shall surely be questioned about bliss.

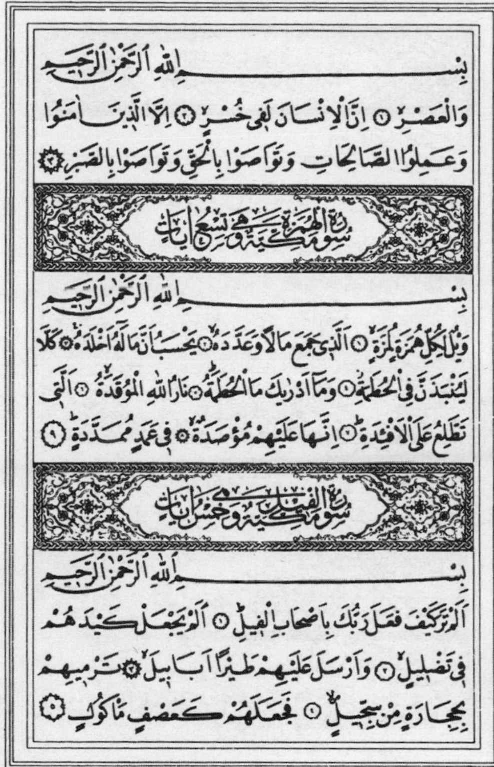
بسم الله الرحمن الرحيم
والعصر ۝ إن الإنسان لفي خسر ۝ إلا الذين آمنوا
وعملوا الصالحات وتواصوا بالحق وتواصوا بالصبر ۝

سورة الهمزة مكية وهي تسع آيات

بسم الله الرحمن الرحيم
ويل لكل همزة لمزة ۝ الذي جمع مالا وعدده ۝ يحسب أن ماله أخلده ۝ كلا
لينبذن في الحطمة ۝ وما أدراك ما الحطمة ۝ نار الله الموقدة ۝ التي
تطلع على الأفئدة ۝ إنها عليهم مؤصدة ۝ في عمد ممددة ۝

سورة الفيل مكية وهي خمس آيات

بسم الله الرحمن الرحيم
ألم تر كيف فعل ربك بأصحاب الفيل ۝ ألم يجعل كيدهم
في تضليل ۝ وأرسل عليهم طيرا أبابيل ۝ ترميهم
بحجارة من سجيل ۝ فجعلهم كعصف مأكول ۝

THE DECLINING DAY

In the Name of God,
the Merciful, the Compassionate

I SWEAR by the declining day 103:1
that perdition shall be the lot
of Man, except for those who 103:3
believe and do good works;
who exhort each other to justice and to fortitude.

THE SLANDERER

In the Name of God,
the Merciful, the Compassionate

WOE BETIDE every backbiting slanderer who amasses riches and sedulously 104:1
hoards them, thinking his wealth will render him immortal!
By no means! He shall be flung into the Destroying Flame.
Would that you knew what the Destroying Flame is like!
It is God's own kindled fire, which will rise up to the hearts. It will close
in upon them, in towering columns. 104:9

THE ELEPHANT

In the Name of God, the Merciful, the Compassionate

HAVE YOU not considered how your Lord dealt with the Army of the Elephant?[1] 105:1
Did He not confound their stratagem and send against them flocks of birds
which pelted them with clay-stones, so that they became like the withered 105:5
stalks of plants which cattle had devoured?

1. The allusion is to the expedition of Abraha, the Christian king of Ethiopia, against Mecca, said to have taken place in the year of Muḥammad's birth.

QURAYSH[1]

In the Name of God,
the Merciful, the Compassionate

106:1 FOR THE protection of Quraysh: their protection in their
winter and summer journey-
ings.
Therefore let them worship
106:4 the Lord of this House who
fed them when there was famine and shielded them from
fear.

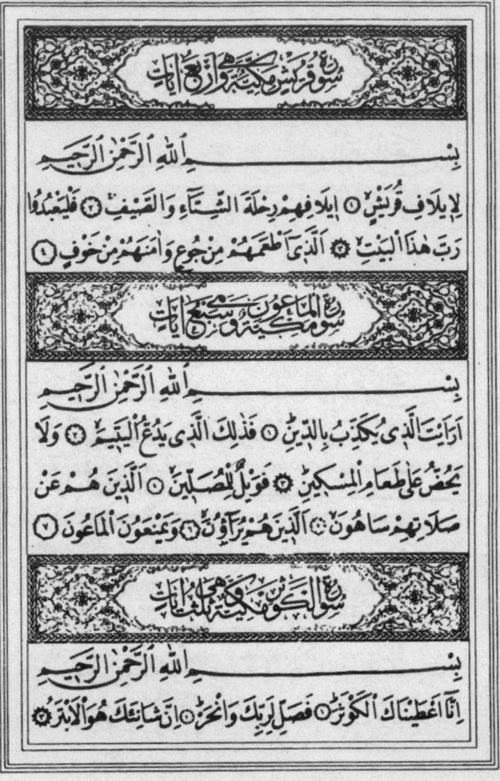
سورة قريش مكية وهي اربع آيات
بسم الله الرحمن الرحيم
لإيلاف قريش ۝ إيلافهم رحلة الشتاء والصيف ۝ فليعبدوا
رب هذا البيت ۝ الذي أطعمهم من جوع وآمنهم من خوف ۝
سورة الماعون مكية وهي سبع آيات
بسم الله الرحمن الرحيم
أرأيت الذي يكذب بالدين ۝ فذلك الذي يدع اليتيم ۝ ولا
يحض على طعام المسكين ۝ فويل للمصلين ۝ الذين هم عن
صلاتهم ساهون ۝ الذين هم يراءون ۝ ويمنعون الماعون ۝
سورة الكوثر مكية وهي ثلث آيات
بسم الله الرحمن الرحيم
إنا أعطيناك الكوثر ۝ فصل لربك وانحر ۝ إن شانئك هو الأبتر ۝

ALMS

In the Name of God,
the Merciful, the Compassionate

107:1 HAVE YOU considered him that denies the Last Judgement? It is he who
turns away the orphan and does not urge the feeding of the destitute.
Woe betide those who pray but are heedless of their prayer; who make a
107:7 show of piety and forbid almsgiving.

ABUNDANCE

In the Name of God, the Merciful, the Compassionate

108:1 WE HAVE given you[2] abundance. So pray to your Lord and sacrifice to Him.
108:3 He that hates you shall remain childless.

1. Muḥammad's own clan. Some commentators connect this *sūrah* with the preceding one.
2. Muḥammad.

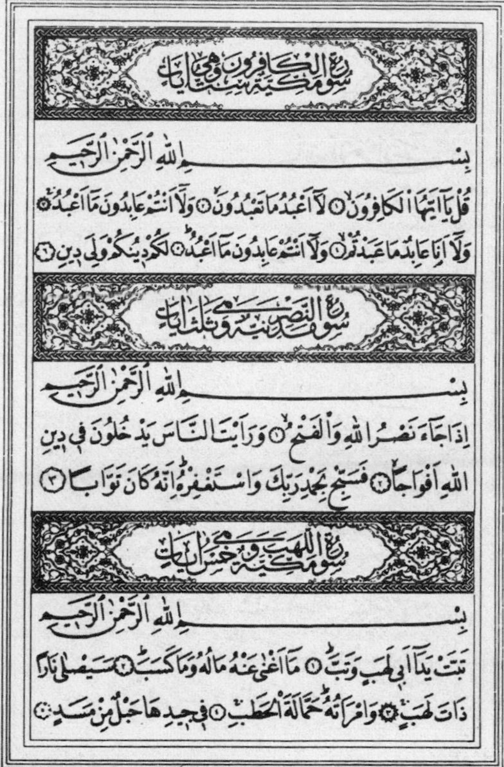

سورة الكافرون مكية وهي ست آيات

بسم الله الرحمن الرحيم

قل يا أيها الكافرون ١ لا أعبد ما تعبدون ٢ ولا أنتم عابدون ما أعبد ٣
ولا أنا عابد ما عبدتم ٤ ولا أنتم عابدون ما أعبد ٥ لكم دينكم ولي دين ٦

سورة النصر مدنية وهي ثلاث آيات

بسم الله الرحمن الرحيم

إذا جاء نصر الله والفتح ١ ورأيت الناس يدخلون في دين
الله أفواجا ٢ فسبح بحمد ربك واستغفره إنه كان توابا ٣

سورة اللهب مكية وهي خمس آيات

بسم الله الرحمن الرحيم

تبت يدا أبي لهب وتب ١ ما أغنى عنه ماله وما كسب ٢ سيصلى نارا
ذات لهب ٣ وامرأته حمالة الحطب ٤ في جيدها حبل من مسد ٥

THE UNBELIEVERS

In the Name of God,
the Merciful, the Compassionate

SAY: 'YOU blasphemers! I do 109:1
not worship what you wor-
ship, nor do you worship what
I worship. I shall never worship what you worship, nor
will you ever worship what I
worship. You have your reli- 109:6
gion, and I have my religion.'

HELP

In the Name of God,
the Merciful, the Compassionate

WHEN GOD'S help and victory come, and you see people embrace God's 110:1
Religion in multitudes, give praise and glory to your Lord and seek His 110:3
forgiveness. He is ever disposed to forgive.

AL-LAHAB[1]

In the Name of God, the Merciful, the Compassionate

MAY THE hands of Abu-Lahab[2] perish! And may he himself perish! Noth- 111:1
ing shall his wealth and gains avail him. He shall be burnt in a flaming fire,[3]
and his wife, laden with firewood, shall have a rope of fibre round her neck! 111:5

1. This *sūrah* is also known by another title: 'Al-Masad' (Fibre).
2. The Prophet's uncle, and one of his staunchest opponents.
3. A pun on the meaning of Abu-Lahab, 'father of flame'.

ONENESS

In the Name of God,
the Merciful, the Compassionate

112:1 Say: 'God is One, the Eternal
God. He begot none, nor was
112:4 He begotten. And none is
equal to Him.'

سورة الإخلاص مكية وهي أربع آيات

بسم الله الرحمن الرحيم

قل هو الله أحد ١ الله الصمد ٢ لم يلد ولم يولد ٣ ولم يكن له كفوا أحد ٤

سورة الفلق مدنية وهي خمس آيات

بسم الله الرحمن الرحيم

قل أعوذ برب الفلق ١ من شر ما خلق ٢ ومن شر غاسق إذا وقب ٣
ومن شر النفاثات في العقد ٤ ومن شر حاسد إذا حسد ٥

سورة الناس مدنية وهي ست آيات

بسم الله الرحمن الرحيم

قل أعوذ برب الناس ١ ملك الناس ٢ إله الناس ٣ من
شر الوسواس الخناس ٤ الذي يوسوس في صدور الناس ٥
من الجنة والناس ٦

DAYBREAK

In the Name of God,
the Merciful, the Compassionate

113:1 Say: 'I seek refuge in the Lord
of Daybreak from the mis-
chief of His creation; from the
mischief of the night when she
spreads her darkness; from the
113:5 mischief of conjuring witches;[1] from the mischief of the envier, when he
envies.'

MANKIND

In the Name of God, the Merciful, the Compassionate

114:1 Say: 'I seek refuge in the Lord of mankind, the King of mankind, the God
of mankind, from the mischief of the slinking prompter who whispers in
114:6 the hearts of mankind; from jinn and mankind.'

1. Literally, the women who blow on knots.

INDEX

This index is designed to be of help to the general reader rather than to provide a comprehensive concordance to the text. References are to page numbers; those followed by 'n' are to footnotes. Headings and references in square brackets are mentioned by allusion, not by name. Names beginning with 'al-' are indexed under the letter immediately following.